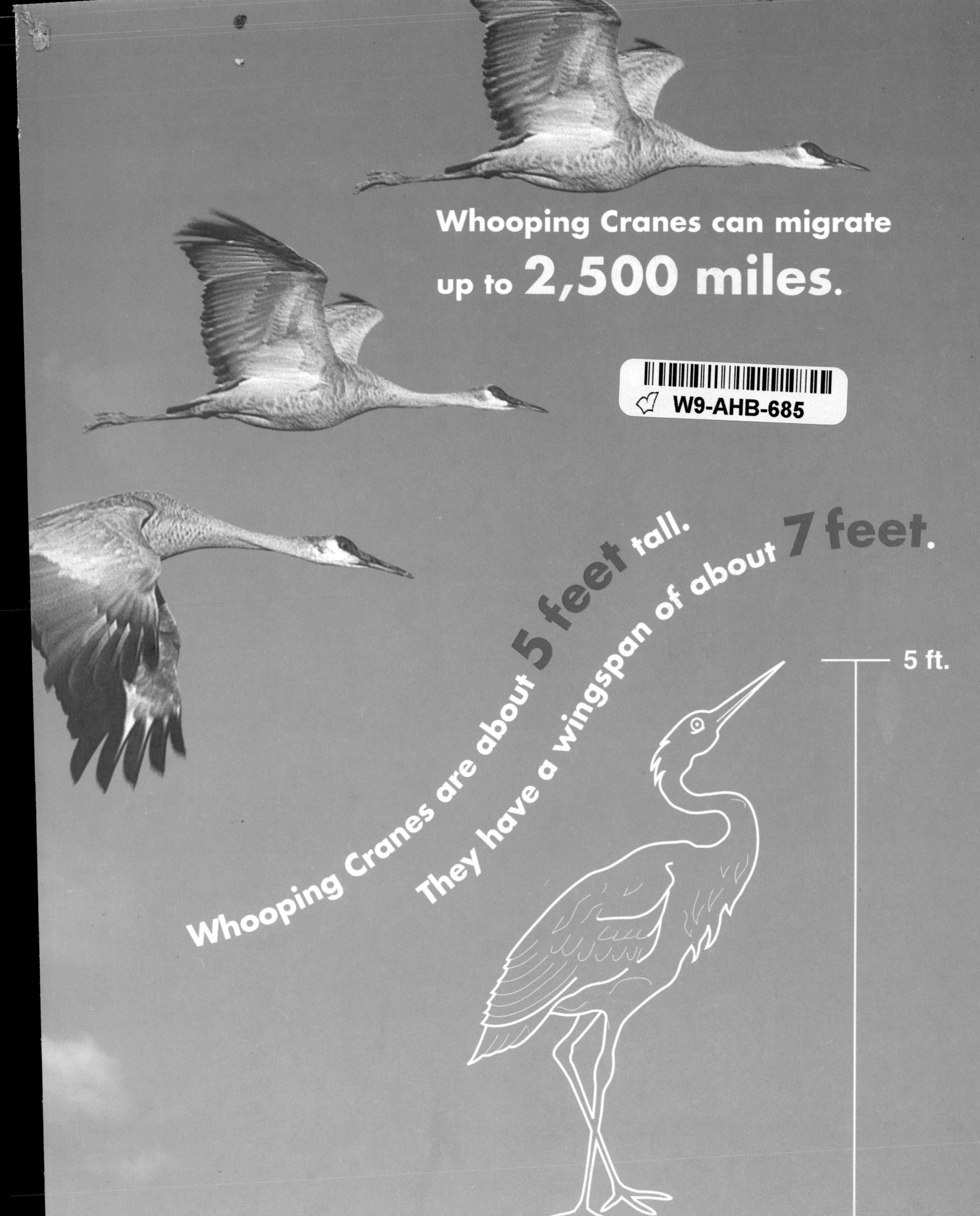
Whooping Cranes can migrate
up to 2,500 miles.
W9-AHB-685
Whooping Cranes are about 5 feet tall.
They have a wingspan of about 7 feet.
5 ft.

Thirty years ago, there were about 1,000 West African Crowned Cranes in Nigeria.

Today, there are fewer than 25.

HSP Math

ILLINOIS EDITION

SCHOOL PUBLISHERS

Visit *The Learning Site!*
www.harcourtschool.com

Printed in the United States of America

ISBN 13: 978-0-15-372487-9
ISBN 10: 0-15-372487-0

1 2 3 4 5 6 7 8 9 10 032 16 15 14 13 12 11 10 09 08 07

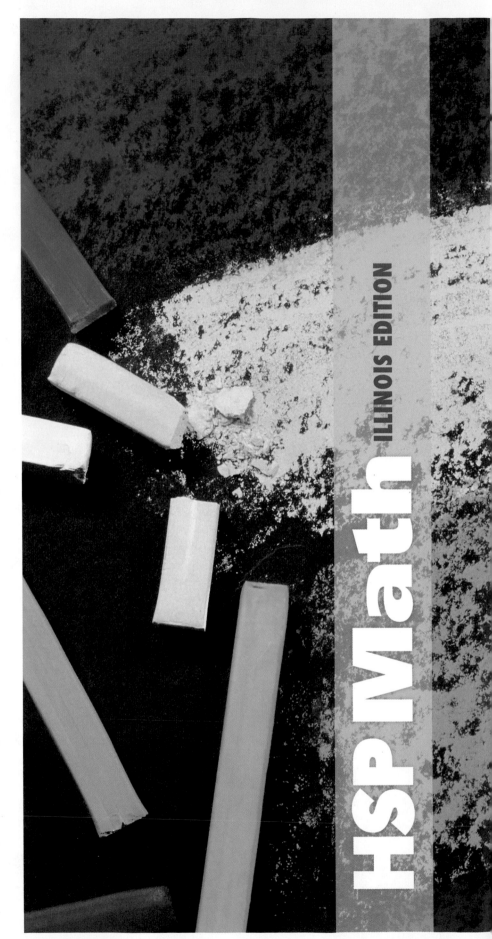

HSP Math
ILLINOIS EDITION

Mathematics Advisors

James A. Mendoza Epperson
Associate Professor
Department of Mathematics
The University of Texas
at Arlington
Arlington, Texas

David G. Wright
Professor
Department of Mathematics
Brigham Young University
Provo, Utah

Senior Authors

Evan M. Maletsky
Professor Emeritus
Montclair State University
Upper Montclair, New Jersey

Joyce McLeod
Visiting Professor, Retired
Rollins College
Winter Park, Florida

Authors

Angela G. Andrews
Assistant Professor of
Math Education
National Louis University
Lisle, Illinois

Lynda Luckie
Director, K-12 Mathematics
Gwinnett County Public Schools
Suwanee, Georgia

Janet K. Scheer
Executive Director
Create-A-Vision
Foster City, California

Juli K. Dixon
Associate Professor of
Mathematics Education
University of Central Florida
Orlando, Florida

David G. Wright
Professor
Department of Mathematics
Brigham Young University
Provo, Utah

Vicki Newman
Classroom Teacher
McGaugh Elementary School
Los Alamitos Unified
School District
Seal Beach, California

Karen S. Norwood
Associate Professor of
Mathematics Education
North Carolina State University
Raleigh, North Carolina

Jennie M. Bennett
Mathematics Teacher
Houston Independent
School District
Houston, Texas

David D. Molina
Program Director, Retired
The Charles A. Dana Center
The University of Texas
at Austin

James A. Mendoza Epperson
Associate Professor
Department of Mathematics
The University of Texas
at Arlington
Arlington, Texas

Tom Roby
Associate Professor of
Mathematics
Director, Quantitative
Learning Center
University of Connecticut
Storrs, Connecticut

Minerva Cordero-Epperson
Associate Professor of
Mathematics and
Associate Dean of the
Honors College
The University of Texas
at Arlington
Arlington, Texas

Barbara Montalto
Mathematics Consultant
Assistant Director
of Mathematics, Retired
Texas Education Agency
Austin, Texas

Program Consultants and Specialists

Michael DiSpezio
Writer and On-Air Host,
JASON Project
North Falmouth,
Massachusetts

Valerie Johse
Elementary Math Specialist
Office of Curriculum
& Instruction
Pearland I.S.D.
Pearland, Texas

Concepion Molina
Southwest Educational
Development Lab
Austin, Texas

Lydia Song
Program Specialist–Mathematics
Orange County Department
of Education
Costa Mesa, California

Rebecca Valbuena
Language Development
Specialist
Stanton Elementary School
Glendora, California

Robin C. Scarcella
Professor and Director
Program of Academic English
and ESL
University of California,
Irvine
Irvine, California

Tyrone Howard
Assistant Professor
UCLA Graduate School
of Education
Information Studies
University of California
at Los Angeles
Los Angeles, California

Russell Gersten
Director, Instructional
Research Group
Long Beach, California
Professor Emeritus of
Special Education
University of Oregon
Eugene, Oregon

Place Value, Addition, and Subtraction

MATH ON LOCATION

GO ONLINE Technology

The Harcourt Learning Site: www.harcourtschool.com

Multimedia Math Glossary: www.harcourtschool.com/hspmath

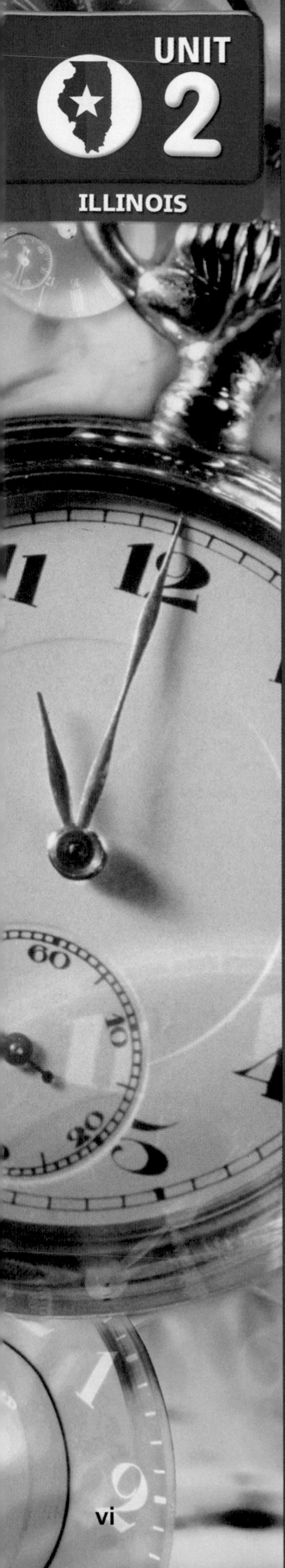

Money and Time, Data and Probability

5 Money and Time 108

GO ONLINE Technology

Harcourt Mega Math: Chapter 5, pp. 112, 126; Chapter 6, pp. 149, 164; Chapter 7, p. 184; Extra Practice, pp. 138–139, 170–171, 192

The Harcourt Learning Site: www.harcourtschool.com

Multimedia Math Glossary: www.harcourtschool.com/hspmath

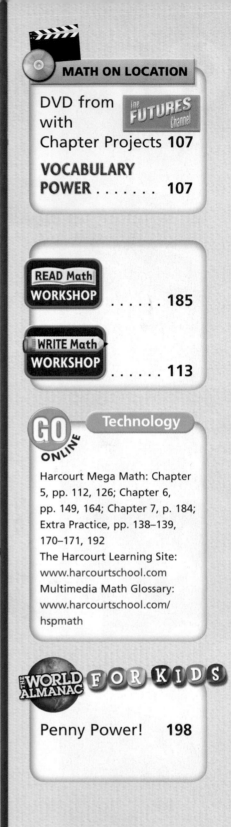

Multiplication Concepts and Facts

8 Understand Multiplication 202

9 Facts and Strategies 230

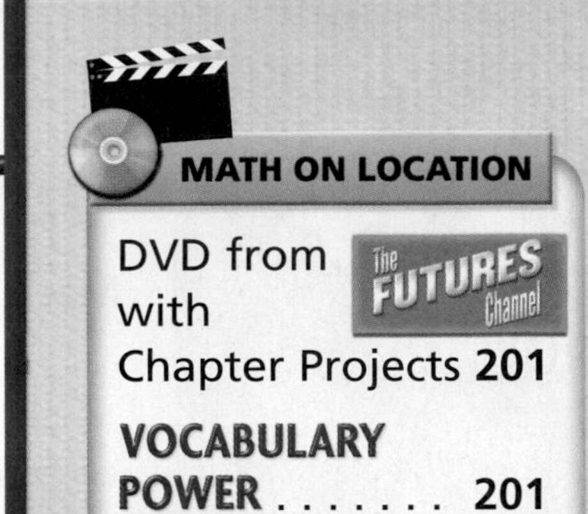

GO ONLINE Technology

Harcourt Mega Math: Chapter 8, p. 208; Chapter 9, p. 239; Chapter 10, p. 259; Extra Practice, pp. 224–225, 248, 266
The Harcourt Learning Site: www.harcourtschool.com
Multimedia Math Glossary: www.harcourtschool.com/hspmath

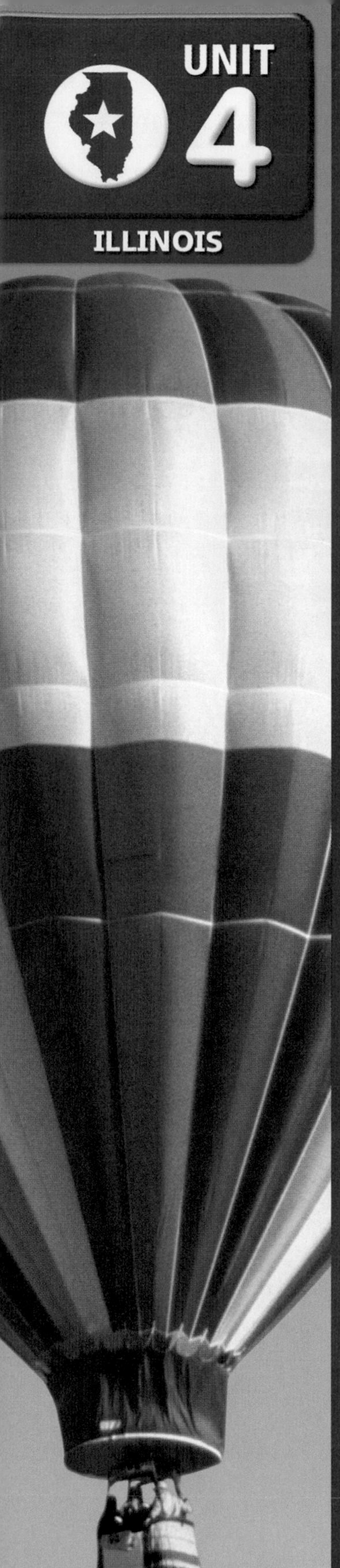

Division Concepts and Facts

13 Facts through 12 320

GO ONLINE Technology

The Harcourt Learning Site: www.harcourtschool.com

Multimedia Math Glossary: www.harcourtschool.com/hspmath

Geometry and Patterns

16 Solid Figures 398

17 Algebra: Patterns 420

GO ONLINE Technology

Harcourt Mega Math: Chapter 14, p. 362; Chapter 15, pp. 385, 387; Chapter 16, p. 402; Chapter 17, p. 423; Extra Practice, pp. 370–371, 392, 414, 434
The Harcourt Learning Site: www.harcourtschool.com
Multimedia Math Glossary: www.harcourtschool.com/hspmath

Fractions and Decimals

19 Understand Decimals 482

GO ONLINE Technology

Harcourt Mega Math: Chapter 18, p. 448; Chapter 19, p. 489; Extra Practice, pp. 476, 500
The Harcourt Learning Site: www.harcourtschool.com
Multimedia Math Glossary: www.harcourtschool.com/hspmath

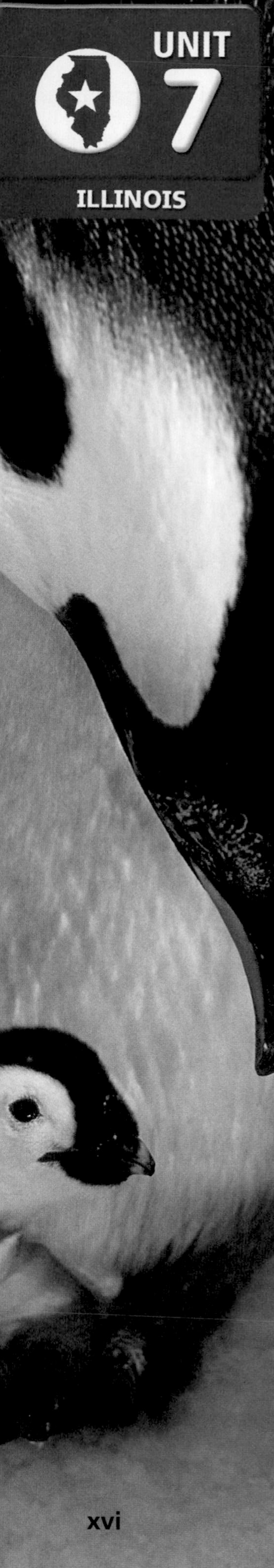

Measurement

20 Customary Measurement 510

21 Metric Measurement 536

22 Perimeter, Area, and Volume 558

GO ONLINE Technology

Harcourt Mega Math: Chapter 20, p. 516; Chapter 21, p. 545; Chapter 22, pp. 562; 566; Extra Practice, pp. 530, 552, 574
The Harcourt Learning Site: www.harcourtschool.com
Multimedia Math Glossary: www.harcourtschool.com/hspmath

Multiply and Divide by 1-Digit

Student Handbook

MATH ON LOCATION

GO ONLINE Technology

Harcourt Mega Math: Chapter 23, p. 597; Chapter 24, p. 621; Extra Practice, pp. 604, 624
The Harcourt Learning Site: www.harcourtschool.com
Multimedia Math Glossary: www.harcourtschool.com/hspmath

TALK, READ, and WRITE About Math

Mathematics is a language of numbers, words, and symbols.

This year, you will learn ways to communicate about math as you **talk**, **read**, and **write** about what you are learning.

The tally table and the bar graph show the number of long-legged wading birds seen along the bay shore of South Padre Island. Marta and her family counted the birds they saw.

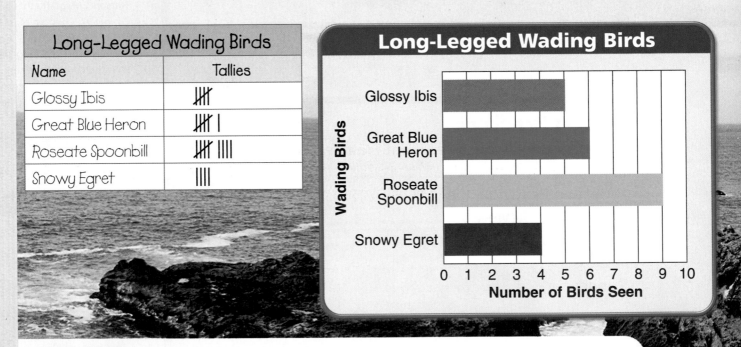

Long-Legged Wading Birds	
Name	Tallies
Glossy Ibis	𝍸
Great Blue Heron	𝍸 |
Roseate Spoonbill	𝍸 ||||
Snowy Egret	||||

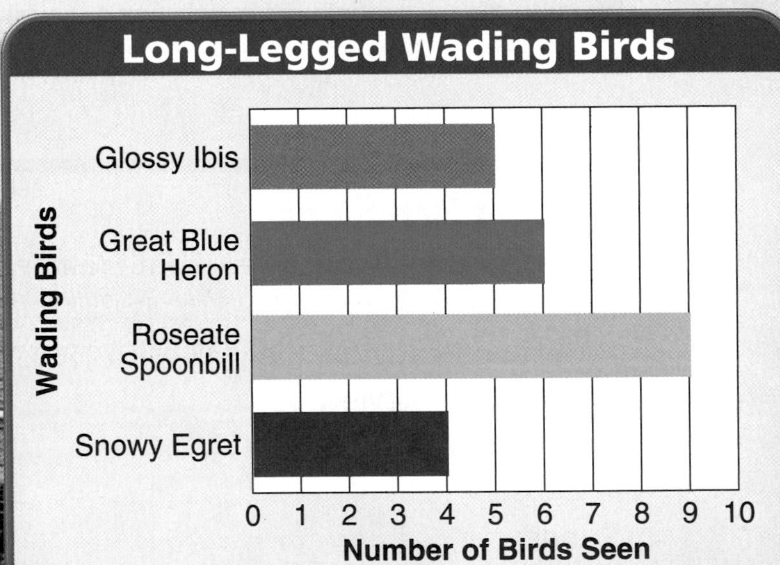

TALK Math

Talk about the tally table and the bar graph.

1. Why are the titles of the tally table and the bar graph the same?
2. How is the information on the tally table and the bar graph alike? How it is different?
3. How do you use the numbers along the bottom of the bar graph?

READ Math

Read the data on the bar graph.

4. How many Snowy Egrets were seen?
5. Were more Glossy Ibises or Snowy Egrets seen?
6. How many more Roseate Spoonbills than Great Blue Herons were seen?
7. How many birds were counted in all?

WRITE Math

Write a problem about the graph.

This year, you will write many problems. When you see **Pose a Problem**, you look at a problem on the page and use it to write your own problem.

In your problem, you can

- change the numbers or some of the information.
- exchange the known and unknown information.
- write an open-ended problem that can have more than one correct answer.

These problems are examples of ways you can pose your own problem. Solve each problem.

Problem How many more Roseate Spoonbills than Snowy Egrets were seen?

- **Change the Numbers or Information.**
  Marta saw 2 more Great Blue Herons, but she forgot to put tally marks on the tally table. How many more Great Blue Herons than Snowy Egrets did she see?
- **Exchange the Known and Unknown Information.**
  Marta tallied a total of 13 Roseate Spoonbills and Snowy Egrets. If she tallied 4 Snowy Egrets, how many Roseate Spoonbills did she tally?
- **Open-Ended**
  Marta visited the seashore again and counted the same birds. She counted a total of 14 birds. She saw 3 Snowy Egrets. How many Glossy Ibises, Great Blue Herons, and Roseate Spoonbills might she have seen?

Pose a Problem Choose one of the three ways to write a new problem. Use the information on the tally table and the bar graph.

UNIT

1 Place Value, Addition, and Subtraction

Math on Location

with
Chapter Projects

1

The biologist visits thousands of acres of refuges by airboat to keep track of birds and other animals.

2

The biologist counts and records the number of egrets to tell if the number is increasing or decreasing.

3

Great numbers of birds and ducks arrive daily so totals are estimated.

VOCABULARY POWER

TALK Math

What math do you see in the **Math on Location** photographs? How can you tell if the number of egrets is increasing or decreasing?

READ Math

REVIEW VOCABULARY You learned the words below when you learned about place value last year. How do these words relate to **Math on Location**?

compare to describe whether numbers are equal to, less than, or greater than each other

estimate to find about how many or how much

place value the value of each digit in a number, based on the location of the digit

WRITE Math

Copy and complete a Word Association Tree Diagram like the one below. Use what you know about place value to fill in the blanks.

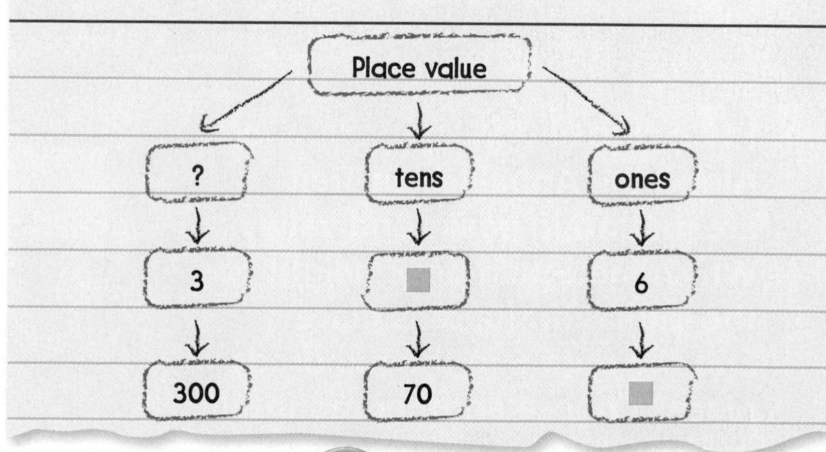

Technology
Multimedia Math Glossary link at
www.harcourtschool.com/hspmath

CHAPTER 1
Understand Place Value

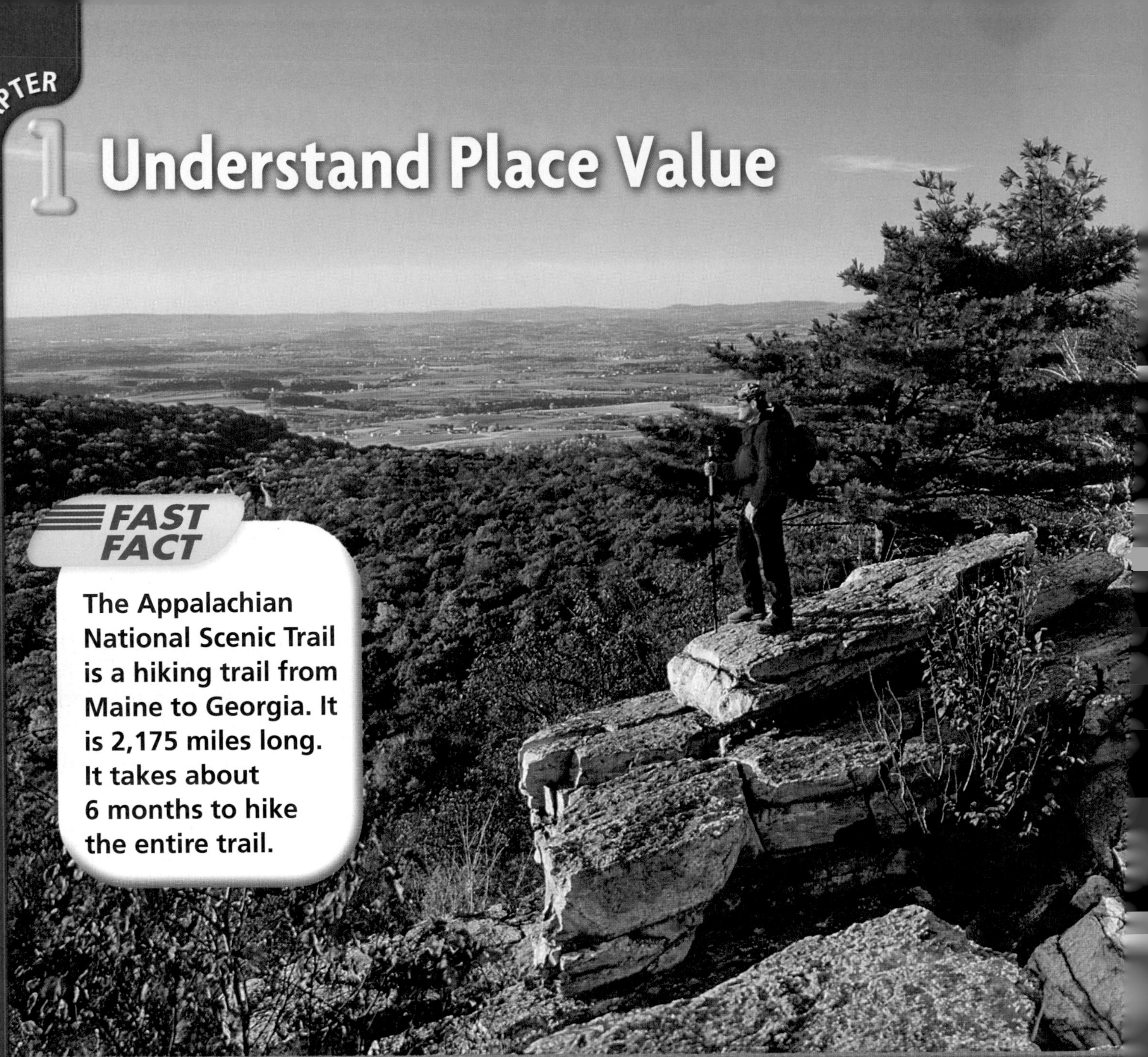

FAST FACT

The Appalachian National Scenic Trail is a hiking trail from Maine to Georgia. It is 2,175 miles long. It takes about 6 months to hike the entire trail.

Investigate

Along the Appalachian Trail are mountain peaks and valleys. Which mountain peak height has the digit 8 in the tens place and the digit 6 in the hundreds place? Choose another mountain peak and describe its height by using place value.

GO ONLINE **Technology**
Student pages are available in the Student eBook.

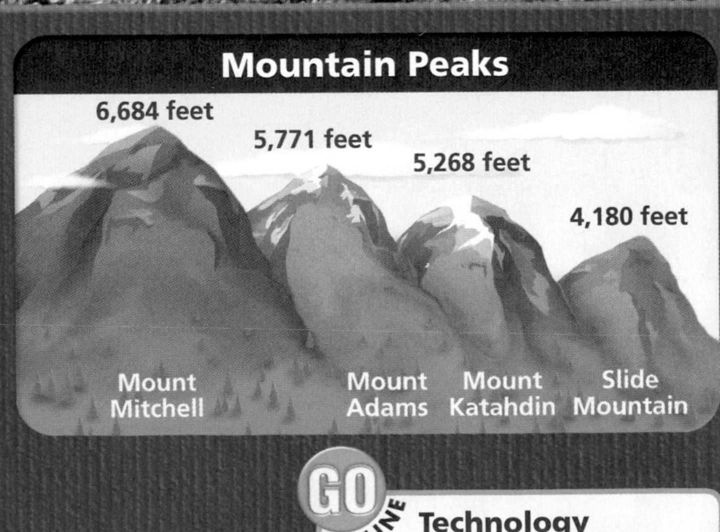

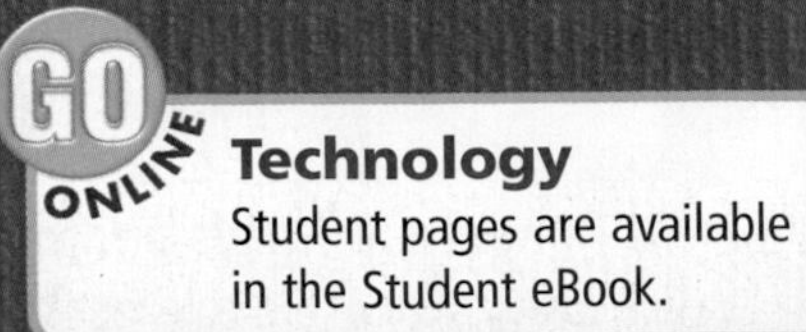

Show What You Know

Check your understanding of important skills needed for success in Chapter 1.

▶ Place Value: Tens and Ones to 100

Write the value of the blue digit.

1. 37 **2.** 81 **3.** 53 **4.** 29 **5.** 14

▶ Understand Place Value

Write the number shown.

6. 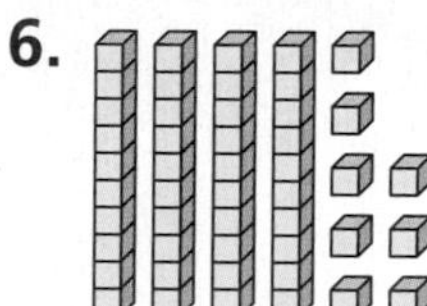

7. 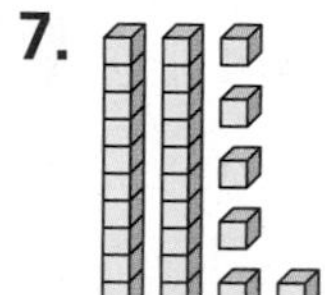

8. 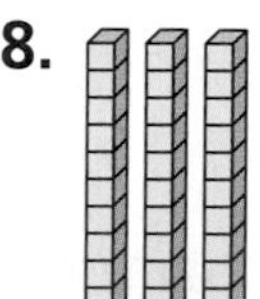

9. 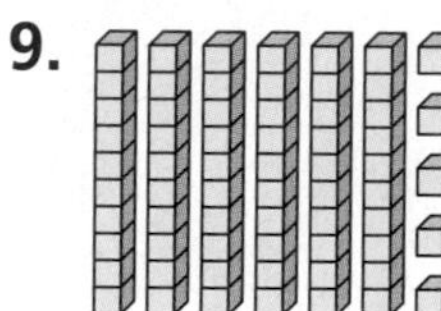

10. 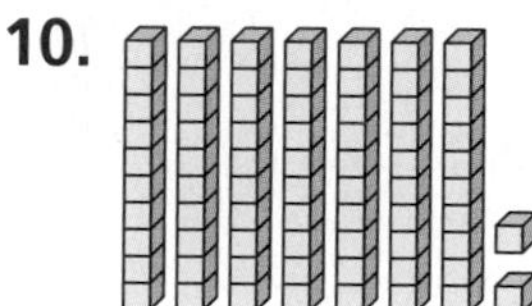

11. 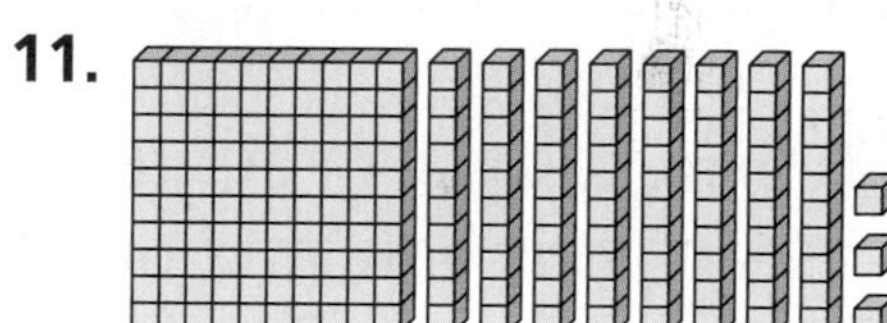

▶ Tens and Ones

Write each number.

12. $90 + 3$

13. $20 + 6$

14. seventeen

15. thirty-one

VOCABULARY POWER

CHAPTER VOCABULARY

digits
even
expanded form
odd
standard form
word form

WARM-UP WORDS

digits The symbols 0, 1, 2, 3, 4, 5, 6, 7, 8, and 9

even A whole number that has a 0, 2, 4, 6, or 8 in the ones place

odd A whole number that has a 1, 3, 5, 7, or 9 in the ones place

LESSON 1 HANDS ON

Algebra: Patterns on a Hundred Chart

OBJECTIVE: Find number patterns on a hundred chart.

Quick Review

Find the sum.

1. 5 + 5
2. 10 + 5
3. 15 + 5
4. 20 + 5
5. 25 + 5

Vocabulary

even **odd**

Investigate

Materials ■ hundred chart

You can use a hundred chart to find number patterns.

A Choose a number from 2 through 5.

B Shade that box on the hundred chart.

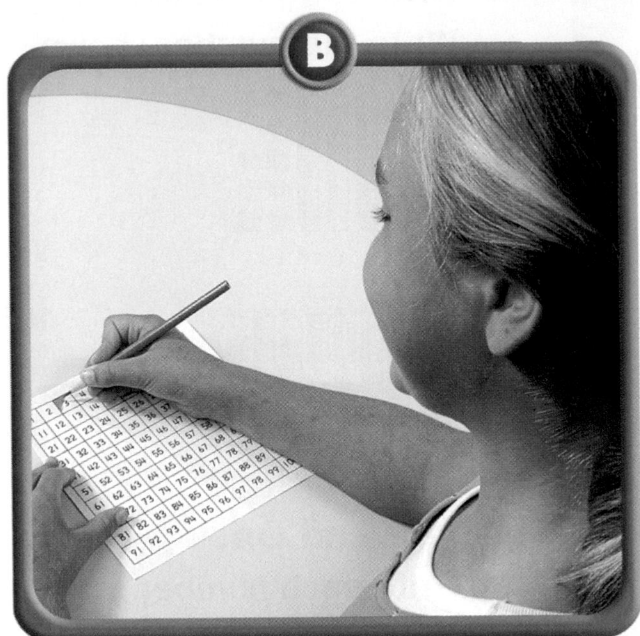

C Skip-count by your number and shade each box you land on.

Draw Conclusions

1. Describe the pattern you see on your hundred chart.
2. Compare your hundred chart with those of other classmates. What do you notice about the patterns? How are they alike? How are they different?
3. **Analysis** Look at a hundred chart. What pattern will you get if you start at 10 and skip-count by tens?

Connect

You can use a hundred chart to identify even and odd numbers.

Step 1

Start at 2. Shade the box on the hundred chart.

1	2	3	4	5	6	7	8	9	10
11	12	13	14	15	16	17	18	19	20
21	22	23	24	25	26	27	28	29	30
31	32	33	34	35	36	37	38	39	40
41	42	43	44	45	46	47	48	49	50
51	52	53	54	55	56	57	58	59	60
61	62	63	64	65	66	67	68	69	70
71	72	73	74	75	76	77	78	79	80
81	82	83	84	85	86	87	88	89	90
91	92	93	94	95	96	97	98	99	100

Step 2

Skip-count by twos. Shade each box you land on. What pattern do you see?

1	2	3	4	5	6	7	8	9	10
11	12	13	14	15	16	17	18	19	20
21	22	23	24	25	26	27	28	29	30
31	32	33	34	35	36	37	38	39	40
41	42	43	44	45	46	47	48	49	50
51	52	53	54	55	56	57	58	59	60
61	62	63	64	65	66	67	68	69	70
71	72	73	74	75	76	77	78	79	80
81	82	83	84	85	86	87	88	89	90
91	92	93	94	95	96	97	98	99	100

The numbers that are shaded are **even** numbers. Even numbers end in 2, 4, 6, 8, or 0.

The numbers that are not shaded are **odd** numbers. Odd numbers end in 1, 3, 5, 7, or 9.

- How does a hundred chart help you identify even and odd numbers?

TALK Math

How can you tell whether a number is odd or even?

Practice

Use the hundred chart. Find the next number in the pattern.

1. 10, 20, 30, 40, ■
2. 5, 10, 15, 20, ■
3. 77, 75, 73, 71, ■
4. 3, 6, 9, 12, ■

Use the hundred chart. Tell whether each number is *odd* or *even*.

5. 16
6. 25
7. 34
8. 23
9. 81
10. 92
11. 47
12. 78
13. **WRITE Math** If you start at 3 and skip-count by twos, will the pattern include even numbers, odd numbers, or both? **Explain.**

LESSON 2

Locate Points on a Number Line

OBJECTIVE: Locate and name points on a number line.

Quick Review

Write the next number in the pattern.

1. 2, 4, 6, 8, ■
2. 5, 10, 15, 20, ■
3. 1, 3, 5, 7, ■
4. 10, 20, 30, 40, ■
5. 4, 8, 12, 16, ■

Learn

PROBLEM Ryan is playing a game that uses a number line. His game piece is on the point labeled *X*. What number does point *X* represent?

A number line shows numbers in order from least to greatest.

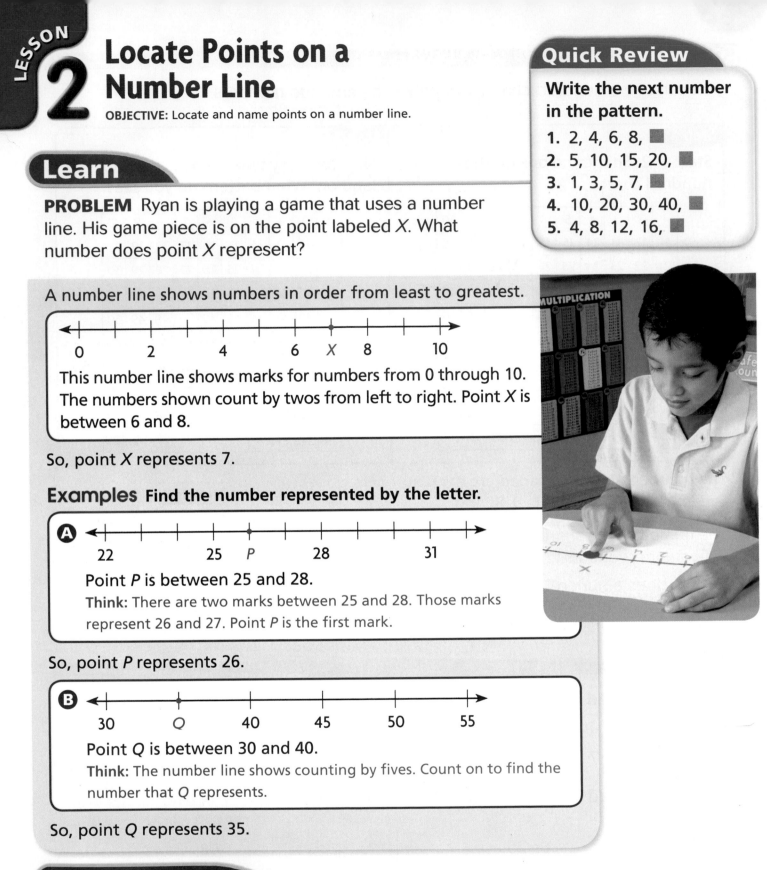

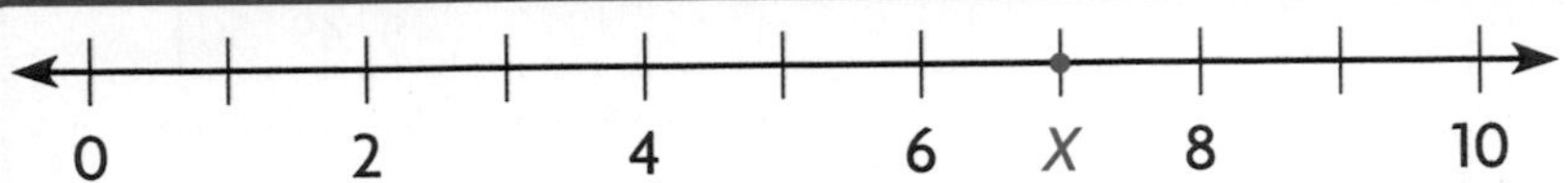

This number line shows marks for numbers from 0 through 10. The numbers shown count by twos from left to right. Point *X* is between 6 and 8.

So, point *X* represents 7.

Examples **Find the number represented by the letter.**

A

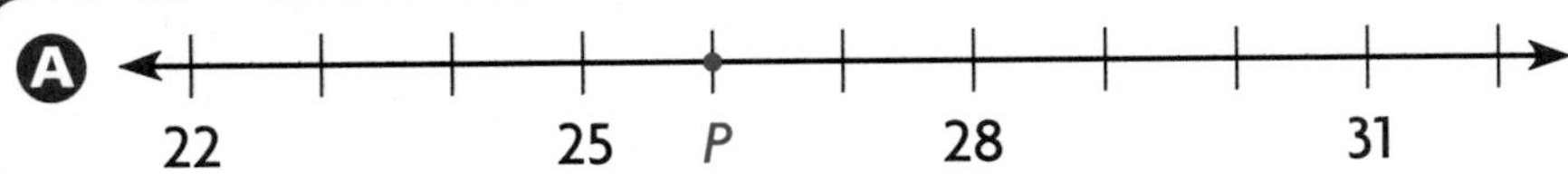

Point *P* is between 25 and 28.

Think: There are two marks between 25 and 28. Those marks represent 26 and 27. Point *P* is the first mark.

So, point *P* represents 26.

B

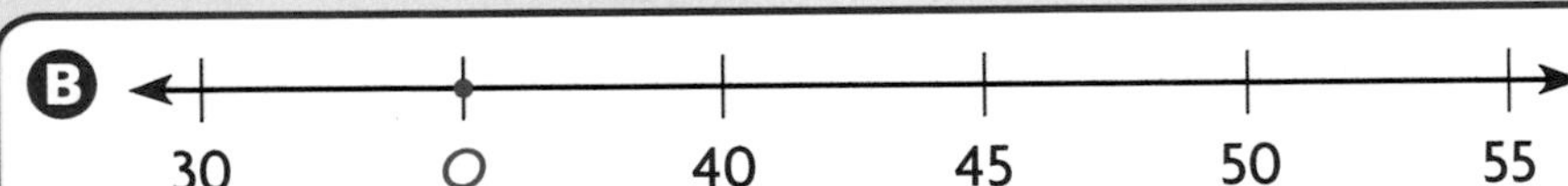

Point *Q* is between 30 and 40.

Think: The number line shows counting by fives. Count on to find the number that *Q* represents.

So, point *Q* represents 35.

Guided Practice

1. Skip-count by threes to find the number that point *Z* represents on the number line.

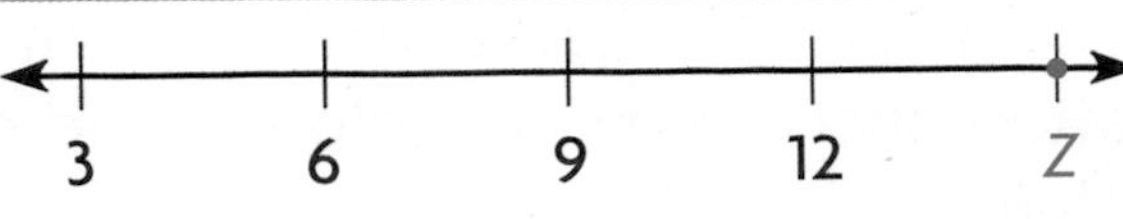

Find the number that point *X* represents on the number line.

2. 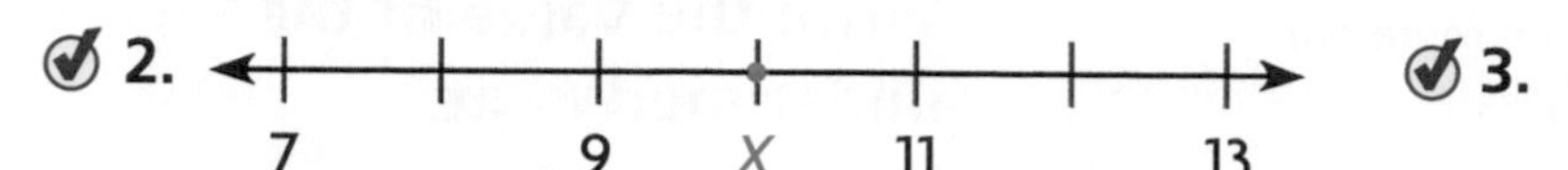

3. 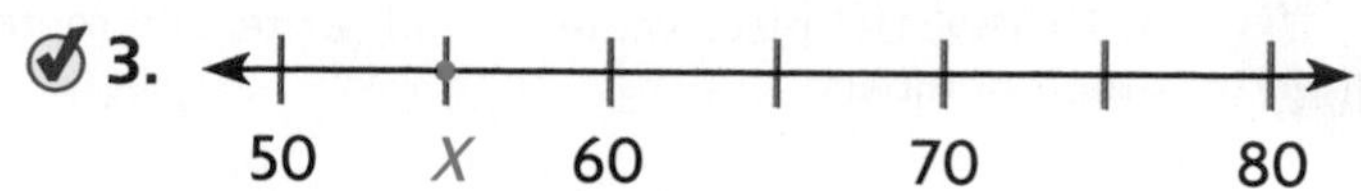

4. **TALK Math** **Explain** how you can use the numbers and marks that are on a number line to find the missing numbers.

Independent Practice and Problem Solving

Find the number that point *X* represents on the number line.

5. 17 20 *X* 23 26 29

6. 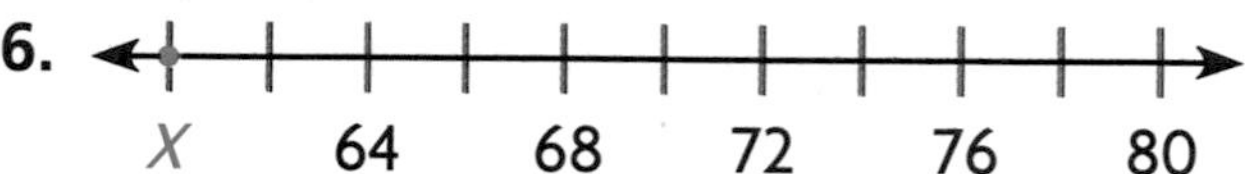

For 7–8, use the number line.

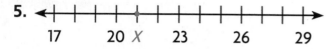

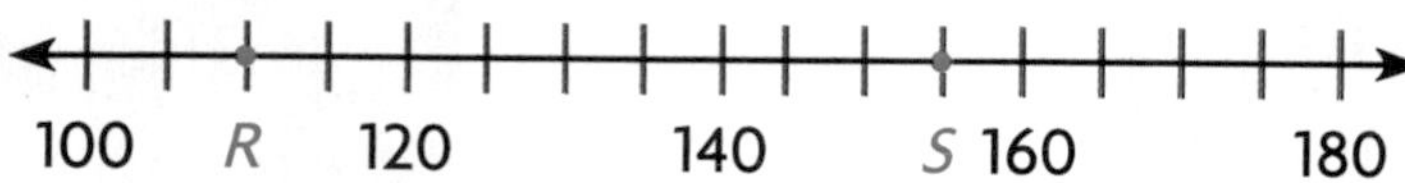

7. Robin's score is shown by point *R* on the number line above. What is her score?

8. **Reasoning** Steve's score is shown by point *S*. What will Steve's next score be if he gets 10 more points? 5 fewer points?

9. **What's the Error?** On the number line below, Laura says that the difference between point *X* and point *Y* is 10. What error did Laura make?

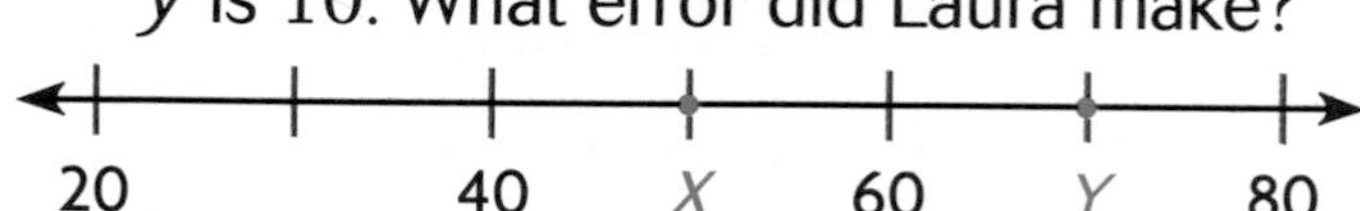

10. **WRITE Math** **Sense or Nonsense** Brian says every other whole number on every number line is an even number. Does Brian's statement make sense?

Mixed Review and Test Prep

11. What is the next number in this pattern? (p. 5)

12, 15, 18, 21, ■

12. Each pen costs $4. What is the total cost of 5 pens? (Grade 2)

13. **Test Prep** What number does point *X* represent?

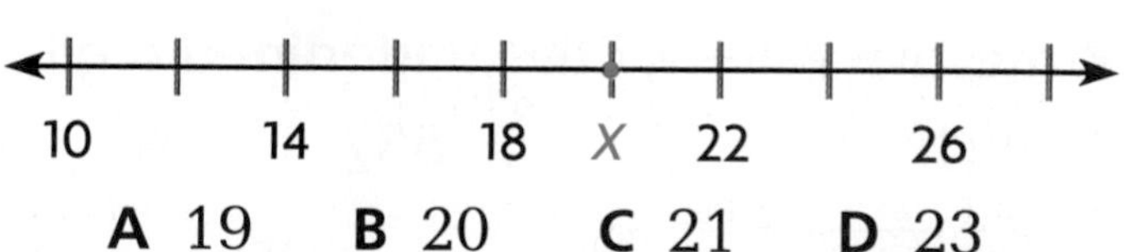

A 19 **B** 20 **C** 21 **D** 23

Extra Practice on page 20, Set A

LESSON 3

Place Value: 3 Digits

OBJECTIVE: Use place value to read, write, and represent 3-digit numbers.

Quick Review

Write the value of the underlined digit.

1. $1\underline{8}$ **2.** $\underline{2}5$
3. $\underline{1}0$ **4.** $\underline{6}1$
5. $4\underline{2}$

Vocabulary

digits
expanded form
standard form
word form

Learn

The symbols 0, 1, 2, 3, 4, 5, 6, 7, 8, and 9 are **digits**. Numbers are made up of digits.

PROBLEM The Otto family visited the world's longest cave at Mammoth Cave National Park. The cave is 367 miles long. What is the value of the digit 6 in 367?

Show 367 with base-ten blocks and a place-value chart.

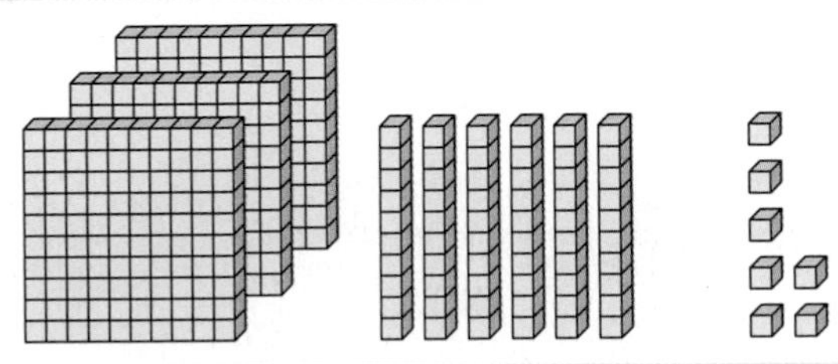

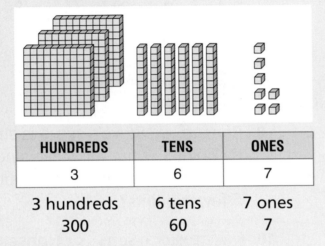

HUNDREDS	TENS	ONES
3	6	7
3 hundreds	6 tens	7 ones
300	60	7

So, the value of the digit 6 in 367 is 6 tens, or 60.

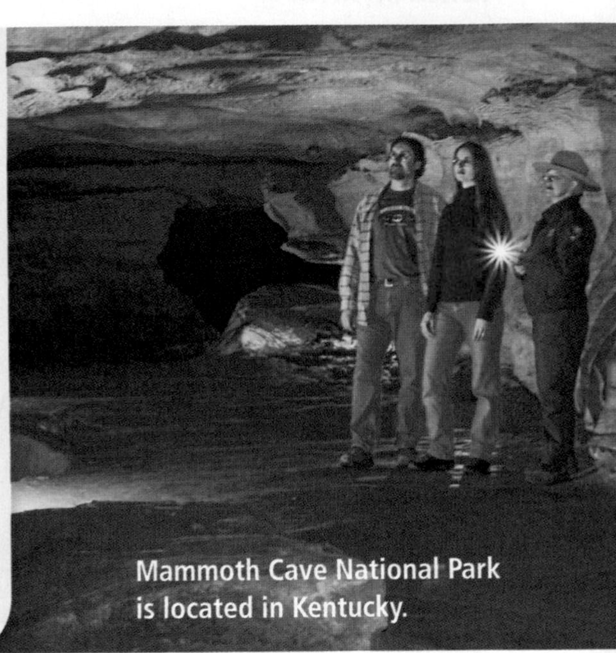

Mammoth Cave National Park is located in Kentucky.

You can write a number in different ways.
Standard form: 367
Expanded form: 300 + 60 + 7
Word form: three hundred sixty-seven

READ Math

When you read whole numbers, do not say "and." The number 367 is read "three hundred sixty-seven."

Guided Practice

1. Write the value of each digit in the chart.

HUNDREDS	TENS	ONES
4	9	5

Write the value of the underlined digit.

2. $9\underline{2}1$ **3.** $53\underline{7}$ ✓**4.** $\underline{6}24$ ✓**5.** $75\underline{0}$

6. **TALK Math** The campground has 109 campsites. **Explain** what the zero in 109 means.

Independent Practice and Problem Solving

Write the value of the underlined digit.

7. $58\underline{1}$ **8.** $6\underline{7}2$ **9.** $\underline{1}20$ **10.** $\underline{2}08$

11. $91\underline{4}$ **12.** $\underline{8}45$ **13.** $7\underline{1}3$ **14.** $6\underline{9}3$

Write each number in standard form.

15. 700 + 80 + 1 **16.** 200 + 10 + 9 **17.** 600 + 40 + 3

18. three hundred eighty-five **19.** 5 hundreds 4 ones **20.** eight hundred nine

Write each number in expanded form.

21. 842 **22.** 329 **23.** four hundred fifty-four

USE DATA For 24–25, use the table.

24. What is the length of Fisher Ridge Cave written in expanded form?

25. Which cave's length has a 1 in the tens place?

United States Caves

Cave	Length in Miles
Jewel Cave	129
Wind Cave	116
Fisher Ridge Cave	107

26. ***FAST FACT*** Jewel Cave in South Dakota has a depth of 632 feet. What is the value of the digit 3 in 632?

27. **WRITE Math** **What's the Error?** Tanya wrote four hundred seven as 470. Explain her error. Write the number in standard form.

28. **Reasoning** Write as many 3-digit numbers as you can with the digits 1, 2, and 3 in each number. Write the greatest number in expanded form.

29. I am an odd number between 21 and 40. The sum of my digits is 8. What number am I?

Mixed Review and Test Prep

30. Cory read 43 pages. Blake read 28 pages. How many more pages did Cory read than Blake? (Grade 2)

31. Jordan has three dollar bills and one quarter. How much money does he have? (Grade 2)

32. **Test Prep** Which shows 806 written in expanded form?

A 800 + 60

B 800 + 6

C 80 + 60

D 80 + 6

Extra Practice on page 20, Set B

Place Value: 4 Digits

OBJECTIVE: Use place value to read, write, and represent 4-digit numbers.

Quick Review

Write the value of the underlined digit.

1. $8\underline{2}5$ **2.** $\underline{4}17$
3. $\underline{2}51$ **4.** $19\underline{8}$
5. $6\underline{3}4$

Learn

PROBLEM Most peanuts grown in the United States are used to make peanut butter. It takes about 1,000 peanuts to make a jar of peanut butter! What does 1,000 of an object look like?

▲ Did you know that the peanut is not a nut? The peanut is actually a vegetable.

Activity

Materials ■ paper clips

Model 1,000 using paper clips.

Step 1
Make a chain of 10 linked paper clips. Then make 9 more chains of 10 paper clips.

Step 2
Skip-count by tens.
How many paper clips have you used?

Step 3
Now link your 10 chains to make one long chain of 100 paper clips.

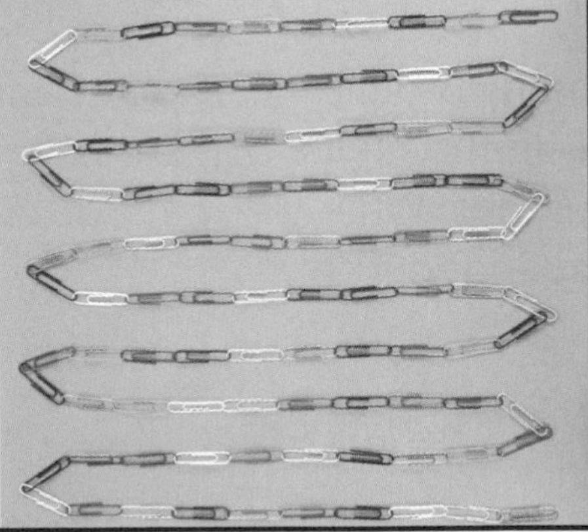

Step 4
Combine your chain of 100 paper clips with the chains from 9 other groups.

- How many chains of 100 paper clips did it take to make 1,000?

So, now you know what 1,000 looks like.

Understand Thousands

Base-ten blocks can help you understand thousands.

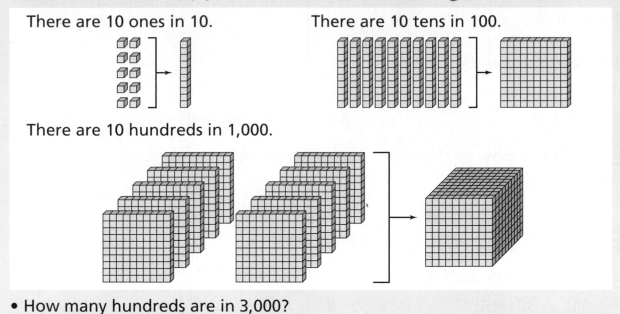

There are 10 ones in 10.

There are 10 tens in 100.

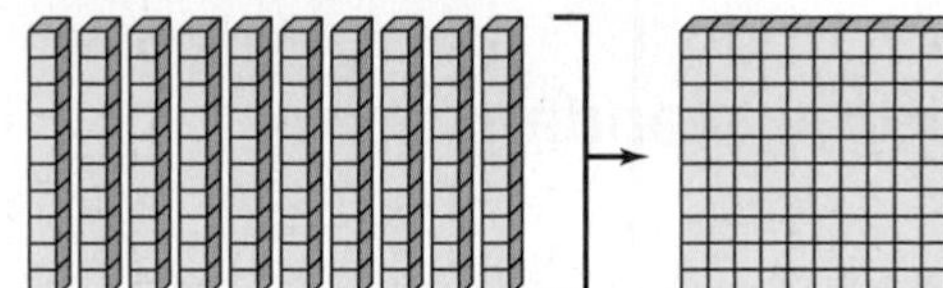

There are 10 hundreds in 1,000.

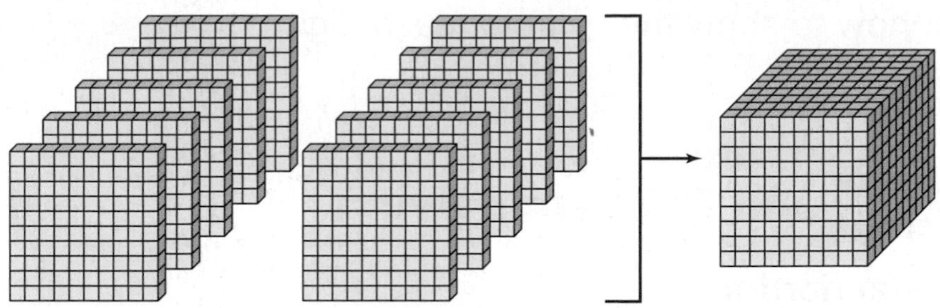

• How many hundreds are in 3,000?

Mr. Jackson sold 2,186 jars of homemade peanut butter. What is the value of the digit 2 in 2,186?

Model the number with base-ten blocks.

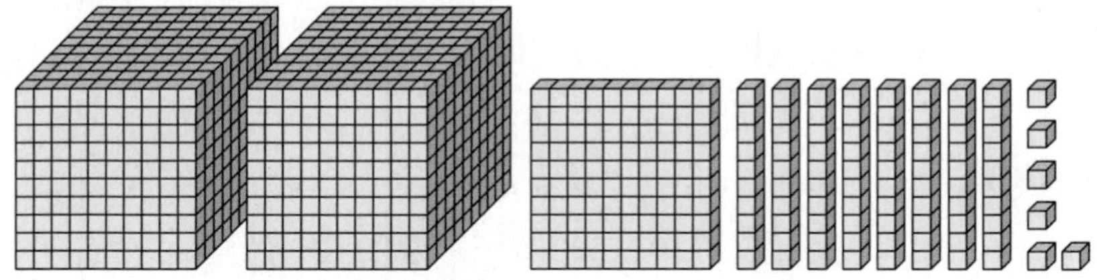

Write the number in a place-value chart.

THOUSANDS	HUNDREDS	TENS	ONES
2,	1	8	6
2 thousands	1 hundred	8 tens	6 ones
2,000	100	80	6

Math Idea
A comma is used to separate the thousands and the hundreds.

So, the value of the digit 2 in 2,186 is 2 thousands, or 2,000.

Here are three ways to write this number.

Standard form: 2,186
Expanded form: 2,000 + 100 + 80 + 6
Word form: two thousand, one hundred eighty-six

Guided Practice

1. Write this number in standard form and in expanded form.

THOUSANDS	HUNDREDS	TENS	ONES
1,	3	4	7

Write each number in standard form.

2. 8,000 + 200 + 50 + 8
3. three thousand, one hundred fourteen
4. 1,000 + 300 + 8
5. two thousand, thirty-four
6. TALK Math **Explain** how to show the value of each digit in the number 9,248.

Independent Practice and Problem Solving

Write each number in standard form.

7. 9,000 + 700 + 30 + 1
8. 1,000 + 20 + 4
9. eight thousand, five hundred two
10. seven thousand, three hundred ninety-one

Write each number in expanded form.

11. 2,389
12. 7,241
13. 6,170
14. 4,502
15. one thousand, eighteen
16. six thousand, four

Write the value of the underlined digit.

17. $\underline{6},452$
18. $3,\underline{8}01$
19. $\underline{5},018$
20. $7,3\underline{1}4$

Algebra Find the missing number.

21. 1,000 + ■ + 40 + 8 = 1,748
22. 3,000 + 200 + ■ + 6 = 3,296
23. 4,000 + 600 + ■ = 4,620
24. ■ + 50 + 4 = 8,054
25. Write a 4-digit number that has a 7 in the hundreds place.
26. Write a number that is 1,000 more than 6,243.
27. How many hundreds are in 6,000? How many tens?
28. WRITE Math **Sense or Nonsense** Brett says that the greatest possible 4-digit number is 9,000. Does Brett's statement make sense? **Explain.**

CD ROM **Technology**
Use Harcourt Mega Math, The Number Games, *Tiny's Think Tank*, Level A; Country Countdown, *Block Busters*, Level T.

Extra Practice on page 20, Set C

Learn About Names For Numbers

You can name numbers in many different ways. Here are some of the different names for 78, 152, and 2,046.

78	152	2,046
70 + 8	100 + 50 + 2	2,000 + 40 + 6
25 + 25 + 25 + 3	50 + 50 + 52	2,000 + 46
80 − 2	155 − 3	2,100 − 54
100 − 22	200 − 48	1,000 + 1,000 + 20 + 20 + 6

Try It

Write two other names for each number.

29. 45 **30.** 215 **31.** 698 **32.** 1,523 **33.** 4,267

34. 61 **35.** 992 **36.** 457 **37.** 29 **38.** 3,514

39. 2,199 **40.** 53 **41.** 95 **42.** 722 **43.** 816

44. 375 **45.** 6,358 **46.** 186 **47.** 74 **48.** 163

Mixed Review and Test Prep

49. Maggie wants to buy a kite that costs 63¢ and a tablet that costs 24¢. She has 85¢. How much more money does she need? (Grade 2)

50. Test Prep Which number shows eight thousand ninety?

A 890

B 8,009

C 8,090

D 8,900

51. In a class survey of favorite pets, 6 students chose dogs, 7 students chose cats, and 3 students chose fish. How many students in all voted? (Grade 2)

52. Test Prep What is the value of the underlined digit in 6,4<u>7</u>2?

A 7

B 70

C 700

D 7,000

Place Value: 5 and 6 Digits

OBJECTIVE: Use place value to read and write 5- and 6-digit numbers.

Quick Review

Write each number in expanded form.

1. 672
2. 1,056
3. 980
4. 2,362
5. 9,005

Learn

PROBLEM The highest peak in California is Mount Whitney. It has a height of 14,494 feet. What is the value of the digit 1 in 14,494?

Use a place-value chart. The place to the left of the thousands place is the ten-thousands place.

TEN THOUSANDS	THOUSANDS	HUNDREDS	TENS	ONES
1	4,	4	9	4

So, the value of the digit 1 in 14,494 is 10,000.

▲ Mount Whitney is part of the mountain range called the Sierra Nevada.

You can write this number in different ways.
Standard form: 14,494
Expanded form: 10,000 + 4,000 + 400 + 90 + 4
Word form: fourteen thousand, four hundred ninety-four

Mount Whitney is in Sequoia National Park, which is next to Kings Canyon National Park. These parks have a total area of 865,952 acres.

Look at this number in a place-value chart. The place to the left of the ten-thousands place is the hundred-thousands place.

HUNDRED THOUSANDS	TEN THOUSANDS	THOUSANDS	HUNDREDS	TENS	ONES
8	6	5,	9	5	2

You can write this number in different ways.
Standard form: 865,952
Expanded form: 800,000 + 60,000 + 5,000 + 900 + 50 + 2
Word form: eight hundred sixty-five thousand, nine hundred fifty-two

Remember
Put a comma between the thousands place and the hundreds place.
865,952
↑
comma

Guided Practice

1. Complete the expanded form for 17,598.   10,000 + ■ + 500 + 90 + ■

Write the value of the underlined digit.

2. 140,278 3. 52,167 4. 23,890 5. 574,302

6. TALK Math **Explain** how to show the value of each digit in the number 623,714.

Independent Practice and Problem Solving

Write the value of the underlined digit.

7. 72,180 8. 826,351 9. 265,817 10. 19,342

Write each number in standard form.

11. 200,000 + 500 + 90 + 4

12. 60,000 + 8,000 + 700 + 40 + 3

13. nine hundred twelve thousand, two hundred six

USE DATA For 14–15, use the graph.

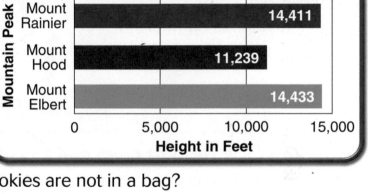

Mountain Heights

Mountain Peak	Height in Feet
Mount Rainier	14,411
Mount Hood	11,239
Mount Elbert	14,433

Height in Feet: 0, 5,000, 10,000, 15,000

14. Write the height of Mount Rainier in expanded form.

15. Find the height of Mount Hood. What is the value of the digit in the hundreds place?

16. **Reasoning** Tammy baked 21 cookies. She ate 2 cookies and put the rest in bags with 3 cookies in each bag. How many cookies are not in a bag?

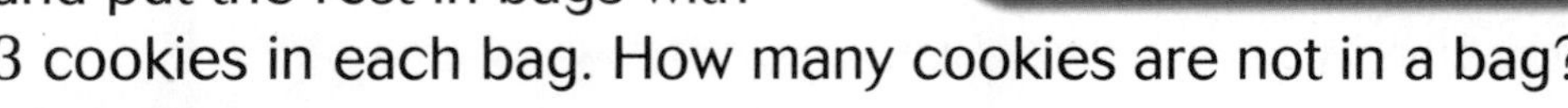

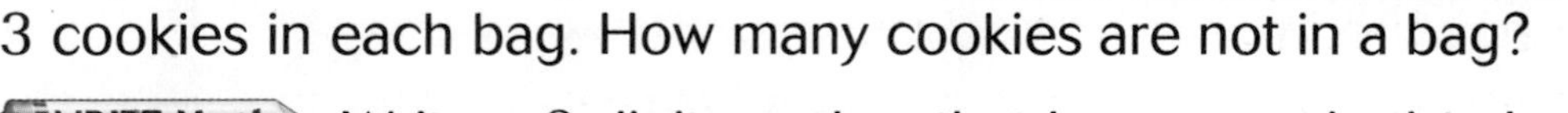

17. WRITE Math Write a 6-digit number that has a zero in the thousands place. **Explain** how to write your number in expanded form.

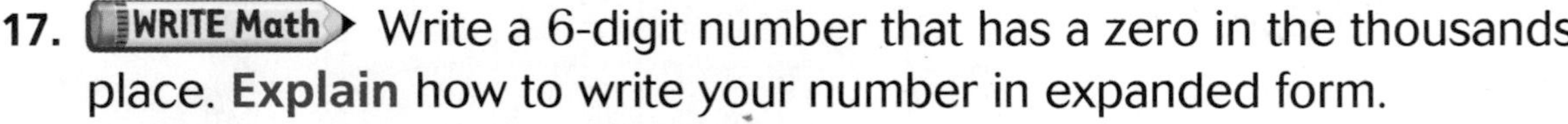

Mixed Review and Test Prep

18. Derek walks home from school in 15 minutes. School gets out at 3:30. At what time does Derek get home? (Grade 2)

19. Beth's dog weighs 18 pounds more than her cat. Her cat weighs 9 pounds. How much does Beth's dog weigh? (Grade 2)

20. **Test Prep** How is 43,867 written in expanded form?

A 4,000 + 800 + 60 + 7

B 40,000 + 800 + 60 + 7

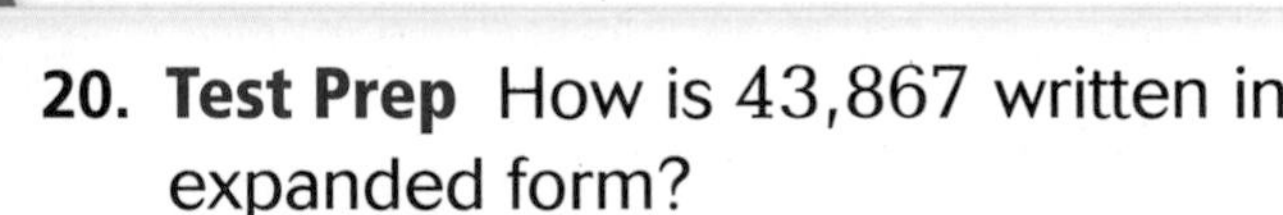

C 40,000 + 3,000 + 60 + 7

D 40,000 + 3,000 + 800 + 60 + 7

Extra Practice on page 20, Set D

Problem Solving Workshop
Strategy: Use Logical Reasoning

OBJECTIVE: Solve problems by using the strategy *use logical reasoning*.

Learn the Strategy

Logical reasoning can help you solve problems. When you use logical reasoning, you compare facts and think about clues.

Sometimes the facts or clues can be organized in a list.

Vince plays soccer. The players on his team have the numbers 1 to 11 on their uniforms.

Vince's uniform has an odd number.

His number is greater than 6.

You can skip-count by threes to find his number.

What is Vince's number?

1 2 3 4 5 6 7 8 9 10 11

Sometimes the facts or clues can be put in a table or chart.

Sue, Rick, and Heather were in a race.

Sue finished first.

Rick did not finish second.

In what position did Heather finish?

	1st	2nd	3rd
Sue	yes	no	no
Rick	no	no	yes
Heather	no	yes	no

TALK Math

Explain why there is a *yes* for Heather in the second column.

Use the Strategy

PROBLEM Anna used a riddle for the invitations to her birthday party. Her friends had to use the clues at the right to find her address on Pine Street.

My address is a 2-digit number. The number is greater than 80. The sum of the digits is 15. The ones digit is 1 less than the tens digit.

What is my address?

You're Invited!

Read to Understand
Plan
Solve
Check

Read to Understand

- **Use a graphic aid to understand the clues.**
- **What information is given?**

Plan

- **What strategy can you use to solve the problem?**
  You can use logical reasoning.

Solve

- **How can you use the strategy to solve the problem?**
  Look at one clue at a time. Use a hundred chart.

  The number has two digits, so cross out 1 through 9 and 100. The number is greater than 80, so cross out 80 and all the numbers less than 80.

1	2	3	4	5	6	7	8	9	10
11	12	13	14	15	16	17	18	19	20
21	22	23	24	25	26	27	28	29	30
31	32	33	34	35	36	37	38	39	40
41	42	43	44	45	46	47	48	49	50
51	52	53	54	55	56	57	58	59	60
61	62	63	64	65	66	67	68	69	70
71	72	73	74	75	76	77	78	79	80
81	82	83	84	85	86	87	88	89	90
91	92	93	94	95	96	97	98	99	100

  Add the digits of each number that is not crossed out. Circle the numbers with digits whose sum is 15.

81	82	83	84	85	86	87	88	89	90
91	92	93	94	95	96	97	98	99	100

  Find the circled number with a ones digit that is 1 less than its tens digit.

  96 → 9 − 6 = 3 ✗

  87 → 8 − 7 = 1 ✓

  So, Anna's address is 87 Pine Street.

Check

- **How do you know your answer is correct?**

Guided Problem Solving

Read to Understand
Plan
Solve
Check

1. Anna wants to mail an invitation to Steve. He gave her his address on Oak Road in the riddle below.

- My address is a 2-digit number between 46 and 64.
- The sum of the digits is 12.
- The ones digit is 2 more than the tens digit.

What is Steve's address?

First, use a copy of a hundred chart and read the first clue. Cross out numbers less than 46 and greater than 64.

Then, add the digits of each number not crossed out. Circle the numbers whose sum is 12.

Finally, use the last clue to find Steve's address.

1	2	3	4	5	6	7	8	9	10
11	12	13	14	15	16	17	18	19	20
21	22	23	24	25	26	27	28	29	30
31	32	33	34	35	36	37	38	39	40
41	42	43	44	45	46	47	48	49	50
51	52	53	54	55	56	57	58	59	60
61	62	63	64	65	66	67	68	69	70
71	72	73	74	75	76	77	78	79	80
81	82	83	84	85	86	87	88	89	90
91	92	93	94	95	96	97	98	99	100

2. **What if** the sum of the digits is 10? What is Steve's address?

3. Julie is thinking of an even number between 12 and 29. The sum of the digits is the same as the digit in the tens place. What is Julie's number?

Problem Solving Strategy Practice

Use logical reasoning to solve.

4. Use the hundred chart and the clues. Cary is thinking of an odd number between 32 and 48. The sum of the digits is 5. What is Cary's number?

5. Copy the chart and use the clues. Andy, Beth, Mary, and Rod brought Anna gifts.

Rod's gift had to be put together.
Beth's gift was not the teddy bear or the soccer ball.
Andy's gift was not the skates.
Mary's gift was the soccer ball.

What was Andy's gift?

	Skates	Puzzle	Teddy Bear	Soccer Ball
Andy	?	no	?	?
Beth	?	no	?	?
Mary	?	no	?	?
Rod	no	yes	no	no

Mixed Strategy Practice

USE DATA For 6–11, use the calendars.

6. Jami's birthday is on a Saturday in July. It is not July 7. It is not an even number. What date is Jami's birthday?

7. Carl's birthday invitations have a riddle theme. He wants his friends to find the date of his party. He gave them the following clues.

> My party is on a Friday in July.
> The date of my party is a two-digit even number.

   What date is Carl's party?

8. Michelle's birthday is June 22. Kim's birthday is 9 days before Michelle's birthday. What date is Kim's birthday?

9. Jon's birthday is June 30. Rachel's birthday is 12 days after Jon's. What date is Rachel's birthday?

10. **Open-Ended** Shawn's birthday is June 16. Mark's birthday is two weeks later. Tell two ways you could find the date of Mark's birthday.

11. **Pose a Problem** Look back at Problem 9. Write a similar problem by changing the date of Rachel's birthday.

Choose a STRATEGY

- Draw a Diagram or Picture
- Make a Model or Act It Out
- Make an Organized List
- Find a Pattern
- Make a Table or Graph
- Predict and Test
- Work Backward
- Solve a Simpler Problem
- Write a Number Sentence
- Use Logical Reasoning

June

Sun	Mon	Tue	Wed	Thu	Fri	Sat
					1	2
3	4	5	6	7	8	9
10	11	12	13	14	15	16
17	18	19	20	21	22	23
24	25	26	27	28	29	30

July

Sun	Mon	Tue	Wed	Thu	Fri	Sat
1	2	3	4	5	6	7
8	9	10	11	12	13	14
15	16	17	18	19	20	21
22	23	24	25	26	27	28
29	30	31				

CHALLENGE YOURSELF

Thirteen children in Kim's class have a birthday in either June, July, or August.

12. Two more children have a birthday in July than in June. In July and August there are the same number of birthdays. How many children have a birthday in August?

13. Michael's birthday falls on a Thursday in August. The sum of the digits of his birthday is 5. **Explain** how you know when Michael's birthday is.

Extra Practice

Set A Find the number that point *X* represents on the number line. (pp. 6–7)

1. 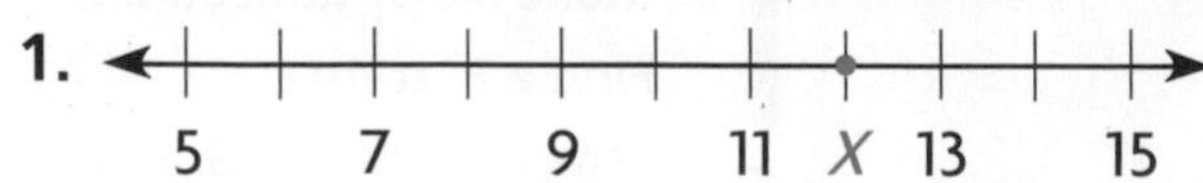

2. 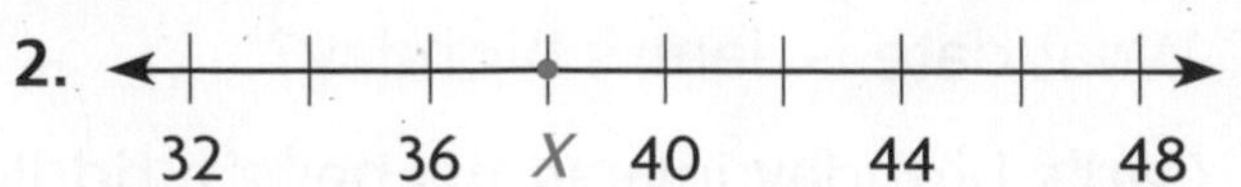

Set B Write the value of the underlined digit. (pp. 8–9)

1. 67$\underline{2}$
2. $\underline{1}$58
3. 8$\underline{9}$0
4. $\underline{4}$35
5. There are 253 students in Talia's school. How do you write the number in expanded form?
6. There are 922 seats in the theater. What is the value of the digit 9 in 922?

Set C Write each number in standard form. (pp. 10–13)

1. 4,000 + 800 + 10 + 3
2. 9,000 + 600 + 50 + 2
3. 7,000 + 20 + 2
4. Mr. Price drove 2,947 miles in one week. What is the value of the digit 2 in 2,947?
5. The library has 7,163 children's books. How do you write 7,163 in expanded form?

Write each number in expanded form.

6. 2,064
7. 5,839
8. 6,127
9. 3,905

Set D Write the value of the underlined digit. (pp. 14–15)

1. 1$\underline{3}$,781
2. 8$\underline{4}$0,526
3. $\underline{5}$71,903
4. 7$\underline{1}$4,200

Write each number in standard form.

5. eighty thousand, seven hundred ninety-six
6. two hundred fifteen thousand, thirty
7. 10,000 + 6,000 + 400 + 90 + 7
8. 400,000 + 5,000 + 800 + 2

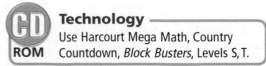

Technology
CD ROM
Use Harcourt Mega Math, Country Countdown, *Block Busters*, Levels S, T.

TECHNOLOGY CONNECTION

*i*Tools: Base-Ten Blocks

Use Base-Ten Blocks to Show Numbers.

Bob has 6 hundreds, 8 tens, and 16 ones. What number does this show?

Step 1	Click on *Base-Ten Blocks*. Then click on the third tab at the bottom. Click on *Hide*.
Step 2	Click on the hundreds block at the left. Click 6 times in the hundreds column. Do the same thing with 8 tens and 16 ones. If you make a mistake, click on the eraser.
Step 3	Click on *Line Up* at the bottom. Then click on the *Regroup* arrow in the **ones** column. Ten **ones** blocks will group together and move to the tens column.
Step 4	Count the hundreds, tens, and ones blocks. Write the 3-digit number. Click on *Show* to check your answer.

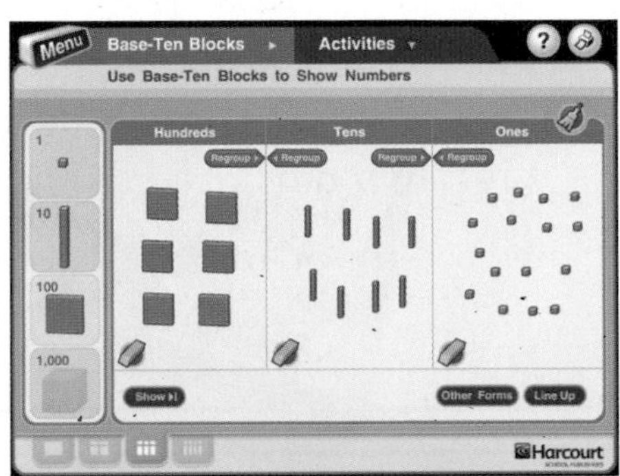

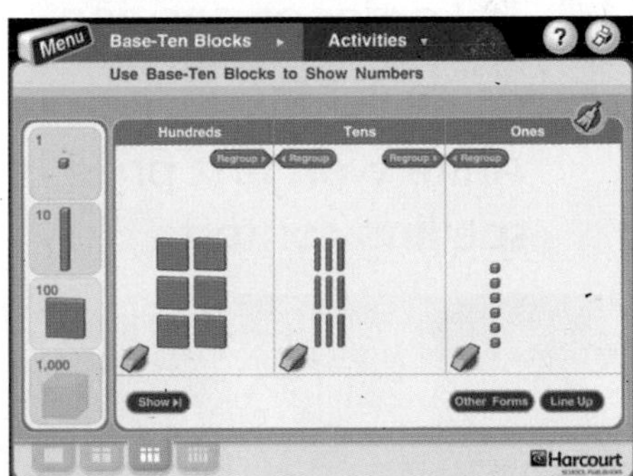

So, Bob's number is 696.
Click on the broom to clear the workspace.

Try It

Follow the steps above to make each 3-digit number.

1. 7 hundreds, 12 tens, 6 ones
2. 3 hundreds, 5 tens, 14 ones

Use Base-Ten Blocks to show each number.

3. 825
4. 917
5. 256
6. 379
7. 568
8. **Explore More** Karen has 4 hundreds, 9 tens, and 11 ones. Benson has 3 hundreds, 19 tens, and 12 ones. Use Base-Ten Blocks to show the numbers. Who has the greater number? **Explain.**

Technology
*i*Tools available online or on CD-Rom

MATH POWER Ways to Use Numbers

Numbers are used in many ways.

Examples

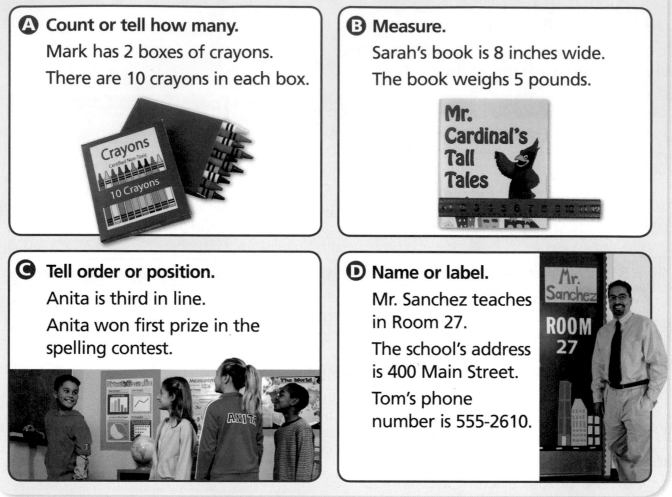

A Count or tell how many.

Mark has 2 boxes of crayons.

There are 10 crayons in each box.

B Measure.

Sarah's book is 8 inches wide.

The book weighs 5 pounds.

C Tell order or position.

Anita is third in line.

Anita won first prize in the spelling contest.

D Name or label.

Mr. Sanchez teaches in Room 27.

The school's address is 400 Main Street.

Tom's phone number is 555-2610.

Try It

Tell how each number is used. Write *count, measure, position,* or *label*.

1. 

2. 

3. 

4. **WRITE Math** Write a list of things you did to get ready for school this morning. In your list, use numbers that tell order.

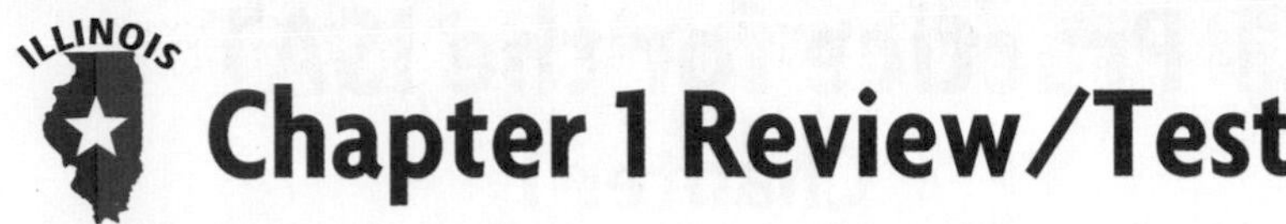

Chapter 1 Review/Test

Check Vocabulary and Concepts

VOCABULARY
digits even odd
standard form
expanded form

Choose the best term from the box.

1. Numbers ending with 2, 4, 6, 8, or 0 are __?__ numbers. IL 6.3.08 (p. 5)
2. There are five __?__ in the number 57,390. IL 6.3.01 (p. 14)
3. Numbers ending with 1, 3, 5, 7, or 9 are __?__ numbers. IL 6.3.08 (p. 5)
4. The __?__ of three hundred seventeen is 317. IL 6.3.02

Check Skills

Use a hundred chart. Find the next number in the pattern. IL 8.3.01 (pp. 4–5)

5. 3, 6, 9, 12, ■
6. 65, 70, 75, 80, ■

Find the number that point *X* represents on each number line. IL 6.3.07 (pp. 6–7)

7. 11 13 *X* 15 17 19

8. 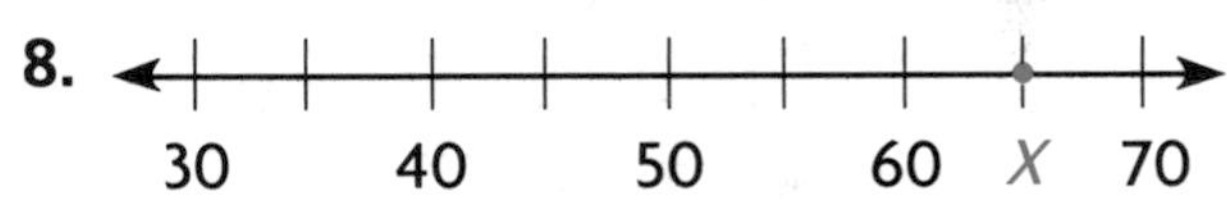

Write the value of the underlined digit. IL 6.3.01 (pp. 8–9, 10–13, 14–15)

9. $\underline{7}$6,521
10. 1,$\underline{9}$64
11. 3$\underline{8}$,795
12. 63,4$\underline{2}$8

Write each number in standard form. IL 6.3.02 (pp. 8–9, 10–13, 14–15)

13. five hundred thirty-two
14. seven thousand, three hundred five
15. 5,000 + 100 + 40 + 8
16. 60,000 + 2,000 + 10 + 7
17. eighty-four thousand, sixteen
18. 3,000 + 900 + 20 + 6

Check Problem Solving

For 19, use the table. Solve. IL 6.03.01 (pp. 16–19)

19. Jack's score is a 4-digit number. The hundreds digit is an even number. The tens digit is odd. What is his score?

Game Scores	
Players	**Scores**
Player A	4,602
Player B	897
Player C	3,415

20. **WRITE Math** Beth, Sasha, Jake, and Tyrone ran in a race. Tyrone finished first. Sasha did not finish second. Beth finished last. **Explain** how you can tell in which place Jake finished.

GO ONLINE **Technology** Use *Online Assessment.*

Practice for the ISAT
Chapter 1

Number and Operations

1. Lily put 43 marbles in a jar. Joe put 28 marbles in the jar. How many marbles did Lily and Joe put in the jar all together? Grade 2

   A 15

   B 25

   C 61

   D 71

Choose the answer.

See item 2. If your answer doesn't match one of the choices, check your computation.

2. $53 - 26 =$ Grade 2

   A 23 C 33

   B 27 D 77

3. Which fraction of this shape is shaded? Grade 2

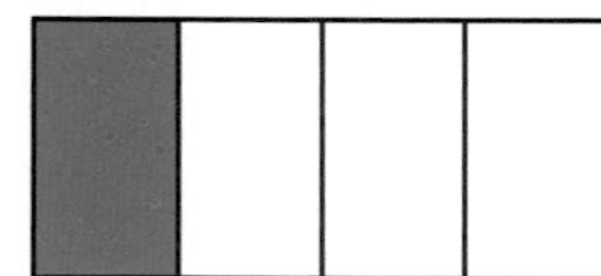

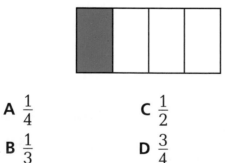

   A $\frac{1}{4}$ C $\frac{1}{2}$

   B $\frac{1}{3}$ D $\frac{3}{4}$

4. WRITE Math **Explain** how you can find the value of the digit 6 in the number 16,782. IL 6.3.01 (p. 14)

Algebra

5. Which addition fact helps you find the difference? Grade 2

$$17 - 9 = \blacksquare$$

   A $10 + 10 = 20$

   B $8 + 9 = 17$

   C $4 + 4 = 8$

   D $1 + 7 = 8$

6. What is the next number in the pattern? IL 8.3.01 (p. 4)

$$20, 24, 28, 32, \blacksquare$$

   A 30 C 36

   B 34 D 37

7. What number makes this number sentence true? Grade 2

$$9 + \blacksquare = 14$$

   A 7 C 5

   B 6 D 4

8. WRITE Math Find the difference. Grade 2

$$70¢ - 24¢$$

   Explain how you can check your answer by using addition.

Measurement

9. What is the area of the figure? Grade 2

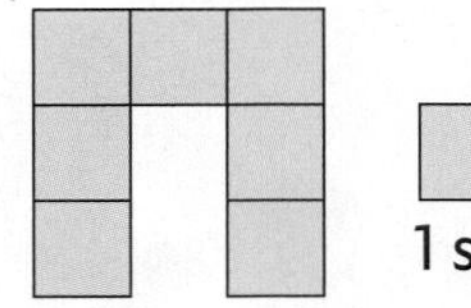

A 6 units

B 7 units

C 8 units

D 9 units

10. Use the inch ruler. About how long is the nail? Grade 2

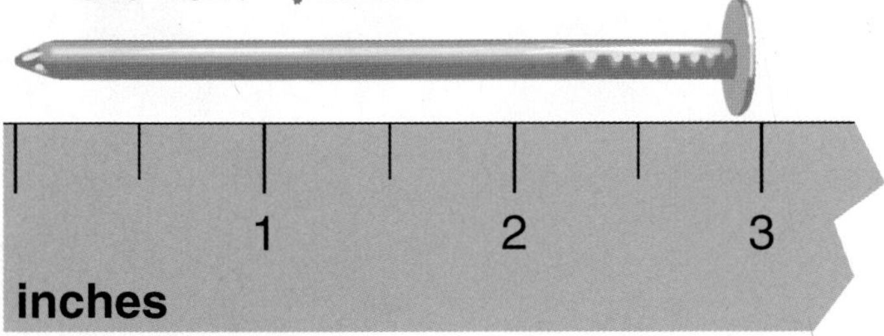

A 1 inch

B 2 inches

C 3 inches

D 4 inches

11. WRITE Math Does a bag of apples weigh about 5 ounces or about 5 pounds? **Explain** how you know. Grade 2

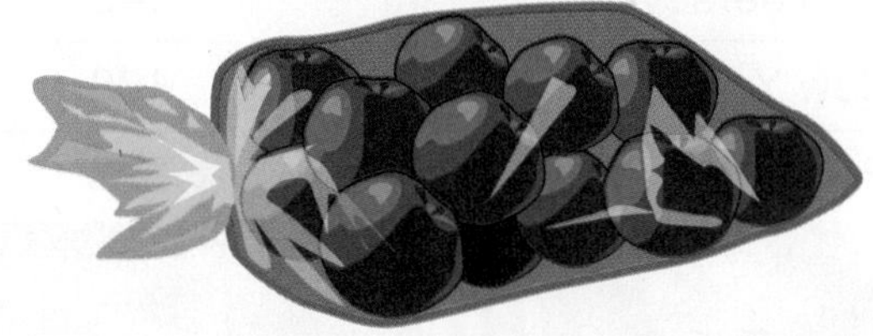

Data Analysis and Probability

12. How many more boxes of cookies were sold in Week 2 than Week 3? Grade 2

Cookie Sales	
Week	**Number of Boxes Sold**
1	15
2	25
3	20
4	10

A 5

B 10

C 15

D 20

13. How many students voted for their favorite fruit all together? Grade 2

Favorite Fruit	
Place	**Votes**
Banana	卌 卌 I
Grapes	卌 卌 卌
Apple	卌 卌 III

A 21

B 26

C 28

D 39

14. WRITE Math From which bag is it more likely to pull a red tile than a blue tile? **Explain.** Grade 2

Bag A

Bag B

CHAPTER 2

Compare, Order, and Round Numbers

FAST FACT

The Ohio State Capitol building, in Columbus, Ohio, is 158 feet tall and is about 150 years old. The floor in one of its rooms is covered with about 5,000 pieces of marble.

Investigate

How does the height of each capitol building compare to the height of the Ohio State Capitol? Round the height of each building to the nearest hundred, and then compare. Explain why you may not want to compare rounded heights.

Heights of State Capitol Buildings

State	Height in Feet
Michigan	267
Mississippi	180
New Jersey	145
New York	108
Pennsylvania	272

Technology
Student pages are available in the Student eBook.

Show What You Know

Check your understanding of important skills needed for success in Chapter 2.

▶ Order on a Number Line to 100

Write the numbers in order from least to greatest.

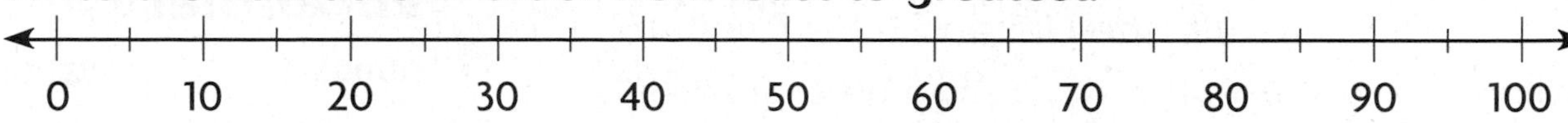

1. 27, 34, 22
2. 41, 38, 50
3. 80, 90, 60
4. 83, 86, 72
5. 20, 14, 19
6. 61, 52, 68

▶ Compare 2-Digit Numbers Using Place Value

Write <, >, or = for each ●.

7. 15 ● 23
8. 77 ● 58
9. 31 ● 34
10. 82 ● 82
11. 91 ● 19
12. 46 ● 61
13. 27 ● 28
14. 45 ● 40
15. 53 ● 63

VOCABULARY POWER

CHAPTER VOCABULARY

compare
equal to =
greater than >
less than <
order
round

WARM-UP WORDS

greater than > A symbol used to compare two numbers, with the greater number given first

less than < A symbol used to compare two numbers, with the lesser number given first

round To replace a number with another number that tells about how many or how much

LESSON 1

Compare Numbers

OBJECTIVE: Use models, place value, and number lines to compare 3-, 4-, and 5-digit numbers.

Quick Review

Write the greater number.

1. 9 or 12
2. 8 or 3
3. 22 or 25
4. 29 or 39
5. 68 or 91

Vocabulary

compare **equal to =** **less than <** **greater than >**

Learn

PROBLEM The State Capitol Building in Springfield, Illinois, is 361 feet tall. The United States Capitol Building in Washington, D.C., is 288 feet tall. Which building is taller?

You can **compare** numbers in different ways to find which number is greater.

greater than > **less than <** **equal to =**

ONE WAY **Use base-ten blocks.**

Compare from left to right.

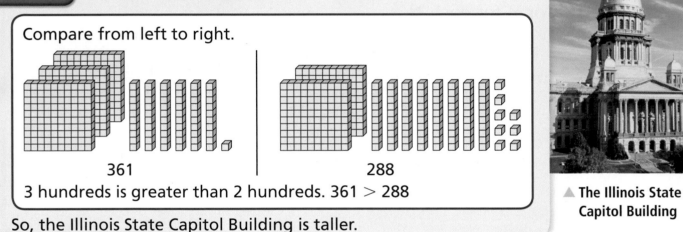

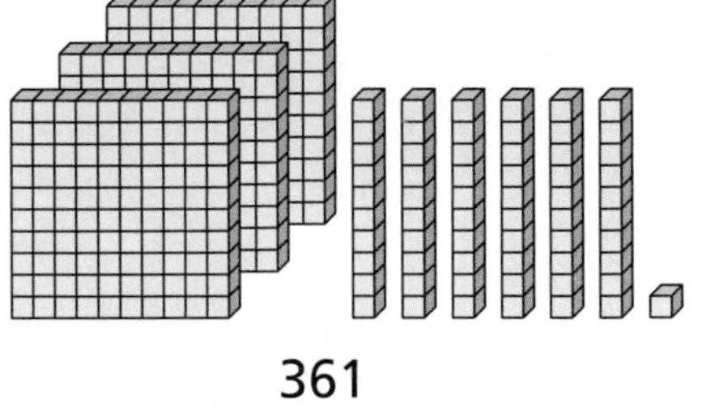

361 288

3 hundreds is greater than 2 hundreds. 361 > 288

So, the Illinois State Capitol Building is taller.

▲ The Illinois State Capitol Building

OTHER WAYS

A Use a number line.

The numbers are in order from least to greatest.

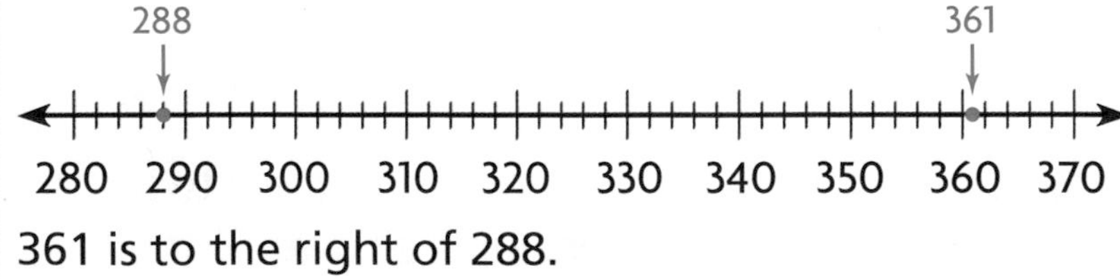

361 is to the right of 288.
361 > 288

B Use a place-value chart.

Compare digits in the same place-value position from left to right.

HUNDREDS	TENS	ONES
3	6	1
2	8	8

↑

3 hundreds is greater than 2 hundreds. 361 > 288.

Compare 4- and 5-Digit Numbers

Example

Compare 1,324 and 1,249.

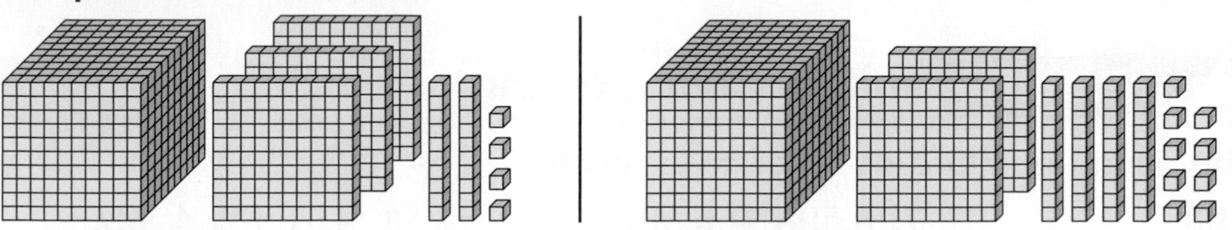

The thousands are the same, so compare the hundreds.
3 hundreds is greater than 2 hundreds. So, 1,324 > 1,249.

More Examples

Ⓐ Compare 3,158 and 3,372.

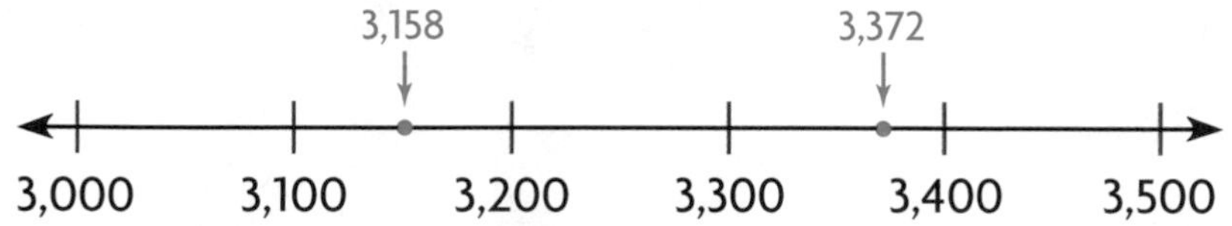

3,158 is to the left of 3,372. So 3,158 < 3,372.

Ⓑ Compare 27,468 and 27,513.

TEN THOUSANDS	THOUSANDS	HUNDREDS	TENS	ONES
2	7,	4	6	8
2	7,	5	1	3
↑ Ten thousands are the same.	↑ Thousands are the same.	↑ 5 > 4		

So, 27,468 < 27,513.

- In Example B, what if you were comparing 27,468 and 9,563? Explain why you do not need to compare the thousands, the hundreds, the tens, and the ones.

Guided Practice

1. Which number has more hundreds? Which number is greater?

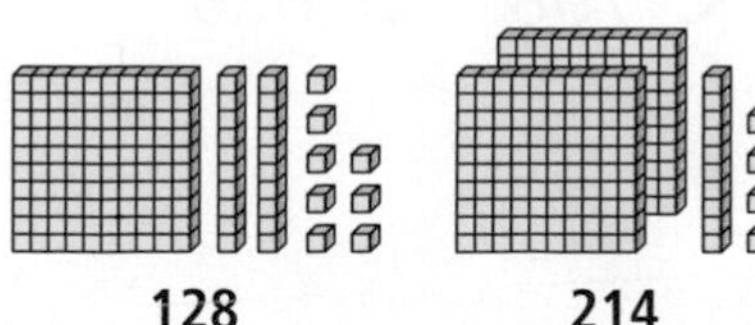

Compare the numbers. Write <, >, or = for each ●.

2. 567 ● 567 ✓3. 5,228 ● 5,628 ✓4. 1,004 ● 789

5. TALK Math **Explain** two ways to compare 368 and 386.

Independent Practice and Problem Solving

Compare the numbers. Write <, >, or = for each ●.

6. 485 ● 98
7. 6,598 ● 6,587
8. 4,165 ● 4,327
9. 2,000 ● 487
10. 521 ● 521
11. 75,362 ● 73,659
12. 3,446 ● 3,446
13. 38,047 ● 39,102
14. 8,389 ● 8,398

USE DATA For 15–17, use the table.

15. Compare the heights of the tallest buildings in Texas and California.
16. Compare the heights of the Key Tower and One Liberty Place.
17. WRITE Math **What's the Error?** Dana compared 947 and 1,002. She says 947 is greater than 1,002 because 9 is greater than 1. What was Dana's error?
18. ***FAST FACT*** • The tallest building in Indiana, the Chase Tower, is 830 feet tall. The tallest building in New Jersey, the Goldman Sachs Tower, is 781 feet tall. Compare the heights.

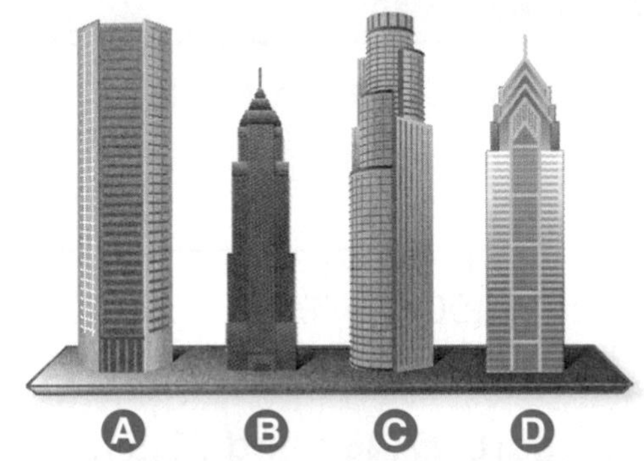

Tallest Buildings in 4 States

State	Building	Height in Feet
Texas	Ⓐ JPMorgan Chase Tower	1,002
Ohio	Ⓑ Key Tower	947
California	Ⓒ U.S. Bank Tower	1,018
Pennsylvania	Ⓓ One Liberty Place	945

Mixed Review and Test Prep

19. Sarah said that it is 278 days until her birthday. What is 278 written in expanded form? (p. 8)
20. **Test Prep** Which number is greater than 822?

    A 637 **B** 743 **C** 798 **D** 826

21. Karen read a book that had 1,028 pages. Is 1,028 an even number or an odd number? What is the value of the 2 in 1,028? (pp. 5, 11)

Technology
Use Harcourt Mega Math, Country Countdown, *Harrison's Comparisons,* Levels L and M; Fraction Action, *Number Line Mine,* Level B.

Extra Practice on page 40, Set A

Write to Explain

Justin is using data from the table to compare the heights of the Chrysler Building and the John Hancock Center. He wants to find out which building is taller.

This is how Justin explained how he compared the heights of the buildings.

Aon Center Empire State Building Chrysler Building John Hancock Sears Tower

First, I looked at the table to find the heights of the Chrysler Building and John Hancock Center.

Next, I recorded the heights of the buildings.

Chrysler Building	*1,046 feet*
John Hancock Center	*1,127 feet*

Tall Buildings in the United States

Building	City	Height in feet
Aon Center	Chicago	1,136
Chrysler Building	New York	1,046
Empire State Building	New York	1,250
John Hancock Center	Chicago	1,127
Sears Tower	Chicago	1,450

Then, I compared the heights. Since both numbers have a 1 in the thousands place, I compared the hundreds digits. The John Hancock Center has a 1 and the Chrysler Building has a 0 in the hundreds place. Since $1 > 0$, I know that the John Hancock Center is taller than the Chrysler Building.

Tips

To write an explanation:

- Write the steps you took to solve the problem.
- Use words such as *first*, *next*, and *then*.
- State your answer in the last sentence of your explanation.

Problem Solving Use the data in the table. Explain how to solve each problem.

1. Is the Aon Center or the John Hancock Center taller?
2. Is the Sears Tower or the Empire State Building taller?

LESSON 2

Order Numbers

OBJECTIVE: Use a number line and place value to order 3-, 4-, and 5-digit numbers.

Quick Review

Compare. Write <, >, or = for each ●.

1. 435 ● 657
2. 319 ● 310
3. 858 ● 886
4. 5,498 ● 5,498
5. 2,000 ● 999

Vocabulary

order

Learn

When you **order** numbers, you write them from least to greatest or from greatest to least.

PROBLEM For a science project, Ben listed in a table the number of bones in a cat, a human, and a dog. Which animal has the greatest number of bones?

Bones	
Animal	**Number**
Cat	230
Human	206
Dog	321

ONE WAY Use a number line.

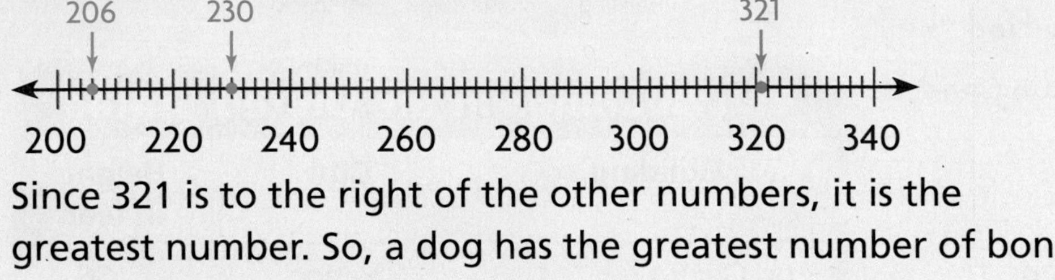

Since 321 is to the right of the other numbers, it is the greatest number. So, a dog has the greatest number of bones.

ANOTHER WAY Use place value.

Example 1 **Order 2,387; 2,475; and 2,190 from least to greatest.**

Step 1	Step 2
2,387 2,475 2,190 Compare the thousands. 2 = 2 = 2	2,387 2,475 2,190 Compare the hundreds. 1 < 3 < 4

So, the order is 2,190; 2,387; 2,475.

Example 2 **Order 54,926; 56,718; and 55,302 from greatest to least.**

Step 1	Step 2
54,926 56,718 55,302 Compare the ten thousands. 5 = 5 = 5	54,926 56,718 55,302 Compare the thousands. 6 > 5 > 4

So, the order is 56,718; 55,302; 54,926.

ERROR ALERT

Compare the digits with the greatest place value first.

Guided Practice

1. Use the number line to order 851, 912, and 796 from least to greatest.

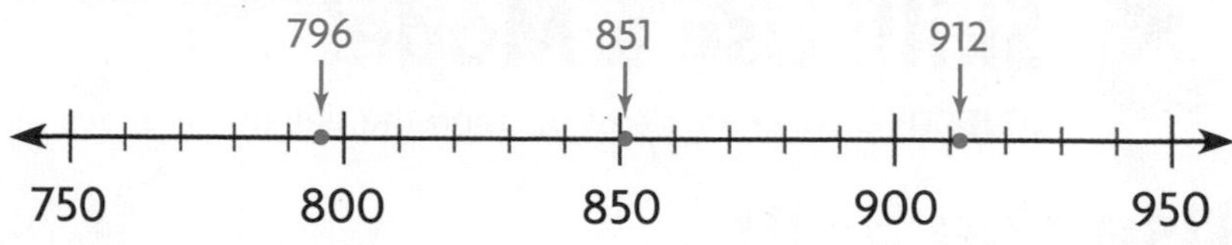

Write the numbers in order from greatest to least.

2. 540, 527, 536
3. 2,079; 2,178; 2,122
4. 20,794; 21,786; 21,157

5. TALK Math **Explain** how you know that 458, 572, and 613 are in order from least to greatest.

Independent Practice and Problem Solving

Write the numbers in order from greatest to least.

6. 310, 440, 390
7. 914, 896, 910
8. 993; 1,399; 949
9. 5,091; 5,136; 5,109
10. 3,403; 3,430; 3,034
11. 79,880; 79,188; 78,899

Write the numbers in order from least to greatest.

12. 645, 456, 654
13. 372, 452, 289
14. 898; 3,786; 3,981
15. 4,570; 4,550; 4,660
16. 9,223; 9,280; 9,275
17. 63,215; 63,149; 62,768

For 18–19, use the pictures.

18. Order the weights of the tiger, lion, and giant panda from greatest to least.
19. WRITE Math **What's the Error?** Alex ordered the three animal weights from least to greatest. He wrote 220, 330, 250. What is Alex's error? Write the weights in the correct order.

Mixed Review and Test Prep

20. Sixty thousand, seventy-eight people attended a football game. Write this number in standard form. (p. 14)
21. Casey, Ben, and Ted ran a race. Casey did not finish last. Ted finished before Casey. Who finished first? (p. 16)
22. **Test Prep** Which number is less than 408 but greater than 390?

    A 400 **C** 410
    B 408 **D** 480

Extra Practice on page 40, Set B

Problem Solving Workshop
Skill: Use a Model

OBJECTIVE: Solve problems by using the skill *use a model.*

Read to Understand
Plan
Solve
Check

Use the Skill

PROBLEM A zoo has a rhinoceros that weighs 2,812 pounds, a camel that weighs 1,520 pounds, a giraffe that weighs 2,233 pounds, and a polar bear that weighs 1,450 pounds. Which animal has the second-greatest weight?

The animal weights are shown on the number line.

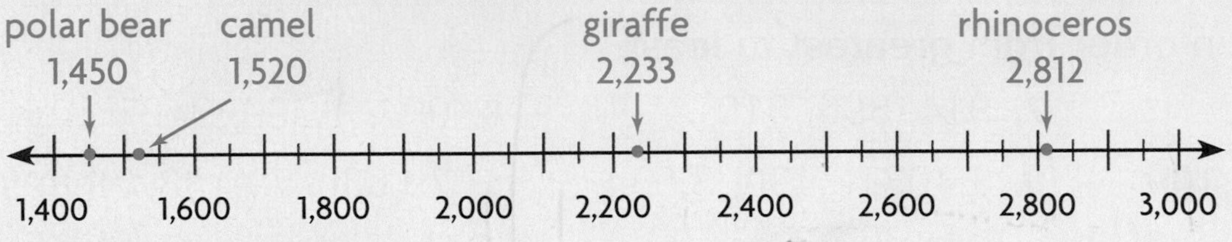

The animal with the greatest weight is on the right.

The rhinoceros has the greatest weight.
So, the giraffe has the second-greatest weight.

Think and Discuss

Use the number line to solve the problem.

a. The zoo concession stand sold 399 sodas, 438 bags of popcorn, 384 candy apples, and 420 ice-cream cones. Which item had the second-least sales?

b. The petting zoo had 1,038 visitors in May, 1,240 in June, 1,287 in July, and 952 in August. List the number of petting zoo visitors in order from greatest to least.

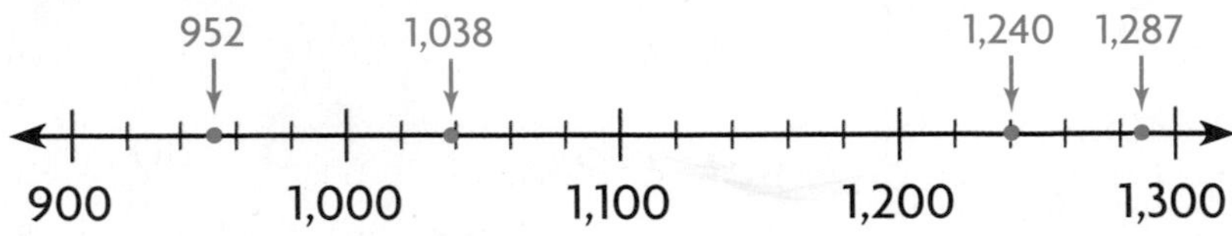

Guided Problem Solving

Use the number line to solve the problem.

1. The zoo had 2,918 visitors in May, 3,976 in June, 3,298 in July, and 2,287 in August. Which month had the least number of visitors?

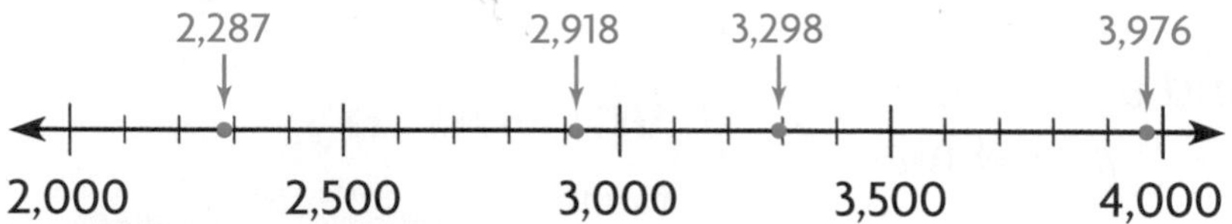

Use the number line.

Think: Where would the least number be on the number line?

2. **What if** there were 2,283 visitors in September? Which month would have had the least number of visitors?

3. The bird show had 2,498 visitors in June, 2,675 visitors in July, and 2,189 visitors in August. Write the number of visitors at the bird show in order from greatest to least.

Mixed Applications

USE DATA For 4–5, use the table.

4. Write the names of the animals in order from least to greatest number of minutes of sleep each day.

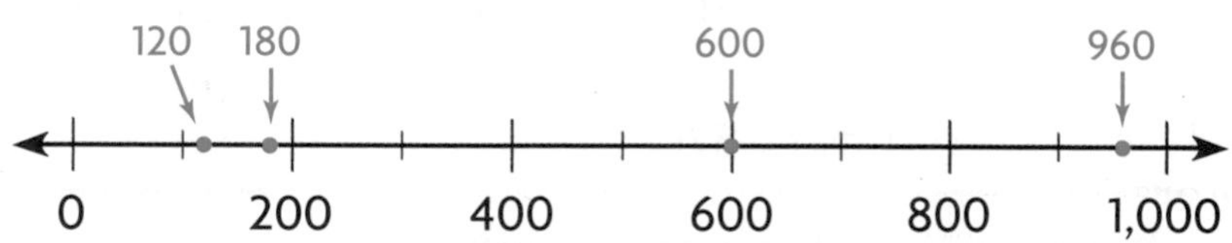

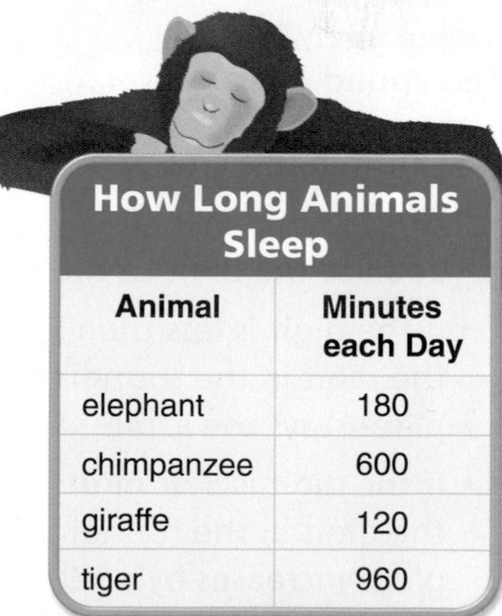

How Long Animals Sleep

Animal	Minutes each Day
elephant	180
chimpanzee	600
giraffe	120
tiger	960

5. How many more minutes each day does a tiger sleep than a chimpanzee?

6. Kelly bought 2 pencils for 25¢ each and an eraser for 50¢ in the zoo gift shop. How much did Kelly spend in all?

7. Hector's family lives 46 miles from the zoo. They have driven 28 miles. How many more miles do they have to drive to reach the zoo?

Round to the Nearest Ten and Hundred

OBJECTIVE: Use the number line and rounding rules to round numbers to the nearest ten and nearest hundred.

Quick Review

1. Is 17 closer to 10 or to 20?
2. Is 42 closer to 40 or to 50?
3. Is 66 closer to 60 or to 70?
4. Is 33 closer to 30 or to 40?
5. Is 77 closer to 70 or to 80?

Vocabulary

round

Learn

When you **round** a number, you find a number that tells you *about* how much or *about* how many.

PROBLEM Carlos has collected 317 baseball cards. To the nearest ten and to the nearest hundred, about how many baseball cards does Carlos have?

ONE WAY Use a number line.

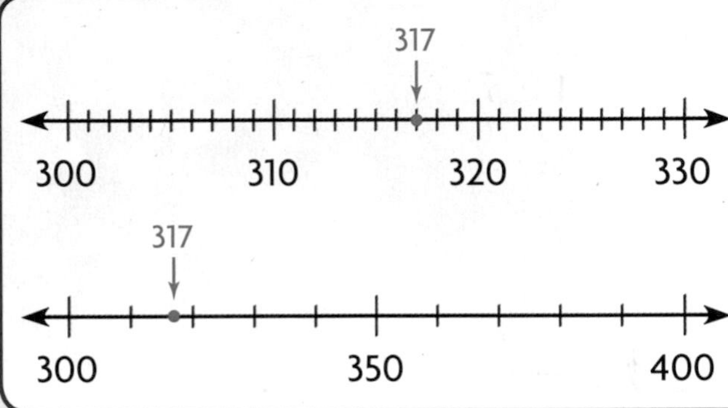

317 is closer to 320 than to 310.
So, to the nearest ten, 317 rounds to 320.

317 is closer to 300 than to 400.
So, to the nearest hundred, 317 rounds to 300.

ANOTHER WAY **Use rounding rules.**

- Find the place to which you want to round.
- Look at the digit to the right.
- If the digit is less than 5, the digit in the rounding place stays the same.
- If the digit is 5 or more, the digit in the rounding place increases by one.
- Write a zero for the digit to the right.

Examples

Round 672 to the nearest ten.

672
↑ (ones digit)

Look at the ones digit.

Since the ones digit is less than 5, the tens digit stays the same. Write a zero for the digit to the right.
So, 672 rounds to 670.

Round 672 to the nearest hundred.

672
↑ (tens digit)

Look at the tens digit.

Since the tens digit is greater than 5, the hundreds digit increases by 1. Write a zero for each digit to the right.
So, 672 rounds to 700.

Guided Practice

1. Use the number line. Is 458 closer to 450 or to 460?

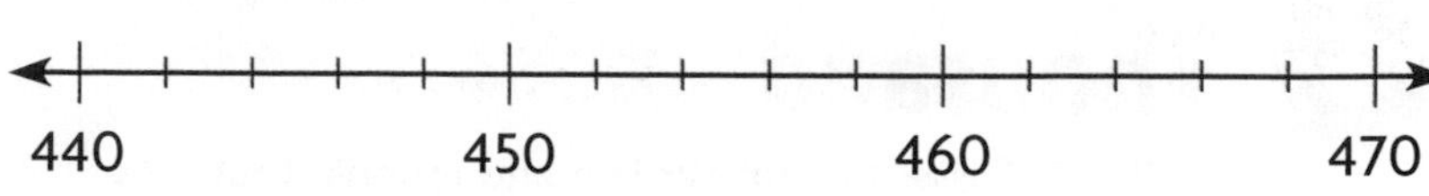

Round the number to the nearest ten and to the nearest hundred.

2. 128 3. 361 4. 835 5. 657 ✓6. 232 ✓7. 944

8. TALK Math **Explain** how you would round 726 to the nearest ten and to the nearest hundred.

Independent Practice and Problem Solving

Round the number to the nearest ten and to the nearest hundred.

9. 152 10. 576 11. 298 12. 663 13. 791 14. 499

15. 283 16. 364 17. 519 18. 455 19. 844 20. 172

USE DATA For 21–22 and 26, use the table.

21. What is the number of dog stickers rounded to the nearest ten?

22. Round the number of horse stickers to the nearest ten and to the nearest hundred.

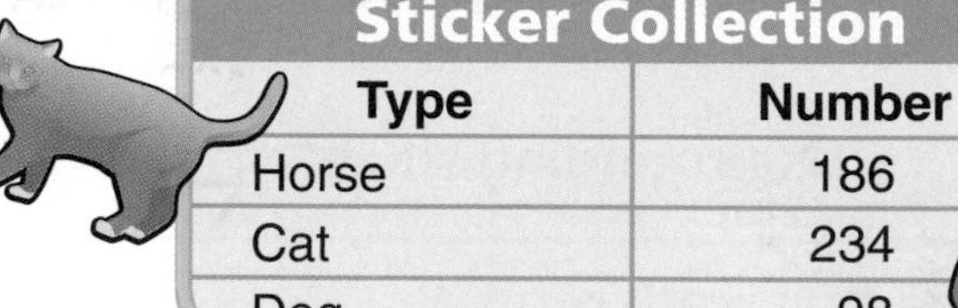

Hannah's Animal Sticker Collection

Type	Number
Horse	186
Cat	234
Dog	98

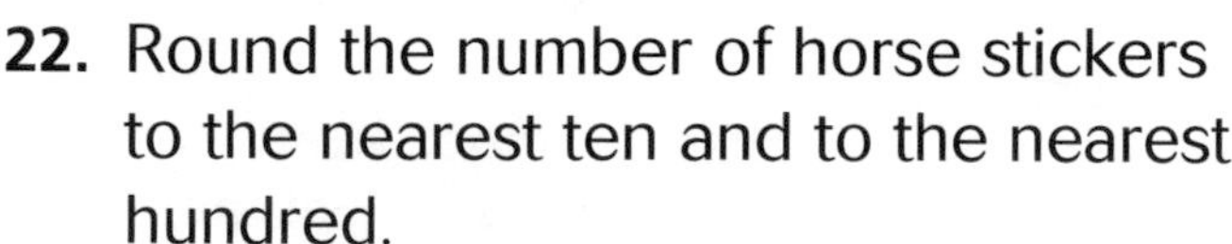

23. WRITE Math **Explain** how rounding 296 to the nearest ten and to the nearest hundred are alike.

24. **Reasoning** A 3-digit number has the digits 3, 7, and 9. To the nearest hundred, it rounds to 1,000. What is the number?

Mixed Review and Test Prep

25. Order the numbers 6,598; 6,782; and 6,516 from least to greatest. (p. 32)

26. Compare the number of horse stickers and cat stickers in Hannah's collection. (p. 28)

27. **Test Prep** The number of seashells in Stella's collection, rounded to the nearest ten, is 520. How many seashells could Stella have?

A 552 **C** 527

B 531 **D** 522

Extra Practice on page 40, Set C

LESSON

5 Round to the Nearest Thousand

OBJECTIVE: Use the number line and rounding rules to round numbers to the nearest thousand.

Quick Review

Round to the nearest hundred.

1. 514
2. 459
3. 4,387
4. 7,428
5. 3,982

Learn

PROBLEM There were 2,773 people in the world's largest pillow fight in 2004. To the nearest thousand, about how many people were in the pillow fight?

Round 2,773 to the nearest thousand.

▲ World's largest pillow fight in 2004 in Dodgeville, Wisconsin

ONE WAY **Use a number line.**

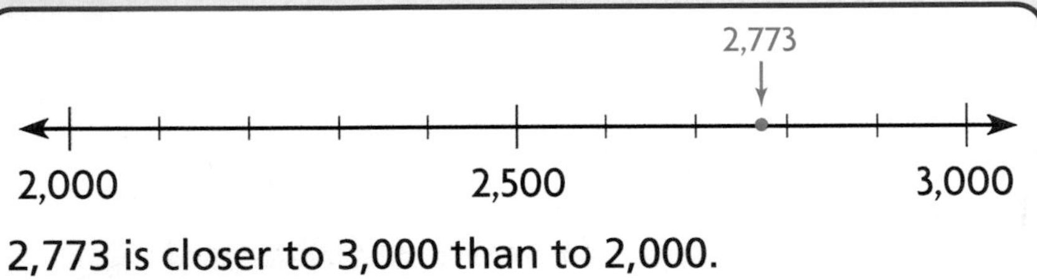

2,773 is closer to 3,000 than to 2,000.
2,773 rounds to 3,000.

So, there were about 3,000 people in the pillow fight.

ANOTHER WAY **Use rounding rules.**

Look at the hundreds digit.

2,773
↑

Since 7 > 5, the thousands digit increases by 1.
Write a zero for each digit to the right.

So, 2,773 rounds to 3,000.

Math Idea
Always look at the digit to the right of the rounding digit.

Examples

A **Round 6,429 to the nearest thousand.**

Look at the hundreds digit.

6,429
↑

Since 4 < 5, the thousands digit stays the same.

So, 6,429 rounds to 6,000.

B **Round 4,591 to the nearest ten, hundred, and thousand.**

Look at the ones digit. 1 < 5, so 4,591 rounds to 4,590.

Look at the tens digit. 9 > 5, so 4,591 rounds to 4,600.

Look at the hundreds digit. 5 = 5, so 4,591 rounds to 5,000.

Guided Practice

1. Between which two thousands is 8,714? To which thousand is it closer?

Round to the nearest thousand.

2. 1,403
3. 5,148
4. 8,747
5. 2,501
6. 3,274

7. **TALK Math** **Explain** how to round 4,681 to the nearest thousand.

Independent Practice and Problem Solving

Round to the nearest thousand.

8. 5,484
9. 8,273
10. 4,593
11. 1,935
12. 2,222

Round to the nearest thousand, to the nearest hundred, and to the nearest ten.

13. 1,376
14. 2,632
15. 6,648
16. 7,051
17. 8,475

USE DATA For 18–19, use the table.

18. To the nearest thousand, about how many people played musical chairs?

19. To the nearest thousand, about how many people had a snowball fight?

Guinness World Records

Most people....	
playing musical chairs	8,238
having a snowball fight	2,473
doing a tap-dance routine	6,952

20. **WRITE Math** **What's the Question?** A total of 1,927 people performed sign language at the same time to the same song. The answer is 2,000.

21. **Reasoning** When rounding to the nearest thousand, what is the greatest number that rounds to 6,000? What is the least number?

Mixed Review and Test Prep

22. What is six thousand, two hundred eight written in standard form? (p. 10)

23. What tool would Kevin use to measure how much juice his glass holds? (Grade 2)

24. **Test Prep** What is 6,871 rounded to the nearest thousand?

A 6,000 **C** 6,900

B 6,870 **D** 7,000

Extra Practice on page 40, Set D

Extra Practice

Set A **Compare the numbers. Write <, >, or = for each ●.** (pp. 28–31)

1. 867 ● 904
2. 3,281 ● 3,281
3. 43,208 ● 39,756
4. 1,882 ● 1,828
5. 71,023 ● 70,968
6. 5,618 ● 6,158
7. 65,358 ● 59,970
8. 8,945 ● 9,217
9. 14,306 ● 41,306

Set B **Write the numbers in order from least to greatest.** (pp. 32–33)

1. 526; 589; 564
2. 1,728; 1,717; 1,731
3. 8,015; 9,317; 6,273
4. 3,956; 1,516; 3,870
5. 27,990; 38,185; 19,654
6. 8,102; 5,973; 7,318
7. A farm produced 1,099 pounds of cherries in June. It produced 998 pounds of cherries in July, and another 901 pounds in August. During which month did the farm produce the most cherries?
8. Ryan saved 359 pennies. His brother Allen saved 368 pennies, and his sister Marla saved 360 pennies. Order the numbers from least to greatest.

Set C **Round the number to the nearest ten and to the nearest hundred.** (pp. 36–37)

1. 657
2. 518
3. 642
4. 109
5. 756
6. 235
7. 456
8. 313
9. 711
10. 544
11. There were 546 people at the summer concert. To the nearest hundred, about how many people attended the concert?
12. Sarah rounded 495 to the nearest hundred. Lee rounded it to another place and got the same answer. To what place did Lee round 495?

Set D **Round to the nearest thousand.** (pp. 38–39)

1. 3,333
2. 2,590
3. 4,938
4. 1,296
5. 7,557
6. 8,432
7. 5,356
8. 4,209
9. 6,750
10. 9,917
11. 1,848
12. 6,172
13. 2,691
14. 7,415
15. 8,763

CD ROM **Technology**
Use Harcourt Mega Math, Fraction Action, *Number Line Mine,* Levels B, C.

PRACTICE GAME

Building Numbers

Prepare!
3 players

Plan!
- Number cube numbered 1–6
- 1 gameboard for each player

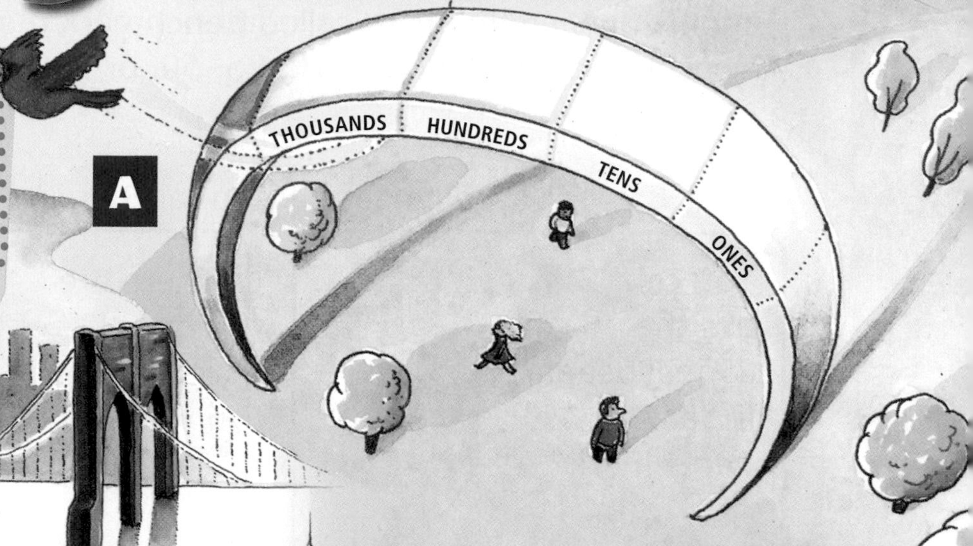

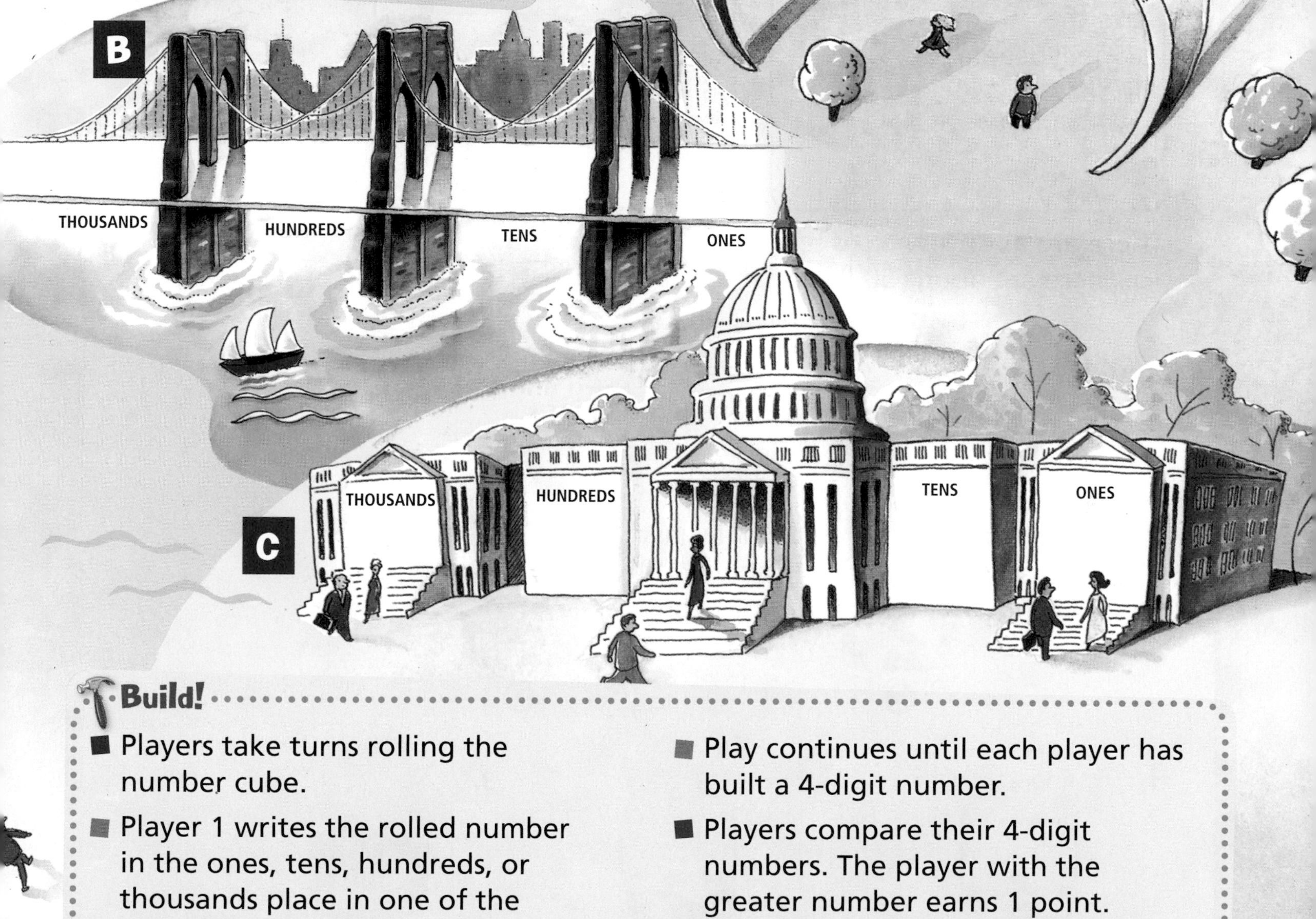

A

THOUSANDS HUNDREDS TENS ONES

B

THOUSANDS HUNDREDS TENS ONES

C

THOUSANDS HUNDREDS TENS ONES

Build!

- Players take turns rolling the number cube.
- Player 1 writes the rolled number in the ones, tens, hundreds, or thousands place in one of the place-value charts.
- Once a number is placed in a chart, it cannot be moved to another place-value position.
- Play continues until each player has built a 4-digit number.
- Players compare their 4-digit numbers. The player with the greater number earns 1 point.
- The game continues until each player has built a 4-digit number in each place-value chart.
- The player with more points wins.

MATH POWER Benchmark Numbers

Numbers that help you estimate a number of objects without counting them are called **benchmark numbers**. Any useful number, such as 10, 25, 50, or 100, can be a benchmark.

About how many jellybeans are in Jar B?

You can use the 25 jellybeans in Jar A as a benchmark.

A

There are about ■ jellybeans in Jar B.

B

There are about twice as many jellybeans in Jar B. So, there are about 50 jellybeans in Jar B.

Try It

Estimate the number of jellybeans in each jar. Use Jars C and D as benchmarks.

Jar C has 10 jellybeans.

C

Jar D has about 100 jellybeans.

D

1.

10 or 50?

2.

25 or 50?

3.

100 or 200?

4. WRITE Math **Explain** how you might use a benchmark of 25 jellybeans to fill a jar that will hold about 100 jellybeans.

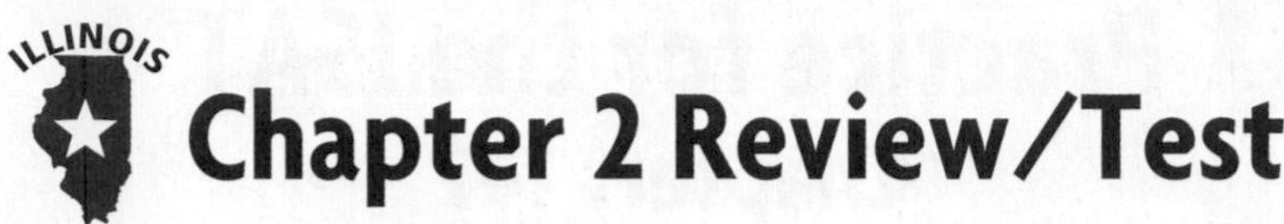

Chapter 2 Review/Test

Check Vocabulary and Concepts

Choose the best term from the box.

VOCABULARY	
compare	
order	round
greater than	
less than	

1. One way to _?_ numbers is to use $<$, $>$, or $=$. IL 6.3.05 (p. 28)
2. The symbol $>$ means _?_. IL 6.3.05 (p. 28)
3. The symbol $<$ means _?_. IL 6.3.05 (p. 28)

Check Skills

Compare the numbers. Write $<$, $>$, or $=$ for each ●. IL 6.3.05 (pp. 28–31)

4. 5,329 ● 5,498
5. 879 ● 1,001
6. 3,867 ● 3,867
7. 980 ● 890
8. 1,226 ● 1,490
9. 9,694 ● 6,949

Write the numbers in order from greatest to least. IL 6.3.05 (pp. 32–33)

10. 498, 569, 389
11. 1,267; 1,098; 1,330
12. 4,013; 4,031; 4,310
13. 8,780; 8,870; 8,078
14. 843, 627, 762
15. 6,636; 6,950; 5,910

Round to the nearest thousand, to the nearest hundred, and to the nearest ten. IL 6.3.01 (pp. 36–39)

16. 8,687
17. 2,341
18. 7,924
19. 4,567
20. 1,212
21. 6,478
22. 3,633
23. 5,295
24. 9,526
25. 2,877

Check Problem Solving

Solve. Use a number line. IL 6.3.05; 6.3.07 (pp. 34–35)

26. The zoo sold 378 tickets on Monday, 389 tickets on Tuesday, 403 tickets on Wednesday, and 369 tickets on Thursday. On which day was the least number of tickets sold?

27. The zoo concession stand sold 1,483 juice drinks, 1,347 fruit smoothies, and 1,429 sandwiches. Order the numbers from least to greatest.

28. WRITE Math Jenny, Todd, and Gene collect stamps. Jenny has 220 stamps, Todd has 216 stamps, and Gene has 261 stamps. **Explain** how you can find who has the second-greatest number of stamps.

GO ONLINE **Technology** Use *Online Assessment.*

Practice for the ISAT
Chapters 1–2

Number and Operations

1. How is twenty thousand, five hundred four written in standard form? IL 6.3.01 (p. 14)

   A 20,540

   B 20,054

   C 20,004

   D 25,504

   E 20,504

2. Use the number line to order these numbers from greatest to least: 3,350; 3,240; 3,150; 3,260 IL 6.3.07 (p. 32)

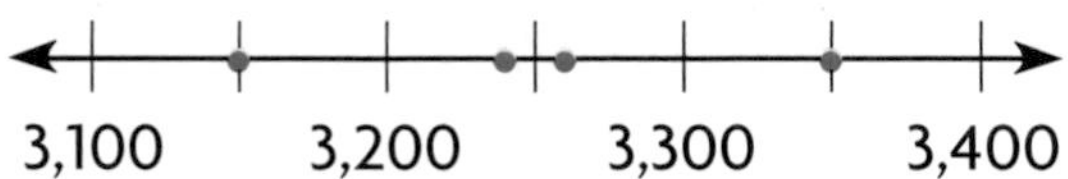

   A 3,150; 3,230; 3,260; 3,350

   B 3,350; 3,230; 3,260; 3,150

   C 3,350; 3,260; 3,240; 3,150

   D 3,260; 3,240; 3,350; 3,150

3. **WRITE Math** Cara has 187 photos and Molly has 178 photos. Who has more photos? Write a number sentence that compares the number of photos. **Explain** how place value can help you solve the problem. IL 6.3.05 (p. 28)

Algebra

4. What is the next number in the pattern? IL 8.3.01 (p. 4)

   33, 36, 39, 42, ■

   A 40

   B 43

   C 45

   D 55

5. Which addition fact helps you find the difference? Grade 2

   $13 - 6 = ■$

   A $7 + 6 = 13$

   B $3 + 3 = 6$

   C $4 + 2 = 6$

   D $13 + 6 = 19$

Check your work.

See item 6. Use subtraction to check your answer.

6. **WRITE Math** Which number makes the number sentence true? **Explain** your answer. Grade 2

   $8 + ■ = 14$

Geometry

7. Mary has three triangles. Which figure can be made from the three triangles? Grade 2

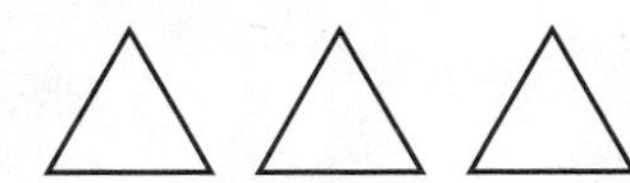

A 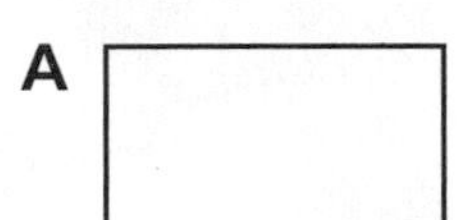

B 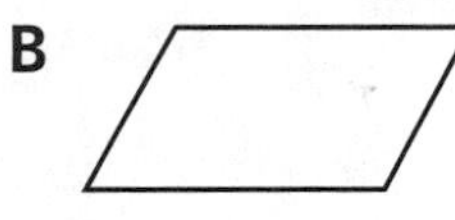

C

D 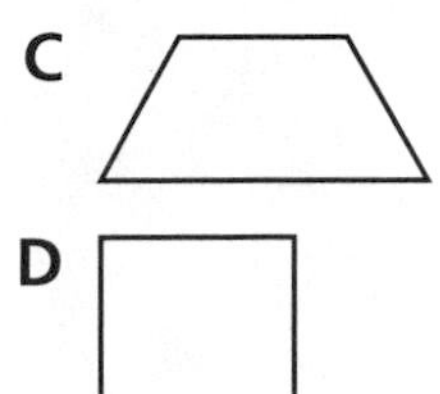

8. How many faces does a rectangular prism have? Grade 2

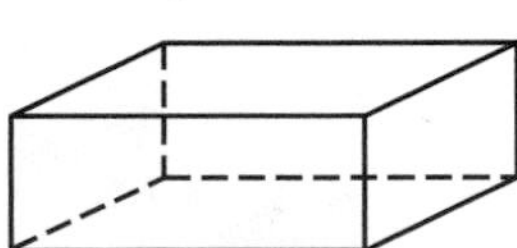

A 4

B 6

C 7

D 8

9. WRITE Math Which solid figure has more faces, a square pyramid or a cube? **Explain** how you know. Grade 2

Data Analysis and Probability

For 10–11, use the Favorite Juice graph.

10. Ms. Parker's class made a bar graph to show the results of their class survey. Which juice did the most students choose? Grade 2

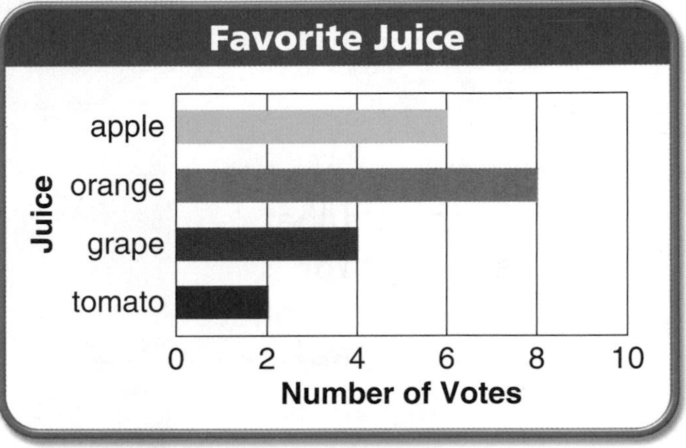

A apple   C grape

B orange   D tomato

11. How many more students chose apple than grape juice? Grade 2

A 8

B 6

C 4

D 2

12. WRITE Math What is the difference between the greatest number of votes and the least number of votes? **Explain** how you found your answer. Grade 2

CHAPTER 3 Addition

FAST FACT

Honeybees are the only insects that make food for people. They collect pollen and nectar from flowers to make honey.

Investigate

Honey is used in a variety of recipes. The pictograph shows the amount of honey used in five different recipes. Choose three of the recipes. Tell how much honey you would need to make all three of those recipes.

Honey Recipes	
Honey muffins	🥄🥄
Honey BBQ chicken	🥄🥄
Honey baked apples	🥄🥄🥄🥄
Honey mustard dressing	🥄
Honey banana pops	🥄🥄🥄🥄
Key: Each 🥄 = 2 tablespoons.	

Technology
Student pages are available in the Student eBook.

Show What You Know

Check your understanding of important skills needed for success in Chapter 3.

▶ Add 1-Digit Numbers

Add.

1. $\begin{array}{r} 5 \\ +2 \\ \hline \end{array}$ **2.** $\begin{array}{r} 3 \\ +7 \\ \hline \end{array}$ **3.** $\begin{array}{r} 8 \\ +6 \\ \hline \end{array}$ **4.** $\begin{array}{r} 9 \\ +4 \\ \hline \end{array}$ **5.** $\begin{array}{r} 1 \\ +8 \\ \hline \end{array}$

▶ Model 2-Digit Addition

Use the models. Find each sum.

6. 15 + 18 = ■

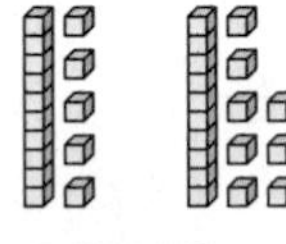

7. 27 + 31 = ■

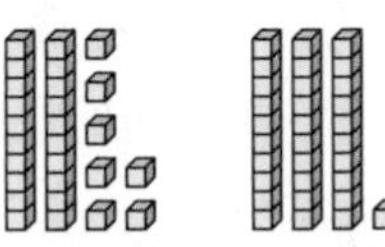

8. 45 + 19 = ■

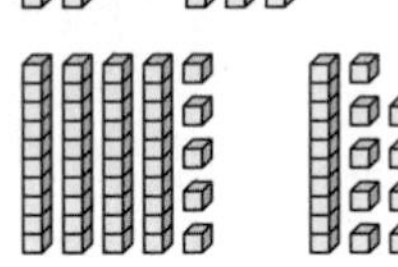

9. 50 + 24 = ■

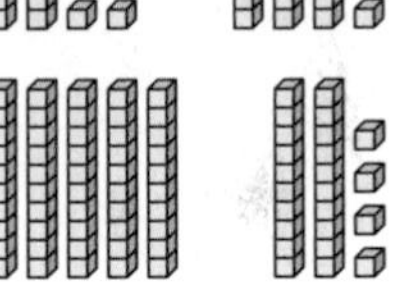

▶ 2-Digit Addition Without Regrouping

Add.

10. $\begin{array}{r} 14 \\ +11 \\ \hline \end{array}$ **11.** $\begin{array}{r} 32 \\ +24 \\ \hline \end{array}$ **12.** $\begin{array}{r} 27 \\ +62 \\ \hline \end{array}$ **13.** $\begin{array}{r} 48 \\ +30 \\ \hline \end{array}$ **14.** $\begin{array}{r} 34 \\ +15 \\ \hline \end{array}$

VOCABULARY POWER

CHAPTER VOCABULARY

Associative Property of Addition
Commutative Property of Addition
compatible numbers
estimate
Identity Property of Addition
missing addend
number sentence

WARM-UP WORDS

Associative Property of Addition The property that states that you can group addends in different ways and still get the same sum

Commutative Property of Addition The property that states that you can add two or more numbers in any order and get the same sum

Identity Property of Addition The property that states that when you add zero to a number, the result is that number

ALGEBRA

Addition Properties

OBJECTIVE: Use properties of addition to solve problems.

Quick Review

1. 5 + 8
2. 6 + 6
3. 7 + 3
4. 8 + 7
5. 9 + 6

Vocabulary

Commutative Property of Addition

Identity Property of Addition

Associative Property of Addition

Learn

PROBLEM Ana saw 9 seagulls on Monday and 5 seagulls on Tuesday. How many seagulls did she see in all?

Commutative Property of Addition

You can add numbers in any order and get the same sum.

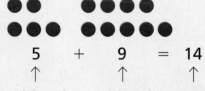

9 + 5 = 14	5 + 9 = 14
addend + addend = sum	addend + addend = sum

So, 9 + 5 = 5 + 9. Ana saw 14 birds.

Identity Property of Addition

Ana saw 8 fish. Beth did not see any. How many fish did the girls see in all?

If you add zero to any number, the sum is that number.

8 + 0 = 8

So, the girls saw 8 fish in all.

Associative Property of Addition

Ana collected 7 brown shells, 4 white shells, and 6 gray shells. How many shells did she collect in all?

You can group addends in different ways, and the sum will be the same.

$$(7 + 4) + 6 = 7 + (4 + 6)$$
$$11 + 6 = 7 + 10$$
$$17 = 17$$

So, Ana collected 17 shells in all.

Math Idea
Parentheses ( ) show which numbers to add first.

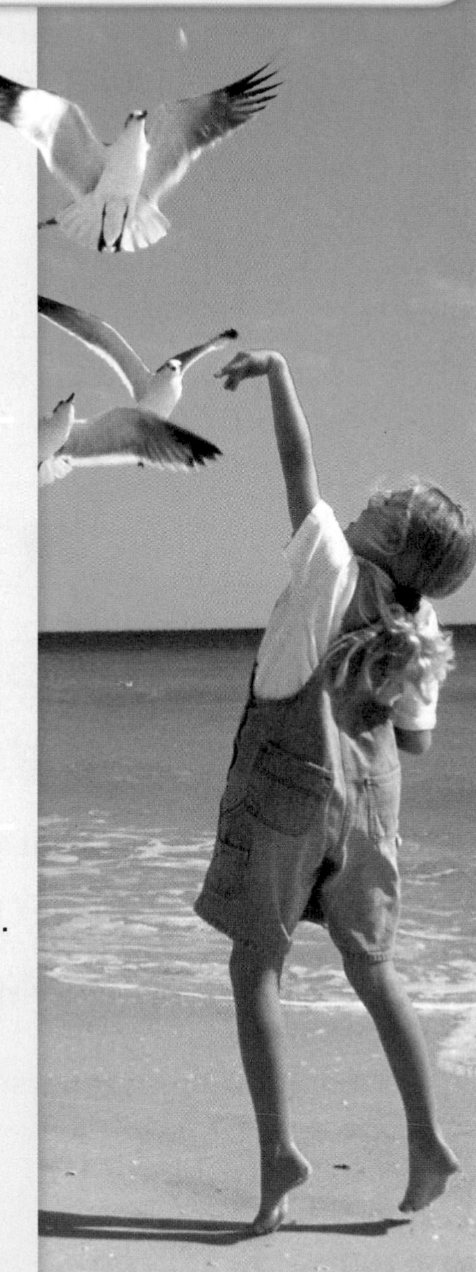

Guided Practice

1. What is the sum when you add 0 to 6?
6 turtles + 0 turtles = ■ turtles

Find each sum. Name the property used.

2. $8 + 4 =$ ■
$4 + 8 =$ ■

3. $0 + 23 =$ ■
$23 + 0 =$ ■

✓4. $6 + 3 =$ ■
$3 + 6 =$ ■

✓5. $(2 + 7) + 1 =$ ■
$2 + (7 + 1) =$ ■

6. TALK Math **Explain** how you can use the Associative Property of Addition to find $15 + 7 + 3$.

Independent Practice and Problem Solving

Find each sum. Name the property used.

7. $10 + 2 =$ ■
$2 + 10 =$ ■

8. $1 + (16 + 4) =$ ■
$(1 + 16) + 4 =$ ■

9. $6 + 0 =$ ■
$0 + 6 =$ ■

10. $3 + (5 + 9) =$ ■
$(3 + 5) + 9 =$ ■

Find each sum two different ways. Use parentheses to show which numbers you added first.

11. $8 + 9 + 1 =$ ■

12. $25 + 25 + 15 =$ ■

13. $30 + 70 + 15 =$ ■

14. A saltwater fishtank has 2 starfish, 3 sea horses, and 5 clown fish. How many animals are in the tank in all? Draw a picture and write a number sentence.

15. **What if** 4 of each animal are added to the tank? How many animals are there in all now?

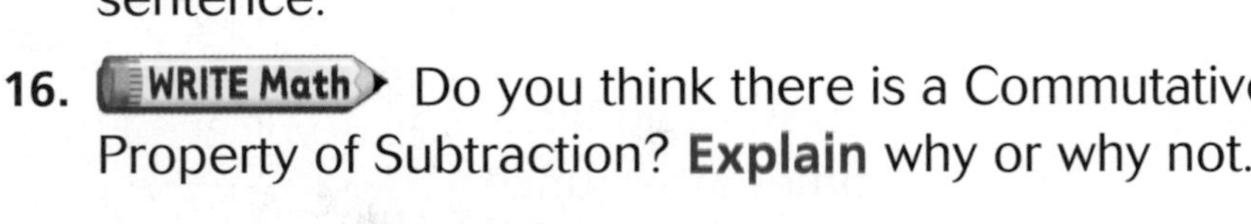

16. WRITE Math Do you think there is a Commutative Property of Subtraction? **Explain** why or why not.

Mixed Review and Test Prep

17. What is 759 rounded to the nearest hundred? (p. 36)

18. There are 2 red marbles and 5 green marbles in a bag. Which color marble are you more likely to choose? (Grade 2)

19. **Test Prep** Which is the sum?

$(6 + 6) + 7 =$ ■

A 12 **C** 19

B 13 **D** 20

Extra Practice on page 68, Set A

LESSON 2

ALGEBRA

Missing Addends

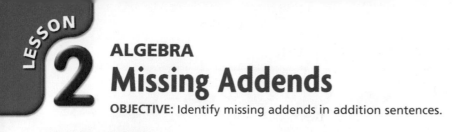

OBJECTIVE: Identify missing addends in addition sentences.

Quick Review

1. 4 + 7
2. 5 + 9
3. 8 + 4
4. 9 + 3
5. 7 + 6

Learn

PROBLEM Nick's family spent the day at an amusement park. They rode roller coasters a total of 12 times. They rode roller coasters 7 times before lunch. How many times did they ride roller coasters after lunch?

ONE WAY **Use an addition fact.**

7 + 5 = 12

ANOTHER WAY **Use a related subtraction fact.**

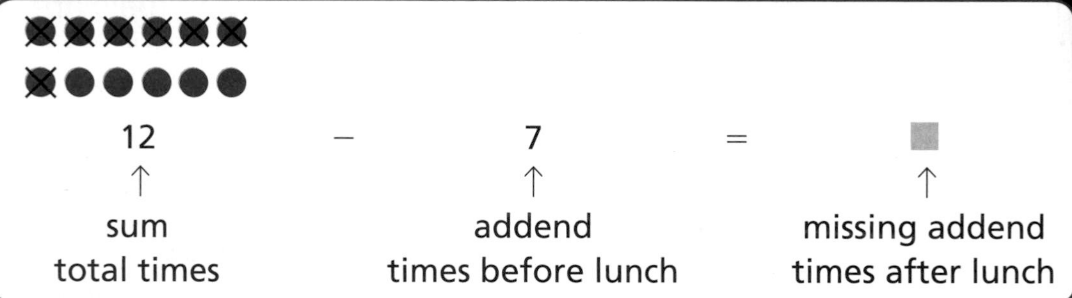

12 − 7 = 5

So, Nick's family rode roller coasters 5 times after lunch.

- **What if** Nick's family had ridden roller coasters 3 times before lunch? How many times would they have ridden roller coasters after lunch?

Guided Practice

1. What addition fact can help you find 3 + ■ = 10? What related subtraction fact can help you?

Find the missing addend. You may want to use counters.

2. $4 + \blacksquare = 12$ **3.** $\blacksquare + 6 = 6$ ✓**4.** $8 + \blacksquare = 10$ ✓**5.** $\blacksquare + 5 = 11$

6. TALK Math **Explain** how to use a related subtraction fact to find $8 + \blacksquare = 13$.

Independent Practice and Problem Solving

Find the missing addend. You may want to use counters.

7. $6 + \blacksquare = 16$ **8.** $\blacksquare + 5 = 12$ **9.** $\blacksquare + 9 = 9$ **10.** $\blacksquare + 17 = 17 + 6$

11. $6 + \blacksquare = 20$ **12.** $5 + \blacksquare = 13$ **13.** $\blacksquare + 3 = 18$ **14.** $19 + 12 = 12 + \blacksquare$

Find the missing number.

15. $7 + 8 = \blacksquare$ **16.** $9 + \blacksquare = 18$ **17.** $\blacksquare + 8 = 14$ **18.** $10 + 0 = \blacksquare$

USE DATA For 19–21, use the table.

19. The table shows the amount of food sold at an amusement park on Friday. How many more hot dogs and nachos were sold than hamburgers?

Food Sold

Food	Number Sold
Hamburgers	41
Hot dogs	29
Nachos	35

20. Pose a Problem Look back at Problem 19. Write a similar problem by changing the number of items sold to numbers less than 20 and by changing the question.

21. WRITE Math If Sue's family bought 8 hot dogs, how many hot dogs were bought by other people? **Explain** how you know.

Mixed Review and Test Prep

22. Leah wrote eight thousand, three hundred four. What is Leah's number in standard form? (p. 10)

23. Dan caught 12 baseballs. Jim didn't catch any. Which addition property is shown by this example? $12 + 0 = 12$ (p. 48)

24. Test Prep Which is the missing addend for $12 + \blacksquare = 17$?

A 3

B 4

C 5

D 6

Extra Practice on page 68, Set B

LESSON 3

Estimate Sums

OBJECTIVE: Estimate sums of 2- and 3-digit numbers by using rounding and compatible numbers.

Quick Review

Round each number to the nearest ten.

1. 83 **2.** 96
3. 55 **4.** 19
5. 74

Vocabulary

estimate
compatible numbers

Learn

PROBLEM There are many types of birds at Lake Whitney, in Texas. One day Jacob counted 128 birds. Paul counted 73 birds. About how many birds did Jacob and Paul count in all?

To find *about* how many, you can **estimate**.

Example Estimate. 128 + 73

ONE WAY Use rounding.

Round each number to the nearest ten. Then add.

$$\begin{array}{rcr} 128 & \rightarrow & 130 \\ +\ 73 & \rightarrow & +\ 70 \\ \hline & & 200 \end{array}$$

ANOTHER WAY Use compatible numbers.

Compatible numbers are close numbers that are easy to compute mentally.

$$\begin{array}{rcr} 128 & \rightarrow & 125 \\ +\ 73 & \rightarrow & +\ 75 \\ \hline & & 200 \end{array}$$

So, 200 is a reasonable estimate of how many birds were counted.

- What other compatible numbers could be used to estimate the sum?

More Examples

A Use rounding.

$$\begin{array}{rcr} 19 & \rightarrow & 20 \\ +66 & \rightarrow & +70 \\ \hline & & 90 \end{array}$$

B Use rounding.

$$\begin{array}{rcr} 492 & \rightarrow & 500 \\ +219 & \rightarrow & +200 \\ \hline & & 700 \end{array}$$

C Use compatible numbers.

$$\begin{array}{rcr} 306 & \rightarrow & 300 \\ +286 & \rightarrow & +285 \\ \hline & & 585 \end{array}$$

Guided Practice

1. Copy the problem at the right. Round both 324 and 48 to the nearest ten. Then estimate their sum.

$$\begin{array}{r} 324 \\ +\ 48 \\ \hline \end{array}$$

Use rounding or compatible numbers to estimate each sum.

2. 37 + 51

3. 307 + 181

4. 476 + 239

✓5. 29 + 44

✓6. 148 + 151

7. TALK Math Use rounding and then use compatible numbers to estimate 128 + 381. Which way do you think gives an answer closer to the exact sum for this problem? **Explain.**

Independent Practice and Problem Solving

Use rounding to estimate each sum.

8. 42 + 35

9. 61 + 95

10. 319 + 54

11. 289 + 407

12. 526 + 361

Use compatible numbers to estimate each sum.

13. 42 + 37

14. 51 + 48

15. 172 + 27

16. 326 + 176

17. 248 + 121

USE DATA For 18–20, use the table.

Shorelines of Texas Lakes

Lake	Distance in Miles
Lake Fork	315
Lake Conroe	157
Lake Buchanan	124

18. **Reasoning** If you went along the shoreline of Lake Conroe two times, would that distance be about the same as going one time along Lake Fork? **Explain** using compatible numbers.

19. WRITE Math Some lakes in Texas have shorelines along which people hike and fish. **Explain** how you would estimate the sum of Lake Fork's and Lake Conroe's shorelines.

20. ***FAST FACT*** Lake Livingston is the second-largest lake in Texas. It has 450 miles of shoreline. Estimate the sum of Lake Livingston's and Lake Buchanan's shorelines.

Mixed Review and Test Prep

21. Write the numbers in order from least to greatest. (p. 32)

2,219; 2,178; 2,198

22. What is the missing addend? (p. 50)

9 + ■ = 18

23. **Test Prep** A plane flew 732 miles and then flew 476 miles. About how many miles did the plane fly in all?

A 200 miles

B 1,000 miles

C 1,200 miles

D 2,000 miles

Extra Practice on page 68, Set C

LESSON 4

Add 2-Digit Numbers

OBJECTIVE: Add 2-digit numbers with and without regrouping.

Quick Review

1. 6 + 8
2. 8 + 9
3. 7 + 7
4. 8 + 4
5. 6 + 4 + 5

Learn

PROBLEM Shannon picked 29 red apples at the orchard. Katrina picked 57 green apples. How many apples did Shannon and Katrina pick in all?

Example 1 **Add.** 29 + 57

Estimate. 30 + 60 = 90

ONE WAY **Use place value.**

Step 1

Add the ones.
9 + 7 = 16 ones
Regroup 16 ones as 1 ten 6 ones.

$$\begin{array}{r} {}^{1} \\ 29 \\ +57 \\ \hline 6 \end{array}$$

Step 2

Add the tens.
1 + 2 + 5 = 8 tens

$$\begin{array}{r} {}^{1} \\ 29 \\ +57 \\ \hline 86 \end{array}$$

ANOTHER WAY **Use mental math.**

	Add the tens.	Add the ones.	Add the sums.
29 + 57	20 + 50 = 70	9 + 7 = 16	70 + 16 = 86

So, Shannon and Katrina picked 86 apples in all. Since 86 is close to the estimate of 90, the answer is reasonable.

Sometimes when you add 3 addends, you can make a ten.

Example 2 **Add.** 35 + 26 + 54

Step 1

Add the ones.
5 + 6 + 4 = 15 ones
Regroup 15 ones as 1 ten 5 ones.

$$\begin{array}{r} {}^{1} \\ 35 \\ 26 \\ +54 \\ \hline 5 \end{array}$$

Make a ten.

Step 2

Add the tens.
1 + 3 + 2 + 5 = 11 tens
Regroup 11 tens as 1 hundred 1 ten.

$$\begin{array}{r} {}^{1} \\ 35 \\ 26 \\ +54 \\ \hline 115 \end{array}$$

ERROR ALERT

Remember to add the regrouped ten.

• How can you use mental math to find 43 + 22 + 18?

Guided Practice

1. Find 45 + 68 using mental math. Complete the number sentences.

$$\begin{array}{r} 45 \\ +\,68 \\ \hline \end{array}$$

40 + 60 = ■
5 + 8 = ■

Estimate. Then find each sum using place value or mental math.

2. $\begin{array}{r} 17 \\ +\,54 \\ \hline \end{array}$

3. $\begin{array}{r} 22 \\ 48 \\ +\,13 \\ \hline \end{array}$

4. $\begin{array}{r} 84 \\ +\,35 \\ \hline \end{array}$

✓5. $\begin{array}{r} 24 \\ +\,39 \\ \hline \end{array}$

✓6. $\begin{array}{r} 47 \\ 23 \\ +\,28 \\ \hline \end{array}$

7. **TALK Math** **Explain** how you would use place value to find 56 + 19 + 31.

Independent Practice and Problem Solving

Estimate. Then find each sum using place value or mental math.

8. $\begin{array}{r} 98 \\ +\,36 \\ \hline \end{array}$

9. $\begin{array}{r} 19 \\ +\,42 \\ \hline \end{array}$

10. $\begin{array}{r} 53 \\ +\,29 \\ \hline \end{array}$

11. $\begin{array}{r} 16 \\ 12 \\ +\,28 \\ \hline \end{array}$

12. $\begin{array}{r} 33 \\ 10 \\ +\,85 \\ \hline \end{array}$

13. 66 + 35 = ■

14. 21 + 46 = ■

15. 18 + 18 = ■

16. 21 + 37 + 19 = ■

USE DATA For 17–19, use the picture.

17. For the class party, Carlos brought 2 gallons of apple juice. How many cups can he pour?

18. Kate brought 2 dozen apples for the class party. Only 22 apples were eaten. How many apples were left?

19. **WRITE Math** Sarah bought 3 dozen apples to make applesauce. How many apples did Sarah buy? **Explain** how you know.

Mixed Review and Test Prep

20. What is 576 rounded to the nearest hundred? (p. 36)

21. Kyle cut apart a square. What figures did he make? (Grade 2)

22. **Test Prep** Which is the sum?

56 + 41 + 73 = ■

A 160
B 161
C 170
D 171

Extra Practice on page 68, Set D

LESSON 5 HANDS ON

Model 3-Digit Addition

OBJECTIVE: Explore adding 3-digit numbers with and without regrouping.

Quick Review

Regroup.

1. 10 ones = ■ ten 0 ones
2. 17 ones = 1 ten ■ ones
3. ■ ones = 1 ten 4 ones
4. 12 tens = ■ hundred 2 tens
5. 19 tens = 1 hundred ■ tens

Investigate

Materials ■ base-ten blocks

You can use base-ten blocks to help add numbers.

A Model the numbers 246 and 175.

Use your model to find the sum of 246 and 175.
Add the ones, tens, and hundreds.
Regroup the blocks when needed.

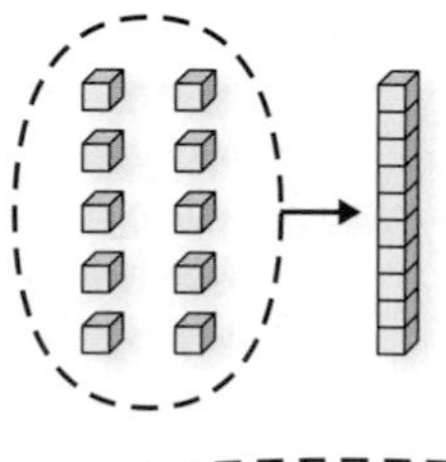

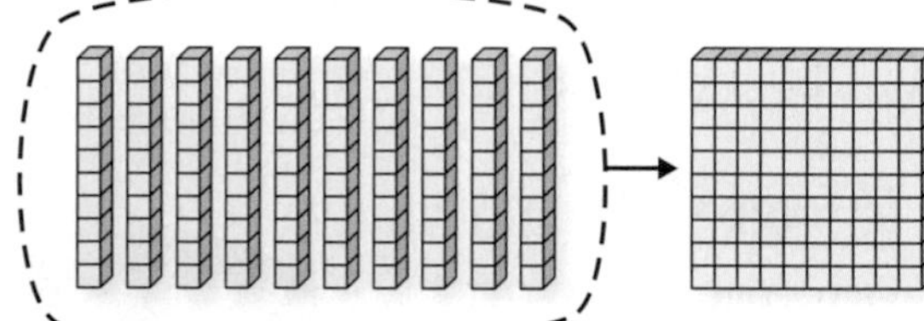

B Draw a picture to show the sum.
Record your answer.

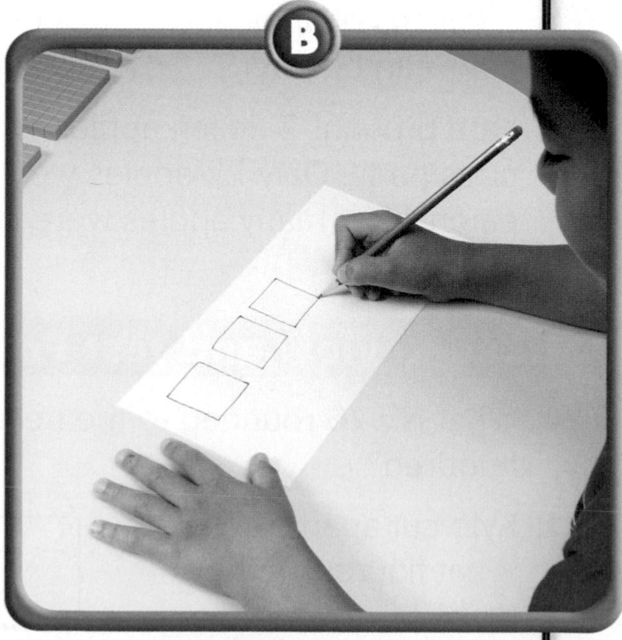

Draw Conclusions

1. Explain how your model helped you find the sum.
2. When do you need to regroup?
3. **Analysis** Can the sum of two 3-digit numbers equal a 4-digit number? Explain. Give an example.

Connect

Here is a way to record addition.

To add 138 and 267, first line up the hundreds, tens, and ones.

H	T	O
1	3	8
+2	6	7

Step 1

Add the ones.
8 + 7 = 15 ones
Regroup.
15 ones = 1 ten 5 ones

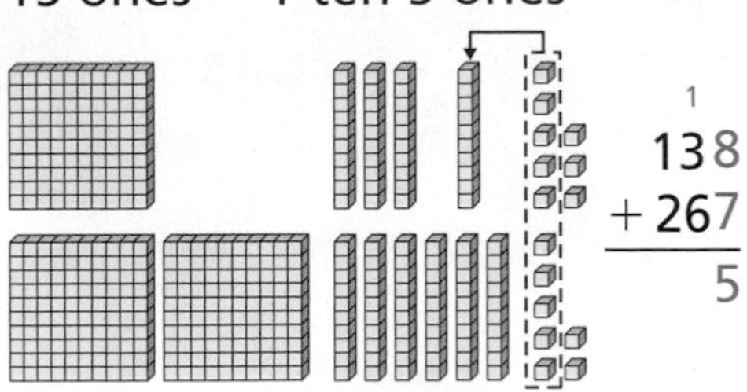

$$\begin{array}{r} \scriptstyle 1 \\ 138 \\ +267 \\ \hline 5 \end{array}$$

Step 2

Add the tens.
1 + 3 + 6 = 10 tens
Regroup.
10 tens = 1 hundred 0 tens

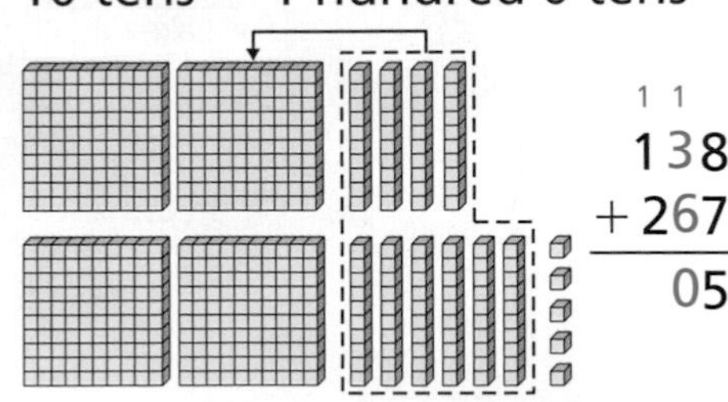

$$\begin{array}{r} \scriptstyle 1\,1 \\ 138 \\ +267 \\ \hline 05 \end{array}$$

Step 3

Add the hundreds.
1 + 1 + 2 =
4 hundreds

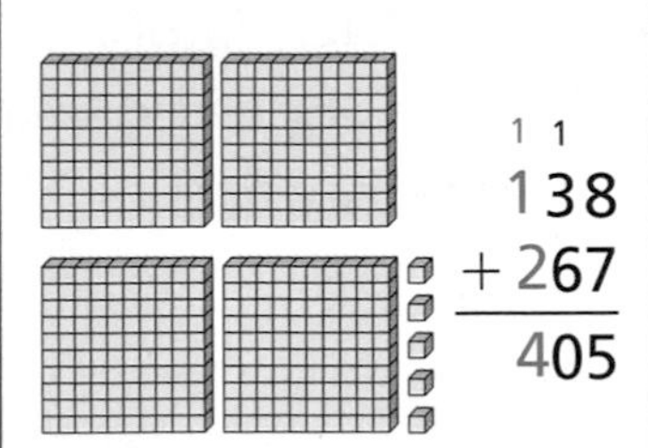

$$\begin{array}{r} \scriptstyle 1\,1 \\ 138 \\ +267 \\ \hline 405 \end{array}$$

So, 138 + 267 = 405.

TALK Math

Explain how to find the sum of 485 and 429. Tell if you need to regroup.

Practice

Use base-ten blocks to find each sum.

1. 511 + 253 = ■
2. 183 + 214 = ■
3. 455 + 346 = ■
4. 268 + 258 = ■
5. 123 + 155 = ■
6. ✓ 352 + 191 = ■

Find each sum.

7. $\begin{array}{r} 434 \\ +517 \\ \hline \end{array}$
8. $\begin{array}{r} 185 \\ +309 \\ \hline \end{array}$
9. $\begin{array}{r} 594 \\ +156 \\ \hline \end{array}$
10. $\begin{array}{r} 233 \\ +128 \\ \hline \end{array}$
11. ✓ $\begin{array}{r} 457 \\ +465 \\ \hline \end{array}$
12. $\begin{array}{r} 193 \\ +796 \\ \hline \end{array}$
13. $\begin{array}{r} 216 \\ +261 \\ \hline \end{array}$
14. $\begin{array}{r} 377 \\ +140 \\ \hline \end{array}$
15. $\begin{array}{r} 615 \\ +284 \\ \hline \end{array}$
16. $\begin{array}{r} 545 \\ +389 \\ \hline \end{array}$

17. **Reasoning** Will the sum of 625 and 718 be greater than or less than 1,000? How do you know?

18. **WRITE Math** **Explain** how to use base-ten blocks to model 182 + 376. What is the sum?

Technology
Use Harcourt Mega Math, Country Countdown, *Block Busters,* Levels U, V.

LESSON 6

Add Greater Numbers

OBJECTIVE: Add 3- and 4-digit numbers with and without regrouping.

Quick Review

1. 12 + 14
2. 13 + 18
3. 20 + 35
4. 36 + 17
5. 68 + 29

Learn

PROBLEM Mia is planning a trip to Los Angeles, California. Her airplane leaves from New York City and stops in Salt Lake City, Utah. Then it flies from Salt Lake City to Los Angeles. What is the total distance of Mia's flight?

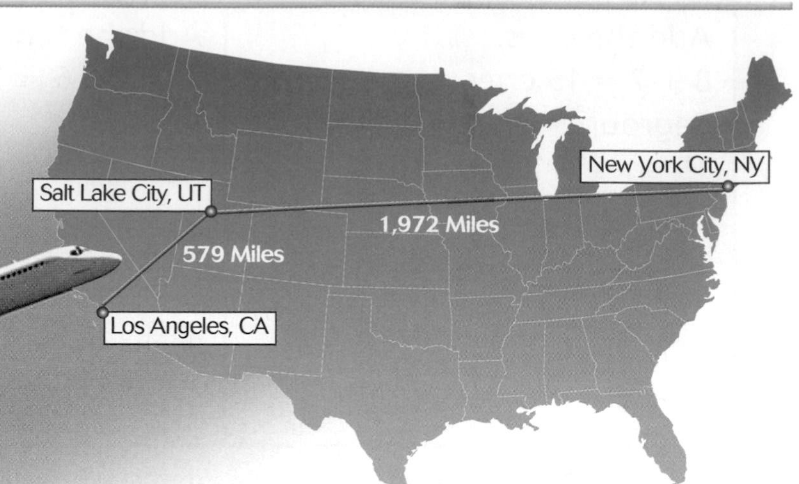

Example **Add.** 1,972 + 579 **Estimate.** 2,000 + 600 = 2,600

Step 1	Step 2	Step 3	Step 4
Add the ones. Regroup. 11 ones = 1 ten 1 one	Add the tens. Regroup. 15 tens = 1 hundred 5 tens	Add the hundreds. Regroup. 15 hundreds = 1 thousand 5 hundreds	Add the thousands.
1,972 + 579 = 1 (regrouped: 1)	1,972 + 579 = 51 (regrouped: 1 1)	1,972 + 579 = 551 (regrouped: 1 1 1)	1,972 + 579 = 2,551 (regrouped: 1 1 1)

So, the total distance of Mia's flight is 2,551 miles. Since 2,551 is close to the estimate of 2,600, the answer is reasonable.

More Examples

A Regrouping

$$\begin{array}{r} {}^{1} \\ 436 \\ +\,182 \\ \hline 618 \end{array}$$

B No regrouping

$$\begin{array}{r} 5,242 \\ +\;\;654 \\ \hline 5,896 \end{array}$$

C Regrouping

$$\begin{array}{r} {}^{1}\;\;{}^{1}{}^{1} \\ 2,764 \\ +\,6,648 \\ \hline 9,412 \end{array}$$

Guided Practice

1. Copy the problem at the right. Do you need to regroup? Find the sum.

$$\begin{array}{r} 534 \\ +319 \\ \hline \end{array}$$

Estimate. Then find each sum.

2. $\begin{array}{r} 604 \\ +263 \\ \hline \end{array}$ 3. $\begin{array}{r} 532 \\ +419 \\ \hline \end{array}$ 4. $\begin{array}{r} 3,163 \\ +3,644 \\ \hline \end{array}$ ✓5. $\begin{array}{r} 2,833 \\ +\ \ 175 \\ \hline \end{array}$ ✓6. $\begin{array}{r} 1,825 \\ +4,617 \\ \hline \end{array}$

7. TALK Math **Explain** how to use place value to add 1,258 and 1,376.

Independent Practice and Problem Solving

Estimate. Then find each sum.

8. $\begin{array}{r} 479 \\ +352 \\ \hline \end{array}$ 9. $\begin{array}{r} 241 \\ +325 \\ \hline \end{array}$ 10. $\begin{array}{r} 5,963 \\ +\ \ 778 \\ \hline \end{array}$ 11. $\begin{array}{r} 2,071 \\ +1,985 \\ \hline \end{array}$ 12. $\begin{array}{r} 3,729 \\ +4,541 \\ \hline \end{array}$

13. $643 + 167 = ■$ 14. $469 + 860 = ■$ 15. $9,514 + 2,858 = ■$

USE DATA For 16–17, use the table.

16. Ms. Sloan flies from Boston to Washington, D.C. Then she flies from Washington, D.C., to Atlanta. She flies the same distance to return home. What is the total distance she flies?

17. WRITE Math **What's the Error?** A plane flies from Philadelphia to Chicago and then to Las Vegas. Keith says the total flight distance is 1,191 miles. Describe his error. Find the correct distance.

Flight Distances Between Cities

Cities	Distance in Miles
Boston to Washington, D.C.	394
Washington, D.C. to Atlanta	541
Philadelphia to Chicago	665
Chicago to Las Vegas	1,526

Mixed Review and Test Prep

18. What is the mode? (Grade 2)

4, 3, 9, 6, 3, 2, 8

19. Write <, >, or = to compare. (p. 28)

2,178 ● 2,187

20. **Test Prep** Which is the sum of 3,579 and 453?

A 4,032
B 3,932
C 3,922
D 3,126

Extra Practice on page 68, Set E

Problem Solving Workshop
Strategy: Predict and Test

OBJECTIVE: Solve problems by using the strategy *predict and test.*

Learn the Strategy

Sometimes, the best way to solve a problem is to predict and test. After reading the problem, you predict, or guess, what the answer might be. Then you use information in the problem to test, or check, if your answer is too low, too high, or just right.

Predict and test to find numbers whose sum is 39.

Three numbers in a row have a sum of 39. What are the numbers?

Predict	Test	Notes
9, 10, 11	9 + 10 + 11 = 30	too low
13, 14, 15	13 + 14 + 15 = 42	too high
12, 13, 14	12 + 13 + 14 = 39	just right

Predict and test to find the number of books each boy has.

Mark has 3 more books than Chad. Together, they have 25 books. How many books does each boy have?

Predict: 12 and 9	Predict: 16 and 13	Predict: 14 and 11
Test: 12 + 9 = 21	Test: 16 + 13 = 29	Test: 14 + 11 = 25
too low	too high	just right

Predict and test to find the amount of time spent on each activity.

Melanie spends 60 minutes reading and exercising. She exercises 10 minutes more than she reads. How much time does Melanie spend doing each activity?

Predict		Test	
Read	Exercise	Total	Notes
30	30 + 10 = 40	30 + 40 = 70	too high
20	20 + 10 = 30	20 + 30 = 50	too low
25	25 + 10 = 35	25 + 35 = 60	just right

TALK Math

Explain how you can use the results from one guess to make another guess.

Use the Strategy

PROBLEM Jacob and Gabe play on different football teams. Jacob's team scored 7 more points than Gabe's team. There were 35 points total scored in the game. How many points did each team score?

Read to Understand
Plan
Solve
Check

Read to Understand

- **Use graphic aids to organize your predictions and test the results.**
- **What information is given?**
- **Is there information you will not use? If so, what?**

Plan

- **What strategy can you use to solve the problem?**
  You can predict and test to help you solve the problem.

Solve

- **How can you use the strategy to solve the problem?**
  Make a table to organize your predictions and test the results.

  Predict the number of points scored by Gabe's team. Add 7 to that number to find the points scored by Jacob's team. Then test to see if the sum of the numbers is 35.

  So, Gabe's team scored 14 points, and Jacob's team scored 21 points.

Predict		Test	
Gabe's Team	Jacob's Team	Total	Notes
11	11 + 7 = 18	11 + 18 = 29	too low
16	16 + 7 = 23	16 + 23 = 39	too high
14	14 + 7 = 21	14 + 21 = 35	just right

Check

- **How do you know your answer is correct?**

Guided Problem Solving

Read to Understand
Plan
Solve
Check

1. Fifty children signed up for the youth basketball league. There were 20 more boys than girls. How many girls and how many boys signed up for the basketball league?

   First, predict the number of girls.

   Then, add 20 to that number to find the number of boys.

   Finally, test to see if the sum is 50. If the sum is not 50, try other numbers.

Predict		Test	
Girls	Boys	Total	Notes
20	20 + 20 = 40	20 + 40 = 60	too high
10	10 + 20 =		

2. **What if** 72 children signed up for the league and there were still 20 more boys than girls? How many girls and how many boys would have signed up?

3. In a survey, 100 students were asked to choose swimming or soccer as their favorite sport. Of those, 14 more chose soccer than swimming. How many students chose soccer?

Problem Solving Strategy Practice

Predict and test to solve.

4. For a volleyball game, 200 tickets were sold. There were 70 more student tickets sold than adult tickets. How many of each type of ticket were sold?

5. The snack bar at the football field has 500 cups. There are 80 more small cups than large cups. How many small cups are there?

6. The youth softball league ordered 48 T-shirts in two colors. There were 10 fewer red shirts ordered than blue shirts. How many of each color were ordered?

7. WRITE Math During basketball practice, Jacob attempted 40 free-throw shots. He made 6 more than he missed. How many free-throw shots did Jacob make? **Explain** how you know.

Mixed Strategy Practice

USE DATA For 8–10, use the graph.

8. For Game 1, the number of fans for the home team was 200 more than the number of fans for the visiting team. How many visiting fans were at Game 1?

9. The coach said that the number of fans at Game 2 was 235 fewer than he expected. How many fans did the coach expect at Game 2?

10. **Pose a Problem** Look back at Problem 9. Write a similar problem by changing the number of fans the coach expected to a number greater than 300.

11. **Open-Ended** At Game 3, each fan was given a 3-digit number for a prize drawing. Justin's number had three even digits. The digit in the tens place was greater than the digit in the ones place. The digit in the hundreds place was greater than the digit in the tens place. What could Justin's number have been?

CHALLENGE YOURSELF

In the first three games of the season, Sam scored 23, 18, and 26 points.

12. In Game 4, Sam scored 5 more points than he did in one of the first three games. He scored fewer than 94 points in all for the first four games. How many points did he score in Game 4?

13. Sam scored more than 100 points over the first 5 games. He scored the same number of points in Games 4 and 5. What is the least number of points he could have scored in Game 5?

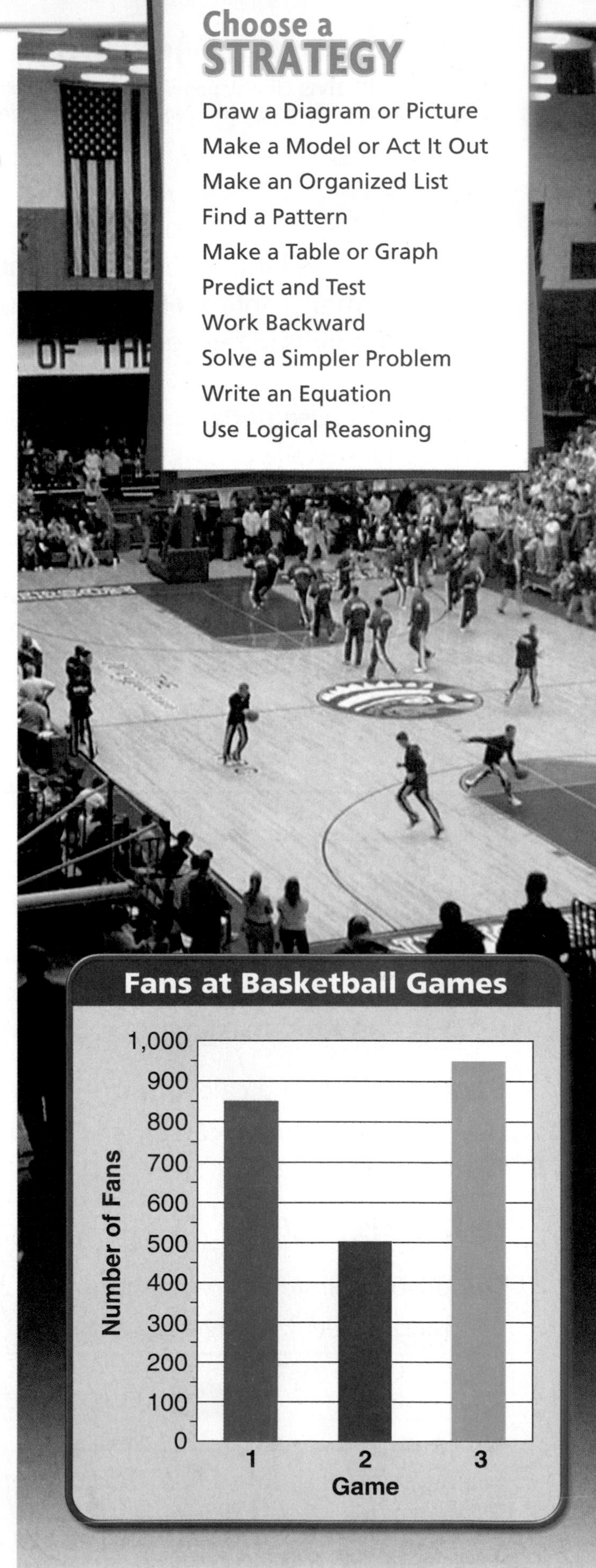

LESSON 8

Choose a Method

OBJECTIVE: Choose paper and pencil, a calculator, or mental math to add 3- and 4-digit numbers.

Quick Review

There are 130 students at Prairie School. There are 275 students at Lincoln School. What is the total number of students at both schools?

Learn

PROBLEM The table shows the number of vegetable seeds a farmer planted. How many cucumber and bean seeds did the farmer plant?

Seeds Planted

Seed	Number Planted
Cucumber	3,317
Carrot	875
Bean	1,754
Lettuce	2,612

Example 1 Use paper and pencil.

Add. 3,317 + 1,754 = ■

Estimate. 3,000 + 2,000 = 5,000

The problem involves regrouping and adding two numbers. So, using paper and pencil is a good choice.

Step 1

Add the ones.
Regroup.
11 ones = 1 ten 1 one

$$\begin{array}{r} \scriptstyle 1 \\ 3{,}317 \\ +\,1{,}754 \\ \hline 1 \end{array}$$

Step 2

Add the tens.

$$\begin{array}{r} \scriptstyle 1 \\ 3{,}317 \\ +\,1{,}754 \\ \hline 71 \end{array}$$

Step 3

Add the hundreds.
Regroup. 10 hundreds = 1 thousand 0 hundreds

$$\begin{array}{r} \scriptstyle 1\ \ 1 \\ 3{,}317 \\ +\,1{,}754 \\ \hline 071 \end{array}$$

Step 4

Add the thousands.

$$\begin{array}{r} \scriptstyle 1\ \ 1 \\ 3{,}317 \\ +\,1{,}754 \\ \hline 5{,}071 \end{array}$$

So, the farmer planted 5,071 cucumber and bean seeds. Since 5,071 is close to the estimate of 5,000, the answer is reasonable.

Example 2 Use a calculator.

How many cucumber, carrot, and lettuce seeds did the farmer plant?

3,317 + 875 + 2,612 = ■

The problem involves regrouping and adding three large numbers. So, using a calculator is a good choice.

Math Idea
Since you may enter a wrong number when using a calculator, it is important to check your answer.

So, the farmer planted 6,804 cucumber, carrot, and lettuce seeds.

Example 3 **Use mental math.**

Pete and Michael bought vegetable plants for their farm. They bought 120 radish plants and 438 broccoli plants. How many plants did they buy?

$$120 + 438 = \blacksquare$$

No regrouping is needed. So, using mental math is a good choice.

Think: Add the hundreds. $100 + 400 = 500$
Add the tens. $20 + 30 = 50$
Add the ones. $0 + 8 = 8$
Find the sum. $500 + 50 + 8 = 558$

So, Pete and Michael bought 558 plants.

More Examples

A **Use paper and pencil.**

$$\begin{array}{r} {}^{1} \\ 581 \\ +\ 495 \\ \hline 1{,}076 \end{array}$$

B **Use a calculator.**

$$\begin{array}{r} 4{,}835 \\ 2{,}462 \\ +\ 1{,}684 \\ \hline 8{,}981 \end{array}$$

C **Use mental math.**

$$\begin{array}{r} 503 \\ +\ 324 \\ \hline 827 \end{array}$$

- What is another method you could use to find the sum in Example B?

Guided Practice

1. Find 247 + 230 using mental math. Use the number sentences to help you.

$$\begin{array}{r} 247 \\ +\ 230 \\ \hline \end{array}$$

$200 + 200 = \blacksquare$
$40 + 30 = \blacksquare$
$7 + 0 = \blacksquare$

Find the sum. Tell which method you used.

2. $\begin{array}{r} 898 \\ +\ 365 \\ \hline \end{array}$ **3.** $\begin{array}{r} 1{,}650 \\ +\ 4{,}103 \\ \hline \end{array}$ **4.** $\begin{array}{r} 5{,}784 \\ 2{,}257 \\ +\ 836 \\ \hline \end{array}$ **5.** $\begin{array}{r} 135 \\ +\ 610 \\ \hline \end{array}$ ✓**6.** $\begin{array}{r} 3{,}862 \\ +\ 2{,}839 \\ \hline \end{array}$

7. $611 + 156 = \blacksquare$ **8.** $2{,}754 + 4{,}526 = \blacksquare$ ✓**9.** $3{,}722 + 4{,}180 + 1{,}359 = \blacksquare$

10. TALK Math **Explain** which strategy would be a good choice to use to add 457 and 963. Then find the sum.

Independent Practice and Problem Solving

Find the sum. Tell which method you used.

11. $608 + 241$

12. $1,895 + 1,542$

13. $456 + 372$

14. $1,211 + 3,849 + 1,970$

15. $968 + 453$

16. $5,570 + 2,695$

17. $786 + 274$

18. $1,054 + 622$

19. $110 + 373$

20. $4,545 + 3,687$

21. $2,904 + 1,418 + 675$

22. $4,103 + 2,865$

23. $324 + 510 + 143$

24. $3,908 + 2,712$

25. $293 + 862$

26. $942 + 528 + 896 = ■$

27. $859 + 364 = ■$

28. $463 + 216 = ■$

29. $309 + 185 = ■$

30. $6,214 + 1,305 = ■$

31. $5,285 + 3,789 = ■$

USE DATA For 32–35, use the table.

Vegetables on Sarah's Farm

Vegetable	Number of Acres
Corn	206
Broccoli	374
Lettuce	2,139
Peas	133

▲ An acre of land is about the size of a football field.

32. Sarah's family owns a farm that is 2,852 acres. How many acres planted with corn, broccoli, and lettuce does the family have?

33. Eric's family plants 878 more acres of lettuce than Sarah's family does. How many acres of lettuce does Eric's family plant?

34. **Reasoning** Is the total number of acres planted with corn and peas greater than or less than the number of acres planted with broccoli? **Explain** your answer.

35. WRITE Math **What's the Question?** Jessica used the data in the table. The answer is 507.

36. On Friday, Dan and his father picked some tomatoes. On Saturday, they picked 36 more tomatoes. Now they have 89 tomatoes. How many tomatoes did they pick on Friday?

Extra Practice on page 68, Set F

Learn About MENTAL MATH Addition Riddle

Copy and find each sum. Use mental math.

S $216 + 153$	B $352 + 617$	O $750 + 248$	A $332 + 504$	I $425 + 250$
E $793 + 206$	T $526 + 361$	R $319 + 320$	G $182 + 607$	C $453 + 116$
H $853 + 134$	N $630 + 230$	K $445 + 424$	y $223 + 513$	

To answer the riddle, match the letters from the sums above to the numbers below.

What food likes to listen to music? Why?

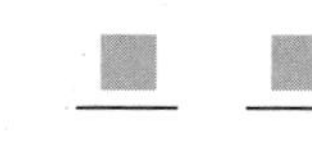

__ __ __ __. __ __ __ __ __ __ __ __ __!

569 998 639 860 675 887 987 836 369 999 836 639 369

Mixed Review and Test Prep

37. Write the numbers in order from least to greatest. (p. 32)

245, 278, 236

38. Test Prep Drew's family drove 512 miles to his uncle's farm. Then they drove 173 miles to Drew's grandmother's house. How many miles did Drew's family drive in all?

A 339 miles

B 456 miles

C 572 miles

D 685 miles

39. What is the greatest whole number you can make by using the digits 4, 7, 3, and 5? Use each digit only once. (p. 10)

40. Test Prep Junie's father runs a shipping business. He shipped 870 boxes on Tuesday. He shipped 765 boxes on Wednesday. How many boxes did he ship on both days? **Explain** what method you used.

Extra Practice

Set A Find each sum. Name the property used. (pp. 48–49)

1. $8 + 3 = ■$
$3 + 8 = ■$
2. $0 + 14 = ■$
$14 + 0 = ■$
3. $13 + 5 = ■$
$5 + 13 = ■$
4. $(4 + 2) + 3 = ■$
$4 + (2 + 3) = ■$

Set B Find the missing addend. You may want to use counters. (pp. 50–51)

1. $■ + 2 = 8$
2. $9 + ■ = 17$
3. $■ + 5 = 22$
4. $15 + ■ = 2 + 15$

Set C Use rounding to estimate each sum. (pp. 52–53)

1. $51 + 47$
2. $89 + 56$
3. $22 + 72$
4. $678 + 113$
5. $487 + 391$

Use compatible numbers to estimate each sum.

6. $49 + 52$
7. $63 + 21$
8. $354 + 126$
9. $477 + 226$
10. $761 + 131$

Set D Estimate. Then find each sum using place value or mental math. (pp. 54–55)

1. $43 + 31 + 22$
2. $38 + 93$
3. $86 + 64 + 54$
4. $27 + 18$
5. $53 + 67$

Set E Estimate. Then find each sum. (pp. 58–59)

1. $367 + 243$
2. $5{,}742 + 2{,}961$
3. $890 + 539$
4. $502 + 319$
5. $2{,}670 + 6{,}529$

6. Andy's family drove 214 miles on Friday and 329 miles on Saturday. How many miles did they drive in all?
7. Becky sold 1,587 shirts one month and 1,703 shirts the next month. How many shirts did she sell in all?

Set F Find the sum. Tell which method you used. (pp. 64–67)

1. $329 + 693$
2. $258 + 640$
3. $965 + 711 + 179$
4. $1{,}404 + 7{,}294$
5. $4{,}433 + 5{,}376$

CD ROM **Technology**
Use Harcourt Mega Math, Country Countdown, *Block Busters,* Levels M, U, V.

PRACTICE GAME

Auto Addition

Get in the Car!

2 players

Start Your Engines!

- 2 two-color counters

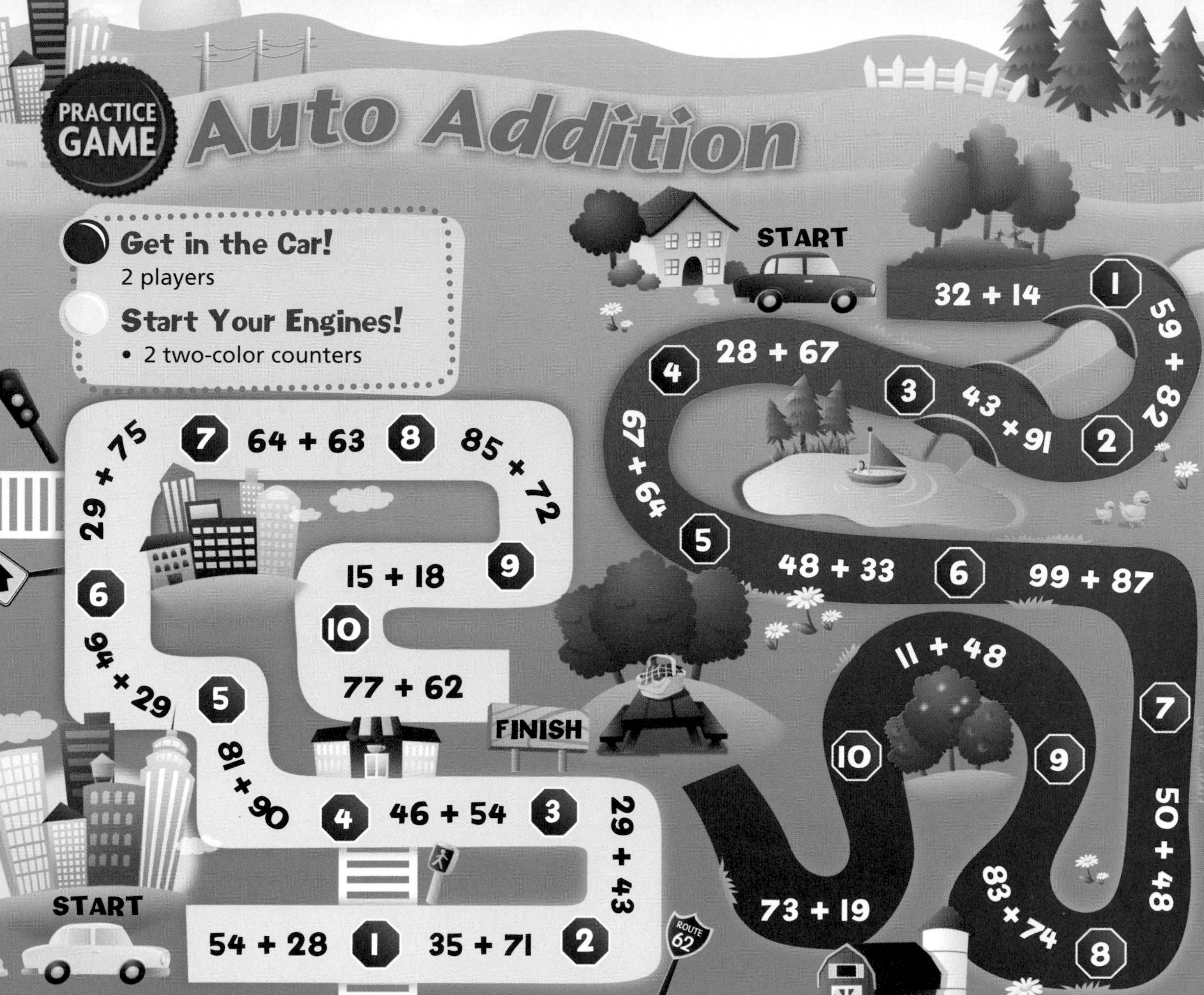

Drive to the Picnic!

- Each player selects a different color counter and places it on the matching START color.
- Players follow the highway color that matches the color of their counter.
- Players complete the addition problem to get to the first Stop Sign. Use paper and pencil to solve. Players will check each other's answers.
- If the player's answer to a problem is wrong, the player does not move forward. The player must wait until his or her next turn to try to solve the problem again.
- Players take turns solving addition problems in order to move to the next Stop Sign.
- The first player to reach the picnic wins the game.

MATH POWER Finding Sums

Magic SQUARES

Magic Squares are a fun way to practice finding sums. In a Magic Square, the sums of each column, row, and diagonal are the same.

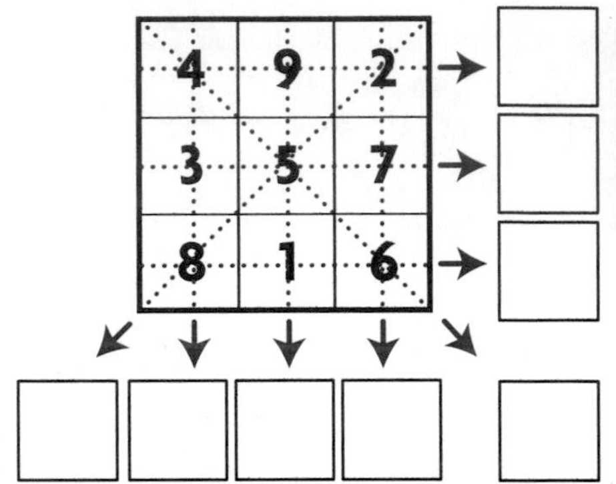

Example

The Magic Square to the right is called the *Lo Shu* Magic Square. To find the answer to this Magic Square, follow these steps.

Step 1 Find the sums of the horizontal rows.

$4 + 9 + 2 = ■, 3 + 5 + 7 = ■, 8 + 1 + 6 = ■$

Step 2 Find the sums of the vertical columns.

$4 + 3 + 8 = ■, 9 + 5 + 1 = ■, 2 + 7 + 6 = ■$

Step 3 Find the sums of the diagonals.

$4 + 5 + 6 = ■, 2 + 5 + 8 = ■$

So, the answer to the Magic Square is 15.

Try It

1. Copy and complete the Magic Square by using the numbers below. The answer is 18.

2 3 5 6 9 10

■	■	7
4	■	8
■	■	■

2. WRITE Math Work with a partner to find the sum of one row in Benjamin Franklin's Magic Square. **Explain** how you found your answer.

Benjamin Franklin's Magic Square

14	3	62	51	46	35	30	19
52	61	4	13	20	29	36	45
11	6	59	54	43	38	27	22
53	60	5	12	21	28	37	44
55	58	7	10	23	26	39	42
9	8	57	56	41	40	25	24
50	63	2	15	18	31	34	47
16	1	64	49	48	33	32	17

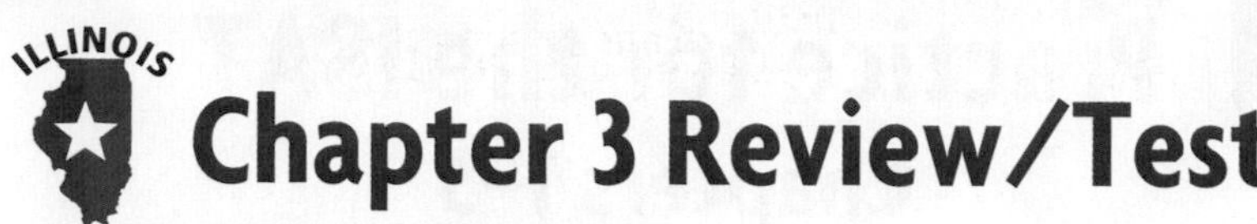

Chapter 3 Review/Test

Check Vocabulary and Concepts

Choose the best term from the box.

VOCABULARY
Associative Property of Addition
Commutative Property of Addition
Identity Property of Addition
estimate

1. The __?__ says that if you add zero to any number, the sum is that number. IL 6.3.13 (p. 48)
2. To find about how many, you can __?__. IL 6.3.14 (p. 52)

Check Skills

Find each sum. Name the property used. IL 6.3.13 (pp. 48–49)

3. $4 + 0 = \blacksquare$
   $0 + 4 = \blacksquare$
4. $8 + (2 + 4) = \blacksquare$
   $(8 + 2) + 4 = \blacksquare$
5. $7 + 6 = \blacksquare$
   $6 + 7 = \blacksquare$

Find the missing addend. IL 8.3.04 (pp. 50–51)

6. $\blacksquare + 8 = 13$
7. $5 + \blacksquare = 9 + 5$
8. $6 + \blacksquare = 12$
9. $\blacksquare + 3 = 12$

Estimate each sum. IL 6.3.14 (pp. 52–53)

10. $57 + 24$
11. $782 + 131$
12. $34 + 59$
13. $542 + 279$

Estimate. Then find each sum. IL 6.3.09; 6.3.14 (pp. 54–55, 58–59)

14. $57 + 24$
15. $782 + 119$
16. $4{,}213 + 1{,}732$
17. $27{,}394 + 61{,}278$

Check Problem Solving

Solve. IL 8.3.03 (pp. 60–63)

18. There were 150 fans at a soccer game. There were 30 more children than parents. How many children were at the game?
19. Caleb and Mary scored a total of 14 points at the basketball game. Mary scored 6 more points than Caleb. How many points did each player score?
20. WRITE Math **Sense or Nonsense** Three numbers in a row have a sum of 45. Kathy says the numbers are 15, 16, and 17. Does her statement make sense? **Explain.**

Technology Use *Online Assessment.*

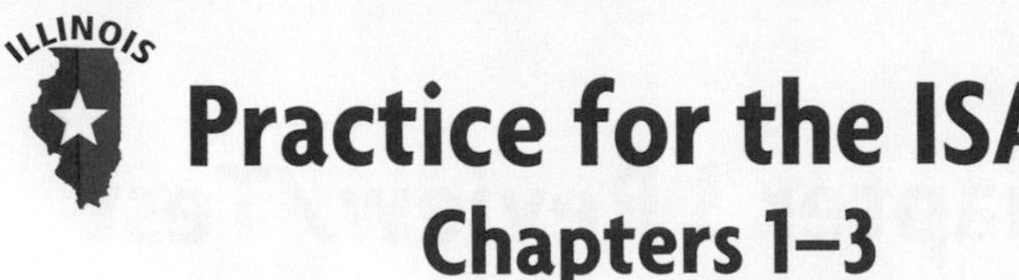

Practice for the ISAT
Chapters 1–3

Number and Operations

1. Which numeral means the same as $500 + 30 + 7$? IL 6.3.01 (p. 8)

   A 537

   B 573

   C 5,037

   D 5,307

Test Tip **Eliminate choices.**

See item 2. First, estimate the sum. Then, find the answer choices that are close to your estimate. Finally, add to find the correct answer choice.

2. The school library has 289 science books and 332 animal books. How many science and animal books does the library have altogether? IL 6.3.09 (p. 58)

   A 511

   B 521

   C 611

   D 621

3. **WRITE Math** On Sunday there were 643 visitors at the amusement park. Rounded to the nearest hundred, about how many people were at the park? **Explain** how to find the answer using the tens digit. IL 6.3.14 (p. 36)

Algebra

4. Cars have 4 wheels. Greg wants to find out how many wheels are on 5 cars. Use the table below to find the answer. Grade 2

number of cars	1	2	3	4	5
number of wheels	4	8	12	16	■

   A 24 C 20

   B 22 D 18

5. Which are the next two figures in the pattern below? Grade 2

□ △ ○ □ △ ○ □ △ ○ ? ?

   A □ △

   B □ ○

   C ○ □

   D △ ○

6. **WRITE Math** Brad had 4 toy cars and got 3 more. Pete had 3 toy cars and got 4 more. Who has more toy cars now? **Explain** which addition property helps you to solve the problem. IL 8.3.03 (p. 48)

Measurement

7. Which time is shown on the clock? Grade 2

A 3:30
B 6:15
C 6:30
D 7:15

8. Which temperature does the thermometer show? Grade 2

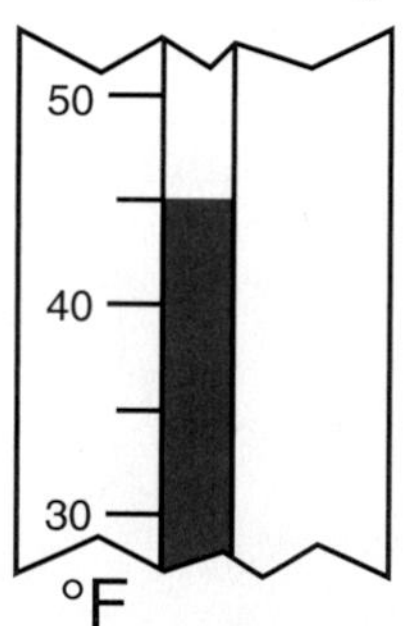

A 50°F
B 45°F
C 40°F
D 35°F

9. WRITE Math Keith ate a snack at three forty. **Explain** where the hands of the clock point at three forty. Grade 2

Data Analysis and Probability

10. Betty has 10 crayons in a bag. There are 2 blue, 5 red, 1 yellow, and 2 green crayons. Which color crayon is Betty more likely to choose? Grade 2

A Blue
B Red
C Yellow
D Green

11. Mrs. Totten's class made a tally table to show the number of books they read in each subject. How many science and social studies books did they read altogether? Grade 2

Books Read	
Subject	**Number of Books**
Social Studies	||||
Science	~~||||~~ |||
Music	||

A 4
B 6
C 11
D 12

12. WRITE Math If Mrs. Totten's class wanted to make a picture graph using the data shown in Problem 11, how many pictures would they use? **Explain.** Grade 2

CHAPTER 4

Subtraction

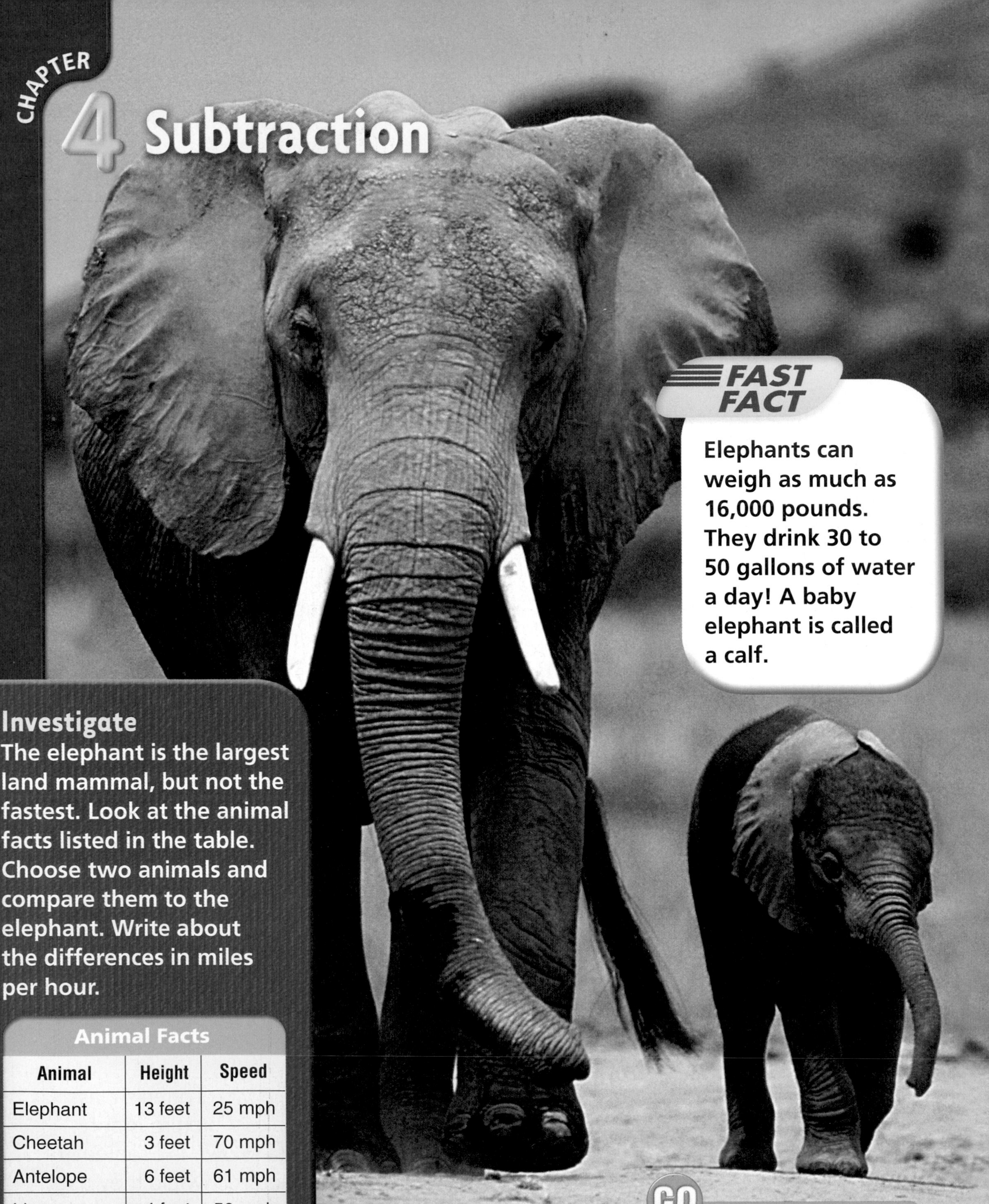

FAST FACT

Elephants can weigh as much as 16,000 pounds. They drink 30 to 50 gallons of water a day! A baby elephant is called a calf.

Investigate

The elephant is the largest land mammal, but not the fastest. Look at the animal facts listed in the table. Choose two animals and compare them to the elephant. Write about the differences in miles per hour.

Animal Facts

Animal	Height	Speed
Elephant	13 feet	25 mph
Cheetah	3 feet	70 mph
Antelope	6 feet	61 mph
Lion	4 feet	50 mph

GO ONLINE **Technology** Student pages are available in the Student eBook.

Show What You Know

Check your understanding of important skills needed for success in Chapter 4.

▶ Subtract 1-Digit from 2-Digit Numbers

Subtract.

1. $12 - 8$

2. $17 - 7$

3. $15 - 6$

4. $11 - 0$

5. $18 - 9$

▶ Model 2-Digit Subtraction

Use the models. Find the difference.

6. $35 - 12 = \blacksquare$

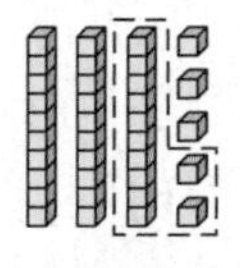

7. $48 - 26 = \blacksquare$

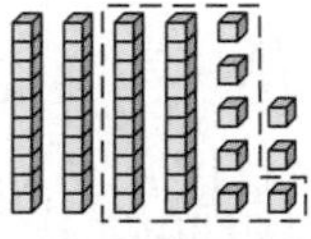

8. $53 - 43 = \blacksquare$

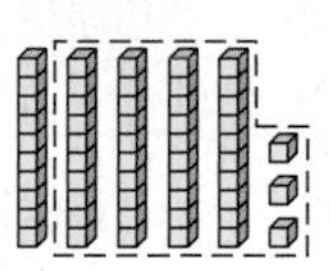

9. $69 - 23 = \blacksquare$

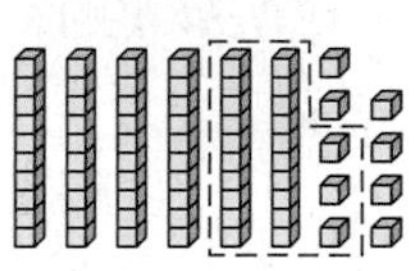

▶ 2-Digit Subtraction Without Regrouping

Subtract.

10. $76 - 32$

11. $29 - 13$

12. $65 - 54$

13. $92 - 50$

14. $38 - 18$

VOCABULARY POWER

CHAPTER VOCABULARY

fact family
inverse operations

WARM-UP WORDS

fact family A set of related addition and subtraction, or multiplication and division, number sentences

inverse operations Opposite operations, or operations that undo each other, such as addition and subtraction or multiplication and division

LESSON 1

ALGEBRA

Fact Families

OBJECTIVE: Identify and write addition and subtraction fact families.

Quick Review

1. 4 + 5
2. 12 − 4
3. 3 + 8
4. 5 + 6
5. 13 − 7

Vocabulary

fact family

inverse operations

Learn

PROBLEM Rory is baking a cake. She has 12 eggs. She uses 3 eggs to make the cake. How many eggs does Rory have left?

You can write a number sentence to solve the problem.

12 − 3 = 9 So, Rory has 9 eggs left.

The numbers 3, 9, and 12 can be used to make a fact family. A **fact family** is a group of related number sentences that use the same numbers.

Addition and subtraction are opposite, or **inverse operations**. Fact families are examples of inverse operations.

Fact Family for 3, 9, and 12

3 + 9 = 12 9 + 3 = 12

12 − 9 = 3 12 − 3 = 9

If both addends are the same, there are only two facts in the fact family.

Fact Family for 4, 4, and 8

4 + 4 = 8 8 − 4 = 4

Guided Practice

1. Copy and complete the fact family.

8 + 5 = 13 5 + 8 = ■ 13 − 5 = 8 13 − 8 = ■

Complete.

2. 12 − 6 = 6, so 6 + 6 = ■.

3. 4 + 3 = 7, so ■ − 3 = 4.

Write the fact family for each set of numbers.

4. 4, 5, 9 5. 5, 9, 14 6. 1, 6, 7 7. 5, 7, 12

8. TALK Math **Explain** why some fact families have four facts and others have only two facts.

Independent Practice and Problem Solving

Complete.

9. $11 - 2 = 9$, so $2 + \blacksquare = 11$.
10. $4 + 8 = 12$, so $\blacksquare - 8 = 4$.
11. $6 + 9 = 15$, so $15 - 6 = \blacksquare$.
12. $10 - 5 = 5$, so $5 + \blacksquare = 10$.
13. $16 - 5 = 11$, so $\blacksquare + \blacksquare = 16$.
14. $7 + 6 = 13$, so $\blacksquare - 7 = \blacksquare$.

Write the fact family for each set of numbers.

15. 2, 8, 10 16. 4, 7, 11 17. 3, 6, 9 18. 7, 7, 14

USE DATA For 19–21, use the picture.

19. Write a number sentence that shows the total number of muffins sold. Then write the fact family for the number sentence.

20. On Tuesday, 3 blueberry muffins and 4 apple muffins were sold. How many more muffins were sold on Monday than on Tuesday?

21. **Pose a Problem** Look back at Problem 20. Write a similar problem by changing the day and the numbers of muffins sold.

22. WRITE Math Draw and label four pictures to show the fact family for 2, 4, and 6. **Explain** how you used inverse operations to find the facts.

Mixed Review and Test Prep

23. The school store has 325 black pens and 115 blue pens. How many pens are there altogether? (p. 58)

24. What is the name of a figure with 6 sides? (Grade 2)

25. **Test Prep** Which number sentence is in the same fact family as $3 + 4 = 7$?

A $3 + 5 = 8$
B $7 + 3 = 10$
C $4 + 7 = 11$
D $4 + 3 = 7$

Extra Practice on page 98, Set A

LESSON 2

Estimate Differences

OBJECTIVE: Estimate differences of 2- and 3-digit numbers by using rounding and compatible numbers.

Quick Review

Round each number to the greatest place value.

1. 24 **2.** 65
3. 391 **4.** 847
5. 588

Learn

PROBLEM The largest Mekong giant catfish caught by fishers weighed 646 pounds. The largest blue catfish caught weighed 124 pounds. About how much more did the Mekong giant catfish weigh than the blue catfish?

To find *about* how much more, you can estimate.

▲ The Mekong giant catfish is the largest known freshwater fish and is an endangered species.

Example **Estimate.** 646 − 124

ONE WAY **Use rounding.**

Round each number to the nearest hundred. Then subtract.

$$\begin{array}{r} 646 \\ -\,124 \\ \hline \end{array} \rightarrow \begin{array}{r} 600 \\ -\,100 \\ \hline 500 \end{array}$$

ANOTHER WAY **Use compatible numbers.**

$$\begin{array}{r} 646 \\ -\,124 \\ \hline \end{array} \rightarrow \begin{array}{r} 650 \\ -\,125 \\ \hline 525 \end{array}$$

So, both 500 and 525 are reasonable estimates of how much more the Mekong giant catfish weighed.

- Why are 650 and 125 compatible numbers?

Remember
Compatible numbers are numbers that are easy to compute mentally.

More Examples

A **Use compatible numbers.**

$$\begin{array}{r} 73 \\ -\,22 \\ \hline \end{array} \rightarrow \begin{array}{r} 75 \\ -\,25 \\ \hline 50 \end{array}$$

B **Use compatible numbers.**

$$\begin{array}{r} 476 \\ -\,248 \\ \hline \end{array} \rightarrow \begin{array}{r} 475 \\ -\,250 \\ \hline 225 \end{array}$$

C **Use rounding.**

$$\begin{array}{r} 87 \\ -\,19 \\ \hline \end{array} \rightarrow \begin{array}{r} 90 \\ -\,20 \\ \hline 70 \end{array}$$

Guided Practice

1. Copy the problem at the right. Round both 319 and 133 to the nearest hundred. Then estimate their difference.

$$\begin{array}{r} 319 \\ -\,133 \\ \hline \end{array}$$

Use rounding or compatible numbers to estimate each difference.

2. $52 - 24$
3. $94 - 56$
4. $691 - 137$
✓5. $736 - 327$
✓6. $487 - 248$

7. **TALK Math** **Explain** ways you could estimate $567 - 209$.

Independent Practice and Problem Solving

Use rounding or compatible numbers to estimate each difference.

8. $88 - 41$
9. $65 - 19$
10. $98 - 67$
11. $378 - 312$
12. $42 - 19$
13. $774 - 349$
14. $936 - 421$
15. $415 - 187$
16. $587 - 208$
17. $86 - 24$
18. $694 - 593$
19. $94 - 42$
20. $798 - 726$
21. $561 - 349$
22. $63 - 37$

Algebra Estimate to compare. Write $<$, $>$, or $=$ for each ●.

23. $456 - 162$ ● 200
24. $798 - 726$ ● 10
25. $542 - 331$ ● 300

USE DATA For 26–27, use the table.

26. About how much more is the total weight of the Pacific halibut and conger than the weight of the yellowfin tuna?

27. **WRITE Math** About how much more did the yellowfin tuna weigh than the conger? **Explain** how you know.

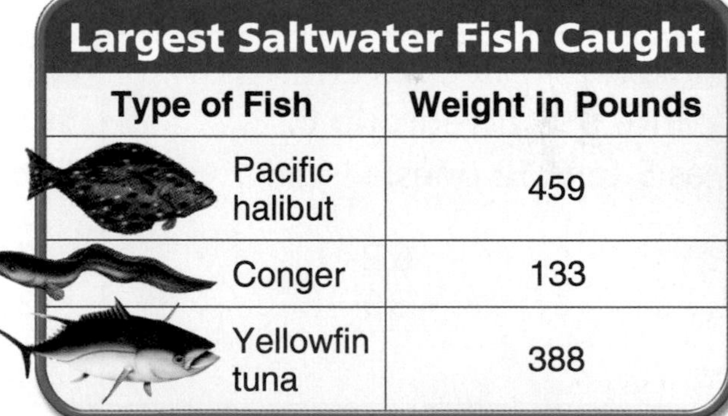

Largest Saltwater Fish Caught

Type of Fish	Weight in Pounds
Pacific halibut	459
Conger	133
Yellowfin tuna	388

Mixed Review and Test Prep

28. Use the Associative Property to complete the number sentence. (p. 48)

$$3 + (2 + 5) = (■ + ■) + 5$$

29. Which color marble is more likely to be pulled from the bag? (Grade 2)

30. **Test Prep** Fred estimated $591 - 128$. He rounded each number to the nearest hundred. Then he subtracted. What was Fred's estimate?

A 400 **C** 600

B 500 **D** 700

Extra Practice on page 98, Set B

LESSON 3

Subtract 2-Digit Numbers

OBJECTIVE: Subtract 2-digit numbers with and without regrouping.

Quick Review

1. 9 − 4 **2.** 12 − 5
3. 18 − 9 **4.** 7 − 3
5. 15 − 7

Learn

PROBLEM Ken saw a grizzly bear that was 39 inches tall. He saw a polar bear that was 62 inches tall. How much taller was the polar bear than the grizzly bear?

▲ When standing on all four legs, a polar bear can be up to 64 inches tall.

Example 1 Subtract. 62 − 39 Estimate. 60 − 40 = 20

ONE WAY Use mental math.

Step 1
Add to the lesser number to make a ten.
$$\begin{array}{r} 62 \\ -39 \to 40 \\ \hline \end{array}$$
Think: 39 + 1 = 40

Step 2
Add the same number to the greater number.
$$\begin{array}{rcl} 62 & \to & 63 \\ -39 & \to & 40 \end{array}$$
Think: 62 + 1 = 63

Step 3
Subtract your answers.
$$\begin{array}{rcr} 62 & \to & 63 \\ -39 & \to & -40 \\ & & \hline 23 \end{array}$$

ANOTHER WAY Use place value.

Step 1
Since 9 > 2, regroup 62 as 5 tens 12 ones.
$$\begin{array}{r} \overset{5}{\cancel{6}}\overset{12}{\cancel{2}} \\ -39 \\ \hline \end{array}$$

Step 2
Subtract the ones.
Subtract the tens.
$$\begin{array}{r} \overset{5}{\cancel{6}}\overset{12}{\cancel{2}} \\ -39 \\ \hline 23 \end{array} \qquad \begin{array}{r} 23 \\ +39 \\ \hline 62 \end{array}$$
Add to check.

So, the polar bear was 23 inches taller than the grizzly bear.

Since 23 is close to the estimate of 20, the answer is reasonable.

Math Idea
Adding the same amount to both numbers does not change the difference.

Example 2 Subtract. 43 − 16

Use mental math.
Think: 16 + 4 = 20
43 + 4 = 47
$$\begin{array}{rcr} 43 & \to & 47 \\ -16 & \to & -20 \\ \hline & & 27 \end{array}$$

Use place value.
Regroup 43 as 3 tens 13 ones.
Subtract the ones.
Subtract the tens.
$$\begin{array}{r} \overset{3}{\cancel{4}}\,\overset{13}{\cancel{3}} \\ -1\,6 \\ \hline 2\,7 \end{array}$$

Guided Practice

1. To find 31 − 17 by using mental math, what number should you add to both 17 and 31?

Estimate. Then find each difference.

2. $94 - 15$
3. $58 - 29$
4. $87 - 54$
5. $72 - 24$
6. $79 - 36$

7. TALK Math **Explain** how to use place value to find 93 − 68.

Independent Practice and Problem Solving

Estimate. Then find each difference.

8. $61 - 48$
9. $46 - 23$
10. $77 - 19$
11. $51 - 34$
12. $45 - 27$

Find each difference. Use addition to check.

13. $55 - 31 = \blacksquare$
14. $86 - 28 = \blacksquare$
15. $68 - 14 = \blacksquare$
16. $93 - 76 = \blacksquare$

USE DATA For 17–18, use the graph.

17. A brown bear grew 6 inches more than the average height. An American black bear grew 3 inches more than the average height. What is the difference between their heights?

18. WRITE Math **Explain** how you can use mental math to find how much taller the polar bear is than the brown bear.

Mixed Review and Test Prep

19. What is 5,399 rounded to the nearest thousand? (p. 38)

20. There are 324 girls and 271 boys at school. About how many students are at school? (p. 52)

21. **Test Prep** Craig sold 54 shirts to raise money for the swim team. He has delivered 17 of them. How many shirts does he have left to deliver?

A 17 **B** 37 **C** 47 **D** 71

Extra Practice on page 98, Set C

LESSON 4 HANDS ON

Model 3-Digit Subtraction

OBJECTIVE: Explore subtracting 3-digit numbers with and without regrouping.

Quick Review

Write the numbers in expanded form.

1. 656 **2.** 703
3. 182 **4.** 599
5. 250

Investigate

Materials ■ base-ten blocks

You can use base-ten blocks to subtract numbers.

A Model the number 345.

B Use your model to find $345 - 158$. Subtract the ones, tens, and hundreds. Regroup the blocks when needed.

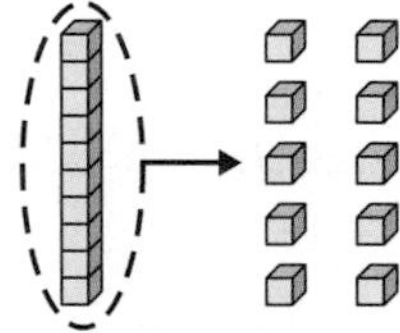

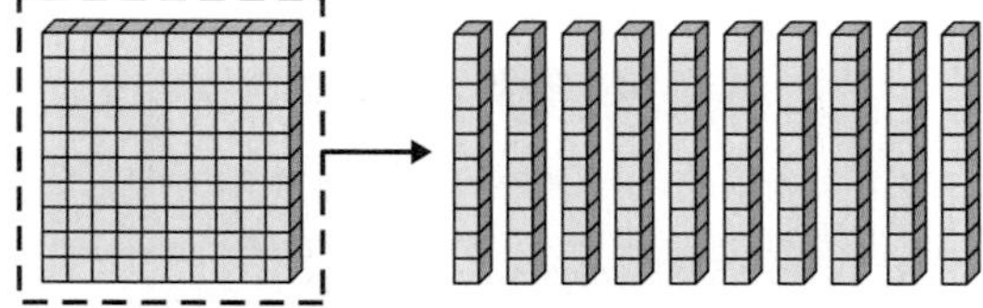

C Look at the base-ten blocks that are left. These blocks represent the difference. Draw a picture to record your answer.

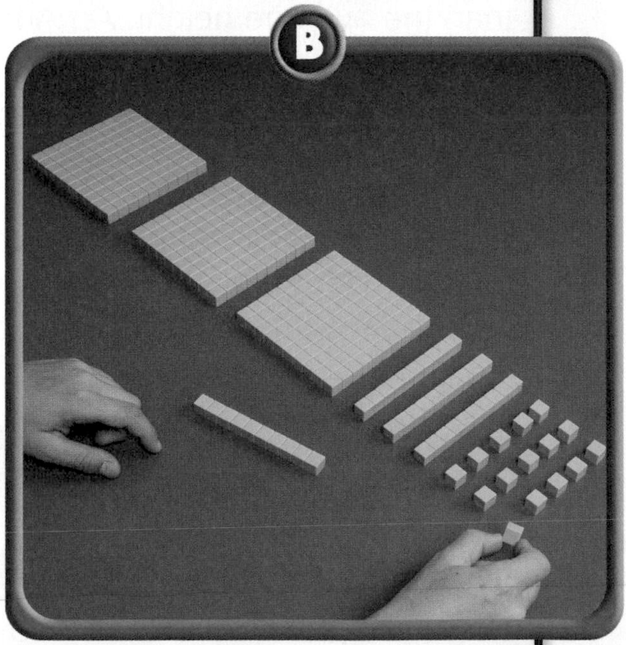

Draw Conclusions

1. **Explain** why there are 3 hundreds, 3 tens, and 15 ones in Picture B.
2. How did you know you had to regroup one of the hundreds?
3. **Synthesis** How could you use base-ten blocks and addition to check your answer?

Connect

You can record your steps with paper and pencil.

Example **Subtract.** 221 − 146

Step 1

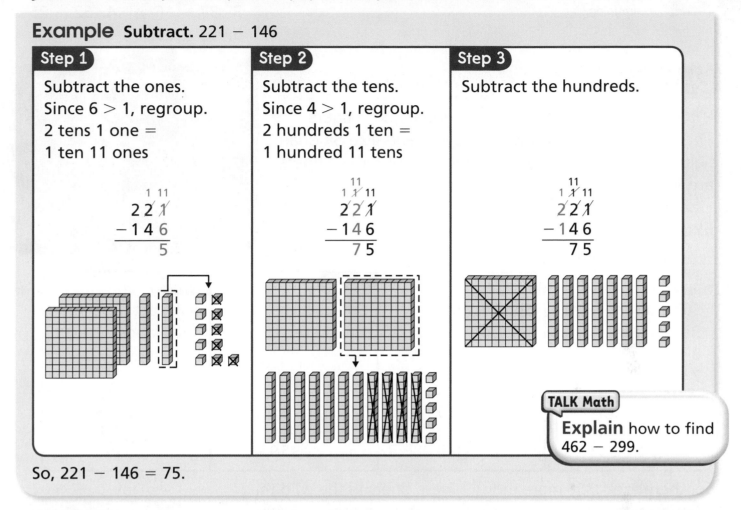

Subtract the ones.
Since 6 > 1, regroup.
2 tens 1 one =
1 ten 11 ones

$$\begin{array}{r} \scriptstyle 1\ 11 \\ 2\,\not{2}\,\not{1} \\ -\,1\,4\,6 \\ \hline 5 \end{array}$$

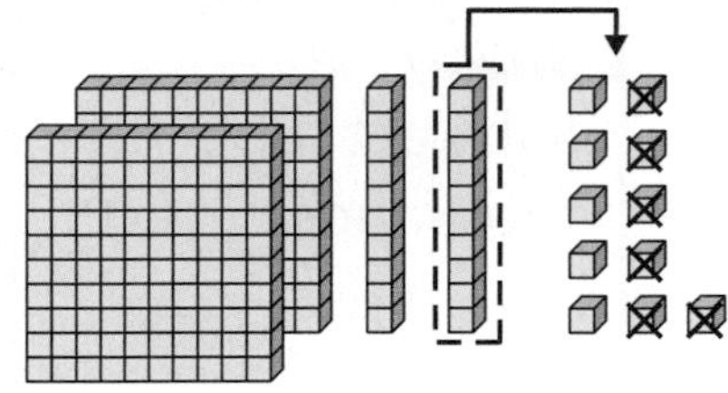

Step 2

Subtract the tens.
Since 4 > 1, regroup.
2 hundreds 1 ten =
1 hundred 11 tens

$$\begin{array}{r} \scriptstyle 11 \\ \scriptstyle 1\ \not{1}\ 11 \\ \not{2}\,\not{2}\,\not{1} \\ -\,1\,4\,6 \\ \hline 7\,5 \end{array}$$

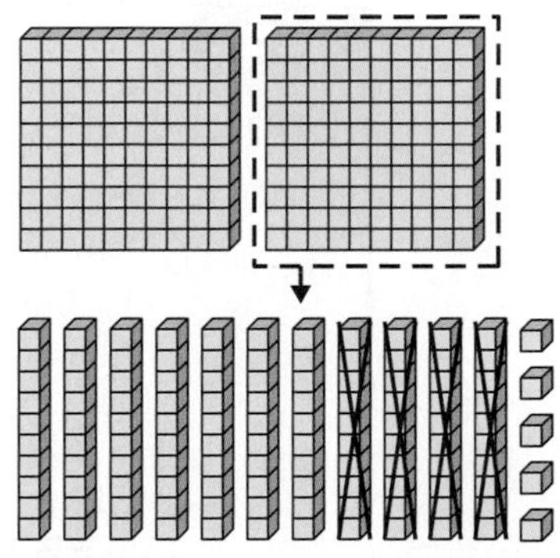

Step 3

Subtract the hundreds.

$$\begin{array}{r} \scriptstyle 11 \\ \scriptstyle 1\ \not{1}\ 11 \\ \not{2}\,\not{2}\,\not{1} \\ -\,1\,4\,6 \\ \hline 7\,5 \end{array}$$

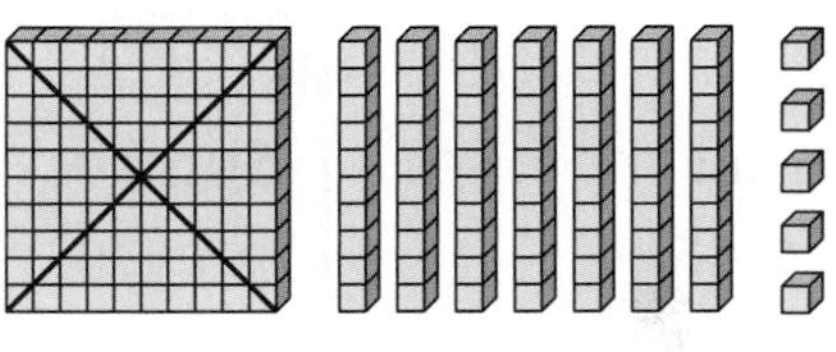

TALK Math

Explain how to find 462 − 299.

So, 221 − 146 = 75.

Practice

Use base-ten blocks to find each difference.

1. 299 − 186 = ■
2. 309 − 281 = ■
3. 443 − 267 = ■

Find each difference.

4. $\begin{array}{r} 435 \\ -319 \\ \hline \end{array}$
5. $\begin{array}{r} 585 \\ -124 \\ \hline \end{array}$
6. $\begin{array}{r} 458 \\ -283 \\ \hline \end{array}$
7. $\begin{array}{r} 796 \\ -435 \\ \hline \end{array}$
8. $\begin{array}{r} 851 \\ -615 \\ \hline \end{array}$
9. $\begin{array}{r} 909 \\ -350 \\ \hline \end{array}$
10. $\begin{array}{r} 374 \\ -126 \\ \hline \end{array}$
11. $\begin{array}{r} 614 \\ -327 \\ \hline \end{array}$
12. $\begin{array}{r} 451 \\ -286 \\ \hline \end{array}$
13. $\begin{array}{r} 640 \\ -337 \\ \hline \end{array}$

14. **WRITE Math** **Explain** how modeling with base-ten blocks helps you see when you need to regroup for subtraction.

CD ROM **Technology**
Use Harcourt Mega Math, Country Countdown, *Block Busters,* Levels X, Y.

LESSON 5

Subtract Greater Numbers

OBJECTIVE: Subtract 3- and 4-digit numbers with and without regrouping.

Quick Review

1. 25 − 12
2. 68 − 34
3. 37 − 16
4. 52 − 25
5. 83 − 59

▲ Indo-Chinese tigers live in the tropical forests of seven different countries.

Learn

PROBLEM Lena is researching endangered tigers. There are 1,785 Indo-Chinese tigers and 426 Siberian tigers in the wild. How many more Indo-Chinese tigers are in the wild than Siberian tigers?

Example

Subtract. 1,785 − 426

Estimate. 1,800 − 400 = 1,400

Step 1

Subtract the ones. Regroup.
8 tens 5 ones = 7 tens 15 ones

$$\begin{array}{r} {\scriptstyle 7\ 15} \\ 1{,}7\not{8}\not{5} \\ -\ 426 \\ \hline 9 \end{array}$$

Step 2

Subtract the tens.

$$\begin{array}{r} {\scriptstyle 7\ 15} \\ 1{,}7\not{8}\not{5} \\ -\ 426 \\ \hline 59 \end{array}$$

Step 3

Subtract the hundreds.

$$\begin{array}{r} {\scriptstyle 7\ 15} \\ 1{,}7\not{8}\not{5} \\ -\ 426 \\ \hline 359 \end{array}$$

Step 4

Subtract the thousands.

$$\begin{array}{r} {\scriptstyle 7\ 15} \\ 1{,}7\not{8}\not{5} \\ -\ 426 \\ \hline 1{,}359 \end{array}$$

So, there are 1,359 more Indo-Chinese tigers in the wild than Siberian tigers. Since 1,359 is close to the estimate of 1,400, the answer is reasonable.

More Examples

A Regrouping

$$\begin{array}{r} {\scriptstyle 4\ 14} \\ \not{5}\not{4}8 \\ -383 \\ \hline 165 \end{array}$$

B No Regrouping

$$\begin{array}{r} 6{,}896 \\ -1{,}524 \\ \hline 5{,}372 \end{array}$$

C Regrouping

$$\begin{array}{r} {\scriptstyle 12} \\ {\scriptstyle 8\ \not{2}\ 15} \\ 4{,}\not{9}\not{3}\not{5} \\ -2{,}277 \\ \hline 2{,}658 \end{array}$$

Guided Practice

1. Copy the problem at the right. Do you have to regroup? Find the difference.

$$\begin{array}{r} 562 \\ -295 \\ \hline \end{array}$$

Estimate. Then find each difference.

2. 654 − 544

3. 425 − 248

4. 5,867 − 2,998

5. 7,404 − 781

6. 8,153 − 4,322

7. TALK Math **Explain** how to find the difference between 3,695 and 1,486.

Independent Practice and Problem Solving

Estimate. Then find each difference.

8. 518 − 305

9. 304 − 124

10. 671 − 268

11. 948 − 659

12. 1,632 − 546

13. 2,519 − 1,400

14. 6,187 − 2,275

15. 4,710 − 2,547

16. 9,346 − 4,419

17. 659 − 424

Algebra **Compare. Write <, >, or = for each ●.**

18. 732 − 284 ● 824 − 392

19. 5,476 − 2,132 ● 8,288 − 4,502

20. 481 − 256 ● 629 − 404

21. 9,109 − 8,387 ● 3,637 − 2,543

USE DATA For 22–24, use the table.

22. What is the difference between the number of Bengal tigers and the number of Indo-Chinese tigers?

23. What if the number of each type of tiger increased by 150? How many tigers would there be in all?

24. WRITE Math **Explain** how you would find how many more Bengal tigers there are than Siberian tigers.

Endangered Tigers in the Wild

Type	Number
Sumatran tiger	500
Bengal tiger	4,556
Indo-Chinese tiger	1,785
Siberian tiger	426

Mixed Review and Test Prep

25. Find the missing addend. (p. 50)

23 + ■ = 41

26. A bookmobile has 327 books. Amy ordered 156 more books. How many books will there be in all? (p. 58)

27. **Test Prep** What is the difference between 2,345 and 1,695?

A 1,650 **C** 750

B 1,350 **D** 650

Extra Practice on page 98, Set D

Problem Solving Workshop
Skill: Estimate or Exact Answer

OBJECTIVE: Solve problems by using the skill *estimate or exact answer.*

Read to Understand
Plan
Solve
Check

Use the Skill

PROBLEM A Boeing 757 airplane that can carry 208 passengers flies from Dallas to St. Louis several times each day. The 547-mile trip takes 95 minutes.

Sometimes, you need an exact answer to solve a problem. Sometimes, an estimate is all you need.

Examples

A Can the airplane carry 418 passengers in 2 trips?

Since the question asks if the airplane can carry an exact number of passengers, an exact answer is needed.

$$\begin{array}{r} 208 \\ +\,208 \\ \hline 416 \end{array}$$

So, the airplane cannot carry 418 passengers in 2 trips.

B About how many minutes will 2 trips take?

Since the question asks *about* how many, you can estimate to solve.

$$\begin{array}{rcr} 95 & \rightarrow & 100 \\ +\,95 & \rightarrow & +\,100 \\ \hline & & 200 \end{array}$$

So, 2 trips will take about 200 minutes.

Think and Discuss

Tell whether you need an exact answer or an estimate. Then solve.

a. A Boeing 747 has 416 seats. A Boeing 767 has 245 seats. What is the greatest number of passengers the two airplanes can carry altogether?

b. Wendy and her family flew on a Boeing 727 last week. They flew 422 miles to Tulsa, Oklahoma, from Jackson, Mississippi. About how many miles is a round trip?

Guided Problem Solving

1. Woodfield Mall is the largest mall in Illinois. It has 294 stores. The nation's largest mall is the Mall of America in Minnesota. It has 520 stores. About how many more stores does the Mall of America have than Woodfield Mall?

   Do you need an estimate or an exact answer? To find out, see if the problem is asking for about how many or an exact answer.

2. **What if** the Mall of America had 568 stores? About how many more stores would the Mall of America have than Woodfield Mall?

3. A Boeing 777 that can carry 368 passengers is traveling from Dallas to Chicago. A one-way trip is 803 miles. Can the airplane carry 1,080 people in 3 one-way trips? Explain.

Mixed Applications

4. Randy wrote a 2-page story for a contest. His story must be 1,250 words or less. Randy's first page has 572 words. How many words can his second page have?

5. The Sunnyville Tree Nursery has 782 oak trees. The Lakeview Tree Nursery has 319 oak trees. About how many fewer oak trees does The Lakeview Tree Nursery have than The Sunnyville Tree Nursery?

6. **Reasoning** The picture shows three houses on Main Street. Hank, Derek, and Jill live in the houses. Derek does not live next to Jill. The sum of the digits in Jill's house number is 12. Who lives at 2041 Main Street? **Explain** your answer.

7. Joel read 10 pages of his book on Monday, 15 pages on Tuesday, and 20 pages on Wednesday. If the pattern continues, how many pages will he read on Friday?

8. **WRITE Math** For social studies, each student wrote about a year in history. Katie picked 1812. Josh's year was 96 years later. What year did Josh pick? **Explain** how you know.

Subtract Across Zeros

OBJECTIVE: Subtract 3- and 4-digit numbers across zeros.

Quick Review

1. 700 − 200
2. 516 − 300
3. 324 − 102
4. 479 − 281
5. 815 − 347

Learn

PROBLEM Colin is playing arcade games to win tickets. He wants to collect 300 tickets to exchange for a coloring book. He already has 184 tickets. How many more tickets does Colin need?

Example 1 **Subtract.** 300 − 184 **Estimate.** 300 − 200 = 100

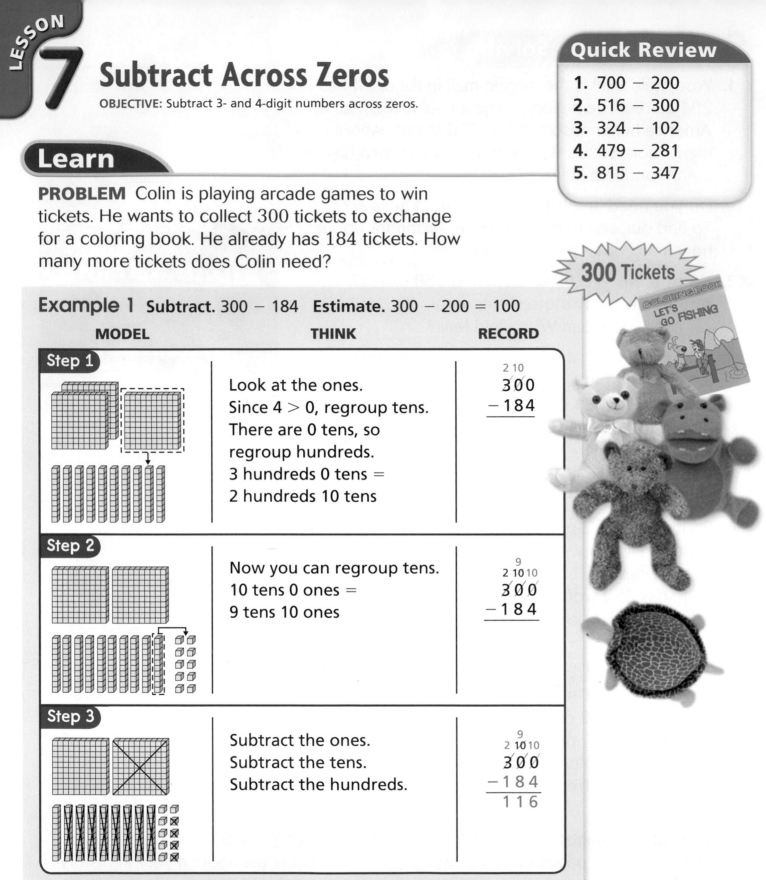

	MODEL	THINK	RECORD
Step 1	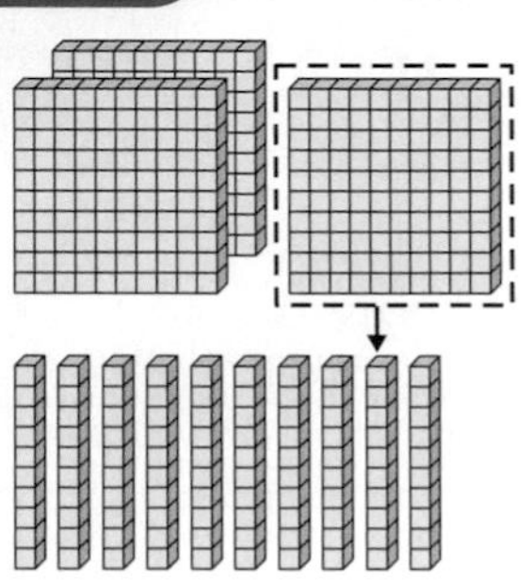	Look at the ones. Since 4 > 0, regroup tens. There are 0 tens, so regroup hundreds. 3 hundreds 0 tens = 2 hundreds 10 tens	2 10 ~~3~~~~0~~0 − 184
Step 2	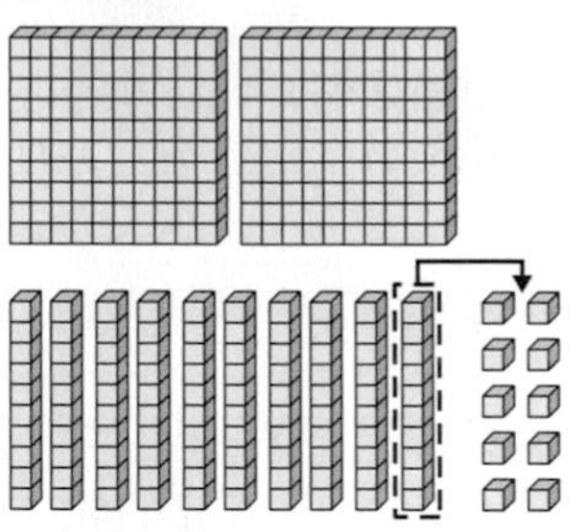	Now you can regroup tens. 10 tens 0 ones = 9 tens 10 ones	9 2 ~~10~~ 10 ~~3~~~~0~~~~0~~ − 184
Step 3	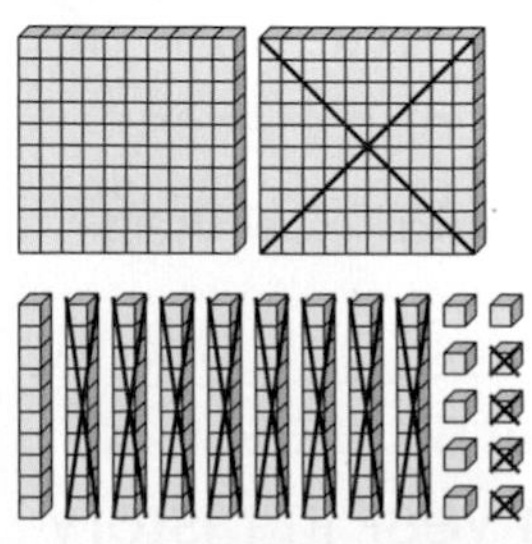	Subtract the ones. Subtract the tens. Subtract the hundreds.	9 2 ~~10~~ 10 ~~3~~~~0~~~~0~~ − 184 116

So, Colin needs to collect 116 more tickets. Since 116 is close to the estimate of 100, the answer is reasonable.

- Explain why you need to regroup twice to find 300 − 184.

Example 2

Anita and Jim need 2,000 tickets to get a board game. They have 1,273 tickets. How many more tickets do they need?

Subtract. 2,000 − 1,273 **Estimate.** 2,000 − 1,300 = 700

Step 1

Since 3 > 0, regroup tens. There are no tens or hundreds, so regroup thousands.
2 thousands 0 hundreds = 1 thousand 10 hundreds

```
  1 10
  2,000
− 1,273
```

Step 2

Regroup hundreds.
10 hundreds 0 tens = 9 hundreds 10 tens

```
     9
  1 10 10
  2,0 0 0
− 1,2 7 3
```

Step 3

Regroup tens.
10 tens 0 ones = 9 tens 10 ones

```
     9  9
  1 10 10 10
  2,0  0  0
− 1,2  7  3
```

Step 4

Subtract the ones.
Subtract the tens.
Subtract the hundreds.
Subtract the thousands.

```
     9  9
  1 10 10 10
  2,0  0  0
− 1,2  7  3
    7  2  7
```

So, Anita and Jim need 727 more tickets. Since 727 is close to the estimate of 700, the answer is reasonable.

More Examples

A

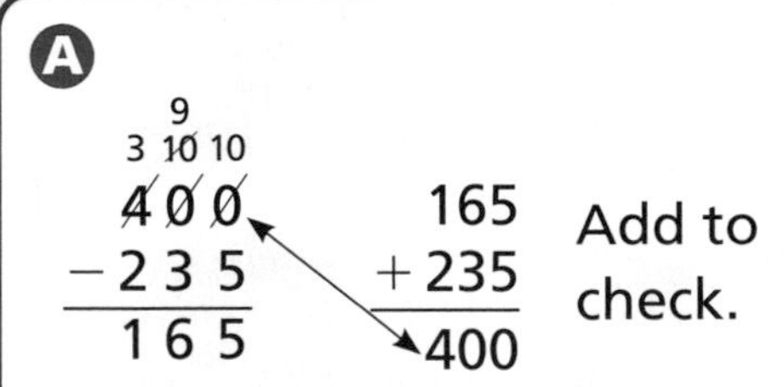

B

```
   9  9
  8 10 10 18
  9,0  0  8
− 4,5  6  9
  4,4  3  9
```

C

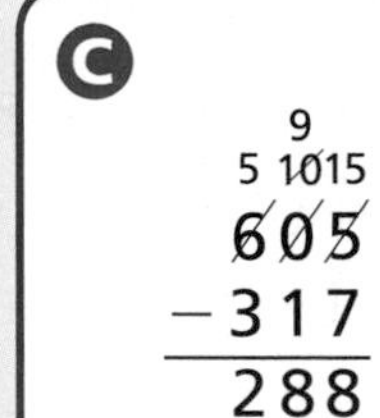

ERROR ALERT

Don't forget to regroup the tens after regrouping the hundreds.

Guided Practice

1. Look at the model for 203. What do you need to do to find 203 − 174?

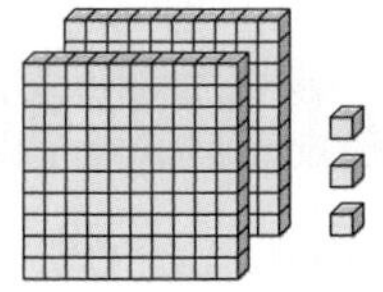

Estimate. Then find each difference.

2. 506 − 457
3. 700 − 374
4. 3,070 − 1,832
5. 5,004 − 1,286
6. 6,500 − 2,144

7. **TALK Math** **Explain** how to find 900 − 658.

Independent Practice and Problem Solving

Estimate. Then find each difference.

8. $\begin{array}{r} 402 \\ -165 \\ \hline \end{array}$ **9.** $\begin{array}{r} 758 \\ -442 \\ \hline \end{array}$ **10.** $\begin{array}{r} 600 \\ -227 \\ \hline \end{array}$ **11.** $\begin{array}{r} 4,400 \\ -3,215 \\ \hline \end{array}$ **12.** $\begin{array}{r} 8,000 \\ -2,480 \\ \hline \end{array}$

13. $\begin{array}{r} 5,075 \\ -2,012 \\ \hline \end{array}$ **14.** $\begin{array}{r} 201 \\ -173 \\ \hline \end{array}$ **15.** $\begin{array}{r} 3,711 \\ -3,520 \\ \hline \end{array}$ **16.** $\begin{array}{r} 900 \\ -677 \\ \hline \end{array}$ **17.** $\begin{array}{r} 6,070 \\ -1,463 \\ \hline \end{array}$

Find each difference. Use addition to check.

18. $805 - 346 = \blacksquare$ **19.** $4,002 - 2,105 = \blacksquare$ **20.** $7,000 - 2,259 = \blacksquare$

Algebra Copy and complete each table.

	Subtract 436.	
21.	957	■
22.	708	■
23.	500	■

	Subtract 3,045.	
24.	5,179	■
25.	4,000	■
26.	8,450	■

	Subtract 1,823.	
27.	3,902	■
28.	6,456	■
29.	2,000	■

USE DATA For 30–31, use the picture.

30. How many more tickets are needed for a backpack than for a puzzle?

31. Sheila has 100 tickets. Tim gives her 54 tickets. How many more tickets does Sheila need to get a hat?

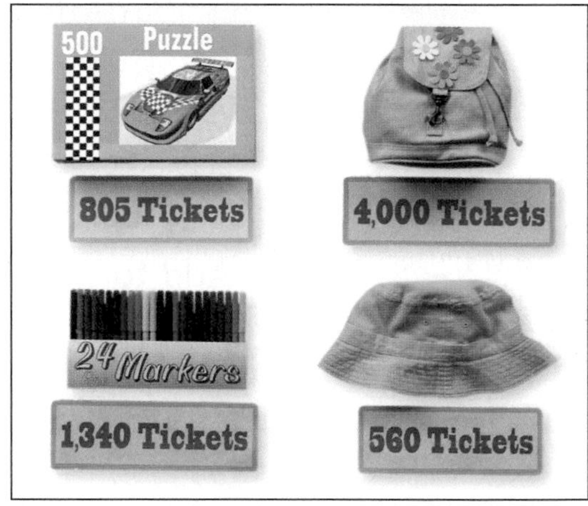

32. WRITE Math **What's the Error?** Oscar wrote this subtraction problem. **Explain** his error. Find the correct difference.

$\begin{array}{r} \scriptstyle 9 \\ \scriptstyle 10\,10 \\ 8\not{0}\not{0} \\ -579 \\ \hline 321 \end{array}$

Mixed Review and Test Prep

33. Kelly had 435 trading cards. She gave away 118 cards. How many cards does she have left? (p. 84)

34. How many vertices does a hexagon have? (Grade 2)

35. **Test Prep** Which number will make the number sentence true?

$5,002 - 3,416 = \blacksquare$

A 2,696 **C** 1,696

B 2,414 **D** 1,586

 Extra Practice on page 98, Set E

The World's Largest Birds

Reading Skill **Compare and Contrast**

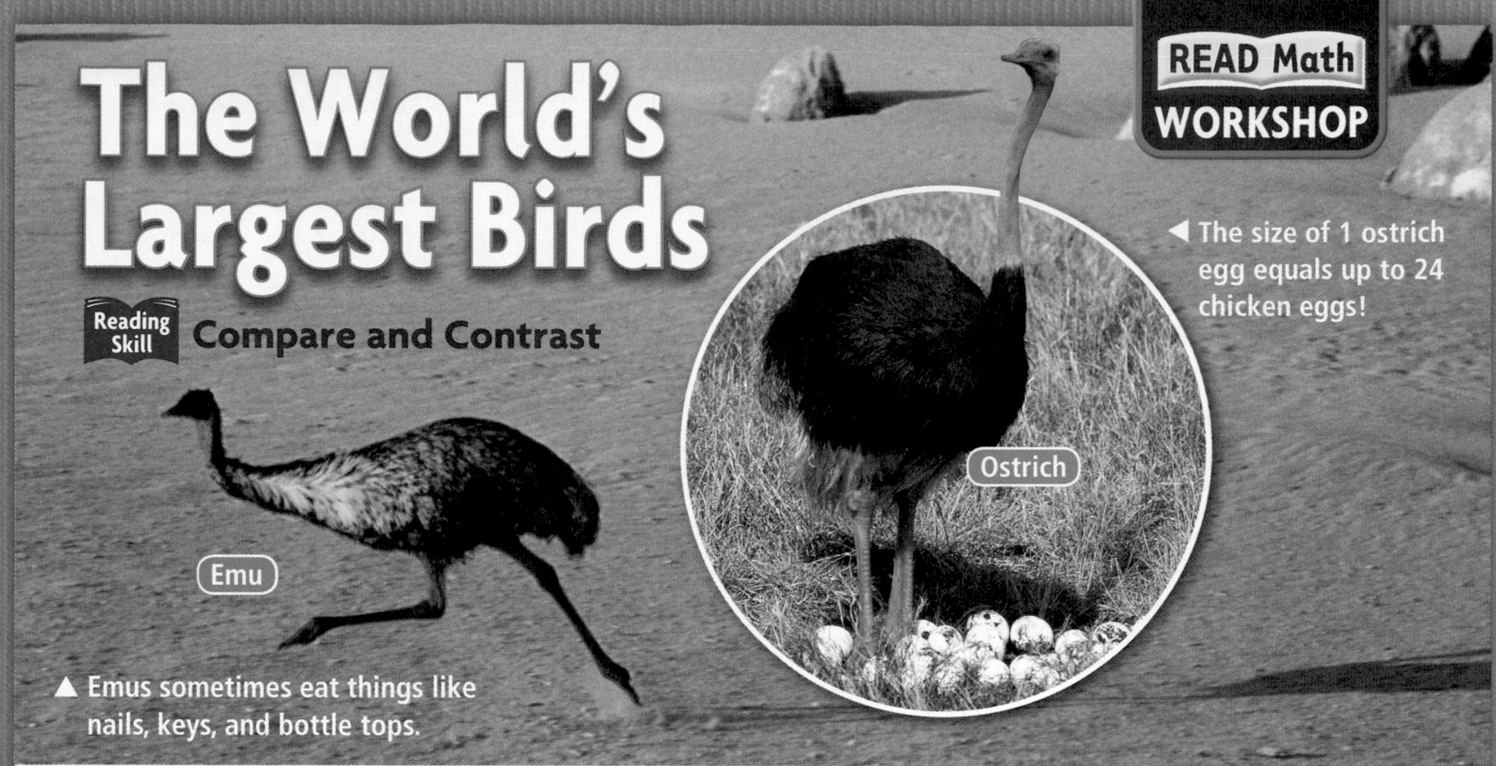

▲ Emus sometimes eat things like nails, keys, and bottle tops.

◀ The size of 1 ostrich egg equals up to 24 chicken eggs!

Emus live in Australia and weigh about 120 pounds. They can grow to be about 6 feet tall and can run as fast as 40 miles per hour.

Ostriches live in Africa and weigh about 300 pounds. They can grow to be about 9 feet tall and can run as fast as 40 miles per hour.

When you compare things, you decide how they are alike. When you contrast things, you decide how they are different. Use the table to compare and contrast the birds. How are they different?

	Emus	Ostriches
Where do they live?	Australia	Africa
How much do they weigh?	120 pounds	300 pounds
How tall are they?	6 feet tall	9 feet tall
How fast can they run?	40 miles per hour	40 miles per hour

Problem Solving **Compare and contrast to solve.**

1. Solve the problem above by using the table to tell how the birds are different.
2. Ostriches have 2 toes on each foot. They protect themselves by kicking with their toes. Emus have 3 toes on each foot. They use them for protection. How are the birds alike?

LESSON 8

Choose a Method

OBJECTIVE: Choose paper and pencil, a calculator, or mental math to subtract 3- and 4-digit numbers.

Quick Review

1. 120 − 110
2. 365 − 50
3. 436 − 241
4. 3,785 − 2,483
5. 4,268 − 1,209

Learn

PROBLEM For her science project, Ella compared the weights of different animals that she saw at the zoo. How much more does the rhinoceros weigh than the walrus?

White rhinoceros
weight: 4,750 pounds

Walrus
weight: 2,840 pounds

Elephant
weight: 9,000 pounds

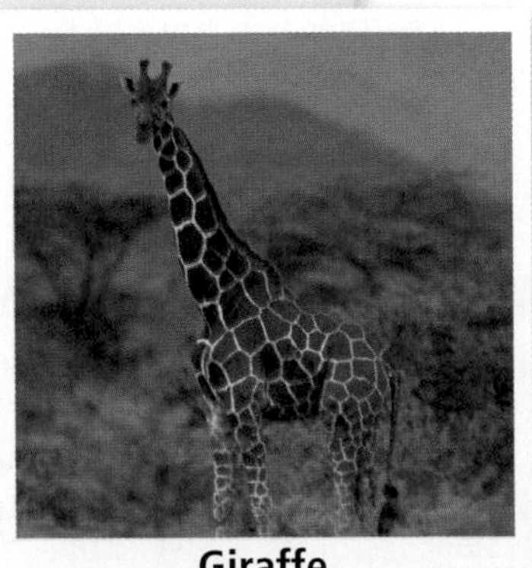
Giraffe
weight: 2,765 pounds

Example 1 Use paper and pencil.

Subtract. 4,750 − 2,840 = ■ **Estimate.** 5,000 − 3,000 = 2,000

The problem involves one regrouping. So, using paper and pencil is a good choice.

Step 1	Subtract the ones. 0 − 0 = 0	4,750 − 2,840 = 0
Step 2	Subtract the tens. 5 − 4 = 1	4,750 − 2,840 = 10
Step 3	Subtract the hundreds. Since 8 > 7, regroup. 17 − 8 = 9	(3 17) 4,750 − 2,840 = 910
Step 4	Subtract the thousands. 3 − 2 = 1	(3 17) 4,750 − 2,840 = 1,910

So, the rhinoceros weighs 1,910 pounds more than the walrus. Since 1,910 is close to the estimate of 2,000, the answer is reasonable.

Example 2 Use a calculator.

How much more does the elephant weigh than the giraffe?

9,000 − 2,765 = ■

The problem involves subtracting across zeros. So, using a calculator is a good choice.

So, the elephant weighs 6,235 pounds more than the giraffe.

- How can you use addition to check your answer?

Example 3 **Use mental math.**

A giraffe can be 218 inches tall.
An ostrich can be 108 inches tall.
How much taller is the giraffe than the ostrich?

$218 - 108 = \blacksquare$

There is no regrouping. So, using mental math is a good choice.

Think: Subtract the hundreds. $200 - 100 = 100$
Subtract the tens. $10 - 0 = 10$
Subtract the ones. $8 - 8 = 0$
110

So, the giraffe is 110 inches taller than the ostrich.

▲ The tallest bird is the ostrich.

▲ The tallest mammal is the giraffe.

More Examples

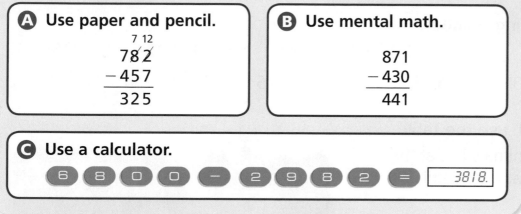

A **Use paper and pencil.**

$$\begin{array}{r} \overset{7\ 12}{7\not{8}\not{2}} \\ -457 \\ \hline 325 \end{array}$$

B **Use mental math.**

$$\begin{array}{r} 871 \\ -430 \\ \hline 441 \end{array}$$

C **Use a calculator.**

Guided Practice

1. Find $561 - 120$ by using mental math. Use the number sentences to help you.

$$\begin{array}{r} 561 \\ -120 \\ \hline \end{array}$$

$500 - 100 = \blacksquare$
$60 - 20 = \blacksquare$
$1 - 0 = \blacksquare$

Find the difference. Tell which method you used.

2. $\begin{array}{r} 748 \\ -205 \\ \hline \end{array}$

3. $\begin{array}{r} 8{,}165 \\ -4{,}823 \\ \hline \end{array}$

4. $\begin{array}{r} 9{,}120 \\ -3{,}576 \\ \hline \end{array}$

5. $\begin{array}{r} 400 \\ -267 \\ \hline \end{array}$

✓6. $\begin{array}{r} 1{,}790 \\ -1{,}218 \\ \hline \end{array}$

7. $357 - 189 = \blacksquare$

8. $6{,}051 - 4{,}370 = \blacksquare$

✓9. $895 - 722 = \blacksquare$

10. **TALK Math** **Explain** what method you would use to subtract 1,612 from 5,294. Then find the difference.

Independent Practice and Problem Solving

Find the difference. Tell which method you used.

11. $\begin{array}{r} 6{,}000 \\ -\,2{,}781 \\ \hline \end{array}$ **12.** $\begin{array}{r} 428 \\ -\,311 \\ \hline \end{array}$ **13.** $\begin{array}{r} 7{,}194 \\ -\,3{,}720 \\ \hline \end{array}$ **14.** $\begin{array}{r} 317 \\ -\,105 \\ \hline \end{array}$ **15.** $\begin{array}{r} 520 \\ -\,419 \\ \hline \end{array}$

16. $\begin{array}{r} 570 \\ -\,269 \\ \hline \end{array}$ **17.** $\begin{array}{r} 8{,}952 \\ -\,4{,}743 \\ \hline \end{array}$ **18.** $\begin{array}{r} 9{,}543 \\ -\,6{,}221 \\ \hline \end{array}$ **19.** $\begin{array}{r} 650 \\ -\,376 \\ \hline \end{array}$ **20.** $\begin{array}{r} 4{,}737 \\ -\,3{,}259 \\ \hline \end{array}$

21. $\begin{array}{r} 904 \\ -\,418 \\ \hline \end{array}$ **22.** $\begin{array}{r} 3{,}983 \\ -\,1{,}720 \\ \hline \end{array}$ **23.** $\begin{array}{r} 1{,}324 \\ -\,193 \\ \hline \end{array}$ **24.** $\begin{array}{r} 6{,}241 \\ -\,5{,}719 \\ \hline \end{array}$ **25.** $\begin{array}{r} 875 \\ -\,233 \\ \hline \end{array}$

26. 900 − 500 = ■ **27.** 2,214 − 1,702 = ■ **28.** 8,522 − 2,789 = ■

29. 5,415 − 3,002 = ■ **30.** 736 − 228 = ■ **31.** 400 − 162 = ■

Algebra **Find the missing number.**

32. 683 − ■ = 331 **33.** ■ − 165 = 164 **34.** 397 − ■ = 255

35. ■ − 1,379 = 2,463 **36.** 5,721 − ■ = 3,575 **37.** ■ − 4,784 = 1,601

USE DATA **For 38–40, use the table.**

38. How many more animals live at the National Zoo than at the Miami Metrozoo?

39. **Reasoning** If 1,786 of the animals at the San Diego Zoo are male, how many of the animals are female?

40. How many fewer animals live at the Minnesota Zoo than at the Miami Metrozoo and the San Diego Zoo?

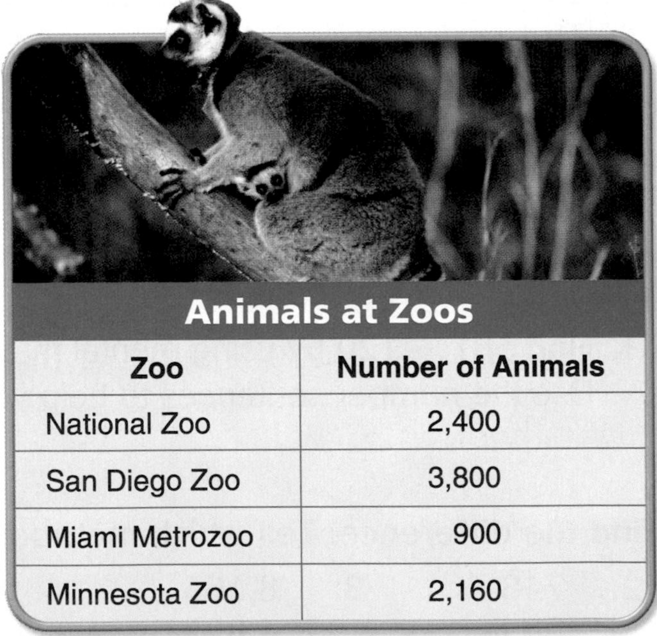

Animals at Zoos

Zoo	Number of Animals
National Zoo	2,400
San Diego Zoo	3,800
Miami Metrozoo	900
Minnesota Zoo	2,160

41. WRITE Math **What's the Question?** There are 359 fish in a large fish tank at a zoo. A zookeeper adds more fish to the tank for a total of 524 fish. The answer is 165 fish.

42. ***FAST FACT*** The heaviest African lion in the wild weighed 690 pounds. The heaviest African lion at a zoo weighed 826 pounds. What is the difference in their weights?

 Extra Practice on page 98, Set F

Learn About

MENTAL MATH

Subtract Across Zeros

Using mental math can make subtracting across zeros easy.

Example

Sharon went to 4 different zoos in June. She saw 300 animals in all. Of the animals, 138 were babies. How many animals were not babies?

Subtract. 300 − 138

You can use addition. To find 300 − 138 = ■, think: 138 + ■ = 300. Count on from 138 to make 300.

Step 1	Step 2	Step 3
Add to make a ten. Think: 138 + 2 = 140	Add to make a hundred. Think: 140 + 60 = 200	Add to make 300. Think: 200 + 100 = 300

Now add the numbers to find 300 − 138. 2 + 60 + 100 = 162

So, 162 animals were not babies.

Try It

Use mental math to subtract.

43. 500 − 265 **44.** 800 − 311 **45.** 400 − 23 **46.** 700 − 541

47. 600 − 417 **48.** 800 − 348 **49.** 500 − 276 **50.** 300 − 79

Mixed Review and Test Prep

51. Kay spun the pointer. Which color is the pointer less likely to land on? (Grade 2)

52. Test Prep An elephant is 136 inches tall. A giraffe is 212 inches tall. What is the difference in their heights?

A 348 inches **C** 124 inches

B 176 inches **D** 76 inches

53. On Friday, 1,689 adults and 2,784 children visited the zoo. How many people visited the zoo in all? (p. 58)

54. Test Prep A white rhinoceros weighs 4,505 pounds, and a giraffe weighs 2,680 pounds. How much more does the white rhinoceros weigh?

A 1,825 pounds **C** 2,185 pounds

B 1,925 pounds **D** 2,825 pounds

Problem Solving Workshop
Skill: Choose the Operation

OBJECTIVE: Solve problems by using the skill *choose the operation.*

Read to Understand
Plan
Solve
Check

Use the Skill

PROBLEM Ms. Wells counted books in the school library. She counted 123 animal books in one section. She counted 305 sports books in another section. How many more sports books did Ms. Wells count than animal books?

This chart will help you decide which operation you can use to solve the problem.

Add	Join groups to find how many in all, or the total.
Subtract	Take away, or compare, to find how many more, how many fewer, or how many are left.

Since the question asks you to find how many more sports books Ms. Wells counted than animal books, you can subtract.

number of sports books		number of animal books		how many more sports books than animal books
↓		↓		↓
305	−	123	=	182

$$\begin{array}{r} \scriptstyle 2\ 10 \\ \not{3}\not{0}5 \\ -\ 123 \\ \hline 182 \end{array}$$

So, Ms. Wells counted 182 more sports books than animal books.

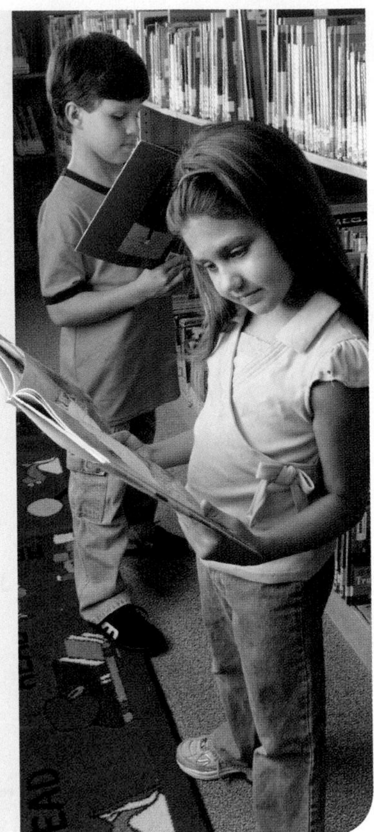

Think and Discuss

Tell which operation you would use. Then solve the problem.

a. Gina's family has 165 books on shelves. They also have 277 books in the attic. How many books does Gina's family have in all?

b. Carlos likes word puzzles. He bought a puzzle book that has 275 word puzzles. He has 132 puzzles left to complete. How many puzzles has Carlos already completed?

Guided Problem Solving

1. Zack has 65 photos of his vacation and 48 photos of his family in his photo album. He has room for 137 more photos. How many photos can Zack's album hold in all?

   Copy and complete the table.

Clues	Meaning
has ■ photos of vacation and ■ photos of family	has a total of ■ photos
has room for ■ more photos	■ more photos can go in the album
How many photos can Zack's album hold in all?	What is the total number of ___?___ the album holds?

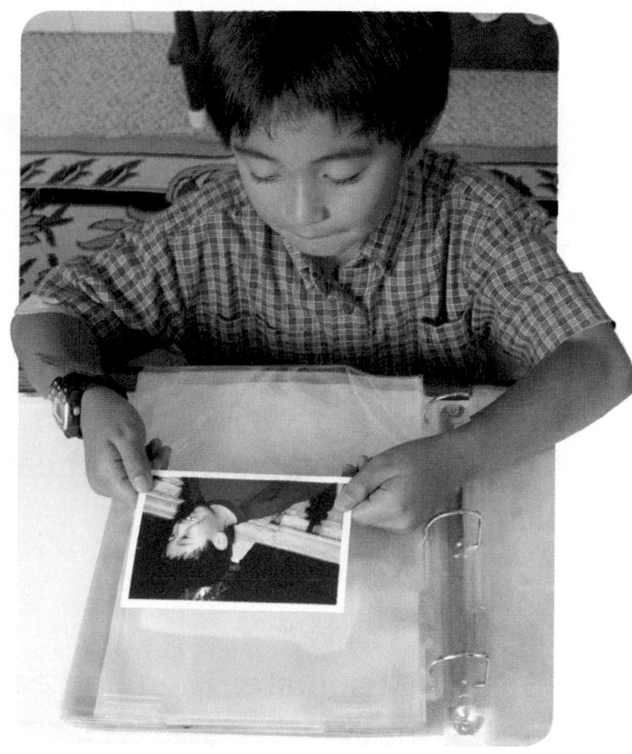

   Which operation can you use to find how many in all? Write a number sentence that shows the answer.

2. **What if** Zack had room for 175 more photos? How many photos would Zack's album hold in all?

3. Brad has room for 100 baseball cards in his binder. He has 64 cards already. How many more cards does he need to fill his binder?

Mixed Applications

4. Erin collects stamps. She has 279 stamps in an album. She gives away 47 stamps to her friends. How many stamps does Erin have left?

5. Kyle and Josh have a total of 64 CDs. Kyle has 12 more CDs than Josh. How many CDs does each boy have?

6. Joseph has 2 coins in his pocket. Their total is 30¢. What are the two coins?

7. Mrs. Gregory has 189 books in her office. Mrs. Moore has 168 books in her office. Who has more books? How many more?

8. **WRITE Math** Kim is reading a book that has 382 pages. She reads 28 pages each night. How many more pages will she have left to read after 3 nights? **Explain** how you know.

9. **Reasoning** Brad's album can hold 225 photos. He has 144 photos in the album. He wants to put 79 more photos in the album. **Explain** how to tell if he has enough space left for the photos.

Extra Practice

Set A **Write the fact family for each set of numbers.** (pp. 76–77)

1. 4, 9, 13
2. 2, 5, 7
3. 6, 8, 14
4. 3, 8, 11
5. 6, 6, 12
6. 1, 7, 8
7. 4, 6, 10
8. 7, 9, 16

Set B **Use rounding or compatible numbers to estimate each difference.** (pp. 78–79)

1. $76 - 24$
2. $89 - 12$
3. $506 - 354$
4. $795 - 133$
5. $448 - 227$
6. Maggie read 87 pages of her book. Alan read 51 pages of his book. About how many more pages did Maggie read?

Set C **Estimate. Then find each difference.** (pp. 80–81)

1. $93 - 59$
2. $78 - 37$
3. $56 - 11$
4. $85 - 26$
5. $62 - 44$

Set D **Estimate. Then find each difference.** (pp. 84–85)

1. $386 - 107$
2. $519 - 185$
3. $865 - 378$
4. $4{,}786 - 2{,}432$
5. $2{,}429 - 1{,}236$
6. Sue is saving money to buy a bike for $220. So far she has saved $136. How much more money does Sue need to save?

Set E **Estimate. Then find each difference.** (pp. 88–91)

1. $600 - 328$
2. $402 - 238$
3. $330 - 119$
4. $7{,}800 - 4{,}183$
5. $5{,}906 - 2{,}557$

Set F **Find the difference. Tell which method you used.** (pp. 92–95)

1. $580 - 461$
2. $792 - 521$
3. $1{,}843 - 376$
4. $6{,}900 - 1{,}263$
5. $9{,}478 - 4{,}105$

CD ROM **Technology**
Use Harcourt Mega Math, Country Countdown, *Block Busters,* Levels R, X, Y.

PRACTICE GAME

Time to Subtract

On Your Mark!
2 players

Get Set!
- Timer

12 27 35 59 68 84

16 29 41 54 73 87

18 33 46 61 80 98

24 38 50 65 76 92

Play!

- Each player chooses a type of animal. Each player uses the 6 numbers on his or her animals to write and solve problems.
- Using their 6 numbers, players write and solve as many subtraction problems as they can in 2 minutes.
- When both players are ready, set the timer for 2 minutes and begin.
- After the 2 minutes are up, players trade papers and check each other's answers.
- The player with more correct answers receives a point.
- Each player chooses a different animal and continues to play.
- The first player to reach 3 points wins.

MATH POWER **Sums and Differences**

Odd or EVEN?

Every number is either **odd** or **even**.

Odd numbers end in 1, 3, 5, 7, or 9.

41, 197, and 1,433 are odd.

Even numbers end in 0, 2, 4, 6, or 8.

28, 374, and 4,562 are even.

You can look for clues to predict if the sum or difference of two numbers will be odd or even.

▲ **Mancala is one of the oldest board games in the world. The game has 6 small holes on each side. Is the total number of small holes an odd or even number?**

Examples

Addition Complete the table to find each answer.

NUMBERS	EXAMPLE	SUM	ODD OR EVEN?
even + even	2 + 6	8	even
odd + odd	73 + 7	■	■
odd + even	45 + 30	■	■
even + odd	2,116 + 517	■	■

Subtraction Complete the table to find each answer.

NUMBERS	EXAMPLE	DIFFERENCE	ODD OR EVEN?
even − even	8 − 4	4	even
odd − odd	87 − 49	■	■
odd − even	835 − 22	■	■
even − odd	474 − 367	■	■

Remember

The ones digit helps you see if a number is even or odd.

Try It

Find the sum or difference. Write *odd* or *even*.

1. 7 + 3 **2.** 1 + 12 **3.** 84 + 18 **4.** 734 + 15 **5.** 565 + 259

6. 10 − 5 **7.** 33 − 12 **8.** 196 − 80 **9.** 775 − 401 **10.** 9,827 − 6,378

11. WRITE Math Choose two numbers to add. Is the sum of your numbers an odd or even number? **Explain** how you know.

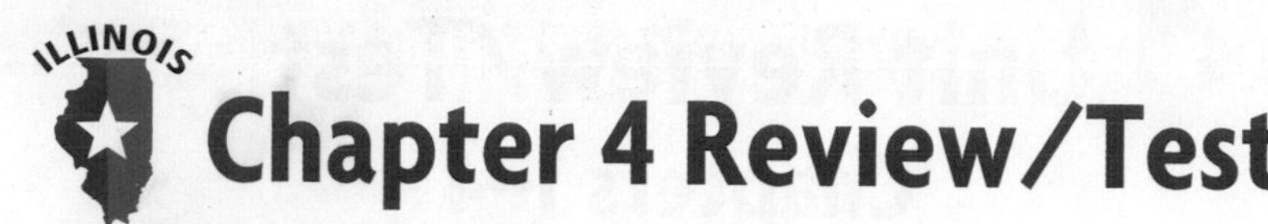

Chapter 4 Review/Test

Check Vocabulary and Concepts

Choose the best term from the box.

VOCABULARY
fact family
inverse operations
regrouping

1. Addition and subtraction are opposite, or __?__. IL 6.3.12 (p. 76)
2. A group of related number sentences that use the same numbers is a __?__. IL 6.3.12 (p. 76)

Check Skills

Write the fact family for each set of numbers. IL 6.3.12 (pp. 76–77)

3. 2, 8, 10
4. 6, 6, 12
5. 3, 4, 7
6. 7, 8, 15

Estimate each difference. IL 6.3.14 (pp. 78–79)

7. $56 - 19$
8. $64 - 23$
9. $661 - 185$
10. $942 - 316$

Estimate. Then find each difference. IL 6.3.09; 6.3.14 (pp. 80–81, 84–85, 88–91)

11. $48 - 17$
12. $77 - 49$
13. $80 - 35$
14. $374 - 253$
15. $507 - 230$
16. $583 - 179$
17. $97 - 58$
18. $7{,}800 - 3{,}567$
19. $8{,}605 - 6{,}386$
20. $7{,}004 - 4{,}112$
21. $96{,}864 - 29{,}775$
22. $38{,}624 - 16{,}248$

Check Problem Solving

Solve. IL 6.3.09; 6.3.14 (pp. 86–87, 96–97)

23. Mr. Patrick read 216 pages of his book. Mrs. Wu read 197 pages of her book. How many pages have they read in all?
24. A car show had 559 visitors. Of the visitors, 165 were children and the rest were adults. About how many of the visitors were adults?
25. **WRITE Math** Did you need an estimate or an exact answer for Problem 24? **Explain** how you know.

GO ONLINE **Technology** Use *Online Assessment.*

Unit Review/Test
Chapters 1–4

Multiple Choice

1. The distance between Chicago, IL, and Carbondale, IL, is 333 miles. The distance from Carbondale, IL, to Peoria, IL, is 269 miles. The distance between Peoria, IL, and Chicago, IL, is 170 miles. Which shows the distances ordered from greatest to least? IL 6.3.05 (p. 32)

   A 170, 333, 269

   B 333, 170, 269

   C 269, 170, 333

   D 333, 269, 170

2. There were 600 students and 432 adults going to a play. How many more students went to the play than adults? IL 6.3.09 (p. 88)

   A 278 C 178

   B 268 D 168

3. The state of Illinois covers 57,914 square miles. What is the value of the digit 9 in 57,914? IL 6.3.01 (p. 14)

   A 9

   B 90

   C 900

   D 9,000

4. Caroline collected 15 shells on the beach yesterday. She collected 6 shells in the morning. She wrote the equation below to find out how many shells she collected in the afternoon. Which number completes the equation? IL 8.3.04 (p. 50)

   $$6 + ■ = 15$$

   A 7 C 9

   B 8 D 10

5. Which addition sentence is related to the subtraction sentence? IL 6.3.12 (p. 76)

   $$7 - 3 = ■$$

   A $3 + 7 = 10$

   B $7 + 7 = 14$

   C $3 + 4 = 7$

   D $4 + 7 = 11$

6. Lilly is using a number line to keep track of her points in a computer game. The number of points she has is shown by point *P*. How many points does Lilly have? IL 6.3.07 (p. 6)

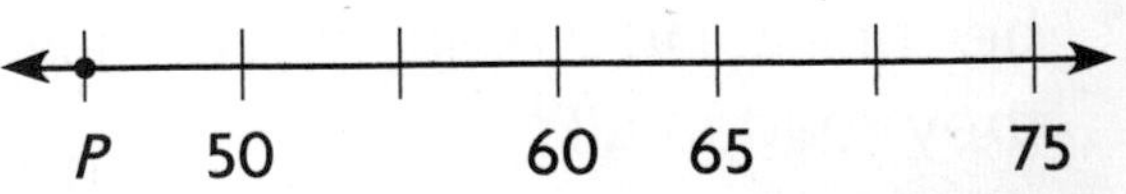

   A 60 C 50

   B 55 D 45

GO ONLINE Technology Use *Online Assessment.*

7. In 2000, the population of Benton, IL, was 6,880. The population of East Alton, IL, was 6,830. Compare the populations. Which symbol makes the sentence true? IL 6.3.08 (p. 28)

6,880 ■ 6,830

A $>$ C $=$

B $\div$ D $<$

8. In 2000, Bedford Park, IL, had a population of 574. Which shows 574 written in expanded form? IL 6.3.01 (p. 8)

A 5,000 + 70 + 4

B 500 + 70 + 4

C 50 + 7 + 4

D 5 + 7 + 4

9. The highest point in Illinois is Charles Mound. It is 1,235 feet above sea level. Which shows 1,235 written in word form? IL 6.3.02 (p. 10)

A one hundred twenty-three thousand, five

B twelve thousand thirty-five

C one thousand, two hundred five

D one thousand, two hundred thirty-five

10. Derek has 484 baseball cards. Finn has 321 baseball cards. About how many more baseball cards does Derek have than Finn? IL 6.3.14 (p. 78)

A about 100 C about 300

B about 200 D about 400

Short Response

11. Marlie and Jake washed a total of 9 cars at the car wash. Jake washed 4 cars. Which is the missing number? IL 8.3.01 (p. 50)

12. Baki sold 200 boxes of greeting cards for a fundraiser. Paula sold 143 boxes of cards. How many more boxes of greating cards did Baki sell than Paula? IL 6.3.09 (p. 84)

Extended Response WRITE Math

13. Sadie, her brother, and sister planted sunflower seeds. Sadie planted 125 seeds. Her brother planted 25 fewer seeds than Sadie. Her sister planted 14 more seeds than her brother. How many seeds did Sadie's sister plant? Show all your work. IL 8.3.05 (p. 96)

14. On Saturday, 1,283 adults and 2,029 children visited the fair. On Sunday, 1,478 adults and 1,924 children visited the fair. How many more people visited the fair on Sunday than on Saturday? Show all your work. IL 6.3.09 (p. 58)

15. A farmer planted 57 acres of corn. He planted 28 acres of soybeans. About how many acres of corn and soybeans did he plant in all? Show all your work. IL 6.3.14 (p. 52)

THE WORLD ALMANAC FOR KIDS

Rivers of the World

Winding Water

There are rivers on every continent. Rivers can be used for transportation, to generate electricity, to water crops, for water to drink, and for fun. Over many thousands of years, rivers can even cut through rock. In the United States, the Colorado River carved out the Grand Canyon, which is about one mile deep.

Mediterranean Sea

The Nile River flows north through Africa from Lake Victoria to the Mediterranean Sea.

Africa

Nile River

Lake Victoria

FACT • ACTIVITY

For 1–4, use the data in the table.

Longest Rivers on Six Continents

Continent	River	Length
Africa	Nile	4,160 miles
Asia	Chang (Yangtze)	3,964 miles
Australia	Murray-Darling	2,310 miles
Europe	Volga	2,290 miles
North America	Mississippi	2,340 miles
South America	Amazon	4,000 miles

1. How many rivers are longer than the Mississippi River?
2. Which river is more than 1,800 miles longer than the Mississippi River?
3. Write the lengths of the rivers in order from the longest to the shortest.
4. Two different rivers have a combined length of exactly 4,600 miles. Which two rivers are they?

River Riddles

A river has a mouth. At its mouth, a river flows into another body of water. A river begins at its source, which may be an underground spring or a place high in the mountains where rain or melting snow collects to form a small stream.

ALMANAC Fact

The Mississippi River is the longest in the United States. It touches 10 different states: Arkansas, Illinois, Iowa, Kentucky, Louisiana, Minnesota, Mississippi, Missouri, Tennessee, and Wisconsin. Many other rivers flow into the Mississippi River.

Facts About Some U.S. Rivers

Name of River	Source State	Mouth	Length
Arkansas	Colorado	Mississippi River	1,459 miles
Colorado	Colorado	Gulf of California	1,450 miles
Delaware	New York	Delaware Bay	390 miles
Hudson	New York	Upper New York Bay	306 miles
Mississippi	Minnesota	Gulf of Mexico	2,340 miles
Missouri	Montana	Mississippi River	2,315 miles
Ohio	Pennsylvania	Mississippi River	981 miles
Potomac	Maryland	Chesapeake Bay	383 miles
Wabash	Ohio	Ohio River	512 miles

FACT · ACTIVITY

For 1–3, use the data in the table.

1. I have four i's, but I can't see. My length has a 0 in the ones place. Which river am I?

2. My name is not a state name. When rounded to the nearest ten, my length is 380 miles. Which river am I?

3. **Pose a Problem** Write three riddles using the river lengths. Have a classmate solve your riddles.

UNIT

2 Money and Time, Data and Probability

with
Chapter Projects

1

Maria checks that there will be enough gallons of each flavor to meet the needs for that day.

2

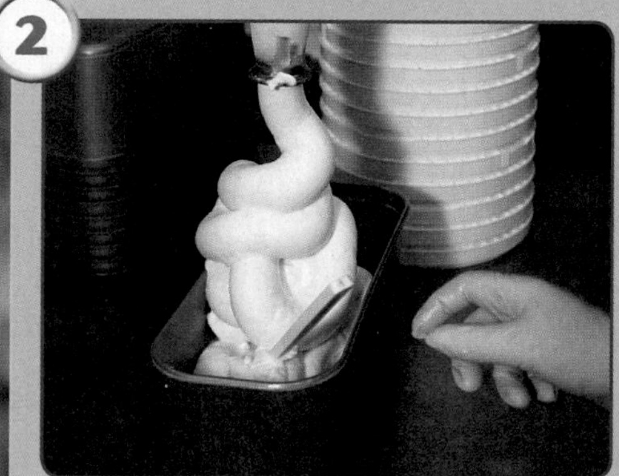

The elapsed time is recorded from cleaning the machine to filling the containers with the ice cream.

3

The cost of the ice cream is affected by the cost of the ingredients.

VOCABULARY POWER

TALK Math

What information is collected and talked about in the **Math on Location** photographs? How can you find the time between cleaning the machine and filling the containers?

READ Math

REVIEW VOCABULARY You learned the words below when you learned about time and data. How do these words relate to **Math on Location**?

graph a picture that represents a mathematical relationship

hour a unit used to measure time; in one hour, the hour hand on a clock moves from one number to the next

WRITE Math

Copy and complete a Freyer Model like the one below. Use what you know about data to add more words.

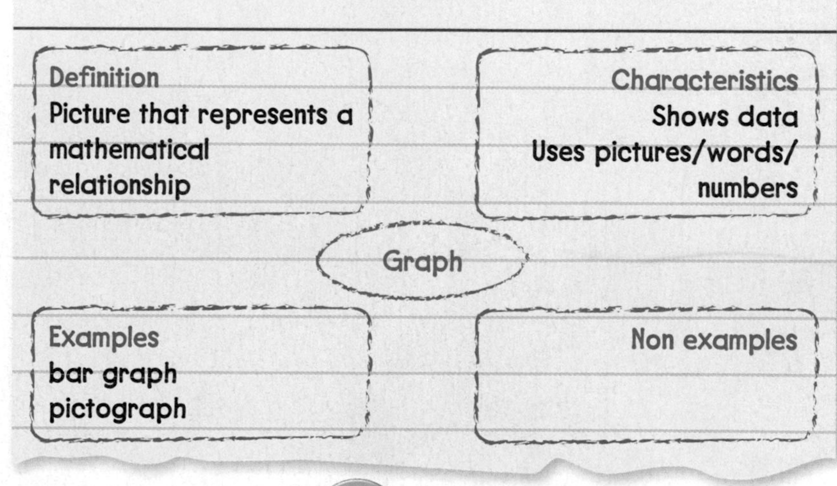

CHAPTER 5 Money and Time

Investigate

Watches come in many different shapes and sizes. Look at the four watches. Write the time shown on each. Then name an activity that you do at that time of day.

FAST FACT

The first pocket watch was invented in the 1500's by Peter Henlein. It only had an hour hand. The minute hand was added in the late 1600's.

GO ONLINE **Technology** Student pages are available in the Student eBook.

Show What You Know

Check your understanding of important skills needed for success in Chapter 5.

▶ Count Coins

Count and write the amount.

1.

2.

3.

4.

▶ Quarters

Count and write the amount.

5.

6.

7.

8.

9.

10.

VOCABULARY POWER

CHAPTER VOCABULARY

change
decimal point
dollar
equivalent

WARM-UP WORDS

change The money you get back if you have paid for an item with coins or bills that have a value greater than the cost of the item

decimal point A symbol used to separate dollars from cents in money

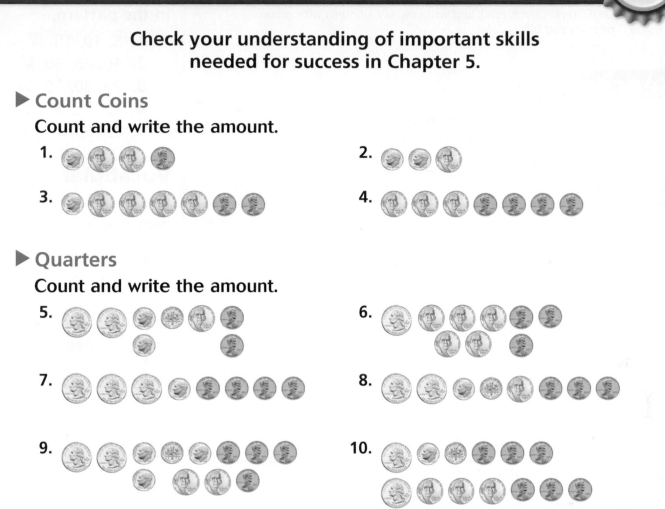

equivalent Two or more sets that name the same amount

LESSON 1 Count Bills and Coins

OBJECTIVE: Count, read, and write money amounts with groups of coins and bills.

Quick Review

Find the next number in the pattern.

1. 5, 10, 15, ■
2. 10, 20, 30, ■
3. 25, 30, 35, ■
4. 15, 25, 35, ■
5. 25, 50, 75, ■

Vocabulary

equivalent **dollar**
decimal point

Learn

PROBLEM Brian has some coins in his piggy bank. How much money does he have?

Brian's Money

half dollar	quarter	dime	nickel	penny
50¢	25¢	10¢	5¢	1¢

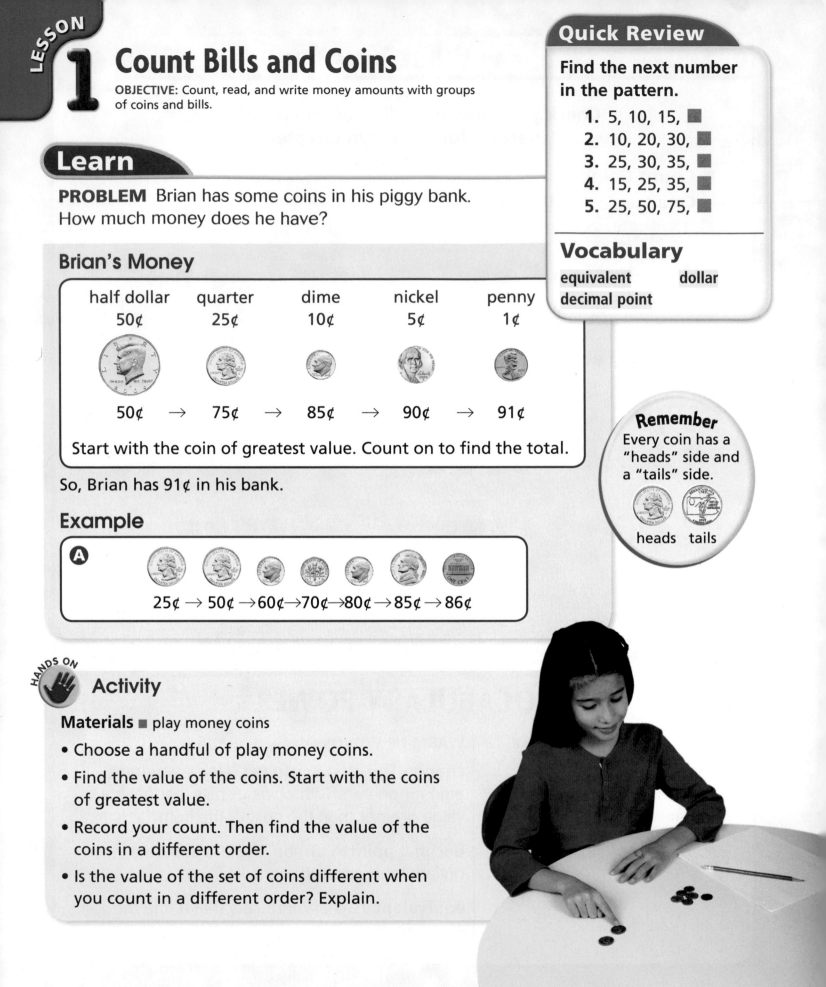

50¢ → 75¢ → 85¢ → 90¢ → 91¢

Start with the coin of greatest value. Count on to find the total.

So, Brian has 91¢ in his bank.

Remember
Every coin has a "heads" side and a "tails" side.

heads

tails

Example

25¢ → 50¢ → 60¢ → 70¢ → 80¢ → 85¢ → 86¢

HANDS ON

Activity

Materials ■ play money coins

- Choose a handful of play money coins.
- Find the value of the coins. Start with the coins of greatest value.
- Record your count. Then find the value of the coins in a different order.
- Is the value of the set of coins different when you count in a different order? Explain.

Equivalent Amounts

Sets of money that have the same value are **equivalent**.

Example 1 Show $1.06 two different ways.

ONE WAY

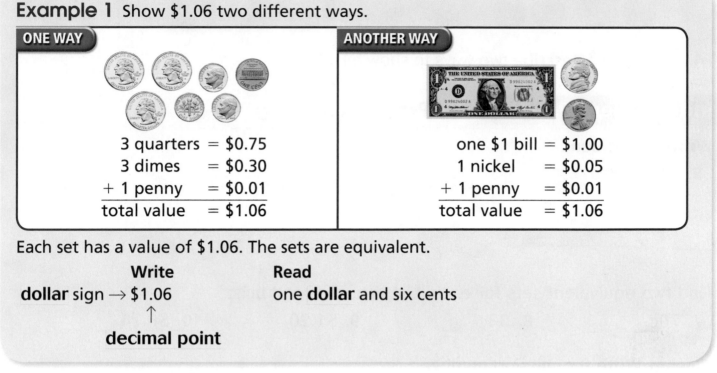

3 quarters	=	$0.75
3 dimes	=	$0.30
+ 1 penny	=	$0.01
total value	=	$1.06

ANOTHER WAY

one $1 bill	=	$1.00
1 nickel	=	$0.05
+ 1 penny	=	$0.01
total value	=	$1.06

Each set has a value of $1.06. The sets are equivalent.

	Write	Read
dollar sign →	$1.06	one **dollar** and six cents

↑ **decimal point**

• What does the 0 in $1.06 mean?

Example 2 Juanita and Tony have the money shown below.

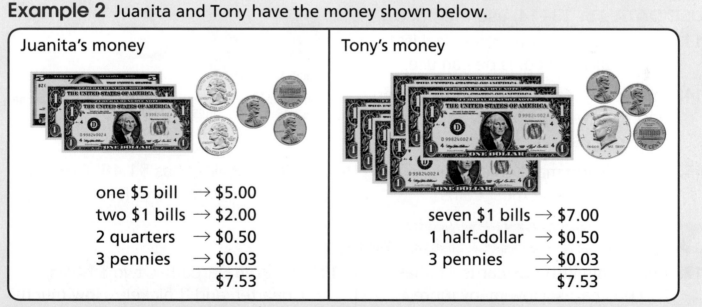

Juanita's money

one $5 bill	→ $5.00
two $1 bills	→ $2.00
2 quarters	→ $0.50
3 pennies	→ $0.03
	$7.53

Tony's money

seven $1 bills	→ $7.00
1 half-dollar	→ $0.50
3 pennies	→ $0.03
	$7.53

So, Juanita and Tony each have $7.53. The amounts are equivalent.

Guided Practice

1. What is the value of 5 nickels?     

Write the amount.

2. 

3.  

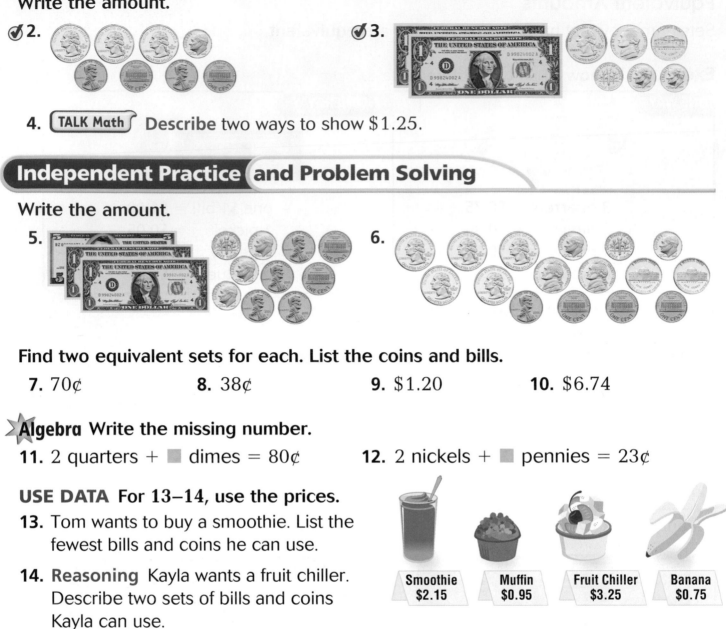

4. TALK Math Describe two ways to show $1.25.

Independent Practice and Problem Solving

Write the amount.

5. 

6. 

Find two equivalent sets for each. List the coins and bills.

7. 70¢ 8. 38¢ 9. $1.20 10. $6.74

Algebra Write the missing number.

11. 2 quarters + ■ dimes = 80¢

12. 2 nickels + ■ pennies = 23¢

USE DATA For 13–14, use the prices.

13. Tom wants to buy a smoothie. List the fewest bills and coins he can use.

14. **Reasoning** Kayla wants a fruit chiller. Describe two sets of bills and coins Kayla can use.

15. How can you make 87¢ by using the fewest coins? the most coins?

16. WRITE Math Alex has $1.48. **Explain** how you know he has at least six coins.

Mixed Review and Test Prep

17. Josh wants 200 postcards. He has 159 postcards. How many more does he need? (p. 88)

18. What number goes in the ■ to make the number sentence true?
63 + ■ = 89 (p. 50)

19. **Test Prep** Jared has two $1 bills, 1 quarter, and 3 nickels. How much money does Jared have in all?

Technology
Use Harcourt Mega Math, The Number Games, *Buggy Bargains,* Levels A and B.

 Extra Practice on page 138, Set A

Write a Conclusion

WRITE Math
WORKSHOP

Writing a conclusion helps you use the information you are given and what you find out to make a decision.

Jessica and Alex are comparing the bills and coins they have. Do they have equivalent amounts of money?

Jessica's Money

Alex's Money

Jessica wrote this paragraph to explain her answer.

First, I counted my money. I have \$3.00 + \$1.00 + \$0.20 + \$0.05. I have \$4.25.

Next, I counted Alex's money. He has \$2.00 + \$2.00 + \$0.10 + \$0.15. He has \$4.25.

Then, I compared the two amounts of money. Alex and I have equivalent amounts.

Tips

- To write a conclusion, first, study the information you are given.
- Then, write the steps you took to help you make a decision.
- Use words such as first and next.
- Then state your conclusion in the last sentence.

Problem Solving Write a conclusion for each problem.

1. Tina has 2 quarters, 2 dimes, and 2 pennies. Jacob has 5 dimes, 5 nickels, and 2 pennies. Do they have equivalent amounts of money?
2. Ron has two \$1 bills, 3 dimes, and 4 nickels. Lois has one \$1 bill, 4 quarters, and 5 dimes. Do they have equivalent amounts of money?

LESSON 2

Compare Money Amounts

OBJECTIVE: Compare money amounts with bills and coins.

Quick Review

Compare. Use $<$, $>$, or $=$ for each.

1. 6 ● 8
2. 11 ● 13
3. 15 ● 12
4. 134 ● 145
5. 229 ● 226

Learn

PROBLEM Sarah and Zoey each bought a pair of sunglasses. They paid the amounts shown below. Who spent more money?

Example 1 Count and compare the money amounts.

Sarah

Sarah spent \$5.27.

Zoey

Zoey spent \$5.30.

$\$5.27 < \$5.30$, or $\$5.30 > \$5.27$

So, Zoey spent more money.

- If you have a greater number of bills and coins than someone else, do you always have the greater amount of money? Explain.

Remember

$<$ means is less than.

$>$ means is greater than.

Example 2 Use place value to compare \$3.56 and \$3.54.

DOLLARS	.	DIMES	PENNIES
\$3	.	5	6
\$3	.	5	4

The number of dollars and dimes are equal.
Compare the number of pennies.
$6 > 4$, so $\$3.56 > \$3.54$.

Guided Practice

1. Which is the greater money amount, 2 quarters or 6 dimes?

Use $<$, $>$, or $=$ to compare the amounts of money.

2.  

3.  

4. TALK Math **Explain** how to compare $5.28 and $5.41 by using place value.

Independent Practice and Problem Solving

Use $<$, $>$, or $=$ to compare the amounts of money.

5.  

Which amount is greater?

6. $6.82 or $6.90
7. $1.10 or 5 quarters
8. $1.90 or 7 quarters
9. $3.26 or $2.63
10. 4 dimes or 4 quarters
11. 3 dimes 3 nickels, or 5 dimes

USE DATA For 12–13, use the table.

12. Write the prices in order from greatest to least. What is the difference between the greatest and the least amount?

13. WRITE Math Hayley has $5.00. Which item can she buy at the Beach Shop? **Explain** how you know.

Beach Shop

Item	Price
Towel	$5.82
Water Bottle	$2.87
Sunscreen	$5.12

Mixed Review and Test Prep

14. Marcus poured milk into his glass. What tool should he use to measure how much milk he poured? (Grade 2)

15. Bianca estimated 688 − 432 by rounding each number to the nearest hundred. What was her estimate? (p. 78)

16. **Test Prep** Amber has only quarters. She has more than 75¢. Which amount could Amber have?

A $0.85
B $1.05
C $1.50
D $1.70

Extra Practice on page 138, Set B

LESSON 3

Problem Solving Workshop
Strategy: Make a Table

OBJECTIVE: Solve problems by using the strategy *make a table.*

Learn the Strategy

Using a table can help you understand the information in some problems.

A table can help you see how items in a problem are related. This table shows a number pattern.

Matt and his dad build wagons. Each wagon has 4 wheels.

Wagons	1	2	3
Wheels	4	8	12

A table can help you record choices. This table shows how students voted.

Mika asked his classmates to vote for their favorite meal.

Favorite Meal	
Meal	Votes
Breakfast	卌 II
Lunch	卌 IIII
Dinner	卌 卌

A table can help you find possible answers. This table shows equivalent sets of money.

Opal has a $1 bill, some dimes, and some nickels. She uses it all to buy a fruit drink for $1.50.

$1 bills	Dimes	Nickels	Total Value
1	2	6	$1.50
1	3	4	$1.50
1	4	2	$1.50

TALK Math

What questions can be answered by using each of the tables above?

Use the Strategy

PROBLEM Damon has the bills and coins pictured below. He wants to rent ice skates for $3.25. How many different ways can Damon make $3.25?

Read to Understand

- **What information is given in the graphic aid?**
- **Is any information not needed?**

Plan

- **What strategy can you use to solve the problem?**
  You can make a table to help you solve the problem.

Solve

- **How can you use the strategy to solve the problem?**
  Make a table to show all the equivalent sets of bills and coins that equal $3.25.

$1 bills	Quarters	Dimes	Nickels	Pennies	Total Value
3	1	0	0	0	$3.25
3	0	2	1	0	$3.25
3	0	2	0	5	$3.25
2	4	2	1	0	$3.25
2	4	2	0	5	$3.25

So, there are 5 equivalent sets Damon can make to equal $3.25.

Check

- **How can you make sure each set of bills and coins equals $3.25?**
- **What other way could you solve the problem?**

Guided Problem Solving

1. Amy has six $1 bills, 4 quarters, 3 dimes, and 4 nickels. She needs to pay $6.85 to ice skate for an hour. How many different ways can Amy make $6.85?

Copy and complete the table. Find all the equivalent sets that equal $6.85. Make sure Amy has enough bills and coins for each set.

$1 bills	Quarters	Dimes	Nickels	Total Value
6	3		0	$6.85
6	3	0		$6.85
6		3		$6.85

2. **What if** Amy had one $5 bill, two $1 bills, 3 quarters, 3 dimes, and 3 nickels? Name two ways Amy could make $6.85.

3. Tyler has 7 quarters, 4 dimes, and 6 nickels. He wants to buy a hot dog for $1.45. How many different ways can Tyler make $1.45?

Problem Solving Strategy Practice

USE DATA For 4–6, use the list. Make a table to solve.

List your favorite juice.

grape apple apple berry
grape berry apple grape
berry grape grape berry
apple apple berry grape
berry berry apple
grape berry berry
apple grape grape grape

4. Kim had a class skating party for her birthday. Each student chose one juice flavor. How many students were at Kim's party? How many students chose each flavor?

5. How many more students chose grape juice than chose apple juice?

6. Kim's mother bought 2 juice boxes for each student at the party. How many juice boxes did she buy in all?

7. Eric has five $1 bills, 3 quarters, 5 dimes, 1 nickel, and 5 pennies. How many different equivalent sets of bills and coins can he use to pay for earmuffs that cost $5.75?

Mixed Strategy Practice

USE DATA For 8–10, use the table below.

8. Jen and Tina sold lemonade and cookies to raise money for an ice-skating class. On Friday, they counted 11 coins. List the coins they could have on Friday.

9. On Saturday, Taylor bought 4 cookies. He gave Jen and Tina 5 dimes and 8 pennies. How much more than that did the girls earn on Saturday?

10. After selling the lemonade and cookies on Sunday, the girls had 2 bills and 6 coins. What bills and coins did the girls have?

Friday	$2.75
Saturday	$5.58
Sunday	$6.30
Monday	$3.65

11. **WRITE Math** Duane scored 2 goals during ice hockey practice. Robbie scored 2 more goals than Duane. Jack scored 1 less goal than Robbie. **Explain** how you can find the number of goals each boy scored.

12. Casey bought ice hockey supplies. She spent $5 and bought 3 items. Which items did she buy?

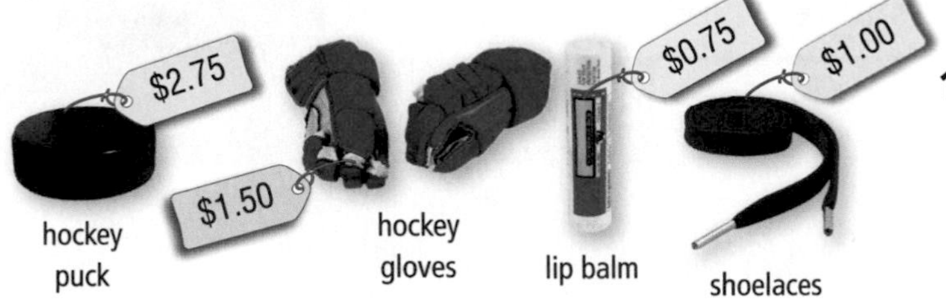

13. **Pose a Problem** Look back at Problem 9. Write a similar problem by changing the amount of money the girls had on Saturday.

14. **Open-Ended** Becca dropped her coins on the ice. The coins were four different sizes. There were more of the smallest coin than of any other coin. What coins could Becca have dropped? How much money would that be?

Choose a STRATEGY

- Draw a Diagram or Picture
- Make a Model or Act It Out
- Make an Organized List
- Find a Pattern
- Make a Table or Graph
- Predict and Test
- Work Backward
- Solve a Simpler Problem
- Write an Equation
- Use Logical Reasoning

CHALLENGE YOURSELF

The Snow Cats are playing against the Polar Bears in ice hockey. Tickets for the game are $8.00 for adults and $5.00 for children.

15. Mr. Meyers buys 1 adult ticket. He pays with 3 bills and 6 coins. What bills and coins does he use?

16. Mr. Hall pays $31 for tickets. **Explain** how you can find the number of adult tickets and the number of children's tickets that he buys.

LESSON 4 Model Making Change

OBJECTIVE: Make change by counting on.

Quick Review

Jody has a $1 bill, 3 pennies, and 1 quarter. How much money does Jody have in all?

Vocabulary

change

Learn

PROBLEM Marla buys a kitten toy for $3.68. She pays with a $5 bill. How much change should she get?

Change is the money you get back if you have paid for an item with coins or bills that have a value greater than the cost of the item.

Activity 1 Make change from $5.00.

Materials ■ play money

Start with the cost of the item.
Count up with coins and bills to the amount Marla paid.

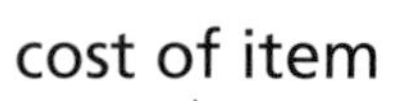
cost of item ↓     

$3.68 → $3.69 → $3.70 → $3.75 → $4.00 → $5.00 ← amount paid

Then count the value of the bills and coins she received.

So, Marla should get $1.32 in change.

Activity 2 Make change from $10.00.

Alex buys a leash for his dog for $7.70. He pays with a $10 bill. What change should Alex get?

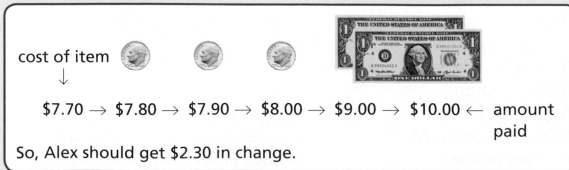

cost of item ↓    

$7.70 → $7.80 → $7.90 → $8.00 → $9.00 → $10.00 ← amount paid

So, Alex should get $2.30 in change.

Guided Practice

1. Count up from $5.18 to $6.00. Name the coins that are missing.

Find the amount of change. Use play money to help.

2. Brenda buys a comic book for $3.42. She pays with a $5 bill.

3. Ivy buys a sandwich for $5.25. She pays with a $10 bill.

4. TALK Math **Explain** how to count up from $2.09 to $5.00.

Independent Practice and Problem Solving

Find the amount of change. Use play money to help.

5. Pete buys a new dictionary for $4.59. He pays with a $5 bill.

6. Rose buys a carton of yogurt for $0.68. She pays with a $5 bill.

7. Omar buys a dog collar for $7.22. He pays with a $10 bill.

8. Morgan buys a stuffed animal for $3.85. She pays with a $10 bill.

USE DATA For 9–11, use the picture.

9. Ed buys a yo-yo. He pays with a $5 bill. How much change should he receive?

10. WRITE Math Mena buys a stuffed bear. She pays with a $10 bill. How much is Mena's change? What bills and coins does she get? **Explain** how you know.

11. Valerie buys a jump rope. She pays with a $5 bill and 4 quarters. How much change should she receive?

12. **Reasoning** Jane bought a book. She paid with $3.00. She got 2 quarters, 2 dimes, and 3 pennies in change. What did her book cost?

Mixed Review and Test Prep

13. A year usually has 365 days. What is the value of the digit 3 in 365? (p. 8)

14. There are 328 boys and 182 girls at camp. Estimate the total number of campers. (p. 52)

15. **Test Prep** Kim buys lunch for $4.17. She pays with a $5 bill. How much change does she get?

   A $0.75
   B $0.78
   C $0.81
   D $0.83

Extra Practice on page 138, Set C

LESSON 5 Add and Subtract Money Amounts

OBJECTIVE: Add and subtract money amounts.

Quick Review

1. 31 + 57 = ■
2. 309 + 112 = ■
3. 450 − 200 = ■
4. 305 − 47 = ■
5. 1,251 + 3,070 = ■

Learn

PROBLEM Tony bought a robot for $12.42 and a book for $13.82. How much did Tony spend?

Example 1 **Add.** $12.42 + $13.82

Estimate to the nearest dollar. $12 + $14 = $26

Step 1	Step 2	Step 3
Line up the decimal points.	Add money like whole numbers.	Write the sum in dollars and cents.
$\begin{array}{r} \$12.42 \\ +\ \$13.82 \\ \hline \end{array}$	$\begin{array}{r} {}^{1} \\ \$12.42 \\ +\ \$13.82 \\ \hline 26\ 24 \end{array}$	$\begin{array}{r} \$12.42 \\ +\ \$13.82 \\ \hline \$26.24 \end{array}$

So, Tony needs $26.24. Since $26.24 is close to the estimate of $26, the answer is reasonable.

- How would you line up the decimal points to find $12.42 + $3.82?

Example 2 Megan bought a jacket for $28.19. She paid with $40.00. How much change did she get?

Estimate to the nearest ten dollars. $40 − $30 = $10

Step 1	Step 2	Step 3
Line up the decimal points.	Subtract money like whole numbers	Write the difference in dollars and cents.
$\begin{array}{r} \$40.00 \\ -\ \$28.19 \\ \hline \end{array}$	$\begin{array}{r} {}^{3\ \not{10}\ \not{10}10} \\ \$\not{4}\not{0}.\not{0}\not{0} \\ -\ \$28.19 \\ \hline 11\ 81 \end{array}$ (regrouped: 9 9 over 3 10 10 10)	$\begin{array}{r} {}^{3\ \not{10}\ \not{10}10} \\ \$\not{4}\not{0}.\not{0}\not{0} \\ -\ \$28.19 \\ \hline \$11.81 \end{array}$ (regrouped: 9 9 over 3 10 10 10)

So, Megan got $11.81 in change. Since $11.81 is close to the estimate of $10, the answer is reasonable.

$13.82

Guided Practice

1. How would you line up the decimal points to find $8.64 + $7.22? Find the sum.

Estimate. Then find the sum or difference.

✓2. $\begin{array}{r} \$45.76 \\ -\$31.28 \\ \hline \end{array}$ ✓3. $\begin{array}{r} \$16.25 \\ +\$13.12 \\ \hline \end{array}$ 4. $\begin{array}{r} \$3.81 \\ -\$1.29 \\ \hline \end{array}$ 5. $\begin{array}{r} \$20.51 \\ -\$16.84 \\ \hline \end{array}$

6. TALK Math **Explain** how you would find $2.43 − $1.25.

Independent Practice and Problem Solving

Estimate. Then find the sum or difference.

7. $\begin{array}{r} \$2.57 \\ +\$7.21 \\ \hline \end{array}$ 8. $\begin{array}{r} \$52.94 \\ -\$21.52 \\ \hline \end{array}$ 9. $\begin{array}{r} \$4.00 \\ -\$3.51 \\ \hline \end{array}$ 10. $\begin{array}{r} \$32.50 \\ -\$14.75 \\ \hline \end{array}$ 11. $\begin{array}{r} \$0.62 \\ +\$1.87 \\ \hline \end{array}$

12. $22.15 + $18.39
13. $50.00 − $42.38
14. $1.23 + $6.50 + $4.27
15. $3.61 + $0.41
16. $46.87 − $29.19
17. $6.50 + $4.12 + $4.12

Algebra **Find the missing number.**

18. $6.50 − ■ = $2.50
19. $10.00 + ■ = $15.20
20. $10.70 + ■ = $50.00

USE DATA **For 21–22, use the pictures.**

21. Eric paid for glitter and glue with a $5 bill. How much change did he get?

22. WRITE Math **What's the Question?** Shelly bought construction paper and craft sticks. The answer is $2.06.

Mixed Review and Test Prep

23. A bag has 7 red cubes and 2 blue cubes. Which color cube are you more likely to choose? (Grade 2)

24. A cafeteria has 253 seats. One hundred sixteen seats are being used. How many seats are not being used? (p. 84)

25. **Test Prep** Ron buys a book for $6.12. He pays with a $10 bill. How much change does Ron get?

A $3.58 **C** $3.88
B $3.86 **D** $3.98

Extra Practice on page 138, Set D

LESSON 6

Tell Time

OBJECTIVE: Read, write, and tell time on analog and digital clocks to the nearest half hour, quarter hour, and minute.

Quick Review

Roberto skip-counted to 60 by fives. What numbers did Roberto count?

Vocabulary

half hour
quarter hour
hour
minute
analog clock
digital clock
second

Learn

In one **hour**, the hour hand on a clock moves from one number to the next. In one **minute**, the minute hand on a clock moves from one mark to the next.

PROBLEM Carrie fed her puppy, Buster, at the 3 times shown below. At what times did she feed Buster?

Example In the morning

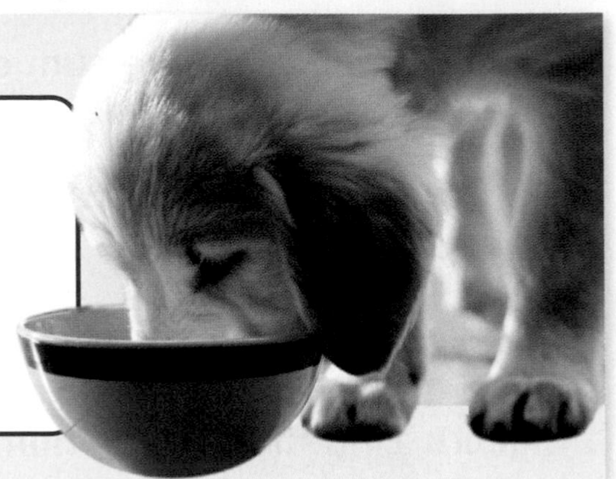

A **half hour** has 30 minutes.

Write: 7:30

Read:

- seven thirty
- thirty minutes after seven
- half past seven

In the afternoon

A **quarter hour** has 15 minutes.

Write: 12:45

Read:

- twelve forty-five
- fifteen minutes before one
- quarter to one

In the evening

An **hour** has 60 minutes.
The hour hand is pointing to the 6.
The minute hand is pointing to the 12.

Write: 6:00

Read:

- six o'clock

So, Carrie fed Buster at 7:30, 12:45, and 6:00.

- Describe how the minute hand moves when the time goes from 8:00 to 9:00.

READ Math

An **analog clock** has a minute hand and an hour hand. Some clocks have second hands.

A **digital clock** shows the time by using numbers. The numbers to the left of the colon show the hour. The numbers to the right show the minutes after the hour.

Time to the Minute

Example 1
Minutes after the hour

To find the number of minutes after the hour, count by fives and ones to where the minute hand is pointing.

Write: 11:23

Read:
- eleven twenty-three
- twenty-three minutes after eleven

Example 2
Minutes before the hour

When a clock shows 31 or more minutes *after* the hour, you can read the time as a number of minutes *before* the next hour.

Write: 2:48

Read:
- twelve minutes before three
- two forty-eight

More Examples

A Minutes after the hour

Write: 3:26

Read:
- three twenty-six
- twenty-six minutes after three

Think: 3:26 is almost half past 3.

B Minutes before the hour

Write: 4:52

Read:
- four fifty-two
- eight minutes before five

Think: 52 minutes after an hour is 8 minutes before the next hour.

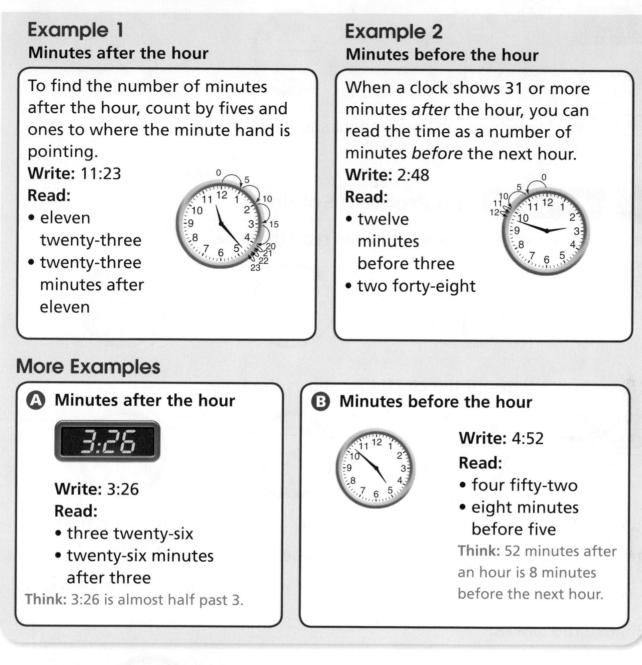

Guided Practice

1. How would you read the time shown on this clock two different ways?

Write the time. Then write two ways you can read the time.

2. 

3. 

4. 

5. 

6. TALK Math Explain where the hour and minute hands are on a clock when it is 15 minutes after 9.

Independent Practice and Problem Solving

Write the time. Then write two ways you can read the time.

7. 

8. 

9. 

10. 

For 11–18, write the letter of the clock that shows the time.

a. 

b. 

c. 

d. 

11. seven fifty
12. quarter past four
13. three twenty-seven
14. ten minutes before eight
15. sixteen minutes before ten
16. 3:27
17. 9:44
18. four fifteen
19. 50 minutes past 7

For 20–22, use the clocks.

20. Bryan woke up at 8:30. Does this clock show that time? Explain how you know.

21. Tanya went home at a quarter after 10. Does this clock show that time? Explain how you know.

22. Art class ends at 5 minutes before 2. Does this clock show that time? Explain how you know.

Technology Use Harcourt Mega Math, Country Countdown, *Clock-a-Doodle-Doo,* Levels I and J.

 Extra Practice on page 139, Set E

USE DATA For 23–25, use the chart of Buster's Feeding Times.

23. When Buster is 6 months old, Carrie will feed him twice each day at the times shown on the clocks. At what times will Carrie feed Buster?

24. Suppose Carrie fed Buster 5 minutes earlier than the evening time shown on the clock. At what time did she feed Buster?

25. WRITE Math **What's the Error?** Carrie says the clock for the morning feeding shows quarter past seven. **Explain** her error. Write the correct time.

Learn About Seconds

A **second** is a very short time. It takes about 1 second to take a step, clap your hands, or hop on one foot. Some clocks have second hands.

Math Idea
60 seconds = 1 minute
60 minutes = 1 hour
24 hours = 1 day

Try It

Write the time.

26. 

27. 

28. 

29. 

Write: 5:45:20
Read: 20 seconds after 5:45 **or** 5:45 and 20 seconds

Mixed Review and Test Prep

30. Bryan's mother bought a television set for \$394. What is 394 rounded to the nearest hundred? (p. 36)

31. **Test Prep** Laura ate lunch at quarter to one. Which shows her lunch time?
A 12:15 **B** 12:45 **C** 1:15 **D** 1:45

32. Three numbers are 46, 48, and 50. If the pattern continues, what is the next number? (p. 4)

33. **Test Prep** Write the time as it would look on Alex's digital watch at five minutes after six.

A.M. and P.M.

OBJECTIVE: Read, write, and tell time in the A.M. and P.M.

Quick Review

Tom sees this time on his clock. What time is it?

Vocabulary

midnight **A.M.**
noon **P.M.**

Learn

PROBLEM Kendra's family is going hiking tomorrow at 8:00. They are going in the morning, not in the evening. How should Kendra write the time?

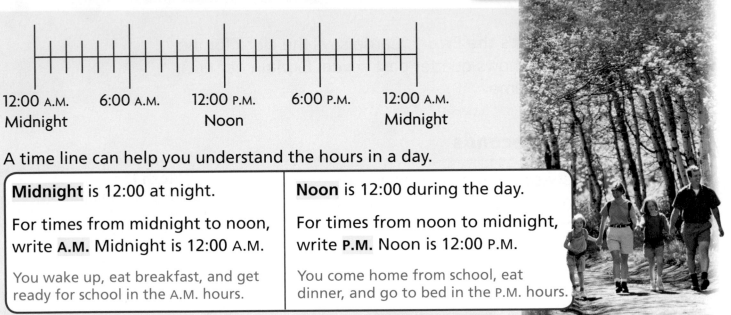

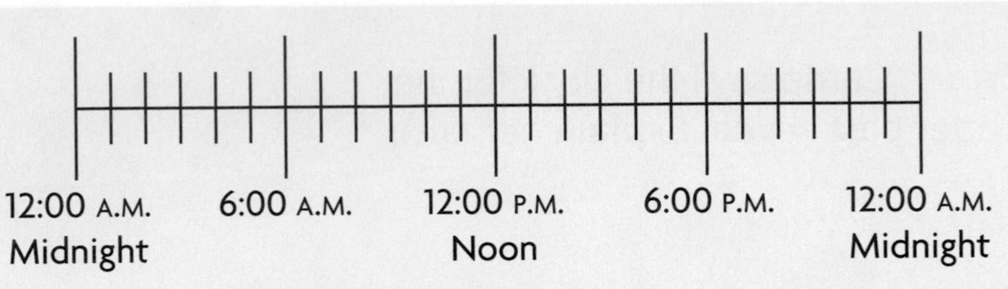

A time line can help you understand the hours in a day.

Midnight is 12:00 at night.	**Noon** is 12:00 during the day.
For times from midnight to noon, write **A.M.** Midnight is 12:00 A.M.	For times from noon to midnight, write **P.M.** Noon is 12:00 P.M.
You wake up, eat breakfast, and get ready for school in the A.M. hours.	You come home from school, eat dinner, and go to bed in the P.M. hours.

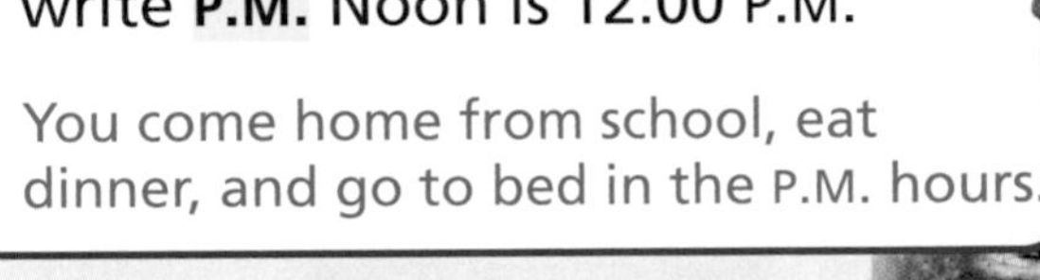

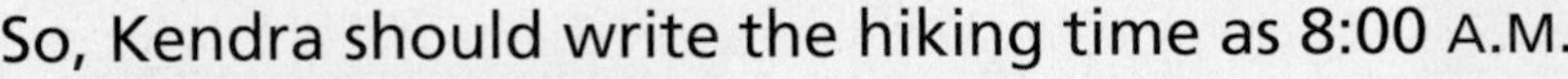

So, Kendra should write the hiking time as 8:00 A.M.

- How do you write the time when it is one minute after noon?

Guided Practice

1. Name something you do in the A.M. hours. Name something you do in the P.M. hours.

Write the time for each activity. Use A.M. or P.M.

2. play soccer

3. go shopping

4. look up at the stars

5. put on pajamas

6. TALK Math **Explain** how you decide whether to use A.M. or P.M. when you write the time.

Independent Practice and Problem Solving

Write the time for each activity. Use A.M. or P.M.

7. eat breakfast

8. have math class

9. play outside

10. watch a sunset

Write the time by using numbers. Use A.M. or P.M.

11. quarter after 8 in the morning

12. 5 minutes before 9 at night

13. one half hour past midnight

14. 20 minutes before noon

15. ***FAST FACT*** Daylight Saving Time begins on the second Sunday in March at 2:00 in the morning. Write the time, and use A.M. or P.M.

USE DATA For 16–18, use the table.

16. Ken wants to go to the tile art class. Write the time for the class, using A.M. or P.M.

17. Brad took the earliest classes in the morning and afternoon. Which classes did he take?

18. **WRITE Math** Mary eats lunch at noon. What classes are before Mary's lunch? **Explain** how you know.

Morning and Afternoon Craft Classes	
Scrapbooking	8:50
Tile Art	10:30
Stamp a Card	1:00
Make Soap	2:45

Mixed Review and Test Prep

19. Use $<$, $>$, or $=$ to make this number sentence true.

$14 - 2$ ■ $10 + 2$ (p. 28)

20. Carlos had 17 markers. He found 4 more. Then he gave Louis 9 markers. How many does Carlos have now? (p. 80)

21. **Test Prep** At which of the times shown are most third graders asleep?

A 8 A.M.

B 12:00 P.M.

C 7:00 P.M.

D 12:00 A.M.

LESSON 8

Model Elapsed Time

OBJECTIVE: Use a clock to measure elapsed time.

Learn

Elapsed time is the amount of time that passes from the start of an activity to the end of the activity.

PROBLEM The Library of Congress in Washington, D.C., is the largest library in the world. One of its buildings is the Thomas Jefferson building. It opens at 10:00 A.M. and closes at 5:30 P.M. For how long is the building open each day?

Quick Review

Write the time, using A.M. or P.M.

1. 7:50 breakfast
2. 4:45 piano lesson
3. 3:10 play ball
4. 7:15 wake up
5. 10:30 sleeping

Vocabulary

elapsed time

Hands On Activity

Materials ■ clock with moveable hands

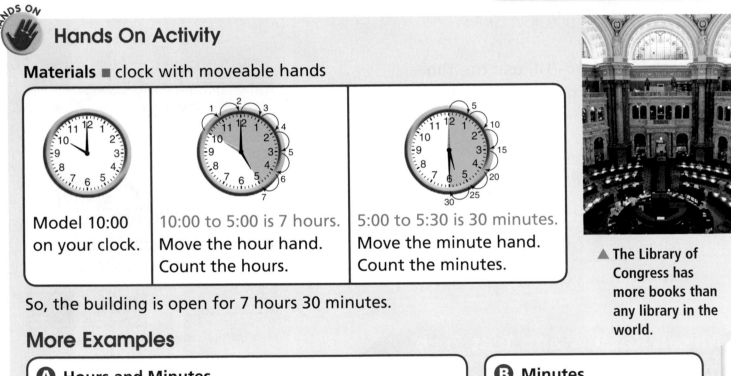

Model 10:00 on your clock.

10:00 to 5:00 is 7 hours.
Move the hour hand. Count the hours.

5:00 to 5:30 is 30 minutes.
Move the minute hand. Count the minutes.

So, the building is open for 7 hours 30 minutes.

▲ The Library of Congress has more books than any library in the world.

More Examples

A Hours and Minutes

Start: 1:00
End: 3:30

Move the hour hand. Count the hours.

Move the minute hand. Count the minutes.

Elapsed time: 2 hours 30 minutes

B Minutes

Start: 5:10
End: 5:38

Move the minute hand. Count the minutes.
Elapsed time: 28 minutes

Guided Practice

1. How much time elapses from 4:15 P.M. until 7:15 P.M.?

Use a clock to find the elapsed time.

✓2. Start: 8:30 A.M.
End: 10:30 A.M.

✓3. Start: 4:20 A.M.
End: 5:00 A.M.

4. Start: 11:50 A.M.
End: 2:30 P.M.

5. **TALK Math** **Explain** how to use a clock to find the elapsed time from noon until 3:45 P.M.

Independent Practice and Problem Solving

Use a clock to find the elapsed time.

6. Start: 2:20 A.M.
End: 5:30 A.M.

7. Start: 8:45 A.M.
End: 2:00 P.M.

8. Start: 10:30 A.M.
End: 6:15 P.M.

Tell what time it will be.

9. 15 minutes after 12:45 P.M.

10. 2 hours 30 minutes after 1:10 A.M.

11. 4 hours after 10:22 A.M.

12. 3 hours 10 minutes after 11:30 A.M.

13. Sam and his family arrived at the Library of Congress at 10:30 A.M. They took a sixty-minute tour. At what time was their tour over?

14. **WRITE Math** Sam's family toured the White House from 2:15 P.M. until 3:20 P.M. **Explain** how you know that the tour was less than 2 hours.

Mixed Review and Test Prep

15. Tim saw a very large sea turtle. About how much does it weigh? (Grade 2)
779 pounds   779 ounces

16. Olivia has 12 nickels and 4 pennies. Toby has 5 dimes and 15 pennies. Who has more money? How much more? (p. 114)

17. **Test Prep** What time is 2 hours 30 minutes after 5:15 P.M.?
A 7:15 P.M.
B 7:18 P.M.
C 7:30 P.M.
D 7:45 P.M.

Extra Practice on page 139, Set G

LESSON 9

Use a Calendar

OBJECTIVE: Use a calendar to determine elapsed time.

Quick Review

Charles skip-counted by sevens from 0 to 35. What numbers did Charles count?

Vocabulary

calendar

Learn

A **calendar** shows the days, weeks, and months of a year. There are 12 months in one year. You can use a calendar to find elapsed time that is more than one day.

PROBLEM Sunrise Elementary School is having a school play. Tom's class begins practicing for the play on October 3. The play is in 3 weeks. On what date is the school play?

October						
Sun	Mon	Tue	Wed	Thu	Fri	Sat
			1	2	(3)	4
5	6	7	8	9	10	11
12	13	14	15	16	17	18
19	20	21	22	23	(24)	25
26	27	28	29	30	31	

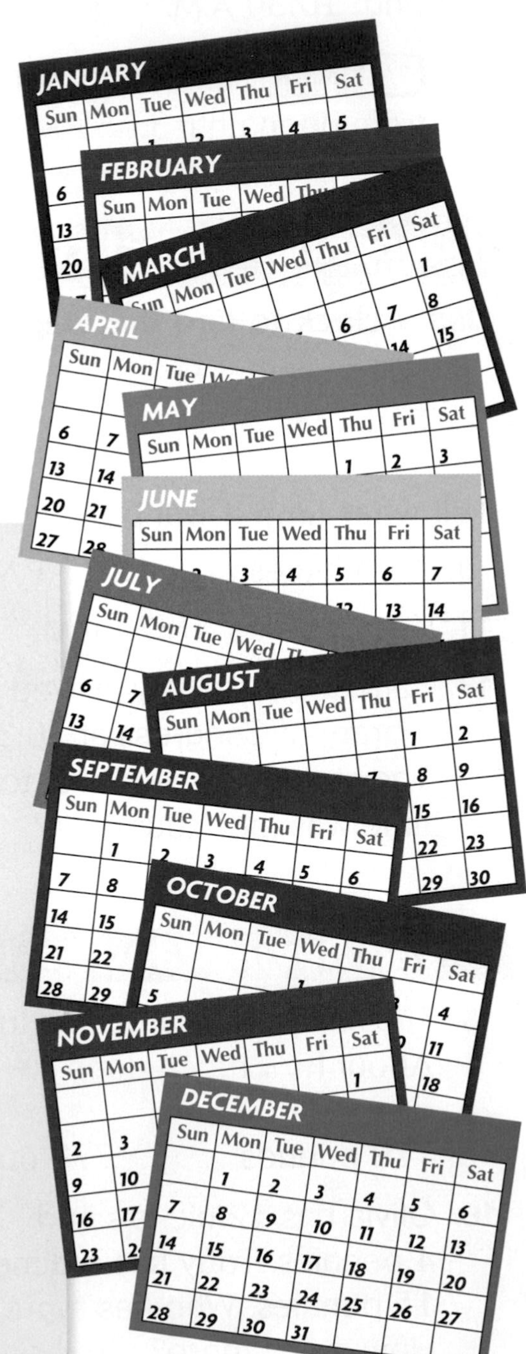

ONE WAY

Count by days.

Start on October 3, and count on one day to October 4, two days to October 5, and so on.

Count all the days that are shaded.
There are 21 days. 21 days = 3 weeks.

So, the school play is on October 24.

ANOTHER WAY

Count by weeks.

Start on October 3. Count down the Friday column one week to October 10, two weeks to October 17, and three weeks to October 24.

So, the school play is on October 24.

- How would you find the number of weeks from October 1 until October 29?

Units of Time

Time can be measured in small units, such as minutes and hours, by using a clock. Time can also be measured in larger units, such as days, weeks, and months, by using a calendar.

Units of Time
60 minutes = 1 hour
24 hours = 1 day
7 days = 1 week
12 months = 1 year
365 days = 1 year
52 weeks = 1 year

Example 1 Abby is visiting her cousin. The first day of her visit is June 18. The last day of her visit is July 10. How long is Abby's visit?

Count each day of her visit. The first day of the visit is June 18. The second day of the visit is June 19, and so on. Count all the days that are shaded. There are 23 days.

June

Sun	Mon	Tue	Wed	Thu	Fri	Sat
1	2	3	4	5	6	7
8	9	10	11	12	13	14
15	16	17	(18)	19	20	21
22	23	24	25	26	27	28
29	30					

July

Sun	Mon	Tue	Wed	Thu	Fri	Sat
		1	2	3	4	5
6	7	8	9	(10)	11	12
13	14	15	16	17	18	19
20	21	22	23	24	25	26
27	28	29	30	31		

So, the visit is 23 days, or 3 weeks and 2 days.

- How many days are in 3 weeks and 4 days?

Example 2 Eric loves baseball. Suppose it is Monday, August 4, at 3:00 P.M. Eric's next baseball game is on Tuesday, August 5, at 5:00 P.M. How long does Eric have to wait until his next baseball game?

August

Sun	Mon	Tue	Wed	Thu	Fri	Sat
					1	2
3	4	5	6	7	8	9
10	11	12	13	14	15	16
17	18	19	20	21	22	23
24/31	25	26	27	28	29	30

Think:

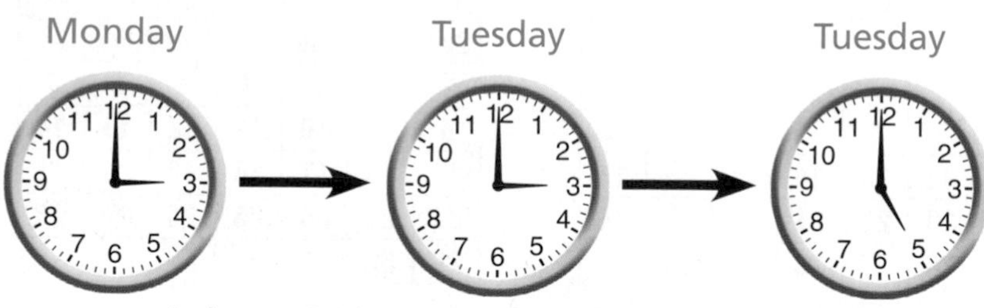

1 day = 24 hours   3:00 P.M. to 5:00 P.M. = 2 hours

24 hours + 2 hours = 26 hours

So, Eric has to wait 26 hours, or 1 day and 2 hours.

- How many hours are in 1 day and 6 hours?

Guided Practice

1. The school's book fair runs for 5 days beginning on September 15. What is the last day of the book fair?

September						
Sun	Mon	Tue	Wed	Thu	Fri	Sat
	1	2	3	4	5	6
7	8	9	10	11	12	13
14	15	16	17	18	19	20
21	22	23	24	25	26	27
28	29	30				

For 2–5, use the calendars.

January						
Sun	Mon	Tue	Wed	Thu	Fri	Sat
		1	2	3	4	5
6	7	8	9	10	11	12
13	14	15	16	17	18	19
20	21	22	23	24	25	26
27	28	29	30	31		

February						
Sun	Mon	Tue	Wed	Thu	Fri	Sat
					1	2
3	4	5	6	7	8	9
10	11	12	13	14	15	16
17	18	19	20	21	22	23
24	25	26	27	28	29	

March						
Sun	Mon	Tue	Wed	Thu	Fri	Sat
						1
2	3	4	5	6	7	8
9	10	11	12	13	14	15
16	17	18	19	20	21	22
23/30	24/31	25	26	27	28	29

2. Today is January 3. Bob's birthday is January 12. How long is it until Bob's birthday? Write your answer two ways.

3. Today is February 11. Nikki began reading her book on January 30. She reads her book every day. Counting today, for how many days has Nikki been reading her book?

4. Suppose it is 8:00 A.M. on March 6. Julie is leaving on vacation at 11:00 A.M. on March 7. How long must Julie wait for her vacation to begin?

5. TALK Math **Explain** how to find the number of days from January 10 through January 25.

Independent Practice and Problem Solving

For 6–8, use the calendars.

April						
Sun	Mon	Tue	Wed	Thu	Fri	Sat
		1	2	3	4	5
6	7	8	9	10	11	12
13	14	15	16	17	18	19
20	21	22	23	24	25	26
27	28	29	30			

May						
Sun	Mon	Tue	Wed	Thu	Fri	Sat
				1	2	3
4	5	6	7	8	9	10
11	12	13	14	15	16	17
18	19	20	21	22	23	24
25	26	27	28	29	30	31

June						
Sun	Mon	Tue	Wed	Thu	Fri	Sat
1	2	3	4	5	6	7
8	9	10	11	12	13	14
15	16	17	18	19	20	21
22	23	24	25	26	27	28
29	30					

6. On April 11, Ms. Hines announced that there would be a class picnic in 2 weeks. On what date will the class have its picnic?

7. Manny began practicing the piano on May 26. He practiced for 1 hour every day through June 10. For how many days did Manny practice the piano?

8. **Reasoning** Jon and his family went camping at noon on May 20. They returned home at 5:00 P.M. on May 22. For how long did Jon's family camp? Write your answer in two ways.

Extra Practice on page 139, Set H

USE DATA **For 9–10, use the calendar.**

9. Suppose today is the second Monday in February. How many weeks is it until Presidents' Day?

10. WRITE Math **What's the Error?** Rob says that Valentine's Day is the third Thursday in February. Describe Rob's error. What correct statement could Rob make?

February						
Sun	Mon	Tue	Wed	Thu	Fri	Sat
					1	2
3	4	5	6	7	8	9
10	11	12	13	14 Valentine's Day	15	16
17	18 Presidents' Day	19	20	21	22	23
24	25	26	27	28	29	

Learn About Visual Thinking

You can use the knuckles on your hands to help you remember the number of days in each month.

The months on the knuckles have 31 days. The months in between have 30 days, except February.

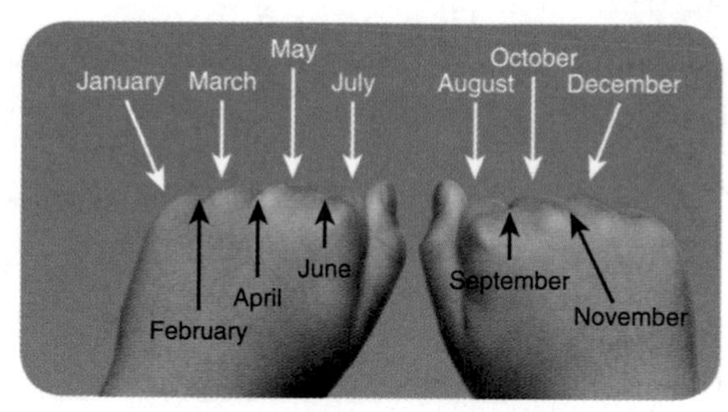

Try It

Write the number of days in each month.

11. September

12. August

13. November

Mixed Review and Test Prep

14. Beth is playing a game with a number line. Her game piece is on 505. If she moves 10 to the right, what number will she be on? (p. 34)

15. Della and Jasmine collected 98 shells at the beach. Della counted 46 shells and then found 4 more in her pocket. How many shells did Jasmine collect? (p. 80)

16. **Test Prep** Suppose it is 10:00 A.M. on Friday. Maggie's party will be at 1:00 P.M. on Saturday. How long is it until Maggie's party?

17. **Test Prep** Tim's birthday is February 13. Jena's birthday is February 20. How many days after Tim's birthday is Jena's birthday?

A 5 days **C** 10 days

B 7 days **D** 13 days

LESSON 10

Sequence Events

OBJECTIVE: Use a clock, a calendar, and a time line to determine a sequence of events.

Quick Review

Which is greater?

1. 13 or 24
2. 92 or 98
3. 334 or 343
4. 1,981 or 1,971
5. 2,000 or 1,999

Vocabulary

sequence

Learn

PROBLEM Ben drew a time line to show some events in the life of his kitten, Pogo. Did Pogo begin to walk before or after his weight doubled?

A time line shows the **sequence,** or order, of events. Read a time line from left to right. Events on the left happened before, or earlier than, events on the right.

Example Use a time line.

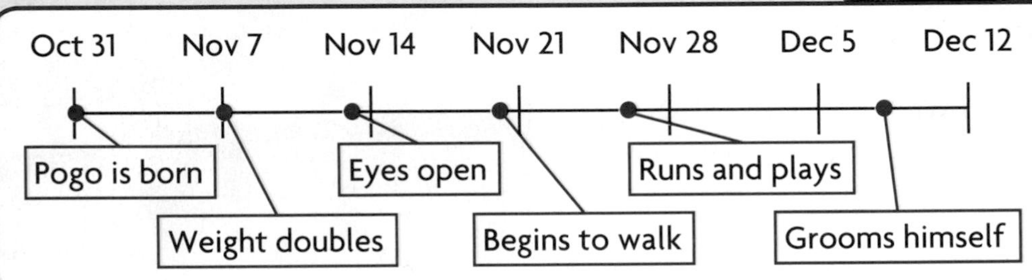

"Begins to walk" is to the right of "weight doubles." So, Pogo began to walk after his weight doubled.

- Pogo was 3 weeks old when he started getting his teeth. What other event on the time line happened about the same time?

More Examples

A Use a calendar.

April						
Sun	Mon	Tue	Wed	Thu	Fri	Sat
		1	2	3 Soccer	4	5 Party
6	7	8 Music	9	10	11	12
13	14 Zoo	15	16	17	18	19
20	21	22	23	24	25	26
27	28	29	30			

The order of Judy's activities: soccer game, birthday party, music lesson, and trip to the zoo.

B Use a clock.

4:20	6:15	7:00
Soccer practice	dinner	homework

Todd uses a clock to order his activities.

Which activity will Todd do first?

Guided Practice

For 1–4 use the time line.

1. *The Lion King* is to the right of the other movies on this time line. Was it first shown before or after the other movies?

Years in Which Movies Were First Shown

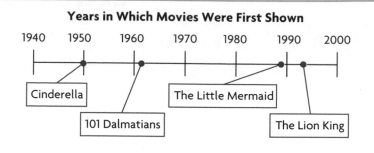

Which movie was shown earlier?

2. *The Little Mermaid* or *Cinderella*
3. *101 Dalmatians* or *The Lion King*
4. TALK Math **Explain** how to use the time line to tell which movie was shown before any of the others.

Independent Practice and Problem Solving

Use the calendar and the clocks. Which activity is earlier?

5. tennis or swimming
6. music or kickball
7. movie or book report

May						
Sun	Mon	Tue	Wed	Thu	Fri	Sat
				1 Book Report	2	3 Movie
4	5	6	7	8	9 Swim	10 Tennis

music	1:00
lunch	11:30
kickball	10:15

USE DATA For 8–9, use the table.

8. Sal's puppy was born on May 2. Which event was likely to happen on May 16?
9. WRITE Math Make a time line and explain how to show the events for Sal's puppy on it.

How a Puppy Grows

Event	Age
eyes open	2 weeks
walks	3 weeks
plays with puppies	4 weeks
eats puppy food	8 weeks

Mixed Review and Test Prep

10. Heath has 8 coins in his pocket. Six are pennies. Is he likely or unlikely to choose a penny? (Grade 2)
11. Jen left at 8 A.M. It took her 12 minutes to walk to the bus stop. The bus arrived at 8:20 A.M. For how many minutes did Jen wait for the bus? (p. 130)
12. **Test Prep** Use the calendar. Which event is Justin going to do last?

June						
Sun	Mon	Tue	Wed	Thu	Fri	Sat
1	2	3	4 Soccer	5	6	7
8 Swimming	9	10	11	12 Library	13	14 Camping

Extra Practice on page 139, Set I

Extra Practice

Set A Write the amount. (pp. 110–113)

1.      

2. 

Find two equivalent sets for each. List the coins and bills.

3. 68¢
4. 80¢
5. $2.57
6. $1.14

Set B Use <, >, or = to compare the amounts of money. (pp. 114–115)

1.    

Which amount is greater?

2. $8.61 or $8.60
3. $3.25 or 3 one-dollar bills
4. $4.32 or $4.23
5. $1.10 or $1.01
6. $7.69 or $9.76
7. $5.15 or $5.51

Set C Find the amount of change. Use play money to help. (pp. 120–121)

1. Sofia buys a sandwich for $3.42. She pays with a $5 bill.
2. Kim buys a fruit salad for $4.74. She pays with a $5 bill.
3. Grace buys a calculator for $8.37. She pays with a $10 bill.
4. Brett buys a puzzle book for $7.99. He pays with a $10 bill.
5. Tony buys a model for $6.70. He pays with a $10 bill.
6. Matt buys a dog toy for $5.59. He pays with a $10 bill.

Set D Estimate. Then find the sum or difference. (pp. 122–123)

1. $6.21 + $5.72
2. $3.65 + $2.17
3. $27.18 − $18.43
4. $70.00 − $58.96
5. $48 + $39
6. $5.37 + $0.83
7. $21.76 − $14.19
8. $1.19 − $0.63

CD ROM **Technology**
Use Harcourt Mega Math, The Number Games, *Buggy Bargains*, Levels D, G, I.

Set E **Write the time. Then write two ways you can read the time.** (pp. 124–127)

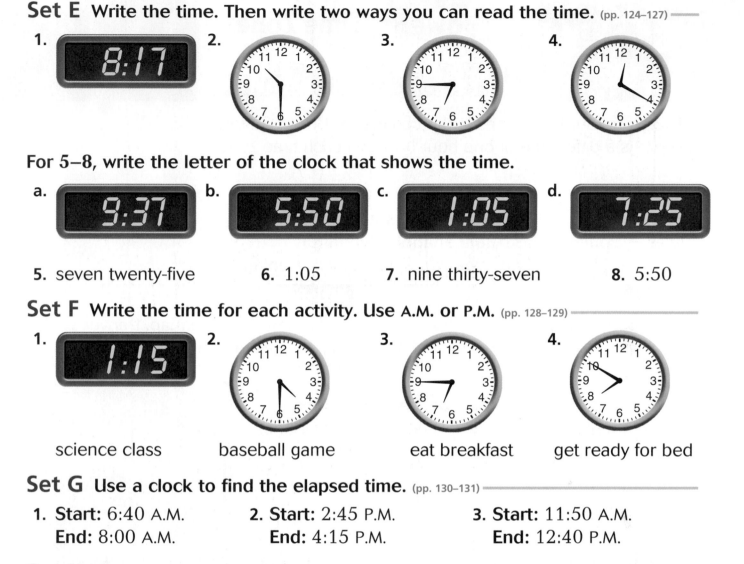

1. 
2. 
3. 
4. 

For 5–8, write the letter of the clock that shows the time.

a. 
b. 
c. 
d. 

5. seven twenty-five
6. 1:05
7. nine thirty-seven
8. 5:50

Set F **Write the time for each activity. Use A.M. or P.M.** (pp. 128–129)

1. 
science class
2. 
baseball game
3. 
eat breakfast
4. 
get ready for bed

Set G **Use a clock to find the elapsed time.** (pp. 130–131)

1. **Start:** 6:40 A.M.
End: 8:00 A.M.
2. **Start:** 2:45 P.M.
End: 4:15 P.M.
3. **Start:** 11:50 A.M.
End: 12:40 P.M.

Set H **For 1–2, use the calendar.** (pp. 132–135)

1. Marcie is going on vacation in 18 days from today. Today is June 3. On what date is Marcie going on vacation?
2. Rosa is visiting her aunt from June 16 through June 25. How many days is Rosa visiting her aunt?

June						
Sun	**Mon**	**Tue**	**Wed**	**Thu**	**Fri**	**Sat**
1	2	3	4	5	6	7 parade
8	9	10	11	12	13 visit cousin	14
15	16	17	18	19	20	21
22 beach	23	24	25 soccer	26	27	28
29	30					

Set I **Use the calendar. Which activity is earlier?** (pp. 136–137)

1. go to the beach or to the parade?
2. play soccer or go to the beach?
3. visit cousins or play soccer?

MATH POWER **Time Zones**

Telephone Time

There are four time zones in the continental United States. There is a difference of one hour between each time zone.

Dial the Phone

Beth lives in San Francisco and her sister Shannon lives in Denver. If Beth calls Shannon when it is 9 A.M. in San Francisco, what time will it be in Denver?

Step 1

Find San Francisco on the map. San Francisco is in the Pacific time zone.

Step 2

Find Denver on the map. Denver is in the Mountain time zone.

Step 3

Find the difference in hours between the Pacific and Mountain time zones. It is one hour later in the Mountain time zone than in the Pacific time zone.

So, when it is 9 A.M. in San Francisco, it will be 10 A.M. in Denver.

Try It

Use the map to solve.

1. Beth's cousin Randy lives in Dallas. If Beth calls him when it is 3:00 P.M. in San Francisco, what time will it be in Dallas?
2. Beth calls her grandmother at 8:00 A.M. each Sunday. Beth's grandmother lives in Miami. What time is it in Miami when Beth calls?
3. Beth calls her brother Mike when it is 4:00 P.M. in Chicago. What time is it in San Francisco when Beth calls her brother?
4. Beth's parents live in Seattle. If they call Beth at 7:00 P.M. once a week, what time is it in San Francisco?
5. WRITE Math Beth's brother Lewis lives in Boston. If Lewis calls Beth at 9:00 P.M. Eastern time, what time will it be in San Francisco? **Explain** how you know.

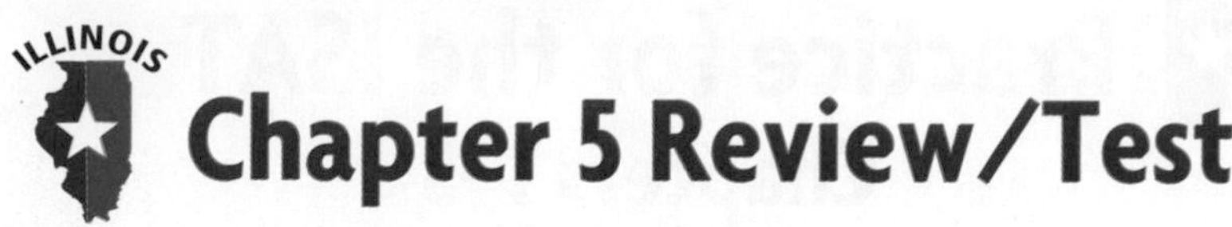

Chapter 5 Review/Test

Check Vocabulary and Concepts

Choose the best term from the box.

VOCABULARY
change
elapsed time
equivalent
half hour
P.M.

1. The money you get back after you paid for an item is called ? . IL 6.3.10 (p. 120)
2. A ? is thirty minutes. IL 7.3.02 (pp. 124–127)
3. The amount of time that passes is called ? . IL 7.3.01 (pp. 130–131)
4. Sets of money that have the same value are ? . IL 6.3.10 (pp. 110–113)

Check Skills

Find two equivalent sets for each. List the coins and bills. IL 6.3.10 (pp. 110–113)

5. 72¢
6. 43¢
7. $3.35

Which amount is greater? IL 6.3.06 (pp. 114–115)

8. $7.52 or $7.58
9. $1.00 or $1.25
10. $6.82 or $5.86
11. $2.15 or $2.52

Write the time using numbers. Use A.M. or P.M. IL 7.3.01 (pp. 128–129)

12. 25 minutes after two in the afternoon
13. one half hour past five in the evening
14. 40 minutes after nine in the morning
15. 50 minutes after one in the afternoon
16. 10 minutes after noon
17. 15 minutes before three in the afternoon

Check Problem Solving

Solve. IL 6.3.10 (pp. 116–119)

18. Ryan wants to buy a snow globe for $2.17. What are two ways to use coins and bills to show $2.17?
19. Ava has 1 $5 bill, 4 $1 bills, 5 quarters, 6 dimes, and 2 nickels. She has to pay $5.95 for a new calculator. What are two ways Ava can make $5.95?
20. WRITE Math Yolanda bought a map for $1.50, sunblock for $4.75, and a bottle of water for $2.25. Write two ways Yolanda can pay for all three items. **Explain** how you found your answers.

GO ONLINE **Technology** Use *Online Assessment.*

Practice for the ISAT
Chapters 1–5

Number and Operations

1. The deepest part of the Gulf of Mexico is Sigsbee Deep. It is 12,714 feet deep. What is the value of the digit 2 in 12,714? IL 6.3.01 (p. 14)

   A 20 C 2,000
   B 200 D 20,000

2. Lucy's book has 39 pages. Angela's book has 48 pages. How many more pages are in Angela's book? IL 6.3.09 (p. 80)

   A 6 C 8
   B 7 D 9

Understand the problem.

See item 3. What is the question? What information do you need to answer the question? Write down all of the numbers in the problem and solve.

3. **WRITE Math** Jaime and Kathy bought maps at a yard sale. Jaime's map cost $8.05. Kathy's map cost $7.95. Who spent the most money? **Explain** how you know. IL 6.3.06 (p. 114)

Algebra

4. Which number completes the fact family? Grade 2

   $6 + \blacksquare = 13$ $\blacksquare + 6 = 13$
   $13 - 6 = \blacksquare$ $13 - \blacksquare = 6$

   A 6
   B 7
   C 13
   D 19

5. How many wheels are on 6 bicycles? IL 8.3.01 (p. 4)

Bicycles	1	2	3	4	5	6
Wheels	2	4	6	8	10	■

   A 11
   B 12
   C 14
   D 18

6. **WRITE Math** Describe the pattern unit and draw the next two shapes. **Explain** how to continue the pattern. Grade 2

   ☆ ○ ☆ ☆ ○ ☆ ☆ ○ ☆

Measurement

7. What is the correct temperature? Grade 2

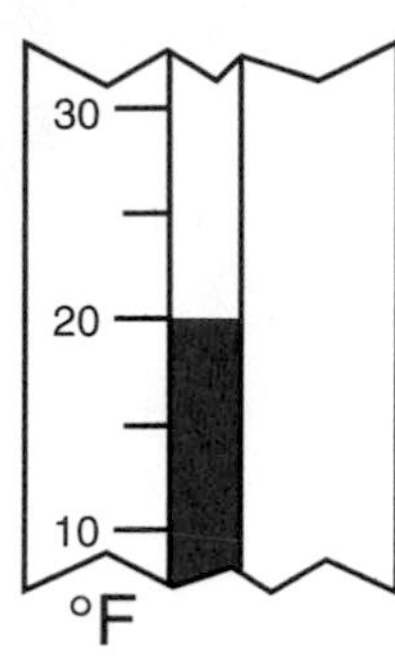

A 20°F **C** 30°F

B 25°F **D** 35°F

8. The clock shows the time Michael and his family eat dinner. At what time do they eat? IL 7.3.02 (p. 124)

A 5:00

B 5:30

C 6:25

D 6:30

9. WRITE Math **Explain** where the hands on the clock will be when the time is 9:25. IL 7.3.02 (p. 124)

Data Analysis and Probability

10. How many more students chose orange juice than apple juice? Grade 2

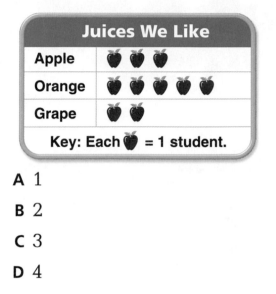

Juices We Like	
Apple	🍎🍎🍎
Orange	🍎🍎🍎🍎🍎
Grape	🍎🍎
Key: Each 🍎 = 1 student.	

A 1

B 2

C 3

D 4

11. Which pizza topping did the most students choose? Grade 2

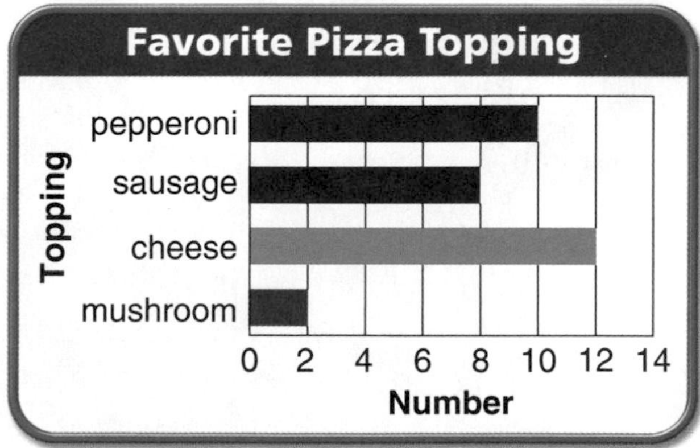

A Pepperoni **C** Cheese

B Sausage **D** Mushroom

12. WRITE Math A bag has 4 green tiles, 3 yellow tiles, and 7 red tiles. Which color are you most likely to pull? **Explain** how you know. Grade 2

CHAPTER 6

Data

FAST FACT

The Mississippi River is the longest river in the United States. It begins at Lake Itasca, in Minnesota, and flows to the Gulf of Mexico.

Investigate

Many rivers flow into the Mississippi River. Look at the map. Show another way you can display the data about the river lengths.

Technology
Student pages are available in the Student eBook.

Show What You Know

Check your understanding of important skills needed for success in Chapter 6.

▶ Read a Tally Table

For 1–3, use the tally table.

1. How many students have a dog?
2. How many students have fish?
3. How many students answered the question?

Which pet do you have?	
Dog	𝍸 𝍸 𝍷𝍷𝍷𝍷
Cat	𝍸 𝍸 𝍷𝍷
Bird	𝍷𝍷𝍷𝍷
Fish	𝍸 𝍷𝍷𝍷

▶ Column Addition

Find the sum.

4. $\begin{array}{r}3\\2\\5\\+7\\\hline\end{array}$

5. $\begin{array}{r}9\\3\\1\\+4\\\hline\end{array}$

6. $\begin{array}{r}6\\2\\8\\+3\\\hline\end{array}$

7. $\begin{array}{r}8\\1\\4\\+6\\\hline\end{array}$

8. $\begin{array}{r}7\\9\\2\\+7\\\hline\end{array}$

▶ Read a Chart

For 9–11, use the bar graph.

9. How many students ate a sandwich?
10. Which food did most students eat?
11. How many students ate lunch?

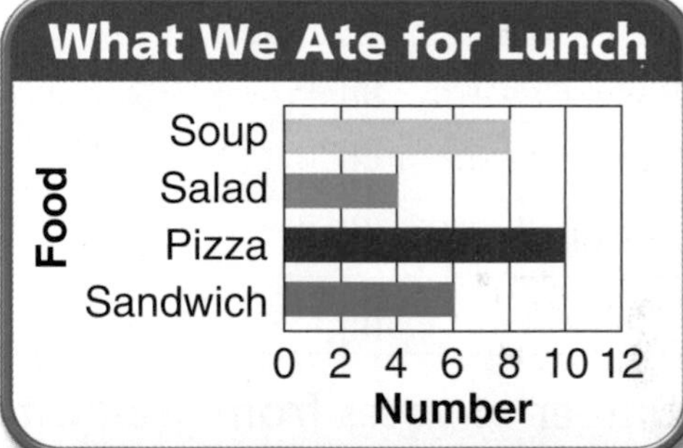

VOCABULARY POWER

CHAPTER VOCABULARY

bar graph
classify
data
frequency table
grid
horizontal bar graph
key
line graph
line plot
mode
ordered pair
pictograph
range
results
scale
survey
tally table
trends
vertical bar graph

WARM-UP WORDS

bar graph A graph that uses bars to show data

data Information that is collected about people or things

tally table A table that uses tally marks to record data

Collect Data

OBJECTIVE: Collect, organize, and record data in tally tables and frequency tables.

Quick Review

Write numbers for the tally marks.

1. 𝍸 |
2. |||
3. ||||
4. 𝍸
5. 𝍸 |||

Vocabulary

data
tally table
frequency table

Learn

Data is information that is collected about people or things.

PROBLEM The students in Moira's class voted for their favorite ice cream flavors. Moira showed the results two ways. Which flavor got the greatest number of votes? Which flavor got the least number of votes?

You can record data in a **tally table** by making tally marks as you gather data.

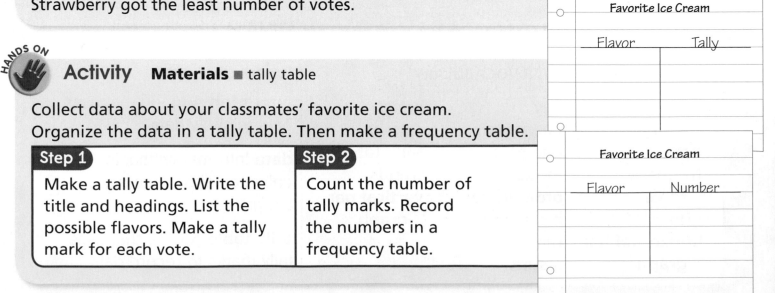

Favorite Ice Cream	
Flavor	**Tally**
Rocky Road	𝍸 |
Vanilla	𝍸 ||
Chocolate	𝍸 |||
Strawberry	||||

You can show the number of tally marks in a **frequency table** to make the data easier to read.

Favorite Ice Cream	
Flavor	**Number**
Rocky Road	6
Vanilla	7
Chocolate	8
Strawberry	4

The number of votes from greatest to least is 8, 7, 6, and 4.

So, chocolate got the greatest number of votes.
Strawberry got the least number of votes.

HANDS ON Activity

Materials ■ tally table

Collect data about your classmates' favorite ice cream. Organize the data in a tally table. Then make a frequency table.

Step 1

Make a tally table. Write the title and headings. List the possible flavors. Make a tally mark for each vote.

Step 2

Count the number of tally marks. Record the numbers in a frequency table.

Favorite Ice Cream

Flavor	Tally

Favorite Ice Cream

Flavor	Number

Guided Practice

1. What number would you write in a frequency table to show 𝍸 𝍸 |||?

For 2–3, use the Favorite Sport table.

2. How many students in all voted for soccer and baseball?
3. How many students voted in all?
4. **TALK Math** **Explain** why a frequency table can be a good way to show data.

Favorite Sport	
Sport	**Tally**
Basketball	𝍸 ||
Soccer	𝍸 ||||
Baseball	𝍸 |

Independent Practice and Problem Solving

For 5–6, use the Shirt Color list.

5. Kelly made this list of the shirt colors the students in her class were wearing. Make a tally table and a frequency table to organize her data.
6. How many more students are wearing white or blue shirts than red or green shirts?

Shirt Color			
Jen	white	Kim	blue
Patty	red	Lee	red
Matt	blue	Pam	white
Jared	white	Brad	red
Carl	green	Jake	blue

For 7–8, use the Favorite Juice table.

7. How many students voted for their favorite juice in this survey?
8. **What if** 13 more students voted for orange juice? How would the table change?
9. **WRITE Math** How are a tally table and a frequency table alike? How are they different?

Favorite Juice	
Flavor	**Number**
Grape	16
Orange	4
Berry	5
Apple	6

Mixed Review and Test Prep

10. Julie had 45 inches of ribbon. She cut 9 inches off each end. How many inches of ribbon are left? (p. 80)
11. A play began at 1:10 P.M. and ended at 3:20 P.M. How long did the play last? (p. 130)
12. **Test Prep** Jen made a tally table to record her friends' votes for their favorite pet. Her chart shows 𝍸 𝍸 || next to Dog. How many voted for dog?

A 7
B 10
C 12
D 15

Extra Practice on page 170, Set A

LESSON 2

Read a Pictograph

OBJECTIVE: Read and interpret data in a pictograph.

Quick Review

Use the tally table.

Favorite Pet	
Pet	**Tally**
Dog	𝍸 𝍸 |
Cat	𝍸 ||||
Bird	||||

How many people voted for cat?

Vocabulary

pictograph **key**

Learn

A **pictograph** uses pictures to show information.

PROBLEM Areas that are part of the national park system are good places to vacation and to learn about plants and animals. The pictograph shows the number of those areas in some states. How many are there in Pennsylvania?

National Parks	
Massachusetts	🌲🌲🌲🌲🌲
Michigan	🌲 half 🌲
New Jersey	🌲🌲 half 🌲
New York	🌲🌲🌲🌲🌲🌲🌲
Pennsylvania	🌲🌲🌲🌲🌲🌲
Key: Each 🌲 = 4 national parks.	

Math Idea
In this graph, 🌲 = 4 parks, so half 🌲 = 2 parks.

The title tells that the pictograph is about national parks.

Each row has a label that tells the name of a state.

The **key** tells that each picture stands for 4 national parks.

To find the number of national parks in Pennsylvania, count the number of 🌲 by fours.

$4 + 4 + 4 + 4 + 4 + 4 = 24$

So, there are 24 national parks in Pennsylvania.

- Which state in the pictograph has the most national parks? How many parks does it have?
- Explain how many national parks are in New Jersey.

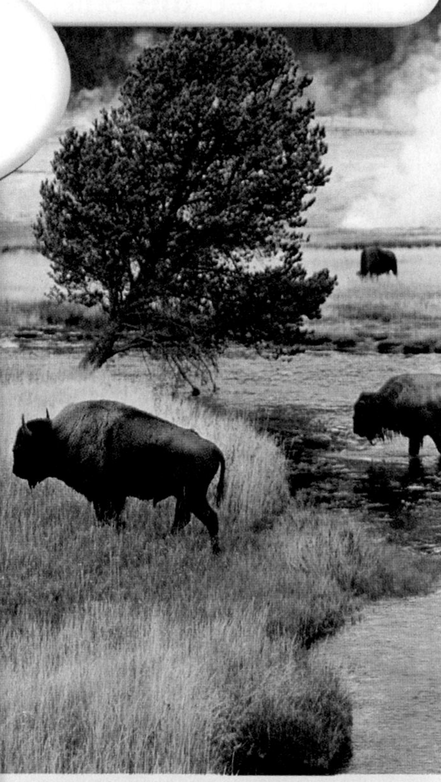

▲ Yellowstone National Park, in Wyoming, was the first named national park in the United States.

Guided Practice

1. How many national parks are in Massachusetts?

$4 + 4 + 4 + 4 + 4 + \blacksquare$

For 2–3, use the National Parks pictograph on page 148.

2. Which state in the pictograph has the fewest national parks?

3. How many more national parks are there in Pennsylvania than in Massachusetts?

4. TALK Math **Explain** why you need a key to read a pictograph.

Independent Practice and Problem Solving

For 5–7, use the National Parks pictograph at the right.

National Parks	
Arizona	🌲🌲🌲🌲🌲
Colorado	🌲🌲🌲
Kansas	🌲🌲
Oregon	🌲🌲
Key: Each 🌲 = 5 national parks.	

5. Kyle has visited every national park in Arizona. How many parks has he visited?

6. Which two states combined have the same number of national parks as Arizona?

7. **Pose a Problem** Look back at problem 5. Write a similar problem by changing the name of the state.

For 8–10, use the Favorite Park Activity pictograph.

Favorite Park Activity	
Biking	☼ ☼ ☼ ◐
Hiking	☼ ☼ ☼ ☼
Boating	☼ ☼ ☼
Fishing	☼ ◐
Key: Each ☼ = 10 votes.	

8. How many people in all voted?

9. How many more people voted for hiking and fishing than for biking?

10. WRITE Math **What if** 25 people had voted for swimming? How would you show this in the pictograph?

Mixed Review and Test Prep

11. Find the missing addend.

$19 + \blacksquare = 32$ (p. 50)

12. Wendy bought a book for $7.59. She paid with a $10 bill. How much change did she receive? (p. 120)

13. **Test Prep** Lester made a pictograph to show how many books he has. This is his key.

Each 📗 = 10 books.

How many books does  stand for?

A 7 **B** 8 **C** 35 **D** 40

Technology CD ROM
Use Harcourt Mega Math, The Number Games, *ArachnaGraph,* Level A.

Extra Practice on page 170, Set B

LESSON 3

Problem Solving Workshop
Strategy: Make a Graph

OBJECTIVE: Solve problems by using the strategy *make a graph*.

Learn the Strategy

There are many ways to show data. Some ways are lists, tables, and graphs.

You can show the data in this table in a pictograph.

Students' Pets	
Type of Pet	**Number**
Cat	9
Dog	12
Fish	4
Hamster	3

Step 1

Write the title at the top of the graph. Write a label for each row.

Students' Pets	
Cat	
Dog	
Fish	
Hamster	

Step 2

Look at the numbers. Choose a key that tells how many each picture represents.

Write the key at the bottom of the graph.

Students' Pets	
Cat	
Dog	
Fish	
Hamster	
Key: Each 🐾 = 2 students.	

Step 3

Draw the correct number of pictures for each type of pet.

Students' Pets	
Cat	🐾🐾🐾🐾½
Dog	🐾🐾🐾🐾🐾🐾
Fish	🐾🐾
Hamster	🐾½
Key: Each 🐾 = 2 students.	

TALK Math

What do the pictures in the row for Dog in the pictograph tell you?

Remember

A half picture has half the value of a whole picture.

🐾 = 2 students

½🐾 = 1 student

Use the Strategy

PROBLEM Mrs. Keller asked all the third grade students where they would like to go for a field trip. Eight students voted for the art museum, 26 students voted for the science center, 28 students voted for the aquarium, and 14 students voted for the zoo. What is one way the votes could be shown in a graph?

Read to Understand
Plan
Solve
Check

Read to Understand

- **Is there any information you will not use? If so, what?**

Plan

- **What graphic aid could help you solve the problem?**
- **What strategy can you use?**
  You can make a pictograph.

Solve

- **How can you use the strategy to solve the problem?**
  Make a pictograph.

  Choose a title.
  Write a label for each row.
  Choose a key to tell how many votes each picture stands for.
  Decide how many pictures should be placed next to each field trip choice.
  Show the correct number of pictures beside each field trip choice.

Field Trip Choices

Art museum	☺☺
Science center	☺☺☺☺☺☺◐
Aquarium	☺☺☺☺☺☺☺
Zoo	☺☺☺◐
Key: Each ☺ = 4 votes.	

Check

- **How do you know whether each row has the correct number of pictures? Give an example.**
- **Could you have used another number for the key? Explain.**

Guided Problem Solving

Read to Understand
Plan
Solve
Check

1. The science center gift shop sold 20 stuffed animals, 30 books, 15 stickers, and 10 T-shirts. How can you display the data?

   Copy the pictograph. Complete it by using the data. In your key, let each [ticket] stand for 10 items.

2. **What if** the gift shop sold 25 posters? Explain how you would display that on the pictograph.

3. Which item at the gift shop was bought the most? The least?

Science Center Gift Shop	
Stuffed Animals	[ticket] [ticket]
Key: Each [ticket] = 10 items.	

Problem Solving Strategy Practice

Make a pictograph to solve.

4. Some students voted for their favorite science center exhibit. The results are in the table at the right. Make a pictograph for the data. Let each picture stand for 3 students.

5. WRITE Math **Explain** how you knew how many pictures to draw for the light and sound exhibit.

6. **Reasoning** If the key is changed so that each picture stands for 6 students, how many pictures should be used for the number of students who voted for the nature exhibit?

Favorite Exhibit	
Nature	𝍸 ||||
Solar system	𝍸 |
Light and sound	𝍸 𝍸 𝍸
Human body	𝍸 𝍸 ||

Mixed Strategy Practice

For 7–10, use the information about the constellations.

7. Make a pictograph to show the number of stars in each constellation. Which constellation has the fewest stars?

8. How many more stars are in Orion than in Ursa Minor? Write a number sentence that shows your answer.

9. **Pose a Problem** Look back at problem 8. Write a similar problem about Ursa Major and Ursa Minor.

10. **WRITE Math** **What's the Error?** Gina says that Ursa Minor has 2 fewer stars than Cassiopeia. What error did Gina make? **Explain.**

11. **Open-Ended** After the constellation show, Rick bought a poster for $1.45. He gave the clerk $2.00. What are three combinations of coins Rick could have received as change?

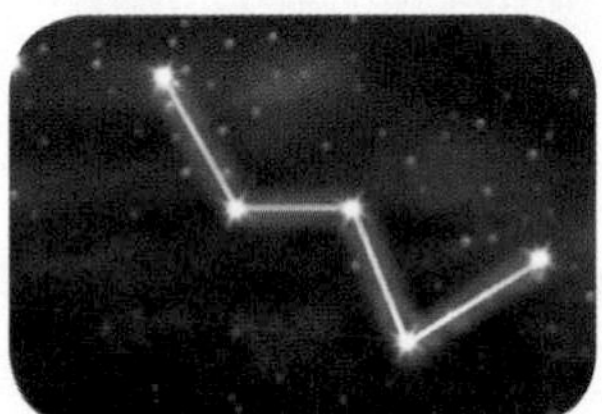

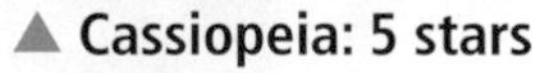

▲ Cassiopeia: 5 stars

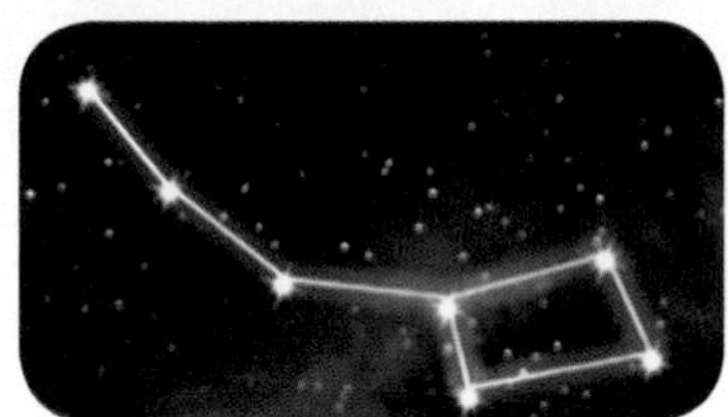

▲ Ursa Minor: 7 stars

▲ Ursa Major: 18 stars

▲ Orion: 20 stars

Choose a STRATEGY

- Draw a Diagram or Picture
- Make a Model or Act It Out
- Make an Organized List
- Find a Pattern
- Make a Table or Graph
- Predict and Test
- Work Backward
- Solve a Simpler Problem
- Write a Number Sentence
- Use Logical Reasoning

CHALLENGE YOURSELF

The seats in the science center's planetarium are divided into 3 sections. Each section has 48 seats. The table shows the numbers of third grade students from Cypress Park School who are visiting the planetarium.

Third Grade Students from Cypress Park School

Teacher	Number of Students
Mrs. Parker	31
Mr. Daniels	28
Ms. McCarthy	26

12. Mrs. Parker's students took their seats first, followed by Mr. Daniels's students. After the first section was filled, how many of Mr. Daniels's students sat in the second section of seats?

13. Ms. McCarthy's class was seated last. Explain how you can find the number of empty seats in the planetarium after everyone, including the teachers, took a seat.

LESSON 4

Read a Bar Graph

OBJECTIVE: Read and interpret data in a bar graph.

Quick Review

Write the numbers that are between:

1. 8 and 10
2. 14 and 18
3. 28 and 32
4. 54 and 60
5. 36 and 40

Vocabulary

bar graph scale
horizontal bar graph
vertical bar graph

Learn

PROBLEM Erin's family is planning to visit an amusement park. They want to ride as many roller coasters as possible. Which amusement park has the greatest number of roller coasters?

A **bar graph** uses bars to show data. A **scale** of numbers helps you read the number each bar shows. On the bar graphs below, the scale shows the numbers 0, 4, 8, 12, and 16. Each space between the numbers represents 4 roller coasters.

These bar graphs show the same data.

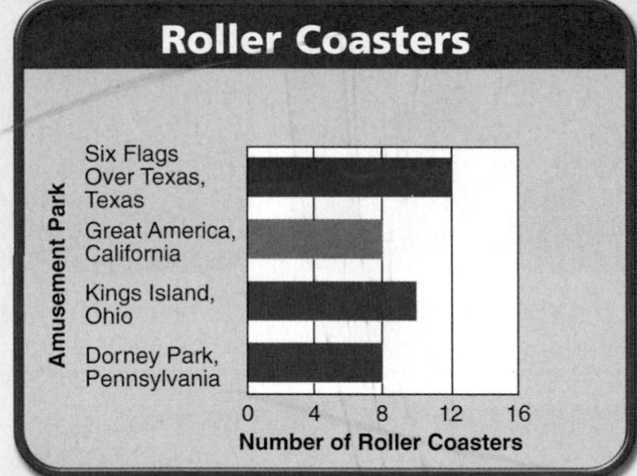

In a **horizontal bar graph**, the bars go across from left to right.

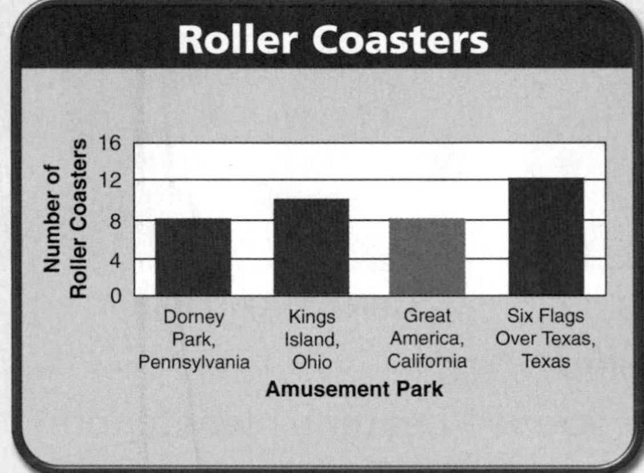

In a **vertical bar graph**, the bars go up from the bottom.

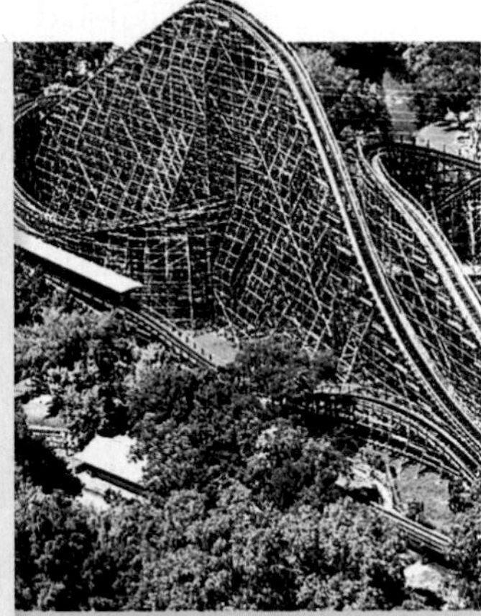

▲ The Texas Giant is a wooden roller coaster. It has 81,370 bolts holding it together!

The longest bar ends at 12. It is for Six Flags Over Texas.

So, Six Flags Over Texas has the greatest number of roller coasters.

Guided Practice

For 1–4, use the Roller Coasters graphs above.

1. Which amusement parks have the same number of roller coasters? **Think:** Which bars have the same length?

✓ **2.** How many roller coasters does Dorney Park have?

✓ **3.** How many more roller coasters does Six Flags Over Texas have than Great America?

4. TALK Math **Explain** how you would use the bar graph to tell how many roller coasters Kings Island has.

Independent Practice and Problem Solving

For 5–7, use the Favorite Ride graph.

5. How many students voted for roller coaster?

6. Did more students vote for ferris wheel and merry-go-round or for roller coaster and bumper cars? **Explain** your answer.

7. How many students voted in all?

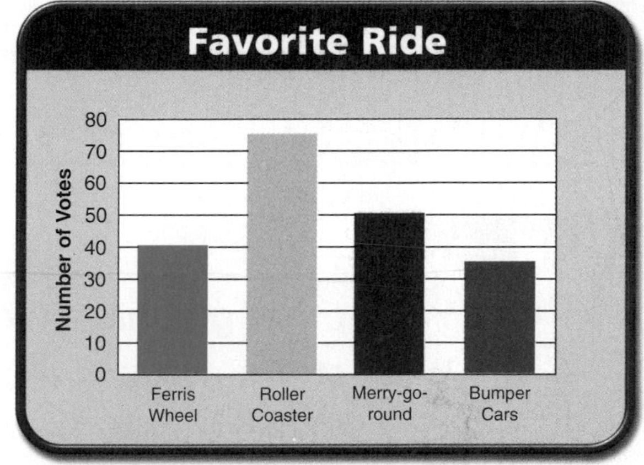

For 8–10, use the Roller Coaster Speed graph.

8. How much faster is Superman, The Escape than Nitro?

9. Which roller coaster has a bar that is twice as long as the bar for Gemini?

10. WRITE Math **Sense or Nonsense?** Jane says that Gemini is faster than Nitro. Does her statement make sense? **Explain.**

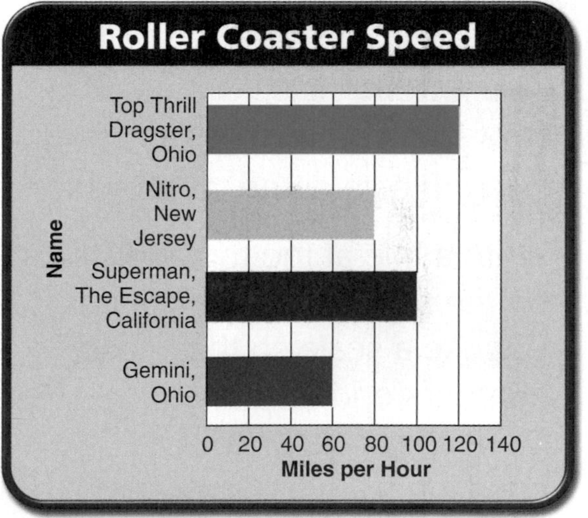

Mixed Review and Test Prep

11. Ty and his friends spent 7 hours at an amusement park. They arrived at 10:30 A.M. At what time did they leave? (p. 130)

12. Arthur placed two squares together side-by-side. What shape did Arthur make? (Grade 2)

13. **Test Prep** Melinda made a bar graph to show how many pets her friends have. Which pet has the shortest bar?

A 8 dogs

B 4 hamsters

C 6 cats

D 3 birds

Extra Practice on page 170, Set C

Problem Solving Workshop
Strategy: Make a Graph

OBJECTIVE: Solve problems by using the strategy *make a graph*.

PROBLEM Ella and Lou played a game with a spinner. Lou recorded the result of each spin in a tally table. What is another way he can show the results?

Spinner Results

Color	Tally
Red	𝍸 𝍸 |||
Blue	𝍸 𝍸
Yellow	𝍸 |||
Green	𝍸 𝍸 ||

Read to Understand

- **What information is given?**

Plan

- **What other graphic aid could you use?**
- **What strategy can you use to solve the problem?**
  You can make a bar graph.

Solve

- **How can you use the strategy to solve the problem?**
  Use the data in the table to make a bar graph.

Write a title at the top and labels on the side and at the bottom. Choose a scale so that most numbers end on a line. Make the scale 0 to 14, counting by twos. Red has 13 tally marks, so the bar for red ends halfway between 12 and 14.

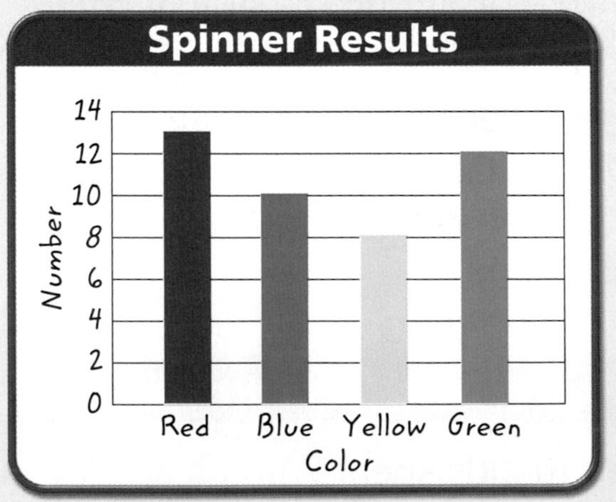

Check

- **How can you check your bar graph?**

Guided Problem Solving

1. Marta and Jordan took a survey of their classmates' favorite types of games. Jordan recorded the results in a table. Show the results in a bar graph.

Favorite Type of Game

Type	Number
Board games	7
Card games	5
Puzzles	8
Playground games	10

First, write the title and labels. Write the types of games on the bottom and the number of votes on the side.

Then, choose a scale so that most bars end on a line.

Finally, draw the bars.

2. **What if** 3 students chose board games instead of playground games as their favorite type of game? How would the graph change?

3. Adrienne pulled her stuffed animals out of her toy box. She pulled out 5 bears, 8 frogs, and 4 rabbits. Make a bar graph to show Adrienne's results. Which bar is twice as long as the bar for rabbits?

Choose a STRATEGY

- Draw a Diagram or Picture
- Make a Model or Act It Out
- Make an Organized List
- Find a Pattern
- Make a Table or Graph
- Predict and Test
- Work Backward
- Solve a Simpler Problem
- Write an Equation
- Use Logical Reasoning

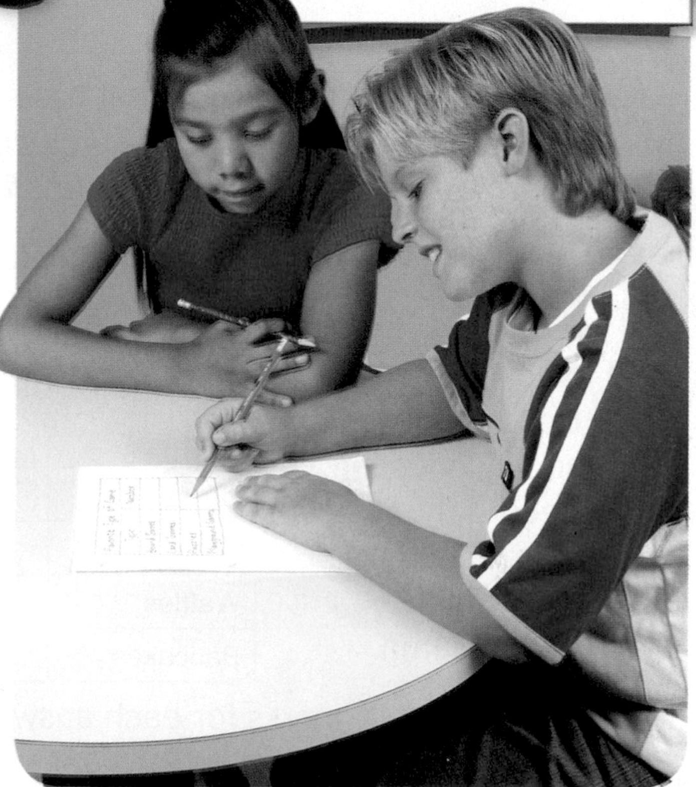

Mixed Strategy Practice

USE DATA For 4–5, use the Team Sports table.

Favorite Team Sports

Sport	Number
Soccer	12
Basketball	4
Baseball	9
Football	10

4. Use the data in the table to make a bar graph. Which sport received the fewest votes?

5. Write a number sentence that shows how many more people chose soccer than baseball.

6. Ed scored more points than Amy but fewer points than Darren. Who scored the fewest points?

6 Hands On: Take a Survey

OBJECTIVE: Take a survey, and record the results in a tally table, pictograph, and bar graph.

Quick Review

Write numbers for the tally marks.

1. 𝍸 ||
2. 𝍸 𝍸
3. 𝍸 𝍸 ||||
4. 𝍸 𝍸 𝍸 |
5. 𝍸 𝍸 𝍸 𝍸 |||

Vocabulary

survey **results**

Investigate

Materials ■ tally table

A **survey** is a way of collecting information or data. The answers collected are the **results** of the survey.

Take a survey in your classroom. Record the results in a tally table.

A Think of a survey question that has several answer choices. For example, you could ask, *What is your favorite breakfast food?*

B Make a tally table. Write a title and labels. List the answer choices.

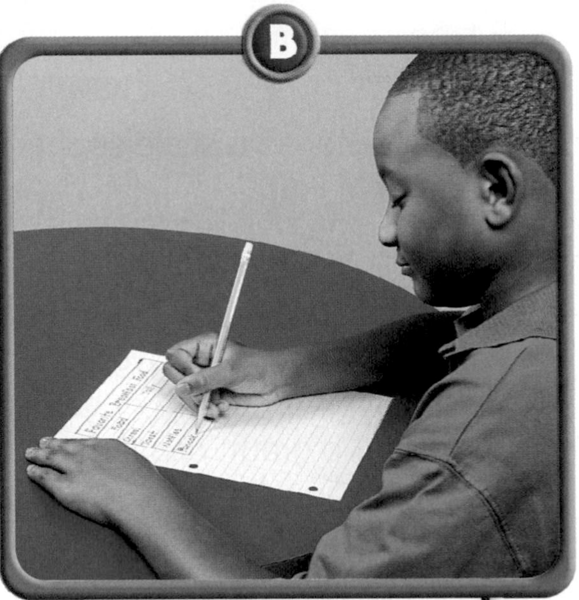

C Ask your classmates the survey question. Record the results by making tally marks in the *Tally* column.

Favorite Breakfast Food

Food	Tally
Cereal	
Toast	
Waffles	
Pancakes	

D Count the tally marks for each answer. Share the results with the class.

Draw Conclusions

1. What answer choices did you use for your survey?
2. Which answer choice for your survey has the most tally marks? Which has the fewest?
3. **Analysis** Do you think each classmate collected the same results in his or her survey? **Explain.**

Connect

You can show the data you collected by making a pictograph and a bar graph.

ONE WAY **Make a pictograph.**

Write a title and a label for each row.
Choose a key to tell how many each picture stands for.
Write the key at the bottom.
Copy and complete your pictograph.

Favorite Breakfast Food	
Cereal	
Toast	
Waffles	
Pancakes	
Key: Each ■ = ■ students.	

ANOTHER WAY **Make a bar graph.**

Write a title and labels.
Write the answer choices.
Choose a scale to show the number of answers.
Copy and complete your bar graph.

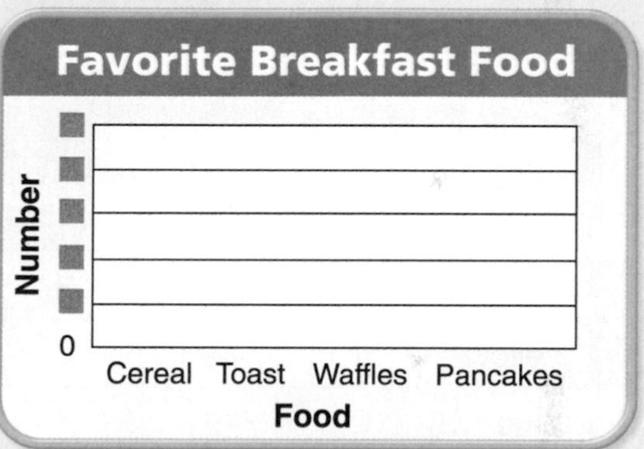

TALK Math

How do your graphs show the choice with the fewest tally marks? The most tally marks?

Practice

For 1–2, use your tally table and graph.

1. What is the title of your tally table and your graph?
2. How many classmates in all answered your survey?
3. Think of another survey question. Write several possible answer choices. Ask your classmates your survey question. Show the results in a pictograph and in a bar graph.
4. **WRITE Math** How are the data in your pictograph and bar graph alike? How are they different?

LESSON 7

Classify Data

OBJECTIVE: Use a table to organize data.

Quick Review

Find the sum.

1. 2 + 3 + 4
2. 4 + 6 + 3
3. 2 + 7 + 5
4. 3 + 5 + 8
5. 7 + 6 + 5

Vocabulary

classify

Learn

To **classify** is to group pieces of data according to how they are the same. You can classify by shape, color, or size.

PROBLEM Cathy and Tom are playing a game. Their game pieces are shown below. What are some ways Cathy and Tom can classify the game pieces?

Data can be organized into a table. A table can show two ways at a time to classify the data.

ONE WAY **By shape and color**

Game Pieces

	triangle	circle	square
red	3	2	3
yellow	4	2	2
blue	2	2	4

ANOTHER WAY **By shape and size**

Game Pieces

	triangle	circle	square
small	2	2	4
medium	3	2	3
large	4	2	2

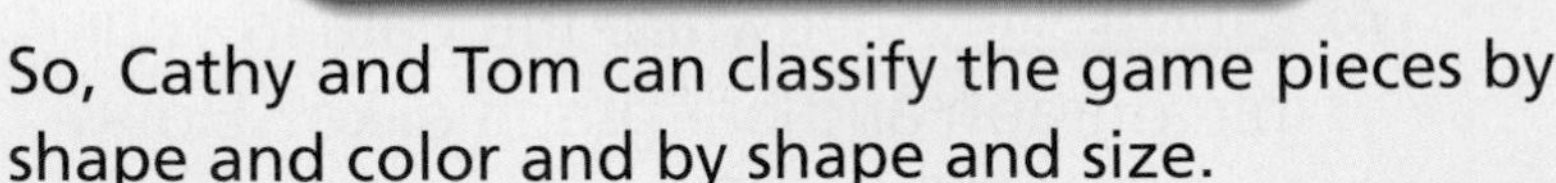

So, Cathy and Tom can classify the game pieces by shape and color and by shape and size.

- What other way can Cathy and Tom classify the game pieces?

Guided Practice

For 1–5, use the Juice Boxes table.

Juice Boxes	orange	apple	grape
small	4	5	6
medium	5	4	4
large	5	5	4

1. How are the juice boxes classified?
2. How many large apple juice boxes are there?
3. How many grape juice boxes are there?
4. How many more small juice boxes than large juice boxes are there?
5. TALK Math **Explain** how to find the total number of juice boxes.

Independent Practice and Problem Solving

For 6–9, use the Class Shoe Color table.

Class Shoe Color	girls	boys
white	4	5
blue	3	2
black	2	3

6. How many girls are wearing black shoes?
7. How many students are wearing blue shoes?
8. How many more boys than girls were surveyed?
9. How many students were surveyed in all?
10. Look at the stars at the right. Make a table to classify them two ways. **Explain** how you classified them.

11. WRITE Math **Explain** three ways you can classify the students in your class.

Mixed Review and Test Prep

12. Susan had $3.45. Then her sister gave her some money. Now Susan has $5.90. How much money did Susan's sister give her? (p. 122)
13. Alex is making a pictograph. His key is [book] = 10 books. How many books are represented by [book] [book] [book] [book] [half book]? (p. 150)
14. **Test Prep** Which shows two ways to classify a group of hats?
    - **A** happy or sad
    - **B** quiet or loud
    - **C** size or color
    - **D** sweet or salty

Extra Practice on page 170, Set D

LESSON 8

Line Plots

OBJECTIVE: Read and make line plots, and find the range and mode.

Quick Review

Find the difference.

1. 7 − 2
2. 16 − 9
3. 24 − 18
4. 35 − 27
5. 51 − 42

Vocabulary

line plot **mode** **range**

Learn

A **line plot** shows each piece of data on a number line.

PROBLEM The students in Mrs. Young's class planted lima bean seeds for a science project. The line plot below shows the heights of the seedlings after 4 weeks. What height was recorded most often?

In this line plot, each ***x*** stands for 1 seedling. The numbers show the heights of the seedlings in inches.

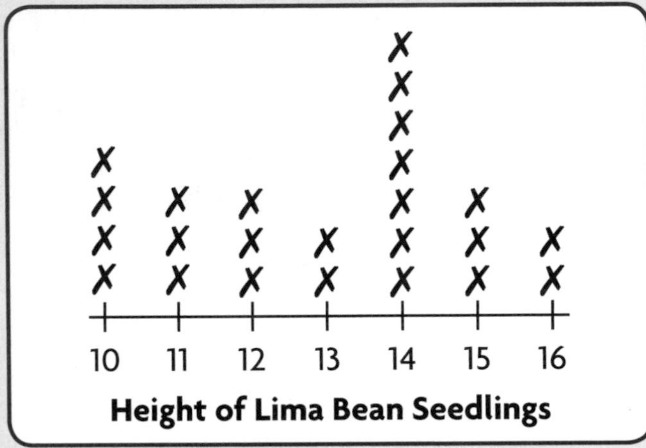

▲ Fordhook lima bean plants can reach about 20 inches in height.

The **mode** is the number or item found most often in a set of data.

Find the number on the line plot with the most ***x***'s above it. There are 7 ***x***'s above 14 inches.

So, the height recorded most often was 14 inches tall.

- How many seedlings were taller than 14 inches?
- **What if** 4 more lima bean seedlings were 10 inches tall? Would that change the mode? Explain.

The **range** is the difference between the greatest number and the least number in a set of data.

greatest number		least number		range
16	−	10	=	6

Activity

Materials ■ number line

Sarah rolled a number cube 20 times. She recorded the number rolled each time in a tally table.

You can also show these data in a line plot.

Sarah's Experiment	
Number rolled	**Tally**
1	||||
2	|||
3	||
4	|||
5	~~||||~~
6	|||

Step 1

Copy the line plot. Write a title. Label the numbers from 1 to 6 to show the numbers on the number cube.

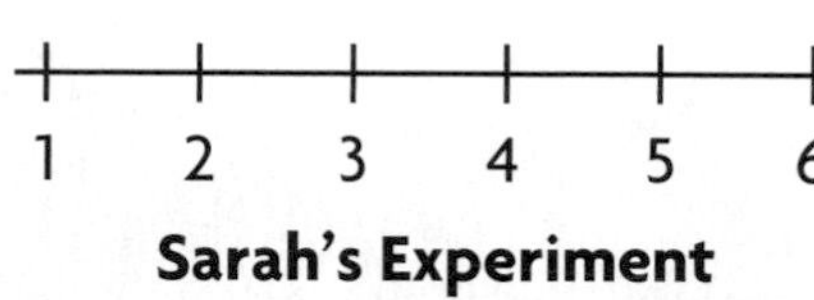

Step 2

Draw *x*'s above the number line to show how many times Sarah rolled each number.

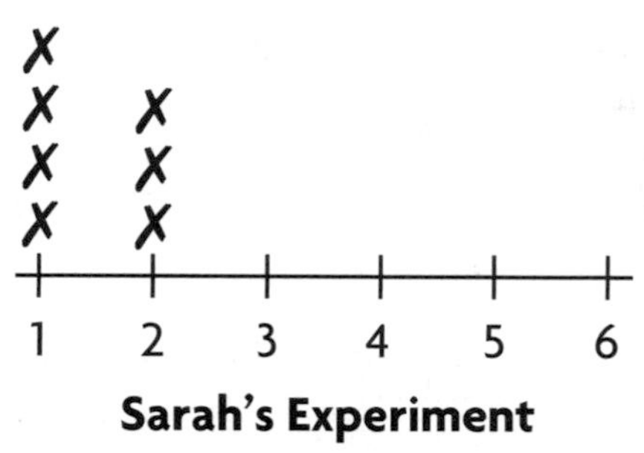

- How are the tally table and the line plot alike? How are they different?

Guided Practice

For 1–5, use your line plot.

1. How can you find the mode in Sarah's experiment?
   Think: Which number did Sarah roll most often?
2. How many times did Sarah roll a 1?
3. What is the range of Sarah's data?
4. Which number did Sarah roll the fewest times?
5. How many more times did Sarah roll a 5 than a 3?
6. TALK Math **Explain** why you would use a line plot to show data.

Independent Practice and Problem Solving

For 7–12, use the Gallons of Sap Collected line plot.

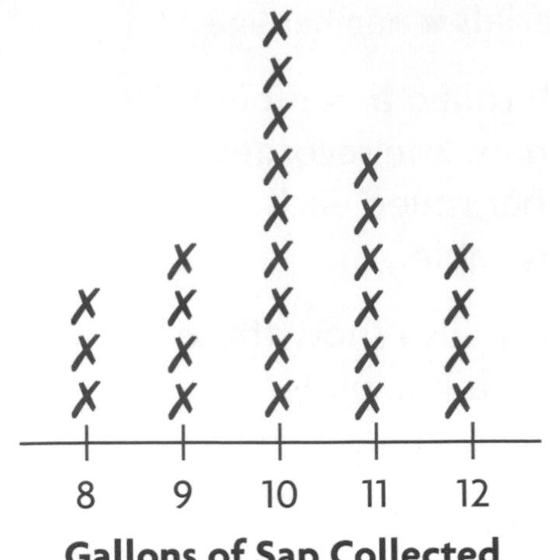

7. **FAST FACT** Sap is collected from sugar maple trees to make maple syrup. The line plot shows how many gallons of sap Blake collected from some of the trees on his farm. From how many trees did Blake collect fewer than 10 gallons of sap?
8. From how many trees did Blake collect more than 10 gallons of sap?
9. What is the range of the data?
10. **WRITE Math** **What's the Error?** Julie says the mode of the data is 9. Describe her error. What is the mode?
11. **Pose a Problem** Look back at problem 7. Write a similar problem by changing the number of gallons.
12. **Reasoning** Suppose Blake collected 11 gallons of sap from 4 more trees. Will the range of the data change? **Explain.**

Mixed Review and Test Prep

13. The Missouri River is 2,315 miles long. The Mississippi River is 2,340 miles long. Which river is longer? (p. 28)
14. Matt has one \$5 bill and 6 nickels. Peter has four \$1 bills, 6 quarters, and 1 nickel. Compare the amounts of money. (p. 114)
15. **Test Prep** Madeline made the line plot below.

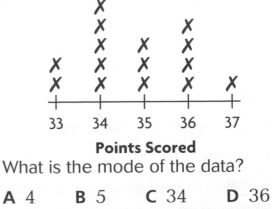

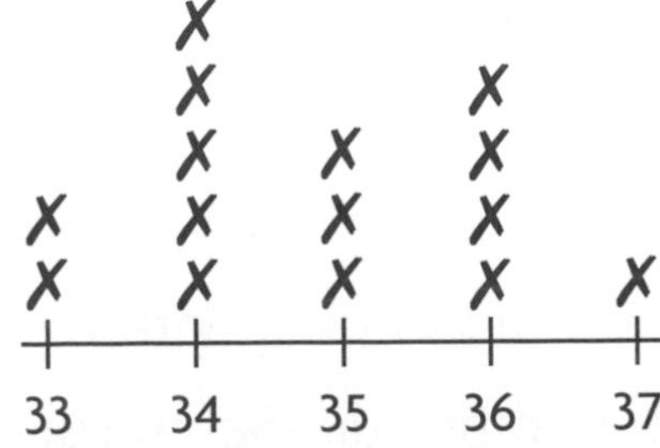

What is the mode of the data?

A 4 **B** 5 **C** 34 **D** 36

Technology
CD ROM
Use Harcourt Mega Math, The Number Games, *ArachnaGraph*, Level F

Extra Practice on page 171, Set E

Learn About Matching Data to Graphs

The table shows the average life spans of different animals. Which graph shows the data in the table correctly?

Compare Graphs A and B to the data in the table.

Animal Life Spans	
Animal	**Years**
chipmunk	6
mouse	3
opossum	1
squirrel	10

Graph A

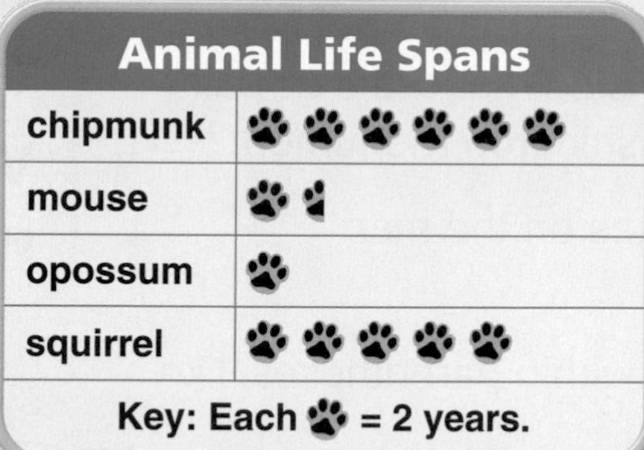

Graph B

Animal Life Spans

Number of Years

12
10
8
6
4
2
0

chipmunk
mouse
opossum
squirrel

Animal

Graph A shows 1 picture, or 2 years, for the opossum and 6 pictures, or 12 years, for the chipmunk. This does not match the data in the table.

Each bar in Graph B correctly shows the data in the table. So, Graph B matches the data.

Try It

1. Which graph shows the data in the table correctly?

Animal Life Spans	
Animal	**Years**
elephant	40
box turtle	100
bear	25
lion	15

Graph C

Animal Life Spans	
elephant	
box turtle	
bear	
lion	

Key: Each = 10 years.

Graph D

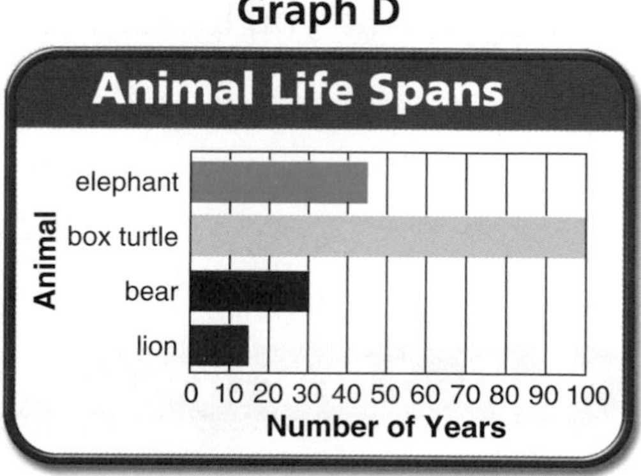

2. **WRITE Math** **Explain** how you know which graph does NOT show the data in the table correctly.

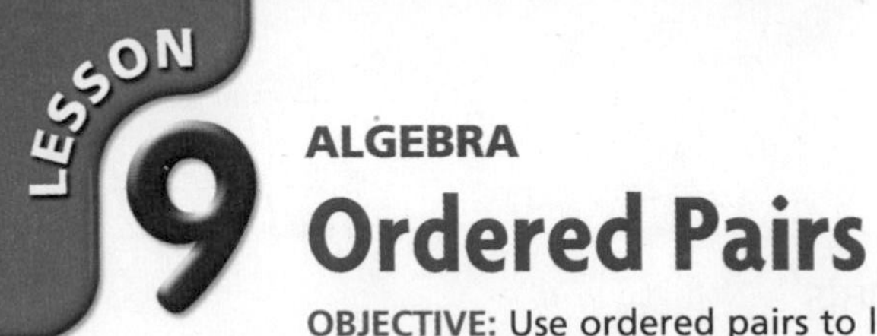

ALGEBRA

Ordered Pairs

OBJECTIVE: Use ordered pairs to locate points on a grid.

Quick Review

Identify the number named by each point.

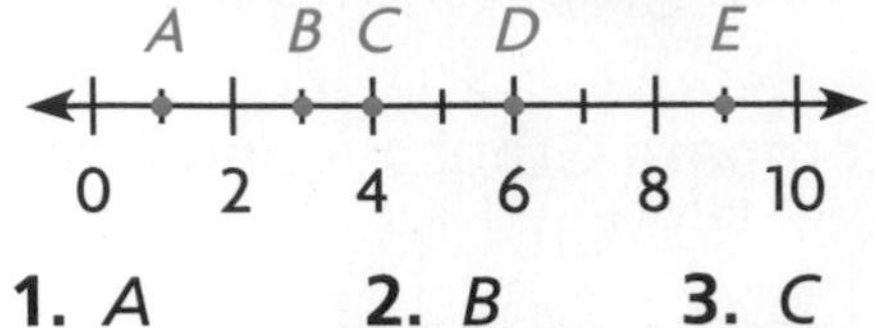

1. *A* **2.** *B* **3.** *C*
4. *D* **5.** *E*

Vocabulary

grid **ordered pair**

Learn

PROBLEM Myra and her family are visiting Washington, D.C. They are using the map below to find the places they want to visit. What ordered pair names the location of the Washington Monument?

The horizontal and vertical lines on the map make a **grid**.

An **ordered pair** of numbers within parentheses, like (2,3), names a point on a grid.

Washington, D.C.

N, S, W, E; White House; Reflecting Pool; Washington Monument; Lincoln Memorial; Jefferson Memorial; 0, 1, 2, 3, 4, 5, 6

Find the Washington Monument on the grid.

Start at 0.
Move 4 spaces to the right.
Then move 3 spaces up.

So, the ordered pair (4,3) names the location for the Washington Monument.

The first number tells how many spaces to move from 0 to the right. → (4,3) ← The second number tells how many spaces to move up.

- How would you locate the Lincoln Memorial?
- What is located at (4,1)?

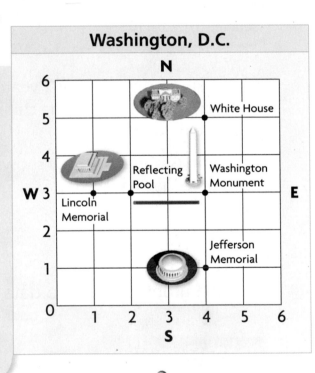

Math Idea
Another way to write *up, down, left,* and *right* is *north, south, west,* and *east.*

Guided Practice

1. Use the Washington, D.C. map. What is located at (4,5)?
Think: Start at 0. Move 4 spaces to the right. Then move 5 spaces up.

For 2–5, use the school grid at the right.

2. What ordered pair names the point between the music room and the art room?

3. What ordered pair names the location of the cafeteria?

4. What is located at (6,1)?

5. **TALK Math** **Explain** how to locate the computer lab.

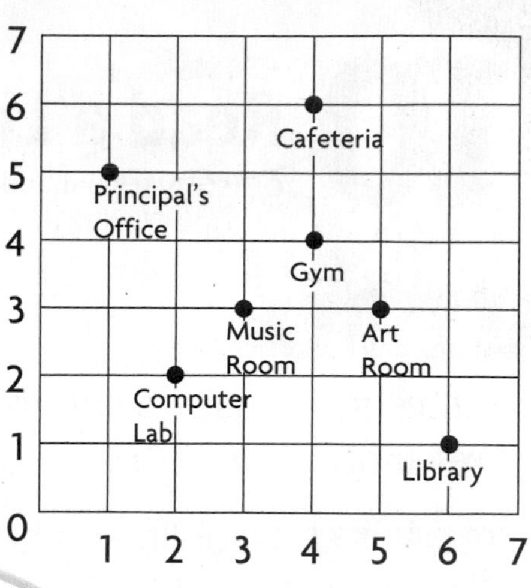

Independent Practice and Problem Solving

Write the ordered pair for each letter.

6. *J* 7. *B* 8. *G* 9. *K* 10. *C*

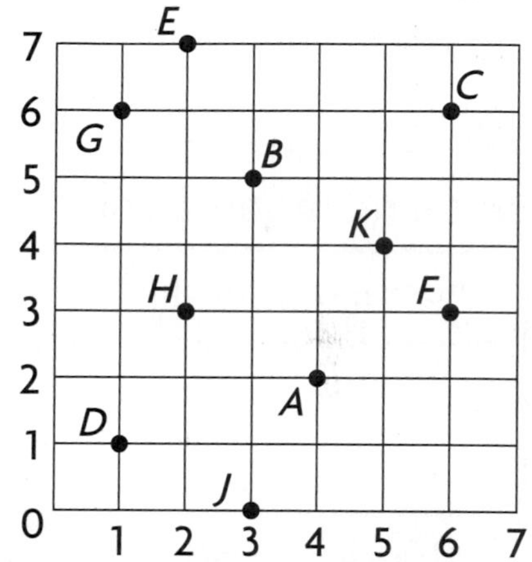

Write the letter that names the point for each ordered pair.

11. (4,2) 12. (1,1) 13. (2,7) 14. (6,3) 15. (2,3)

For 16–19 use the garden grid below.

16. What ordered pair names the location of the corn?

17. What is located at (4,3)?

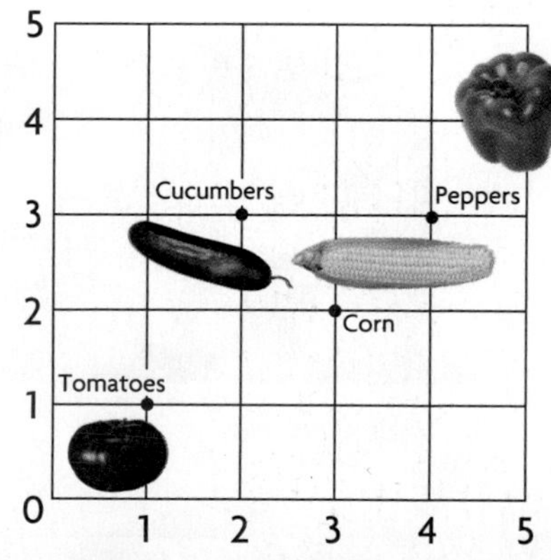

18. **Reasoning** What if Geoff planted lettuce at (1,4) and Janna planted carrots at (3,4)? What ordered pair would name the point between the lettuce and the carrots?

19. **WRITE Math** **Explain** how a point located at (2,3) is different than a point located at (3,2).

Mixed Review and Test Prep

20. Sergio practiced soccer for 1 hour and 25 minutes. For how many minutes did he practice? (p. 124)

21. What number is missing in Jon's pattern? (p. 4)

17, 27, 37, ■, 57

22. **Test Prep** Margie drew a grid. She started at 0, moved 4 spaces to the right and 6 spaces up. At what point did Margie end?

A (0,4) **C** (4,6)
B (6,4) **D** (10,0)

Extra Practice on page 171, Set F

LESSON 10

Read a Line Graph

OBJECTIVE: Read and interpret data in a line graph.

Quick Review

Find the difference.

1. 15 − 9
2. 25 − 8
3. 39 − 22
4. 47 − 29
5. 125 − 109

Vocabulary

line graph   trends

Learn

A **line graph** uses a line to show how data change over time.

PROBLEM Isabella and her mother did an experiment to see how long it took water to boil. The line graph shows the data they collected. What was the water temperature at 2 minutes?

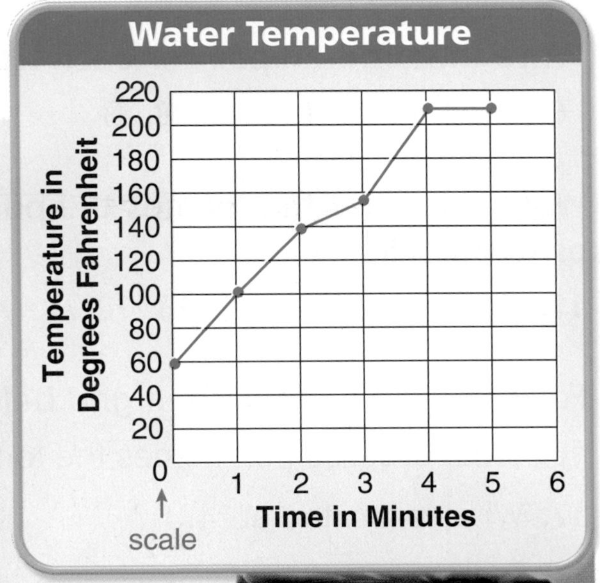

You can locate points on a line graph as you locate points on a grid.

Find the vertical line for 2 minutes. Move up to the point. Follow the horizontal line left to the scale showing degrees.

The point for 2 minutes is at 140 degrees.

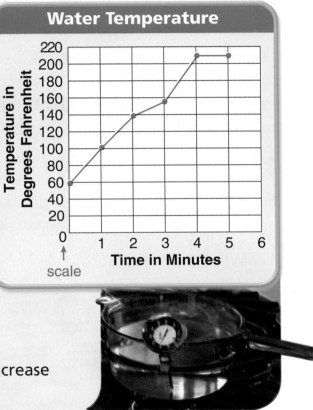

So, the temperature of the water at 2 minutes was 140 degrees.

On a line graph, you can see **trends**, or areas where data increase, decrease, or stay the same over time.

- What does the blue line tell you?
- Between which two minutes did the temperature increase the most?

Guided Practice

For 1–4 use the Water Temperature graph.

1. What was the water temperature at 1 minute?

   Think: Find the vertical line for 1 minute. Move up to the point, and follow the horizontal line left to the scale.

2. What was the water temperature at 3 minutes?

3. By about how many degrees did the temperature increase between 2 minutes and 3 minutes?

4. TALK Math **Explain** a trend you see in the line graph.

Independent Practice and Problem Solving

For 5–7, use the Depth of Water graph.

Matthew measured the depth of the water in an outside bucket each day for 6 days.

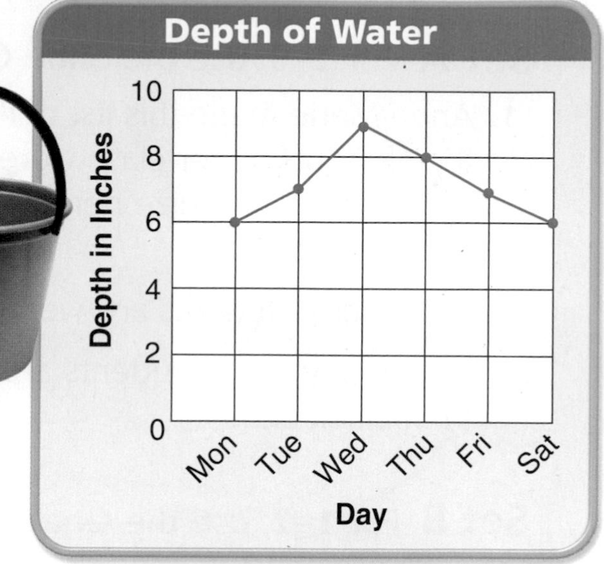

5. How deep was the water on Friday?
6. Between which two days did the depth of the water increase 3 inches?
7. When the sun warms water, the water evaporates, or changes from a liquid to a gas. Suppose it did not rain and Matthew's bucket did not have a leak. How much water evaporated between Thursday and Saturday? **Explain** how you know.

For 8–10, use the Plant Growth graph.

8. How tall was the plant at 2 weeks?
9. How did the height of the plant change every week?
10. **WRITE Math** **Sense or Nonsense?** Sam thinks that the plant will be 7 inches tall at week 6. Does Sam's statement make sense? Explain.

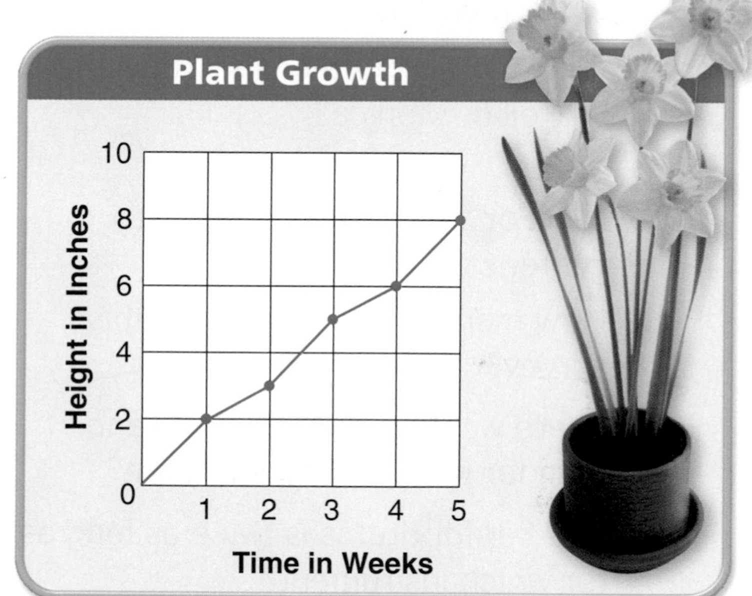

Mixed Review and Test Prep

11. What is the name of this shape? (Grade 2)
12. The heights in inches of six students are: 36, 40, 38, 40, 39, and 40. What is the mode? (p. 162)
13. **Test Prep** How many books did Scott read in February?
    - **A** 2 books
    - **B** 3 books
    - **C** 4 books
    - **D** 6 books

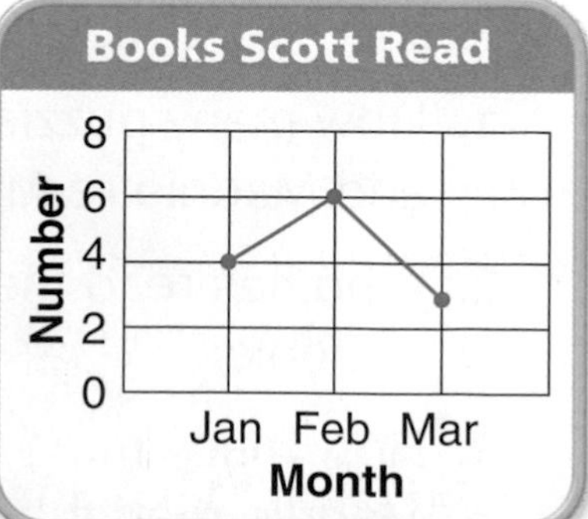

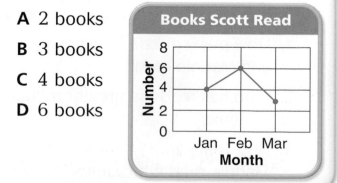

Extra Practice on page 171, Set G

Extra Practice

Set A For 1–3, use the Shoe Color list. (pp. 146–147)

1. Anne Marie made this list of the shoe colors the students in her class were wearing. Make a tally table to organize her data. Then make a frequency table.
2. How many students are wearing brown shoes?
3. How many more students are wearing blue shoes than black shoes?

Shoe Color	
Jack	blue
Mike	brown
Trisha	black
Shelly	blue
Greta	white
Manuel	brown
Tyler	brown
Samantha	black
Hunter	blue
Morgan	brown

Set B For 1–2, use the Goals Scored pictograph. (pp. 148–149)

1. How many more goals did Monica score than Tony?
2. Who scored more goals—Tony and Darrell or Monica?

Goals Scored	
Tony	⚽ ⚽ ⚽ ⚽
Darrell	⚽ ⚽
Monica	⚽ ⚽ ⚽ ⚽ ⚽
Key: Each ⚽ = 2 goals.	

Set C For 1–4, use the Favorite Instrument graph. (pp. 154–155)

1. How many students voted in this survey?
2. There was 1 more vote for piano than for what other instrument?
3. The bar for drums is twice as long as for which instrument?
4. How many more students voted for drums than for piano?

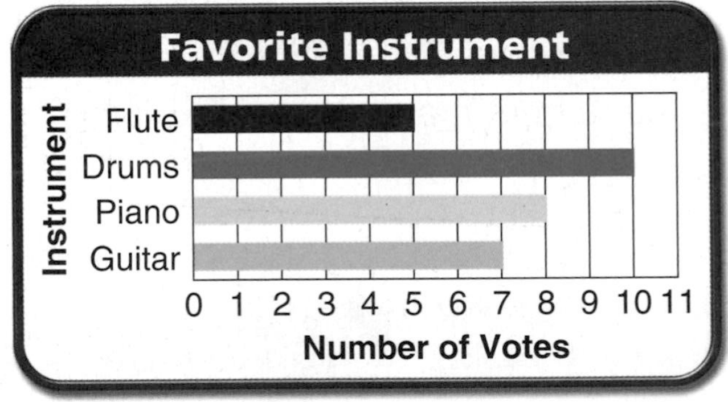

Set D For 1–3, use the Types of Books Read table. (pp. 160–161)

1. How many puzzle books have James and Maddie read?
2. Who has read the greater number of books?
3. How many more sports books has Maddie read than James?

Types of Books Read		
	James	Maddie
animal	4	1
puzzle	6	3
sports	6	9

Set E For 1–5, use the Baskets of Blueberries Picked line plot. (pp. 162–165)

1. How many people picked 9 baskets of blueberries?
2. What is the range of the data?
3. What is the mode of the data?
4. How many people picked fewer than 7 baskets of blueberries?
5. How many people picked more than 6 baskets of blueberries?

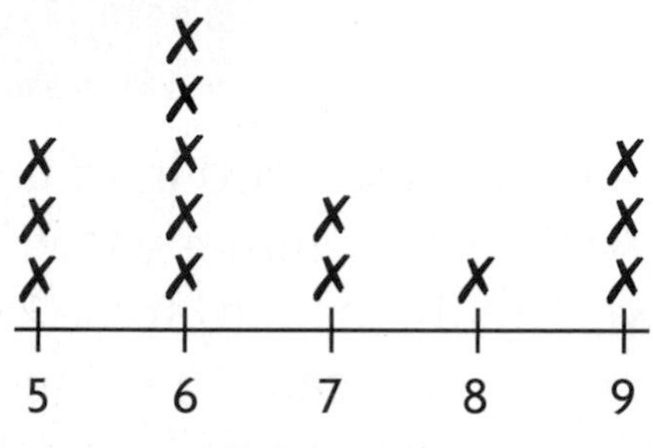

Set F For 1–4, use the classroom grid. (pp. 166–167)

1. What is located at (2,2)?
2. What is located at (1,1)?
3. What ordered pair names the location of the computer?
4. The teacher put a rug between the reading area and the bookshelf. What ordered pair names the point where the rug is?

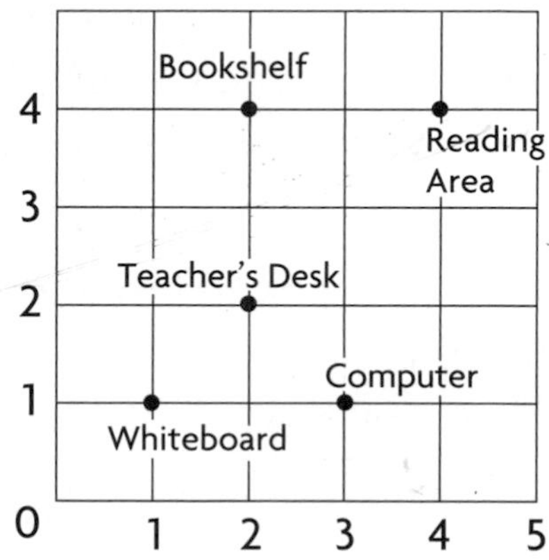

Set G For 1–3, use the Plants Sold graph. (pp. 168–169)

1. How many plants were sold on Monday?
2. How many more plants were sold on Saturday than on Sunday?
3. There were 5 more plants sold on Wednesday than on Tuesday. How many plants were sold on Wednesday?

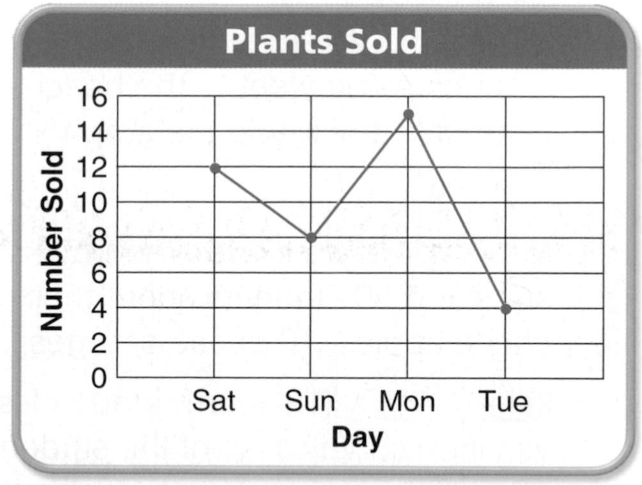

CD ROM **Technology**
Use Harcourt Mega Math, The Number Games, *ArachnaGraph*, Levels A, B, C, F, G, J.

Circle Graphs

Mr. Spear's class asked 100 third grade students where they went for summer vacation. Some students went to the beach, some went to a theme park, and some went camping. The class showed the data in a circle graph. A **circle graph** shows data as parts of a whole circle.

Example

- The whole circle represents all 100 students in the survey.
- The section for beach is half of the circle. Since $50 + 50 = 100$, 50 students went to the beach.
- The sections for camping and theme park are the same size. Since $25 + 25 = 50$, 25 students went camping, and 25 students went to a theme park.

Try It

For 1–2, use the Third Grade Vacations graph.

1. What if the 25 students who went camping went to the beach instead? How would the graph change?
2. What if 25 of the students who went to the beach went to a family reunion instead? How would the graph change?
3. Make your own circle graph by using these data: Robbie surveyed 60 students about their favorite fruit. Half chose apples, 10 chose oranges, and 20 chose grapes.
4.  WRITE Math The fourth grade classes did their own vacation survey. Half of the students went camping. If 120 students were surveyed, how many went camping? **Explain.**

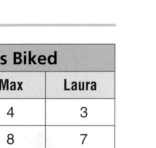

Chapter 6 Review/Test

Check Vocabulary and Concepts

Choose the best term from the box.

VOCABULARY
pictograph
bar graph
frequency table
classify

1. When you __?__, you group pieces of data by color or size. IL 10.3.01 (p. 160)
2. A __?__ uses pictures to show information. IL 10.3.01 (p. 148)
3. A way to record the number of tally marks is in a __?__. IL 10.3.01 (p. 146)

Check Skills

For 4–6, use the Miles Biked table. IL 10.3.01 (pp. 160–161)

Miles Biked		
	Max	Laura
Friday	4	3
Saturday	8	7
Sunday	9	10

4. How many miles did Max bike on Saturday and Sunday?
5. Who biked the greater number of miles?
6. On which day did Laura bike more miles than Max?

For 7–9, use the Number of Goals Scored line plot. IL 10.3.03 (pp. 162–165)

7. How many soccer players scored 4 goals?
8. What is the mode of the data?
9. How many soccer players scored fewer than 2 goals?

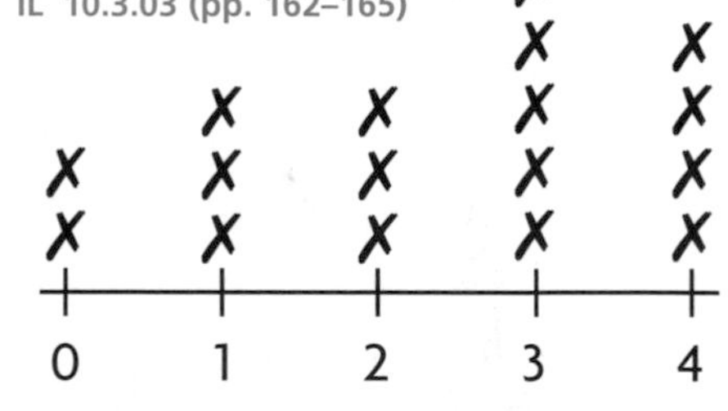

Number of Goals Scored

Check Problem Solving

Make a pictograph to solve. IL 10.3.02 (pp. 150–153)

Field Trip Locations	
Location	Number of Votes
Zoo	16
Amusement park	20
Nature museum	8
Science center	24

10. The third grade classes voted on locations for their field trip. The results are shown in the tally table. Make a pictograph for the data. Let each picture stand for 4 votes.
11. How many pictures did you draw for amusement park?
12. **WRITE Math** When Randy made his pictograph, he let each picture stand for 8 votes. **Explain** how the votes for the science center look different than on your pictograph.

GO ONLINE **Technology** Use *Online Assessment.*

Practice for the ISAT
Chapters 1–6

Number and Operations

Check the answer.

See Item 1. Subtract to find the answer. If the difference does not match one of the answer choices, check your subtraction.

1. On Tuesday, the cafeteria at Ramon's school served 300 lunches. On Wednesday, the cafeteria served 257 lunches. How many more lunches were served on Tuesday? IL 6.3.09 (p. 88)

   A 42 **C** 52

   B 43 **D** 53

2. Meredith and her friend James live 182 miles apart. What is the value of the digit 8 in 182? IL 6.3.01 (p. 8)

   A 8,000 **C** 80

   B 800 **D** 8

3. WRITE Math Cheryl has a collection of 413 stamps. Patty has a collection of 329 stamps. How many stamps do they have altogether? Which method did you use to solve the problem? **Explain.** IL 6.3.09 (p. 64)

Algebra

4. Look at the pattern. What are the next two shapes? Grade 2

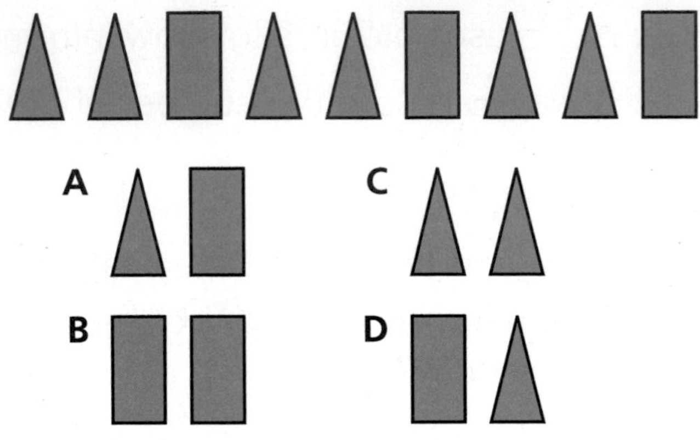

5. Look at the pattern. What comes next? Grade 2

6. WRITE Math Sarah has 4 puzzle books. She got 9 more. Her sister Emily has 9 puzzle books. She got 4 more. Who has more puzzle books? **Explain.** IL 8.3.03 (p. 48)

Geometry

7. What is the name of the shape? Grade 2

A Square

B Hexagon

C Rectangle

D Triangle

8. Look at the solid figure. Which plane figure is one face of the solid figure? Grade 2

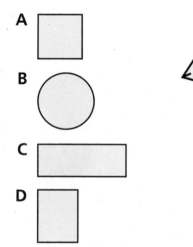

A

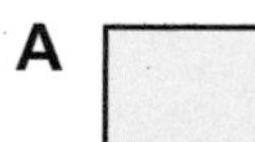

B

C

D

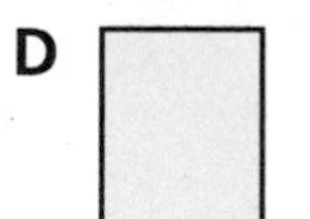

9. WRITE Math **Explain** how this cube and rectangular prism are alike. Grade 2

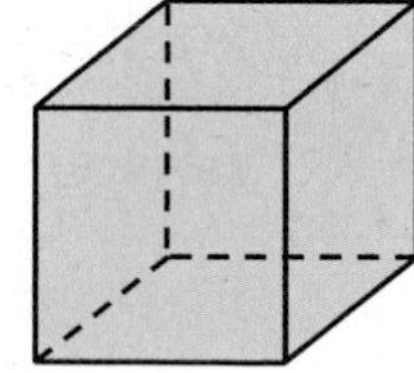

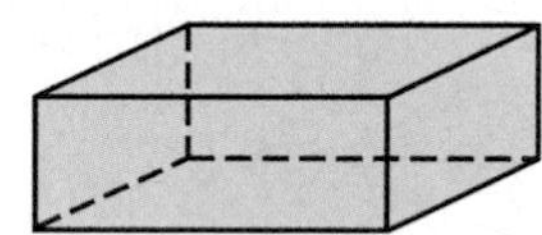

Data Analysis and Probability

10. Students voted for their favorite ice cream topping. How many students in all voted? IL 10.3.01 (p. 154)

A 16 **C** 26

B 20 **D** 30

11. Which color marble is least likely to be pulled? Grade 2

A Yellow

B Blue

C Green

D Red

12. WRITE Math Sherri is making a pictograph to show the number of books the students in her class have read. Each [book] = 5 books. This is her key. There are 3 books next to Eric's name. How many books has he read? **Explain.** IL 10.3.01 (p. 148)

TER

7 Probability

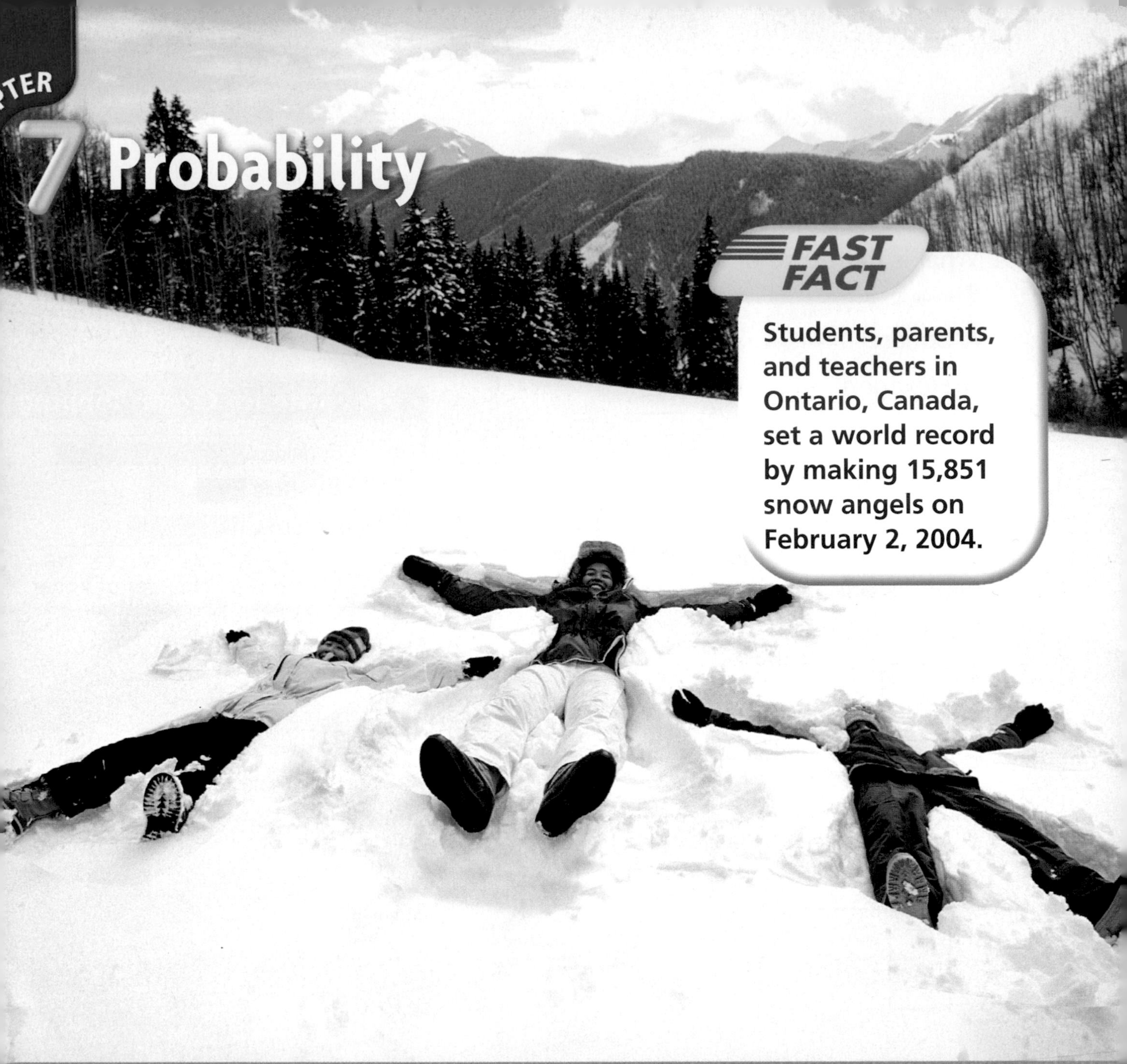

FAST FACT

Students, parents, and teachers in Ontario, Canada, set a world record by making 15,851 snow angels on February 2, 2004.

Investigate

Suppose you want to break the world record for the most snow angels. Use the line graph of normal monthly snowfall amounts to choose a month for your event. Explain your choice.

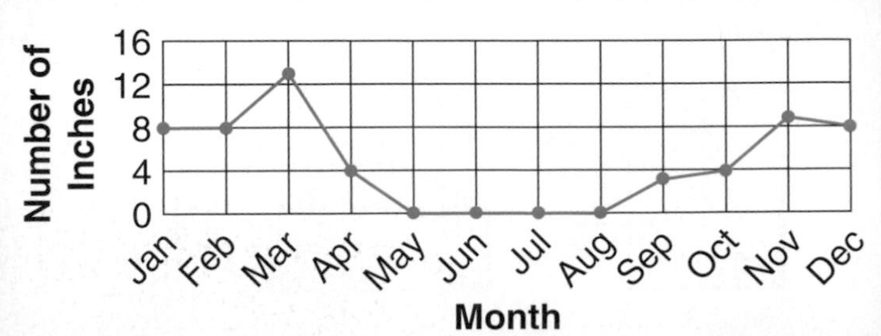

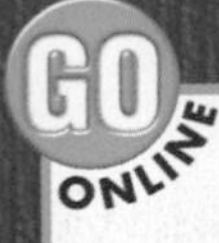

Normal Monthly Snowfall Amounts

GO ONLINE **Technology**
Student pages are available in the Student eBook.

Show What You Know

Check your understanding of important skills needed for success in Chapter 7.

▶ Read a Tally Table

For 1–4, use the tally table.

1. How many students play baseball?
2. How many students play football?
3. How many students answered the question?
4. How many more students play soccer than basketball?

Which sport do you play?	
Baseball	卌 卌 I
Soccer	卌 卌 III
Football	卌 III
Basketball	卌 IIII

▶ Compare Parts of a Whole

For 5–8, write the color shown by the largest part of each spinner.

5. 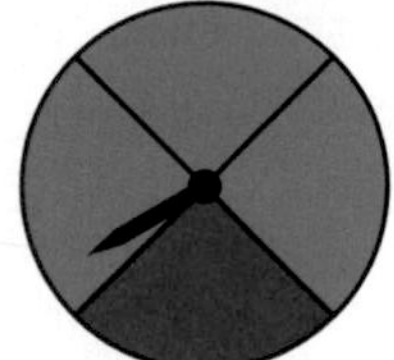
6. 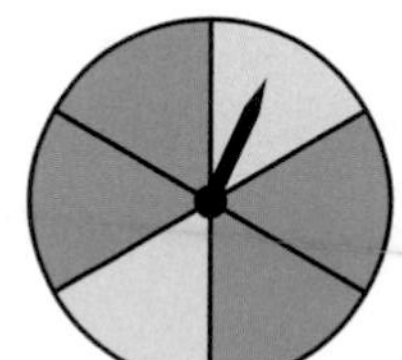
7. 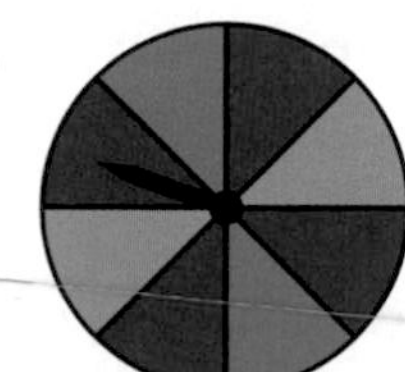
8. 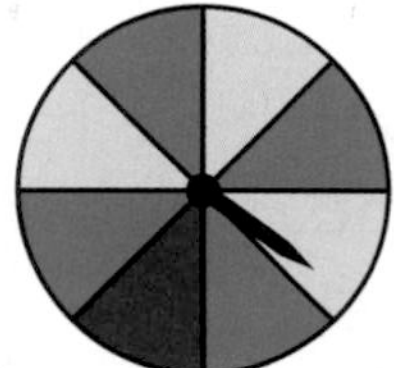

VOCABULARY POWER

CHAPTER VOCABULARY

certain
combination
equally likely
event
experiment
impossible
likely
outcome
predict
probability
tree diagram
unlikely

WARM-UP WORDS

event Something that might happen

outcome A possible result of an experiment

probability The chance that a given event will occur

Probability: Likelihood of Events

OBJECTIVE: Decide if an event is likely, unlikely, certain, or impossible.

Quick Review

What color marbles can Sarah pull from this bag?

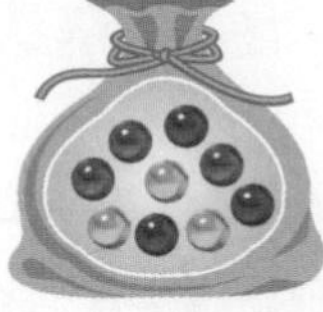

Vocabulary

event	probability
likely	unlikely
impossible	certain

Learn

An **event** is something that might happen. **Probability** is the chance that an event will happen.

PROBLEM Ted is going to pull a marble out of this bag without looking. Is it likely, unlikely, certain, or impossible that Ted will pull a red marble?

Use these examples.

Pulling red is **likely**. It has a good chance of happening.

Pulling yellow is **unlikely**. It does not have a good chance of happening.

Pulling green is **impossible**. It will never happen.

In this bag, pulling red is **certain**. It will always happen.

Ted's bag has more red marbles than blue or yellow marbles.

So, it is likely that Ted will pull a red marble.

- Is Ted more likely to pull a blue marble or a yellow marble?

Guided Practice

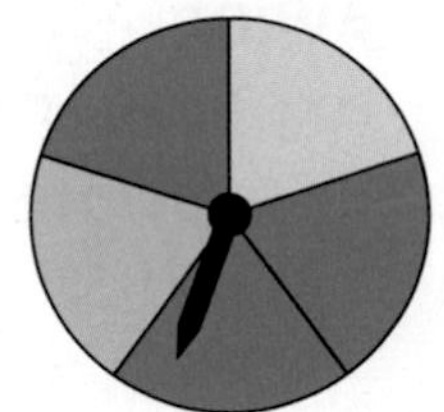

1. Which color marble are you unlikely to pull?

If you spin the pointer one time, tell whether each event is *likely, unlikely, certain,* or *impossible*.

2. The pointer will land on green.
3. The pointer will land on red.
4. The pointer will land on blue.
5. The pointer will land on blue, yellow, or green.
6. TALK Math **Explain** why landing on yellow is unlikely.

Independent Practice and Problem Solving

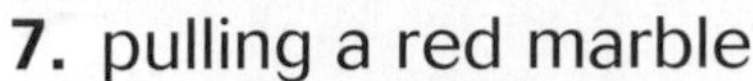

If you pull one marble, tell whether each event is *likely, unlikely, certain,* or *impossible*.

7. pulling a red marble

8. pulling a yellow marble

9. pulling a blue marble

10. pulling a yellow, green, or red marble

For 11–12, use the spinner.

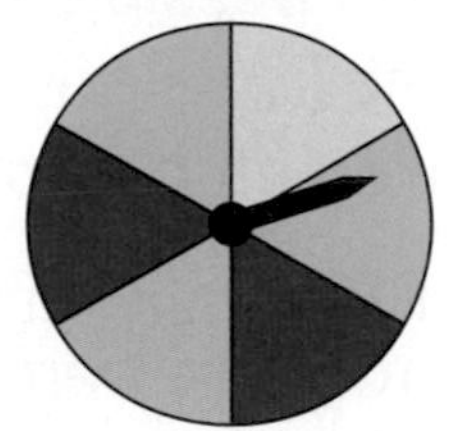

11. Which color are you likely to spin?

12. Which color are you unlikely to spin?

Algebra **Find the missing addend.**

13. $18 + \blacksquare = 24$

14. $\blacksquare + 79 = 92$

15. $205 + \blacksquare = 472$

USE DATA For 16–19, use the table. Tom pulls one sock from his drawer without looking.

Tom's Socks	
Color	**Number**
Black	14
Brown	12
White	2

16. Is it likely or unlikely that Tom will pull a white sock?

17. Is it certain or impossible that Tom will pull a blue sock?

18. **What if** Tom had 16 more black socks? How many more black socks than brown socks would he have?

19. WRITE Math **What if** Tom had 30 more white socks? **Explain** how your answer to Problem 16 would change.

Mixed Review and Test Prep

20. Morgan took a survey of her friends' favorite kind of snack. She recorded the results in a tally table. Her table shows 𝍸 || next to popcorn. How many friends chose popcorn? (p. 146)

21. Laura has 20 marbles in her collection. There are 5 green, 4 red, 9 white, and 2 blue marbles. She wants to make a bar graph to show her marble collection. Which color will have the shortest bar? (p. 156)

22. **Test Prep** Pulling a green marble from this bag is __?__.

A likely

B unlikely

C certain

D impossible

Extra Practice on page 192, Set A

LESSON 2 HANDS ON

Possible Outcomes

OBJECTIVE: Find the possible outcomes for simple events.

Quick Review

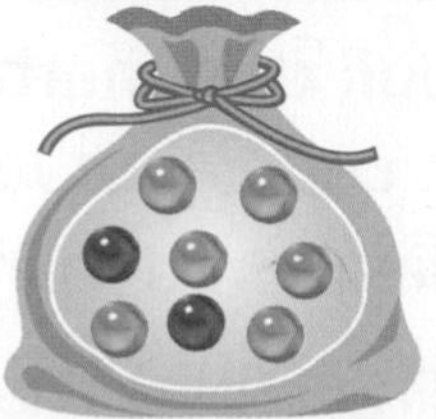

Without looking, Roz pulls one marble from the bag. Name a likely event and an impossible event.

Vocabulary

outcome **equally likely** **predict**

When you toss a coin, there are two possible results. In probability, a possible result is called an **outcome**.

The possible outcomes in a coin toss are *heads up* and *tails up*.

The outcomes *heads up* and *tails up* are **equally likely** because each has the same chance of happening.

Investigate

Materials ■ coin, tally table

Record the outcomes of tossing a coin. Before the first toss, **predict** the results, or tell what you think they will be.

A Predict the number of times the coin will land heads up.

B Toss the coin. Record the outcome in a tally table.

C Toss the coin 25 times. Record each outcome.

Draw Conclusions

1. How many times did the coin land heads up? tails up?
2. How did your prediction compare to the results?
3. **Synthesis** Would you predict the same number if you were going to toss the coin 25 more times? **Explain.**

Connect

You can display the results of the coin toss in a bar graph.

Step 1

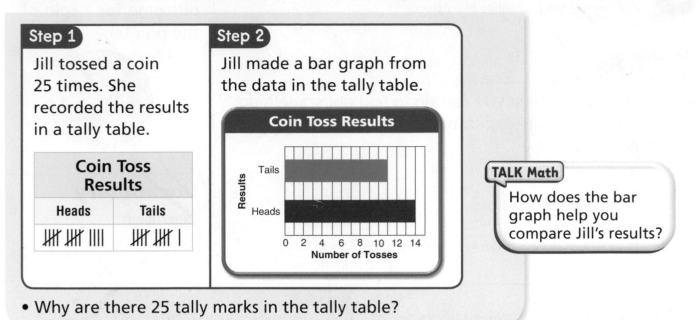

Jill tossed a coin 25 times. She recorded the results in a tally table.

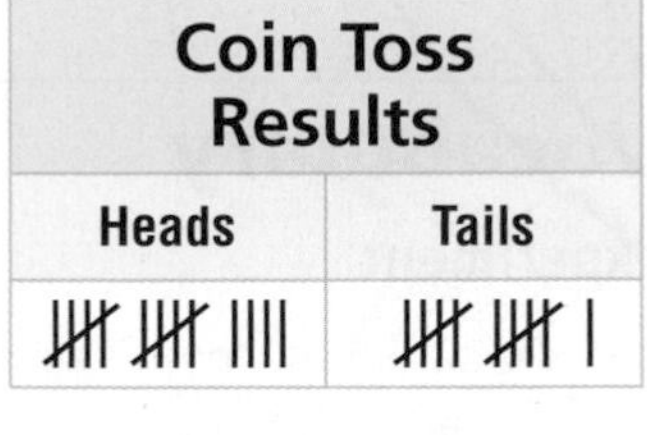

Coin Toss Results	
Heads	**Tails**
卌 卌 ||||	卌 卌 |

Step 2

Jill made a bar graph from the data in the tally table.

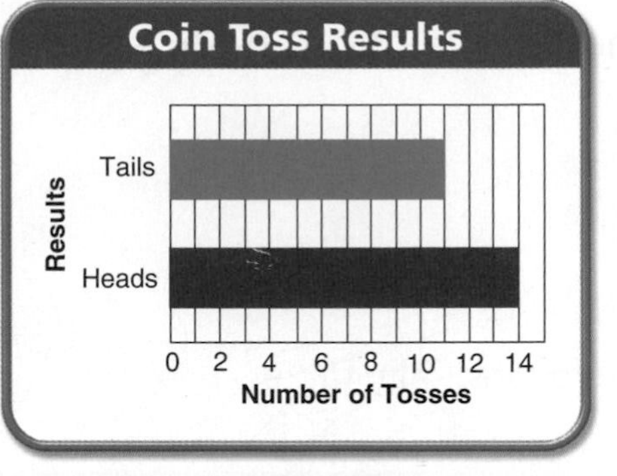

- Why are there 25 tally marks in the tally table?

TALK Math

How does the bar graph help you compare Jill's results?

Practice

For 1–2, list a possible outcome for each.

1. Henry will toss a quarter.

✓ 2. Marsha will use the spinner.

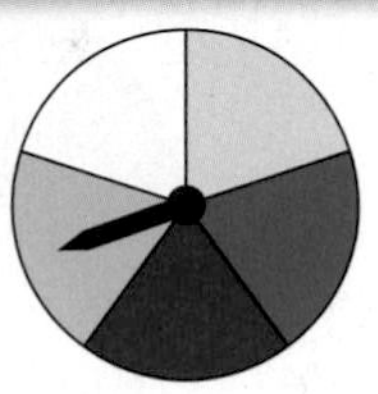

For 3–4, use the bag of marbles.

✓ 3. Billy is going to pull 1 marble from the bag. What are the possible outcomes for 1 pull?

4. **WRITE Math** **Sense or Nonsense** Billy says that pulling a red marble is equally likely as pulling a green marble. Does his statement make sense? **Explain.**

5. What are the possible outcomes for tossing a number cube? Which outcomes are equally likely?

6. **Reasoning** Mario drew a spinner with 8 equal sections. Three sections are yellow. Landing on yellow and landing on red are equally likely. How many sections are red? **Explain.**

LESSON 3

Experiments

OBJECTIVE: Conduct probability experiments, record the results, and describe the probability of outcomes.

Quick Review

Name a possible outcome for 1 spin of the pointer.

Vocabulary

experiment

Learn

An **experiment** is a test you can do to find out something. You can do probability experiments to explore how likely outcomes are.

Activity

Materials ■ 5-part spinner pattern, crayons, tally table, bar graph pattern

Step 1

Make a spinner that has 5 equal parts. Color the parts yellow, red, green, purple, and blue.

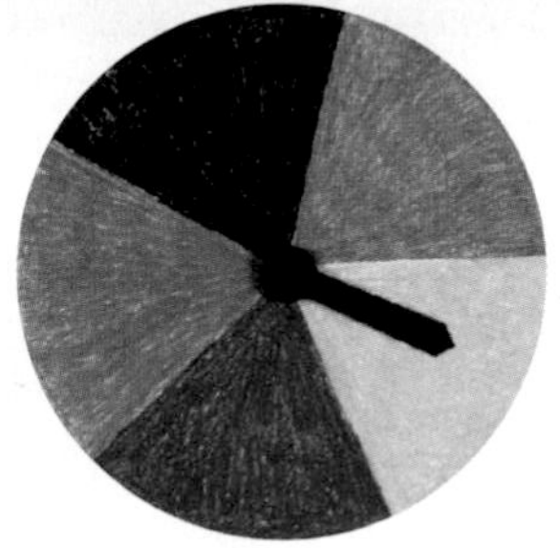

Step 2

Make a tally table. List all the possible outcomes. Spin 20 times. Record the results in the table.

Spinner Experiment	
Color	Tallies
Yellow	
Red	
Green	
Purple	
Blue	

Step 3

Make a bar graph of your data to show the results of your experiment.

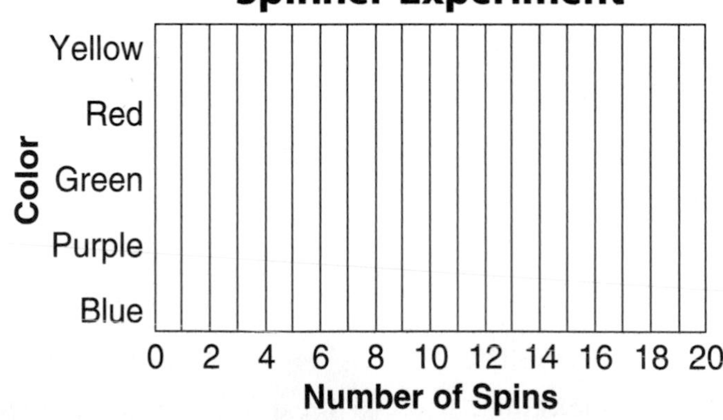

- Did the pointer land on each color about the same number of times?
- **What if** 2 sections of the spinner were blue? How would the results of your experiment change?

More About Experiments

Look at Spinner A. There are 5 possible outcomes: green, red, blue, purple, or yellow. Each outcome is equally likely.	Look at Spinner B. There are 5 possible outcomes: yellow, yellow, blue, blue, or green.
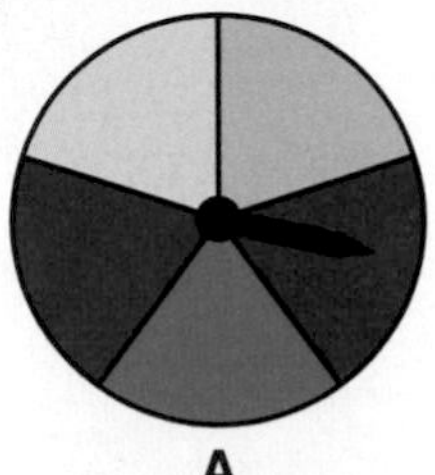 A	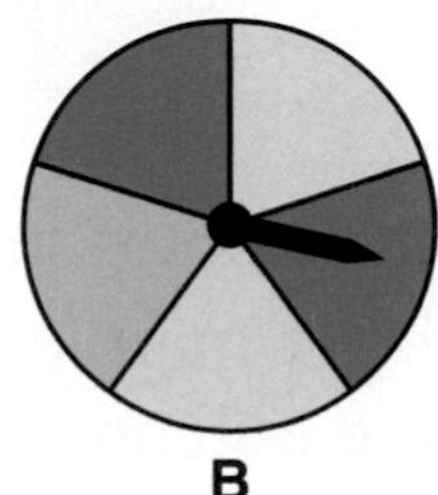 B
The probability of spinning blue is 1 out of 5. You can write the probability as the fraction $\frac{1}{5}$.	The probability of spinning blue is 2 out of 5. You can write the probability as the fraction $\frac{2}{5}$.

- For Spinner B, what is the probability of spinning green?
- For Spinner B, which outcomes are equally likely?

If an event is certain, the probability that it will happen is 1.
If an event is impossible, the probability that it will happen is 0.

The probability that you will pull a red marble from this bag is 8 out of 8, the fraction $\frac{8}{8}$, or 1.

The probability that you will pull any other color is 0 out of 8, the fraction $\frac{0}{8}$, or 0.

Guided Practice

1. In spinner C, which outcome is most likely? Think: Which color is shown most often?

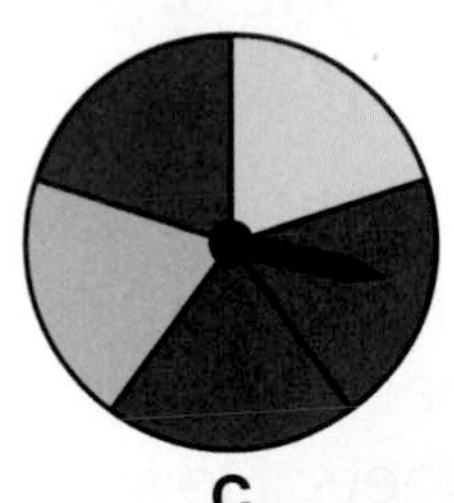
C

For 2–5, use the bags of tiles at the right.

2. For Bag D, which outcomes are equally likely?
3. What are the possible outcomes if you pull 1 tile from Bag E?
4. What is the probability of pulling a green tile from Bag D?
5. TALK Math **Explain** why the outcomes in Bag E are equally likely.

Bag D

Bag E

Independent Practice and Problem Solving

6. Which outcome is most likely?
7. What is the probability of spinning red?

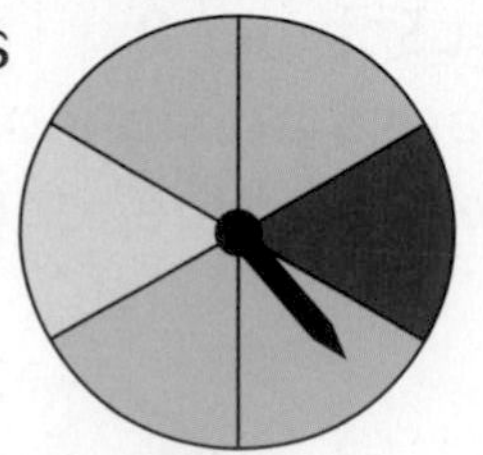

8. Which outcome is least likely?
9. What is the probability of pulling a green tile?

For 10–13, use the bag of marbles.

10. Cheryl is pulling 1 marble from this bag. What are the possible outcomes?
11. Which outcomes are equally likely?
12. What is the probability that Cheryl will pull a red marble?
13. **Pose a Problem** Look back at Problem 12. Write a similar problem by changing the color of the marble.
14. **WRITE Math** There are 6 red, 1 green, 2 blue, and 3 yellow tiles in a bag. **Explain** how to find the probability of pulling a yellow tile.
15. Predict the number of times a coin will land tails up in an experiment. Toss the coin 30 times. Then make a tally table to record the results.
16. ***FAST FACT*** The first machine-made glass marbles were produced in Akron, Ohio, in 1905. How many years ago was that?

Mixed Review and Test Prep

17. Is it likely, unlikely, certain, or impossible to pull a red tile from a bag of 1 blue, 2 green, 1 yellow, and 6 red tiles? (p. 178)
18. Dale bought a package of paper for his printer. The package had 500 sheets of paper. Dale used 112 sheets. How many sheets of paper are left? (p. 88)
19. **Test Prep** What is the probability of pulling a blue tile from this bag?

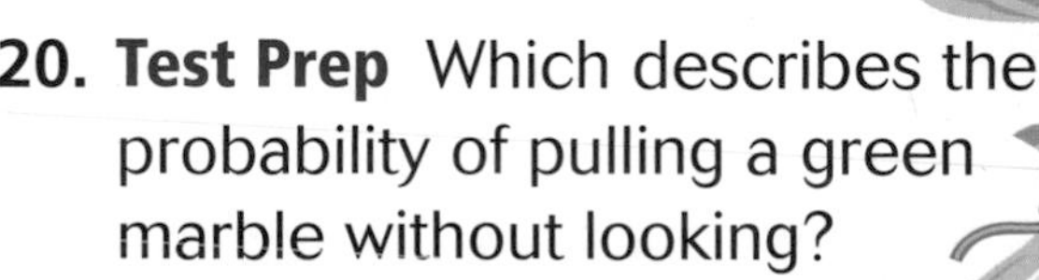

20. **Test Prep** Which describes the probability of pulling a green marble without looking?

   A likely **C** certain

   B unlikely **D** impossible

CD ROM Technology
Use Harcourt Mega Math, Fraction Action, *Last Chance Canyon,* Level D.

Extra Practice on page 192, Set B

Spinning Around

Make an Inference

The tables below show the results of 30 spins on each person's spinner. What inference can you make about the yellow section of Eve's spinner? When you make an inference, you develop ideas based on information given in a problem.

Julie's Results

Color	Times
Orange	5
Yellow	4
Blue	6
Green	6
Red	5
Purple	4

Eve's Results

Color	Times
Orange	5
Yellow	15
Blue	6
Green	0
Red	4
Purple	0

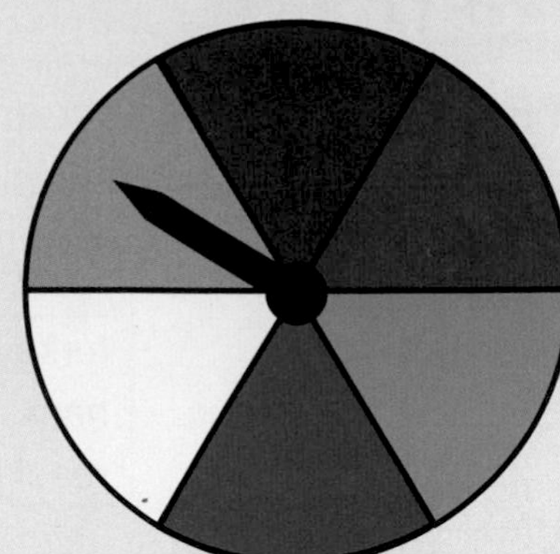
Julie's Spinner

Eve's Spinner

Use what you know about probability and the data in the tables to make an inference about the yellow section of Eve's spinner.

On Julie's spinner, the pointer landed on each color about an equal number of times. On Eve's spinner the pointer landed on yellow about 3 times more often than it landed on the other colors.

So, you can infer that the yellow section of Eve's spinner is larger than the other sections.

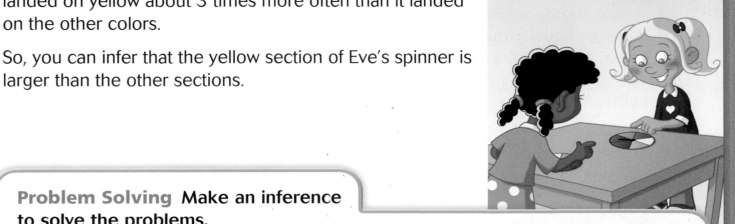

Problem Solving Make an inference to solve the problems.

1. How many times did the pointer on Eve's spinner land on purple or green? What inference can you make?

2. How many times did the pointer on Eve's spinner land on orange, blue, or red? What inference can you make? **Explain.**

LESSON 4

Combinations

OBJECTIVE: Use a tree diagram to find all the possible combinations.

Quick Review

Judy wants a piece of fruit for a snack. She has an apple, a banana, and an orange. How many snack choices does Judy have? What are they?

Vocabulary

tree diagram combination

Learn

PROBLEM Each soccer player will have the choices of sandwich and drink shown below for lunch.

Sandwich	Drink
turkey	juice
ham	milk
roast beef	

A **combination** is a result of joining two or more things. How many different combinations of 1 sandwich and 1 drink are possible?

You can use a **tree diagram** to find the possible combinations.

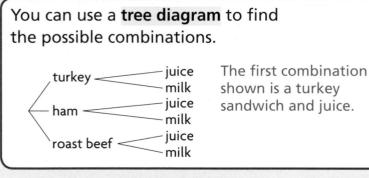

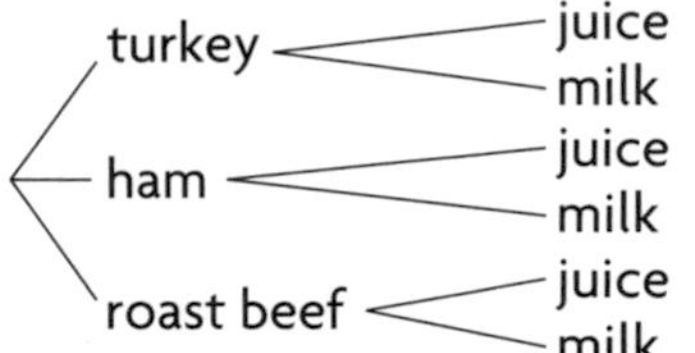

The first combination shown is a turkey sandwich and juice.

So, there are 6 possible combinations of 1 sandwich and 1 drink.

When there are equal groups, you can multiply to find how many in all. There are 3 groups with 2 in each group. Multiply 3×2 to find how many combinations of sandwich and drink are possible. $3 \times 2 = 6$

- **What if** cheese was added to the sandwich choices? How many combinations of 1 sandwich and 1 drink would be possible?

Guided Practice

1. What are the possible combinations of vanilla yogurt and 1 topping? Look at the tree diagram at the right.

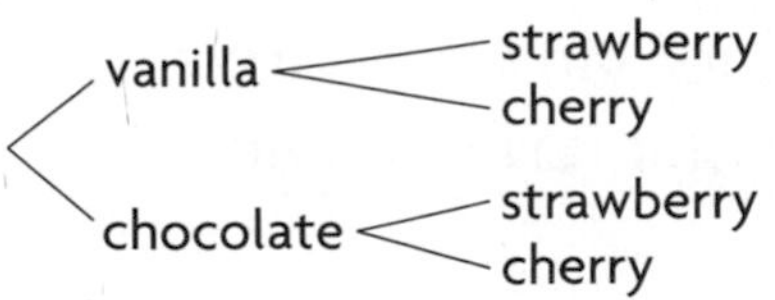

Make a tree diagram to show all the combinations.
Tell the number of combinations.

2.

Soup	Fruit
tomato chicken noodle chili	banana apple

3.

Shoes	Colors
sneakers sandals boots	red black white

4. **TALK Math** Eric has blue, yellow, and red shirts and black and brown shorts. **Explain** how he can use a tree diagram to find the number of possible shirt and shorts combinations.

Independent Practice and Problem Solving

Make a tree diagram to show all the combinations.
Tell the number of combinations.

5. side orders: grits, potatoes
   meats: ham, bacon, sausage

6. shirts: yellow, green, striped, plaid
   pants: jeans, shorts

USE DATA For 7–8, use the table.

7. John has the bills and coins shown in the table. How many combinations of 1 coin and 1 bill can he make?

8. **What if** John also had a $10 bill? How many combinations of 1 coin and 1 bill could he make?

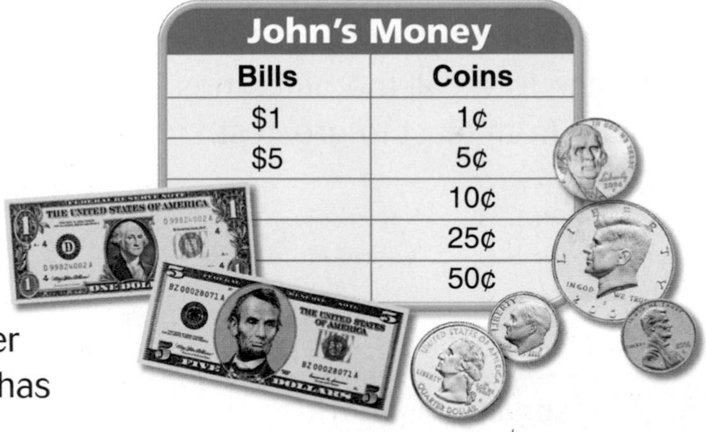

John's Money

Bills	Coins
$1	1¢
$5	5¢
	10¢
	25¢
	50¢

9. **WRITE Math** **What's the Error?** Oliver has 2 hats and 4 jackets. He says he has 6 combinations of 1 hat and 1 jacket. Describe his error.

Mixed Review and Test Prep

10. What shape is each face of a number cube? (Grade 2)

11. Jill is doing a coin toss experiment. How many possible outcomes are there? (p. 180)

12. **Test Prep** Zach's printer has 3 colors of paper and 3 colors of ink. How many combinations of paper and ink color are possible?

A 1 **B** 5 **C** 6 **D** 9

Extra Practice on page 192, Set C

LESSON 5

Problem Solving Workshop
Strategy: Make an Organized List

OBJECTIVE: Solve problems by using the strategy *make an organized list.*

Learn the Strategy

You can make an organized list to help solve problems.

Joy has 5 pennies, 5 nickels, and 5 dimes. She listed some of the different ways she can make 20¢.

Ways to make 20¢

20¢ 2 dimes
20¢ 1 dime, 2 nickels
20¢ 1 dime, 1 nickel, 5 pennies
20¢ 3 nickels, 5 pennies
20¢ 4 nickels

Allie is doing a number cube experiment. She found the possible outcomes of 1 toss. Then she listed all the outcomes in order from least to greatest.

Allie

1
2
3
4
5
6

Scott is serving his friends snacks and drinks after school. He listed the possible snack and drink combinations.

pretzels, juice
pretzels, water

popcorn, juice
popcorn, water

chips, juice
chips, water

TALK Math

Look at Scott's list. How many combinations of 1 snack and 1 drink are possible?

Use the Strategy

PROBLEM Sonya is having a birthday party. She is planning to serve chocolate cupcakes and yellow cupcakes at her party. Her guests can choose chocolate, vanilla, or strawberry frosting. How many combinations of a cupcake and frosting are there?

Read to Understand
Plan
Solve
Check

Read to Understand

Reading Skill

- **Identify the details of the problem.**
- **Is there any information you will not use? If so, what?**

Plan

- **What strategy can you use to solve the problem?** You can make an organized list of the combinations.

Solve

- **How can you use the strategy to solve the problem?**

  Make a list of the possible combinations. Start with one cupcake flavor. Match the cupcake flavor to each frosting flavor.

  Match the other cupcake to each frosting.

  Then, count the combinations.

  So, there are 6 combinations of a cupcake and frosting.

chocolate, chocolate
chocolate, vanilla
chocolate, strawberry

yellow, chocolate
yellow, vanilla
yellow, strawberry

Check

- **Is your answer reasonable? Explain.**

Guided Problem Solving

Read to Understand
Plan
Solve
Check

1. Sonya has prizes for her guests. Each guest will get 1 T-shirt and 1 hat. Sonya has blue, red, and white T-shirts. She has purple, blue, and green hats. How many combinations of 1 T-shirt and 1 hat are there?

   First, start with 1 T-shirt color. Match the T-shirt color to each hat color.

   Next, repeat until you have listed each hat color next to each T-shirt color.

   Finally, count the T-shirt and hat combinations.

blue, purple
blue, blue
blue, green

red, purple
red, blue
red, green

white, purple
white, blue
white, green

2. **What if** Sonya also had yellow T-shirts? How would the number of combinations of 1 T-shirt and 1 hat change?

3. Lana's class is having a contest. Each student can choose 1 pencil and 1 notebook as a prize. There are smiley-face and animal pencils. The notebooks are blue and red. How many combinations of 1 pencil and 1 notebook are there?

Problem Solving Strategy Practice

USE DATA For 4–6, use the table.

4. There are 3 bags of party prizes. Marty pulls out 1 prize from the balloon bag and 1 prize from the trading-card bag. How many combinations of 1 balloon and 1 trading card are there?

5. Rico pulls out 1 prize from the bookmark bag and 1 prize from the trading card bag. How many combinations of 1 bookmark and 1 trading card are there?

6. **WRITE Math** Sheree will pull 1 bookmark and 1 balloon. **Explain** how to find the number of bookmark and balloon combinations there are.

Party Prizes

Balloons	Bookmarks	Trading Cards
red	ribbon	baseball
white	paper	superhero
blue		

Mixed Strategy Practice

USE DATA For 8 and 10, use the pictures and prices.

7. Sonya is buying lollipops and yo-yos as party favors. She wants every guest to have one of each. She can buy orange or cherry lollipops and green or blue yo-yos. Make a list to show how many combinations of 1 lollipop and 1 yo-yo Sonya can buy.

8. **Pose a Problem** Look back at Problem 7. Write a similar problem by adding another color yo-yo.

9. **WRITE Math** **What's the Question?** Jared had $5.00 to spend at the store. He bought 1 item. The answer is $3.45.

10. **Open-Ended** Suppose you have $10.00 to spend on party favors. There will be 10 guests, and each guest will receive 2 favors. Choose the favors you would give, and find the total cost.

11. **Reasoning** A party store sold 86 packs of party hats in one day. There were 22 more packs sold in the afternoon than in the morning. How many packs were sold in the morning?

Choose a STRATEGY

- Draw a Diagram or Picture
- Make a Model or Act It Out
- Make an Organized List
- Find a Pattern
- Make a Table or Graph
- Predict and Test
- Work Backward
- Solve a Simpler Problem
- Write an Equation
- Use Logical Reasoning

CHALLENGE YOURSELF

Ted invited 12 friends to his party. He bought whistles for party favors. Each friend will get 1 whistle. The whistles come in packs of 4 for $2 or packs of 10 for $3.

12. Ted wants to buy the whistles in a way that will cost the least amount of money. Explain how you can find which packs Ted should buy and how many of each pack.

13. Each friend brought Ted a stamp for his collection. Now he has 40 stamps. There are 12 more stamps in his second album than there are in his first album. How many stamps are in each album?

Extra Practice

Set A If you spin the pointer one time, tell whether each event is *likely, unlikely, certain,* or *impossible.* (pp. 178–179)

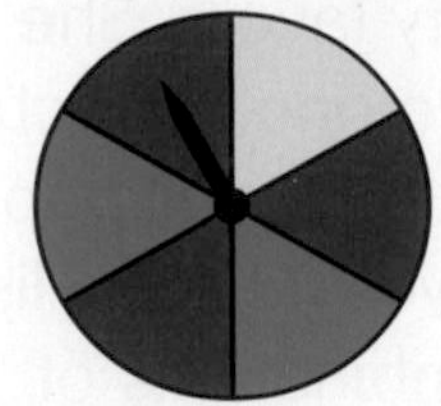

1. The pointer will land on yellow.
2. The pointer will land on green.
3. The pointer will land on red, blue, or yellow.
4. The pointer will land on red.

Set B For 1–2, use the spinner. For 3–4, use the bag of marbles. (pp. 182–185)

1. Which outcomes are equally likely?
2. What is the probability of spinning red?
3. What are the possible outcomes if you pull 1 tile?
4. What is the probability of pulling a red tile?

5. Rebecca made this tally table to show the results of a number cube experiment. What was the probability of tossing an odd number?

<table>
<tr><th colspan="2">Experiment</th></tr>
<tr><th>Number</th><th>Tallies</th></tr>
<tr><td>1</td><td>||||</td></tr>
<tr><td>2</td><td>||||</td></tr>
<tr><td>3</td><td>|||</td></tr>
<tr><td>4</td><td>卌 |</td></tr>
<tr><td>5</td><td>卌</td></tr>
<tr><td>6</td><td>|||</td></tr>
</table>

Set C Make a tree diagram to show all the combinations. Tell the number of combinations. (pp. 186–187)

1. **ice cream:** vanilla, chocolate
   toppings: marshmallow, chocolate, caramel
2. **sandwich bread:** white, wheat, rye
   meats: turkey, ham, salami
3. **place to go:** school, store, park
   transportation: bike, walk
4. **what to read:** book, magazine
   where to read: bedroom, library, family room, school
5. Jeff has 4 sweaters and 2 pairs of jeans. Explain how many combinations of 1 sweater and 1 pair of jeans there are.

Technology
Use Harcourt Mega Math, Fraction Action, *Last Chance Canyon,* Levels A–D.

TECHNOLOGY CONNECTION

Computer: Spreadsheet

Use a Spreadsheet to Show Data

Carol studied humpback whales during June, July, and August. She looked for 3 humpback whales. Then she recorded how many times she saw each of the whales each month. Carol's findings are shown below.

BANDIT
June ||||
July ||
August |

MIDNIGHT
June |||
July |||| |
August ||||

OWEN
June ||||
July |||| |||
August |||| |||

Record Carol's data on a spreadsheet.

Step 1	Type labels in Row 1. Tab across the row, or use the mouse or arrow keys to move. Type *Name* in Column A, *June* in Column B, *July* in Column C, and *August* in Column D.
Step 2	Use the mouse or arrow keys to move to Row 2. Type *Bandit* in Column A. Then type the data for Bandit in Columns B, C, and D.
Step 3	Fill in the data for the other whales in the same way in Rows 3 and 4.

	A	B	C	D
1	Name	June	July	August
2				
3				

	A	B	C	D
1	Name	June	July	August
2	Bandit	5	2	1
3				

Try It

1. Ed kept track of how many food pellets his fish ate on 4 days. Fin ate 1, 0, 2, and 3 pellets. Flip ate 2, 1, 0, and 3. Stripe ate 0, 2, 2, and 2. Make a spreadsheet to show the amount of food eaten by each fish on the 4 days.

2. **Explore More** Record how many pages of homework you had on each day of one week. Ask four friends to do the same. Enter all the data on a spreadsheet. **Explain** what labels you need on the spreadsheet.

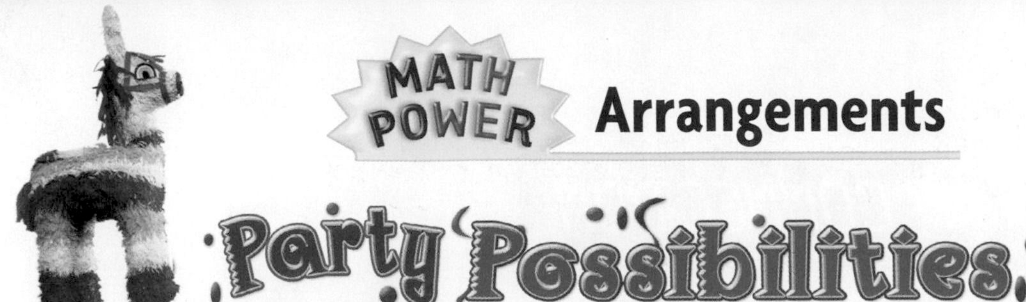

Arrangements

Party Possibilities

Rory is planning her birthday party. Her guests will play games, eat birthday cake, and break a piñata. In how many different ways can Rory plan the order of the 3 activities?

When the order is important, you need an **arrangement**.

To solve the problem, select each activity and then combine it with each of the other activities.

Examples

Step 1 Choose **games** to be first. Write down all the ways to do the 3 activities with games first.

Step 2 Next, choose **cake** to be first. Write down all the ways to do the 3 activities with cake first.

Step 3 Then, choose the **piñata** to be first. Write down all the ways to do the 3 activities with piñata first.

Now count the ways. The order of the activities can be arranged 6 ways.

FIRST	SECOND	THIRD
games	cake	piñata
games	piñata	cake
cake	games	piñata
cake	piñata	games
piñata	cake	games
piñata	games	cake

Try It

Make a chart or list to solve.

1. Paula is arranging her stuffed animals on a shelf. She has a tiger, a lion, and an elephant. In how many ways can Paula arrange her animals?

2. Choose 4 numbers from 1 through 9. Using each number once, in how many ways can you arrange the numbers in a 4-digit number?

3. WRITE Math Jillian and Molly are visiting New York City. They want to visit the places on the list at the right. In how many different ways can they visit the places? **Explain.**

PLACES TO VISIT

Empire State Building
Times Square
Statue of Liberty
Central Park

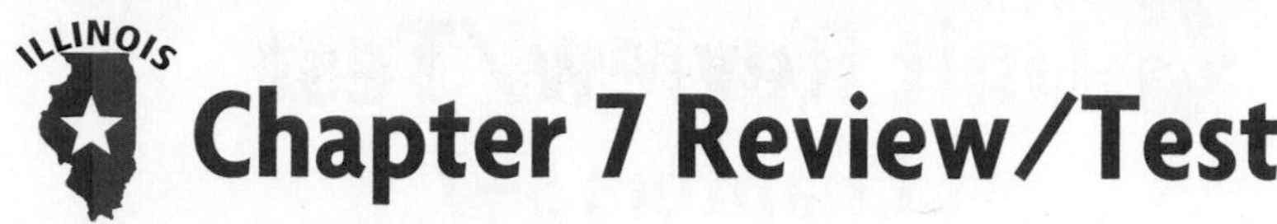

Chapter 7 Review/Test

Check Vocabulary and Concepts

Choose the best term from the box.

VOCABULARY
probability
experiment
outcome
predict

1. An __?__ is a possible result. IL 10.3.04 (p. 180)
2. __?__ is the chance that an event will happen. IL 10.3.04 (p. 178)
3. An __?__ is a test you can do to find out something. IL 10.3.04 (p. 182)

Check Skills

For 4–6, if you pull one marker, tell whether each event is *likely, unlikely, certain,* or *impossible.* IL 10.3.04 (pp. 178–179)

4. You will pull an orange marker.
5. You will pull a blue marker.
6. You will pull a red marker.

For 7–9, use the spinner. IL 10.3.05 (pp. 182–185)

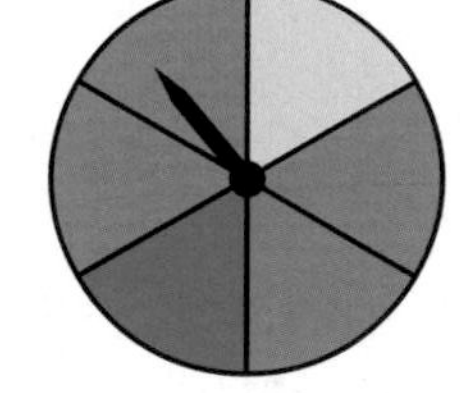

7. What are the possible outcomes of spinning the pointer one time?
8. What is the probability of spinning green?
9. Which outcomes are equally likely?

For 10–11, list a possible outcome for each. IL 10.3.04 (pp. 180–181)

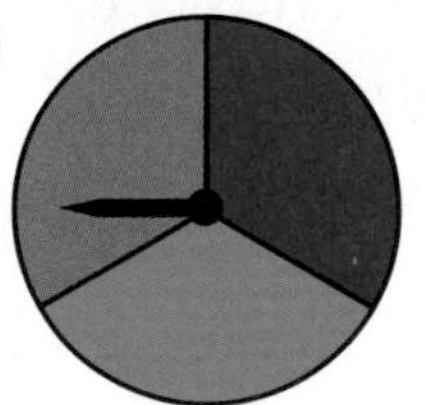

10. Sarah will use the spinner.
11. Randy will toss a nickel.

Check Problem Solving

For 12–14, use the table. IL 10.3.04 (pp. 178–179)

12. Is it certain or impossible that Linda will pull a purple clip?
13. WRITE Math Linda puts 10 purple clips in the box. **Explain** how your answer to Problem 12 would change?

Linda's Clips in a Box

Color	Number
Blue	5
White	2
Yellow	4

GO ONLINE **Technology** Use *Online Assessment.*

Unit Review/Test
Chapters 5–7

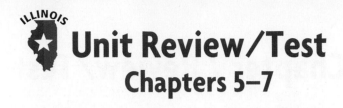

Multiple Choice

1. Which shows the number of students who voted for basketball? IL 10.3.01 (p. 154)

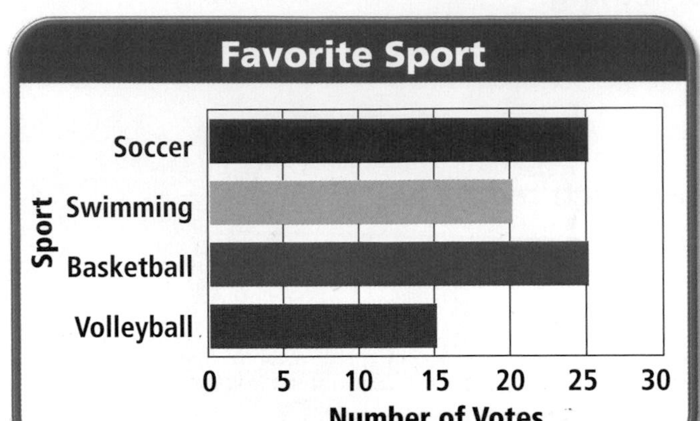

A 30 **C** 20

B 25 **D** 15

2. Jacob went to the Illinois State Fair. He bought a caramel apple for \$4.65. He paid with a \$10 bill. Which shows the amount of change Jacob received? IL 6.3.10 (p. 120)

A \$6.45 **C** \$5.45

B \$6.35 **D** \$5.35

3. Mara fell asleep at 9:30 P.M. She woke up at 7:15 A.M. Which shows the amount of time Mara slept? IL 7.3.01 (p. 130)

A 9 hours 45 minutes

B 9 hours 15 minutes

C 8 hours 45 minutes

D 8 hours 15 minutes

4. Cordelia bought a book for \$7.95. Abby bought a different book for \$9.75. Compare the money amounts. Which makes the sentence true? IL 6.3.06 (p. 114)

\$7.95 ● \$9.75

A $=$ **C** $<$

B $>$ **D** $\div$

5. Alexis took a survey of her classmates' favorite attractions in Chicago. She recorded the results in the table. Then Alexis began to make the pictograph using the data from the table.

Favorite Chicago Attractions

Attraction	Number
Field Museum	24
Art Institute	15
Shedd Aquarium	27
Navy Pier	18

Which shows the number of symbols Alexis should draw in the row for Shedd Aquarium if each symbol equals 3 tickets? IL 10.3.02 (p. 150)

A 27 **C** 9

B 18 **D** 3

GO ONLINE **Technology** Use *Online Assessment.*

6. The distance from Rockford, IL, to Metropolis, IL, is 415 miles. The distance from Taylorville, IL, to Metropolis, IL, is 193 miles. About how much further from Metropolis is Rockford than Taylorville? IL 6.3.14 (p. 78)

A about 400 miles

B about 300 miles

C about 200 miles

D about 100 miles

7. Clara will pull one marble from this bag. What is the probability that she will pull a red marble? IL 10.3.05 (p. 182)

A 5 out of 10

B 3 out of 8

C 3 out of 5

D 1 out of 3

8. In 2000, the population of Walnut, IL, was 1,461. The population of Winnebago, IL, was 2,958. Compare the populations. Which symbol makes the sentence true? IL 6.3.05 (p. 28)

1,461 ● 2,958

A $>$

B $<$

C $=$

D $\div$

Short Response

9. Megan emptied her coin purse after a shopping trip. She had one \$5 bill, three \$1 bills, 5 quarters, and 8 pennies. How much money does she have? IL 6.3.10 (p. 112)

Extended Response WRITE Math

For 10–11, use the spinner.

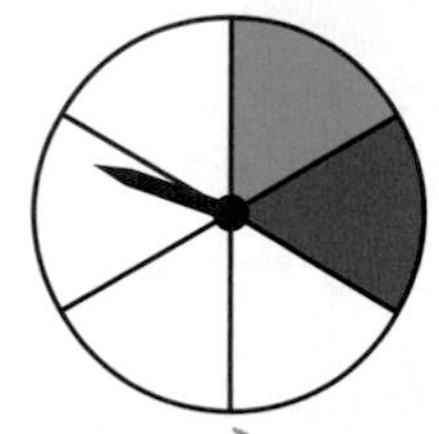

10. Julia will spin the spinner one time. Which outcomes are equally likely? **Explain.**

11. Is it likely or unlikely that Julia will spin white? **Explain.** IL 10.3.04 (p. 182)

12. Start on number 4 and skip-count by fours. Are the numbers in your pattern odd, even, or both? **Explain.** IL 8.3.01 (p. 4)

1	2	3	4	5	6	7	8	9	10
11	12	13	14	15	16	17	18	19	20
21	22	23	24	25	26	27	28	29	30
31	32	33	34	35	36	37	38	39	40
41	42	43	44	45	46	47	48	49	50
51	52	53	54	55	56	57	58	59	60
61	62	63	64	65	66	67	68	69	70
71	72	73	74	75	76	77	78	79	80
81	82	83	84	85	86	87	88	89	90
91	92	93	94	95	96	97	98	99	100

THE WORLD ALMANAC FOR KIDS

Penny Power!

Pennies Yesterday and Today

The penny is the oldest coin made by the United States Mint. The first copper penny was made in 1793.

What would life be like without pennies?

FACT • ACTIVITY

If we did not have pennies, prices might be higher. Sellers might raise prices to the next higher nickel. Something that now sells for 72 cents might sell for 75 cents.

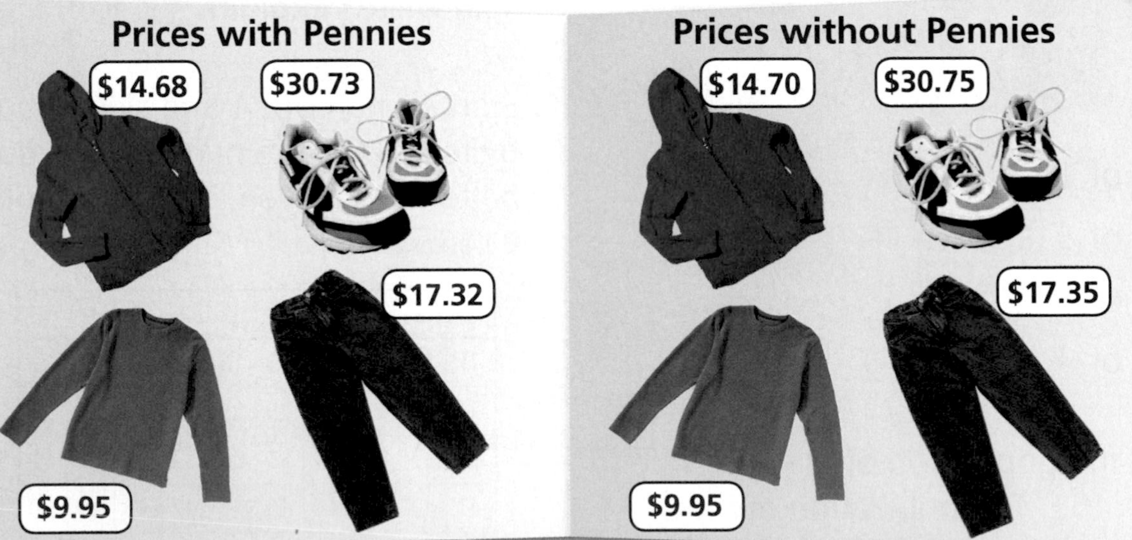

Use the information from the pictures.

1. Which items have higher prices when pennies are not used?
2. What is the total cost of the jacket and pants with pennies? Without pennies? Which total cost is greater? How much greater?
3. You want to buy a long-sleeved T-shirt for $9.95. How would you pay the exact amount for the shirt, using the fewest bills and coins?

Survey: Pennies

Some people think it is time to stop making and using pennies. The idea was talked about in Congress, but members voted to keep making and using pennies.

The table shows what some people think about getting rid of pennies.

ALMANAC **Fact**

A coin usually lasts for about 30 years.

A one-dollar bill usually lasts about 2 years.

Should We Stop Making and Using Pennies?

Yes	No
1. Vending machines don't take pennies.	1. Pennies keep prices down.
2. Pennies get lost in sofas and car seats.	2. Rolls of pennies can be exchanged for dollars.
3. Pennies are too heavy to carry around.	3. Pennies have been around for a long time.

FACT • ACTIVITY

Do you think it is time to stop making and using pennies? What do other students think? Survey 10 students.

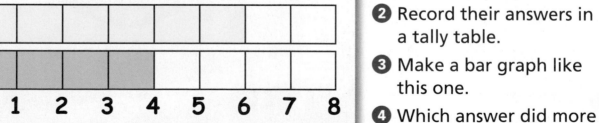

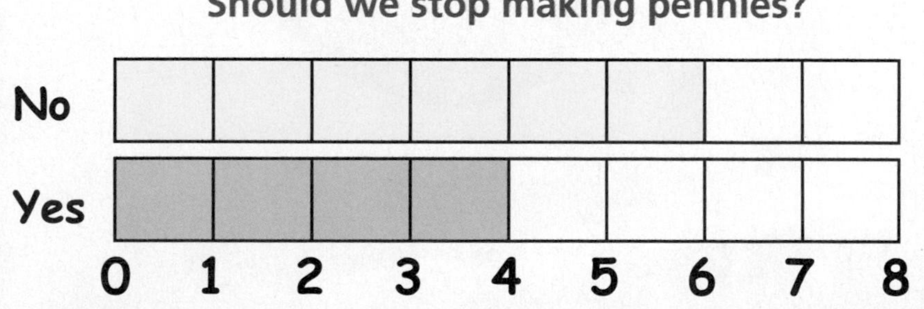

1. Make a list of 10 students to survey.
2. Record their answers in a tally table.
3. Make a bar graph like this one.
4. Which answer did more students choose?

WRITE Math If we stop using pennies, what could be done with the ones we already have? Make a list of three or more ideas.

UNIT 3

Multiplication Concepts and Facts

Math on Location

with
Chapter Projects

1

A new toy is invented by starting with an idea, making a drawing, and combining pieces for a kit.

2

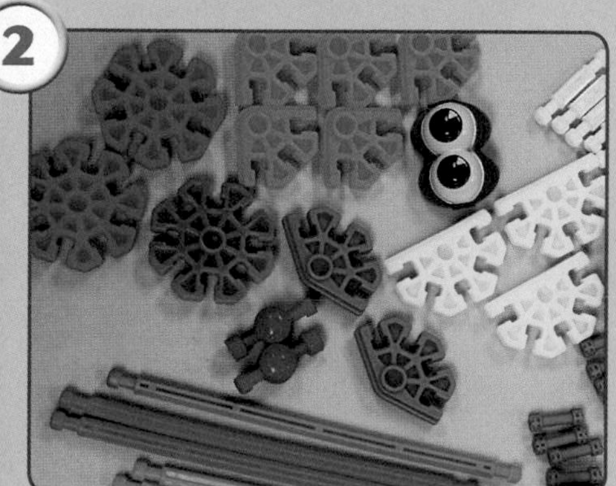

The unassembled kit shows multiple numbers of each different piece.

3

The designers use imagination and creativity when designing small toys or large, movable toys.

VOCABULARY POWER

TALK Math

What math is shown in the **Math on Location** photographs? How can you use multiplication to tell how many pieces there are?

READ Math

REVIEW VOCABULARY You learned the words below when you learned about multiplication last year. How do these words relate to **Math on Location**?

factor a number that is multiplied by another number to find a product

multiply to combine equal groups to find how many in all

product the answer in a multiplication problem

WRITE Math

Copy and complete a Word Definition Map like the one below. Use what you know about multiplication.

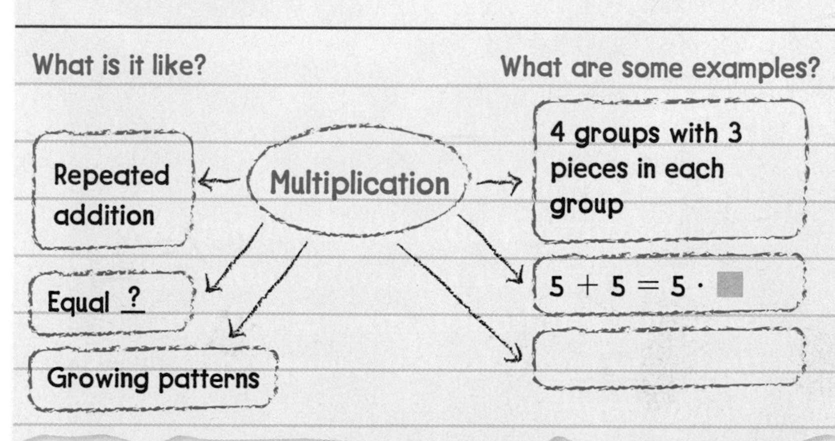

Technology
Multimedia Math Glossary link at
www.harcourtschool.com/hspmath

CHAPTER

8 Understand Multiplication

The Eastern Bluebird is the state bird of Missouri and New York. Its nest is made out of grass. Bluebirds usually lay 3 to 6 light blue eggs at a time.

Investigate

You can attract bluebirds to your yard by putting up a bluebird house. Suppose you want to make more than one birdhouse. How could you find how many feet of wood you would need?

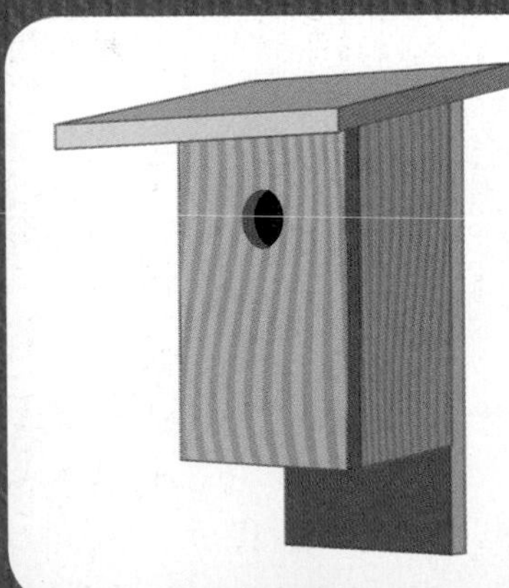

Materials:
6-foot piece of wood
nails
1 eye screw
wood screws

GO ONLINE **Technology** Student pages are available in the Student eBook.

Show What You Know

Check your understanding of important skills needed for success in Chapter 8.

▶ Skip-Count

Skip-count to find the missing numbers.

1. 2, 4, 6, 8, ■, ■, ■ **2.** 3, 6, 9, ■, ■, ■

3. 5, 10, 15, ■, 25, ■, ■ **4.** 10, 20, ■, ■, 50, ■, ■

▶ Equal Groups

Write how many there are in all.

5.

4 groups of 3 = ■

6.

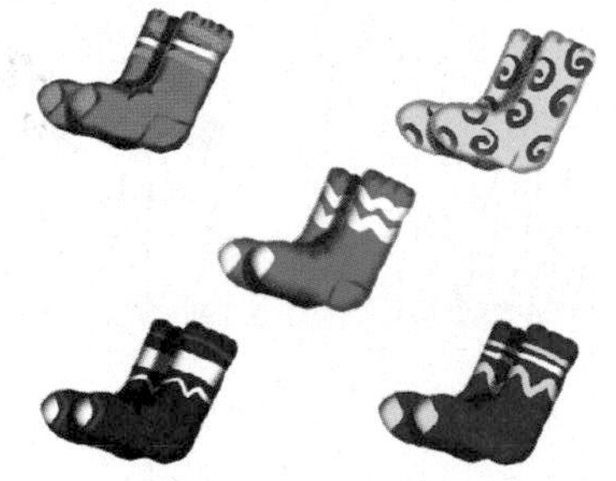

5 groups of 2 = ■

7.

2 groups of 4 = ■

Find how many in all. You may wish to draw a picture.

8. 3 groups of 6 **9.** 2 groups of 2 **10.** 4 groups of 5

11. 2 groups of 4 **12.** 4 groups of 3 **13.** 5 groups of 6

VOCABULARY POWER

CHAPTER VOCABULARY

array
Commutative Property of Multiplication
factor
Identity Property of Multiplication
multiplication
multiply
product
Zero Property of Multiplication

WARM-UP WORDS

array An arrangement of objects in rows and columns

factor A number that is multiplied by another number to find a product

product The answer in a multiplication problem

LESSON 1

ALGEBRA

Relate Addition to Multiplication

OBJECTIVE: Relate addition and multiplication.

Quick Review

Add.

1. 4 + 4 + 4
2. 5 + 5 + 5 + 5
3. 7 + 7 + 7
4. 2 + 2 + 2
5. 3 + 3 + 3

Vocabulary

multiplication multiply

Learn

PROBLEM Jasmine needs 3 bananas to make 1 loaf of banana bread. The same number of bananas are in each loaf. How many bananas does Jasmine need to make 4 loaves?

ONE WAY **Use addition.**

Use counters to show the bananas.
Show 3 counters for each loaf of bread.
Make 4 groups to show the 4 loaves.

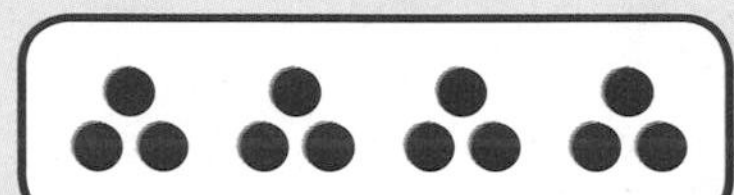

Find the total number of counters.
Write the addition sentence.

3 + 3 + 3 + 3 = 12

So, Jasmine needs 12 bananas to make 4 loaves of bread.

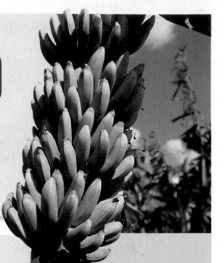

▲ There are about 200 bananas in some bunches.

ANOTHER WAY **Use multiplication.**

When groups are equal, you can use **multiplication** to find the total. When you **multiply**, you combine equal groups to find how many in all.

Think: 4 groups of 3

Write: $4 \times 3 = 12$ **Read:** 4 times 3 equals 12.

A table can show the addition and multiplication.

Equal Groups	Think:	Addition Sentence	Multiplication Sentence
●●● ●●● ●●● ●●●	4 groups of 3	$3 + 3 + 3 + 3 = 12$	$4 \times 3 = 12$

- **What if** Jasmine makes 5 loaves of bread? How many bananas will she need? Use multiplication to show your answer.

Guided Practice

1. Write a multiplication sentence that shows $2 + 2 + 2 + 2 + 2 = 10$.

Use counters to model. Then write an addition sentence and a multiplication sentence for each.

2. 2 groups of 4
3. 3 groups of 2
4. 5 groups of 4
5. 3 groups of 3

6. TALK Math **Explain** how you know that both $3 + 3$ and 2×3 equal 6.

Independent Practice and Problem Solving

Use counters to model. Then write an addition sentence and a multiplication sentence for each.

7. 3 groups of 4
8. 2 groups of 5
9. 4 groups of 6
10. 3 groups of 7

Write a multiplication sentence for each.

11.

12.

13. 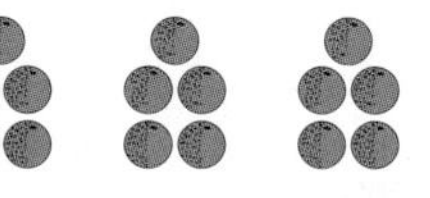

14. 

15. $2 + 2 + 2 + 2 = 8$
16. $4 + 4 + 4 + 4 = 16$
17. $9 + 9 + 9 = 27$

USE DATA For 18–19, use the table.

18. John bought 3 oranges. How much do the oranges weigh in all?

19. Which weighs more, 3 apples or 4 bananas? How much more?

Weight of Fruit

Fruit	Weight in ounces
Apple	6
Orange	5
Banana	4

20. WRITE Math **Sense or Nonsense** Jared says that he can write a multiplication sentence and an addition sentence for $5 + 4 + 4$. Does Jared's statement make sense? **Explain.**

Mixed Review and Test Prep

21. Tell whether the event is certain or impossible. Next year, May 2 will come before May 3. (p. 178)

22. Drew pulls 1 marble from the bag. List the possible outcomes. (p. 180)

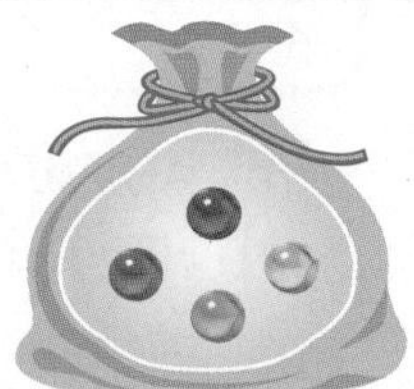

23. **Test Prep** What is another way to show $2 + 2 + 2 + 2$?

A 2×2 **B** 6×2 **C** 4×2 **D** 2×8

Extra Practice on page 224, Set A

ALGEBRA

Model with Arrays

OBJECTIVE: Use arrays to understand multiplication and the Commutative Property of Multiplication.

Quick Review

Find how many in all.

1. 3 groups of 2
2. 2 groups of 6
3. 4 groups of 3
4. 3 groups of 5
5. 5 groups of 2

Vocabulary

array

factor

product

Commutative Property of Multiplication

Learn

PROBLEM Mark has a garden. He planted 2 rows of tomato plants with 3 plants in each row. How many tomato plants did Mark put in his garden?

An **array** is a group of objects in rows and columns.

Activity

Materials ■ square tiles

Make an array with 2 rows and 3 columns to show Mark's tomato plants.

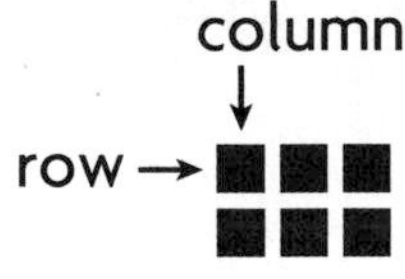

2 rows of 3 = ■

Now find the total number of tiles.

Add.	Multiply.
$3 + 3 = 6$	$2 \times 3 = 6$

So, Mark put 6 tomato plants in his garden.

You can turn your array to show 3 rows of 2.

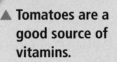

3 rows of 2 = ■

Find the total number of tiles.

Add.	Multiply.
$2 + 2 + 2 = 6$	$3 \times 2 = 6$

- What happened to the number of tiles in the array when you turned it?

▲ Tomatoes are a good source of vitamins.

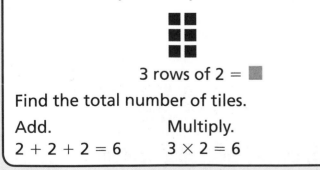

Commutative Property of Multiplication

In multiplication, the numbers you multiply are called **factors**. The answer is called the **product**.

2 × 3 = 6
↑ factor ↑ factor ↑ product

The **Commutative Property of Multiplication**, or Order Property of Multiplication, states that factors can be multiplied in any order and their product is the same.

You can use a table to see the Commutative Property.

Model	Draw	Write a Multiplication Sentence
2 rows of 3		$2 \times 3 = 6$
3 rows of 2		$3 \times 2 = 6$
2 rows of 5		$2 \times 5 = 10$
5 rows of 2		$5 \times 2 = 10$
3 rows of 4		$3 \times 4 = 12$
4 rows of 3		$4 \times 3 = 12$

Guided Practice

1. Write the multiplication sentences these arrays show.

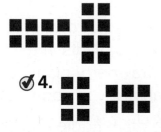

Write a multiplication sentence for each array.

2. 

3. 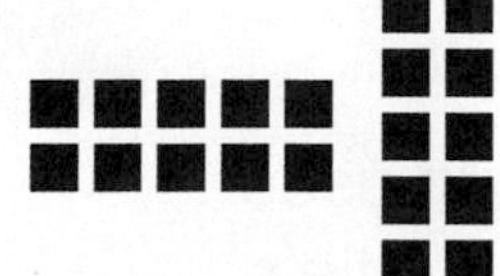

4.

5. TALK Math **Explain** why the Commutative Property is also called the Order Property.

Independent Practice and Problem Solving

Write a multiplication sentence for each array.

6.

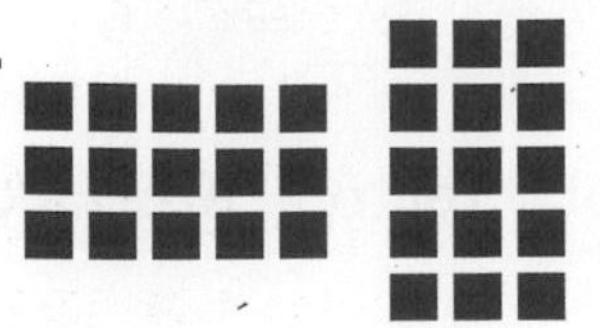

7.

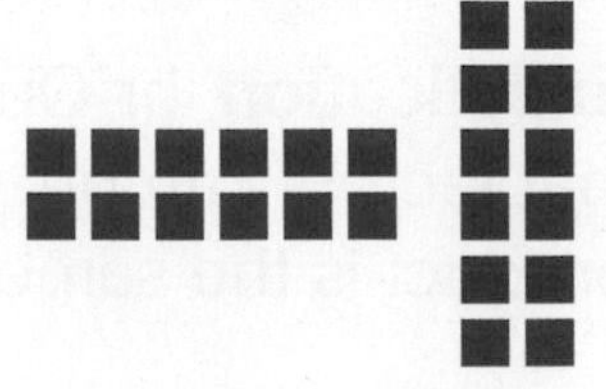

8.

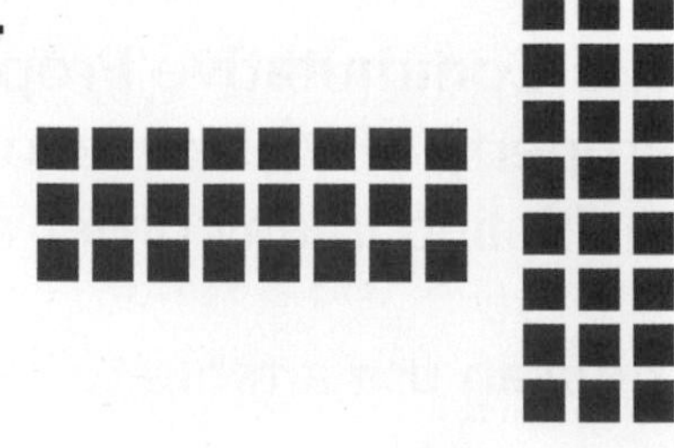

9.

10.

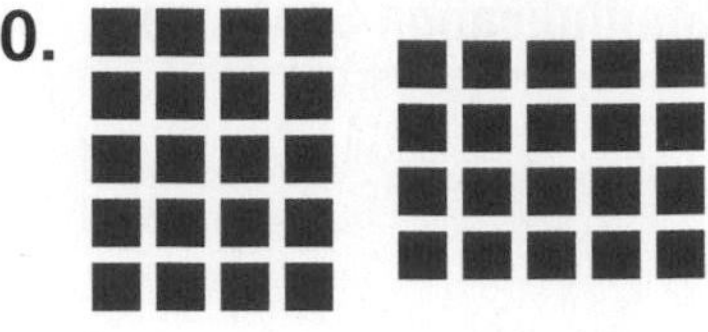

11.

**Write the multiplication sentence for each array.
Then draw the array that shows the Commutative Property.**

12.

13.

14.

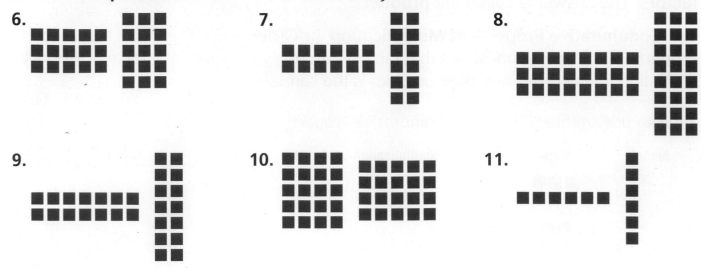

15. Mary placed 24 cans of tomato sauce in 6 rows. How many cans were in each row?

6 rows of ■ = 24

16. Mark picked 5 peppers from each of the 2 rows in his garden. He used 3 peppers to make a salad. How many peppers does he have left?

17. Reasoning Jenna and her mother baked apple pies. They picked 18 apples and put the same number of apples in each of 3 pies. Draw an array to show how many apples they put in each pie.

18. John planted 4 rows of strawberries. There are 8 plants in each row. How many strawberry plants did John grow? Draw an array to show your answer.

19. WRITE Math Eddie and Jackie both used 12 square tiles to make an array. Eddie's array had 4 rows. Jackie's array had 3 rows. Is this possible? **Explain.**

CD ROM **Technology**
Use Harcourt Mega Math, Country Countdown, *Counting Critters*, Level W.

Extra Practice on page 224, Set B

Learn About Square Numbers

If both factors are the same, the product is called a **square number**. When you use the factors to make an array, the array is a square.

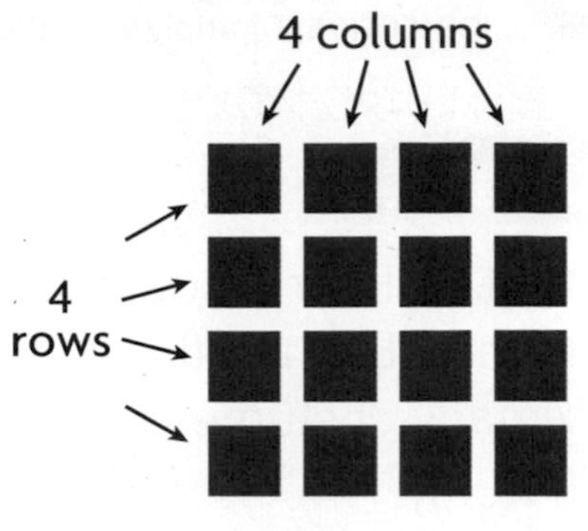

$4 \times 4 = 16$
16 is a square number.

Work with a partner to draw arrays that show square numbers.

Use tiles to make a square array with 3 rows and 3 columns.

Draw the array and write the multiplication sentence.

$3 \times 3 = 9$

So, 9 is a square number.

Try It

Draw each array. Write the multiplication sentence. Then circle the square number in each sentence.

20. 5×5 **21.** 7×7 **22.** 8×8

23. 6×6 **24.** 9×9

25. WRITE Math Is 10 a square number? **Explain** how you know.

Mixed Review and Test Prep

26. *FAST FACT* The world's largest Catsup Bottle is one hundred seventy feet tall. Write this number in standard form. (p. 8)

27. A notebook has 2 pockets for loose paper. Write an addition sentence and a multiplication sentence to show how many pockets 4 notebooks would have. (p. 204)

28. **Test Prep** Which is an example of the Commutative Property of Multiplication?

A $6 + 4 = 2 + 4$
B $4 \times 6 = 4 + 6$
C $4 \times 6 = 6 \times 4$
D $4 \times 6 = 3 \times 8$

29. **Test Prep** The art students hung up their paintings. There are 5 rows with 6 paintings in each row. How many paintings are there in all?

LESSON 3

Multiply with 2

OBJECTIVE: Multiply with the factor 2.

Quick Review

1. 3 + 3
2. 4 + 4
3. 8 + 8
4. 6 + 6
5. 9 + 9

Learn

PROBLEM Four students are putting on a play for their class. Each of the 4 students has 2 costumes. How many costumes do the students have in all?

Find 4 × 2 = ■.

Activity **Materials** ■ counters

Use counters.

MODEL	THINK	RECORD
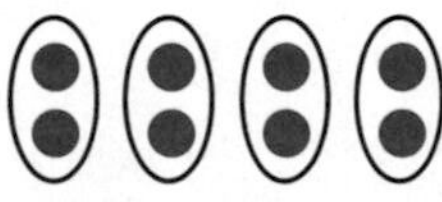	4 groups of 2 2 + 2 + 2 + 2	4 × 2 = 8 $\begin{array}{r} 2 \\ \times 4 \\ \hline 8 \end{array}$

Draw a picture.

DRAW	THINK	RECORD
  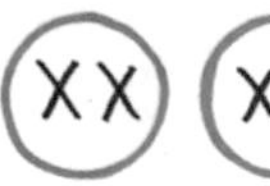 	4 groups of 2 2 + 2 + 2 + 2	4 × 2 = 8 $\begin{array}{r} 2 \\ \times 4 \\ \hline 8 \end{array}$

So, the students have 8 costumes in all.

Example

You can also multiply by 2 by doubling the other factor.

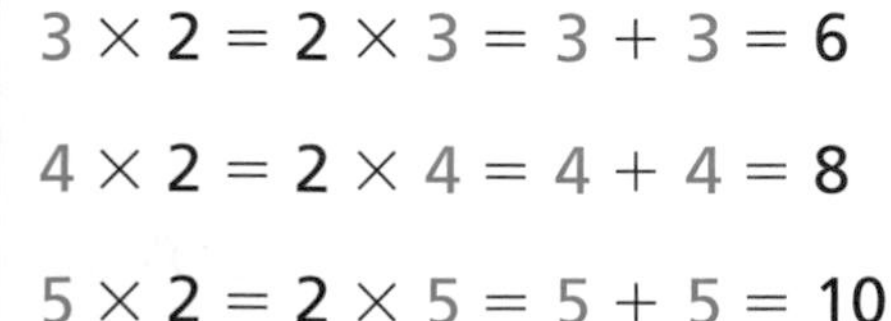

3 × 2 = 2 × 3 = 3 + 3 = 6

4 × 2 = 2 × 4 = 4 + 4 = 8

5 × 2 = 2 × 5 = 5 + 5 = 10

Guided Practice

1. Write the multiplication sentence the drawing shows.

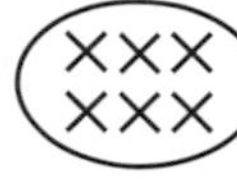 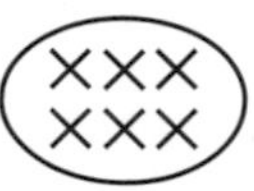

Write the multiplication sentence for each.

2. ●●●●●●●●●●　　3. ●●●●●●●●●●　　4. ●●●●●●●●

5. TALK Math Explain how 6×2 can help you find the product for 2×6.

Independent Practice and Problem Solving

Write a multiplication sentence for each.

6. ●●●●●●　　7. ●●●●●●●●●●●●●●●●　　8. ●●●●●●●●●●●●●●●●●●

Find the product.

9. $\begin{array}{r} 1 \\ \times 2 \\ \hline \end{array}$　10. $\begin{array}{r} 2 \\ \times 2 \\ \hline \end{array}$　11. $\begin{array}{r} 4 \\ \times 2 \\ \hline \end{array}$　12. $\begin{array}{r} 2 \\ \times 9 \\ \hline \end{array}$　13. $\begin{array}{r} 6 \\ \times 2 \\ \hline \end{array}$　14. $\begin{array}{r} 2 \\ \times 7 \\ \hline \end{array}$

Copy and complete.

15.

×	1	2	3	4	5	6	7	8	9	10
2	■	■	■	■	■	■	■	■	■	■

USE DATA For 16–17, use the graph.

16. How many tickets did Tyrone and Julia sell in all?

17. WRITE Math **Explain** how you find out how many tickets Lee sold for the school play.

Play Tickets

Name	Tickets Sold
Tyrone	🎟🎟🎟🎟
Julia	🎟🎟🎟🎟🎟🎟🎟
Lee	🎟🎟🎟🎟🎟🎟🎟🎟🎟

Key: Each 🎟 = 2 tickets.

Mixed Review and Test Prep

18. What is the next number in Tom's pattern? (p. 4)

6, 12, 18, 24, ■

19. Write 2 multiplication sentences that use the factors 3 and 6. What property do the sentences show? (p. 206)

20. **Test Prep** Jenna and Matt each wear 5 costumes in the play. Which number sentence shows their total number of costumes?

A $2 + 5 = 7$　　C $2 \times 2 = 4$

B $5 + 2 = 7$　　D $2 \times 5 = 10$

Extra Practice on page 224, Set C

Multiply with 4

OBJECTIVE: Multiply with the factor 4.

Quick Review

1. 2 × 3
2. 2 × 5
3. 8 × 2
4. 2 × 6
5. 10 × 2

Learn

PROBLEM Matchbox® cars were invented by Jack Odell in 1952. Caleb has 3 Matchbox cars. Each car has 4 wheels. What is the total number of wheels on Caleb's cars?

Find 3 × 4 = ■.

Activity

Materials ■ counters, number line

ONE WAY Use counters.

MODEL	THINK	RECORD
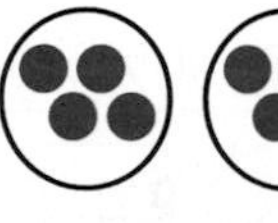 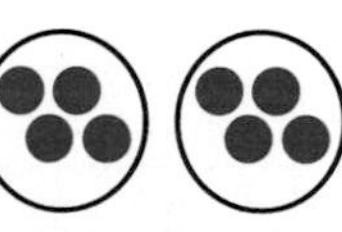	3 groups of 4 4 + 4 + 4	3 × 4 = 12 $\begin{array}{r} 4 \\ \times 3 \\ \hline 12 \end{array}$

So, Caleb's cars have a total of 12 wheels.

OTHER WAYS Use a number line.

MODEL	THINK	RECORD
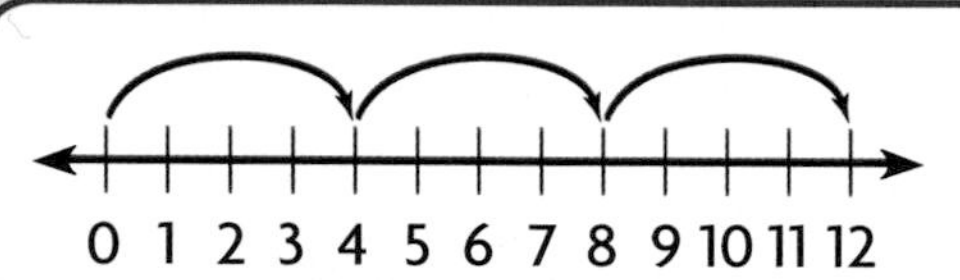	Skip-count by 4. 4, 8, 12	3 × 4 = 12 $\begin{array}{r} 4 \\ \times 3 \\ \hline 12 \end{array}$

Use doubles.

Multiplying with 4 is the same as multiplying by 2 and doubling the product.

	Multiply by 2.	Double the product.
3 × 4 = ■ Think: 2 + 2	3 × 2 = 6	6 + 6 = 12, so 3 × 4 = 12
5 × 4 = ■ Think: 2 + 2	5 × 2 = 10	10 + 10 = 20, so 5 × 4 = 20

- How can you double a 2's fact to find 6 × 4?

Guided Practice

1. How can you use this number line to find 4×4?

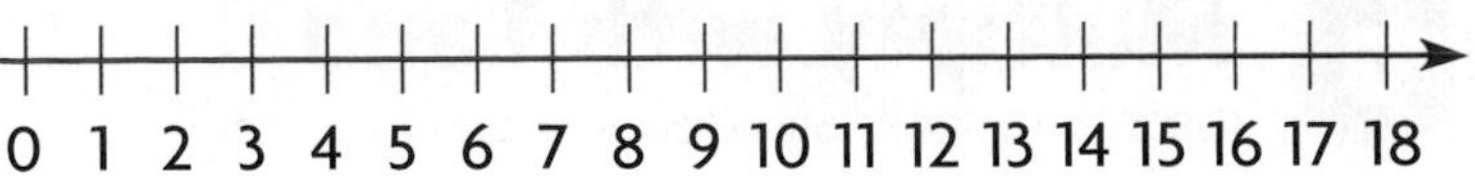

Find the product.

2. $6 \times 4 = ■$
3. $3 \times 4 = ■$
4. $5 \times 4 = ■$
5. $8 \times 4 = ■$
6. TALK Math **Explain** how knowing the product of 2×8 helps you find the product of 4×8.

Independent Practice and Problem Solving

Find the product.

7. $4 \times 4 = ■$
8. $7 \times 4 = ■$
9. $6 \times 4 = ■$
10. $4 \times 5 = ■$

Copy and complete.

	×	1	2	3	4	5	6	7	8	9	10
11.	2	■	■	■	■	■	■	■	■	■	■
12.	4	■	■	■	■	■	■	■	■	■	■

USE DATA For 13–14, use the graph.

13. Tina, Charlie, and Amber have Matchbox cars. How many wheels do their cars have altogether?
14. WRITE Math **What's the Error?** Charlie says that since $5 \times 2 = 10$, his cars have a total of 10 wheels. What is Charlie's error?

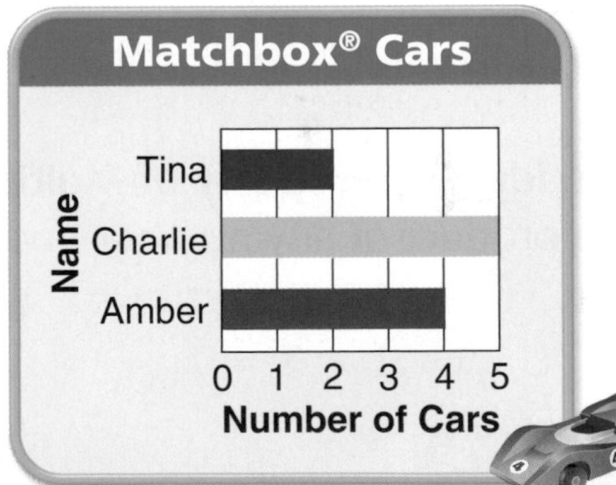

Mixed Review and Test Prep

15. In a pictograph, how would you show 9 votes using the key each ☺ = 3 votes? (p. 148)
16. What shape has 4 equal sides and 4 square corners? (Grade 2)
17. **Test Prep** There are 4 rows of 5 cars on the toy shelf. How many cars are there in all?

    A $4 + 5 = 9$
    B $4 \times 4 = 16$
    C $4 \times 5 = 20$
    D $5 \times 5 = 25$

Extra Practice on page 225, Set D

LESSON 5

ALGEBRA

Multiply with 1 and 0

OBJECTIVE: Multiply with the factors 1 and 0.

Quick Review

1. 6 + 1
2. 5 + 0
3. 1 + 4
4. 7 + 0
5. 9 + 1

Vocabulary

Identity Property of Multiplication

Zero Property of Multiplication

Learn

PROBLEM Luke saw 4 doghouses. Each doghouse had 1 dog in it. How many dogs were there in all?

ONE WAY Draw a picture.

Step 1

Step 2

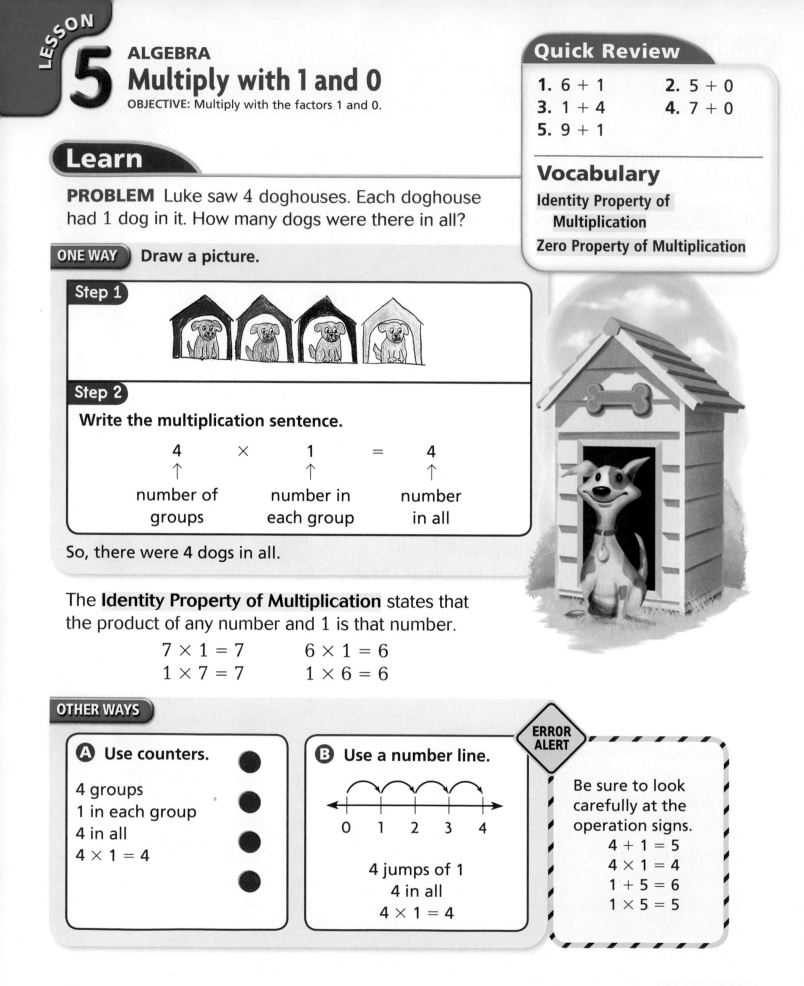

Write the multiplication sentence.

4	×	1	=	4
↑		↑		↑
number of groups		number in each group		number in all

So, there were 4 dogs in all.

The **Identity Property of Multiplication** states that the product of any number and 1 is that number.

$7 \times 1 = 7$ $\quad$ $6 \times 1 = 6$

$1 \times 7 = 7$ $\quad$ $1 \times 6 = 6$

OTHER WAYS

A Use counters.

4 groups
1 in each group
4 in all
$4 \times 1 = 4$

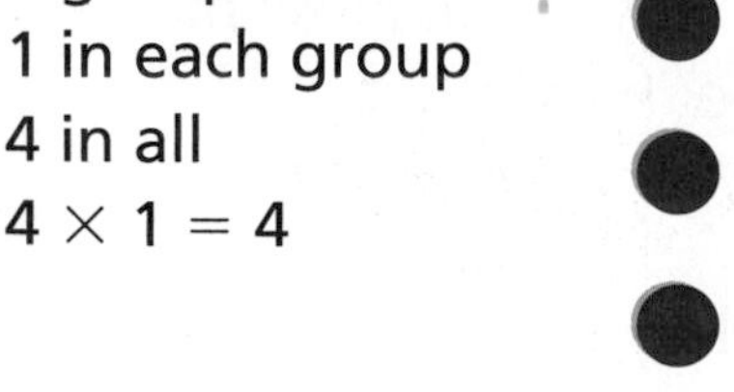

B Use a number line.

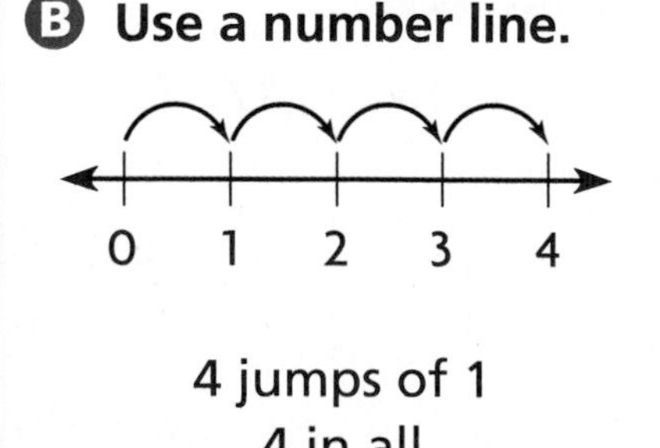

4 jumps of 1
4 in all
$4 \times 1 = 4$

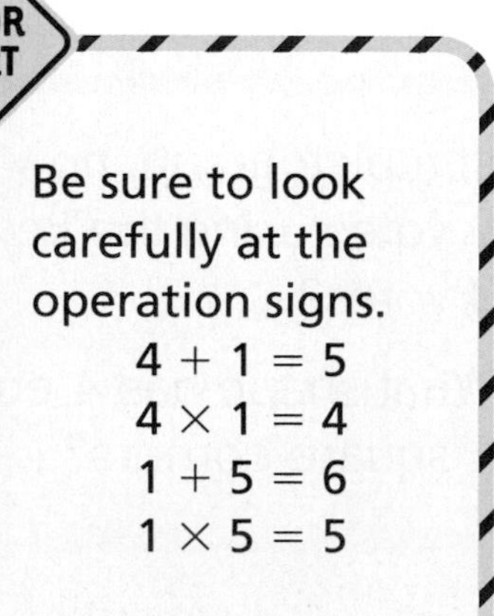

Be sure to look carefully at the operation signs.

$4 + 1 = 5$
$4 \times 1 = 4$
$1 + 5 = 6$
$1 \times 5 = 5$

Multiply with Zero

Lilly saw 4 doghouses. There were 0 dogs in each doghouse. How many dogs were there in all?

ONE WAY **Draw a picture.**

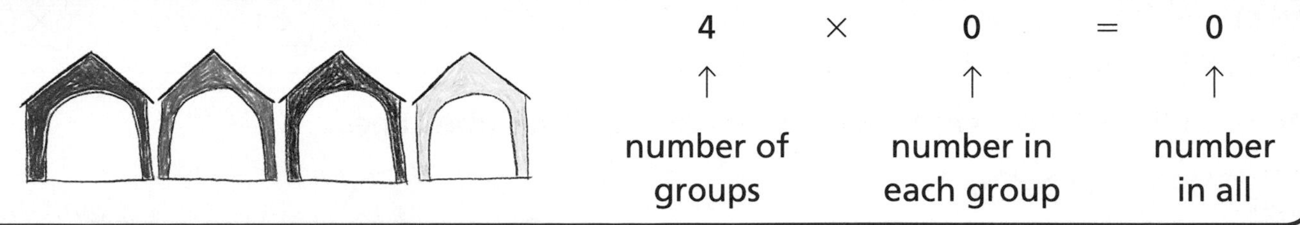

So, there were 0 dogs in all.

The **Zero Property of Multiplication** states that the product of zero and any number is zero.

$0 \times 10 = 0 \qquad 5 \times 0 = 0$

ANOTHER WAY **Use a multiplication table.**

Look at the row and column for 0.

- What do you notice about the products that have 0 as a factor?

Look at the row and column for 1.

- What do you notice about the products that have 1 as a factor?

×	0	1	2	3	4	5	6	7	8	9	10
0	0	0	0	0	0	0	0	0	0	0	0
1	0	1	2	3	4	5	6	7	8	9	10
2	0	2									
3	0	3									
4	0	4									
5	0	5									
6	0	6									
7	0	7									
8	0	8									
9	0	9									
10	0	10									

Guided Practice

1. What multiplication sentence is shown in this picture? Find the product.

2. $3 \times 1 = ■$
3. $0 \times 2 = ■$
4. $4 \times 0 = ■$
5. $1 \times 6 = ■$
6. **TALK Math** **Explain** how 3×1 and $3 + 1$ are different. Draw a picture to show your answer.

Independent Practice and Problem Solving

Find the product.

7. $5 \times 1 = ■$ **8.** $8 \times 0 = ■$ **9.** $1 \times 9 = ■$ **10.** $0 \times 7 = ■$ **11.** $1 \times 1 = ■$

12. $\begin{array}{r} 1 \\ \times 0 \\ \hline \end{array}$ **13.** $\begin{array}{r} 1 \\ \times 7 \\ \hline \end{array}$ **14.** $\begin{array}{r} 0 \\ \times 6 \\ \hline \end{array}$ **15.** $\begin{array}{r} 2 \\ \times 1 \\ \hline \end{array}$ **16.** $\begin{array}{r} 8 \\ \times 1 \\ \hline \end{array}$ **17.** $\begin{array}{r} 0 \\ \times 5 \\ \hline \end{array}$

Write a multiplication sentence shown on each number line.

18. 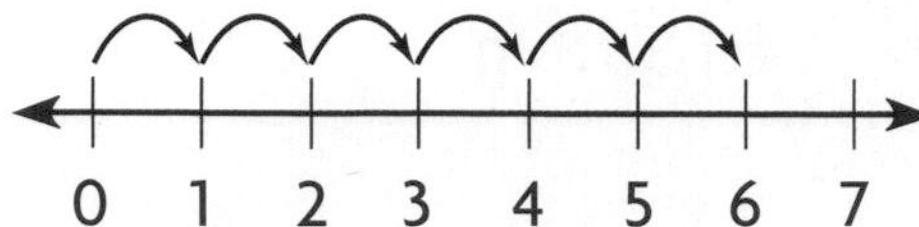

19. 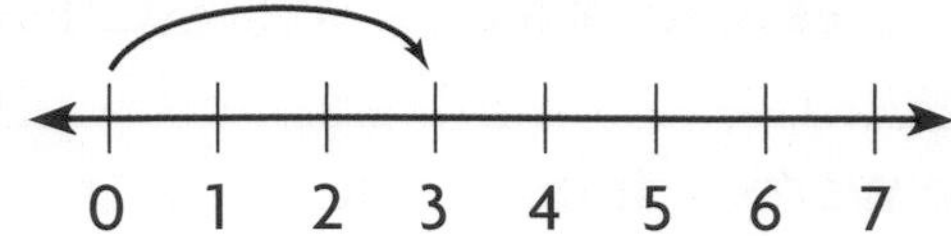

Find the missing number.

20. $3 \times ■ = 0$ **21.** $5 \times 1 = ■ \times 5$ **22.** $■ \times 28 = 28$ **23.** $0 \times 46 = ■$

USE DATA For 24–26, use the table.

Vehicle	Number of Wheels
Car	4
Tricycle	3
Bicycle	2
Unicycle	1

24. At the circus Jon saw 5 unicycles. How many wheels are on the unicycles in all? Draw a picture and write a multiplication sentence.

25. Brian's family has 3 bicycles and 1 tricycle. How many wheels are there in all?

26. WRITE Math **What's the Question?** Josh used multiplication by 1 and the information in the table. The answer is 6.

Mixed Review and Test Prep

27. There are 5 marbles in a bag. There are 4 orange marbles and 1 green marble. What color marble are you likely to choose? (p. 178)

28. Amy earned $9.75 raking leaves for a neighbor. Michelle earned $9.25 selling lemonade. How much more did Amy earn? (p. 122)

29. Test Prep Eric has 6 boxes. He has 1 pencil in each box. Which number sentence shows how many pencils Eric has?

A $6 + 1 = 7$ **C** $0 \times 6 = 0$

B $6 - 1 = 5$ **D** $6 \times 1 = 6$

Extra Practice on page 225, Set E

Pose a Problem

Writing a problem helps you become a better problem solver. Sarah is learning how to multiply with 1 and 0. Her teacher asked her to write a problem about multiplying with 1 and another problem about multiplying with 0. Sarah wrote the problems below.

Marcos bought 1 box of crayons. There are 8 crayons in the box. How many crayons does Marcos have?

Each box of crayons has 8 crayons in it. James did not get a box. How many crayons does James have?

Tips

To pose a problem, think about these things:

- the information you will give
- the question you will ask
- the math idea your problem will be about
- the numbers you will use in your problem
- how to solve the problem

Problem Solving Write problems to show that you understand how to multiply with 1 and 0.

1. Multiply with 1.

2. Multiply with 0.

LESSON 6

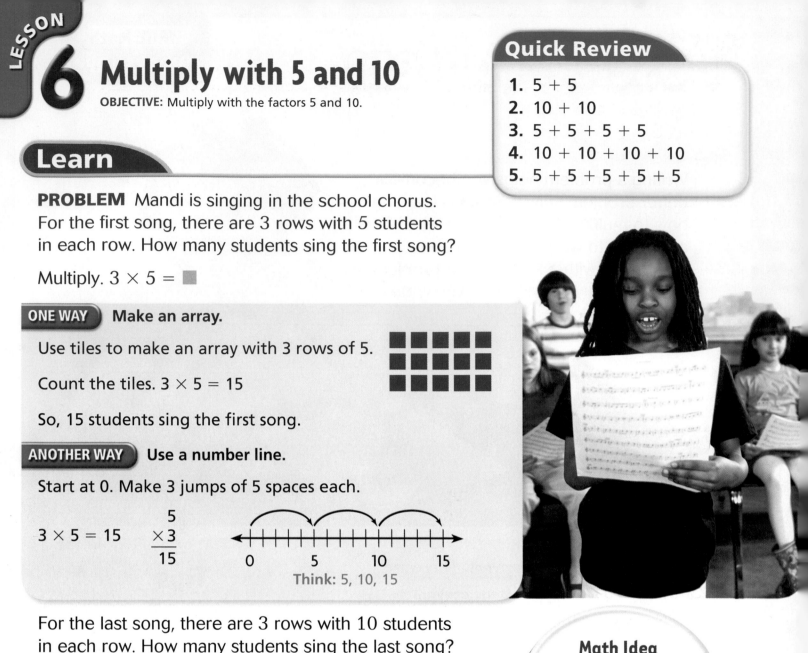

Multiply with 5 and 10

OBJECTIVE: Multiply with the factors 5 and 10.

Quick Review

1. 5 + 5
2. 10 + 10
3. 5 + 5 + 5 + 5
4. 10 + 10 + 10 + 10
5. 5 + 5 + 5 + 5 + 5

Learn

PROBLEM Mandi is singing in the school chorus. For the first song, there are 3 rows with 5 students in each row. How many students sing the first song?

Multiply. $3 \times 5 = \blacksquare$

ONE WAY **Make an array.**

Use tiles to make an array with 3 rows of 5.

Count the tiles. $3 \times 5 = 15$

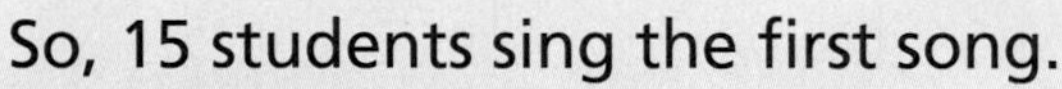

So, 15 students sing the first song.

ANOTHER WAY **Use a number line.**

Start at 0. Make 3 jumps of 5 spaces each.

$3 \times 5 = 15$ $\quad \begin{array}{r} 5 \\ \times 3 \\ \hline 15 \end{array}$

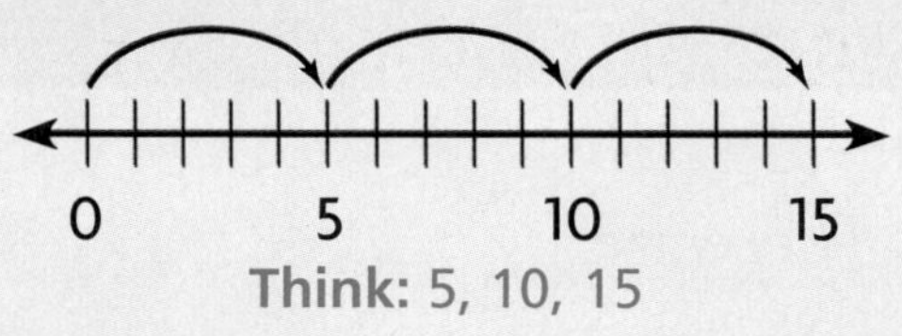

Think: 5, 10, 15

For the last song, there are 3 rows with 10 students in each row. How many students sing the last song?

Multiply. $3 \times 10 = \blacksquare$

Math Idea
The product of 10 and any factor always looks like the other factor followed by a zero.

ONE WAY **Use zeros.**

To find a 10's product, write a zero after the 1's product.	$1 \times 1 = 1$	$1 \times 10 = 10$
	$2 \times 1 = 2$	$2 \times 10 = 20$
	$3 \times 1 = 3$	$3 \times 10 = 30$

So, 30 students sing the last song.

ANOTHER WAY **Use doubles.**

Find the 5's product. $3 \times 5 = 15$
Double that product. $15 + 15 = 30$
So, $3 \times 10 = 30$.

Guided Practice

1. How can you use this number line to find 4×10?

Find the product.

2. $2 \times 5 = ■$
3. $■ = 6 \times 10$
✓4. $■ = 5 \times 5$
✓5. $10 \times 7 = ■$
6. **TALK Math** **Explain** how 4×5 can help you find 4×10.

Independent Practice and Problem Solving

Find the product.

7. $10 \times 2 = ■$
8. $■ = 5 \times 3$
9. $■ = 10 \times 10$
10. $6 \times 5 = ■$
11. $10 \times 5 = ■$
12. $9 \times 5 = ■$
13. $■ = 2 \times 10$
14. $■ = 5 \times 9$
15. 10×0
16. 7×5
17. 5×8
18. 10×9
19. 5×6
20. 10×8

USE DATA **For 21–22, use the table.**

21. Draw a picture to show how many strings are on 4 banjos. Then write a multiplication sentence.
22. Mr. Case has 2 guitars, 4 banjos, and 1 mandolin. What is the total number of strings on Mr. Case's instruments?

Stringed Instruments

Instrument	Number of Strings
Guitar	6
Banjo	5
Mandolin	8
Violin	4

Mandolin

23. **WRITE Math** When you multiply by 5, are the products odd or even? **Explain** how you know.

Mixed Review and Test Prep

24. A music store sold 586 guitar books and 297 piano books. How many more guitar books were sold? (p. 84)
25. Which symbol makes this number sentence true?

    $7 \bullet 4 = 28$ (p. 212)

26. **Test Prep** A music store has guitars displayed on 5 shelves. There are 5 guitars on each shelf. How many guitars are there in all?

    A 10
    B 15
    C 20
    D 25

Extra Practice on page 225, Set F

Problem Solving Workshop
Strategy: Draw a Picture

OBJECTIVE: Solve problems by using the strategy *draw a picture*.

Learn the Strategy

Drawing a picture can help you understand a problem and see how to solve it. You can draw pictures to solve different types of problems.

A picture can show how many in all.

There are 4 flower pots on the Langs' front porch. Mrs. Lang wants to plant 3 flowers in each pot. How many flowers will she plant in all?

A picture can show how to divide a whole.

Lucy bought a sub sandwich. She wants to share it with 3 friends for lunch. Into how many pieces should Lucy cut the sandwich? How many cuts will she need to make?

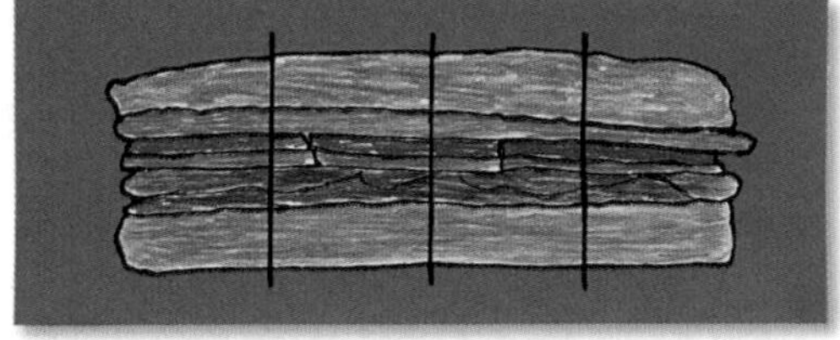

A picture can show order.

Morgan built a snowman. She put 5 buttons on it. The blue button was below the red button. The green button was above the red one. The black button was between the red and blue buttons. The yellow button was just above the green button. Which button was at the top?

To draw a picture, carefully read the information in the problem. Keep your drawing simple.

TALK Math

Choose one of the problems. Tell how the picture helps you solve it.

Use the Strategy

PROBLEM There are 2 rows of drummers in the drum section of a marching band. There are 7 drummers in each row. How many drummers are there in all?

Read to Understand
Plan
Solve
Check

Read to Understand

- **Summarize what you are asked to find.**
- **What information will you use?**

Plan

- **What strategy can you use to solve the problem?**
  You can draw a picture to help you solve the problem.

Solve

- **How can you use the strategy to solve the problem?**
  Draw a picture with stick people to show the drummers.

  Draw 2 rows.
  Show 7 stick people in each row.

  Add or multiply to find the total number of drummers in all.

$7 + 7 = 14$
$2 \times 7 = 14$

So, there are 14 drummers in all in the drum section.

Check

- **How can you check your answer?**
- **What other ways could you solve the problem?**

Guided Problem Solving

Read to Understand
Plan
Solve
Check

1. The marching band has 6 groups of 4 people who play the trumpet. How many people play the trumpet?

   First, draw a picture of the problem. Show 6 circles with 4 dots in each circle.

   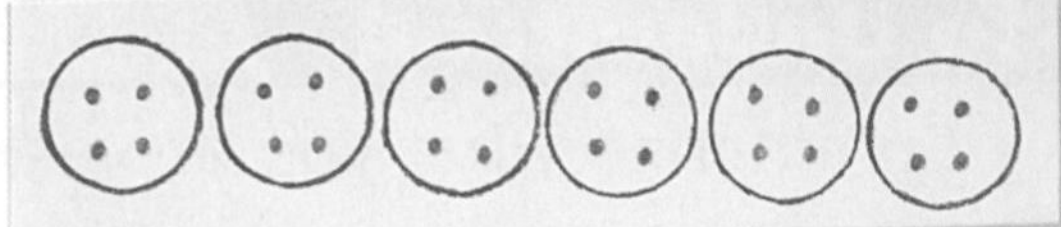

   Next, find the total number of dots.

   $6 \times 4 = ■$

2. **What if** there are 5 groups instead of 6 in Problem 1? How many people would play the trumpet?

3. There are 3 rows of flute players in the marching band. There are 7 people in each row. How many flute players are in the marching band?

Problem Solving Strategy Practice

For 4–6, draw a picture to solve.

4. Each drummer needs 2 drumsticks. How many drumsticks do 6 drummers need?

5. During band practice, 7 students each twirled 1 flag. How many total flags did the students twirl?

6. Twelve students in Mrs. Taylor's class want to start a band. Seven of the students made drums. The rest made 2 maracas each. How many maracas in all were made?

USE DATA For 7–8, use the table.

7. How many rubber bands will seven students need to make their drums?

8. **WRITE Math** Three students want to use maracas in the class band. How many water bottles do they need in all to make their maracas? Explain how you can draw a picture to find the answer.

9. **Reasoning** The class band has 12 students. Show two different ways the band members can stand in equal rows to march.

Materials Needed for Making Instruments

Drum	Maracas
1 coffee can	2 plastic water bottles
1 large rubber band	1 roll of tape
1 trash bag	Dried beans

Mixed Strategy Practice

USE DATA For 10–12, use the Favorite Instrument Survey.

10. The table shows how students in Jillian's class voted. How many students voted for the guitar? Draw a picture to show your answer.

11. On the day of Jillian's survey, two students in the class were absent. The table shows the votes of all other students in the class, including Jillian. How many students in all are in Jillian's class?

12. **Reasoning** Jillian added the number of votes for two instruments and got a total of 12 students. Which two instruments did she add?

13. ***FAST FACT*** The electric guitar was invented in 1931. How many years ago was that?

14. **Open-Ended** Tony and Mike surveyed 50 students about their favorite instrument: flute, trumpet, drum, or guitar. Choose a key and show a possible survey result in a table like the one at the right.

Choose a STRATEGY

- Draw a Diagram or Picture
- Make a Model or Act It Out
- Make an Organized List
- Find a Pattern
- Make a Table or Graph
- Predict and Test
- Work Backward
- Solve a Simpler Problem
- Write an Equation
- Use Logical Reasoning

Favorite Instrument Survey

Instrument	Number of Children
Flute	☺ ☺
Trumpet	☺ ☺ ☺
Drums	☺ ☺ ☺ ☺
Guitar	☺ ☺ ☺ ☺ ☺

Key: Each ☺ = 2 children.

CHALLENGE YOURSELF

Ari, Beth, Corey, and Dan each play a different instrument. One plays the flute, one plays the trumpet, one plays the drum, and one plays the guitar. Read the clues to find out who plays which instrument.

	Clues
a.	Ari's instrument does not have strings.
b.	Beth uses her mouth to play her instrument.
c.	Corey does not use sticks with his instrument.
d.	Dan's instrument is shaped like a cylinder.
e.	Ari's instrument is wider at one end than at the other.

15. Who plays the guitar? Who plays the trumpet?

16. Explain how you know which instrument Ari plays.

Extra Practice

Set A **Use counters to model. Then write an addition sentence and a multiplication sentence for each.** (pp. 204–205)

1. 3 groups of 4
2. 2 groups of 2
3. 2 groups of 3
4. 5 groups of 2
5. 6 groups of 1
6. 4 groups of 5
7. 3 groups of 6
8. 7 groups of 3

Write a multiplication sentence for each.

9. $3 + 3 + 3 = 9$
10. $2 + 2 + 2 + 2 = 8$
11. $4 + 4 = 8$
12. $7 + 7 + 7 + 7 = 28$
13. $1 + 1 + 1 = 3$
14. $6 + 6 + 6 + 6 = 24$
15. $5 + 5 + 5 = 15$
16. $3 + 3 = 6$
17. $8 + 8 + 8 = 24$

Set B **Write a multiplication sentence for each array.** (pp. 206–209)

1. 
2.  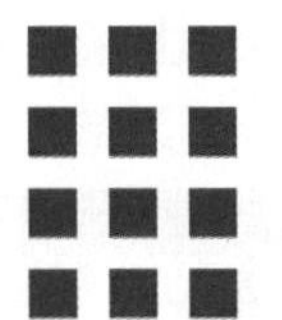
3.  

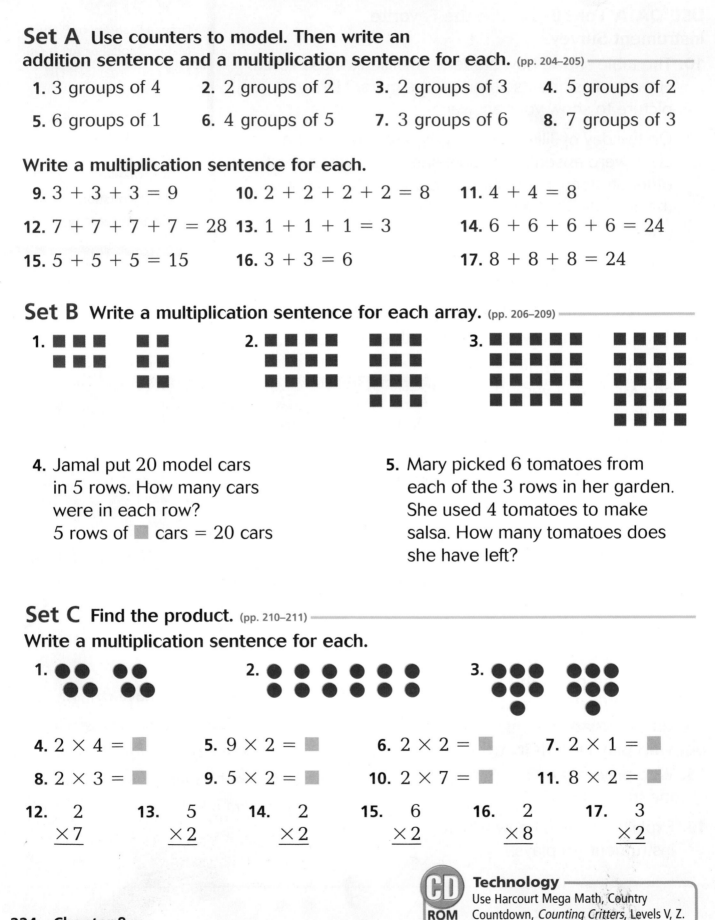

4. Jamal put 20 model cars in 5 rows. How many cars were in each row?
   5 rows of ■ cars = 20 cars

5. Mary picked 6 tomatoes from each of the 3 rows in her garden. She used 4 tomatoes to make salsa. How many tomatoes does she have left?

Set C **Find the product.** (pp. 210–211)

Write a multiplication sentence for each.

1. 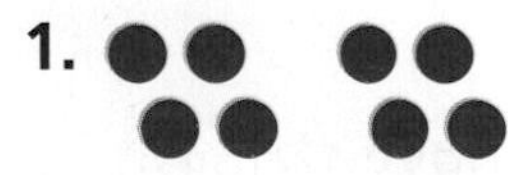
2. 
3. 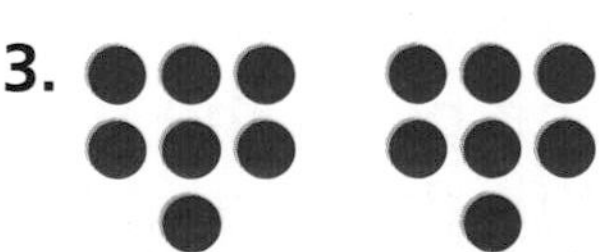

4. $2 \times 4 =$ ■
5. $9 \times 2 =$ ■
6. $2 \times 2 =$ ■
7. $2 \times 1 =$ ■
8. $2 \times 3 =$ ■
9. $5 \times 2 =$ ■
10. $2 \times 7 =$ ■
11. $8 \times 2 =$ ■

12. $\begin{array}{r} 2 \\ \times 7 \\ \hline \end{array}$
13. $\begin{array}{r} 5 \\ \times 2 \\ \hline \end{array}$
14. $\begin{array}{r} 2 \\ \times 2 \\ \hline \end{array}$
15. $\begin{array}{r} 6 \\ \times 2 \\ \hline \end{array}$
16. $\begin{array}{r} 2 \\ \times 8 \\ \hline \end{array}$
17. $\begin{array}{r} 3 \\ \times 2 \\ \hline \end{array}$

CD ROM **Technology**
Use Harcourt Mega Math, Country Countdown, *Counting Critters*, Levels V, Z.

Set D Find the product. (pp. 212–213)

1. $2 \times 4 = $ ■ 2. $9 \times 4 = $ ■ 3. $4 \times 4 = $ ■ 4. $4 \times 1 = $ ■

5. $4 \times 3 = $ ■ 6. $5 \times 4 = $ ■ 7. $4 \times 7 = $ ■ 8. $8 \times 4 = $ ■

9. $\begin{array}{r} 9 \\ \times 4 \\ \hline \end{array}$ 10. $\begin{array}{r} 2 \\ \times 4 \\ \hline \end{array}$ 11. $\begin{array}{r} 7 \\ \times 4 \\ \hline \end{array}$ 12. $\begin{array}{r} 8 \\ \times 4 \\ \hline \end{array}$ 13. $\begin{array}{r} 1 \\ \times 4 \\ \hline \end{array}$ 14. $\begin{array}{r} 6 \\ \times 4 \\ \hline \end{array}$

Copy and complete.

	×	1	2	3	4	5	6	7	8	9	10
15.	2	■	■	■	■	■	■	■	■	■	■
16.	4	■	■	■	■	■	■	■	■	■	■

Set E Find the product. (pp. 214–217)

1. $6 \times 0 = $ ■ 2. $4 \times 1 = $ ■ 3. $3 \times 0 = $ ■ 4. $0 \times 1 = $ ■

5. $1 \times 5 = $ ■ 6. $0 \times 9 = $ ■ 7. $1 \times 1 = $ ■ 8. $4 \times 0 = $ ■

9. $\begin{array}{r} 2 \\ \times 0 \\ \hline \end{array}$ 10. $\begin{array}{r} 7 \\ \times 1 \\ \hline \end{array}$ 11. $\begin{array}{r} 8 \\ \times 0 \\ \hline \end{array}$ 12. $\begin{array}{r} 6 \\ \times 1 \\ \hline \end{array}$ 13. $\begin{array}{r} 0 \\ \times 3 \\ \hline \end{array}$ 14. $\begin{array}{r} 9 \\ \times 1 \\ \hline \end{array}$

Find the missing number.

15. $5 \times$ ■ $= 0$ 16. $3 \times 1 = $ ■ $\times 3$ 17. ■ $\times 14 = 14$ 18. $0 \times 89 = $ ■

19. ■ $\times 8 = 8$ 20. $24 \times 0 = $ ■ 21. $11 \times$ ■ $= 11$ 22. $1 \times 7 = $ ■ $\times 1$

23. Tom had 4 boxes. He put 1 car in each box. How many cars does he have in all?

24. Lucy has 2 fish bowls. There are no fish in the bowls. How many fish does she have in all?

Set F Find the product. (pp. 218–219)

1. $4 \times 5 = $ ■ 2. ■ $= 3 \times 10$ 3. ■ $= 5 \times 2$ 4. ■ $= 6 \times 10$

5. $10 \times 7 = $ ■ 6. ■ $= 2 \times 5$ 7. ■ $= 5 \times 10$ 8. $5 \times 5 = $ ■

9. $\begin{array}{r} 9 \\ \times 5 \\ \hline \end{array}$ 10. $\begin{array}{r} 10 \\ \times 0 \\ \hline \end{array}$ 11. $\begin{array}{r} 8 \\ \times 5 \\ \hline \end{array}$ 12. $\begin{array}{r} 10 \\ \times 2 \\ \hline \end{array}$ 13. $\begin{array}{r} 5 \\ \times 6 \\ \hline \end{array}$ 14. $\begin{array}{r} 3 \\ \times 10 \\ \hline \end{array}$

15. A music store has CDs in 10 boxes. There are 8 CDs in each box. How many CDs are there in all?

16. A grocery store has boxes of cereal on 5 shelves. There are 6 boxes on each shelf. How many boxes of cereal are there in all?

MATH POWER **Value of Shapes**

Shape Solvers

Using shapes instead of numbers can help you practice addition, subtraction, and multiplication facts.

Find the value of the ♥ and ✿ by answering the questions.

♥ − ✿ = 3

✿ × ✿ = 16

Step 1

The ✿ is in both problems, so find the value of the ✿ first.

Think: What number multiplied by itself equals 16?

4 × 4 = 16, so ✿ = 4.

Step 2

Now you can find the value of the ♥.

Using the value of the ✿, you know that ♥ − 4 = 3.

Find the value of ♥ by adding.

4 + 3 = 7.

7 − 4 = 3, so ♥ = 7.

So, ✿ = 4 and ♥ = 7.

Try It

Find the value for each shape in the puzzles below.

1. ▲ + ⬢ = 8

⬢ × ▲ = 12

▲ = ■

⬢ = ■

2. ⬟ + ⬟ = 6

⬟ × ⬟ = 9

⬟ = ■

3. 🍁 − 🌳 = 5

🍁 × 🌳 = 24

🍁 = ■

🌳 = ■

4. WRITE Math How can knowing ★ = 3 help you to solve the puzzle below? **Explain.**

★ + ⏢ = 12

★ × ★ = ⏢

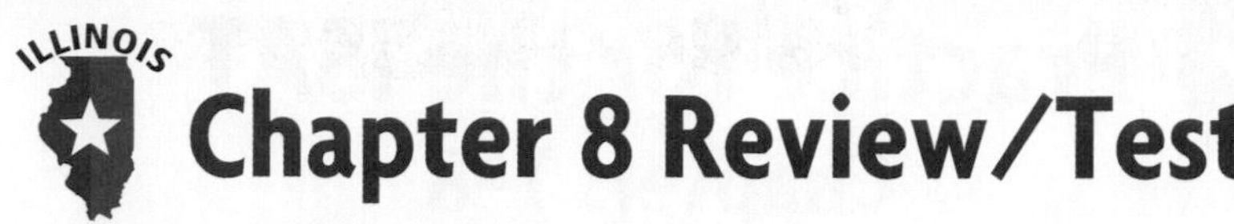

Chapter 8 Review/Test

Check Vocabulary and Concepts

Choose the best term from the box.

1. When you __?__, you combine equal groups to find how many in all. IL 6.3.11 (p. 204)
2. The __?__ states that the product of any number and 1 is that number. IL 6.3.13 (p. 214)

VOCABULARY
array
Identity Property of Multiplication
multiply
Zero Property of Multiplication

Check Skills

Use counters to model. Then write an addition sentence and a multiplication sentence for each. IL 6.3.04 (pp. 204–205)

3. 7 groups of 3
4. 3 groups of 6
5. 4 groups of 5
6. 2 groups of 8

Write a multiplication sentence for each array. IL 6.3.11 (pp. 206–209)

7\. 8\. 9\.

Find the product. IL 6.3.11 (pp. 210–211, 212–213, 214–217, 218–219)

10. $5 \times 2 = \blacksquare$
11. $4 \times 1 = \blacksquare$
12. $0 \times 7 = \blacksquare$
13. $4 \times 4 = \blacksquare$
14. $2 \times 8 = \blacksquare$
15. $9 \times 0 = \blacksquare$
16. $1 \times 1 = \blacksquare$
17. $9 \times 5 = \blacksquare$
18. $\begin{array}{r} 2 \\ \times 2 \\ \hline \end{array}$
19. $\begin{array}{r} 10 \\ \times \ 6 \\ \hline \end{array}$
20. $\begin{array}{r} 7 \\ \times 1 \\ \hline \end{array}$
21. $\begin{array}{r} 6 \\ \times 2 \\ \hline \end{array}$
22. $\begin{array}{r} 10 \\ \times \ 4 \\ \hline \end{array}$
23. $\begin{array}{r} 8 \\ \times 4 \\ \hline \end{array}$

Check Problem Solving

Solve. IL 6.3.11, 8.3.05 (pp. 220–223)

24. Ten students are in the school play. Three students will play instuments and one student will sing a song. The rest of the students will make 2 props each. How many props will the students make in all?
25. WRITE Math Three students sold tickets for the play. They sold 10 tickets each. How many tickets did they sell in all? **Explain** how you know.

GO ONLINE **Technology** Use *Online Assessment.*

Practice for the ISAT
Chapters 1–8

Number and Operations

1. How many miles did Larry and Mike walk altogether? IL 10.3.01 (p. 148)

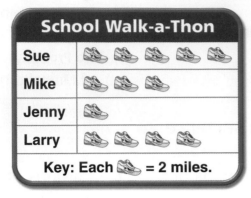

School Walk-a-Thon	
Sue	
Mike	
Jenny	
Larry	
Key: Each = 2 miles.	

A 18 miles

B 16 miles

C 14 miles

D 12 miles

2. Order the numbers from greatest to least. IL 6.3.05 (p. 33)

3,403; 3,430; 3,034

A 3,430; 3,403; 3,034

B 3,403; 3,430; 3,034

C 3,034; 3,403; 3,403

D 3,034; 3,430; 3,403

3. WRITE Math **Explain** how knowing the product 9×2 can help you to find the product 9×4. IL 6.3.11 (p. 212)

Algebra

4. Which array shows the product 6×3? IL 6.3.11 (p. 206)

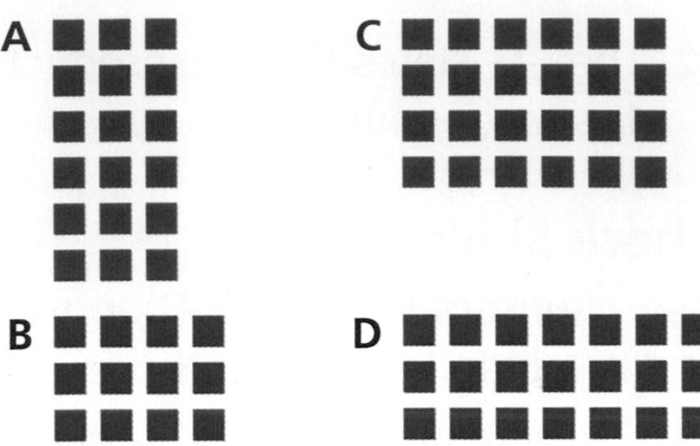

5. Which multiplication sentence is shown by the counters? IL 8.3.03 (p. 204)

A $6 \times 3 = 18$

B $4 \times 3 = 12$

C $2 \times 6 = 12$

D $4 \times 2 = 8$

6. WRITE Math Write the addition sentence $5 + 5 + 5 + 5 = 20$ as a multiplication sentence. **Explain** how you know. IL 6.3.04 (p. 204)

Measurement

Eliminate choices.

See item 7. First find the time that names the correct hour shown on the clock. Then find the time that names the correct minutes.

7. Walter's swim practice ends at the time shown on the clock. What time does Walter's swim practice end? IL 7.3.02 (p. 124)

A 5:15

B 4:45

C 4:15

D 3:45

8. Jim is playing outside in the snow. Which temperature does the thermometer show? Grade 2

A 5° F

B 15° F

C 25° F

D 35° F

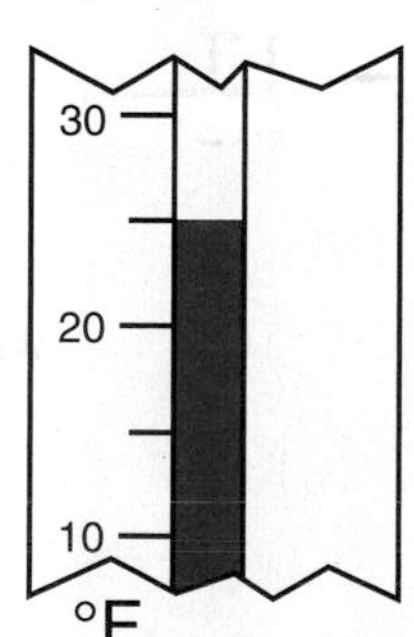

9. 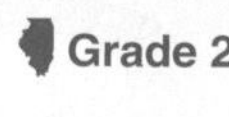

Would you use inches, feet, or yards to measure the door? **Explain.** Grade 2

Data Analysis and Probability

10. Randy pulled marbles from a bag and recorded the results for a probability experiment. How many marbles did Randy pull in all? IL 10.3.01 (p. 182)

A 12

B 13

C 14

D 15

Marbles Pulled

Marble	Number of Times Pulled
orange	III
red	II
green	~~IIII~~ III
blue	II

11. How many more red shirts than blue shirts does Matt have? IL 10.3.01 (p. 154)

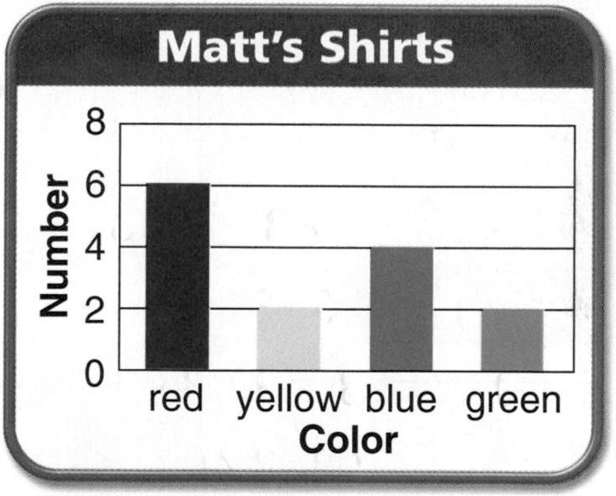

A 4

B 3

C 2

D 1

12. WRITE Math List the possible outcomes for this spinner. **Explain** how you know. IL 10.3.04 (p. 180)

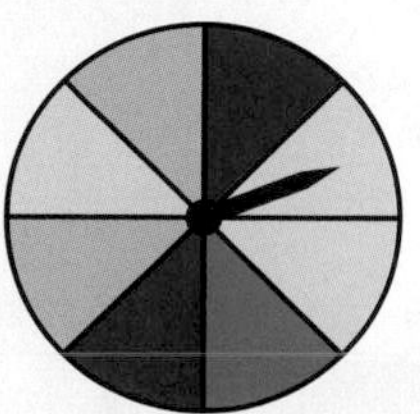

CHAPTER 9 Facts and Strategies

Investigate

Each train in the Manhattan Express roller coaster has 4 cars that hold 4 riders each for a total of 16 riders. Choose a roller coaster. How many cars and riders per car could the roller coaster have? Make a list of the possible combinations.

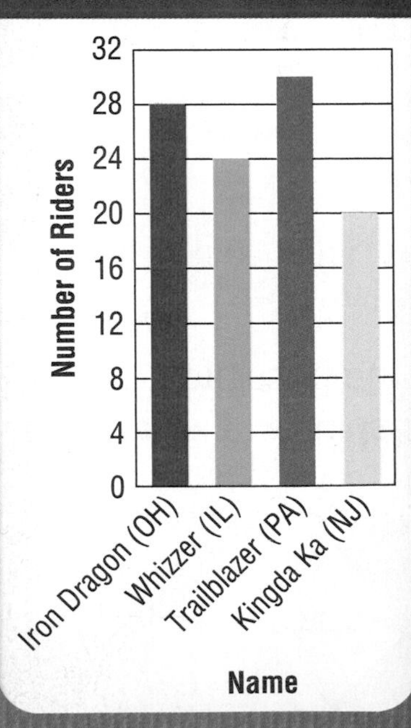

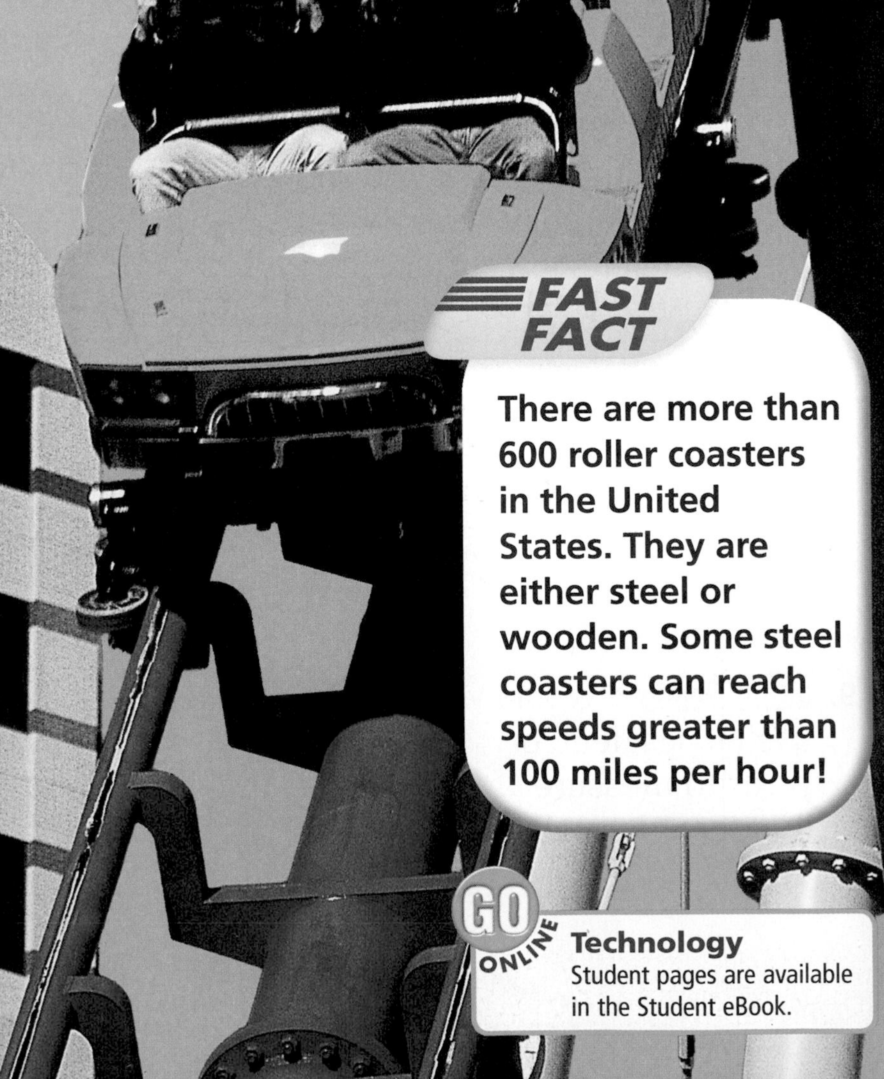

FAST FACT

There are more than 600 roller coasters in the United States. They are either steel or wooden. Some steel coasters can reach speeds greater than 100 miles per hour!

GO ONLINE **Technology** Student pages are available in the Student eBook.

Show What You Know

Check your understanding of important skills needed for success in Chapter 9.

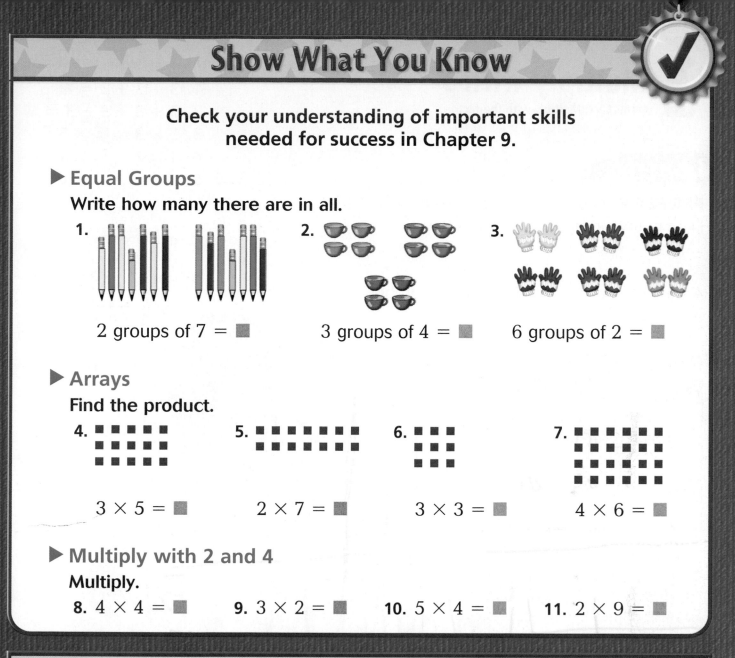

Equal Groups

Write how many there are in all.

1. 

2 groups of 7 = ■

2. 

3 groups of 4 = ■

3. 

6 groups of 2 = ■

Arrays

Find the product.

4. 

$3 \times 5 =$ ■

5. ■ ■ ■ ■ ■ ■ ■ / ■ ■ ■ ■ ■ ■ ■

$2 \times 7 =$ ■

6. ■ ■ ■ / ■ ■ ■ / ■ ■ ■

$3 \times 3 =$ ■

7. ■ ■ ■ ■ ■ ■ / ■ ■ ■ ■ ■ ■ / ■ ■ ■ ■ ■ ■ / ■ ■ ■ ■ ■ ■

$4 \times 6 =$ ■

Multiply with 2 and 4

Multiply.

8. $4 \times 4 =$ ■
9. $3 \times 2 =$ ■
10. $5 \times 4 =$ ■
11. $2 \times 9 =$ ■

VOCABULARY POWER

CHAPTER VOCABULARY

array
factor
multiple
multiplication
multiply
product

WARM-UP WORDS

multiple A number that is the product of a given number and a counting number

multiply When you combine equal groups, you can multiply to find how many in all.

product The answer in a multiplication problem

LESSON 1

Multiply with 3

OBJECTIVE: Multiply with the factor 3.

Quick Review

1. 3 + 3 + 3 = ■
2. 3 + 3 + 3 + 3 = ■
3. 5 × 3 = ■ × 5
4. 1 × 7 = ■ × 1
5. ■ × 2 = 2 × 6

Learn

PROBLEM Paula is making a design with 4 triangles. How many sides do 4 triangles have?

$4 \times 3 = \blacksquare$

equilateral triangle

3 inches 3 inches

3 inches

A triangle has 3 sides. To find the number of sides in 4 triangles, find 4 × 3.

ONE WAY **Draw a picture.**

Step 1 **Draw 4 triangles.**

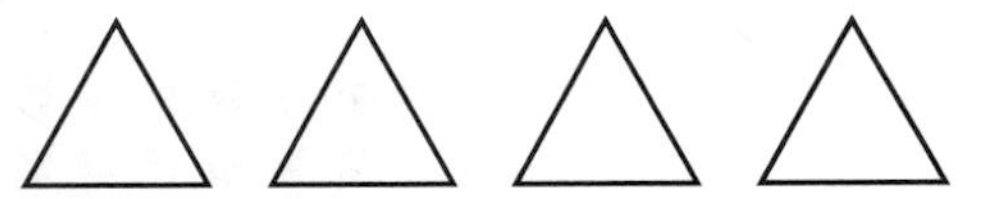

Step 2 **Count the sides.**

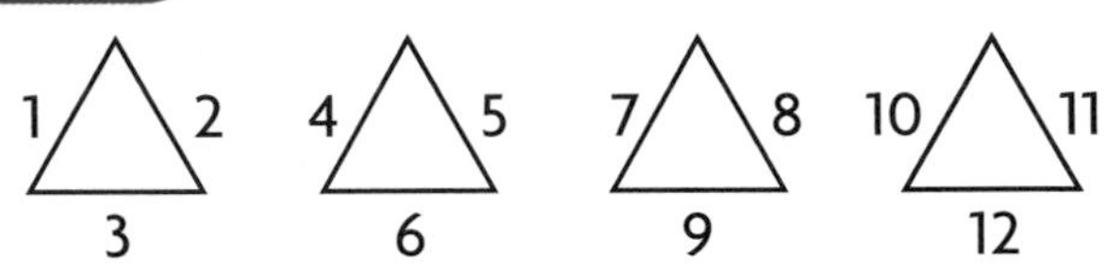

4 × 3 = 12

So, 4 triangles have 12 sides.

OTHER WAYS

A **Use counters.**

Make 4 groups of 3.

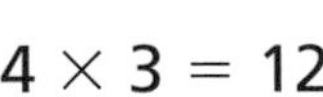

4 × 3 = 12

B **Look for a pattern.**

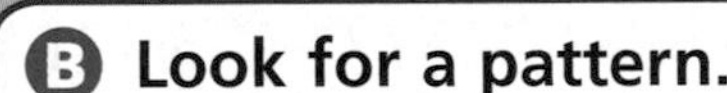

Triangles	Sides	Total
1	3	3
2	3	6
3	3	9
4	3	12

4 × 3 = 12

Guided Practice

1. Use the picture and tell how to find the number of sides in 6 triangles.

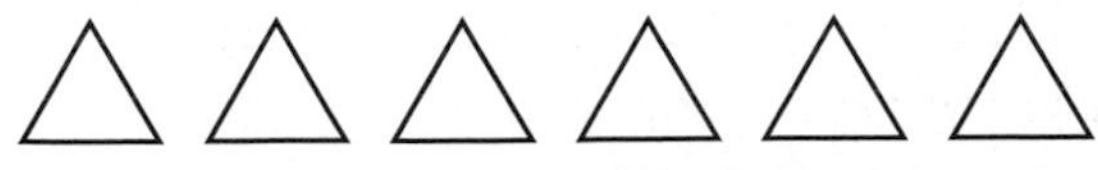

Find the product.

2. $3 \times 5 = ■$
3. $■ = 3 \times 6$
✓4. $■ = 7 \times 3$
✓5. $9 \times 3 = ■$

6. TALK Math **Explain** how you can use counters to find 5×3.

Independent Practice and Problem Solving

Find the product.

7. $6 \times 3 = ■$
8. $■ = 8 \times 3$
9. $■ = 3 \times 0$
10. $3 \times 3 = ■$
11. $2 \times 3 = ■$
12. $■ = 9 \times 3$
13. $■ = 3 \times 1$
14. $3 \times 7 = ■$

15. $\begin{array}{r} 3 \\ \times 6 \\ \hline \end{array}$
16. $\begin{array}{r} 8 \\ \times 3 \\ \hline \end{array}$
17. $\begin{array}{r} 5 \\ \times 3 \\ \hline \end{array}$
18. $\begin{array}{r} 3 \\ \times 2 \\ \hline \end{array}$
19. $\begin{array}{r} 7 \\ \times 3 \\ \hline \end{array}$
20. $\begin{array}{r} 3 \\ \times 9 \\ \hline \end{array}$

Algebra Complete.

21. $2 \times 3 = ■ \times 2$
22. $8 \times 1 = ■ \times 8$
23. $5 \times 2 = ■ \times 5$
24. $2 \times 3 = ■ + 1$
25. $8 \times 1 = ■ + 1$
26. $5 \times 2 = ■ + 1$

27. A square has 4 sides. Which have more sides, 5 squares or 6 triangles? Show your work.

28. **Reasoning** Use the factors 3 and 4 to show the Commutative Property of Multiplication. Draw a picture.

USE DATA For 29–30, use the table.

29. How many squares are there in 3 pieces of the quilt pattern? Draw a picture to show your answer.

30. WRITE Math **Explain** how to find the total number of sides of all the shapes in the quilt pattern. Some sides will be counted more than once.

Quilt Pattern

Shape	Number in 1 pattern piece
Square	6
Triangle	4
Rectangle	4

Amish pattern used ▶ in making quilts.

Mixed Review and Test Prep

31. Jon has 2 quarters, 2 dimes, and 3 nickels. Tom has 1 quarter, 5 nickels, and 27 pennies. Who has more money? How much more? (p. 114)

32. Ryan has 2 sheets of stickers. Each sheet has 8 stickers. How many stickers does Ryan have? (p. 210)

33. **Test Prep** There are 9 color pencils in each of 3 packages. How many color pencils are there in all?

A 6 **B** 12 **C** 24 **D** 27

Extra Practice on page 248, Set A

LESSON 2

Multiply with 6

OBJECTIVE: Multiply with the factor 6.

Quick Review

1. 3×2
2. 9×3
3. 5×3
4. 3×4
5. 6×3

Vocabulary

multiple

Learn

PROBLEM A lightning bug has 6 legs. How many legs do 5 lightning bugs have?

$$5 \times 6 = ■$$

ONE WAY Use an array.

Make 5 rows with 6 tiles in each row.

Count the tiles.

$5 \times 6 = 30$

$$\begin{array}{r} 6 \\ \times 5 \\ \hline 30 \end{array}$$

So, 5 lightning bugs have 30 legs.

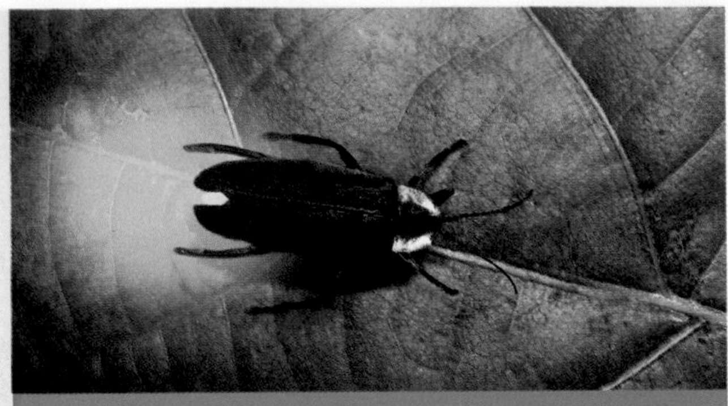

▲ Lightning bugs are also called fireflies.

OTHER WAYS

A **Use a number line.**

Make 5 jumps of 6 spaces each.

$5 \times 6 = 30$

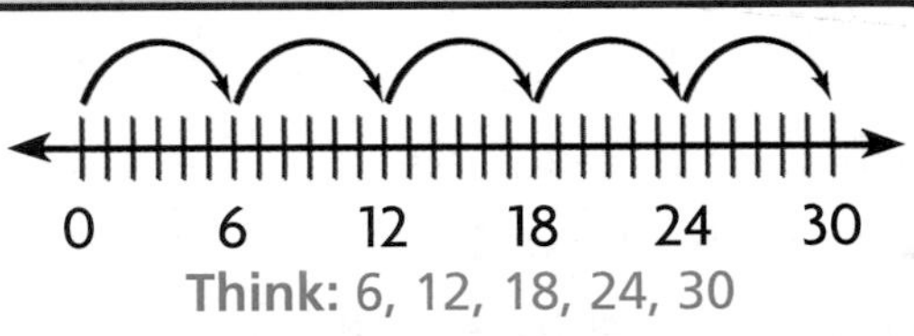

Think: 6, 12, 18, 24, 30

A **multiple** of 6 is any product that has a 6 as one of its factors. Some multiples of 6 are 6, 12, 18, 24, and 30.

B **Use a multiplication table.**

Find the product for 5×6 where row 5 and column 6 meet. $5 \times 6 = 30$

column ↓

row →

×	0	1	2	3	4	5	6	7	8	9
0	0	0	0	0	0	0	0	0	0	0
1	0	1	2	3	4	5	6	7	8	9
2	0	2	4	6	8	10	12	14	16	18
3	0	3	6	9	12	15	18	21	24	27
4	0	4	8	12	16	20	24	28	32	36
5	0	5	10	15	20	25	30	35	40	45
6	0	6	12	18	24	30	36	42	48	54
7	0	7	14	21	28	35	42	49	56	63
8	0	8	16	24	32	40	48	56	64	72
9	0	9	18	27	36	45	54	63	72	81

C **Use doubles.**

First, find the 3s product. $5 \times 3 = 15$

Then double that product. $15 + 15 = 30$

So, $5 \times 6 = 30$.

- Look at the columns for 3 and 6 in the table. What do you notice about their products?

Guided Practice

1. Use the array to find 3 × 6.

Find the product.

2. 6 × 1 = ■ 3. ■ = 3 × 6 ✓4. ■ = 6 × 4 ✓5. 6 × 8 = ■

6. **TALK Math** Name a product that is a multiple of 3 and 6. **Explain** how you know.

Independent Practice and Problem Solving

Find the product.

7. 6 × 5 = ■ 8. ■ = 8 × 6 9. ■ = 6 × 6 10. 0 × 6 = ■

11. 10 × 6 = ■ 12. 4 × 5 = ■ 13. ■ = 1 × 6 14. ■ = 5 × 5

15. $\begin{array}{r} 6 \\ \times 5 \\ \hline \end{array}$ 16. $\begin{array}{r} 3 \\ \times 5 \\ \hline \end{array}$ 17. $\begin{array}{r} 9 \\ \times 6 \\ \hline \end{array}$ 18. $\begin{array}{r} 6 \\ \times 7 \\ \hline \end{array}$ 19. $\begin{array}{r} 6 \\ \times 6 \\ \hline \end{array}$ 20. $\begin{array}{r} 6 \\ \times 3 \\ \hline \end{array}$

Algebra Copy and complete each table.

	Multiply by 3.	
21.	6	■
22.	■	30

	Multiply by 6.	
23.	3	■
24.	7	■

25.

Multiply by ■.	
6	30
5	25

USE DATA For 26–28, use the table.

26. How many wings do 6 honeybees have?

27. How many more wings do 6 beetles have than 6 flies?

28. **WRITE Math** Write a number sentence that shows how many wings 3 flies have. **Explain** how this fact can help you find the number of wings 6 flies have.

Winged Insects

Insect	Number of Wings
Fly	2
Beetle	4
Honeybee	4

Mixed Review and Test Prep

29. Ten flies each had 2 wings. How many wings did they have in all? (p. 210)

30. Write the time shown on the clock. (p. 124)

31. **Test Prep** Sean saw 8 ladybugs while he was camping. Each one had 6 legs. How many legs did the 8 ladybugs have in all?

A 12 **B** 16 **C** 48 **D** 54

Extra Practice on page 248, Set B

LESSON 3

Multiply with 8

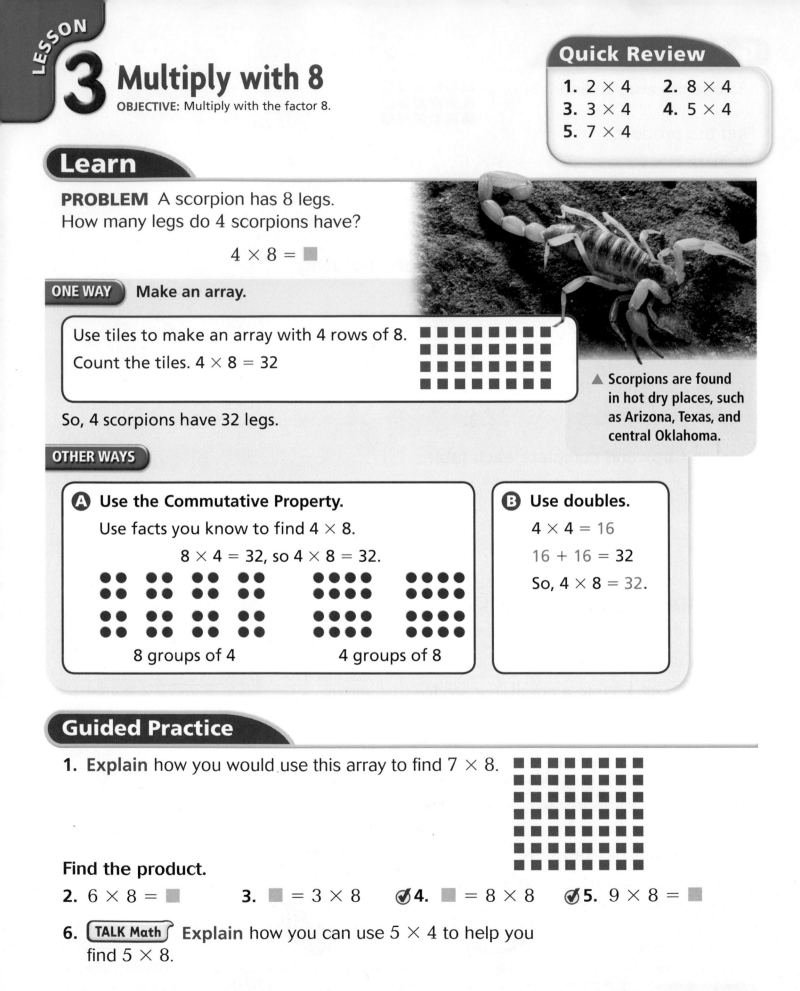

OBJECTIVE: Multiply with the factor 8.

Quick Review

1. 2×4 **2.** 8×4
3. 3×4 **4.** 5×4
5. 7×4

Learn

PROBLEM A scorpion has 8 legs. How many legs do 4 scorpions have?

$4 \times 8 = \blacksquare$

▲ Scorpions are found in hot dry places, such as Arizona, Texas, and central Oklahoma.

ONE WAY **Make an array.**

Use tiles to make an array with 4 rows of 8.

Count the tiles. $4 \times 8 = 32$

So, 4 scorpions have 32 legs.

OTHER WAYS

A Use the Commutative Property.

Use facts you know to find 4×8.

$8 \times 4 = 32$, so $4 \times 8 = 32$.

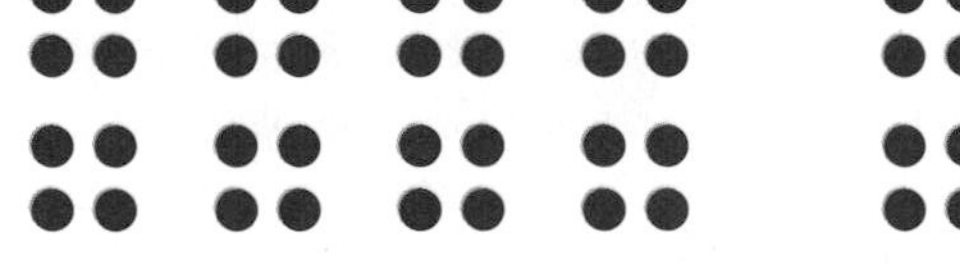

8 groups of 4

4 groups of 8

B Use doubles.

$4 \times 4 = 16$

$16 + 16 = 32$

So, $4 \times 8 = 32$.

Guided Practice

1. Explain how you would use this array to find 7×8.

Find the product.

2. $6 \times 8 = \blacksquare$ **3.** $\blacksquare = 3 \times 8$ ✓**4.** $\blacksquare = 8 \times 8$ ✓**5.** $9 \times 8 = \blacksquare$

6. TALK Math **Explain** how you can use 5×4 to help you find 5×8.

Independent Practice and Problem Solving

Find the product.

7. $10 \times 8 = \blacksquare$ 8. $2 \times 8 = \blacksquare$ 9. $\blacksquare = 3 \times 8$ 10. $\blacksquare = 8 \times 7$

11. $8 \times 4 = \blacksquare$ 12. $\blacksquare = 6 \times 8$ 13. $\blacksquare = 0 \times 8$ 14. $5 \times 8 = \blacksquare$

15. 8×8 16. 10×3 17. 9×8 18. 1×8 19. 8×2 20. 5×7

21. 6×4 22. 7×3 23. 5×5 24. 3×8 25. 6×5 26. 7×8

Algebra Copy and complete each table.

	Multiply by 4.	
27.	9	■
28.	3	■
29.	5	■

	Multiply by 8.	
30.	4	■
31.	■	56
32.	■	24

33.	Multiply by ■.	
	3	18
	6	36
34.	9	■

USE DATA For 35–37 use the table.

35. About how much rain falls in the Chihuahuan Desert in 4 years? **Explain** how you can use doubles to find the answer.

36. In 2 years, how many more inches of rainfall are there in the Sonoran Desert than in the Mojave Desert?

37. WRITE Math **Explain** how you can find about how many inches of rain fall in the Chihuahuan Desert in 5 years.

Average Yearly Rainfall in North American Deserts

Desert	Inches
Chihuahuan	8
Great Basin	9
Mojave	4
Sonoran	9

Mixed Review and Test Prep

38. About 460 inches of rain falls on Mt. Waialeale, Hawaii, each year. What is the value of the 4 in 460? (p. 8)

39. Carrie has 3 bags of oranges. Each bag has 4 oranges. How many oranges is that? (p. 212)

40. **Test Prep** A black widow spider has 8 legs. How many legs do 7 black widow spiders have?

A 1 **C** 48

B 15 **D** 56

Extra Practice on page 248, Set C

LESSON 4

ALGEBRA

Patterns with 9

OBJECTIVE: Multiply with the factor 9.

Quick Review

1. 9×4
2. 7×10
3. 6×10
4. 9×2
5. 9×3

Learn

PROBLEM Melissa's class is studying the solar system. Students are making models of 9 planets that orbit, or revolve around, the sun. How many planets are in 5 solar system models?

$$5 \times 9 = \blacksquare$$

▲ Planets orbit the sun.

 Use patterns of 9.

Look at the products in the table of 9s facts.

The tens digit is 1 less than the factor that is multiplied by 9.

$5 \times 9 = 4\blacksquare$

$5 - 1 = 4$

The sum of the digits in the product equals 9.

$4 + 5 = 9$

So, $5 \times 9 = 45$

So, there are 45 planets in 5 solar system models.

- How can you use patterns of 9 to complete the table?

Table of 9s	
Factors	**Product**
$1 \times 9 =$	9
$2 \times 9 =$	18
$3 \times 9 =$	27
$4 \times 9 =$	36
$5 \times 9 =$	■
$6 \times 9 =$	54
$7 \times 9 =$	63
$8 \times 9 =$	■
$9 \times 9 =$	■
$10 \times 9 =$	■

ANOTHER WAY Use a related 10s fact.

To multiply by 9, first multiply by 10.

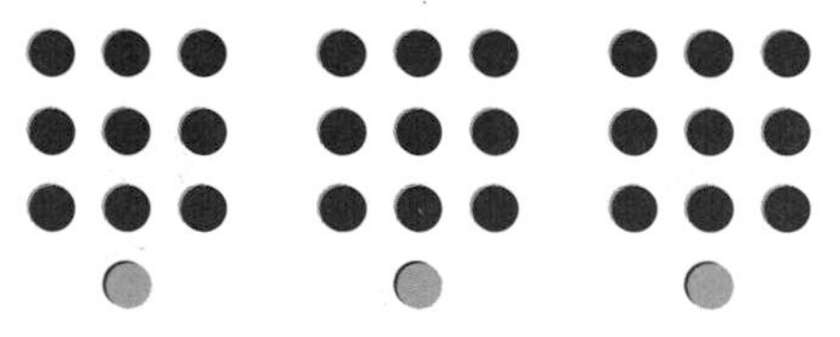

$3 \times 10 = 30$

Then subtract the first factor.

$30 - 3 = 27$

So, $3 \times 9 = 27$

Guided Practice

1. How can you use a related 10s fact to find 4×9?

Find each product.

2. $9 \times 8 = $ ■ 3. ■ $= 2 \times 9$ ✓4. ■ $= 9 \times 6$ ✓5. $9 \times 1 = $ ■

6. **TALK Math** **Explain** how to use the 9s pattern to find 7×9.

Independent Practice and Problem Solving

Find each product.

7. ■ $= 9 \times 0$ 8. $5 \times 9 = $ ■ 9. ■ $= 6 \times 9$ 10. ■ $= 1 \times 9$

11. $9 \times 2 = $ ■ 12. ■ $= 9 \times 9$ 13. $9 \times 4 = $ ■ 14. $3 \times 9 = $ ■

15. $\begin{array}{r} 9 \\ \times 8 \\ \hline \end{array}$ 16. $\begin{array}{r} 9 \\ \times 7 \\ \hline \end{array}$ 17. $\begin{array}{r} 10 \\ \times\ 5 \\ \hline \end{array}$ 18. $\begin{array}{r} 4 \\ \times 6 \\ \hline \end{array}$ 19. $\begin{array}{r} 8 \\ \times 4 \\ \hline \end{array}$ 20. $\begin{array}{r} 9 \\ \times 5 \\ \hline \end{array}$

Algebra Compare. Write $<$, $>$, or $=$ for each ●.

21. 2×9 ● 3×6 22. 5×9 ● 6×7 23. 1×9 ● 3×3

24. 9×4 ● 7×5 25. 9×0 ● 2×3 26. 5×8 ● 3×9

USE DATA For 27–29, use the table.

27. The number of moons of one of the planets can be found by multiplying 7×9. Which planet is it?

28. **Reasoning** This planet has 9 times as many moons as Mars and Earth together have. Which planet is it? **Explain** your answer.

29. **WRITE Math** Nine groups of students made models of Mars and its moons. How many moons were made in all? **Explain** how to find the answer.

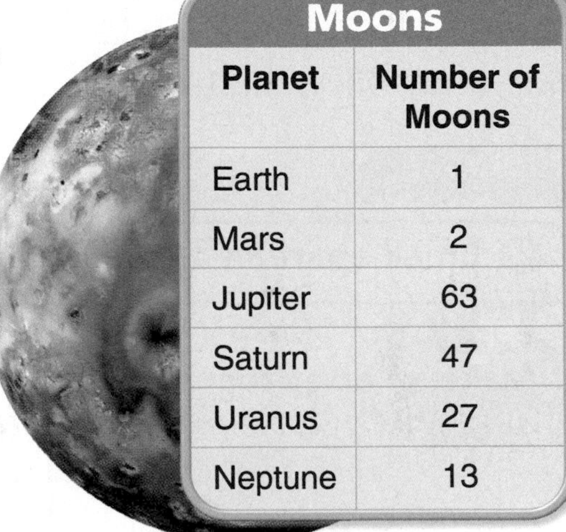

Moons

Planet	Number of Moons
Earth	1
Mars	2
Jupiter	63
Saturn	47
Uranus	27
Neptune	13

Mixed Review and Test Prep

30. The school library has 87 books about space. John checked out 9 of them. How many books about space does the library have left? (p. 80)

31. Ten students each checked out 3 books from the library. How many books did the students check out? (p. 232)

32. **Test Prep** Maddie has 5 sheets of star stickers. Each sheet has 9 stars on it. How many star stickers are there in all?

A 50 **C** 36

B 45 **D** 14

Extra Practice on page 248, Set D

CD ROM **Technology**
Use Harcourt Mega Math, The Number Games, *Up, Up, and Array*, Level B and C.

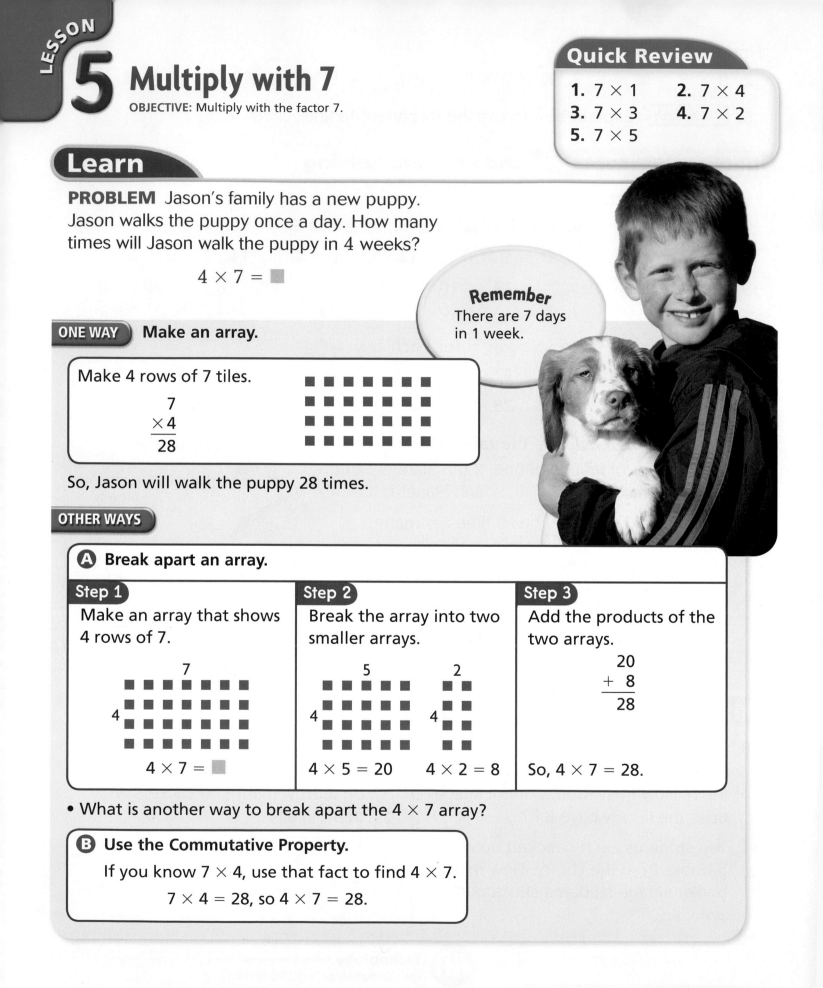

LESSON 5

Multiply with 7

OBJECTIVE: Multiply with the factor 7.

Quick Review

1. 7×1
2. 7×4
3. 7×3
4. 7×2
5. 7×5

Learn

PROBLEM Jason's family has a new puppy. Jason walks the puppy once a day. How many times will Jason walk the puppy in 4 weeks?

$4 \times 7 = \blacksquare$

Remember
There are 7 days in 1 week.

ONE WAY **Make an array.**

Make 4 rows of 7 tiles.

$$\begin{array}{r} 7 \\ \times 4 \\ \hline 28 \end{array}$$

So, Jason will walk the puppy 28 times.

OTHER WAYS

A Break apart an array.

Step 1

Make an array that shows 4 rows of 7.

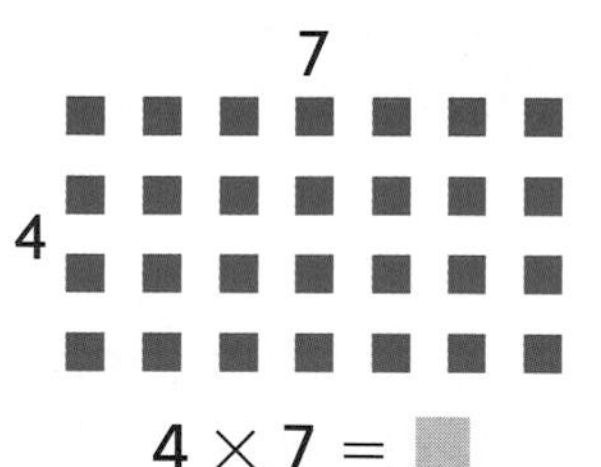

$4 \times 7 = \blacksquare$

Step 2

Break the array into two smaller arrays.

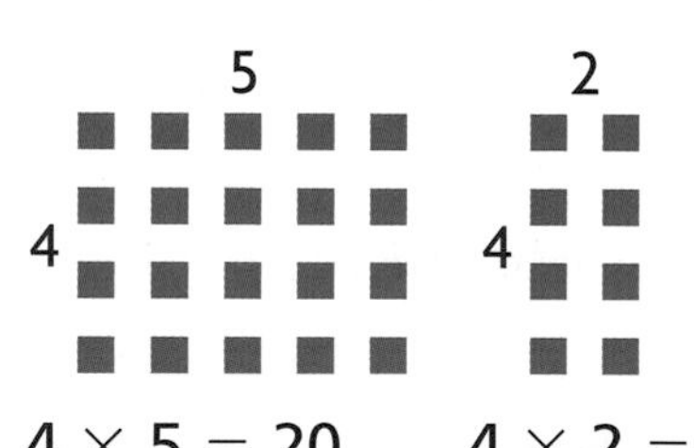

$4 \times 5 = 20$ $4 \times 2 = 8$

Step 3

Add the products of the two arrays.

$$\begin{array}{r} 20 \\ +\ 8 \\ \hline 28 \end{array}$$

So, $4 \times 7 = 28$.

- What is another way to break apart the 4×7 array?

B Use the Commutative Property.

If you know 7×4, use that fact to find 4×7.

$7 \times 4 = 28$, so $4 \times 7 = 28$.

Guided Practice

1. **Explain** how you could break apart 8×7 into two arrays to help you find the product. Use tiles to help.

Find the product.

2. $9 \times 7 = ■$
3. $■ = 6 \times 7$
4. $■ = 3 \times 7$
5. $7 \times 1 = ■$

6. TALK Math How could you use the Commutative Property to find 6×7?

Independent Practice and Problem Solving

Find the product.

7. $■ = 7 \times 7$
8. $7 \times 6 = ■$
9. $■ = 1 \times 8$
10. $■ = 7 \times 2$

11. 7×3
12. 10×6
13. 9×7
14. 5×7
15. 6×8
16. 7×6

17. 8×9
18. 0×7
19. 8×8
20. 7×4
21. 3×6
22. 8×7

USE DATA For 23 and 25, use the table.

Midnight's Care	
Food	3 cups a day
Water	4 cups a day
Bath	2 times a month

23. Lori has a dog named Midnight. How many baths will Midnight have in 7 months?

24. **FAST FACT** A dog's heartbeat depends on its size. Some dogs' hearts beat 70 times a minute. What 7s fact equals 70?

25. WRITE Math Jose's dog, Sunny, eats 4 cups of food a day. In 7 days, does Sunny eat more or less than Midnight eats? **Explain.**

Mixed Review and Test Prep

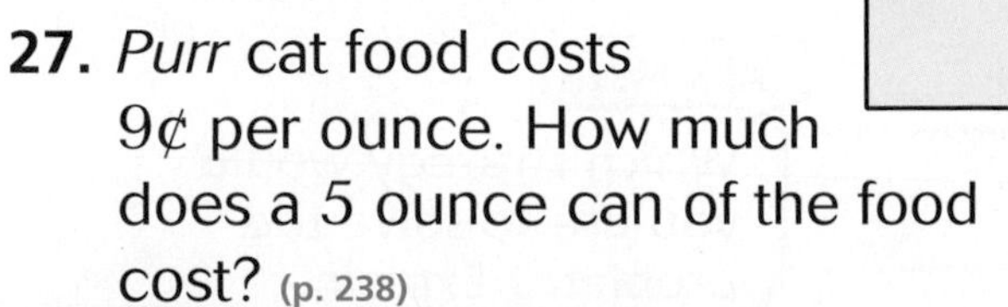

26. How many faces does a cube have? (Gr. 2)

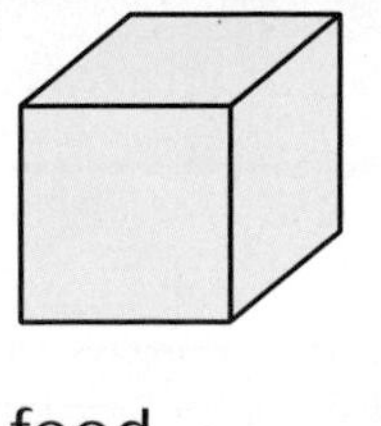

27. *Purr* cat food costs 9¢ per ounce. How much does a 5 ounce can of the food cost? (p. 238)

28. **Test Prep** Sam walks 3 miles a day. How many miles does he walk in one week?

A 3 miles
B 10 miles
C 21 miles
D 28 miles

Extra Practice on page 248, Set E

Problem Solving Workshop
Strategy: Compare Strategies

OBJECTIVE: Compare different strategies to solve problems.

Read to Understand
Plan
Solve
Check

PROBLEM The nine-banded armadillo usually has 9 bands across its back. How many bands would 4 armadillos have?

Read to Understand

- **Summarize what you are asked to find.**
- **What information is given?**

Plan

- **What strategy can you use to solve the problem?**
  Many times you can use more than one strategy to solve a problem. For example, you can *draw a picture* or *make a table* to solve this problem.

Solve

- **How can you use each strategy to solve the problem?**

Draw a picture of 4 armadillos with 9 bands on each one.

$4 \times 9 = 36$

So, 4 armadillos will have 36 bands.

Make a table to show the number of bands on four armadillos.

Armadillo Bands				
Number of armadillos	1	2	3	4
Number of bands	9	18	27	36

Check

- **How do you know your answer is correct?**

TALK Math

Which strategy would you use to solve the problem? Explain.

Guided Problem Solving

1. Julie saw 6 robins each time she went bird-watching. How many robins did Julie see in 5 days?

Draw a picture.

First, draw a picture of 6 birds.

Next, draw 4 more groups of 6 birds so there are 5 groups in all.

Last, count to find the total number of birds.

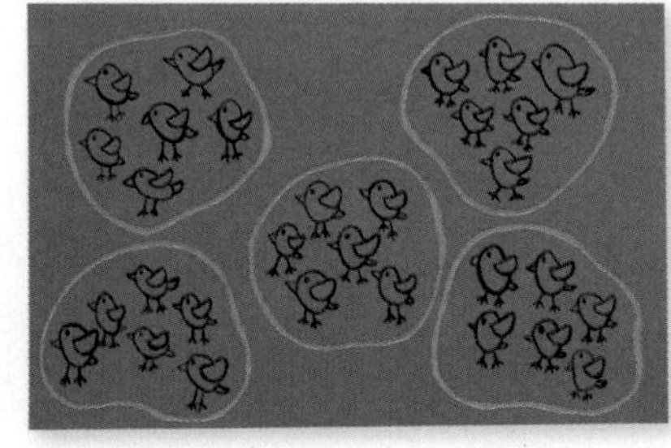

$5 \times 6 = \blacksquare$

Make a table.

First, decide what information should be in each row.

Next, write the information from the problem in the table.

Last, fill in the table through 5 days.

Bird-Watching					
Day	1	2	3	4	5
Number of birds	6	12	18	24	

Choose a STRATEGY

- Make a Model or Act It Out
- Draw a Diagram or Picture
- Make an Organized List
- Find a Pattern
- Make a Table or Graph
- Predict and Test
- Work Backward
- Solve a Simpler Problem
- Write an Equation
- Use Logical Reasoning

2. What if Julie saw 6 robins every day for 6 days? How many would she have seen in all?

3. Mark hiked a trail every day for 5 days. Each day he saw 9 cactus plants. How many cactus plants did he see in all?

Mixed Strategy Practice

USE DATA For 4–6, use the recipe.

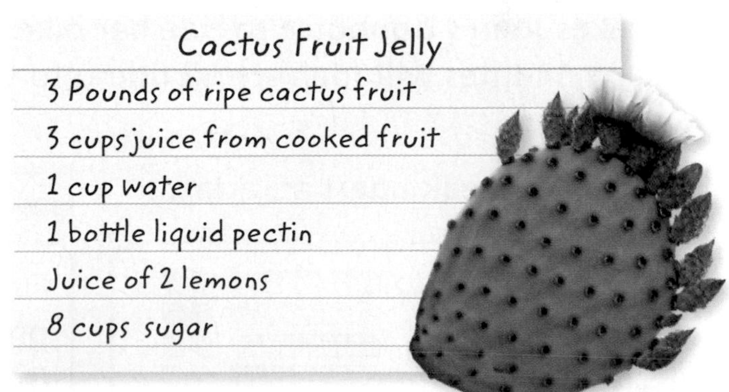

Cactus Fruit Jelly

3 Pounds of ripe cactus fruit
3 cups juice from cooked fruit
1 cup water
1 bottle liquid pectin
Juice of 2 lemons
8 cups sugar

4. Jane doubles the cactus jelly recipe. How many lemons does she need?

5. Joan, Michelle, Samantha, and Gerri each use the recipe to make cactus fruit jelly. How many cups of sugar do they use in all?

6. Reasoning Joel has 7 pounds of ripe cactus fruit. How many pounds will he have left if he makes 2 batches of jelly? **Explain** your answer.

7. Lilly took a 4-mile walk every day for 9 days. How many miles in all did Lilly walk?

8. **WRITE Math** Louis planted a cactus garden. He bought 48 cactus. He planted 8 cactus each day. How many days did it take Louis to plant all of the cactus? **Explain** how you know.

ALGEBRA

Multiplication Facts through 12

OBJECTIVE: Multiply with the factors 11 and 12 and practice multiplication facts by using various strategies.

Quick Review

1. 11 + 11 **2.** 12 + 12
3. 1 × 10 **4.** 2 × 10
5. 11 + 11 + 11

Learn

PROBLEM It takes Bobby 11 minutes to walk to school each morning. How many minutes will Bobby spend walking to school in 5 days?

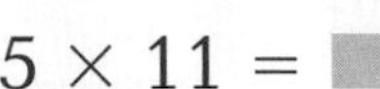

$5 \times 11 = \blacksquare$

ONE WAY Break apart an array.

Make 5 rows of 11.

Use the 10s facts and the 1s facts to multiply by 11.

$5 \times 10 = 50$ $5 \times 1 = 5$

$5 \times 11 = 50 + 5 = 55$

5 × 10 5 × 1

So, Bobby will spend 55 minutes walking to school.

ANOTHER WAY

Look at the table of 11s facts.

To find 5 × 11, write the first factor twice.

$5 \times 11 = 55$

- What pattern do you see in the 11s facts through 9?

11s Facts
1 × 11 = 11
2 × 11 = 22
3 × 11 = 33
4 × 11 = 44
5 × 11 = ■
6 × 11 = 66
7 × 11 = 77
8 × 11 = 88
9 × 11 = 99
10 × 11 = 110

It takes Joan 12 minutes to ride her bike to school. How many minutes will Joan spend riding to school in 5 days?

$5 \times 12 = \blacksquare$

ONE WAY Break apart an array.

Make 5 rows of 12.

Use the 10s facts and the 2s facts to multiply by 12.

5 × 10 5 × 2

$5 \times 10 = 50$ $5 \times 2 = 10$

$5 \times 12 = 50 + 10 = 60$

So, Joan will spend 60 minutes riding to school.

ANOTHER WAY Double a 6s fact.

Find the 6s product. $5 \times 6 = 30$

Double that product. $30 + 30 = 60$

So, $5 \times 12 = 60$.

12s Facts
0 × 12 = 0
1 × 12 = 12
2 × 12 = 24
3 × 12 = 36
4 × 12 = 48
5 × 12 = 60
6 × 12 = 72
7 × 12 = 84
8 × 12 = 96
9 × 12 = 108
10 × 12 = 120
11 × 12 = 132
12 × 12 = 144

Practice the Facts

You can multiply by using a variety of strategies.

OTHER WAYS

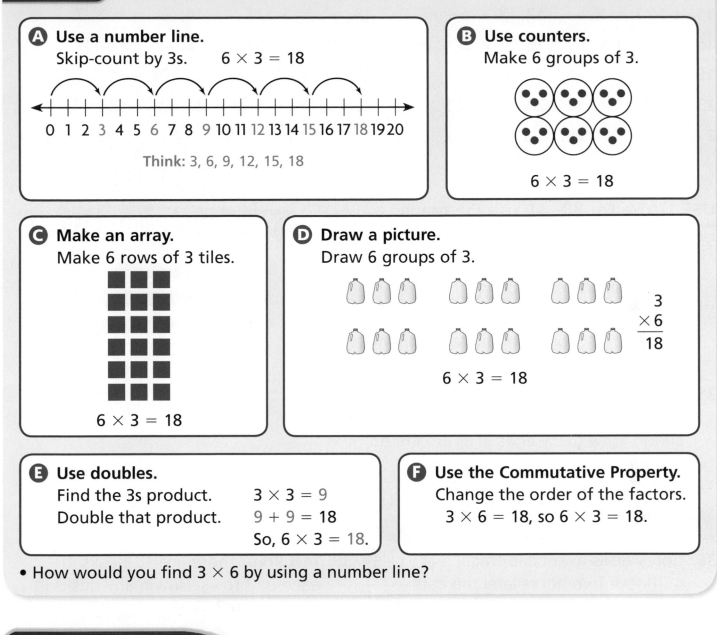

A Use a number line.

Skip-count by 3s. $6 \times 3 = 18$

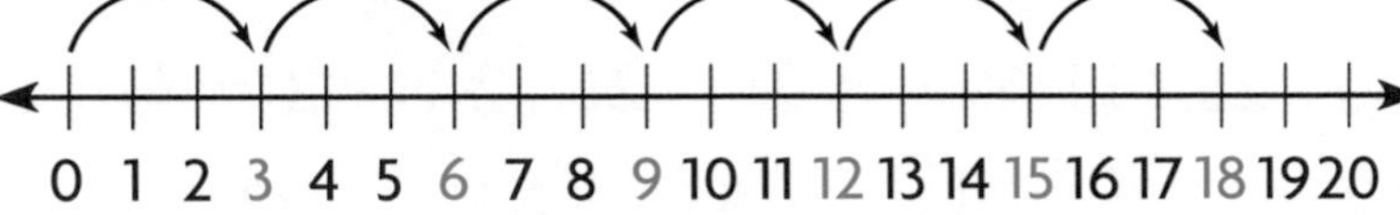

Think: 3, 6, 9, 12, 15, 18

B Use counters.

Make 6 groups of 3.

$6 \times 3 = 18$

C Make an array.

Make 6 rows of 3 tiles.

$6 \times 3 = 18$

D Draw a picture.

Draw 6 groups of 3.

$$\begin{array}{r} 3 \\ \times 6 \\ \hline 18 \end{array}$$

$6 \times 3 = 18$

E Use doubles.

Find the 3s product. $3 \times 3 = 9$

Double that product. $9 + 9 = 18$

So, $6 \times 3 = 18$.

F Use the Commutative Property.

Change the order of the factors.

$3 \times 6 = 18$, so $6 \times 3 = 18$.

- How would you find 3×6 by using a number line?

Guided Practice

1. How can you use the 10s facts and the 2s facts to find 4×12?

Find the product.

2. $9 \times 11 = ■$
3. $■ = 12 \times 7$
4. $■ = 4 \times 11$
5. $12 \times 3 = ■$
6. **TALK Math** How does knowing $11 \times 6 = 66$ help you find 11×12?

Independent Practice and Problem Solving

Find the product.

7. $6 \times 8 = $ ■
8. ■ $= 5 \times 6$
9. ■ $= 4 \times 2$
10. $0 \times 9 = $ ■
11. $4 \times 7 = $ ■
12. $2 \times 6 = $ ■
13. ■ $= 5 \times 5$
14. ■ $= 6 \times 7$
15. ■ $= 10 \times 1$
16. $7 \times 2 = $ ■
17. $8 \times 3 = $ ■
18. $6 \times 9 = $ ■
19. ■ $= 11 \times 11$
20. $6 \times 12 = $ ■
21. ■ $= 10 \times 9$
22. ■ $= 0 \times 12$
23. $10 \times 11 = $ ■
24. ■ $= 11 \times 8$
25. $11 \times 3 = $ ■
26. $2 \times 12 = $ ■
27. $\begin{array}{r} 11 \\ \times\ 4 \\ \hline \end{array}$
28. $\begin{array}{r} 12 \\ \times\ 9 \\ \hline \end{array}$
29. $\begin{array}{r} 12 \\ \times\ 0 \\ \hline \end{array}$
30. $\begin{array}{r} 11 \\ \times\ 9 \\ \hline \end{array}$
31. $\begin{array}{r} 12 \\ \times\ 7 \\ \hline \end{array}$
32. $\begin{array}{r} 12 \\ \times\ 6 \\ \hline \end{array}$

USE DATA For 33–34, use the graph.

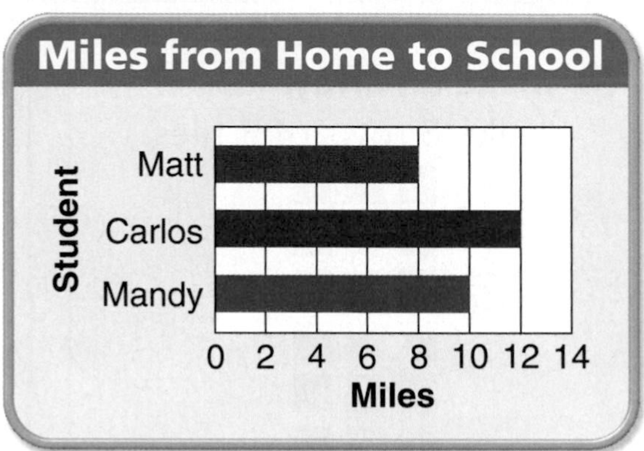

33. The graph shows the number of miles some students travel to school. How many miles will Carlos travel to school in 10 days?
34. Mandy takes 11 trips to school. Matt takes 12 trips to school. Who travels more miles? **Explain** your answer.
35. **WRITE Math** Mr. Lane is putting 6 cartons of eggs on the shelf. There are 12 eggs in each carton. How many eggs in all are there? **Explain** two ways to find the answer.

Mixed Review and Test Prep

36. Corey goes to soccer practice at 4:30 P.M. Two hours later, he eats dinner. At what time does Corey eat dinner? (p. 130)
37. There are 9 red marbles and 1 blue marble in a bag. Sam pulls a marble without looking. Is it certain, likely, unlikely, or impossible that Sam will pull a red marble from the bag? (p. 178)
38. **Test Prep** There are 12 desks in each of 3 rows. How many desks in all are there?

    A 8 **B** 16 **C** 36 **D** 48
39. **Test Prep** Sharon has 4 necklaces. There are 12 beads on each necklace. **Explain** how you would find the total number of beads on all of Sharon's necklaces.

Healthy Foods for Good Health

Use Graphic Aids

▶ The food pyramid shows amounts of different food groups people need for good health. The person climbing up the stairs reminds us that it is important to exercise as well as eat healthy foods.

To help you stay healthy, you should eat a balanced diet and exercise every day. The table shows the recommended daily servings for third graders. For good health, you should eat the right amounts of each food group. To stay healthy, you also need to limit the amount of foods you eat that have a lot of fat and sugar in them.

Recommended Daily Servings

Food Group	Servings
Whole grains (bread, cereal)	6 ounces
Vegetables (beans, corn)	2 cups
Fruits (apples, oranges)	1 cup
Dairy products (milk, cheese)	3 cups
Meat, beans, fish, eggs, nuts	5 ounces
8 ounces = 1 cup	

Problem Solving **Look at the graphic aids. Use the information to solve the problems.**

1. A slice of wheat bread weighs about 1 ounce. How many ounces of whole grains, such as bread and cereal, should a third grader eat in 1 week? Think: 1 week = 7 days
2. How many cups of vegetables and fruits should a third grader eat in 1 day? In 1 week?
3. How many cups of dairy products, such as milk and cheese, should a third grader have in 1 day? In 10 days?
4. **WRITE Math** **What's the Question?** Kendra ate the recommended number of vegetable servings each day for 7 days. The answer is 14 cups.

Extra Practice

Set A Find the product. (pp. 232–233)

1. $3 \times 5 = \blacksquare$ 2. $\blacksquare = 4 \times 3$ 3. $\blacksquare = 3 \times 10$ 4. $7 \times 3 = \blacksquare$

5. $3 \times 9 = \blacksquare$ 6. $\blacksquare = 3 \times 2$ 7. $\blacksquare = 4 \times 6$ 8. $3 \times 3 = \blacksquare$

Set B Find the product. (pp. 234–235)

1. $7 \times 6 = \blacksquare$ 2. $\blacksquare = 3 \times 6$ 3. $\blacksquare = 5 \times 6$ 4. $6 \times 2 = \blacksquare$

5. $4 \times 6 = \blacksquare$ 6. $1 \times 7 = \blacksquare$ 7. $\blacksquare = 2 \times 5$ 8. $\blacksquare = 1 \times 6$

9. $\begin{array}{r} 6 \\ \times 6 \\ \hline \end{array}$ 10. $\begin{array}{r} 5 \\ \times 6 \\ \hline \end{array}$ 11. $\begin{array}{r} 6 \\ \times 8 \\ \hline \end{array}$ 12. $\begin{array}{r} 6 \\ \times 4 \\ \hline \end{array}$ 13. $\begin{array}{r} 1 \\ \times 6 \\ \hline \end{array}$ 14. $\begin{array}{r} 10 \\ \times\ 6 \\ \hline \end{array}$

Set C Find the product. (pp. 236–237)

1. $3 \times 8 = \blacksquare$ 2. $1 \times 8 = \blacksquare$ 3. $5 \times 8 = \blacksquare$ 4. $8 \times 0 = \blacksquare$

5. $\begin{array}{r} 6 \\ \times 6 \\ \hline \end{array}$ 6. $\begin{array}{r} 0 \\ \times 8 \\ \hline \end{array}$ 7. $\begin{array}{r} 7 \\ \times 8 \\ \hline \end{array}$ 8. $\begin{array}{r} 2 \\ \times 7 \\ \hline \end{array}$ 9. $\begin{array}{r} 4 \\ \times 8 \\ \hline \end{array}$ 10. $\begin{array}{r} 8 \\ \times 9 \\ \hline \end{array}$

Set D Find each product. (pp. 238–239)

1. $3 \times 9 = \blacksquare$ 2. $9 \times 5 = \blacksquare$ 3. $0 \times 9 = \blacksquare$ 4. $9 \times 7 = \blacksquare$

Compare. Write $<$, $>$, or $=$ for each $\bullet$.

5. $9 \times 3 \bullet 7 \times 4$ 6. $4 \times 3 \bullet 2 \times 6$ 7. $9 \times 2 \bullet 6 \times 3$

Set E Find the product. (pp. 240–241)

1. $7 \times 10 = \blacksquare$ 2. $3 \times 7 = \blacksquare$ 3. $5 \times 7 = \blacksquare$ 4. $7 \times 4 = \blacksquare$

5. A photo album has 7 pictures on 8 pages. How many photos are there in all?

6. Malik rides his bike 7 miles every day. How many miles does he ride in one week?

Set F Find the product. (pp. 244–247)

1. $11 \times 9 = \blacksquare$ 2. $3 \times 11 = \blacksquare$ 3. $12 \times 2 = \blacksquare$ 4. $11 \times 8 = \blacksquare$

5. $7 \times 11 = \blacksquare$ 6. $3 \times 12 = \blacksquare$ 7. $6 \times 12 = \blacksquare$ 8. $8 \times 12 = \blacksquare$

Technology
Use Harcourt Mega Math, The Number Games, *Up, Up, and Array,* Levels B, C, and D.

TECHNOLOGY CONNECTION

*i*Tools: Counters

Use Counters to Multiply

Trading cards come in packs of 6. If Seth has 8 packs, how many cards does he have in all?

Step 1 Click on *Counters.* Then click on *Multiply* in the *Activities* menu.

Step 2 Click on the workmat 6 times to show 6 counters.

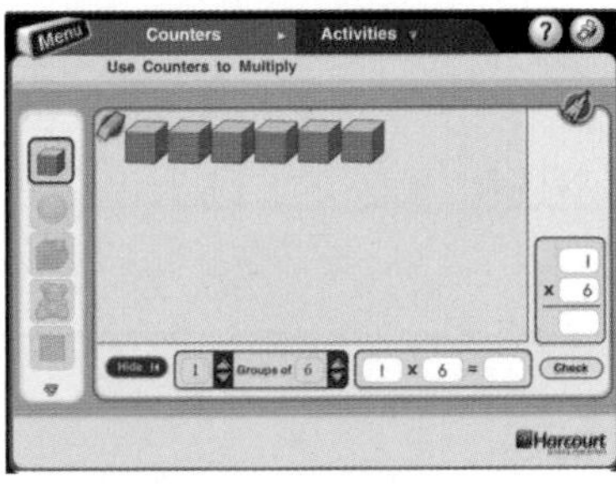

Step 3 Click on the up arrow before *Groups of* to set the number of groups. There should be 8 groups of 6.

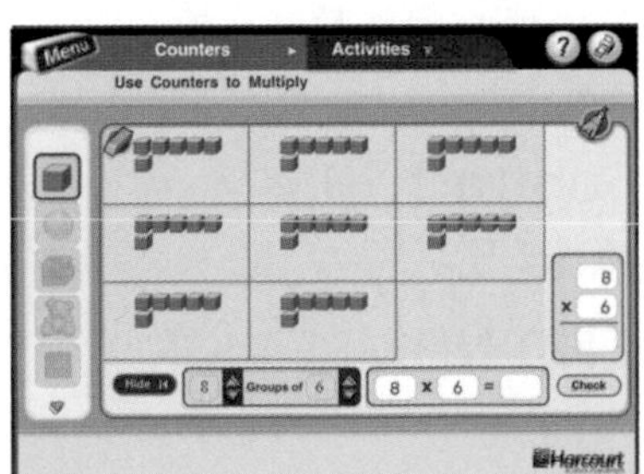

Step 4 Count or multiply the counters. Type your answer in one of the answer boxes. Click on *Check.*

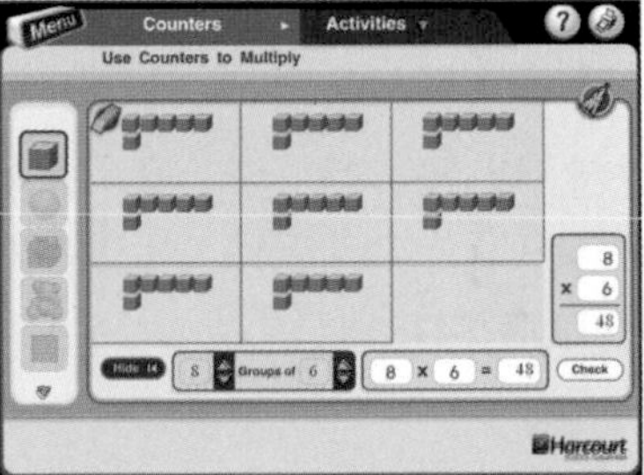

Try It

Follow the same steps to solve these problems.

1. $3 \times 9 = \blacksquare$
2. $5 \times 6 = \blacksquare$
3. $6 \times 4 = \blacksquare$
4. $10 \times 8 = \blacksquare$
5. $4 \times 7 = \blacksquare$
6. $2 \times 8 = \blacksquare$
7. $4 \times 9 = \blacksquare$
8. $6 \times 7 = \blacksquare$
9. $5 \times 8 = \blacksquare$
10. $6 \times 3 = \blacksquare$
11. **Explore More** Eighteen students went apple picking. Half of them picked 6 apples each. The other half picked 5 apples each. **Explain** how you can find out how many apples were picked by the whole class.

Technology
*i*Tools available online or on CD-ROM

MATH POWER **Number Riddles**

MATH MYSTERY

Everybody loves a good mystery! Use addition, subtraction, and multiplication to solve the riddle below.

Follow the steps to begin solving the riddle.

Start with 5.	5	**A**
Add 4.	$5 + 4 = 9$	
Multiply by 2.	$9 \times 2 = 18$	
Subtract 3.	$18 - 3 = 15$	
END NUMBER: ■	15	
	So, **A** $= 15$.	

Try It

Copy the riddle below. Find the value of each letter. Then write the letters in the correct spaces.

1. Start with 9. **Q**
Subtract 3.
Multiply by 4.
Subtract 4.
END NUMBER: ■

2. Start with 4. **C**
Add 2.
Subtract 3.
Multiply by 6.
END NUMBER: ■

3. Start with 8. **K**
Multiply by 3.
Subtract 10.
Add 5.
END NUMBER: ■

4. Start with 7. **U**
Subtract 3.
Multiply by 9.
Add 4.
END NUMBER: ■

5. Start with 10. **E**
Multiply by 5.
Subtract 6.
Add 11.
END NUMBER: ■

6. Start with 6. **R**
Multiply by 8.
Add 9.
Subtract 22.
END NUMBER: ■

7. What is a duck's favorite food?

A	?	?	?	?	?	?	?!
15	20	40	15	18	19	55	35

8. WRITE Math Create a riddle with at least 4 steps. **Explain** your riddle.

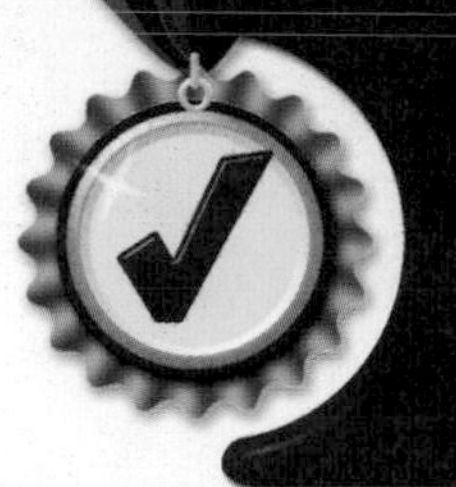

Chapter 9 Review/Test

Check Concepts

1. **Explain** how you can use the picture to find how many sides 4 triangles have. IL 6.3.11 (pp. 232–233)

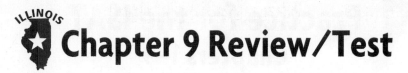

Make an array to solve. IL 6.3.11 (pp. 236–237, 240–241)

2. Maria puts 8 ice cubes into each of 3 glasses for her friends. How many ice cubes has she used in all?

3. There are 7 days in a week. How many days are there in 4 weeks?

Check Skills

Find the product. IL 6.3.11 (pp. 232–233, 234–235, 236–237, 238–239, 240–241, 244–247)

4. $2 \times 10 = ■$
5. $8 \times 4 = ■$
6. $3 \times 9 = ■$
7. $5 \times 7 = ■$
8. $7 \times 8 = ■$
9. $7 \times 5 = ■$
10. $9 \times 8 = ■$
11. $6 \times 4 = ■$
12. $9 \times 10 = ■$
13. $■ = 3 \times 4$
14. $6 \times 6 = ■$
15. $■ = 3 \times 7$
16. 5×4
17. 3×8
18. 5×6
19. 9×9
20. 10×3
21. 8×4

Compare. Write <, >, or = for each ●. IL 6.3.11 (pp. 238–239)

22. 4×3 ● 5×2
23. 6×5 ● 7×4
24. 4×5 ● 10×2
25. 8×2 ● 5×3
26. 8×3 ● 10×2
27. 7×5 ● 9×4

Check Problem Solving

Solve. IL 6.3.11 (pp. 242–243)

28. Linda can paint 4 pictures in one day. How many pictures can she paint in 5 days?

Number of days	1	2	3	4	5
Pictures painted	4	8	■	■	■

29. Jerod buys 4 packages of markers and 5 packages of paper. Each package of markers costs \$5, and each package of paper costs \$3. How much does Jerod spend in all?

30. **WRITE Math** What if each package of paper costs \$6? How much does Jerod spend in all for paper and markers then? **Explain** how you found your answer.

Technology Use *Online Assessment.*

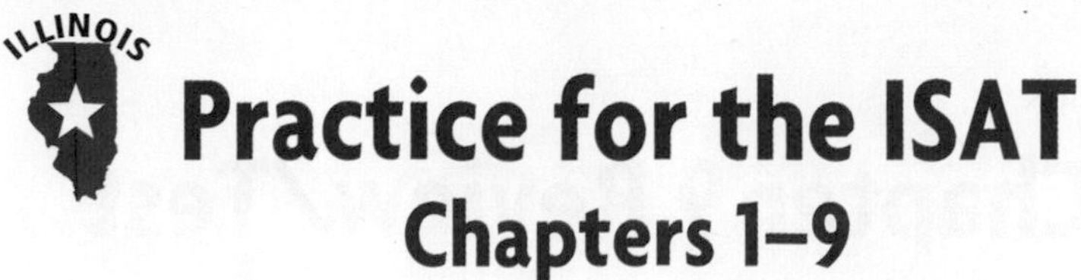

Practice for the ISAT
Chapters 1–9

Number and Operations

1. Jody's school is having a craft fair. There are 7 rows of tables with 5 tables in each row. How many tables are set up for the craft fair? IL 6.3.11 (p. 218)

   A 25   C 35

   B 30   D 40

Test Tip **Understand the problem.**

See item 2. What is the question asking you to find? Read the problem again to find the information you need to answer the question.

2. There was a talent show at Wanda's school on Friday and Saturday. On Friday, 495 people saw the talent show. In all, 867 people saw the talent show. How many people saw the talent show on Saturday? IL 6.3.09 (p. 84)

   A 262   C 362

   B 272   D 372

3. **WRITE Math** How can this picture help you find 5×6? **Explain.** IL 6.3.11 (p. 234)

Algebra

4. What is the ordered pair for the post office? IL 9.3.03 (p. 166)

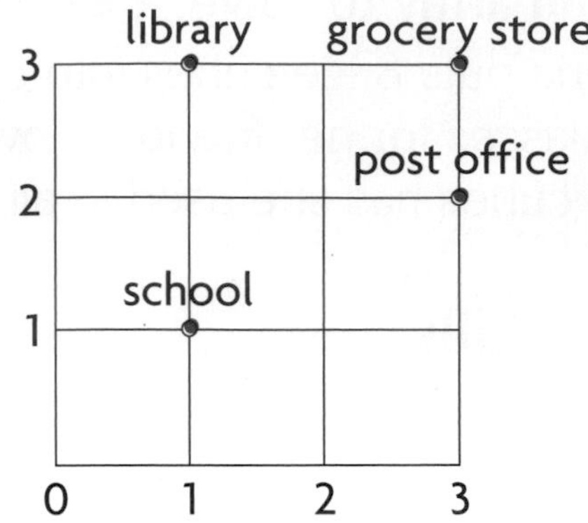

   A (3, 3)

   B (3, 2)

   C (1, 3)

   D (2, 3)

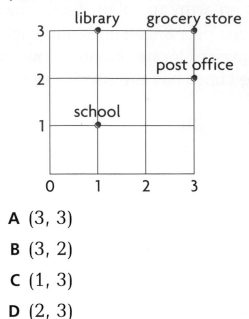

5. Which array shows 6×2? IL 6.3.11 (p. 206)

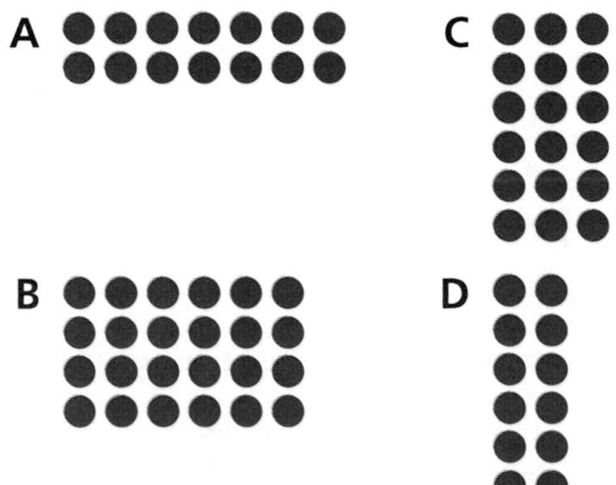

6. **WRITE Math** What is one way to find 8×4? **Explain.** IL 6.3.11 (p. 212)

Geometry

7. These faces can be put together to make which solid figure? Grade 2

A Rectangular prism

B Cylinder

C Cube

D Square pyramid

8. Which solid figure has exactly 5 faces? Grade 2

A 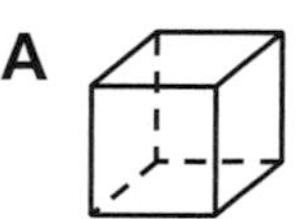

B 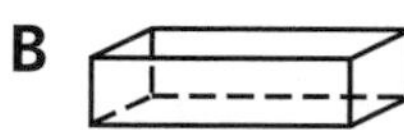

C 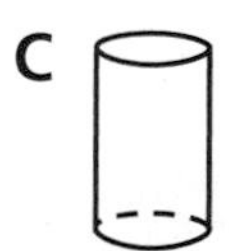

D 

9. WRITE Math **Explain** how this square and this rectangle are alike. Grade 2

Data Analysis and Probability

10. How many more students chose blue than green as their favorite color? IL 10.3.01 (p. 154)

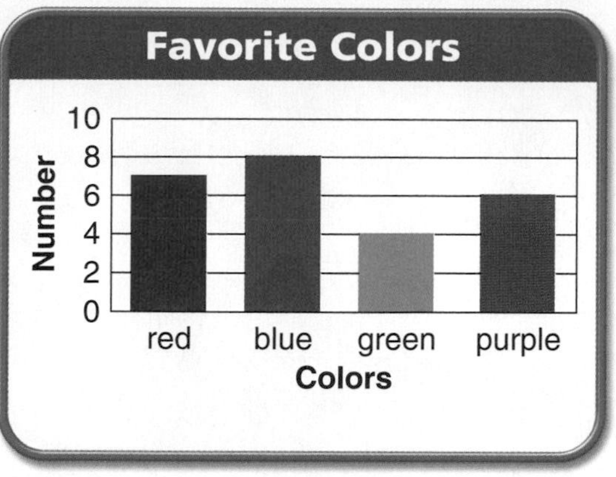

A 1
B 2
C 3
D 4

11. Which color block is Brian least likely to pull? IL 10.3.04 (p. 178)

A Blue

B Green

C Red

D Yellow

12. WRITE Math What if Brian's bag had 10 yellow blocks and 2 green blocks. Which color would he be more likely to pull? **Explain** your answer. IL 10.3.04 (p. 178)

CHAPTER

10 Algebra: Facts and Properties

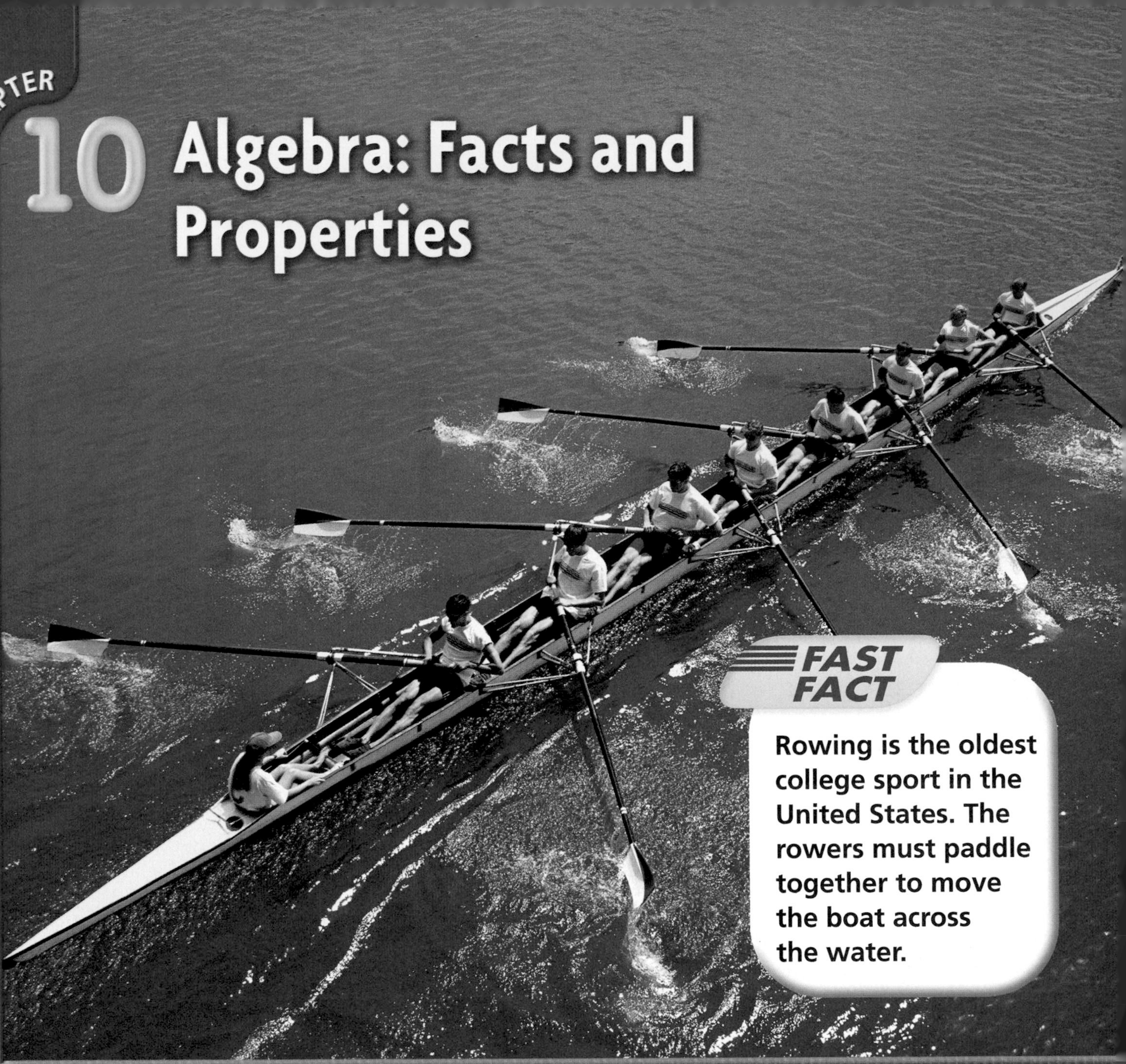

FAST FACT

Rowing is the oldest college sport in the United States. The rowers must paddle together to move the boat across the water.

Investigate

The boat used in sport rowing is called a shell. Other types of boats also use oars or paddles. Choose a boat from the graph. Explain how you can use multiplication to find how many boats you would need for your whole class to go boating.

GO ONLINE **Technology**
Student pages are available in the Student eBook.

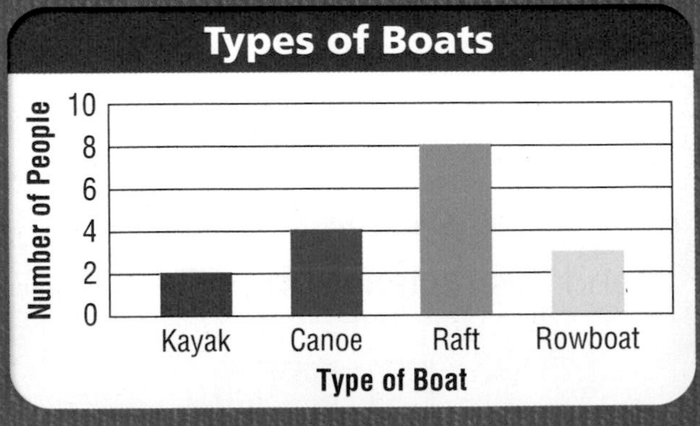

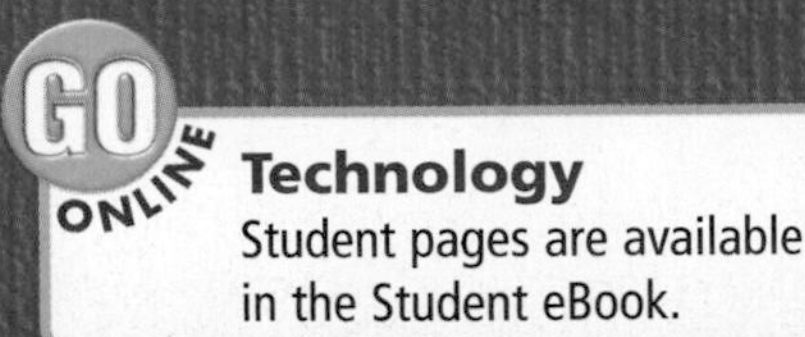

Show What You Know

Check your understanding of important skills needed for success in Chapter 10.

▶ Arrays

Complete.

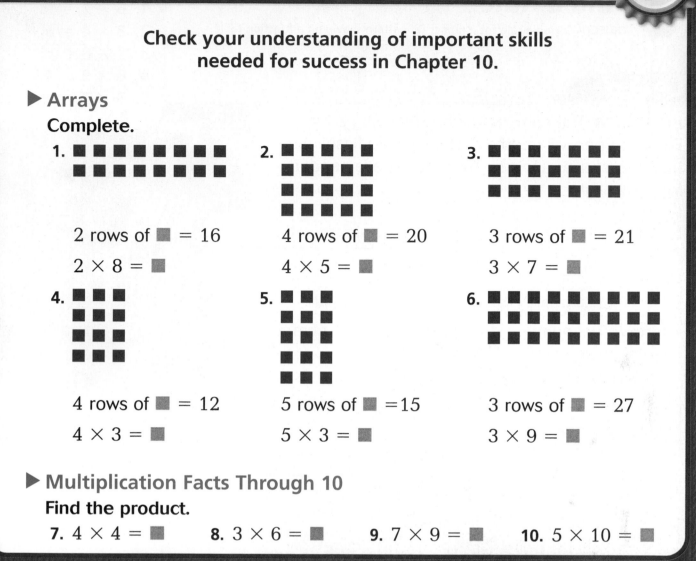

1. 

2 rows of ■ = 16

$2 \times 8 =$ ■

2. 

4 rows of ■ = 20

$4 \times 5 =$ ■

3.

3 rows of ■ = 21

$3 \times 7 =$ ■

4. 

4 rows of ■ = 12

$4 \times 3 =$ ■

5. 

5 rows of ■ =15

$5 \times 3 =$ ■

6. 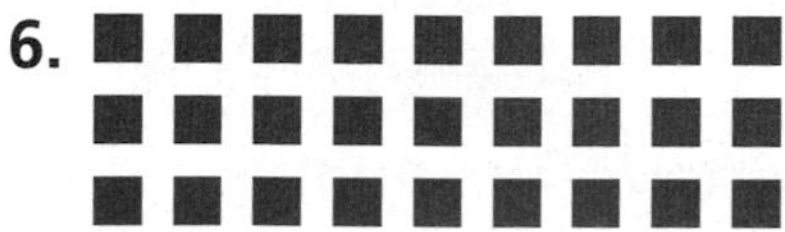

3 rows of ■ = 27

$3 \times 9 =$ ■

▶ Multiplication Facts Through 10

Find the product.

7. $4 \times 4 =$ ■ **8.** $3 \times 6 =$ ■ **9.** $7 \times 9 =$ ■ **10.** $5 \times 10 =$ ■

VOCABULARY POWER

CHAPTER VOCABULARY

Associative Property of Multiplication
Commutative Property of Multiplication
Identity Property of Multiplication
variable
Zero Property of Multiplication

WARM-UP WORDS

Associative Property of Multiplication The property that states that when the grouping of factors is changed, the product remains the same

variable A symbol or a letter that stands for an unknown number

Zero Property of Multiplication The property that states that the product of zero and any number is 0

LESSON 1

Find a Rule

OBJECTIVE: Find a rule for a numerical pattern shown on a function table.

Quick Review

1. 6 × 7 = ■
2. 8 × 4 = ■
3. 1 × 8 = ■
4. 6 × 9 = ■
5. 8 × 7 = ■

Learn

PROBLEM The camping club is planning a trip. Each camper will need a flashlight. One flashlight uses 3 batteries. How many batteries are needed for 7 flashlights?

▲ The flashlight was invented in 1896.

Example Look for a pattern. Write a rule.

Flashlights	1	2	3	4	5	6	7
Batteries	3	6	9	12	15	18	■

Pattern: The number of batteries equals the number of flashlights times 3.

Rule: Multiply the number of flashlights by 3.

To find how many batteries are needed for 7 flashlights, multiply 7 times 3.

$$7 \times 3 = 21$$

So, 21 batteries are needed for 7 flashlights.

More Examples Describe the pattern. Write a rule.

Packs of batteries	1	2	3	4	5
Number of batteries	4	8	■	16	■

Pattern: The number of batteries equals the number of packs times 4.

Rule: Multiply the number of packs of batteries by 4.

- How many batteries are in 3 packs? 5 packs?

Packs of batteries	1	2	3	4
Cost	$5	$10	$15	■

Pattern: The cost equals the number of packs times $5.

Rule: Multiply the number of packs of batteries by $5.

- How much do 4 packs cost? 7 packs?

- How does knowing the pattern rule help you find the next number in the pattern?

Guided Practice

1. **Explain** how to use a rule to find how many batteries are needed for 9 flashlights.

Flashlights	1	2	3
Batteries	3	6	9

Write a rule for each table. Then copy and complete the table.

✓2.

Tents	2	3	4	5	6	7
Campers	4	6	8	10	■	■

✓3.

Campers	1	2	3	4	5
Flashlights	1	2	3	■	■

4. TALK Math **Explain** how you can make a table to find how many plates on 6 tables. Pattern: The number of plates equals the number of tables times 4.

Independent Practice and Problem Solving

Write a rule for each table. Then copy and complete the table.

5.

Hours	1	2	3	4	5
Miles Hiked	2	4	■	■	■

6.

Cabins	3	4	5	6	7
Campers	27	36	■	■	■

USE DATA For 7–10, use the table.

7. Write a rule for the table at the right. What pattern do you see?

Rafts	1	2	3	4
People	6	12	18	■

8. The camping club rents 4 rafts. How many people can 4 rafts hold?

9. The cost to rent a raft is $10 per person. There is a $2 launch fee per raft. What is the cost for a group of 6 people?

10. WRITE Math **What's the Question?** The answer is 30 people. What is the question?

Mixed Review and Test Prep

11. Are you more likely or less likely to spin blue on this spinner? (p. 178)

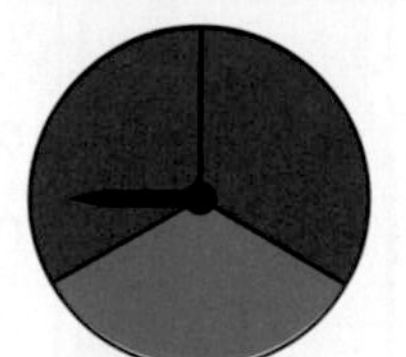

12. Tim bought 4 boxes of granola bars. There are 6 bars in each box. How many bars did Tim buy? (p. 234)

13. **Test Prep** At the store, two notebooks cost $4 and three notebooks cost $6. Jenny wants to buy 6 notebooks. How much will she spend?

A $6 **B** $10 **C** $12 **D** $24

Extra Practice on page 266, Set A

LESSON 2

Missing Factors

OBJECTIVE: Use an array and a multiplication table to find missing factors.

Quick Review

1. $7 \times 3 = \blacksquare$
2. $9 \times 6 = \blacksquare$
3. $8 \times 5 = \blacksquare$
4. $5 \times 7 = \blacksquare$
5. $2 \times 0 = \blacksquare$

Vocabulary

variable

Learn

PROBLEM Brandy plans to invite 24 people to a picnic. The invitations come in packs of 8. How many packs of invitations does Brandy need to buy?

$$\blacksquare \times 8 = 24$$

A **variable** is a letter or symbol that stands for an unknown number.

ONE WAY **Make an array.**

Activity **Materials** ■ square tiles

Make an array with 24 tiles.
Use 8 tiles in each row.

Count the rows of 8 tiles.

column

row →

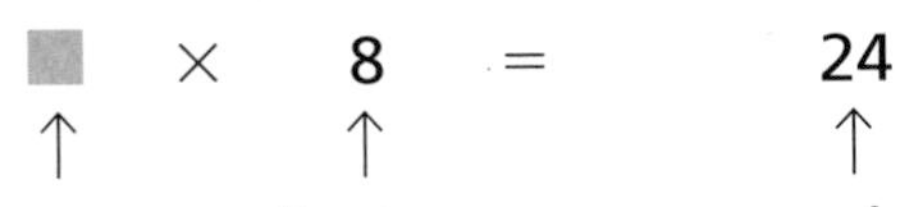

There are 3 rows of 8 tiles. The missing factor is 3.

$$3 \times 8 = 24$$

So, Brandy needs 3 packs of invitations.

ANOTHER WAY **Use a multiplication table.**

Start at the column for 8.
Look down to the product, 24.
Look left across the row from 24.
The missing factor is 3.

$a \times 8 = 24$

$3 \times 8 = 24$

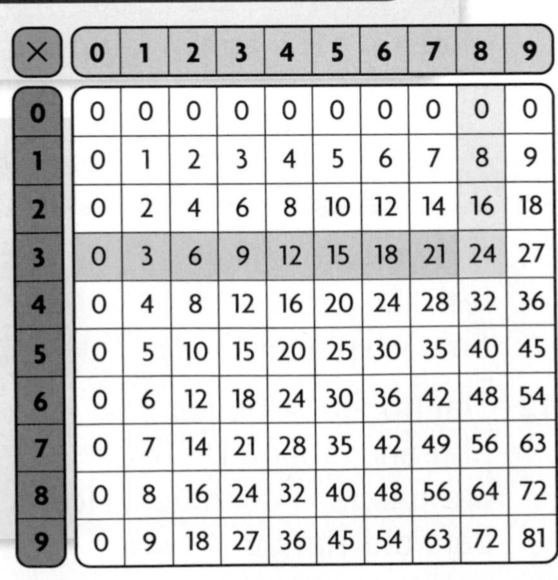

×	0	1	2	3	4	5	6	7	8	9
0	0	0	0	0	0	0	0	0	0	0
1	0	1	2	3	4	5	6	7	8	9
2	0	2	4	6	8	10	12	14	16	18
3	0	3	6	9	12	15	18	21	24	27
4	0	4	8	12	16	20	24	28	32	36
5	0	5	10	15	20	25	30	35	40	45
6	0	6	12	18	24	30	36	42	48	54
7	0	7	14	21	28	35	42	49	56	63
8	0	8	16	24	32	40	48	56	64	72
9	0	9	18	27	36	45	54	63	72	81

Guided Practice

1. What is the missing factor shown by this array?

$5 \times ■ = 35$

Find the missing factor.

2. $■ \times 3 = 27$ 3. $6 \times b = 30$ ✓4. $c \times 5 = 20$ ✓5. $■ \times 2 = 14$

6. **TALK Math** **Explain** how to use the multiplication table on page 258 to find the missing factor in $■ \times 6 = 42$.

Independent Practice and Problem Solving

Find the missing factor.

7. $■ \times 2 = 18$ 8. $4 \times ■ = 28$ 9. $■ \times 3 = 9$ 10. $■ \times 7 = 63$

11. $5 \times ■ = 40$ 12. $8 \times ■ = 56$ 13. $■ \times 6 = 36$ 14. $9 \times ■ = 72$

15. $a \times 4 = 24$ 16. $7 \times y = 7$ 17. $m \times 3 = 15$ 18. $b \times 8 = 48$

19. $3 \times 6 = n \times 9$ 20. $9 \times d = 70 + 2$ 21. $5 \times g = 35 - 5$

USE DATA For 22–24, use the table.

22. Brandy needs 48 bowls for the picnic. How many packs of bowls should she buy?

23. What is the total cost for 3 tablecloths and 2 packs of napkins?

24. **WRITE Math** **What's the Error?** Brandy needs 5 packs of cups. She gives the cashier $8. What is Brandy's error?

Picnic Supplies

Item	Number per pack	Cost
Bowls	6	$4
Cups	8	$3
Tablecloth	1	$2
Napkins	36	$6
Forks	50	$3

Mixed Review and Test Prep

25. Eric bounced the ball 170 times. What is 170 in expanded notation? (p. 8)

26. The gym teacher divides the class into 4 teams. There are 9 students on each team. How many students are in the class? (p. 238)

27. **Test Prep** What is the missing factor?

$■ \times 6 = 12$

A 18 **C** 3

B 6 **D** 2

CD ROM **Technology**
Use Harcourt Mega Math, Ice Station Exploration, *Arctic Algebra,* Level C.

Extra Practice on page 266, Set B

LESSON 3

Multiply 3 Factors

OBJECTIVE: Multiply with three factors using the Associative (Grouping) Property of Multiplication.

Quick Review

1. $6 + 3 + 5$
2. $8 + 4 + 8$
3. $5 + 2 + 7$
4. $2 + 6 + 9$
5. $4 + 8 + 1$

Vocabulary

Associative Property of Multiplication

Learn

PROBLEM The Mr. Freeze Roller Coaster in Texas has 5 cars. Each car has 2 rows of seats. Each row has 2 seats. How many seats in all are on the ride?

ONE WAY Multiply $5 \times (2 \times 2) = \blacksquare$.

Make an array to show 5 groups of 2 times 2.

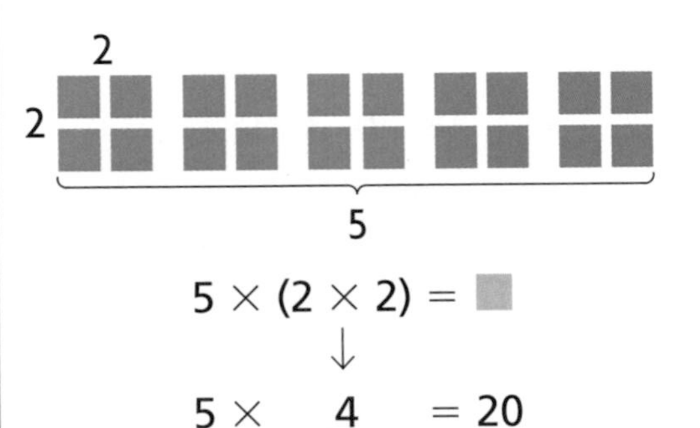

$5 \times (2 \times 2) = \blacksquare$

↓

$5 \times 4 = 20$

Multiply the numbers in parentheses first.

ANOTHER WAY Multiply $(5 \times 2) \times 2 = \blacksquare$.

Make an array to show 2 groups of 5 times 2.

$(5 \times 2) \times 2 = \blacksquare$

↓

$10 \times 2 = 20$

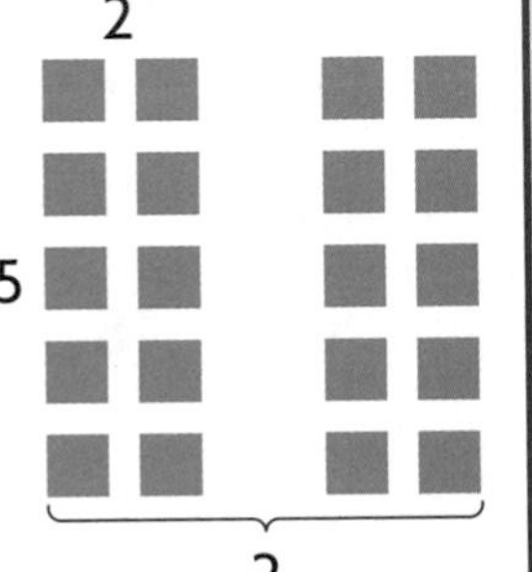

So, there are 20 seats in all on the roller coaster.

The **Associative Property of Multiplication**, or Grouping Property, states that when the grouping of factors is changed, the product remains the same.

- What if you change the order of the factors and multiply $(2 \times 5) \times 2$? What will the product be?

▲ Mr. Freeze Roller Coaster in Arlington, Texas, can go from 0 to 70 miles per hour in 4 seconds!

Guided Practice

1. What number sentence does this array represent? Use tiles. Write another way to group the factors.

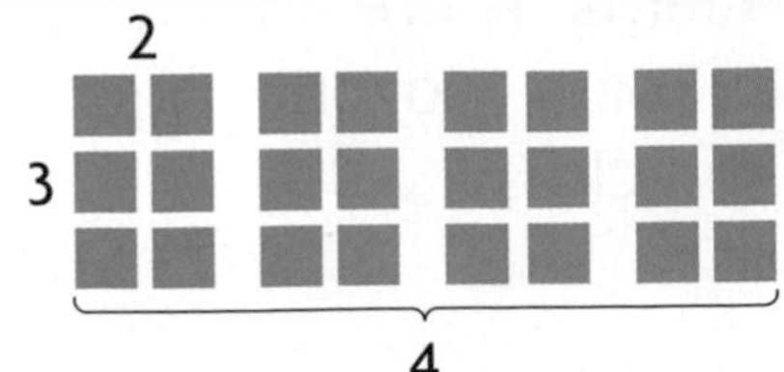

Find the product. Write another way to group the factors.

2. $(2 \times 1) \times 7$
3. $3 \times (5 \times 2)$
4. $4 \times (3 \times 3)$
5. $(3 \times 2) \times 6$

6. TALK Math Heidi multiplies $(3 \times 2) \times 5$, and Jesse multiplies $3 \times (2 \times 5)$. Will they get the same product? **Explain.**

Independent Practice and Problem Solving

Find the product. Write another way to group the factors.

7. $(5 \times 2) \times 2$
8. $8 \times (3 \times 2)$
9. $(1 \times 3) \times 2$
10. $(3 \times 2) \times 7$
11. $(6 \times 1) \times 4$
12. $(2 \times 2) \times 7$
13. $9 \times (3 \times 3)$
14. $5 \times (2 \times 4)$

Use parentheses. Find the product.

15. $3 \times 1 \times 9$
16. $1 \times 3 \times 5$
17. $4 \times 2 \times 6$
18. $2 \times 3 \times 6$

Find the missing factor.

19. $(2 \times ■) \times 7 = 28$
20. $6 \times (5 \times ■) = 30$
21. $■ \times (3 \times 2) = 54$

USE DATA For 22–23, use the graph.

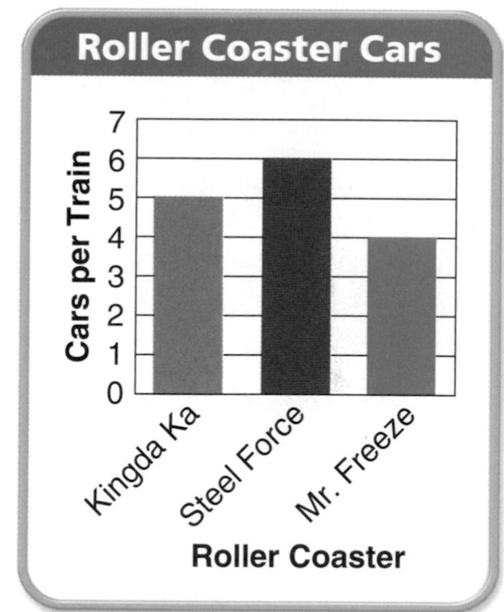

22. Each car on Steel Force has 3 rows with 2 seats in each row. How many seats are on a train?

23. **Reasoning** A Kingda Ka train has 4 seats per car but the last car has only 2 seats. How many people can ride in one Kingda Ka train?

24. WRITE Math **Sense or Nonsense** Ken works 2 days for 4 hours each day and earns \$5 an hour. Len works 5 days for 2 hours each day and earns \$4 an hour. Ken says they both earn the same. Does his statement make sense? **Explain.**

Mixed Review and Test Prep

25. Renee is 3 times as old as Jim. Jim is 5 years old. Write a number sentence to show Renee's age. (p. 218)

26. The product of two factors is 24. One factor is 4. What is the other factor? (p. 258)

27. **Test Prep** Multiply. $3 \times 2 \times 5 = ■$

A 11

B 13

C 16

D 30

Extra Practice on page 266, Set C

LESSON 4

Multiplication Properties

OBJECTIVE: Use the Identity, Zero, Commutative, and Associative Properties of Multiplication to find products.

Quick Review

1. 9×1
2. 0×5
3. 4×2
4. 2×4
5. $(2 \times 3) \times 5$

Vocabulary

Identity Property

Zero Property

Commutative Property

Associative Property

Learn

PROBLEM Mandy knit 3 scarves. She used 1 ball of yarn for each scarf. How many balls of yarn did she use in all?

You can use multiplication properties to help you find products.

Example Multiply 3×1.

The **Identity Property** states that the product of 1 and any number equals that number.

$3 \times 1 = 3$ ■ ■ ■

So, Mandy used 3 balls of yarn.

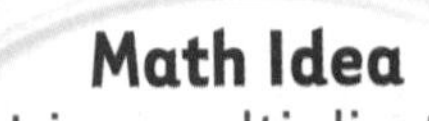

Math Idea
Using multiplication properties makes finding products easier.

More Examples

Zero Property The product of zero and any number equals 0.

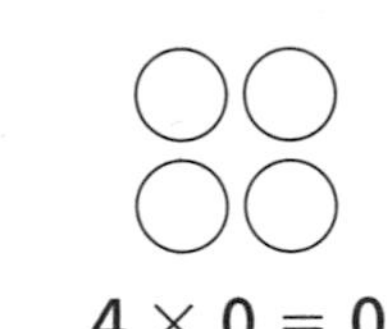

$4 \times 0 = 0$

Commutative Property When you multiply two factors in any order the product is the same.

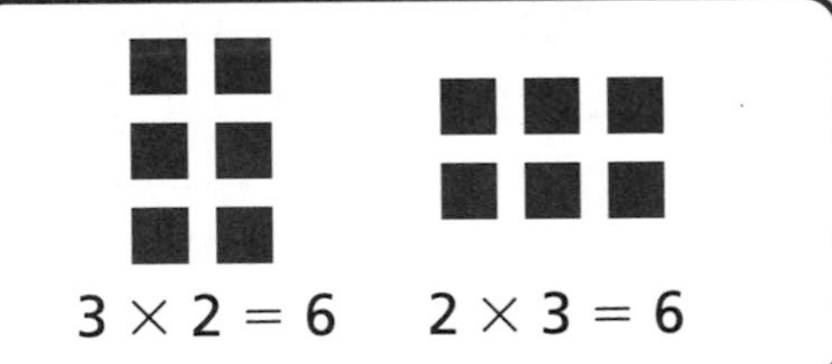

$3 \times 2 = 6$ $2 \times 3 = 6$

Associative Property
When you group factors in different ways the product is the same.

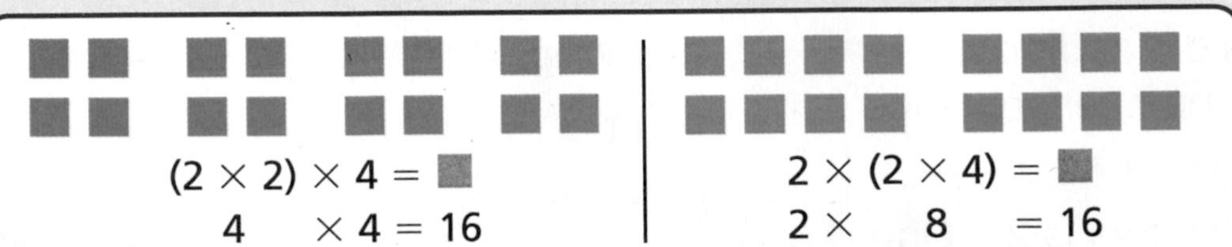

$(2 \times 2) \times 4 = ■$
$4 \times 4 = 16$

$2 \times (2 \times 4) = ■$
$2 \times 8 = 16$

• Which multiplication property can you use to find 85×0?

Guided Practice

1. Which property is shown in this array?

Find the product. Tell which property you could use.

2. 5×1
3. 8×4
4. 0×9
5. $3 \times (3 \times 7)$

6. TALK Math Which costs more—5 balls of yarn for \$3 each or 3 balls of yarn for \$5 each? **Explain** your answer.

Independent Practice and Problem Solving

Find the product. Tell which property you could use.

7. 0×7
8. 8×1
9. 9×2
10. 7×2
11. $(5 \times 2) \times 7$
12. 9×3
13. 6×0
14. $(3 \times 3) \times 8$

Algebra Find the missing factor.

15. $5 \times \blacksquare = 6 \times 5$
16. $3 \times (2 \times 4) = (\blacksquare \times 2) \times 4$
17. $\blacksquare \times 3 = 3 \times 9$

USE DATA For 18–19 and 21, use the pictograph.

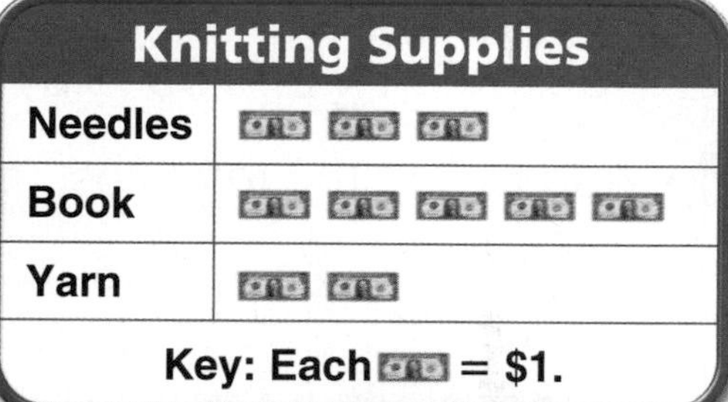

Knitting Supplies	
Needles	💵 💵 💵
Book	💵 💵 💵 💵 💵
Yarn	💵 💵
Key: Each 💵 = \$1.	

18. Amy bought 3 balls of yarn. How much did she spend?

19. Katie bought one pack of needles, a knitting book, and 2 balls of yarn. What was the total cost?

20. **Reasoning** What is the missing number? **Explain** your answer.

$$\blacksquare \times 0 = 0$$

21. WRITE Math Sandy bought 8 balls of yarn. **Explain** how you can use the Commutative Property to find the cost.

Mixed Review and Test Prep

22. Kevin has 3 packs of baseball cards. Each pack has 9 cards. How many baseball cards does he have? (p. 238)

23. A school's auditorium has 950 seats. There were 843 students who attended an assembly. How many seats were empty? (p. 84)

24. **Test Prep** Which is an example of the Identity Property?

A $5 \times 3 = 3 \times 5$

B $0 \times 6 = 0$

C $7 \times 1 = 7$

D $(8 \times 1) \times 4 = 8 \times (1 \times 4)$

Extra Practice on page 266, Set D

Problem Solving Workshop
Skill: Multistep Problems

OBJECTIVE: Solve problems by using the skill multistep problems.

Use the Skill

PROBLEM The circus is in town! Tickets cost $7 for adults and $5 for children. Mr. Kimble buys 5 tickets for his family. He buys 2 adult tickets and 3 child tickets. How much does it cost for the Kimble family to go to the circus?

Use the tickets to help you solve the problem.

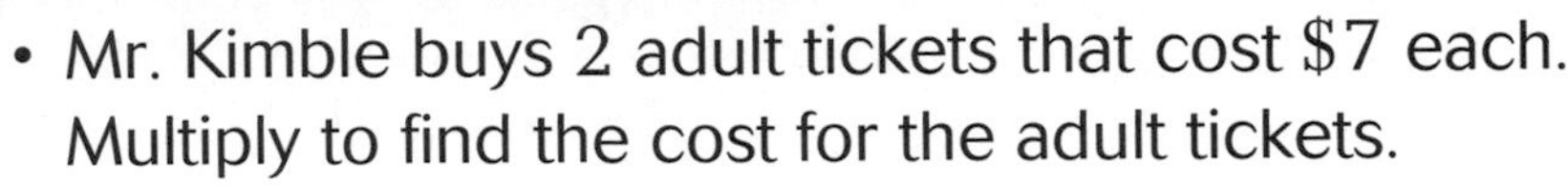

- Mr. Kimble buys 2 adult tickets that cost $7 each. Multiply to find the cost for the adult tickets.

$$2 \times \$7 = \$14$$

- He buys 3 child tickets that cost $5 each. Multiply to find the cost for the child tickets.

$$3 \times \$5 = \$15$$

- Add to find the total cost.

$14	+	$15	=	$29
↑		↑		↑
Cost of adult tickets		Cost of child tickets		Total cost

So, the total cost is $29.

TALK Math

Why did you multiply in this problem?

Think and Discuss

Reading Skill **Visualize Draw a picture to show the problem. Solve the problem. Explain the steps you used.**

a. There are 5 clowns with balloons. Four of the clowns have 8 balloons each. One clown has only 6 balloons. How many balloons in all do the clowns have?

b. Sam has a $20 bill. He buys 4 sheets of circus stickers. Each sheet costs $3. How much money does Sam have left?

Guided Problem Solving

1. Maddie and Sasha buy 2 boxes of popcorn and 4 balloons. The popcorn costs $5 a box. Each balloon costs $2. How much do Maddie and Sasha spend in all?

   Visualize the problem.

   Which operation combines equal amounts?

   Which operation can you use to find the total cost?

   Solve the problem.

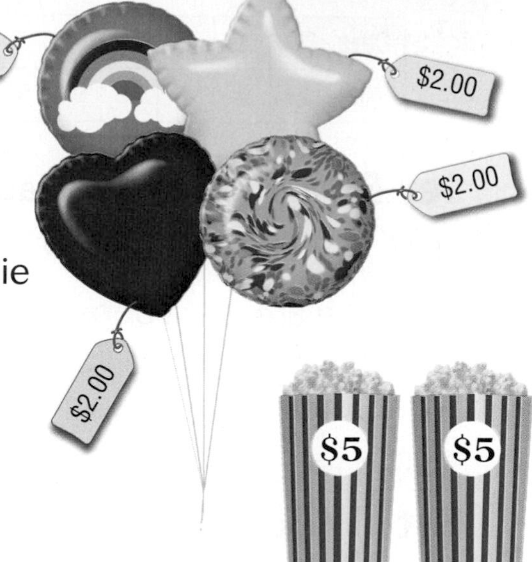

2. **What if** each balloon costs $3? How much do Maddie and Sasha spend in all for balloons and popcorn?
3. The animal trainers give 6 horses apples as rewards. The trainers reward each with 3 apples. If the trainers started with 30 apples, how many apples are left?

Mixed Applications

4. Mr. Brown's four children all have pets. Three of his children have 2 hamsters each. One child has 3 goldfish. How many pets in all do Mr. Brown's children have?
5. Jodi is saving money to buy a new bike. The bike costs $127. She has saved $75. How much more does Jodi need to buy the bike?

USE DATA For 6–8 use the menu.

6. Mr. Werner ordered turkey on rye, a salad, and juice. He paid with a $20 bill. How much change did he get back?
7. The baseball team went to David's Deli after the game. Each player ordered a hamburger and milk. There are 9 players on the team. What was the total cost of the team's order?
8. WRITE Math Mrs. Quigley bought twice as many apples as bananas. She bought 4 bananas. How much did Mrs. Quigley spend on fruit? **Explain** how you got your answer.

David's Deli

Hot Roast Beef Sandwich	**$8**
Turkey on Rye	**$6**
Hamburger	**$4**
Macaroni and Cheese	**$5**
Salad	**$2**
Fruit per piece banana, apple, orange	**$1**
Juice	**$3**
Milk	**$2**

Extra Practice

Set A **Write a rule for each table. Then copy and complete the table.** (pp. 256–257)

1.

Cars	1	2	3	4	5
Wheels	4	8	■	■	■

2.

Weeks	3	4	5	6	7
Days	21	28	■	■	■

Set B **Find the missing factor.** (pp. 258–259)

1. $3 \times ■ = 21$
2. $b \times 5 = 35$
3. $a \times 3 = 30$
4. $5 \times ■ = 25$
5. There are 18 scoops of ice cream. If there are 6 bowls, how many scoops will go in each bowl?
6. There are 32 children and 8 slides on the playground. If the students are divided evenly into groups, how many can play on each slide?

Set C **Find the product. Write another way to group the factors.** (pp. 260–261)

1. $(2 \times 2) \times 4 = ■$
2. $(1 \times 3) \times 3 = ■$
3. $(5 \times 2) \times 3 = ■$
4. $8 \times (1 \times 2) = ■$

Use parentheses. Find the product.

5. $3 \times 3 \times 1 = ■$
6. $2 \times 4 \times 5 = ■$
7. $1 \times 7 \times 4 = ■$
8. $2 \times 2 \times 2 = ■$
9. For Arbor Day, Nora wants to plant 3 groups of 3 trees in 4 different parks. How many trees in all will she plant?
10. Nora's friend Dion plants 2 groups of 4 trees in 7 different parks. How many trees will he plant?

Find the missing factor.

11. $(1 \times ■) \times 2 = 8$
12. $4 \times (2 \times ■) = 16$
13. $■ \times (5 \times 2) = 80$

Set D **Find the product. Tell which property you used.** (pp. 262–263)

1. $(2 \times 1) \times 5$
2. $(3 \times 3) \times 5$
3. 8×3
4. 6×1

Find the missing factor.

5. $2 \times ■ = 10 \times 1$
6. $(2 \times 2) \times ■ = 6 \times 2$
7. $0 \times 7 = 7 \times ■$
8. $7 \times ■ = 5 \times 7$
9. $(4 \times ■) \times 3 = 4 \times 6$
10. $■ \times 9 = 9$

CD ROM **Technology**
Use Harcourt Mega Math, Ice Station Exploration, *Arctic Algebra,* Level C.

TECHNOLOGY CONNECTION

Calculator: Multiplication Facts

Use a Calculator for Multiplication

Eleanor is making a food mix for her hamsters. She wants equal numbers of sunflower seeds, corn kernels, peanuts, round pellets, and flat pellets. If she uses 12 of each item, how many items will be in the mix?

Write a number sentence for the word problem.

$5 \times 12 = ■$

Use a calculator to solve.

So, Eleanor will use 60 items in the food mix.

Try It

Use a calculator to multiply.

1. $11 \times 7 = ■$
2. $8 \times 4 = ■$
3. $12 \times 6 = ■$
4. $7 \times 4 = ■$
5. $8 \times 5 = ■$
6. $12 \times 8 = ■$
7. $10 \times 11 = ■$
8. $9 \times 4 = ■$
9. $3 \times 12 = ■$
10. $7 \times 3 = ■$
11. $6 \times 9 = ■$
12. $2 \times 11 = ■$
13. Ferris went bird watching 7 times in May. On each trip, he wrote about 9 new bird sightings in his journal. How many new birds did he see in May?
14. Carter collects old coins. He has 6 dimes, 6 quarters, and 6 half dollars. How many coins does he have in all? Write a number sentence, and then use a calculator to multiply.
15. Maria has 12 pennies, 12 nickels, 12 dimes, and 12 silver dollars in her wallet. How many coins does she have in all? Write a number sentence, and then use a calculator to multiply.
16. **Explore More** Yvette has invited 8 friends to her party. She plans to give each friend 4 party favors. She has 35 favors in all. How many will she have left over? **Explain.**

MATH POWER

Multiplication Table Parts

Little Pieces

Jake's baby sister tore his multiplication table into little pieces. Where in the table does this piece belong?

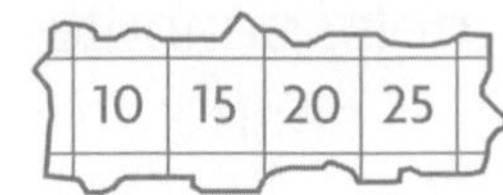

Example

Step 1 Find the pattern.
Five is added to each number.

Step 2 Describe the pattern using multiplication.
The numbers 10, 15, 20, and 25 are all multiples of 5.

Step 3 Look at the first and last numbers.

$10 = \mathbf{2} \times 5$

$25 = \mathbf{5} \times 5$

So, this piece is from row 5 between columns 2 and 5.

X	0	1	2	3	4	5	6	7	8	9
0										
1										
2										
3										
4										
5			10	15	20	25				
6										
7										
8										
9										

Try It

Below are parts of a multiplication table. In which row or column is each part found?

1. 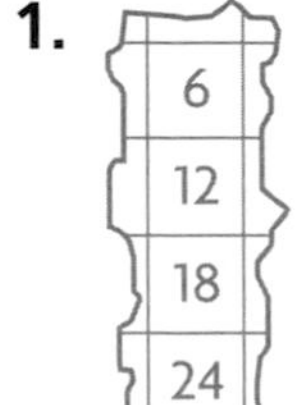

2. 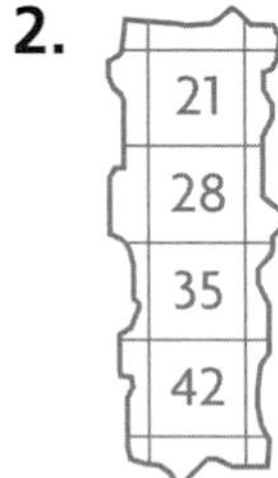

3. 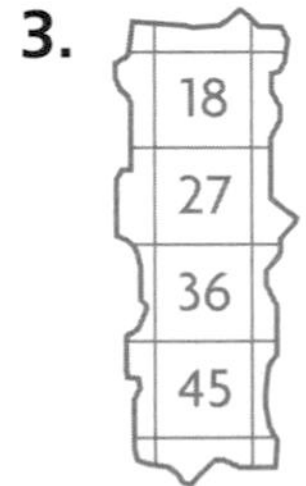

4. 

5. 

6. WRITE Math In what part of the table is this piece found? **Explain.**

Chapter 10 Review/Test

Check Vocabulary and Concepts

Choose the best term from the box.

VOCABULARY
Associative Property of Multiplication
Zero Property
Identity Property
variable

1. A _?_ is a letter or symbol that stands for an unknown number. IL 6.3.11 (p. 258)
2. The _?_ states that the product of 1 and any number equals that number. IL 6.3.13 (p. 262)
3. The _?_ states that when the grouping of factors is changed, the product remains the same. IL 6.3.11 (p. 260)

Check Skills

Find the missing factor. IL 6.3.11 (pp. 258–259)

4. $7 \times a = 28$
5. $\blacksquare \times 5 = 45$
6. $6 \times \blacksquare = 30$
7. $d \times 3 = 9$
8. $8 \times \blacksquare = 64$
9. $\blacksquare \times 4 = 20$
10. $g \times 10 = 40$
11. $9 \times b = 27$

Find the product. IL 6.3.11 (pp. 260–261)

12. $3 \times (5 \times 2) = \blacksquare$
13. $(2 \times 4) \times 8 = \blacksquare$
14. $(1 \times 9) \times 5 = \blacksquare$
15. $6 \times (3 \times 3) = \blacksquare$
16. $7 \times (2 \times 2) = \blacksquare$
17. $(4 \times 2) \times 3 = \blacksquare$

Find the missing factor. IL 6.3.11 (pp. 262–263)

18. $3 \times (3 \times \blacksquare) = 27$
19. $\blacksquare \times (4 \times 2) = 40$
20. $5 \times (\blacksquare \times 10) = 50$
21. $3 \times 4 = \blacksquare \times 2$
22. $\blacksquare \times 5 = 3 \times 10$
23. $6 \times \blacksquare = 9 \times 2$

Check Problem Solving

Solve. IL 8.3.05 (pp. 264–265)

24. Michelle bought 2 necklaces for \$3 each and 3 rings for \$4 each. How much money did Michelle spend in all?
25. **WRITE Math** Rick put 5 baseball cards on each of 2 pages, and 8 cards on each of 4 pages. How many baseball cards did he put in the book altogether? **Explain** how you solved the problem.

Technology Use *Online Assessment.*

ILLINOIS Unit Review/Test
Chapters 8–10

Multiple Choice

1. There are 9 teams in a gymnastics tournament. There are 4 people on each team. How many people are in the tournament altogether? IL 6.3.11 (p. 238)

   A 35 C 45
   B 36 D 46

2. There are 4 students in the library. Each student checks out 5 books. Which addition sentence shows a way to find the number of books they checked out altogether? IL 6.3.04 (p. 204)

   A $4 + 5 = 9$
   B $4 + 4 + 4 + 4 = 16$
   C $5 + 5 + 5 + 5 = 20$
   D $5 + 5 + 5 + 5 + 5 = 25$

3. Aidan and David are going to the beach at Rock Cut State Park. Before they go, they buy a beach ball and 4 sand toys. Each sand toy costs \$2.00. They spend \$12.00 in all. Which shows how much the beach ball costs? IL 8.3.05 (p. 264)

   A \$4.00
   B \$6.00
   C \$10.00
   D \$14.00

4. Trisha worked 2 hours each day for 3 days. She earned \$7 for each hour she worked. How much money did Trisha earn in all? IL 6.3.11 (p. 260)

   A \$6 C \$36
   B \$21 D \$42

5. Danshay made some sandwiches to bring on a picnic. She put 3 slices of cheese on each sandwich. She used 24 slices of cheese in all. Which shows the number of sandwiches Danshay made? IL 8.3.05 (p. 220)

   A 3 C 8
   B 6 D 12

6. Karsten has some bunches of bananas. She wrote this addition sentence to find out how many bananas she has in all. Which multiplication sentence could Karsten use to help solve the problem? IL 6.3.04 (p. 204)

   $$6 + 6 + 6 = \blacksquare$$

   A $6 \times 6 = 36$
   B $6 \times 3 = 18$
   C $3 \times 3 = 9$
   D $2 \times 9 = 18$

GO ONLINE **Technology** Use *Online Assessment.*

7. Allison has 7 carrot sticks in her lunch. Sam has 0 carrot sticks in his lunch. How many carrot sticks do Allison and Sam have together?
IL 6.3.13 (p. 76)

A 0 **C** 7
B 1 **D** 8

8. Olivia bought a sandwich for $2.79 and a drink for $1.49. How much money did Olivia spend? IL 6.3.10 (p. 122)

A $4.28 **C** $3.28
B $4.18 **D** $3.18

9. In 2003, the population of Bloomington, IL, was 68,507. What is the value of the 6 in 68,507?
IL 6.3.01 (p. 10)

A 60
B 600
C 6,000
D 60,000

10. Which shows a way to write the time? IL 7.3.02 (p. 124)

A quarter past six
B five thirty
C fifteen minutes before six
D four forty-five

Short Response

11. Juan went to stay with his grandparents. He left at 10:00 A.M. on August 3. He returned home at 2:00 P.M. on August 5. How long was Juan away from home?
IL 7.3.01 (p. 132)

August

Sun	Mon	Tue	Wed	Thu	Fri	Sat
			1	2	3	4
5	6	7	8	9	10	11
12	13	14	15	16	17	18
19	20	21	22	23	24	25
26	27	28	29	30	31	

12. Jaden went on a 7-day camping trip. He hiked 2 miles each day. How many total miles did Jaden hike?
IL 6.3.11 (p. 242)

Extended Response WRITE Math

13. Tara went on 2 biking trips with her family. They biked 8 miles each day for 5 days on each trip. Use repeated addition and a multiplication sentence to find how many miles they biked in all.
IL 6.3.04; 6.3.11 (p. 242)

14. **Explain** all of the different ways that you can show the product 16 using arrays of counters. IL 6.3.11 (p. 236)

THE WORLD ALMANAC FOR KIDS

All About Animals

Strange Animal Parts

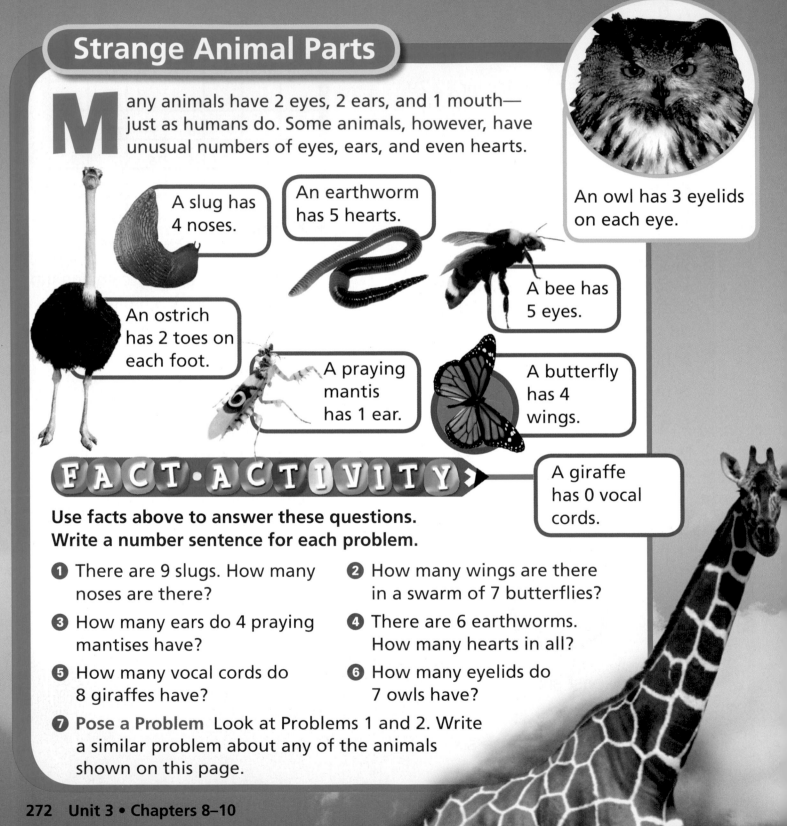

Many animals have 2 eyes, 2 ears, and 1 mouth—just as humans do. Some animals, however, have unusual numbers of eyes, ears, and even hearts.

An owl has 3 eyelids on each eye.

A slug has 4 noses.

An earthworm has 5 hearts.

A bee has 5 eyes.

An ostrich has 2 toes on each foot.

A praying mantis has 1 ear.

A butterfly has 4 wings.

A giraffe has 0 vocal cords.

FACT·ACTIVITY

Use facts above to answer these questions. Write a number sentence for each problem.

1. There are 9 slugs. How many noses are there?
2. How many wings are there in a swarm of 7 butterflies?
3. How many ears do 4 praying mantises have?
4. There are 6 earthworms. How many hearts in all?
5. How many vocal cords do 8 giraffes have?
6. How many eyelids do 7 owls have?
7. **Pose a Problem** Look at Problems 1 and 2. Write a similar problem about any of the animals shown on this page.

Names of Some Animal Groups

army of frogs
band of gorillas
pack of wolves
kindle of kittens
pod of whales
pride of lions
troop of monkeys

Problem Solving

Strange Names

Have you ever seen a *gaggle* fly overhead or a *school* in the water? *Gaggle* and *school* are strange names for groups of animals: a *gaggle* of geese, a *school* of fish. You might shiver from fright if you saw some sharks in the water, but did you know that a group of sharks is called a *shiver*?

FACT · ACTIVITY

Write multiplication sentences to solve.

1. A kitten has 4 paws. How many paws are in a kindle of 8 kittens?
2. A goose has 2 wings. How many wings are in a gaggle of 9 geese?
3. Design an animal that has an unusual number of parts. Think about the number of legs, tails, wings, eyes, noses, ears, or other parts that your animal has.
   - Draw your animal, and label its parts.
   - Copy the chart. You may include more parts. Remember, you may choose 0 for some parts.
   - Complete the table to show how many parts there are in 1, 2, and 3 animals.
   - Suppose there are 10 of your animal in a group. Make up a name for the group.

My Animal

Part	Number of parts		
	In 1 animal	In 2 animals	In 3 animals
eyes			
legs			
tails			
wings			
noses			
ears			

UNIT

4 Division Concepts and Facts

Math on Location

with
Chapter Projects

1

Each batch of dough is cut into the same number of triangular shapes.

2

The croissants are rolled and placed in rows on baking trays to form an array.

3

The baker divides 18 croissants onto 3 trays to put in the oven to bake.

VOCABULARY POWER

TALK Math

What math do you see in the **Math on Location** photographs? How can you use division to tell how many croissants are in each row?

READ Math

REVIEW VOCABULARY You learned the words below when you learned about division in grade 2. How do these words relate to **Math on Location**?

division the operation that separates objects into equal groups

equal shares equal groups of items

WRITE Math

Copy and complete a Semantic Map like the one below. Use Math on Location and what you know about division to fill in the blanks.

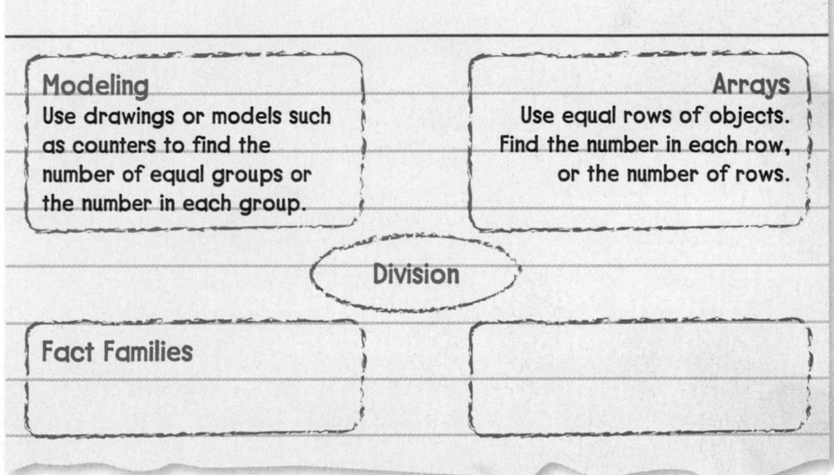

Modeling
Use drawings or models such as counters to find the number of equal groups or the number in each group.
Arrays
Use equal rows of objects. Find the number in each row, or the number of rows.
Division
Fact Families

Technology
Multimedia Math Glossary link at
www.harcourtschool.com/hspmath

CHAPTER 11

Understand Division

FAST FACT

Skateboarding was once called "sidewalk surfing." The first skateboards were made by attaching roller skate wheels to a piece of wood.

Investigate

A skateboard has 4 wheels. Suppose you want to make your own skateboards. Choose a wheel color from the table. Tell how many skateboards you could make using only that wheel color.

Wheels in Skate Shop

Color	Number of Wheels
Red	24
White	40
Black	12
Green	36
Blue	28

Technology
Student pages are available in the Student eBook.

Show What You Know

Check your understanding of important skills needed for success in Chapter 11.

▶ Counting Equal Groups

Complete.

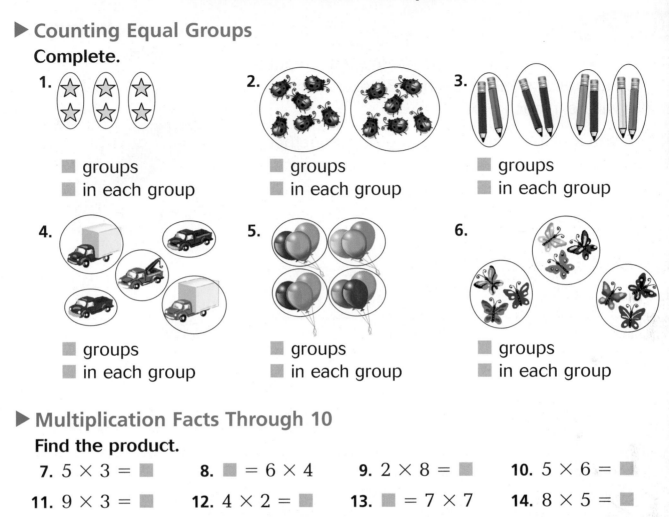

1. 

■ groups
■ in each group

2. 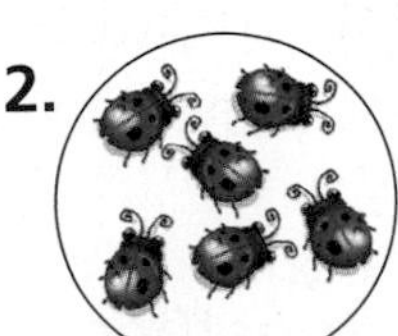

■ groups
■ in each group

3. 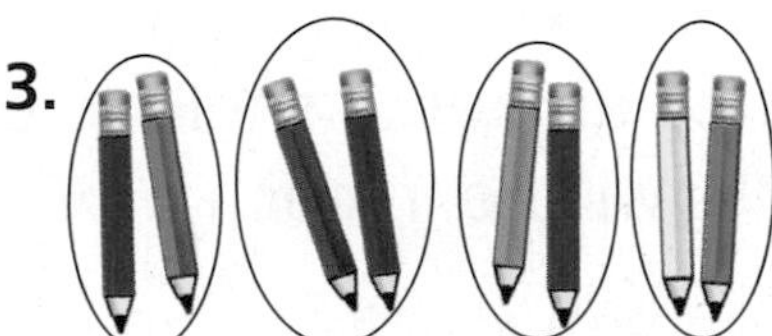

■ groups
■ in each group

4. 

■ groups
■ in each group

5. 

■ groups
■ in each group

6. 

■ groups
■ in each group

▶ Multiplication Facts Through 10

Find the product.

7. $5 \times 3 = $ ■ **8.** ■ $= 6 \times 4$ **9.** $2 \times 8 = $ ■ **10.** $5 \times 6 = $ ■

11. $9 \times 3 = $ ■ **12.** $4 \times 2 = $ ■ **13.** ■ $= 7 \times 7$ **14.** $8 \times 5 = $ ■

VOCABULARY POWER

CHAPTER VOCABULARY

array
divide
dividend
divisor
fact family
quotient

WARM-UP WORDS

divide To separate into equal groups; the opposite operation of multiplication

fact family A set of related addition and subtraction, or multiplication and division, number sentences

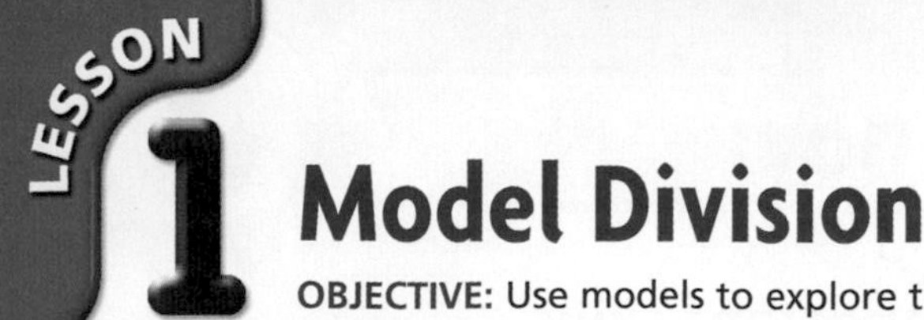

Model Division

OBJECTIVE: Use models to explore the meaning of division.

Quick Review

1. 2 × 3
2. 5 × 7
3. 4 × 5
4. 3 × 6
5. 7 × 4

Vocabulary

divide

Learn

PROBLEM William has 12 shells. He wants to put the same number of shells in each of 3 boxes. How many shells will be in each box?

When you multiply, you put equal groups together. When you **divide**, you separate into equal groups.

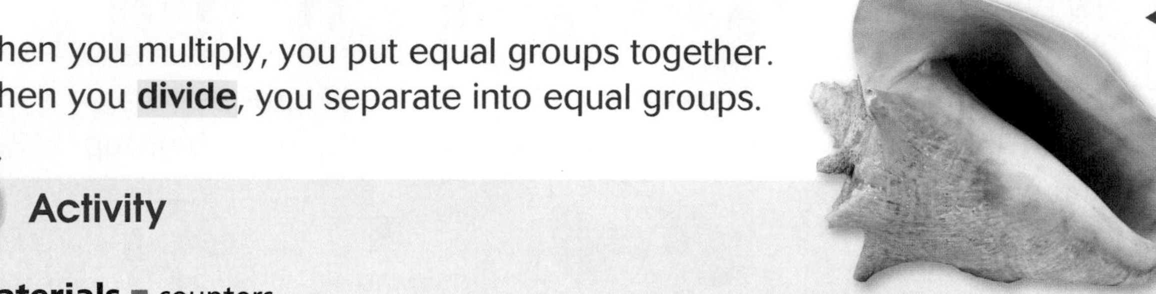

◀ A pink conch shell can be as long as 1 foot!

HANDS ON

Activity

Materials ■ counters

Example 1 You can divide to find the number in each group.

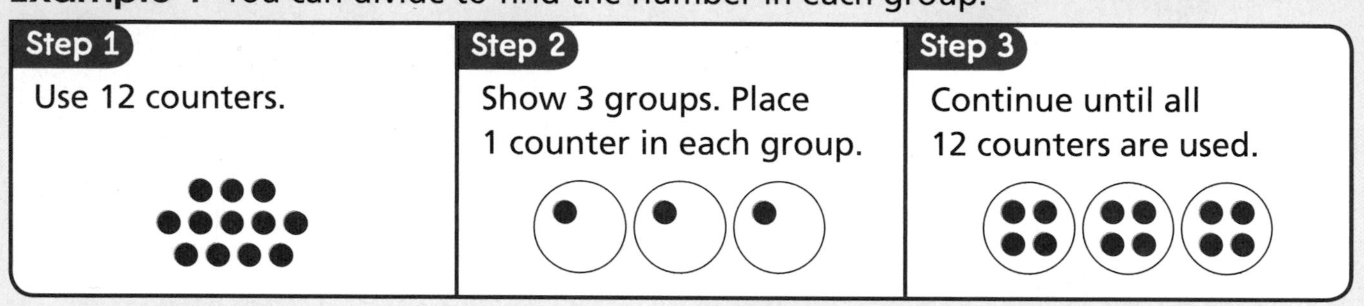

Step 1
Use 12 counters.
Step 2
Show 3 groups. Place 1 counter in each group.
Step 3
Continue until all 12 counters are used.

So, there will be 4 shells in each box.

William has decided that he wants to put his 12 shells in groups of 3. How many boxes will he need for his shells?

Example 2 You can divide to find the number of equal groups.

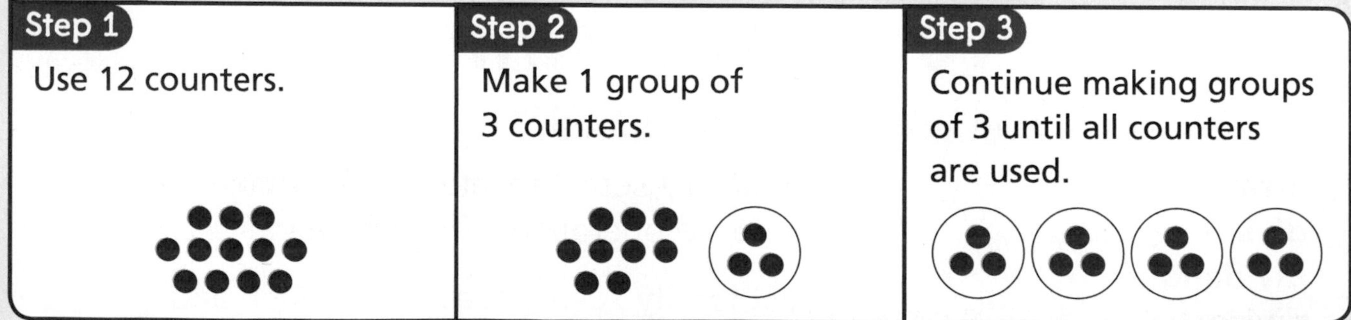

Step 1
Use 12 counters.
Step 2
Make 1 group of 3 counters.
Step 3
Continue making groups of 3 until all counters are used.

So, William will need 4 boxes for his shells.

Guided Practice

1. Jon has 8 counters. He wants to put 2 in each group. Draw a picture to show the groups.

Copy and complete the table. Use counters to help.

	Counters	Number of Equal Groups	Number in Each Group
✓2.	10	2	■
✓3.	24	■	4

4. TALK Math **Explain** two ways you could divide 18 counters into equal groups. Draw a picture to show each way.

Independent Practice and Problem Solving

Copy and complete the table. Use counters to help.

	Counters	Number of Equal Groups	Number in Each Group
5.	14	7	■
6.	21	■	3
7.	20	5	■

8. Jackie has 28 stamps. She put an equal number of her stamps on each of 4 pages. How many stamps are on each page?

9. Joe has 25 stamps and Martha has 15 stamps. They put their stamps in the same book. Each page has 5 stamps. How many pages did they fill?

10. WRITE Math Elijah has 16 stamps. He put 4 stamps each on 4 pages. **Explain** another way to arrange his stamps with an equal number of stamps on each page.

Mixed Review and Test Prep

11. What is the missing factor? (p. 258)

$$6 \times ■ = 48$$

12. Lee has 3,943 coins. What is the value of the 9 in 3,943? (p. 10)

13. **Test Prep** Zana has 9 rocks. She put 3 rocks in each bag. How many bags did she use in all?

A 27
B 12
C 6
D 3

Extra Practice on page 294, Set A

LESSON 2

Relate Division and Subtraction

OBJECTIVE: Relate division to repeated subtraction.

Quick Review

How many are there in all?

1. 2 groups of 5
2. 5 groups of 3
3. 3 groups of 4
4. 4 groups of 2
5. 3 groups of 3

Learn

PROBLEM Sarah and Mandy take a total of 12 newspapers to school for the recycling program. Each girl takes the same number. How many newspapers does each girl take?

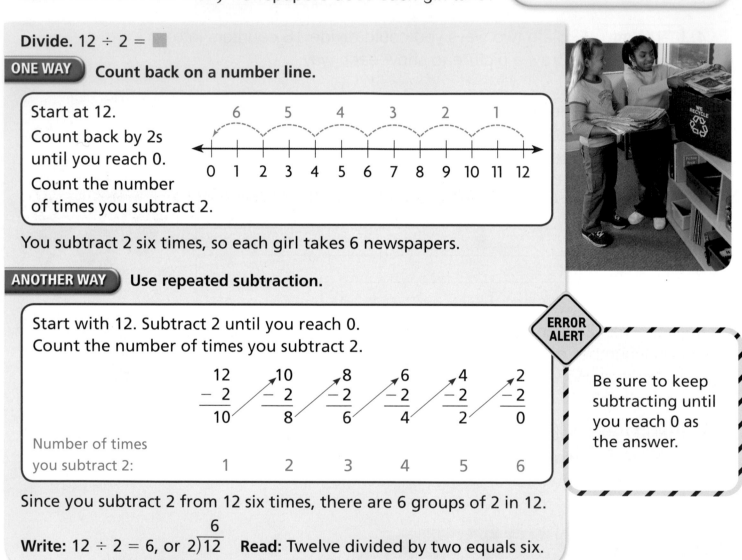

Divide. $12 \div 2 = ■$

ONE WAY **Count back on a number line.**

Start at 12.
Count back by 2s until you reach 0.
Count the number of times you subtract 2.

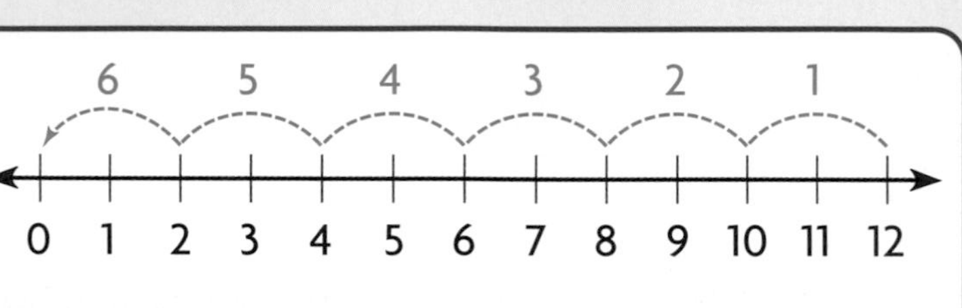

You subtract 2 six times, so each girl takes 6 newspapers.

ANOTHER WAY **Use repeated subtraction.**

Start with 12. Subtract 2 until you reach 0.
Count the number of times you subtract 2.

	$12 - 2 = 10$	$10 - 2 = 8$	$8 - 2 = 6$	$6 - 2 = 4$	$4 - 2 = 2$	$2 - 2 = 0$
Number of times you subtract 2:	1	2	3	4	5	6

ERROR ALERT

Be sure to keep subtracting until you reach 0 as the answer.

Since you subtract 2 from 12 six times, there are 6 groups of 2 in 12.

Write: $12 \div 2 = 6$, or $2\overline{)12}$ with quotient 6 **Read:** Twelve divided by two equals six.

Guided Practice

1. Use the number line to complete the number sentence. $12 \div 4 = ■$

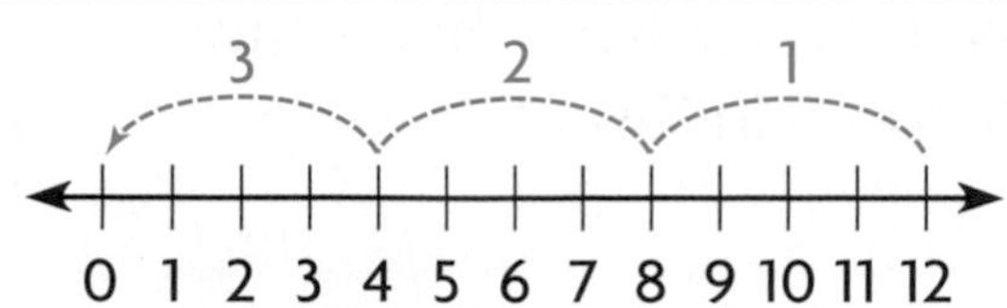

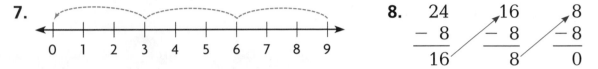

Use a number line or repeated subtraction to solve.

2. $16 \div 4 = $ ■ **3.** $10 \div 5 = $ ■ ✓**4.** $3\overline{)21}$ ✓**5.** $8\overline{)32}$

6. TALK Math **Explain** how you can use subtraction to find $18 \div 3$.

Independent Practice and Problem Solving

Write a division sentence for each.

7.

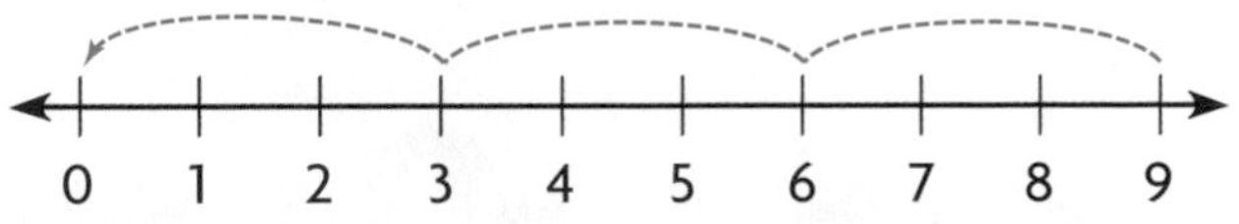

8. $\begin{array}{r} 24 \\ -\ 8 \\ \hline 16 \end{array} \quad \begin{array}{r} 16 \\ -\ 8 \\ \hline 8 \end{array} \quad \begin{array}{r} 8 \\ -\ 8 \\ \hline 0 \end{array}$

Use a number line or repeated subtraction to solve.

9. $14 \div 7 = $ ■ **10.** $35 \div 5 = $ ■ **11.** $27 \div 9 = $ ■ **12.** $20 \div 4 = $ ■

13. $4\overline{)28}$ **14.** $6\overline{)24}$ **15.** $2\overline{)16}$ **16.** $9\overline{)36}$

USE DATA For 17–19, use the graph.

17. Carl put his box tops in 6 equal piles. How many box tops were in each pile?

18. Reasoning Miguel brought an equal number of box tops to school each day for 5 days. Jane also brought an equal number of box tops each day for 5 days. How many box tops did they bring in altogether in 1 day? **Explain.**

19. WRITE Math **What's the Question?** Genna put an equal number of box tops in each of 3 bins. The answer is 5.

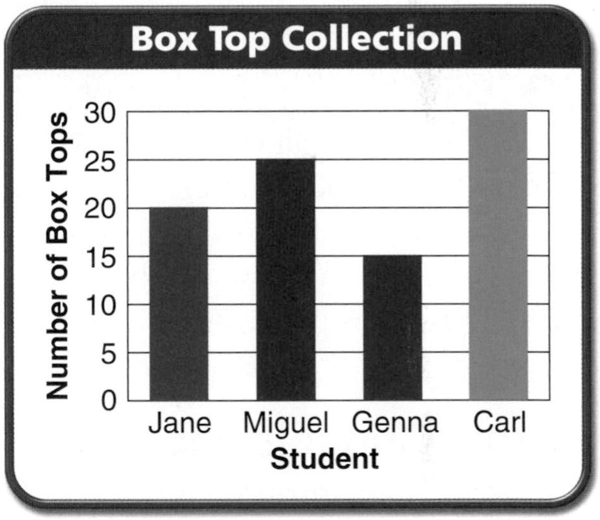

Mixed Review and Test Prep

20. Kara has 3 packs of paintbrushes. Each pack has 8 brushes. How many brushes does Kara have? (p. 236)

21. A figure has 4 vertices and 4 equal sides. What is the figure? (Grade 2)

22. Test Prep Mya collected 7 shells each day. She collected 21 shells in all. For how many days did Mya collect shells?

A 2 days **C** 4 days

B 3 days **D** 6 days

Extra Practice on page 294, Set B

LESSON 3 HANDS ON

Model with Arrays

OBJECTIVE: Model division by using arrays.

Quick Review

1. 3 × 5
2. 5 × 7
3. 5 × 5
4. 4 × 5
5. 5 × 6

Investigate

Materials ■ square tiles

You can use arrays to model division and find equal groups.

A Count out 30 tiles. Make an array to find how many groups of 5 are in 30.

B Make a row of 5 tiles.

C Continue to make rows of 5 tiles until all of the tiles have been used.

Draw Conclusions

1. How many groups of 5 are in 30?
2. Explain how you used the tiles to find the number of groups of 5 in 30.
3. **Application** Tell how to use an array to find how many groups of 6 are in 30.

Connect

You can write a division sentence to show what you did.

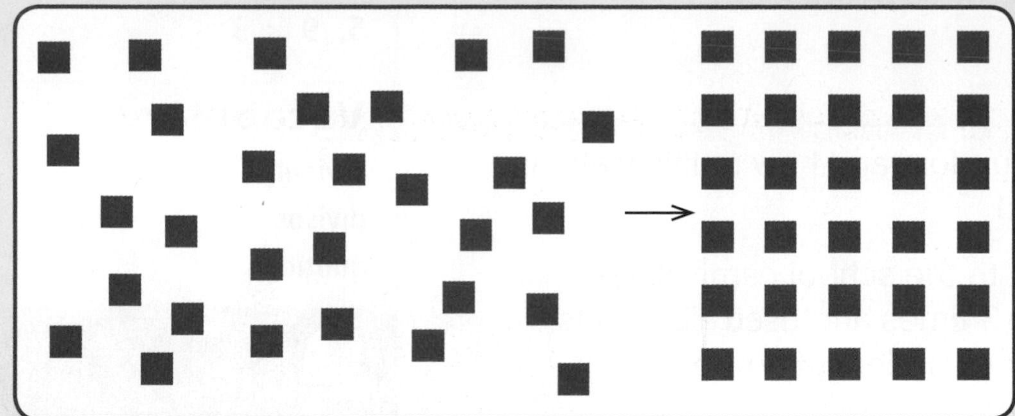

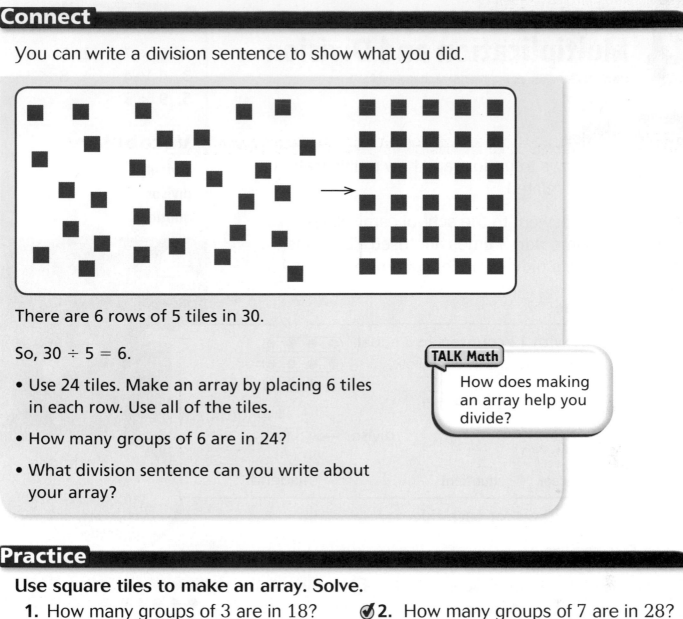

There are 6 rows of 5 tiles in 30.

So, $30 \div 5 = 6$.

- Use 24 tiles. Make an array by placing 6 tiles in each row. Use all of the tiles.
- How many groups of 6 are in 24?
- What division sentence can you write about your array?

TALK Math

How does making an array help you divide?

Practice

Use square tiles to make an array. Solve.

1. How many groups of 3 are in 18?
2. How many groups of 7 are in 28?
3. How many groups of 9 are in 27?
4. How many groups of 8 are in 24?
5. How many groups of 5 are in 20?
6. How many groups of 6 are in 36?

Make an array. Write a division sentence for each one.

7. 16 tiles in 4 groups
8. 21 tiles in 3 groups
9. 24 tiles in 8 groups
10. 14 tiles in 2 groups
11. 25 tiles in 5 groups
12. 12 tiles in 4 groups
13. Reggie made an array with 32 tiles. He placed 8 tiles in each row. How many rows did he make?
14. WRITE Math **Explain** how to use an array to find $18 \div 6$.

LESSON 4

ALGEBRA
Multiplication and Division

OBJECTIVE: Relate multiplication and division.

Quick Review

1. 2×7 **2.** 5×6
3. 4×4 **4.** 8×1
5. 9×3

Vocabulary

dividend
divisor
quotient

Learn

You can use arrays to understand how multiplication and division are related.

PROBLEM Mark went to the school carnival. He went on the same ride 3 times and used 12 tickets. How many tickets did he use for each ride?

Example Divide. $12 \div 3 = \blacksquare$

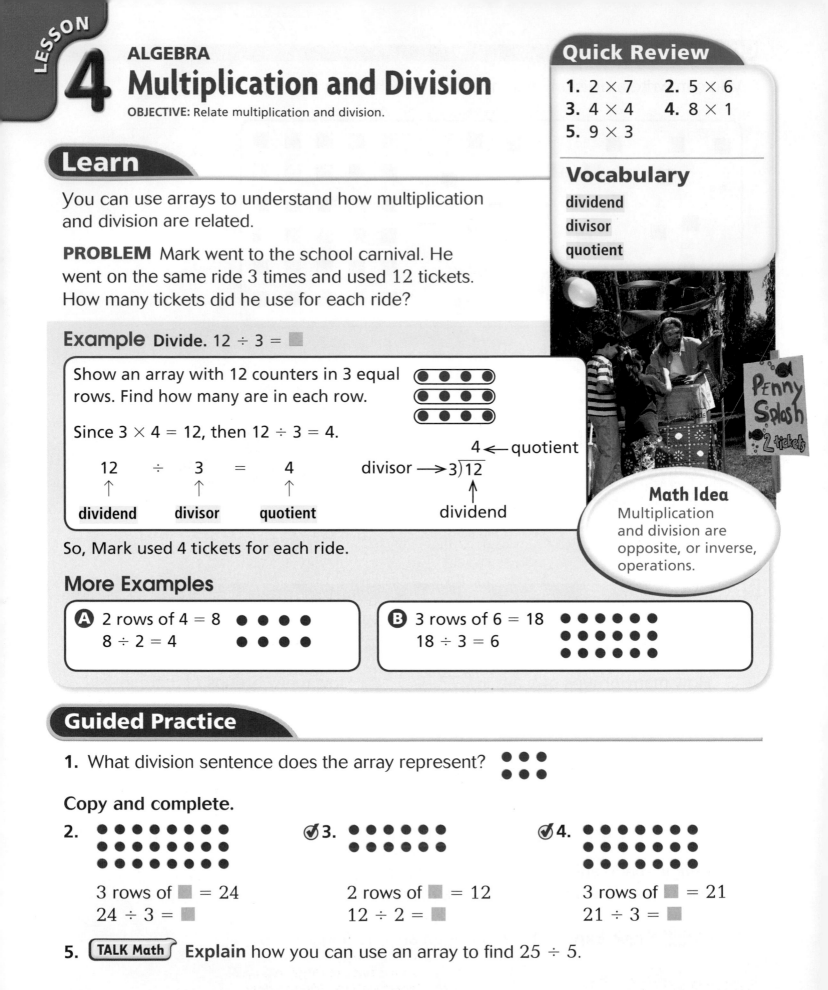

Show an array with 12 counters in 3 equal rows. Find how many are in each row.

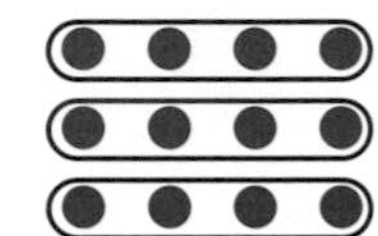

Since $3 \times 4 = 12$, then $12 \div 3 = 4$.

12	÷	3	=	4
↑		↑		↑
dividend		**divisor**		**quotient**

$$\text{divisor} \rightarrow 3\overline{)12} \quad 4 \leftarrow \text{quotient}, \quad 12 \uparrow \text{dividend}$$

So, Mark used 4 tickets for each ride.

Math Idea
Multiplication and division are opposite, or inverse, operations.

More Examples

A 2 rows of 4 = 8
$8 \div 2 = 4$

B 3 rows of 6 = 18
$18 \div 3 = 6$

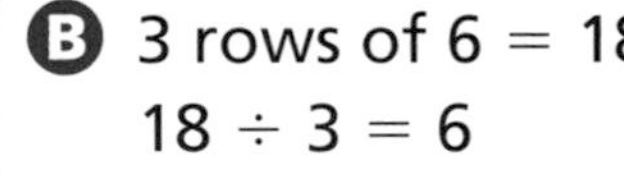

Guided Practice

1. What division sentence does the array represent?

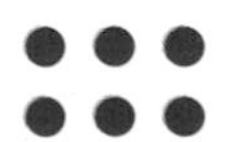

Copy and complete.

2.

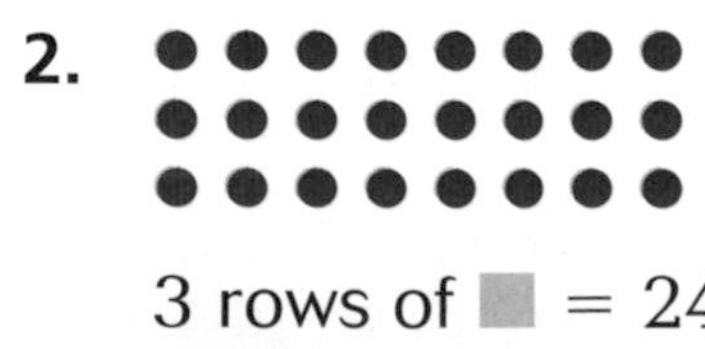

3 rows of $\blacksquare$ = 24
$24 \div 3 = \blacksquare$

✓3.

2 rows of $\blacksquare$ = 12
$12 \div 2 = \blacksquare$

✓4.

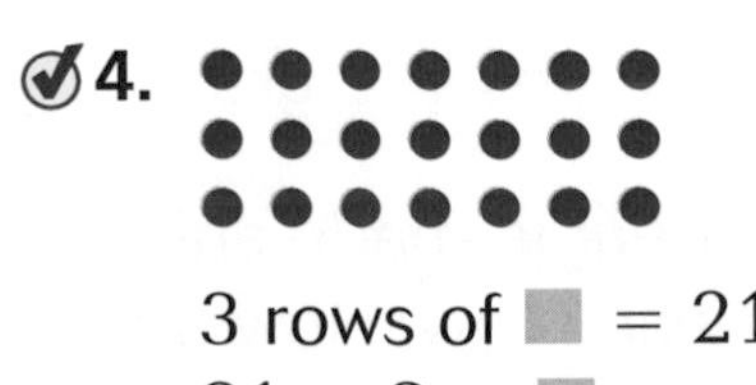

3 rows of $\blacksquare$ = 21
$21 \div 3 = \blacksquare$

5. TALK Math **Explain** how you can use an array to find $25 \div 5$.

Independent Practice and Problem Solving

Copy and complete.

6. ● ● ● ●
● ● ● ●
● ● ● ●
● ● ● ●

4 rows of $\blacksquare = 16$
$16 \div 4 = \blacksquare$

7. ● ● ● ● ●
● ● ● ● ●
● ● ● ● ●

3 rows of $\blacksquare = 15$
$15 \div 3 = \blacksquare$

8. 

4 rows of $\blacksquare = 28$
$28 \div 4 = \blacksquare$

Complete each number sentence. Draw an array to help.

9. $6 \times \blacksquare = 24$ $24 \div 6 = \blacksquare$

10. $5 \times \blacksquare = 35$ $35 \div 5 = \blacksquare$

11. $8 \times \blacksquare = 32$ $32 \div 8 = \blacksquare$

12. $9 \times \blacksquare = 18$ $18 \div 9 = \blacksquare$

Complete.

13. $3 \times 3 = 27 \div \blacksquare$

14. $16 \div 2 = \blacksquare \times 2$

15. $\blacksquare \times 1 = 25 \div 5$

USE DATA For 16–19, use the signs.

16. Jill has 15 tickets. How many times can she ride the Scooter?

17. Philip bought 8 tickets for the Wildcat ride 3 different times. How many times did he ride the Wildcat?

18. **Reasoning** Joe rode the Scooter 3 times, and Kate rode the Crazy Sub 4 times. Who used more tickets? **Explain.**

19. WRITE Math **Sense or Nonsense** Scott has 13 tickets. He says that to ride the Scooter 4 times, he needs more tickets. Is he correct? **Explain.**

Mixed Review and Test Prep

20. What is a possible outcome of using a spinner with 2 red and 2 blue sections? (p. 180)

21. A ticket to the zoo costs $4. How much do 9 tickets cost? (p. 238)

22. **Test Prep** At a game booth, there are 32 prizes in 4 equal rows. How many prizes are in each row?

A 36 **C** 8
B 28 **D** 6

Extra Practice on page 294, Set C

CD ROM **Technology**
Use Harcourt Mega Math, Ice Station Exploration, *Arctic Algebra,* Level E.

LESSON 5
ALGEBRA
Fact Families

OBJECTIVE: Use multiplication and division fact families.

Quick Review

Complete.

1. ■ × 5 = 15
2. 3 × ■ = 15
3. 15 ÷ 5 = ■
4. 5 × ■ = 25
5. 25 ÷ 5 = ■

Vocabulary

fact family

Learn

A **fact family** is a set of related multiplication and division number sentences.

PROBLEM Kim's pack of modeling clay has 2 rows of 5 colors. What is the fact family for 2, 5, and 10?

Activity

Materials ■ square tiles

Step 1

Count the number of rows and the number of colors in each row in the pack of clay.

There are 2 rows with 5 colors in each row.

Step 2

Make an array with 2 rows of 5. Count the total number of tiles.

There are 10 tiles.

Step 3

Write two multiplication sentences and two division sentences that describe the array.

2 × 5 = 10	10 ÷ 5 = 2
5 × 2 = 10	10 ÷ 2 = 5

So, these related number sentences make the fact family for 2, 5, and 10.

Example

The array shows the fact family for 4, 4, and 16.

4 × 4 = 16   16 ÷ 4 = 4

Since both factors are the same, there are only two number sentences in this fact family.

Remember

4 × 4 = 16
factor, factor, product

• Write another set of numbers that has only two number sentences in the fact family for it.

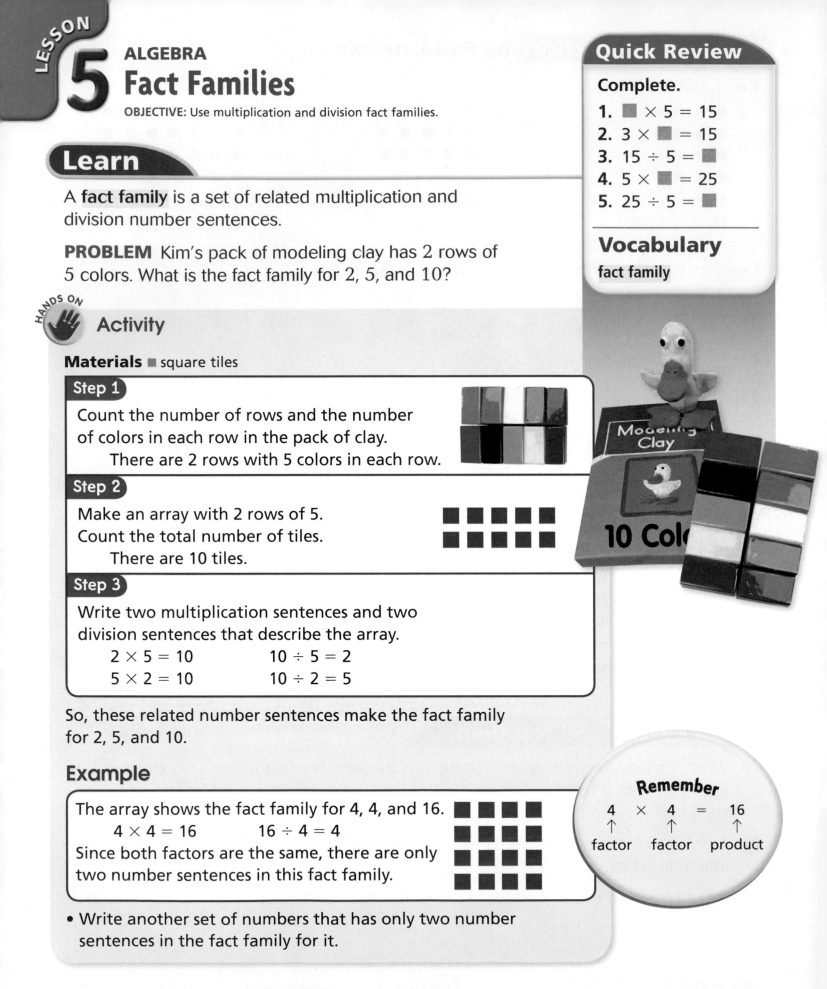

Use a Multiplication Table to Divide

Since division is the opposite of multiplication, you can use a multiplication table to find a quotient or a missing divisor.

Examples

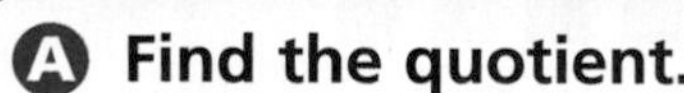

A Find the quotient.

$20 \div 4 = \blacksquare$

Think: $4 \times \blacksquare = 20$

Find the row for the factor 4. Look to the right to find the product 20. Look up to find the missing factor, 5.

$4 \times 5 = 20$
So, $20 \div 4 = 5$.

B Find the missing divisor.

$18 \div \blacksquare = 3$

Think: $\blacksquare \times 3 = 18$

Find the factor 3 in the top row. Look down to find the product 18. Look left to find the missing factor, 6.

$6 \times 3 = 18$
So, $18 \div 6 = 3$.

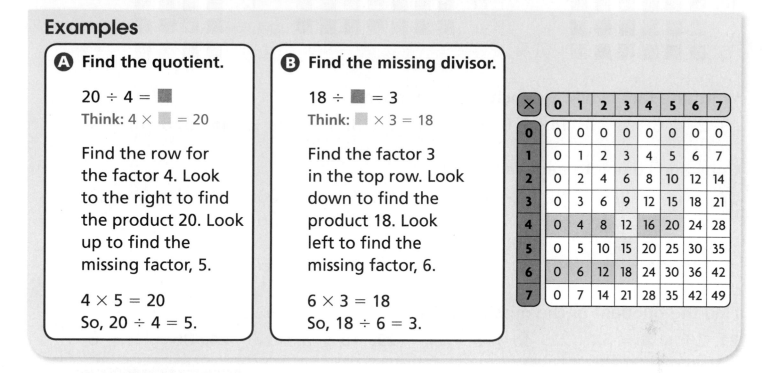

×	0	1	2	3	4	5	6	7
0	0	0	0	0	0	0	0	0
1	0	1	2	3	4	5	6	7
2	0	2	4	6	8	10	12	14
3	0	3	6	9	12	15	18	21
4	0	4	8	12	16	20	24	28
5	0	5	10	15	20	25	30	35
6	0	6	12	18	24	30	36	42
7	0	7	14	21	28	35	42	49

Guided Practice

1. Complete the fact family for this array.

$3 \times 8 = 24$ $\quad$ $24 \div 3 = 8$

Write the fact family for each array.

2. 

3. 

✓4. 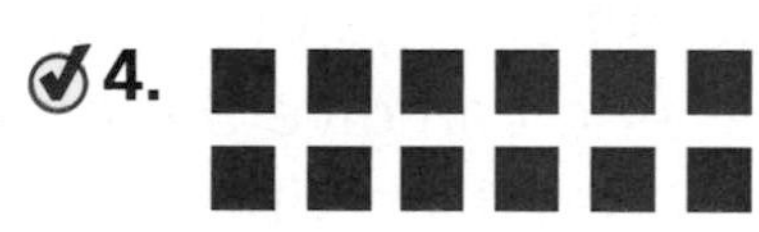

Write the fact family for each set of numbers.

5. 6, 7, 42

6. 2, 3, 6

7. 4, 8, 32

✓8. 5, 5, 25

9. TALK Math **Explain** how you can use a multiplication table to find the missing divisor in $36 \div \blacksquare = 6$.

Independent Practice and Problem Solving

Write the fact family for each array.

10. ■■■■■■ / ■■■■■■ / ■■■■■■

11. ■■■■■■■ / ■■■■■■■

12. ■■■■ / ■■■■ / ■■■■

Write the fact family for each set of numbers.

13. 2, 4, 8 14. 4, 6, 24 15. 3, 3, 9 16. 5, 8, 40

Copy and complete each fact family.

17. $4 \times 7 = 28$
$7 \times ■ = 28$
$28 \div ■ = 4$
$28 \div 4 = ■$

18. $5 \times 6 = ■$
$6 \times ■ = 30$
$30 \div 6 = ■$
$30 \div 5 = ■$

19. $4 \times ■ = 36$
$9 \times ■ = 36$
$36 \div 4 = ■$
$36 \div 9 = ■$

20. $■ \times 9 = 27$
$■ \times 3 = 27$
$■ \div 9 = 3$
$27 \div ■ = 9$

Find the quotient or the missing divisor.

21. $20 \div ■ = 5$ 22. $45 \div 5 = ■$ 23. $15 \div 3 = ■$ 24. $36 \div ■ = 6$

USE DATA For 25–26, use the table.

Clay Supplies

Item	Number in Package
Clay	12 sections
Clay tool set	11 tools
Glitter dough	36 sections

25. Mrs. Lee divides one package of clay and one package of glitter dough equally among 4 students. How many more glitter dough sections does each student have than clay sections?

26. WRITE Math **What's the Error?** Ty has a package of glitter dough. He says he can give 9 friends 5 equal sections. Describe his error.

27. **Pose a Problem** Write a division word problem using $35 \div 5 = 7$. Solve your problem.

Mixed Review and Test Prep

28. What is the missing factor? (p. 258)

$$6 \times ■ = 42$$

29. Jake has 57 pens and 49 pencils. How many more pens than pencils does Jake have? (p. 80)

30. **Test Prep** Which number sentence is not included in the same fact family as $9 \times 4 = 36$?

A $4 \times 9 = 36$
B $36 \div 6 = 6$
C $36 \div 4 = 9$
D $36 \div 9 = 4$

 Extra Practice on page 294, Set D

Justify an Answer

Tamara is making a recipe that calls for 15 teaspoons of milk. She doesn't have a teaspoon measure. She knows that 3 teaspoons equal 1 tablespoon. So, she uses 5 tablespoons of milk. How do you know whether she used the right amount of milk?

Jamal wrote this paragraph to justify Tamara's solution to her problem.

I know that a teaspoon is a smaller unit than a tablespoon. First, I use a teaspoon to fill a tablespoon of water. It takes 3 teaspoons of water to fill 1 tablespoon.

Then, I divide 15 by 3 to find out if 5 tablespoons is the correct amount of milk. I use the fact family for 5, 3, and 15 to check my answer.

$5 \times 3 = 15$ $\quad$ $3 \times 5 = 15$

$15 \div 5 = 3$ $\quad$ $15 \div 3 = 5$

I know that Tamara used the right amount of milk because $3 \times 5 = 15$.

Tips

To justify an answer:

- First, check that the information given in the problem is correct.
- Next, check whether the answer given is correct.
- Last, write a sentence to justify the answer, or explain why it is correct.

Problem Solving Write a paragraph to justify each answer.

1. Tara says, "I can share 12 crackers evenly with 3 friends."
2. Darin says, "I can share 6 sports cards evenly with 2 friends."

Problem Solving Workshop
Strategy: Write a Number Sentence

OBJECTIVE: Solve problems by using the strategy *write a number sentence*.

Learn the Strategy

Writing a number sentence can help you understand how the numbers in a problem are related.

You can write an addition number sentence.

Joe has 14 crayons. He gets 12 more crayons. Now he has 26 crayons.

$14 + 12 = 26$

- 14 ↑ crayons Joe has
- 12 ↑ crayons Joe got
- 26 ↑ crayons Joe has now

You can write a subtraction number sentence.

Kat has 23 shells. She gives 10 shells to her brother. She has 13 shells left.

$23 - 10 = 13$

- 23 ↑ shells Kat has
- 10 ↑ shells Kat gave away
- 13 ↑ shells Kat has left

You can write a multiplication number sentence.

April has 4 boxes of books. Each box has 8 books in it. There are 32 books in all.

$4 \times 8 = 32$

- 4 ↑ boxes April has
- 8 ↑ books in each box
- 32 ↑ books in all

You can write a division number sentence.

Scott has 40 stickers. There are 8 stickers on each sheet. He has 5 sheets of stickers.

$40 \div 8 = 5$

- 40 ↑ stickers Scott has
- 8 ↑ stickers on each sheet
- 5 ↑ sheets of stickers

TALK Math

What question could you ask about each number sentence above?

Use the Strategy

PROBLEM In Michelle's third grade class, the desks are in 4 equal rows. There are 24 desks in all. How many desks are in each row?

Read to Understand

- **Identify the details in the problem.**
- **What information is given?**

Plan

- **What strategy can you use to solve the problem?**

  You can *write a number sentence* to help you solve the problem.

Solve

- **How can you use the strategy to solve the problem?**

  The desks are divided into equal rows.
  This helps you know to use division.
  Write a division sentence. Find the quotient.

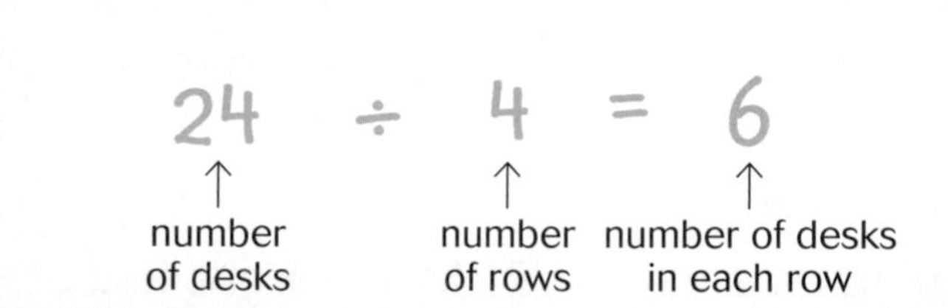

So, there are 6 desks in each row.

Check

- **How can you check your answer?**
- **What other strategy could you use to solve the problem?**

Read to Understand
Plan
Solve
Check

Guided Problem Solving

1. Mrs. Partin gave each student at Jenna's table 5 sheets of paper. She gave out 20 sheets of paper in all. How many students are at Jenna's table?

First, decide what operation to use. The 20 sheets of paper are divided into equal groups.

Then, write the number sentence.

Finally, solve the number sentence.

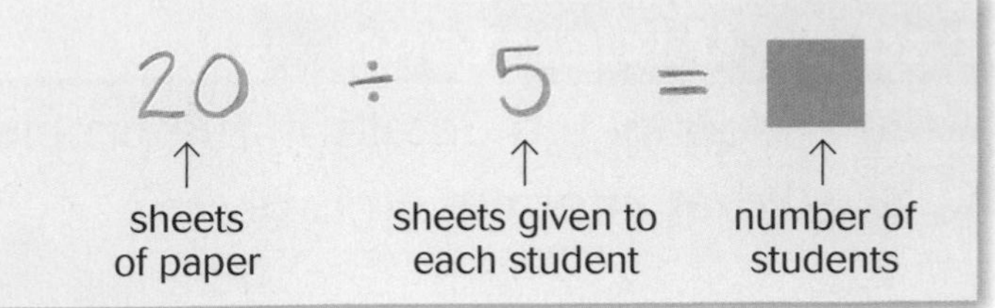

2. **What if** Mrs. Partin gave each student 6 sheets of paper and there were 6 students? How many sheets of paper would she have given out?

3. Jack read for 20 minutes on Monday. He read 15 minutes more on Tuesday than on Monday. For how many minutes did Jack read on Tuesday?

Problem Solving Strategy Practice

For 4–5, choose the number sentence from the box. Solve.

$4 \times 10 = ■$ $10 + 4 = ■$ $27 - 3 = ■$ $27 \div 3 = ■$

4. One eraser costs 3¢. Lizzie spends 27¢ on erasers. How many erasers does Lizzie have?

5. Jeremy has 10 pencils. His teacher gives him 4 more pencils. How many pencils does Jeremy have now?

Write a number sentence to solve.

6. Elizabeth reads for 360 minutes each week. She has read for 215 minutes so far this week. How many more minutes will Elizabeth read this week?

7. Mrs. Vargas has 30 students in her math class. There are 5 tables in her classroom. The same number of students sit at each table. How many students sit at each table?

8. WRITE Math At a store, there are 6 notebooks on each of 7 shelves. There are 5 notebooks on the 8th shelf. How many notebooks are on the shelves altogether? **Explain.**

Mixed Strategy Practice

USE DATA For 9–12, use the table.

9. Mr. Clark buys a pack of pencils for his students. He gives the same number of pencils to 8 students. How many pencils does each student get?
10. **Pose a Problem** Look back at Problem 9. Write a similar problem by changing the number of students.
11. Min bought 3 packs of erasers. She kept 8 erasers and divided the rest of them equally among 4 of her classmates. How many erasers did Min give to each of her 4 classmates? **Explain** your answer.
12. There are blue pencils and red pencils in a pencil pack. There are twice as many red pencils as blue pencils. How many red pencils are there?
13. **Open-Ended** ***FAST FACT*** The first box of Crayola® crayons was sold in 1903 for 5¢. List two different groups of coins you could use to pay for 7 boxes of crayons.

CHALLENGE YOURSELF

The school store has these items for sale:

pencil	**25¢**	**ruler**	**75¢**
marker	**45¢**	**sharpener**	**15¢**
pen	**65¢**	**notebook**	**95¢**

14. Amy spends $1.25 on 3 different items. What items does she buy?
15. Frank buys 4 different items. He pays with three $1 bills, and receives two dimes in change. What items does Frank buy?

Choose a STRATEGY

- Draw a Diagram or Picture
- Make a Model or Act It Out
- Make an Organized List
- Find a Pattern
- Make a Table or Graph
- Predict and Test
- Work Backward
- Solve a Simpler Problem
- Write an Equation
- Use Logical Reasoning

Items Sold

Items	Number
Crayons	8 per pack
Erasers	12 per pack
Pencils	24 per pack
Stickers	100 per roll

Extra Practice

Set A Copy and complete the table. Use counters to help. (pp. 278–279)

	Counters	Number of Equal Groups	Number in Each Group
1.	30	5	■
2.	28	■	7
3.	24	8	■
4.	12	4	■

Set B Write a division sentence for each. (pp. 280–281)

1. 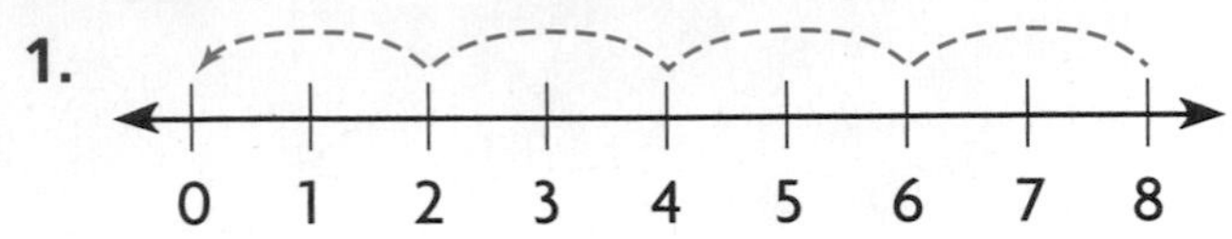

2. $\begin{array}{r} 12 \\ -\ 4 \\ \hline 8 \end{array}$ → $\begin{array}{r} 8 \\ -4 \\ \hline 4 \end{array}$ → $\begin{array}{r} 4 \\ -4 \\ \hline 0 \end{array}$

Use a number line or repeated subtraction to solve.

3. $15 \div 3 =$ ■ **4.** $4\overline{)16}$ **5.** $12 \div 2 =$ ■ **6.** $5\overline{)20}$

7. If Desiree can make 6 necklaces in 36 minutes, how long does it take her to make each necklace?

8. Desiree can make 5 bracelets in 25 minutes. How long does it take to make each bracelet?

Set C Copy and complete. (pp. 284–285)

1. ●●●●
●●●●
●●●●

3 rows of ■ = 12
$12 \div 3 =$ ■

2. ●●●●●●●●●
●●●●●●●●●

2 rows of ■ = 18
$18 \div 2 =$ ■

3. 

3 rows of ■ = 18
$18 \div 3 =$ ■

Complete each number sentence. Draw an array to help.

4. $5 \times$ ■ $= 30$ $30 \div 5 =$ ■ **5.** $8 \times$ ■ $= 40$ $40 \div 8 =$ ■

Set D Write the fact family for each set of numbers. (pp. 286–289)

1. 3, 5, 15 **2.** 4, 7, 28 **3.** 2, 8, 16 **4.** 3, 7, 21

CD ROM **Technology**
Use Harcourt Mega Math, Ice Station Exploration, *Arctic Algebra*, Level E.

PRACTICE GAME

All in the Family

Draw Your Cards
2–4 players

Are They a Family?
- Gameboard
- Counter for each player
- Number cards
- Paper and pencils

6 2 12

$2 \times 6 = 12$
$6 \times 2 = 12$
$12 \div 2 = 6$
$12 \div 6 = 2$

Coming Home

- Players place their counter on any number on the gameboard.
- Each player is dealt 5 number cards. The remaining cards are placed facedown in a pile.
- Player 1 tries to make a fact family, either by using 3 of his or her cards or by using 2 cards and the number on which the counter lies. The player writes down the fact family, and the other players check it.
- Player 1 then discards the cards used, draws cards to replace them, and advances 1 space, clockwise, on the gameboard. It is then the next player's turn.
- If a player cannot make a fact family, he or she exchanges some or all of his or her cards with the cards from the pile, and his or her turn is over.
- The first player to return to his or her start space is the winner.

Finding Factor Pairs

SPY GAMES

Use the Decoder to help Sam Sleuth solve the secret message. Match the symbol to the correct factor pair and letter in the Decoder.

      ?

The clues used are:

♥ Their product is odd. Their difference is 6.	△ Their product ends in zero and is less than 30.
▽ Their product equals 21 + 21.	□ Their product is a single digit.
∴ Their product is equal to 18 + 18.	∅ Their product is 18. The larger factor is odd.
✕ Their product is between 20 and 25. Their sum is 11.	👍 Their product is equal to 30 – 9.
~ Their product is 18. The smaller factor is odd.	✓ Their product is equal to 16 – 4.
≈ Their product is 24. Both factors are even.	◊ Their product is odd. Their difference is 2.

DECODER			
4, 5	**A**	4, 6	**G**
6, 7	**R**	2, 6	**W**
3, 8	**M**	2, 9	**N**
4, 9	**E**	3, 6	**I**
5, 7	**X**	3, 7	**S**
3, 9	**H**	2, 4	**T**

Example

A Read the clue for the first symbol. Their product is equal to 16 – 4.

B Find the factor pair that satisfies the clue. 2, 6

C Write the letter for the symbol. W

Try It

1. Solve the rest of the secret message.
2. **WRITE Math** Sam Sleuth sent this message: ∴ ~ ≈ ♥ □ ∴ ∴ ∅. What does it mean? **Explain** how you know.

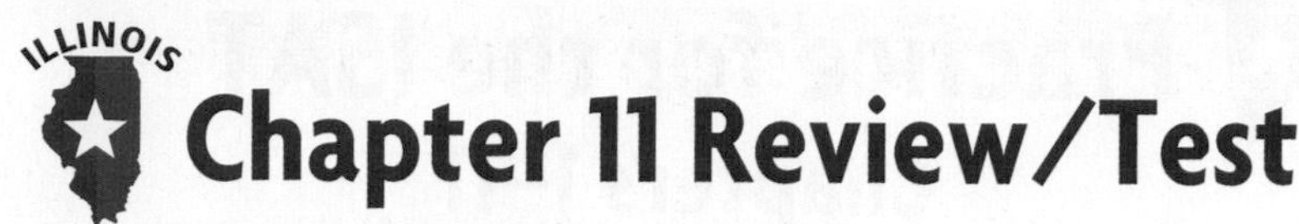

Chapter 11 Review/Test

Check Vocabulary and Concepts

Choose the best term from the box.

VOCABULARY
divide
divisor
fact family
quotient

1. You __?__ when you separate into equal groups. IL 6.4.12 (p. 280)
2. A __?__ is a set of related multiplication and division number sentences. IL 6.4.12 (p. 288)
3. How many times a divisor goes into a dividend is the __?__. IL 6.4.12 (p. 286)

Check Skills

Copy and complete the table. Use counters to help. IL 6.4.12 (pp. 280–281)

	Counters	Number of Equal Groups	Number in Each Group
4.	21	3	■
5.	16	■	4
6.	36	9	■

Use a number line or repeated subtraction to solve. IL 6.4.12 (pp. 282–283)

7. $28 \div 7 = ■$
8. $2\overline{)10}$
9. $8 \div 4 = ■$
10. $7\overline{)35}$

Complete each number sentence. Draw an array to help. IL 6.4.15 (pp. 286–287)

11. $5 \times ■ = 15$ $\quad 15 \div 5 = ■$
12. $3 \times ■ = 24$ $\quad 24 \div 3 = ■$
13. $6 \times ■ = 42$ $\quad 42 \div 6 = ■$
14. $6 \times ■ = 30$ $\quad 30 \div 6 = ■$

Write the fact family for each set of numbers. IL 6.4.15 (pp. 288–291)

15. 3, 9, 27
16. 3, 4, 12
17. 6, 6, 36
18. 3, 6, 18

Check Problem Solving

Solve. IL 6.4.12 (pp. 292–295)

19. At a party, Dolly the Clown gave each child 4 balloons. She gave out 36 balloons in all. How many children were at the party?
20. WRITE Math There were 5 students at a table. Each student drew 5 pictures. How many pictures did the students draw in all? **Explain** how you know.

GO ONLINE **Technology** Use *Online Assessment.*

ILLINOIS Practice for the ISAT
Chapters 1–11

Number and Operations

1. There were 1,457 people at a play. What is the value of the 4 in 1,457? IL 6.3.01 (p. 10)

   A 4

   B 40

   C 400

   D 4,000

Test Tip **Eliminate choices.**

See item 2. Since you need to subtract to find the answer, you can eliminate the answer choices that are greater than 312 and 259. Then subtract carefully, remembering to regroup.

2. Katie and Juan are reading books. Katie has read 312 pages in her book. Juan has read 259 pages in his book. How many more pages has Katie read than Juan? IL 6.3.09 (p. 84)

   A 571

   B 153

   C 147

   D 53

3. **WRITE Math** **Explain** how to use the number line to find 4×3. IL 6.3.11 (p. 212)

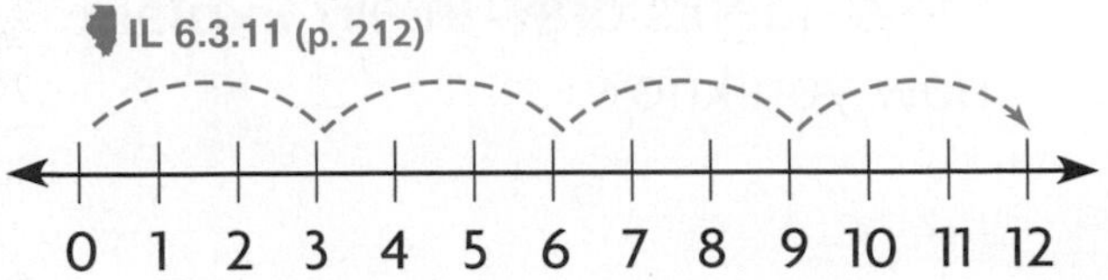

Algebra

4. Spiders have 8 legs. Marcy wants to find out how many legs are on 5 spiders. Use the table below to find the answer. IL 8.3.01 (p. 256)

Spiders	1	2	3	4	5
Legs	8	16	24	32	■

   A 36

   B 38

   C 40

   D 42

5. Which number sentence is in the same fact family as $4 \times 8 = 32$? IL 8.3.03 (p. 286)

   A $32 \div 8 = 4$

   B $8 \div 4 = 2$

   C $4 \times 4 = 16$

   D $4 \times 2 = 8$

6. **WRITE Math** Sammy wrote the pattern below. Grade 2

   4, 7, 10, 13, 16

   Write a rule for Sammy's pattern. **Explain** how to find the next number in his pattern.

Geometry

7. Which figure is a cone? Grade 2

A 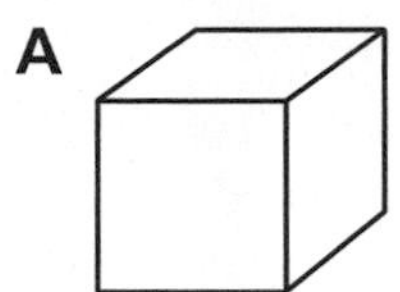

B 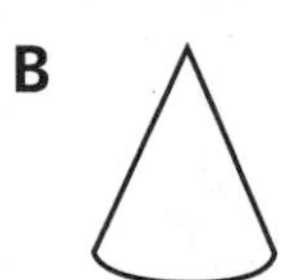

C 

D 

8. How many faces does a cube have? Grade 2

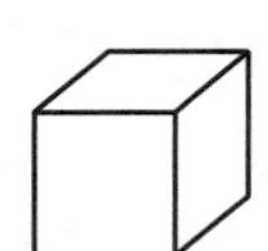

A 3 C 6

B 4 D 8

9. WRITE Math Are the two figures below congruent? **Explain** how you know. Grade 2

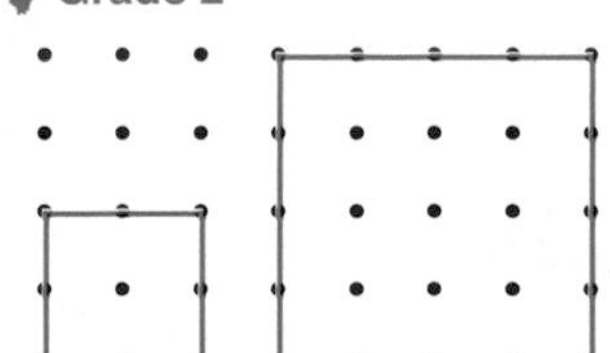

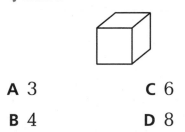

Data Analysis and Probability

10. How many more points does Drake need to score to equal the number of points Tio scored? IL 10.3.01 (p. 154)

A 10 C 20

B 15 D 30

11. On which color is the spinner more likely to stop? IL 10.3.04 (p. 178)

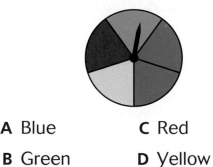

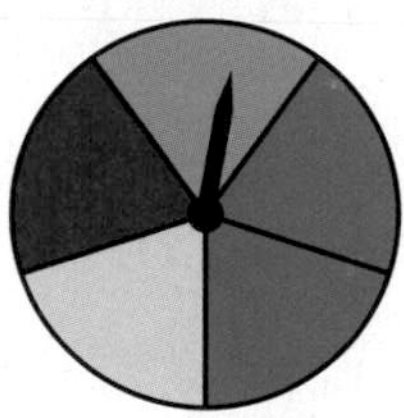

A Blue C Red

B Green D Yellow

12. WRITE Math Tina made a pictograph to show how many books she owns.

Each [book] = 10 books.

How many books does [book][book][book][book][half book] stand for? **Explain.** IL 10.3.01 (p. 148)

CHAPTER 12

Division Facts

FAST FACT

A candy company in Bethlehem, Pennsylvania, makes Marshmallow Peeps®. It takes about 6 minutes to make one Marshmallow Peep®.

Investigate

Choose a candy from the table that you could share equally among the people who live at your house. Tell how you would find how many pieces to give to each person and if you would have any pieces left over.

Candy	Number of Pieces Per Package
Peeps®	10
Gobstoppers®	32
Mike and Ike®	36
M&M's®	54
Skittles®	63

GO ONLINE **Technology**
Student pages are available in the Student eBook.

Show What You Know

Check your understanding of important skills needed for success in Chapter 12.

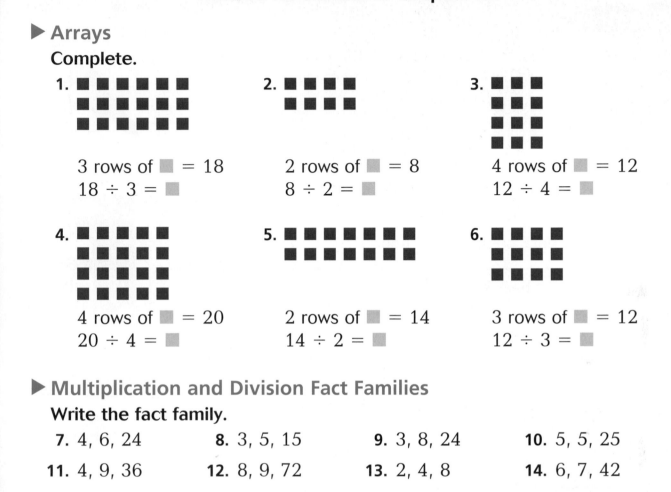

▶ Arrays

Complete.

1. 

3 rows of ■ = 18
18 ÷ 3 = ■

2. 

2 rows of ■ = 8
8 ÷ 2 = ■

3. 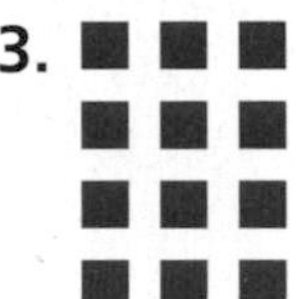

4 rows of ■ = 12
12 ÷ 4 = ■

4.

4 rows of ■ = 20
20 ÷ 4 = ■

5.

2 rows of ■ = 14
14 ÷ 2 = ■

6.

3 rows of ■ = 12
12 ÷ 3 = ■

▶ Multiplication and Division Fact Families

Write the fact family.

7. 4, 6, 24 **8.** 3, 5, 15 **9.** 3, 8, 24 **10.** 5, 5, 25

11. 4, 9, 36 **12.** 8, 9, 72 **13.** 2, 4, 8 **14.** 6, 7, 42

VOCABULARY POWER

CHAPTER VOCABULARY

divide
dividend
divisor
fact family
quotient

WARM-UP WORDS

dividend The number that is to be divided in a division problem

divisor The number that divides the dividend

quotient The number, not including the remainder, that results from division

LESSON 1

Divide by 2 and 5

OBJECTIVE: Divide by 2 and 5.

Quick Review

1. ■ × 2 = 10
2. 5 × ■ = 15
3. 3 × ■ = 6
4. ■ × 2 = 18
5. 5 × ■ = 25

Learn

PROBLEM Mrs. Benson needs feeders for 12 hummingbirds. If there will be 2 birds at each feeder, how many feeders does she need?

12 ÷ 2 = ■
(12 = dividend, 2 = divisor, ■ = quotient)

divisor → $2\overline{)12}$ ← dividend, with ■ ← quotient above

▲ A hummingbird can beat its wings as many as 80 times per second and can fly at a speed of 25 miles per hour!

Example 1 Divide. 12 ÷ 2 = ■

ONE WAY Count back on a number line.

Start at 12. Count back by 2s until you reach 0. Count the number of times you subtract 2.

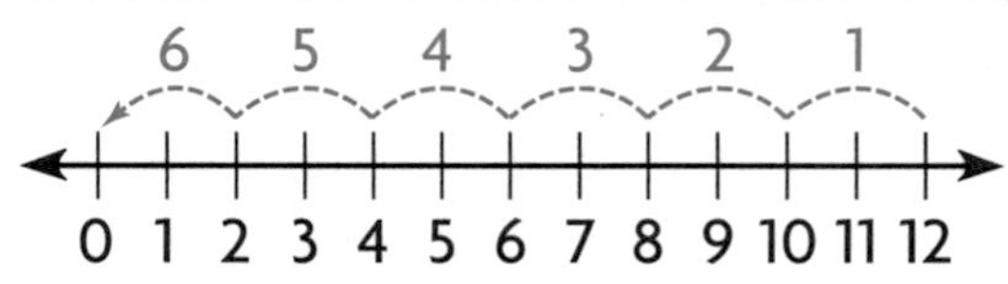

You subtract 2 six times. So, Mrs. Benson needs 6 feeders.

ANOTHER WAY Use a related multiplication fact.

12 ÷ 2 = ■   Think: ■ × 2 = 12
6 × 2 = 12
So, 12 ÷ 2 = 6, or $2\overline{)12}$ with quotient 6.

Example 2 Divide. 20 ÷ 5 = ■

ONE WAY Count back on a number line.

Start at 20. Count back by 5s until you reach 0. Count the number of times you subtract 5.

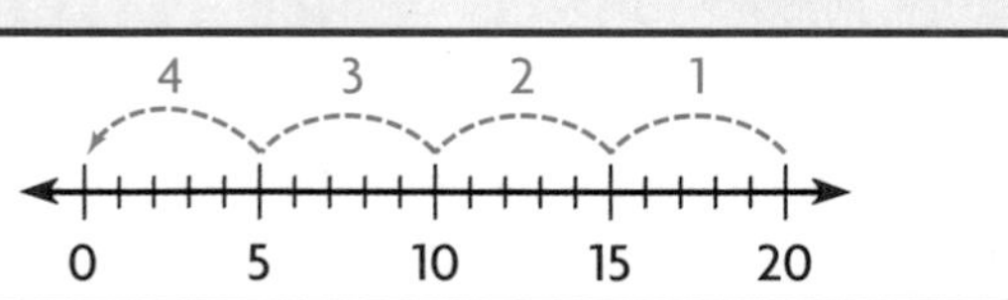

You subtract 5 four times. So, 20 ÷ 5 = 4.

ANOTHER WAY Use a related multiplication fact.

20 ÷ 5 = ■   Think: ■ × 5 = 20
4 × 5 = 20
So, 20 ÷ 5 = 4, or $5\overline{)20}$ with quotient 4.

Guided Practice

1. Use the number line to find $25 \div 5$.

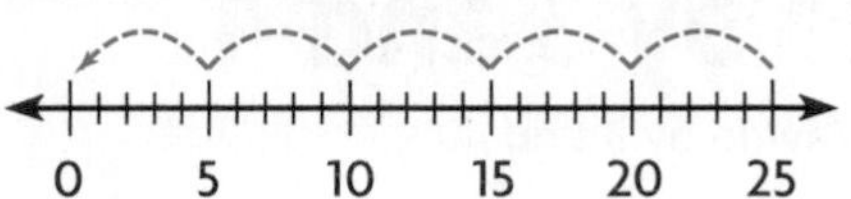

Find each quotient.

2. $16 \div 2 = \blacksquare$
3. $\blacksquare = 30 \div 5$
4. $20 \div 2 = \blacksquare$
5. $\blacksquare = 15 \div 5$
6. TALK Math **Explain** how $5 \times 8 = 40$ can help you find $40 \div 5$.

Independent Practice and Problem Solving

Find each quotient.

7. $6 \div 2 = \blacksquare$
8. $\blacksquare = 35 \div 5$
9. $10 \div 5 = \blacksquare$
10. $\blacksquare = 18 \div 2$
11. $\blacksquare = 45 \div 5$
12. $\blacksquare = 10 \div 2$
13. $8 \div 2 = \blacksquare$
14. $5 \div 5 = \blacksquare$
15. $5\overline{)15}$
16. $2\overline{)16}$
17. $5\overline{)35}$
18. $2\overline{)2}$

Algebra Copy and complete each table.

19.

÷	25	30	35	40
5	■	■	■	■

20.

÷	12	14	16	18
2	■	■	■	■

USE DATA For 21–22, use the table.

Hummingbirds

Type	Mass in Grams
Magnificent	7
Rubythroat	3
Anna's	4

21. The total mass of 2 hummingbirds of the same type is 8 grams. Which type of hummingbird are they? Write a division sentence to show the answer.
22. WRITE Math Five hummingbirds of the same type have a total mass of 15 grams. What type are they? **Explain** how to find the answer.

Mixed Review and Test Prep

23. What is 5×7? (p. 240)
24. What is the missing number? (p. 262)

$$3 \times 8 = \blacksquare \times 3$$

25. **Test Prep** Jo sees the same number of birds each hour for 2 hours. She sees 16 birds in all. How many birds does Jo see each hour?

A 6 **B** 7 **C** 8 **D** 9

Extra Practice on page 314, Set A

LESSON 2

Divide by 3 and 4

OBJECTIVE: Divide by 3 and 4.

Quick Review

1. $\blacksquare \times 3 = 18$
2. $4 \times \blacksquare = 12$
3. $6 \times \blacksquare = 24$
4. $\blacksquare \times 9 = 36$
5. $3 \times \blacksquare = 21$

Learn

PROBLEM For field day, 15 students have signed up for the relay race. Each relay team needs 3 students. How many teams can be made?

Example 1 Divide. $15 \div 3 = \blacksquare$

ONE WAY Draw a picture.

Draw 15 counters in groups of 3.
Count the number of equal groups.
There are 5 groups of 3.
So, 5 teams can be made.

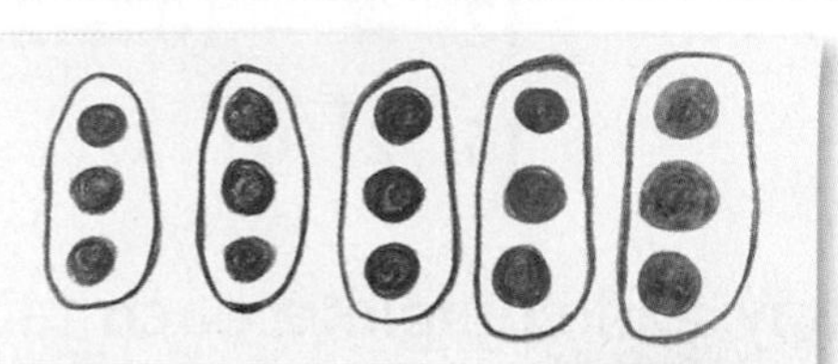

ANOTHER WAY Use a related multiplication fact.

$15 \div 3 = \blacksquare$ Think: $\blacksquare \times 3 = 15$
$5 \times 3 = 15$
So, $15 \div 3 = 5$, or $3\overline{)15}$ with quotient 5.

Math Idea
You can divide to find the number of equal groups or to find how many are in each group.

Example 2 Divide. $12 \div 4 = \blacksquare$

ONE WAY Draw a picture.

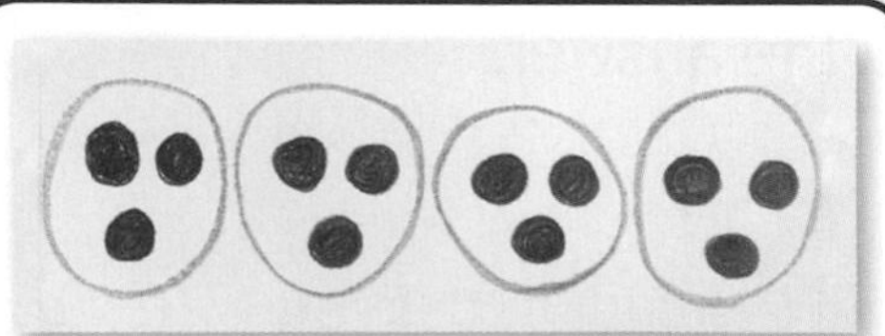

There are 3 counters in each group. So, $12 \div 4 = 3$.

ANOTHER WAY Use a related multiplication fact.

Think: $4 \times \blacksquare = 12$
$4 \times 3 = 12$
So, $12 \div 4 = 3$, or $4\overline{)12}$ with quotient 3.

Guided Practice

1. Use the picture to find $21 \div 3 = \blacksquare$.

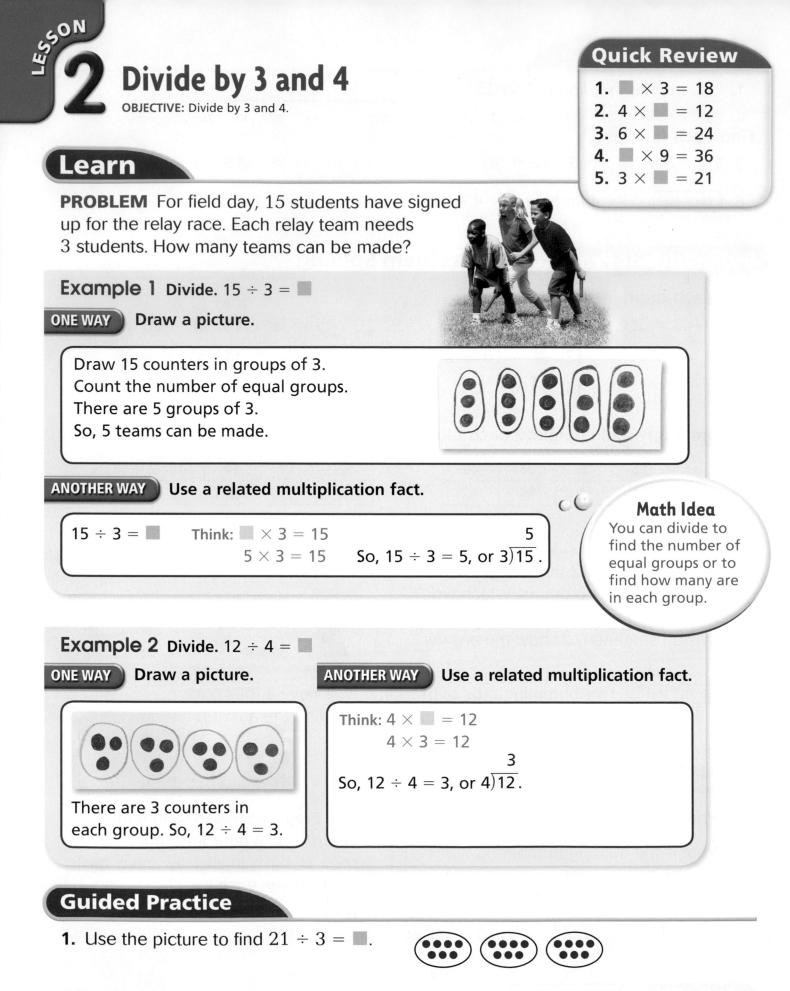

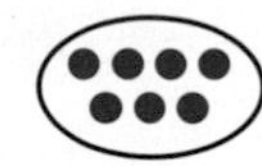 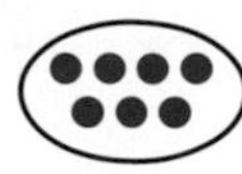 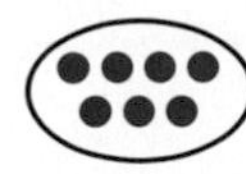

Find each quotient.

2. $9 \div 3 = ■$
3. $28 \div 4 = ■$
✓4. $32 \div 4 = ■$
✓5. $24 \div 3 = ■$

6. TALK Math **Explain** how you can use multiplication to find $20 \div 4$.

Independent Practice and Problem Solving

Find each quotient.

7. $30 \div 3 = ■$
8. $8 \div 4 = ■$
9. $■ = 27 \div 3$
10. $16 \div 4 = ■$
11. $24 \div 4 = ■$
12. $■ = 35 \div 5$
13. $6 \div 3 = ■$
14. $■ = 14 \div 2$
15. $3\overline{)12}$
16. $4\overline{)36}$
17. $5\overline{)20}$
18. $3\overline{)18}$

Algebra Copy and complete each table.

19.

÷	6	9	12	15
3	■	■	■	■

20.

÷	20	24	28	32
4	■	■	■	■

USE DATA For 21–22, use the table.

Field Day Events

Activity	Number of Students
Relay race	28
Beanbag toss	18
Jump-rope race	27

21. **Reasoning** Students doing the beanbag toss and the jump-rope race competed in groups of 3. How many more groups participated in the jump-rope race than in the beanbag toss? **Explain** how you know.

22. **What if** students ran the relay race in groups of 4? Write a number sentence to show the number of groups that would have competed.

23. WRITE Math **What's the Question?** Cara put 36 sports cards into 4 equal piles. The answer is 9 sports cards.

Mixed Review and Test Prep

24. Lee used 35 beads to make 5 bracelets. How many beads did she use for each bracelet? (p. 302)

25. A bag has 5 red tiles and 2 blue tiles. Are you likely or unlikely to pull a blue tile? (p. 178)

26. **Test Prep** Carlos has 24 pretzels. He puts 4 pretzels in each bag. How many bags does Carlos fill?

A 4
B 5
C 6
D 7

Extra Practice on page 314, Set B

LESSON 3

Division Rules for 1 and 0

OBJECTIVE: Divide using the rules for 1 and 0.

Quick Review

1. 6 × ■ = 6
2. ■ × 9 = 0
3. 1 × ■ = 3
4. 8 × ■ = 0
5. ■ × 1 = 5

Learn

These division rules can help you divide with 1 and 0.

RULE A: Any number divided by 1 equals that number.

4 ÷ 1 = 4

number of birds ↑ number of cages ↑ number in each cage ↑

If there is only 1 cage, then all of the birds must go in that cage.

RULE B: Any number (except 0) divided by itself equals 1.

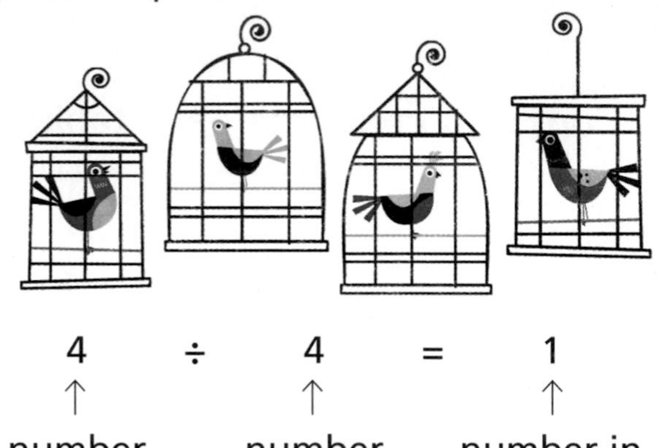

4 ÷ 4 = 1

number of birds ↑ number of cages ↑ number in each cage ↑

If there are the same number of birds and cages, then 1 bird goes in each cage.

RULE C: Zero divided by any number (except 0) equals 0.

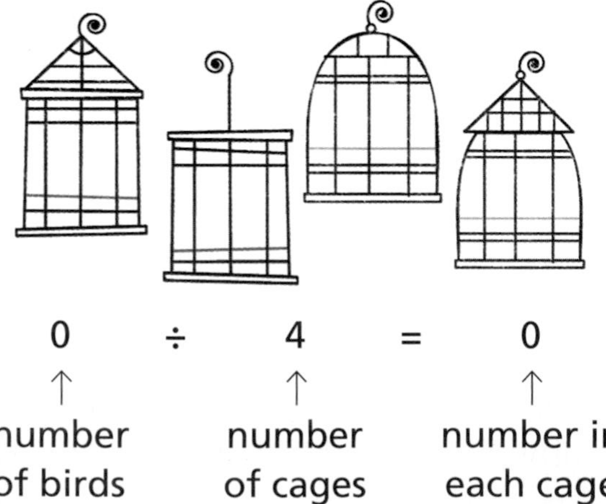

0 ÷ 4 = 0

number of birds ↑ number of cages ↑ number in each cage ↑

If there are 0 birds and 4 cages, there will not be any birds in the cages.

RULE D: You cannot divide by 0.

If there are 0 cages, then you cannot separate the birds into equal groups. Dividing by 0 is not possible.

Guided Practice

1. Use the picture to find $3 \div 3 = \blacksquare$.

Find each quotient.

2. $7 \div 1 = \blacksquare$
3. $2 \div 2 = \blacksquare$
4. $0 \div 5 = \blacksquare$
5. $6 \div 6 = \blacksquare$
6. TALK Math **Explain** why it is easy to find $9 \div 1$. Solve.

Independent Practice and Problem Solving

Find each quotient.

7. $0 \div 8 = \blacksquare$
8. $5 \div 5 = \blacksquare$
9. $\blacksquare = 2 \div 1$
10. $0 \div 7 = \blacksquare$
11. $6 \div 1 = \blacksquare$
12. $\blacksquare = 25 \div 5$
13. $\blacksquare = 0 \div 10$
14. $18 \div 3 = \blacksquare$
15. $14 \div 2 = \blacksquare$
16. $\blacksquare = 9 \div 9$
17. $32 \div 4 = \blacksquare$
18. $\blacksquare = 8 \div 1$
19. $4\overline{)24}$
20. $5\overline{)10}$
21. $3\overline{)0}$
22. $10\overline{)10}$

Algebra Compare. Write <, >, or = for each ●.

23. $7 \div 7$ ● $7 \div 1$
24. 9×1 ● $9 \div 1$
25. $2 \div 2$ ● $0 \div 2$

26. Angie has 7 parakeets. She put 4 of them in a cage. She let 3 friends hold the other parakeets. How many parakeets did each friend get to hold?

27. **Pose a Problem** Look back at Problem 26. Change the number of parakeets and friends so you can use the division sentence $6 \div 6 = 1$.

28. ***FAST FACT*** There are more than 340 different types of parrots. Mary has 5 different parrots. She gives each parrot 1 grape. How many grapes does she give to her parrots?

29. WRITE Math Suppose a zoo has 59 birds in each of 59 cages. Use what you know to find the number of birds in each cage. **Explain** your answer.

Mixed Review and Test Prep

30. A flower shop sold 795 flowers last week. What is the value of the 9? (p. 8)

31. Use a related multiplication fact to find the quotient. $18 \div 3 = \blacksquare$ (p. 304)

32. **Test Prep** Farmer Joe has 4 stables. There is 1 horse in each stable. How many horses are there?

A 0 **B** 1 **C** 2 **D** 4

Extra Practice on page 314, Set C

LESSON 4

ALGEBRA

Practice the Facts

OBJECTIVE: Practice division facts through 5 using various strategies.

Quick Review

1. $4 \times \square = 32$
2. $\square \times 7 = 21$
3. $\square \times 5 = 10$
4. $2 \times \square = 12$
5. $1 \times \square = 9$

Learn

PROBLEM Tory made cottonball snowmen for her friends. She glued 3 cottonballs together to make each snowman. She used a total of 24 cottonballs. How many snowmen did Tory make?

Divide. $24 \div 3 = \square$

There are many ways to find the quotient.

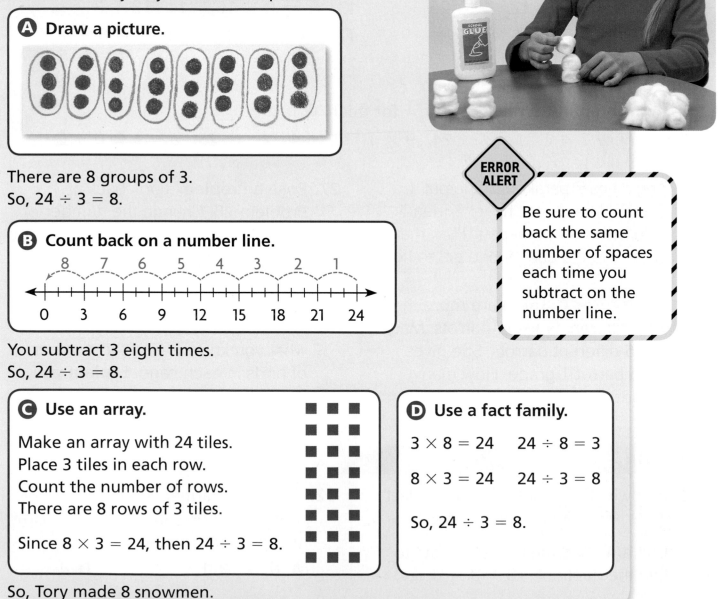

A Draw a picture.

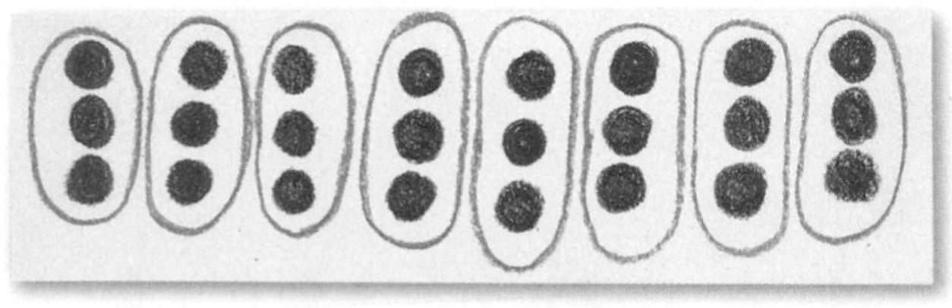

There are 8 groups of 3.
So, $24 \div 3 = 8$.

B Count back on a number line.

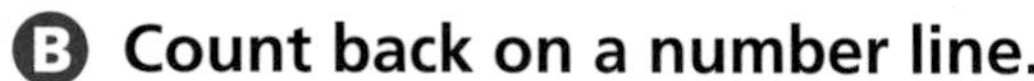

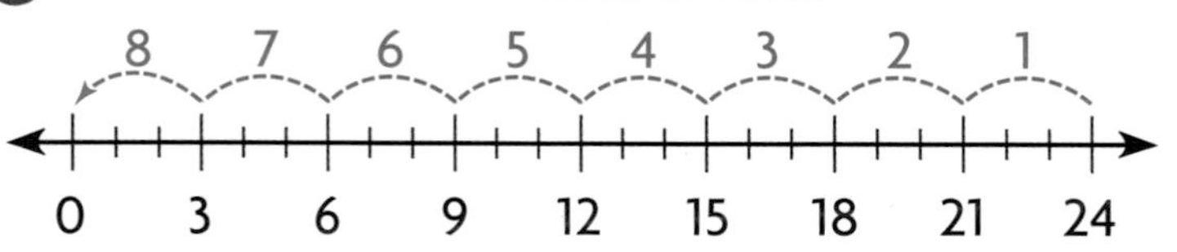

You subtract 3 eight times.
So, $24 \div 3 = 8$.

ERROR ALERT

Be sure to count back the same number of spaces each time you subtract on the number line.

C Use an array.

Make an array with 24 tiles.
Place 3 tiles in each row.
Count the number of rows.
There are 8 rows of 3 tiles.

Since $8 \times 3 = 24$, then $24 \div 3 = 8$.

D Use a fact family.

$3 \times 8 = 24$ $24 \div 8 = 3$

$8 \times 3 = 24$ $24 \div 3 = 8$

So, $24 \div 3 = 8$.

So, Tory made 8 snowmen.

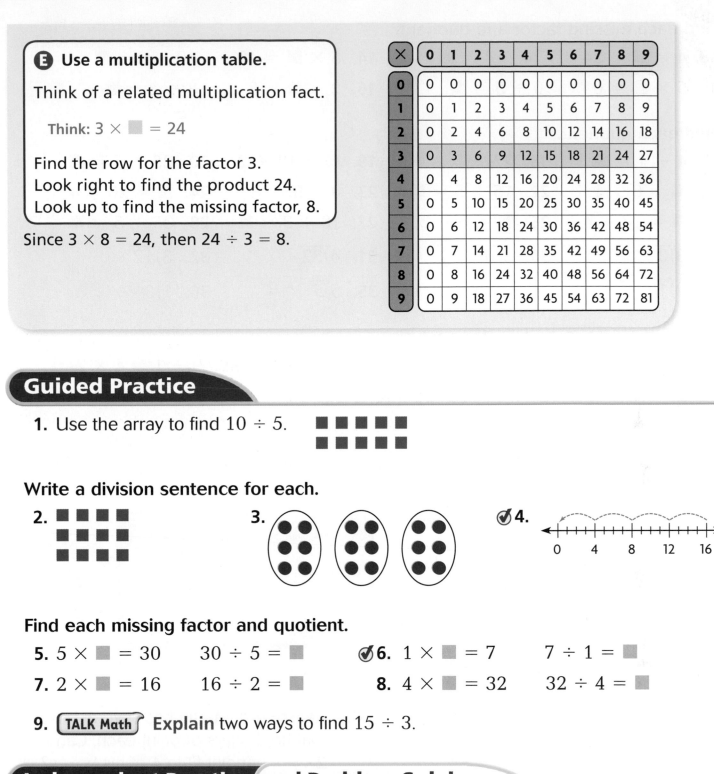

E **Use a multiplication table.**

Think of a related multiplication fact.

Think: $3 \times ■ = 24$

Find the row for the factor 3.
Look right to find the product 24.
Look up to find the missing factor, 8.

Since $3 \times 8 = 24$, then $24 \div 3 = 8$.

×	0	1	2	3	4	5	6	7	8	9
0	0	0	0	0	0	0	0	0	0	0
1	0	1	2	3	4	5	6	7	8	9
2	0	2	4	6	8	10	12	14	16	18
3	0	3	6	9	12	15	18	21	24	27
4	0	4	8	12	16	20	24	28	32	36
5	0	5	10	15	20	25	30	35	40	45
6	0	6	12	18	24	30	36	42	48	54
7	0	7	14	21	28	35	42	49	56	63
8	0	8	16	24	32	40	48	56	64	72
9	0	9	18	27	36	45	54	63	72	81

Guided Practice

1. Use the array to find $10 \div 5$.

Write a division sentence for each.

2. 

3. 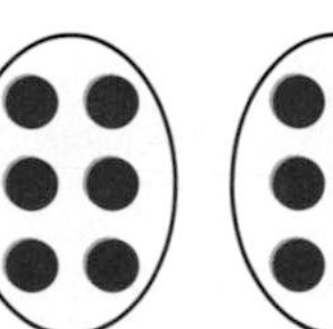 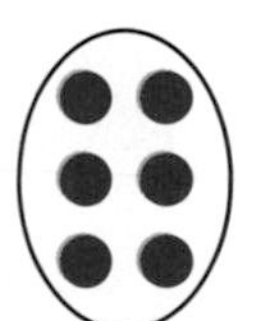 

✓4. 

Find each missing factor and quotient.

5. $5 \times ■ = 30$ $30 \div 5 = ■$
✓6. $1 \times ■ = 7$ $7 \div 1 = ■$
7. $2 \times ■ = 16$ $16 \div 2 = ■$
8. $4 \times ■ = 32$ $32 \div 4 = ■$

9. **TALK Math** **Explain** two ways to find $15 \div 3$.

Independent Practice and Problem Solving

Write a division sentence for each.

10. 

11. 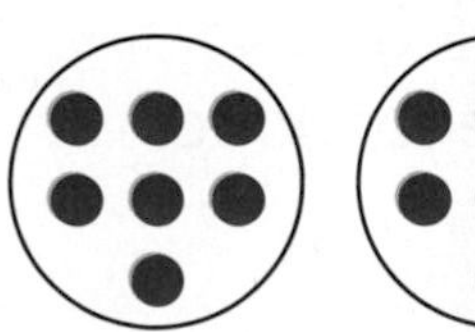

12. 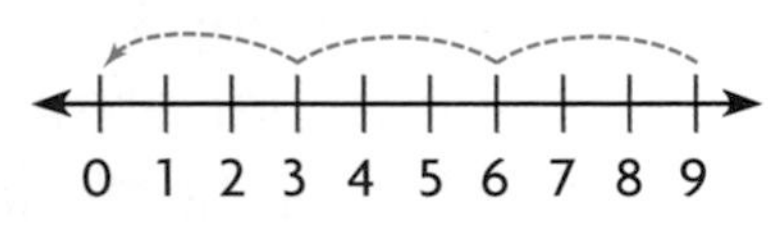

Extra Practice on page 314, Set D

Find each missing factor and quotient.

13. $4 \times ■ = 24$ $\quad 24 \div 4 = ■$

14. $5 \times ■ = 40$ $\quad 40 \div 5 = ■$

15. $5 \times ■ = 0$ $\quad 0 \div 5 = ■$

16. $2 \times ■ = 8$ $\quad 8 \div 2 = ■$

Find each quotient.

17. $4 \div 4 = ■$

18. $27 \div 3 = ■$

19. $■ = 12 \div 2$

20. $25 \div 5 = ■$

21. $■ = 6 \div 1$

22. $15 \div 5 = ■$

23. $0 \div 9 = ■$

24. $■ = 20 \div 4$

25. $■ = 36 \div 4$

26. $■ = 6 \div 2$

27. $18 \div 3 = ■$

28. $35 \div 5 = ■$

29. $8\overline{)0}$

30. $3\overline{)6}$

31. $4\overline{)32}$

32. $3\overline{)12}$

33. $2\overline{)18}$

34. $5\overline{)45}$

35. $5\overline{)5}$

36. $1\overline{)3}$

Compare. Write <, >, or = for each ●.

37. $30 \div 5$ ● 2×3

38. $12 \div 2$ ● $21 \div 3$

39. $9 \div 1$ ● 4×2

40. $27 \div 3$ ● $45 \div 5$

41. $24 \div 4$ ● 4×2

42. $16 \div 2$ ● $28 \div 4$

Write +, −, ×, or ÷ for each ●.

43. 14 ● $2 = 6 \times 2$

44. $12 \div 4 = 27$ ● 9

45. $21 \div 3 = 5$ ● 2

USE DATA For 46–47, use the table.

Snowman Craft Supplies

Item	Number per Bag
Carrot noses	6
Buttons	30
Mittens	12
Bead eyes	4

46. Each snowman gets 2 bead eyes. How many bags of bead eyes do you need for 8 snowmen?

47. If you use 5 buttons for each snowman, how many snowmen can you decorate with one bag of buttons?

48. **Pose a Problem** Write a word problem for the number sentence.

$$12 \div 2 = 6$$

49. **Reasoning** Martin has several boxes that hold 6 jars of paint each. Can 25 jars of paint fit in 4 of his boxes? **Explain** how you know.

50. WRITE Math **What's the Error?** Kim drew 3 equal groups of 9 to model $24 \div 3$. Describe her error. Draw a picture to model the division sentence.

CD ROM **Technology**
Use Harcourt Mega Math, The Number Games, *Up, Up, and Array,* Level E.

ALGEBRA

Learn About Finding the Cost

You can use multiplication to find the cost of multiple items.
You can use division to find the cost of one item.

Example 1 Mr. Lee buys 8 poster boards. Each poster board costs $2. How much does Mr. Lee spend?

8	×	$2	=	$16
↑		↑		↑
number of poster boards		cost of one		total spent

So, Mr. Lee spends $16.

Example 2 Courtney buys a pack of 5 paintbrushes. A pack costs $10. How much does each paintbrush cost?

$10	÷	5	=	$2
↑		↑		↑
total spent		number of paintbrushes		cost of one

So, each paintbrush costs $2.

Try It

Write a number sentence. Then solve.

51. Ms. Jenkins spends $28 on 4 picture frames. How much does each frame cost?

52. Glenn buys 4 rubber stamps. Each rubber stamp costs $5. How much does he spend?

53. The craft store sells baskets for $7 each. Karen buys 4 baskets. How much does she spend?

54. Books are on sale 3 for $12. What is the cost of one book?

Mixed Review and Test Prep

55. How many sides and vertices does this figure have? (Grade 2)

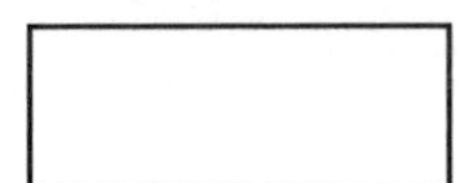

56. Test Prep Which division sentence is related to $6 \times 2 = 12$?

A $12 \div 3 = 4$
B $12 \div 6 = 2$
C $6 \div 2 = 3$
D $6 \div 3 = 2$

57. Mr. Lowry put 36 chairs in equal rows. He put 4 chairs in each row. How many rows did he make? (p. 304)

58. Test Prep Mrs. Kapp has 18 students in her class. She needs to divide them into groups of 3 for a project. **Explain** how you could use a number line to find how many groups there will be.

Problem Solving Workshop Skill: Choose the Operation

OBJECTIVE: Solve problems by using the skill *choose the operation.*

Read to Understand
Plan
Solve
Check

Use the Skill

PROBLEM Miss Kent's class went to the science center to visit the new water and animal exhibits.

Sometimes, you need to decide which operation to use to solve a problem.

Examples

A Add to join groups of different sizes. The water exhibit has 26 displays, and the animal exhibit has 18 displays. How many displays are in the exhibits in all?

$$\begin{array}{rl} 26 & \leftarrow \text{water displays} \\ +18 & \leftarrow \text{animal displays} \\ \hline 44 & \leftarrow \text{total number of displays} \end{array}$$

B Subtract to find the number left or to compare amounts. Three of the 26 displays in the water exhibit were closed. How many were open?

$$\begin{array}{rl} 26 & \leftarrow \text{total water displays} \\ -\ 3 & \leftarrow \text{closed displays} \\ \hline 23 & \leftarrow \text{open displays} \end{array}$$

C Multiply to join equal amounts. The gift shop has world map puzzle books for $8 each. What is the cost of 5 puzzle books?

$$5 \times \$8 = \$40$$

5 ↑ number of books; $8 ↑ cost of one book; $40 ↑ total cost

D Divide to separate into equal groups or to find the number in each group. The 24 students who went on the trip were separated into 4 equal groups. How many were in each group?

$$24 \div 4 = 6$$

24 ↑ number of students; 4 ↑ number of groups; 6 ↑ students in each group

Think and Discuss

Choose the operation. Write a number sentence. Then solve.

a. The Davis family spent $30 for 5 tickets to the ocean show. How much did each ticket cost?

b. There were 24 students and 13 adults on the bus for the science center trip. How many people rode on the bus?

Guided Problem Solving

Solve.

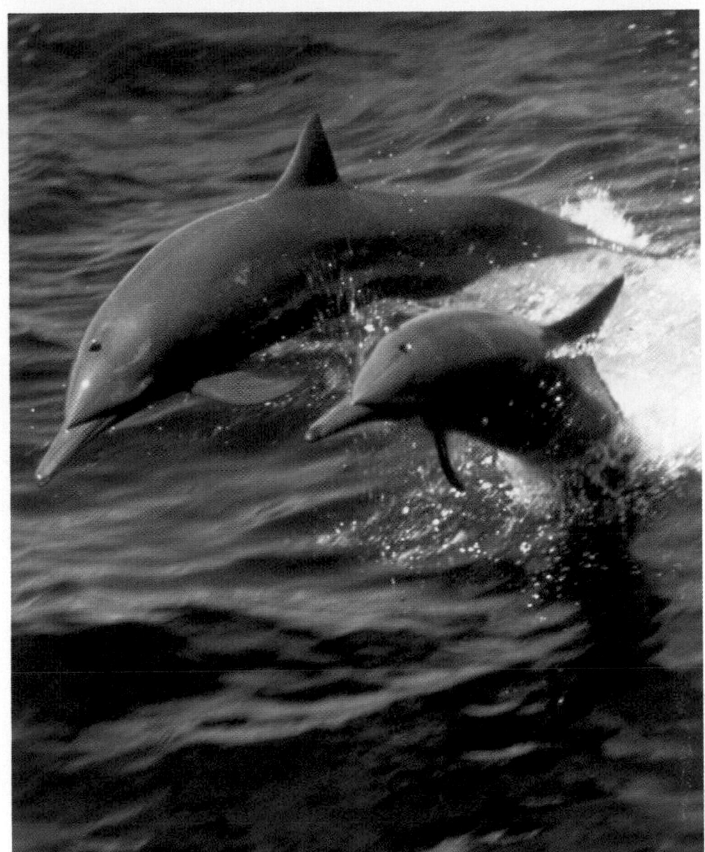

1. The show about the ocean was 17 minutes long, and the show about dolphins was 32 minutes long. How much longer was the dolphin show than the ocean show?

   Which operation can you use to compare amounts? Write a number sentence and solve.

2. **What if** Problem 1 asked you to find the total time of the two shows? What operation would you use? Write a number sentence and solve.

3. T-shirts are sold for $9 each at the gift shop. What is the cost of 3 T-shirts?

Mixed Applications

4. There are 45 books in the gift shop. There are an equal number of books on each of 5 shelves. How many books are on each shelf?

5. There are 54 fourth graders and 62 third graders who will enter projects in the science fair. Each project will be set up on its own table. How many tables are needed?

USE DATA For 6–8, use the table.

6. After visiting the science center, Miss Kent's class made this table about water use. In two days, how much water would a family of 4 use for brushing teeth in the morning and at bedtime?

7. Jonas took a bath, and his sister took a shower. How much more water did Jonas use than his sister?

8. **WRITE Math** Mr. Foster washed his clothes, washed his car, and ran the dishwasher. How much water did he use? **Explain** how you found your answer.

Water Use

Activity	Amount in Gallons
Brush teeth	1
Wash clothes	30
Take a shower	30
Take a bath	40
Wash car	20
Run dishwasher	15

Extra Practice

Set A **Find each quotient.** (pp. 302–303)

1. $6 \div 2 = ■$
2. $■ = 25 \div 5$
3. $18 \div 2 = ■$
4. $■ = 40 \div 5$
5. $5\overline{)30}$
6. $2\overline{)12}$
7. $5\overline{)15}$
8. $2\overline{)4}$
9. Gina bought movie tickets for $20. Each ticket cost $5. How many tickets did she buy?
10. Carl placed a total of 14 chairs in 2 equal rows. How many chairs were in each row?

Set B **Find each quotient.** (pp. 304–305)

1. $■ = 21 \div 3$
2. $28 \div 4 = ■$
3. $■ = 18 \div 3$
4. $36 \div 4 = ■$
5. $4\overline{)12}$
6. $3\overline{)24}$
7. $4\overline{)32}$
8. $3\overline{)9}$

Set C **Find each quotient.** (pp. 306–307)

1. $3 \div 1 = ■$
2. $■ = 0 \div 9$
3. $■ = 5 \div 1$
4. $7 \div 7 = ■$
5. $4\overline{)0}$
6. $5\overline{)5}$
7. $2\overline{)0}$
8. $1\overline{)9}$
9. Dena has 3 fish. She divides them equally among 3 fishbowls. How many fish are in each bowl?
10. Steve has 4 flowers. He puts all of his flowers in 1 vase. How many flowers are in the vase?

Set D **Write a division sentence for each.** (pp. 308–311)

1. 
2.  
3. 0 1 2 3 4 5 6

Find each missing factor and quotient.

4. $5 \times ■ = 45$ $45 \div 5 = ■$
5. $1 \times ■ = 6$ $6 \div 1 = ■$

Find each quotient.

6. $8 \div 2 = ■$
7. $35 \div 5 = ■$
8. $0 \div 7 = ■$
9. $16 \div 2 = ■$
10. $9\overline{)9}$
11. $3\overline{)15}$
12. $1\overline{)8}$
13. $4\overline{)24}$

CD ROM **Technology**
Use Harcourt Mega Math, The Number Games, *Up, Up, and Array*, Level E.

PRACTICE GAME

Division Cover-Up

Shuffle!
2 players

Draw!
- Division fact cards
- 10 counters for each player

1	27	14	6	15	5
21	8	7	32	12	2
16	0	18	30	10	24
9	3	45	35	4	36
40	4	28	50	8	3

Cover Them Up!

- Players shuffle the division fact cards and place them facedown in a pile.
- Player 1 draws the card from the top of the pile and says the number that is missing from the division number sentence on that card.
- Player 1 finds the missing number on the gameboard and places a counter on it.
- Players take turns. If a player cannot place a counter on the gameboard because the number is already covered, that player's turn ends.
- The first player to place all 10 of his or her counters on the gameboard wins the game.

MATH POWER **Odd and Even**

Beat the Odds

Marco and his brother choose pairs of numbers and guess if their products are odd or even. What is the best guess for Marco—will most of the products be odd or even?

Example

Marco made a table to decide.

Step 1 Find the product of each example.

Step 2 Determine if each product is even or odd.

NUMBERS	EXAMPLE	PRODUCT	ODD OR EVEN?
odd × odd	3 × 9	■	odd
even × even	4 × 8	32	■
odd × even	5 × 8	■	even
even × odd	2 × 7	14	■

Step 3 Make a conclusion based on the table results.
Three of the four possibilities result in an even product.

So, Marco should guess that the product will usually be even.

Try It

Complete the table.

	NUMBERS	EXAMPLE	QUOTIENT	ODD OR EVEN?
1.	odd ÷ odd	21 ÷ 3	■	■
2.	odd ÷ odd	35 ÷ 5	■	■
3.	even ÷ even	10 ÷ 2	■	■
4.	even ÷ even	24 ÷ 4	■	■
5.	even ÷ odd	20 ÷ 5	■	■
6.	even ÷ odd	18 ÷ 3	■	■

7. **WRITE Math** Make a conclusion based on the table results. **Explain** how you reached that conclusion.

Chapter 12 Review/Test

Check Concepts

Write a division sentence for each. IL 6.4.12 (pp. 308–311)

1. 

2. 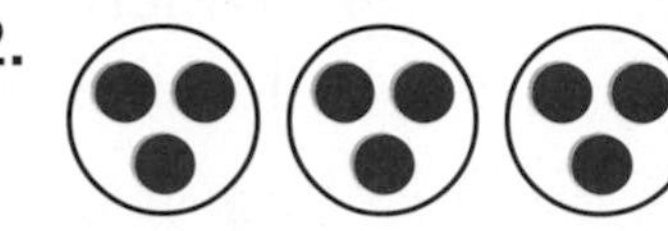

3. 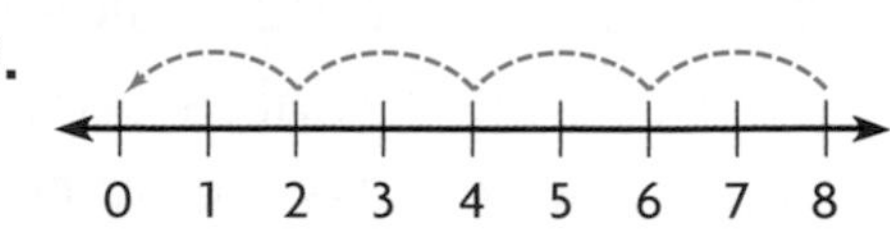

Check Skills

Find each quotient. IL 6.4.12 (pp. 302–303, 304–305, 306–307, 308–311)

4. $14 \div 2 = \blacksquare$
5. $8 \div 8 = \blacksquare$
6. $20 \div 5 = \blacksquare$
7. $\blacksquare = 0 \div 3$
8. $5 \div 1 = \blacksquare$
9. $\blacksquare = 20 \div 2$
10. $12 \div 3 = \blacksquare$
11. $16 \div 4 = \blacksquare$
12. $\blacksquare = 30 \div 5$
13. $24 \div 3 = \blacksquare$
14. $\blacksquare = 6 \div 6$
15. $12 \div 2 = \blacksquare$
16. $4\overline{)36}$
17. $6\overline{)0}$
18. $5\overline{)45}$
19. $3\overline{)6}$
20. $5\overline{)25}$
21. $4\overline{)28}$
22. $1\overline{)9}$
23. $2\overline{)18}$

Find each missing factor and quotient. IL 6.4.15 (pp. 308–311)

24. $4 \times \blacksquare = 8$ $\quad 8 \div 4 = \blacksquare$
25. $3 \times \blacksquare = 27$ $\quad 27 \div 3 = \blacksquare$
26. $1 \times \blacksquare = 7$ $\quad 7 \div 1 = \blacksquare$
27. $2 \times \blacksquare = 10$ $\quad 10 \div 2 = \blacksquare$

Check Problem Solving

Solve. IL 8.3.05 (pp. 312–313)

28. Mark put all of his shirts in 4 equal stacks. There are 6 shirts in each stack. How many shirts does Mark have altogether?

29. Beverly has 6 apples, 8 oranges, and 12 bananas. How many pieces of fruit does Beverly have in all?

30. WRITE Math Mike scored 18 points in the flag football game. He scored only touchdowns, and each touchdown he made scored 3 points. How many touchdowns did Mike make? **Explain** how you know which operation to use to solve the problem.

GO ONLINE **Technology** Use *Online Assessment.*

Practice for the ISAT
Chapters 1–12

Number and Operations

1. Sarah is setting tables for a party. She puts 8 plates on each of 5 tables. How many plates did Sarah set in all? IL 6.3.11 (p. 218)

   A 3

   B 13

   C 40

   D 85

Look for important words.

See item 2. Key words can help you solve a problem. The word *altogether* indicates that you should find a total. Since there are two numbers that are different, find the total by adding.

2. There are 346 books on the first shelf in a library. There are 299 books on the second shelf. How many books are on both shelves altogether? IL 6.3.09 (p. 58)

   A 535 C 635

   B 545 D 645

3. WRITE Math How you can use the counters to find 4×5. **Explain.** IL 6.3.11 (p. 234)

Algebra

4. Which number completes the fact family? IL 8.3.03 (p. 286)

   $■ \times 9 = 63$ $63 \div ■ = 9$
   $9 \times ■ = 63$ $63 \div 9 = ■$

   A 6

   B 7

   C 8

   D 9

5. Which number is missing in the pattern below? Grade 2

   98, 85, 72, 59, 46, 33, ■

   A 22

   B 21

   C 20

   D 19

6. WRITE Math **Explain** how the array shows the Identity Property of Multiplication. IL 6.3.13 (p. 260)

Measurement

7. Which figure has an area of 15 square units? Grade 2

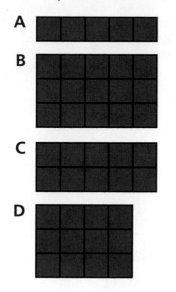

A

B

C 

D

8. Which temperature does the thermometer show? Grade 2

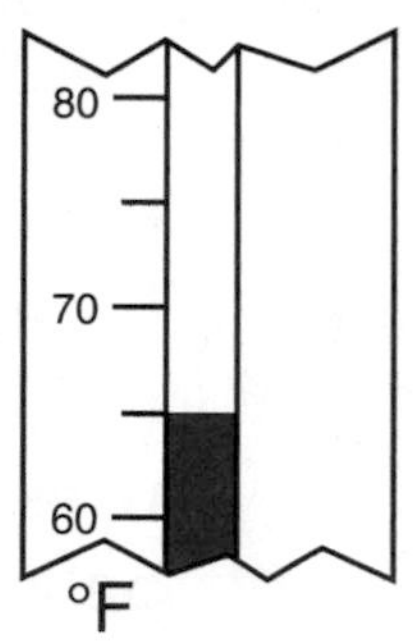

A 70°F

B 65°F

C 60°F

D 55°F

9. WRITE Math A paper clip is about 1 inch long. **Explain** how you could use a paper clip to measure the length of your pencil. Grade 2

Data Analysis and Probability

10. Jerry pulls a marble out of the bag without looking. Which color marble is he more likely to pull? IL 10.3.04 (p. 178)

A Green

B Yellow

C Red

D Blue

11. How many letters did Thomas send? IL 10.3.01 (p. 148)

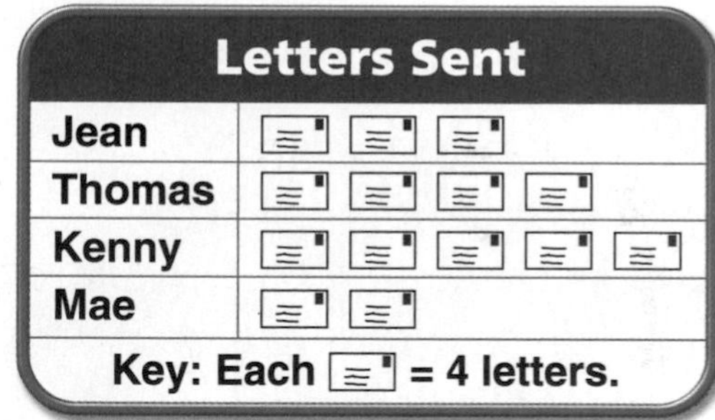

A 4

B 12

C 16

D 20

12. WRITE Math A bar graph shows the number of students in each grade at Faber School. The bars for third grade and fourth grade are the same height. What does this mean? **Explain.** IL 10.3.01 (p. 154)

CHAPTER 13 Facts Through 12

Investigate

A hot-air balloon carries passengers in a basket. The size of the basket determines the number of passengers. Choose a balloon from the pictograph. How many balloon rides would be needed for all the students in your class to ride in that balloon?

Hot-Air Balloon Rides	
Balloon A	🎈 🎈
Balloon B	🎈
Balloon C	🎈 🎈 🎈 🎈 🎈
Balloon D	🎈 🎈 🎈
Key: Each 🎈 = 2 passengers.	

FAST FACT

Hot-air balloons fly because the hot air inside the balloon rises and lifts the balloon. Over 4,000 people in the United States are pilots of hot-air balloons.

Technology
Student pages are available in the Student eBook.

Show What You Know

Check your understanding of important skills needed for success in Chapter 13.

▶ Multiplication Facts Through 12

Find the product.

1. $7 \times 3 = \blacksquare$ **2.** $4 \times 9 = \blacksquare$ **3.** $\blacksquare = 5 \times 6$ **4.** $\blacksquare = 10 \times 3$

5. $11 \times 8 = \blacksquare$ **6.** $\blacksquare = 6 \times 4$ **7.** $2 \times 12 = \blacksquare$ **8.** $\blacksquare = 8 \times 7$

▶ Missing Factors

Find the missing factor.

9. $4 \times \blacksquare = 32$ **10.** $18 = \blacksquare \times 3$ **11.** $\blacksquare \times 9 = 54$ **12.** $49 = 7 \times \blacksquare$

▶ Multiplication Properties

Use the properties of multiplication to help you find each product.

13. $6 \times 8 = \blacksquare$ $8 \times 6 = \blacksquare$ **14.** $(3 \times 2) \times 4 = \blacksquare$ $3 \times (2 \times 4) = \blacksquare$

15. $7 \times 1 = \blacksquare$ **16.** $0 \times 12 = \blacksquare$

▶ Division Facts Through 5

Find the quotient.

17. $28 \div 4 = \blacksquare$ **18.** $12 \div 3 = \blacksquare$ **19.** $\blacksquare = 30 \div 5$ **20.** $8 \div 1 = \blacksquare$

21. $\blacksquare = 18 \div 2$ **22.** $20 \div 4 = \blacksquare$ **23.** $27 \div 3 = \blacksquare$ **24.** $40 \div 5 = \blacksquare$

VOCABULARY POWER

CHAPTER VOCABULARY

array
divide
dividend
divisor
equation
expression
fact family
quotient

WARM-UP WORDS

equation A number sentence that uses the equal sign to show that two amounts are equal

expression The part of a number sentence that combines numbers and operation signs, but does not have an equal sign

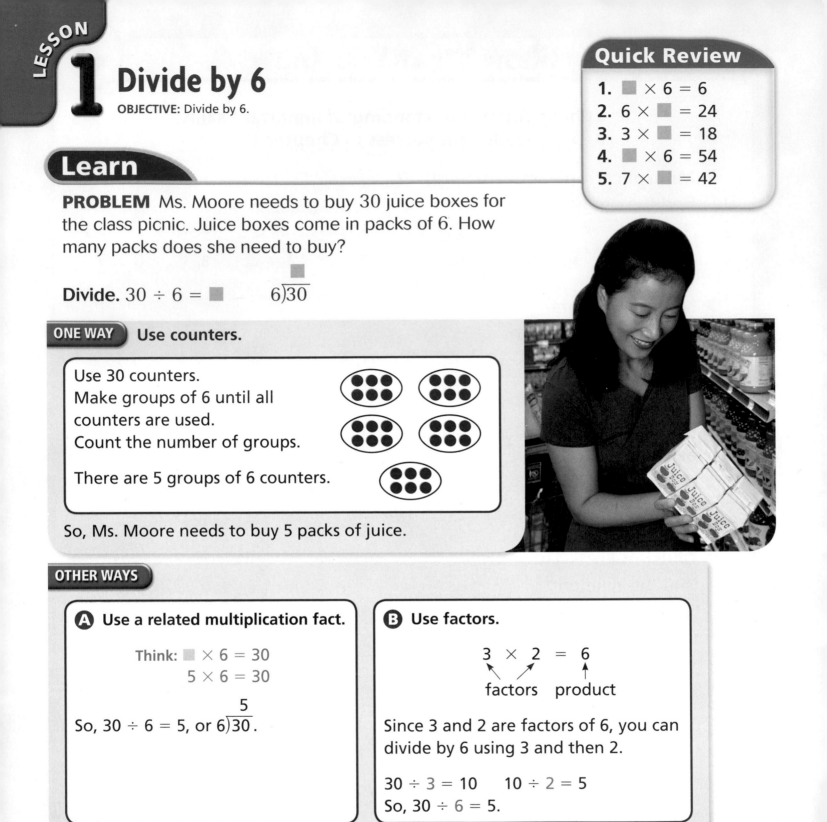

LESSON 1

Divide by 6

OBJECTIVE: Divide by 6.

Quick Review

1. ■ × 6 = 6
2. 6 × ■ = 24
3. 3 × ■ = 18
4. ■ × 6 = 54
5. 7 × ■ = 42

Learn

PROBLEM Ms. Moore needs to buy 30 juice boxes for the class picnic. Juice boxes come in packs of 6. How many packs does she need to buy?

Divide. $30 \div 6 = ■$ $6\overline{)30}$ (quotient ■)

ONE WAY Use counters.

Use 30 counters.
Make groups of 6 until all counters are used.
Count the number of groups.

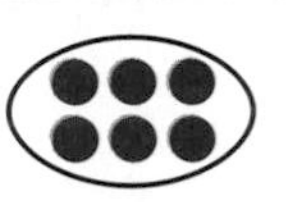
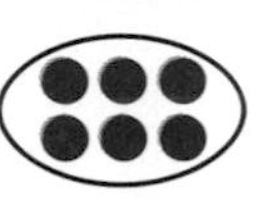

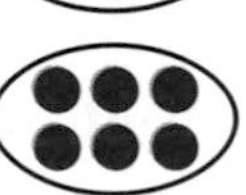

There are 5 groups of 6 counters.

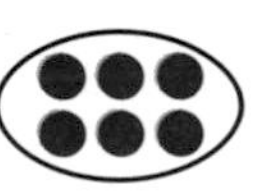

So, Ms. Moore needs to buy 5 packs of juice.

OTHER WAYS

A Use a related multiplication fact.

Think: ■ × 6 = 30
5 × 6 = 30

So, 30 ÷ 6 = 5, or $6\overline{)30}$ with quotient 5.

B Use factors.

3 × 2 = 6
(3 and 2: factors; 6: product)

Since 3 and 2 are factors of 6, you can divide by 6 using 3 and then 2.

30 ÷ 3 = 10   10 ÷ 2 = 5
So, 30 ÷ 6 = 5.

- How can you solve 24 ÷ 6 by using the factors 3 and 2?

Guided Practice

1. Use the model to find 18 ÷ 6.

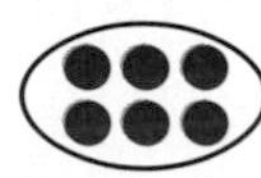
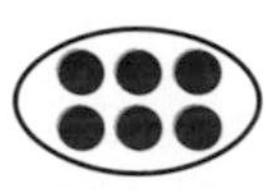

Find each missing factor and quotient.

2. $6 \times ■ = 36$ $36 \div 6 = ■$
3. $6 \times ■ = 12$ $12 \div 6 = ■$
4. $6 \times ■ = 6$ $6 \div 6 = ■$
5. $6 \times ■ = 42$ $42 \div 6 = ■$
6. TALK Math **Explain** how $6 \times 9 = 54$ helps you find $54 \div 6$.

Independent Practice and Problem Solving

Find each missing factor and quotient.

7. $6 \times ■ = 30$ $30 \div 6 = ■$
8. $6 \times ■ = 48$ $48 \div 6 = ■$
9. $6 \times ■ = 18$ $18 \div 6 = ■$
10. $6 \times ■ = 24$ $24 \div 6 = ■$

Find each quotient.

11. $12 \div 6 = ■$
12. $■ = 6 \div 2$
13. $■ = 42 \div 6$
14. $15 \div 5 = ■$
15. $■ = 60 \div 6$
16. $20 \div 4 = ■$
17. $7 \div 1 = ■$
18. $■ = 54 \div 6$
19. $4\overline{)28}$
20. $6\overline{)36}$
21. $6\overline{)0}$
22. $3\overline{)21}$

Algebra Find the missing number.

23. $6 \div ■ = 6$
24. $27 \div ■ = 9$
25. $16 \div ■ = 8$
26. $42 \div ■ = 7$

27. Ms. Moore bought a bag of 12 apples for the class picnic. How many apples can each of 6 students have if they each get the same number?
28. There are 30 students in a relay race at the picnic. The students are divided into 6 equal teams. How many students are on each team?
29. **Reasoning** Cody baked 24 muffins. He ate 6 of them. How many muffins does he have left? How many can he give to each of 6 friends if they each get the same number? **Explain.**
30. WRITE Math **What's the Error?** Mary has 36 stickers to give to 6 friends. She says she can give each friend only 5 stickers. Use a division sentence to describe Mary's error.

Mixed Review and Test Prep

31. What is the missing number? (p. 262)

$$7 \times 8 = 8 \times ■$$

32. What is 8,024 written in expanded form? (p. 10)
33. **Test Prep** The same number of students are at each of 6 tables. There are 48 students in all. How many students are at each table?

A 9 **B** 8 **C** 7 **D** 6

Extra Practice on page 338, Set A

LESSON

2 Divide by 7 and 8

OBJECTIVE: Divide by 7 and 8.

Quick Review

1. ■ × 7 = 21
2. 3 × ■ = 24
3. 2 × ■ = 14
4. ■ × 7 = 42
5. 8 × ■ = 16

Learn

PROBLEM Firewood is sold in bundles of 7 logs. Steve has 28 logs. How many bundles of firewood can he make?

Example 1 Divide. 28 ÷ 7 = ■

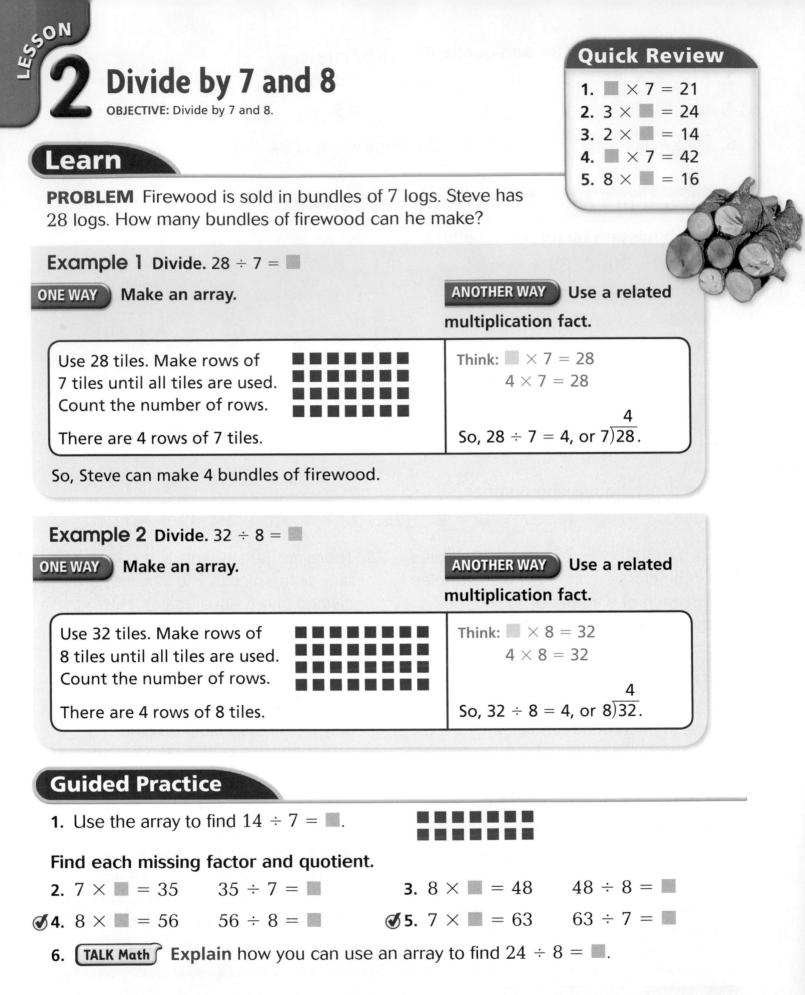

ONE WAY Make an array.

Use 28 tiles. Make rows of 7 tiles until all tiles are used. Count the number of rows.

There are 4 rows of 7 tiles.

ANOTHER WAY Use a related multiplication fact.

Think: ■ × 7 = 28
4 × 7 = 28

So, 28 ÷ 7 = 4, or $7\overline{)28}$ = 4.

So, Steve can make 4 bundles of firewood.

Example 2 Divide. 32 ÷ 8 = ■

ONE WAY Make an array.

Use 32 tiles. Make rows of 8 tiles until all tiles are used. Count the number of rows.

There are 4 rows of 8 tiles.

ANOTHER WAY Use a related multiplication fact.

Think: ■ × 8 = 32
4 × 8 = 32

So, 32 ÷ 8 = 4, or $8\overline{)32}$ = 4.

Guided Practice

1. Use the array to find 14 ÷ 7 = ■.

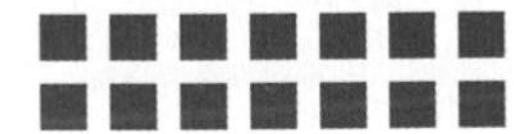

Find each missing factor and quotient.

2. 7 × ■ = 35 35 ÷ 7 = ■
3. 8 × ■ = 48 48 ÷ 8 = ■
4. 8 × ■ = 56 56 ÷ 8 = ■
5. 7 × ■ = 63 63 ÷ 7 = ■
6. **TALK Math** **Explain** how you can use an array to find 24 ÷ 8 = ■.

Independent Practice and Problem Solving

Find each missing factor and quotient.

7. $8 \times$ ■ $= 40$ $40 \div 8 =$ ■

8. $7 \times$ ■ $= 49$ $49 \div 7 =$ ■

9. $7 \times$ ■ $= 7$ $7 \div 7 =$ ■

10. $8 \times$ ■ $= 64$ $64 \div 8 =$ ■

Find each quotient.

11. $21 \div 7 =$ ■

12. ■ $= 8 \div 8$

13. $18 \div 2 =$ ■

14. ■ $= 25 \div 5$

15. $24 \div 6 =$ ■

16. ■ $= 15 \div 3$

17. ■ $= 16 \div 8$

18. $56 \div 7 =$ ■

19. ■ $= 36 \div 4$

20. $70 \div 7 =$ ■

21. ■ $= 6 \div 1$

22. $72 \div 8 =$ ■

23. $8\overline{)80}$

24. $5\overline{)40}$

25. $7\overline{)14}$

26. $6\overline{)54}$

Algebra **Copy and complete each table.**

27.

÷	48	56	64	72
8	■	■	■	■

28.

÷	35	42	49	56
7	■	■	■	■

USE DATA For 29–31, use the table.

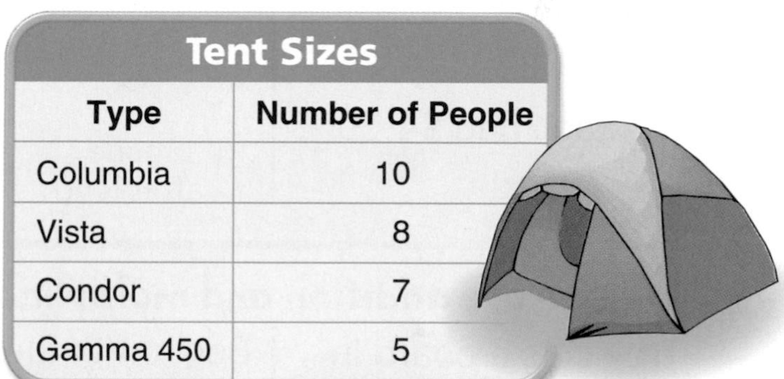

Tent Sizes

Type	Number of People
Columbia	10
Vista	8
Condor	7
Gamma 450	5

29. **Reasoning** There are 58 people camping at Zoe's family reunion. They have Columbia tents and Vista tents. How many of each type of tent do they need to sleep 58 people? **Explain.**

30. **Pose a Problem** Look back at Problem 29. Write a similar problem by changing the number of people and the types of tents used.

31. **WRITE Math** There are 42 people going camping. How many Condor tents do they need? **Explain.**

Mixed Review and Test Prep

32. A Columbia tent costs $286. Mrs. Kent has $177. How much more money does she need to buy the tent? (p. 84)

33. There are 30 tents set up in groups with 5 tents in each group. How many groups are there? (p. 302)

34. **Test Prep** There are 24 benches in 8 equal rows at a picnic area. How many benches are in each row?

A 32 **C** 4

B 16 **D** 3

Extra Practice on page 338, Set B

LESSON 3

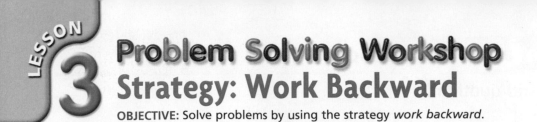

Problem Solving Workshop
Strategy: Work Backward

OBJECTIVE: Solve problems by using the strategy *work backward*.

Learn the Strategy

When you know the final amount, you can work backward to solve a problem.

You can use subtraction and addition.

Zach paid $1.70 for lunch. Then his mom gave him $5.00. Now, Zach has $7.50. How much money did Zach have to start?

Begin with the final amount of money.

Subtract the money Zach's mom gave him.

$7.50	−	$5.00	=	$2.50
↑		↑		↑
final amount		money from mom		money after lunch

Add the amount Zach spent on lunch.

$2.50	+	$1.70	=	$4.20
↑		↑		↑
money after lunch		money spent on lunch		money to start

So, Zach had $4.20 to start.

You can use addition and multiplication.

Troy cuts a board in 2 equal pieces. Then he cuts 4 inches off one piece. The piece is now 6 inches long. What was the length of the original board?

Begin with the final length of the board.

Add the number of inches Troy cut off.

6	+	4	=	10
↑		↑		↑
final length		inches cut off		length of one piece

Multiply to find the length of the original board.

10	×	2	=	20
↑		↑		↑
length of one piece		number of pieces		length of board

So, the board was 20 inches long.

TALK Math

In the last problem, why did you use multiplication when you worked backward?

Use the Strategy

PROBLEM Chad bought 4 packs of T-shirts. He gave 5 T-shirts to his brother. Now Chad has 19 shirts. How many T-shirts were in each pack?

Read to Understand
Plan
Solve
Check

Read to Understand

- **What information is given?**
- **How can you sequence the information?**

Plan

- **What strategy can you use to solve the problem?**
  You can work backward to help you solve the problem.

Solve

- **How can you use the strategy to solve the problem?**
  Work backward from the number of T-shirts Chad has now.

  Begin with the final number of T-shirts. Add the number of T-shirts Chad gave away.

19	+	5	=	24
↑		↑		↑
final number of T-shirts		T-shirts given away		T-shirts in 4 packs

Then divide to find the number of T-shirts in each pack.

24	÷	4	=	6
↑		↑		↑
T-shirts in 4 packs		number of packs		number in each pack

So, each pack had 6 T-shirts.

Check

- **How can you check your answer?**

Guided Problem Solving

1. Mac collects Matchbox® cars. He bought 4 packs of cars. Then his friend gave him 9 cars. Now Mac has 21 cars. How many cars are in each pack?

   Work backward from the total number of cars Mac has now.

   First, subtract the cars Mac's friend gave him.

21	−	9	=	12
↑		↑		↑
total cars		cars given to Mac		cars in 4 packs

   Then, divide to find the number of cars in each pack.

12	÷	4	=	■
↑		↑		↑
cars in 4 packs		number of packs		number in each pack

2. **What if** Mac bought 8 packs of cars and then his friend gave him 3 cars? If Mac has 19 cars now, how many cars are in each pack?

3. Ryan collects model cars. He gave half of his model car collection to a friend. Then he bought 6 more cars. Now Ryan has 14 cars. How many cars did Ryan have to start?

Problem Solving Strategy Practice

USE DATA For 4–6, use the table. Work backward to solve.

4. After lunch, 16 bracelets were sold. Then 2 bracelets were returned. How many bracelets were sold before lunch?

5. During the day, 9 customers each bought the same number of key chains. Then 9 more key chains were sold. How many key chains did each of the 9 customers buy?

6. WRITE Math First, Jan bought half of the total number of one item shown in the table. Then she bought 2 craft books. She bought 12 items in all. Which item did she buy first? **Explain.**

Items Sold in One Day

Item	Number
bracelets	25
craft books	30
key chains	45
model car kits	20

Mixed Strategy Practice

USE DATA For 7–10, use the table.

7. Tim and Erica have eaten at all of the restaurants. Tim's restaurants are all different from Erica's. He has eaten at 10 more of the restaurants than Erica. How many restaurants has Tim eaten at?

8. ***FAST FACT*** The Mall of America is the largest mall in the United States. Suppose there are 6 food stores on each level of the mall. How many levels would there be?

9. **Pose a Problem** Look back at Problem 8. Write a similar problem by using a different fact from the table and changing the number on each level.

10. **Open-Ended** Mark visited every food store. He visited the same number of food stores each day. List 3 different ways he could have done this.

11. Rose saw a movie, shopped in a store, and ate at a restaurant. She did not see the movie first. She shopped last. In what order did Rose do these activities?

12. Mr. Acosta went to the same number of stores each day for 4 days. On the fifth day, he went to 10 stores. He visited 34 stores in all. How many stores did he visit each of the 4 days?

Choose a STRATEGY

- Draw a Diagram or Picture
- Make a Model or Act It Out
- Make an Organized List
- Find a Pattern
- Make a Table or Graph
- Predict and Test
- Work Backward
- Solve a Simpler Problem
- Write an Equation
- Use Logical Reasoning

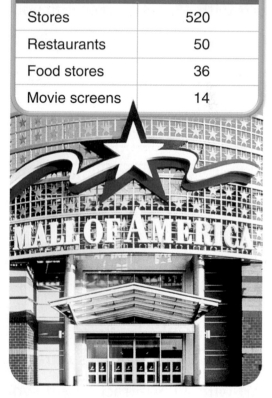

Mall of America Facts	
Stores	520
Restaurants	50
Food stores	36
Movie screens	14

CHALLENGE YOURSELF

A store sells pants for $12. The store also gives shoppers one free shirt for each $9 shirt they buy.

13. Dillon paid $30 for pants and shirts. How many pairs of pants did he buy? How many shirts did he get?

14. Pants usually sell for $16. Anna saved a total of $8 on her pants. She received 3 free shirts. How much did Anna spend?

Divide by 9 and 10

OBJECTIVE: Divide by 9 and 10.

Quick Review

1. 2 × ■ = 20
2. ■ × 10 = 50
3. 9 × ■ = 36
4. ■ × 7 = 70
5. 6 × ■ = 54

Learn

PROBLEM Mateo's class goes to the aquarium. They have 45 minutes to visit 9 exhibits. How much time can they spend at each exhibit if they spend the same amount of time at each one?

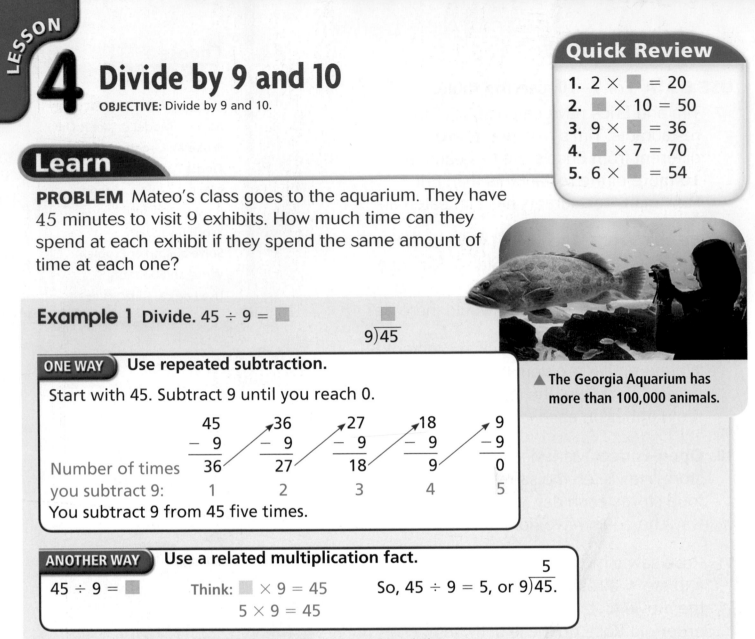

▲ The Georgia Aquarium has more than 100,000 animals.

Example 1 Divide. 45 ÷ 9 = ■

$9\overline{)45}$ ■

ONE WAY **Use repeated subtraction.**

Start with 45. Subtract 9 until you reach 0.

	45 − 9 = 36	36 − 9 = 27	27 − 9 = 18	18 − 9 = 9	9 − 9 = 0
Number of times you subtract 9:	1	2	3	4	5

You subtract 9 from 45 five times.

ANOTHER WAY **Use a related multiplication fact.**

45 ÷ 9 = ■

Think: ■ × 9 = 45
5 × 9 = 45

So, 45 ÷ 9 = 5, or $9\overline{)45}$ with quotient 5.

So, Mateo's class can spend 5 minutes at each exhibit.

Example 2 Divide. 40 ÷ 10 = ■

ONE WAY **Use repeated subtraction.**

Start with 40. Subtract 10 until you reach 0.

40 − 10 = 30	30 − 10 = 20	20 − 10 = 10	10 − 10 = 0
1	2	3	4

Count the number of times you subtract 10. You subtract 10 from 40 four times.

ANOTHER WAY **Use a related multiplication fact.**

40 ÷ 10 = ■

Think: ■ × 10 = 40
4 × 10 = 40

So, 40 ÷ 10 = 4, or $10\overline{)40}$ with quotient 4.

Guided Practice

1. Use the related multiplication fact to find $27 \div 9$.
   $3 \times 9 = 27$

Find each quotient.

2. $80 \div 10 = ■$
3. $36 \div 9 = ■$
4. $63 \div 9 = ■$
5. $30 \div 10 = ■$
6. **TALK Math** **Explain** how to use repeated subtraction to find $60 \div 10$.

Independent Practice and Problem Solving

Find each quotient.

7. $18 \div 9 = ■$
8. $■ = 30 \div 5$
9. $50 \div 10 = ■$
10. $■ = 81 \div 9$
11. $■ = 20 \div 10$
12. $9 \div 9 = ■$
13. $■ = 12 \div 6$
14. $28 \div 7 = ■$
15. $4\overline{)32}$
16. $9\overline{)72}$
17. $10\overline{)10}$
18. $8\overline{)56}$

Algebra **Copy and complete each table.**

19.

÷	36	45	54	63
9	■	■	■	■

20.

÷	70	80	90	100
10	■	■	■	■

USE DATA **For 21–23, use the table.**

21. Which jellyfish is four times the length of the sea wasp?
22. A marlin can be 87 inches long. This is 6 inches more than 9 times the length of which jellyfish?
23. **WRITE Math** **What's the Question?** A striped bass is 45 inches long. The answer is sea wasp. What is the question?

Lengths of Jellyfish

Type	Length
Moon jelly	9 inches
Mushroom jelly	20 inches
Sea wasp	5 inches

Mixed Review and Test Prep

24. What is the quotient? $45 \div 5 = ■$ (p. 302)
25. Compare the numbers. Write <, >, or =. 3,346 ● 3,374 (p. 28)
26. **Test Prep** Fifty people form 10 equal lines. How many people are in each line?

    A 500 **B** 50 **C** 5 **D** 1

LESSON 5

ALGEBRA

Division Facts Through 12

OBJECTIVE: Practice division facts through 12 using various strategies.

Quick Review

1. $12 \times ■ = 24$
2. $■ \times 11 = 55$
3. $2 \times ■ = 22$
4. $■ \times 12 = 72$
5. $10 \times ■ = 120$

Learn

PROBLEM Kenny collects model cars. Each shelf in his room can hold 11 cars. Kenny has 44 cars. How many shelves will Kenny use to display his cars?

Example 1 Divide. $44 \div 11 = ■$

Think of a related multiplication fact.

Think: $■ \times 11 = 44$

- Find the factor 11 in the top row.
- Look down to find the product, 44.
- Look left to find the missing factor, 4.

Since $4 \times 11 = 44$, then $44 \div 11 = 4$.

So, Kenny will use 4 shelves.

×	0	1	2	3	4	5	6	7	8	9	10	11	12
0	0	0	0	0	0	0	0	0	0	0	0	0	0
1	0	1	2	3	4	5	6	7	8	9	10	11	12
2	0	2	4	6	8	10	12	14	16	18	20	22	24
3	0	3	6	9	12	15	18	21	24	27	30	33	36
4	0	4	8	12	16	20	24	28	32	36	40	44	48
5	0	5	10	15	20	25	30	35	40	45	50	55	60
6	0	6	12	18	24	30	36	42	48	54	60	66	72
7	0	7	14	21	28	35	42	49	56	63	70	77	84
8	0	8	16	24	32	40	48	56	64	72	80	88	96
9	0	9	18	27	36	45	54	63	72	81	90	99	108
10	0	10	20	30	40	50	60	70	80	90	100	110	120
11	0	11	22	33	44	55	66	77	88	99	110	121	132
12	0	12	24	36	48	60	72	84	96	108	120	132	144

Tara collects postcards. She has 108 postcards that she wants to divide equally among 12 boxes. How many postcards will Tara put in each box?

Example 2 Divide. $108 \div 12 = ■$

Think of a related multiplication fact.

Think: $■ \times 12 = 108$

- Find the factor 12 in the top row.
- Look down to find the product, 108.
- Look left to find the missing factor, 9.

Since $9 \times 12 = 108$, then $108 \div 12 = 9$.

So, Tara will put 9 postcards in each box.

- What if Tara had 72 postcards to divide equally among 12 boxes? How many postcards would she put in each box?

Practice the Facts

There are many ways to solve division problems.

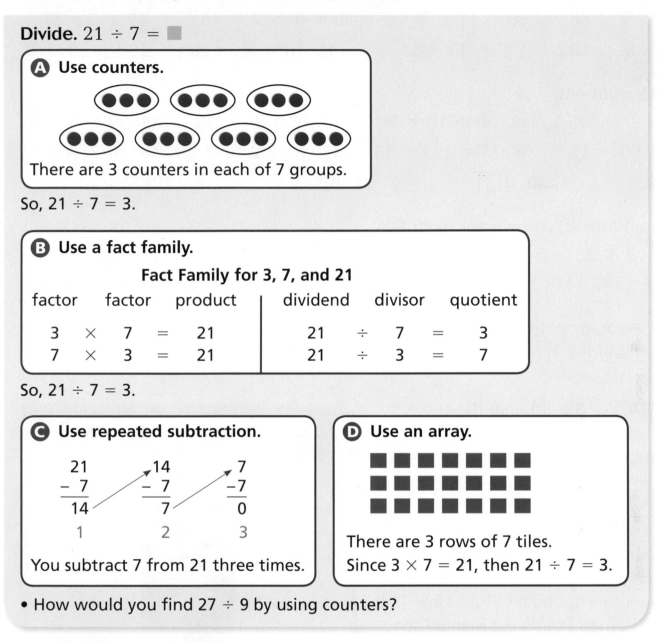

Divide. $21 \div 7 = \blacksquare$

Ⓐ Use counters.

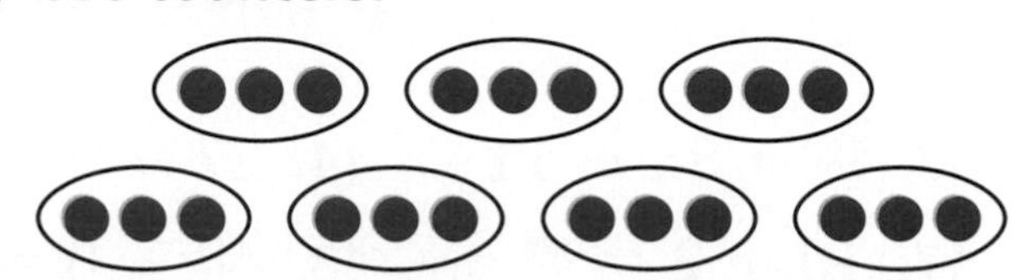

There are 3 counters in each of 7 groups.

So, $21 \div 7 = 3$.

Ⓑ Use a fact family.

Fact Family for 3, 7, and 21

factor		factor		product	dividend		divisor		quotient
3	×	7	=	21	21	÷	7	=	3
7	×	3	=	21	21	÷	3	=	7

So, $21 \div 7 = 3$.

Ⓒ Use repeated subtraction.

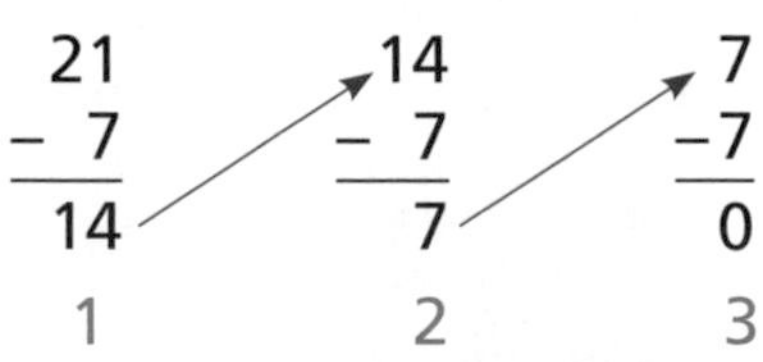

1 2 3

You subtract 7 from 21 three times.

Ⓓ Use an array.

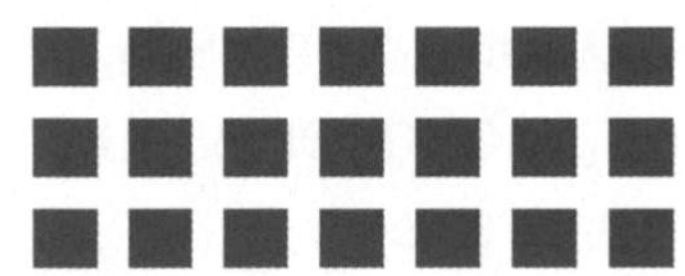

There are 3 rows of 7 tiles.
Since $3 \times 7 = 21$, then $21 \div 7 = 3$.

- How would you find $27 \div 9$ by using counters?

Guided Practice

1. Use the multiplication table on page 332 to find $88 \div 11$.

Find each missing factor and quotient.

2. $11 \times \blacksquare = 55$ $55 \div 11 = \blacksquare$
3. $12 \times \blacksquare = 24$ $24 \div 12 = \blacksquare$
4. $12 \times \blacksquare = 48$ $48 \div 12 = \blacksquare$
5. $11 \times \blacksquare = 99$ $99 \div 11 = \blacksquare$
6. TALK Math **Explain** how to use multiplication to find $84 \div 12 = \blacksquare$.

Independent Practice and Problem Solving

Find each missing factor and quotient.

7. 11 × ■ = 66 66 ÷ 11 = ■ **8.** 9 × ■ = 45 45 ÷ 9 = ■

9. 12 × ■ = 132 132 ÷ 12 = ■ **10.** 10 × ■ = 100 100 ÷ 10 = ■

Find each quotient.

11. 45 ÷ 5 = ■ **12.** 50 ÷ 10 = ■ **13.** ■ = 88 ÷ 11 **14.** 27 ÷ 9 = ■

15. ■ = 96 ÷ 12 **16.** ■ = 121 ÷ 11 **17.** 10 ÷ 2 = ■ **18.** 48 ÷ 6 = ■

19. $7\overline{)42}$ **20.** $3\overline{)21}$ **21.** $8\overline{)56}$ **22.** $12\overline{)72}$

Compare. Write <, >, or = for each ●.

23. 49 ÷ 7 ● 35 ÷ 5 **24.** 100 − 16 ● 9 × 9 **25.** 96 ÷ 8 ● 4 + 9

26. 49 + 12 ● 11 × 6 **27.** 120 ÷ 12 ● 23 − 13 **28.** 6 × 7 ● 4 × 10

Write +, −, ×, or ÷ for each ●.

29. 3 ● 3 = 72 ÷ 8 **30.** 9 ● 2 = 63 ÷ 9 **31.** 10 × 3 = 6 ● 5

USE DATA For 32–34, use the table.

Animals Hannah Saw in the Davis Mountains

Animal	Number
Rattlesnakes	14
Deer	12
Horned lizards	45
Quails	42
Elk	18

32. Hannah likes to visit the Davis Mountains in Texas. During her visits, she saw 4 equal groups of deer eating grass. How many deer were in each group?

33. The number of horned lizards Hannah saw is 9 times the number Manuel saw during his visits. How many horned lizards did Manuel see?

34. WRITE Math When Todd visited the Davis Mountains, he saw half as many elk and half as many deer as Hannah saw. How many elk and deer did Todd see in all? **Explain** your answer.

35. Reasoning Hannah took 60 photos of animals. She put 4 photos in a picture frame and put the rest in her photo album. Each page in the album holds 8 photos. How many pages did Hannah fill? **Explain.**

CD ROM **Technology**
Use Harcourt Mega Math, The Number Games, *Up, Up, and Array,* Levels H, T.

Extra Practice on page 338, Set D

Learn About MENTAL MATH Near Facts

You can use *near facts* to help you find quotients for division problems that do not come out evenly.

Example Rosa wants to share 25 cookies equally among 4 friends. How many cookies should each friend get?

Divide. $25 \div 4 = \blacksquare$

To find the quotient, look for a *near fact*. A near fact for this problem is a multiplication fact with 4 as a factor and a product as close to 25 as possible without going over.

Think: $4 \times 5 = 20$ (too low)
$4 \times 6 = 24$ (close)
$4 \times 7 = 28$ (too high)

Since $4 \times 6 = 24$ gives the closest product without going over, the quotient is 6. Since $25 - 24 = 1$, 1 is left over.
$25 \div 4 = 6$ with 1 left over

So, each friend should get 6 cookies. There will be 1 cookie left over.

Try It

Use near facts to solve. Write the near fact you used.

36. Mrs. Hart wants to put 33 desks in 4 equal rows. How many desks will be in each row? How many desks will be left over?

37. Keisha has 47 plates. She sets tables with 5 plates each. How many tables can she set? How many plates will she have left over?

Mixed Review and Test Prep

38. Gabe walked 3 miles each day for a total of 27 miles. What multiplication fact can you use to find the number of days Gabe walked? Solve. (p. 304)

39. **Test Prep** There are 80 miles of trails at a mountain. Each trail is 10 miles long. How many trails are there?

A 8 **B** 10 **C** 70 **D** 90

40. Sarah has a purple shirt, a blue shirt, and a pink shirt. She has brown pants, black pants, and tan pants. How many outfits can Sarah make with these shirts and pants? (p. 186)

41. **Test Prep** What is $77 \div 11$?

A 9 **B** 8 **C** 7 **D** 6

LESSON 6

ALGEBRA

Expressions and Equations

OBJECTIVE: Write expressions and equations that represent situations and find missing operation signs.

Quick Review

1. 15 ÷ 5
2. 28 ÷ 7
3. 32 ÷ 4
4. 40 ÷ 10
5. 48 ÷ 8

Vocabulary

expression equation

Learn

PROBLEM There are 20 children at a bowling party. They are divided into 5 equal teams. How many children are on each team?

You can write an expression for this problem. An **expression** is part of a number sentence. It combines numbers and operation signs but does not have an equal sign.

20	÷	5
↑	↑	↑
20 children	divided into	5 teams

An **equation** is a number sentence. It uses an equal sign to show that two amounts are equal. You can use the expression above to write an equation to solve the problem.

20	÷	5	=	4
↑	↑	↑	↑	↑
20 children	divided into	5 teams	is equal to	4 children on each team.

So, there are 4 children on each team.

You need to know what operation symbol to use in an equation.

There are 3 children eating pizza at each of 5 tables. There are 15 children eating pizza.

5 ● 3 = 15

Which symbol correctly completes the equation?

Try +. 5 + 3 = 15 is false.
Try −. 5 − 3 = 15 is false.
Try ÷. 5 ÷ 3 = 15 is false.
Try ×. 5 × 3 = 15 is true.

So, the correct symbol is ×.

Guided Practice

1. Write an expression to show 6 children bowling and 5 more children joining the game.

Write an expression. Then write an equation to solve.

2. There were 7 children who each paid \$4 to bowl. How much did the children pay in all?

3. There were 28 slices of pizza. The children ate 19 slices. How many slices of pizza were left?

4. TALK Math **Explain** how you know which operation symbol will complete the equation 26 ● 13 = 39.

Independent Practice and Problem Solving

Write an expression. Then write an equation to solve.

5. There were 42 children and 23 adults at a roller-skating rink. How many people were at the rink in all?

6. There were 45 balloons tied in 9 equal bunches at a party. How many balloons were in each bunch?

Write +, −, ×, or ÷ to complete each equation.

7. $3 \bullet 2 = 48 \div 8$

8. $16 \bullet 12 = 4 \times 1$

9. $11 \bullet 10 = 7 \times 3$

USE DATA For 10–12, use the graph and the equations in the box.

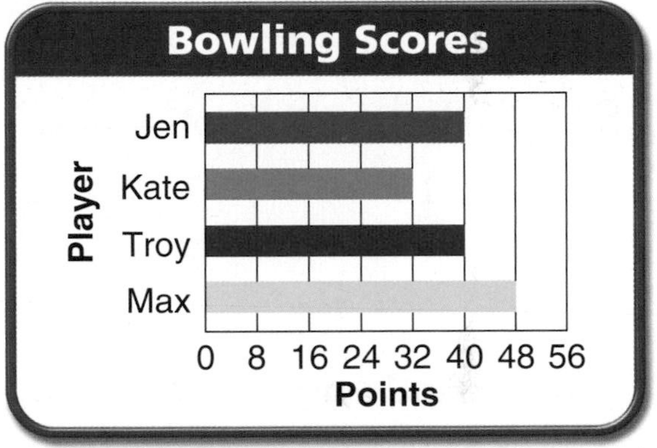

$8 \times 5 = 40$	$48 + 10 = 58$
$40 \div 8 = 5$	$48 - 10 = 38$

10. Troy scored 8 points each time it was his turn to bowl. Which equation shows how many turns Troy had?

11. John scored 10 more points than Max. Which equation shows how many points John scored?

12. WRITE Math Who scored more points during the bowling games—the boys or girls? **Explain** how you know.

Mixed Review and Test Prep

13. There are 36 score sheets in 9 packages. How many score sheets are in each package? (p. 330)

14. How many sides does a triangle have? (Grade 2)

15. **Test Prep** There are 4 pizzas each with 8 slices. Which equation shows the number of slices in all?

A $4 + 8 = 12$

B $8 - 4 = 4$

C $4 \times 8 = 32$

D $8 \div 4 = 2$

Extra Practice on page 338, Set E

Extra Practice

Set A Find each missing factor and quotient. (pp. 322–323)

1. $6 \times ■ = 36$ $36 \div 6 = ■$ 2. $6 \times ■ = 54$ $54 \div 6 = ■$

Find each quotient.

3. $12 \div 6 = ■$ 4. $■ = 42 \div 6$ 5. $30 \div 6 = ■$ 6. $■ = 24 \div 6$

7. $6\overline{)48}$ 8. $6\overline{)6}$ 9. $6\overline{)60}$ 10. $6\overline{)18}$

Set B Find each missing factor and quotient. (pp. 324–325)

1. $7 \times ■ = 28$ $28 \div 7 = ■$ 2. $8 \times ■ = 40$ $40 \div 8 = ■$

Find each quotient.

3. $■ = 56 \div 7$ 4. $16 \div 8 = ■$ 5. $■ = 72 \div 8$ 6. $21 \div 7 = ■$

7. $8\overline{)48}$ 8. $7\overline{)35}$ 9. $8\overline{)32}$ 10. $7\overline{)63}$

Set C Find each quotient. (pp. 330–331)

1. $70 \div 10 = ■$ 2. $■ = 27 \div 9$ 3. $■ = 50 \div 10$ 4. $81 \div 9 = ■$

5. $9\overline{)54}$ 6. $10\overline{)20}$ 7. $10\overline{)100}$ 8. $9\overline{)36}$

Set D Find each quotient. (pp. 332–335)

1. $■ = 32 \div 4$ 2. $60 \div 12 = ■$ 3. $45 \div 9 = ■$ 4. $■ = 88 \div 11$

5. $12\overline{)108}$ 6. $8\overline{)56}$ 7. $11\overline{)110}$ 8. $12\overline{)84}$

9. Mr. Jones divided 33 students into 11 equal groups. How many students were in each group?

10. Marie has 72 CDs. She has them arranged in stacks of 12. How many stacks of CDs does she have?

Set E Write an expression. Then write an equation to solve. (pp. 336–337)

1. There are 35 seeds planted equally among 7 pots. How many seeds are in each pot?

2. Daniel earned $75 mowing lawns. Pat earned $90. How much more money did Pat earn than Daniel?

CD ROM **Technology**
Use Harcourt Mega Math, The Number Games, *Up, Up, and Array,* Levels F, G, H.

TECHNOLOGY CONNECTION

Calculator: Division Facts

Use a Calculator for Division

Ms. Andrews bought 56 new books for her class library. There are 7 shelves on her bookshelf. If she divides the books evenly on the shelves, how many will go on each shelf?

Write a number sentence for the word problem. $56 \div 7 =$ ■

Use a calculator to solve.

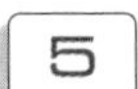     

So, Ms. Andrews can put 8 books on each shelf.

What if Ms. Andrews bought 58 books? How many books would go on each shelf? How many would be left over?

A calculator gives the remainder as a decimal. A remainder is the amount left over when a number cannot be divided evenly.

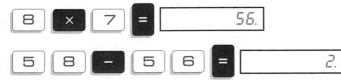

To find out how many books are left over, use a *near fact*.

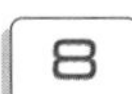    

   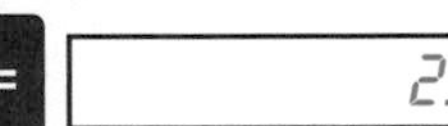

So, Ms. Andrews can put 8 books on each shelf and have 2 left over.

Try It

Use a calculator to divide.

1. $63 \div 7 =$ ■
2. $60 \div 12 =$ ■
3. $54 \div 9 =$ ■
4. $48 \div 6 =$ ■

Use a calculator to divide. Then use a near fact to find the remainder.

5. $32 \div 5 =$ ■ remainder ■
6. $65 \div 9 =$ ■ remainder ■
7. $76 \div 8 =$ ■ remainder ■
8. $68 \div 11 =$ ■ remainder ■

MATH POWER Order of Operations

Getting the SAME Answer

Find $6 - 2 \div 2$.

ONE WAY

Think: $6 - 2 = 4$

$6 - 2 \div 2 = 4 \div 2$

$4 \div 2 = 2$

ANOTHER WAY

Think: $2 \div 2 = 1$

$6 - 2 \div 2 = 6 - 1$

$6 - 1 = 5$

There seem to be two correct answers. Over the years, mathematicians have created rules so that everyone solves the problem the same way and gets the same answer.

Order of Operations

1. Solve operations inside parentheses first.
2. When there are no parentheses, multiply and divide from left to right.
3. Then, add and subtract from left to right.

So, the correct answer to $6 - 2 \div 2$ is 5.

Examples

A Find $12 \div (4 - 1)$

Think: Subtract inside the parentheses first. Then divide.

$12 \div (4 - 1) = 12 \div 3$

$12 \div 3 = 4$

B Find $6 + 4 \times 5$

Think: There are no parentheses. So, multiply first. Then add.

$6 + 4 \times 5 = 6 + 20$

$6 + 20 = 26$

Try It

Find the sum or difference.

1. $(8 - 2) \times 6 = \blacksquare$ **2.** $5 + 10 \div 5 = \blacksquare$ **3.** $3 \times (4 + 6) = \blacksquare$

4. $6 + 4 \div 2 = \blacksquare$ **5.** $(15 - 3) \times 2 = \blacksquare$ **6.** $14 - 7 \times 2 = \blacksquare$

7. WRITE Math **Explain** how to find $8 - 2 \times 3$.

Chapter 13 Review/Test

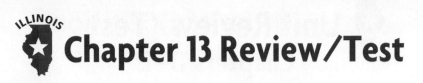

Check Concepts

Write a division sentence for each. IL 8.4.06 (pp. 332–335)

1. 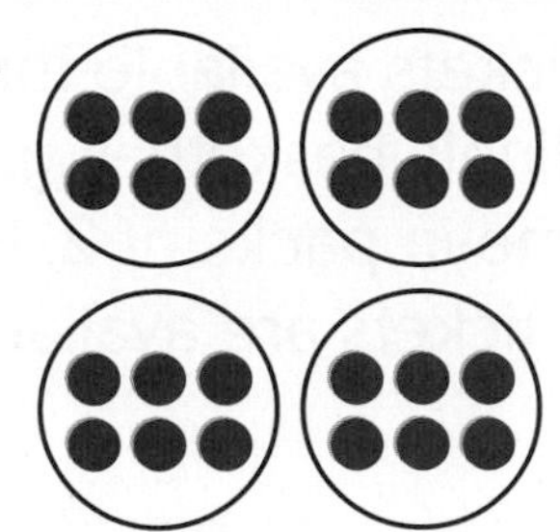

2. 

3.

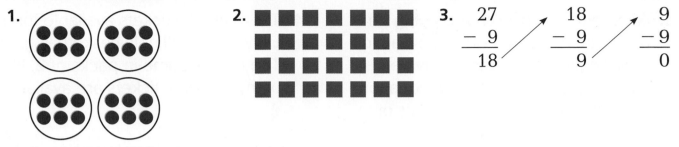

$$\begin{array}{r} 27 \\ -\ 9 \\ \hline 18 \end{array} \nearrow \begin{array}{r} 18 \\ -\ 9 \\ \hline 9 \end{array} \nearrow \begin{array}{r} 9 \\ -9 \\ \hline 0 \end{array}$$

Check Skills

Find each quotient. IL 6.4.12 (pp. 322–323, 324–325, 330–331, 332–335)

4. $32 \div 8 = \blacksquare$ **5.** $70 \div 10 = \blacksquare$ **6.** $21 \div 3 = \blacksquare$ **7.** $\blacksquare = 45 \div 5$

8. $99 \div 11 = \blacksquare$ **9.** $54 \div 9 = \blacksquare$ **10.** $60 \div 12 = \blacksquare$ **11.** $0 \div 2 = \blacksquare$

12. $16 \div 2 = \blacksquare$ **13.** $\blacksquare = 48 \div 6$ **14.** $20 \div 4 = \blacksquare$ **15.** $\blacksquare = 63 \div 7$

16. $100 \div 10 = \blacksquare$ **17.** $35 \div 5 = \blacksquare$ **18.** $121 \div 11 = \blacksquare$ **19.** $81 \div 9 = \blacksquare$

20. $9\overline{)36}$ **21.** $1\overline{)7}$ **22.** $3\overline{)9}$ **23.** $8\overline{)24}$

24. $7\overline{)28}$ **25.** $6\overline{)36}$ **26.** $8\overline{)0}$ **27.** $12\overline{)144}$

28. $1\overline{)4}$ **29.** $11\overline{)55}$ **30.** $4\overline{)24}$ **31.** $2\overline{)10}$

Write an expression. Then write an equation to solve. IL 8.3.02 (pp. 336–337)

32. There were 30 students in each of 6 groups. How many students were in each group?

33. There were 54 girls and 47 boys in line for a ride. How many students were in line?

Check Problem Solving

Solve. IL 8.3.05 (pp. 326–329)

34. Mary gave half of her markers to a friend. Then she bought 8 more markers. Now Mary has 21 markers. How many markers did she have to start?

35. WRITE Math Tim bought 3 packs of baseball cards. He gave 4 cards to his friend. Now Tim has 14 cards. How many cards were in each pack? **Explain** how you know.

Unit Review/Test
Chapters 11–13

Multiple Choice

1. A class of 24 children are going on a field trip to the Illinois State Capitol in Springfield. The class is divided into 6 equal groups. Which equation can you use to find the number of children in each group? IL 8.3.03 (p. 336)

   A $24 - 6 = 18$

   B $24 + 6 = 30$

   C $24 \div 6 = 4$

   D $24 \times 6 = 144$

2. Greson has 18 toy cars. He put the toy cars into equal groups with 3 cars in each group. Which shows how many groups Greson made? IL 8.3.05 (p. 312)

   A 54 **C** 6

   B 9 **D** 3

3. In Mr. Jenkin's classroom, there are 4 rows of desks with 5 desks in each row. Which number sentence could you solve to find total number of desks in the classroom? IL 8.3.03 (p. 290)

   A $4 \times 5 = \blacksquare$

   B $4 + 5 = \blacksquare$

   C $5 - 4 = \blacksquare$

   D $9 - 5 = \blacksquare$

4. There are 10 tickets available for a University of Illinois basketball game. The tickets come in packs of 2. How many packs of tickets are available? IL 9.3.11 (p. 280)

   A 6 **C** 4

   B 5 **D** 3

5. Kevin practiced piano for 35 minutes on Saturday. He practiced 5 songs for an equal number of minutes. Which number sentence shows how many minutes Kevin spent practicing each song? IL 8.3.05 (p. 290)

   A $35 \div 5 = 7$

   B $35 - 5 = 30$

   C $35 + 5 = 40$

   D $35 \times 5 = 175$

6. There were 58 adults and 23 children at Shedd Aquarium on Tuesday afternoon. Which equation can you use to find how many total people were at the aquarium Tuesday afternoon? IL 8.3.03 (p. 336)

   A $58 - 23 = 35$

   B $58 + 23 = 81$

   C $23 + 35 = 58$

   D $58 - 35 = 23$

GO ONLINE **Technology** Use *Online Assessment.*

7. Allie bought 4 packages of hot dog buns for a picnic. The hot dog buns come in packages of 8. How many hot dog buns did Allie buy in all? IL 6.3.11 (p. 260)

A 24 C 40

B 32 D 48

8. Derek, Amanda, and Connor told a total of 12 jokes at a school talent show. Each of them told the same number of jokes. Which expression represents the number of jokes each person told? IL 8.3.03 (p. 290)

A 12×4

B 3×12

C $4 \div 3$

D $12 \div 3$

9. A movie theater sold 2,467 tickets on Friday, 3,527 tickets on Saturday, 3,984 tickets on Sunday, and 2,057 tickets on Monday. On which day did they sell the second-greatest number of tickets? IL 6.3.07 (p. 34)

A Thursday

B Friday

C Saturday

D Sunday

Extended Response WRITE Math

10. Mrs. Morris has a box of oranges. There are 6 rows of oranges with the same number of oranges in each row. After she takes 4 oranges out, there are 14 oranges left in the box. How many oranges were in each row? IL 8.3.05 (p. 326)

11. Sandra bought 5 bags of peaches. She gave 12 peaches to her neighbor. Now Sandra has 8 peaches. How many peaches were in each bag? IL 8.3.05 (p. 326)

Use the spinner for 12–13. Alex will spin the spinner one time.

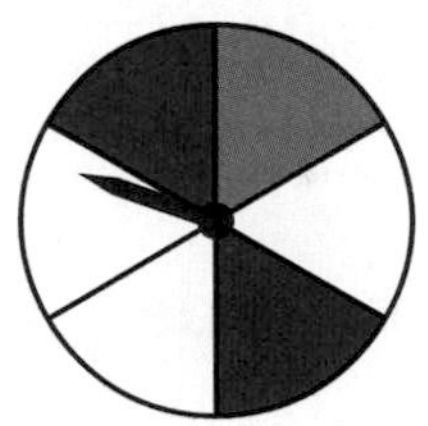

12. On which color is the pointer most likely to land? On which color is it least likely to land? **Explain.**

13. Name an impossible outcome for one spin. **Explain.** IL 10.3.04 (p. 182)

14. Daria says that $7 \times 1 = 8$. **Explain** her error and give the correct answer. IL 10.3.04 (p. 182)

THE WORLD ALMANAC FOR KIDS

The Wheel Is a Big Deal

Around the Wheel

Think about the wheel. Without it, almost no one could travel anywhere. Buses, trains, cars, skateboards, and even planes and space shuttles use wheels.

FACT • ACTIVITY

Vehicles with Different Numbers of Wheels

	Vehicle	Number of Wheels
	unicycle	1
	bicycle	2
	tricycle	3
	car	4
	space shuttle	6
	tractor trailer	18

School teams are making models of vehicles with a given number of wheels. Use the table to answer the questions.

1. Team A has 22 wheels. How many bicycles can they make?
2. Team B has 48 wheels. How many space shuttles can they make?
3. Team A wants to make cars instead of bicycles. How many cars can they make? What can they make with the extra wheels?
4. Make your own vehicle.
   - Invent a new vehicle that uses 7 wheels.
   - Draw your vehicle and name it.
   - How many of these new vehicles could you make if you had 21 wheels?

ALMANAC
Fact

The first pedaled bicycle was invented in Scotland in 1839.

Today, bicycles are used all over the world.

Reusing Tired Tires

Trucks, motorcycles, and cars all use tires. These tires are strong, but they do wear out. What happens to old tires? Ground-up tires can be used to make roads, playground surfaces, and jogging tracks. Some tires are even made into park benches and waste containers. Whole tires can be used to make playground equipment.

FACT·ACTIVITY

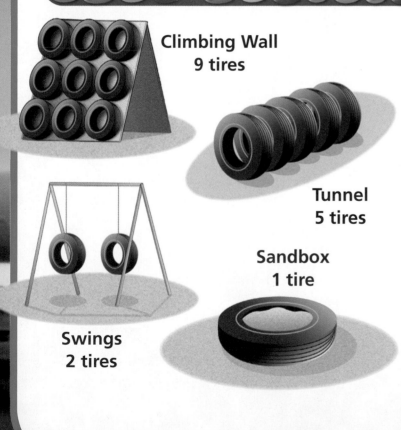

Climbing Wall
9 tires

Tunnel
5 tires

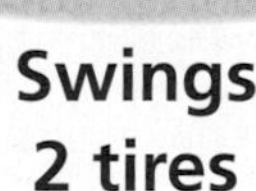

Swings
2 tires

Sandbox
1 tire

Some playgrounds use tires for swings, tunnels, and climbing walls. Use the data from the playground pictures to answer the questions.

1. How many tires are needed for this playground?
2. How many climbing walls can be made from 63 tires?
3. **WRITE Math** Are 19 tires enough to make 4 tire tunnels? **Explain.**
4. It takes 6 tires to make the tunnel and sandbox combined. How many sets of these can be made from 30 tires?

UNIT

5 Geometry and Patterns

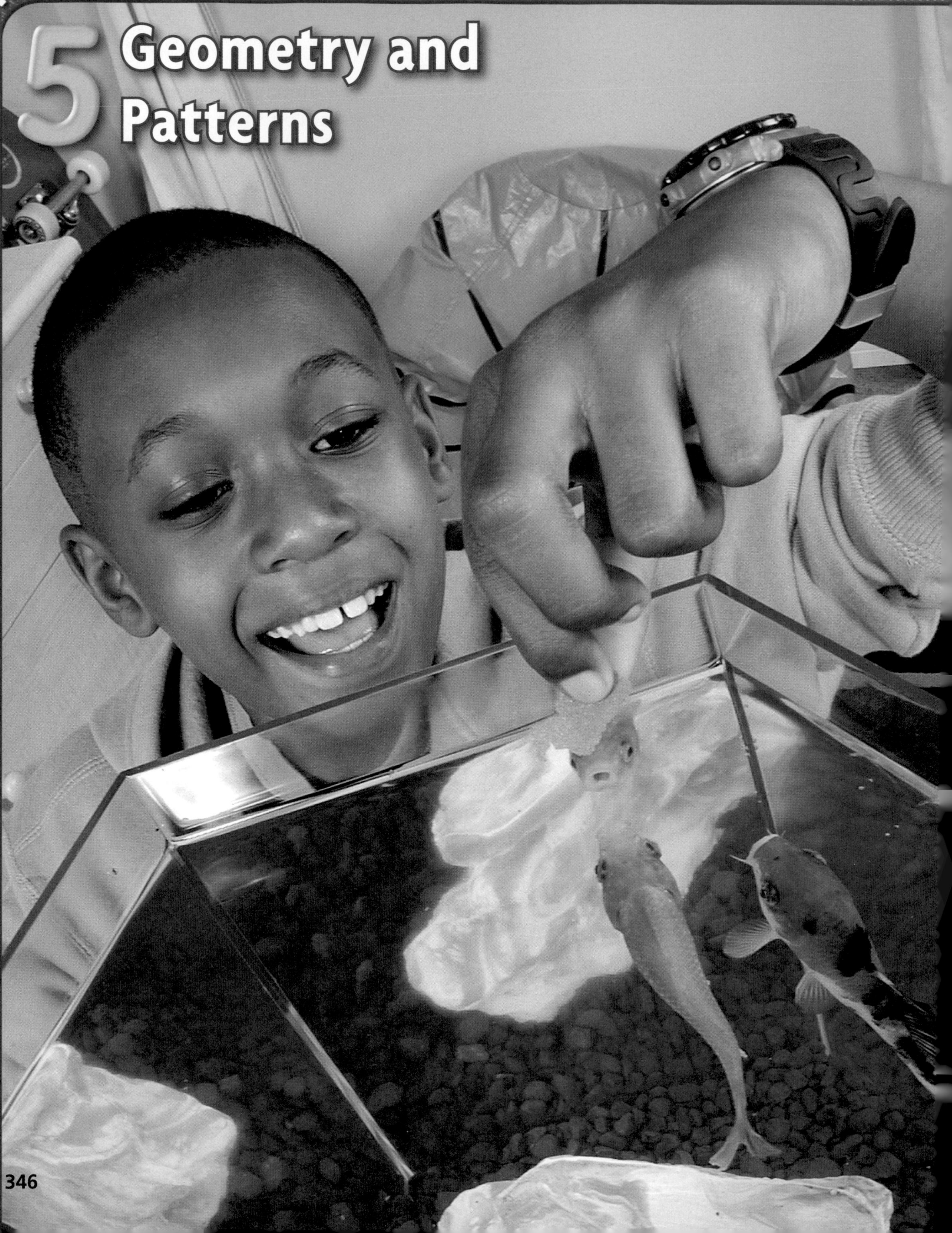

Math on Location

with
Chapter Projects

1

Fresh or saltwater aquariums of all shapes and sizes bring nature into a home or office.

2

This large tank, a rectangular prism, will hold 32,000 pounds of water. It needs thick acrylic faces!

3

Some customers want curved-shaped aquariums like the half-cylinder surface that is being polished.

VOCABULARY POWER

TALK Math

What math ideas do you see in the **Math on Location** photographs? How many faces does the large rectangular tank have?

READ Math

REVIEW VOCABULARY You learned the words below when you learned about geometry last year. How do these words relate to **Math on Location**?

rectangle

square

solid figure a figure such as a sphere, a cube, a rectangular prism, a cylinder, a cone, or a pyramid

WRITE Math

Copy and complete a Degree of Meaning Grid like the one below. Use what you know about geometry.

General	Less General	Specific	More Specific
Plane figure	Lines	Line segment	Yarn
Polygon	Quadrilateral	Square	Napkin
Solid figure			

Technology
Multimedia Math Glossary link at
www.harcourtschool.com/hspmath

CHAPTER 14 Plane Figures

FAST FACT

The Flatiron Building is one of the oldest skyscrapers in New York City. The sides of the three-sided building connect to form a right triangle!

Investigate

Each side of the Flatiron Building is in the shape of a rectangle. Below are pictures of other skyscrapers. Make a list of the plane figures you see.

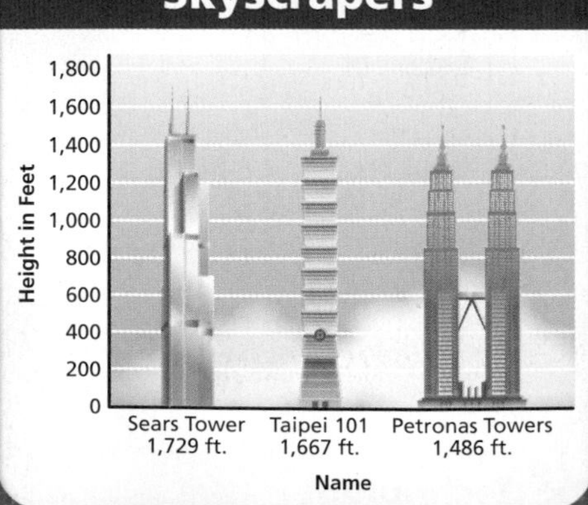

GO ONLINE **Technology**
Student pages are available in the Student eBook.

Show What You Know

Check your understanding of important skills needed for success in Chapter 14.

▶ Plane Figures

Name each figure.

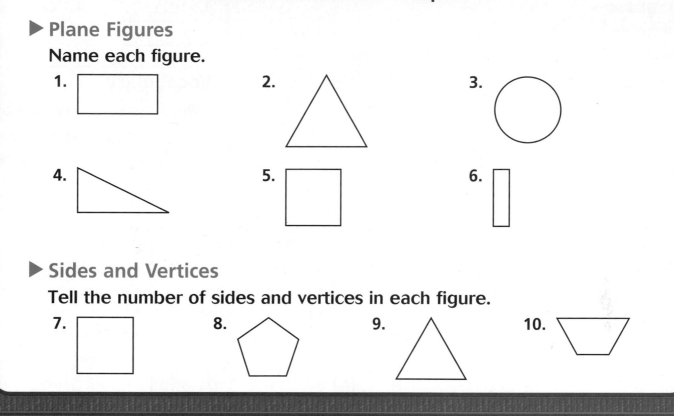

1. 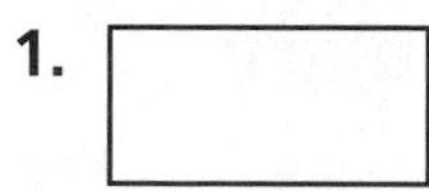
2. 
3. 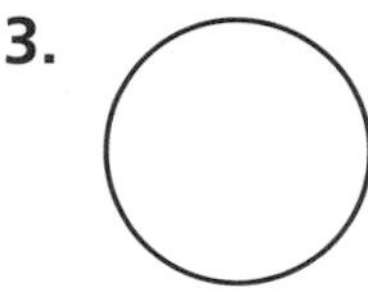
4. 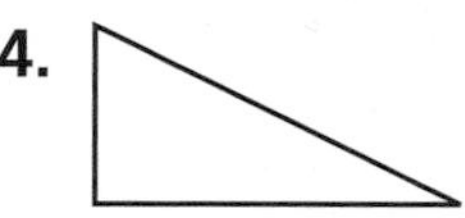
5. 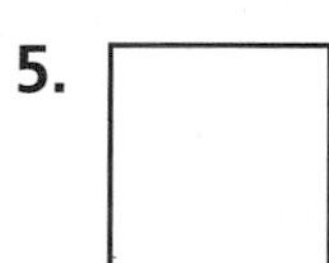
6. 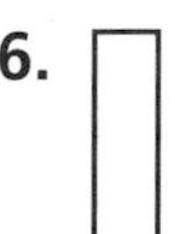

▶ Sides and Vertices

Tell the number of sides and vertices in each figure.

7. 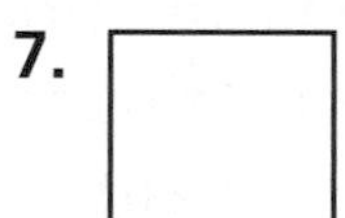
8. 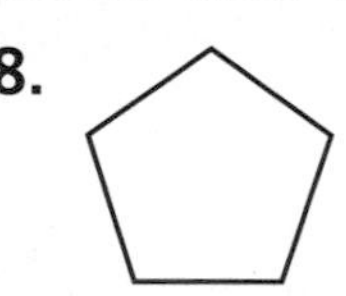
9. 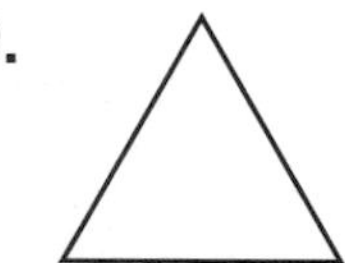
10. 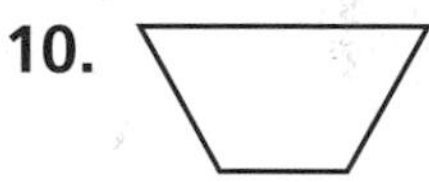

VOCABULARY POWER

CHAPTER VOCABULARY

acute angle
acute triangle
angle
center
circle
circumference
diameter
equilateral triangle
hexagon
intersecting lines
isosceles triangle
line
line segment
obtuse angle
obtuse triangle
octagon
parallel lines
parallelogram
pentagon
perpendicular lines
plane figure
point
polygon
quadrilateral
radius
ray
rhombus
right angle
right triangle
scalene triangle
straight angle
trapezoid
2-dimensional figures
vertex

WARM-UP WORDS

angle A figure formed by two rays that share an endpoint

line A straight path extending in both directions with no endpoints

quadrilateral A polygon with four sides

LESSON 1

Line Segments and Angles

OBJECTIVE: Identify points, lines, line segments, rays, and angles.

Quick Review

Write the number of sides.

1. □
2. △
3. ▱
4. ⬡
5. ▭

Vocabulary

point, line, line segment, ray, angle, vertex, right angle, acute angle, obtuse angle, straight angle

Learn

PROBLEM Carmen drew this figure. What math words can you use to describe the figure?

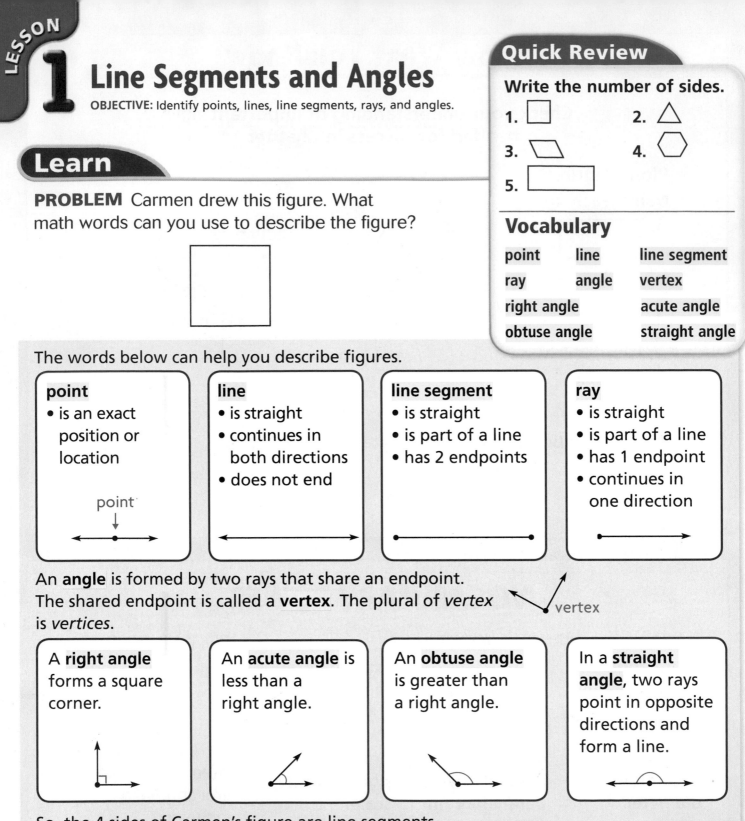

The words below can help you describe figures.

point	**line**	**line segment**	**ray**
• is an exact position or location	• is straight • continues in both directions • does not end	• is straight • is part of a line • has 2 endpoints	• is straight • is part of a line • has 1 endpoint • continues in one direction
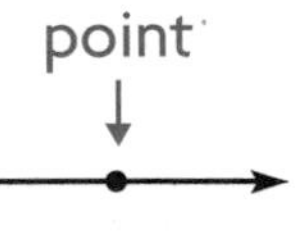			

An **angle** is formed by two rays that share an endpoint. The shared endpoint is called a **vertex**. The plural of *vertex* is *vertices*.

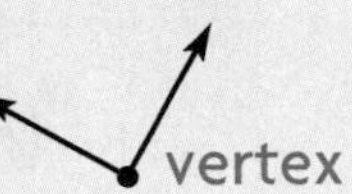

A **right angle** forms a square corner.	An **acute angle** is less than a right angle.	An **obtuse angle** is greater than a right angle.	In a **straight angle**, two rays point in opposite directions and form a line.
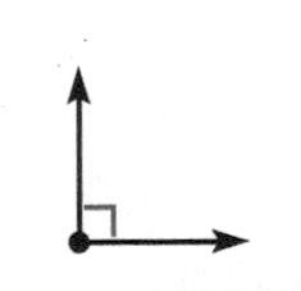	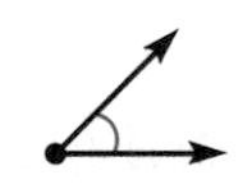	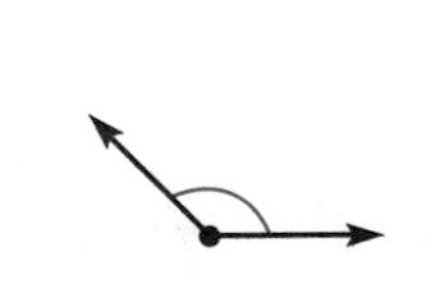	

So, the 4 sides of Carmen's figure are line segments. There are 4 right angles and 4 vertices.

- How are lines and line segments alike? How are they different?

Activity Draw Angles

Materials ■ dot paper, ruler

Step 1
Draw a point.

Step 2
Use a ruler to draw 2 rays that meet at the point.

Step 3
Label your angle.

right angle

- Draw and label an acute angle, an obtuse angle, and a straight angle.
- Explain how you can use the corner of a sheet of paper to check the angles you drew.

Guided Practice

1. How many line segments are in this figure?

Tell whether each is a *point, line, line segment,* or *ray*.

2.
3.
4.
5.

Use the corner of a sheet of paper to tell whether each angle is *right, acute, obtuse,* or *straight*.

6.
7.
8.
9.

10. TALK Math **Explain** the difference between a ray and a line segment.

Independent Practice and Problem Solving

Tell whether each is a *point, line, line segment,* or *ray.*

11. ←→

12. •→

13. •

14. 

Use the corner of a sheet of paper to tell whether each angle is *right, acute, obtuse,* or *straight.*

15. 

16. 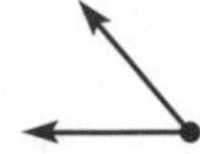

17. 

18. 

19. Katie made the figure on the right on grid paper. How many angles does Katie's figure have? Tell how many are right, acute, and obtuse.

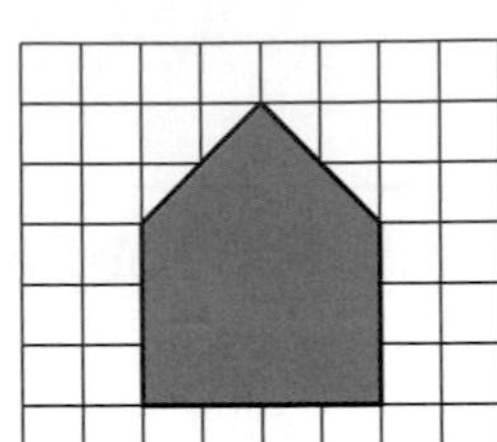

20. Use a ruler and dot paper to draw an acute angle.

21. ***FAST FACT*** The first pocket watch was invented in 1524. What time is shown? What type of angle do the hands form?

22. WRITE Math **What's the Error?** Zoey says this angle is an acute angle. Is she correct? **Explain.**

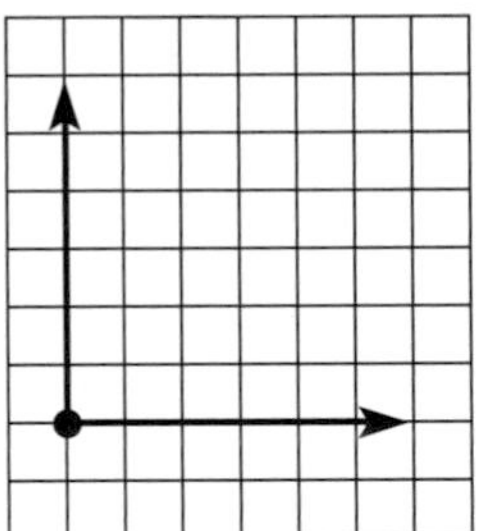

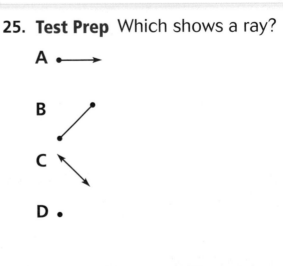

Mixed Review and Test Prep

23. Bruce has 8 bags of marbles. There are the same number of marbles in each bag. He has a total of 56 marbles. How many marbles are in each bag? (p. 324)

24. The drama club sold 3,500 tickets for three shows. They sold 987 tickets for the Thursday show and 1,215 tickets for the Friday show. How many tickets did they sell for the Saturday show? (p. 58, 88)

25. Test Prep Which shows a ray?

A •→

B •—•

C ←→

D •

Extra Practice on page 370, Set A

Write to Explain

One way to explain two different things is to write about ways they are alike and ways they are different. In doing so, you compare the things.

Allen is learning about line segments, rays, and angles. He compares two angles by explaining how they are alike and how they are different.

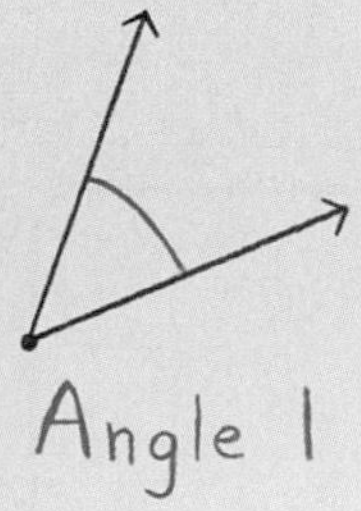

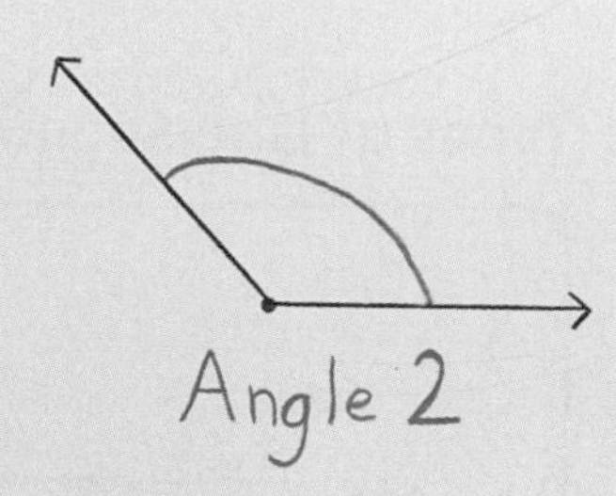

The two angles are alike. They are both made of two rays that share one endpoint.

The two angles are different. The angles are different sizes. Angle 1 is an acute angle. It is smaller than a right angle. Angle 2 is an obtuse angle. It is larger than a right angle.

Tips

To compare two drawings:

- First, describe the ways the drawings are alike.
- Then, describe the ways the drawings are different.
- Use correct definitions of math words.

Problem Solving **Write a paragraph to explain how the drawings are alike and how they are different.**

1. 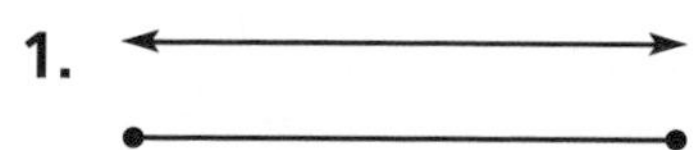

2. 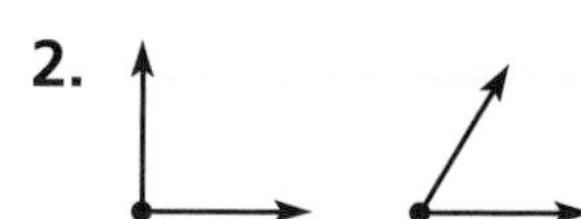

LESSON

2 Types of Lines

OBJECTIVE: Identify and classify lines as intersecting, perpendicular, or parallel.

Quick Review

Name each figure.

1\.

2\.

3\.

4\.

5\.

Vocabulary

intersecting lines

perpendicular lines

parallel lines

Learn

PROBLEM What kinds of line segments are in this figure?

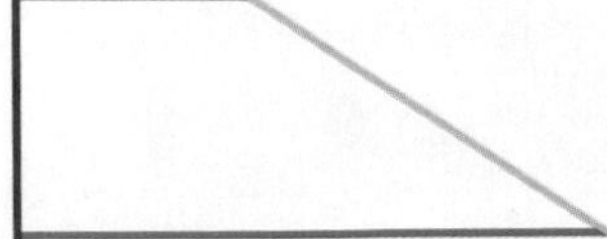

There are different ways to describe lines and line segments.

Types of Lines

Lines that cross are **intersecting lines**. Intersecting lines form angles.

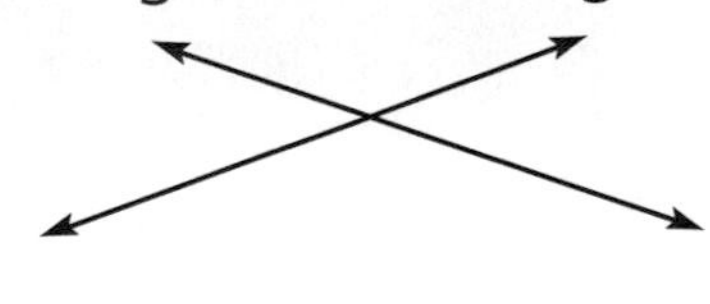

Intersecting lines that cross to form right angles are **perpendicular lines**.

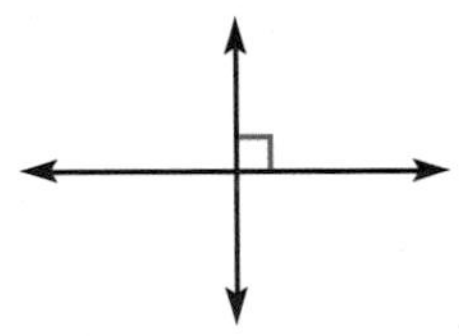

Lines that appear never to cross are **parallel lines**. They are always the same distance apart. They do not form any angles.

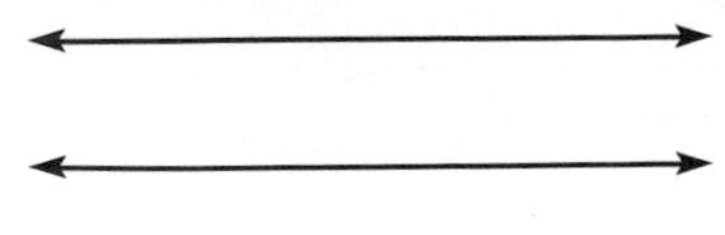

Types of Line Segments

The yellow and blue line segments meet. So, they form an angle.

The red and blue line segments meet at a right angle. So, they are perpendicular.

The green and blue line segments never cross. They are always the same distance apart. So, they appear to be parallel.

Guided Practice

1. The lines cross to form angles. Are they perpendicular lines or intersecting lines?

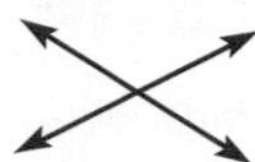

Describe the green line segments. Tell if the line segments appear to be *perpendicular* or *parallel*.

2. 

✓ 3. 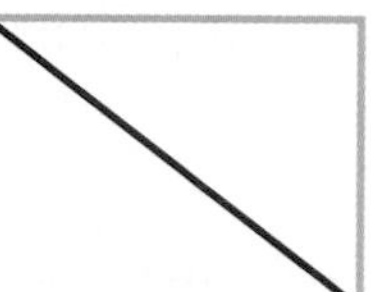

✓ 4. 

5. TALK Math **Explain** the difference between parallel lines and perpendicular lines.

Independent Practice and Problem Solving

Describe the lines. Tell if the lines appear to be *intersecting, perpendicular,* or *parallel*.

6.

7. 

8. 

Describe the green line segments. Tell if the line segments appear to be *perpendicular* or *parallel*.

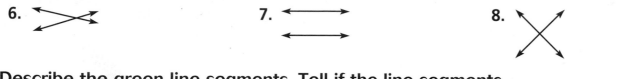

9. 

10. 

11. 

12. Use a ruler to draw pairs of intersecting, parallel, and perpendicular lines. Label each pair of lines.

13. WRITE Math **What's the Error?** Katie says the lines below appear to be parallel. **Explain** her error.

Mixed Review and Test Prep

14. Which operation sign goes in the box to make this number sentence true?

$12 \bullet 4 = 3$ (p. 304)

15. Name this angle. (p. 350)

16. **Test Prep** Which of these pairs of lines appear to be perpendicular?

A C

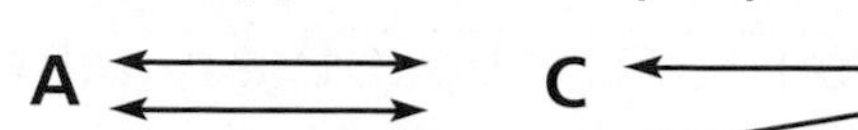

B

D

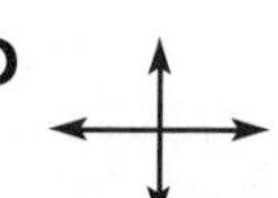

Extra Practice on page 370, Set B

LESSON 3

Identify Plane Figures

OBJECTIVE: Identify, classify, and describe plane figures.

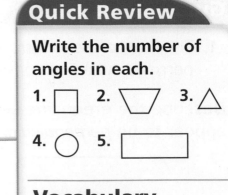

Quick Review

Write the number of angles in each.

1. 2. 3.

4. 5.

Vocabulary

plane figure
polygon
quadrilateral
two-dimensional figure
pentagon
hexagon
octagon

Learn

A **plane figure** is a figure on a flat surface. It is formed by lines that are curved, straight, or both.

A **polygon** is a closed plane figure with straight sides that are line segments.

Polygons have length and width, so they are called **two-dimensional figures**.

Polygons can be named by the number of sides or number of angles they have.

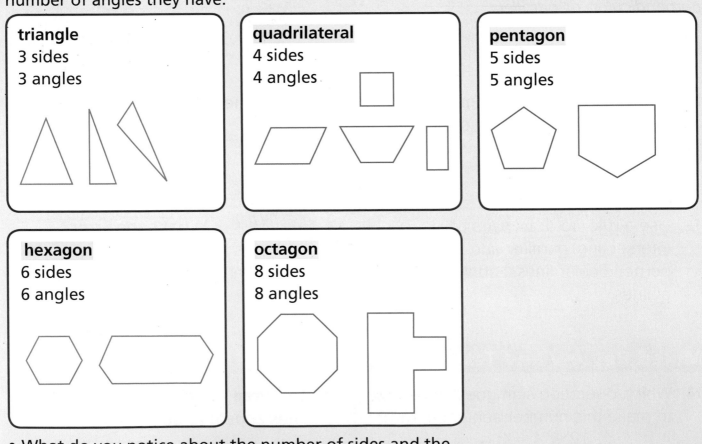

triangle
3 sides
3 angles

quadrilateral
4 sides
4 angles

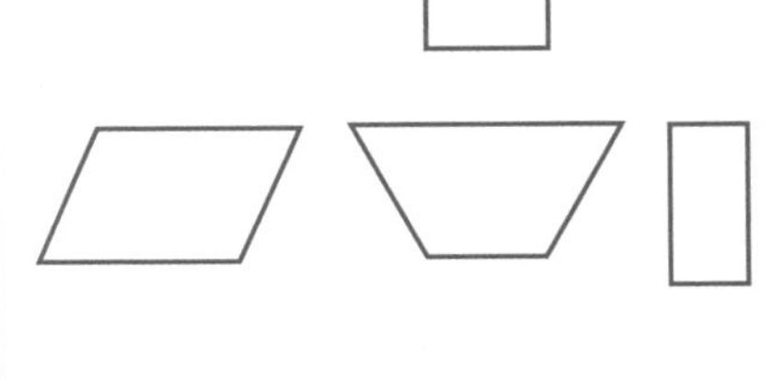

pentagon
5 sides
5 angles

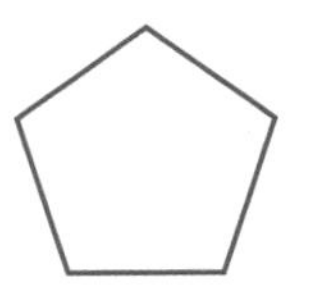

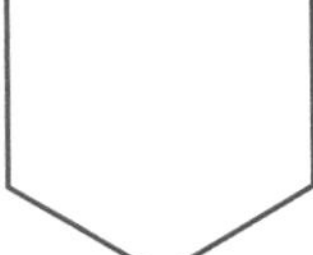

hexagon
6 sides
6 angles

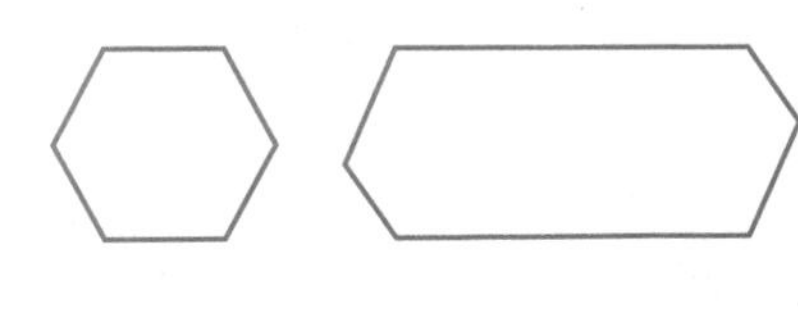

octagon
8 sides
8 angles

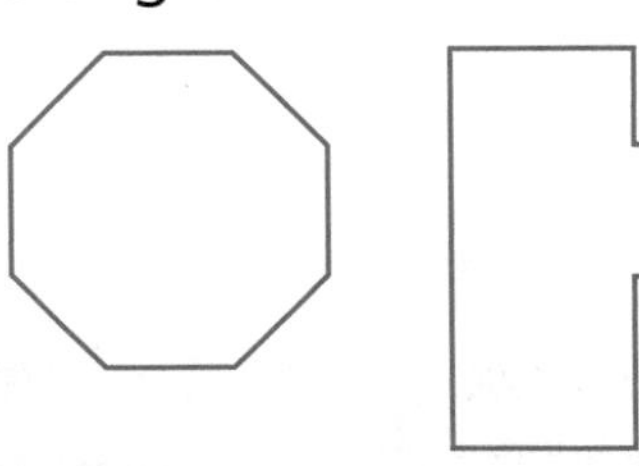

- What do you notice about the number of sides and the number of angles in each of the polygons shown above?

Guided Practice

1. Tell why the figure at the right is not a polygon.

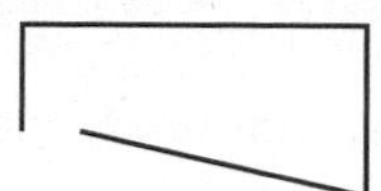

Name each polygon. Tell how many sides.

2. 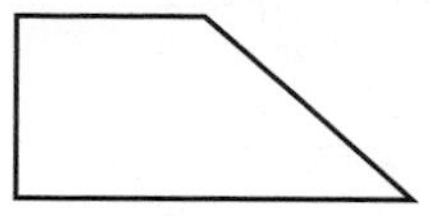

3. 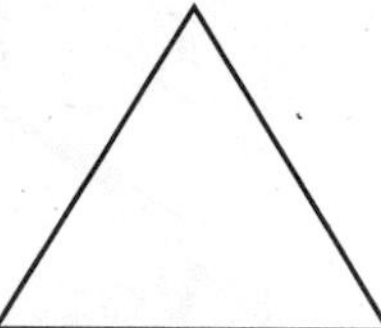

✓ 4. 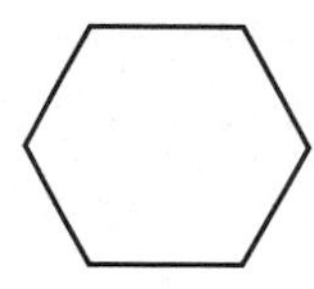

✓ 5. 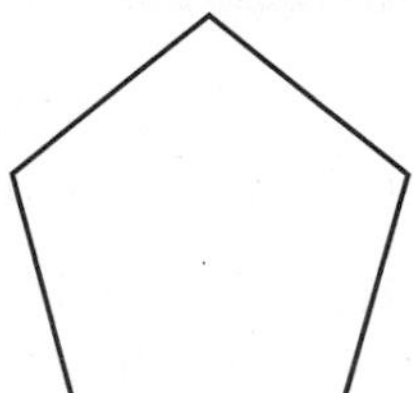

6. TALK Math **Explain** why a pentagon is a polygon.

Independent Practice and Problem Solving

Name each polygon. Tell how many sides.

7. 

8. 

9. 

10. 

Tell whether each figure is a polygon. Write *yes* or *no*.

11. 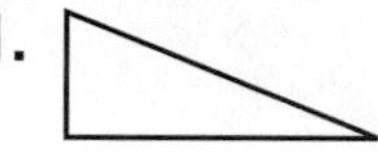

12. 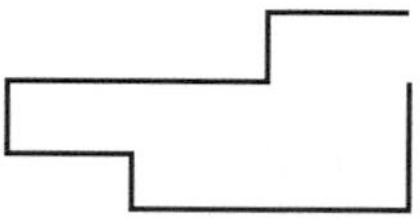

13. 

14. 

15. Draw a polygon with 4 sides and 4 angles. Then name the polygon.

16. Val has 25 craft sticks. She glues some sticks together to make 6 triangles. How many sticks does she have left?

17. WRITE Math Are figures *A–E* all polygons? **Explain** why or why not.

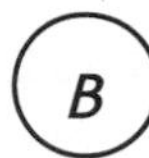

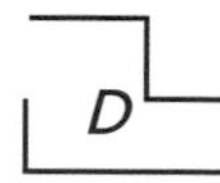

Mixed Review and Test Prep

18. Is this angle *right, acute, obtuse,* or *straight*? (p. 350)

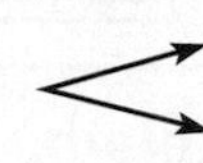

19. How many endpoints does a ray have? (p. 350)

20. **Test Prep** How many sides does a pentagon have?

A 4 **B** 5 **C** 6 **D** 8

Extra Practice on page 370, Set C

LESSON 4 Triangles

OBJECTIVE: Identify, describe, and classify triangles.

Quick Review

Is the angle a right angle? Write *yes* or *no*.

1. ↑→ **2.** ↗→ **3.** ↖→

4. ↙↗ **5.** ↗→

Vocabulary

equilateral triangle
isosceles triangle
scalene triangle
right triangle
obtuse triangle
acute triangle

Learn

PROBLEM The sculpture in the photo is called *Moondog*. The artist used triangles and other polygons. Name the types of triangles outlined in the sculpture.

ONE WAY You can name triangles by their equal sides.

equilateral triangle	isosceles triangle	scalene triangle
3 equal sides	2 equal sides	0 equal sides
3 cm, 3 cm, 3 cm	2 cm, 3 cm, 3 cm	3 cm, 4 cm, 2 cm

So, the red and white triangles are equilateral triangles, the yellow, purple, and green triangles are isosceles triangles, and the blue triangles are scalene triangles.

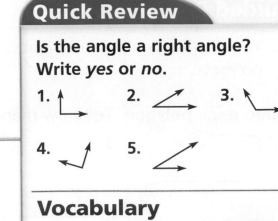

▲ The sculpture *Moondog*, by Tony Smith, is at the National Gallery of Art in Washington, D.C.

ANOTHER WAY You can name triangles by their angles.

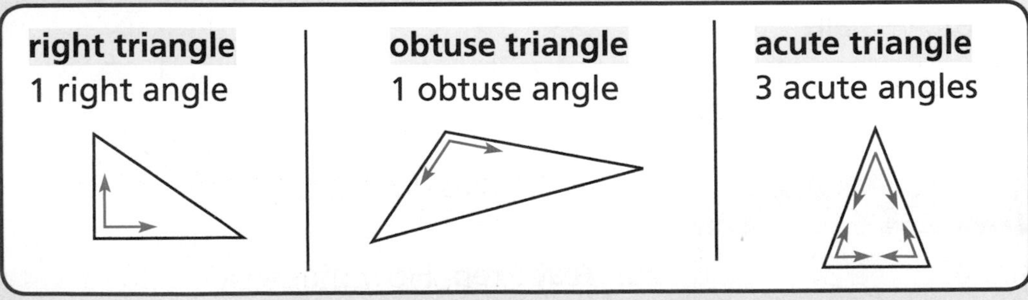

right triangle	obtuse triangle	acute triangle
1 right angle	1 obtuse angle	3 acute angles

• Can a right triangle also be an isosceles triangle? **Explain.**

Remember

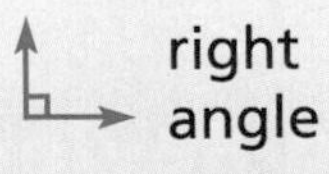
right angle

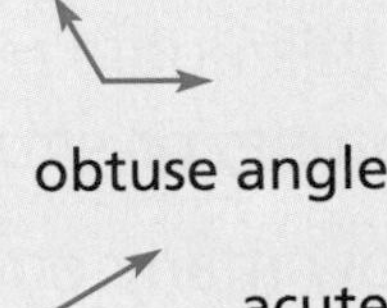
obtuse angle

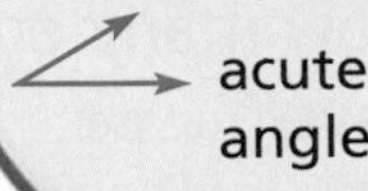
acute angle

Guided Practice

1. Name each triangle.
   Write *equilateral, isosceles,* or *scalene.*
   Think: How many equal sides does each triangle have?

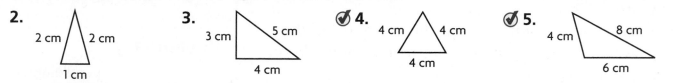

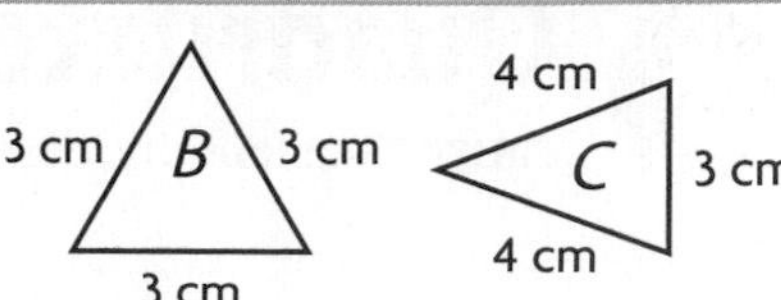

Name each triangle. Write *right, obtuse,* or *acute.*

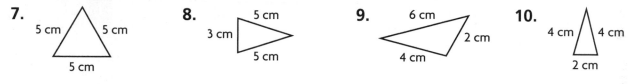

2. 2 cm, 2 cm, 1 cm
3. 3 cm, 5 cm, 4 cm
4. 4 cm, 4 cm, 4 cm
5. 4 cm, 8 cm, 6 cm

6. **TALK Math** **Describe** how a triangle can be both equilateral and acute.

Independent Practice and Problem Solving

Name each triangle. Write *equilateral, isosceles,* or *scalene.*

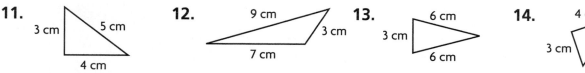

7. 5 cm, 5 cm, 5 cm
8. 5 cm, 3 cm, 5 cm
9. 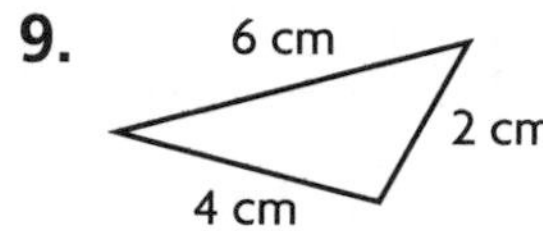

10. 4 cm, 4 cm, 2 cm

Name each triangle. Write *right, obtuse,* or *acute.*

11. 3 cm, 5 cm, 4 cm
12. 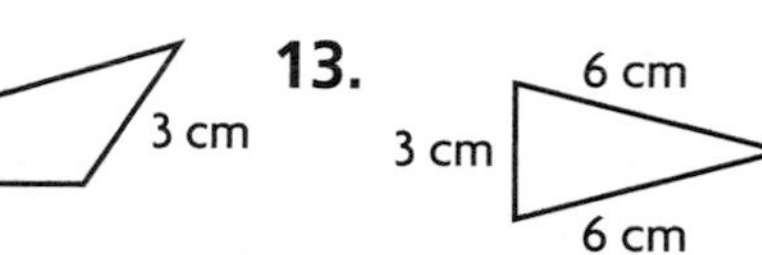

13. 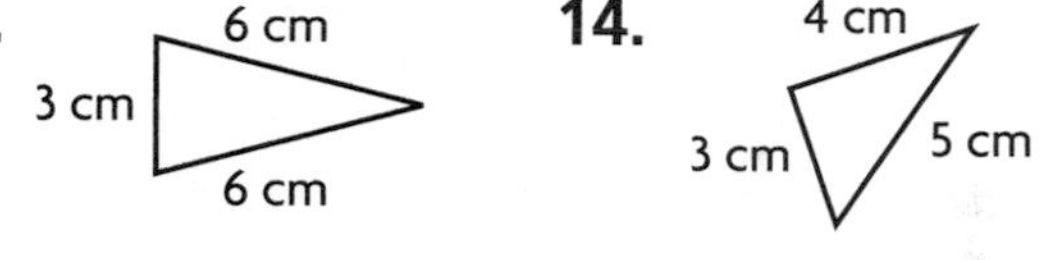

14. 4 cm, 3 cm, 5 cm

15. Two of my sides are 5 inches long. My third side is shorter. All of my angles are less than a right angle. What kind of triangle am I?

16. **WRITE Math** How are an equilateral triangle and a scalene triangle alike? How are they different? **Explain.**

Mixed Review and Test Prep

17. Aaron drew a plane figure with 5 sides and 5 angles. Name the figure Aaron drew. (p. 356)

18. You toss a coin. What are the possible outcomes? (p. 180)

19. **Test Prep** Which correctly names this triangle?

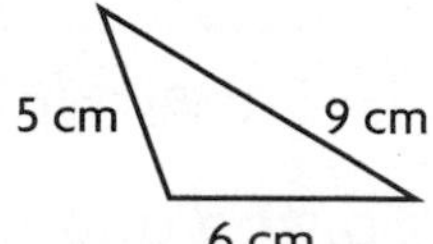

A scalene and obtuse
B isosceles and acute
C scalene and acute
D isosceles and obtuse

Extra Practice on page 371, Set D

LESSON 5

Quadrilaterals

OBJECTIVE: Identify, describe, and classify quadrilaterals.

Quick Review

Write the number of sides.

1.  **2.** 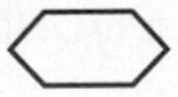 **3.** 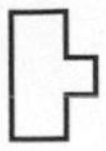

4.  **5.** 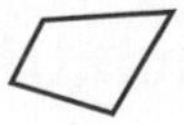

Vocabulary

rhombus **parallelogram**

trapezoid

Learn

PROBLEM Lynn's aunt sent her this postcard of the Eiffel Tower, in Paris, France. What type of quadrilateral do you see in the tower?

Some quadrilaterals are named by their sides and their angles.

Examples

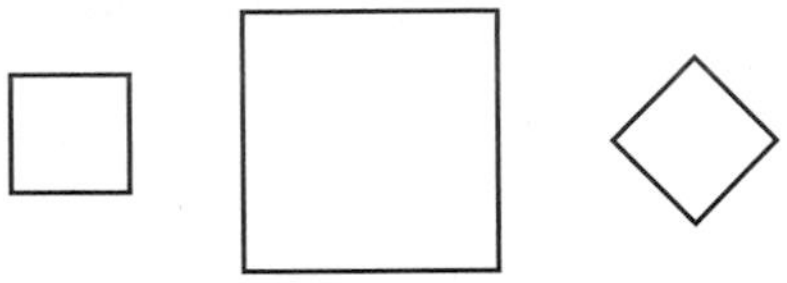

Square

- 2 pairs of parallel sides
- 4 equal sides
- 4 right angles

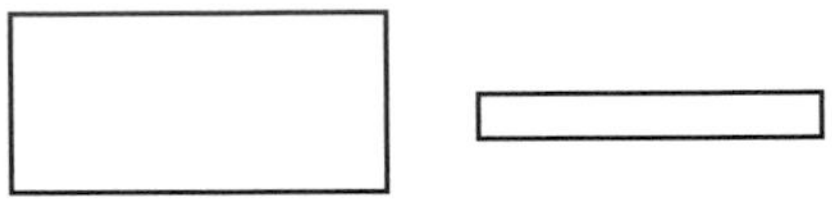

Rectangle

- 2 pairs of parallel sides
- 2 pairs of equal sides
- 4 right angles

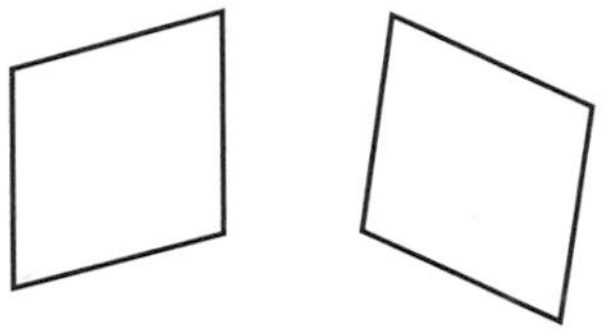

Rhombus

- 2 pairs of parallel sides
- 4 equal sides

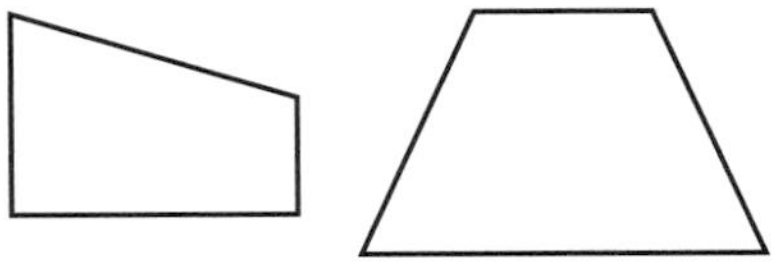

Trapezoid

- exactly 1 pair of parallel sides
- lengths of sides may not be the same
- sizes of angles may not be the same

The quadrilateral in the tower has 1 pair of parallel sides.

So, the quadrilateral in the Eiffel Tower is a trapezoid.

- What types of angles are in the trapezoid?

▲ The Eiffel Tower is 984 feet high. From the top you can see the city of Paris.

Another Example

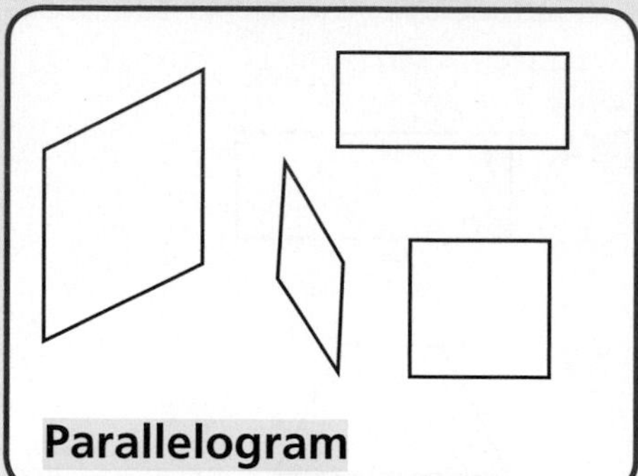

Parallelogram

- 2 pairs of parallel sides
- 2 pairs of equal sides

- Explain why a trapezoid is not a parallelogram.
- Explain why a square is a parallelogram, a rectangle, a quadrilateral, and a rhombus.

Guided Practice

Look at the quadrilateral at the right.

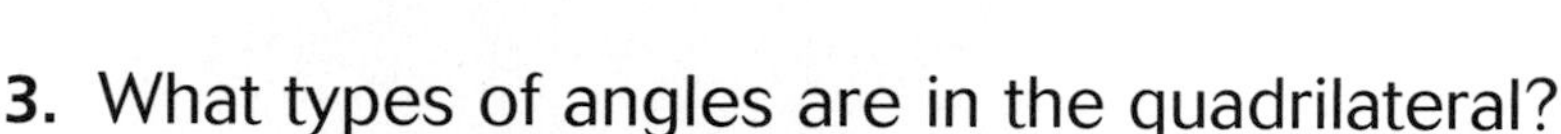

1. How many pairs of sides are parallel?
2. How many pairs of sides are equal?
3. What types of angles are in the quadrilateral?
4. Name the quadrilateral.

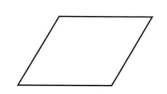

Write as many names for each quadrilateral as you can.

5. 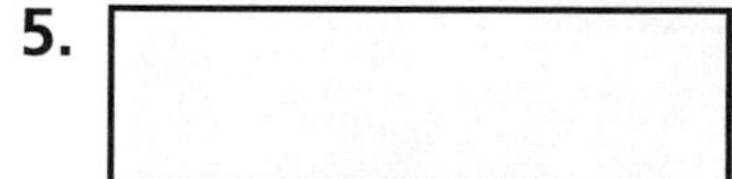

6. 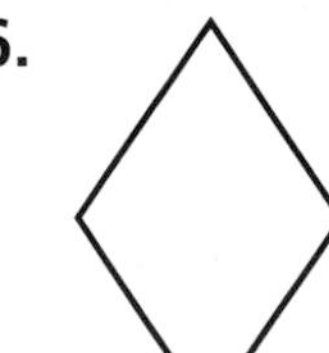

7. 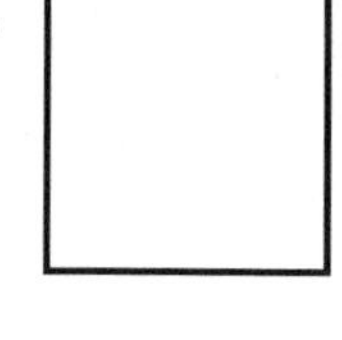

8. 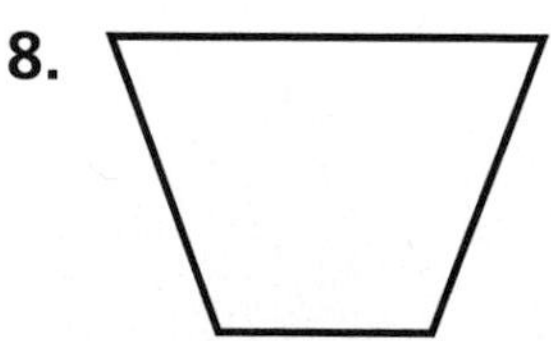

9. 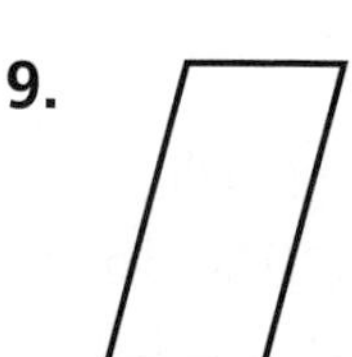

10. 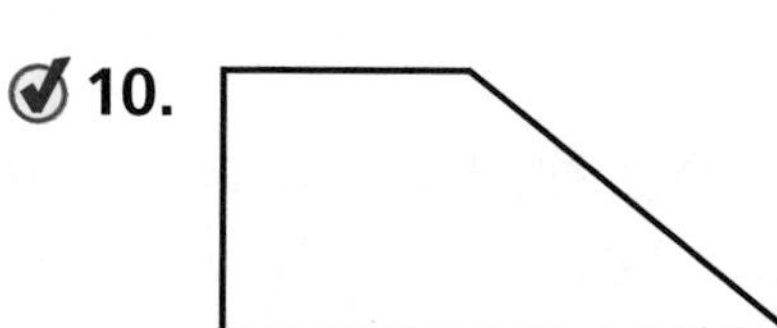

11. TALK Math **Describe** a square by its sides and by its angles.

Independent Practice and Problem Solving

Write as many names for each quadrilateral as you can.

12. 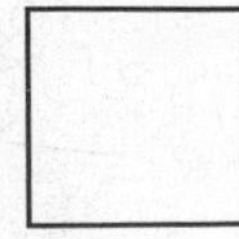

13. 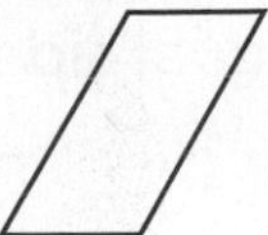

14. 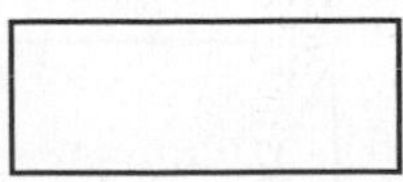

15. 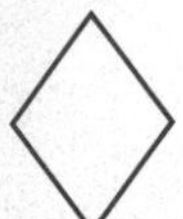

16. 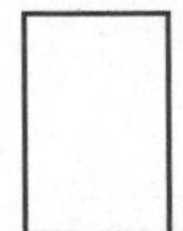

17. 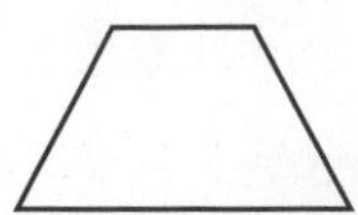

For 18–21, use the quadrilaterals at the right.

18. Which quadrilaterals have 4 right angles?

19. Which quadrilaterals have 2 pairs of parallel sides?

20. Which quadrilaterals have no right angles?

21. How are quadrilateral B and quadrilateral C alike? How are they different?

22. Describe the quadrilaterals you see in the flag of France below.

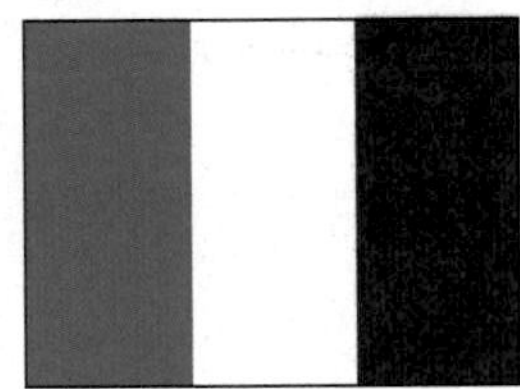

23. Below is a diagram of Jay's bedroom. His bedroom is a rectangle. What is the length of the side labeled *s*?

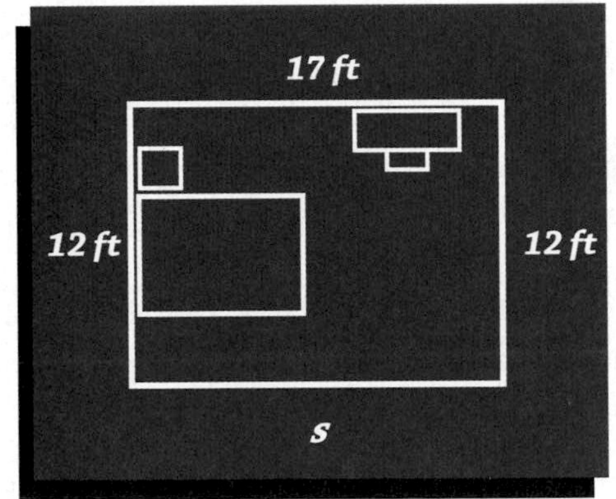

24. I am a quadrilateral with 1 pair of parallel sides. My sides may not be the same length. What figure am I?

25. I am a quadrilateral with 2 pairs of parallel sides and 2 pairs of equal sides. What figure am I?

26. **Reasoning** Describe how a rhombus is like a square and how it is different.

27. WRITE Math **Sense or Nonsense** Joe said all parallelograms have 4 equal sides. Does his statement make sense? **Explain.**

CD ROM **Technology**
Use Harcourt Mega Math, Ice Station Exploration, *Polar Planes*, Level G.

 Extra Practice on page 371, Set E

Learn About Venn Diagrams

A Venn diagram shows how sets of things are related. Look at the Venn diagram below. One circle shows figures that are rectangles. The other circle shows figures that are rhombuses. The figures inside the area where the circles overlap are both rectangles and rhombuses.

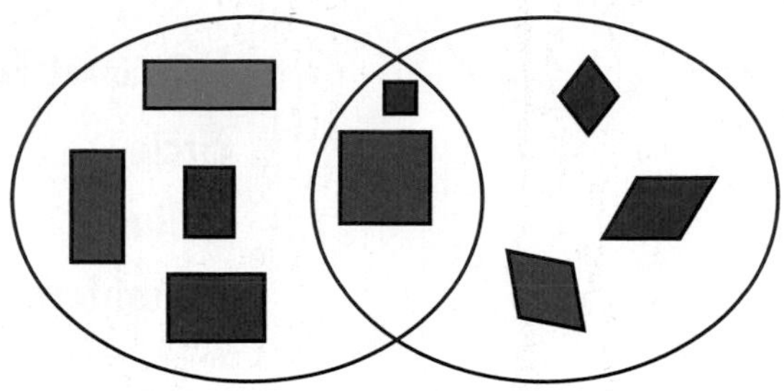

Try It

Use the Venn diagram.

28. How many rectangles are there?

29. How many rhombuses are there?

30. How many figures are both rectangles and rhombuses?

31. What type of quadrilateral is in both circles?

32. Where in the Venn diagram would you put this figure? ■

Mixed Review and Test Prep

33. Chris, Lee, and Jill played a video game. Chris scored 6,852 points. Lee scored 6,781 points and Jill scored 6,917 points. Write the scores in order from least to greatest. (p. 32)

34. Name this triangle by its sides. (p. 358)

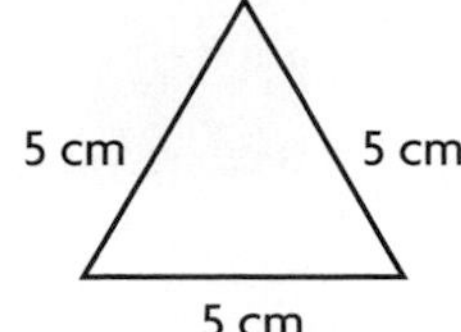

35. **Test Prep** What figure has 2 pairs of parallel sides, no right angles, and 4 equal sides?

36. **Test Prep** Rita glued craft sticks together to make this shape. Which best describes the quadrilateral Rita made?

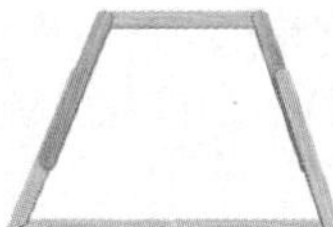

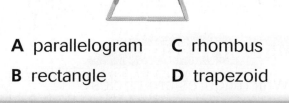

A parallelogram **C** rhombus
B rectangle **D** trapezoid

LESSON 6

Circles

OBJECTIVE: Identify and draw the parts of a circle.

Quick Review

Name each figure.

1.
2.
3.
4.
5.

Vocabulary

circle, center, radius, diameter, circumference

Learn

A **circle** is a closed plane figure made of points that are the same distance from the center. The **center** is the point in the middle of a circle.

Parts of a Circle

A **radius** is a line segment. Its endpoints are the center of the circle and any point on the circle.	A **diameter** is a line segment. It passes through the center of the circle. It has endpoints on the circle.	The **circumference** is the distance around the circle.
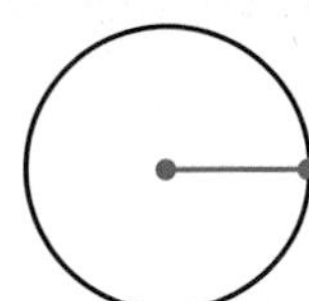	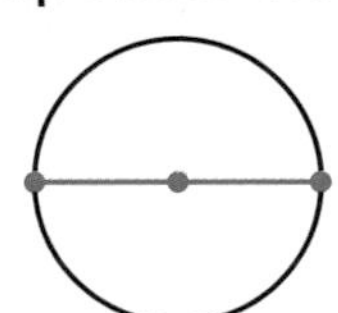	

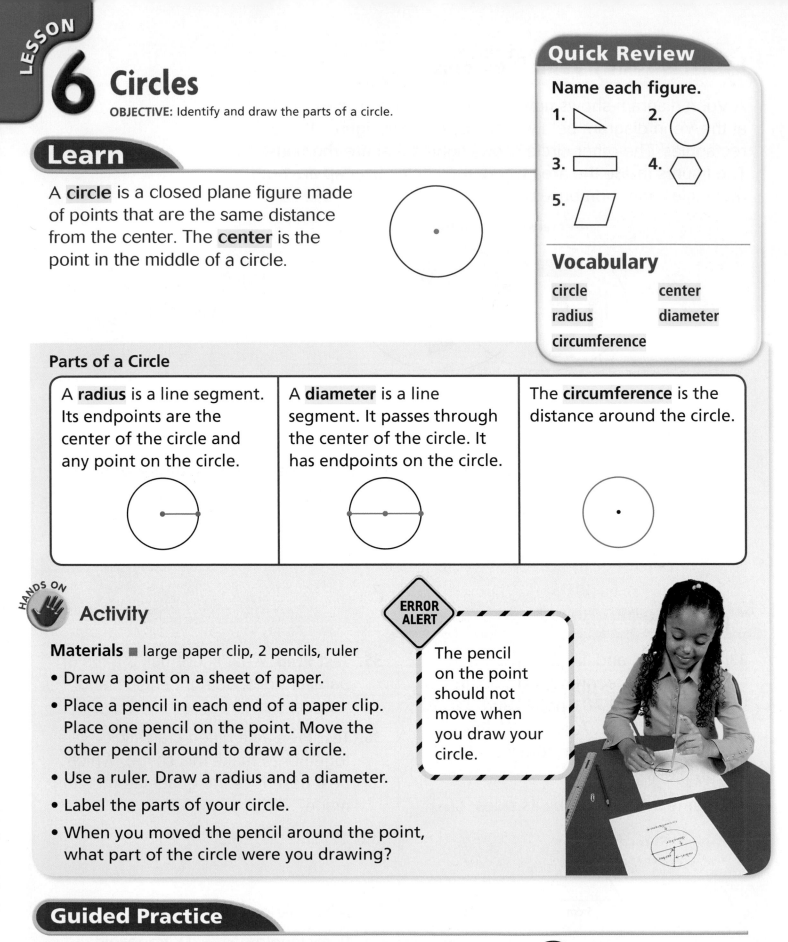

Activity

Materials ■ large paper clip, 2 pencils, ruler

- Draw a point on a sheet of paper.
- Place a pencil in each end of a paper clip. Place one pencil on the point. Move the other pencil around to draw a circle.
- Use a ruler. Draw a radius and a diameter.
- Label the parts of your circle.
- When you moved the pencil around the point, what part of the circle were you drawing?

ERROR ALERT

The pencil on the point should not move when you draw your circle.

Guided Practice

1. Which figures are circles?

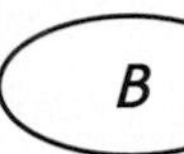

Name the blue part in each circle.

2. 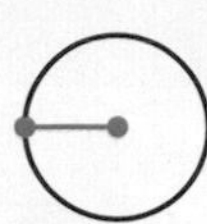
3. 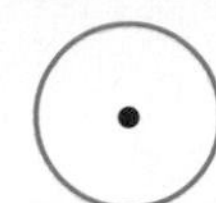
4. 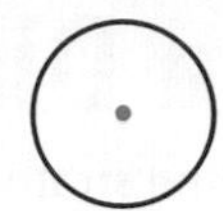
5. 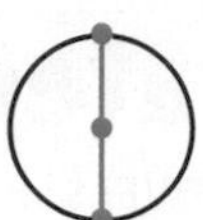

6. **TALK Math** How are the radius and diameter of a circle related? **Explain.**

Independent Practice and Problem Solving

Name the blue part in each circle.

7. 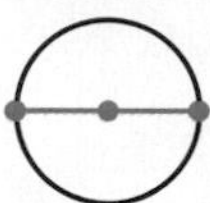
8. 
9. 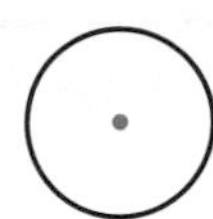
10. 

Is the blue part a diameter? Write *yes* or *no*.

11. 
12. 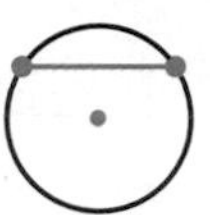
13. 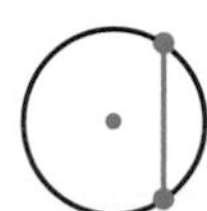
14. 

15. Darcy's swimming pool is in the shape of a circle. She swims the diameter of the pool. Draw Darcy's pool. Label the part Darcy swims.

16. **Reasoning** If the diameter of a circle is 4 inches, what is the radius? How do you know?

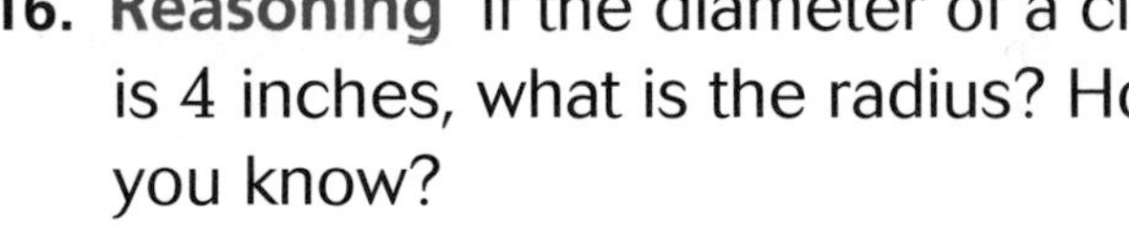

17. **WRITE Math** Cindy and Reggie drew the figures at the right. How are their figures alike? How are they different?

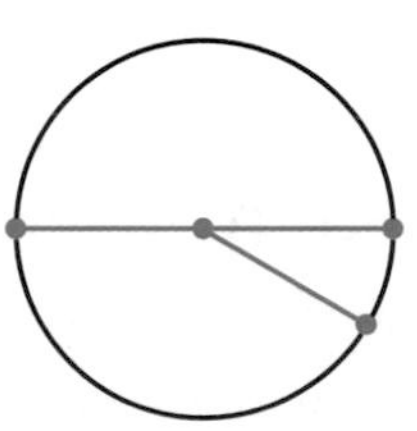

Cindy's circle

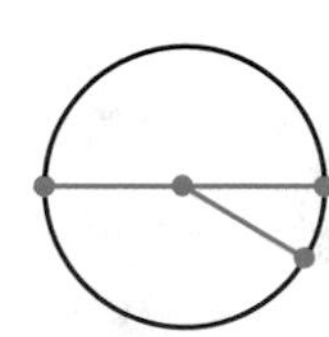

Reggie's circle

Mixed Review and Test Prep

18. What number makes this number sentence true?

$\blacksquare \div 3 = 4 + 3$? (p. 304)

19. A quadrilateral has 2 pairs of parallel sides and no right angles. All sides measure 5 inches. Name the quadrilateral. (p. 360)

20. **Test Prep** Angie drew a circle and colored the diameter red. Which picture is Angie's circle?

A B C D

Extra Practice on page 371, Set F

Problem Solving Workshop
Strategy: Draw a Diagram

OBJECTIVE: Solve problems by using the strategy *draw a diagram*.

Read to Understand
Plan
Solve
Check

Use the Strategy

PROBLEM In art class, Harry used 11 figures to make this train. How can you sort the figures Harry used?

Read to Understand

- **Classify and categorize the figures Harry used.**
- **What information is given?**

Plan

- **What strategy can you use to solve the problem?**
  You can draw a diagram to sort the figures Harry used.

Solve

- **How can you use the strategy to solve the problem?**
  Draw a Venn diagram. A Venn diagram shows how sets of things are related.

  Draw one circle, and label it *Quadrilaterals*.

  Draw another circle that overlaps the first circle. Label this circle *Blue*.

  Sort the figures into the two circles.

  The figures inside the area where the circles overlap are both blue and quadrilaterals.

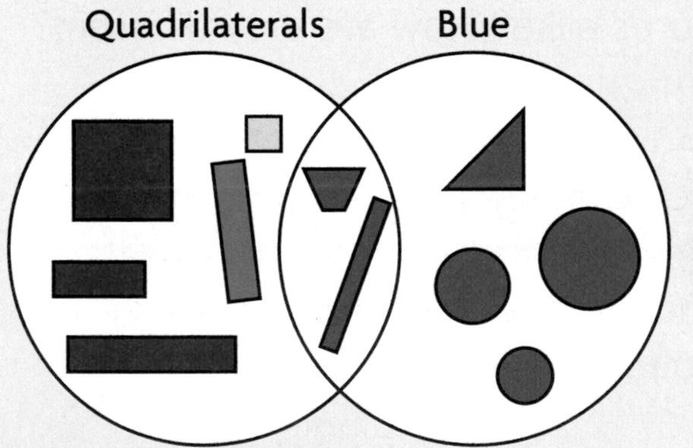

Check

- **What other strategy could you use?**

Guided Problem Solving

1. Georgia used these figures to make a picture.

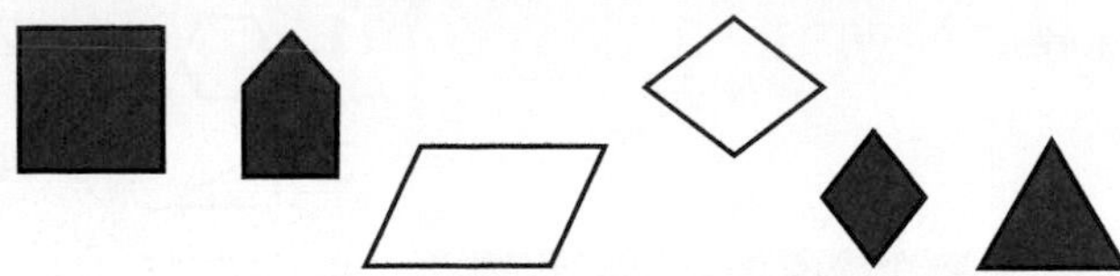

How are the figures alike, and how are they different?

First, draw a Venn diagram with two overlapping circles.

Then, label the circles.

Next, sort the figures.

Last, tell how the figures are alike and how they are different.

Parallelograms   Red

2. **What if** Georgia added this figure to her picture?

Where should it be placed in the Venn diagram?

3. Copy the Venn diagram, showing multiples of 2 and 3. Complete the diagram, using the numbers through 24.

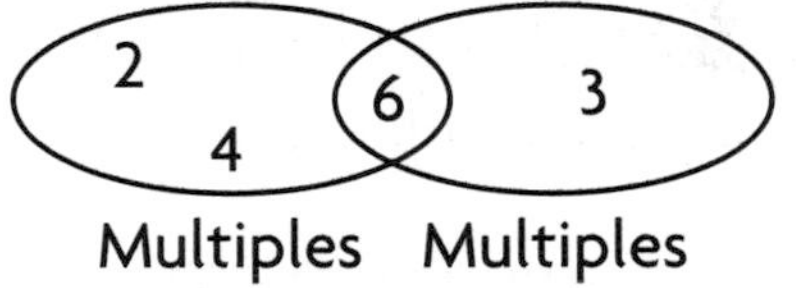

What do the numbers in the overlapping section represent?

Choose a STRATEGY

- Draw a Diagram or Picture
- Make a Model or Act It Out
- Make an Organized List
- Find a Pattern
- Make a Table or Graph
- Predict and Test
- Work Backward
- Solve a Simpler Problem
- Write an Equation
- Use Logical Reasoning

Mixed Strategy Practice

USE DATA For 4–6, use the Venn diagram.

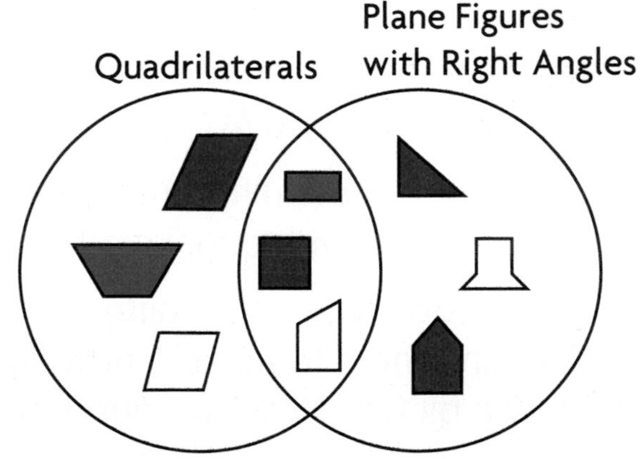

4. The Venn diagram shows the figures Cory used to make a picture. How many quadrilaterals with right angles did he use?

5. How many red figures have right angles but are not quadrilaterals?

6. WRITE Math **Explain** what the figures in the overlapping section represent.

7. **Reasoning** Twenty pictures were entered in an art contest. The pictures were done with either paint or chalk. There were 8 more done with paint than with chalk. How many pictures were done with paint? How many with chalk?

LESSON 8 HANDS ON

Combine Plane Figures

OBJECTIVE: Combine and take apart plane figures.

Quick Review

Name each figure.

1. ⬡
2. ▭
3. ◺
4. ⬠
5. ▱

Investigate

Materials ■ pattern blocks

You can combine plane figures or take them apart to make new figures.

A Combine 2 triangles and record the name of the figure.

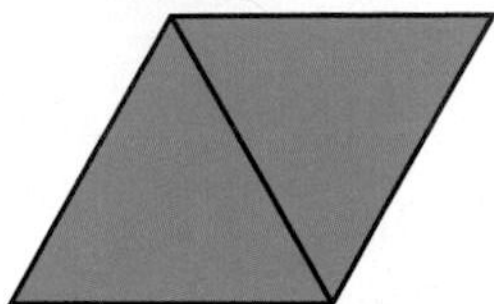

B Predict the new figure that can be made by adding a third triangle. Add it and make a new figure.

C Combine other pattern blocks to make several new figures.

D Trace your figures on paper and label them.

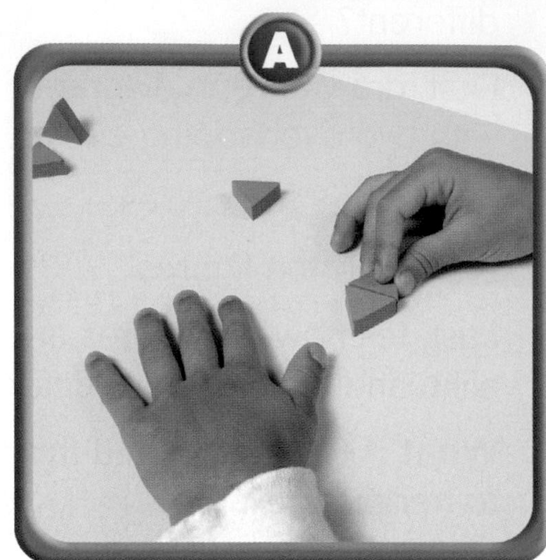

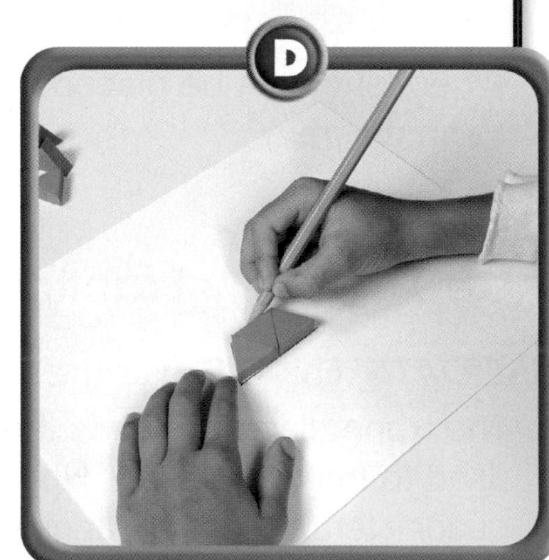

Draw Conclusions

1. What figure can you make by combining 4 triangles in a row?
2. Make a list of the different figures that can be combined to make a trapezoid.
3. **Application** Choose 4 different blocks. Combine them to make a new figure. Draw a picture to show your figure.

Connect

Some figures can be combined to make other figures.
Some figures can be taken apart to become other figures.

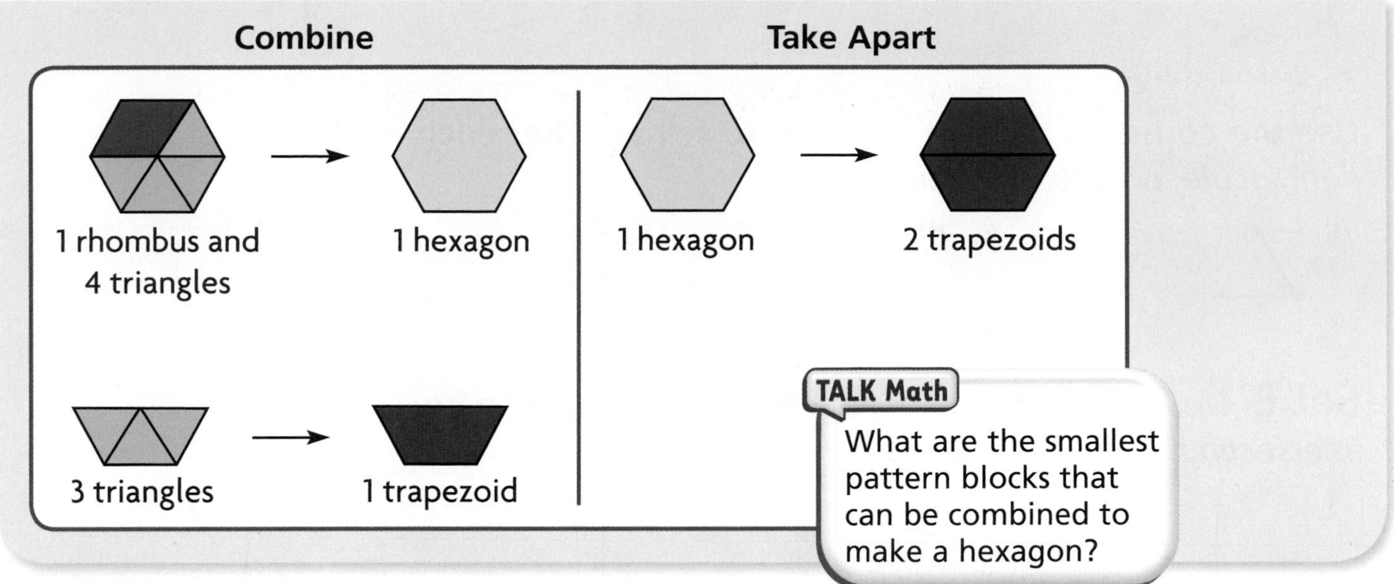

Practice

What figures could have been combined to make each figure?

1. 

2. 

3. 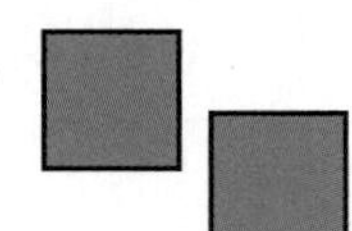

4. 

Draw and name a figure that could be made by using the figures shown.

5.

6.

7.

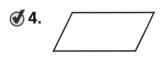

8.

9. Jamie cut a rhombus into 2 equal parts. What plane figures does she have?

10. Violet used two figures to make a trapezoid. One of the figures was a triangle. What was the other figure?

11. WRITE Math Mary has 6 triangles. How many triangles will she have left if she makes 1 trapezoid and 1 rhombus? **Explain** your answer and draw a picture.

Extra Practice

Set A Tell whether each is a *point, line, line segment,* or *ray.* (pp. 350–353)

1.
2.
3.
4.

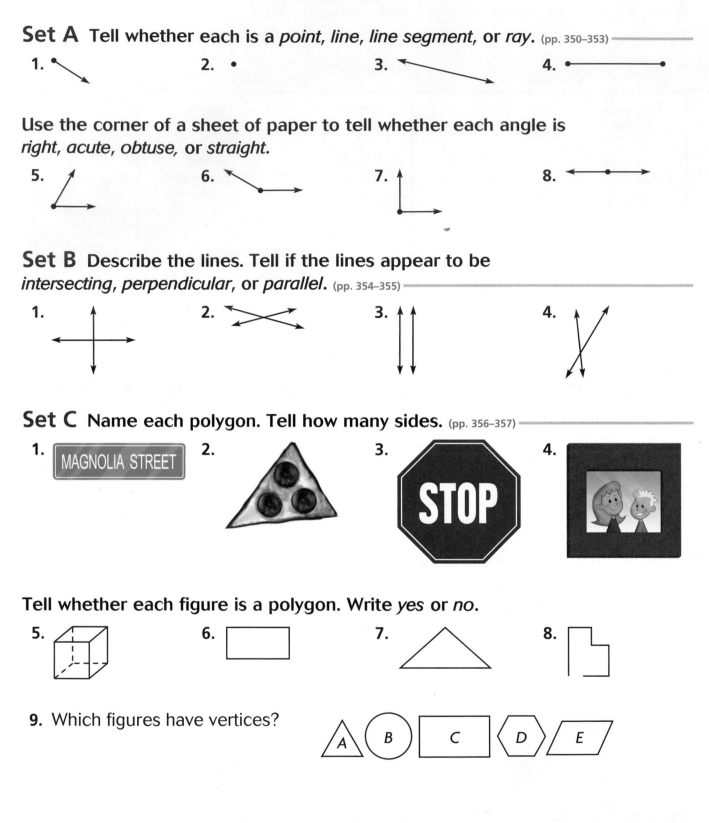

Use the corner of a sheet of paper to tell whether each angle is *right, acute, obtuse,* or *straight.*

5.
6.
7.
8.

Set B Describe the lines. Tell if the lines appear to be *intersecting, perpendicular,* or *parallel.* (pp. 354–355)

1. 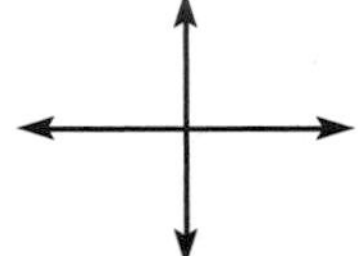
2. 
3. 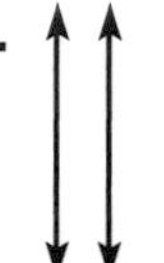
4. 

Set C Name each polygon. Tell how many sides. (pp. 356–357)

1. MAGNOLIA STREET
2. 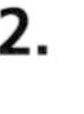 
3. 

4. 

Tell whether each figure is a polygon. Write *yes* or *no.*

5. 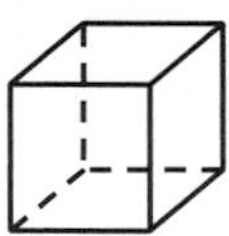
6. 
7. 
8. 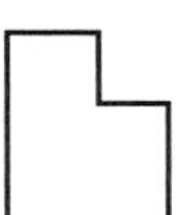

9. Which figures have vertices?

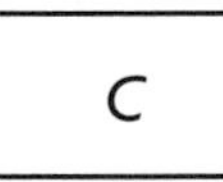

Technology
CD ROM
Use Harcourt Mega Math, Ice Station Exploration, *Polar Planes,* Levels A–G.

Set D Name each triangle. Write *equilateral*, *isosceles*, or *scalene*. (pp. 358–359)

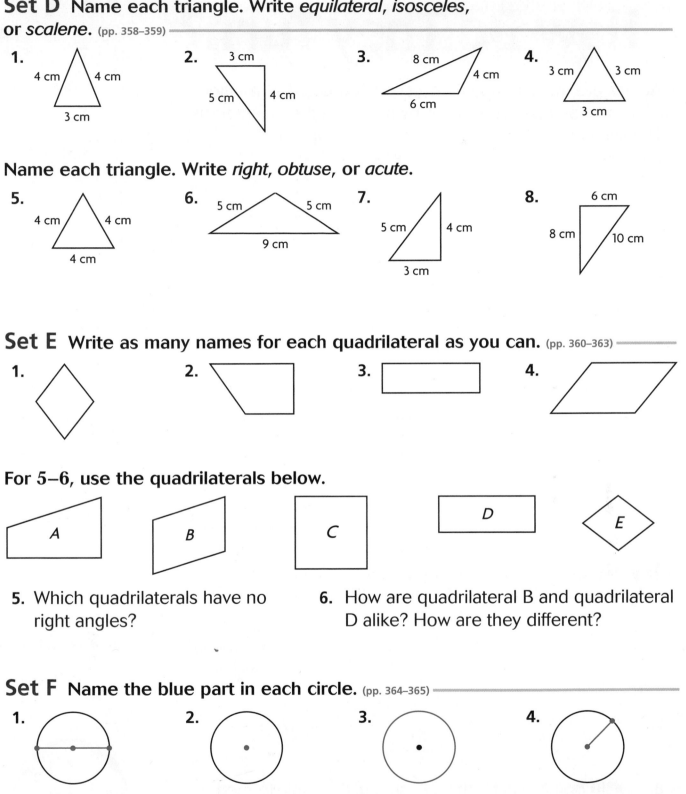

1. 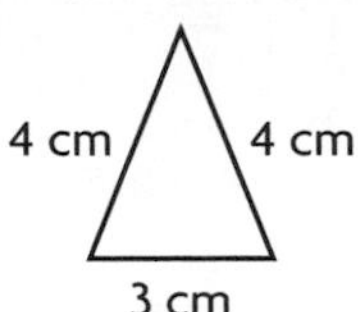

2. 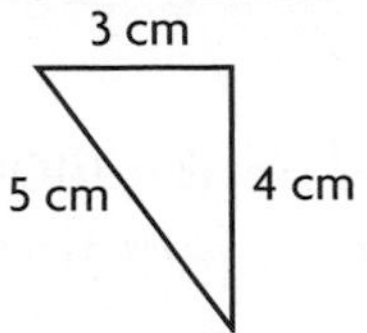

3. 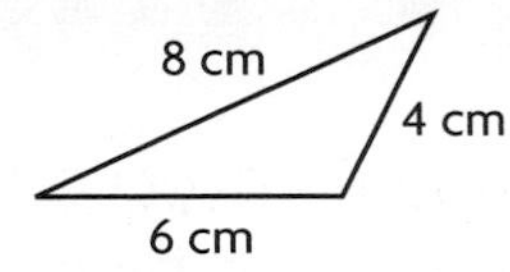

4. 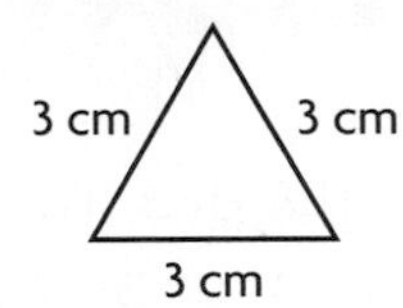

Name each triangle. Write *right*, *obtuse*, or *acute*.

5. 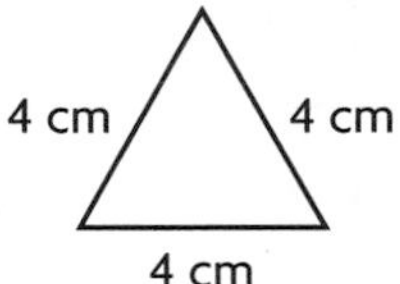

6. 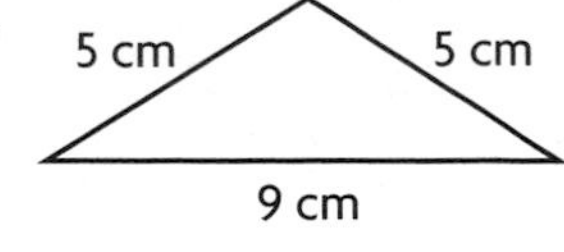

7. 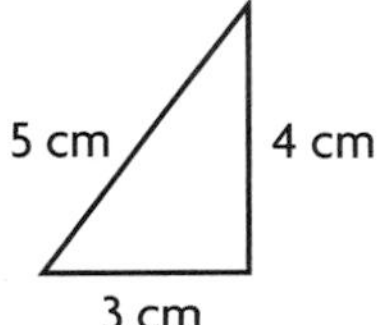

8. 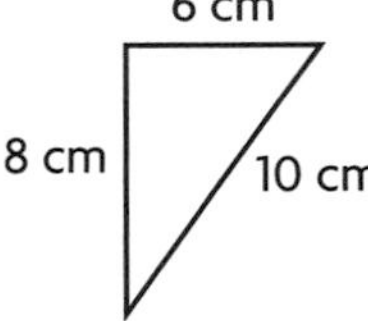

Set E Write as many names for each quadrilateral as you can. (pp. 360–363)

1. 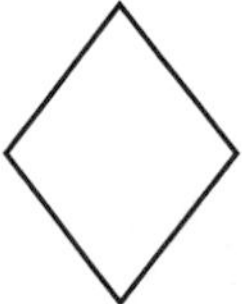

2. 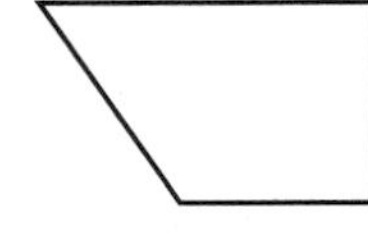

3. 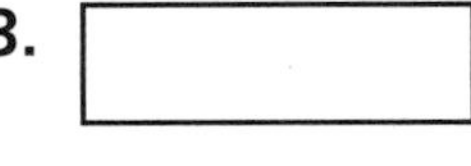

4. 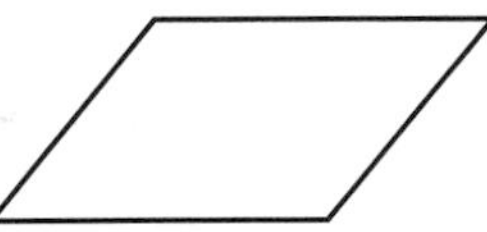

For 5–6, use the quadrilaterals below.

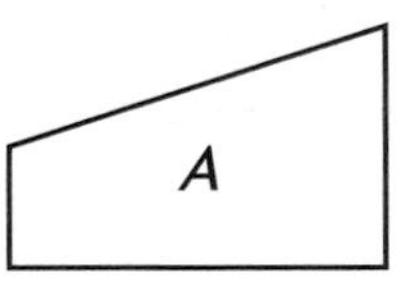

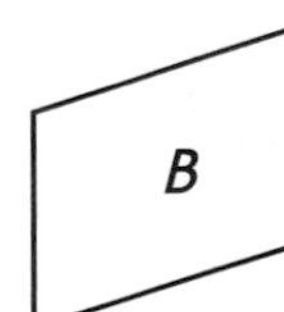

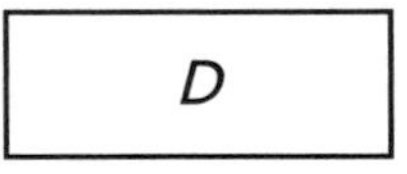

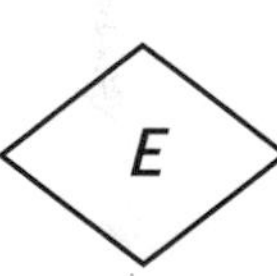

C

5. Which quadrilaterals have no right angles?

6. How are quadrilateral B and quadrilateral D alike? How are they different?

Set F Name the blue part in each circle. (pp. 364–365)

1. 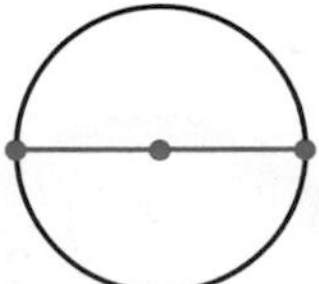

2. 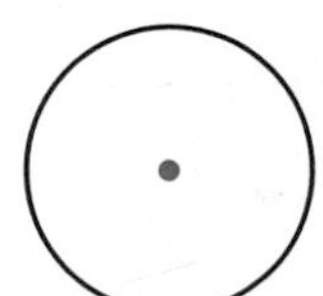

3. 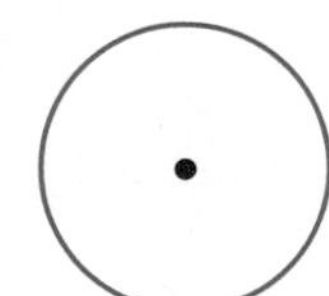

4. 

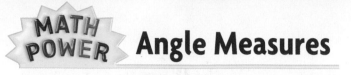

MATH POWER **Angle Measures**

How Do They Turn?

Angles are measured in units called degrees. The rotation, or turn, of an object is named by the angle the object turns. The symbol for degree is °. A circle can help you understand the measure of degrees.

Examples

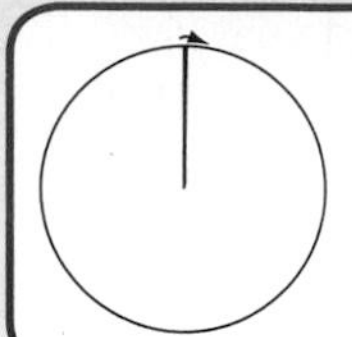

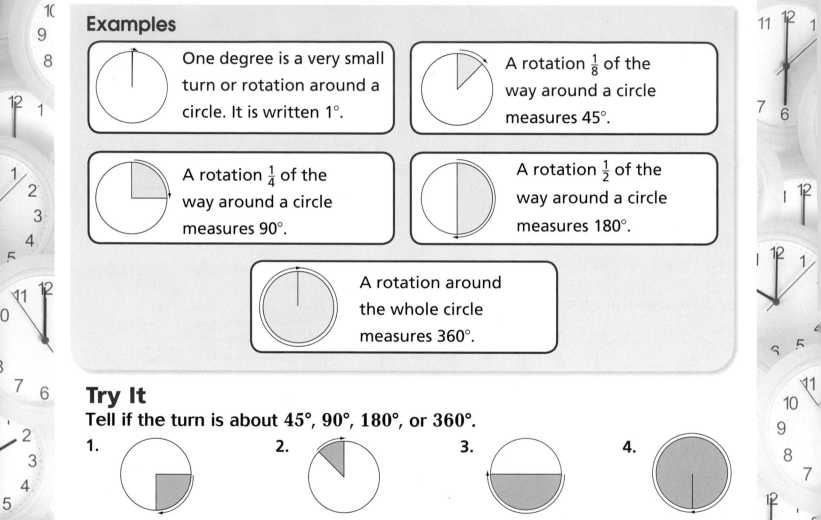

One degree is a very small turn or rotation around a circle. It is written 1°.

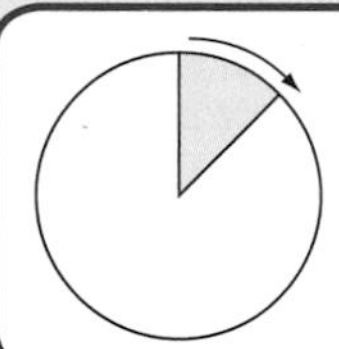

A rotation $\frac{1}{8}$ of the way around a circle measures 45°.

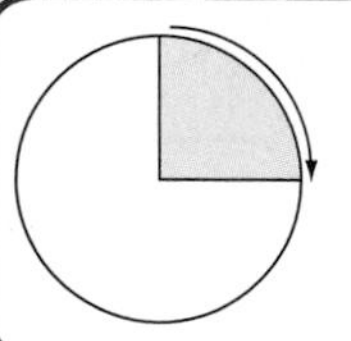

A rotation $\frac{1}{4}$ of the way around a circle measures 90°.

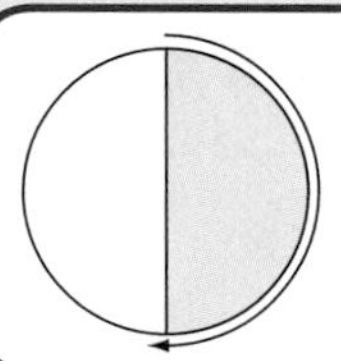

A rotation $\frac{1}{2}$ of the way around a circle measures 180°.

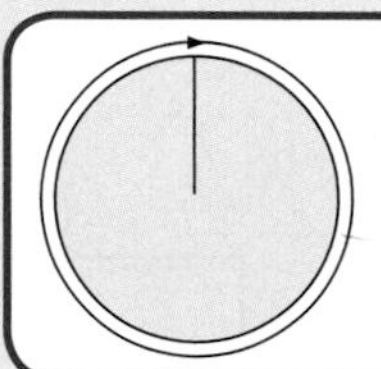

A rotation around the whole circle measures 360°.

Try It

Tell if the turn is about 45°, 90°, 180°, or 360°.

1. 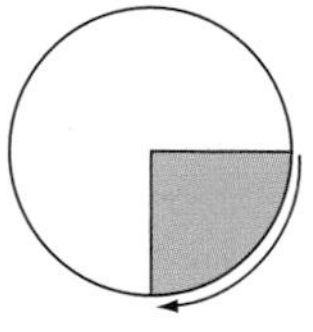

2. 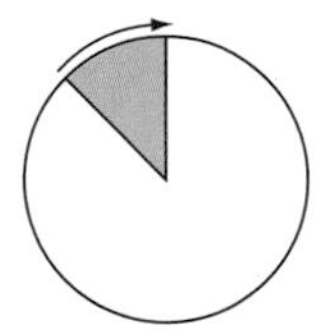

3. 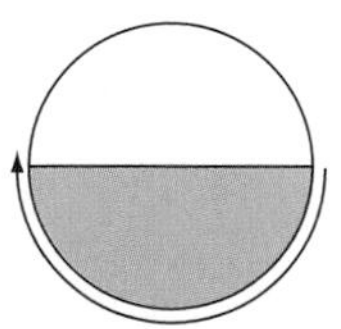

4. 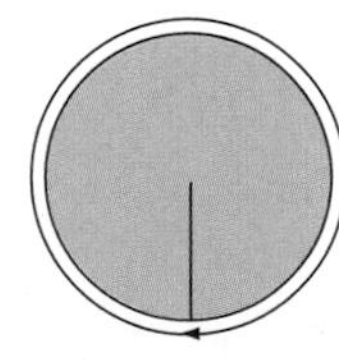

5.

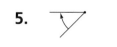

6. 

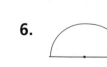

7.

8. WRITE Math What is the measure of the angle formed on a clock when the minute hand points to 12 and the hour hand points to 3? **Explain.**

Chapter 14 Review/Test

Check Vocabulary and Concepts

Choose the best term from the box.

VOCABULARY
diameter
equilateral triangle
hexagon
isosceles triangle
parallelogram
right angle

1. A __?__ has 5 sides and 5 angles. IL 9.3.01 (p. 356)
2. An __?__ is a triangle with 3 equal sides. IL 9.3.01 (p. 358)
3. A __?__ is a quadrilateral with 2 pairs of equal sides and 2 pairs of parallel sides. IL 9.3.01 (p. 360)
4. A __?__ has 6 sides and 6 angles. IL 9.3.01 (p. 356)
5. Lines that never cross are called __?__. IL 9.3.06 (p. 354)

Check Skills

Name each polygon. Tell how many sides. IL 9.3.01 (pp. 356–357)

6. 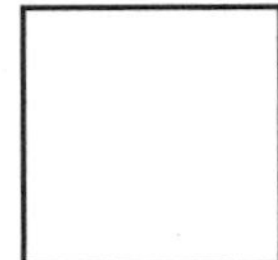

7. 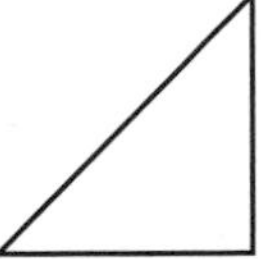

8. 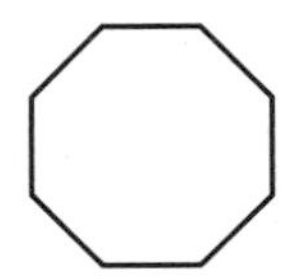

9. 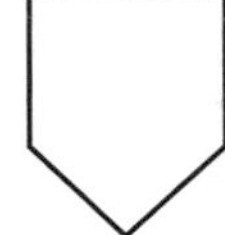

Name each triangle. Write *equilateral*, *isosceles*, or *scalene*. IL 9.3.01 (pp. 358–359)

10. 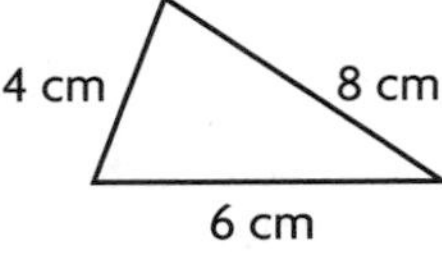

11. 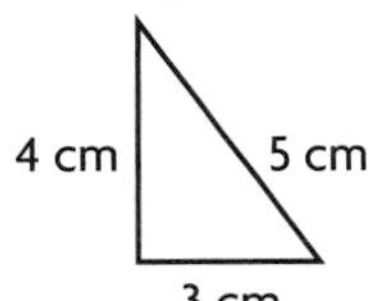

12. 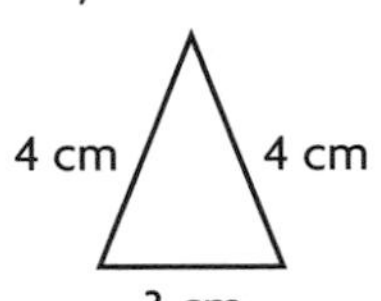

13. 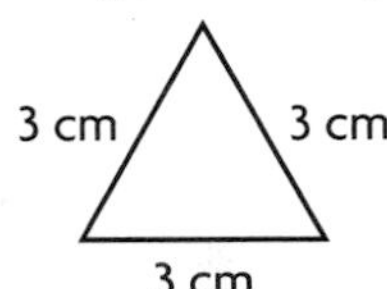

Check Problem Solving

Solve. IL 10.3.01 (pp. 366–367)

14. The Venn diagram shows the figures Ethan used to make a picture. What does the overlapping section represent?

Quadrilaterals   Red

15. WRITE Math Ethan added this figure to his picture. **Explain** where it should be placed in the Venn diagram.

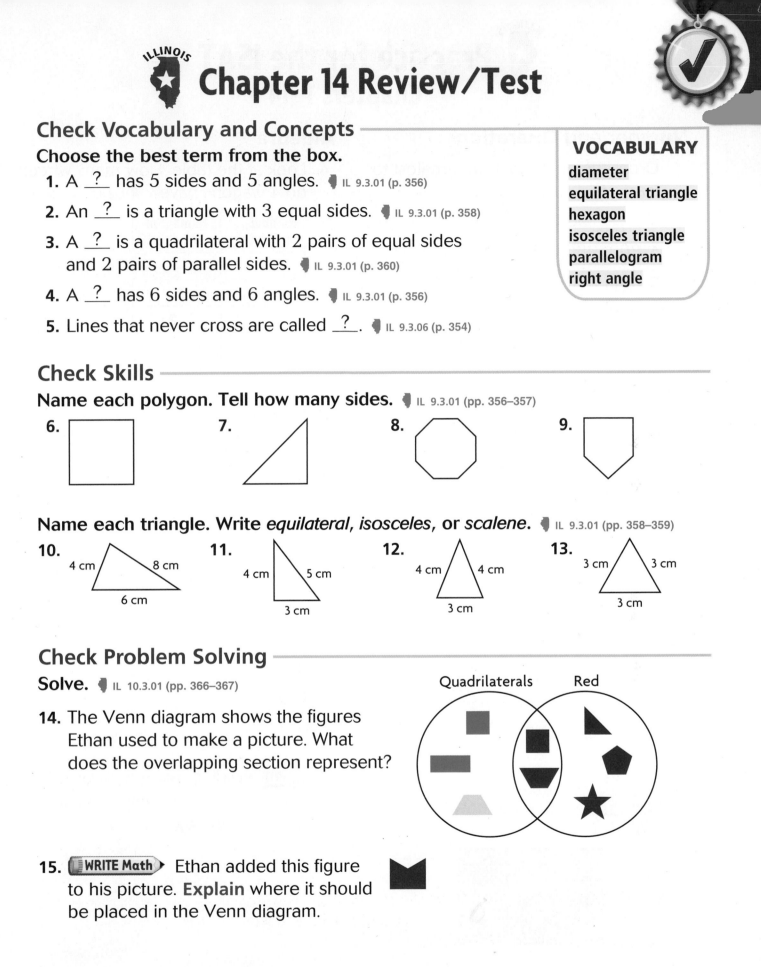

Practice for the ISAT
Chapters 1–14

Number and Operations

1. Order the numbers from greatest to least. IL 6.3.05 (p. 33)

   908; 809; 980

   A 809; 980; 908

   B 980; 908; 809

   C 980; 809; 908

   D 809; 908; 980

Test Tip **Understand the problem.**

See item 2. Read the question again. What are you asked to find? Look in the problem for the information you need to answer the question.

2. Bill is putting his stamps in an album. There are 8 stamps on each page. Bill has filled 8 pages. How many stamps does Bill have? IL 6.3.11 (p. 236)

   A 1

   B 16

   C 56

   D 64

3. **WRITE Math** **Explain** how this array models $6 \times 9 = 54$. IL 6.3.11 (p. 206)

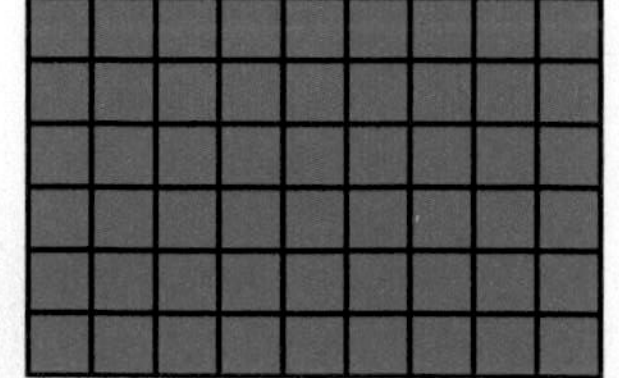

Algebra

4. Look at the table. How many wheels do 4 wagons have? IL 8.3.01 (p. 256)

Number of Wagons	Number of Wheels
1	4
2	8
3	12
4	■

   A 8

   B 16

   C 20

   D 22

5. Which number completes the fact family? IL 8.3.03 (p. 286)

   $4 \times ■ = 32$ $■ \times 4 = 32$

   $32 \div 4 = ■$ $32 \div ■ = 4$

   A 4

   B 8

   C 9

   D 32

6. **WRITE Math** **Explain** how knowing $(2 \times 4) \times 8 = 64$ helps you find $2 \times (4 \times 8)$. IL 8.3.03 (p. 262)

Geometry

7. Look at the figure below. Which does NOT describe the shape? IL 9.3.01 (p. 360)

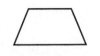

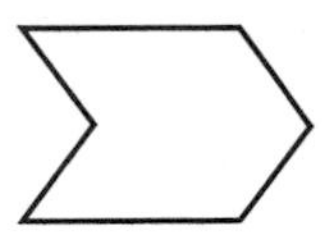

A It is a rhombus.

B It is a trapezoid.

C It is a polygon.

D It is a quadrilateral.

8. Which polygon has more sides than this figure? IL 9.3.01 (p. 356)

A Triangle

B Quadrilateral

C Hexagon

D Octagon

9. WRITE Math **Explain** how parallel lines are different than perpendicular lines. IL 9.3.06 (p. 354)

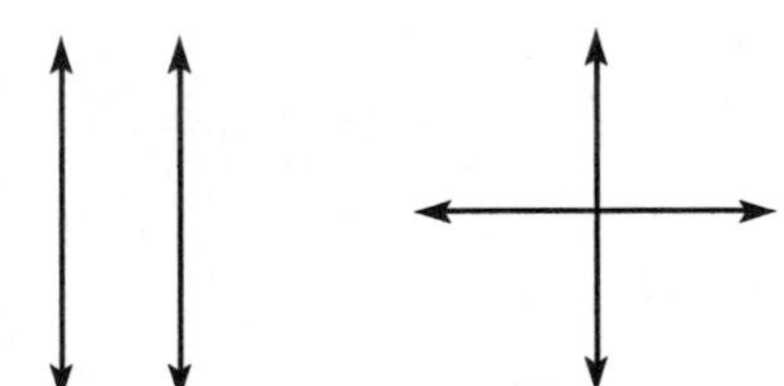

Data Analysis and Probability

10. A tally table shows 卌 卌 卌 || for the number of students who rode bikes to school. How many students rode bikes? IL 10.3.01 (p. 146)

A 20 **C** 15

B 17 **D** 14

11. The graph shows some of the activities Jason did during the day. How many more hours did Jason spend sleeping than reading? IL 10.3.01 (p. 154)

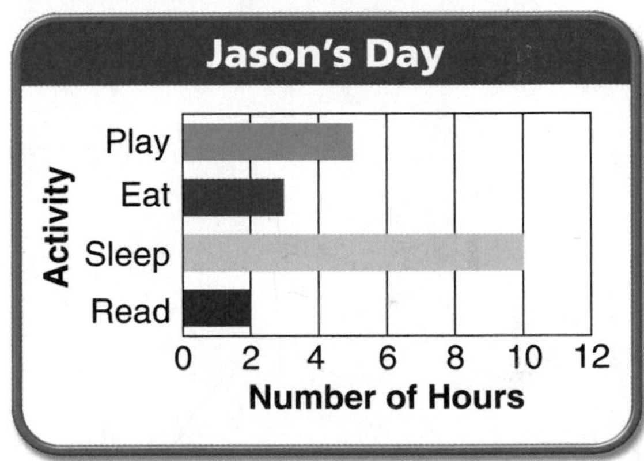

A 2 hours **C** 10 hours

B 8 hours **D** 12 hours

12. WRITE Math Rosanna picks a card from the cards shown. Is she more likely or less likely to pick an *A* than a *B*? **Explain** how you know. IL 10.3.04 (p. 182)

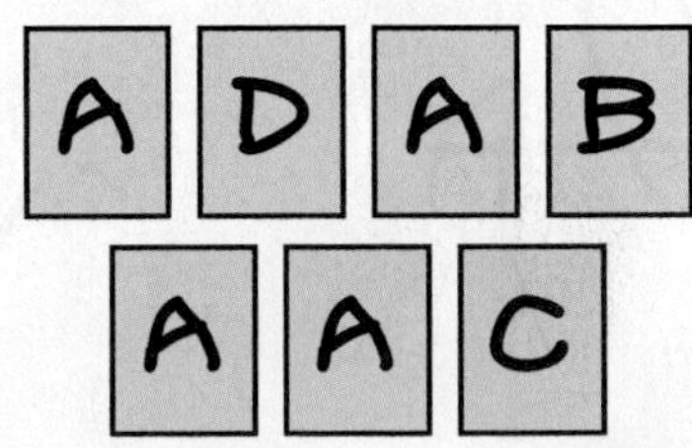

CHAPTER 15

Congruence and Symmetry

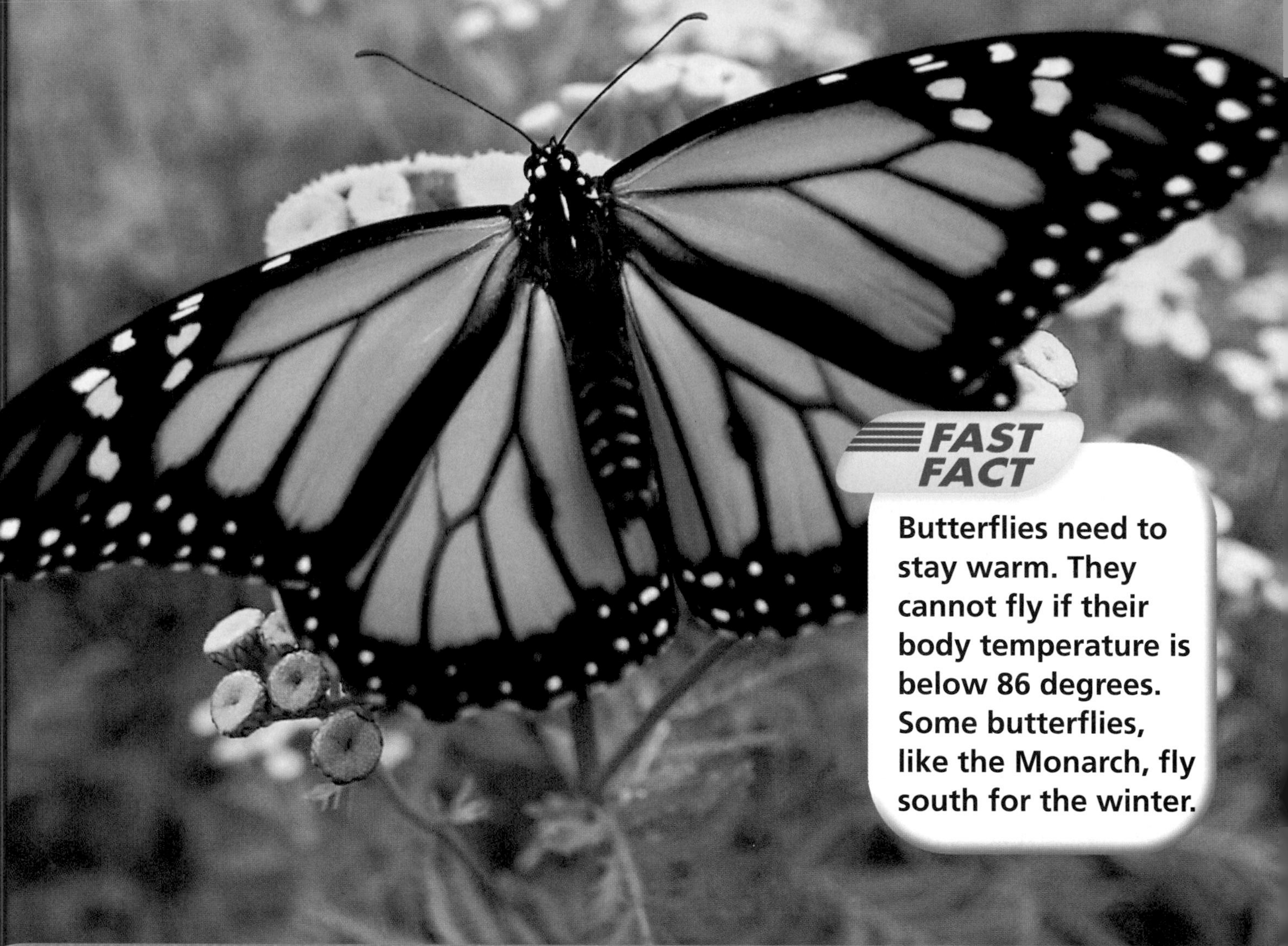

FAST FACT

Butterflies need to stay warm. They cannot fly if their body temperature is below 86 degrees. Some butterflies, like the Monarch, fly south for the winter.

Investigate

All butterflies are symmetrical. Their left and right wings have the same designs and colors. Look at the drawings. Which cannot be real butterflies? How do you know? Draw a butterfly that has a line of symmetry.

GO ONLINE **Technology**
Student pages are available in the Student eBook.

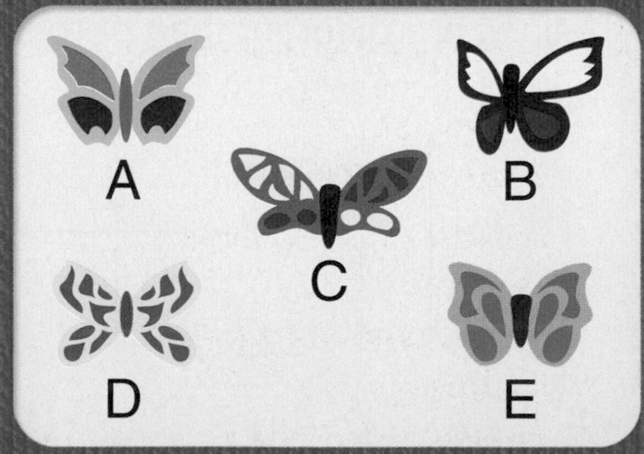

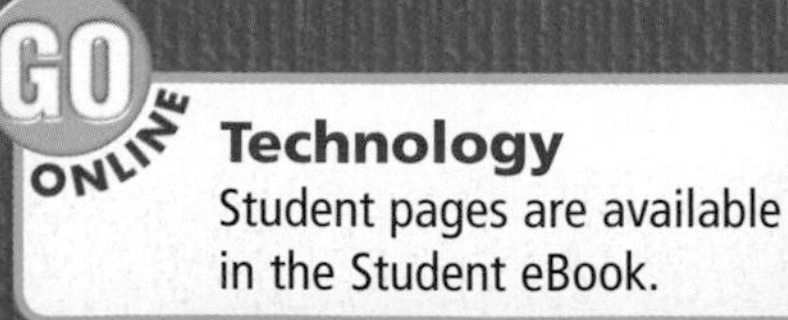

Show What You Know

Check your understanding of important skills needed for success in Chapter 15.

▶ Same Size, Same Shape

Tell whether the figures are the same size and shape.
Write *yes* or *no*.

1. 

2. 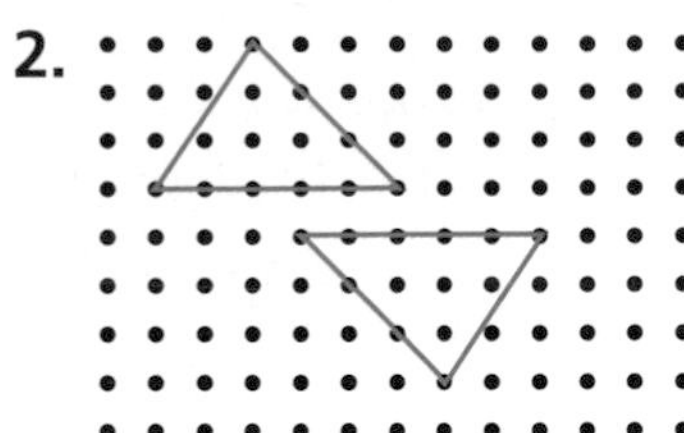

3. 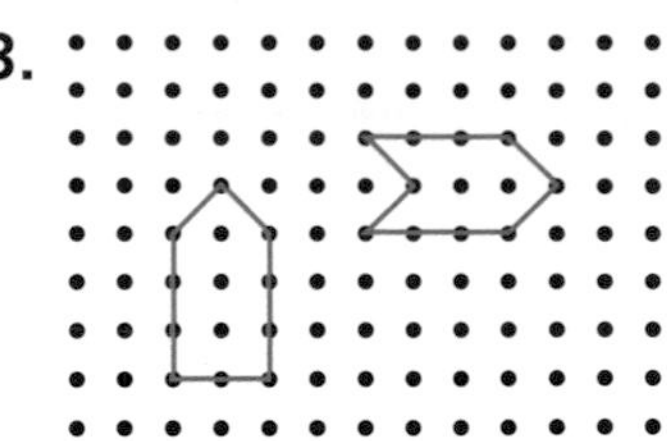

4. 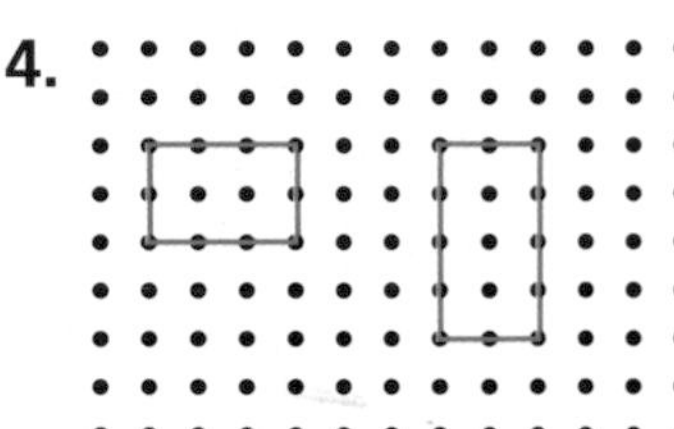

5. 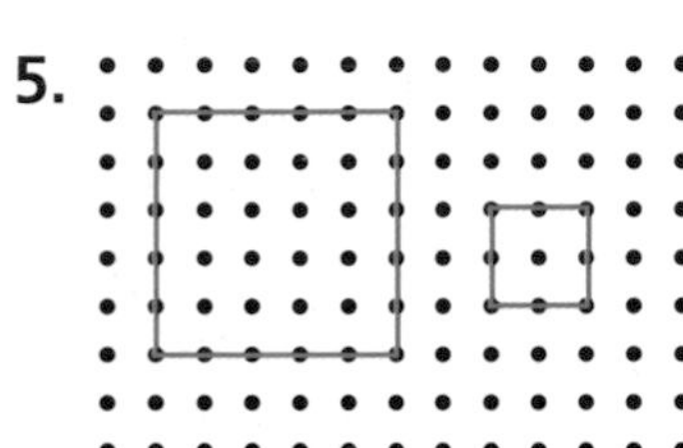

6. 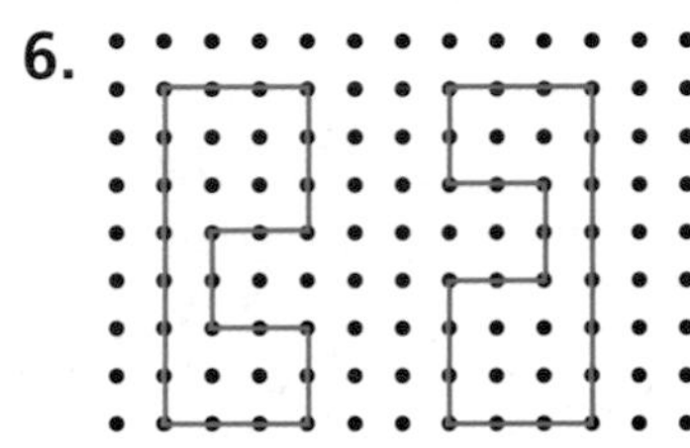

7. 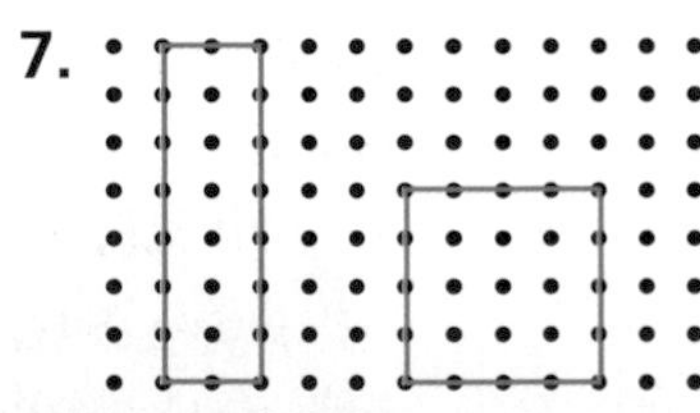

8. 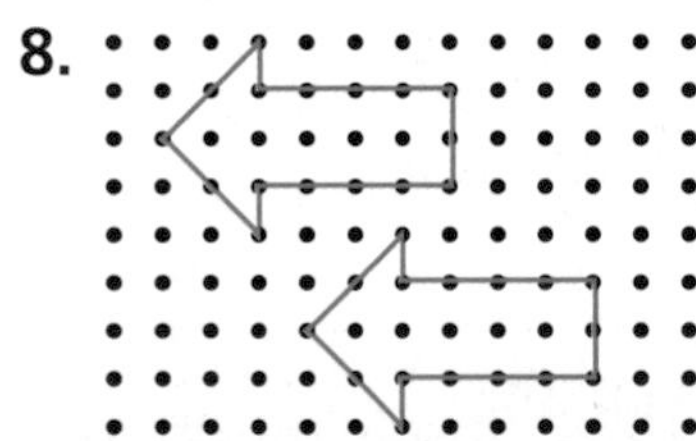

9. 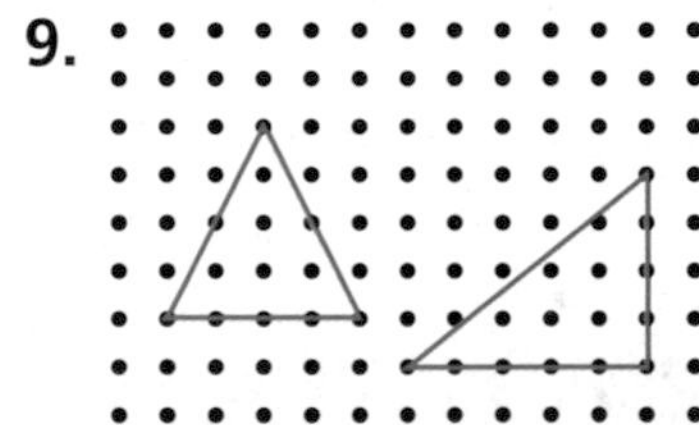

VOCABULARY POWER

CHAPTER VOCABULARY

congruent
flip (reflection)
line of symmetry
similar
slide (translation)
symmetry
turn (rotation)

WARM-UP WORDS

congruent Figures that have the same size and shape

similar Figures that have the same shape and the same or different size

symmetry A figure has symmetry if it can be folded along a line so that the two parts match exactly

LESSON 1 Congruent Figures

OBJECTIVE: Identify 2-dimensional congruent figures.

Quick Review

Name 4 plane figures in this picture.

Vocabulary

congruent

Learn

Figures with the same size and shape are **congruent**. Congruent figures can be in different positions.

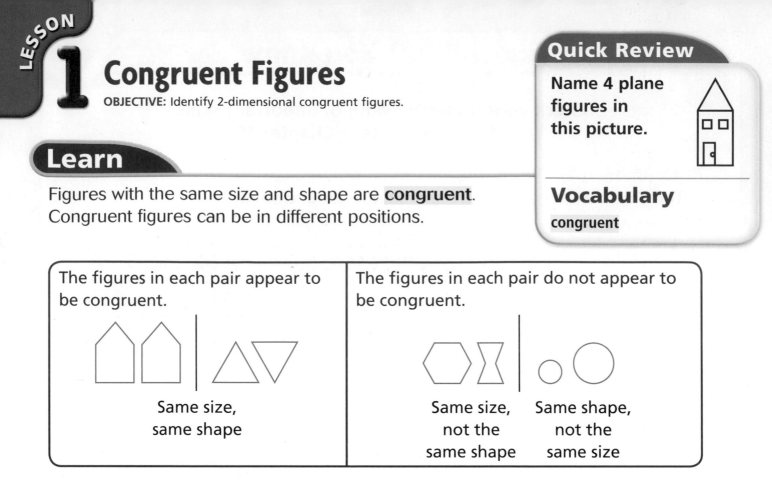

The figures in each pair appear to be congruent.	The figures in each pair do not appear to be congruent.
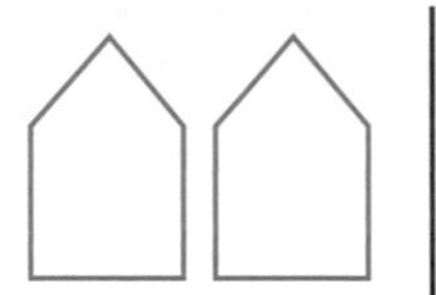  Same size, same shape	 Same size, not the same shape  Same shape, not the same size

PROBLEM Molly put a red hexagon on the front of her scrapbook. She wants to put a congruent figure on the back. Which figure should she use?

Activity **Materials** ■ tracing paper

Use tracing paper to find the congruent figure.

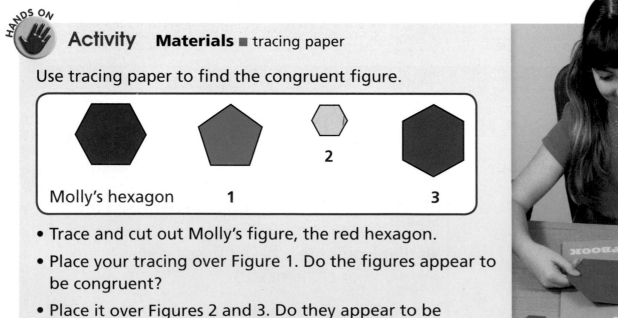

Molly's hexagon

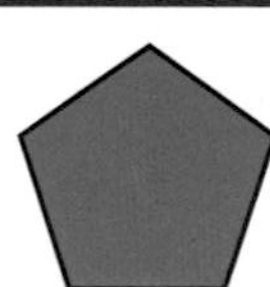

1

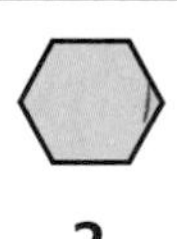

2

3

- Trace and cut out Molly's figure, the red hexagon.
- Place your tracing over Figure 1. Do the figures appear to be congruent?
- Place it over Figures 2 and 3. Do they appear to be congruent?

So, Molly should use Figure 3, the blue hexagon, because it appears to be congruent to her red hexagon.

Guided Practice

1. Trace triangle A. Which triangle appears to be the same size and shape as A?

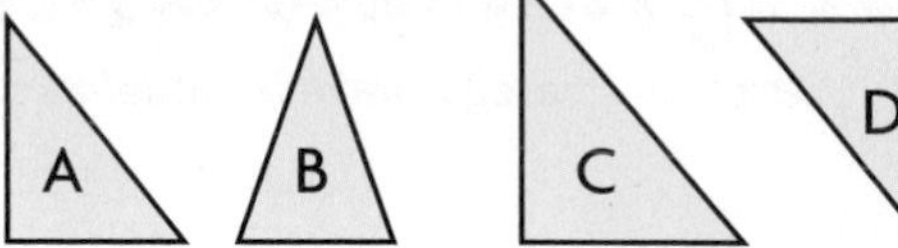

Trace and cut out each pair of figures. Tell if the figures appear to be congruent. Write *yes* or *no*.

2. 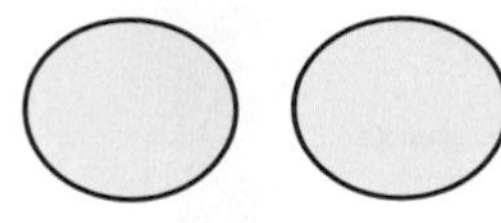

3. 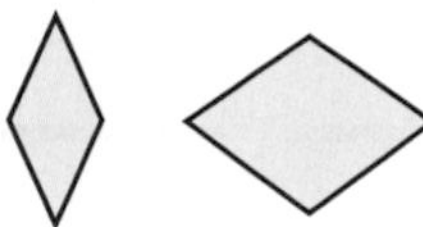

4. 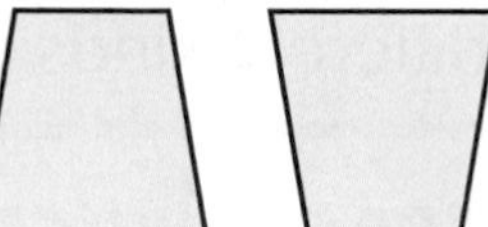

5. TALK Math **Explain** how to tell if two figures appear to be congruent.

Independent Practice and Problem Solving

Trace and cut out each pair of figures. Tell if the figures appear to be congruent. Write *yes* or *no*.

6. 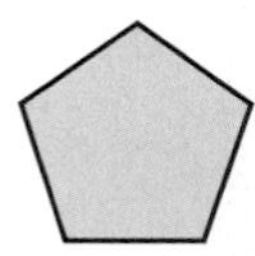 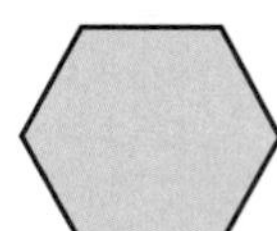

7. 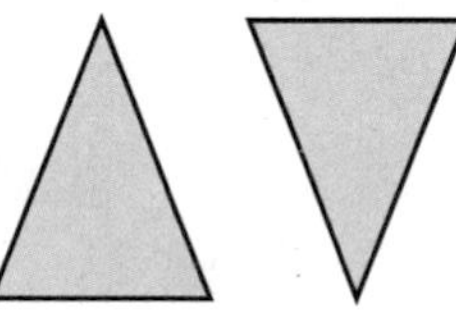

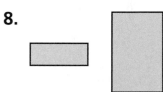

8. 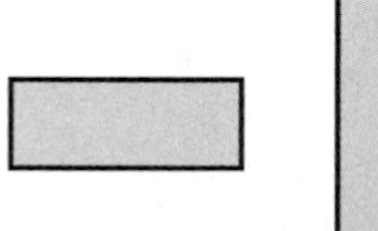 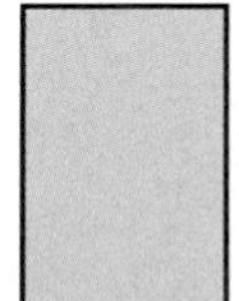

For 9–11, use the figures in the chart.

9. Johnny used two congruent star figures for his picture. Which figures did he use?

10. One of the figures in Mae's picture is triangle F. Which figure appears to be congruent to triangle F?

11. WRITE Math Look at stars A and C. Do they appear to be congruent? **Explain.**

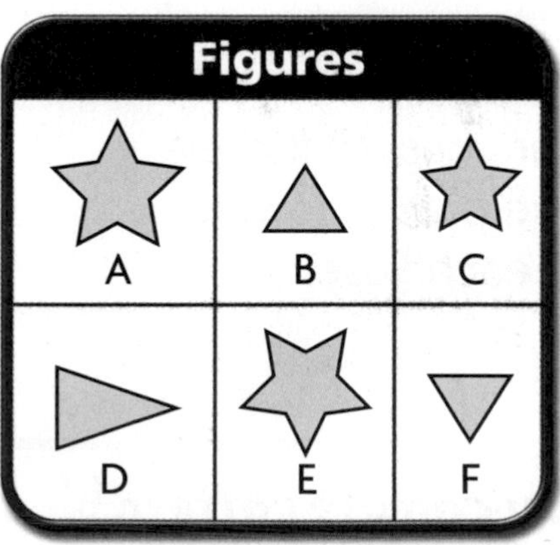

Mixed Review and Test Prep

12. A puzzle in Jill's classroom has 2,039 pieces in it. Write the number 2,039 in expanded form. (p. 10)

13. A figure has 4 equal sides and 4 right angles. What is the figure? (p. 360)

14. **Test Prep** Which figure appears to be congruent to this figure?

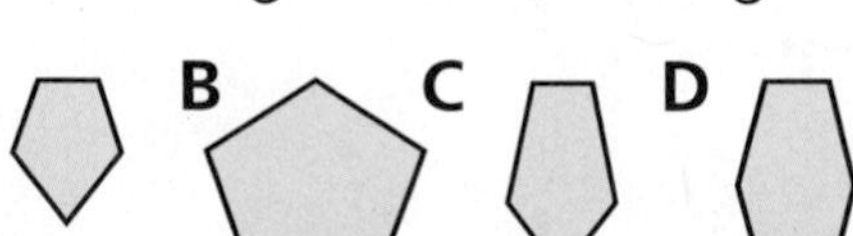

Extra Practice on page 392, Set A

Problem Solving Workshop
Strategy: Make a Model

OBJECTIVE: Use the strategy *make a model* to solve problems.

Learn the Strategy

Making models can help you solve problems. You can use many different kinds of models.

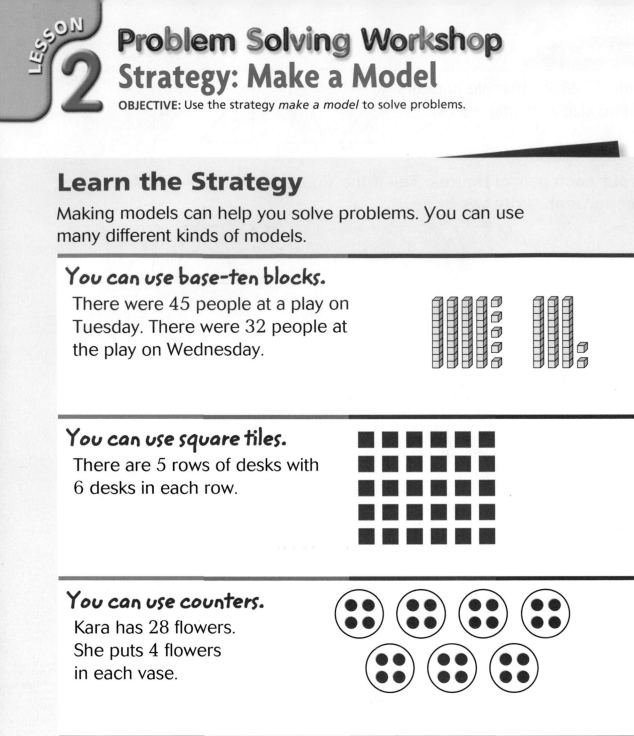

You can use base-ten blocks.

There were 45 people at a play on Tuesday. There were 32 people at the play on Wednesday.

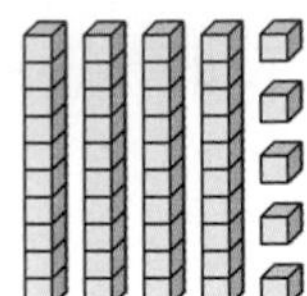
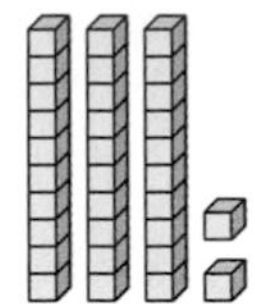

You can use square tiles.

There are 5 rows of desks with 6 desks in each row.

You can use counters.

Kara has 28 flowers. She puts 4 flowers in each vase.

You can use pattern blocks.

Ben is tiling his floor. He uses triangles and squares to make a border.

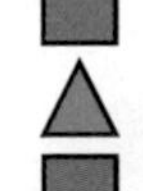
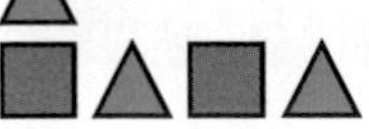

TALK Math

What problem can be solved by using each of the models shown?

Use the Strategy

PROBLEM Mr. Miller is making a path in his garden by using stones that are shaped like hexagons. He needs one more stone to complete the path. How can he use the stone shapes below to make the last stepping stone?

Read to Understand

Reading Skill

- **Visualize a hexagon.**
- **What information is given?**

Plan

- **What strategy can you use to solve the problem?**

  You can *make a model.*

Solve

- **How can you use the strategy to solve the problem?**

  Use pattern blocks to model the problem. Use the yellow hexagon, the green triangles, and the red trapezoid to model the stones.

  Arrange the pattern blocks to make a hexagon.

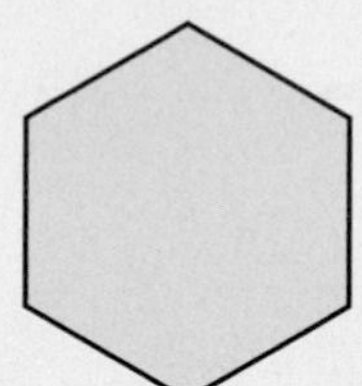

hexagon stone

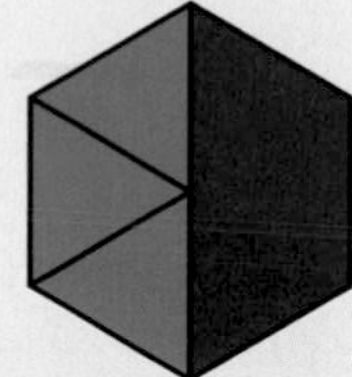

pieces of stone

So, Mr. Miller can put the 3 triangles and 1 trapezoid together to make the last stepping stone.

Check

- **How do you know your answer is correct?**

Guided Problem Solving

Read to Understand
Plan
Solve
Check

1. Jillian is making a pattern. What pieces are missing from her pattern?

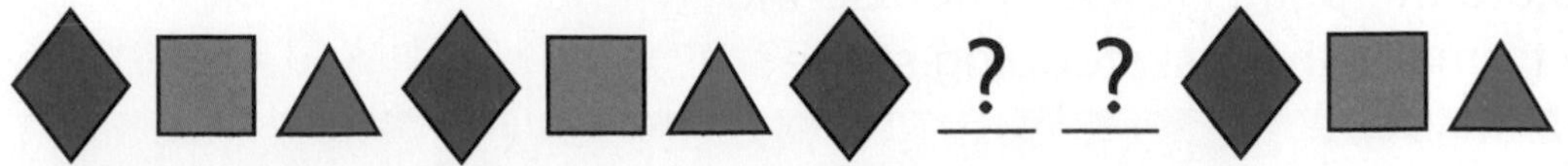

First, decide what model to use.
You can use pattern blocks to make the design.

Then, use the blocks to fill in the missing pieces.
Explain how you completed the pattern.

2. What if Jillian added 1 hexagon after each triangle? How many hexagons would be in her design?

3. Hunter uses square tiles to make an array with 4 rows and 3 columns. How many square tiles does he use?

Problem Solving Strategy Practice

Make a model to solve.

4. Two apples are the same size. Jenna ate $\frac{1}{2}$ of an apple. Caitlin ate $\frac{1}{3}$ of an apple. Who ate the larger part?

5. Mrs. Parker bought 48 muffins. There are 8 muffins in each box. How many boxes are there?

6. Ashley is making a photo album. Each page holds 6 photos. There are 12 pages. How many photos can her album hold?

7. Mary has 24 napkins. She puts the same number of napkins on each of 3 tables. How many napkins does Mary put on 2 of the tables?

8. Jessica is saving money to buy a bike. She saved $4 the first month, $8 the second month, $12 the third month, and $16 the fourth month. If the pattern continues, how much will she save the sixth month?

9. Patrick picked 3 baskets of apples. Each basket held 12 apples. How many apples in all did he pick?

10. WRITE Math John used 1 hexagon and 2 triangles to make this rhombus. What other pattern blocks can be used to make a rhombus congruent to this one?

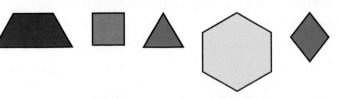

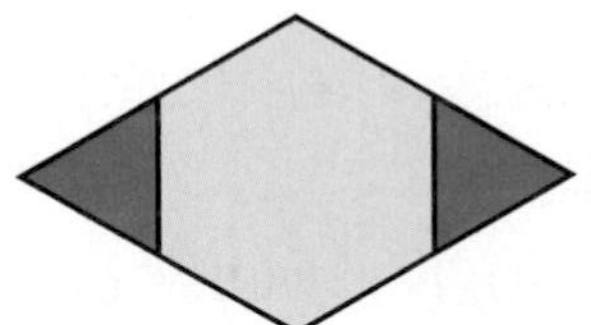

  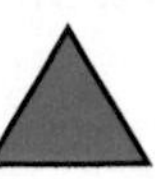 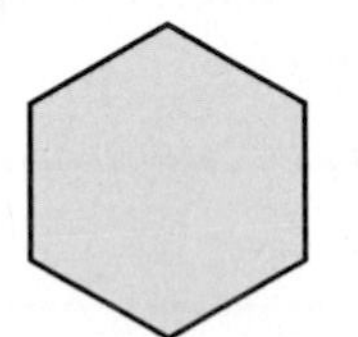 

Mixed Strategy Practice

USE DATA For 11–13, use the table.

11. Tina buys 9 pattern-block stamp kits. How many stamps does Tina have in all?

12. There are 4 fraction circles in each bag. How many bags of fraction circles are in 1 kit?

13. There are 4 different kinds of number cards in a kit. How many of each kind of card are there if there are the same number of each kind?

14. Sierra chose a square, a trapezoid, and a triangle from the pattern blocks. The block she chose first did not have 4 sides. She did not choose the square last. In what order did Sierra choose the blocks?

15. Pose a Problem Look back at problem 14. Write a similar problem using a rhombus, a hexagon, and a square. **Explain** the answer.

16. Open-Ended Choose 6 plane figures. Draw a Venn diagram with two overlapping circles. Label the circles. Sort the figures. Tell how the figures are alike and how they are different.

17. Marti used pattern blocks to make this pattern. What is the twelfth block in her pattern?

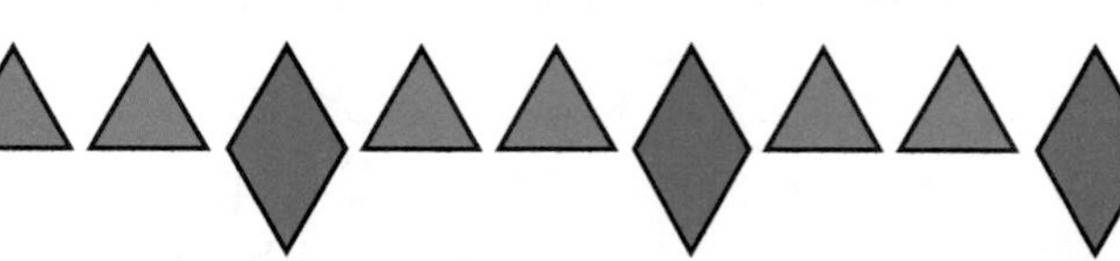

Choose a STRATEGY

- Draw a Diagram or Picture
- Make a Model or Act It Out
- Make an Organized List
- Find a Pattern
- Make a Table or Graph
- Predict and Test
- Work Backward
- Solve a Simpler Problem
- Write an Equation
- Use Logical Reasoning

Math Kit

Item	Number in Each Kit
Pattern blocks	100
Number cards	36
Pattern-block stamps	6
Fraction circles	12

CHALLENGE YOURSELF

Glenn's town has 4 school supply stores.
Each store has 95 pattern-block stamp kits for sale.

18. Two schools each bought 28 pattern-block stamp kits from one store in September. Then one school returned 17 stamp kits. How many pattern-block stamp kits were in stock after the kits were returned?

19. Each pattern-block stamp kit costs $9. On Tuesday, two stores sold 5 kits, and three stores sold 2 kits. How much money was paid for the kits on Tuesday?

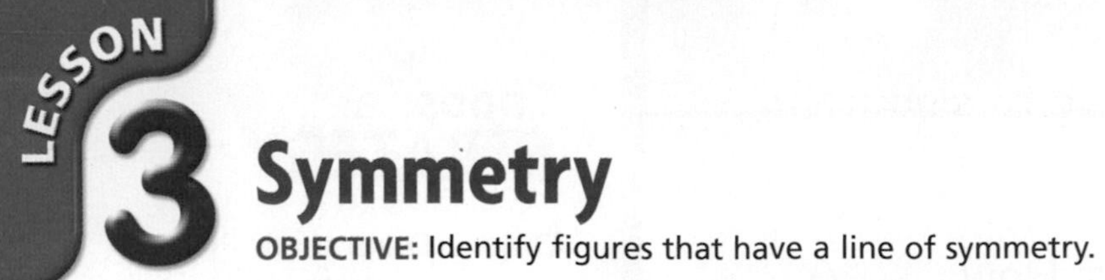

LESSON 3 Symmetry

OBJECTIVE: Identify figures that have a line of symmetry.

Quick Review

Which two figures appear to be congruent?

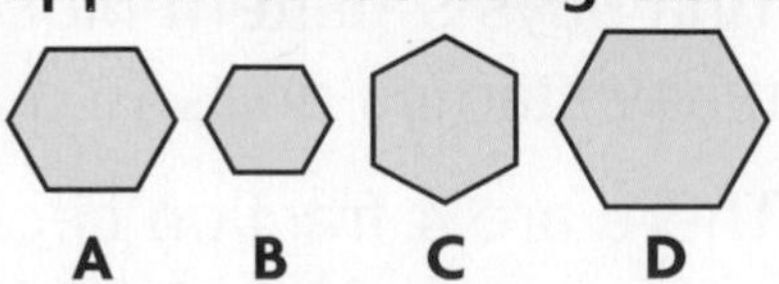

Vocabulary

symmetry

line of symmetry

Learn

A figure has **symmetry** if it can be folded in half so that the halves match exactly.

These figures appear to have a line of symmetry.

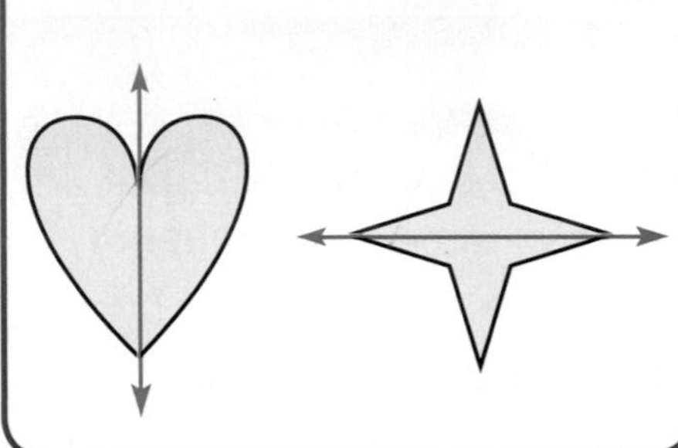

These figures do not appear to have a line of symmetry.

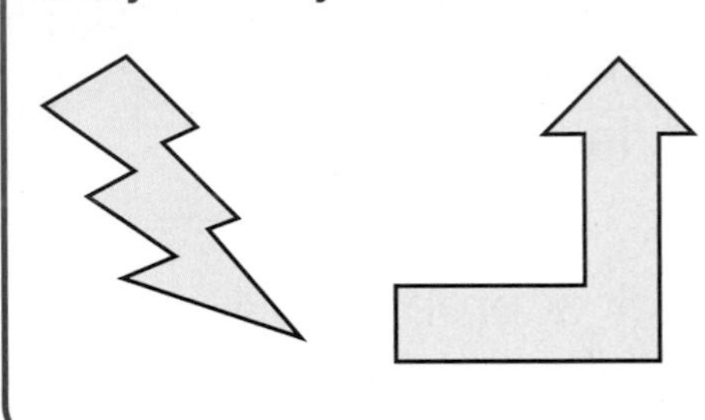

A line that divides a figure into two congruent parts is a **line of symmetry**.

Activity

Materials ■ paper, scissors, crayon or marker

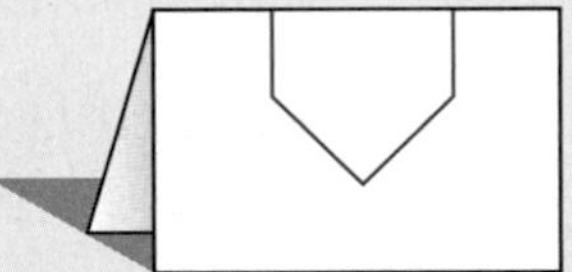

You can fold paper to explore symmetry.

- Fold a sheet of paper in half.
- Draw a figure that begins and ends on the fold. Cut out the figure with the paper still folded.
- Unfold the figure, and draw a line on the fold. The line on the fold is a line of symmetry.
- Do the halves match exactly? Explain.

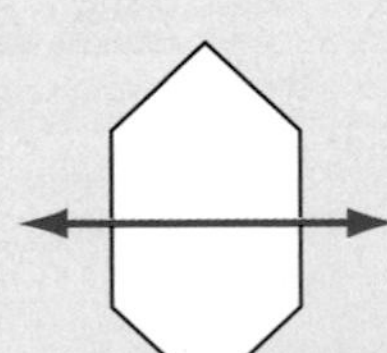

Guided Practice

1. Does the blue line appear to be a line of symmetry? **Explain.**

   Think: Do the halves match exactly?

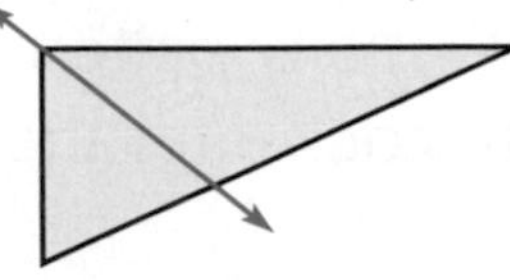

Tell if the blue line appears to be a line of symmetry. Write *yes* or *no*.

2. 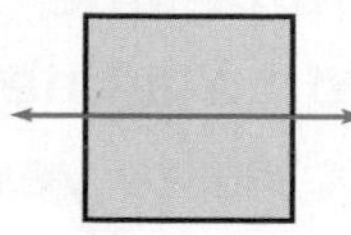

3. 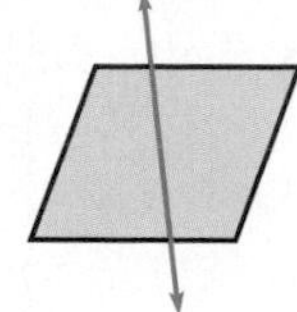

✓4. 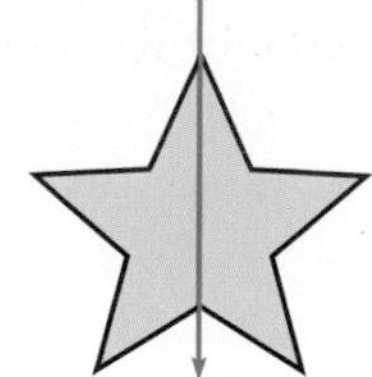

✓5. 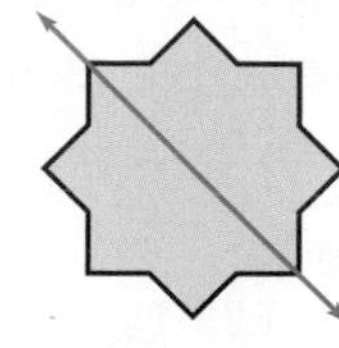

6. TALK Math **Explain** how you can fold paper to find a line of symmetry.

Independent Practice and Problem Solving

Tell if the blue line appears to be a line of symmetry. Write *yes* or *no*.

7. 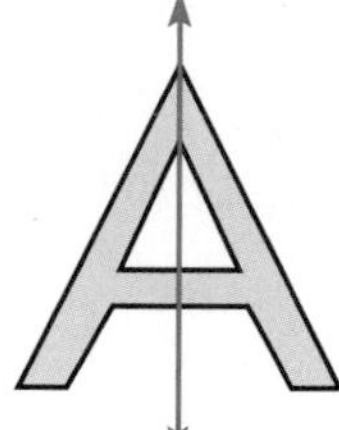

8. 

9. 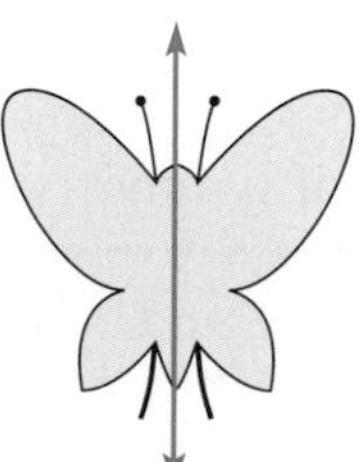

10. 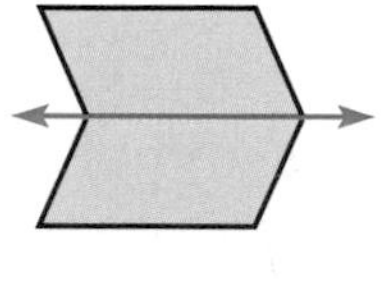

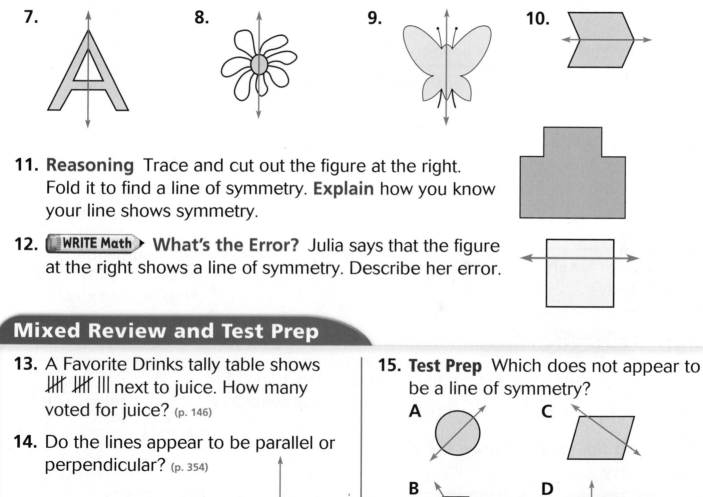

11. **Reasoning** Trace and cut out the figure at the right. Fold it to find a line of symmetry. **Explain** how you know your line shows symmetry.

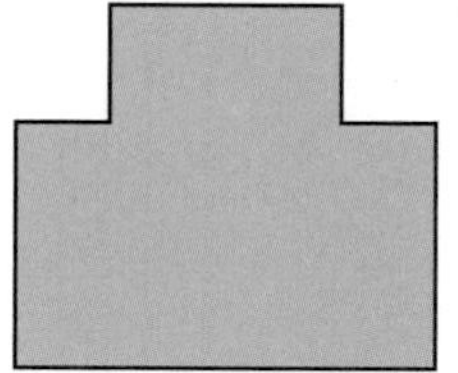

12. WRITE Math **What's the Error?** Julia says that the figure at the right shows a line of symmetry. Describe her error.

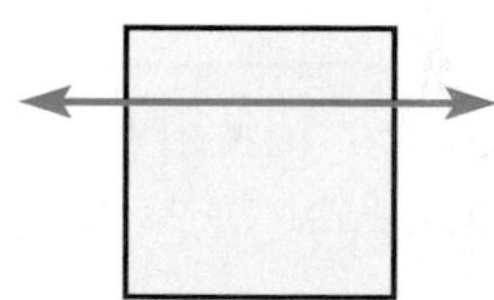

Mixed Review and Test Prep

13. A Favorite Drinks tally table shows 𝍸 𝍸 ||| next to juice. How many voted for juice? (p. 146)

14. Do the lines appear to be parallel or perpendicular? (p. 354)

15. **Test Prep** Which does not appear to be a line of symmetry?

A

C 

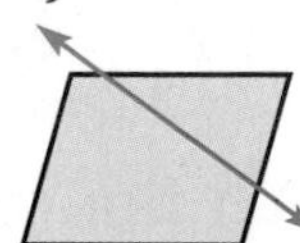

B 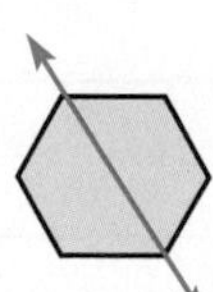

D 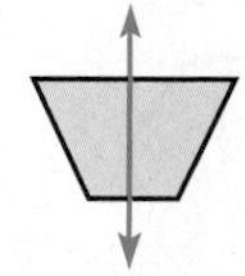

Extra Practice on page 392, Set B

CD ROM **Technology**
Use Harcourt Mega Math, Ice Station Exploration, *Polar Planes*, Level K.

LESSON 4

Lines of Symmetry

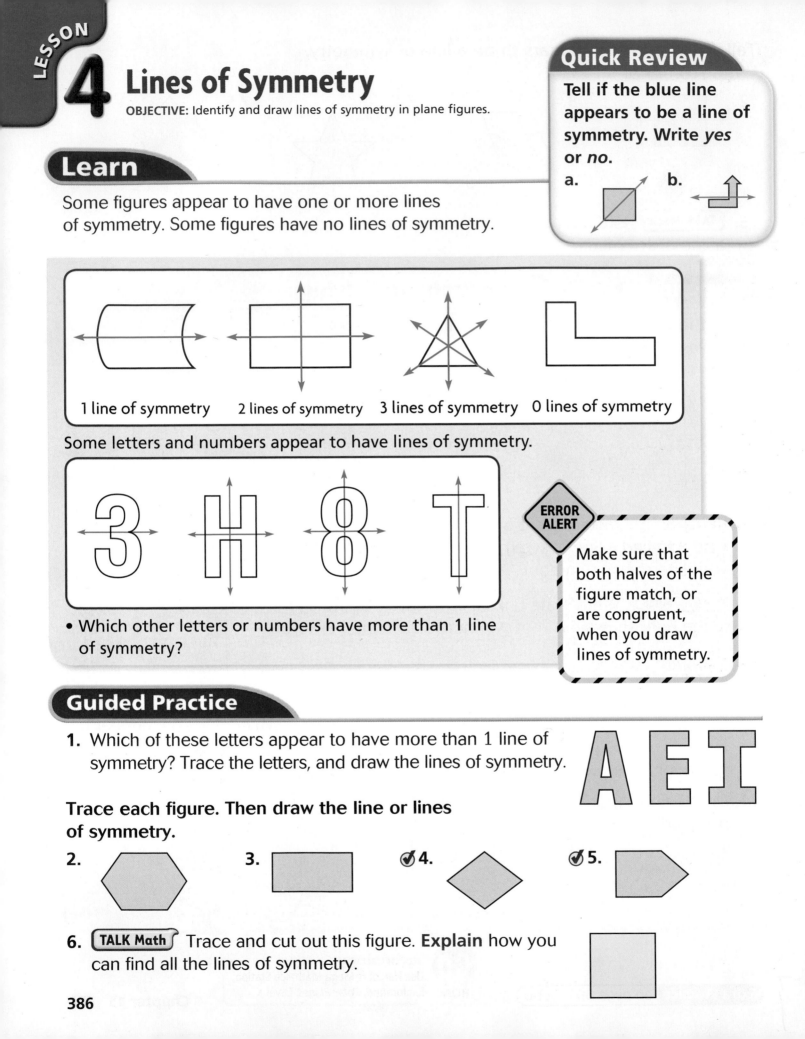

OBJECTIVE: Identify and draw lines of symmetry in plane figures.

Quick Review

Tell if the blue line appears to be a line of symmetry. Write *yes* or *no*.

a. 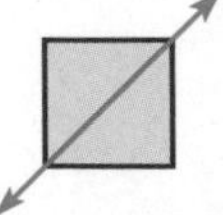

b. 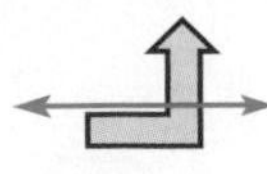

Learn

Some figures appear to have one or more lines of symmetry. Some figures have no lines of symmetry.

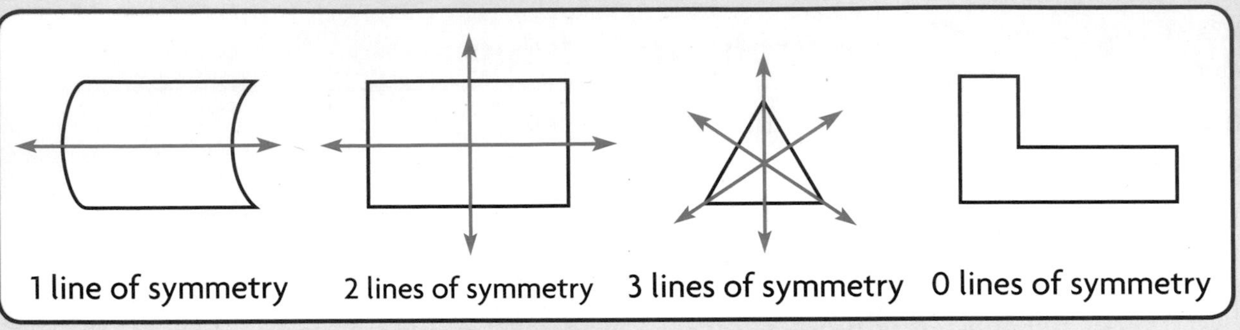

Some letters and numbers appear to have lines of symmetry.

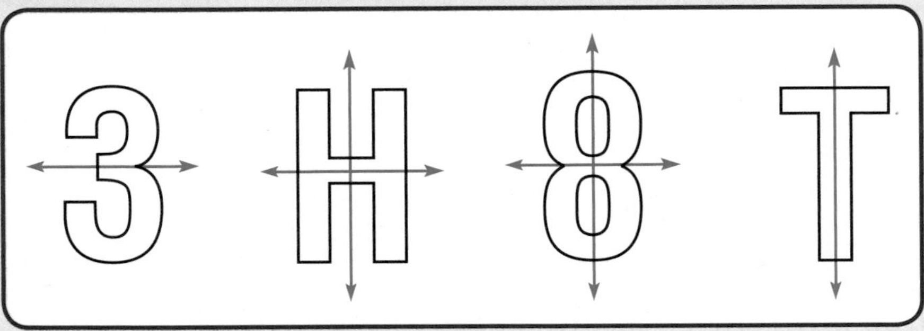

- Which other letters or numbers have more than 1 line of symmetry?

ERROR ALERT

Make sure that both halves of the figure match, or are congruent, when you draw lines of symmetry.

Guided Practice

1. Which of these letters appear to have more than 1 line of symmetry? Trace the letters, and draw the lines of symmetry.

A E I

Trace each figure. Then draw the line or lines of symmetry.

2. 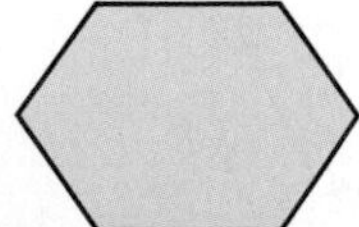

3. 

✓4. 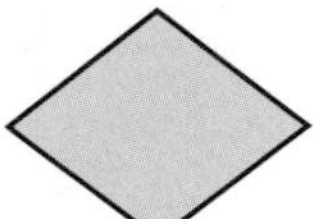

✓5. 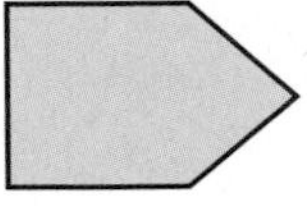

6. **TALK Math** Trace and cut out this figure. **Explain** how you can find all the lines of symmetry.

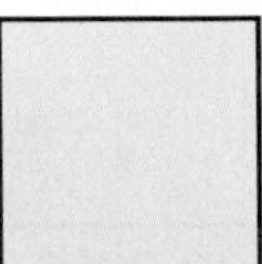

Independent Practice and Problem Solving

Trace each figure. Then draw the line or lines of symmetry.

7. 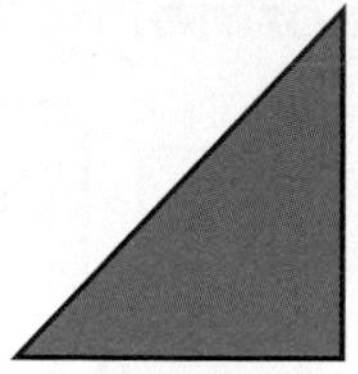

8. 

9. 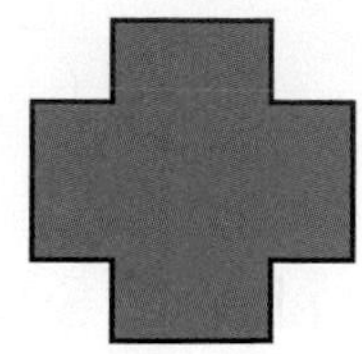

10. 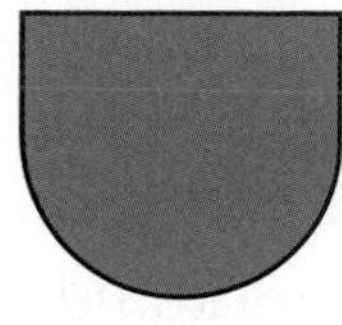

Decide if each figure appears to have 0 lines, 1 line, or more than 1 line of symmetry. Write *0, 1,* or *more than 1.*

11. 

12. 

13. 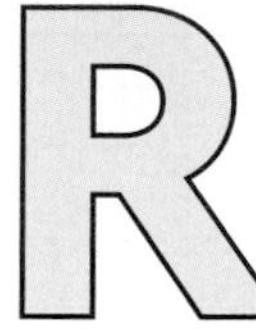

14. 

For 15–16, use shapes A–C.

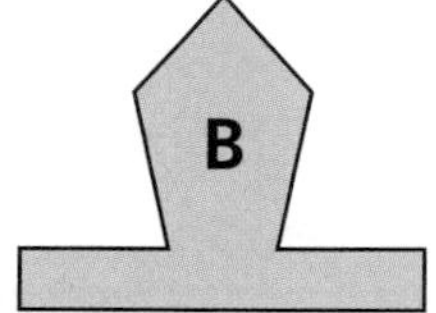

15. Gillian is making a book cover. She drew a figure on it that has 2 lines of symmetry. Which figure did she draw?

16. **FAST FACT** A nonagon is a polygon with 9 sides. Which of Gillian's book cover shapes is a nonagon? How many lines of symmetry does it have?

17. **WRITE Math** **Sense or Nonsense** Sienna says that this pattern block she traced has only 1 line of symmetry. Does her statement make sense? **Explain.**

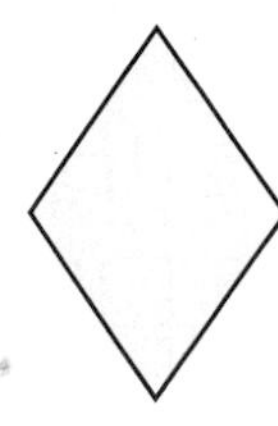

Mixed Review and Test Prep

18. Max drew a figure that is congruent to a hexagon. How many sides does his figure have? (p. 378)

19. What division number sentence is in the same fact family as $2 \times 8 = 16$? (p. 286)

20. **Test Prep** Which letters appear to have only 1 line of symmetry?

A K and X
B X and O
C B and O
D K and B

Extra Practice on page 392, Set C

CD ROM **Technology**
Use Harcourt Mega Math, Ice Station Exploration, *Polar Planes,* Level J.

Similar Figures

OBJECTIVE: Identify and draw similar figures.

Quick Review

Tell if the figures appear to be congruent. Write *yes* or *no*.

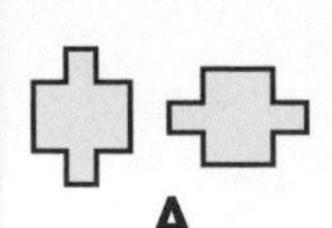

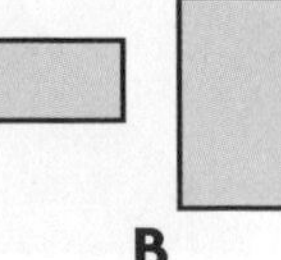

Vocabulary

similar

Learn

Similar figures have the same shape. Sometimes they are different sizes.

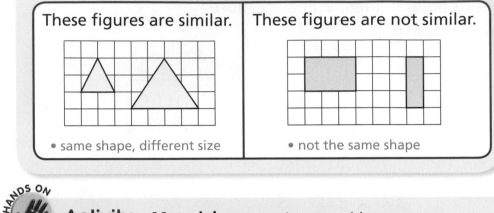

These figures are similar.	These figures are not similar.
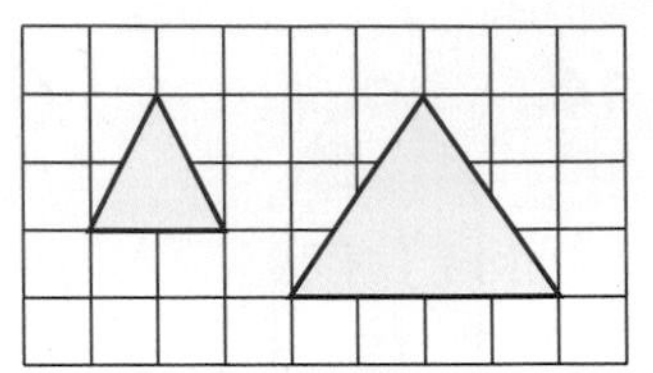	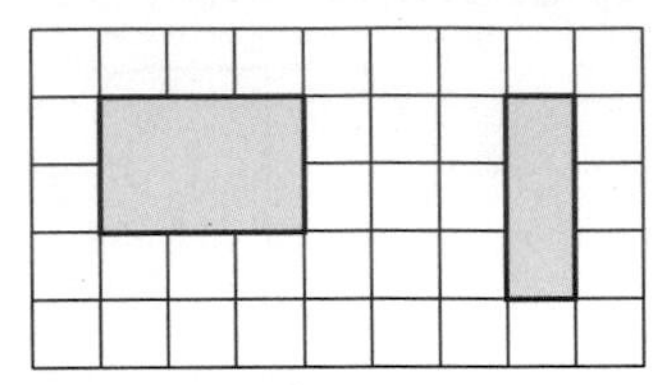
• same shape, different size	• not the same shape

Activity

Materials ■ 1-centimeter grid paper

Explore similar figures on grid paper.

Step 1

Draw a 2 by 2 square on grid paper.

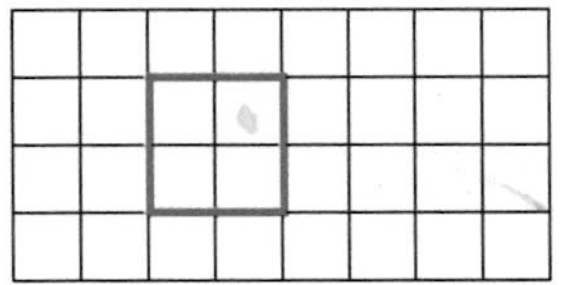

Step 2

On the same grid paper, draw a 3 by 3 square, a 4 by 4 square, and a 1 by 1 square.

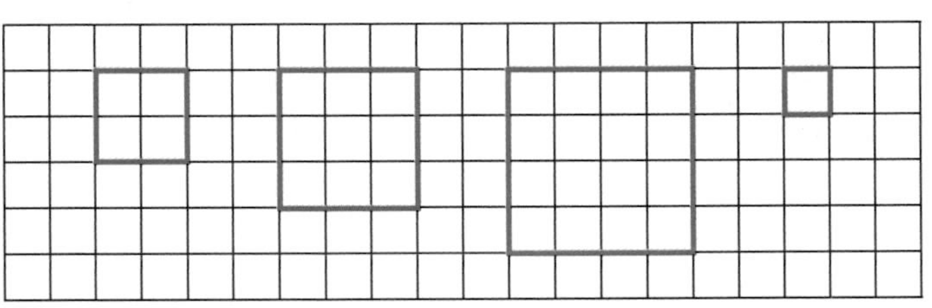

All figures that are the same shape are similar. If the figures are the same size, they are also congruent.

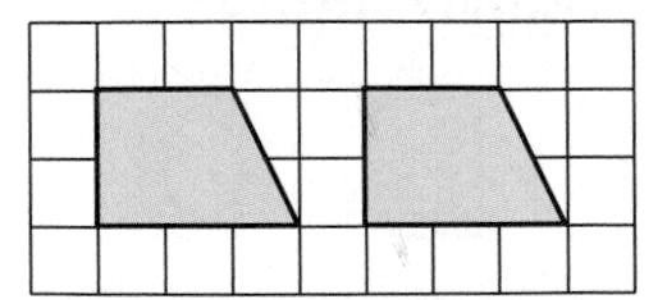	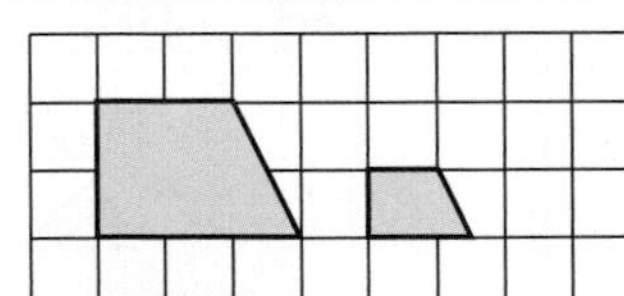	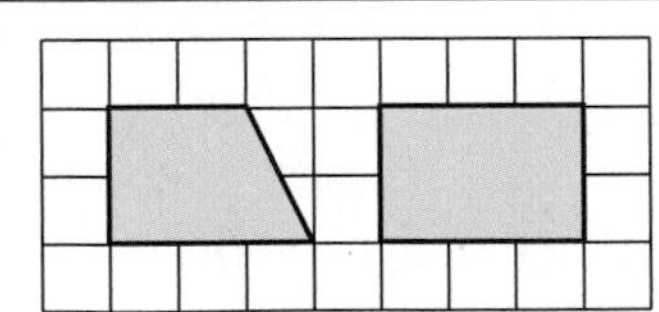
• same size • same shape • similar • congruent	• same shape • not the same size • similar • not congruent	• not the same shape • not similar • not congruent

Guided Practice

1. Look at the figures at the right. Do they appear to be the same shape? the same size?

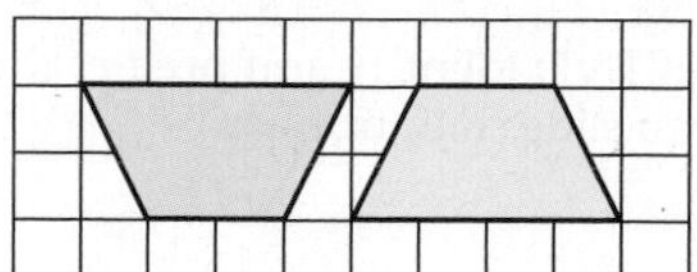

Tell if each pair of figures appears to be similar. Write *yes* or *no*.

2. 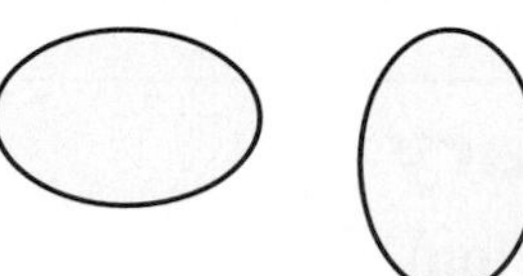

3. 

4.  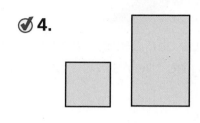

5. TALK Math **Explain** why the figures at the right appear to be similar but not congruent.

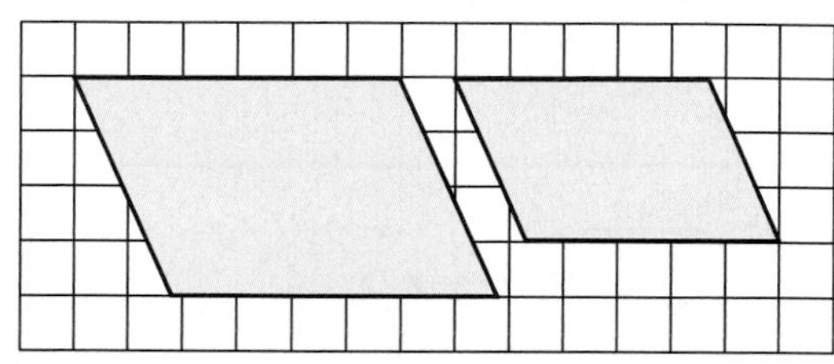

Independent Practice and Problem Solving

Tell if each pair of figures appears to be similar. Write *yes* or *no*.

6.  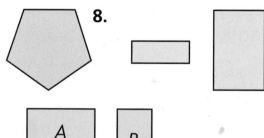

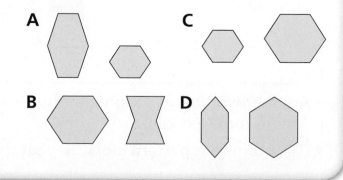

7. 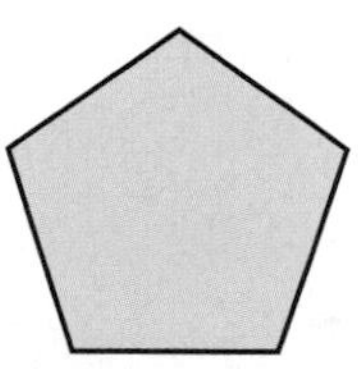

8.  

9. WRITE Math **What's the Error?** Joanna says that rectangles *A* and *B* appear to be similar. **Explain** her error.

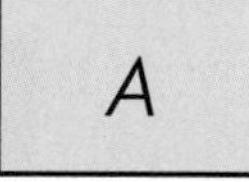

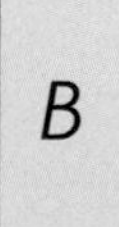

Mixed Review and Test Prep

10. Tonya has 15 crayons. She gives 3 crayons to each of her cousins. How many cousins does Tonya have? Multiply to check your answer. (p. 304)

11. Erin measured a rug. She measured the line segment shown. Did she measure the diameter or the radius? (p. 364)

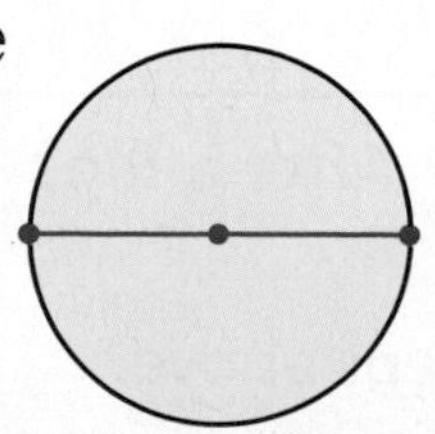

12. **Test Prep** Which pair of hexagons appears to be similar?

A 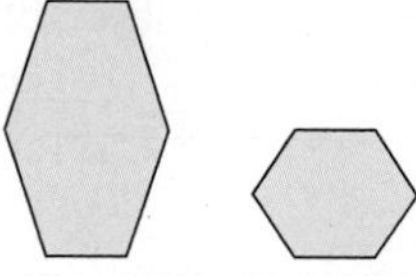

C 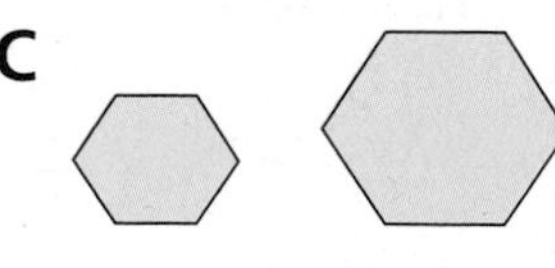

B 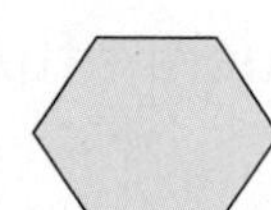

D 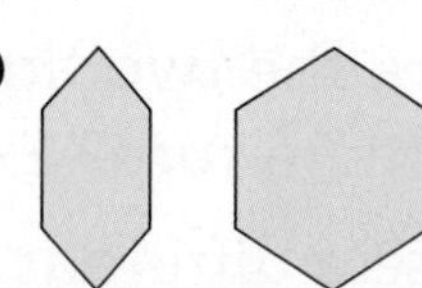

Extra Practice on page 392, Set D

Slides, Flips, and Turns

OBJECTIVE: Identify and predict the position of a figure after a slide, flip, or turn.

Quick Review

Tell if the figures appear to be congruent. Write *yes* or *no*.

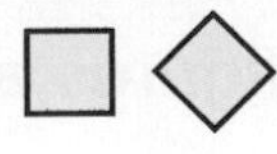
A

B

Vocabulary

slide (translation)
flip (reflection)
rotation (turn)

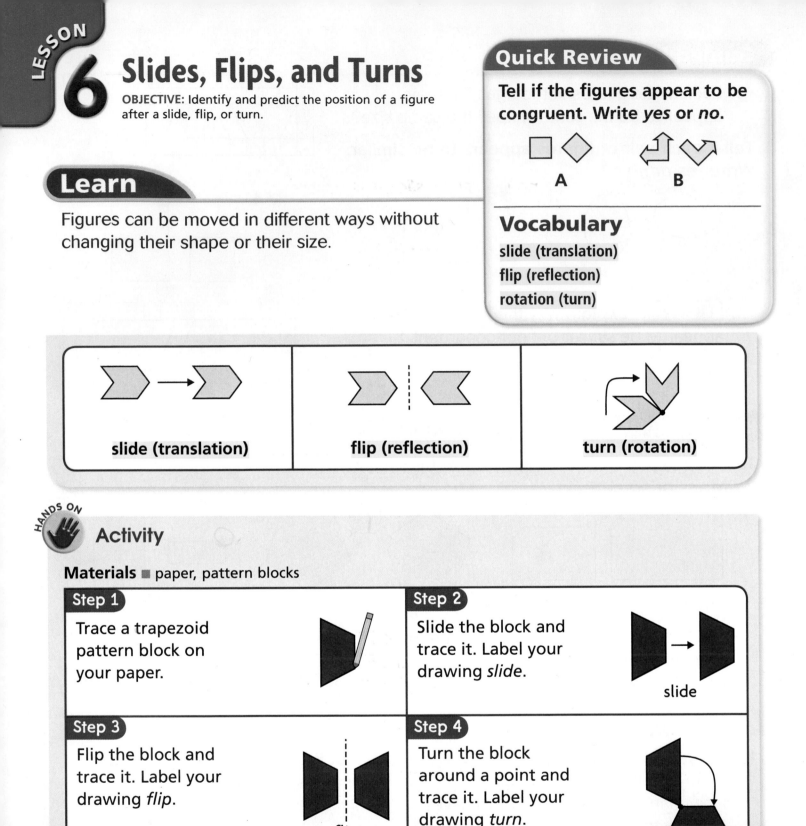

Learn

Figures can be moved in different ways without changing their shape or their size.

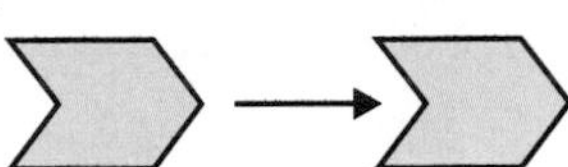 **slide (translation)**	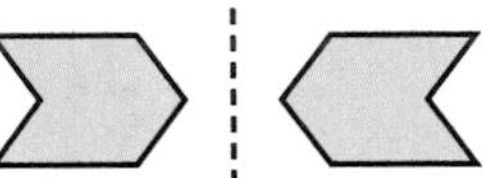 **flip (reflection)**	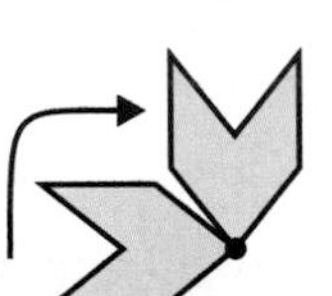 **turn (rotation)**

Activity

Materials ■ paper, pattern blocks

Step 1
Trace a trapezoid pattern block on your paper.

Step 2
Slide the block and trace it. Label your drawing *slide*.

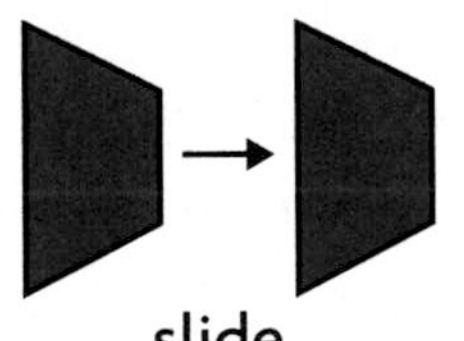

Step 3
Flip the block and trace it. Label your drawing *flip*.

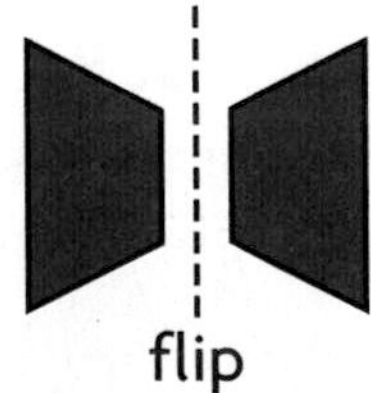

Step 4
Turn the block around a point and trace it. Label your drawing *turn*.

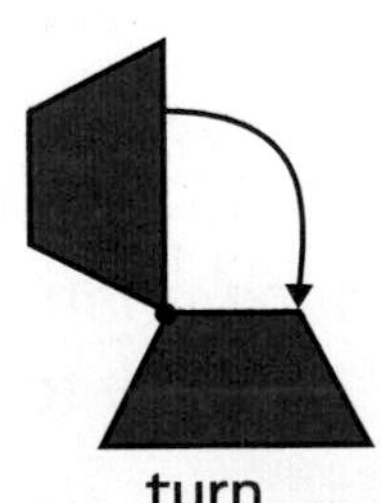

- Are the two figures congruent after a slide? After a flip? After a turn? Explain.
- Use a different pattern block. Repeat the steps above.

Guided Practice

1. How was this figure moved?

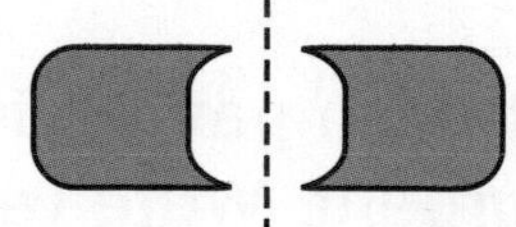

Tell how each figure was moved. Write *slide, flip,* or *turn*.

2. 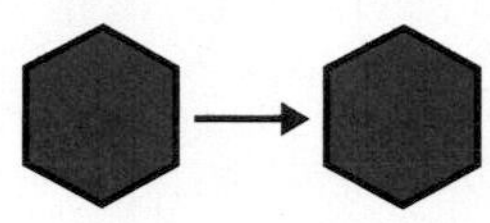

3. 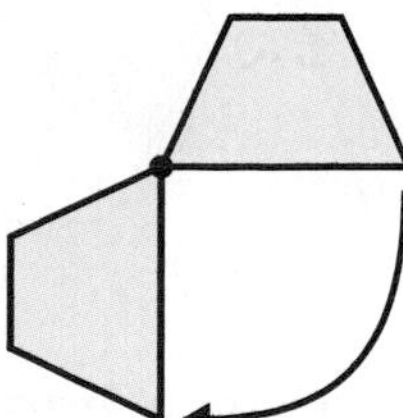

4. 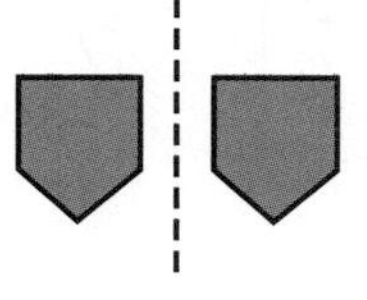

5. **TALK Math** Does the size or shape of a plane figure change after a slide, flip, or turn? **Explain.**

Independent Practice and Problem Solving

Tell how each figure was moved. Write *slide, flip,* or *turn*.

6. 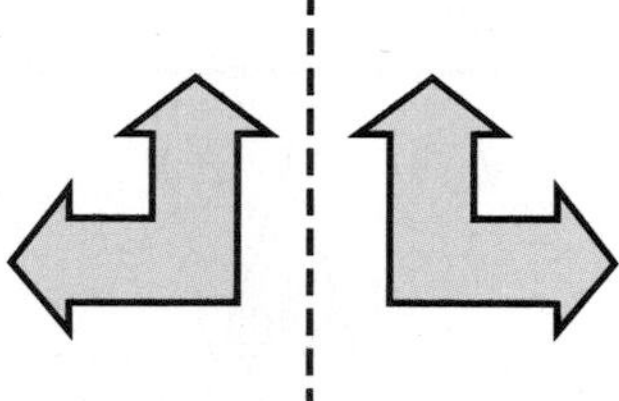

7. 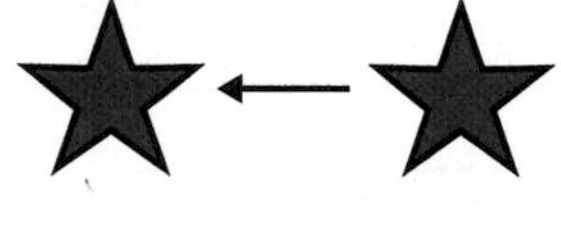

8. 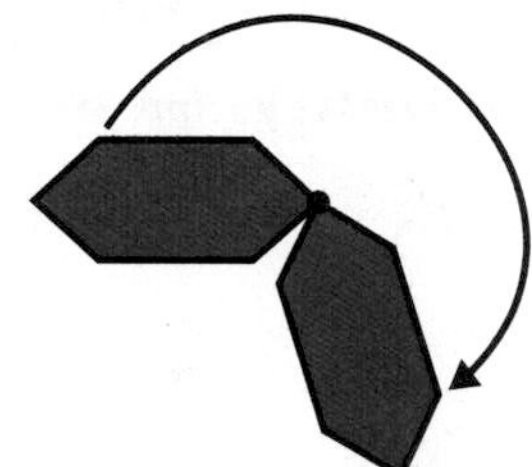

9. **WRITE Math** **What's the Error?** Mike traced Figure A. Then he moved it twice and traced it again. Figure B shows the new position. He said he slid the figure. What's his error?

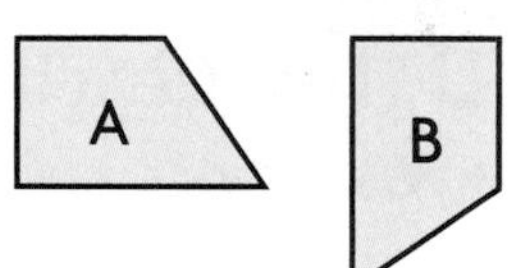

Mixed Review and Test Prep

10. What is the missing number in Jack's pattern? (Grade 2)

    26, 37, ■, 59, 70

11. A quadrilateral has 2 pairs of parallel sides and no right angles. Name the quadrilateral. (p. 360)

12. **Test Prep** Which shows a turn?

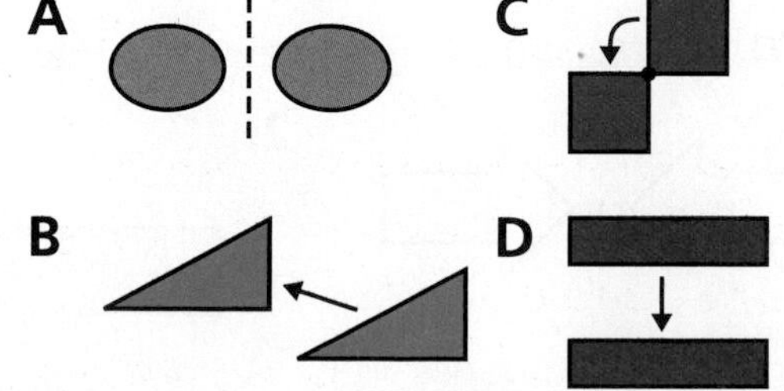

Extra Practice on page 392, Set E

Extra Practice

Set A Trace and cut out each pair of figures. Tell if the figures appear to be congruent. Write *yes* or *no*. (pp. 378–379)

1. 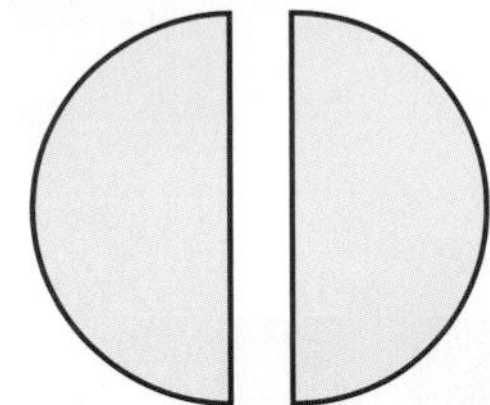
2. 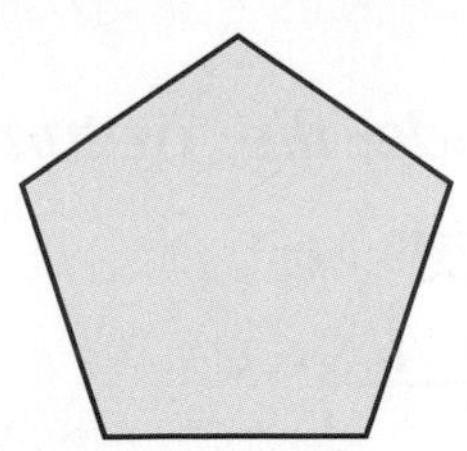
3. 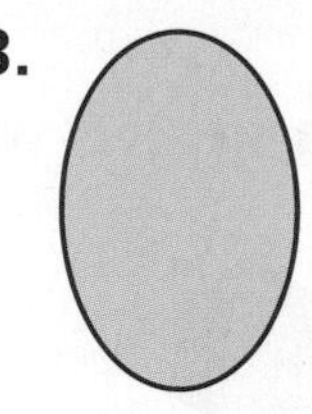 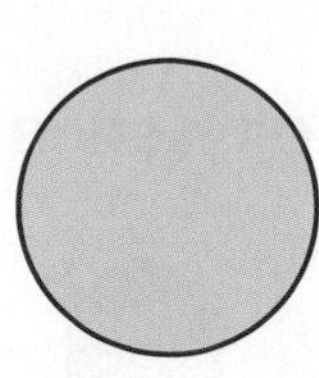

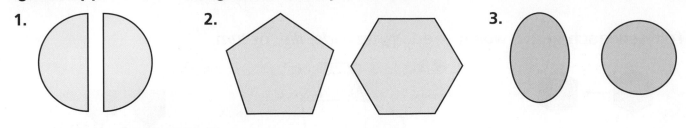

Set B Tell if the blue line appears to be a line of symmetry. Write *yes* or *no*. (pp. 384–385)

1. 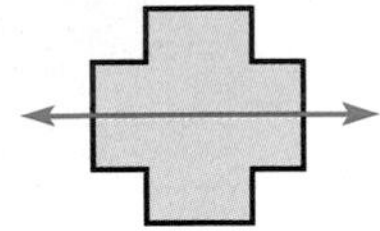
2. 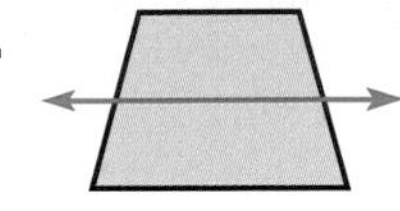
3. 
4. 

Set C Trace each figure. Then draw the line or lines of symmetry. (pp. 386–387)

1. 
2. 
3. 
4. 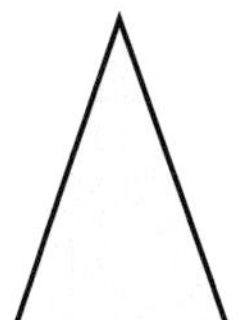

Set D Tell if each pair of figures appears to be similar. Write *yes* or *no*. (pp. 388–389)

1.  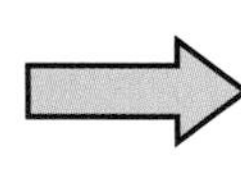
2. 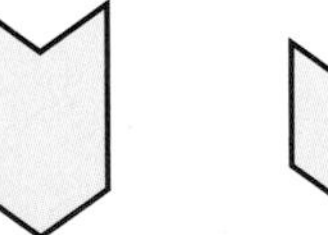
3.  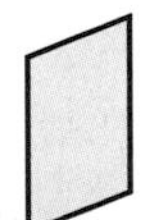

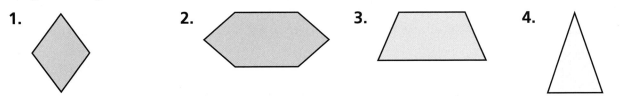

Set E Tell how each figure was moved. Write *slide, flip,* or *turn*. (pp. 390–391)

1. 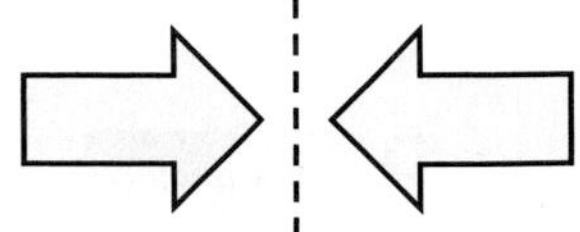
2. 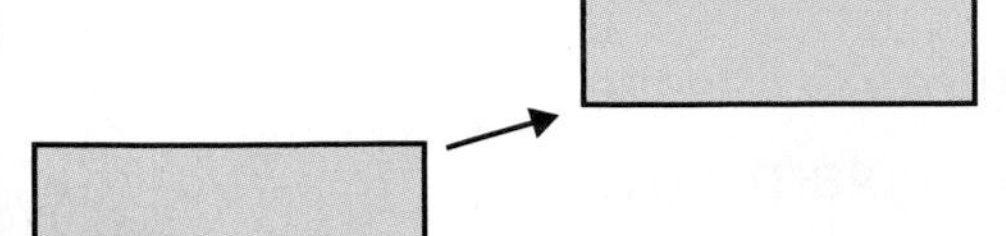
3. 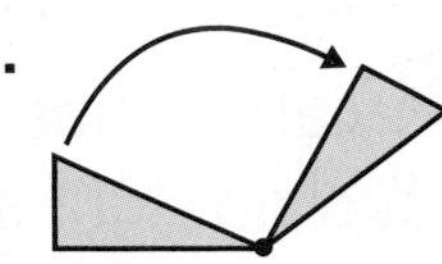

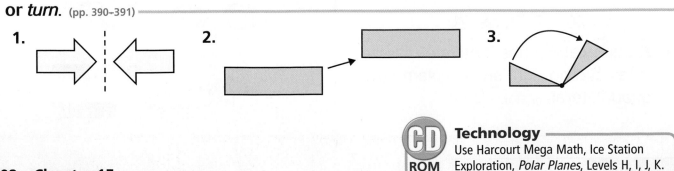

Technology
Use Harcourt Mega Math, Ice Station Exploration, *Polar Planes*, Levels H, I, J, K.

TECHNOLOGY CONNECTION

*i*Tools: Geometry

Find out if a Plane Figure has Symmetry

Jane made invitations for her party. She used figures that had lines of symmetry and then folded them to make cards.

Step 1	Click on *Geometry*. Then click on *Plane Figures* in the *Activities* menu. Now click on the second tab at the bottom.
Step 2	Click on the square on the left to place it on the grid.
Step 3	Click on the arrows at the top of the screen to make the sentence true. Then click on *Check*.
Step 4	Click on *Line of Symmetry*.

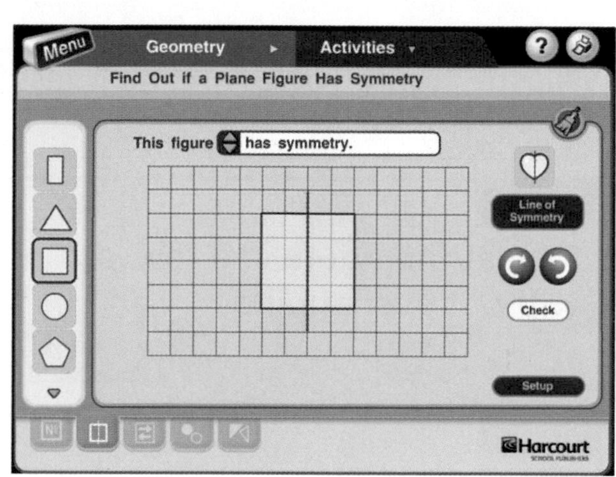

Click on the broom to clear the workspace.

Try It

1. Look at the figures on the left of the screen. Find a figure that has 2 lines of symmetry. Then find a figure with more than 2 lines of symmetry.

2. Click on the arrow below the figures. Find a figure that has no lines of symmetry.

3. **Explore More** How many lines of symmetry does the hexagon have? Use the *i*Tool to show the lines of symmetry, and then draw what you see. **Explain** the lines of symmetry.

Technology
*i*Tools available online or on CD-ROM

MATH POWER **Tessellations**

Make a Pattern

Some geometric figures can make a tessellation. A **tessellation** is a repeating pattern made of a closed plane figure that covers a surface with no overlapping or empty space.

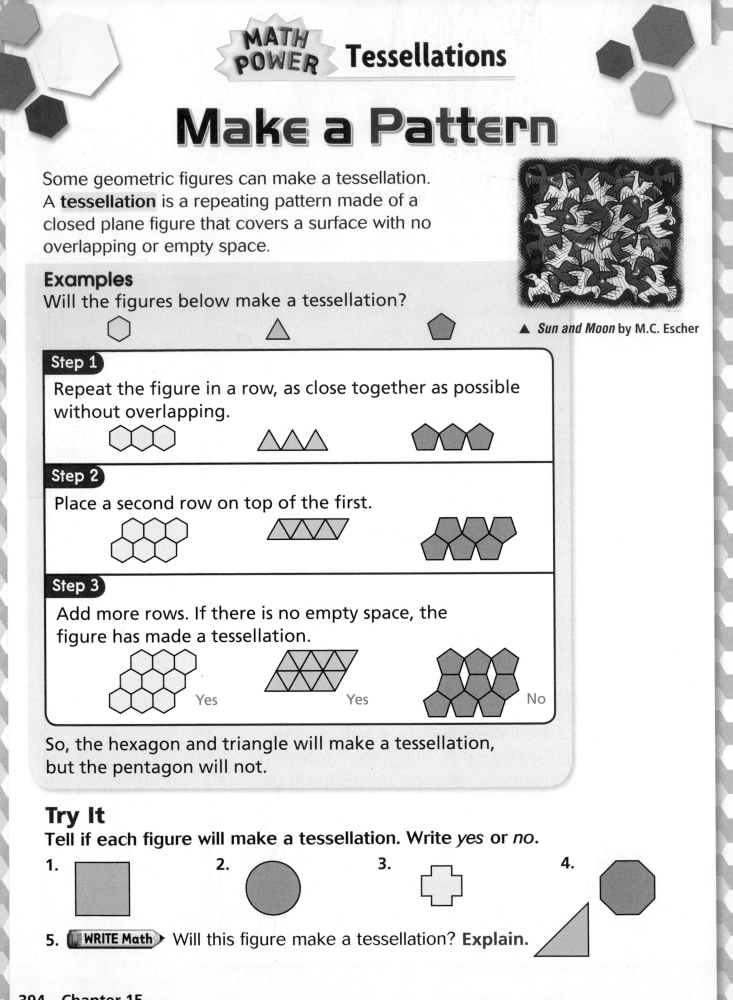

▲ *Sun and Moon* by M.C. Escher

Examples

Will the figures below make a tessellation?

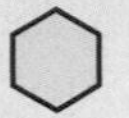  

Step 1

Repeat the figure in a row, as close together as possible without overlapping.

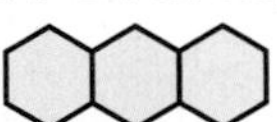  

Step 2

Place a second row on top of the first.

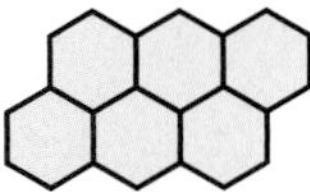 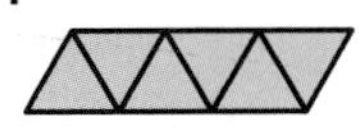 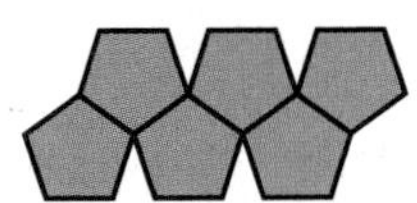

Step 3

Add more rows. If there is no empty space, the figure has made a tessellation.

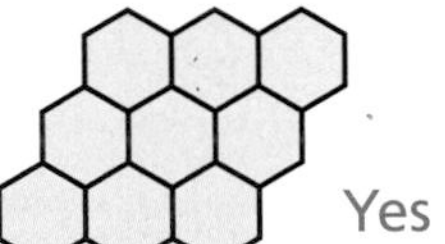

Yes

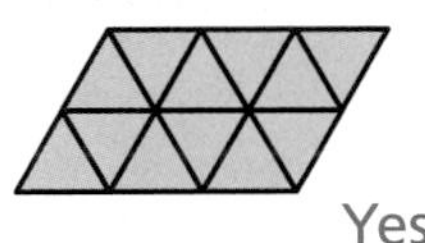

Yes

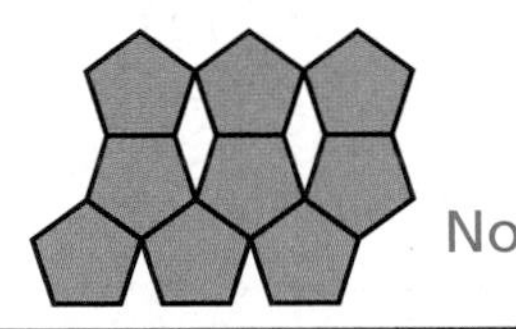

No

So, the hexagon and triangle will make a tessellation, but the pentagon will not.

Try It

Tell if each figure will make a tessellation. Write *yes* or *no*.

1. 

2. 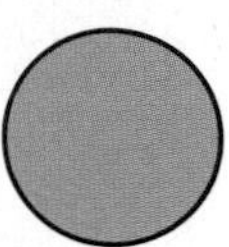

3. 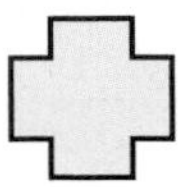

4. 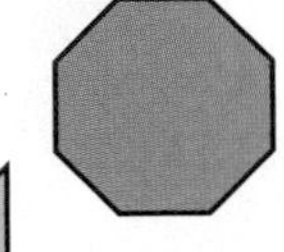

5. WRITE Math Will this figure make a tessellation? **Explain.**

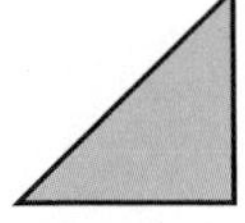

Chapter 15 Review/Test

Check Vocabulary and Concepts

Choose the best term from the box.

VOCABULARY
symmetry
line of symmetry
similar
congruent

1. Figures with the same size and shape are _?_. IL 9.3.10 (p. 378)
2. Figures that have the same shape and may have the same size are _?_. IL 9.3.10 (p. 388)
3. A _?_ divides a figure into two congruent parts. IL 9.3.04 (p. 384)

Check Skills

For 4–7, tell if the blue line appears to be a line of symmetry. Write *yes* or *no*. IL 9.3.04 (pp. 384–385)

4. 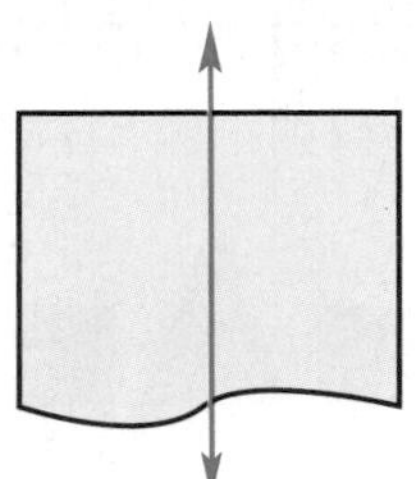
5. 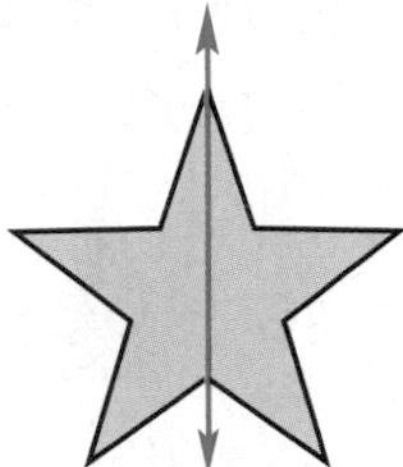
6. 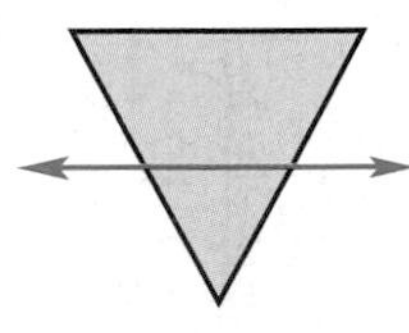
7. 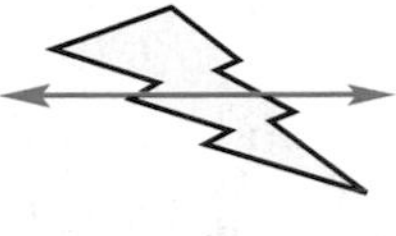

For 8–10, tell if each pair of figures appears to be similar. Write *yes* or *no*. IL 9.3.10 (pp. 388–389)

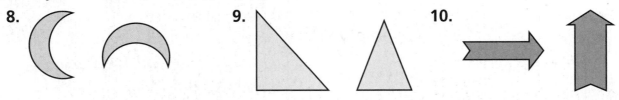

8. 
9. 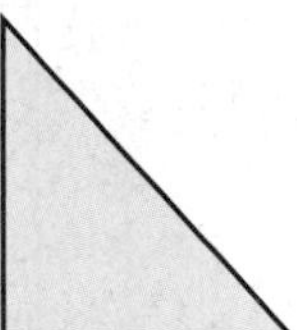
10. 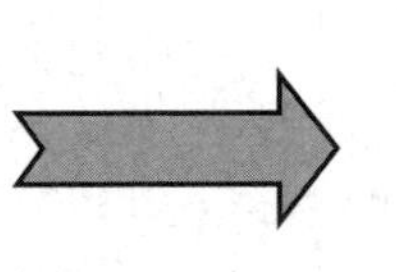

Check Problem Solving

Make a model to solve. IL 9.3.09; 9.3.04 (pp. 380–383)

11. Mrs. Thompson baked 4 apple pies. Each pie is cut into 8 slices. How many pieces of pie are there?
12. WRITE Math Bailey used 2 triangles and 2 trapezoids to make this rhombus. What other pattern blocks can be used to make a rhombus congruent to this one? **Explain.**

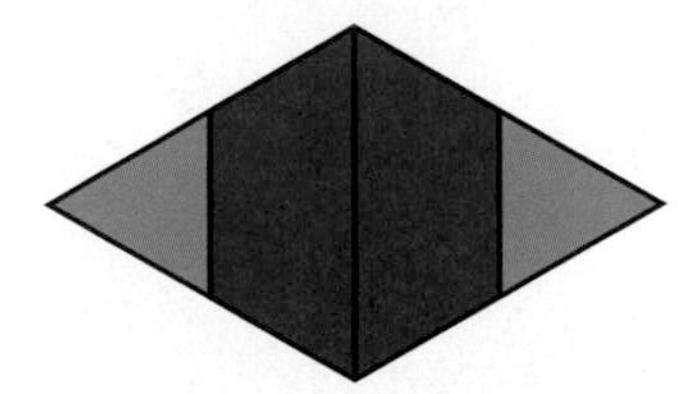

GO ONLINE **Technology** Use *Online Assessment.*

Practice for the ISAT
Chapters 1–15

Number and Operations

1. At *Beads and Things*, there are 447 wooden beads. There are 600 glass beads. How many more glass beads than wooden beads are there? IL 6.3.09 (p. 88)

   A 47
   B 153
   C 247
   D 1,047

2. It takes Eli 10 minutes to read a page in his book. How long would it take Eli to read 5 pages? IL 6.3.11 (p. 218)

   A 5 minutes
   B 15 minutes
   C 50 minutes
   D 105 minutes

3. **WRITE Math** Ben has 2 half dollars, 1 quarter, 5 dimes, and 6 pennies in his bank. How much money does Ben have? **Explain** how you know. IL 6.3.10 (p. 110)

Algebra

4. What related multiplication fact can help you find $132 \div 11$? IL 8.3.03 (p. 244)

   A $10 \times 11 = 110$
   B $11 \times 1 = 11$
   C $66 \times 2 = 132$
   D $12 \times 11 = 132$

5. Which shape comes next in the pattern? IL 8.3.01 (p. 426)

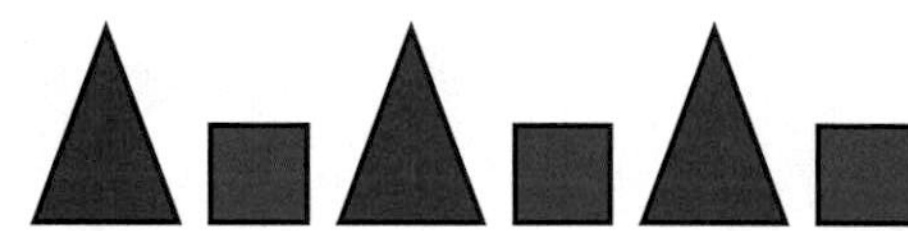

   A blue triangle
   B red triangle
   C blue square
   D red square

6. How many wheels do 4 wagons have? IL 8.3.01 (p. 256)

Wagons	1	2	3	4
Wheels	4	8	12	■

   A 16
   B 15
   C 14
   D 13

7. **WRITE Math** How can you use a fact family to find $32 \div 8$? **Explain** your answer. IL 8.3.03 (p. 286)

Geometry

8. Which figure appears to be congruent to figure A? IL 9.3.10 (p. 378)

A 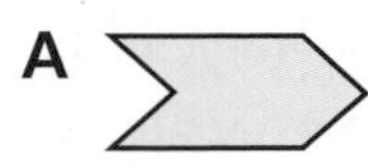

B 

C 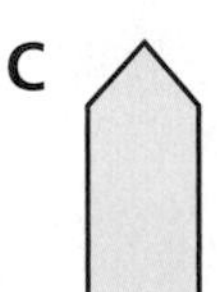

D 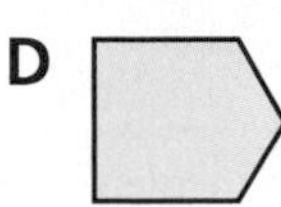

9. How many vertices does a hexagon have? IL 9.3.01 (p. 256)

A 5

B 6

C 7

D 8

10. WRITE Math How many lines of symmetry does this figure appear to have? Draw a picture to help you **explain.** IL 9.3.04 (p. 386)

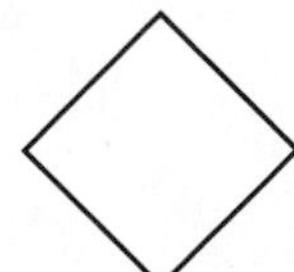

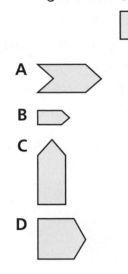

Data Analysis and Probability

11. The pictograph shows the number of trading cards Maria's friends have. Maria has 30 cards. How many symbols are needed to show this on the graph? IL 10.3.01 (p. 148)

A 6

B $7\frac{1}{2}$

C 8

D $8\frac{1}{2}$

12. WRITE Math The graph shows the insects Stephen saw on a walk. How many insects did Stephen see in all? **Explain** how you know. IL 10.3.01 (p. 154)

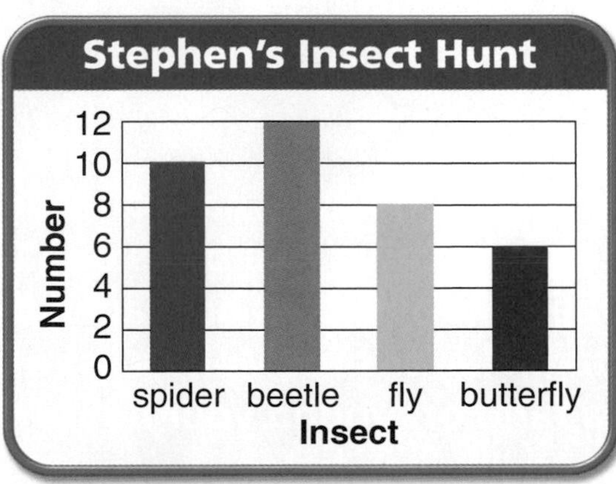

CHAPTER 16

Solid Figures

FAST FACT

At the Missouri State Fair, people can compete in events such as rolling large round bales of hay. Hay bales can weigh up to 2,000 pounds!

Investigate

Farmers use bales of hay to feed horses, sheep, and cows. The bales of hay can be shaped like cylinders or shaped like rectangular prisms. Make a list of other items on a farm or around your house that are shaped like hay bales.

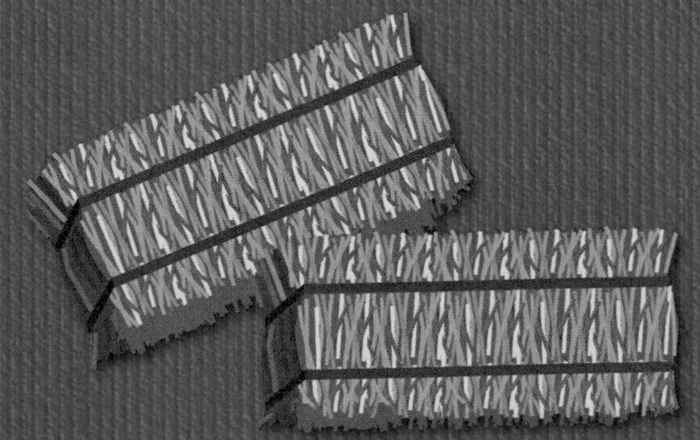

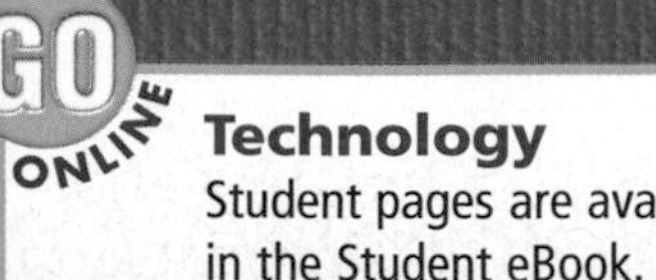

Technology
Student pages are available in the Student eBook.

Show What You Know

Check your understanding of important skills needed for success in Chapter 16.

▶ **Solid Figures**

Choose the best term from the box.

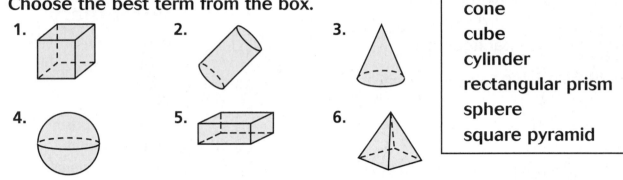

cone
cube
cylinder
rectangular prism
sphere
square pyramid

1. 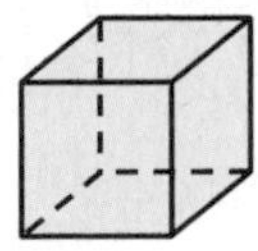
2. 
3. 
4. 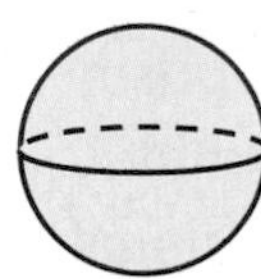
5. 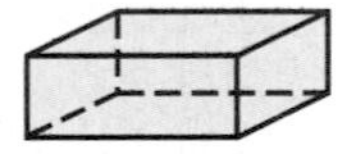
6. 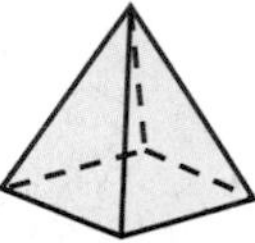

Name the solid figure that each object looks like.

7. 

8. 
9. 
10. 

VOCABULARY POWER

CHAPTER VOCABULARY

cone
cube
cylinder
edge
face
net
rectangular prism
sphere
square pyramid
three-dimensional figure
vertex

WARM-UP WORDS

cube A solid figure with six faces that are all squares

face A flat surface of a solid figure

three-dimensional figure A figure having length, width, and height

Identify Solid Figures

OBJECTIVE: Identify, describe, and classify solid figures.

Quick Review

Name each plane figure.

1. □ **2.** △ **3.** ▭

4. ○ **5.** ▷

Vocabulary

cone
cube
cylinder
sphere
rectangular prism
square pyramid
three-dimensional figure
edge
face
vertex

Learn

Solid figures have length, width, and height. They are also called **three-dimensional figures**.

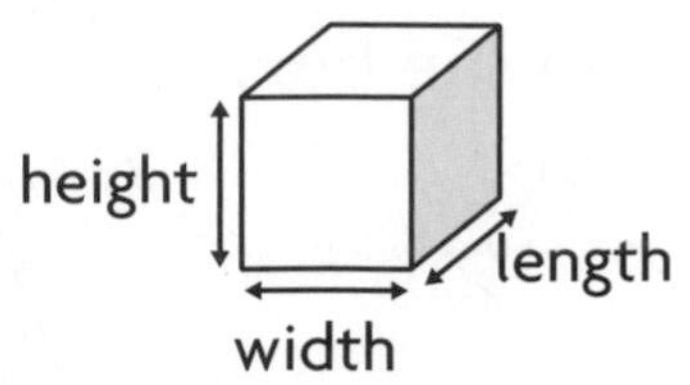

PROBLEM Jodie's grandmother gave her a charm bracelet. Which charm on her bracelet is shaped like a sphere?

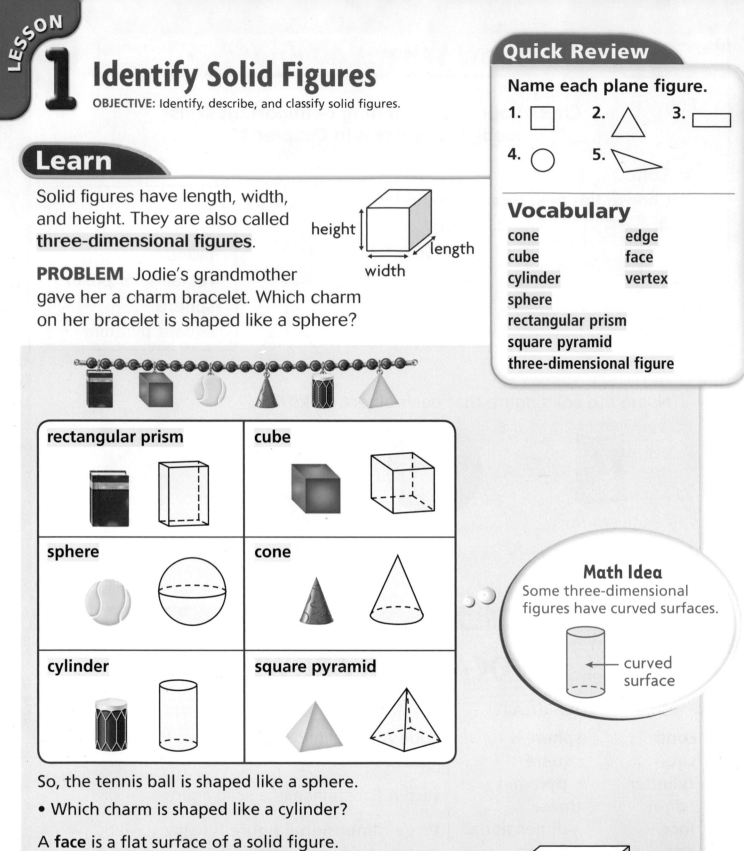

rectangular prism	cube
sphere	**cone**
cylinder	**square pyramid**

Math Idea

Some three-dimensional figures have curved surfaces.

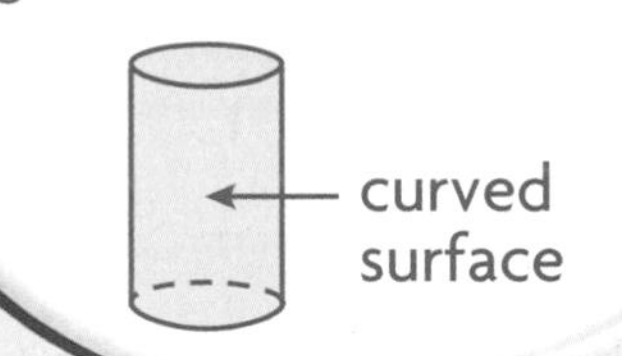

So, the tennis ball is shaped like a sphere.

• Which charm is shaped like a cylinder?

A **face** is a flat surface of a solid figure.

An **edge** is the line segment formed where two faces meet.

A **vertex** is a point where three or more edges meet. The plural of *vertex* is *vertices*.

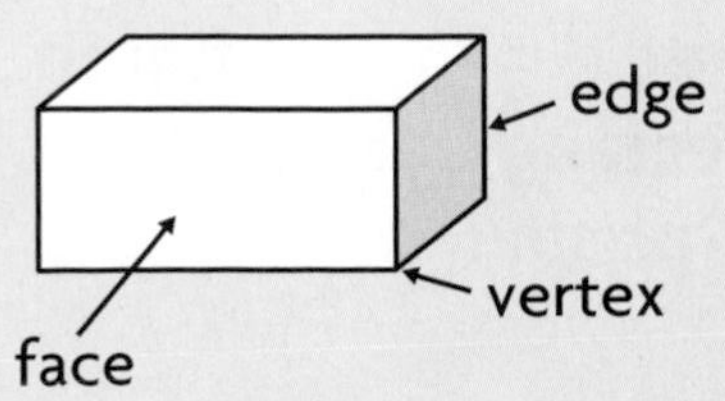

Naming Faces

Activity

Materials ■ solid figures (cube, square pyramid, rectangular prism), paper, crayons

- Copy the table below.
- Trace the faces of a cube. Name the plane figures.
- Count the numbers of faces, edges, and vertices. Record the numbers in the table.

Name of Figure	Shapes of Faces	Names of Faces	Number of		
			Faces	Edges	Vertices
cube	□□ □□ □□	6 squares	6	12	8

- Repeat the steps for a square pyramid and a rectangular prism.
- Describe the faces of a square pyramid.
- How many edges does a rectangular prism have?

Guided Practice

1. Which solid figure has the faces shown?

Name the solid figure that each object is shaped like.

2. 

3. 

✓4. 

✓5. 

6. **TALK Math** **Explain** the difference between a cube and a square.

Independent Practice and Problem Solving

Name the solid figure that each object is shaped like.

7. 

8. 

9. 

10. 

Name the solid figure. Then tell the number of faces, edges, and vertices.

11. 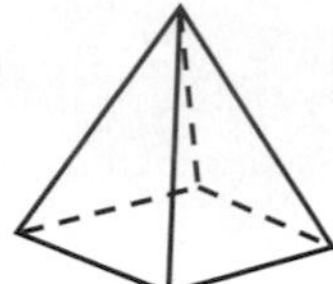

12. 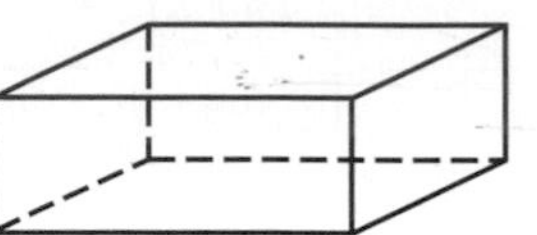

13. 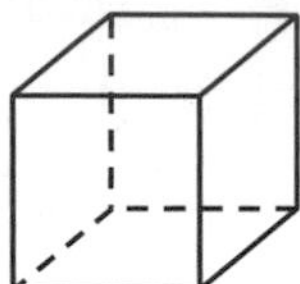

For 14–17, use the grocery items.

14. Which grocery item is shaped like a sphere?

15. Which grocery item has the faces shown below?

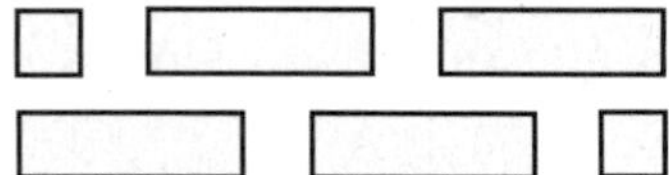

16. Describe the faces of the box of tissues.

17. Which solid figure is the can of soup shaped like?

18. I am a solid figure with 5 faces. One of my faces is a quadrilateral with 4 right angles and 4 sides the same length. What figure am I?

19. **Pose a Problem** Look at Problem 18. Write a similar problem about a different solid figure.

20. Rick built a tower using 7 rectangular prisms, 4 cylinders, 8 cubes, and 1 square pyramid. Half of the figures were blue and half were red. How many figures were blue?

21. ***FAST FACT*** Earth is the third planet from the sun and the fifth-largest planet in our solar system. What solid figure is shaped like Earth?

22. **Reasoning** Explain how a rectangular prism and a cube are alike and how they are different.

23. WRITE Math **What's the Question?** The answer is 6 square faces.

Extra Practice on page 414, Set A

Learn About Parallel Faces

Some solid figures have parallel faces.
Parallel faces are always the same distance apart.

Megan made a jewelry box in the shape of a rectangular prism. She painted the parallel faces the same colors. How many colors did she use?

Remember
Parallel lines are lines that appear never to cross. They are always the same distance apart.

Example Identify the parallel faces.

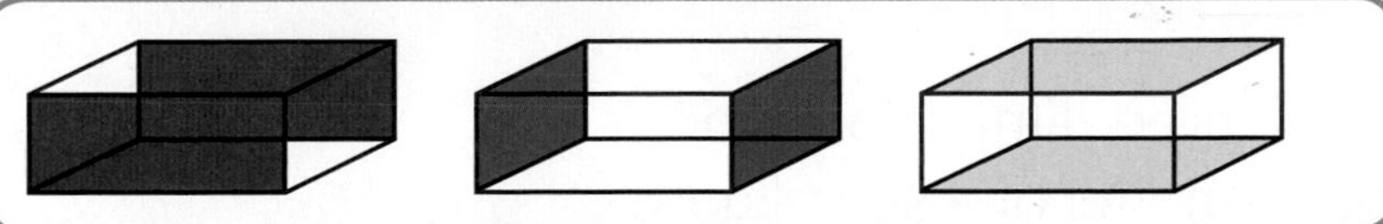

A rectangular prism has 3 pairs of parallel faces.
So, Megan used 3 different colors to paint her jewelry box.

Try It

24. Trace the solid figure below. Color one pair of parallel faces. Write the number of parallel faces.

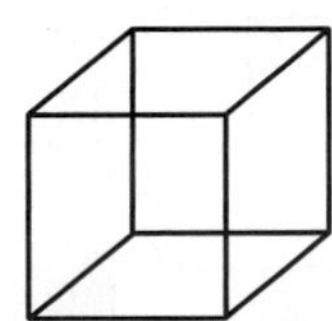

25. Megan said the figure below has 2 pairs of parallel faces. Do you agree? **Explain.**

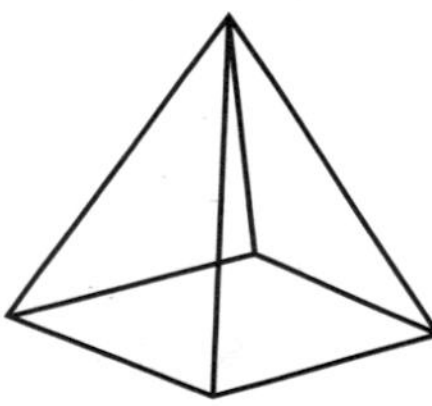

Mixed Review and Test Prep

26. A bag contains 8 balls numbered 1 through 8. You pull 1 ball from the bag. List the possible outcomes. (p. 182)

27. **Test Prep** Which solid figure is shaped like a party hat?

A cone **C** cylinder
B cube **D** prism

28. What kind of motion was used to move this figure? (p. 390)

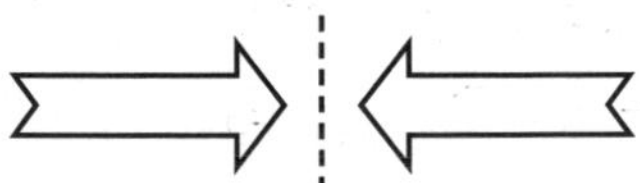

29. **Test Prep** How many faces does a square pyramid have?

A 12 **B** 8 **C** 6 **D** 5

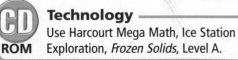

CD ROM Technology
Use Harcourt Mega Math, Ice Station Exploration, *Frozen Solids*, Level A.

Model Solid Figures

OBJECTIVE: Identify and make a model of a solid figure from a net.

Quick Review

Name the figure. Then tell how many faces, edges, and vertices.

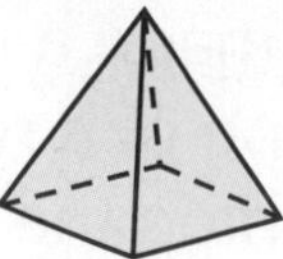

Vocabulary

net

Learn

PROBLEM Lori folded this pattern to make a solid figure. What figure did she make?

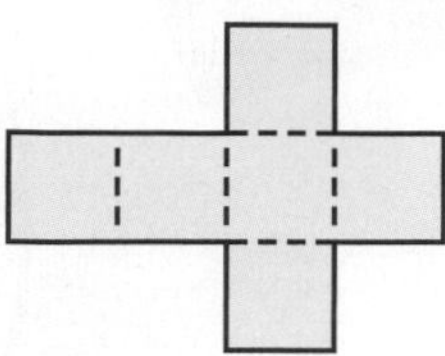

A **net** is a two-dimensional pattern of a three-dimensional, or solid, figure. When folded, it becomes a model of a solid figure.

Activity 1

Materials ■ cube pattern, scissors, tape

- Cut out the net along the solid lines.
- Fold along the dashed lines. Tape the edges together.

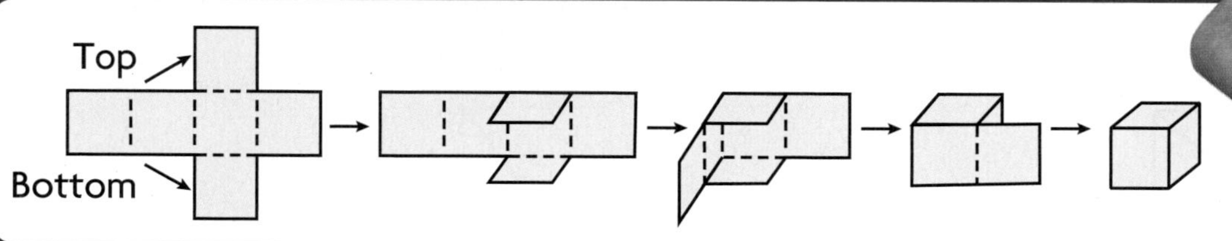

- Identify the solid figure you made.

The net can be folded to make a cube. So, Lori made a cube.

- What plane figures are the faces of a cube?

Examples of Nets

A

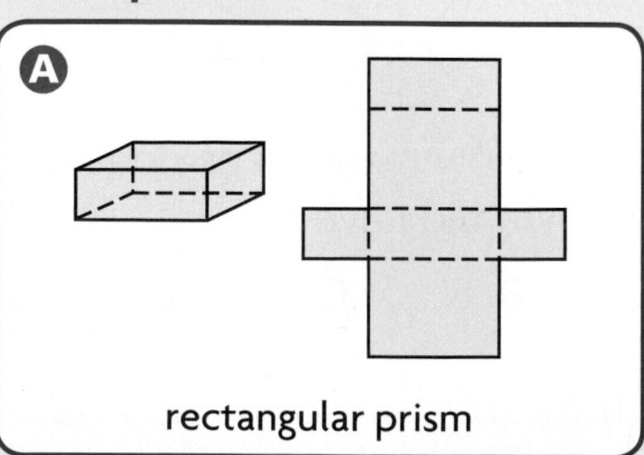

rectangular prism

B

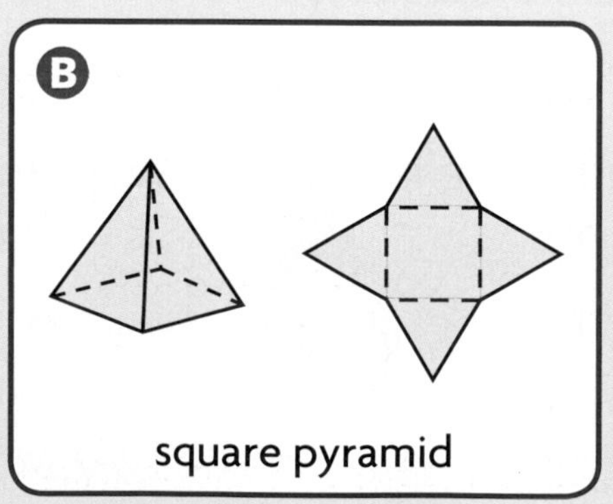

square pyramid

Making a Net

You can cut apart a three-dimensional figure to make a net.

HANDS ON

Activity 2

Materials ■ box, paper, scissors, tape

- Cut along the edges of a box until it is flat. Lay it on a sheet of paper.
- Trace around the flattened box to make a net.
- Cut out the net. Fold it the same way the original box was folded. Tape the edges together.
- What are the plane figures on the net you made?

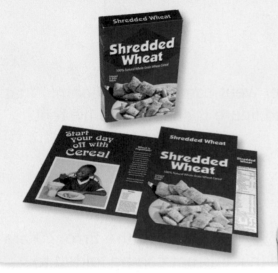

Guided Practice

1. What plane figures are the faces of this net?

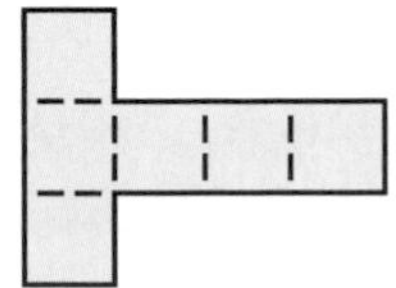

Identify the solid figure that can be made from each net.

2.

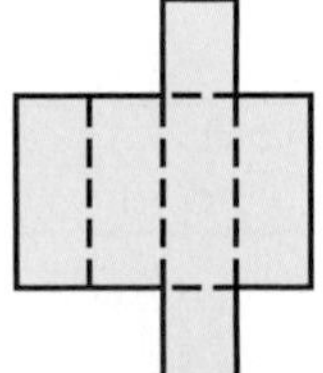

✓3.

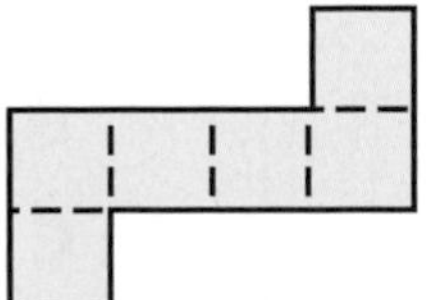

✓4.

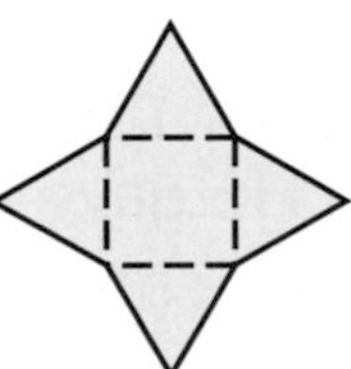

5. TALK Math **Explain** how a net for a cube is different from a net for a rectangular prism.

Independent Practice and Problem Solving

Identify the solid figure that can be made from each net.

6. 

7. 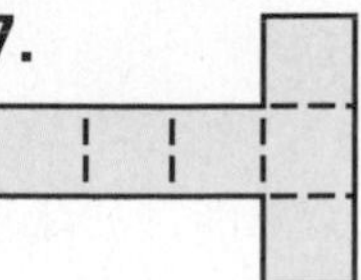

8. 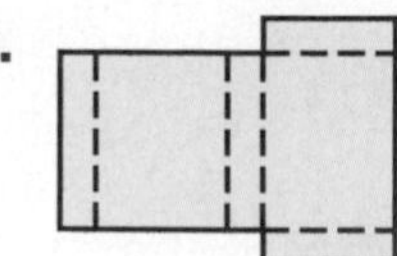

Write the letter of the solid figure that matches each net.

9. 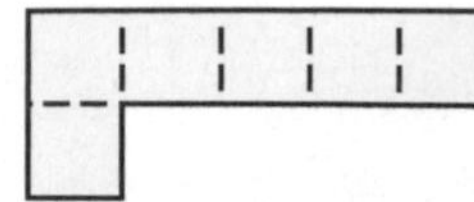

10. 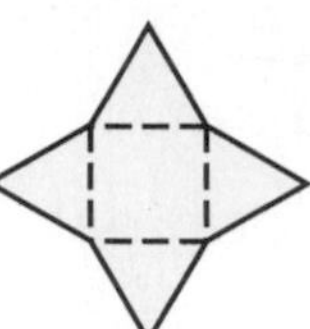

11. 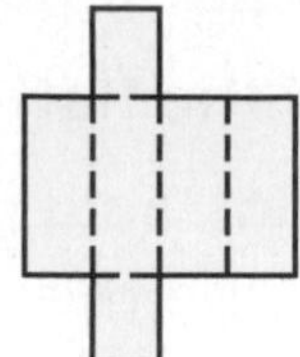

a. 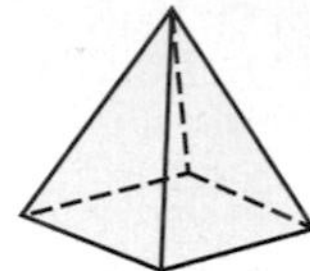

b. 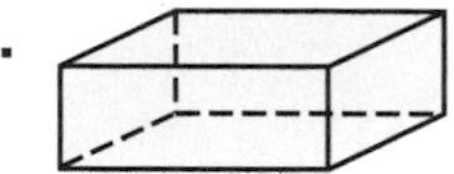

c. 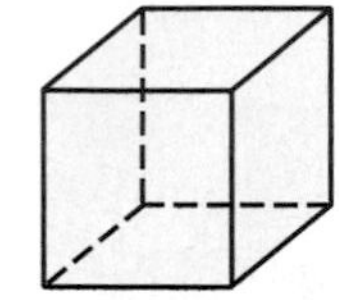

12. Arnie is moving to a new house. He has a cardboard packing box that is now in the shape of the net on the right. What shape will the box be?

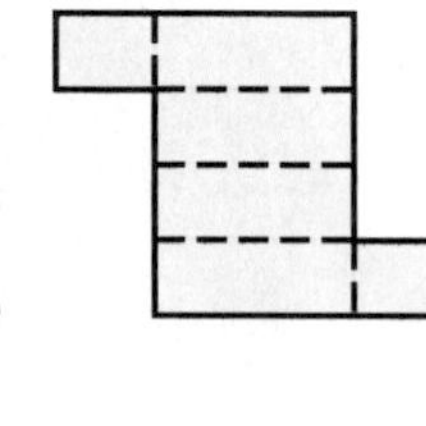

13. Tyler went camping last month. What solid figure is shaped like his tent?

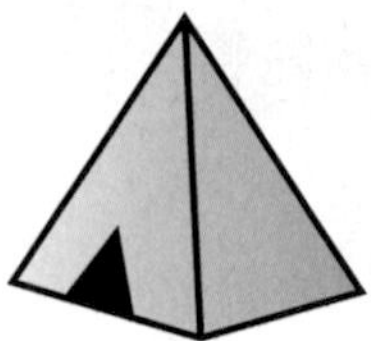

14. **Reasoning** Chris is mailing a basketball to his sister. He has boxes shaped like a cube, a rectangular prism, and a cylinder. Which box should he use? **Explain** your choice.

15. WRITE Math **What's the Error?** Kara said that this net can be folded to make a cube. **Explain** her error.

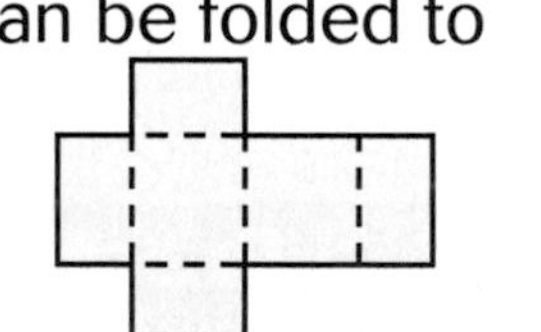

Mixed Review and Test Prep

16. Nick made a model of a rectangular prism. How many faces, edges, and vertices did Nick's model have? (p. 400)

17. Kit bought 3 puzzles. Each puzzle cost $7. He gave the cashier $30. How much change did he receive? (p. 264)

18. **Test Prep** Which solid figure could be made from this net?

A cube

B sphere

C square pyramid

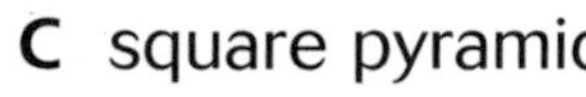

D cylinder

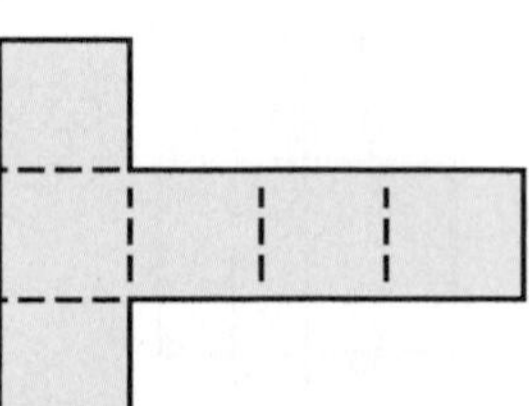

Extra Practice on page 414, Set B

The Art of Origami

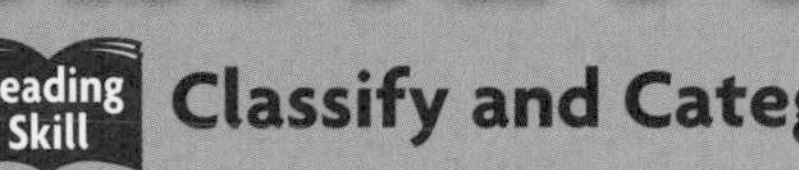

Classify and Categorize

Origami is the art of folding paper. The only material needed is paper. Some people can make models of animals and geometric shapes. Look at the origami models below.

When you classify three-dimensional figures, you organize them into groups by ways they are alike.

▲ The name *origami* comes from the Japanese word "oru," which means to fold, and "kami," which means paper.

Figures that stack	Figures that roll	Figures with flat surfaces	Figures with curved surfaces	Figures with right angles	Figures with no right angles
cylinder rectangular prism cube	cylinder cone sphere	rectangular prism square pyramid cube	cylinder cone sphere	rectangular prism square pyramid cube	cylinder cone sphere

Problem Solving **Use *classify and categorize* to solve.**

1. How are the cube and the square pyramid alike?
2. Teresa sorted the solid figures shown below into two groups. Tell two ways Teresa could classify the models. Which models would you place in each category?

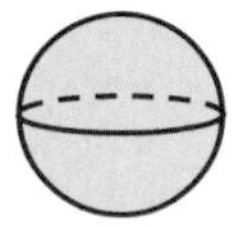
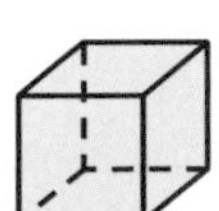

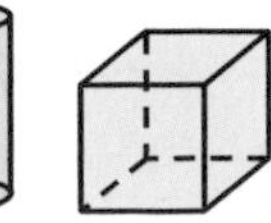
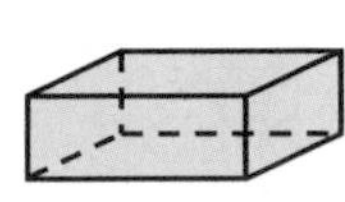
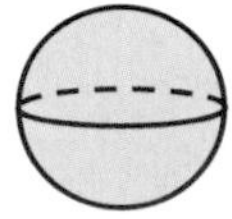
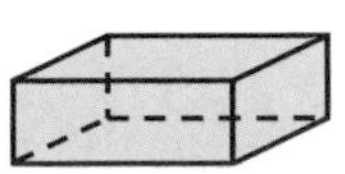

LESSON 3

Combine Solid Figures

OBJECTIVE: Identify common solid figures in complex solid figures.

Quick Review

Name each solid figure.

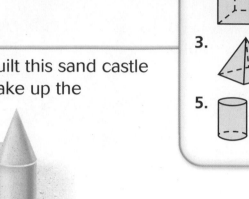

1. 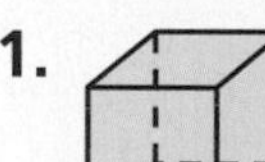
2. 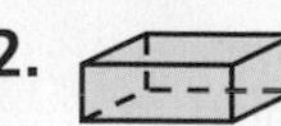
3. 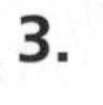 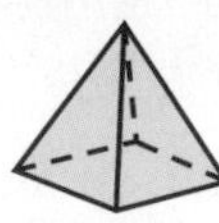
4. 
5. 

Learn

PROBLEM Randy and his sister built this sand castle at the beach. What solid figures make up the sand castle?

Example

Look at each part of the sand castle separately.

So, the sand castle is made up of 2 cones, 2 cylinders, and a rectangular prism.

More Examples

A 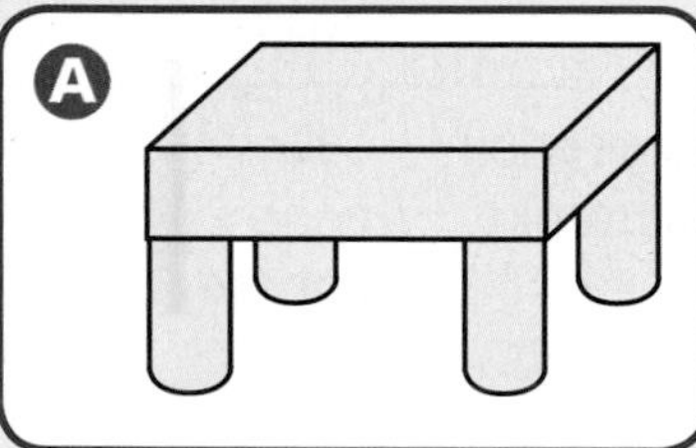

B 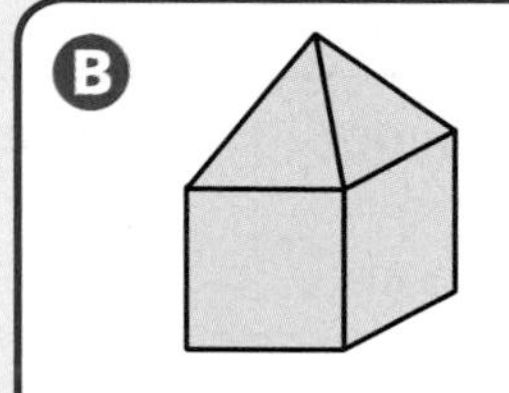

C 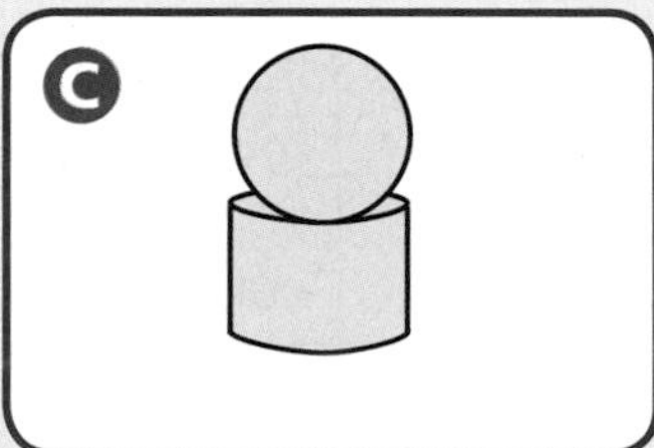

- What solid figures were used to make Object A? Object B? Object C?

Guided Practice

1. How many solid figures were used to make this object?

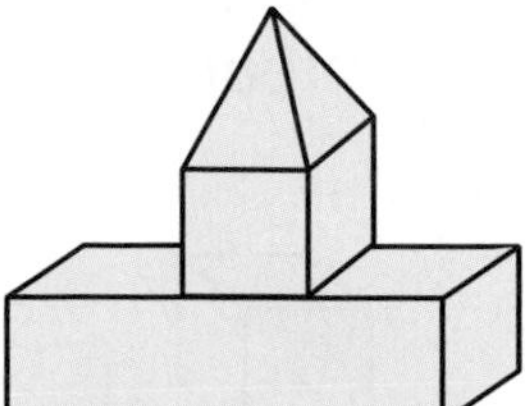

Name the solid figures used to make each object.

2. 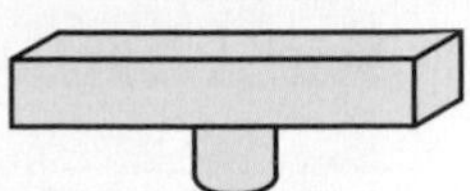

3. 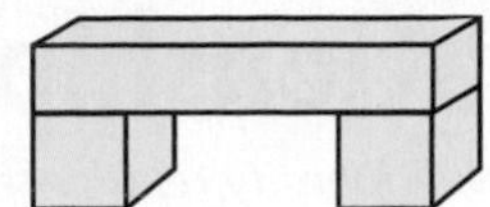

4. 

5. TALK Math **Explain** how to make Object B in More Examples look like this object.

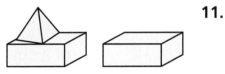

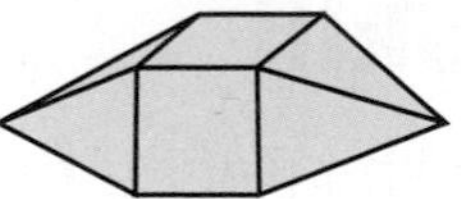

Independent Practice and Problem Solving

Name the solid figures used to make each object.

6. 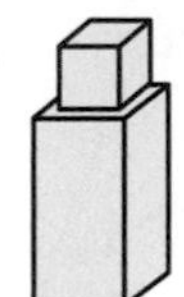

7. 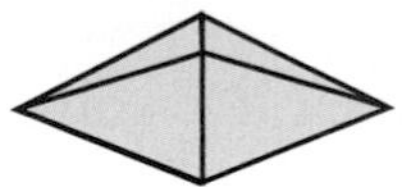

8. 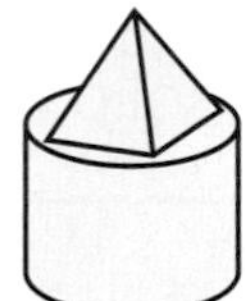

Each pair of objects should be the same.
Name the solid figure that is missing.

9. 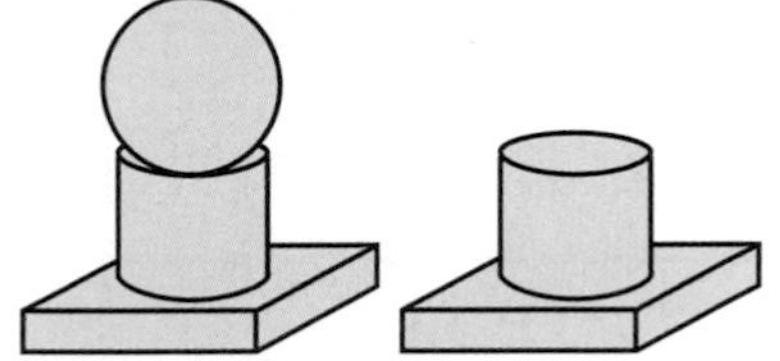

10. 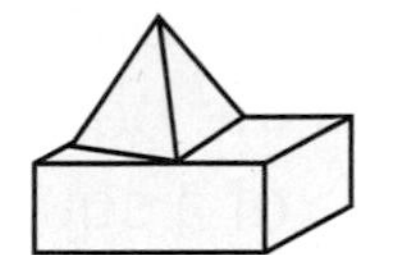

11. 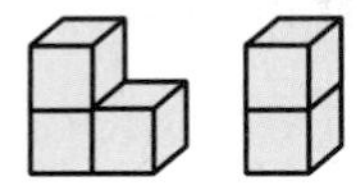

12. **Reasoning** What solid figures would you get if you cut a cube in half like this?

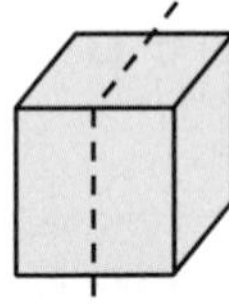

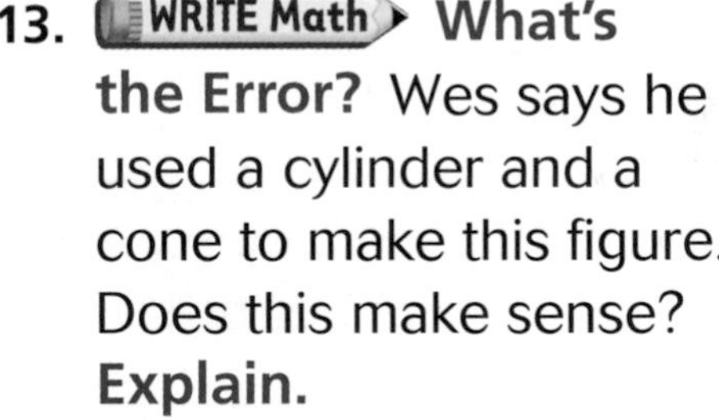

13. WRITE Math **What's the Error?** Wes says he used a cylinder and a cone to make this figure. Does this make sense? **Explain.**

Mixed Review and Test Prep

14. What solid figure can be made from this net? (p. 404)

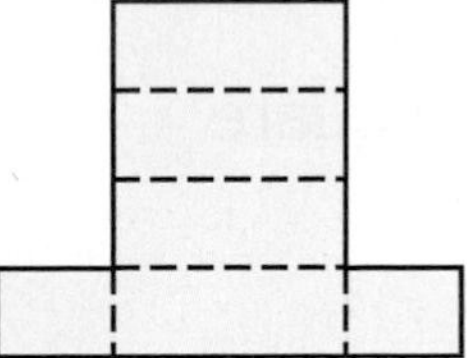

15. Write a rule for the pattern. Then write the next two numbers in the pattern. 3, 7, 11, 15, __, __. (p. 256)

16. **Test Prep** Which object is made by combining a cube and a cylinder?

A 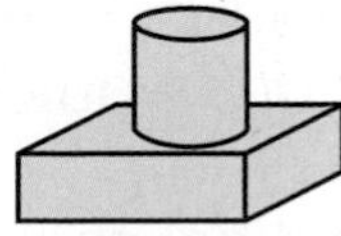

C 

B 

D 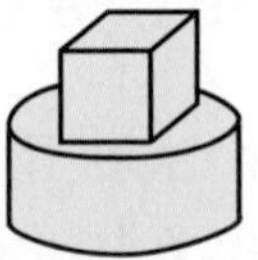

Extra Practice on page 414, Set C

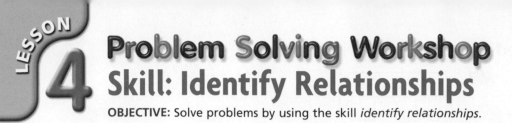

Problem Solving Workshop
Skill: Identify Relationships

OBJECTIVE: Solve problems by using the skill *identify relationships.*

Read to Understand
Plan
Solve
Check

Use the Skill

PROBLEM Trisha traced the face of a solid figure to make this plane figure. Which solid figure did she use?

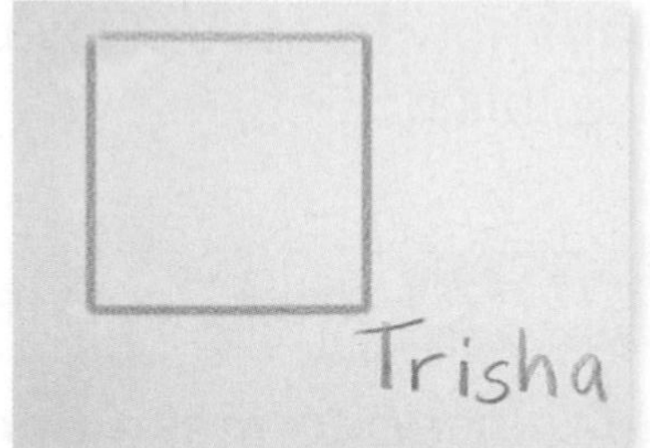

You can identify solid figures by looking at the different views.

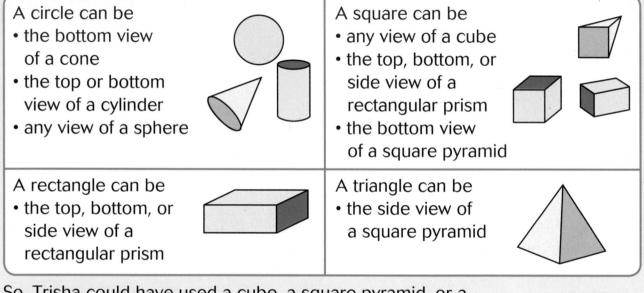

A circle can be • the bottom view of a cone • the top or bottom view of a cylinder • any view of a sphere 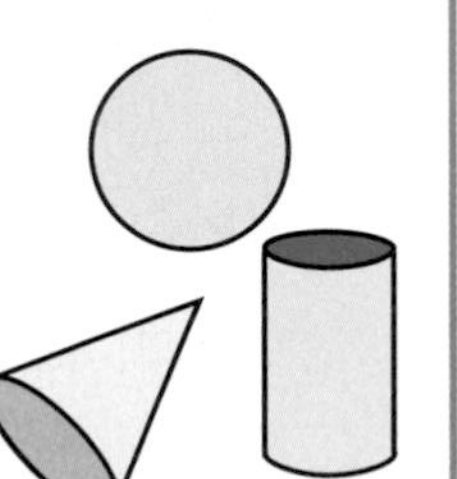	A square can be • any view of a cube • the top, bottom, or side view of a rectangular prism • the bottom view of a square pyramid 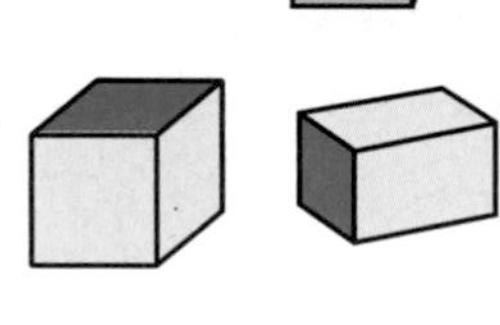
A rectangle can be • the top, bottom, or side view of a rectangular prism 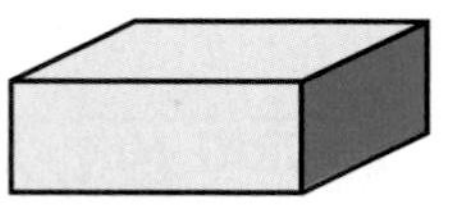	A triangle can be • the side view of a square pyramid 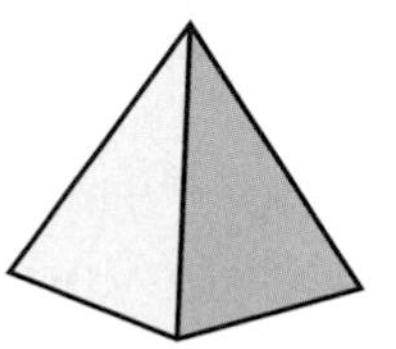

So, Trisha could have used a cube, a square pyramid, or a rectangular prism to make her drawing.

Think and Discuss

Use plane and solid figures to solve.

a. Natalie has a wooden block shaped like a square pyramid. If you look at the bottom view of her block, what plane figure would you see?

b. Eileen pressed a solid figure into clay. It left the outline of a circle. What solid figure did she use?

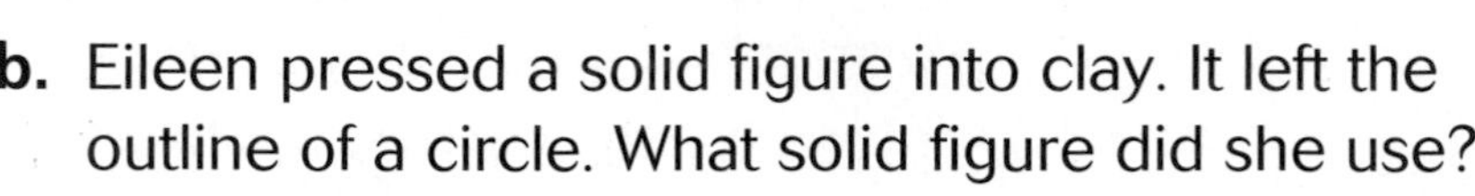

c. Karl made this pattern. Which solid figures could he have traced?

Guided Problem Solving

Solve.

1. Jannelle used a sponge to paint a border of circles around a picture frame. She has three different sponges in the shapes of a cylinder, a cube, and a rectangular prism. Which sponge did she use to make the border?

   Think about the three solid figures from different views.

   Which figure has a circle as the top, bottom, or side view?

   Now solve the problem.

2. **What if** Jannelle made a border of squares? Which sponge could she have used?

3. Casey made a sponge paint border of triangles around a poster. Was his sponge in the shape of a cylinder, a sphere, or a square pyramid?

Mixed Applications

For 4–7, use the pictures.

4. Matt bought an item at the store. He said that if you look at the item from the side, it looks like a rectangle. Which item could Matt have bought?

5. Martin bought some items. He paid with a $20 bill. He got $3 in change. Which items could Martin have bought?

6. Mrs. Garrett bought 6 cans of peanuts and 2 boxes of crayons. Find the total amount she spent.

7. **Pose a Problem** Look at Problem 6. Write a similar problem by changing the items that Mrs. Garrett bought.

8. On Saturday, 482 people visited the aquarium. On Sunday, 621 people visited the aquarium. How many more people visited the aquarium on Sunday?

9. **WRITE Math** Nick painted a fence for 75 minutes in the morning and 90 minutes in the afternoon. How many minutes in all did Nick spend painting? How many hours and minutes? **Explain.**

LESSON 5 HANDS ON

Draw Figures

OBJECTIVE: Draw plane and solid figures.

Quick Review

Name each figure.

1. 2. 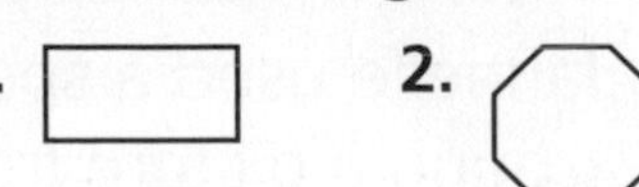

3. 

4. 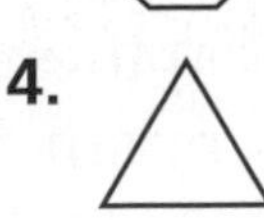

5. 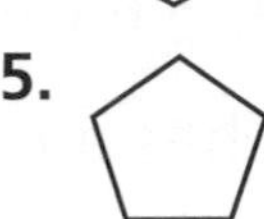

Investigate

Materials ■ dot paper, ruler

You can draw plane figures using line segments.

A Use a ruler. Draw a plane figure on dot paper. Name your figure based on the number of sides.

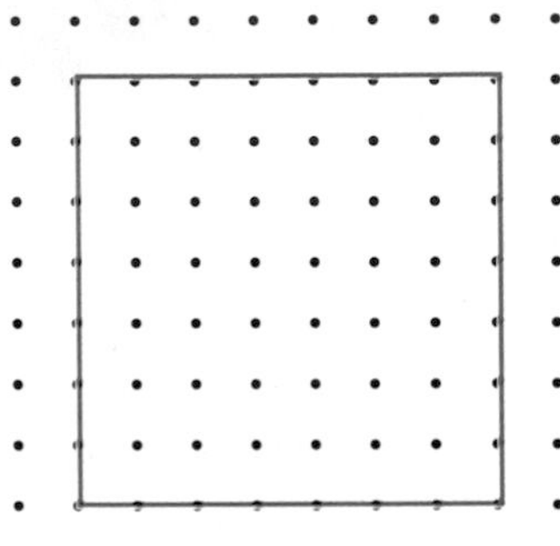

Remember

A closed plane figure with straight sides that are line segments is a polygon.

B Draw different plane figures.

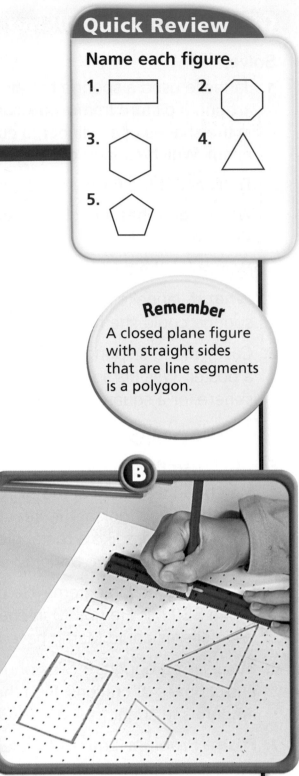

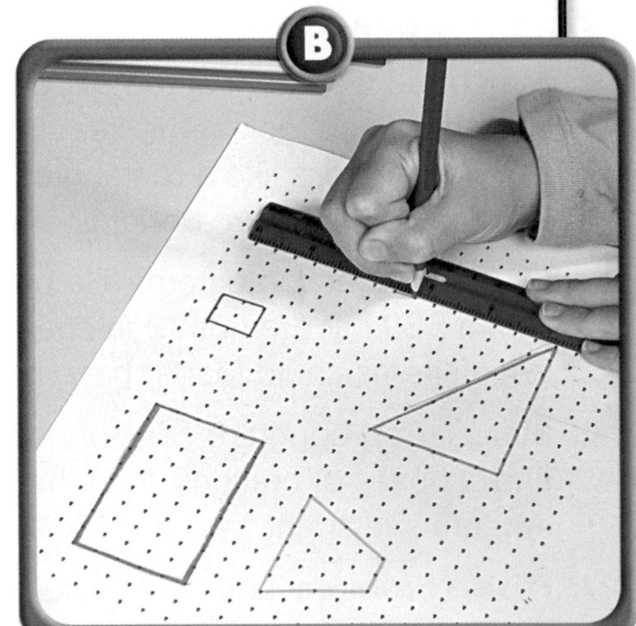

Draw Conclusions

1. How many pairs of parallel sides does each of your plane figures have?
2. Describe the angles in each of your plane figures.
3. **Analysis** Compare your plane figures with those of your classmates. Explain how they are alike and how they are different.

Connect

You can use what you know about faces, edges, and vertices to draw solid figures using line segments.

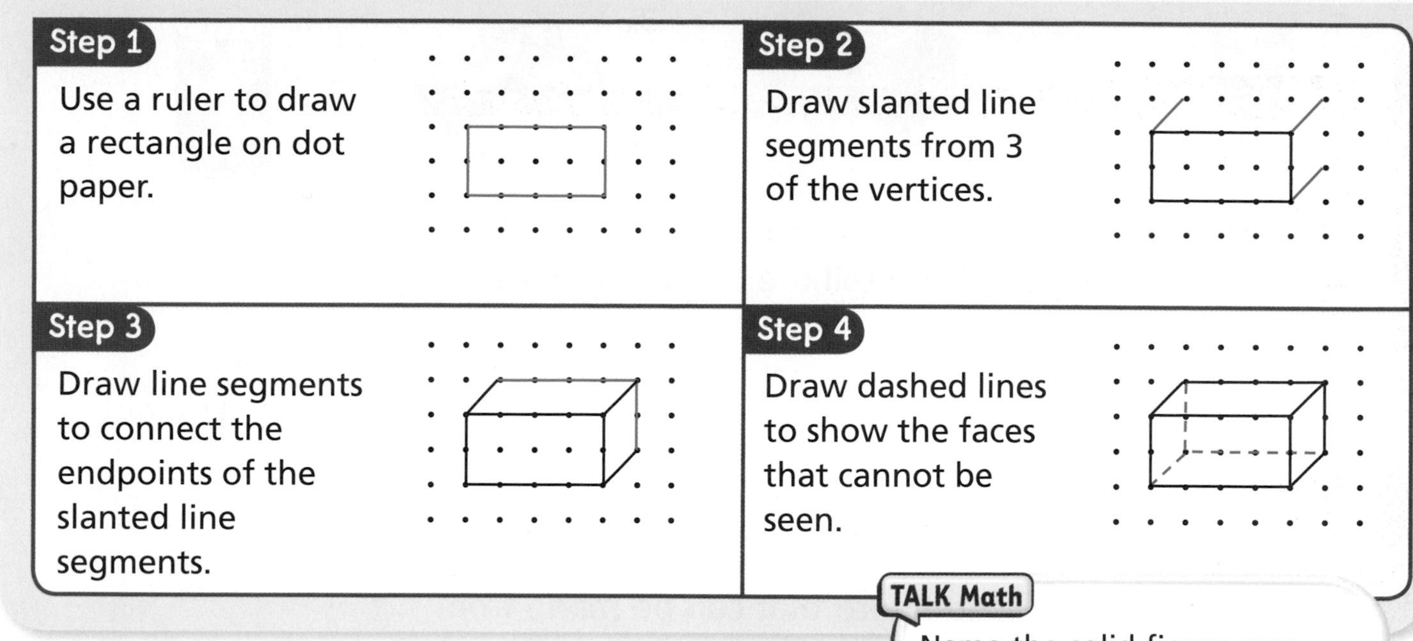

Step 1
Use a ruler to draw a rectangle on dot paper.
Step 2
Draw slanted line segments from 3 of the vertices.
Step 3
Draw line segments to connect the endpoints of the slanted line segments.
Step 4
Draw dashed lines to show the faces that cannot be seen.

TALK Math

Name the solid figure you drew. Then tell how many faces, edges and vertices the figure has.

Practice

For 1–6, copy each figure on dot paper. Then name the figure.

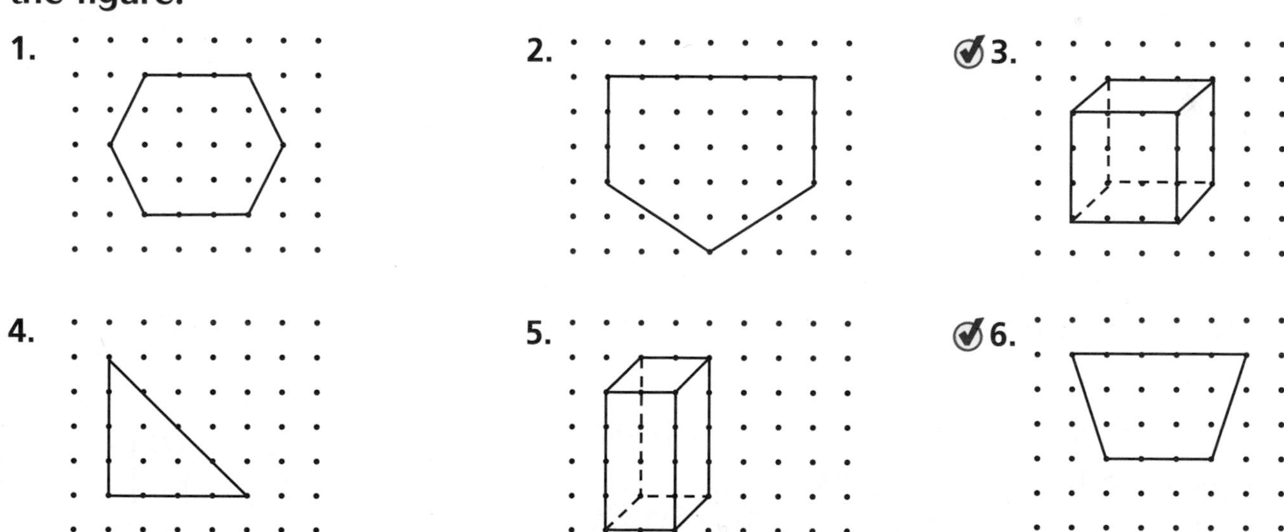

7. **WRITE Math** **Explain** how a square and a cube are alike. Use dot paper to draw each figure.

Extra Practice

Set A Name the solid figure that each object is shaped like. (pp. 400–403)

1. 

2. 

3. 

4. 

Name the solid figure. Then tell the number of faces, edges, and vertices.

5. 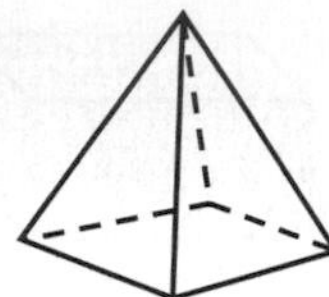

6. 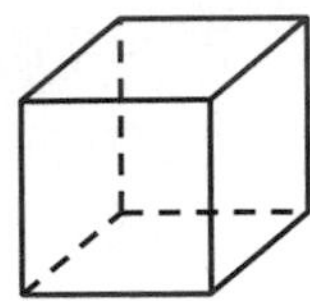

7. 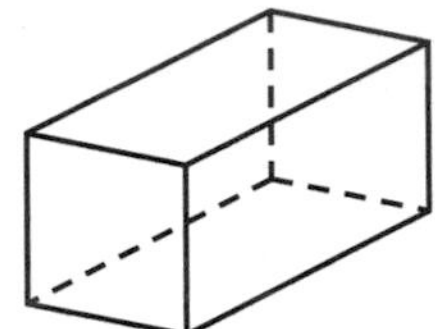

Set B Identify the solid figure that can be made from each net. (pp. 404–407)

1. 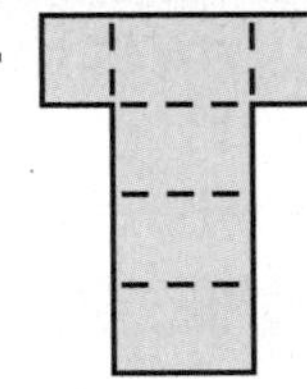

2. 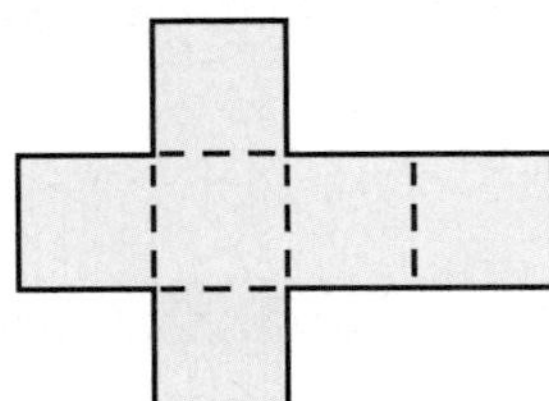

3. 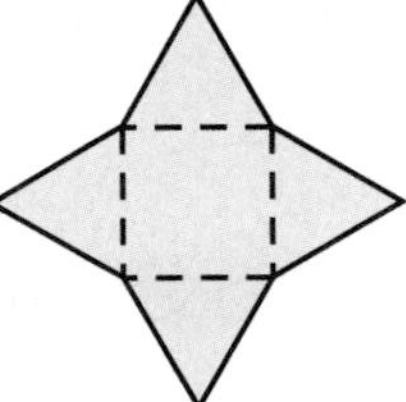

Set C Name the solid figures used to make each object. (pp. 408–409)

1. 

2. 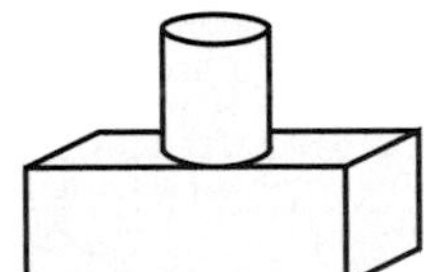

3. 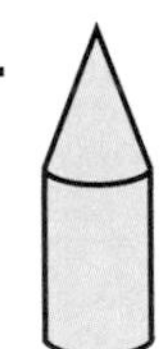

For 4–5, use the wooden shapes.

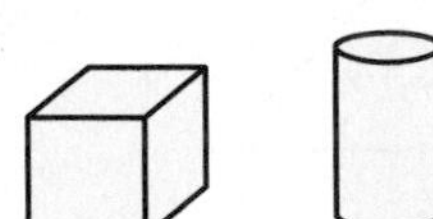

4. Everett made a tower of 2 yellow shapes. What solid figures did he use?

5. Madison used the remaining 3 shapes in her tower. Name the solid figures she used. What shape is probably on the top? Why?

CD ROM **Technology**
Use Harcourt Mega Math, Ice Station Exploration, *Frozen Solids*, Levels A, B, G.

PRACTICE GAME

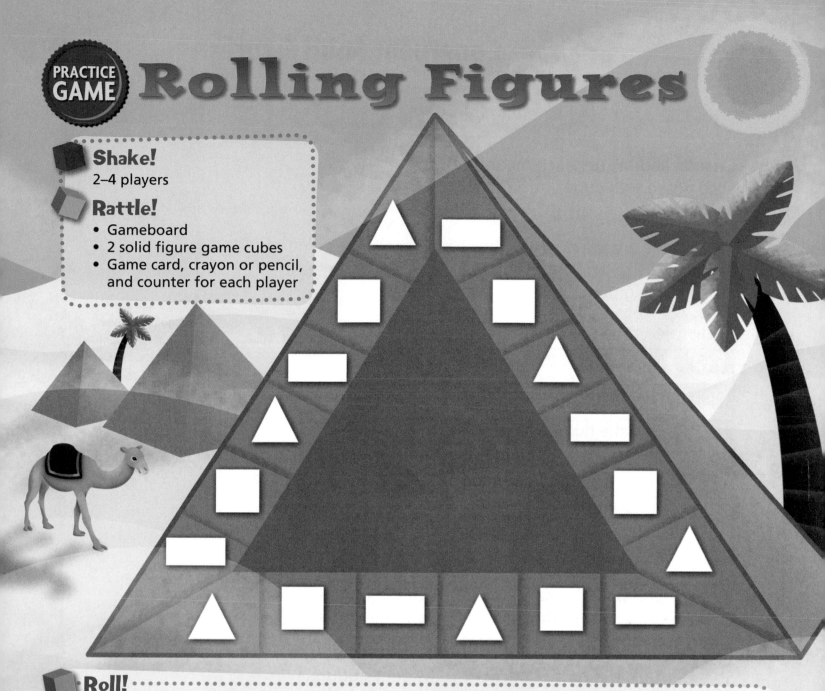

Rolling Figures

Shake!

2–4 players

Rattle!

- Gameboard
- 2 solid figure game cubes
- Game card, crayon or pencil, and counter for each player

Roll!

- Each player places a counter on any space on the gameboard.
- The first player rolls both solid figure cubes and then tells whether the two figures that land face up can be combined.
- If the two figures can be combined, Player 1 shades a face on his or her game card that matches the face on which the counter lies. Player 1 then moves 1 space in any direction.
- Player 2 follows the same steps as Player 1. If the rolled figures cannot be combined, it is the next player's turn.
- The game continues as players roll the cubes, shade faces, and move around the gameboard.
- The first player to shade all the faces of any solid figure on his or her game card wins.

Congruent Solid Figures

Building Blocks

Chantal and Miguel each made a solid figure with cubes. Are the two solid figures congruent?

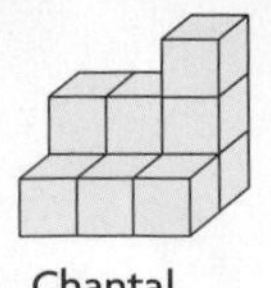
Chantal

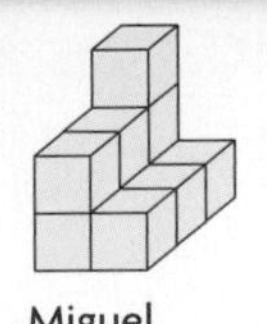
Miguel

▲ The small plastic Lego® bricks were invented in Denmark. There is a LEGOLAND® Park in Carlsbad, California.

Two figures are congruent if they have exactly the same shape and size. Look at each layer of the figures to tell if they are congruent.

Example

Step 1 Make a table to compare the figures.

Step 2 Find the number of cubes in each row.

Step 3 Find the number of cubes in the layer.

	CHANTAL'S FIGURE	NUMBER OF CUBES	MIGUEL'S FIGURE	NUMBER OF CUBES
Layer 1	2 rows of 3 cubes	6	2 rows of 3 cubes	6
Layer 2	1 row of 3 cubes	3	1 row of 3 cubes	3
Layer 3	1 cube	1	1 cube	1

Step 4 Compare the sizes and shapes of the figures at each layer. If all of the sizes and shapes are the same, then the figures are congruent.

So, Chantal's figure is congruent to Miguel's figure.

Try It

Are the solid figures congruent?

1. 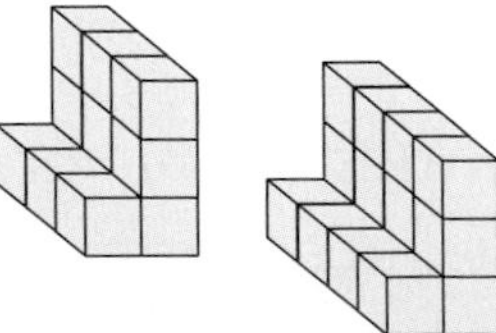

2. 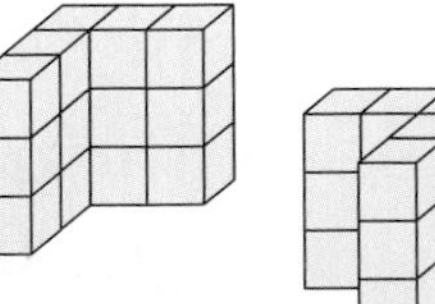

3. 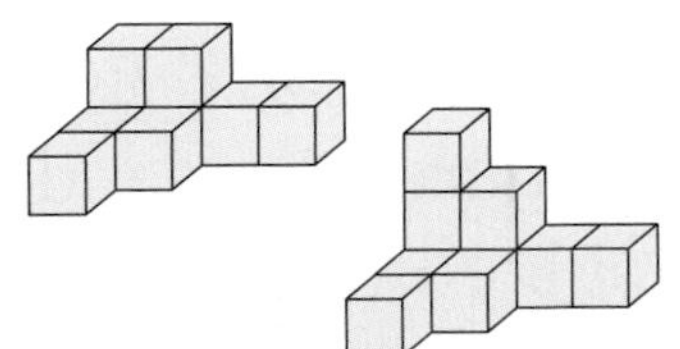

4. WRITE Math ▸ Use cubes to build a figure congruent to the one shown. **Explain** how you know they are congruent.

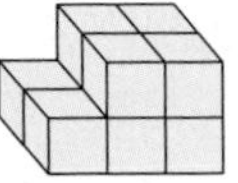

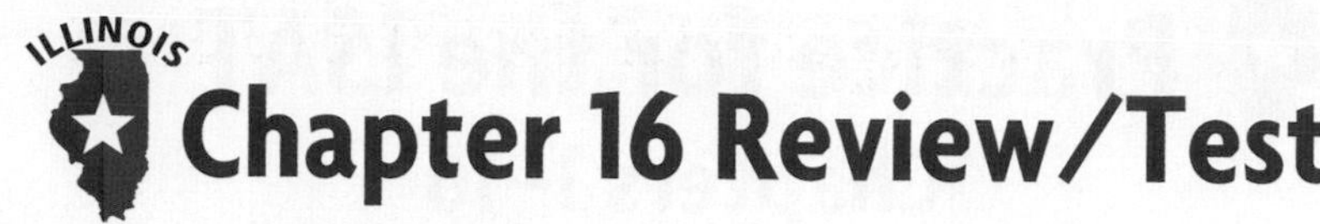

Chapter 16 Review/Test

Check Vocabulary and Concepts

Choose the best term from the box.

VOCABULARY	
edge	face
vertex	net
cube	

1. The line segment formed where two faces meet is an __?__. IL 9.3.02 (p. 400)
2. The flat surface of a solid figure is called a __?__. IL 9.3.02 (p. 400)
3. A __?__ is a two-dimensional pattern used to make a three-dimensional figure. IL 9.3.08 (p. 404)
4. A __?__ is a solid figure with 6 square faces. IL 9.3.08 (p. 400)

Check Skills

Name the solid figure. Then tell the number of faces, edges, and vertices. IL 9.3.02 (pp. 400–403)

5. 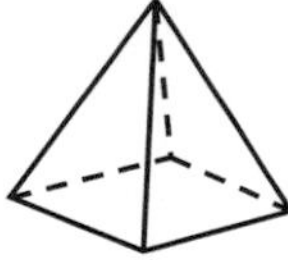

6. 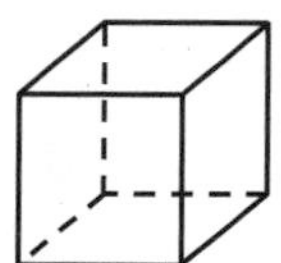

7. 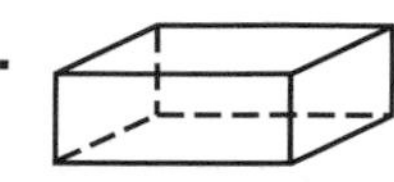

Identify the solid figure that can be made from each net. IL 9.3.08 (pp. 404–407)

8. 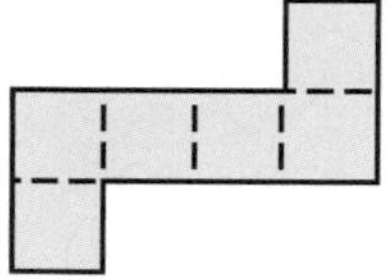

9. 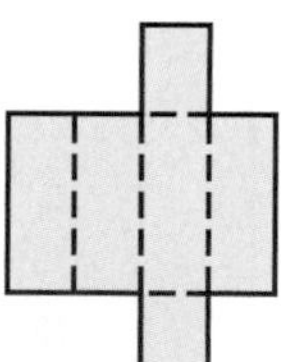

10. 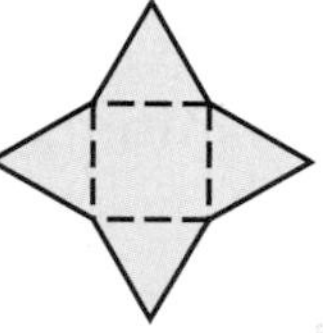

Name the solid figures used to make each object. IL 9.3.09 (pp. 408–409)

11. 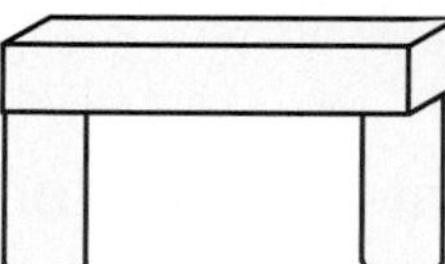

12. 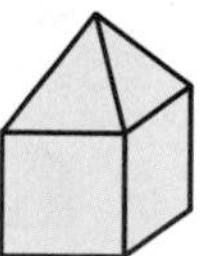

13. 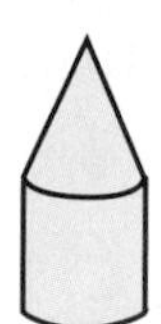

Check Problem Solving

Solve. IL 9.3.07 (pp. 410–411)

14. Paul pressed a solid figure into clay. It left the outline of a square. Name 2 solid figures he could have used.

15. WRITE Math Jenita has 2 cubes, 2 rectangular prisms, and 1 square pyramid. She is painting them all blue. How many faces will she paint in all? **Explain** how you found the answer by writing number sentences.

GO ONLINE **Technology** Use *Online Assessment.*

Practice for the ISAT
Chapters 1–16

Number and Operations

1. At the science center, 299 people visited one exhibit. Another exhibit had 431 visitors. Which is the best estimate of the number of visitors at the exhibits altogether? IL 6.3.14 (p. 52)

A 100

B 600

C 700

D 800

Get the information you need.

See item 2. First, find the information given in the problem. Next, read the question again. Then, decide if there is information that is not needed. Finally, use the needed information to solve the problem.

2. Linda bought 7 packages of hotdog rolls. Each package had 8 hotdog rolls. How many hotdog rolls did Linda buy in all? IL 6.3.11 (p. 218)

A 7   **C** 15

B 8   **D** 56

3. **WRITE Math** What is 5×4? **Explain** two ways to find the product.
IL 6.3.11 (p. 212)

Algebra

4. The students in Charlie's class put tennis balls on the legs of their chairs. How many tennis balls were used for 9 chairs? IL 8.3.01 (p. 256)

Chairs	Tennis Balls
1	4
2	8
3	12
4	16

A 4   **C** 20

B 13   **D** 36

5. Which number sentence belongs to the same fact family as $25 \div 5 = 5$?
IL 8.3.03 (p. 286)

A $5 + 5 = 10$

B $5 \times 5 = 25$

C $5 \div 5 = 1$

D $25 \div 1 = 25$

6. **WRITE Math** What is a rule for this pattern? What is the next number? **Explain** how you got your answer.
IL 8.3.01 (p. 256)

193, 183, 173, 163, ■

Geometry

7. How many edges does the figure have? IL 9.3.02 (p. 400)

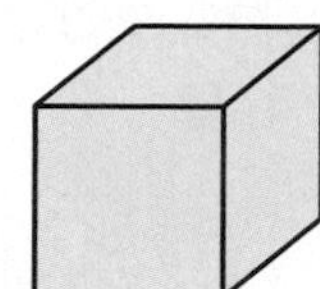

A 4

B 6

C 8

D 12

8. How many faces does this figure have? IL 9.3.07 (p. 402)

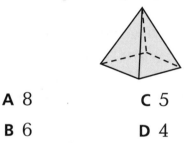

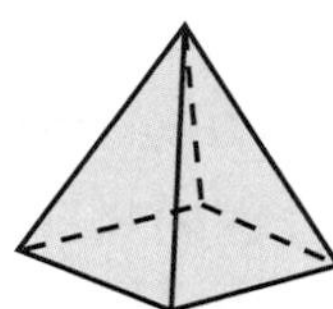

A 8

B 6

C 5

D 4

9. WRITE Math Are these figures similar? **Explain** your answer. IL 9.3.10 (p. 388)

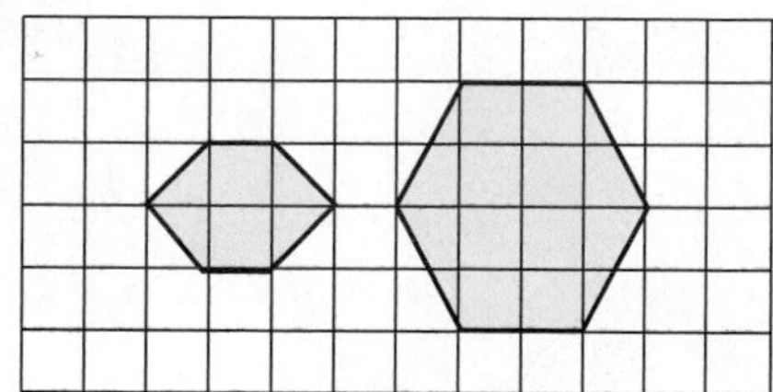

Data Analysis and Probability

10. What is the mode of the following data? IL 10.3.03 (p. 162)

35, 32, 36, 35, 47, 43, 45, 35, 32

A 32

B 35

C 45

D 47

11. Jane made a bar graph of the heights of the students in her class. How many students are 53 inches tall? IL 10.3.01 (p. 154)

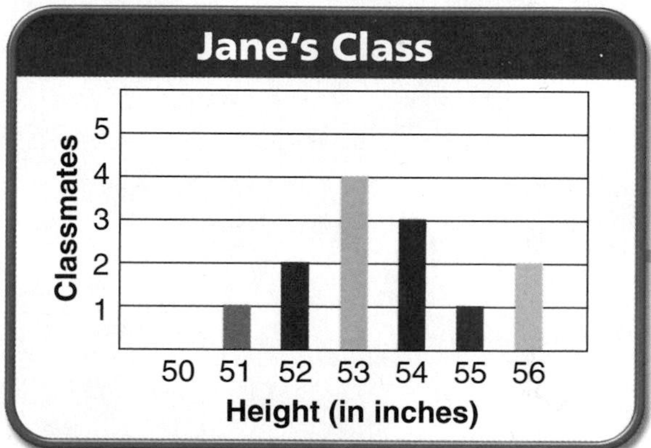

A 15

B 9

C 4

D 2

12. WRITE Math **Explain** how to find the mode of data. IL 10.3.03 (p. 162)

CHAPTER 17

Algebra: Patterns

FAST FACT

Socks were one of the first items that were hand-knitted. In 1589, William Lee invented the first knitting machine in England.

Investigate

Socks can be one color or many colors. Design your own socks. Create a color pattern using two or more colors of yarn. Draw what your socks might look like.

GO ONLINE **Technology**
Student pages are available in the Student eBook.

Show What You Know

Check your understanding of important skills needed for success in Chapter 17.

▶ Find a Number Pattern

Write a rule. Then copy and complete the table.

1.

Boxes	1	2	3	4	5
Pencils	4	8	12	16	■

2.

Bicycles	1	2	3	4	5
Wheels	2	4	6	■	■

3.

T-shirt	1	2	3	4	5
Cost	$5	$10	■	$20	■

4.

Shelf	1	2	3	4	5
Books	10	■	30	40	■

▶ Plane Shape Patterns

Describe the pattern. Then draw the next two shapes.

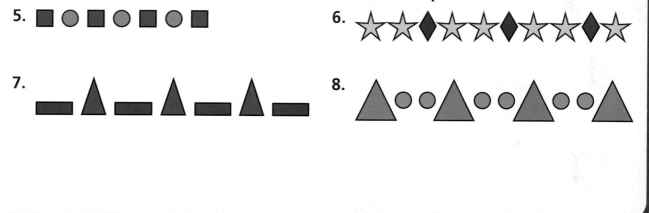

5. ■ ● ■ ● ■ ● ■

6. 

7. ▬ ▲ ▬ ▲ ▬ ▲ ▬

8. 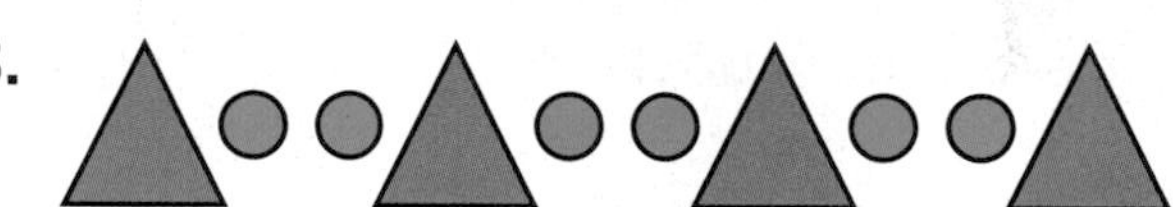

VOCABULARY POWER

CHAPTER VOCABULARY

growing pattern
pattern unit
repeating pattern

WARM-UP WORDS

growing pattern A pattern that increases by the same amount from one figure to the next

pattern unit The part of a pattern that repeats

repeating pattern A pattern that uses the same pattern unit over and over again

Patterns

OBJECTIVE: Identify and extend number and geometric patterns to solve problems.

Quick Review

Name each shape.

1. △
2. ▭
3. ○
4. □
5. ☆

Vocabulary

pattern unit

Learn

A pattern is an ordered set of numbers or objects. A **pattern unit** is the part of a pattern that repeats.

PROBLEM Karen enjoys sewing and making pillows. The chart shows the number of pillows she made each week. If the pattern continues, how many pillows will she make in Week 10?

Week	one	two	three	four	five	six	seven	eight	nine	ten
Number of pillows	3	2	4	3	2	4	3	2	4	■

Example

Look at the number pattern. Find the pattern unit.

The number pattern is 3, 2, 4, 3, 2, 4, 3, 2, 4.

The pattern unit is *3, 2, 4.*

To continue the pattern, repeat the pattern unit.

3, 2, 4, 3, 2, 4, 3, 2, 4, 3, 2, 4

So, Karen will make 3 pillows in Week 10.

Math Idea
Both numbers and shapes can form patterns.

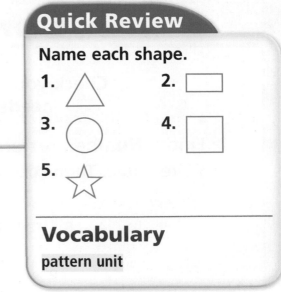

Another Example

Karen sewed shapes across a pillow. Look at the pattern she used. What is the missing shape?

      ?  

The pattern unit is *red circle, blue square.*

So, the missing shape is a red circle.

- Predict what the next two shapes in her pattern will be.
- What if the pattern unit was *red circle, blue square, green circle?* What would the pattern look like?

Guided Practice

1. What are the next two shapes in this pattern? 

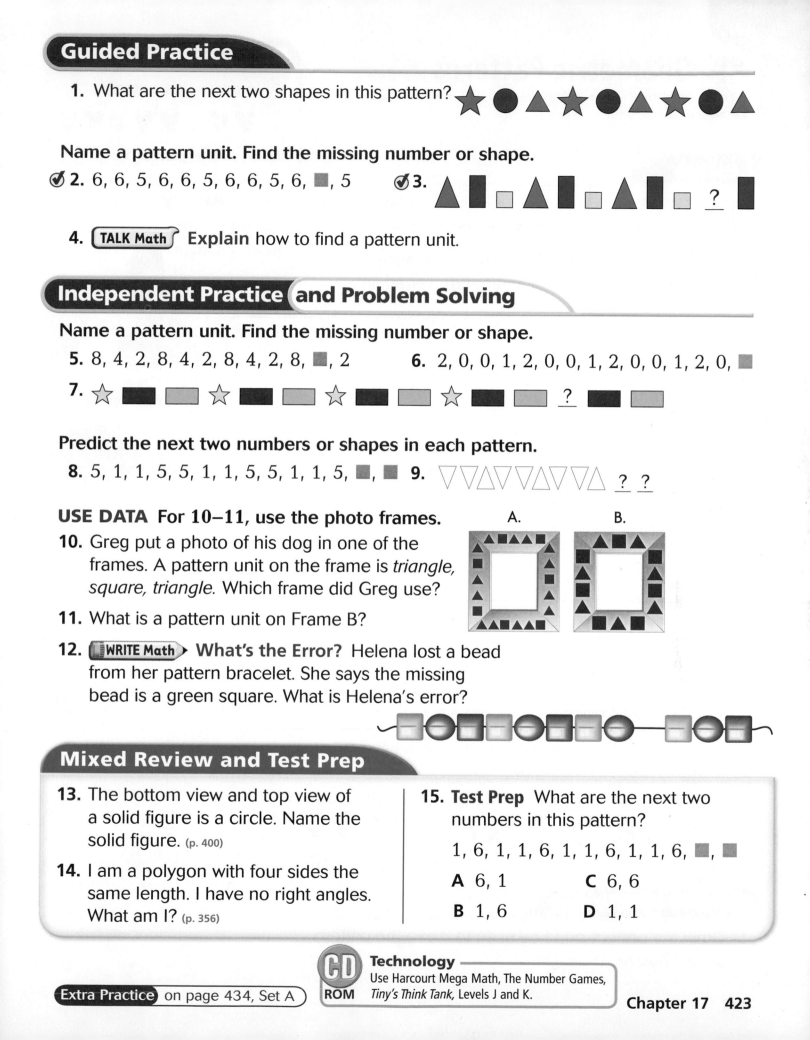

Name a pattern unit. Find the missing number or shape.

✓2. 6, 6, 5, 6, 6, 5, 6, 6, 5, 6, ■, 5

✓3. ?

4. TALK Math **Explain** how to find a pattern unit.

Independent Practice and Problem Solving

Name a pattern unit. Find the missing number or shape.

5. 8, 4, 2, 8, 4, 2, 8, 4, 2, 8, ■, 2

6. 2, 0, 0, 1, 2, 0, 0, 1, 2, 0, 0, 1, 2, 0, ■

7. ?

Predict the next two numbers or shapes in each pattern.

8. 5, 1, 1, 5, 5, 1, 1, 5, 5, 1, 1, 5, ■, ■

9. ? ?

USE DATA For 10–11, use the photo frames.

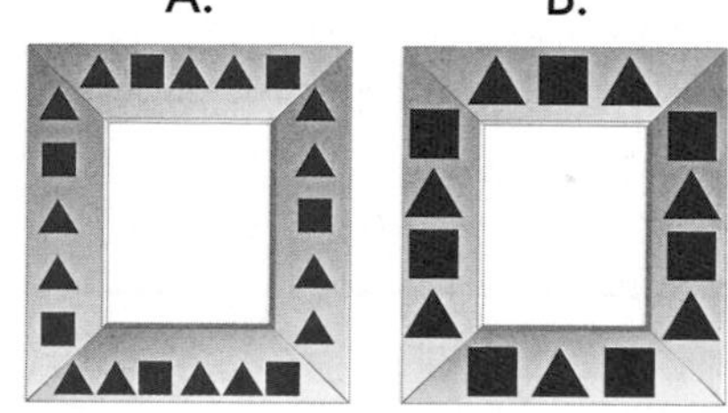

10. Greg put a photo of his dog in one of the frames. A pattern unit on the frame is *triangle, square, triangle*. Which frame did Greg use?

11. What is a pattern unit on Frame B?

12. WRITE Math **What's the Error?** Helena lost a bead from her pattern bracelet. She says the missing bead is a green square. What is Helena's error?

Mixed Review and Test Prep

13. The bottom view and top view of a solid figure is a circle. Name the solid figure. (p. 400)

14. I am a polygon with four sides the same length. I have no right angles. What am I? (p. 356)

15. **Test Prep** What are the next two numbers in this pattern?

1, 6, 1, 1, 6, 1, 1, 6, 1, 1, 6, ■, ■

A 6, 1 **C** 6, 6

B 1, 6 **D** 1, 1

Extra Practice on page 434, Set A

CD ROM **Technology** Use Harcourt Mega Math, The Number Games, *Tiny's Think Tank*, Levels J and K.

LESSON 2

Geometric Patterns

OBJECTIVE: Identify and extend geometric patterns to solve problems.

Quick Review

Kylie drew this pattern.

What is the pattern unit?

Vocabulary

repeating pattern

growing pattern

Learn

PROBLEM Vicky and Will make rubber stamp patterns. What are the next two shapes in each pattern?

Vicky's pattern is a **repeating pattern** because it uses the same pattern unit over and over again.

The pattern unit is *rectangle, triangle, circle, square.*

To continue a repeating pattern, use the pattern unit.

So, the next two shapes in Vicky's pattern are: *rectangle, triangle.*

Will's pattern is called a **growing pattern** because the number of rectangles increases by the same amount from one figure to the next.

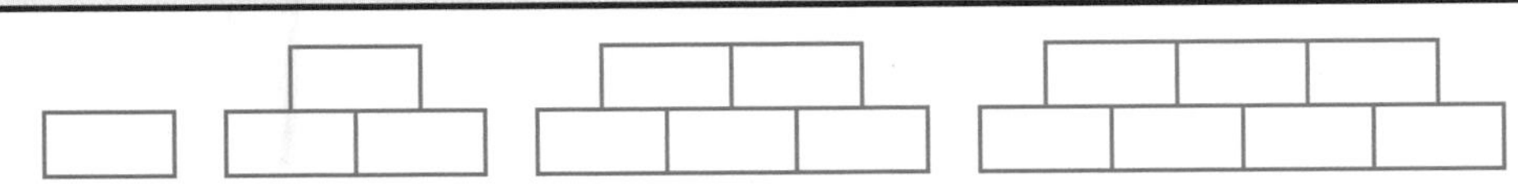

The rule is *add 2 rectangles.*

To continue a growing pattern, use a rule.

So, the next two figures in Will's pattern will have 9 rectangles and 11 rectangles.

- This is Lee's pattern. Is it a repeating or a growing pattern?

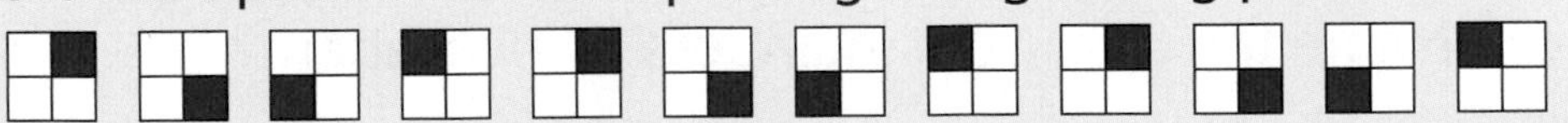

Guided Practice

1. Draw the pattern unit Lee used to make the pattern shown above.

Find the pattern unit or rule. Then name the next figure.

2.

3.

4. TALK Math **Explain** the difference between a repeating pattern and a growing pattern. Draw an example of each.

Independent Practice and Problem Solving

Find the pattern unit or rule. Then name the next figure.

5.

6.

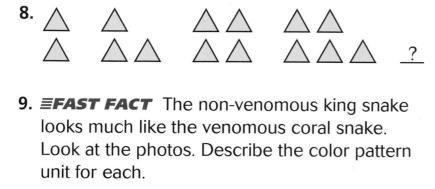

Find the pattern unit or rule. Draw the missing figure.

7. ?

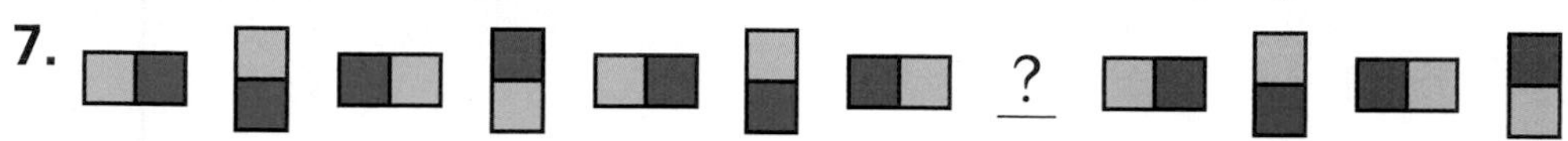

8. ?

9. **FAST FACT** The non-venomous king snake looks much like the venomous coral snake. Look at the photos. Describe the color pattern unit for each.

king snake

coral snake

10. Draw a pattern. Tell whether your pattern is repeating or growing.

11. WRITE Math **What's the Question?** The answer is 9 tiles.

Mixed Review and Test Prep

12. The zoo sold 785 adult tickets and 418 child tickets. To the nearest hundred, how many tickets were sold? (p. 52)

13. What mailbox number is missing? (p. 422)

14. **Test Prep** Which is the missing figure?

?

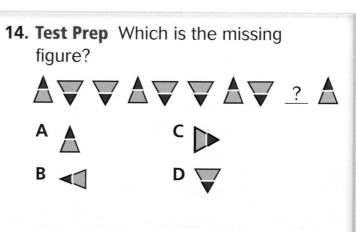

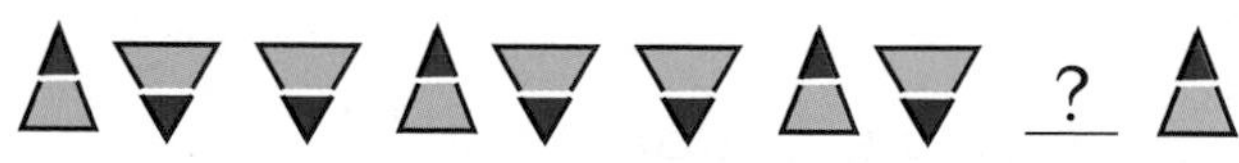

A

B

C

D

Extra Practice on page 434, Set B

LESSON 3

Number Patterns

OBJECTIVE: Identify and extend whole-number patterns to find rules and solve problems.

Quick Review

Skip-count to complete.

1. 3, 6, 9, 12, 15, ■
2. 5, 10, 15, 20, ■
3. 2, 4, 6, 8, 10, ■
4. 10, 20, 30, 40, 50, ■
5. 1, 3, 5, 7, 9, 11, ■

Learn

A rule can be used to describe a pattern.

PROBLEM Mr. Rome wrote a number pattern. What rule describes his pattern? What will the next number be?

Example

Look at the number pattern. Find the rule.

Think: What do I do to 2 to get 5? What do I do to 5 to get 8?

2 →(+3) 5 →(+3) 8 →(+3) 11 →(+3) 14

The numbers increase by 3. So, the rule *add 3* describes the pattern.

Use the rule to extend the pattern.

2 →(+3) 5 →(+3) 8 →(+3) 11 →(+3) 14 →(+3) 17

So, the next number in the pattern is 17.

Math Idea
A rule must be true for all the numbers in the pattern.

More Examples

A

Think: What do I do to 27 to get 23?
What do I do to 23 to get 19?

27 →(−4) 23 →(−4) 19 →(−4) 15 →(−4) ■ →(−4) 7

So, the rule is *subtract 4.*

To find the missing number, subtract 4.

$15 - 4 = 11$

So, the missing number is 11.

B

Think: What do I do to 1 to get 2?
to 2 to get 4? to 4 to get 7?

1 →(+1) 2 →(+2) 4 →(+3) 7 →(+4) 11 →(+5) 16 → ■

So, the rule is *add 1, then add 2, then add 3 and so on.*

To find the next number, add 6.

$16 + 6 = 22$

So, the next number is 22.

Guided Practice

1. What is a rule for this number pattern? 1, 5, 9, 13, 17

Write a rule for each pattern. Then find the next number.

2. 28, 33, 38, 43, 48
3. 52, 45, 38, 31, 24
4. 4, 12, 20, 28, 36
5. TALK Math **Explain** how you can find a rule for a pattern.

Independent Practice and Problem Solving

Write a rule for each pattern. Then find the next number.

6. 7, 16, 25, 34, 43, 52
7. 81, 75, 69, 63, 57, 51
8. 211, 198, 185, 172, 159
9. 3, 5, 8, 10, 13, 15, 18, 20, 23
10. 12, 18, 17, 23, 22, 28, 27, ■

Find the missing numbers.

11. 109, 119, 129, ■, 149, 159, 169
12. 96, 93, 90, 87, ■, ■, 78, 75
13. 5, 15, 13, 23, ■, 31, 29, ■, 37, ■
14. 324, 316, 308, ■, 292, ■, ■, 268, ■

USE DATA For 15–17, use the table.

15. How much money does Erik save each week?
16. How much money is in Erik's account in Week 5?
17. **Reasoning** Erik wants a bike that costs $76. If he continues the savings pattern, will he have enough saved by Week 10? **Explain.**
18. WRITE Math **What's the Error?** Tim wrote this pattern: 5, 12, 15, 22, 25, 32, 35. Louie said the rule is *add* 7. Describe his error. Write a correct rule.

Erik's Savings

Week	Amount
1	$25
2	$31
3	$37
4	$43
5	■
6	$55

Mixed Review and Test Prep

19. Morgan has 2 quarters, 3 dimes, and 6 nickels. How much money does she have in all? (p. 110)
20. Zoey ate breakfast at the time shown on the clock. At what time did she eat? (p. 128)

21. **Test Prep** Valerie wrote the following pattern:

    262, 259, 256, 253, ■, 247, ■

    What numbers are missing?

    A 250, 245 **C** 250, 244
    B 249, 243 **D** 256, 250

Extra Practice on page 434, Set C

Problem Solving Workshop
Strategy: Find a Pattern

OBJECTIVE: Solve problems by using the strategy *find a pattern*.

Learn the Strategy

Finding patterns can help you solve problems. To find a pattern, see whether the numbers in the problem increase or decrease or if the colors or shapes repeat.

Number Patterns

Hannah is saving money to buy a new bike. She saved $3 the first week, $6 the second week, $9 the third week, and $12 the fourth week.

Week	1	2	3	4
Savings	$3	$6	$9	$12

Color Patterns

Josie made this bracelet in art class. She used red and blue beads to make a pattern.

Geometric Patterns

Dan made this pattern with pattern blocks.

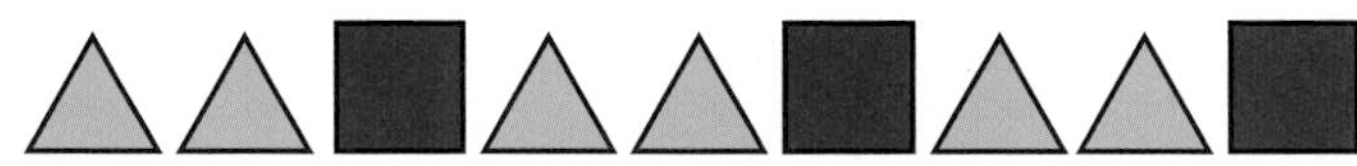

TALK Math

Look at each pattern above. Is the pattern repeating or growing? What number, color, or shape comes next in each pattern?

Use the Strategy

PROBLEM Sean is using square tiles to make patterns. He used 20 tiles to make the 4 rows in the pattern at the right.

How many tiles will he need for the fifth row?

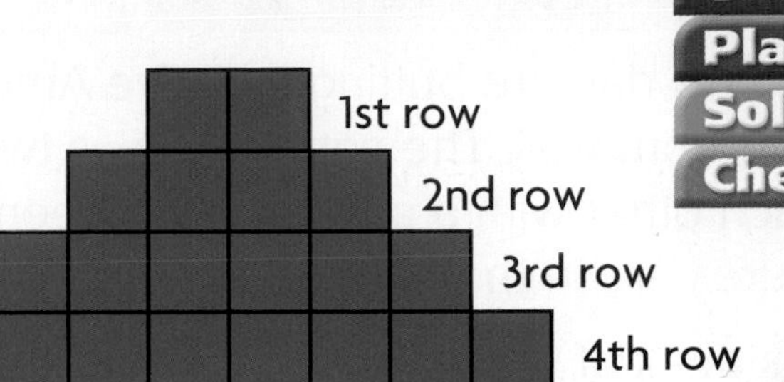

Read to Understand

- **Summarize what you are asked to find.**
- **What information is given?**

Plan

- **What strategy can you use to solve the problem?**
  You can find a pattern.

Solve

- **How can you use the picture of tiles and the strategy to solve the problem?**
  Look at the tile pattern. Is the pattern repeating or growing? How are the rows related?

  The number of tiles increases by 2 from one row to the next. *Add 2 tiles* is a rule that describes the pattern.

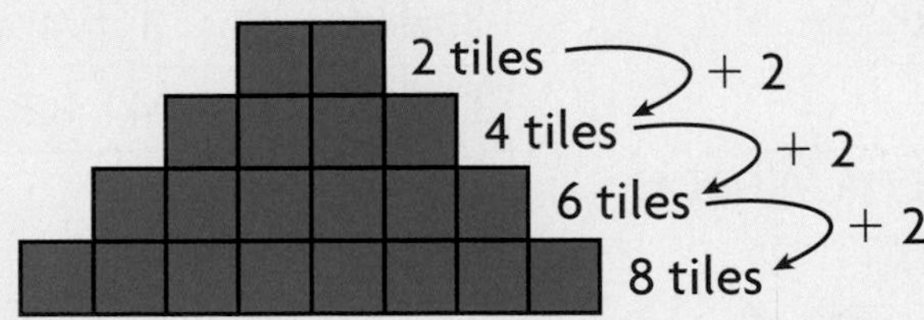

To make the fifth row, add 2 tiles to the number of tiles in the fourth row.

$$8 + 2 = 10$$

So, Sean will need 10 tiles for the fifth row.

Check

- **How can you check your answer?**
- **In what other ways could you solve the problem?**

Guided Problem Solving

Read to Understand
Plan
Solve
Check

1. Dylan and his dad are putting a Native American border on his bedroom wall. The pattern shows two bears facing each other with a paw print between them. How many figures are in the pattern unit?

   First, look at all of the figures in the border.

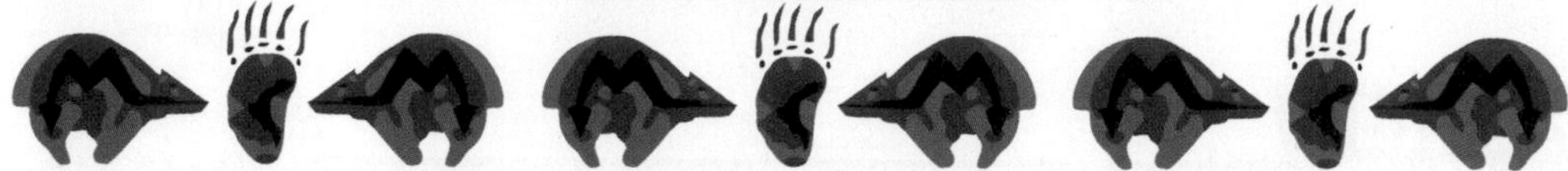

   Next, find the pattern unit where the pattern repeats.

   Then, count the number of figures in the pattern unit.

2. **What if** the border pattern included a right paw print between every other pair of facing bears? How many figures would be in this pattern unit?

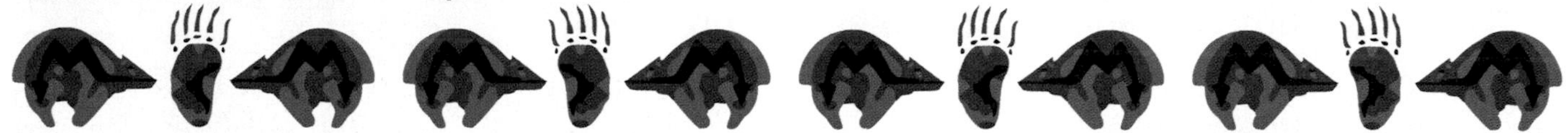

3. Steven painted a border around a picture frame. His pattern unit was *3 circles, 1 triangle.* He painted a total of 24 figures. What shape was the 12th figure?

Problem Solving Strategy Practice

Find a pattern to solve.

4. A spider has 8 legs. How many legs do 7 spiders have?

Spiders	2	3	4	5	6	7
Legs	16	24	32	40	■	■

5. Mr. Tanner wrote this number pattern. What is the rule and the next two numbers?

   385, 381, 377, 373, 369, 365, ■, ■

6. Elise arranged shape cards to make a pattern. Then she turned 2 of the cards face down. What shapes are on those 2 cards?

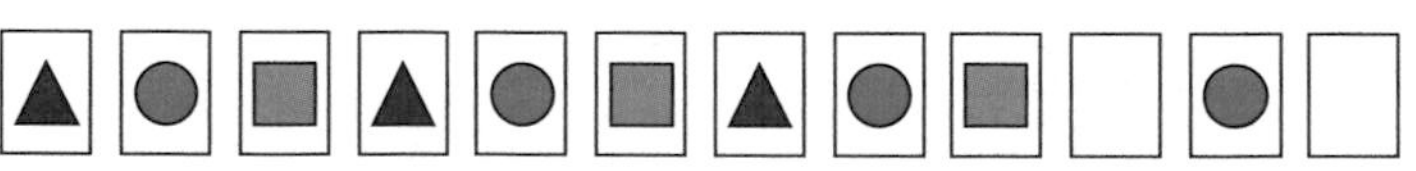

7. WRITE Math Curt is using 35 tiles to make a pattern. The bottom 3 rows are shown at the right. How many rows will Curt make? How many tiles will be in each row? **Explain** how you found the answer.

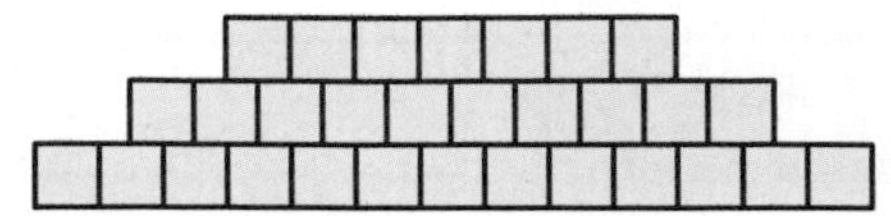

Mixed Strategy Practice

8. Some of the seat numbers in the stadium have worn off. Here is a row of seats. What seat numbers are missing?

9. Abe made a spinner that has 4 colors. The pointer is most likely to land on blue and equally likely to land on red, yellow, and green. What could Abe's spinner look like?

Choose a STRATEGY

- Find a Pattern
- Draw a Diagram or Picture
- Make a Model or Act It Out
- Make an Organized List
- Make a Table or Graph
- Predict and Test
- Work Backward
- Solve a Simpler Problem
- Write an Equation
- Use Logical Reasoning

USE DATA For 10–12, use the jersey information.

10. Some students in Mr. Jenson's class play soccer. They wore their soccer jerseys to school. Write the numbers in order from least to greatest.

11. Lisa's jersey number is a two-digit number. The ones digit is greater than the tens digit. The sum of the digits is less than 6. What is Lisa's jersey number?

12. **Open-Ended** Use all of the numbers on the soccer jerseys to write a pattern. Find a rule for your pattern. Then tell what the next two numbers would be if you continued your pattern.

CHALLENGE YOURSELF

Five teams played in a soccer tournament.
Each team played each other only 1 time.

13. How many games in all were played in the tournament?

14. During the season, Team 1 won 2 fewer games than Team 5. Team 2 won 2 fewer games than Team 1. Team 1 won twice as many games as Team 3. Team 4 won 3 more games than Team 3. Team 5 won 10 games. How many games did Team 4 win?

LESSON 5 HANDS ON

Make a Pattern

OBJECTIVE: Use a rule or a pattern unit to make a pattern.

Quick Review

Identify each rule or pattern unit.

1. 6, 10, 14, 18, 22
2. 97, 91, 85, 79, 73
3. 2, 3, 6, 7, 10, 11, 14
4. ○ ▯ ▯ ○ ▯ ▯ ○ ▯ ▯
5. ★★▲▲★★★★▲▲★★▲▲

Investigate

Materials ■ plane shapes, crayons, paper or index cards

You can make patterns by using a repeating pattern unit.

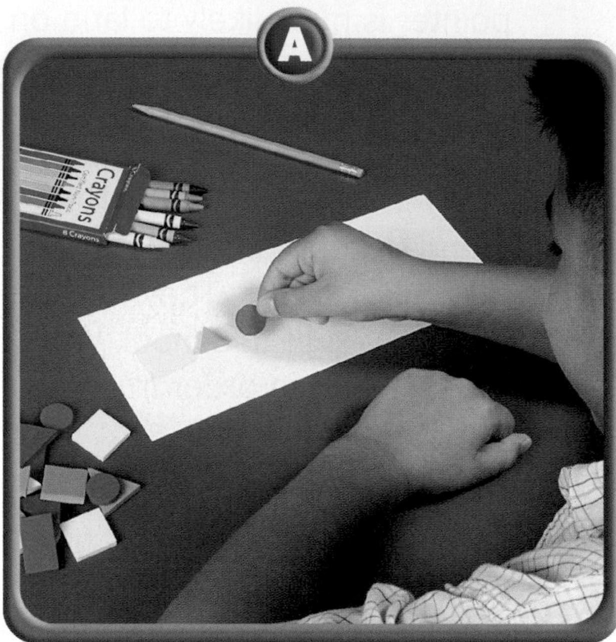

A Choose several shapes from a set of plane shapes. Use the shapes to make a pattern unit.

 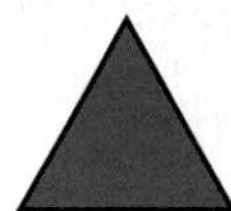 

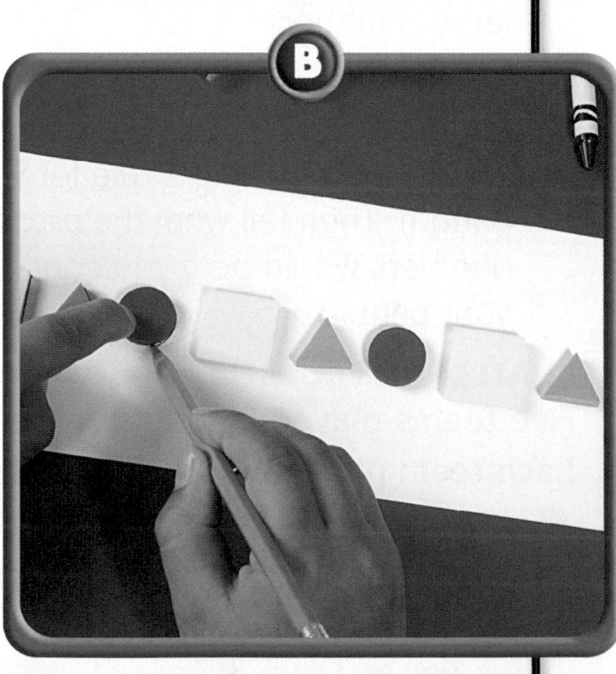

B Repeat your pattern unit at least three times to make a pattern. Trace each shape and color it.

Draw Conclusions

1. Describe your pattern unit.
2. If you continued your pattern, what would be the next two shapes?
3. **Analysis** What will be the 20th figure in your pattern? **Explain** how you know.

Connect

You can use a rule to make a growing number pattern.

A Think of a rule you would like to use for a number pattern.

B Choose a number to begin your pattern.
Write this number on an index card or paper.

C Use your rule to write the next five numbers in your pattern. Make a card for each number.

7	11	15	19	23	27

Describe your number pattern rule. Then write the next three numbers in your pattern.

Practice

Draw each geometric pattern.

1. Use four different shapes to make a pattern unit. Repeat the pattern unit three times. Draw your pattern.

2. Select two different shapes. Trace and color the shapes to make a pattern. Describe your pattern unit.

Make each number pattern.

3. Choose a two-digit number. Write a number pattern that begins with that number and uses addition as the rule.

4. Write the first five numbers of a number pattern. Describe the rule you used.

5. Thomas made a pattern with the pattern unit *red square, blue triangle, red square*. He drew 16 shapes. What figure was the 16th shape?

6. The band director put the band members in rows. The drawing shows the first five rows. Describe the pattern. How many band members will be in the 8th row?

7. **Reasoning** Trish wrote a number pattern. The third number in her pattern is 15. She used the rule *add 2*. What number did Trish choose as the starting number?

8. WRITE Math **Explain** how to find the missing number in this pattern: 12, 17, 22, 27, ■, 37, 42.

Extra Practice

Set A Name a pattern unit. Find the missing number or shape. (pp. 422–423)

1. 7, 6, 3, 7, 6, 3, ■, 6, 3, 7, 6, 3
2. 9, 1, 7, 9, 1, 7, 9, 1, 7, 9, 1, ■
3.   ?

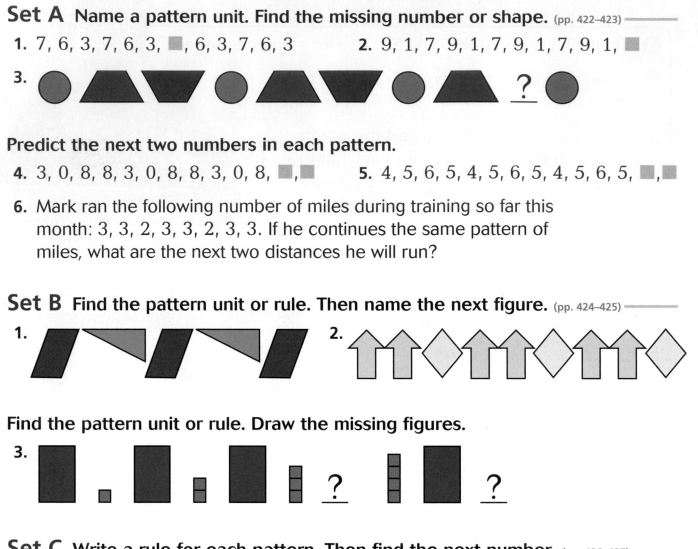

Predict the next two numbers in each pattern.

4. 3, 0, 8, 8, 3, 0, 8, 8, 3, 0, 8, ■, ■
5. 4, 5, 6, 5, 4, 5, 6, 5, 4, 5, 6, 5, ■, ■
6. Mark ran the following number of miles during training so far this month: 3, 3, 2, 3, 3, 2, 3, 3. If he continues the same pattern of miles, what are the next two distances he will run?

Set B Find the pattern unit or rule. Then name the next figure. (pp. 424–425)

1. 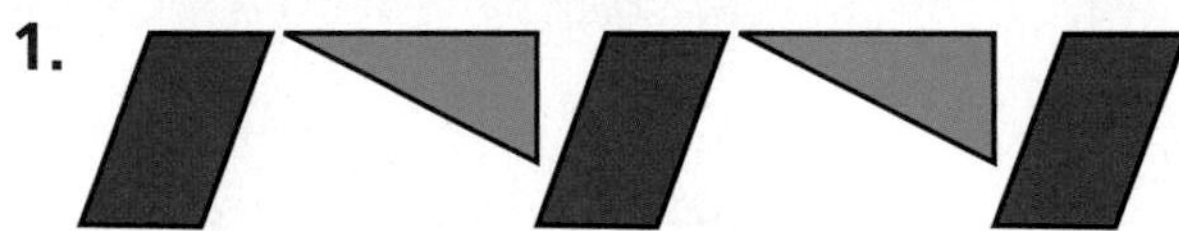
2. 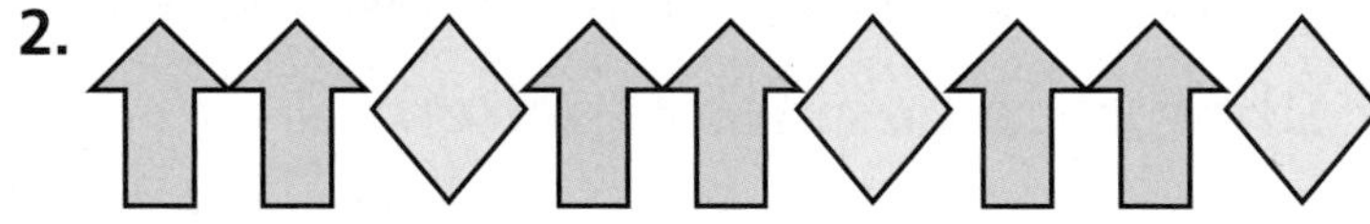

Find the pattern unit or rule. Draw the missing figures.

3.    ?  ?

Set C Write a rule for each pattern. Then find the next number. (pp. 426–427)

1. 25, 37, 49, 61, 73, 85
2. 65, 58, 51, 44, 37, 30
3. 4, 8, 13, 17, 22, 26, 31, 35

Find the missing numbers.

4. 26, 34, 33, 41, 40, 48, 47, ■, 54
5. 5, 10, 8, 13, 11, ■, 14, 19, ■
6. The balances in Vivian's bank account for the last six months were $112, $127, $142, $157, $172, and $187. How much did Vivian save each month?
7. Matt read the first 20 pages of his book on Monday. He reads 3 pages more each day than the day before. How many pages will he read on Friday?

CD ROM Technology
Use Harcourt Mega Math, The Number Games, *Tiny's Think Tank*, Levels J, K.

TECHNOLOGY CONNECTION

Calculator: Number Patterns

Use a calculator to find number patterns.

Elizabeth is taking a bead-making class. In her first lesson, she makes 8 beads. In each of the next lessons, she makes 3 more beads than in the lesson before. How many beads does she make in her fifth lesson?

Identify the first number and a rule for the pattern.

First lesson: 8 beads **Pattern rule:** add 3

Add 3 to find out how many beads Elizabeth made in the second lesson.

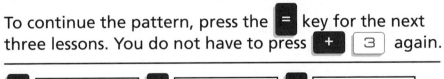

So, Elizabeth made 11 beads in the second lesson.

To continue the pattern, press the = key for the next three lessons. You do not have to press + 3 again.

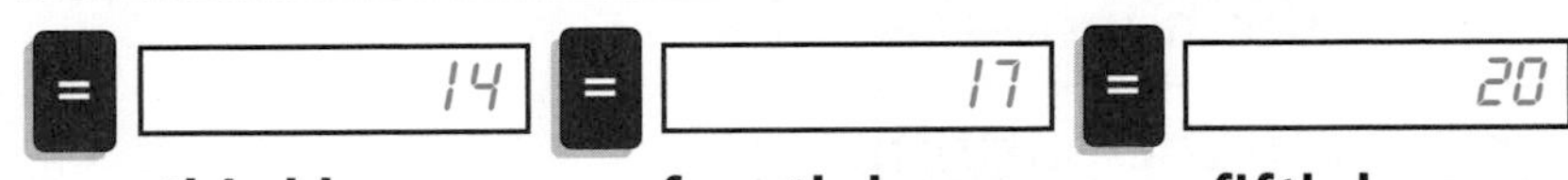

So, Elizabeth made 20 beads in the fifth lesson.

Try It

Use a calculator to find the first five numbers in each number pattern.

1. First number: 5
   Pattern rule: add 9
2. First number: 74
   Pattern rule: subtract 8
3. First number: 15
   Pattern rule: add 12

Use a calculator to find a rule for each pattern. Fill in the missing numbers.

4. 56, 50, ■, 38, 32
5. 26, 39, 52, ■, 78
6. 140, 122, 104, 86, ■
7. **Explore More** Ethan made this table to show how long he read on each day of one week. How many minutes did he read on Friday? **Explain** your answer.

	Monday	Tuesday	Wednesday	Thursday	Friday
minutes	18	31	44	57	■

MATH POWER **Calculator Patterns**

Nifty Numbers

You can use a calculator to find number patterns with large numbers.

Example

Start with 0. Add 99 five times. What patterns do you see?

Step 1 Enter the starting number, 99.

Press the plus key and then the equal key.

Step 2 Record each sum.

99 198 297 396 495 594

Step 3 Look for the patterns.

- What did you notice about the ones digits?
  the tens digits?
  the hundreds digits?

Step 4 Predict the next four numbers in the pattern. Check your predictions on your calculator.

So, you can predict the results of adding 99, using patterns.

Try It

Find a pattern. Write the next 3 numbers in each pattern.

1. Multiply 6×2. Record the product. Press the equal key 10 times. Record the products. What pattern do you notice in the ones digits?

2. Start with 7. Add 6 ten times. What patterns do you notice in the ones digits of the sums?

3. WRITE Math Choose a number from 1 through 9. Then choose a second number from 1 through 9 to add at least 10 times. Record each sum. Describe the patterns you find in the ones digits.

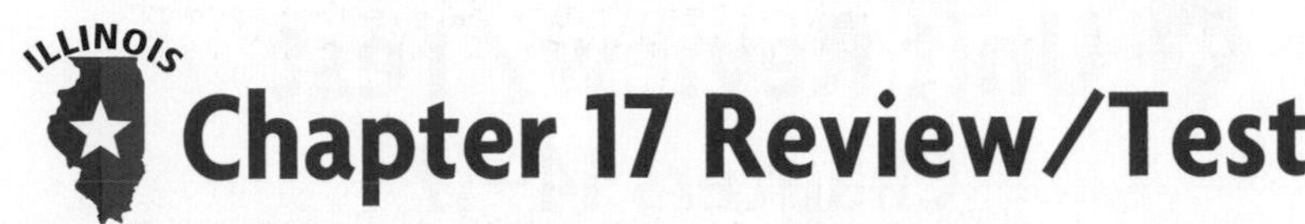

Chapter 17 Review/Test

Check Vocabulary and Concepts

Choose the best term from the box.

VOCABULARY
repeating pattern
pattern unit
growing pattern
geometric pattern

1. A __?__ is a pattern that uses a rule and increases by the same amount from one figure to the next. IL 8.3.01 (p. 426)
2. The part of the pattern that repeats is the __?__. IL 8.3.01 (p. 424)
3. A pattern that uses the same pattern unit over and over is a __?__. IL 8.3.01 (p. 426)

Check Skills

Find the pattern unit or rule. Then draw the missing figure. IL 8.3.01 (pp. 426–427)

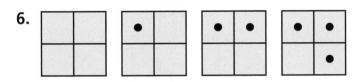

4. △ ▽ △ ▽ △ ▽ △ __?__
5. (2 circles) (4 circles) (6 circles) (8 circles) __?__
6. (squares with 0, 1, 2, 3 dots) __?__ (squares with 5, 6 dots)

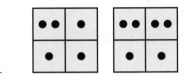

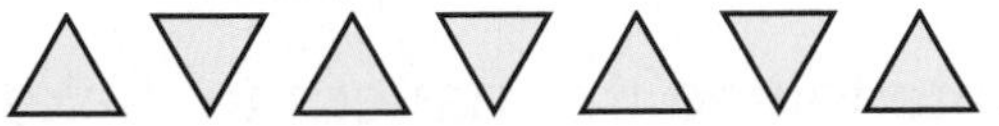

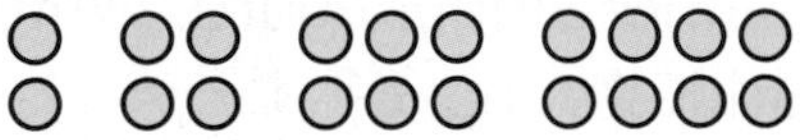

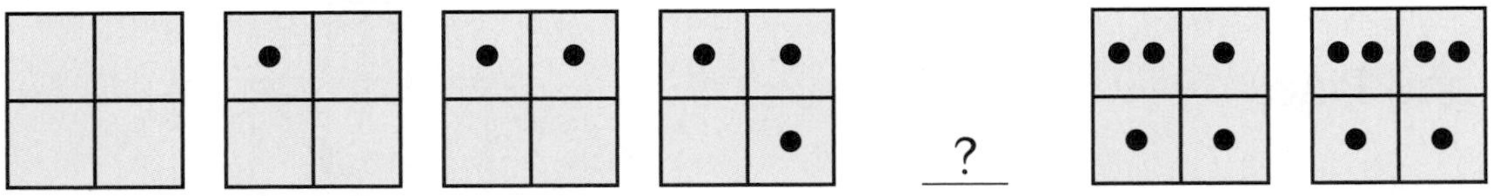

Write a rule for each pattern. Then find the next number. IL 8.3.01 (pp. 428–429)

7. 27, 34, 41, 48, 55, 62, ■
8. 8, 14, 19, 25, 30, 36, ■
9. 7, 9, 13, 19, 27, 37, ■
10. 93, 87, 85, 79, 77, 71, ■
11. 19, 28, 36, 43, 49, 54 ■
12. 1, 2, 4, 7, 11, 16, 22, 29, 37, ■

Check Problem Solving

Solve. IL 8.3.01 (pp. 432–433)

13. Malik has a border on his bedroom wall that follows a pattern unit of two trees, a deer, and a leaf. What is the 14th figure in the pattern?

14. Melissa's rug has this pattern:

What is the pattern unit for the rug? What is the next shape?

15. WRITE Math Keisha is making a necklace with 9 red beads, 6 blue beads, and 3 yellow beads. What pattern can Keisha use so that she includes all the beads in the necklace? **Explain.**

GO ONLINE **Technology** Use *Online Assessment.*

Unit Review/Test
Chapters 14–17

Multiple Choice

1. Xavier used this map to get to his friend's house. Look at the map. Which two streets are parallel? IL 9.3.06 (p. 354)

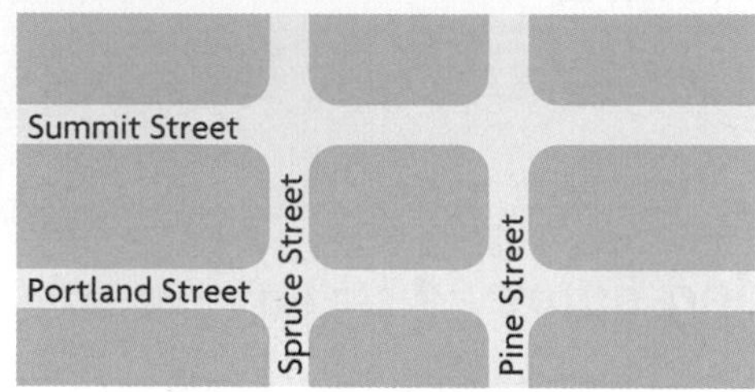

A Spruce and Summit
B Pine and Portland
C Summit and Pine
D Spruce and Pine

2. Which pair of hexagons appear to be congruent? IL 9.3.10 (p. 378)

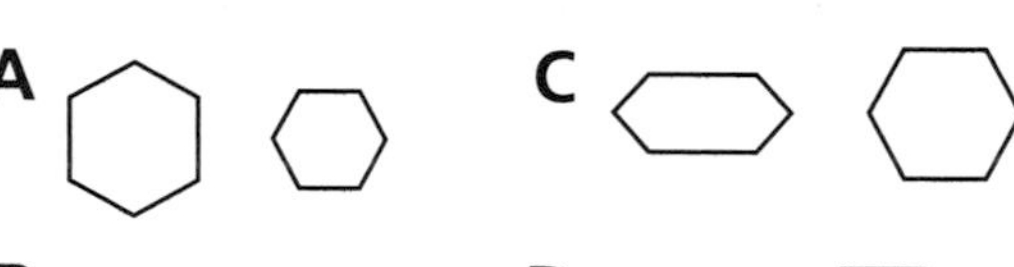
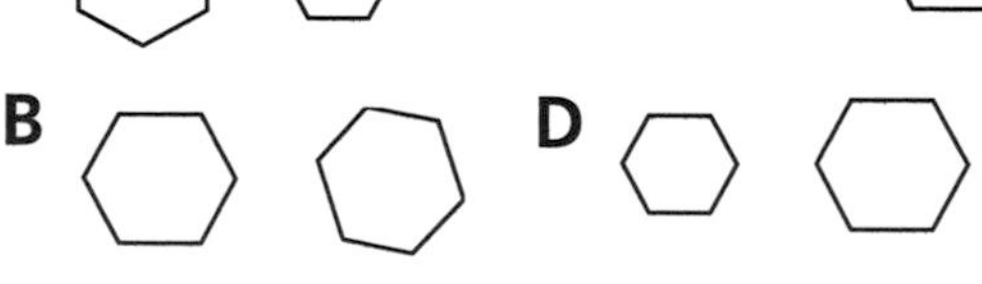

3. Tracy is making a number pattern. Which shows a rule for the pattern? IL 8.3.01 (p. 426)

100, 105, 95, 100, 90, 95, 85, 90

A add 5, subtract 10
B add 5, subtract 5
C add 10, subtract 10
D add 10, subtract 5

4. Chelsea drew a pentagon. Which could be the figure she drew? IL 9.3.01 (p. 356)

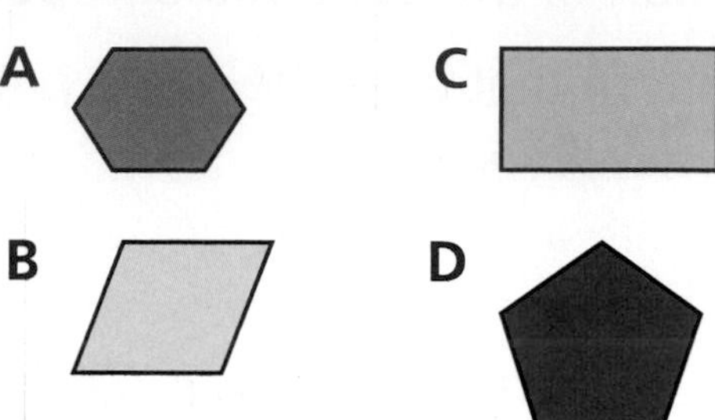

5. Kate folded this pattern to make a three-dimensional figure. Which figure did Kate make? IL 9.3.08 (p. 404)

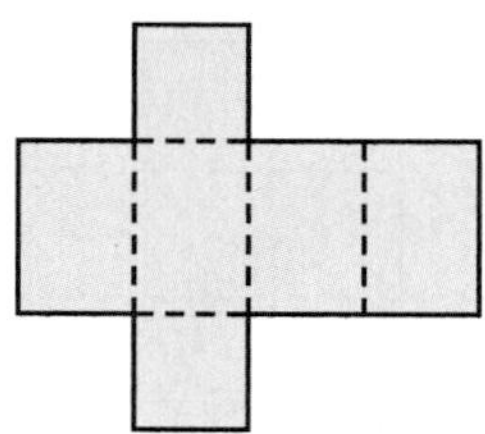

A square pyramid
B cube
C rectangular prism
D cylinder

6. Lucien pulls a box of cereal down from the shelf in his kitchen. What shape will Lucien see when he looks at the box from the side? IL 9.3.07 (p. 410)

A triangle
B trapezoid
C rectangle
D circle

GO ONLINE Technology Use *Online Assessment.*

7. Carly has 39 beads. Her sister has 24 beads. Which expression represents the number of beads that Carly and her sister have together? IL 8.3.02 (p. 336)

A $39 + 24$

B 39×24

C $39 - 24$

D $39 \div 24$

8. Sam has 6 envelopes of stickers. Each envelope has 6 stickers in it. How many stickers does Sam have in all? IL 6.3.11 (p. 234)

A 24 C 32

B 28 D 36

9. Alexandra used 2 figures to make a parallelogram. One of the figures was a triangle. What is the other figure? IL 9.3.09 (p. 368)

A pentagon

B circle

C trapezoid

D hexagon

10. Carter bought a can of tennis balls for \$5.83. He paid with a \$20 bill. Which shows the amount of change Carter received? IL 6.3.10 (p. 120)

A \$6.17

B \$6.27

C \$7.27

D \$14.17

Short Response

11. Johanna is at school each day 8:00 A.M. to 2:30 P.M. How long is Johanna at school each day? IL 7.3.01 (p. 130)

12. Chad made the spinner below and had each of his classmates spin the pointer one time. What is the most likely outcome that the pointer will stop on? IL 10.3.01 (p. 180)

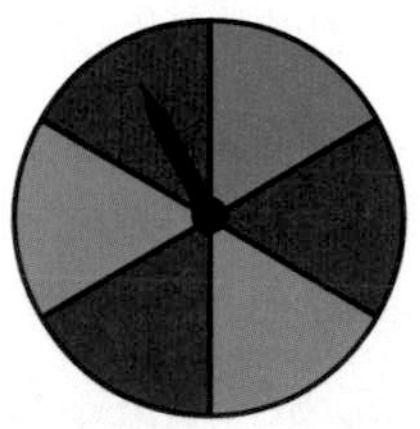

13. Which figure has more sides, a cube or a square pyramid? IL 9.3.01 (p. 400)

Extended Response WRITE Math

14. Draw what the figure will look like after a slide, after a flip, and after a turn. Label your drawings. IL 9.3.05 (p. 390)

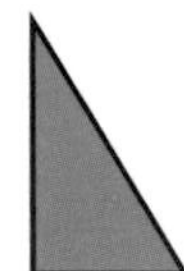

15. Mr. Potter bought 2 bags of 6 pears. Mr. Lakman bought 8 bags of 3 pears. How many pears did Mr. Potter and Mr. Lakman buy together? Show all your work. IL 8.3.03 (p. 290)

THE WORLD ALMANAC FOR KIDS

Native American Culture

Food Symmetry

The Caddo people lived in East Texas. They were farmers, hunters, and builders. They made pottery and carved wood. They grew many types of plants including corn, pumpkins, squash, beans, and sunflowers. Parts of the plants were used for food.

▲ The Caddo people cut pumpkins and squash into long strips and wove the strips together to make a mat. This would make the round vegetables flat and easier to store.

FACT • ACTIVITY

Look at the pictures to answer the questions.

1. Which sunflower pictures appear to have a line of symmetry?

A

B

C

D

2. How can you draw a bean that is congruent to the bean below?

3. How many lines of symmetry does this squash appear to have?

USEFUL CADDO OBJECTS

ALMANAC Fact

Caddo houses were made of grass with domed roofs. Some were large enough to hold 30 people! It only took one day to build a house, because the whole village worked together.

Many objects made by the Caddo people are in museums. Some objects were for everyday use. Others were for decoration or for special occasions. Often these objects tell us a lot about the Caddo people.

FACT • ACTIVITY

Pictures of Caddo objects can be congruent, even if they are moved.

1. Object A shows a turn. Are the objects congruent?
2. Object B shows a flip. Are the objects congruent?
3. Object C shows a slide. Are the objects congruent?
4. Draw 2 congruent objects that are not in the same position.

A

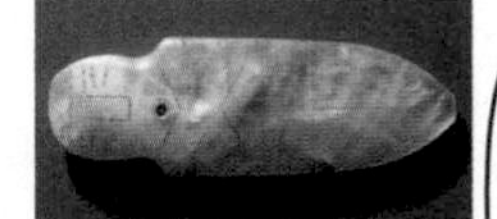

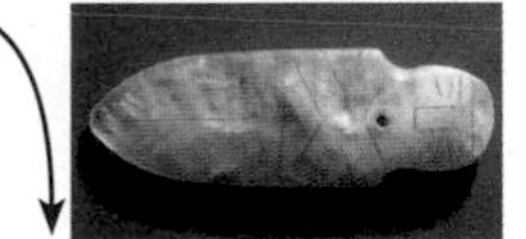

B

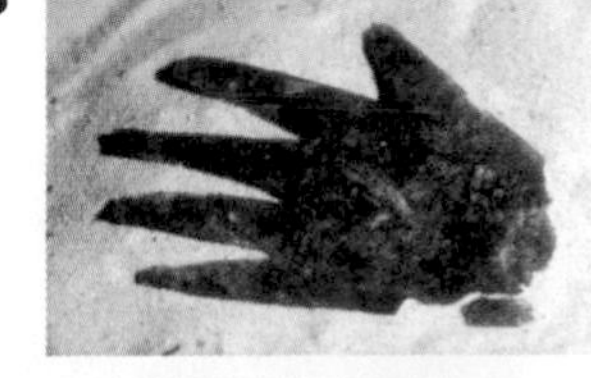

C

UNIT 6

Fractions and Decimals

Math on Location

with
Chapter Projects

1

Some gold coins were cut into 4 or 8 equal pieces to make change in colonial times.

2

Today people buy and sell rare coins, which have values much greater than their face value.

3

If you find an old wheat penny or buffalo nickel, you might be able to sell them for more than 1 cent or 5 cents!

VOCABULARY POWER

TALK Math

What math do you see in the **Math on Location** photographs? If a coin was cut into 4 equal pieces, what fraction of the whole coin would each piece represent?

READ Math

REVIEW VOCABULARY You learned about fractions and money in grade 2. How do these words relate to **Math on Location**?

numerator the part of a fraction above the line, which tells how many parts are being counted

denominator the part of a fraction below the line, which tells how many equal parts there are in the whole or in the group

cent 1 penny; 100 cents equal 1 dollar

WRITE Math

Copy and complete a Word Association Map like the one below. Use **Math on Location** and what you know about fractions to complete the map.

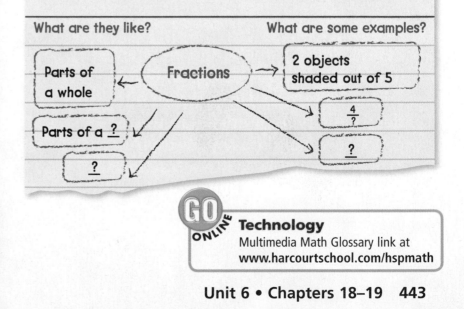

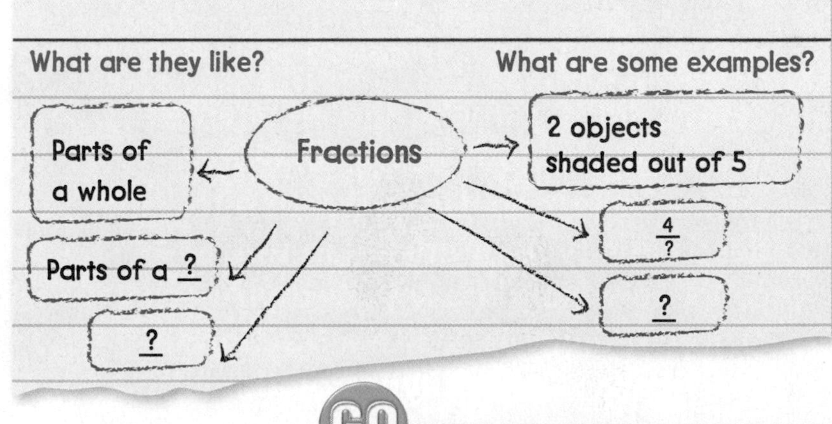

Technology
Multimedia Math Glossary link at
www.harcourtschool.com/hspmath

CHAPTER 18 Understand Fractions

FAST FACT

The stripes on a zebra are like a fingerprint. Zebras can be identified by the color, thickness, and pattern of their stripes.

Investigate

Zebras, lions, camels, and elephants live in Africa. Look at the animal sticker collection. Use a fraction to describe a type of animal in the collection. Now draw your own group of animals. Write a fraction to describe one of the types of animals.

GO ONLINE **Technology** Student pages are available in the Student eBook.

Show What You Know

Check your understanding of important skills needed for success in Chapter 18.

▶ Parts of a Group

Write the number in each set. Then write the number in each set that are striped.

1. 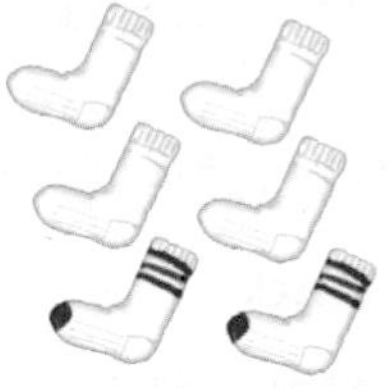
2. 
3. 
4. 
5. 
6. 

▶ Parts of a Whole

Write how many equal parts make up the whole figure. Then write how many parts are shaded.

7. 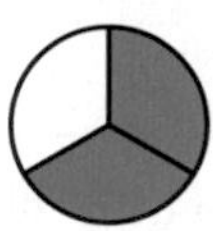
8. 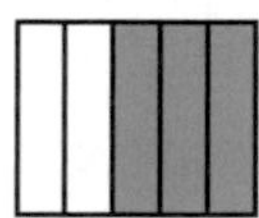
9. 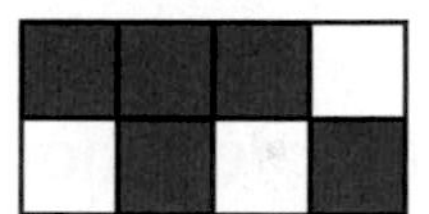
10. 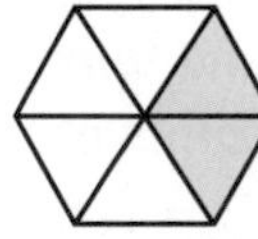
11. 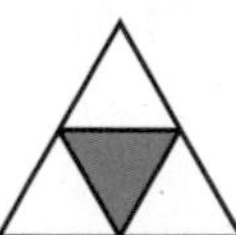
12. 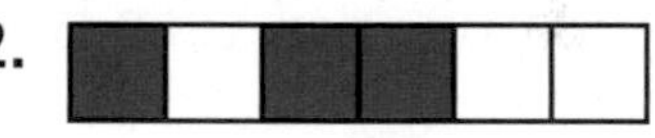

VOCABULARY POWER

CHAPTER VOCABULARY

denominator
equivalent fractions
fraction
like fractions
mixed number
numerator
simplest form

WARM-UP WORDS

fraction A number that names part of a whole or part of a group

numerator The part of a fraction above the line, which tells how many parts are being counted

denominator The part of a fraction below the line, which tells how many equal parts there are in the whole or in the group

LESSON 1 Model Part of a Whole

OBJECTIVE: Read, write, and model fractional parts of a whole.

Quick Review

Tell how many equal parts are in each.

1. 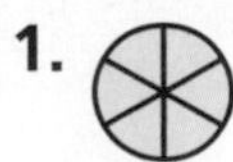
2. 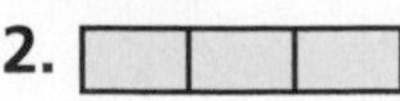
3. 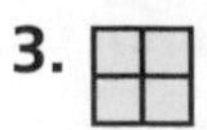
4. 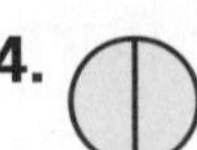
5. 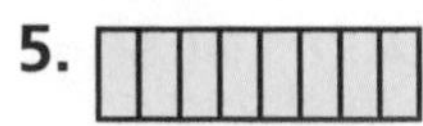

Vocabulary

fraction

numerator

denominator

Learn

PROBLEM The first pizzeria in America opened in New York in 1905. The pizza recipe came from Italy. Look at Italy's flag. What fraction of Italy's flag is red?

A **fraction** is a number that names part of a whole or part of a group.

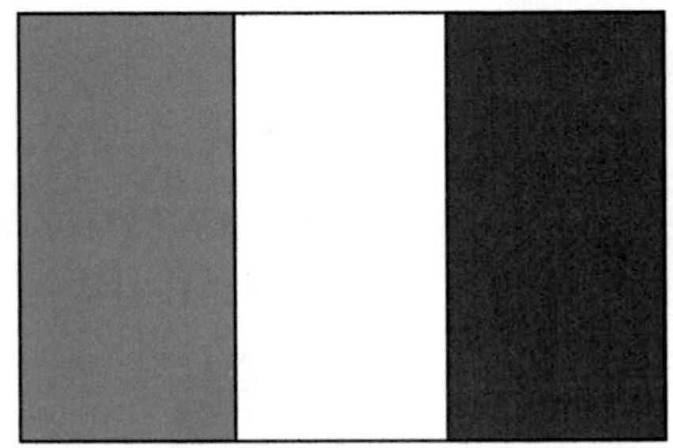

▲ The ingredients of some pizzas—basil, mozzarella, and tomato—show the colors of Italy's flag.

The flag is divided into 3 equal parts, and 1 part is red.

1 red part → $\frac{1}{3}$ ← numerator
3 equal parts in all → ← denominator

Read: one third **Write:** $\frac{1}{3}$

one part out of three equal parts 1 divided by 3

So, $\frac{1}{3}$ of Italy's flag is red.

The **numerator** tells how many parts are being counted.

The **denominator** tells how many equal parts are in the whole or in the group.

HANDS ON Activity Materials ■ fraction circle pieces

Maria ate 2 out of 6 slices of pizza.
Find the fraction of the pizza that is left.

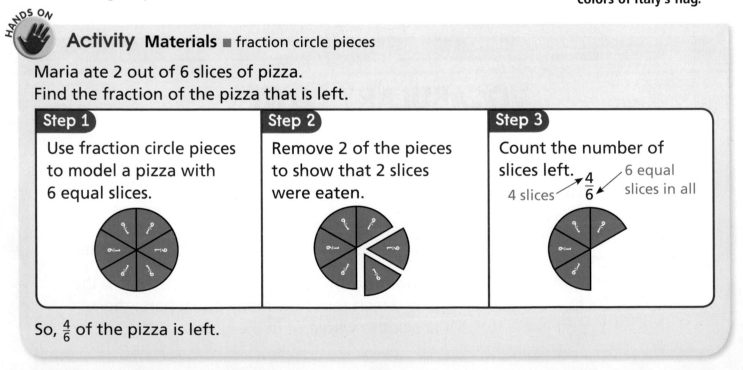

Step 1	Step 2	Step 3
Use fraction circle pieces to model a pizza with 6 equal slices.	Remove 2 of the pieces to show that 2 slices were eaten.	Count the number of slices left. 4 slices → $\frac{4}{6}$ ← 6 equal slices in all
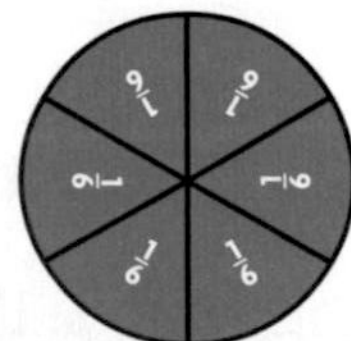	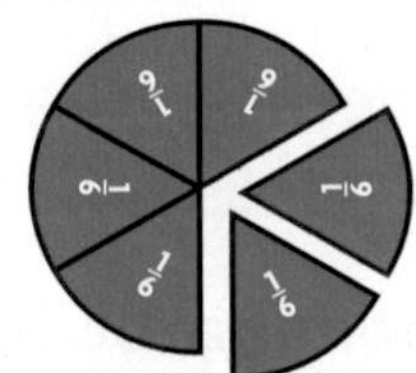	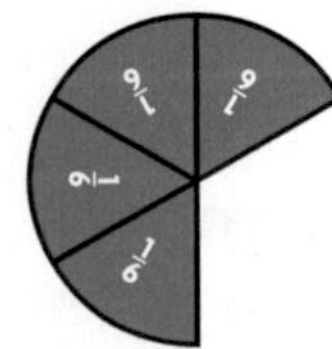

So, $\frac{4}{6}$ of the pizza is left.

A figure or a number line can show parts of a whole.

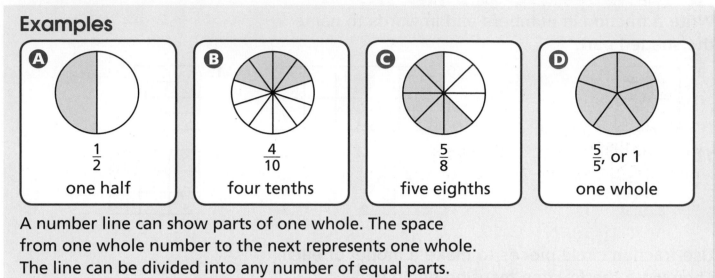

Examples

A

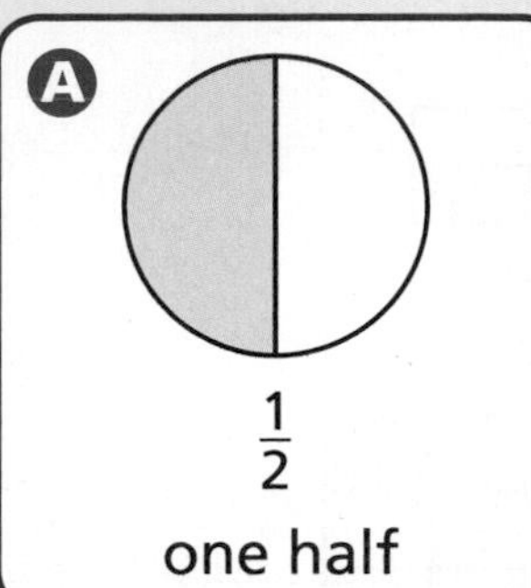

$\frac{1}{2}$

one half

B

$\frac{4}{10}$

four tenths

C

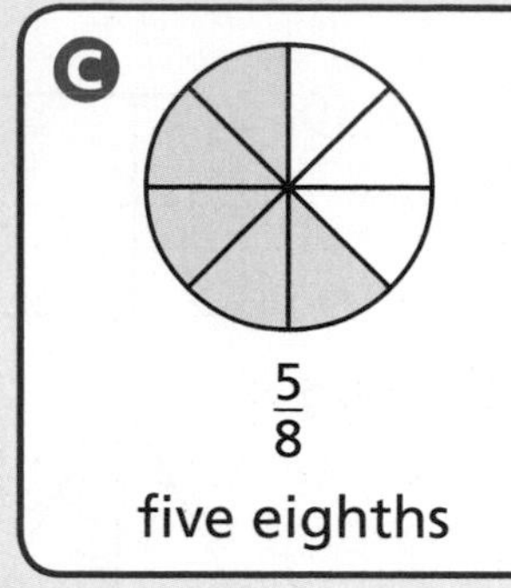

$\frac{5}{8}$

five eighths

D

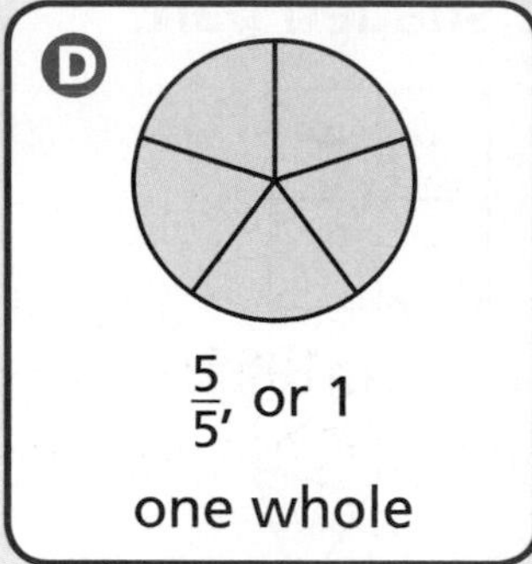

$\frac{5}{5}$, or 1

one whole

A number line can show parts of one whole. The space from one whole number to the next represents one whole. The line can be divided into any number of equal parts.

E This number line shows thirds.

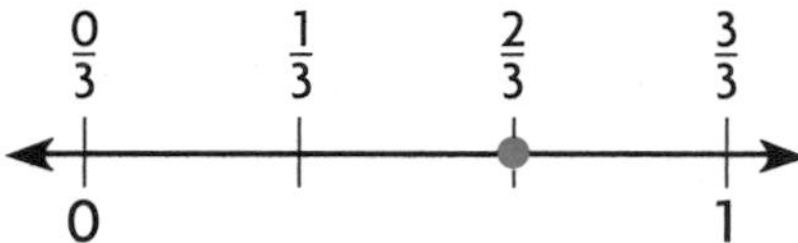

The point shows the location of $\frac{2}{3}$.

F This number line shows fourths.

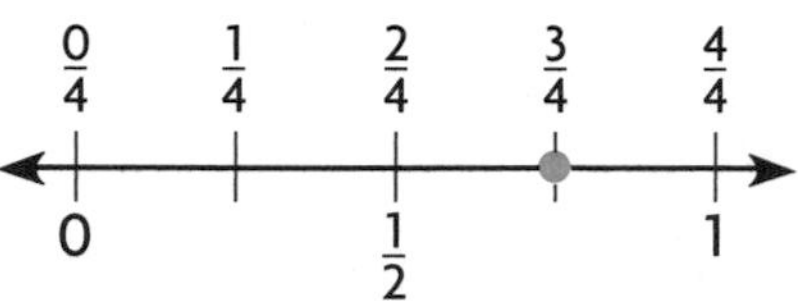

The point shows the location of $\frac{3}{4}$.

Guided Practice

1. What fraction names the point?
   Think: What number comes after 4?

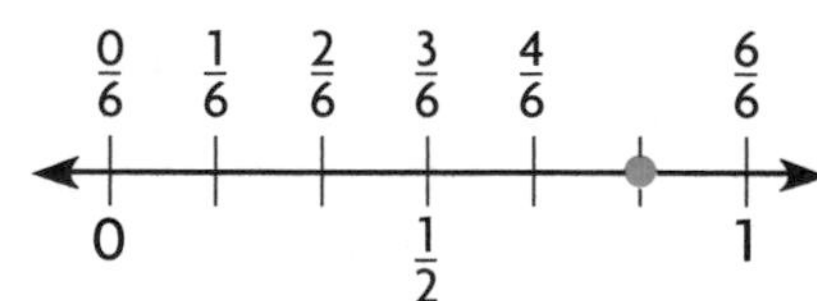

Write a fraction in numbers and in words to name the shaded part.

2. 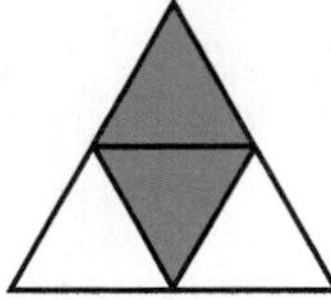

3. 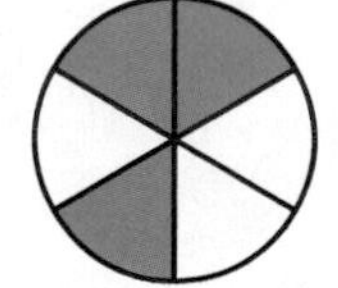

✓4. 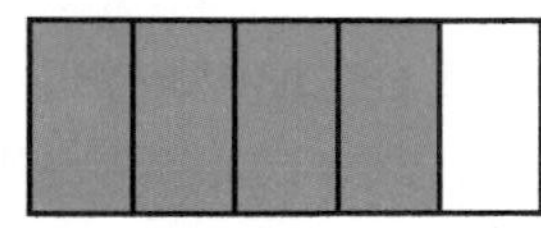

Use fraction circle pieces to make a model of each. Then write the fraction by using numbers.

5. nine twelfths
6. two divided by ten
✓7. seven out of nine

8. **TALK Math** **Explain** how to write a fraction for the part that is not shaded.

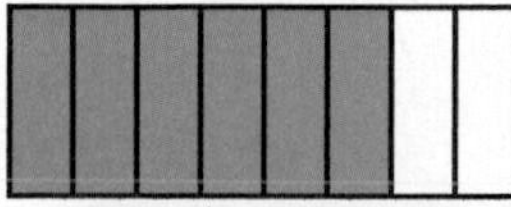

Independent Practice and Problem Solving

Write a fraction in numbers and in words to name the shaded part.

9. 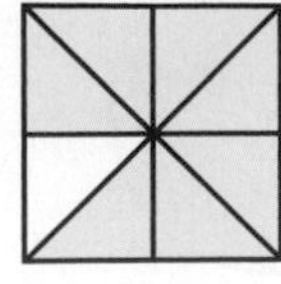

10. 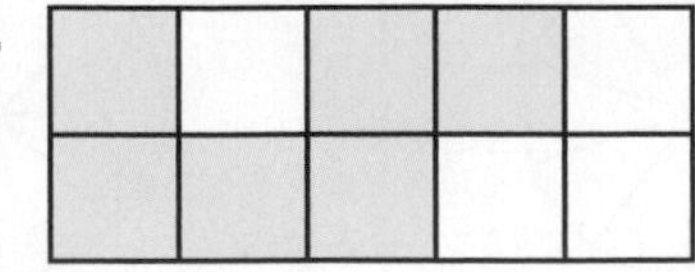

11. 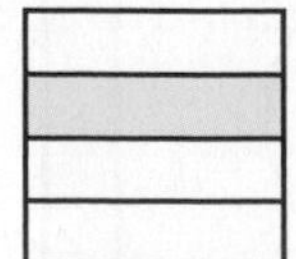

12. 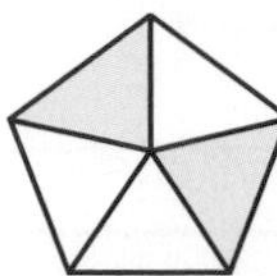

13. 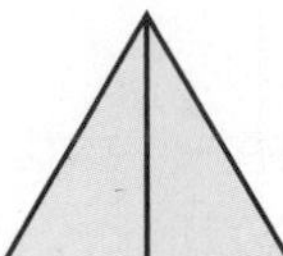

14. 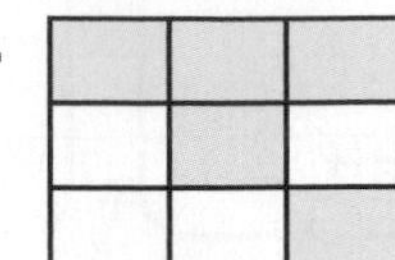

Use fraction circle pieces to make a model of each. Then write the fraction by using numbers.

15. five sixths
16. four out of twelve
17. one divided by three
18. six out of eight
19. two fourths
20. eight tenths

Write a fraction for the shaded part of each figure.

21. 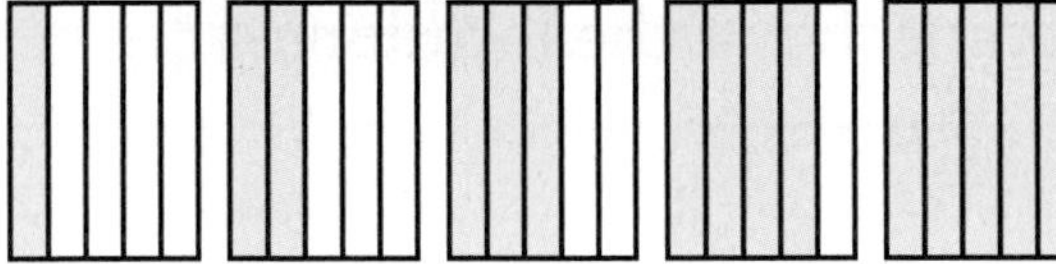

22. 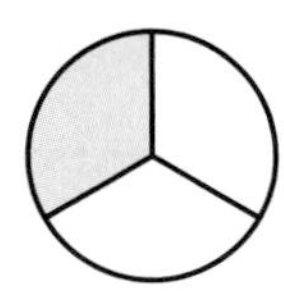 

Write a fraction that names each point.

23. 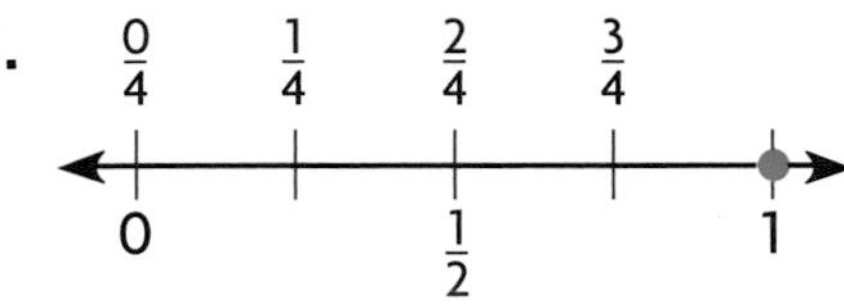

24. 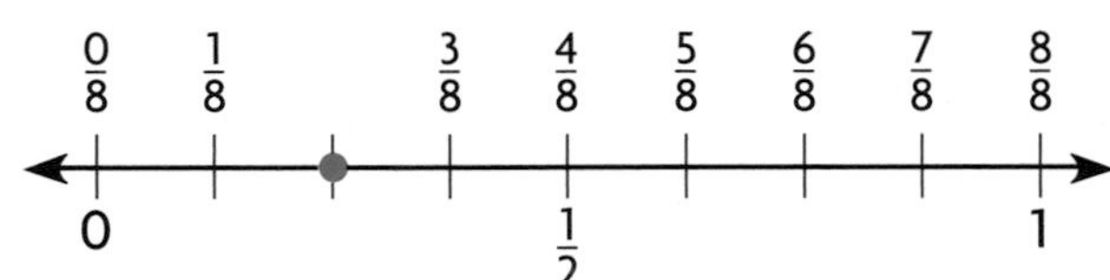

USE DATA For 25–27, use the pizzas.

Pepperoni

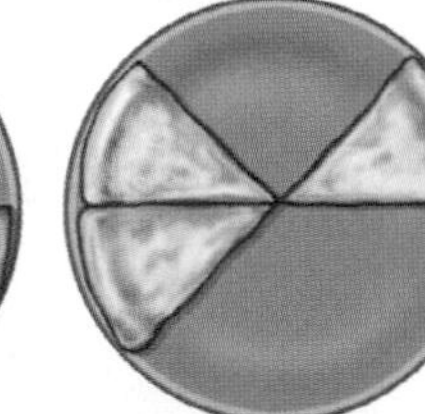
Cheese

Veggie

25. Mrs. Ormond ordered pizza. Each pizza had 8 equal slices. What fraction of the pepperoni pizza is left?

26. What fraction of the cheese pizza is left?

27. **Pose a Problem** Use the picture of the veggie pizza to write a problem that can be answered by using fractions.

28. Randy's family ate six eighths of a pizza. Draw a picture to show the amount that Randy's family ate.

CD ROM Technology
Use Harcourt Mega Math, Fraction Action, *Fraction Flare Up*, Level B.

 Extra Practice on page 476, Set A

29. **Reasoning** Two pizzas are the same size. The cheese pizza is cut into 6 equal slices. The meat pizza is cut into 8 equal slices. Which pizza has larger slices? **Explain.**

30. **WRITE Math** **What's the Error?** Kate says that $\frac{2}{3}$ names the shaded part. Describe her error. Write the correct fraction.

Learn About Fractions on a Clock

The minute hand can divide a clock into equal parts. So, you can use fractions when you tell time.

Example

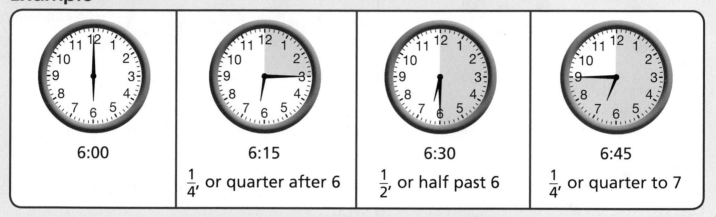

 6:00	 6:15	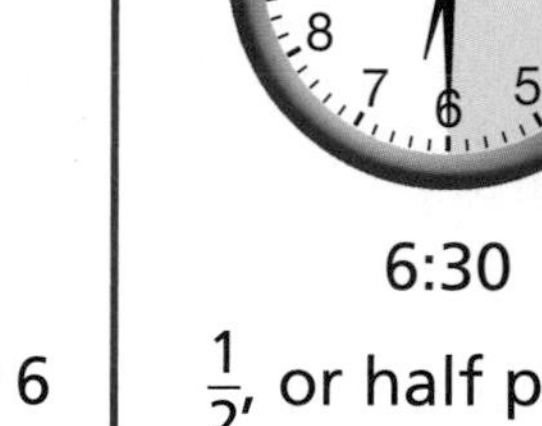 6:30	 6:45
	$\frac{1}{4}$, or quarter after 6	$\frac{1}{2}$, or half past 6	$\frac{1}{4}$, or quarter to 7

Try It

Complete each sentence. Write *one fourth*, *one half*, or *three fourths*.

31. At 6:30, the minute hand has moved __?__ of the way around the clock.
32. At 6:15, the minute hand has moved __?__ of the way around the clock.
33. At 6:45, the minute hand has moved __?__ of the way around the clock.

Mixed Review and Test Prep

34. John said these two figures are congruent. Do you agree? **Explain.** (p. 378)

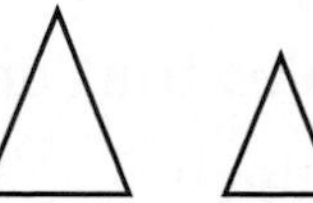

35. **Test Prep** Write in numbers and words the fraction that names the shaded part.

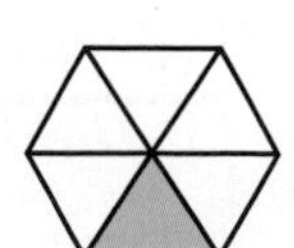

36. What is the area of the figure? (Grade 2)

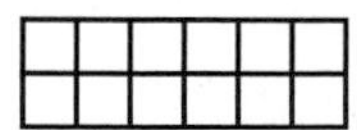

37. **Test Prep** What fraction of the figure is blue?

A $\frac{3}{5}$ B $\frac{8}{5}$ C $\frac{3}{8}$ D $\frac{5}{8}$

LESSON 2

Model Part of a Group

OBJECTIVE: Read, write, and model fractional parts of a group.

Quick Review

Name the fraction for each shaded part.

1. 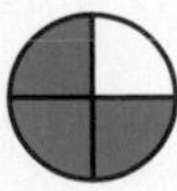 **2.** **3.**

4.  **5.**

Learn

PROBLEM Jake and Emma each have a collection of marbles. What fraction of each collection is blue?

Jake's marbles

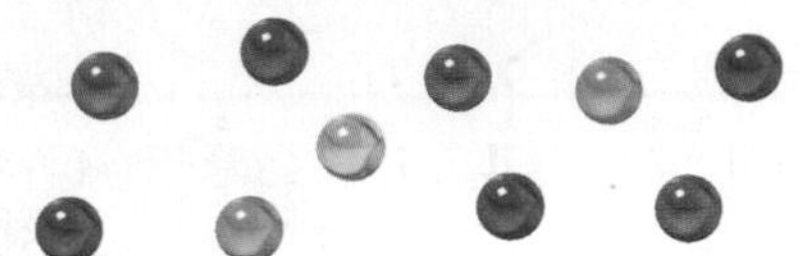

number of blue marbles → 3 ← numerator
total number of marbles → 10 ← denominator

$\frac{3}{10}$

Read: three tenths, or three out of ten

Write: $\frac{3}{10}$

So, $\frac{3}{10}$ of Jake's marbles are blue.

Emma's marbles

 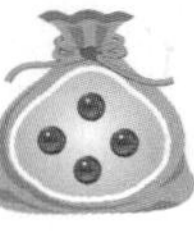 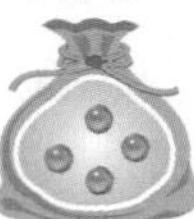 

sets of blue marbles → 1 ← numerator
total number of sets → 4 ← denominator

$\frac{1}{4}$

Read: one fourth, or one out of four

Write: $\frac{1}{4}$

So, $\frac{1}{4}$ of Emma's marbles are blue.

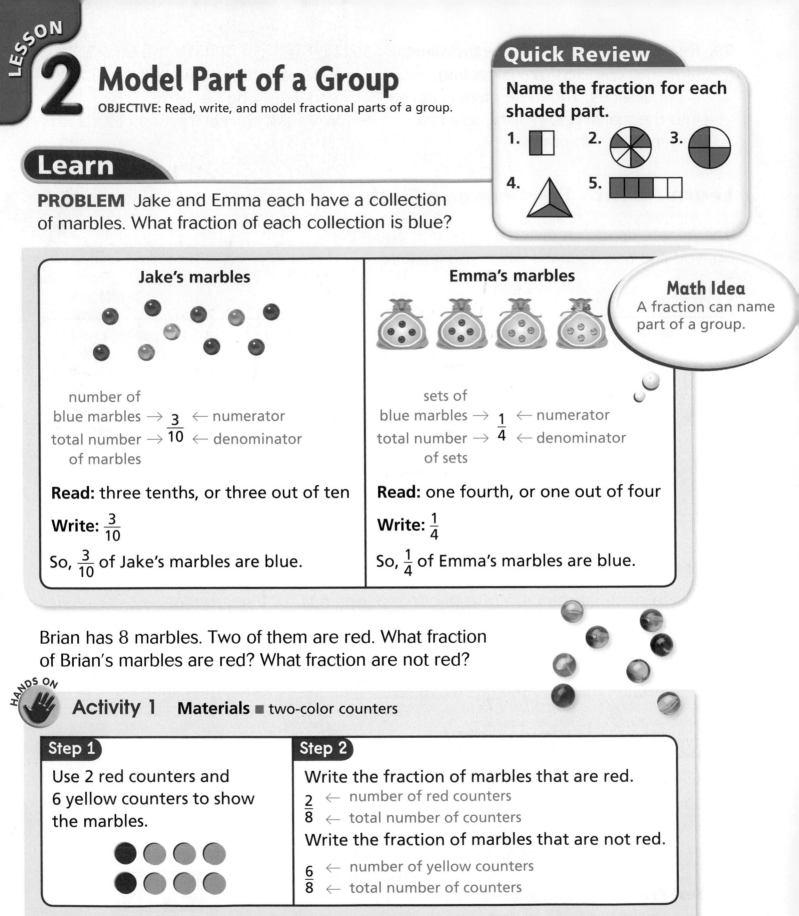

Math Idea
A fraction can name part of a group.

Brian has 8 marbles. Two of them are red. What fraction of Brian's marbles are red? What fraction are not red?

Activity 1 **Materials** ■ two-color counters

Step 1

Use 2 red counters and 6 yellow counters to show the marbles.

Step 2

Write the fraction of marbles that are red.

$\frac{2}{8}$ ← number of red counters / ← total number of counters

Write the fraction of marbles that are not red.

$\frac{6}{8}$ ← number of yellow counters / ← total number of counters

So, $\frac{2}{8}$ of Brian's marbles are red and $\frac{6}{8}$ are not red.

Twelve students signed up to play in a marble tournament. One third of the students who signed up are girls. How many girls will play in the marble tournament?

Find $\frac{1}{3}$ of 12.

Activity 2

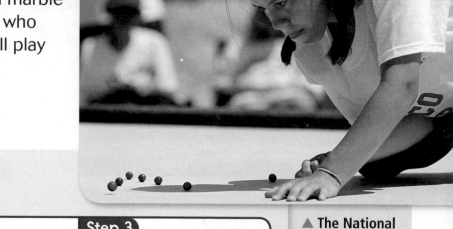

Materials ■ two-color counters

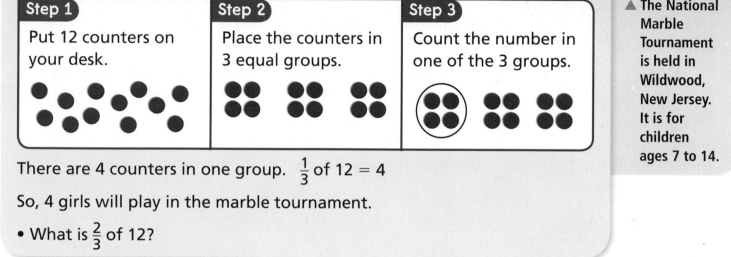

Step 1	Step 2	Step 3
Put 12 counters on your desk. 	Place the counters in 3 equal groups. 	Count the number in one of the 3 groups. 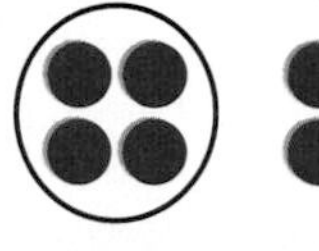 

There are 4 counters in one group. $\frac{1}{3}$ of $12 = 4$

So, 4 girls will play in the marble tournament.

- What is $\frac{2}{3}$ of 12?

▲ The National Marble Tournament is held in Wildwood, New Jersey. It is for children ages 7 to 14.

Guided Practice

1. Use the counters to find $\frac{1}{2}$ of 8. 

Write a fraction that names the red part of each group.

2. 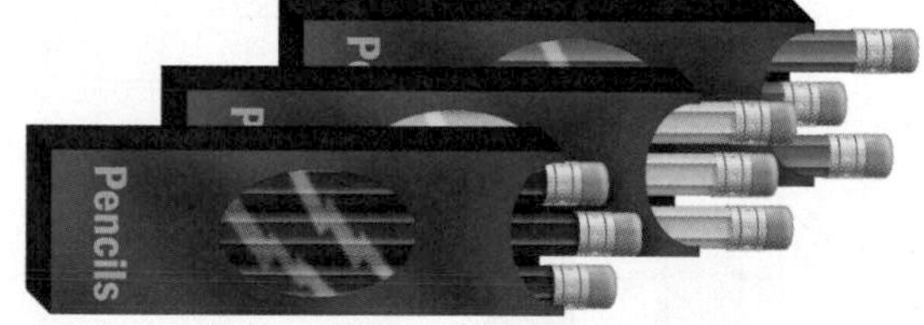

✓3. 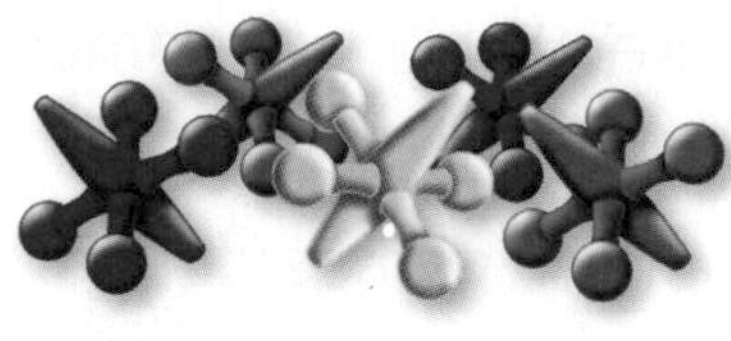

Draw each. Then write a fraction that names the shaded part.

4. Draw 10 squares.
Shade 7 squares.

5. Draw 6 triangles.
Make 2 equal groups.
Shade 1 group.

✓6. Draw 8 circles.
Shade 3 circles.

7. TALK Math **Explain** how to use counters to find $\frac{1}{5}$ of 10.

Independent Practice and Problem Solving

Write a fraction that names the blue part of each group.

8. 

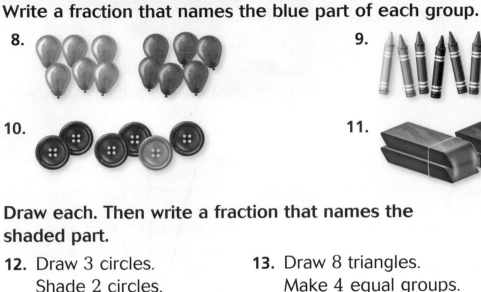

9. 

10. 

11. 

Draw each. Then write a fraction that names the shaded part.

12. Draw 3 circles. Shade 2 circles.

13. Draw 8 triangles. Make 4 equal groups. Shade 2 groups.

14. Draw 4 rectangles. Shade 1 rectangle.

Model each fraction with counters. Then write the fraction in words.

15. $\frac{4}{9}$ **16.** $\frac{1}{5}$ **17.** $\frac{6}{6}$ **18.** $\frac{2}{4}$ **19.** $\frac{5}{8}$

Use counters to solve.

20. $\frac{1}{2}$ of 4 **21.** $\frac{3}{4}$ of 8 **22.** $\frac{1}{3}$ of 9 **23.** $\frac{2}{6}$ of 12 **24.** $\frac{5}{5}$ of 10

USE DATA For 25–27, use the bar graph.

25. The bar graph shows the winners of the Smith Elementary School Marble Tournament. How many games were played? What fraction of the games did Scott win?

26. What fraction of the games did Robyn NOT win?

27. Pose a Problem Use the data from the bar graph. Write a problem that can be answered by using a fraction to name part of a group.

 Extra Practice on page 476, Set B

28. Kevin has 5 blue pens and 3 red pens. What fraction of Kevin's pens are red?

29. Lori has 10 flowers. Four of those flowers are pink. What fraction of the flowers are NOT pink?

30. Jess has a bag of 12 marbles. Of those marbles, $\frac{4}{12}$ are red, $\frac{3}{12}$ are white, and the rest are green. How many green marbles are in the bag?

31. **WRITE Math** **What's the Question?** A bag has 2 yellow cubes, 3 blue cubes, and 1 white cube. The answer is $\frac{5}{6}$.

Learn About Fraction Patterns

You can use the models and patterns to complete the table.

32.	Model	●●●●	●●●●	■	●●●●	●●●●
33.	Total number of parts	4	■	4	4	4
34.	Number of red parts	0	1	2	■	4
35.	Fraction of red parts	$\frac{0}{4}$	$\frac{1}{4}$	$\frac{2}{4}$	$\frac{3}{4}$	■

Mixed Review and Test Prep

36. What fraction of the circle is shaded? (p. 446)

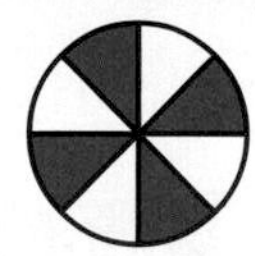

37. **Test Prep** A basket is filled with 8 pieces of fruit. Of the pieces of fruit, $\frac{1}{4}$ are apples. How many apples are there?

A 1
B 2
C 4
D 6

38. Doug can choose ham, turkey, or beef for his sandwich. He can also choose white or wheat bread. How many different types of sandwiches can Doug make? (p. 186)

39. **Test Prep** What fraction of the coins are pennies?

LESSON 3 Equivalent Fractions

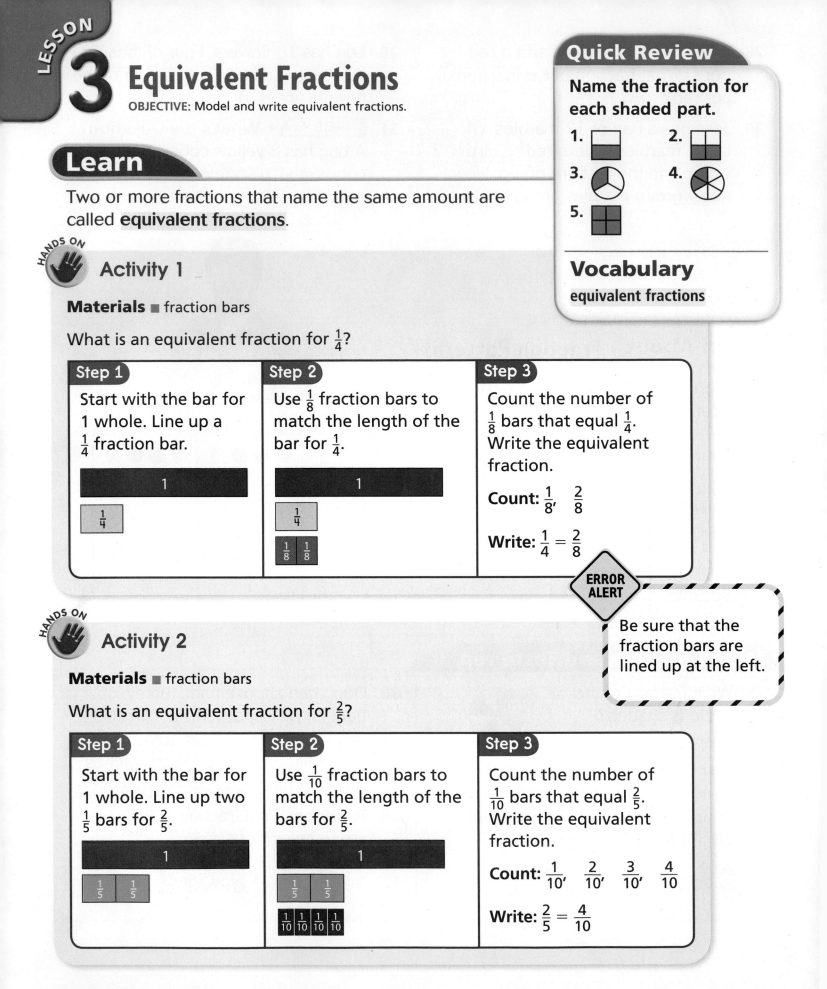

OBJECTIVE: Model and write equivalent fractions.

Quick Review

Name the fraction for each shaded part.

1.
2. 
3.
4.
5.

Vocabulary

equivalent fractions

Learn

Two or more fractions that name the same amount are called **equivalent fractions**.

Activity 1

Materials ■ fraction bars

What is an equivalent fraction for $\frac{1}{4}$?

Step 1

Start with the bar for 1 whole. Line up a $\frac{1}{4}$ fraction bar.

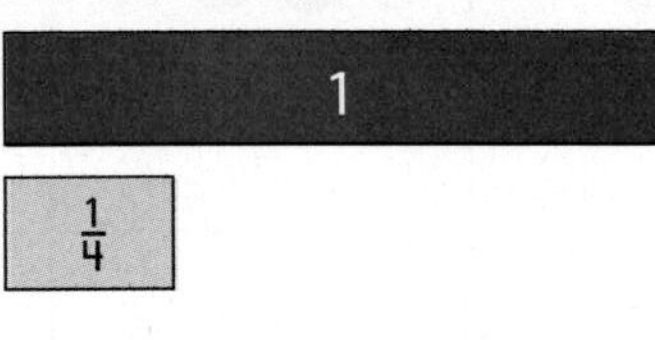

Step 2

Use $\frac{1}{8}$ fraction bars to match the length of the bar for $\frac{1}{4}$.

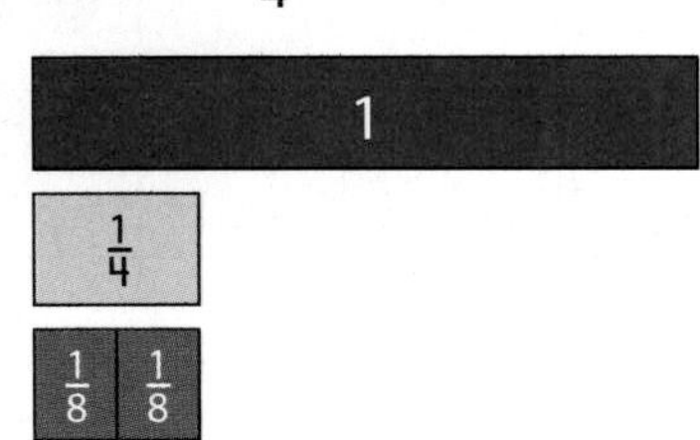

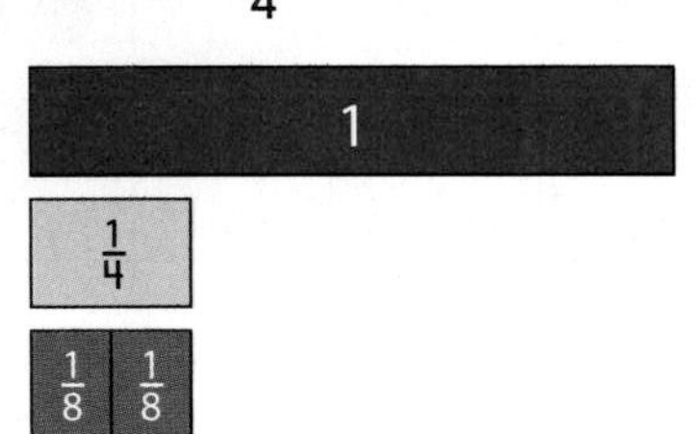

Step 3

Count the number of $\frac{1}{8}$ bars that equal $\frac{1}{4}$. Write the equivalent fraction.

Count: $\frac{1}{8}$, $\frac{2}{8}$

Write: $\frac{1}{4} = \frac{2}{8}$

ERROR ALERT

Be sure that the fraction bars are lined up at the left.

Activity 2

Materials ■ fraction bars

What is an equivalent fraction for $\frac{2}{5}$?

Step 1

Start with the bar for 1 whole. Line up two $\frac{1}{5}$ bars for $\frac{2}{5}$.

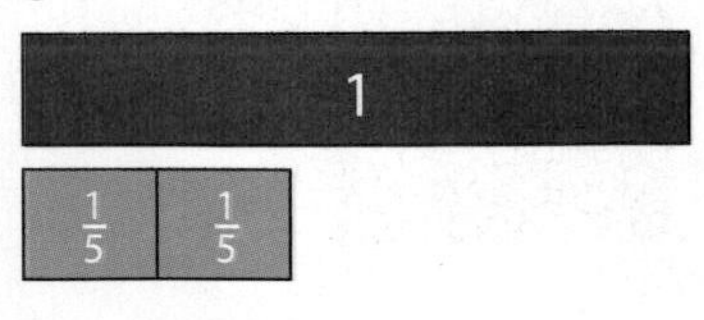

Step 2

Use $\frac{1}{10}$ fraction bars to match the length of the bars for $\frac{2}{5}$.

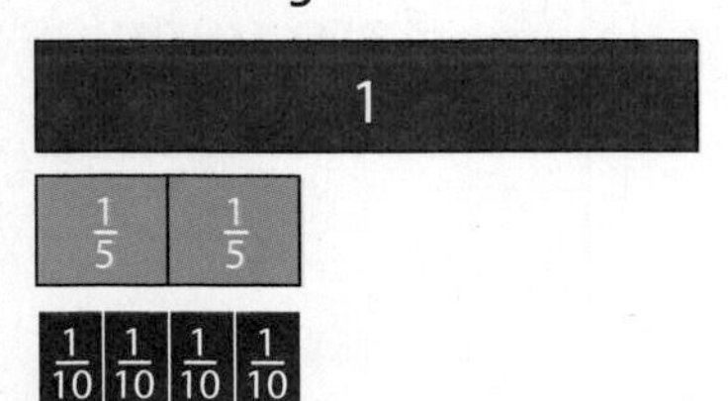

Step 3

Count the number of $\frac{1}{10}$ bars that equal $\frac{2}{5}$. Write the equivalent fraction.

Count: $\frac{1}{10}$, $\frac{2}{10}$, $\frac{3}{10}$, $\frac{4}{10}$

Write: $\frac{2}{5} = \frac{4}{10}$

More Examples

A

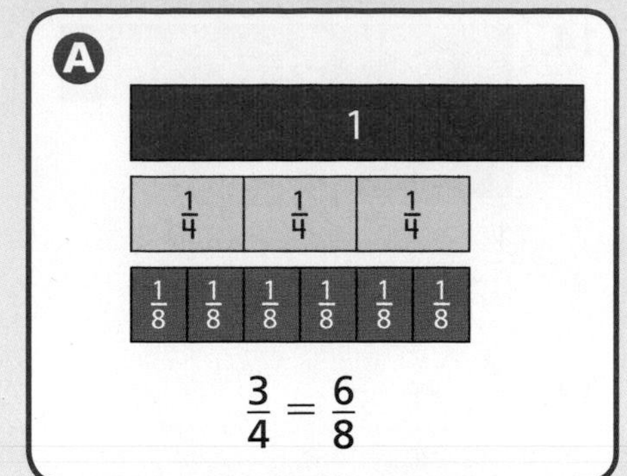

$\frac{3}{4} = \frac{6}{8}$

B

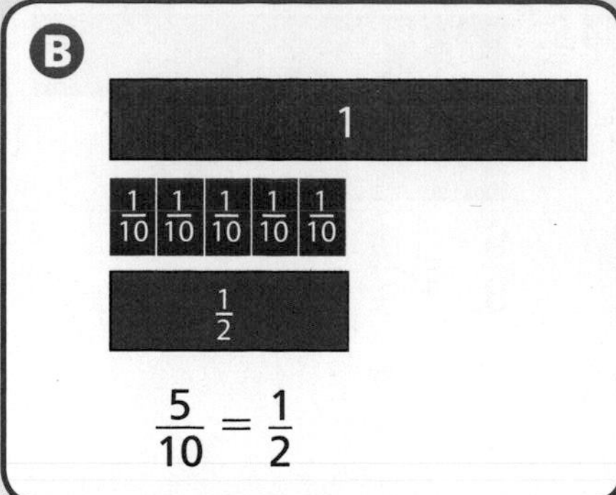

$\frac{5}{10} = \frac{1}{2}$

C

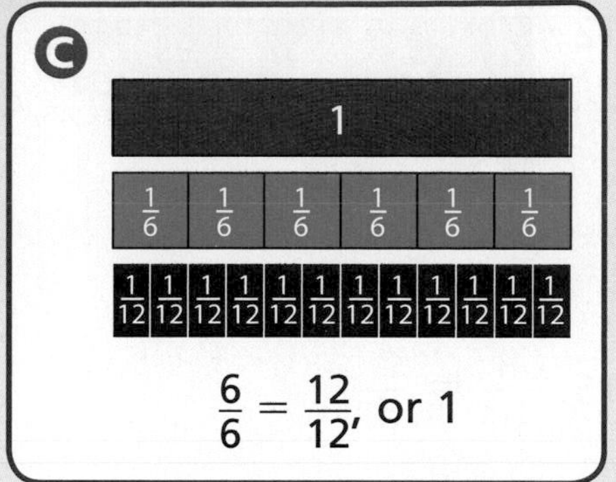

$\frac{6}{6} = \frac{12}{12}$, or 1

Guided Practice

1. What fraction is equivalent to $\frac{2}{3}$?

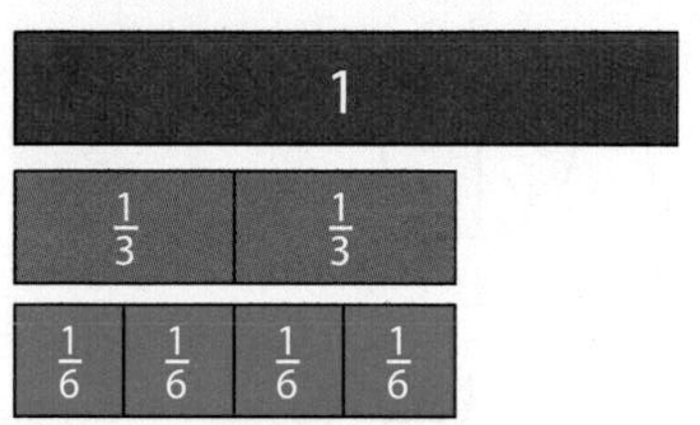

Find an equivalent fraction. Use fraction bars.

2. 1
$\frac{1}{5}$ $\frac{1}{5}$ $\frac{1}{5}$

✓ 3. 1
$\frac{1}{8}$ $\frac{1}{8}$

✓ 4. 1
$\frac{1}{10}$ $\frac{1}{10}$ $\frac{1}{10}$ $\frac{1}{10}$ $\frac{1}{10}$ $\frac{1}{10}$ $\frac{1}{10}$ $\frac{1}{10}$

5. **TALK Math** **Explain** how to use fraction bars to find a fraction that is equivalent to $\frac{3}{4}$.

Independent Practice and Problem Solving

Find an equivalent fraction. Use fraction bars.

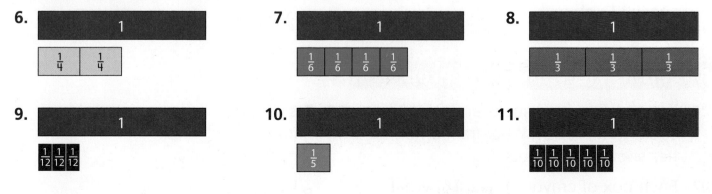

6.
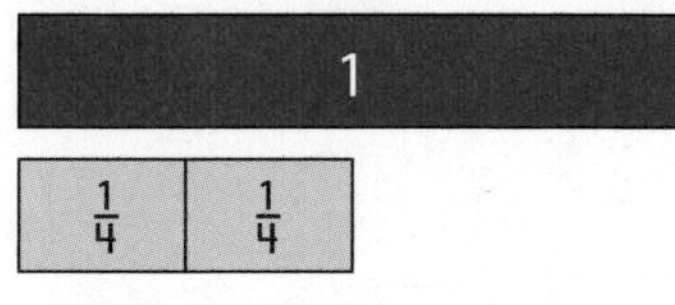

7.
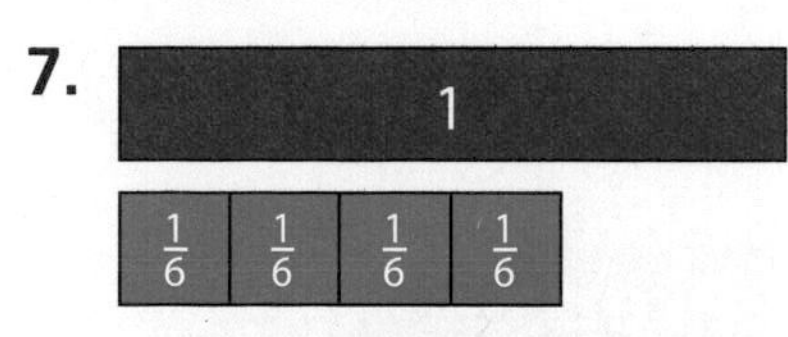

8.
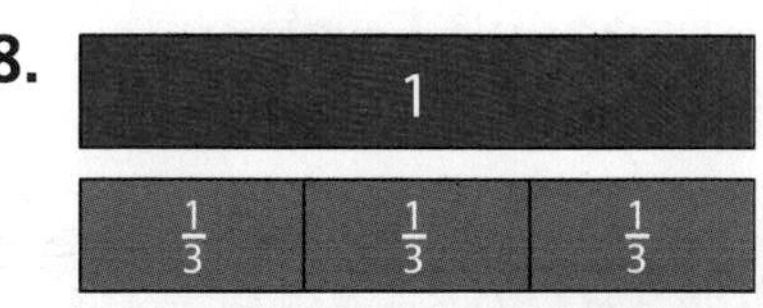

9. 1
$\frac{1}{12}$ $\frac{1}{12}$ $\frac{1}{12}$

10.
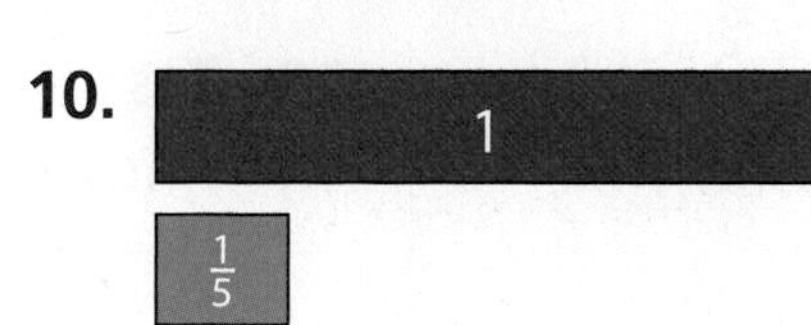

11.
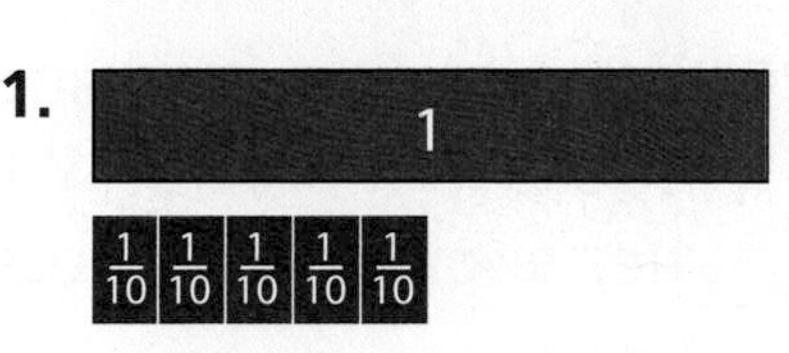

Extra Practice on page 476, Set C

Find the missing numerator. Use fraction bars.

12. 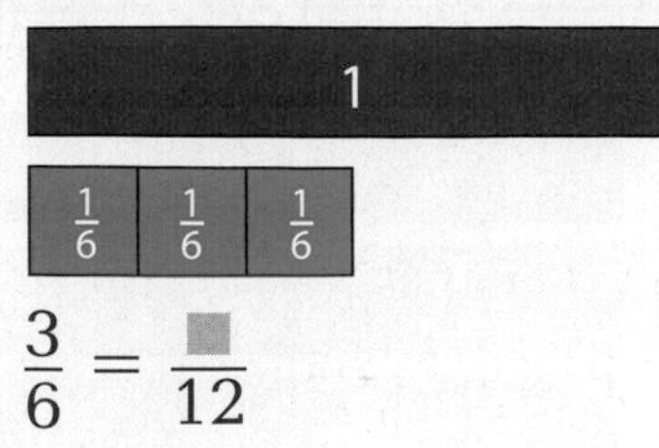

$\frac{3}{6} = \frac{■}{12}$

13. 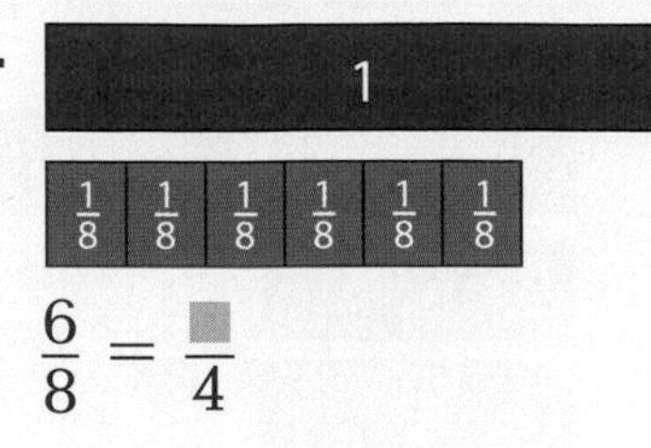

$\frac{6}{8} = \frac{■}{4}$

14. 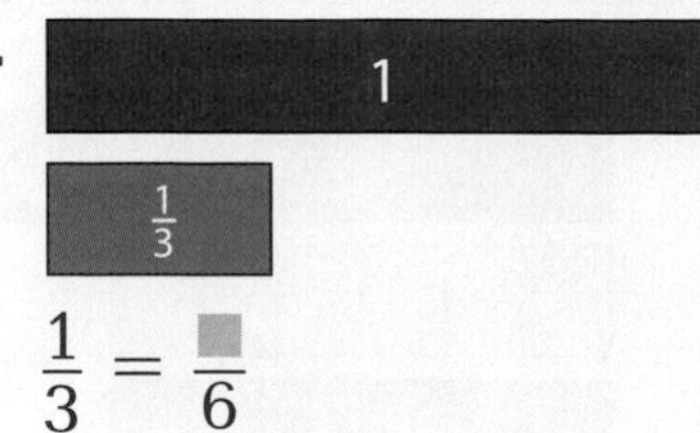

$\frac{1}{3} = \frac{■}{6}$

15. $\frac{8}{10} = \frac{■}{5}$

16. $\frac{1}{2} = \frac{■}{8}$

17. $\frac{4}{12} = \frac{■}{3}$

18. $\frac{2}{4} = \frac{■}{12}$

19. $\frac{5}{5} = \frac{■}{10}$

20. $\frac{4}{8} = \frac{■}{2}$

21. Write the fraction that names the shaded part of each. Then tell which fractions are equivalent.

a.  b. c. 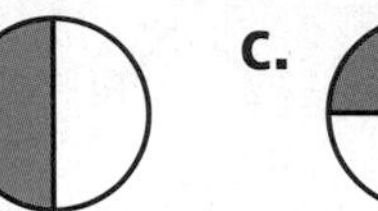 d. 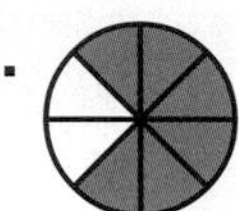 e. 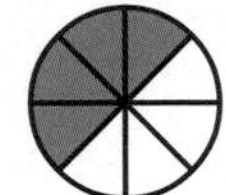

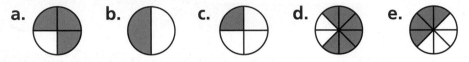

USE DATA For 22–24, use the table.

22. The table shows the lengths of three different types of ants. How many fire ants would it take to equal the length of one carpenter ant?

23. What fraction is equivalent to the length of a bulldog ant?

24. **Reasoning** Are any of the ants in the table the same length? **Explain.**

Ants

Type	Length
Fire ants	about $\frac{1}{4}$ inch
Bulldog ants	about $\frac{4}{5}$ inch
Carpenter ants	about $\frac{1}{2}$ inch

25. **WRITE Math** **Sense or Nonsense** Jay cut an orange into 8 equal pieces and ate 4 of the pieces. He says he ate one half of the orange. Does Jay's statement make sense? **Explain.**

Mixed Review and Test Prep

26. Erin has 6 striped socks and 2 white socks in a drawer. What fraction of her socks are striped? (p. 450)

27. Each box of crayons costs $6. What is the cost of 4 boxes of crayons? (p. 212)

28. **Test Prep** What is the missing numerator? $\frac{5}{6} = \frac{■}{12}$

A 7 **C** 9

B 8 **D** 10

Draw to Explain

WRITE Math WORKSHOP

Sometimes you can best explain your thinking by drawing a picture or diagram.

Marta wants to find two fractions that are equivalent to $\frac{1}{3}$. She uses crayons and strips of paper to make diagrams of equivalent fractions.

She explains her thinking by describing what she did and showing her drawings.

First, I cut three strips of paper that are the same size. Next, I folded the strips by using different numbers of folds to show $\frac{1}{3}$. I drew lines to show the folds and shaded $\frac{1}{3}$ of each strip.

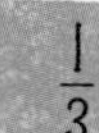

$\frac{1}{3}$	$\frac{1}{3}$	$\frac{1}{3}$

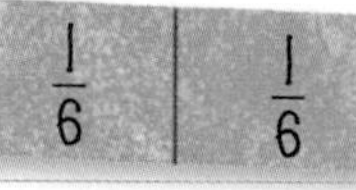

$\frac{1}{6}$	$\frac{1}{6}$	$\frac{1}{6}$	$\frac{1}{6}$	$\frac{1}{6}$	$\frac{1}{6}$

$$\frac{1}{3} = \frac{2}{6}$$

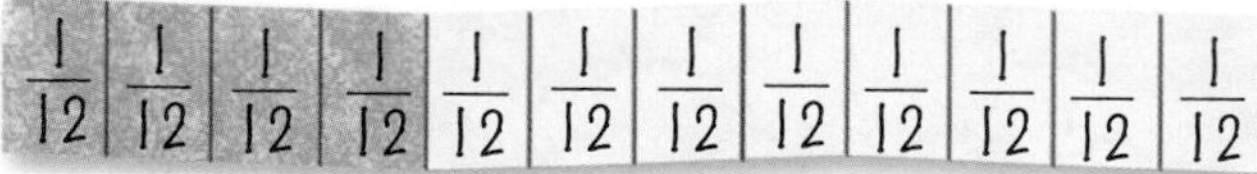

$\frac{1}{12}$	$\frac{1}{12}$	$\frac{1}{12}$	$\frac{1}{12}$	$\frac{1}{12}$	$\frac{1}{12}$	$\frac{1}{12}$	$\frac{1}{12}$	$\frac{1}{12}$	$\frac{1}{12}$	$\frac{1}{12}$	$\frac{1}{12}$

$$\frac{1}{3} = \frac{4}{12}$$

My drawings prove that $\frac{1}{3}$, $\frac{2}{6}$, and $\frac{4}{12}$ are equivalent fractions.

Problem Solving

Fold paper strips to show fractional parts. Draw lines to show the folds. Shade some parts to show the fractions. Then explain what you did. Use your drawings to show your solution.

1. Find an equivalent fraction for $\frac{2}{3}$.
2. Find an equivalent fraction for $\frac{3}{4}$.

LESSON 4

Compare and Order Fractions

OBJECTIVE: Compare and order fractions.

Quick Review

Compare. Write <, >, or = for each ●.

1. 52 ● 48
2. 67 ● 68
3. 183 ● 183
4. 2,594 ● 2,549
5. 5,271 ● 5,712

Learn

You can compare fractions in different ways.

Example 1 Compare $\frac{2}{6}$ and $\frac{3}{6}$.

ONE WAY Use fraction bars.

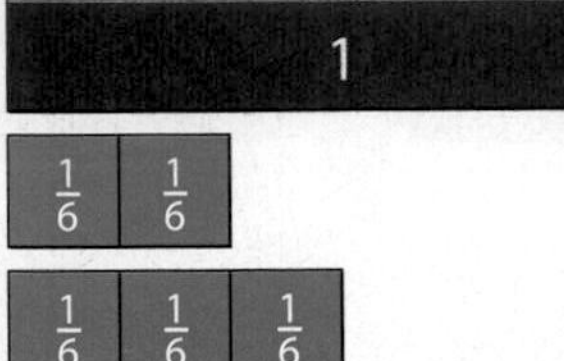

The bars for $\frac{2}{6}$ are shorter than the bars for $\frac{3}{6}$.

So, $\frac{2}{6} < \frac{3}{6}$, or $\frac{3}{6} > \frac{2}{6}$.

ANOTHER WAY Use a number line.

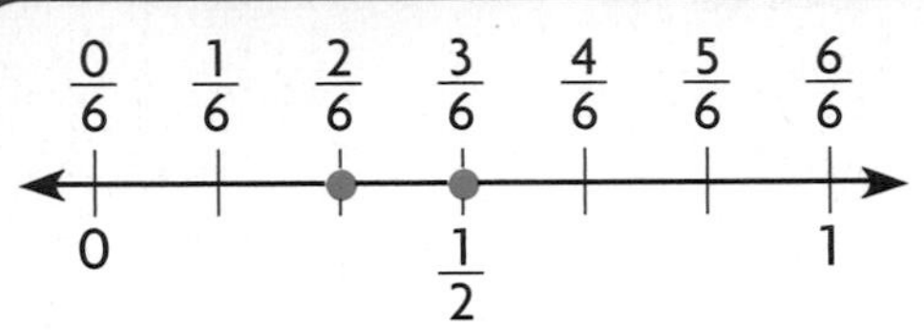

$\frac{3}{6}$ is to the right of $\frac{2}{6}$. It is closer to 1.

So, $\frac{3}{6} > \frac{2}{6}$, or $\frac{2}{6} < \frac{3}{6}$.

- How can you compare fractions with the same denominators but different numerators?

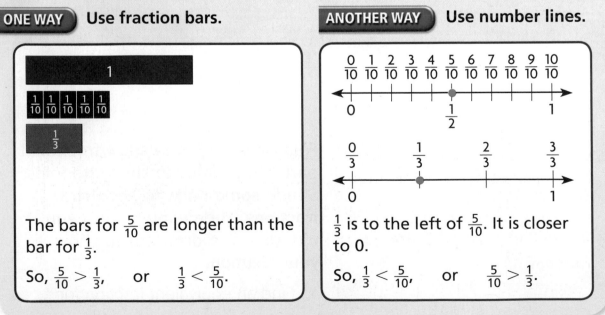

Example 2 Compare $\frac{5}{10}$ and $\frac{1}{3}$.

ONE WAY Use fraction bars.

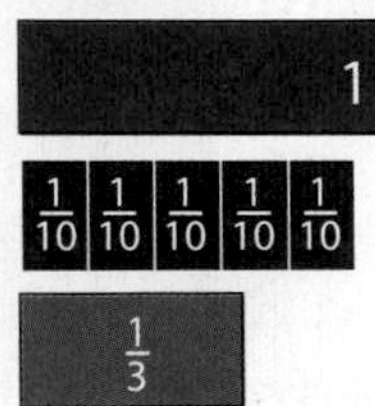

The bars for $\frac{5}{10}$ are longer than the bar for $\frac{1}{3}$.

So, $\frac{5}{10} > \frac{1}{3}$, or $\frac{1}{3} < \frac{5}{10}$.

ANOTHER WAY Use number lines.

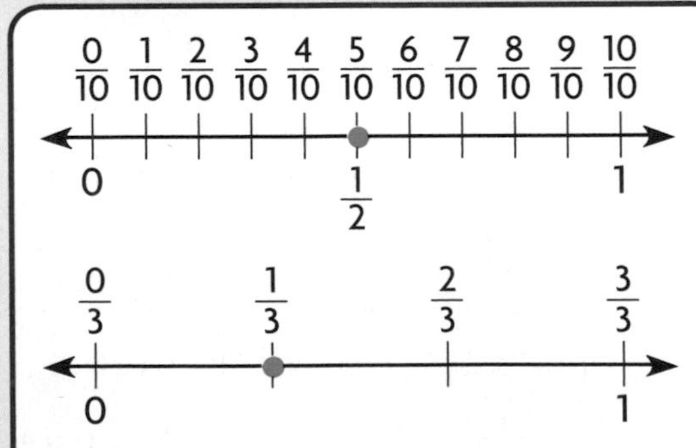

$\frac{1}{3}$ is to the left of $\frac{5}{10}$. It is closer to 0.

So, $\frac{1}{3} < \frac{5}{10}$, or $\frac{5}{10} > \frac{1}{3}$.

You can use fraction bars or number lines to order fractions.

Example **Compare and order $\frac{5}{8}$, $\frac{1}{4}$, and $\frac{4}{5}$.**

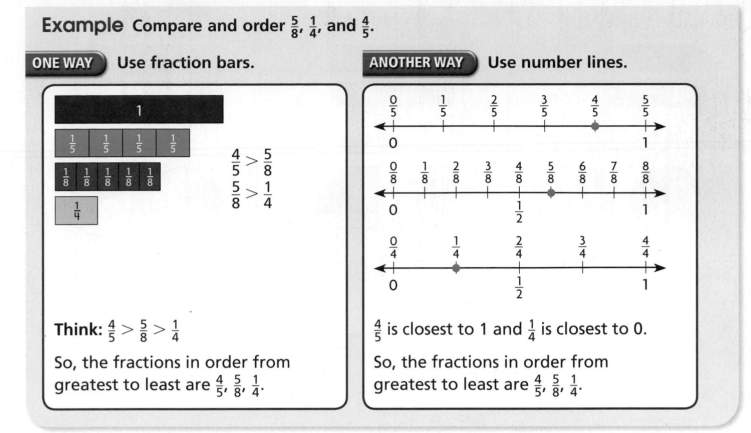

ONE WAY **Use fraction bars.**

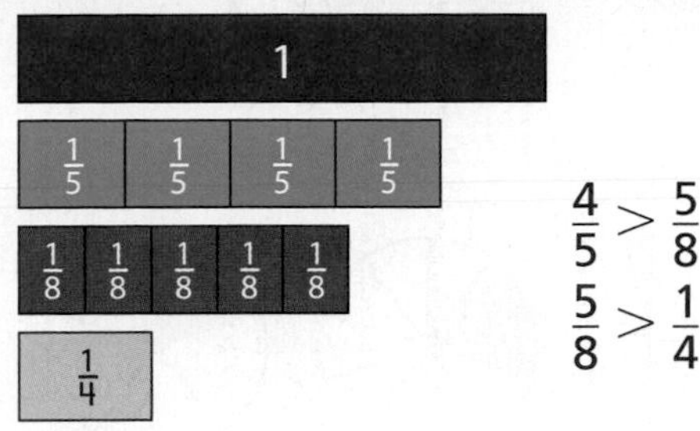

$\frac{4}{5} > \frac{5}{8}$

$\frac{5}{8} > \frac{1}{4}$

Think: $\frac{4}{5} > \frac{5}{8} > \frac{1}{4}$

So, the fractions in order from greatest to least are $\frac{4}{5}$, $\frac{5}{8}$, $\frac{1}{4}$.

ANOTHER WAY **Use number lines.**

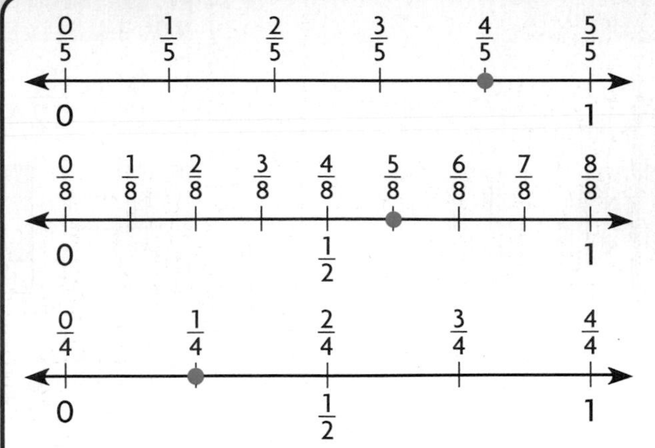

$\frac{4}{5}$ is closest to 1 and $\frac{1}{4}$ is closest to 0.

So, the fractions in order from greatest to least are $\frac{4}{5}$, $\frac{5}{8}$, $\frac{1}{4}$.

- What are the fractions in order from least to greatest?
- Compare and order $\frac{1}{8}$, $\frac{1}{4}$, and $\frac{1}{5}$. When the denominator is greater, are the fraction bars longer or shorter? Why?

Guided Practice

1. Which fraction is greater, $\frac{4}{6}$ or $\frac{2}{5}$?
   Think: The bars for $\frac{4}{6}$ are longer.

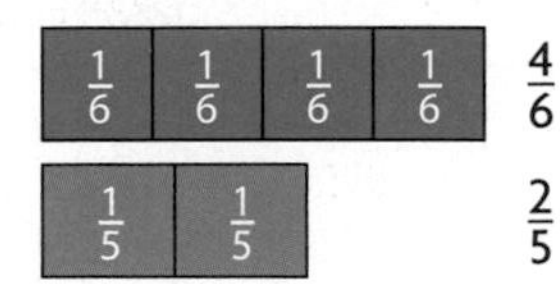

Compare. Write <, >, or = for each ●.

2. 1/8 1/8 1/8 1/8 1/8 1/8
   1/8 1/8 1/8 1/8
   $\frac{6}{8}$ ● $\frac{4}{8}$

✓3. 0/4 1/4 2/4 3/4 4/4
   0 1/2 1
   $\frac{2}{4}$ ● $\frac{3}{4}$

✓4. 1/12 1/12 1/12
   1/10 1/10 1/10 1/10 1/10
   $\frac{3}{12}$ ● $\frac{5}{10}$

5. **TALK Math** **Explain** how to use a number line to order $\frac{5}{6}$, $\frac{1}{6}$, and $\frac{3}{6}$ from least to greatest.

Independent Practice and Problem Solving

Compare. Write <, >, or = for each ●.

6.

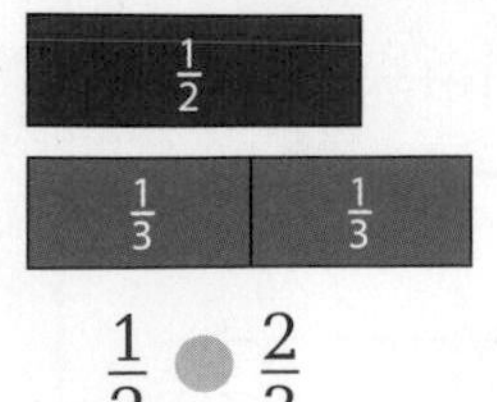

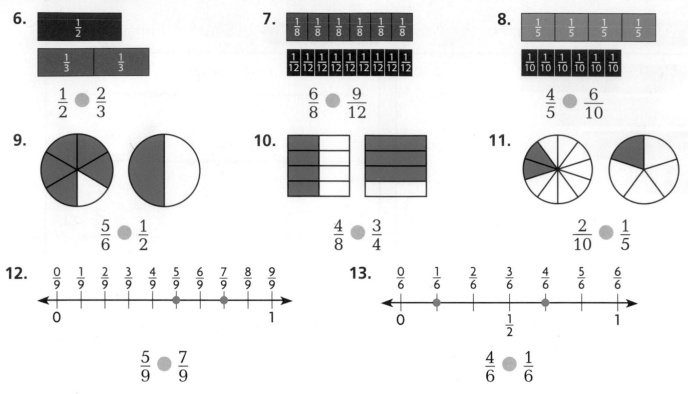

$\frac{1}{2}$ ● $\frac{2}{3}$

7.

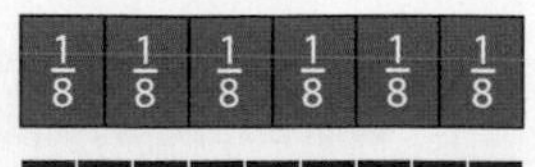

$\frac{6}{8}$ ● $\frac{9}{12}$

8.

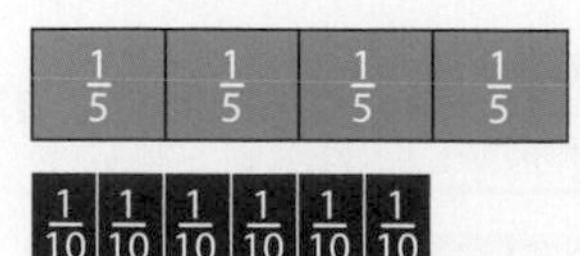

$\frac{4}{5}$ ● $\frac{6}{10}$

9.

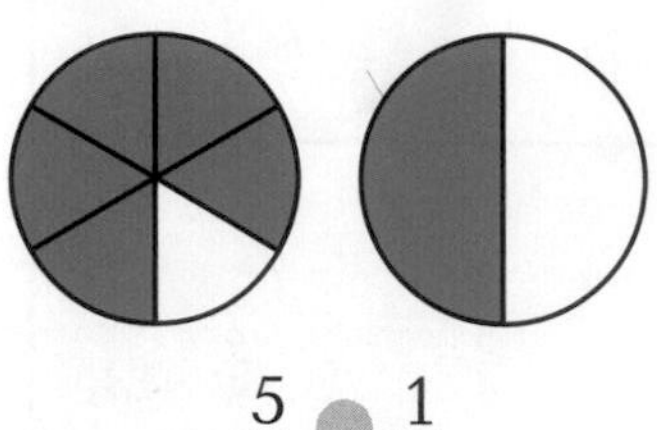

$\frac{5}{6}$ ● $\frac{1}{2}$

10.

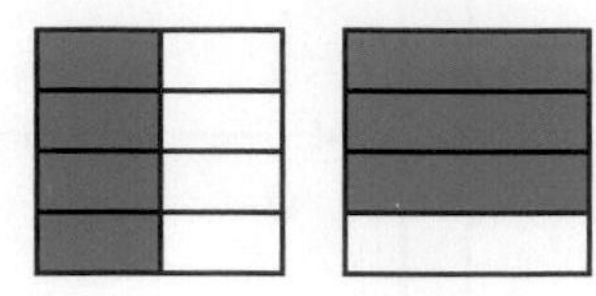

$\frac{4}{8}$ ● $\frac{3}{4}$

11.

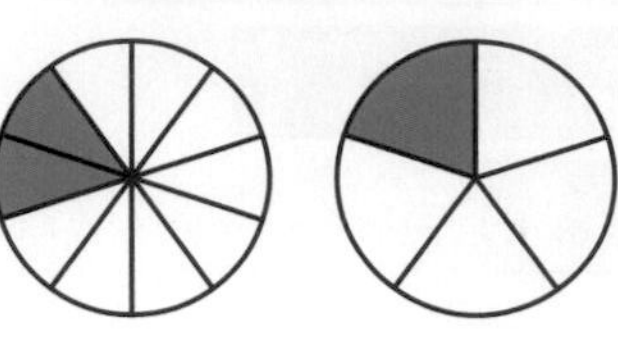

$\frac{2}{10}$ ● $\frac{1}{5}$

12.

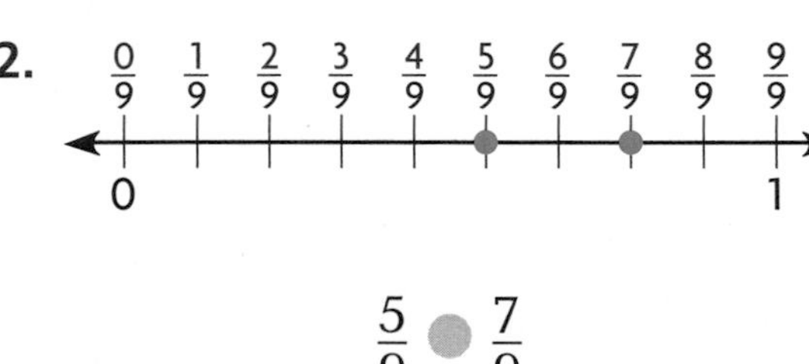

$\frac{5}{9}$ ● $\frac{7}{9}$

13.

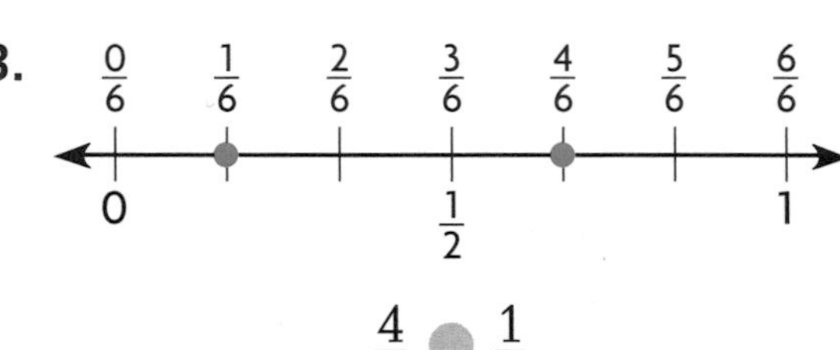

$\frac{4}{6}$ ● $\frac{1}{6}$

Use fraction bars or number lines to compare.
Write <, >, or = for each ●.

14. 1 ● $\frac{3}{3}$

15. $\frac{5}{9}$ ● $\frac{10}{12}$

16. $\frac{1}{2}$ ● $\frac{3}{6}$

17. $\frac{7}{8}$ ● $\frac{3}{4}$

18. Order $\frac{6}{10}$, $\frac{1}{2}$, and $\frac{5}{6}$ from greatest to least.

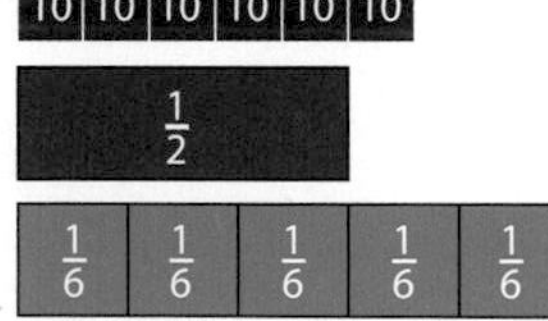

19. Order $\frac{4}{5}$, $\frac{1}{4}$, and $\frac{3}{5}$ from least to greatest.

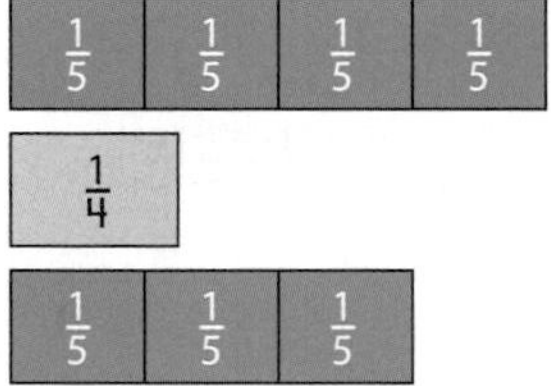

USE DATA For 20–21, use the map.

20. Which pet store is closer to Becky's house, Pet Mart or Super Pet?

21. Becky walked her dog from her house to Super Pet and then from Super Pet to the dog park. Which distance is greater?

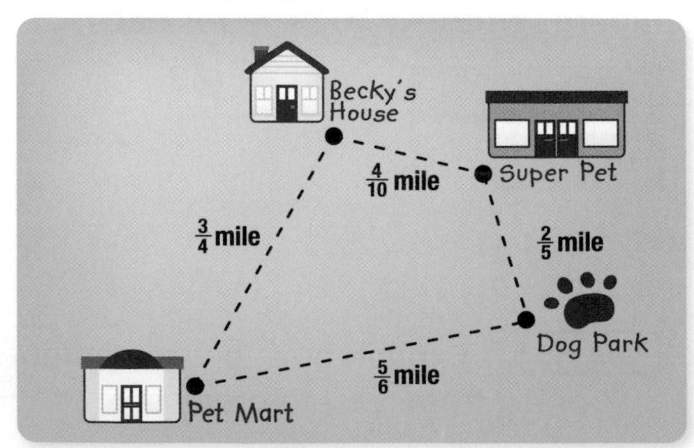

 Extra Practice on page 476, Set D

22. I am greater than $\frac{3}{6}$ and less than $\frac{4}{5}$. My denominator is 4. What fraction am I?

23. I am greater than $\frac{2}{8}$ and less than $\frac{1}{2}$. My denominator is 5. What fraction am I?

24. Jen found a recipe for dog biscuits. She needs $\frac{1}{3}$ cup butter, $\frac{3}{4}$ cup water, and $\frac{1}{2}$ cup powdered milk. Order these ingredients from the least to the greatest amount.

25. WRITE Math **Explain** how you can compare fractions that have different denominators.

Learn About Number Sense

Bobby and Jill went to a pizza restaurant and ordered the pizzas shown. Bobby and Jill each ate $\frac{1}{2}$ of his or her pizza.

Bobby's pizza

Example

Did Bobby and Jill eat the same amount of pizza? Bobby and Jill did not eat the same amount. Since Bobby's pizza is larger, he ate more than Jill.

Try It

Use the pictures of the pizzas to answer the questions below.

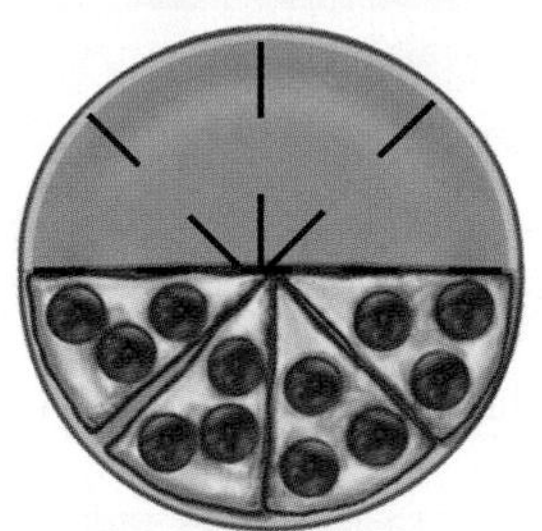

Jill's pizza

26. One slice of each pizza is $\frac{1}{8}$. Explain why Bobby's and Jill's slices aren't the same size.

27. Which pizza slices do you think cost less? Explain.

28. What if the pizzas were divided into thirds? Would Bobby's slices and Jill's slices be the same size?

Mixed Review and Test Prep

29. One jar of jelly costs \$3. Two jars cost \$6, and three jars cost \$9. What is the cost of 7 jars of jelly? (p. 256)

30. **Test Prep** Which fraction is greater than $\frac{5}{8}$?

A $\frac{1}{2}$ B $\frac{4}{10}$ C $\frac{3}{8}$ D $\frac{3}{4}$

31. Write the fact family for 2, 7, and 9. (p. 76)

32. **Test Prep** Rick, Jerry, and Tabitha are all reading the same book. Rick has read $\frac{2}{3}$ of the book, Jerry has read $\frac{2}{5}$, and Tabitha has read $\frac{4}{12}$. Who has read most of the book?

Problem Solving Workshop
Strategy: Compare Strategies

OBJECTIVE: Compare different strategies to solve problems.

Use the Strategy

PROBLEM Emma and her friends climbed a rock wall. Emma climbed $\frac{3}{4}$ of the wall, Elijah climbed $\frac{3}{6}$ of the wall, and Martin climbed $\frac{2}{3}$ of the wall. Who climbed the highest?

Read to Understand

- Visualize the problem.
- What information is given?

Plan

- **What strategy can you use to solve the problem?**

  Sometimes you can use more than one strategy to solve a problem. You can *make a model* or *draw a picture* to solve this problem.

Solve

- **How can you use each strategy to solve the problem?**

Make a Model Use fraction bars to model the problem.

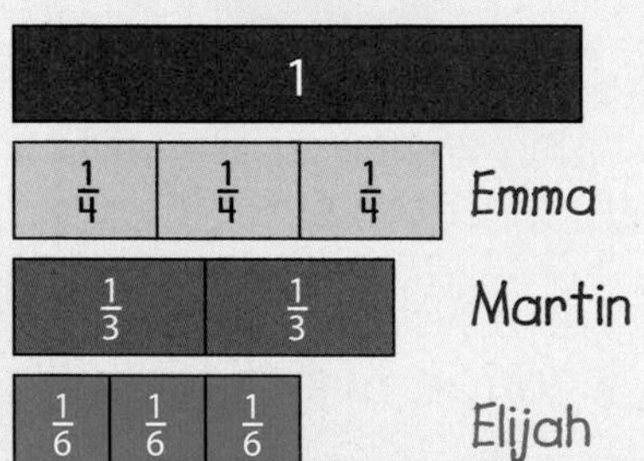

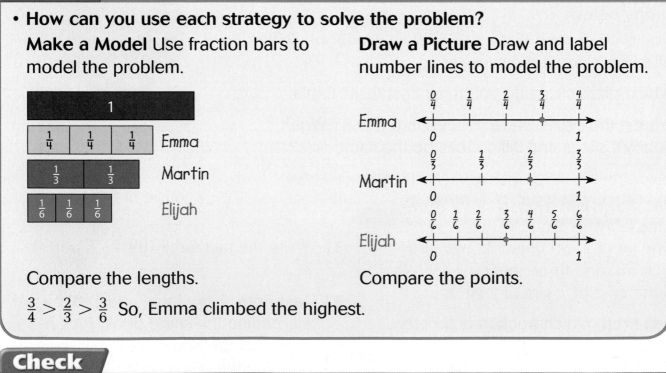

Compare the lengths.

Draw a Picture Draw and label number lines to model the problem.

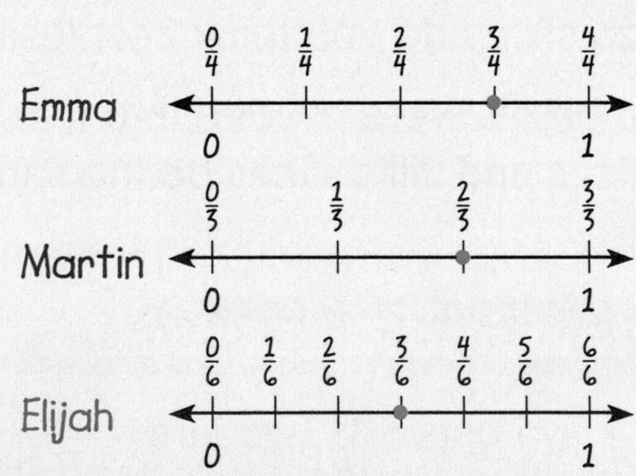

Compare the points.

$\frac{3}{4} > \frac{2}{3} > \frac{3}{6}$ So, Emma climbed the highest.

Check

- **How do you know the answer is correct?**

Guided Problem Solving

1. Tracy and Kim ran on the track to see who could run farther without stopping. Tracy ran $\frac{4}{5}$ of a mile and Kim ran $\frac{8}{10}$ of a mile. Who ran farther?

   First, decide which strategy to use.

   Then, compare the fractions.

   Finally, find the greater fraction.

   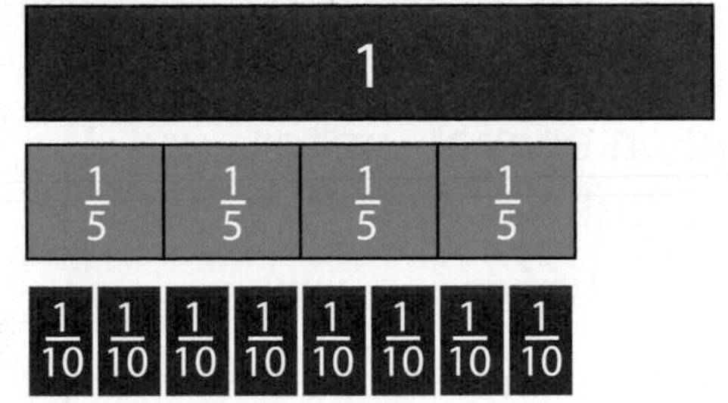

   $\frac{4}{5} \bullet \frac{8}{10}$

Choose a STRATEGY

- Draw a Diagram or Picture
- Make a Model or Act It Out
- Make an Organized List
- Find a Pattern
- Make a Table or Graph
- Predict and Test
- Work Backward
- Solve a Simpler Problem
- Write an Equation
- Use Logical Reasoning

2. **What if** Cara decided to run on the track, too, and she ran $\frac{9}{10}$ of a mile? Who would have run the farthest?

3. Lewis made a wax candle at the carnival. He made $\frac{2}{8}$ of it blue, $\frac{1}{2}$ of it green, and $\frac{1}{4}$ of it yellow. Which color did he use the most?

Mixed Strategy Practice

USE DATA For 4–5, use the table.

4. For the Frisbee toss, players get 12 chances to toss Frisbees through a tire. Who threw the most Frisbees through the tire?

5. Who threw the fewest Frisbees through the tire? Write the fraction for that person in words.

Frisbee® Toss

Name of Player	Fraction Thrown Through Tire
Lisa	$\frac{4}{12}$
Suri	$\frac{5}{6}$
Patrick	$\frac{3}{4}$

6. Malia, Andy, and Jenna are in line for popcorn. Jenna is not first. Malia is last. In what position in line is Andy?

7. Joe and Mark did the balloon toss. Joe caught the balloon 3 more times than Mark. Together they caught the balloon 29 times. How many times did Mark catch the balloon?

8. **WRITE Math** Each team ran 1 lap in a relay race. Byron ran $\frac{1}{4}$ of a lap. Each person on his team ran the same distance. How many runners were on Byron's team? **Explain.**

LESSON 6

Mixed Numbers

OBJECTIVE: Identify, read, and write mixed numbers.

Quick Review

Name the fraction for each shaded part.

1. 2. 3. 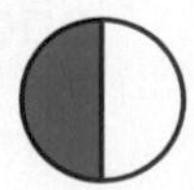

4. 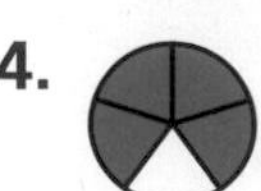 5.

Vocabulary

mixed number

Learn

PROBLEM Sarah volunteers at an animal shelter. She feeds each kitten $\frac{1}{3}$ can of food. How many cans of food will she give to 5 kittens?

Here are two ways to find the total number of cans.

ONE WAY

Make a model.

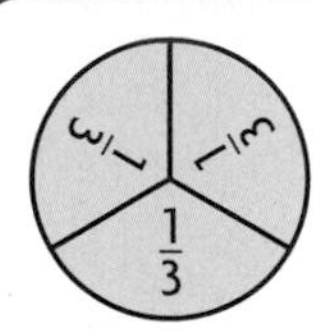

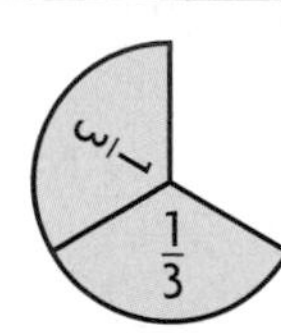

There are $\frac{5}{3}$ in all.

$\frac{3}{3} = 1$ whole

So, $\frac{5}{3} = 1 + \frac{2}{3}$, or $1\frac{2}{3}$.

ANOTHER WAY

Use a number line.

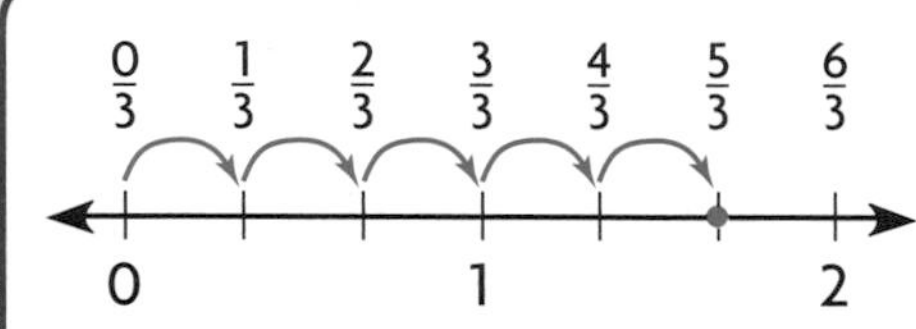

Show one jump for each $\frac{1}{3}$.

Five jumps on the number line is two thirds more than 1.

So, $\frac{5}{3} = 1 + \frac{2}{3}$, or $1\frac{2}{3}$.

So, Sarah will give 5 kittens $1\frac{2}{3}$ cans of food.

The number $1\frac{2}{3}$ is a mixed number. A **mixed number** is made up of a whole number and a fraction.

READ Math

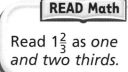

Read $1\frac{2}{3}$ as *one and two thirds.*

Guided Practice

1. Write a mixed number for the model.
Think: There are $\frac{7}{4}$ in all.

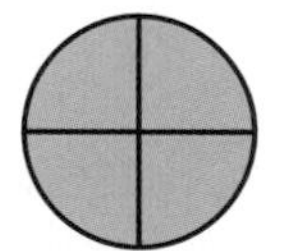 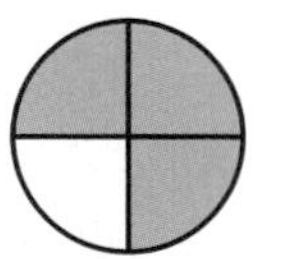

Write a mixed number for the parts that are shaded.

2. 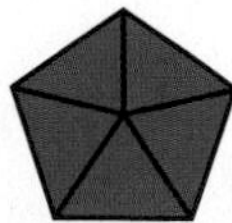 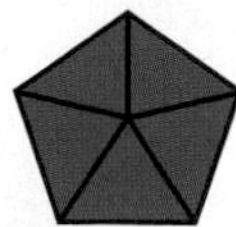 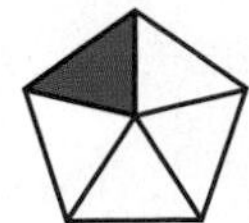

✓3. 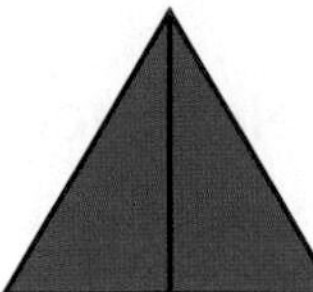 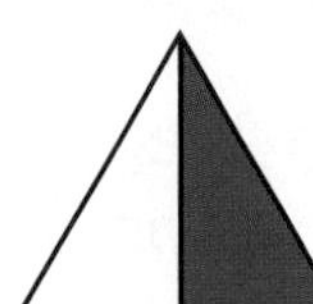

✓4. 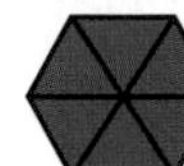 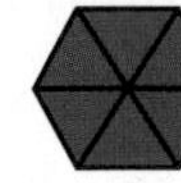 

5. **TALK Math** Is $2\frac{1}{2}$ equal to $\frac{5}{2}$? **Explain** how you know.

Independent Practice and Problem Solving

Write a mixed number for the parts that are shaded.

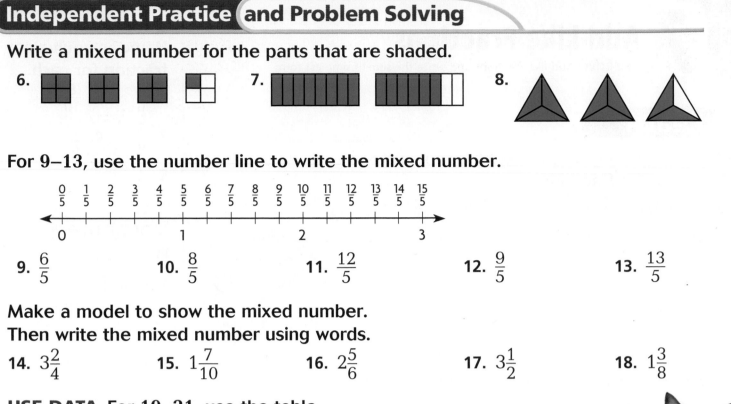

6.  

7. 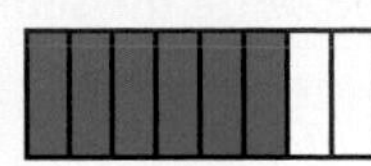

8.  

For 9–13, use the number line to write the mixed number.

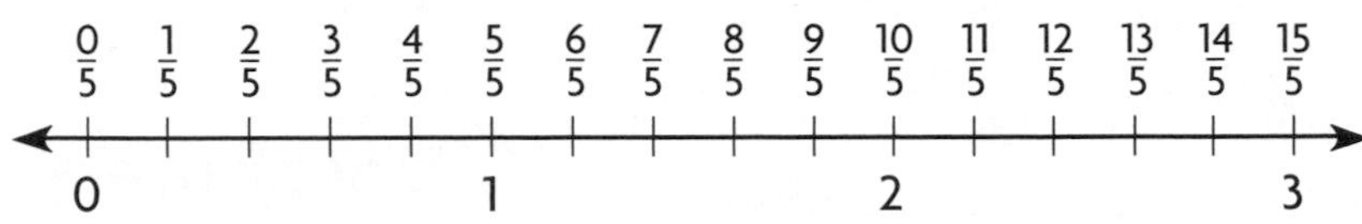

9. $\frac{6}{5}$
10. $\frac{8}{5}$
11. $\frac{12}{5}$
12. $\frac{9}{5}$
13. $\frac{13}{5}$

Make a model to show the mixed number.
Then write the mixed number using words.

14. $3\frac{2}{4}$
15. $1\frac{7}{10}$
16. $2\frac{5}{6}$
17. $3\frac{1}{2}$
18. $1\frac{3}{8}$

USE DATA For 19–21, use the table.

19. The table shows the weights of some kittens. What is Timber's weight written as a mixed number?
20. Which kitten weighs between 1 and $2\frac{1}{2}$ pounds?
21. Order the weights of the kittens from greatest to least. Write the weights as mixed numbers.

Weights of Kittens

Name	Weight
Timber	$\frac{10}{3}$ pounds
Kally	$\frac{9}{6}$ pounds
Tabby	$\frac{11}{4}$ pounds

22. **WRITE Math** Buttercup is a cat at the animal shelter. She weighs $2\frac{5}{8}$ pounds. Is her weight closer to 2 pounds or 3 pounds? **Explain** how you know.

Mixed Review and Test Prep

23. Jasmine drew a polygon that has five sides. Name the polygon she drew. (p. 356)

24. What is the difference? (p. 88)
$3,006 - 1,165 = \blacksquare$

25. **Test Prep** Ms. Adams gave $\frac{1}{4}$ of an apple to each of 10 children. How many apples did she give to the children in all?

A $1\frac{4}{10}$ **B** $1\frac{2}{4}$ **C** $2\frac{1}{4}$ **D** $2\frac{2}{4}$

Extra Practice on page 477, Set E

Add Like Fractions

OBJECTIVE: Add like fractions and write the sum in simplest form.

Quick Review

Name an equivalent fraction for each.

1. $\frac{2}{6}$
2. $\frac{8}{10}$
3. $\frac{3}{4}$
4. $\frac{1}{2}$
5. $\frac{1}{5}$

Vocabulary

like fractions

simplest form

Learn

Fractions that have the same denominator are called **like fractions**.

PROBLEM Jeb cut a pumpkin pie into 6 equal pieces. He ate 2 pieces. Claire ate 1 piece. How much of the pie did they eat altogether?

Add. $\frac{2}{6} + \frac{1}{6}$

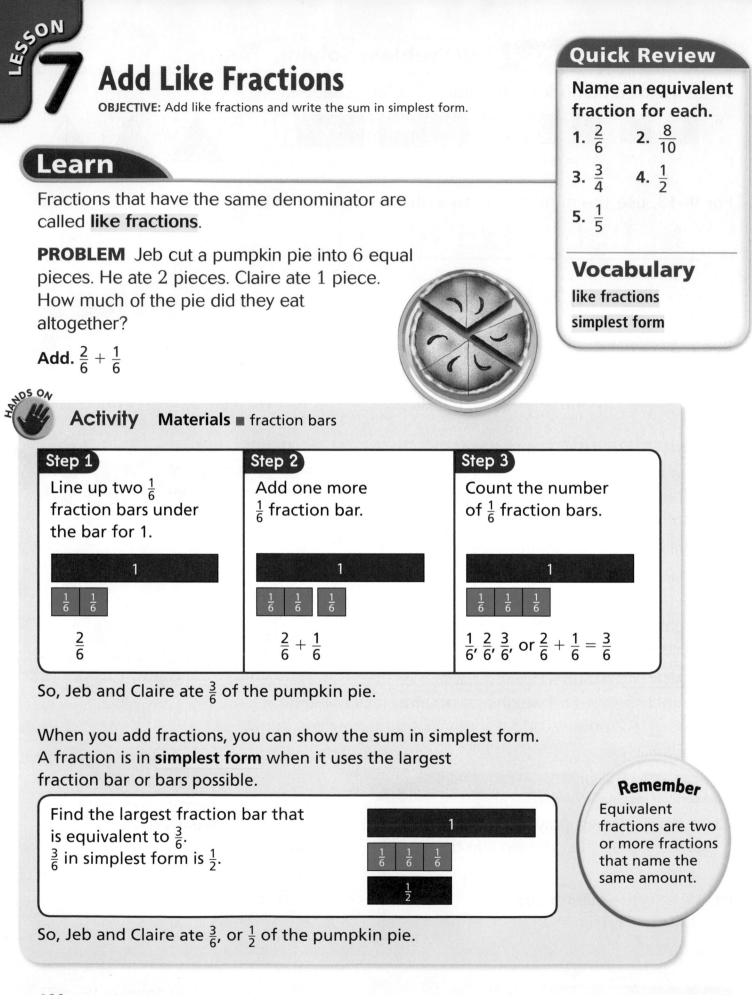

Activity

Materials ■ fraction bars

Step 1

Line up two $\frac{1}{6}$ fraction bars under the bar for 1.

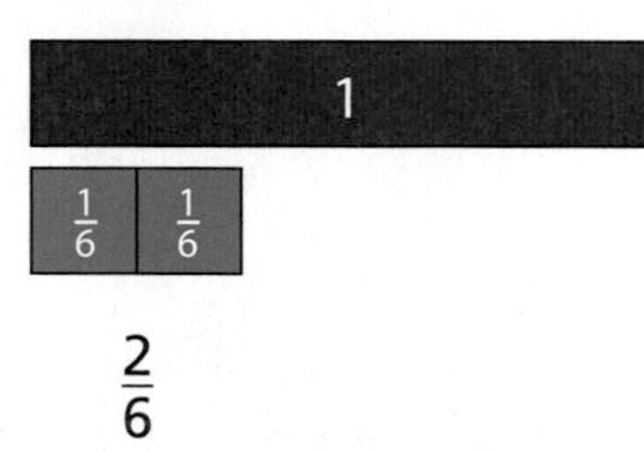

$\frac{2}{6}$

Step 2

Add one more $\frac{1}{6}$ fraction bar.

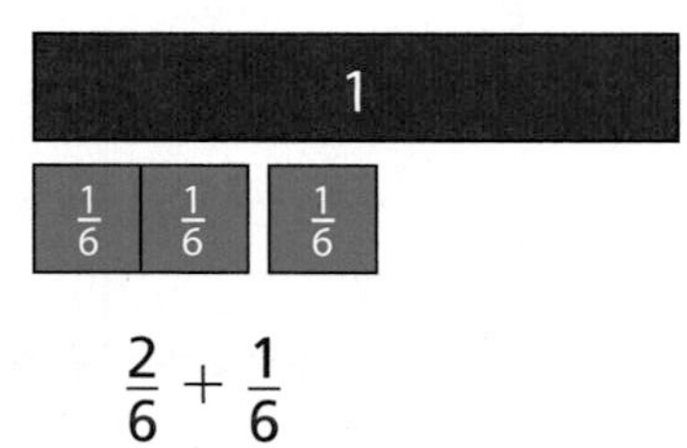

$\frac{2}{6} + \frac{1}{6}$

Step 3

Count the number of $\frac{1}{6}$ fraction bars.

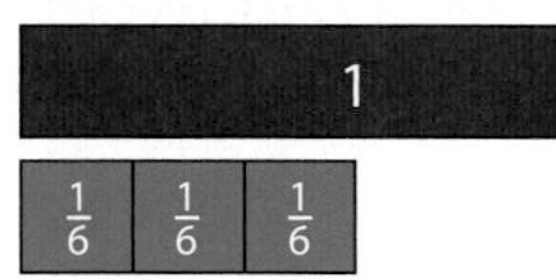

$\frac{1}{6}, \frac{2}{6}, \frac{3}{6}$, or $\frac{2}{6} + \frac{1}{6} = \frac{3}{6}$

So, Jeb and Claire ate $\frac{3}{6}$ of the pumpkin pie.

When you add fractions, you can show the sum in simplest form. A fraction is in **simplest form** when it uses the largest fraction bar or bars possible.

Find the largest fraction bar that is equivalent to $\frac{3}{6}$.
$\frac{3}{6}$ in simplest form is $\frac{1}{2}$.

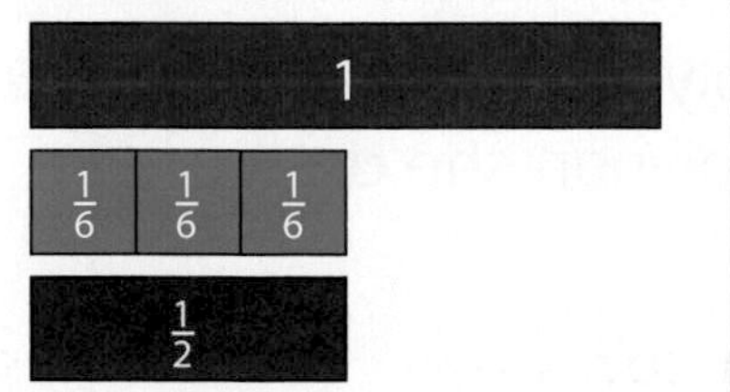

Remember

Equivalent fractions are two or more fractions that name the same amount.

So, Jeb and Claire ate $\frac{3}{6}$, or $\frac{1}{2}$ of the pumpkin pie.

Adding Numerators

You can add like fractions by adding the numerators.

Julie cut a loaf of pumpkin bread into 8 slices. She ate 2 slices, or $\frac{2}{8}$ of the loaf. Caleb ate 3 slices, or $\frac{3}{8}$ of the loaf. What fraction of the loaf did they eat in all?

Example **Add.** $\frac{2}{8} + \frac{3}{8}$

MODEL	**RECORD**
Add the number of $\frac{1}{8}$ slices that Julie and Caleb ate. 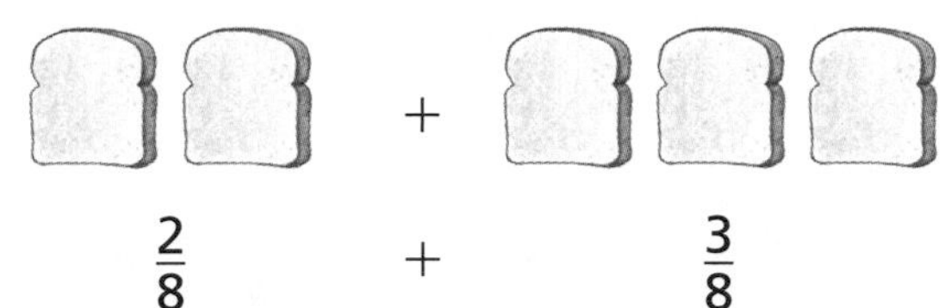 $\frac{2}{8} + \frac{3}{8}$	2 slices + 3 slices = 5 slices ↓ ↓ ↓ $\frac{2}{8} + \frac{3}{8} = \frac{5}{8}$ So, Julie and Caleb ate $\frac{5}{8}$ of the loaf.

Guided Practice

1. What is the sum of $\frac{2}{5}$ and $\frac{2}{5}$?
   Think: 2 + 2 = 4

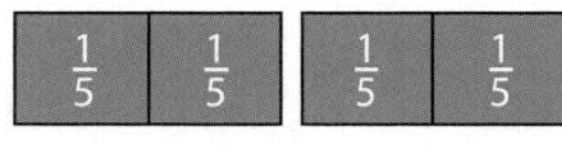

Find each sum.

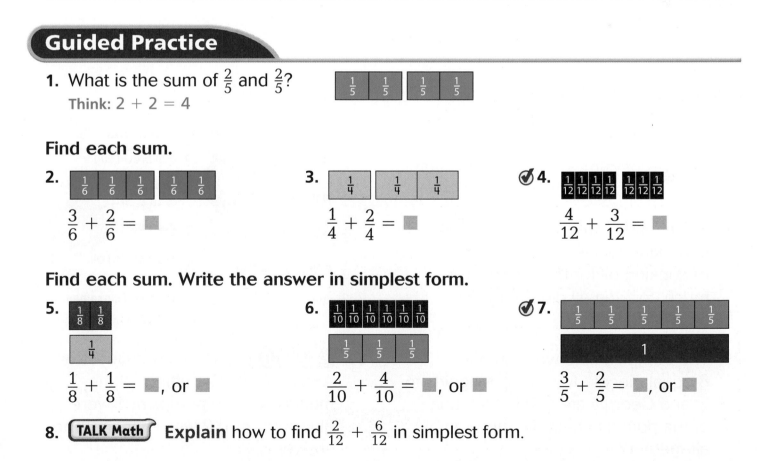

2. $\frac{1}{6}\ \frac{1}{6}\ \frac{1}{6}\ \frac{1}{6}\ \frac{1}{6}$

   $\frac{3}{6} + \frac{2}{6} = ■$

3. $\frac{1}{4}\ \frac{1}{4}\ \frac{1}{4}$

   $\frac{1}{4} + \frac{2}{4} = ■$

✓4. $\frac{1}{12}\ \frac{1}{12}\ \frac{1}{12}\ \frac{1}{12}\ \frac{1}{12}\ \frac{1}{12}\ \frac{1}{12}$

   $\frac{4}{12} + \frac{3}{12} = ■$

Find each sum. Write the answer in simplest form.

5. $\frac{1}{8}\ \frac{1}{8}$ / $\frac{1}{4}$

   $\frac{1}{8} + \frac{1}{8} = ■$, or ■

6. $\frac{1}{10}\ \frac{1}{10}\ \frac{1}{10}\ \frac{1}{10}\ \frac{1}{10}\ \frac{1}{10}$ / $\frac{1}{5}\ \frac{1}{5}\ \frac{1}{5}$

   $\frac{2}{10} + \frac{4}{10} = ■$, or ■

✓7. 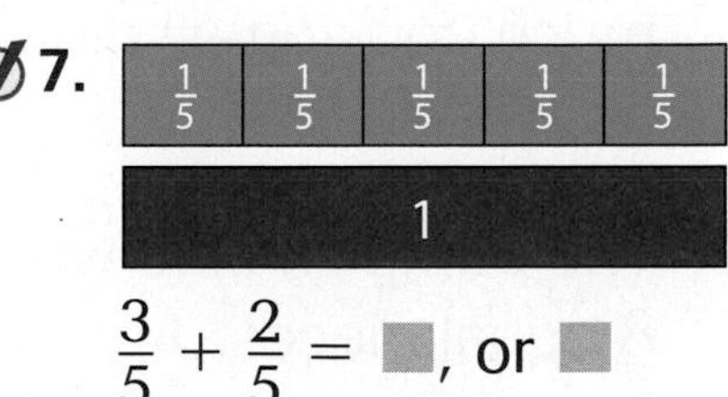

   $\frac{3}{5} + \frac{2}{5} = ■$, or ■

8. **TALK Math** **Explain** how to find $\frac{2}{12} + \frac{6}{12}$ in simplest form.

Independent Practice and Problem Solving

Find each sum.

9. 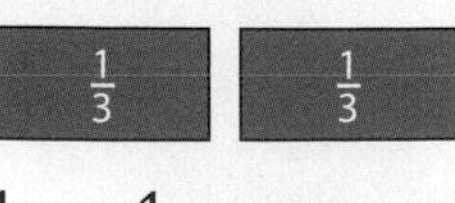

$\frac{1}{3} + \frac{1}{3} =$ ■

10. 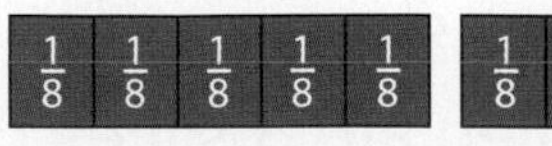

$\frac{5}{8} + \frac{2}{8} =$ ■

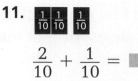

11. $\frac{1}{10}$ $\frac{1}{10}$ $\frac{1}{10}$

$\frac{2}{10} + \frac{1}{10} =$ ■

Find each sum. Write the answer in simplest form.

12. 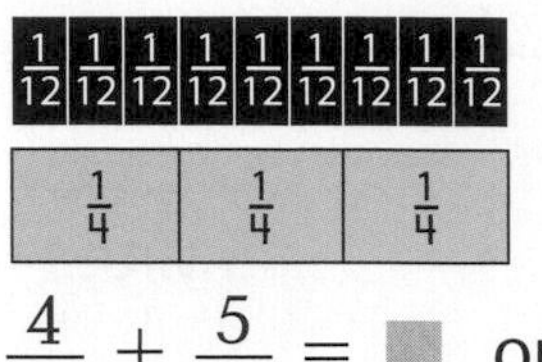

$\frac{4}{12} + \frac{5}{12} =$ ■, or ■

13. 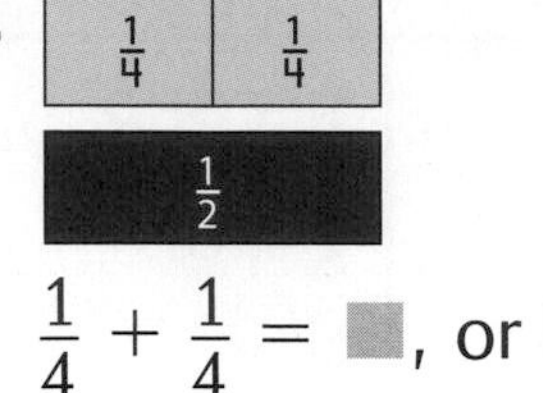

$\frac{1}{4} + \frac{1}{4} =$ ■, or ■

14. 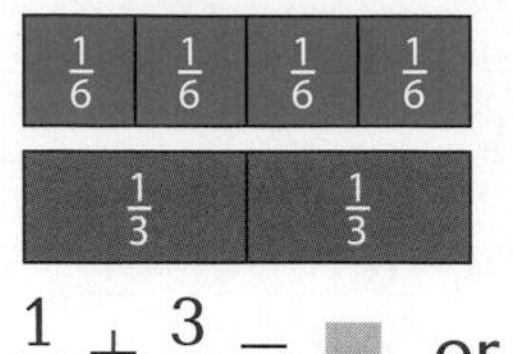

$\frac{1}{6} + \frac{3}{6} =$ ■, or ■

Find each sum.

15. $\frac{1}{5} + \frac{1}{5} =$ ■ **16.** $\frac{2}{10} + \frac{3}{10} =$ ■ **17.** $\frac{1}{3} + \frac{2}{3} =$ ■ **18.** $\frac{6}{12} + \frac{4}{12} =$ ■

19. $\frac{4}{6} + \frac{1}{6} =$ ■ **20.** $\frac{1}{4} + \frac{3}{4} =$ ■ **21.** $\frac{2}{8} + \frac{4}{8} =$ ■ **22.** $\frac{5}{10} + \frac{2}{10} =$ ■

23. $\frac{2}{10} + \frac{2}{10} =$ ■ **24.** $\frac{1}{5} + \frac{2}{5} =$ ■ **25.** $\frac{3}{12} + \frac{8}{12} =$ ■ **26.** $\frac{2}{8} + \frac{1}{8} =$ ■

USE DATA For 27–28, use the list of ingredients.

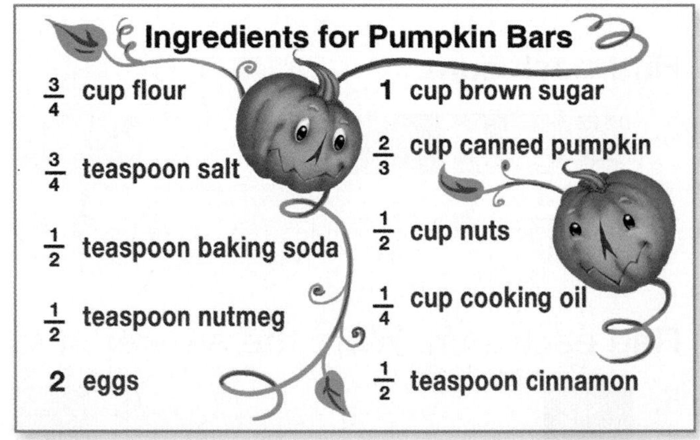

Ingredients for Pumpkin Bars
$\frac{3}{4}$ cup flour
$\frac{3}{4}$ teaspoon salt
$\frac{1}{2}$ teaspoon baking soda
$\frac{1}{2}$ teaspoon nutmeg
2 eggs
1 cup brown sugar
$\frac{2}{3}$ cup canned pumpkin
$\frac{1}{2}$ cup nuts
$\frac{1}{4}$ cup cooking oil
$\frac{1}{2}$ teaspoon cinnamon

27. The ingredients list is for one batch of pumpkin bars. Amy made two batches of pumpkin bars. How much cinnamon did she use altogether?

28. Steve made pumpkin bars and pumpkin muffins. He used $\frac{1}{4}$ cup of cooking oil for the muffins. How much cooking oil did he use for both recipes?

29. The pumpkin bars were cut into 8 equal pieces. Jodi ate $\frac{3}{8}$, Maggie ate $\frac{1}{8}$, and Georgia ate $\frac{2}{8}$. What fraction of the pumpkin bars did they eat altogether?

30. **WRITE Math** **What's the Question?** Anna baked 12 muffins. Of the muffins, 6 were pumpkin, 4 were blueberry, and 2 were banana. The answer is $\frac{10}{12}$.

 Extra Practice on page 477, Set F

Learn About Finding Sums

Find each sum. Write the answer in simplest form.

E	$\frac{1}{6} + \frac{3}{6}$	**H**	$\frac{1}{5} + \frac{1}{5}$	**L**	$\frac{1}{8} + \frac{3}{8}$	**A**	$\frac{2}{10} + \frac{1}{10}$
S	$\frac{2}{4} + \frac{1}{4}$	**T**	$\frac{3}{8} + \frac{2}{8}$	**P**	$\frac{3}{5} + \frac{1}{5}$	**E**	$\frac{5}{8} + \frac{2}{8}$
A	$\frac{4}{10} + \frac{5}{10}$	**N**	$\frac{6}{12} + \frac{4}{12}$	**O**	$\frac{1}{6} + \frac{1}{6}$	**F**	$\frac{4}{12} + \frac{4}{12}$

To answer the riddle, match the answers from above to the fractions below.

What kind of phone does a turtle use?

?		?	?	?	?	?		?	?	?	?	?!
$\frac{9}{10}$		$\frac{3}{4}$	$\frac{2}{5}$	$\frac{7}{8}$	$\frac{1}{2}$	$\frac{1}{2}$		$\frac{4}{5}$	$\frac{2}{5}$	$\frac{1}{3}$	$\frac{5}{6}$	$\frac{7}{8}$

Mixed Review and Test Prep

31. Ernie and Lupe rode along a bike trail. Ernie rode his bike $\frac{4}{5}$ of a mile. Lupe rode her bike $\frac{9}{10}$ of a mile. Who rode farther? (p. 458)

32. Test Prep Mandy is working on a crossword puzzle. Yesterday she filled in $\frac{3}{6}$ of the puzzle. Today she filled in $\frac{1}{6}$ of the puzzle. What fraction of the puzzle has Mandy filled in altogether?

A $\frac{2}{6}$ **C** $\frac{2}{12}$

B $\frac{4}{6}$ **D** $\frac{4}{12}$

33. Megan can choose to wear a blue shirt, a red shirt, or a yellow shirt. She can wear black pants, blue pants, or brown pants. How many different outfits can Megan choose to wear? (p. 186)

34. Test Prep Reilly made a necklace and a bracelet. She used $\frac{6}{10}$ meter of string for the necklace and $\frac{2}{10}$ meter of string for the bracelet. How much string did she use in all? Write the fraction in simplest form.

LESSON 8 Subtract Like Fractions

OBJECTIVE: Subtract like fractions and write the difference in simplest form.

Quick Review

Find each sum. Write the answer in simplest form.

1. $\frac{1}{4} + \frac{1}{4}$

2. $\frac{2}{6} + \frac{3}{6}$

3. $\frac{3}{10} + \frac{5}{10}$

4. $\frac{6}{12} + \frac{1}{12}$

5. $\frac{3}{8} + \frac{3}{8}$

Learn

You can use fraction bars to subtract like fractions.

Subtract. $\frac{8}{10} - \frac{5}{10}$

HANDS ON

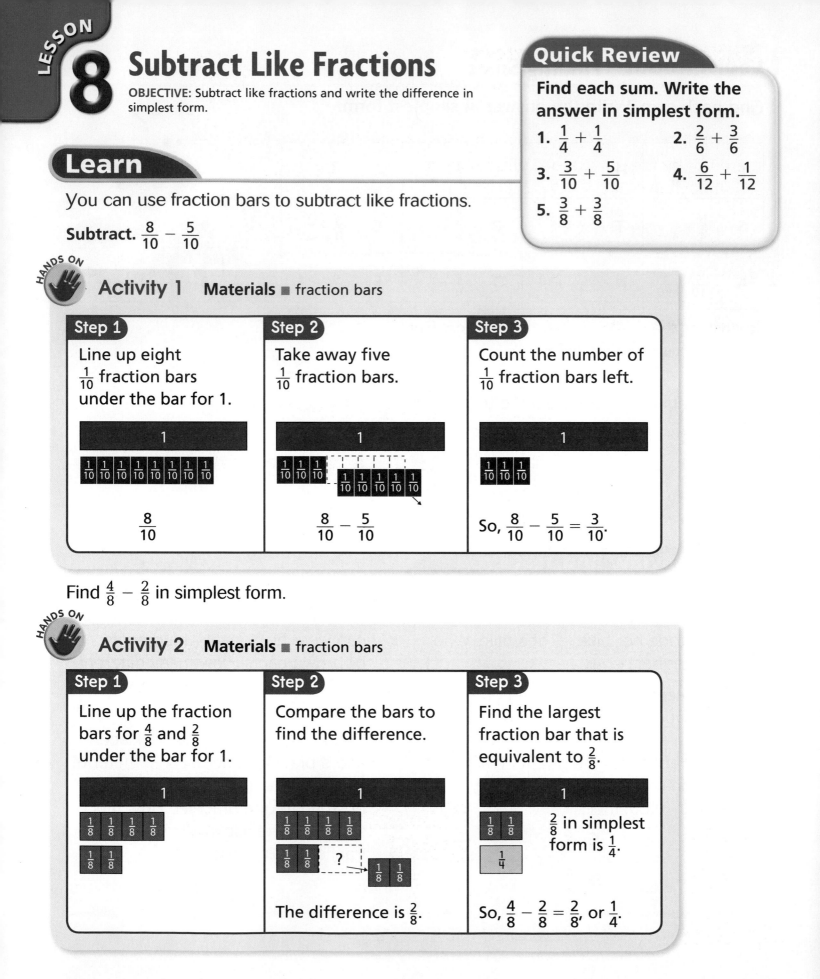

Activity 1 **Materials** ■ fraction bars

Step 1

Line up eight $\frac{1}{10}$ fraction bars under the bar for 1.

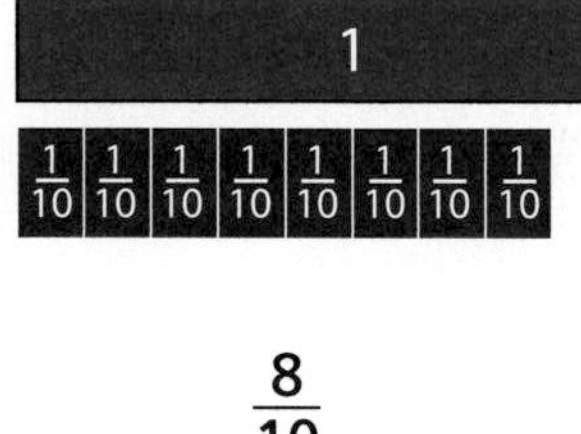

$\frac{8}{10}$

Step 2

Take away five $\frac{1}{10}$ fraction bars.

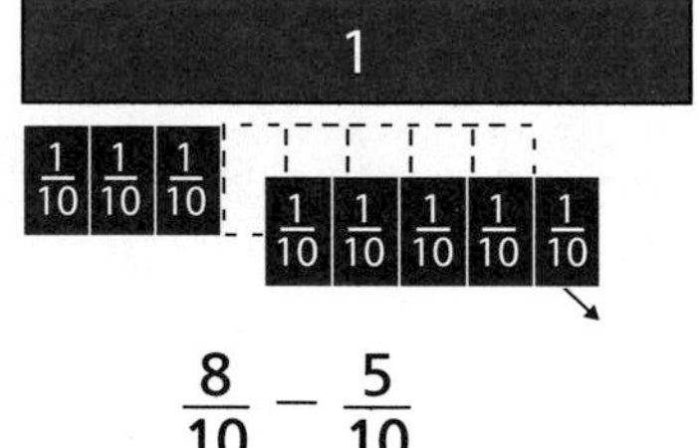

$\frac{8}{10} - \frac{5}{10}$

Step 3

Count the number of $\frac{1}{10}$ fraction bars left.

So, $\frac{8}{10} - \frac{5}{10} = \frac{3}{10}$.

Find $\frac{4}{8} - \frac{2}{8}$ in simplest form.

HANDS ON

Activity 2 **Materials** ■ fraction bars

Step 1

Line up the fraction bars for $\frac{4}{8}$ and $\frac{2}{8}$ under the bar for 1.

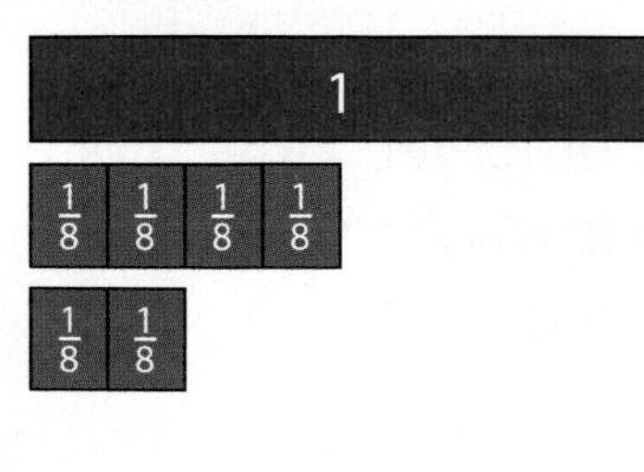

Step 2

Compare the bars to find the difference.

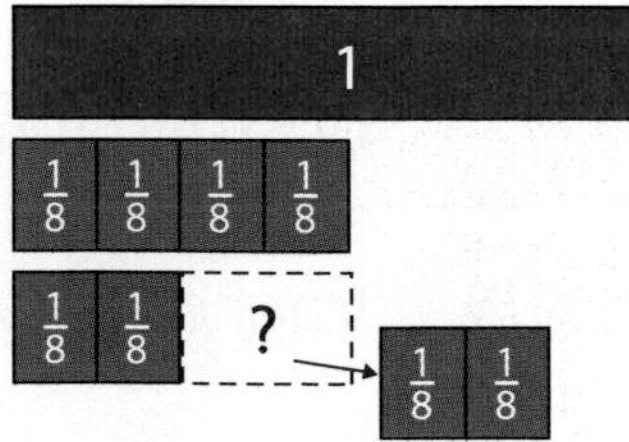

The difference is $\frac{2}{8}$.

Step 3

Find the largest fraction bar that is equivalent to $\frac{2}{8}$.

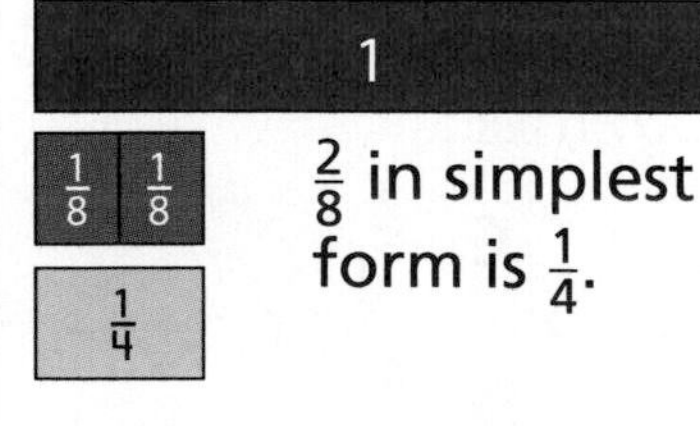

$\frac{2}{8}$ in simplest form is $\frac{1}{4}$.

So, $\frac{4}{8} - \frac{2}{8} = \frac{2}{8}$, or $\frac{1}{4}$.

Subtracting Numerators

You can subtract like fractions by subtracting the numerators.

Molly had $\frac{7}{12}$ of a sub sandwich left to share with her friends. Her friends ate $\frac{6}{12}$ of the sandwich. What fraction of the sandwich is left?

Example **Subtract.** $\frac{7}{12} - \frac{6}{12}$

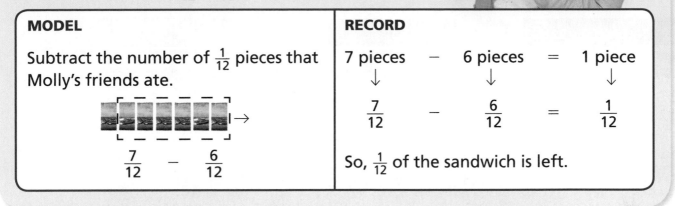

MODEL	RECORD
Subtract the number of $\frac{1}{12}$ pieces that Molly's friends ate. $\frac{7}{12} - \frac{6}{12}$	7 pieces − 6 pieces = 1 piece ↓ ↓ ↓ $\frac{7}{12} - \frac{6}{12} = \frac{1}{12}$ So, $\frac{1}{12}$ of the sandwich is left.

Guided Practice

1. What is the difference? $\frac{4}{5} - \frac{2}{5} = \blacksquare$

   Think: 4 − 2 = 2

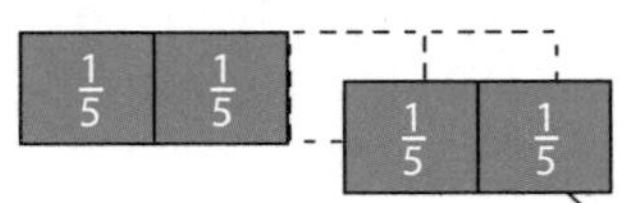

Find each difference.

2. $\frac{7}{8} - \frac{4}{8} = \blacksquare$

3. $\frac{4}{4} - \frac{1}{4} = \blacksquare$

✓4. 

$\frac{9}{12} - \frac{2}{12} = \blacksquare$

Compare. Find each difference. Write the answer in simplest form.

5. 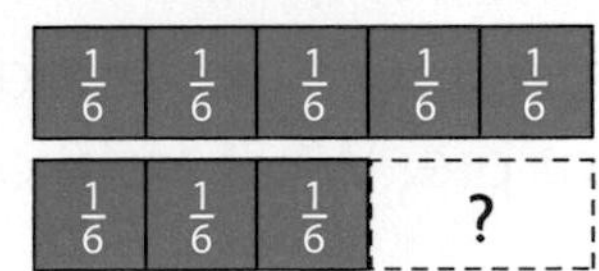

$\frac{5}{6} - \frac{3}{6} = \blacksquare$

6. $\frac{9}{10} - \frac{5}{10} = \blacksquare$

✓7. 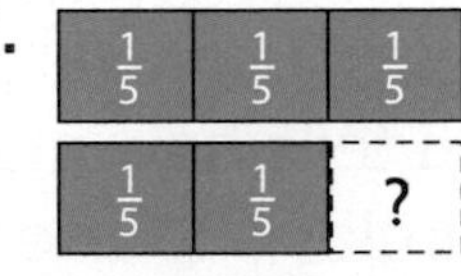

$\frac{3}{5} - \frac{2}{5} = \blacksquare$

8. **TALK Math** Explain how to use fraction bars to find $\frac{6}{8} - \frac{2}{8}$.

Independent Practice and Problem Solving

Find each difference.

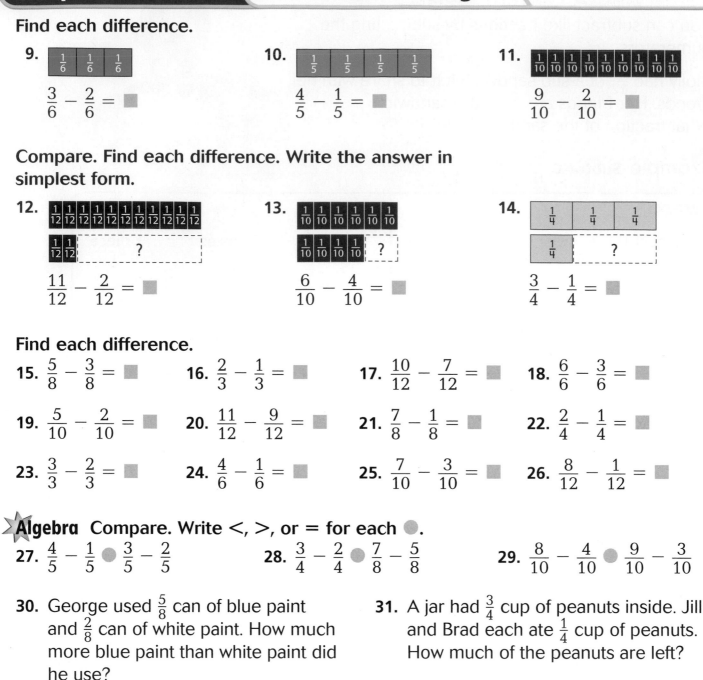

9. 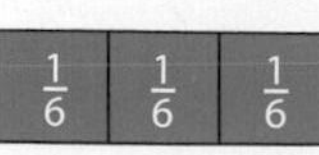

$\frac{3}{6} - \frac{2}{6} = \blacksquare$

10. 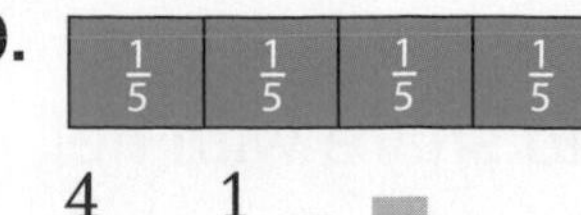

$\frac{4}{5} - \frac{1}{5} = \blacksquare$

11. $\frac{9}{10} - \frac{2}{10} = \blacksquare$

Compare. Find each difference. Write the answer in simplest form.

12. 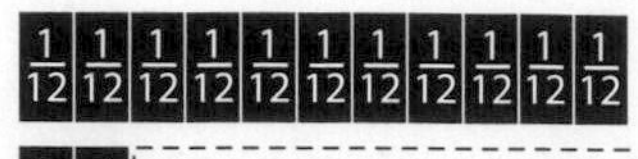

$\frac{11}{12} - \frac{2}{12} = \blacksquare$

13. 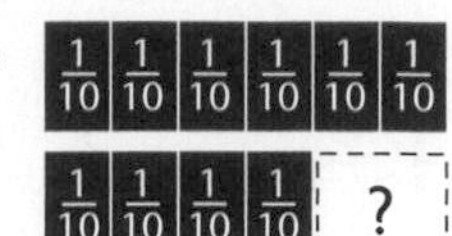

$\frac{6}{10} - \frac{4}{10} = \blacksquare$

14. 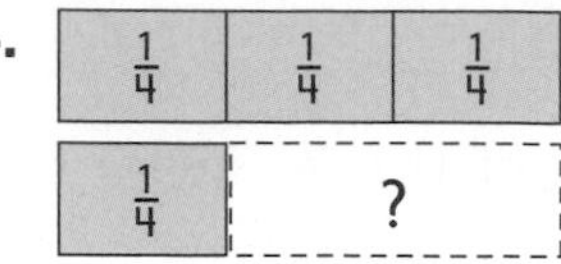

$\frac{3}{4} - \frac{1}{4} = \blacksquare$

Find each difference.

15. $\frac{5}{8} - \frac{3}{8} = \blacksquare$ **16.** $\frac{2}{3} - \frac{1}{3} = \blacksquare$ **17.** $\frac{10}{12} - \frac{7}{12} = \blacksquare$ **18.** $\frac{6}{6} - \frac{3}{6} = \blacksquare$

19. $\frac{5}{10} - \frac{2}{10} = \blacksquare$ **20.** $\frac{11}{12} - \frac{9}{12} = \blacksquare$ **21.** $\frac{7}{8} - \frac{1}{8} = \blacksquare$ **22.** $\frac{2}{4} - \frac{1}{4} = \blacksquare$

23. $\frac{3}{3} - \frac{2}{3} = \blacksquare$ **24.** $\frac{4}{6} - \frac{1}{6} = \blacksquare$ **25.** $\frac{7}{10} - \frac{3}{10} = \blacksquare$ **26.** $\frac{8}{12} - \frac{1}{12} = \blacksquare$

Algebra Compare. Write <, >, or = for each ●.

27. $\frac{4}{5} - \frac{1}{5}$ ● $\frac{3}{5} - \frac{2}{5}$ **28.** $\frac{3}{4} - \frac{2}{4}$ ● $\frac{7}{8} - \frac{5}{8}$ **29.** $\frac{8}{10} - \frac{4}{10}$ ● $\frac{9}{10} - \frac{3}{10}$

30. George used $\frac{5}{8}$ can of blue paint and $\frac{2}{8}$ can of white paint. How much more blue paint than white paint did he use?

31. A jar had $\frac{3}{4}$ cup of peanuts inside. Jill and Brad each ate $\frac{1}{4}$ cup of peanuts. How much of the peanuts are left?

32. Michelle made a pattern by using shapes. Of the shapes, $\frac{9}{12}$ were squares and $\frac{3}{12}$ were circles. What fraction tells how many more squares than circles she used?

33. Jacob cut a pie into 8 equal slices. He shared the pie with 5 of his friends. Jacob and each of his friends each ate 1 piece of pie. What fraction of the pie is left?

34. WRITE Math In a bag of 9 balloons, $\frac{5}{9}$ are blue and $\frac{1}{9}$ are red. The rest of the balloons are green. What fraction of the balloons are green? **Explain.**

 Extra Practice on page 477, Set G

Learn About Visual Thinking

You can use a number line to subtract like fractions.

Example

It is $\frac{9}{10}$ mile from the school to the library. It is $\frac{5}{10}$ mile from the museum to the library. How far is it from the school to the museum?

$\frac{9}{10} - \frac{5}{10} = \blacksquare$

school — museum — library

$\frac{0}{10}$ $\frac{1}{10}$ $\frac{2}{10}$ $\frac{3}{10}$ $\frac{4}{10}$ $\frac{5}{10}$ $\frac{6}{10}$ $\frac{7}{10}$ $\frac{8}{10}$ $\frac{9}{10}$ $\frac{10}{10}$

0 $\frac{1}{2}$ 1

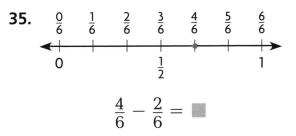

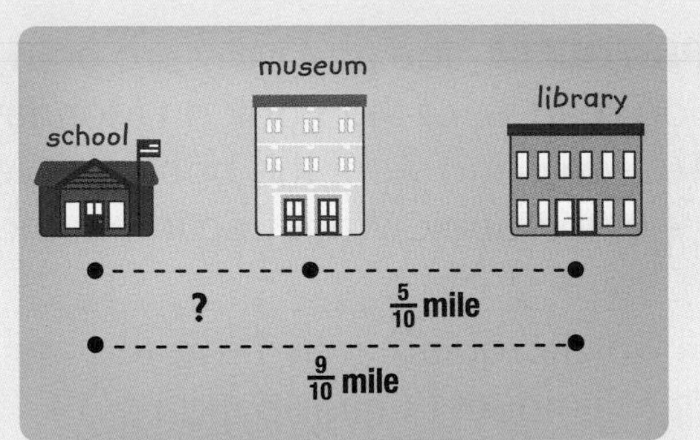

So, it is $\frac{4}{10}$ mile from the school to the museum.

Try It

Use a number line to find each difference.

35. $\frac{0}{6}$ $\frac{1}{6}$ $\frac{2}{6}$ $\frac{3}{6}$ $\frac{4}{6}$ $\frac{5}{6}$ $\frac{6}{6}$

0 $\frac{1}{2}$ 1

$\frac{4}{6} - \frac{2}{6} = \blacksquare$

36.

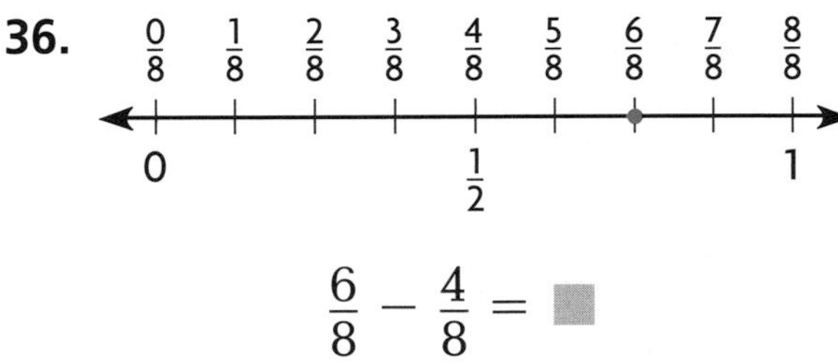

$\frac{6}{8} - \frac{4}{8} = \blacksquare$

Mixed Review and Test Prep

37. Write a rule for the pattern and find the next number. (p. 426)

5, 11, 17, 23, 29, 35, ■

38. Test Prep Kelly has $\frac{8}{8}$ yard of fabric. She uses $\frac{6}{8}$ yard to make a pillow. How much of the yard of fabric is left?

A $\frac{1}{4}$ **B** $\frac{3}{8}$ **C** $\frac{1}{2}$ **D** $\frac{3}{4}$

39. Tia collected 21 stamps. She divided the stamps into 3 groups. How many stamps were in each group? (p. 304)

40. Test Prep A log is $\frac{8}{10}$ meter long. Troy cuts off a piece that is $\frac{3}{10}$ meter long. What is the length of the log now? **Explain** how you know.

Problem Solving Workshop Skill: Too Much/Too Little Information

Read to Understand
Plan
Solve
Check

OBJECTIVE: Solve problems by using the skill *too much/too little information.*

Use the Skill

PROBLEM Joe and Milly are both reading a 100-page book. Joe read $\frac{1}{10}$ of the book on Monday, $\frac{3}{10}$ of the book on Tuesday, and $\frac{2}{10}$ of the book on Wednesday. Milly has read $\frac{7}{10}$ of the book. What fraction of the book has Joe read?

A word problem may have too much, too little, or the right amount of information.

Step 1	Step 2	Step 3
What do you need to find? the fraction of the book that Joe has read	**List the information you need.** Joe read $\frac{1}{10}$ of the book on Monday, $\frac{3}{10}$ on Tuesday, and $\frac{2}{10}$ on Wednesday.	**Is there information you do not need?** The book has 100 pages. Milly has read $\frac{7}{10}$ of the book.

Step 4

Solve the problem.
Add the amounts that Joe has read.

$\frac{1}{10} + \frac{3}{10} + \frac{2}{10} = \frac{6}{10}$ So, Joe has read $\frac{6}{10}$ of the book.

Think and Discuss

Tell whether there is too much or too little information. Solve if there is enough information.

a. Mrs. Charles cut a pie into equal-size pieces. She gave 6 pieces to Mike and his friends. What fraction of the pie is left?

b. In a relay race, Tom ran $\frac{1}{4}$ mile, Lori ran $\frac{3}{4}$ mile, and Raul ran $\frac{2}{4}$ mile. How far did Tom and Lori run altogether?

c. Isaiah bought 8 toy cars and 6 books. He gave 3 toy cars to his brother. What fraction of the toy cars did Isaiah keep?

Guided Problem Solving

Solve.

1. Mary used red, green, and blue ribbons to decorate a card. She used $\frac{5}{12}$ foot of red ribbon and $\frac{3}{12}$ foot of blue ribbon. How much ribbon did she use altogether?
   - **a.** What do you need to find?
   - **b.** What information do you need to solve the problem?
   - **c.** Is there too much information? If so, what?
   - **d.** Is there too little information? If so, what?
   - **e.** Can you solve the problem? Explain.
2. **What if** Mary used $\frac{2}{12}$ foot of green ribbon? How much ribbon did she use altogether?
3. There are 8 books on a shelf. Three of the books are short stories, some are coloring books, and the rest are sports books. What fraction of the books are NOT short stories?

Mixed Applications

4. Some children ate $\frac{4}{12}$ of a veggie pizza, $\frac{9}{12}$ of a pepperoni pizza, and $\frac{11}{12}$ of a cheese pizza. All 3 pizzas were the same size. What fraction tells how much more cheese pizza than veggie pizza the children ate?
5. ***FAST FACT*** The longest suspension bridge in the United States is in New York. Drivers pay $9 to cross in a car and $4 to cross on a motorcycle. What is the total cost for 5 cars and 2 motorcycles?
6. Betty has $25.00. She buys a book for $5.25 and a calendar for $6.50. How much money does she have now?
7. Matt has 129 books and Karly has 153 books. About how many books do they have altogether?
8. A box is filled with 5 books. Each book is 8 inches long and 6 inches wide. What is the perimeter of one book?
9. **WRITE Math** Lee read his book for 80 minutes on Saturday. How many hours and minutes is that? **Explain** how you know.
10. Mrs. Totten has 48 pencils. She keeps 12 pencils and divides the rest equally among 9 students. How many pencils does each student get?

Extra Practice

Set A Write a fraction in numbers and in words to name the shaded part. (pp. 446–449)

1. 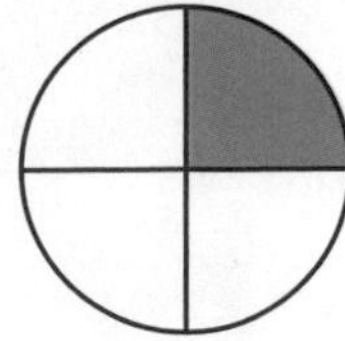

2. 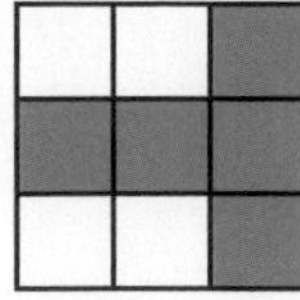

3. 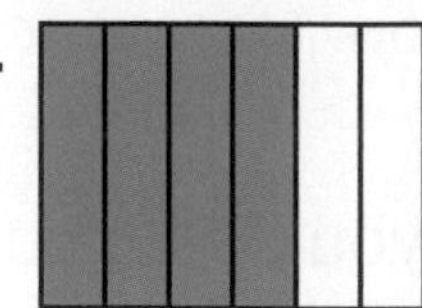

Use fraction circle pieces to make a model of each. Then write the fraction by using numbers.

4. seven eighths
5. one divided by two
6. three out of five

Set B Write a fraction that names the red part of each group. (pp. 450–453)

1. 

2. 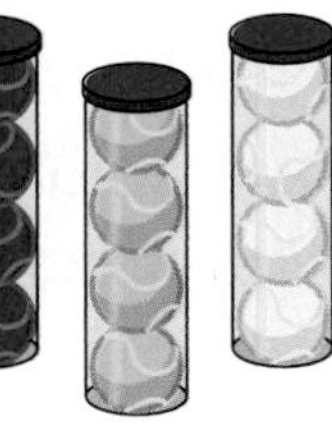

Set C Find an equivalent fraction. Use fraction bars. (pp. 454–457)

1. 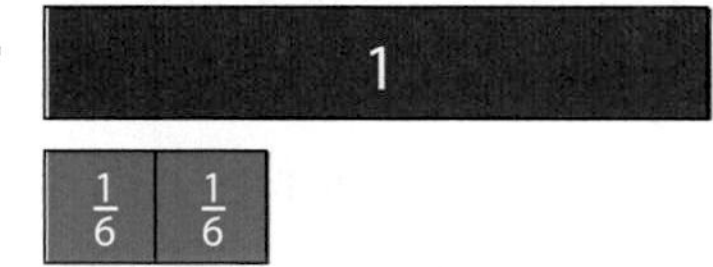

2. 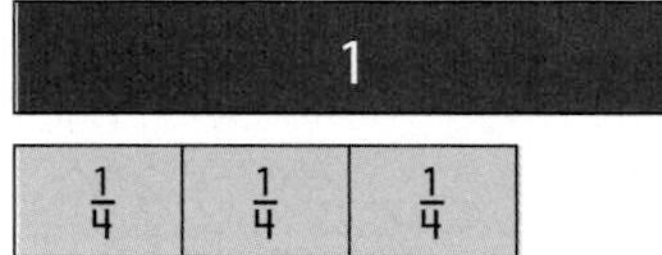

3. 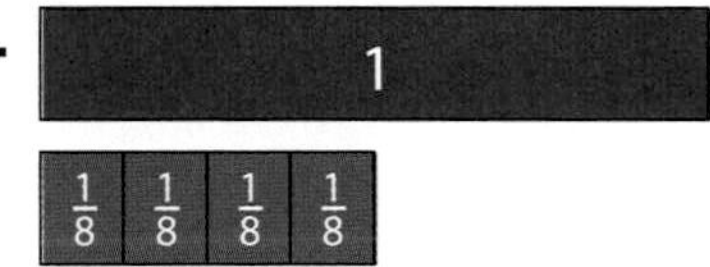

Set D Compare. Write <, >, or = for each ●. (pp. 458–461)

1. 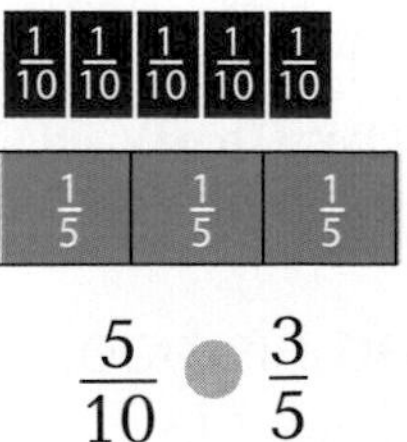

$\frac{5}{10}$ ● $\frac{3}{5}$

2. 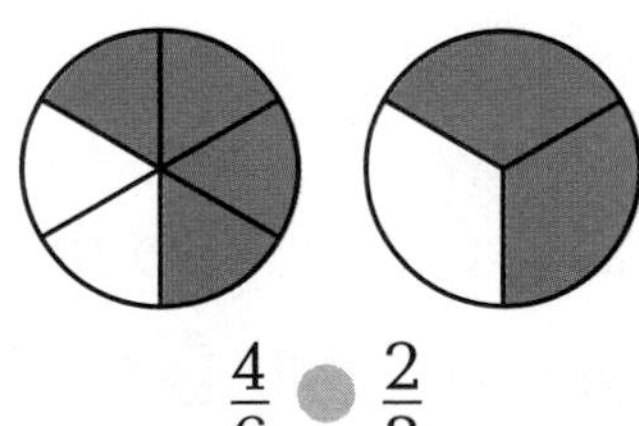

$\frac{4}{6}$ ● $\frac{2}{3}$

3. 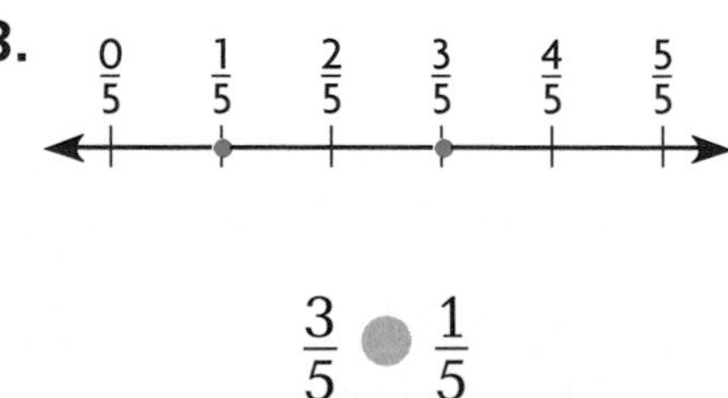

$\frac{3}{5}$ ● $\frac{1}{5}$

4. I am greater than $\frac{1}{2}$ and less than $\frac{3}{4}$. My denominator is 3. What fraction am I?

5. I am greater than $\frac{1}{3}$ and less than $\frac{3}{5}$. My denominator is 4. What fraction am I?

Technology
Use Harcourt Mega Math, Fraction Action, *Fraction Flare Up*, Levels B, C, D, E, F, G, H.

Set E Write a mixed number for the parts that are shaded. (pp. 464–465)

1.

2.

3. 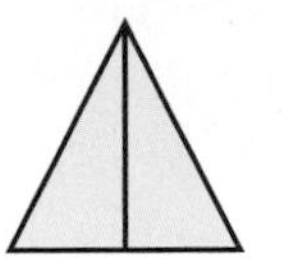 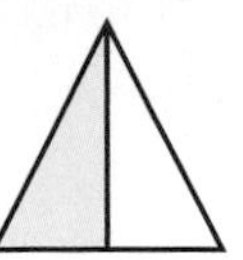

4. 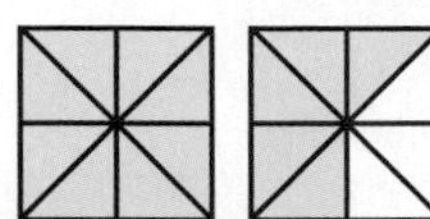

5. 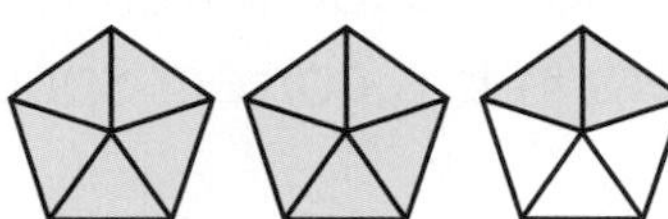

6. 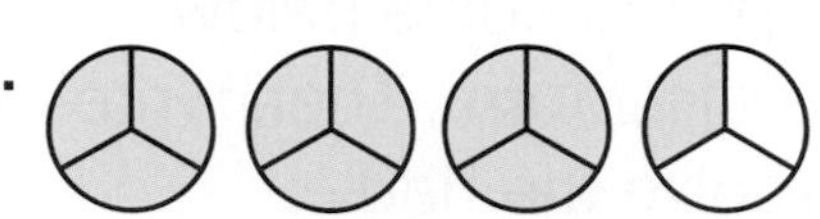

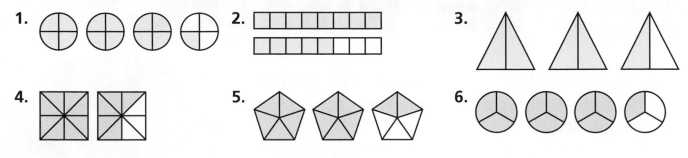

Set F Find each sum. Write the answer in simplest form. (pp. 466–469)

1. 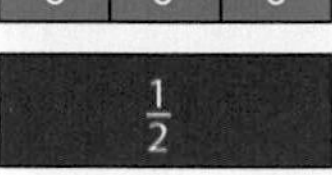

$\frac{2}{6} + \frac{1}{6} = \blacksquare$, or $\blacksquare$

2. 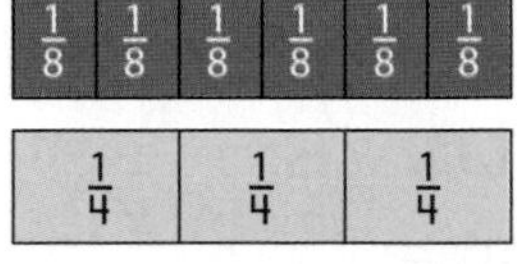

$\frac{3}{8} + \frac{3}{8} = \blacksquare$, or $\blacksquare$

3. 

$\frac{6}{10} + \frac{2}{10} = \blacksquare$, or $\blacksquare$

4. $\frac{1}{3} + \frac{1}{3} = \blacksquare$

5. $\frac{3}{12} + \frac{4}{12} = \blacksquare$

6. $\frac{2}{6} + \frac{2}{6} = \blacksquare$

7. $\frac{1}{4} + \frac{2}{4} = \blacksquare$

8. Bonnie ordered a pizza that was $\frac{1}{4}$ sausage, $\frac{1}{4}$ cheese, $\frac{1}{4}$ pepperoni, and $\frac{1}{4}$ mushroom. What fraction of the pizza had sausage or mushroom?

9. A submarine sandwich was cut into 12 equal pieces. Peter ate $\frac{3}{12}$, Taj ate $\frac{2}{12}$, and Marissa ate $\frac{5}{12}$. What fraction of the sandwich did they eat altogether?

Set G Compare. Find each difference. Write the answer in simplest form. (pp. 470–473)

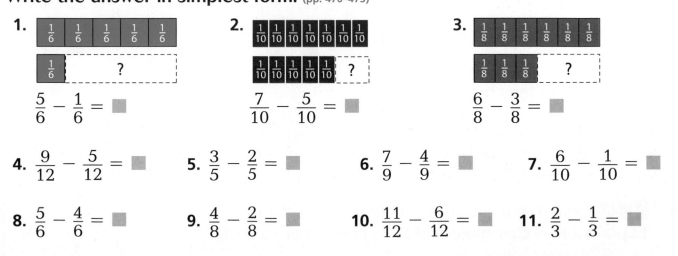

1. $\frac{5}{6} - \frac{1}{6} = \blacksquare$

2. $\frac{7}{10} - \frac{5}{10} = \blacksquare$

3. 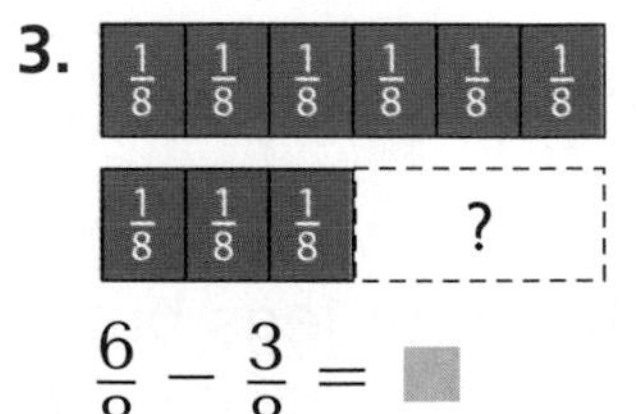

$\frac{6}{8} - \frac{3}{8} = \blacksquare$

4. $\frac{9}{12} - \frac{5}{12} = \blacksquare$

5. $\frac{3}{5} - \frac{2}{5} = \blacksquare$

6. $\frac{7}{9} - \frac{4}{9} = \blacksquare$

7. $\frac{6}{10} - \frac{1}{10} = \blacksquare$

8. $\frac{5}{6} - \frac{4}{6} = \blacksquare$

9. $\frac{4}{8} - \frac{2}{8} = \blacksquare$

10. $\frac{11}{12} - \frac{6}{12} = \blacksquare$

11. $\frac{2}{3} - \frac{1}{3} = \blacksquare$

MATH POWER Fraction Riddles

The Riddler

Copy the riddle below. Find the value of each letter in simplest form. Then write the letters in the correct spaces to solve the riddle.

Which weighs more, a pound of rocks or a pound of feathers? Neither, they both weigh one pound.

Example

$\frac{7}{12} - \frac{5}{12}$ **A**

Step 1 Add or subtract the numerators. $\frac{7}{12} - \frac{5}{12} = \frac{2}{12}$
The denominator stays the same.

Step 2 Simplify the answer. $\frac{2}{12} = \frac{1}{6}$

Step 3 Place the letter in the riddle.
Put the letter A on each line that is above $\frac{1}{6}$.

Try It

Add or subtract to answer the riddle.

1. $\frac{1}{5} + \frac{2}{5} = \blacksquare$ **R**
2. $\frac{7}{10} - \frac{3}{10} = \blacksquare$ **N**
3. $\frac{3}{6} - \frac{1}{6} = \blacksquare$ **O**
4. $\frac{4}{8} + \frac{2}{8} = \blacksquare$ **S**
5. $\frac{5}{9} + \frac{1}{9} = \blacksquare$ **T**
6. $\frac{3}{8} - \frac{1}{8} = \blacksquare$ **I**
7. $\frac{11}{12} - \frac{1}{12} = \blacksquare$ **F**
8. $\frac{4}{8} + \frac{1}{8} = \blacksquare$ **W**
9. $\frac{1}{4} + \frac{1}{4} = \blacksquare$ **P**

10. What has four legs but cannot walk?

$\frac{?}{\frac{2}{3}}$ $\frac{?}{\frac{5}{8}}$ $\frac{?}{\frac{1}{3}}$ $\frac{?}{\frac{1}{2}}$ $\frac{A}{\frac{1}{6}}$ $\frac{?}{\frac{1}{4}}$ $\frac{?}{\frac{3}{5}}$ $\frac{?}{\frac{3}{4}}$ $\frac{?}{\frac{1}{3}}$ $\frac{?}{\frac{5}{6}}$ $\frac{?}{\frac{1}{2}}$ $\frac{A}{\frac{1}{6}}$ $\frac{?}{\frac{2}{5}}$ $\frac{?}{\frac{2}{3}}$ $\frac{?}{\frac{3}{4}}$

11. **WRITE Math** Write your own riddle using fractions. **Explain** it to a classmate and have him or her solve it.

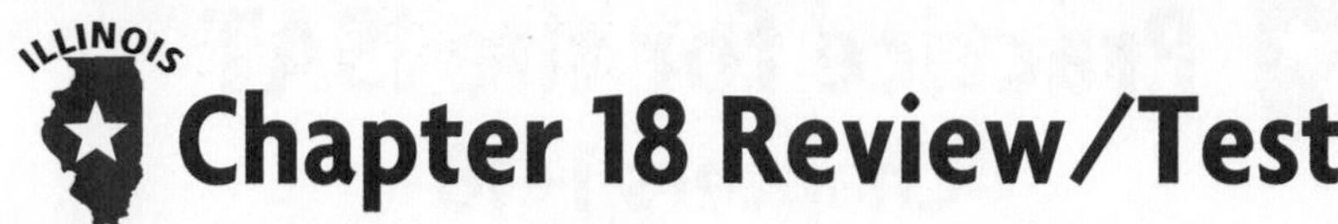

Chapter 18 Review/Test

Check Vocabulary and Concepts

Choose the best term from the box.

VOCABULARY
denominator
equivalent fractions
fraction
numerator

1. The _?_ tells how many parts are being counted. IL 6.3.03 (p. 446)
2. A _?_ is a number that names part of a whole or part of a group. IL 6.3.03 (p. 446)
3. The _?_ tells how many equal parts are in the whole. IL 6.3.03 (p. 446)

Check Skills

Write a fraction in numbers and in words to name the blue part. IL 6.3.03 (pp. 446–449, 450–453)

4. 

5. 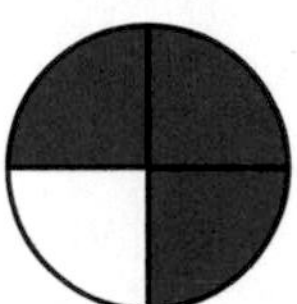

6. 

7.    

8. 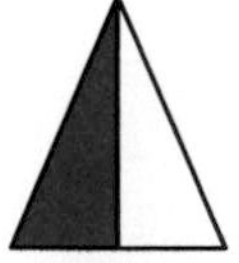

9. 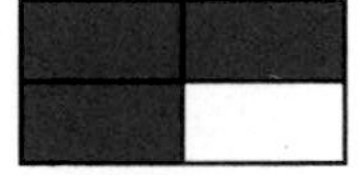

10. 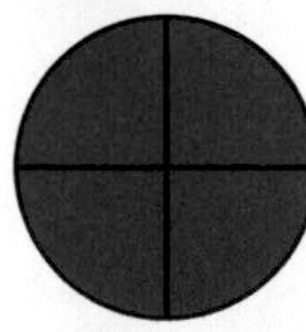

11. 

12. 

13. 

Check Problem Solving

Solve. IL 8.3.05 (pp. 462–463, 474–475)

14. Colby, Fred, and Jim ran for six minutes. Colby ran $\frac{4}{6}$ mile, Fred ran $\frac{8}{10}$ mile, and Jim ran $\frac{8}{12}$ mile. Who ran the farthest?

15. WRITE Math Amy ate $\frac{3}{8}$ of a pizza and Sue ate $\frac{2}{4}$ of it. Who ate more pizza? **Explain** how you know.

GO ONLINE **Technology** Use *Online Assessment.*

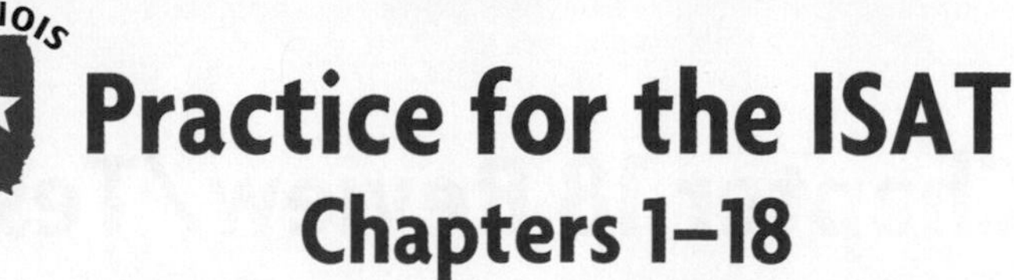

Practice for the ISAT
Chapters 1–18

Number and Operations

1. Which fraction names the shaded part? IL 6.3.03 (p. 446)

A $\frac{1}{7}$

B $\frac{5}{12}$

C $\frac{7}{12}$

D $\frac{7}{10}$

2. Charlie bought 6 packs of notepads. There were 10 notepads in each pack. How many notepads did Charlie buy? IL 6.3.11 (p. 218)

A 4

B 16

C 54

D 60

3. **WRITE Math** What fraction names the green circles? **Explain** your answer. IL 6.3.03 (p. 450)

Algebra

4. Which number sentence is in the same fact family as $27 \div 9 = 3$? IL 8.3.03 (p. 286)

A $9 \div 3 = 3$

B $3 \times 3 = 9$

C $3 \times 9 = 27$

D $6 \times 3 = 18$

Check your work.

See item 5. To check your work, place your answer in the table. Then make sure your number continues the pattern in the table.

5. Which number will complete the table below? IL 8.3.01 (p. 256)

Cars	5	6	7	8	9
Wheels	20	24	28	32	■

A 40

B 38

C 36

D 34

6. **WRITE Math** **Explain** how you can use a related multiplication fact to find $49 \div 7$. IL 8.3.03 (p. 324)

Geometry

7. How many lines of symmetry does the figure below appear to have? IL 9.3.04 (p. 386)

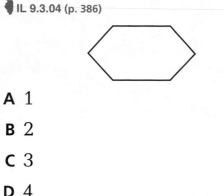

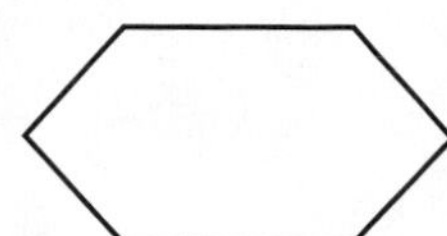

A 1

B 2

C 3

D 4

8. Which best describes how the figure has been moved? IL 9.3.05 (p. 390)

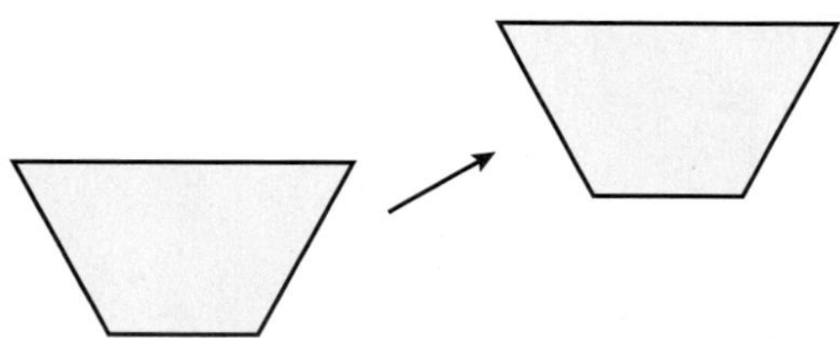

A slide

B turn

C flip

D roll

9. **WRITE Math** What solid figure is shown? **Explain** how you know. IL 9.3.02 (p. 400)

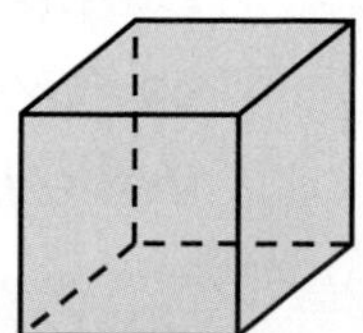

Data Analysis and Probability

10. How many more books did Julie read than Stephen? IL 10.3.01 (p. 154)

A 2

B 3

C 4

D 5

11. Kenny pulls a marble out of the bag without looking. Which color marble is he less likely to pull? IL 10.3.04 (p. 178)

A Green

B Blue

C Red

D Yellow

12. **WRITE Math** Jennifer made a pictograph showing her classmates' favorite colors. The key for the graph is: Each 🚹 = 6 students. How many symbols should she use to show that 15 students chose red as their favorite color? **Explain.** IL 10.3.01 (p. 148)

CHAPTER

19 Understand Decimals

Investigate

The table shows the top 5 runners who ran in the 100-meter race. The race times for runners are in decimals to show 100 parts of a second. Select two of the runners. Write each of their times in word form.

Special Olympics 100-Meter Run

Athlete	Time in Seconds
Rachel	17.24
Tim	17.37
Kayla	17.58
Caleb	18.84
Thomas	19.02

FAST FACT

Special Olympics offers 30 individual and team sports, including gymnastics, roller skating, and volleyball.

GO ONLINE **Technology** Student pages are available in the Student eBook.

Show What You Know

Check your understanding of important skills needed for success in Chapter 19.

▶ Name the Fraction

Write a fraction for the shaded part.

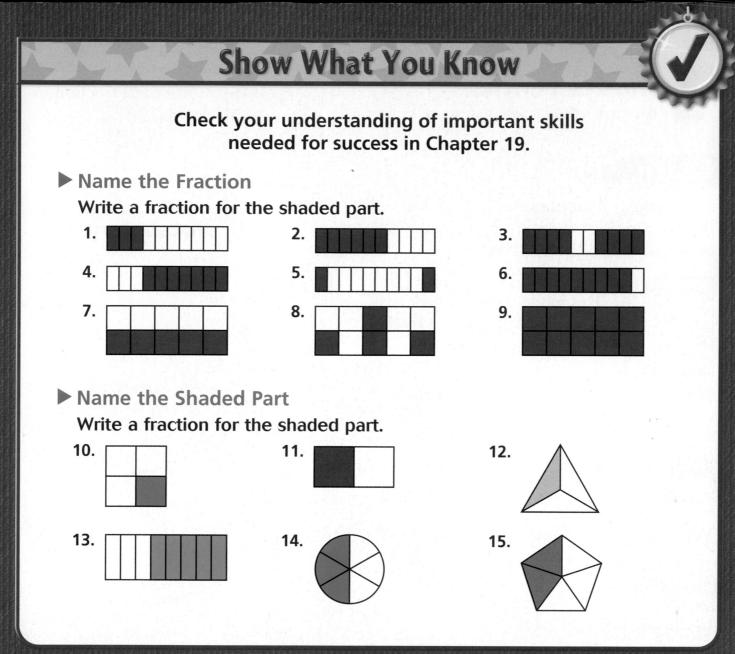

1. **2.** **3.**

4. **5.** **6.**

7. **8.** **9.**

▶ Name the Shaded Part

Write a fraction for the shaded part.

10. 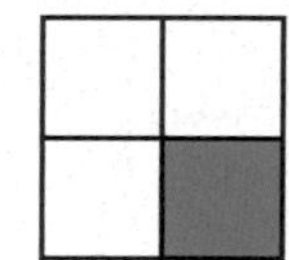

11. 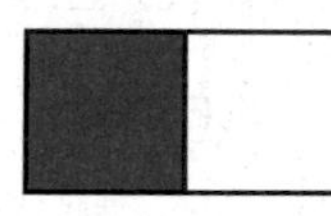

12. 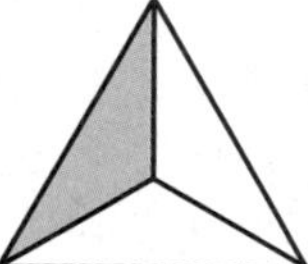

13. 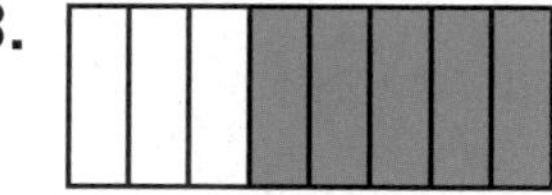

14. 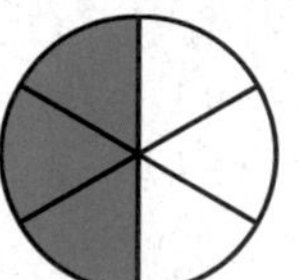

15. 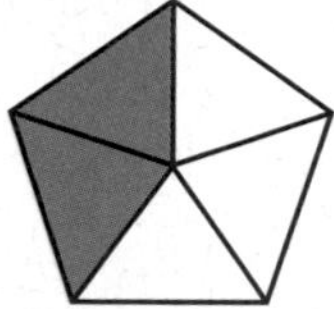

VOCABULARY POWER

CHAPTER VOCABULARY

decimal
hundredth
tenth

WARM-UP WORDS

decimal A number with one or more digits to the right of the decimal point

hundredth One of one hundred equal parts

tenth One of ten equal parts

LESSON 1

Model Tenths

OBJECTIVE: Model and write fractions and decimals in tenths.

Quick Review

Write each fraction in words.

1. $\frac{2}{5}$ 2. $\frac{1}{2}$ 3. $\frac{3}{4}$

4. $\frac{5}{8}$ 5. $\frac{7}{10}$

Vocabulary

decimal

tenth

Learn

A **decimal** is a number with one or more digits to the right of the decimal point. A decimal shows values less than one, such as tenths.

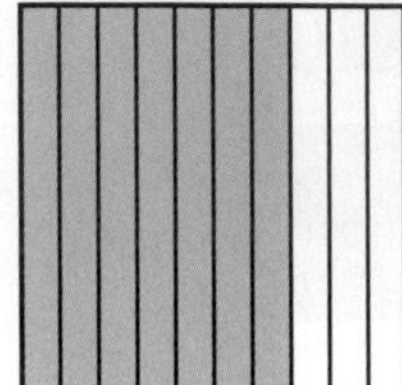

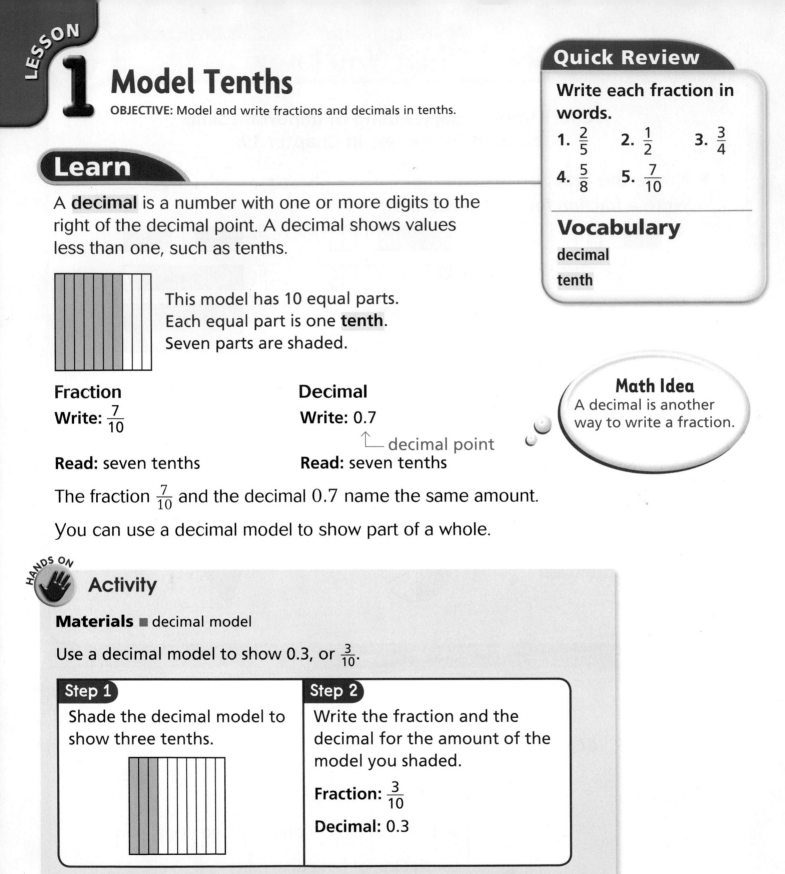

This model has 10 equal parts.
Each equal part is one **tenth**.
Seven parts are shaded.

Fraction	**Decimal**
Write: $\frac{7}{10}$	**Write:** 0.7 (decimal point)
Read: seven tenths	**Read:** seven tenths

Math Idea
A decimal is another way to write a fraction.

The fraction $\frac{7}{10}$ and the decimal 0.7 name the same amount.

You can use a decimal model to show part of a whole.

Activity

Materials ■ decimal model

Use a decimal model to show 0.3, or $\frac{3}{10}$.

Step 1

Shade the decimal model to show three tenths.

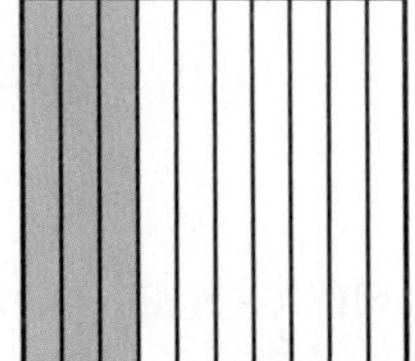

Step 2

Write the fraction and the decimal for the amount of the model you shaded.

Fraction: $\frac{3}{10}$

Decimal: 0.3

- How do you read 0.3?
- **What if** you shaded the model to show 0.6? How many parts would be shaded?

A decimal can name part of a whole or part of a group.

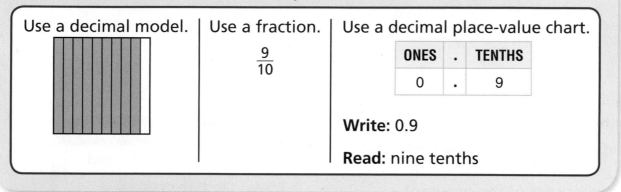

Example

There are 10 beanbags.
Five of the beanbags are red.

What part of the group of beanbags are red?

Fraction	**Decimal**
Write: $\frac{5}{10}$	**Write:** 0.5 (↑ decimal point)
Read: five tenths	**Read:** five tenths

So, $\frac{5}{10}$, or 0.5, of the beanbags are red.

You can show tenths in different ways.

Use a decimal model.

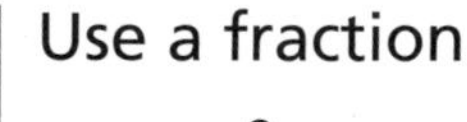

Use a fraction.

$\frac{9}{10}$

Use a decimal place-value chart.

ONES	.	TENTHS
0	.	9

Write: 0.9

Read: nine tenths

Guided Practice

1. What fraction of the square is shaded?
Think: How many tenths are shaded?

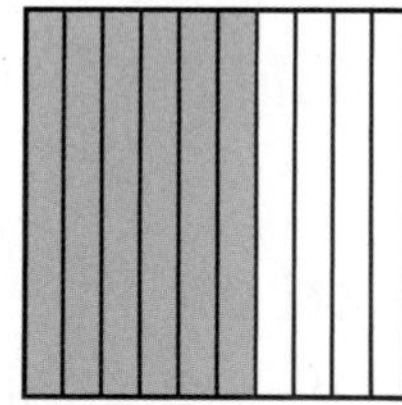

Write the fraction and decimal for the shaded part.

2. 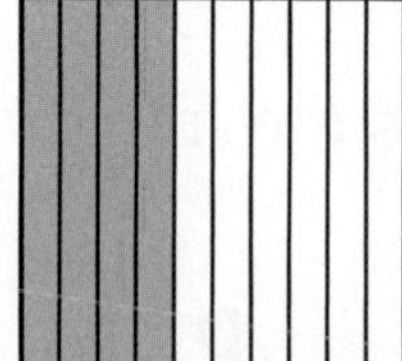

3. 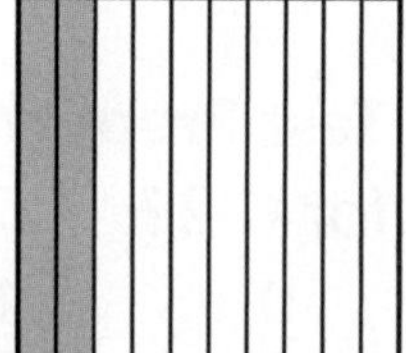

✓4. 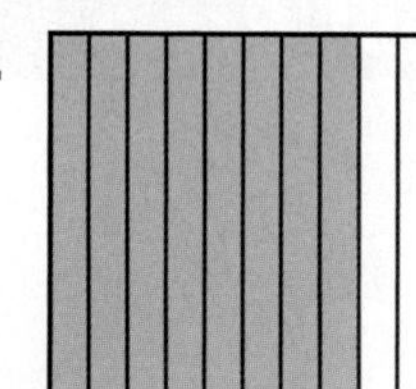

✓5. 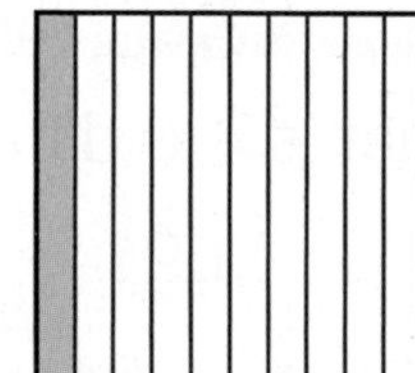

6. TALK Math **Explain** how fractions and decimals are related.

Independent Practice and Problem Solving

Write the fraction and decimal for the shaded part.

7. 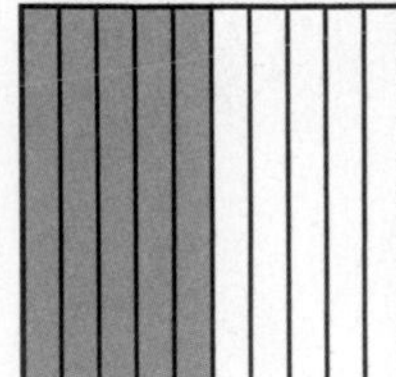

8. 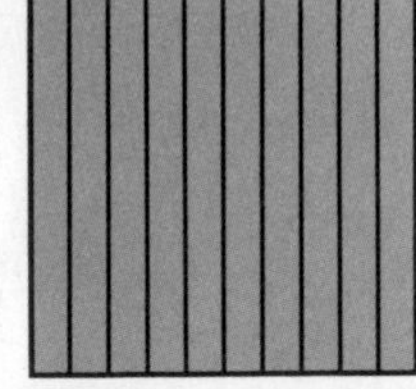

9. 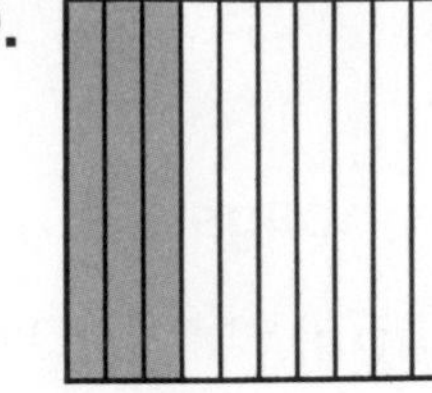

10. 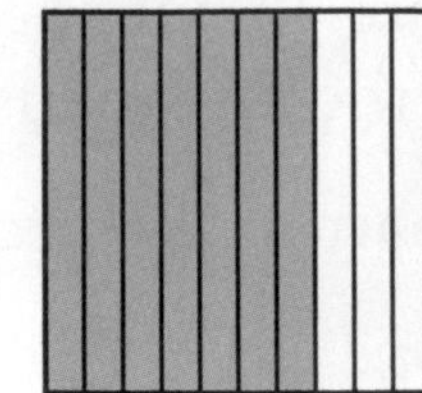

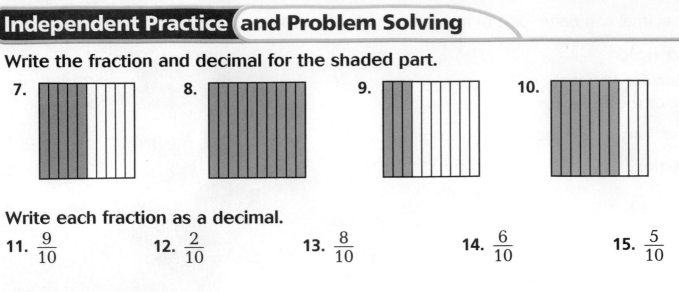

Write each fraction as a decimal.

11. $\frac{9}{10}$

12. $\frac{2}{10}$

13. $\frac{8}{10}$

14. $\frac{6}{10}$

15. $\frac{5}{10}$

Write each decimal as a fraction.

16.

ONES	.	TENTHS
0	.	4

17.

ONES	.	TENTHS
0	.	7

18.

ONES	.	TENTHS
0	.	1

19. 0.5

20. 0.2

21. 0.9

22. 0.3

23. 0.8

USE DATA For 24–26, use the pictograph.

24. Each player tossed 10 beanbags. The pictograph shows how many bags each person got in the goal. Write a decimal to show what part of the group of beanbags Travis tossed in the goal.

25. **Pose a Problem** Look back at Problem 24. Write a similar problem by changing the name of the person who tossed the beanbags.

Beanbag Toss Results

Name	Tosses in Goal
Travis	◇◇◇◇◇
Lee	◇◇◇
Carter	◇◇◇◇◇◇
Trina	◇◇◇◇◇◇◇

Key: Each ◇ = 1 beanbag.

26. Write a decimal for the part of Trina's tosses that did NOT land in the goal.

27. **WRITE Math What's the Question?** Lisa tossed 10 beanbags and missed the goal 4 times. The answer is 0.6.

Mixed Review and Test Prep

28. What is the difference? (p. 84)

$$7{,}691 - 3{,}852 = \blacksquare$$

29. If $6 \times 9 = 54$, then what is 9×6? (p. 262)

30. **Test Prep** Which shows the fraction for 0.2?

A $\frac{0}{2}$ B $\frac{1}{2}$ C $\frac{2}{10}$ D $\frac{8}{10}$

Extra Practice on page 500, Set A

Bowling

Reading Skill **Identify the Details**

Bowling is a game in which players roll a ball to knock down ten pins. Each time you knock down a pin, you earn a point.

A player gets a *strike* when he or she knocks down all ten pins on the first roll. This is shown on the scorecard with an X. A player who knocks down all ten pins by the second roll gets a *spare*. A spare is shown on the scorecard with a /.

1	2	3	4	5	6	7	8	9	10
X	4 3	7 2	6 /	4 4	X	X	9 0	5 /	0 7

▲ A bowling game is divided into ten frames. In each frame, a player is given two chances to knock down all ten pins.

Look at the scorecard above. In what fraction of the ten frames did the bowler score a strike? Write your answer as a fraction and a decimal.

You can identify the details to help you answer the question.

Question: In what fraction of the frames did the bowler score a strike?

Details: A bowling game is divided into 10 frames.
A strike is shown on the scorecard with an X.

Problem Solving Identify the details to solve the problems.

1. Solve the problem above. **Explain** your answer.
2. Harvey went bowling. In his first game, he got two strikes and three spares. Write a decimal to show in what fraction of the ten frames Harvey knocked down all of the pins.

LESSON 2

Model Hundredths

OBJECTIVE: Model and write fractions and decimals in hundredths.

Quick Review

Write each fraction as a decimal.

1. $\frac{3}{10}$ **2.** $\frac{1}{10}$ **3.** $\frac{8}{10}$

4. $\frac{5}{10}$ **5.** $\frac{7}{10}$

Vocabulary

hundredth

Learn

This decimal model has 100 equal parts. Each equal part is one **hundredth**. In the model, 26 parts are shaded.

You can write the shaded parts as a decimal or as a fraction.

Write: 0.26, or $\frac{26}{100}$

Read: twenty-six hundredths

Activity

Materials ■ decimal model

Use a decimal model to show 0.08, or $\frac{8}{100}$.

Step 1

Shade the decimal model to show eight hundredths.

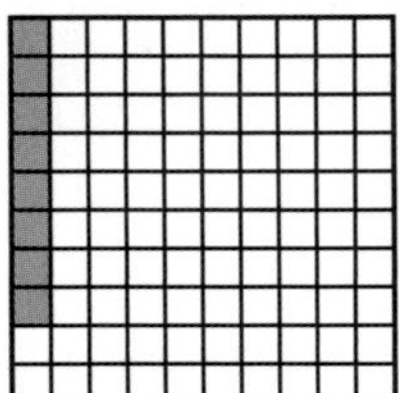

Step 2

Write the fraction and the decimal for the amount you shaded.

Fraction: $\frac{8}{100}$ **Decimal:** 0.08

Read: eight hundredths

You can show hundredths in different ways.

Use a model.

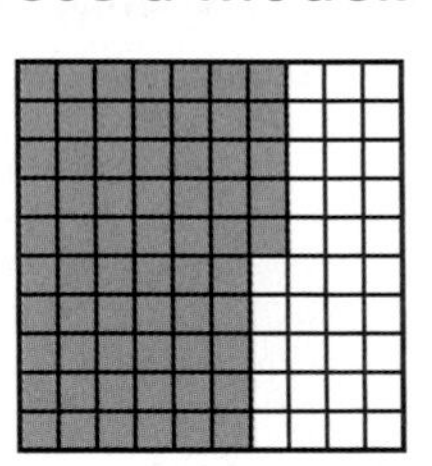

Use a fraction.

$\frac{65}{100}$

Use a place-value chart.

ONES	.	TENTHS	HUNDREDTHS
0	.	6	5

Write: 0.65
Read: sixty-five hundredths
Expanded form: 0.6 + 0.05

Guided Practice

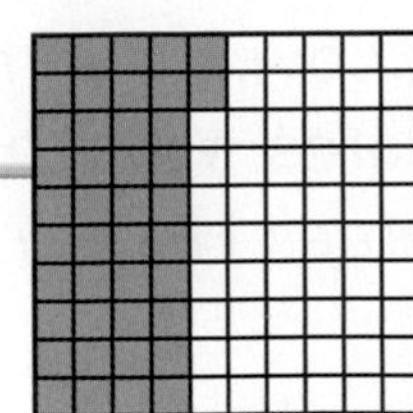

1. Write the fraction and the decimal for the model.
Think: How many of the hundredths are shaded?

Write each fraction as a decimal. Use a decimal model to help.

2. $\frac{16}{100}$ **3.** $\frac{5}{100}$ **4.** $\frac{37}{100}$ ✓**5.** $\frac{60}{100}$ ✓**6.** $\frac{51}{100}$

7. TALK Math **Explain** how to write 0.32 as a fraction.

Independent Practice and Problem Solving

Write each fraction as a decimal. Use a decimal model to help.

8. $\frac{29}{100}$ **9.** $\frac{10}{100}$ **10.** $\frac{75}{100}$ **11.** $\frac{43}{100}$ **12.** $\frac{82}{100}$

Write each decimal as a fraction.

13.

ONES	.	TENTHS	HUNDREDTHS
0	.	1	2

14.

ONES	.	TENTHS	HUNDREDTHS
0	.	5	9

Write each decimal as a fraction and in expanded form.

15. 0.34 **16.** 0.18 **17.** 0.90 **18.** 0.03 **19.** 0.66

20. Reasoning There are 100 centimeters in 1 meter. Measure the paper clip in centimeters. Then write the length as a fraction and as a decimal of a meter.

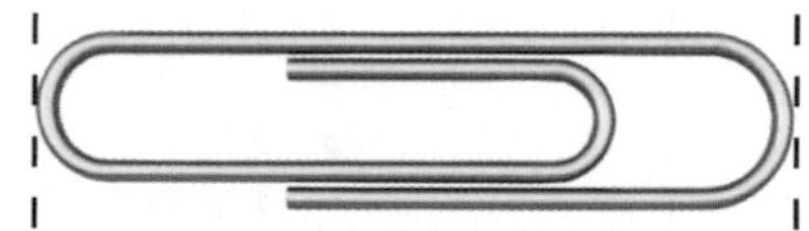

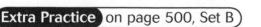

21. Lou surveyed 100 students. Of the 100 students, 0.38 of them have a dog for a pet. How many students have a dog?

22. WRITE Math **What's the Error?** Nikki says 0.20 is equal to $\frac{2}{100}$. Describe her error.

Mixed Review and Test Prep

23. Kim lives $\frac{9}{10}$ of a mile from Lydia. Write the distance as a decimal. (p. 484)

24. A rectangle is 5 units long and 3 units wide. What is the perimeter? (Grade 2)

25. Test Prep Which decimal shows eight hundredths?

A 8.00 **C** 0.08

B 0.80 **D** 0.008

Technology CD ROM Use Harcourt Mega Math, Fraction Action, *Fraction Flare Up*, Levels L, N.

Extra Practice on page 500, Set B

LESSON 3

Decimals Greater Than One

OBJECTIVE: Read and write decimals greater than one.

Quick Review

Write each decimal in word form.

1. 0.5 **2.** 0.9
3. 0.16 **4.** 0.72
5. 0.43

Learn

PROBLEM Mr. Branson is painting the fence around his yard. There are 10 sections. Each section has 10 boards. Mr. Branson has painted 16 boards so far. What decimal shows how many sections he has painted?

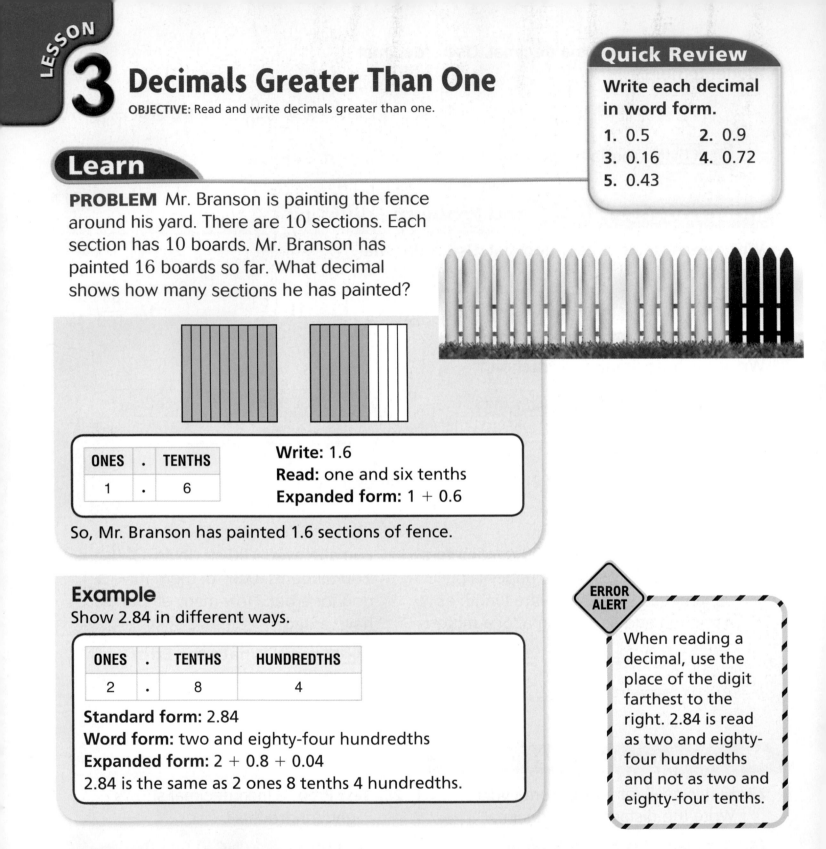

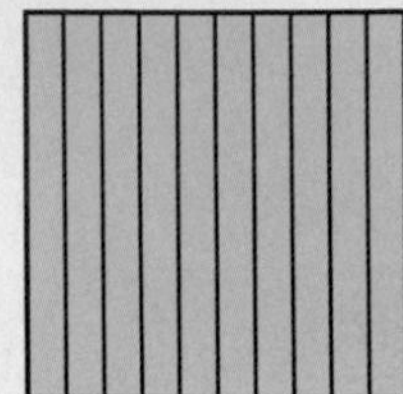

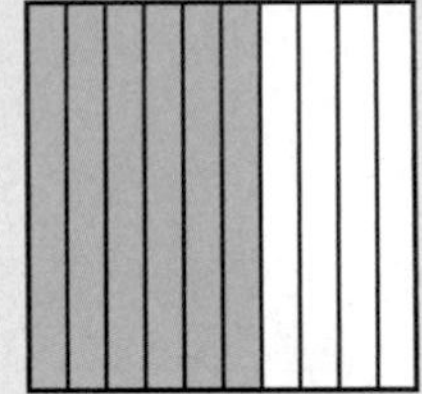

ONES	.	TENTHS
1	.	6

Write: 1.6
Read: one and six tenths
Expanded form: $1 + 0.6$

So, Mr. Branson has painted 1.6 sections of fence.

Example

Show 2.84 in different ways.

ONES	.	TENTHS	HUNDREDTHS
2	.	8	4

Standard form: 2.84
Word form: two and eighty-four hundredths
Expanded form: $2 + 0.8 + 0.04$
2.84 is the same as 2 ones 8 tenths 4 hundredths.

ERROR ALERT

When reading a decimal, use the place of the digit farthest to the right. 2.84 is read as two and eighty-four hundredths and not as two and eighty-four tenths.

Guided Practice

1. Write the decimal in expanded form.

ONES	.	TENTHS
3	.	2

■ + ■

Write the word form and the expanded form for each.

2.

ONES	.	TENTHS
7	.	5

3.

ONES	.	TENTHS	HUNDREDTHS
4	.	9	8

4. TALK Math **Explain** how to write five and thirty-one hundredths as a decimal.

Independent Practice and Problem Solving

Write the word form and the expanded form for each.

5.

ONES	.	TENTHS
6	.	4

6.

ONES	.	TENTHS	HUNDREDTHS
9	.	7	0

7. 1.53 8. 8.6 9. 3.26 10. 5.9 11. 2.48

Write the decimal for each.

12. four and three tenths 13. seven and two hundredths 14. nine and one tenth

15. Ms. Rich shares 2 boxes of markers and $\frac{7}{10}$ of another box of markers with her class. Write a decimal to show the total number of boxes of markers Ms. Rich shares.

16. **Reasoning** I am a decimal greater than 1 but less than 3. All my digits are even. My tenths digit is three times my ones digit. My hundredths digit is 8. What decimal am I?

17. Mr. Vo has 3 full boxes of crayons and $\frac{85}{100}$ of another box of crayons. Write a decimal to show the total number of boxes of crayons Mr. Vo has.

18. WRITE Math Does six and eighty hundredths name the same amount as six and eight tenths? **Explain.**

Mixed Review and Test Prep

19. What is the range of these numbers? (p. 162)

42, 36, 41, 35, 48, 44

20. Trace the figure and draw the line or lines of symmetry. (p. 386)

21. **Test Prep** Which shows 6.05 written in word form?

A six hundred five

B six and five hundredths

C six and five tenths

D six and fifty hundredths

Extra Practice on page 500, Set C

LESSON 4

Compare and Order Decimals

OBJECTIVE: Compare and order decimals.

Quick Review

Write <, >, or = for each ●.

1. 9 ● 5
2. 63 ● 37
3. 449 ● 458
4. 2,698 ● 2,689
5. 1,346 ● 1,463

Learn

You can use models and place value charts to compare decimals. Compare 0.3 and 0.7.

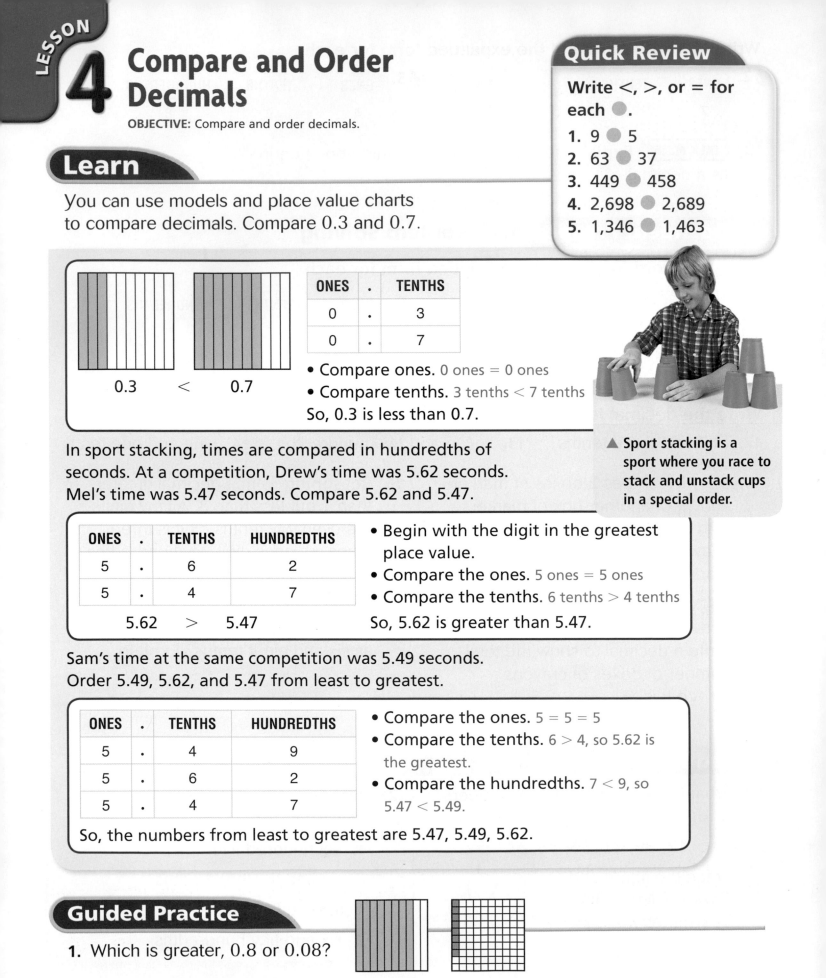

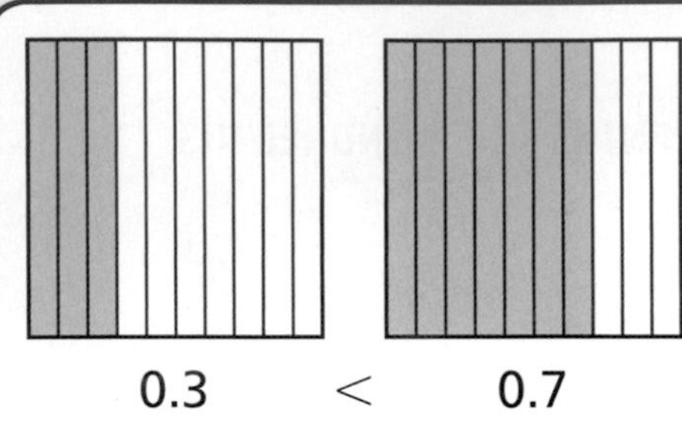

ONES	.	TENTHS
0	.	3
0	.	7

- Compare ones. 0 ones = 0 ones
- Compare tenths. 3 tenths < 7 tenths

So, 0.3 is less than 0.7.

▲ **Sport stacking is a sport where you race to stack and unstack cups in a special order.**

In sport stacking, times are compared in hundredths of seconds. At a competition, Drew's time was 5.62 seconds. Mel's time was 5.47 seconds. Compare 5.62 and 5.47.

ONES	.	TENTHS	HUNDREDTHS
5	.	6	2
5	.	4	7

5.62 > 5.47

- Begin with the digit in the greatest place value.
- Compare the ones. 5 ones = 5 ones
- Compare the tenths. 6 tenths > 4 tenths

So, 5.62 is greater than 5.47.

Sam's time at the same competition was 5.49 seconds. Order 5.49, 5.62, and 5.47 from least to greatest.

ONES	.	TENTHS	HUNDREDTHS
5	.	4	9
5	.	6	2
5	.	4	7

- Compare the ones. 5 = 5 = 5
- Compare the tenths. 6 > 4, so 5.62 is the greatest.
- Compare the hundredths. 7 < 9, so 5.47 < 5.49.

So, the numbers from least to greatest are 5.47, 5.49, 5.62.

Guided Practice

1. Which is greater, 0.8 or 0.08?

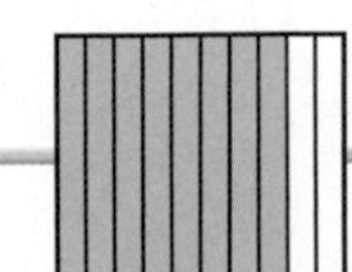
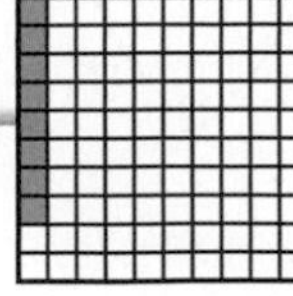

Compare. Write <, >, or = for each ●.

2. 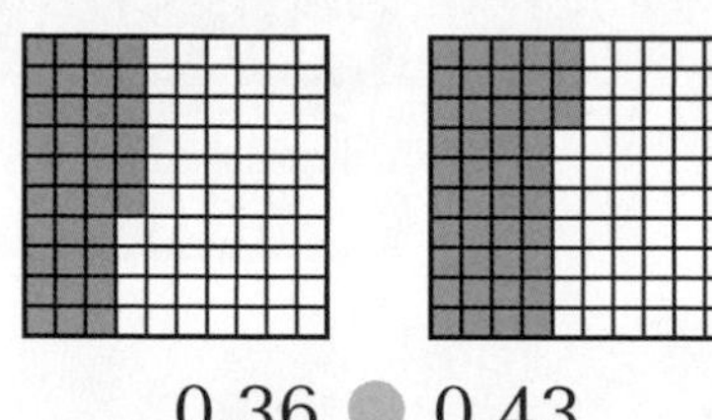

0.36 ● 0.43

3.

ONES	.	TENTHS
1	.	7
1	.	5

1.7 ● 1.5

4. **TALK Math** **Explain** how to order 0.4, 0.7, and 0.2 from least to greatest.

Independent Practice and Problem Solving

Compare. Write <, >, or = for each ●.

5. 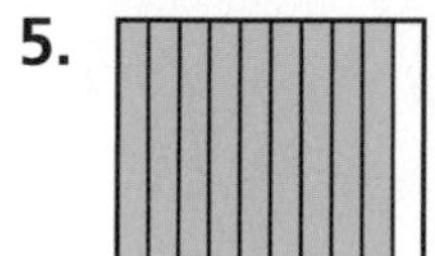 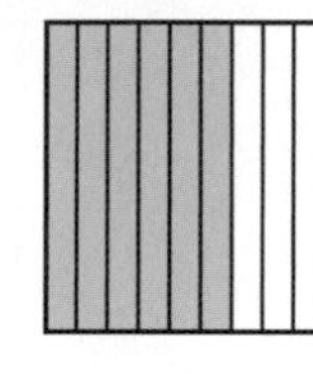

0.9 ● 0.6

6.

ONES	.	TENTHS	HUNDREDTHS
2	.	6	1
2	.	6	4

2.61 ● 2.64

7. 3.1 ● 2.8

8. 4.5 ● 4.3

9. 0.19 ● 0.24

10. 1.75 ● 1.57

Order the decimals from least to greatest.

11. 0.2, 0.5, 0.12

12. 0.6, 0.09, 0.1

13. 1.63, 1.89, 1.78

USE DATA For 14–16, use the table.

3-6-3 Stack Times

Name	Time in Seconds
Robin Stangenberg	2.91
Emily Fox	2.72
Timo Reuhl	2.78

14. The stacker who holds the World Record for the 3-6-3 stack has the least time listed in the table. Who holds the World Record?

15. **Open-Ended** Jay said his time was greater than Timo's, but less than Robin's. What could his time be?

16. **WRITE Math** Brennan Fox did a 3-6-3 stack in 2.81 seconds. **Explain** how 2.81 compares to the times in the table.

Mixed Review and Test Prep

17. What is 428 + 373? (p. 58)

18. What is the value of the 5 in 5,861? (p. 10)

19. **Test Prep** Which is greater than 1.64?

A 1.7 **B** 1.5 **C** 1.47 **D** 1.08

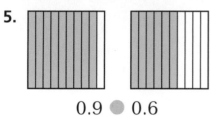

Extra Practice on page 500, Set D

Problem Solving Workshop
Strategy: Compare Strategies

OBJECTIVE: Compare different strategies to solve problems.

Read to Understand
Plan
Solve
Check

Use the Strategy

PROBLEM Lynn was in a gymnastics competition. She scored 8.6 for her floor routine and 8.4 for her uneven bars routine. For which routine did she earn the greater score?

Read to Understand

- What information is given?
- Visualize the information.

Plan

- **What strategy can you use to solve the problem?**
  Sometimes you can use more than one strategy to solve a problem. You can *make a table* or *make a model* to solve this problem.

Solve

- **How can you use the strategies to solve the problem?**

Make a table to compare the decimals.

ONES	.	TENTHS
8	.	6
8	.	4

The ones are the same.
So, compare the tenths.

$0.6 > 0.4$

$8.6 > 8.4$

Make a Model to show and compare the decimals.

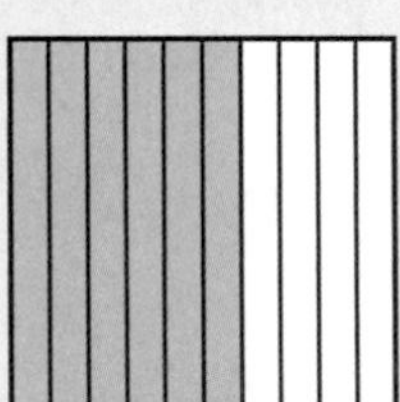
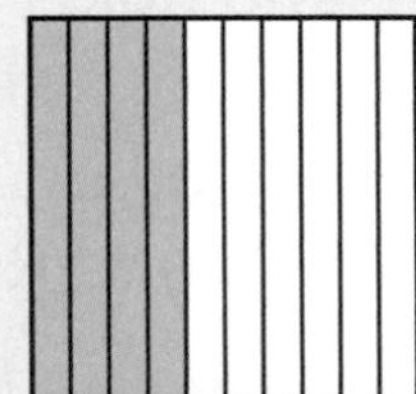

Since the ones are the same, compare the tenths.

$0.6 > 0.4$

$8.6 > 8.4$

So, Lynn earned a greater score for her floor routine.

Check

- **What other ways could you solve the problem?**

Guided Problem Solving

1. Lynn and Shane take gymnastics classes together. Lynn lives 1.30 miles from the gym. Shane lives 1.15 miles from the gym. Who lives the least distance from the gym?

   First, choose a strategy. You can make a table or make a model.

   Then, use the strategy to solve the problem.

ONES	.	TENTHS	HUNDREDTHS
1	.	3	0
1	.	1	5

2. **What if** Nina lives 1.5 miles from the gym? How does this compare to the distances Lynn and Shane live from the gym?

3. In a gymnastics competition, Shane scored 8.39 on the rings, 8.75 on the parallel bars, and 8.7 on his floor routine. For which event did he earn the greatest score?

Choose a STRATEGY

- Draw a Diagram or Picture
- Make a Model or Act It Out
- Make an Organized List
- Find a Pattern
- Make a Table or Graph
- Predict and Test
- Work Backward
- Solve a Simpler Problem
- Write an Equation
- Use Logical Reasoning

Mixed Strategy Practice

USE DATA For 4–8, use the table.

4. The table lists seven gymnasts and their scores in different events. Which gymnast had the greatest score on the vault?

5. Did more gymnasts score greater than 9 points or less than 9 points?

6. Which gymnast's score has a 7 in the hundredths place?

7. **Pose a Problem** Use the scores in the table to write a problem that can be solved by comparing two decimals.

8. **Open-Ended** Gretchen placed first and Beth placed third in the balance beam event. Give a possible score for the gymnast who placed second.

Gymnastics Competition

Name	Event	Points
Tanya	Vault	8.65
Joel	Vault	8.48
Missy	Floor routine	9.20
Gretchen	Balance beam	9.54
Brad	Floor routine	8.95
Beth	Balance beam	9.37
Latesha	Vault	7.90

9. **WRITE Math** Vanessa's score on the uneven bars had the digits 5, 7, and 8. Her score was greater than 6.0 but less than 8.0. **Explain** how to find Vanessa's score.

LESSON 6

Relate Fractions, Decimals, and Money

OBJECTIVE: Relate fractions, decimals, and money.

Quick Review

Write each fraction as a decimal.

1. $\frac{5}{10}$ **2.** $\frac{3}{10}$ **3.** $\frac{75}{100}$

4. $\frac{8}{100}$ **5.** $\frac{60}{100}$

Learn

PROBLEM Julie and Sarah have $1.00 in quarters. They want to share the quarters equally. How many should each girl get? How much money is this?

Math Idea

Amounts less than $1.00 can be written as a fraction of a dollar.

$0.75 = $\frac{75}{100}$

Example You can relate money and fractions.

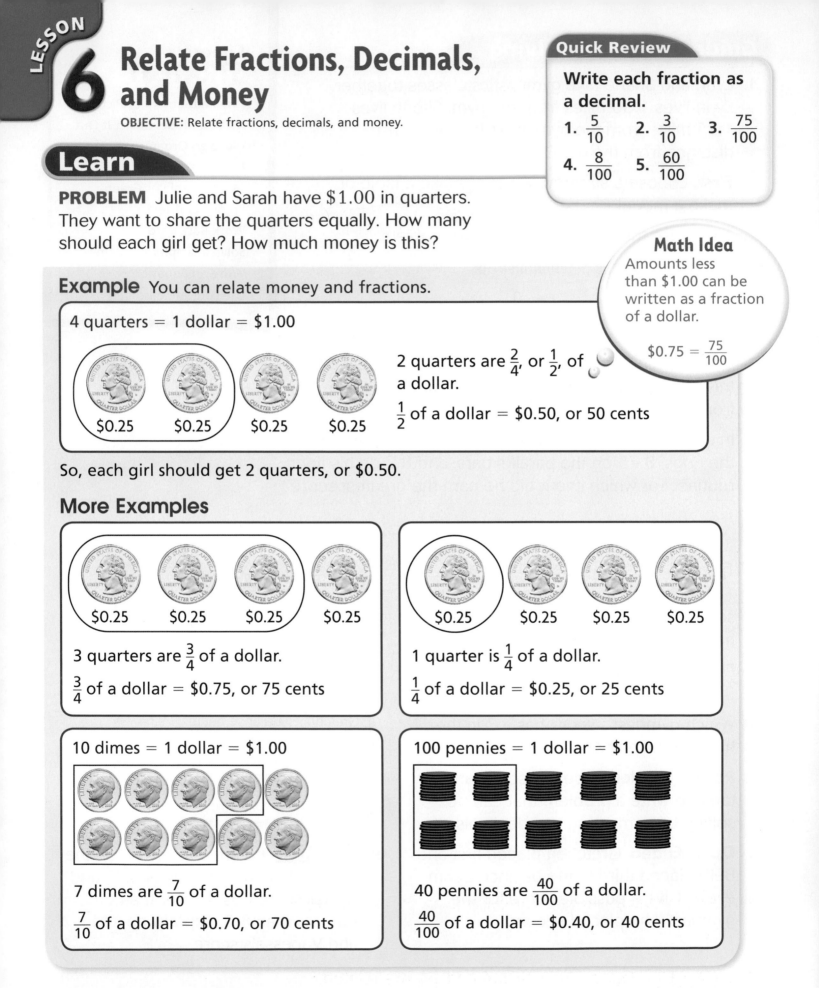

4 quarters = 1 dollar = $1.00

$0.25 $0.25 $0.25 $0.25

2 quarters are $\frac{2}{4}$, or $\frac{1}{2}$, of a dollar.

$\frac{1}{2}$ of a dollar = $0.50, or 50 cents

So, each girl should get 2 quarters, or $0.50.

More Examples

$0.25 $0.25 $0.25 $0.25

3 quarters are $\frac{3}{4}$ of a dollar.

$\frac{3}{4}$ of a dollar = $0.75, or 75 cents

$0.25 $0.25 $0.25 $0.25

1 quarter is $\frac{1}{4}$ of a dollar.

$\frac{1}{4}$ of a dollar = $0.25, or 25 cents

10 dimes = 1 dollar = $1.00

7 dimes are $\frac{7}{10}$ of a dollar.

$\frac{7}{10}$ of a dollar = $0.70, or 70 cents

100 pennies = 1 dollar = $1.00

40 pennies are $\frac{40}{100}$ of a dollar.

$\frac{40}{100}$ of a dollar = $0.40, or 40 cents

Coin Combinations

You can write an amount of money as a decimal and as a fraction of a dollar.

$0.21, or $\frac{21}{100}$ of a dollar

$0.57, or $\frac{57}{100}$ of a dollar

The table shows how to relate money, fractions, and decimals.

Coins	Money Amount	Fraction of a Dollar	Decimal
3 pennies	$0.03	$\frac{3}{100}$	0.03
9 dimes	$0.90	$\frac{90}{100}$ or $\frac{9}{10}$	0.90
1 quarter	$0.25	$\frac{25}{100}$ or $\frac{1}{4}$	0.25
6 nickels	$0.30	$\frac{30}{100}$ or $\frac{3}{10}$	0.30
2 quarters 1 dime	$0.60	$\frac{60}{100}$ or $\frac{6}{10}$	0.60

Guided Practice

1. Write the amount of money as a decimal.
   5 pennies $= \frac{5}{100} = \blacksquare$

Write the amount of money shown. Then write the amount as a fraction of a dollar.

2.

✓3.

Write the money amount for each fraction of a dollar.

4. $\frac{92}{100}$
5. $\frac{7}{100}$
6. $\frac{16}{100}$
7. $\frac{53}{100}$
✓8. $\frac{71}{100}$

9. **TALK Math** **Explain** how $0.84 and $\frac{84}{100}$ are related.

Independent Practice and Problem Solving

Write the amount of money shown. Then write the amount as a fraction of a dollar.

10. 

11. 

12. 

13. 

Write the money amount for each fraction of a dollar.

14. $\frac{27}{100}$ **15.** $\frac{4}{100}$ **16.** $\frac{75}{100}$ **17.** $\frac{98}{100}$ **18.** $\frac{61}{100}$

19. $\frac{83}{100}$ **20.** $\frac{11}{100}$ **21.** $\frac{32}{100}$ **22.** $\frac{9}{100}$ **23.** $\frac{52}{100}$

Write each money amount as a fraction of a dollar.

24. $0.68 **25.** $0.09 **26.** $0.20 **27.** $0.13 **28.** $0.47

29. $0.59 **30.** $0.70 **31.** $0.88 **32.** $0.35 **33.** $0.16

Write the money amount.

34. six hundredths of a dollar

35. fifty-two hundredths of a dollar

36. ninety hundredths of a dollar

USE DATA For 37–38, use the table.

37. The table shows the coins three students have. Write Nick's total amount as a fraction of a dollar.

38. Kim spent $\frac{40}{100}$ of a dollar on a snack. Write the amount she has left as a decimal.

Pocket Change

Name	Quarters	Dimes	Nickels	Pennies
Kim	1	3	2	3
Tony	0	6	1	6
Nick	2	4	0	2

39. **Reasoning** Travis has $\frac{1}{2}$ of a dollar. He has at least two different coins in his pocket. Draw two possible sets of coins that Travis could have.

40. WRITE Math Would you rather have $0.25 or $\frac{3}{10}$ of a dollar? **Explain** why.

 Extra Practice on page 500, Set E

Learn About Showing Money with Decimal Models

You can use decimal models to show parts of a dollar.

Examples

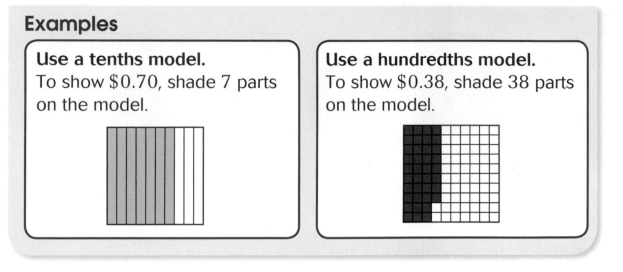

Use a tenths model.
To show $0.70, shade 7 parts on the model.

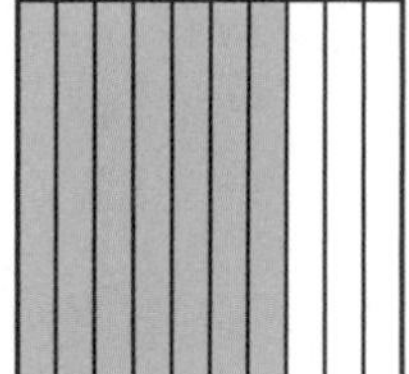

Use a hundredths model.
To show $0.38, shade 38 parts on the model.

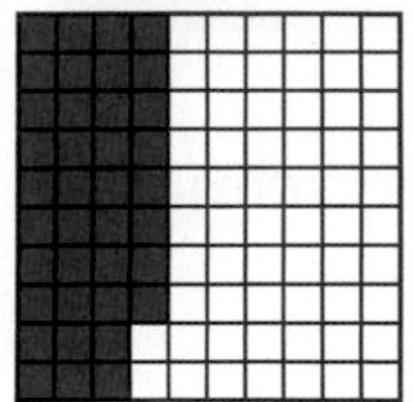

Try It

Write the amount of money shown by each model.

41. 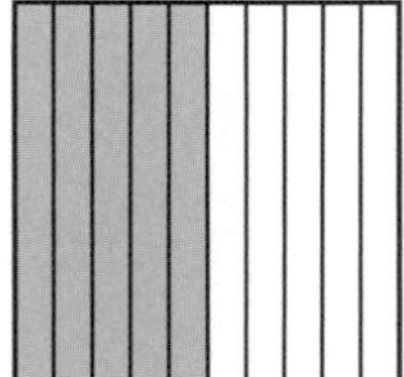

42. 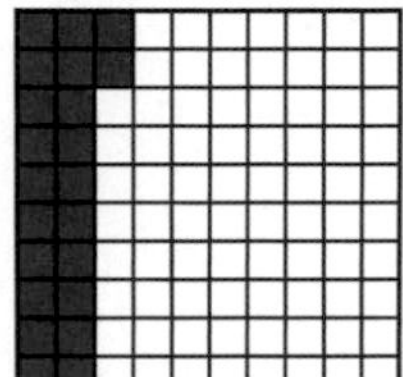

43. 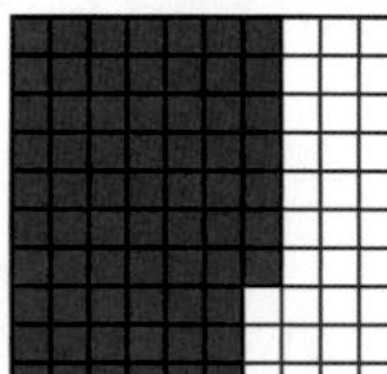

44. 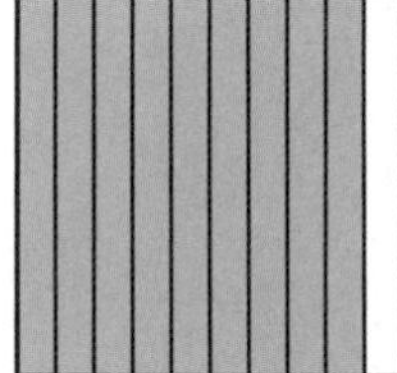

Mixed Review and Test Prep

45. Becky earns $7 an hour. Write a number sentence to find how many hours Becky needs to work to earn $56. (p. 290)

46. On Saturday, Greg rode his bike 4.25 miles and Nate rode his bike 4.40 miles. Who rode farther? (p. 492)

47. **Test Prep** Which amount equals $\frac{7}{10}$ of a dollar?

A $0.07 **C** $0.70

B $0.17 **D** $7.00

48. **Test Prep** Which amount of money shows the decimal $0.55?

A    

B  

C 

D 

Extra Practice

Set A Write the fraction and decimal for the shaded part. (pp. 484–487)

1. 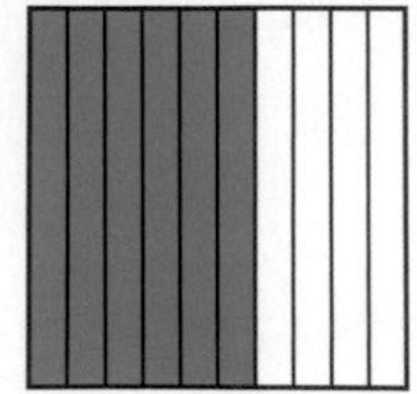
2. 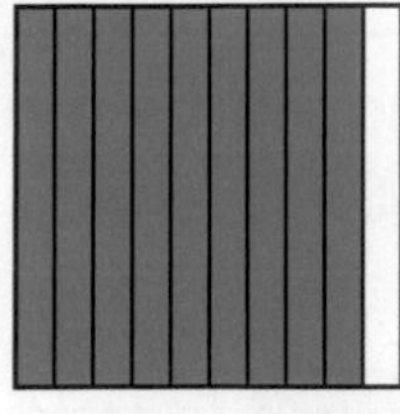
3. 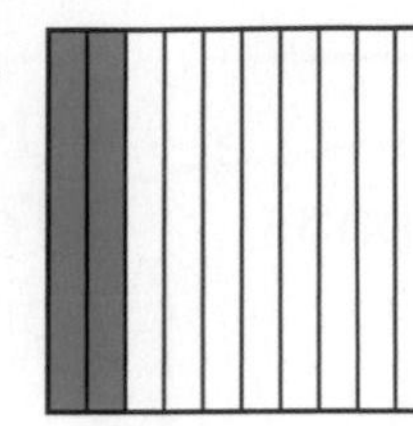
4. 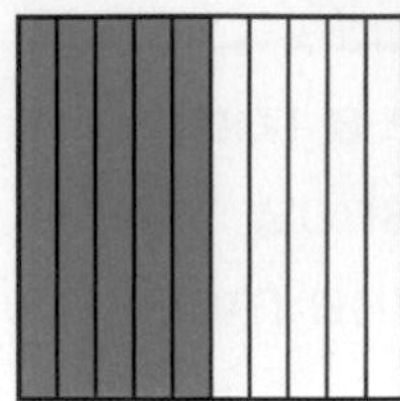

Write each fraction as a decimal.

5. $\frac{7}{10}$
6. $\frac{4}{10}$
7. $\frac{1}{10}$
8. $\frac{9}{10}$
9. $\frac{3}{10}$

Set B Write each fraction as a decimal. Use a decimal model to help. (pp. 488–489)

1. $\frac{35}{100}$
2. $\frac{17}{100}$
3. $\frac{80}{100}$
4. $\frac{62}{100}$
5. $\frac{94}{100}$

Write each decimal as a fraction and in expanded form.

6. 0.55
7. 0.72
8. 0.05
9. 0.40
10. 0.27

Set C Write the word form and the expanded form for each. (pp. 490–491)

1. 2.76
2. 3.15
3. 5.2
4. 9.61
5. 1.74

Set D Compare. Write $<$, $>$, or $=$ for each ●. (pp. 492–493)

1. 1.2 ● 1.3
2. 5.8 ● 4.9
3. 0.27 ● 0.18
4. 2.79 ● 2.97
5. Order 0.5, 0.41, and 0.07 from least to greatest.
6. Order 1.89, 1.86, and 1.91 from greatest to least.

Set E Write the money amount for each fraction of a dollar. (pp. 496–499)

1. $\frac{52}{100}$
2. $\frac{82}{100}$
3. $\frac{14}{100}$
4. $\frac{61}{100}$
5. $\frac{49}{100}$

CD ROM **Technology**
Use Harcourt Mega Math, Fraction Action, *Fraction Flare Up,* Levels L, N.

PRACTICE GAME

Decimal Trains

Draw It!
2 players

Connect It!
- Decimal Trains gameboard for each player
- Game cards

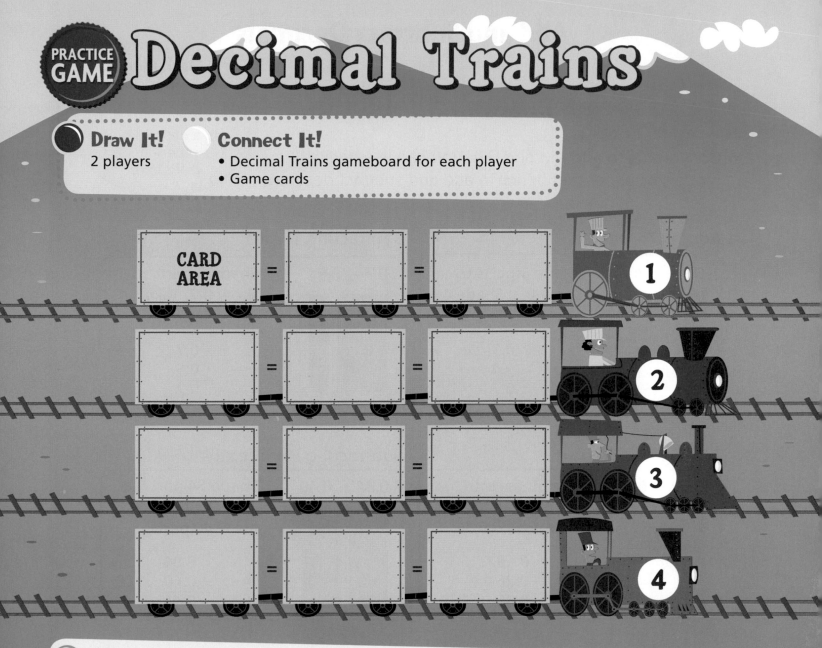

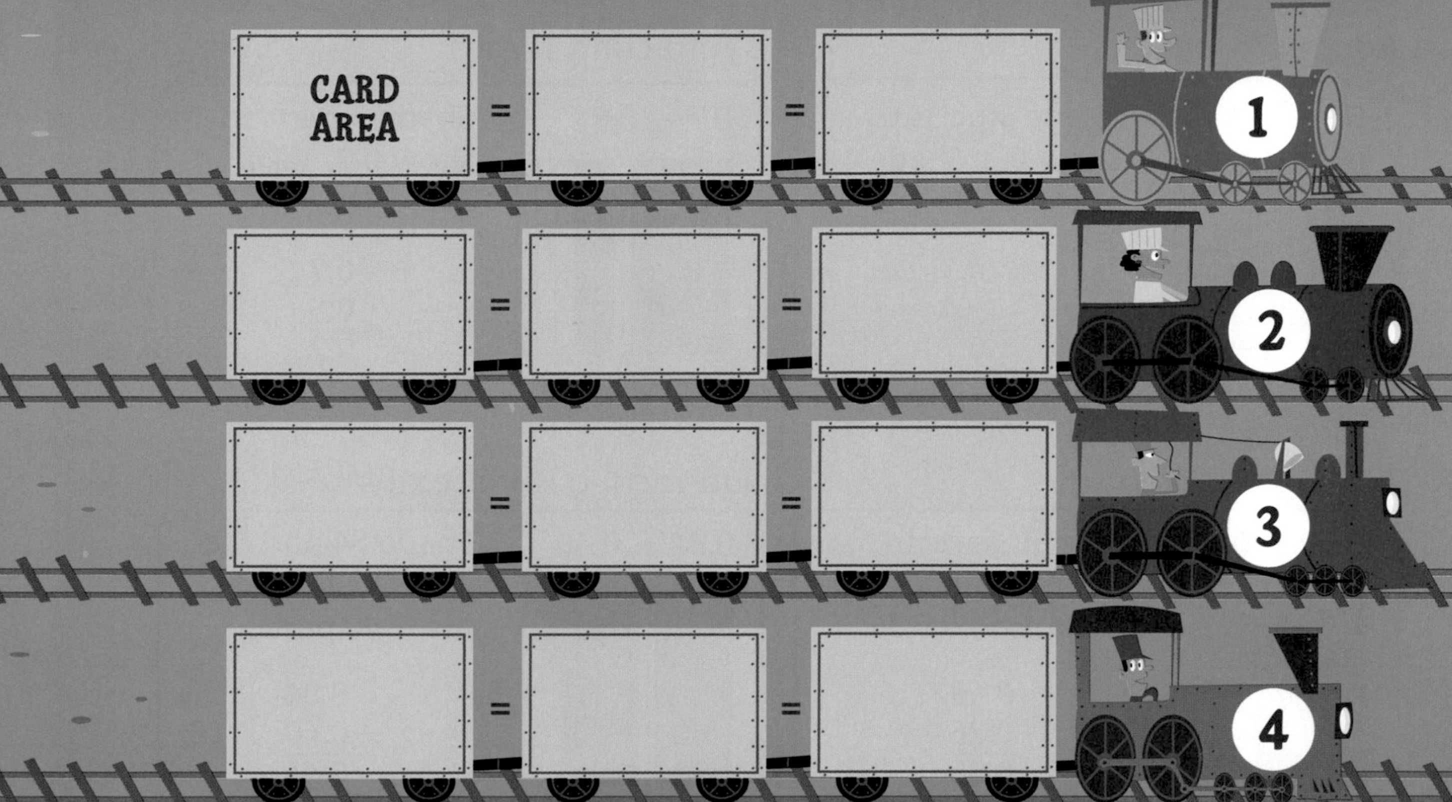

Make a Train!

- Each player receives a gameboard.
- Shuffle the cards. Deal 5 cards to each player. Put remaining cards facedown in a pile.
- Players look at their cards and begin making trains by placing any equivalent fractions, decimals, and money on their gameboards.
- Player 1 draws a card from the pile and may begin a new train with it, add it to a train, or discard it.
- Player 2 may take the top card from the discard pile or draw the next card from the facedown pile. Players draw 1 card per turn.
- Play continues until a player has completed 4 trains. Cards in the same train must have a fraction, decimal, and money amount that are equal.
- The first player to complete all 4 trains wins the game.

MATH POWER

Add and Subtract Decimals

SHADING PARTS

Math Idea
You can add and subtract decimals like whole numbers. Just add a decimal point to the sum or difference.

Cody wants to add 0.3 and 0.4. You can use decimal models or paper and pencil to add and subtract decimals.

Examples

Adding Tenths

0.3 + 0.4

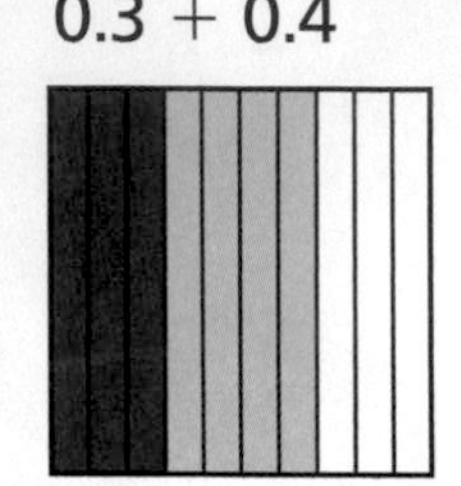

Shade 3 parts to show 0.3. Shade 4 parts to show 0.4.

$$\begin{array}{r} 0.3 \\ +0.4 \\ \hline 0.7 \end{array}$$

Subtracting Tenths

0.7 − 0.5

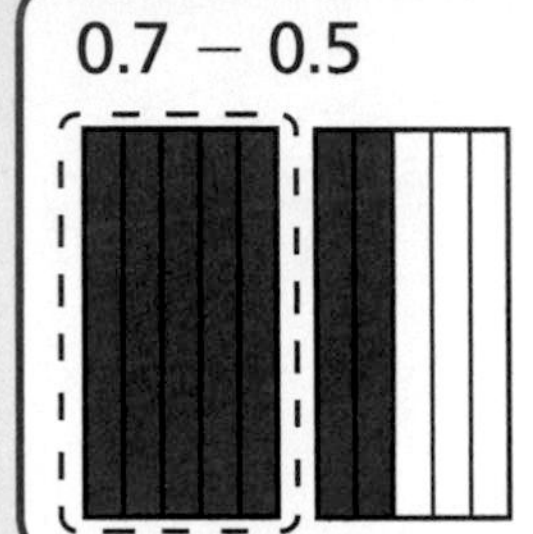

Shade 7 parts to show 0.7. Take away 5 parts.

$$\begin{array}{r} 0.7 \\ -0.5 \\ \hline 0.2 \end{array}$$

Adding Hundredths

0.59 + 0.26

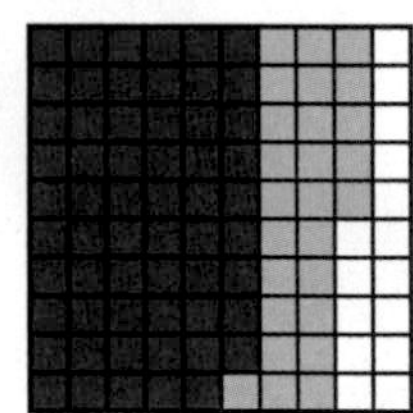

Shade 59 parts to show 0.59. Shade 26 parts to show 0.26.

$$\begin{array}{r} 0.59 \\ +0.26 \\ \hline 0.85 \end{array}$$

Subtracting Hundredths

0.84 − 0.40

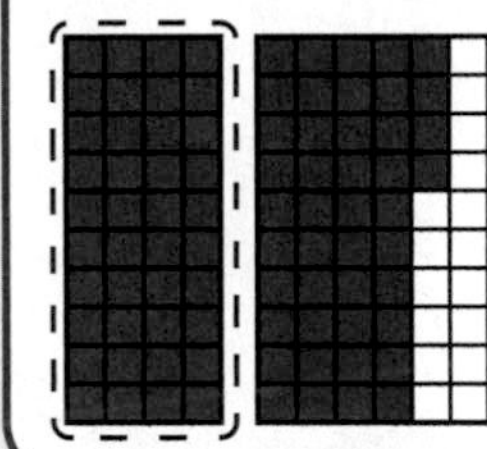

Shade 84 parts to show 0.84. Take away 40 parts.

$$\begin{array}{r} 0.84 \\ -0.40 \\ \hline 0.44 \end{array}$$

Try It

Add or subtract.

1. $\begin{array}{r} 0.54 \\ +0.39 \\ \hline \end{array}$
2. $\begin{array}{r} 0.9 \\ -0.3 \\ \hline \end{array}$
3. $\begin{array}{r} 3.46 \\ +1.44 \\ \hline \end{array}$
4. $\begin{array}{r} 1.75 \\ +0.52 \\ \hline \end{array}$
5. $\begin{array}{r} 5.67 \\ -2.80 \\ \hline \end{array}$
6. $\begin{array}{r} 0.4 \\ +0.6 \\ \hline \end{array}$
7. $\begin{array}{r} 0.87 \\ -0.53 \\ \hline \end{array}$
8. $\begin{array}{r} 6.5 \\ -3.8 \\ \hline \end{array}$
9. $\begin{array}{r} 1.6 \\ +0.8 \\ \hline \end{array}$
10. $\begin{array}{r} 1.57 \\ -1.14 \\ \hline \end{array}$

11. WRITE Math **Explain** how to find the sum of 1.15 and 2.64 by using decimal models or paper and pencil.

Chapter 19 Review/Test

Check Vocabulary and Concepts

Choose the best term from the box.

VOCABULARY
decimal
hundredth
tenth

1. A number with one or more digits to the right of the decimal point is called a __?__. IL 6.5.04 (p. 484)
2. A __?__ is one of one hundred equal parts. IL 6.5.04 (p. 488)

Check Skills

Write each fraction as a decimal. IL 6.5.04 (pp. 484–487, 488–489)

3. $\frac{4}{10}$ 4. $\frac{7}{10}$ 5. $\frac{61}{100}$ 6. $\frac{28}{100}$ 7. $\frac{95}{100}$

Write each decimal as a fraction.

8.

ONES	.	TENTHS
0	.	9

9.

ONES	.	TENTHS	HUNDREDTHS
0	.	3	1

Write the word form and the expanded form for each. IL 6.5.04 (pp. 490–491)

10. 3.16 11. 1.22 12. 6.5 13. 9.93 14. 2.7

Compare. Write <, >, or = for each ●. IL 6.4.06 (pp. 492–493)

15. 3.2 ● 2.3 16. 4.49 ● 4.09 17. 0.01 ● 0.10 18. 1.20 ● 1.25

Write each money amount as a fraction of a dollar. IL 6.5.04 (pp. 496–499)

19. \$0.65 20. \$0.20 21. \$0.84 22. \$0.05 23. \$0.32

Check Problem Solving

Solve. IL 6.4.06 (pp. 494–495)

24. Maria has 3 kittens. Molly is 1.9 pounds, Max is 2.18 pounds, and Toby is 2.05 pounds. What are the weights of the kittens in order from greatest to least?

25. WRITE Math At the long jump competition, Harvey's first jump was 2.97 meters. His second jump was 2.86 meters. **Explain** how to make a model to find which jump was longer.

GO ONLINE **Technology** Use *Online Assessment.*

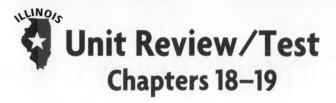

Unit Review/Test
Chapters 18–19

Multiple Choice

1. Trisha drew this figure for an art project. Which fraction names the shaded part of her figure? IL 6.3.03 (p. 446)

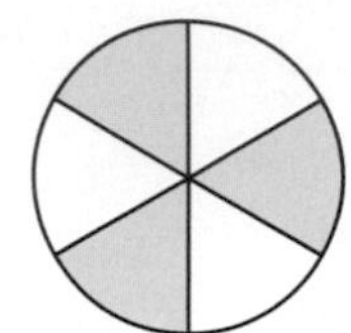

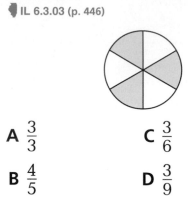

A $\frac{3}{3}$ C $\frac{3}{6}$

B $\frac{4}{5}$ D $\frac{3}{9}$

2. Lara has completed $\frac{1}{2}$ of her homework. Which point on the number line shows $\frac{1}{2}$? IL 6.3.07 (p. 450)

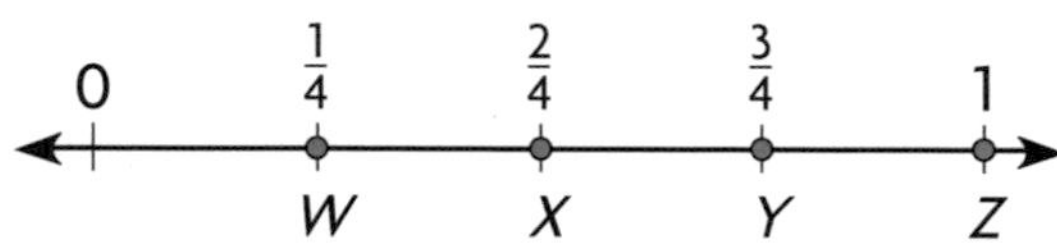

A W C Y

B X D Z

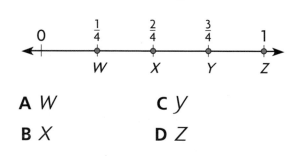

3. Trevor has these marbles. Which shows the fraction of Trevor's marbles that are purple? IL 6.3.03 (p. 450)

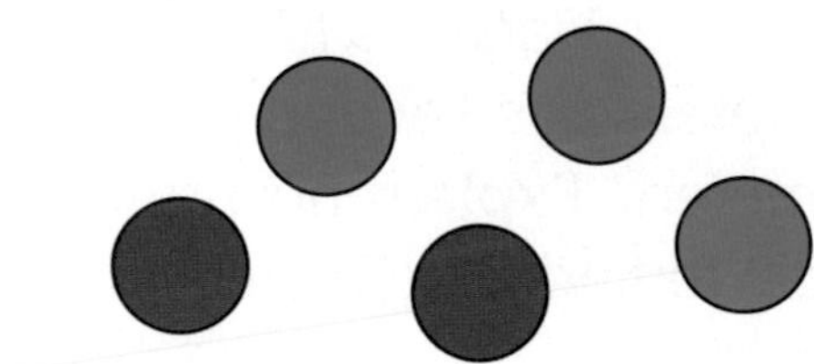

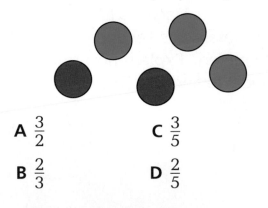

A $\frac{3}{2}$ C $\frac{3}{5}$

B $\frac{2}{3}$ D $\frac{2}{5}$

4. Ellie has these coins. Which shows the value of the coins as a fraction of a dollar? IL 6.3.03 (p. 496)

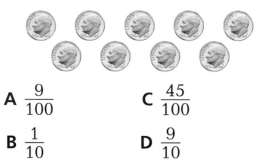

A $\frac{9}{100}$ C $\frac{45}{100}$

B $\frac{1}{10}$ D $\frac{9}{10}$

5. Carl ate $\frac{7}{10}$ of a pizza. Together, he and his sister ate the whole pizza. What fraction of the pizza did Carl's sister eat? IL 8.3.05 (p. 474)

A $\frac{1}{4}$ C $\frac{4}{10}$

B $\frac{3}{10}$ D $\frac{7}{10}$

6. Richard drew a rectangle that shows $\frac{5}{8}$ shaded. Which rectangle might Richard have drawn? IL 6.3.03 (p. 446)

A 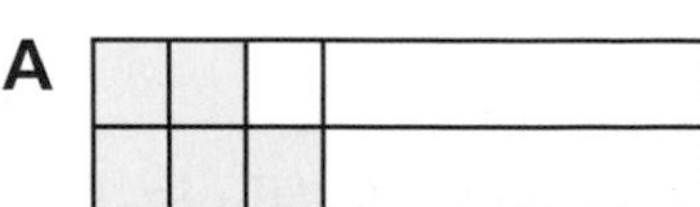

B 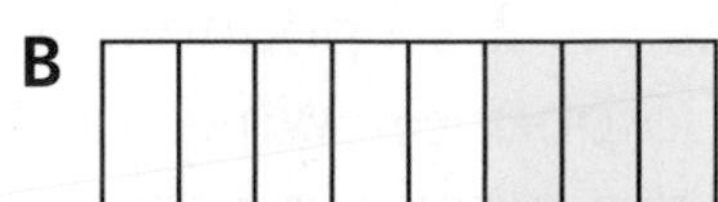

C 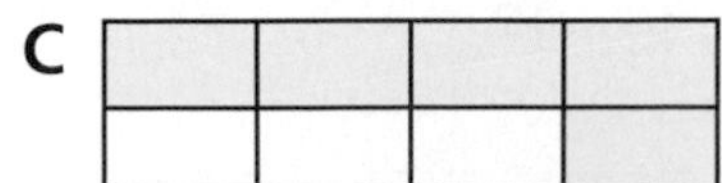

D 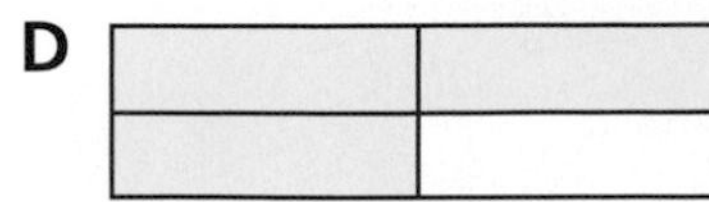

GO ONLINE **Technology** Use *Online Assessment.*

7. Alec bought 7 binders at the school store. He spent $\$49$. Which shows how much each binder cost? IL 8.3.05 (p. 312)

A $\$8$
B $\$7$
C $\$6$
D $\$5$

8. David and his friends are on a treasure hunt. They need to find an object that is shaped like a cylinder. Which of the objects is shaped like a cylinder? IL 9.3.02 (p. 400)

A 

C 

B 

D 

9. Jordan drew a pattern for a quilt. She shaded the squares that will be green. What fraction of the quilt will be green? IL 6.3.03 (p. 488)

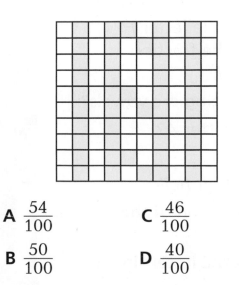

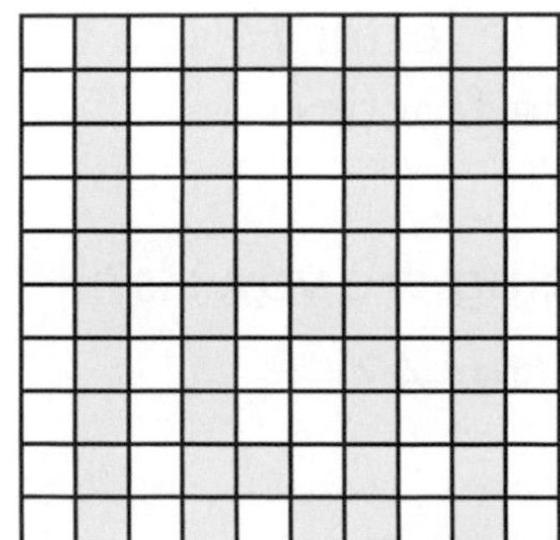

A $\frac{54}{100}$
B $\frac{50}{100}$
C $\frac{46}{100}$
D $\frac{40}{100}$

Short Response

10. Debbie and Joe are at the store. Debbie spent $\$4.27$ and Joe spent $\$4.72$. Who spent a greater amount of money? IL 6.3.06 (p. 116)

11. Write the fraction for the shaded part of the model. IL 6.3.03 (p. 446)

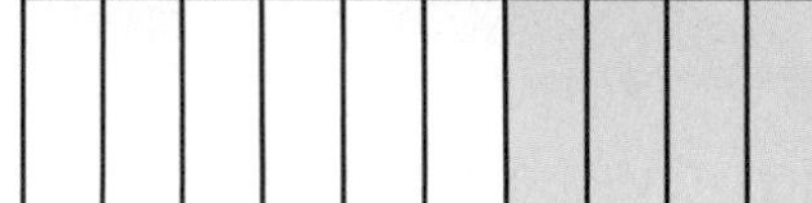

Extended Response WRITE Math

12. Gretta has 3 different figures. She wants to draw a line of symmetry through each one. Write yes or no to tell if each figure has a line of symmetry. If yes, draw the figure and a line of symmetry. IL 9.3.04 (p. 386)

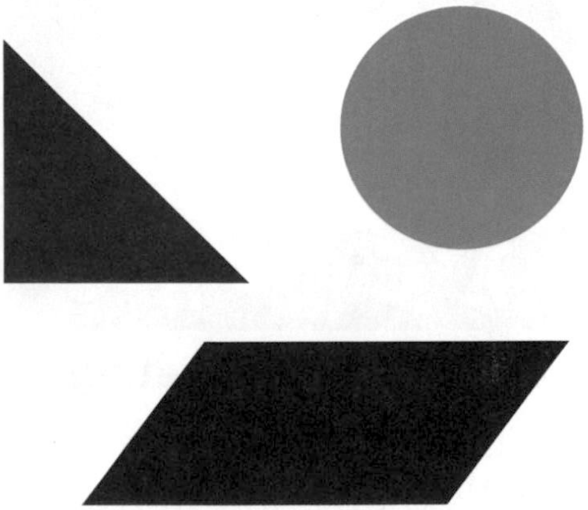

13. Timothy started to make this number pattern. Write a rule for Timothy's pattern. Explain how you found the rule. Then write the next 5 numbers in the pattern. IL 8.3.01 (p. 432)

3, 7, 5, 9, 7, 11, 9, 13, 11, 15, 13

THE WORLD ALMANAC FOR KIDS

Hello, World

Ways to Say Hello

In the United States, about 380 different languages are used, including some signed languages. The most-used spoken languages are shown below. Tagalog is a language from the Philippines that is the sixth-most-used spoken language in the United States.

Saying Hello in Many Ways

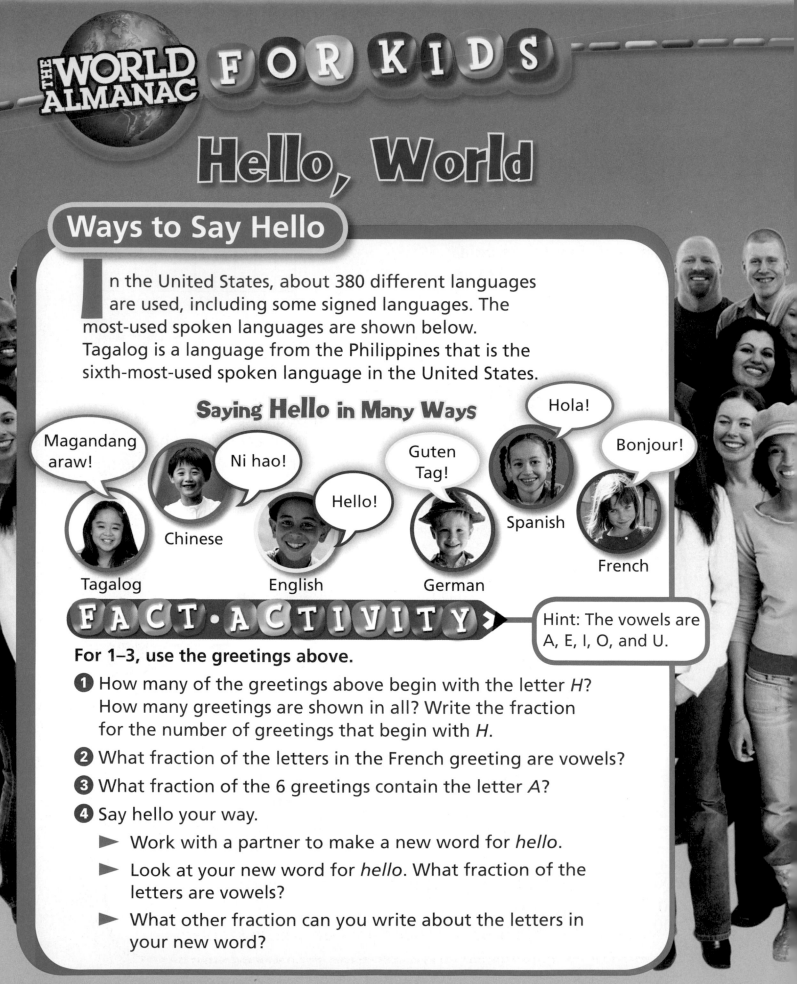

Magandang araw!

Tagalog

Chinese

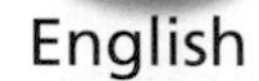

English

German

Hola!

Spanish

French

FACT·ACTIVITY

Hint: The vowels are A, E, I, O, and U.

For 1–3, use the greetings above.

1. How many of the greetings above begin with the letter *H*? How many greetings are shown in all? Write the fraction for the number of greetings that begin with *H*.
2. What fraction of the letters in the French greeting are vowels?
3. What fraction of the 6 greetings contain the letter *A*?
4. Say hello your way.
   - Work with a partner to make a new word for *hello*.
   - Look at your new word for *hello*. What fraction of the letters are vowels?
   - What other fraction can you write about the letters in your new word?

Sign Language

Many people who cannot hear or speak use sign language to communicate. American Sign Language uses movements and positions of the hands and arms and expressions on the face. The American Manual Alphabet uses finger spelling.

ALMANAC Fact

The manual alphabet uses positions of the fingers on one hand to stand for each of the 26 letters in the alphabet.

Thomas Gallaudet and Laurent Clerc introduced sign language in the United States. They also founded the first school for the deaf in Hartford, Connecticut, in 1817.

American Manual Alphabet

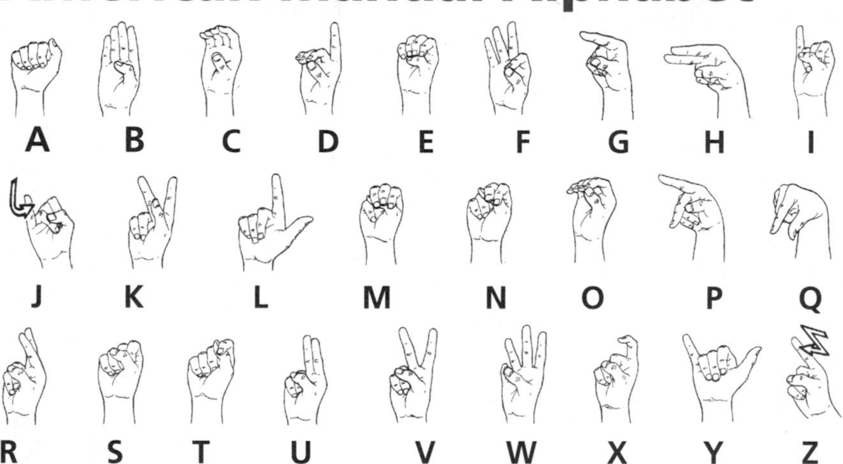

FACT·ACTIVITY

Use the alphabet chart above to help you answer the questions.

1. To sign the letter *F*, what fraction of your fingers on one hand do you have to hold out?
2. Look at the vowels, *A, E, I, O,* and *U*. For which vowel do you hold out $\frac{1}{5}$ of the fingers on your hand? For which vowel do you hold out $\frac{2}{5}$ of your fingers?
3. For what fraction of the letters in *hello* do you need to hold out fingers?
4. WRITE Math **Explain** how you found your answer to Problem 3.

UNIT 7

Measurement

Math on Location

with
Chapter Projects

1

Daily chores at the zoo include cutting, measuring, and mixing food that keeps the animals healthy.

2

The sea lion on the scale weighs 180 pounds. The tank it swims in has more than 1,000 gallons of water.

3

The cougar was measured to make sure its living space was large enough for it to move about easily.

VOCABULARY POWER

TALK Math

What math is being used in the **Math on Location** photographs? How can you find the weight of the sea lion in ounces?

READ Math

REVIEW VOCABULARY You learned the words below when you learned about measurement last year. How do these words relate to **Math on Location**?

gallon a customary unit for measuring capacity

kilogram a metric unit for measuring mass

ounce a customary unit for measuring weight

WRITE Math

Copy and complete a Magic Square like the one below. Use what you know about measurement.

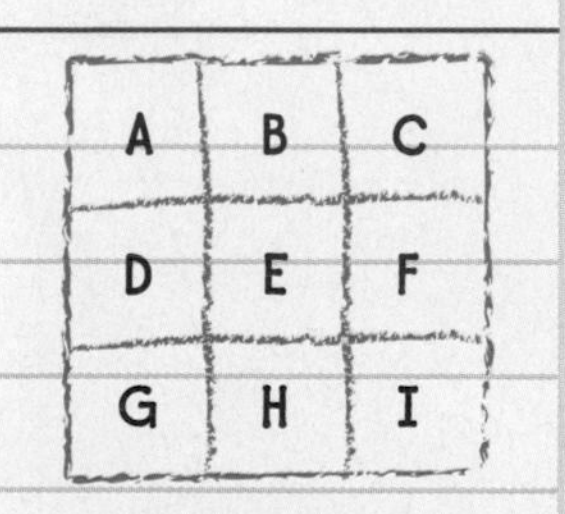

A. liter
B. kilometer
C. quart
D. yard
E. kilogram
F. gallon
G. pint
H. foot
I. meter

1. equals 12 inches
2. equals 1,000 milliliters
3. equals 4 quarts
4. equals 2 pints
5. equals 1,000 grams
6. equals 2 cups
7. equals 3 feet
8. equals 100 cm
9. equals 1,000 meters

Technology
Multimedia Math Glossary link at
www.harcourtschool.com/hspmath

CHAPTER 20 Customary Measurement

Investigate

There are 17 species of penguins. The bar graph shows the heights of some penguin species. Choose a penguin from the graph. Tell its height in inches. Then compare the penguin's height to your height.

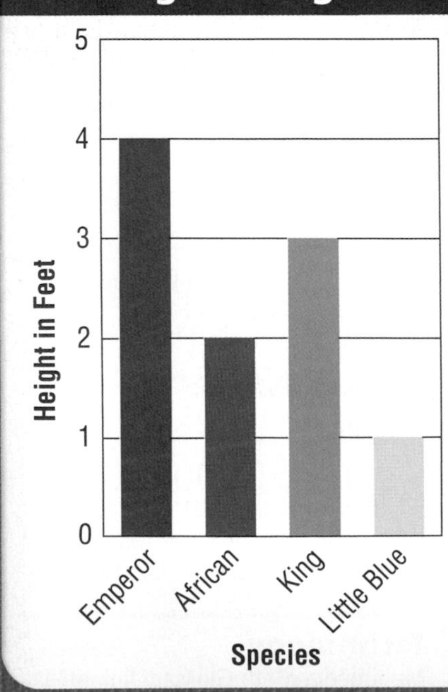

FAST FACT

Penguins are birds, but they spend most of their time underwater. Emperor penguins are the largest of all penguins. They are about 4 feet tall.

GO ONLINE **Technology**
Student pages are available in the Student eBook.

Show What You Know

Check your understanding of important skills needed for success in Chapter 20.

▶ Use a Customary Ruler

Use an inch ruler to measure.

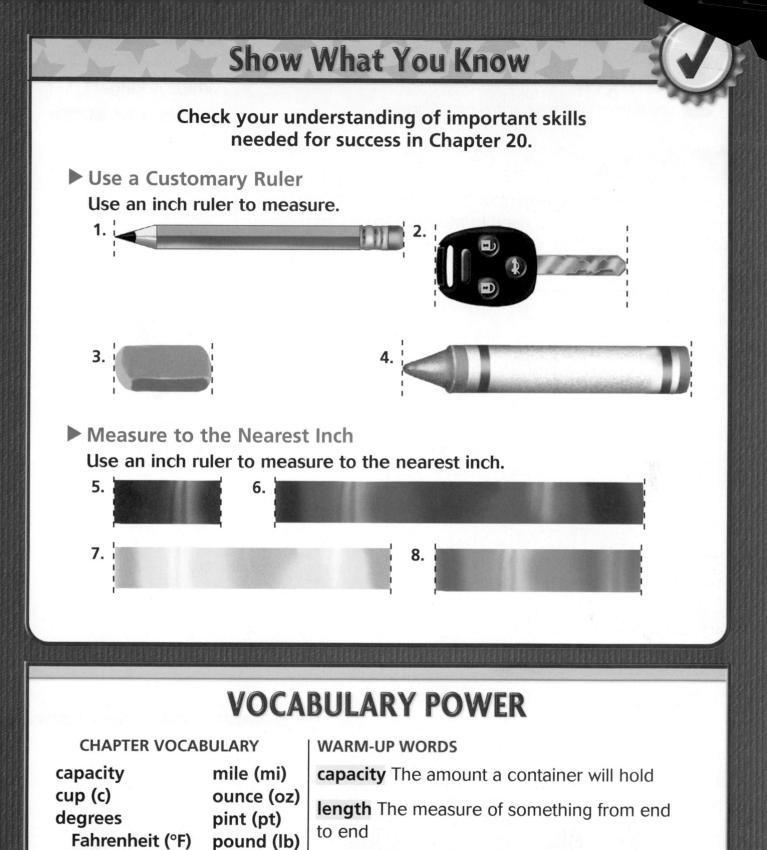

1. **2.**

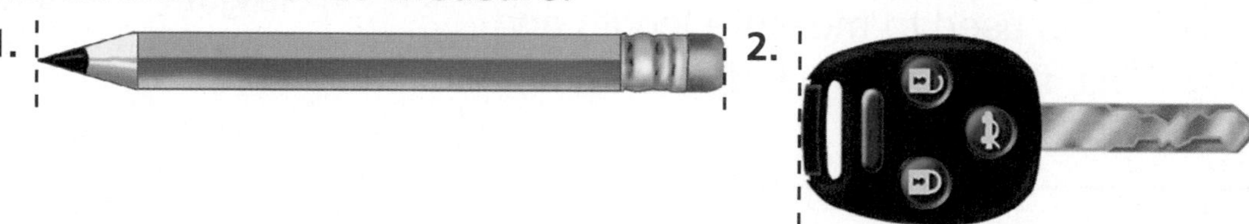

3.

4.

▶ Measure to the Nearest Inch

Use an inch ruler to measure to the nearest inch.

5. **6.** **7.** **8.**

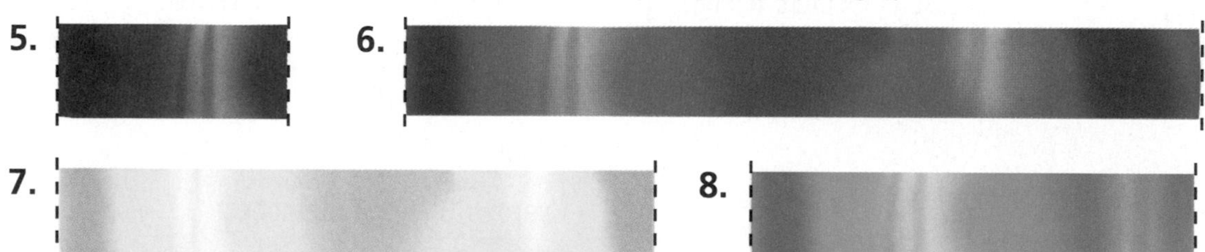

VOCABULARY POWER

CHAPTER VOCABULARY

capacity
cup (c)
degrees Fahrenheit (°F)
foot (ft)
gallon (gal)
length
mile (mi)
ounce (oz)
pint (pt)
pound (lb)
quart (qt)
weight
yard (yd)

WARM-UP WORDS

capacity The amount a container will hold

length The measure of something from end to end

weight The measurement of how heavy an object is

Length

OBJECTIVE: Introduce customary units of length.

Quick Review

Which is longer?

Vocabulary

length
foot (ft)
yard (yd)
mile (mi)

Learn

Length is the measurement of distance between two points. Customary units used to measure length and distance are inch (in.), **foot (ft)**, **yard (yd)**, and **mile (mi)**.

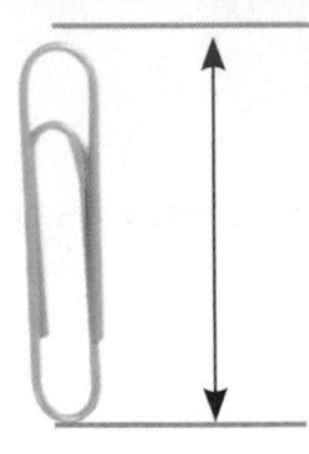

A small paper clip is about 1 inch long.

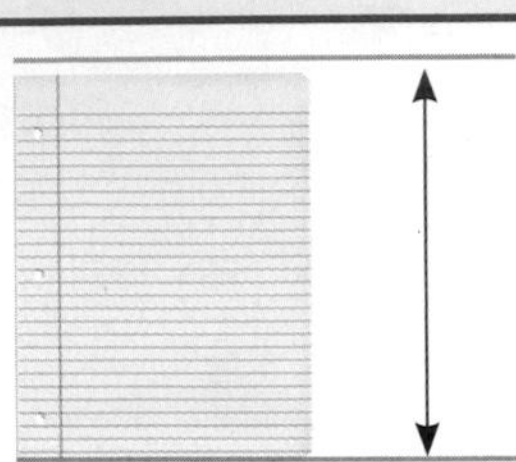

A sheet of notebook paper is about 1 foot long.

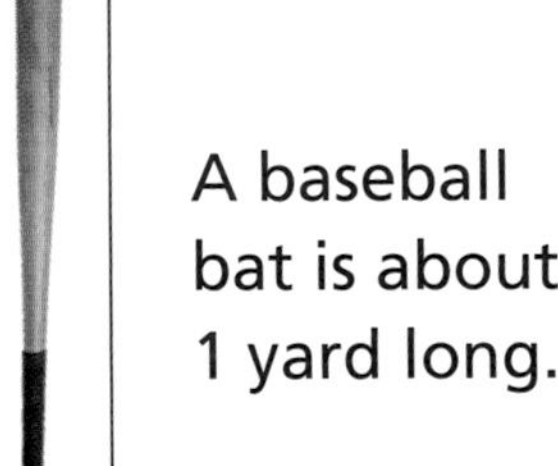

A baseball bat is about 1 yard long.

It takes about 20 minutes to walk 1 mile.

This chart shows how customary units of length are related.

Customary Units of Length
1 foot = 12 inches
1 yard = 3 feet = 36 inches
1 mile = 5,280 feet

Guided Practice

1. Would you measure the length of a pencil in inches or feet? **Think:** Is a pencil longer or shorter than a sheet of notebook paper?

Choose the unit you would use to measure each. Write *inch*, *foot*, *yard*, or *mile*.

2. 

3. 

4. 

5. **TALK Math** **Explain** what unit you would use to measure the length of your classroom.

Independent Practice and Problem Solving

Choose the unit you would use to measure each. Write *inch, foot, yard,* or *mile*.

6. 

7. 

8. 

9. length of a one dollar bill

10. distance between two towns

11. length of a kitchen table

12. distance between two states

13. length of a car

14. length of a watch

15. Annie is going to walk to her friend's house. Her friend lives 3 houses away. What unit best measures how far Annie will have to walk?

16. **Reasoning** Jack is 2 weeks old. Andy is 12 years old. What unit would you use to measure how tall Jack is? Would you use the same unit to measure how tall Andy is? **Explain.**

17. Toni saw a giraffe at the zoo. What unit should Toni use to tell the height of the giraffe?

18. **WRITE Math** Madison visits her grandmother in another city. Does she travel 100 feet, 100 yards, or 100 miles? **Explain** your answer.

Mixed Review and Test Prep

19. There are 3 tennis balls in each of 5 cans. What expression shows the total number of tennis balls? (p. 336)

20. What shape comes next in this pattern? (p. 424)

21. **Test Prep** Kenny uses a large piece of posterboard to draw a picture. About how long is the posterboard?

A 20 inches **C** 20 yards

B 20 feet **D** 20 miles

Extra Practice on page 530, Set A

LESSON 2

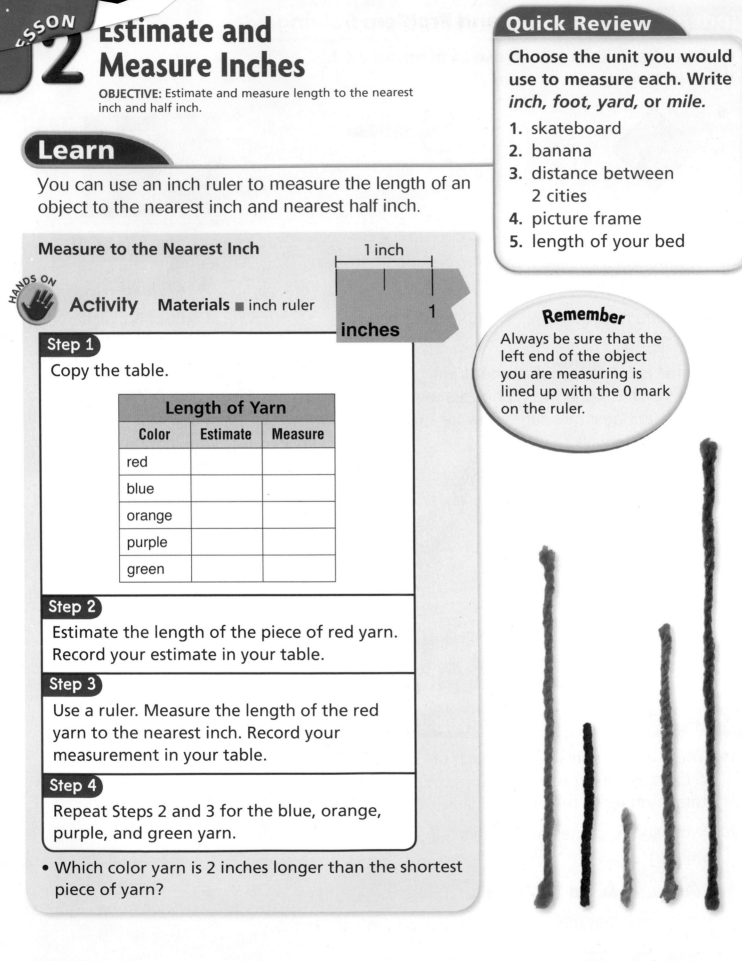

Estimate and Measure Inches

OBJECTIVE: Estimate and measure length to the nearest inch and half inch.

Quick Review

Choose the unit you would use to measure each. Write *inch, foot, yard,* or *mile.*

1. skateboard
2. banana
3. distance between 2 cities
4. picture frame
5. length of your bed

Learn

You can use an inch ruler to measure the length of an object to the nearest inch and nearest half inch.

Measure to the Nearest Inch

1 inch

1

inches

Activity Materials ■ inch ruler

Step 1

Copy the table.

Length of Yarn		
Color	**Estimate**	**Measure**
red		
blue		
orange		
purple		
green		

Step 2

Estimate the length of the piece of red yarn. Record your estimate in your table.

Step 3

Use a ruler. Measure the length of the red yarn to the nearest inch. Record your measurement in your table.

Step 4

Repeat Steps 2 and 3 for the blue, orange, purple, and green yarn.

- Which color yarn is 2 inches longer than the shortest piece of yarn?

Remember

Always be sure that the left end of the object you are measuring is lined up with the 0 mark on the ruler.

Measure to the Nearest Half Inch

You can also measure to the nearest half inch.

Examples

What is the length of each object to the nearest half inch?

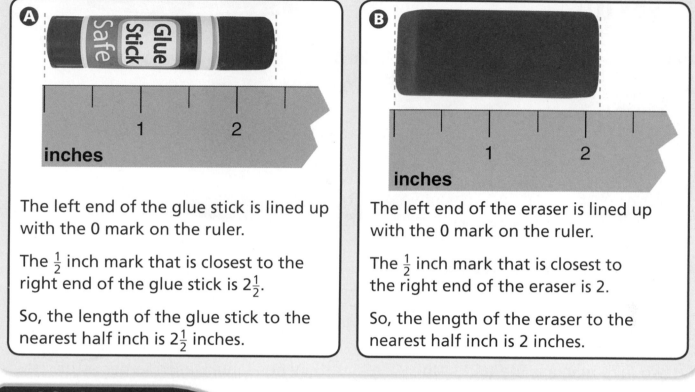

A

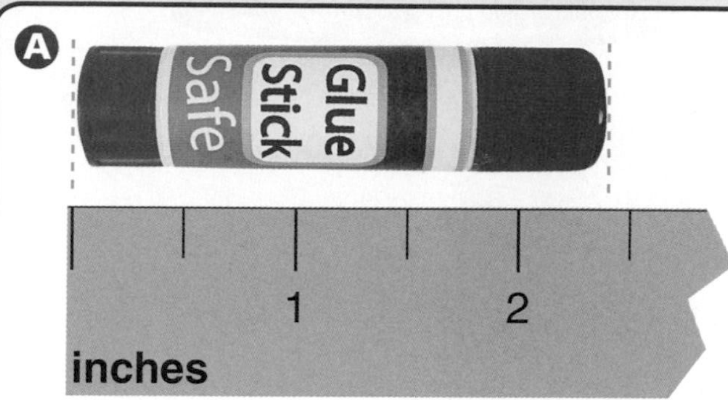

The left end of the glue stick is lined up with the 0 mark on the ruler.

The $\frac{1}{2}$ inch mark that is closest to the right end of the glue stick is $2\frac{1}{2}$.

So, the length of the glue stick to the nearest half inch is $2\frac{1}{2}$ inches.

B

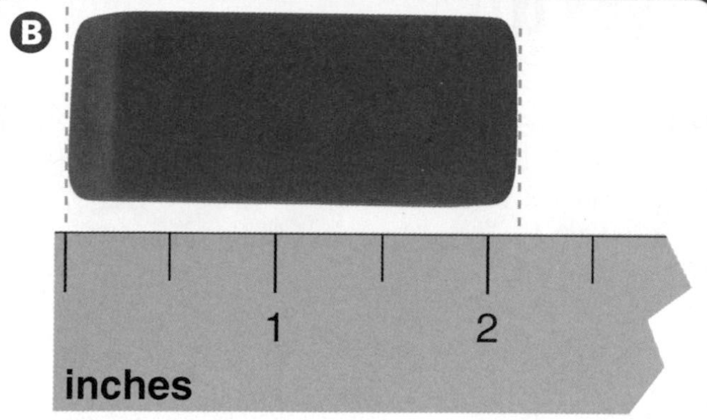

The left end of the eraser is lined up with the 0 mark on the ruler.

The $\frac{1}{2}$ inch mark that is closest to the right end of the eraser is 2.

So, the length of the eraser to the nearest half inch is 2 inches.

Guided Practice

1. Is the key $1\frac{1}{2}$ inches, 2 inches, or $2\frac{1}{2}$ inches long?

Measure the length to the nearest inch.

 2.

Measure the length to the nearest half inch.

3.

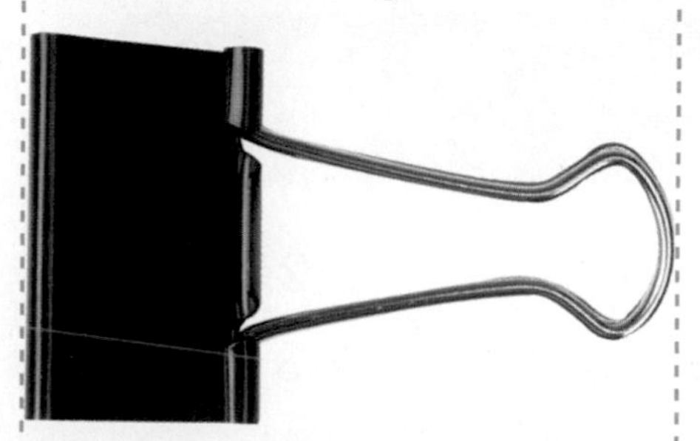

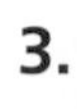 4.

5. TALK Math **Explain** how you measured the shell to the nearest half inch.

Independent Practice and Problem Solving

Measure the length to the nearest inch.

6. 

7. 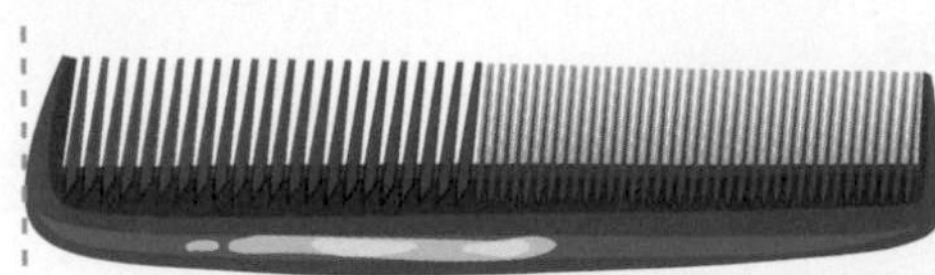

Measure the length to the nearest half inch.

8. 

9. 

10. 

Use a ruler. Draw a line for each length.

11. 3 inches
12. $4\frac{1}{2}$ inches
13. 5 inches
14. $6\frac{1}{2}$ inches

15. Emily is measuring her hairbrush. It is $7\frac{1}{2}$ inches long. Between which two inch marks is the end of the hairbrush?

16. **WRITE Math** **What's the Error?** Joni said this piece of ribbon is 3 inches long. Describe her error.

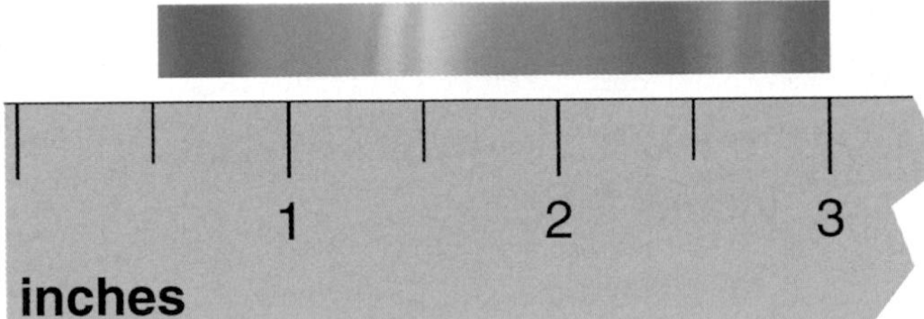

17. Find two different-sized objects in your desk. Measure the length of each object to the nearest half inch. Use $<$ or $>$ to compare the measurements.

Mixed Review and Test Prep

18. Is a football about 1 foot or 1 yard long? (p. 512)

19. Mary spent \$4.25 on a notebook and \$5.15 on some trading cards. She paid with a \$10 bill. How much change did she receive? (pp. 120, 122)

20. **Test Prep** What is the length of the bandage to the nearest half inch?

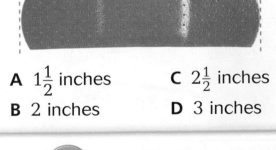

A $1\frac{1}{2}$ inches
B 2 inches
C $2\frac{1}{2}$ inches
D 3 inches

Technology
Use Harcourt Mega Math, Ice Station Exploration, *Linear Lab*, Levels C and D.

 Extra Practice on page 530, Set B

Learn About Measuring to the Nearest Quarter Inch

You learned to measure to the nearest inch and half inch. You can also measure to the nearest quarter inch. When you measure an object to the nearest quarter inch, your measurement is closer to the actual length of the object.

Examples

Measure the length to the nearest quarter inch.

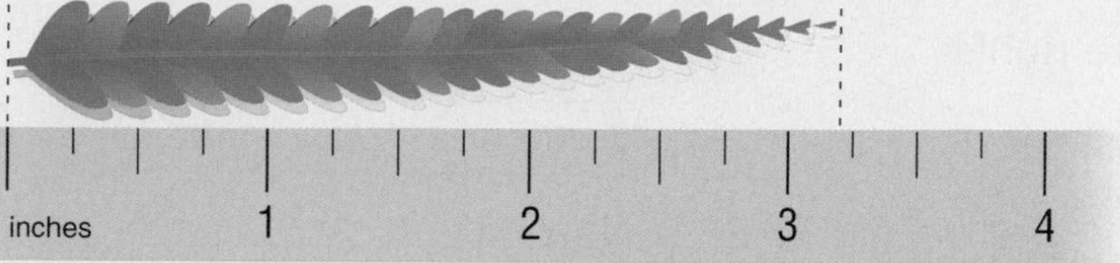

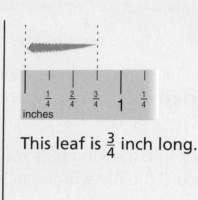

The left end of the leaf is lined up with the 0 mark on the ruler.

The $\frac{1}{4}$ inch mark that is closest to the right end of the leaf is $3\frac{1}{4}$ inches.

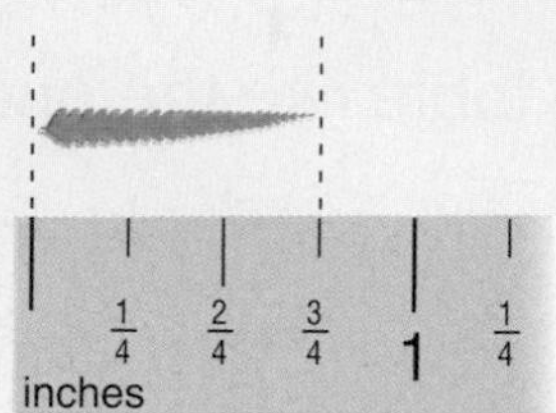

This leaf is $\frac{3}{4}$ inch long.

Try It

Measure the length to the nearest quarter inch.

21. 

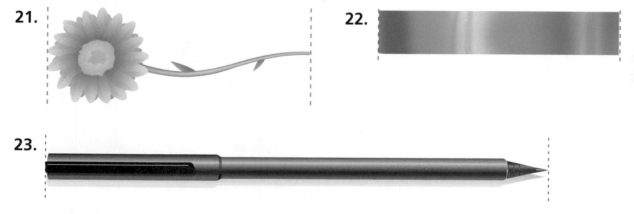

22. 

23. 

24. WRITE Math **Explain** how you can measure the length of the crayon to the nearest quarter inch.

LESSON 3 HANDS ON

Estimate and Measure Feet and Yards

OBJECTIVE: Estimate and measure length to the nearest foot and yard.

Quick Review

Is your math book about 8 feet, 8 inches, or 8 yards wide?

You can use a ruler or yardstick to measure longer lengths.

Investigate

Materials ■ inch ruler and yardstick

A Make a table like the one at the right.

Length of Classroom Objects		
Object	**Estimate**	**Measure**
desk		

B Estimate the length of your desk, and record your estimate in the table.
Think: What unit should you use?

C Measure the length of your desk, and record the measurement in your table.

D Repeat Steps B and C for 2 other objects in your classroom. Some examples are the length of the teacher's desk, the height of the door, and the width of a window.

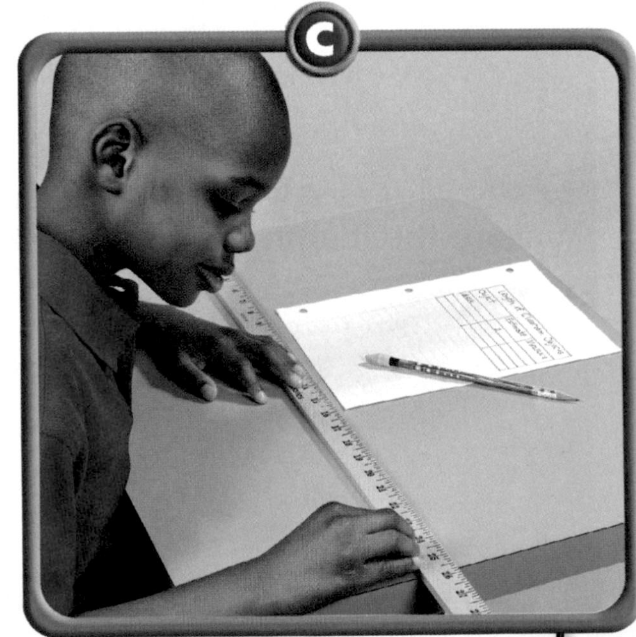

Draw Conclusions

1. When did you use a yardstick instead of a ruler to measure an object?
2. How does the length of your desk compare with another object you measured?
3. **Evaluation** You know about how long 1 foot is. How does that help you estimate the length of an object about 1 yard long? **Explain.**

Connect

Objects that are longer than 12 inches can be measured using a combination of units.

Suppose the length of your desk is 18 inches. You can write the length of the desk in inches or in feet and inches.

18 inches = ■ foot ■ inches

Think: 12 inches = 1 foot

18 inches = 12 inches + 6 inches

So, 18 inches = 1 foot 6 inches.

Table of Measures
1 foot = 12 inches
1 yard = 3 feet
1 yard = 36 inches

TALK Math

Explain how to write 40 inches as a combination of yards and inches.

Practice

Choose the better unit of measure.

1. the width of a small window

   3 feet or 3 yards

2. the length of a car

   9 feet or 9 yards

3. the height of a bookcase

   4 feet or 4 yards

✓4. the length of a bathtub

   2 feet or 2 yards

Use the Table of Measures above. Write the length in feet and inches or in yards and feet.

5. 28 inches = ■ feet ■ inches
6. 8 feet = ■ yards ■ feet
7. 11 feet = ■ yards ■ feet

✓8. 42 inches = ■ feet ■ inches

Algebra Compare. Write <, >, or = for each ●.

9. 4 feet ● 30 inches
10. 70 inches ● 2 yards
11. 24 inches ● 2 feet
12. Karl is building a pen for his rabbit. He needs 8 feet of wire. He has 2 yards of wire. Does he have enough wire to build the pen? **Explain.**
13. **WRITE Math** **What's the Error?** Mary said the length of the soccer field is 100 feet. Describe her error.

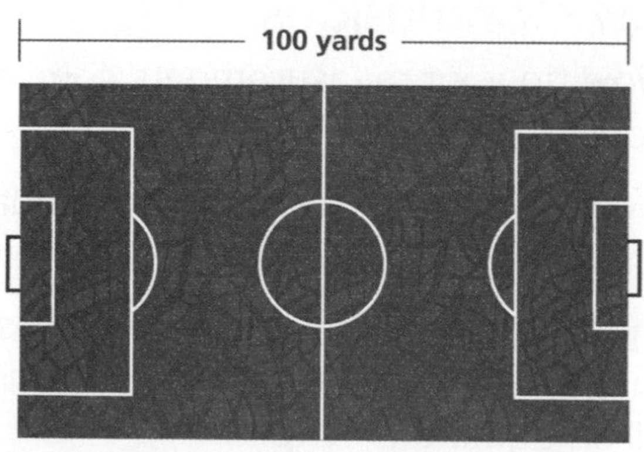

LESSON 4 HANDS ON

Capacity

OBJECTIVE: Estimate and measure capacity.

Capacity is the amount a container will hold. Customary units used to measure capacity are **cup (c)**, **pint (pt)**, **quart (qt)**, and **gallon (gal)**.

 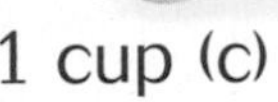 1 cup (c)	 1 pint (pt)	 1 quart (qt)	 1 gallon (gal)

Quick Review

Which container holds more?

Vocabulary

capacity
cup (c)
pint (pt)
quart (qt)
gallon (gal)

Investigate

Materials ■ cup, pint, quart, and gallon containers; water

A Make a table like the one at the right.

B Estimate the number of cups it will take to fill the pint container. Record your estimate.

C Fill a cup and pour it into the pint container. Repeat until the pint container is full.

D Record the number of cups it took to fill the pint container.

E Repeat Steps B–D for the quart and gallon containers.

Number of Cups		
	Estimate	Measure
Cups in a pint		
Cups in a quart		
Cups in a gallon		

E

Draw Conclusions

1. How do your measurements compare to your estimates?
2. How many cups are in a pint? a quart? a gallon?
3. **Synthesis** Which unit would you use to measure the amount of water needed to fill an aquarium? **Explain.**

Connect

How are cups, pints, quarts, and gallons related?

TALK Math

Explain how you can find the number of cups in 3 pints 1 cup.

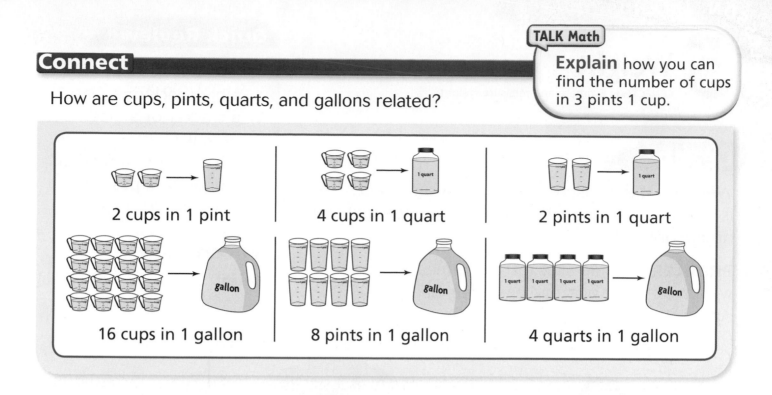

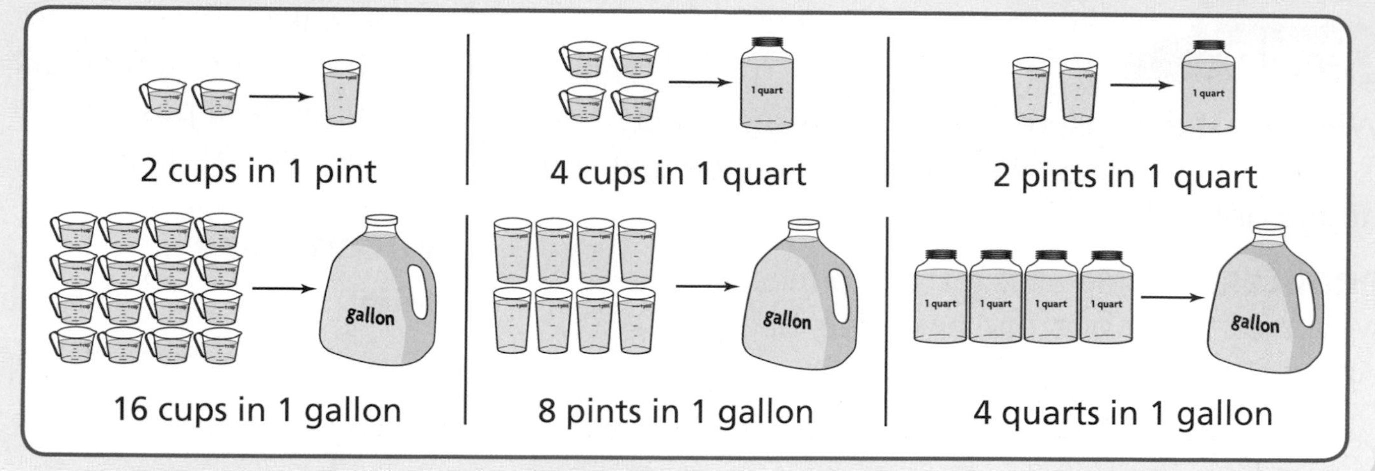

2 cups in 1 pint | 4 cups in 1 quart | 2 pints in 1 quart
16 cups in 1 gallon | 8 pints in 1 gallon | 4 quarts in 1 gallon

Practice

Choose the unit you would use to measure the capacity of each. Write *cup, pint, quart,* or *gallon*.

1. 

2. 

3. 

✓4. 

Tell how the units are related.

5. 8 cups = ■ pints
6. 6 pints = ■ quarts
✓7. 2 gallons = ■ quarts

Algebra **Compare. Write <, >, or = for each ●.**

8. 2 gallons ● 7 quarts
9. 3 cups ● 2 pints
10. 1 quart ● 5 cups

11. Find a container in the classroom that holds about 2 pints. Draw and label the container.

12. Write these amounts in order from greatest to least: 2 quarts, 6 pints, 10 cups.

13. **WRITE Math** **What's the Error?** Connor says it takes 8 cups to fill a 2-gallon container. Is he correct? **Explain.**

14. Lisa made 4 quarts of lemonade. How many cups can she pour?

LESSON 5

Weight

OBJECTIVE: Estimate and measure weight.

Quick Review

Which object is heavier?

1. a backpack or a plate?
2. a cracker or a glass of milk?
3. a baseball or a feather?
4. a book or a postcard?
5. a wristwatch or a TV?

Vocabulary

weight **ounce (oz)** **pound (lb)**

Learn

Weight is the measure of how heavy an object is. Customary units of weight include **ounce (oz)** and **pound (lb)**.

PROBLEM Sophie uses a scale to measure the weight of a slice of bread and a loaf of bread. About how much does each weigh?

about 1 ounce

about 1 pound

So, a slice of bread weighs about 1 ounce, and a loaf of bread weighs about 16 ounces, or 1 pound.

HANDS ON

Activity

Materials ■ scale, classroom objects

Estimate the weight of each object. Then use a scale to measure to the nearest ounce or pound.

- ■ tape dispenser
- ■ book
- ■ apple
- ■ pencil box

- How do your estimates compare to the actual measurements?
- Put the items you weighed in order from least to greatest weight.

Customary Units of Weight
1 pound = 16 ounces

Guided Practice

1. Does a strawberry weigh about 1 ounce or about 1 pound?

Choose the unit you would use to weigh each.
Write *ounce* or *pound*.

2. 
3. 
4. 
5. 

6. **TALK Math** Which weighs more—a key or a baseball bat? **Explain** how you know.

Independent Practice and Problem Solving

Choose the unit you would use to weigh each.
Write *ounce* or *pound*.

7. 
8. 
9. 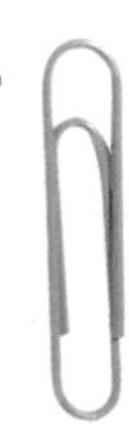
10. 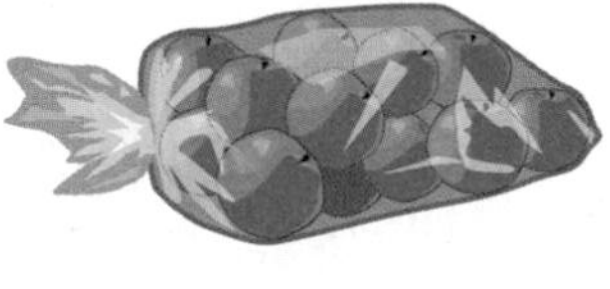

Find an object in the classroom to match each weight.
Draw it, and label its weight.

11. about 2 pounds
12. less than 1 pound
13. greater than 1 pound

14. **WRITE Math** **Sense or Nonsense** Hank says that 20 ounces is the same as 1 pound 4 ounces. Does his statement make sense? **Explain.**

Mixed Review and Test Prep

15. Two lines intersect and form right angles. Do the lines appear to be parallel or perpendicular? (p. 354)

16. $4 \times 3 = \blacksquare \times 6$ (p. 212)

17. **Test Prep** A store sells 4 ball caps. Each cap weighs 8 ounces. How much do the caps weigh in all?

A 8 ounces
B 12 ounces
C 2 pounds
D 4 pounds

Extra Practice on page 530, Set C

LESSON 6

Estimate or Measure

OBJECTIVE: Know when to estimate or when to measure.

Quick Review

1. 1 yard = ■ feet
2. 1 quart = ■ pints
3. 1 foot = ■ inches
4. 1 pint = ■ cups
5. 1 gallon = ■ quarts

Learn

Sometimes you need an exact measurement. Sometimes an estimate is all you need.

Example 1 Theresa's father is making lemonade. The recipe calls for 6 cups of water, $\frac{3}{4}$ cup sugar, and the juice from 4 lemons. Should he estimate or measure the water and sugar?

When you use a recipe, you should accurately measure each ingredient.

So, Theresa's father should measure the water and sugar.

Example 2 Theresa wants to pour 4 glasses of lemonade from a pitcher that holds 2 quarts. Each glass holds 1 cup of lemonade. Should Theresa measure the lemonade she pours into each glass, or can she estimate whether there will be enough?

There are 4 cups in 1 quart, so Theresa can pour about 8 glasses from the 2-quart pitcher.

So, Theresa does not need to measure the lemonade she pours into each glass.

- Why is it necessary to measure accurately when using a recipe?

Guided Practice

1. Ty filled a 1-quart container to water 3 plants. Each plant needs about 1 cup of water. Should he measure the water he gives each plant or can he estimate?

Choose *estimate* or *measure*.

2. Zach fills a water bowl for his kitten each day. Should Zach estimate or measure the water?

3. Morgan needs 36 inches of wire for each side of a rabbit pen. Should she estimate or measure the wire?

4. Jenna is cutting pieces of ribbon to glue on a picture frame. Should she estimate or measure the ribbon?

5. **TALK Math** Marta needs to mix 1 tablespoon of cocoa with 1 cup of milk to make hot chocolate. **Explain** why it is better for Marta to measure these amounts than to estimate them.

Independent Practice and Problem Solving

Choose *estimate* or *measure*.

6. Leigh is making cookies. The recipe calls for $\frac{3}{4}$ cup brown sugar. Should Leigh estimate or measure the brown sugar?

7. Jonas tore a poster when taking it off the wall. He needs 2 pieces of tape to fix the poster. Should Jonas estimate or measure the tape he needs?

8. Nathaniel has to be 48 inches tall to ride the Super Loop roller coaster. Should the theme park estimate or measure his height?

9. **WRITE Math** Sandra and Kailyn are making jump ropes. Should they estimate or measure the rope? **Explain.**

Mixed Review and Test Prep

10. Rory's room is 3 yards 2 feet long. How many feet long is the room? (p. 518)

11. Paula's volleyball practice lasts 90 minutes. It starts at 4:15. At what time does it end? (p. 130)

12. **Test Prep** Which amount should you measure?

    A the distance you can throw a ball

    B the amount of flour in a cake recipe

    C the amount of water in a teapot

    D the weight of a pair of skates

Extra Practice on page 530, Set D

Problem Solving Workshop
Skill: Choose a Unit

OBJECTIVE: Solve problems by using the skill *choose a unit.*

Read to Understand
Plan
Solve
Check

Read to Understand

PROBLEM Ian's class is setting up a freshwater fish tank. What customary unit would Ian use to measure the capacity of the tank?

Remember how customary units of capacity are related.

The smallest customary unit of capacity in Ian's class is a cup.

A pint is larger than a cup.
Think: there are 2 cups in 1 pint.

A quart is larger than a pint.
Think: there are 2 pints in 1 quart.

A gallon is larger than a quart.
Think: there are 4 quarts in 1 gallon.

Since the fish tank holds a lot of water, Ian would use gallons to measure the capacity.

Table of Measures
Length
12 inches = 1 foot
3 feet = 1 yard
Capacity
2 cups = 1 pint
4 cups = 1 quart
2 pints = 1 quart
8 pints = 1 gallon
4 quarts = 1 gallon
Weight
16 ounces = 1 pound

Think and Discuss

Choose the better unit of measure.

a. Marianna measures the length of a black swordtail fish in the classroom fish tank. Is the length closer to 2 inches or 2 feet?

b. It takes Ned 12 minutes to drive from his house to the store. Is the distance he travels about 7 yards or 7 miles?

c. Ben likes to watch the pandas at the zoo. Is the weight of an adult panda measured in ounces or pounds?

TALK Math

How can you decide which unit is better to measure the weight of an object?

Guided Problem Solving

1. About 2 cars, end to end, will fit in Beth's driveway. What customary unit of length should Beth use to measure the length of her driveway?

   Think of the units of length.

   Which unit would be best to measure the length of a car?

   Which unit would be the best to measure a distance that is about 2 car lengths long?

   Solve the problem.

✓2. **What if** Beth helps her dad build a small birdhouse? What customary unit of length could they use to estimate the amount of wood they would need?

✓3. Mary enjoys drinking cocoa in the morning. Does her mug hold about 2 cups or 2 quarts?

Mixed Applications

4. Which unit would you use to measure the amount of water in a bathtub?

5. A bathtub is twice as long as Kia's dog. Kia's dog is 3 feet long. How many yards long is the bathtub?

For 6–8, use the items pictured.

6. Mike bought 2 bags of potting soil and 3 daylily plants. How much did he spend?

7. Which would cost more, 4 black-eyed Susan plants or 6 daisy plants? How much more?

8. Joe has $10. Name two combinations of items he could buy.

9. **WRITE Math** Judy bought 24 daisy plants. She wants to plant them in 4 equal rows. How many daisies will be in each row? **Explain** your answer by drawing an array.

LESSON HANDS ON

8 Fahrenheit Temperature

OBJECTIVE: Estimate and measure temperature in degrees Fahrenheit.

Quick Review

Which is colder?

Vocabulary

degrees Fahrenheit (°F)

Temperature is the measure of how hot or cold something is. **Degrees Fahrenheit (°F)** are customary units of temperature.

To read a thermometer, find the number closest to the top of the red bar. Use the scale along the side like a number line. On the thermometer at the right, each line on the scale stands for 1 degree. The top of the red bar is at 67°F. The temperature shown is 67°F.

Write: 67°F Read: sixty-seven degrees Fahrenheit

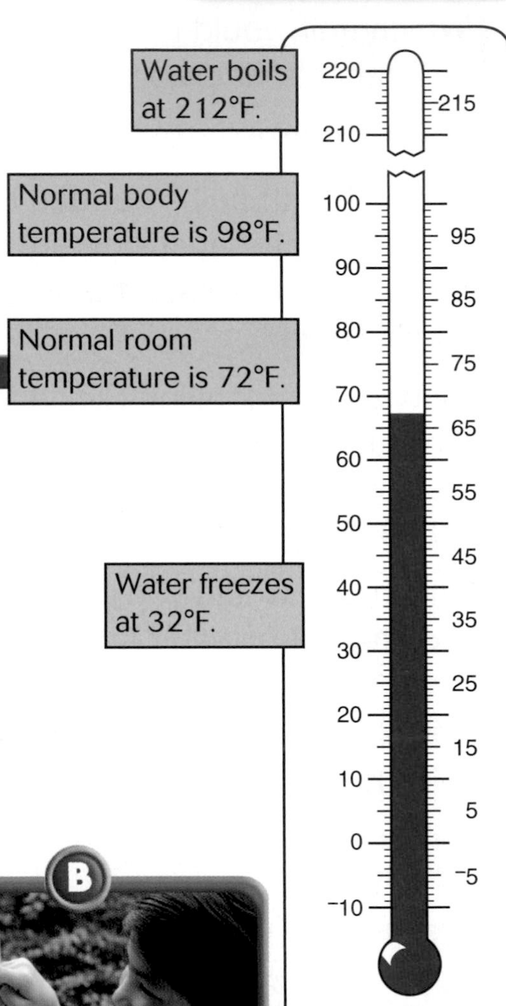

Investigate

Materials ■ Fahrenheit thermometer

A Estimate what you think the outdoor temperature will be, in degrees Fahrenheit, 3 times during the day. Record your estimates.

B Use a Fahrenheit thermometer to measure the outdoor temperature at the listed times. Record the actual temperature.

Draw Conclusions

1. At what time is temperature the coolest? the warmest? **Explain.**
2. How did each of the temperatures compare with normal room temperature?
3. **Analysis** How did knowing the temperature inside your classroom help you estimate the outside temperature? **Explain.**

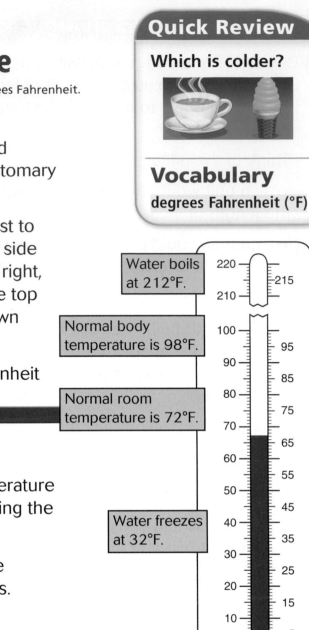

Connect

Below are outside activities you might do at 20°F, 75°F, and 90°F.

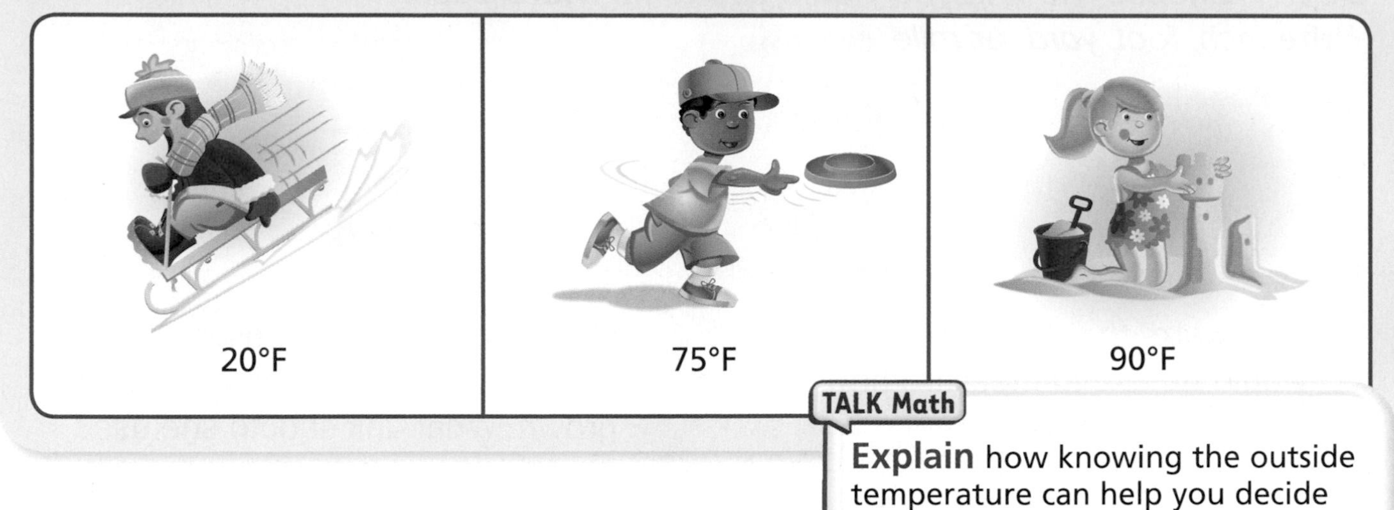

TALK Math

Explain how knowing the outside temperature can help you decide what clothes to wear.

Practice

Write each temperature in °F.

1\. 50 40 30 °F

2\. 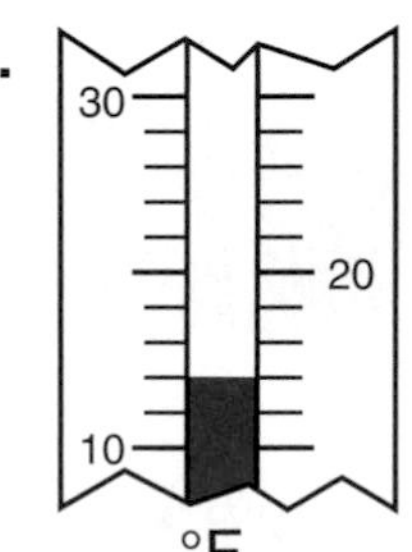

3\. 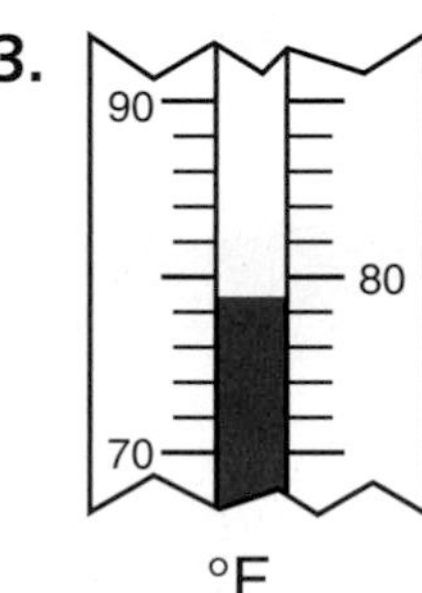

✓4. 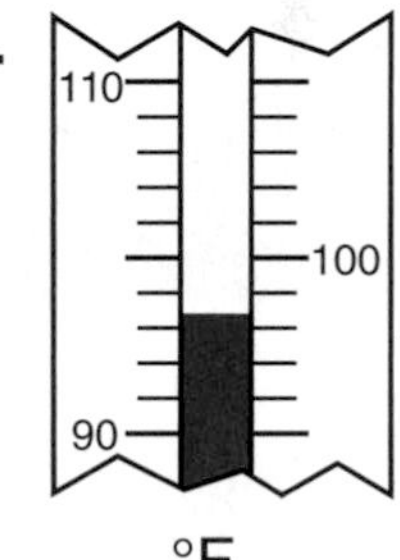

Choose the better temperature for each activity.

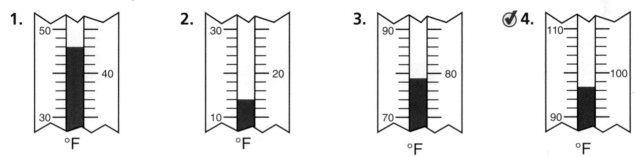

5\. 

58°F or 88°F

6\. 

23°F or 53°F

7\. 

75°F or 105°F

✓8. 

90°F or 30°F

9\. **WRITE Math** Kenny's father is building a fire in the fireplace. About what temperature might it be outside? **Explain.**

10\. It is 85°F outside. What is an activity that Paige might do at this temperature? What clothes do you think she might wear?

Extra Practice

Set A **Choose the unit you would use to measure each.**
Write *inch, foot, yard,* or *mile*. (pp. 512–513)

1. 

2. 

3. 

4. Sam walks to school. What unit would he use to measure how far he has to walk?

5. Helena is going to measure her kitten to see how much he has grown. What unit should she use?

Set B **Measure the length to the nearest inch.** (pp. 514–517)

1. 

2.

Measure the length to the nearest half inch.

3.

4. 

Set C **Choose the unit you would use to measure each.**
Write *ounce* or *pound*. (pp. 522–523)

1. 

2. 

3. 

Set D **Choose *estimate* or *measure*.** (pp. 524–525)

1. Melanie wants to pour each of her 5 friends about 1 cup of orange juice. Her pitcher holds 2 quarts. Should Melanie estimate or measure the orange juice she pours?

2. Melanie is making cookies to serve with the orange juice. The recipe calls for 1 cup of sugar. Should Melanie estimate or measure the sugar?

Technology
Use Harcourt Mega Math, The Number Games, *Tiny's Think Tank*, Levels N, O, P.

PRACTICE GAME

Measure Up!

Set Up the Board!

2 players and 1 reader

Choose Your Question!

- Gameboard
- Money cards
- Answer sheet

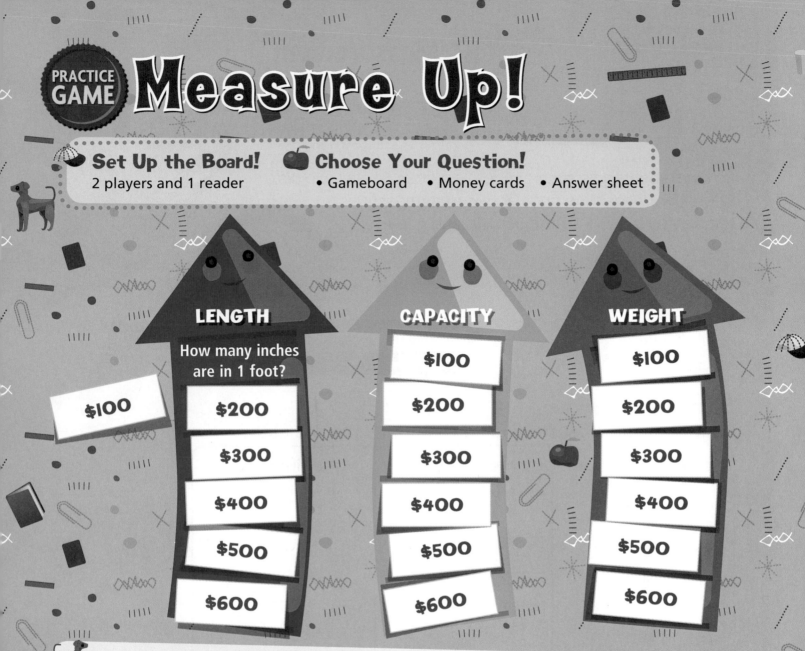

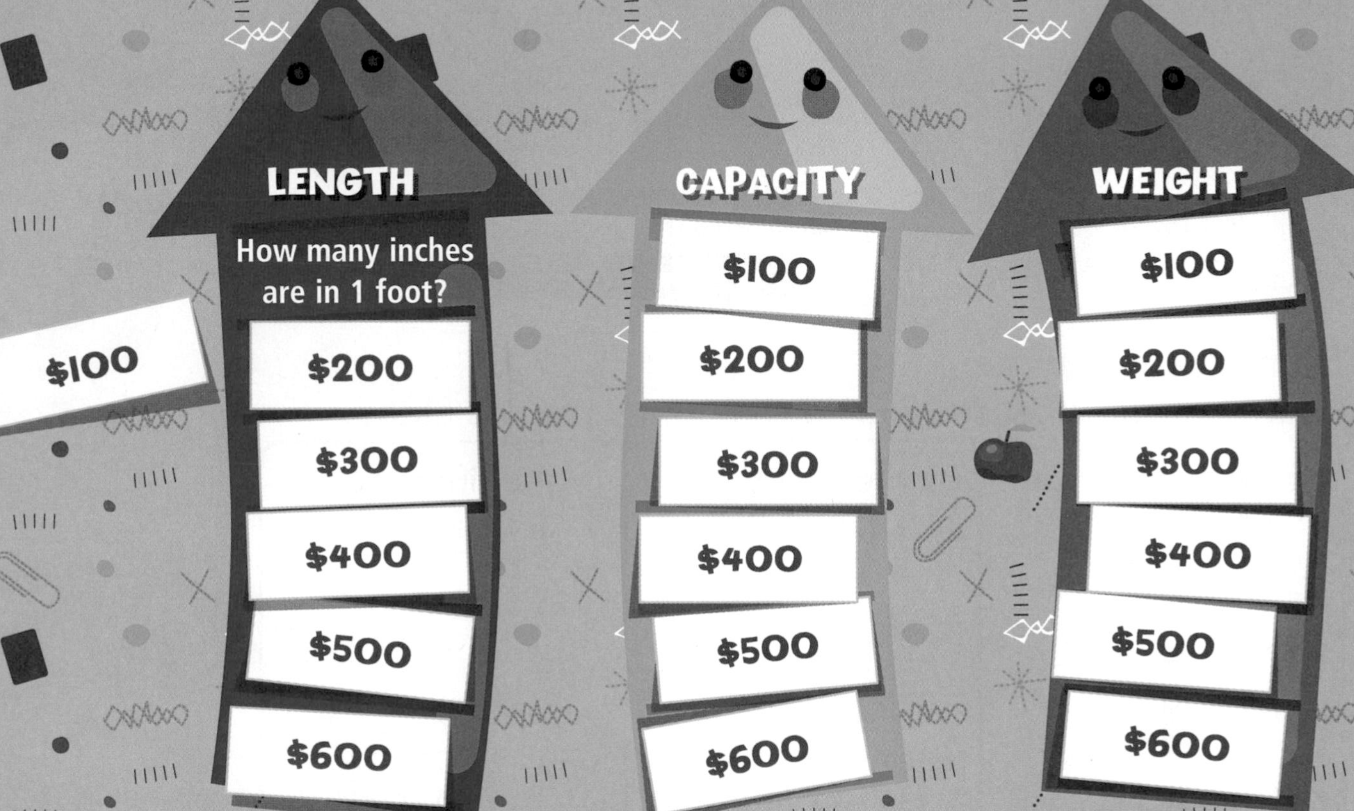

Your Answer, Please!

- Place the money cards over the gameboard sections as shown above.
- The first player chooses Length, Capacity, or Weight, and begins with the $100 question. The reader uncovers the question and reads it aloud.
- Player 1 answers the question. The reader uses the answer sheet to check Player 1's answer.
- If the answer is correct, Player 1 keeps the money card and chooses the next question in the same category. If Player 1's answer is not correct, it is Player 2's turn.
- Player 2 may continue in Player 1's category or begin a new category. Players may answer only 2 questions per turn.
- Play continues until all questions are answered. The player with the greater amount of money wins.

Measurement

CHOOSE A TOOL

Measurement tools such as thermometers, scales, clocks, rulers and measuring cups are used to measure temperature, weight, time, length, and capacity.

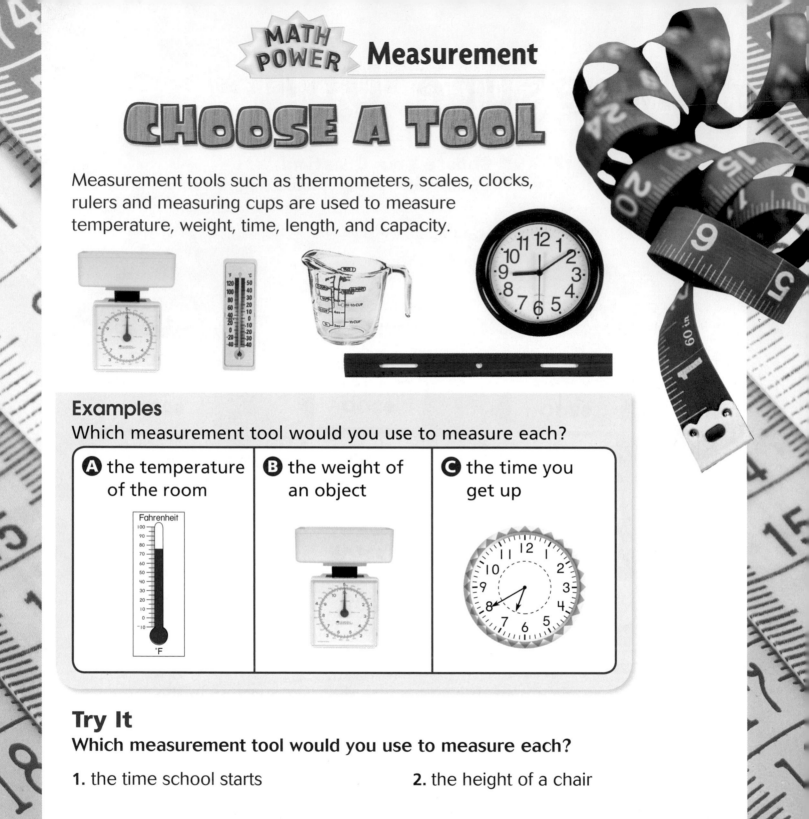

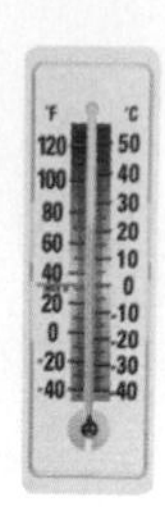

Examples

Which measurement tool would you use to measure each?

A the temperature of the room	B the weight of an object	C the time you get up
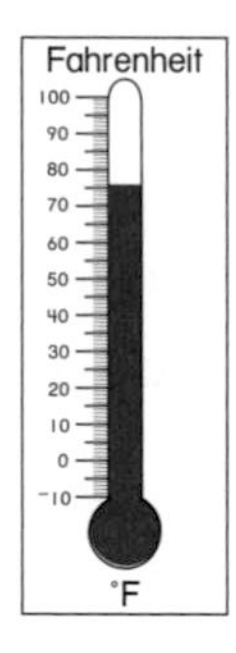		

Try It

Which measurement tool would you use to measure each?

1. the time school starts

2. the height of a chair

3. the weight of a pencil

4. the capacity of a pitcher

5. WRITE Math What measurement tool would you use to find out which of two objects is heavier? **Explain.**

Chapter 20 Review/Test

Check Concepts

Solve.

1. Would you use miles, yards, feet, or inches to measure the distance between two cities? IL 7.3.02 (p. 512)
2. Which weighs more, a baseball or a crayon? IL 7.3.05 (pp. 522–523)

Check Skills

Choose the unit you would use to measure each.
Write *inch*, *foot*, *yard*, or *mile*. IL 7.3.02 (pp. 512–513)

3. 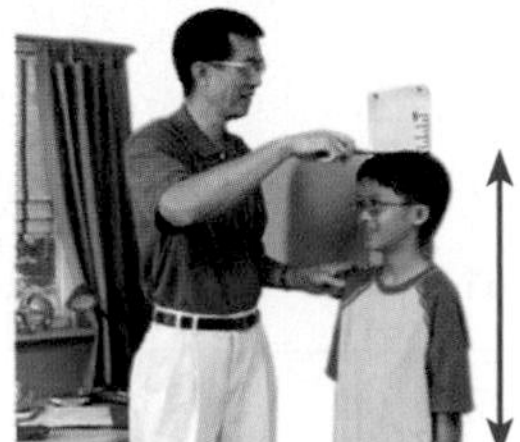
4. 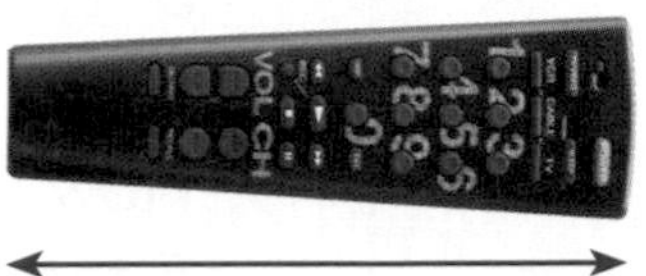
5. 

Measure to the nearest half inch. IL 7.3.02 (pp. 514–517)

6. 
7. 
8. 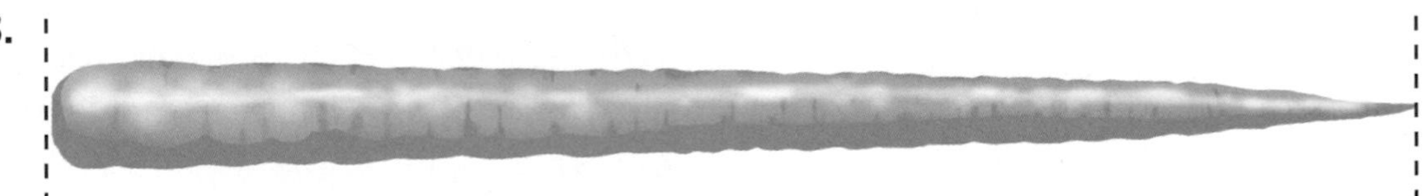

Check Problem Solving

Solve. IL 7.3.02 (pp. 526–527)

9. Christina's garden has 6 rows of corn, with 10 plants in each row. What unit of length should she use to measure the corn section of her garden?
10. WRITE Math Christina's mother is preparing 12 ears of corn. Should she put the corn in a pot that holds 3 cups or 3 gallons of water? **Explain.**

Practice for the ISAT
Chapters 1–20

Number and Operations

1. There are 204 people in the band. There are 289 people in the choir. Which shows the BEST estimate of how many more people are in the choir than in the band? IL 6.3.14 (p. 52)

   A 400 C 50
   B 100 D 0

Test Tip **Choose the answer.**

See item 2. Order the numbers from greatest to least mentally. Then compare your list with the answers given. If your answer does not match any of the answers given, carefully solve the problem again.

2. One of Liz's books has 347 pages. Another book has 299 pages. A third book has 390 pages. Which lists the number of pages in order from greatest to least? IL 6.3.05 (p. 32)

   A 299; 347; 390
   B 347; 390; 299
   C 390; 299; 347
   D 390; 347; 299

3. WRITE Math How can this picture help you find 5×8? **Explain.** IL 6.3.11 (p. 206)

Algebra

4. What is the pattern unit in this number pattern? IL 8.3.01 (p. 422)

   2, 0, 1, 4, 2, 0, 1, 4, 2, 0, 1, 4

   A 0, 1, 4, 2
   B 2, 0, 1, 4
   C 2, 0, 1
   D 1, 4, 2, 0

5. How many players are on 5 teams? IL 8.3.01 (p. 218)

Teams	1	2	3	4	5
Players	5	10	15	20	■

   A 10
   B 15
   C 20
   D 25

6. WRITE Math What is a rule for the number pattern below? **Explain.** IL 8.3.01 (p. 256)

   77, 66, 55, 44, 33

Measurement

7. Marisa used inches to measure an object. Which object did she measure? IL 7.3.02 (p. 512)

A 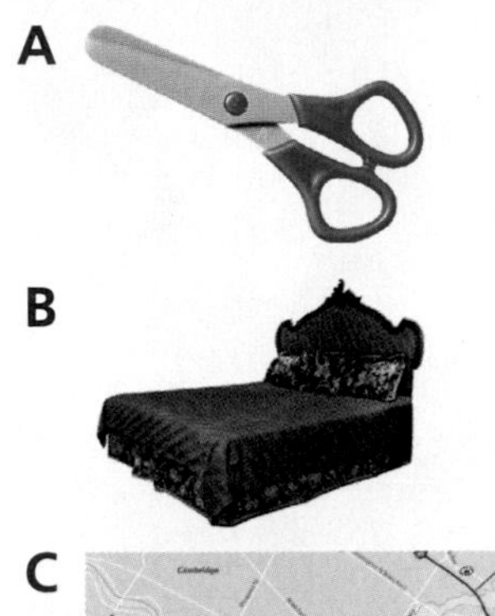

B

C 

D 

8. What temperature does the thermometer show? IL 7.3.02 (p. 528)

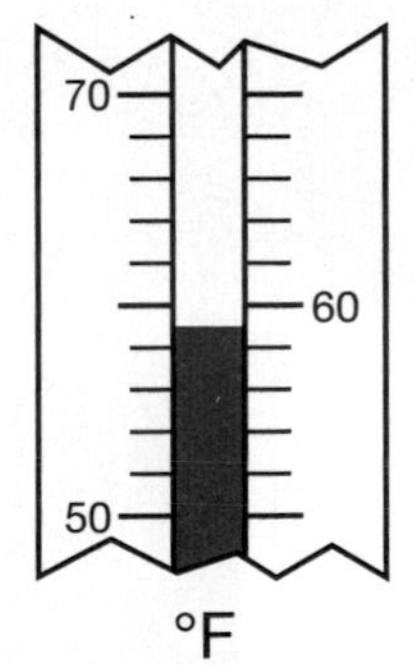

A 51°F
B 54°F
C 59°F
D 61°F

9. **WRITE Math** Would the height of the desk be 28 inches or 28 feet? **Explain.** IL 7.3.05 (p. 512)

Data Analysis and Probability

10. Billy and Eric use this spinner to play a game. Which color are they more likely to spin? IL 10.3.04 (p. 182)

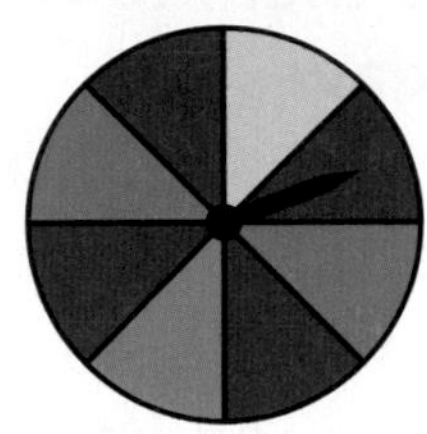

A yellow
B blue
C green
D red

11. John made a pictograph to show how many people played winter sports. He used the key: Each = 8 people. The pictograph shows next to ice-skating. How many people ice-skate? IL 10.3.01 (p. 148)

A 36
B 40
C 44
D 48

12. **WRITE Math** John wants to make a bar graph from the data in his pictograph. The bars for ice-skating and skiing are the same length. **Explain** what this means. IL 10.3.01 (p. 154)

CHAPTER

21 Metric Measurement

FAST FACT

Giraffes' long necks allow them to reach the leaves on treetops. A giraffe is the tallest land mammal. Some giraffes can be as tall as 6 meters!

Investigate

The bar graph shows the heights of several items. Choose an item from the graph and compare it to the height of the giraffe. Find the difference between the two heights.

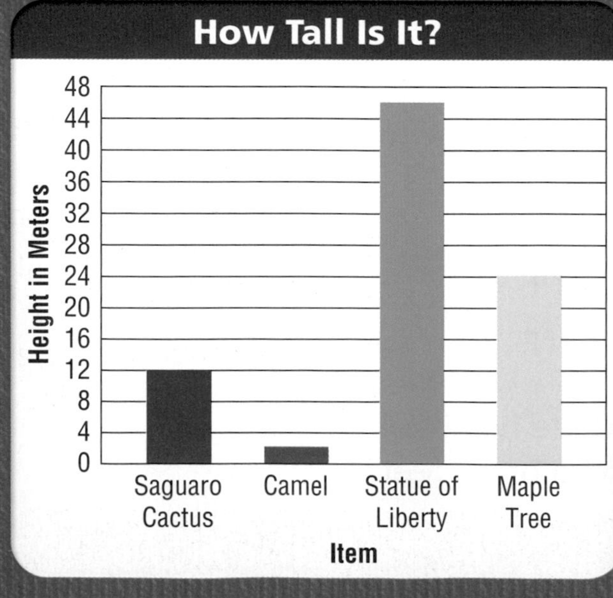

GO ONLINE **Technology** Student pages are available in the Student eBook.

Show What You Know

Check your understanding of important skills needed for success in Chapter 21.

▶ Use a Metric Ruler

Use a centimeter ruler to measure.

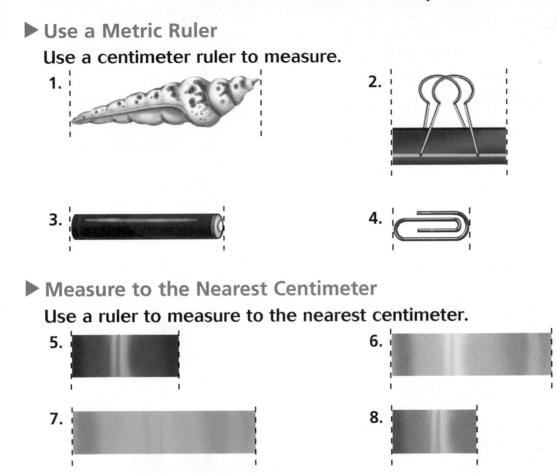

1. 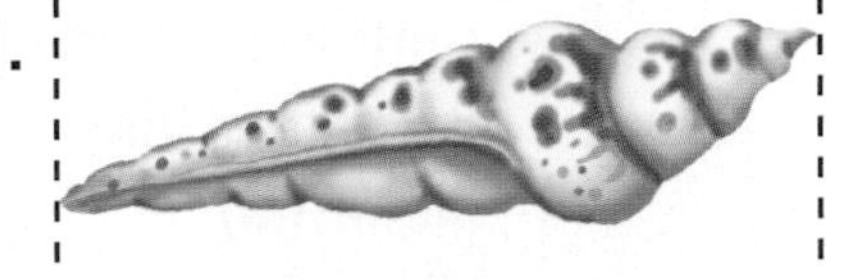

2. 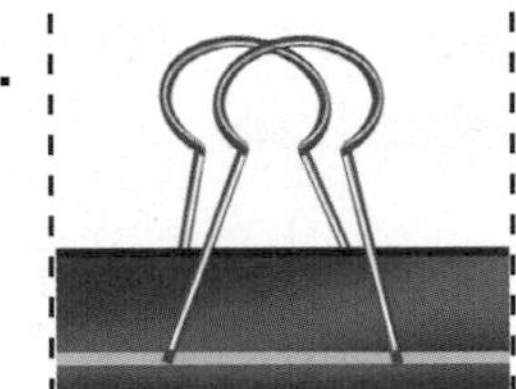

3. 

4. 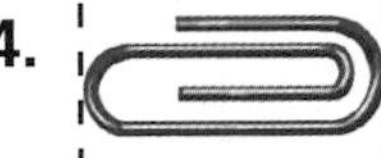

▶ Measure to the Nearest Centimeter

Use a ruler to measure to the nearest centimeter.

5. 

6.

7.

8. 

VOCABULARY POWER

CHAPTER VOCABULARY

centimeter (cm)
decimeter (dm)
gram (g)
kilogram (kg)
kilometer (km)
length
liter (L)
mass
meter (m)
milliliter (mL)

WARM-UP WORDS

centimeter (cm) A metric unit for measuring length or distance

gram A metric unit for measuring mass; 1 kilogram = 1,000 grams

liter A metric unit for measuring capacity; 1 liter = 1,000 milliliters

LESSON 1 Length

OBJECTIVE: Introduce metric units of length.

Quick Review

Would you use an inch ruler or a yardstick to measure the length of a pencil?

Vocabulary

centimeter (cm)
decimeter (dm)
meter (m)
kilometer (km)

Learn

Length and distance can be measured by using metric units such as **centimeter (cm)**, **decimeter (dm)**, **meter (m)**, and **kilometer (km)**.

PROBLEM Aaron plays basketball in college. Is Aaron about 2 centimeters, 2 decimeters, 2 meters, or 2 kilometers tall?

Measure shorter lengths in centimeters and decimeters.

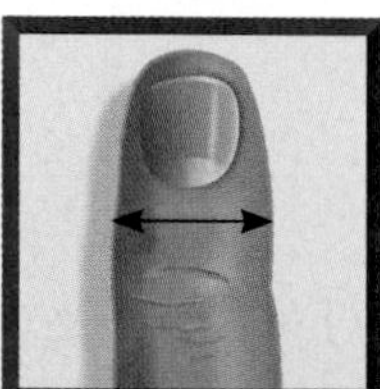

A child's finger is about 1 centimeter wide.

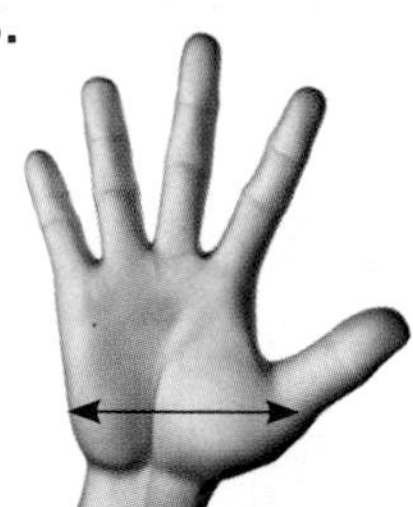

An adult's hand is about 1 decimeter wide.

Measure longer lengths in meters and kilometers.

A doorway is about 1 meter wide.

It takes about 10 minutes to walk 1 kilometer.

So, Aaron is about 2 meters tall.

Guided Practice

1. Would you measure the length of this crayon in centimeters or decimeters?

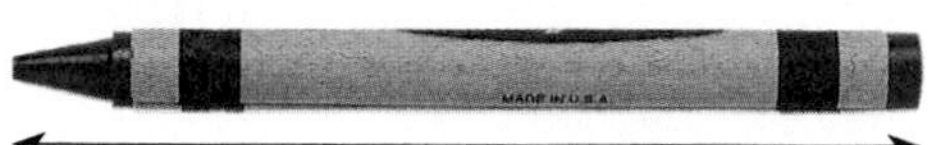

Choose the unit you would use to measure each. Write *cm*, *m*, or *km*.

2. 

3. 

4. 

5. **TALK Math** Would you use centimeters or meters to measure the width of your school picture? **Explain.**

Independent Practice and Problem Solving

Choose the unit you would use to measure each. Write *cm*, *m*, or *km*.

6. 

7. 

8. 

9. distance from your house to school

10. width of a bookshelf

11. height of a skyscraper

12. width of a butterfly

13. height of a flagpole

14. length of a dollar bill

15. Brad walks from his house to the park every afternoon to play basketball. It takes him 20 minutes to get to the park. Is the park 2 dm, 2 m, or 2 km from his house?

16. **WRITE Math** **What's the Error?** Nancy's plant is about the same width as her front door. She says it is about 1 dm wide. Describe Nancy's error.

Mixed Review and Test Prep

17. Theresa has 5 quarters, 3 dimes, and 5 pennies. How much money does she have? (p. 110)

18. The temperature is 30°F. Is Eric planting flowers or shoveling snow? (p. 528)

19. **Test Prep** About how long is this shell?

A 3 cm

B 3 dm

C 3 m

D 3 km

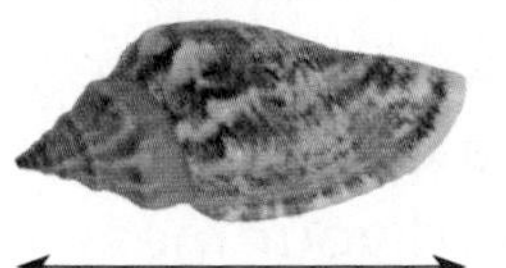

LESSON 2

Estimate and Measure Centimeters, Decimeters, and Meters

OBJECTIVE: Estimate and measure length to the nearest centimeter, decimeter, and meter.

Quick Review

Choose the unit you would use to measure each. Write *cm*, *m*, or *km*.

1. width of a penny
2. height of a bookcase
3. distance to the airport
4. length of a paper clip
5. length of a car

Learn

You can use a centimeter ruler to measure length to the nearest centimeter and decimeter.

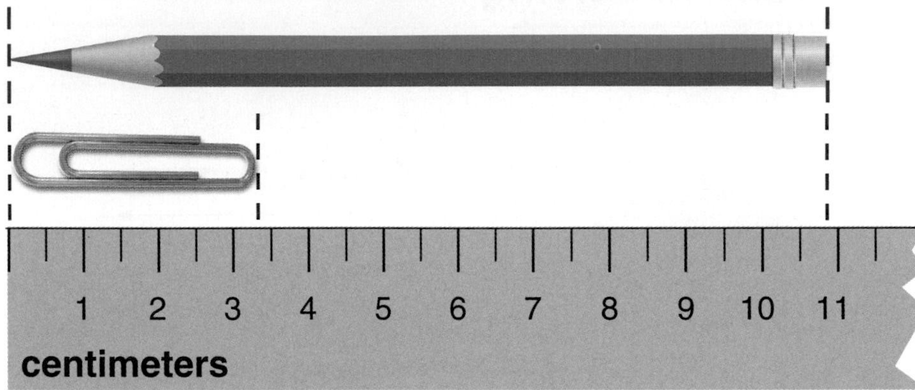

The right end of the paper clip is closest to the 3-centimeters mark. So, the paperclip is 3 centimeters long, to the nearest centimeter.

The right end of the pencil is closest to the 11-centimeters mark. So, the pencil is 11 centimeters long, to the nearest centimeter, and 1 decimeter long, to the nearest decimeter.

Remember

1 decimeter = 10 centimeters

Activity 1 **Materials** ■ centimeter ruler

Step 1

Make a table like the one at the right. Choose three objects to measure. Estimate the length of each object in cm or dm. Record your estimates.

Step 2

Use a centimeter ruler to measure each object. Record your measurements in the table.

Length of Objects

Object	Estimate	Measure

- How did your estimates compare to the actual measurements?
- Write the lengths of the objects in order from least to greatest.

Relating Units

You can measure longer lengths in meters.

Table of Measures
1 decimeter = 10 centimeters
1 meter = 100 centimeters = 10 decimeters
1 kilometer = 1,000 meters

Activity 2

Materials ■ centimeter grid paper, tape, crayons

Step 1
Use the Table of Measures to find the number of decimeters in one meter.

Step 2
Cut enough decimeter strips out of grid paper to make a 1-meter strip. Color each decimeter strip a different color.

Step 3
Tape the decimeter strips together so that the edges do not overlap.

Step 4
Estimate the length of your classroom. Then use your meter strip to find the actual measure.

- How did you know how many decimeter strips were needed to make a meter strip?

Guided Practice

1. To the nearest centimeter, how long is this crayon?

Estimate the length in centimeters. Then use a ruler to measure to the nearest centimeter.

2. the length of your math book
3. the length of your shoe
4. the length of your pencil
5. the length of a marker

Choose the best estimate.

6. height of a fence
   2 cm 2 m 2 km
7. length of a roadrace
   5 dm 5 m 5 km

8. TALK Math **Explain** how you can measure the length of your notebook to the nearest centimeter.

Independent Practice and Problem Solving

Estimate the length in centimeters. Then use a ruler to measure to the nearest centimeter.

9. the length of a piece of chalk

10. the length of a ruler

11. the length of a pencil case

12. the length of an eraser

Use a ruler to measure to the nearest centimeter.

13. 

14.

Choose the best estimate.

15. length of a camera
10 cm 10 dm 10 m

16. length of a banana
2 cm 2 dm 2 m

17. length of a peanut
4 cm 4 dm 40 dm

18. length of a marker
12 cm 12 dm 12 m

19. length of a notebook
3 cm 30 cm 300 cm

20. length of a paintbrush
15 cm 15 dm 15 m

Use a centimeter ruler. Draw a line for each length.

21. 13 centimeters

22. 2 decimeters

23. 18 centimeters

24. **Reasoning** Peter is 8 dm tall. Mary is 86 cm tall. Susan is 9 dm tall and Jack is 84 cm tall. Who is tallest? **Explain.**

25. Suppose you measure your desk in centimeters and then in decimeters. Will there be more centimeters or more decimeters? **Explain.**

26. Choose 3 objects inside your classroom. Estimate and measure the lengths with a centimeter ruler. How do your estimates compare to the actual measurements?

27. WRITE Math **Sense or Nonsense** Justin said that 32 centimeters is the same as 3 decimeters plus 2 centimeters. Do you agree? **Explain.**

Mixed Review and Test Prep

28. Write $<$, $>$, or $=$ to complete.
$8 \div 2$ ● $2 + 2$ (p. 308)

29. Write the fact family for 3, 9, and 27.
(p. 286)

30. **Test Prep** June's book is 40 cm long. How many decimeters long is it?

A 400 dm **B** 40 dm **C** 4 dm **D** 4 cm

CD ROM **Technology**
Use Harcout Mega Math, Ice Station Exploration, *Linear Lab*, Level H.

 Extra Practice on page 552, Set B

How Big is the Collection?

Visualize

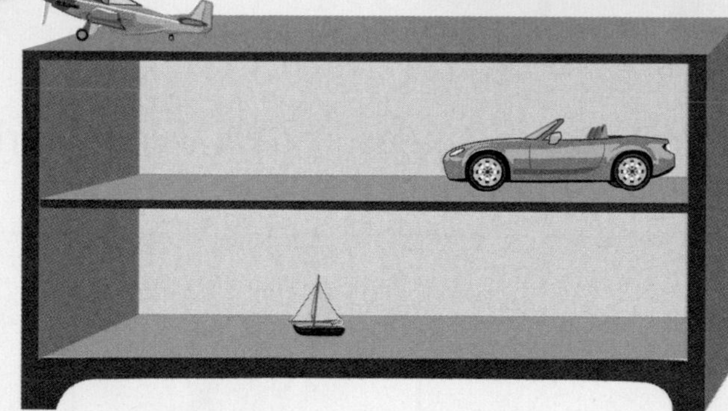

Mike has a collection of model planes, cars, and boats. He wants to display each collection on one of the three shelves shown above. Each shelf is 12 dm long. The cars are about 4 dm long, the boats are about 1 dm long, and the planes are about 3 dm long. How many of each model will fit on one shelf?

You can visualize, or picture in your mind, how the models will fit on the shelves.

To solve the problem, use details from the problem and visualize the size of the models in Mike's collection. Then decide how many of each model will fit on one shelf.

Visualize
Each shelf is 12 dm long, or about 12 hand widths long.
The cars are about 4 dm long, or about 4 hand widths long.
The boats are about 1 dm long, or about 1 hand width long.
The planes are about 3 dm long, or about 3 hand widths long.

Remember
An adult's hand is about one decimeter wide.

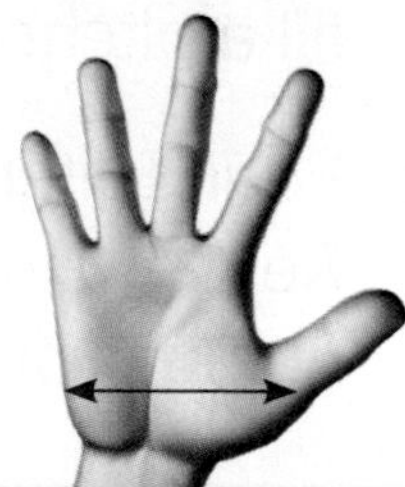

Problem Solving **Visualize to understand the problem.**

1. Solve the problem above. Which model will have the most on one shelf? Which model will have the fewest?
2. Mike also has 2 model trains. Each train is 6 dm long. Would both model trains fit on one shelf?
3. One motorcycle is about 5 dm long. If Mike has 3 motorcycles the same size, would they all fit on one shelf?

LESSON 3 HANDS ON

Capacity

OBJECTIVE: Estimate and measure capacity.

Quick Review

Which container holds more?

Vocabulary

milliliter (mL) **liter (L)**

Capacity can be measured by using metric units such as **milliliter (mL)** and **liter (L)**.

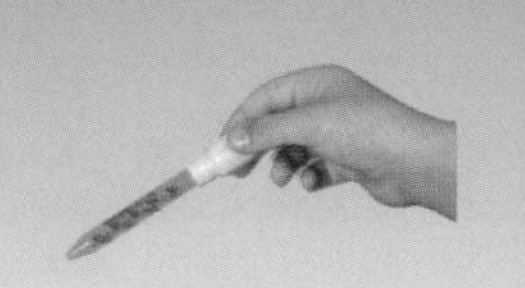

A dropper holds about 1 mL.

A full glass holds about 250 mL.

A water bottle holds about 1 L.

Investigate

Materials ■ 250-mL plastic water glass, liter container, pitcher

Find the Capacity		
How many:	Estimate	Measure
milliliters in a liter?		
liters in a pitcher?		

A Make a table like the one at the right to help find the capacity of different containers.

B Estimate the number of milliliters that are in 1 liter. Use the plastic glass. Pour 250 mL of water into the liter container.

C Repeat until the liter container is full. Record how many milliliters you poured.

D Estimate the number of liters it will take to fill a pitcher.

E Pour 1 liter of water into the pitcher. Repeat until the pitcher is full. Record the number of liters you poured.

B

Draw Conclusions

1. How close were your estimates to the actual capacity of your containers?
2. **Evaluation** Suppose you drank a tall glass of orange juice. Did you drink about 4 mL or 400 mL of orange juice? **Explain.**

Connect

The table helps you see how liters and milliliters are related.

L	1	2	3	4	5
mL	1,000	2,000	3,000	4,000	5,000

1,000 mL = 1 L

TALK Math

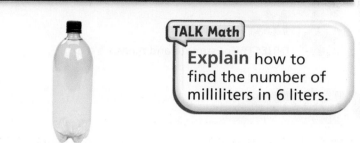

Explain how to find the number of milliliters in 6 liters.

Practice

Choose the unit you would use to measure the capacity of each. Write *mL* or *L*.

1. 

2. 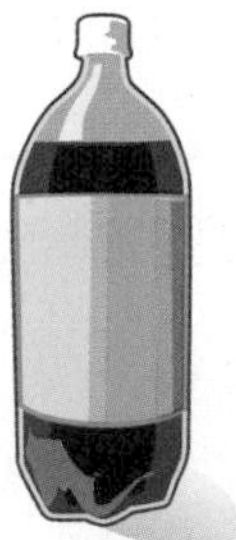

✓3. 

4. 

5. 

✓6. 

Find a container in the classroom that shows each capacity. Draw it and label its capacity.

7. less than 250 mL
8. greater than 1 L
9. greater than 2 L

Algebra Find each missing number.

10. ■ mL = 4 L
11. 12,000 mL = ■ L
12. 8 L = ■ mL
13. **Reasoning** Jason made 1 liter of lemonade. He drank 450 milliliters of it. How much lemonade is left now? **Explain** how you got your answer.
14. **WRITE Math** Patrick's aquarium holds 10 L of water. He fills the aquarium using a 500-mL container. How many times will Patrick have to fill his container? **Explain.**

CD ROM Technology
Use Harcourt Mega Math, The Number Games, *Tiny's Think Tank,* Level N.

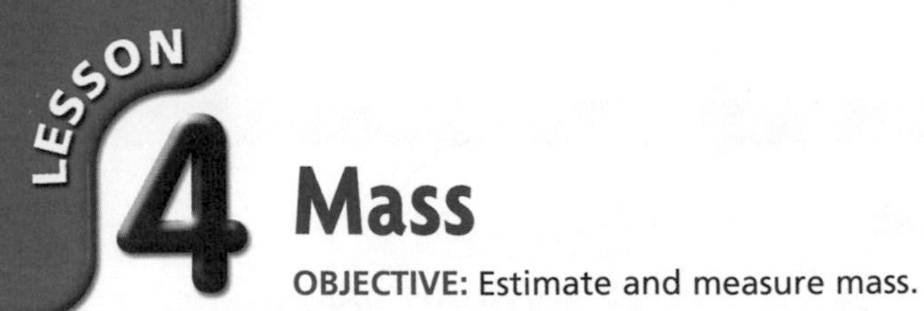

LESSON 4 Mass

OBJECTIVE: Estimate and measure mass.

Quick Review

Which is heavier?

Vocabulary

mass gram (g) kilogram (kg)

Learn

Mass is the amount of matter in an object. Mass can be measured by using metric units such as **gram (g)** and **kilogram (kg)**.

Metric Units of Mass
1 kilogram = 1,000 grams

PROBLEM Ethan uses a balance to find the mass of a paper clip and a box of 1,000 paper clips. What is the mass of each object?

A small paper clip has a mass of about 1 gram.

A box of 1,000 paper clips has a mass of about 1 kilogram.

HANDS ON Activity

Materials ■ balance, gram and kilogram weights, classroom objects

Estimate the mass of each object. Record your estimates in a table. Then find the mass of each object to the nearest gram or kilogram.

- marker
- dictionary
- scissors
- eraser
- notebook
- crayon

- How did your estimates compare with the actual measurements?
- Put the objects in order from greatest to least mass.

Mass		
Object	Estimate	Measure

Guided Practice

1. Does a nickel have a mass of about 5 grams or 5 kilograms?

Choose the unit you would use to find the mass of each. Write *gram* or *kilogram*.

2. 

3. 

4. 

5. 

6. **TALK Math** Would you use grams or kilograms to find the mass of a toothbrush? **Explain.**

Independent Practice and Problem Solving

Choose the unit you would use to find the mass of each. Write *gram* or *kilogram*.

7. 

8. 

9. 

10. 

Find an object in the classroom to match each mass. Draw it and label its mass.

11. less than 50 grams

12. greater than 100 grams

13. greater than 1 kilogram

14. **WRITE Math** Do objects of about the same size always have about the same mass? **Explain** your answer.

Mixed Review and Test Prep

15. Find the missing number.
108, 112, 116, 120, ■, 128 (p. 426)

16. Would you use centimeters or meters to measure the length of a carrot? (p. 538)

17. There are 2 fish in Javier's tank. One fish has a mass of 750 grams and one fish has a mass of 250 grams. What is the total mass of both fish?

   A 500 grams
   B 1 kilogram
   C 5 kilograms
   D 1,000 kilograms

Extra Practice on page 552, Set C

LESSON 5

Problem Solving Workshop
Skill: Choose a Unit

OBJECTIVE: Solve problems by using the skill *choose a unit*.

Read to Understand
Plan
Solve
Check

Read to Understand

PROBLEM Sarah and her father are putting a wallpaper border around her bedroom. Which metric unit of length should Sarah use to measure the wallpaper border?

Think about how metric units of length are related.

Measure shorter lengths in centimeters and decimeters. Measure longer lengths in meters and kilometers.

Sarah's wallpaper border is too long to be measured in centimeters or decimeters, so think of the next largest unit.

Sarah's wallpaper border could be measured in meters.

Sarah's wallpaper border is too short to be measured in kilometers.

So, Sarah should use meters to measure the wallpaper border.

Metric Table of Measures
Length
10 centimeters = 1 decimeter
100 centimeters = 1 meter
1,000 meters = 1 kilometer
Capacity
1,000 milliliters = 1 liter
Mass
1,000 grams = 1 kilogram

TALK Math

How can you decide which metric unit is best to measure the length of an object?

Think and Discuss

Choose the better unit of measure.

a. ***FAST FACT*** A newborn baby rabbit is about 4 cm long. Would you estimate the mass of the baby rabbit in grams or kilograms?

b. Jolene used chalk to draw a large rainbow on her driveway. The height of the rainbow is taller than she is. Is the rainbow about 3 meters or 3 decimeters tall?

c. Judy is making fruit punch for 6 of her friends. Which unit of capacity should she use to estimate the amount of fruit punch she needs: milliliters or liters?

Guided Problem Solving

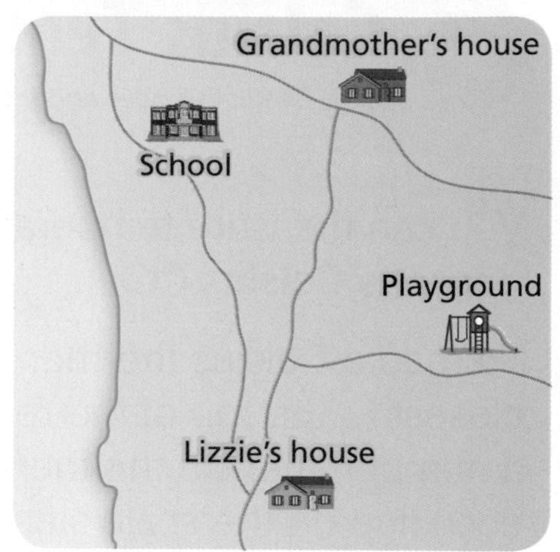

1. It takes about 30 minutes for Lizzie's family to drive from their house to her grandmother's house. Which unit of length should Lizzie use to measure the distance to her grandmother's house?

   Think of the units of length. How are the units related?

   Which unit would be best to measure a distance that takes about 30 minutes to drive? Solve the problem.

2. **What if** Lizzie's grandmother lived across the street? Which unit should Lizzie use to measure the distance to her grandmother's house?

3. George fills a bathtub with water. Does the bathtub hold about 100 L or 100 mL of water?

Mixed Applications

4. Gina collects miniature dolls. Her favorite doll is shorter than the width of her hand. Is the doll 6 cm or 6 dm tall?

5. Sam is making cookies. Should he use grams or kilograms to find the mass of one cookie?

USE DATA For 6–8, use the table.

Costume Items	
Felt for crown	$16.50 per pack
Leather belt	$9.50 each
Velvet for robe	$7.00 per meter

6. Kendra bought 1 pack of felt and 5 meters of velvet fabric to make a costume. How much did she spend?

7. **Reasoning** Ben bought a leather belt and one other item with a $20 bill. How much change did he receive? **Explain.**

8. **WRITE Math** Maddie needs 3 meters of velvet and 2 leather belts. Will Maddie spend more money on the belts or the velvet? **Explain.**

9. Jim's costume comes with a walking stick, which is taller than he is. Is the walking stick 2 cm or 2 m tall?

LESSON 6 HANDS ON

Celsius Temperature

OBJECTIVE: Estimate and measure temperature in degrees Celsius.

Quick Review

Which shows a warmer day?

Vocabulary

degrees Celsius (°C)

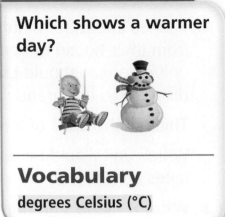

You can measure temperature in metric units as **degrees Celsius (°C)**.

To read a Celsius thermometer, find the number closest to the top of the red bar. Use the scale like a number line. On the thermometer at the right, each line on the scale stands for 5 degrees. The temperature shown is 20°C.

Write: 20°C   Read: twenty degrees Celsius

Investigate

Materials ■ Celsius thermometer

A Estimate what you think the outdoor temperature will be, in degrees Celsius, 3 times during the day. Record your estimates.

B Use a Celsius thermometer to measure the outdoor temperature at the listed times. Record the actual temperature.

Draw Conclusions

1. At what time was the temperature the warmest? the coolest?
2. How did each of the temperatures compare with normal room temperature?
3. **Analysis** How did knowing the temperature inside your classroom help you estimate the outside temperature?

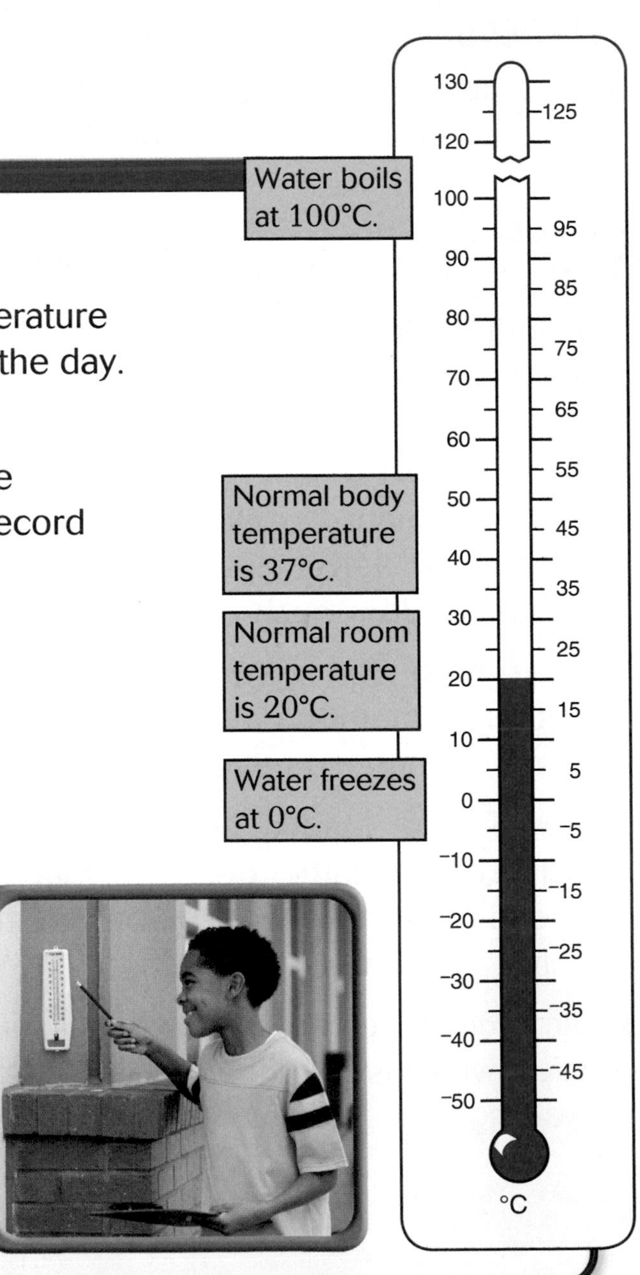

Connect

Below are outside activities you might do at 0°C, 15°C, and 30°C.

TALK Math

Explain how knowing the outside temperature can help you decide what clothes to wear to school.

Practice

Write each temperature in °C.

1. 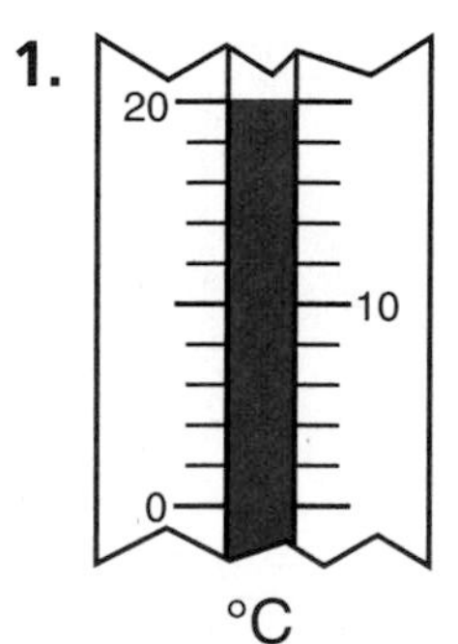

2. 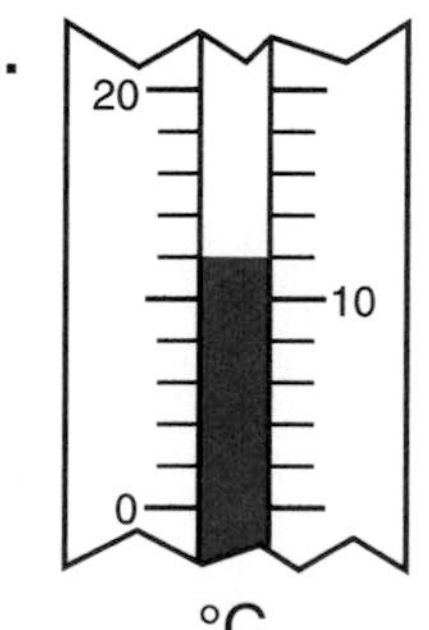

3. 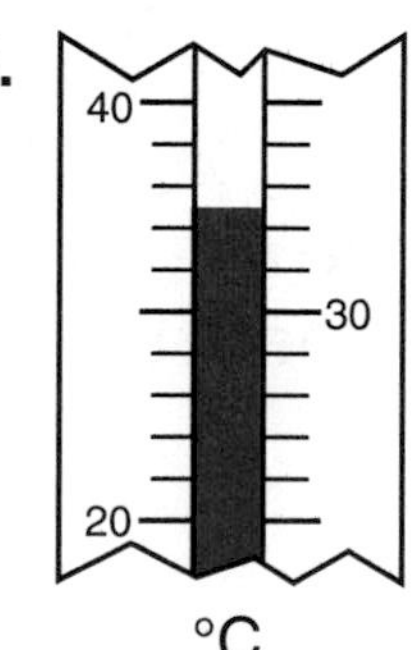

✓4. 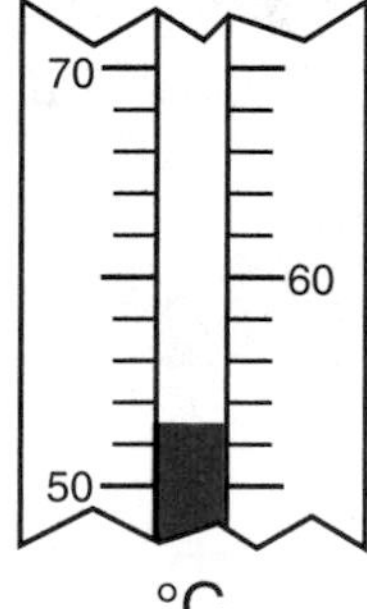

Choose the better temperature for each activity.

5. 
1°C or 33°C?

6. 
24°C or 6°C?

7. 
12°C or 31°C?

✓8. 
17°C or 35°C?

9. Lauren is wearing shorts and a pair of sandals. Is the outdoor temperature 5°C or 25°C?

10. **WRITE Math** It is 3°C outside. What is an activity that Jason might do at this temperature? What clothes do you think he might wear? **Explain.**

Extra Practice

Set A **Choose the unit you would use to measure each. Write *cm*, *m*, or *km*.** (pp. 538–539)

1. 

2. 

3. 

4. height of a drinking glass

5. distance from your home to school

6. length of a skating rink

7. distance from New Jersey to Illinois

8. length of a playground

9. height of a chair

Set B **Estimate the length in centimeters. Then use a ruler to measure to the nearest centimeter.** (pp. 540–543)

1. 

2. 

3. 

Choose the best estimate.

4. height of a window
8 cm   8 dm   8 km

5. length of a safety pin
3 cm   3 dm   3 m

6. length of a cell phone
8 cm   8 dm   8 m

Set C **Choose the unit you would use to find the mass of each. Write *gram* or *kilogram*.** (pp. 546–547)

1. 

2. 

3. 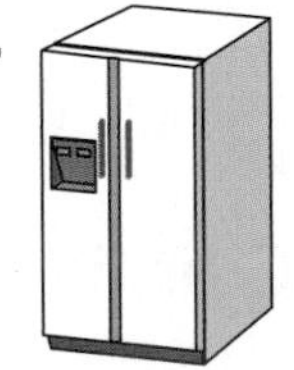

4. 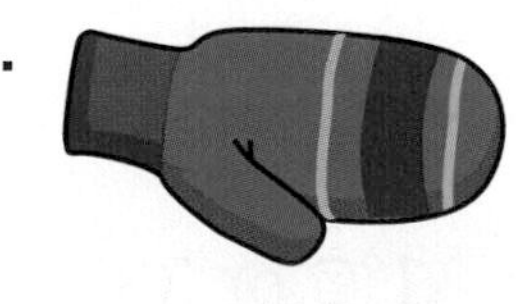

CD ROM **Technology**
Use Harcourt Mega Math, Ice Station Exploration, *Linear Lab*, Levels H, I.

PRACTICE GAME

Collect-a-Meter

Roll 'Em!
2–4 players

Measure 'Em!
- Gameboard
- Centimeter rulers
- Number cube
- Counter, paper, and pencil for each player
- Action cards

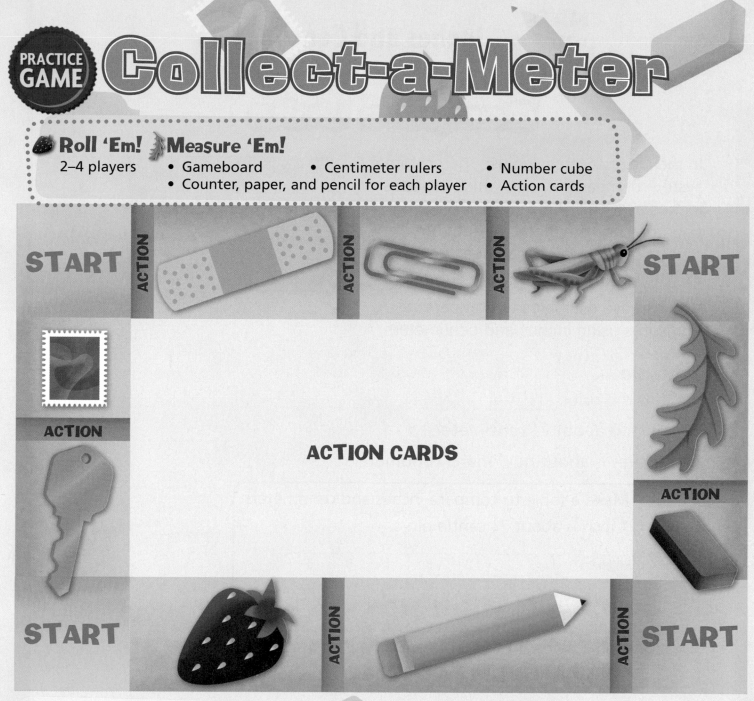

START

ACTION

ACTION

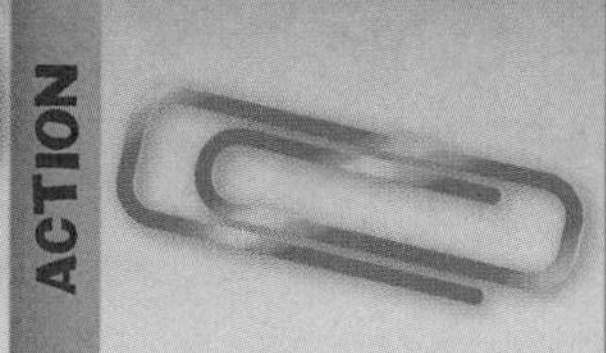

ACTION

START

ACTION

ACTION

Collect 'Em!

- Players shuffle the Action cards and place them facedown in the middle of the gameboard.
- Each player places a counter in one of the START corners.
- Player 1 rolls the number cube, moves the number of spaces rolled, measures the picture of the object on the space where he or she lands, and writes the measurement on a score sheet. It is then Player 2's turn.
- When players land on an Action space, they pick an Action card and follow its directions.
- The first player to score a total of 100 centimeters wins.

MATH POWER Inches and Centimeters

Compare Units

In the United States, we use the customary system of measurement, which includes inches as a unit of measure. Most other countries use the metric system of measurement, which includes centimeters as a unit of measure.

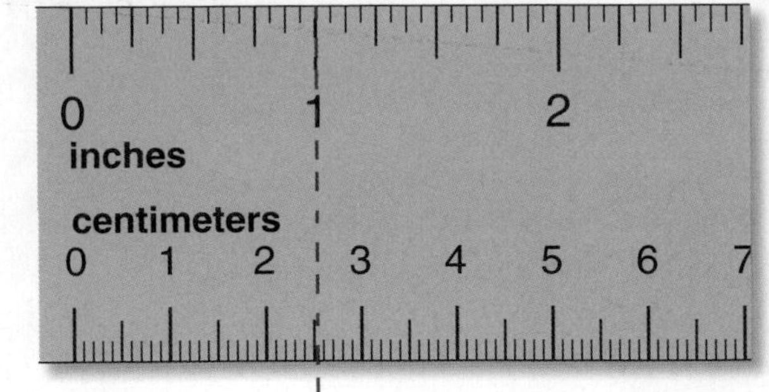

You can use estimates to compare measures using inches and centimeters.

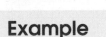

Example

Look at the ruler.

One inch is about $2\frac{1}{2}$ centimeters.

Five inches is about how many centimeters?

Step 1 Make a table to compare inches and centimeters. 1 inch is about $2\frac{1}{2}$ centimeters.

inches	1	2	3	4	5	6
centimeters	$2\frac{1}{2}$	5	$7\frac{1}{2}$	10	$12\frac{1}{2}$	15

Step 2 Find 5 inches in the table and the estimated centimeter measure that matches it.

So, 5 inches is about $12\frac{1}{2}$ centimeters.

Try It

Copy and complete each comparison.

1. 4 inches is about ____ centimeters.
2. 5 centimeters is about ____ inches.
3. $17\frac{1}{2}$ centimeters is about ____ inches.
4. 10 inches is about ____ centimeters.
5. WRITE Math **Explain** how to compare centimeters to 1 foot.

Chapter 21 Review/Test

Check Concepts

Solve.

1. Which is a greater mass, a gram or a kilogram? IL 7.3.05 (p. 546)
2. Which is a greater distance, a centimeter or a decimeter? IL 7.3.02 (p. 538)
3. Which is a greater distance, a kilometer or a meter? IL 7.3.02 (p. 538)

Check Skills

Choose the unit you would use to measure each.
Write *cm*, *m*, or *km*. IL 7.3.02 (pp. 538–539)

4. length of a driveway
5. distance from one city to another
6. length of a carrot

Choose the better estimate. IL 7.3.05 (pp. 538–539)

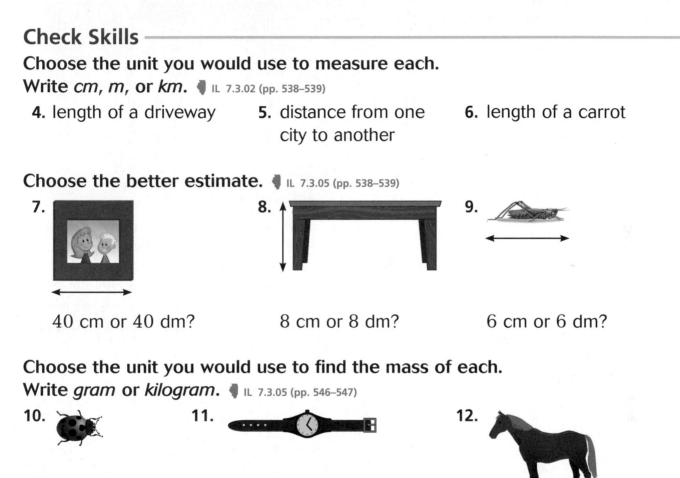

7. 
40 cm or 40 dm?

8. 
8 cm or 8 dm?

9. 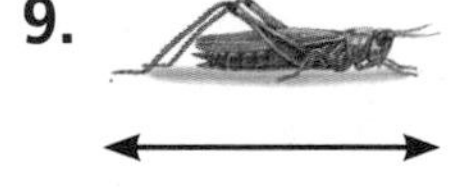
6 cm or 6 dm?

Choose the unit you would use to find the mass of each.
Write *gram* or *kilogram*. IL 7.3.05 (pp. 546–547)

10. 

11. 

12. 

Check Problem Solving

Solve. IL 7.3.07 (pp. 548–549)

13. Ed rides 3,000 meters to get to school. How many kilometers does he ride?
14. Becky's bedroom is 5 meters long. How many decimeters long is her room?
15. WRITE Math Michael's puppy has a mass of 7,000 grams. Pauline's puppy has a mass of 8 kilograms. **Explain** how to find whose puppy has a greater mass.

GO ONLINE **Technology** Use *Online Assessment.*

Practice for the ISAT
Chapters 1–21

Number and Operations

1. Jackie baked cookies. She put 6 cookies in each of 9 bags. How many cookies in all did she bake? IL 6.3.11 (p. 234)

   A 63 C 45
   B 54 D 15

2. The area of Illinois is 57,914 square miles. What is the value of the digit 7 in 57,914? IL 6.3.01 (p. 14)

   A 7
   B 70
   C 700
   D 7,000

3. Which number is between 3,165 and 3,217? IL 6.3.05 (p. 32)

   A 3,098
   B 3,147
   C 3,185
   D 3,240

4. WRITE Math What multiplication fact does this model show? **Explain** your answer. IL 6.3.11 (p. 238)

Algebra

5. Maribele collects coins. If the pattern continues, how many coins will she collect in the fifth month? IL 8.3.01 (p. 256)

Judy's Coins				
Month	1	2	3	4
Coins	6	12	18	24

   A 26 C 30
   B 28 D 32

Test Tip **Decide on a plan.**

See item 6. Make a plan to find the missing number. First, choose a number that completes one of the number sentences. Next, check if it completes the others. Then, find the number in the answers choices. Use the plan to find the answer.

6. Which number completes the fact family? IL 8.3.03 (p. 286)

   $6 \times ■ = 42$ $■ \times 6 = 42$
   $42 \div ■ = 6$ $42 \div 6 = ■$

   A 6 C 8
   B 7 D 36

7. WRITE Math What is a rule in this pattern? **Explain** how you know. IL 8.3.01 (p. 256)

   4, 5, 8, 9, 12, 13, 16

Geometry

8. Which pair of figures appears to be congruent? IL 9.3.10 (p. 378)

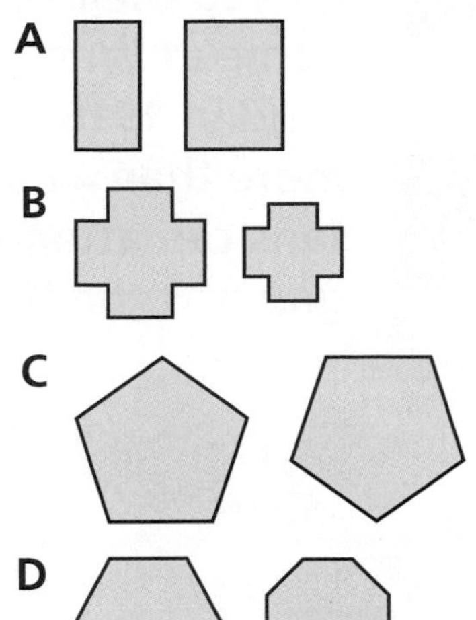

9. Cho drew these figures on the computer. Which figure appears to have a line of symmetry? IL 9.3.04 (p. 384)

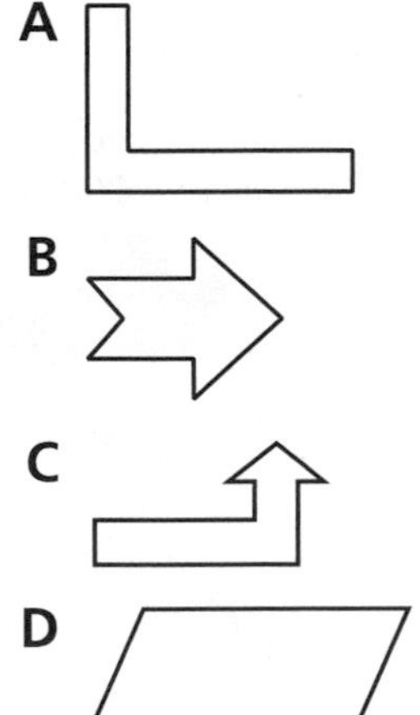

10. WRITE Math What type of lines are shown? **Explain** how you know. IL 9.3.06 (p. 354)

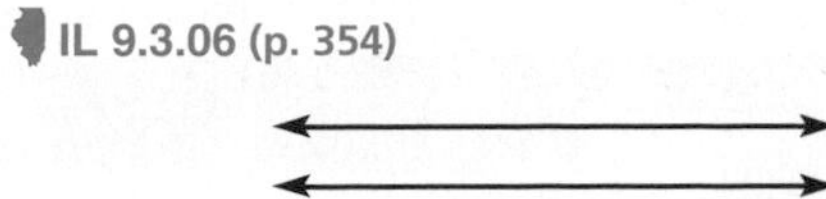

Data Analysis and Probability

11. How much money did the children earn altogether? IL 10.3.01 (p. 148)

Money Earned	
Mia	$ $ $
Jeff	$ $
Carol	$ $ $ $ $
Key: Each $ = $3.	

A $10

B $12

C $30

D $40

12. Which color tile is more likely to be pulled? IL 10.3.04 (p. 182)

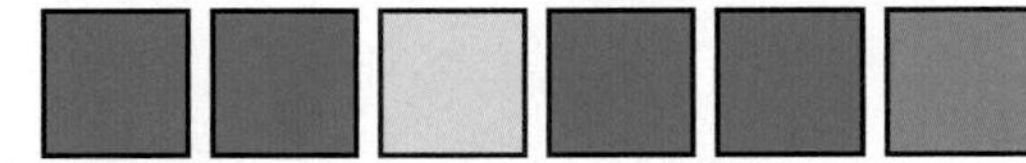

A Yellow

B Blue

C Green

D Red

13. WRITE Math Judy made a bar graph to show the number of pictures she took each day for a week. The bar for Wednesday ends at 12. What does this mean? **Explain.** IL 10.3.01 (p. 156)

CHAPTER 22

Perimeter, Area, and Volume

FAST FACT

The Chicago Cubs played their first game at Wrigley Field in 1916. Today, more than 41,000 fans can attend a game at the field.

Investigate

A Major League baseball infield is similar to a Little League baseball infield. Look at the two drawings. Describe how the infields are alike and how they are different.

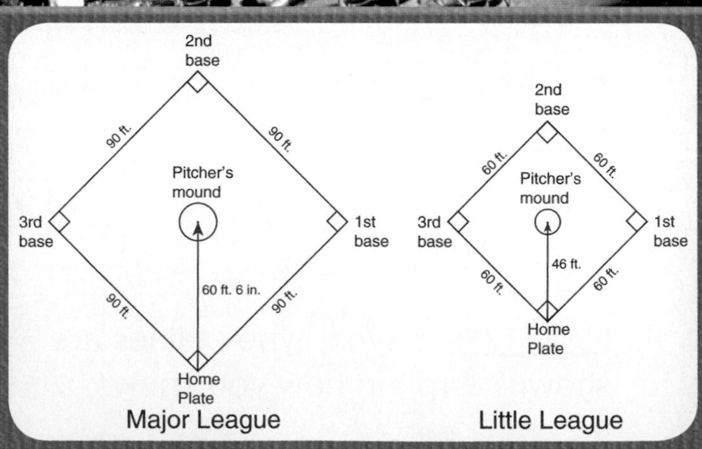

GO ONLINE **Technology** Student pages are available in the Student eBook.

Show What You Know

Check your understanding of important skills needed for success in Chapter 22.

▶ Column Addition

Find the sum.

1. $\begin{array}{r} 1 \\ 8 \\ 9 \\ +4 \\ \hline \end{array}$ **2.** $\begin{array}{r} 2 \\ 6 \\ 7 \\ +6 \\ \hline \end{array}$ **3.** $\begin{array}{r} 5 \\ 5 \\ 8 \\ +3 \\ \hline \end{array}$ **4.** $\begin{array}{r} 4 \\ 2 \\ 2 \\ +7 \\ \hline \end{array}$

5. $\begin{array}{r} 6 \\ 7 \\ 5 \\ +2 \\ \hline \end{array}$ **6.** $\begin{array}{r} 10 \\ 9 \\ 9 \\ +4 \\ \hline \end{array}$ **7.** $\begin{array}{r} 3 \\ 5 \\ 2 \\ +4 \\ \hline \end{array}$ **8.** $\begin{array}{r} 10 \\ 10 \\ 7 \\ +\ 2 \\ \hline \end{array}$

▶ Multiplication Facts Through 10

Find the product.

9. $3 \times 4 = ■$ **10.** $7 \times 5 = ■$ **11.** $8 \times 2 = ■$ **12.** $6 \times 3 = ■$

13. $1 \times 5 = ■$ **14.** $4 \times 9 = ■$ **15.** $3 \times 2 = ■$ **16.** $5 \times 5 = ■$

17. $\begin{array}{r} 3 \\ \times 8 \\ \hline \end{array}$ **18.** $\begin{array}{r} 10 \\ \times\ 7 \\ \hline \end{array}$ **19.** $\begin{array}{r} 6 \\ \times 4 \\ \hline \end{array}$ **20.** $\begin{array}{r} 7 \\ \times 9 \\ \hline \end{array}$

VOCABULARY POWER

CHAPTER VOCABULARY

area
cubic unit
perimeter
square unit
volume

WARM-UP WORDS

area The number of square units needed to cover a flat surface

perimeter The distance around a figure

volume The amount of space a solid figure takes up

LESSON 1

Estimate and Measure Perimeter

OBJECTIVE: Estimate and measure perimeter.

Quick Review

Find the sum.

1. 8 + 8 + 8 + 8
2. 2 + 3 + 4
3. 1 + 1 + 8 + 3
4. 6 + 6 + 5 + 5
5. 3 + 3 + 1 + 4 + 1

Vocabulary

perimeter

Learn

Perimeter is the distance around a figure. You can estimate and measure perimeter in standard units, such as inches and centimeters.

Find the perimeter of a notebook.

HANDS ON **Activity** **Materials** ■ inch ruler

Step 1

Estimate the perimeter of a notebook in inches. Record your estimate.

Step 2

Use an inch ruler to measure the length of each side of the notebook.

Step 3

Add the lengths of the sides.

■ in. + ■ in. + ■ in. + ■ in. = ■ in.

Record the perimeter.

- How does your estimate compare with your measurement?

Examples

Estimate. Then use a ruler to find the length of each side in inches.

Add the lengths of the sides:
1 in. + 2 in. + 1 in. + 2 in. = 6 in.
The perimeter is 6 inches.

Estimate. Then use a ruler to find the length of each side in centimeters.

Add the lengths of the sides:
3 cm + 3 cm + 3 cm + 3 cm = 12 cm
The perimeter is 12 centimeters.

More Examples

Add the lengths of the sides to find the perimeter.

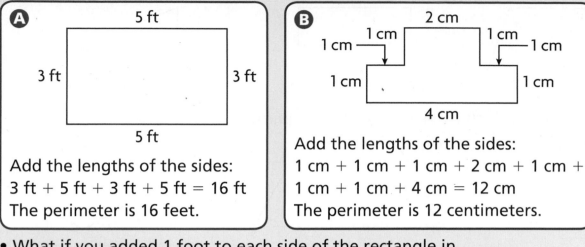

A

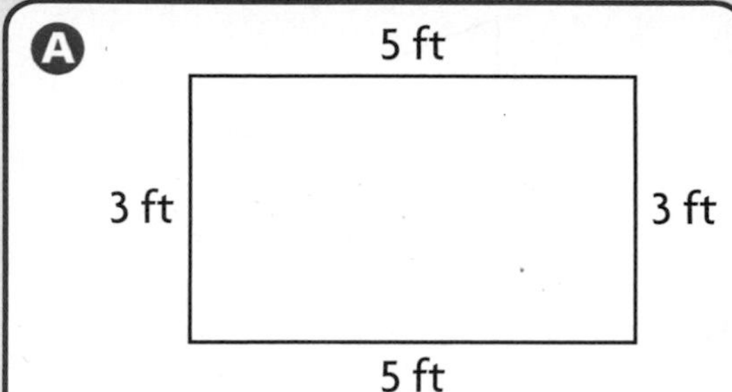

Add the lengths of the sides:
3 ft + 5 ft + 3 ft + 5 ft = 16 ft
The perimeter is 16 feet.

B

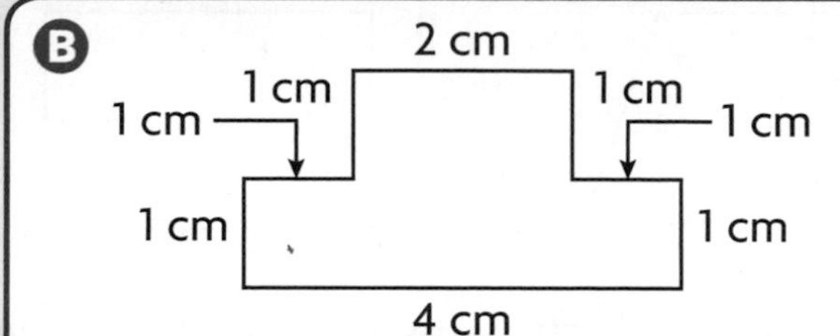

Add the lengths of the sides:
1 cm + 1 cm + 1 cm + 2 cm + 1 cm + 1 cm + 1 cm + 4 cm = 12 cm
The perimeter is 12 centimeters.

- What if you added 1 foot to each side of the rectangle in Example A? How would the perimeter change?

Guided Practice

1. Find the perimeter of the triangle in inches.
   Think: how long is each side?

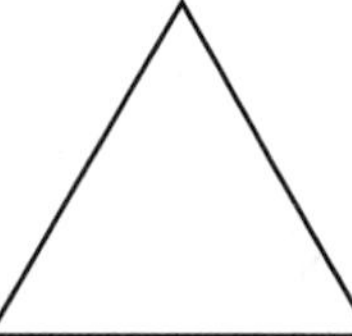

Estimate. Then use a centimeter ruler to find the perimeter.

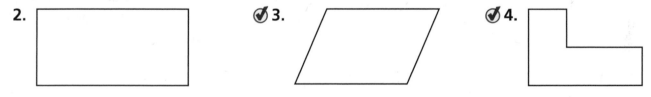

2. 

3. 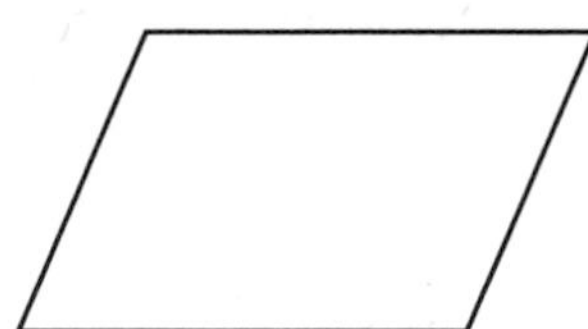

4. 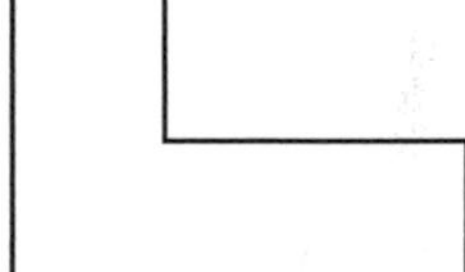

Estimate. Then use an inch ruler to find the perimeter.

5. 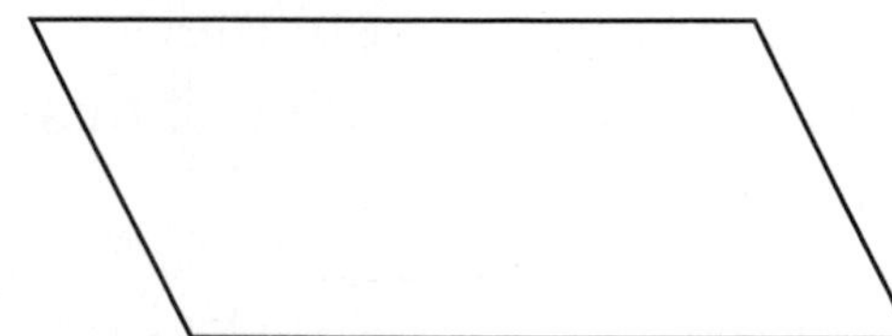

6. 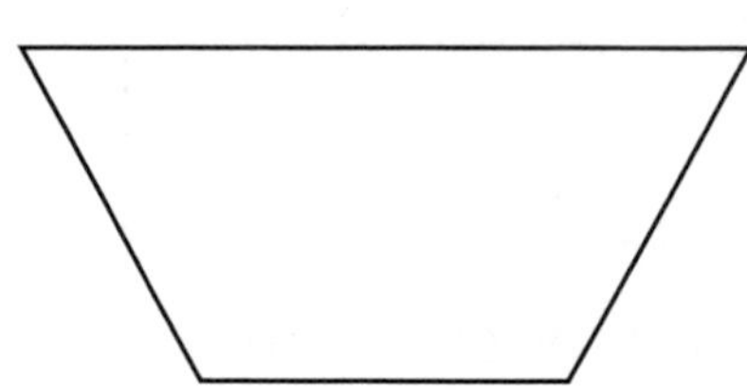

7. TALK Math **Explain** how to find the perimeter of this figure in centimeters.

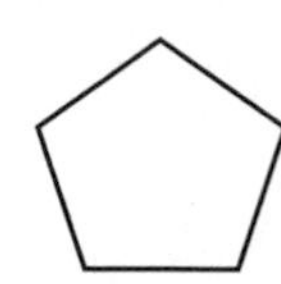

Independent Practice and Problem Solving

Estimate. Then use a centimeter ruler to find the perimeter.

8. 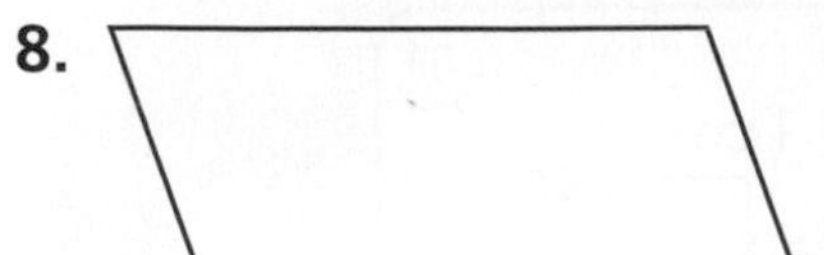

9. 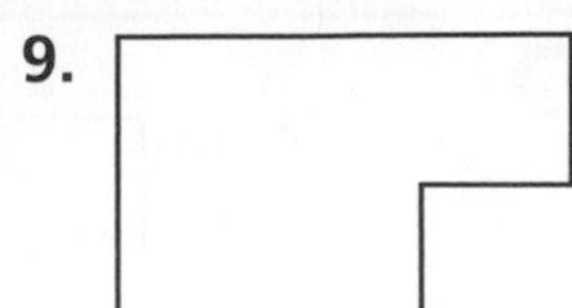

10. 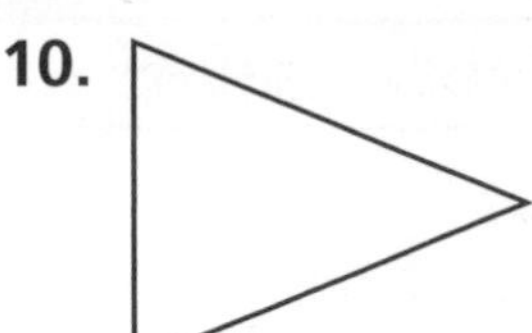

Estimate. Then use an inch ruler to find the perimeter.

11. 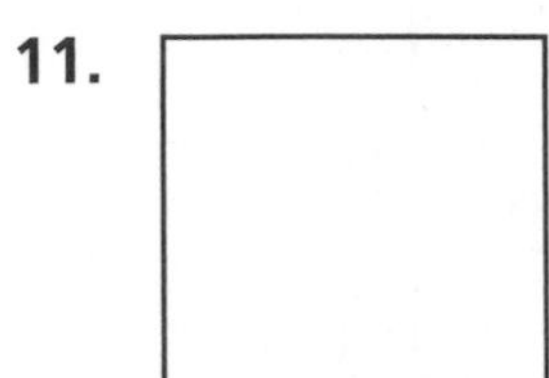

12. 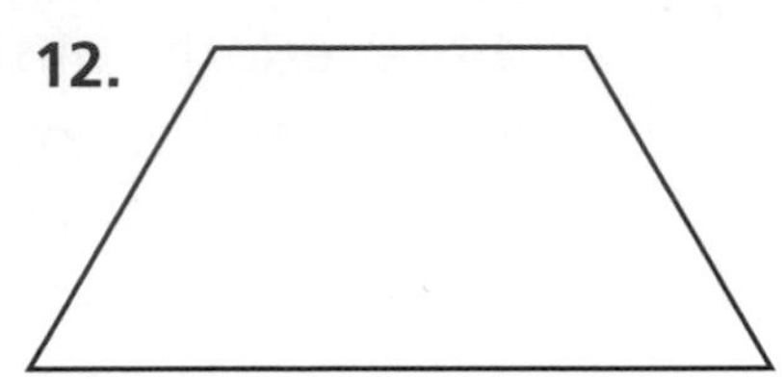

13. 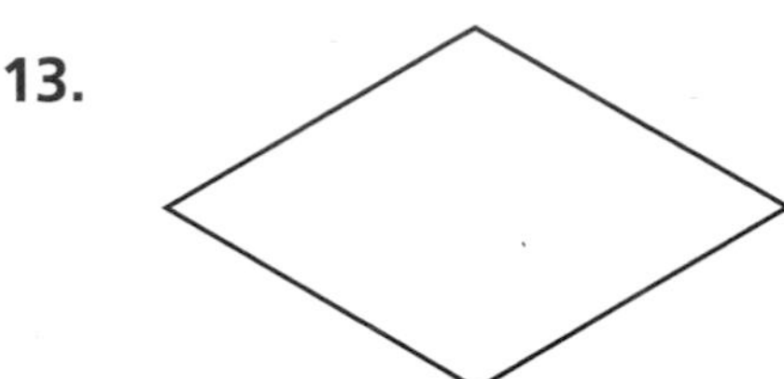

For 14–15, use the photos.

14. Which of the animal photos has a perimeter of 24 inches?

15. How much greater is the perimeter of the bird photo than the perimeter of the cat photo?

16. **Open Ended** Use grid paper or a ruler to draw a polygon with a perimeter of 20 cm. Label the length of each side.

17. Lacy is putting a fence around her square garden. Each side of her garden is 3 yards long. The fence costs $5 for each yard. How much will the fence cost?

18. **WRITE Math** One side of a rectangle is 4 feet long and one side is 10 feet long. What is the perimeter of the rectangle? **Explain.**

Mixed Review and Test Prep

19. A quadrilateral has two pairs of parallel sides and four right angles. Name this quadrilateral. (p. 360)

20. Which is the better estimate for the length of a room: 12 in. or 12 ft? (p. 526)

21. **Test Prep** Use your centimeter ruler to find the perimeter of this rectangle.

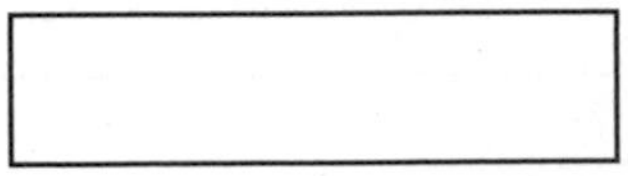

A 8 cm **B** 10 cm **C** 12 cm **D** 16 cm

Technology
CD ROM Use Harcourt Mega Math, Ice Station Exploration, *Polar Planes,* Level P.

 Extra Practice on page 574, Set A

Take My Picture

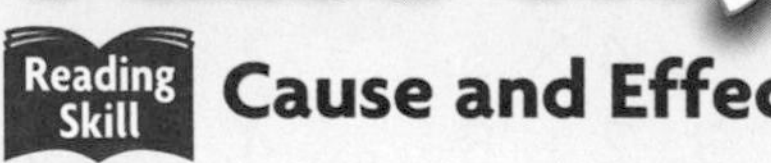

Cause and Effect

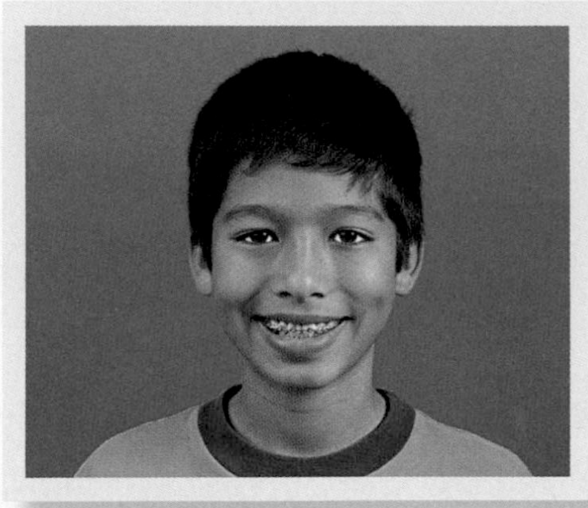

When you take a picture with a digital camera, the picture is stored in the camera's memory. Then you can print your picture later. Before you print the picture, you can choose the size. Look at the photo below. If each side of the photo is increased by 2 inches, how much will the perimeter increase?

Cause and effect is a strategy that can help you understand a problem. A cause is the reason something happens. An effect is the result, or outcome.

Cause	Effect
Increase each side of the photo by 2 inches.	The perimeter increases.

So, if the length of each side changes, then the perimeter will also change.

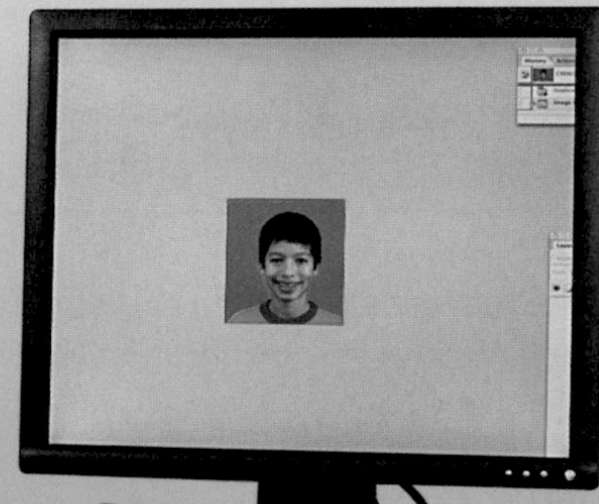

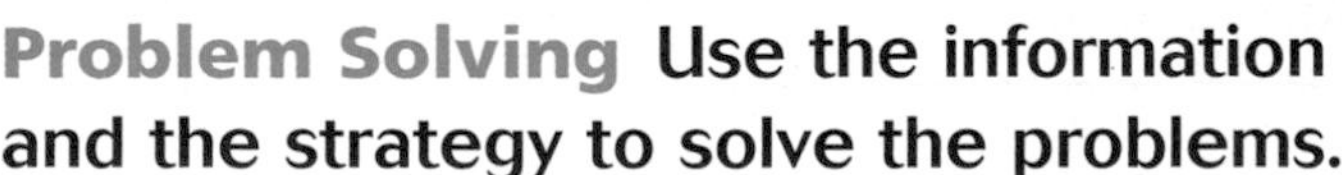

Problem Solving Use the information and the strategy to solve the problems.

1. Solve the problem above. What operation did you use to solve the problem?
2. Courtney has a photo of her dog. The photo is 8 inches wide and 10 inches long. She wants to decrease the length of each side by 3 inches and reprint the photo. What will the new perimeter be? **Explain.**

LESSON 2

Area of Plane Figures

OBJECTIVE: Estimate and measure the area of plane figures.

Quick Review

Multiply.

1. 4 × 5
2. 6 × 3
3. 2 × 8
4. 5 × 7
5. 9 × 9

Vocabulary

area

square unit

Learn

Area is the number of square units needed to cover a flat surface.

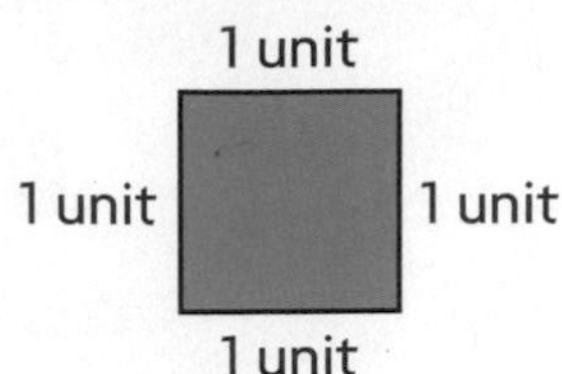

A **square unit** is a square with a side length of 1 unit.

Activity

Materials ■ square tiles, index card, grid paper

Step 1

Estimate how many square tiles it will take to cover an index card. Record your estimate.

Step 2

Use square tiles to cover the surface of an index card.

Step 3

Use grid paper. Draw a picture to show how you covered the index card.

Step 4

Count and record the number of rows of tiles and the number of tiles in each row. The product of these numbers is the area of the index card in square units.

- What is the area of your index card?
- How does your estimate compare with your measurement?
- How is finding the area like making an array?
- **What if** you used larger paper squares to cover the surface of your index card? How would the number of paper squares compare to the number of tiles?

ERROR ALERT

Do not leave any space between the square tiles when you use them to find area.

Examples

You can count or multiply square units to find area.

A Count units.

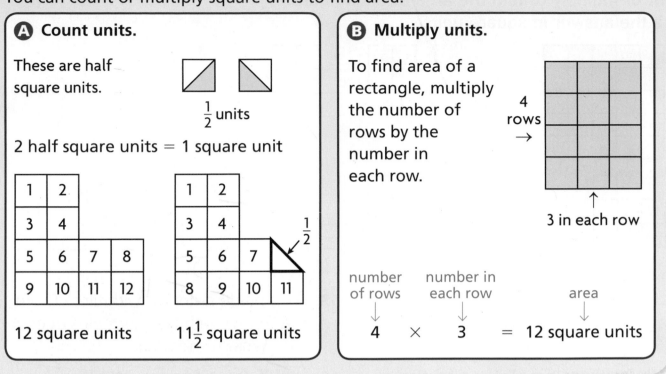

These are half square units.

$\frac{1}{2}$ units

2 half square units = 1 square unit

1	2		
3	4		
5	6	7	8
9	10	11	12

12 square units

1	2		
3	4		$\frac{1}{2}$
5	6	7	
8	9	10	11

$11\frac{1}{2}$ square units

B Multiply units.

To find area of a rectangle, multiply the number of rows by the number in each row.

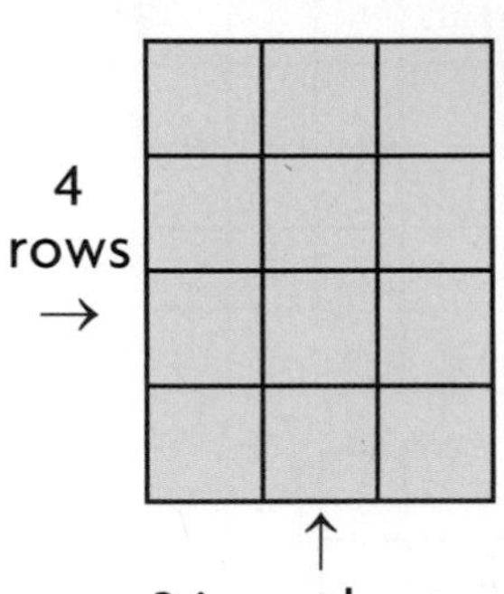

number of rows		number in each row		area
↓		↓		↓
4	×	3	=	12 square units

Guided Practice

1. How many square tiles were used to make this figure? What is the area?

Count or multiply to find the area of each figure. Write the answer in square units.

2. 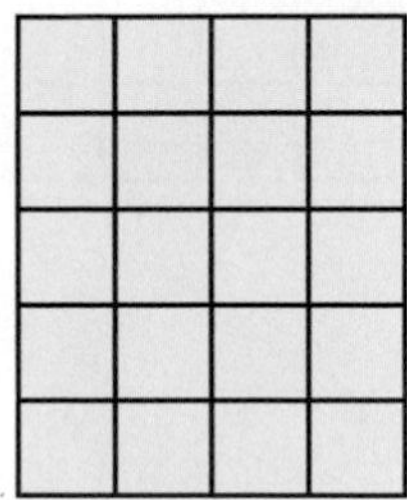

3. 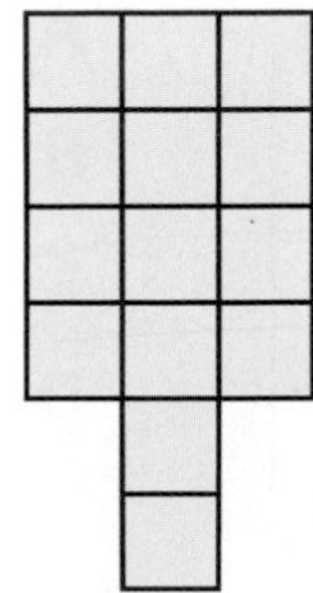

4. 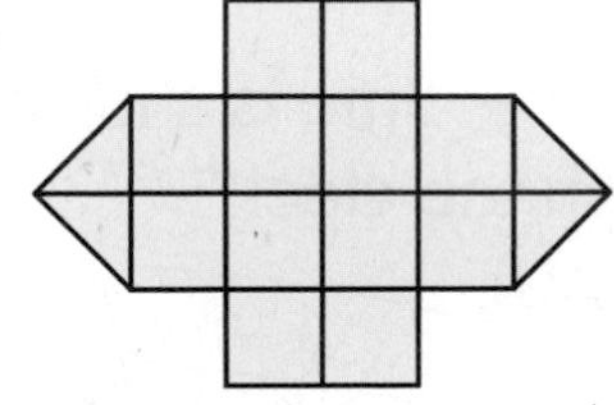

5. **TALK Math** On grid paper, draw a square that has a side length of 5 units. **Explain** two ways to find the area of the square.

Independent Practice and Problem Solving

Count or multiply to find the area of each figure. Write the answer in square units.

6. 

7. 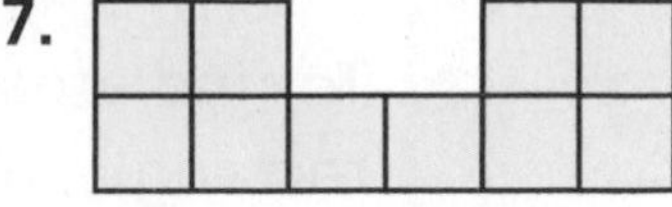

8. 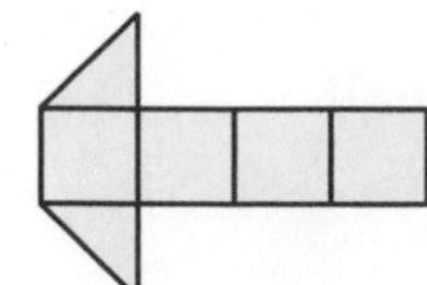

9. 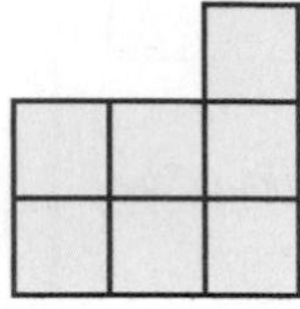

10. 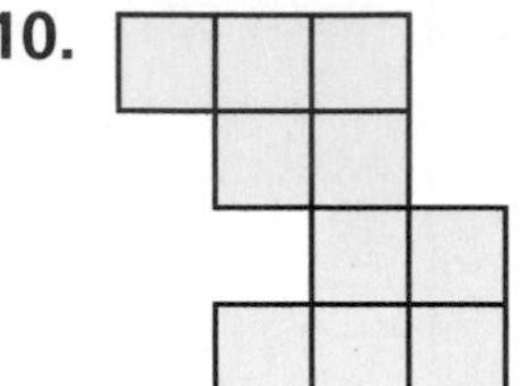

11. 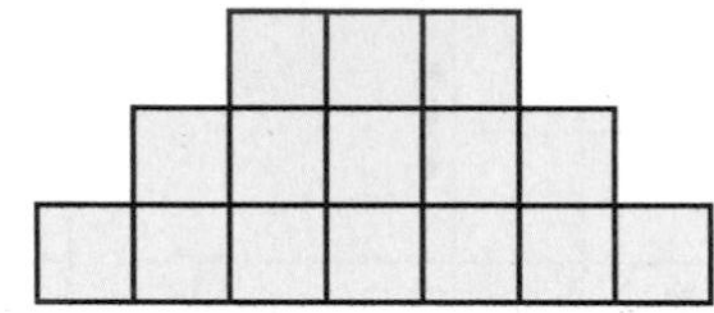

12. Use grid paper to draw a figure with an area of 16 square units.

13. Josh made a design with tiles. There are 6 rows with 6 square tiles in each row. What is the area?

14. Mr. Stephens put tile on a section of his floor. The section had 3 rows with 4 tiles in each row. Each tile cost $3. How much did Mr. Stephens spend?

15. WRITE Math **Sense or Nonsense** Mary says you can find the area of this rectangle by multiplying 2 times 3. Does this make sense? **Explain.**

Mixed Review and Test Prep

16. Jade made a square pillow with 10 inch sides. She sewed a ribbon around the perimeter of the pillow. How much ribbon did she use? (p. 560)

17. What time is shown on the clock? (p. 124)

18. **Test Prep** What is the area of this rectangle?

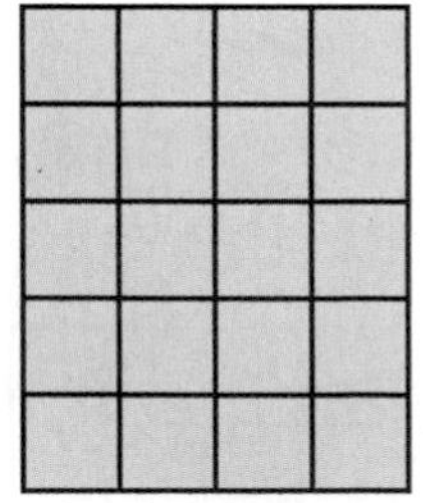

A 9 square units

B 10 square units

C 18 square units

D 20 square units

CD ROM **Technology**
Use Harcourt Mega Math, Ice Station Exploration, *Polar Planes*, Level Q.

 Extra Practice on page 574, Set B

Learn About Comparing Area

Lydia has plans for two different gardens. Each square unit represents 1 square yard. Which garden has the greater area?

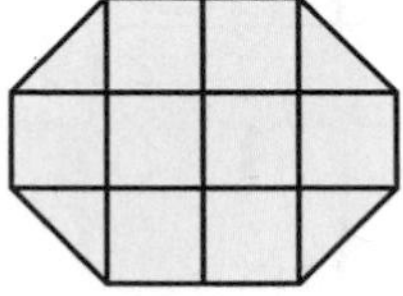

Garden A

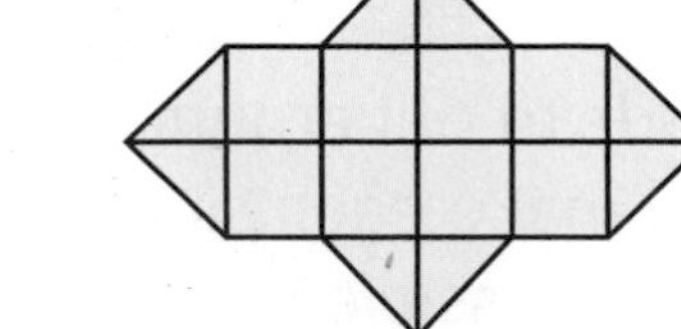

Garden B

Step 1 Count to find the number of whole square units in each garden.	Garden A has 8 whole square units. Garden B has 8 whole square units.
Step 2 Count the number of half square units in each garden.	Garden A has 4 half square units. Garden B has 8 half square units.
Step 3 Find the total area of each garden.	Garden A: $8 + 2 = 10$ square units Garden B: $8 + 4 = 12$ square units
Step 4 Compare the areas.	10 square units $<$ 12 square units

So, Garden B has the greater area.

Try It

For each pair, find the area in square units. Which figure has the greater area?

19.

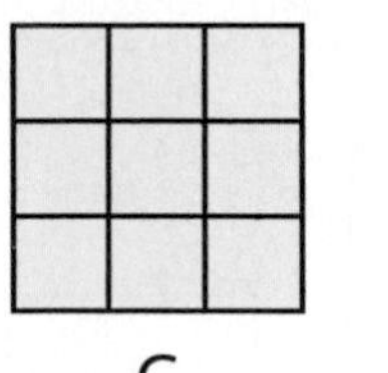

C

D

20.

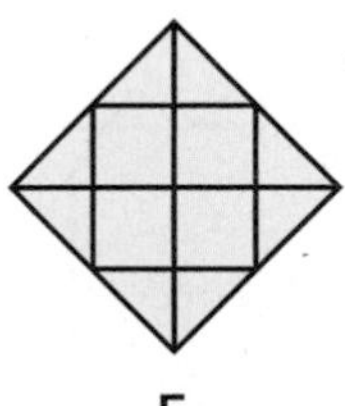

E

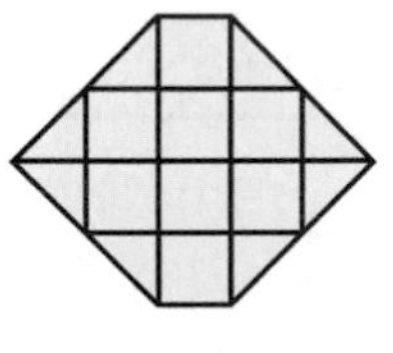

F

21. WRITE Math Can two rectangles with different shapes have the same area? **Explain.**

LESSON 3

Relate Perimeter and Area

OBJECTIVE: Explore the relationship between the area and the perimeter of a figure.

Quick Review

Find the perimeter and the area.

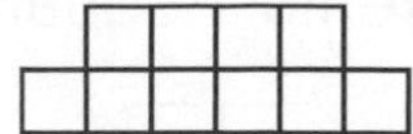

Learn

PROBLEM Cody has 20 feet of wood boards to put around a rectangular sandbox. How long should he make each side so that the area of the sandbox is as large as possible?

Example

Use square tiles. Make all the rectangles you can that have a perimeter of 20. Then find the area of each.

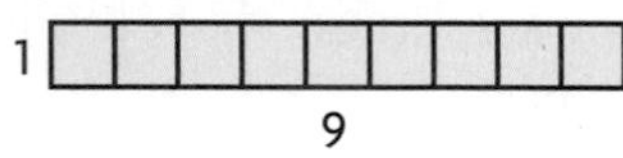

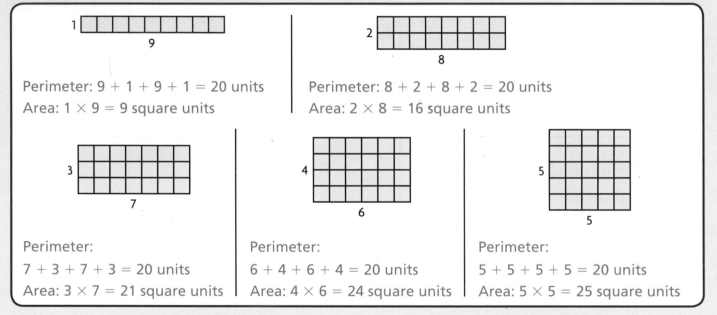

Perimeter: $9 + 1 + 9 + 1 = 20$ units
Area: $1 \times 9 = 9$ square units

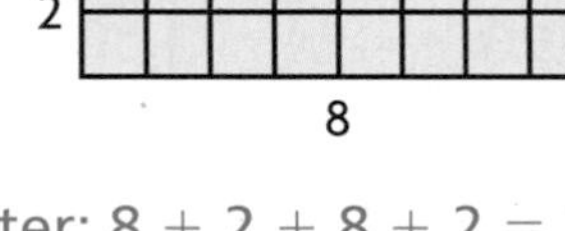

Perimeter: $8 + 2 + 8 + 2 = 20$ units
Area: $2 \times 8 = 16$ square units

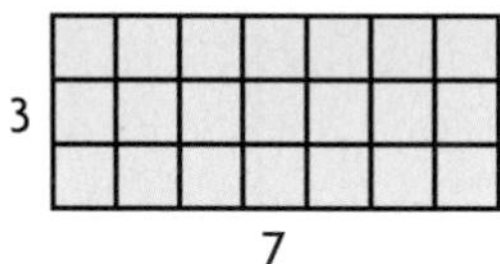

Perimeter:
$7 + 3 + 7 + 3 = 20$ units
Area: $3 \times 7 = 21$ square units

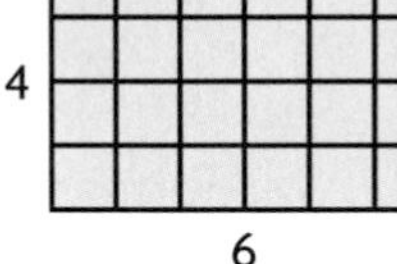

Perimeter:
$6 + 4 + 6 + 4 = 20$ units
Area: $4 \times 6 = 24$ square units

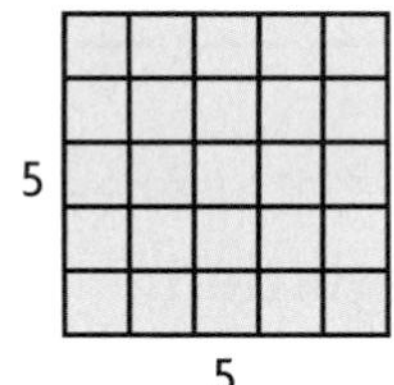

Perimeter:
$5 + 5 + 5 + 5 = 20$ units
Area: $5 \times 5 = 25$ square units

Order the areas: $9 < 16 < 21 < 24 < 25$
25 square units is the greatest area.
So, to have a sandbox with the largest area possible, Cody should make a square with sides 5 feet long.

More Examples

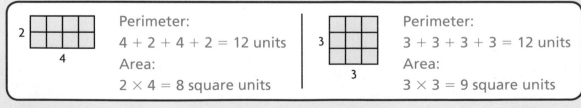

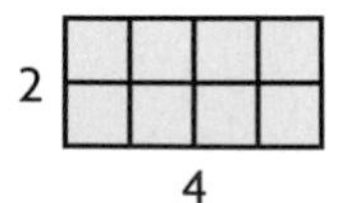

Perimeter:
$4 + 2 + 4 + 2 = 12$ units
Area:
$2 \times 4 = 8$ square units

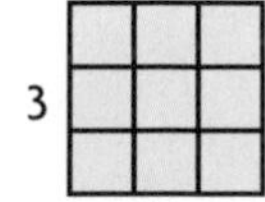

Perimeter:
$3 + 3 + 3 + 3 = 12$ units
Area:
$3 \times 3 = 9$ square units

- What do you notice about the perimeters and areas of the two figures in More Examples?

Guided Practice

1. Use square tiles. Make a rectangle with the same perimeter but a different area as the one on the right. Which figure has the greater area?

For each pair, find the perimeter and the area. Tell which figure has the greater area.

2. A B

3. C D

4. **TALK Math** Figures E and F have the same perimeter. **Explain** which figure has the greater area.

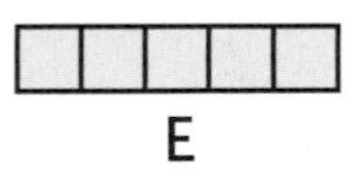

E

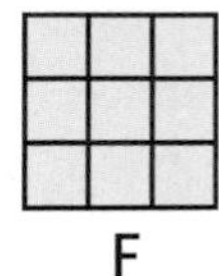

F

Independent Practice and Problem Solving

For each pair, find the perimeter and the area. Tell which figure has the greater area.

5. G

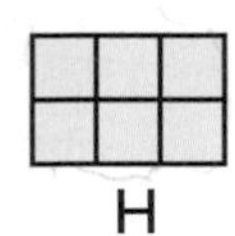

H

6.

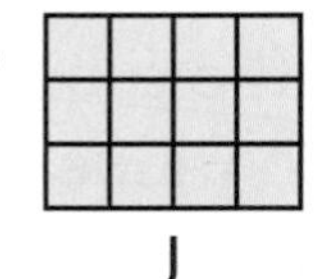

J K

7. Julia made a rectangular flower garden with a perimeter of 16 feet and an area of 15 square feet. What are the lengths of the sides? Draw a picture to show your answer.

8. **WRITE Math** **What's the Question?** Todd's flower garden is 4 feet wide and 8 feet long. The answer is 32 square feet.

Mixed Review and Test Prep

9. A violin has 4 strings. How many strings are on 9 violins? (p. 212)

10. Ann glued strips of felt around the perimeter of a square picture frame. One side is 5 inches. How many inches of felt did she use? (p. 560)

11. **Test Prep** Which figure has an area of 16 square units and a perimeter of 16 units?

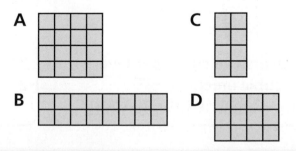

A **C**

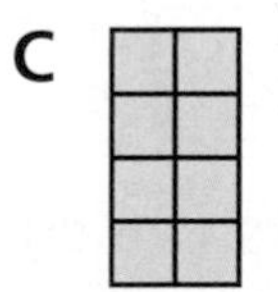

B

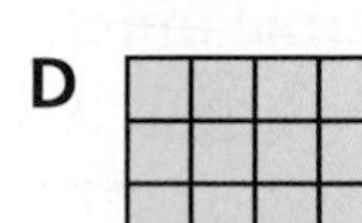

D

Extra Practice on page 574, Set C

4 Estimate and Find Volume

OBJECTIVE: Estimate and find volume.

Quick Review

Multiply.

1. 4×3
2. 2×5
3. 3×2
4. 6×4
5. 5×5

Vocabulary

volume cubic unit

Learn

Volume is the amount of space a solid figure takes up.

A **cubic unit** is used to measure volume. A cubic unit is a cube with a side length of 1 unit.

1 cubic unit

ONE WAY **Count the cubes to find volume.**

HANDS ON **Activity** **Materials** ■ small boxes, cubes

Step 1

Choose a box. Estimate the number of cubes it will take to fill the box. Record your estimate.

Step 2

Count the cubes you use. Place the cubes in rows along the bottom of the box. Continue to make layers of cubes until the box is full.

Step 3

Record how many cubes it took to fill the box. This is the volume of the box in cubic units.

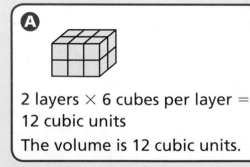

- How does your estimate compare with the actual volume?

ANOTHER WAY **Multiply to find volume.**

When you cannot count each cube, count the number of cubes in the top layer. Then count the number of layers and multiply.

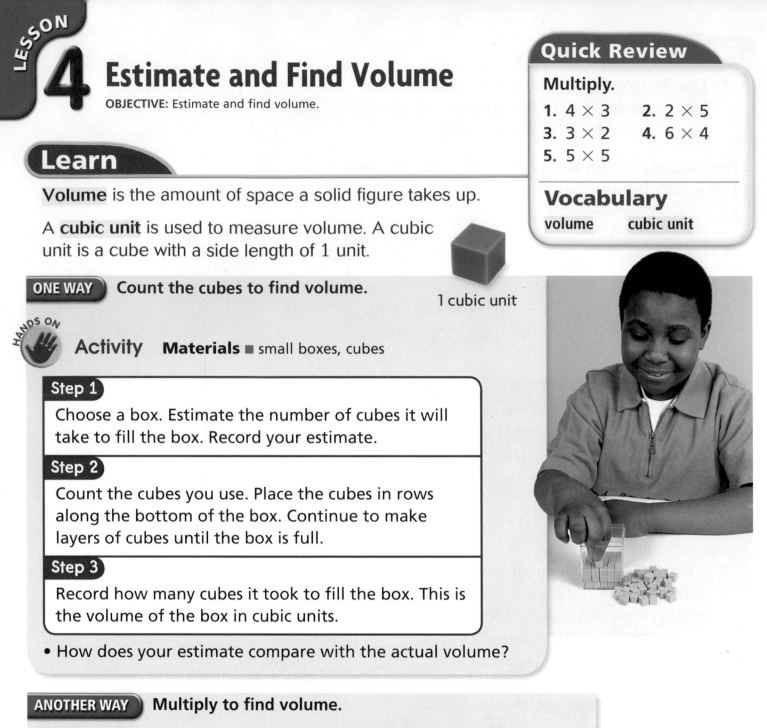

2 layers × 6 cubes per layer = 12 cubic units

The volume is 12 cubic units.

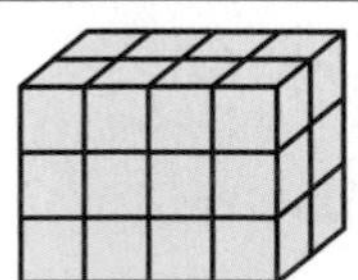

3 layers × 8 cubes per layer = 24 cubic units

The volume is 24 cubic units.

Guided Practice

1. Find the volume of this solid figure.
   Think: How many layers are there? How many cubes are in each layer?

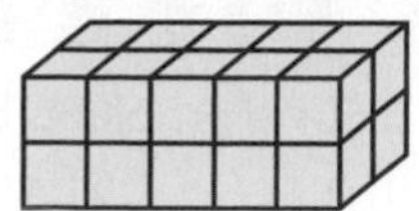

Use cubes to make each solid. Then write the volume in cubic units.

2. 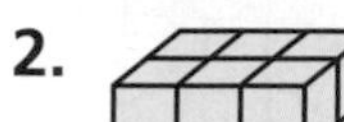

3. 

4. 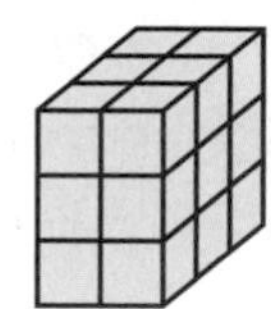

5. **TALK Math** **Explain** one way you can find the volume of a box that has 3 layers with 10 cubes in each layer.

Independent Practice and Problem Solving

Use cubes to make each solid. Then write the volume in cubic units.

6. 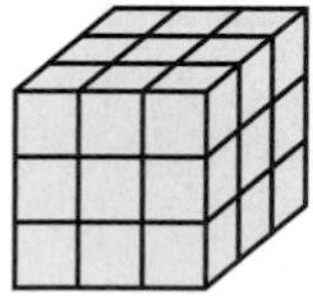

7. 

8. 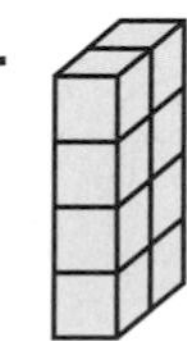

9. The volume of Chad's box is 36 cubic units. There are 4 layers. How many cubes are in each layer?

10. Look at the figure in Exercise 6. Write a multiplication sentence to find the volume of the figure.

11. Each layer of a prism is 6 cubic units. The volume is 24 cubic units. How many layers are in the prism?

12. **WRITE Math** **What's the Error?** Describe the error. Find the correct answer.

    Volume = 6 cubic units

Mixed Review and Test Prep

13. If $(4 \times 2) \times 3 = 24$, what is $(2 \times 3) \times 4$? (p. 260)

14. Find the perimeter and area of this figure. (pp. 560, 564)

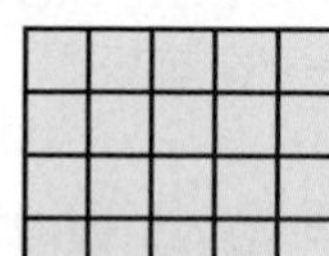

15. **Test Prep** What is the volume of this solid figure?

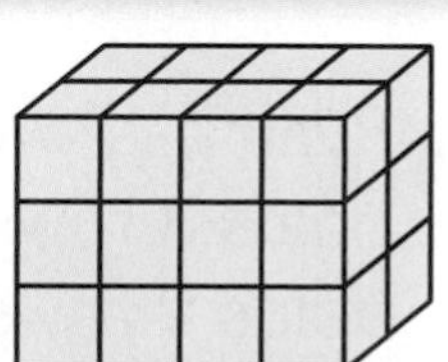

A 9 cubic units
B 12 cubic units
C 24 cubic units
D 36 cubic units

Extra Practice on page 574, Set D

LESSON 5

Problem Solving Workshop
Skill: Use a Model

OBJECTIVE: Solve problems by using the skill *use a model.*

Use the Skill

PROBLEM Mr. Davis bought 12 baseballs. Each baseball comes in a cube-shaped box. He wants to put all the baseballs into one large box. Which box can Mr. Davis use to hold the 12 baseballs?

Box A

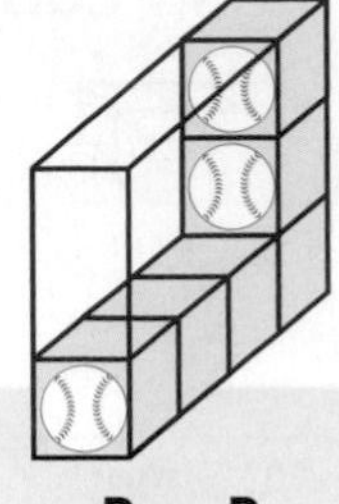
Box B

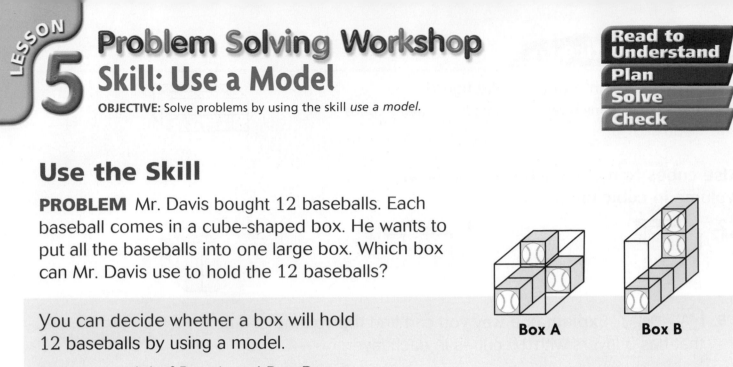

You can decide whether a box will hold 12 baseballs by using a model.

Make a model of Box A and Box B.
Use a cube to represent each baseball.

Box A	Box B
Place 3 rows of 2 cubes in the first layer. Add a second layer. 	Place 1 row of 4 cubes in the first layer. Add two more layers. 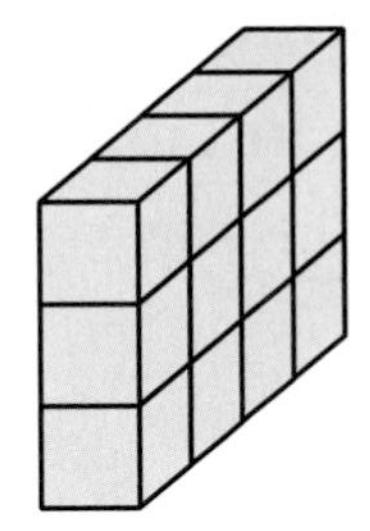
Find the volume: 2 layers × 6 cubes per layer = 12 cubic units	Find the volume: 3 layers × 4 cubes per layer = 12 cubic units

Both containers have a volume of 12 cubic units.

So, Mr. Davis can use Box A or Box B.
Both boxes will hold 12 baseballs.

Think and Discuss

Use a model to solve.

a. Lou filled a box with blocks. There are 2 layers. Each layer has 3 rows of 4 blocks. What is the volume of the box?

b. Ryan has two boxes. The red box has 4 layers. Each layer holds 3 rows of 3 cubes. The blue box has 5 layers. Each layer holds 2 rows of 4 cubes. Which box holds more cubes?

c. A box has a volume of 24 cubic units. There are 3 rows with 2 cubes in each row. How many layers does the box have?

Guided Problem Solving

Solve.

1. Mrs. Spencer collects teacups. She keeps each one in a cube-shaped box. She wants to pack her teacups in a larger box. There are two different-sized boxes she can use. Which box can hold 36 teacups?

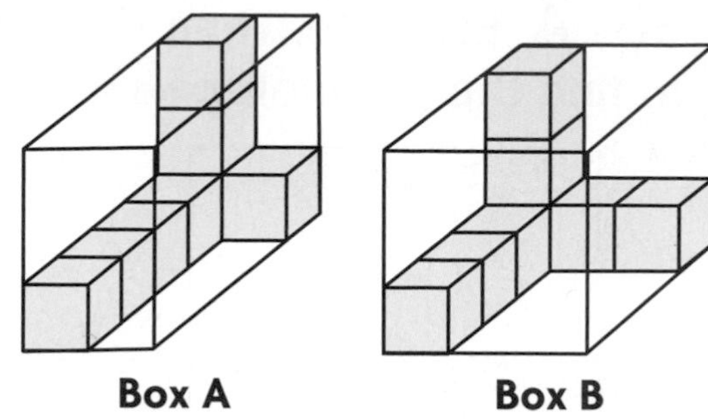

Make a model of each box.
Use a cube to represent each teacup box.
Count the cubes or multiply to find the volume of each box. Solve the problem.

2. **What if** Box A could hold 4 layers of teacups? What would be the volume of Box A in cubic units?

3. A carton is filled with 20 mugs in cube-shaped boxes. The carton has 2 layers. How many mugs are in each layer?

Mixed Applications

USE DATA For 5–6, use the table.

4. Ms. Wagner bought a box full of strawberry yogurt cups. The box has 2 layers. Each layer has 3 rows of 4 cups. How many yogurt cups are in the box?

Strawberry Snacks

Snack	Price
Strawberry yogurt cup	$2.00
Strawberry pie slice	$3.50
Strawberry ice cream cone	$2.75

5. Brandon had $10. He bought 2 slices of strawberry pie and 1 strawberry ice cream cone. How much money does he have left?

6. Tom bought an ice cream cone and a yogurt cup. He did not use any quarters. What bills and coins could he have used?

7. WRITE Math Bob's box has 2 layers with 2 rows of 3 blocks. Tom's box has 3 layers with 2 rows of 2 blocks. Whose box has more blocks? **Explain.**

8. Steve traced around the bottom of a solid figure. He drew a circle. Which could he have traced: a square pyramid, a cone, or a cube?

9. Sandy can run 1 mile in 8 minutes. At that speed, about how long will it take Sandy to run a 3-mile race?

10. Bryanna is washing her dad's car. Is the temperature about 25°F or about 75°F?

Extra Practice

Set A **Estimate. Then use a centimeter ruler to find the perimeter.** (pp. 560–563)

1. 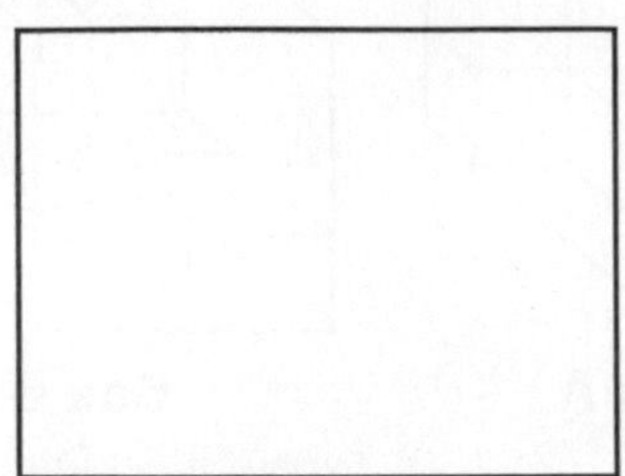

2. 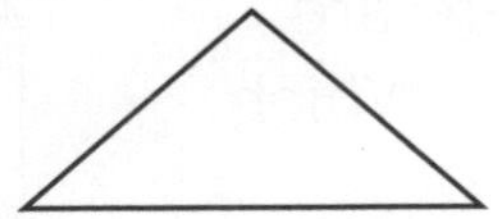

3. 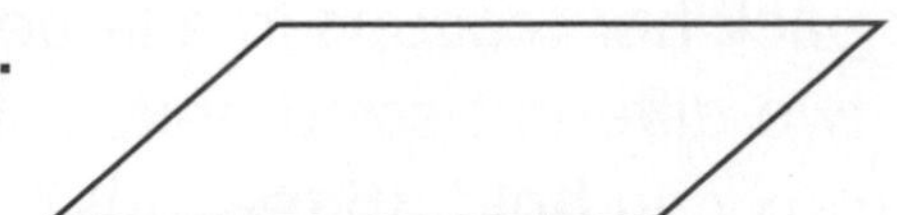

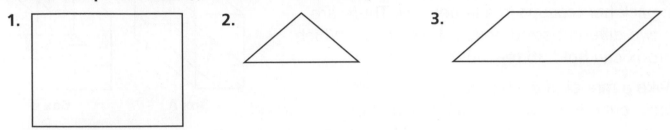

Set B **Count or multiply to find the area of each figure. Write the answer in square units.** (pp. 564–567)

1.

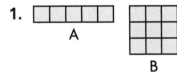

2. 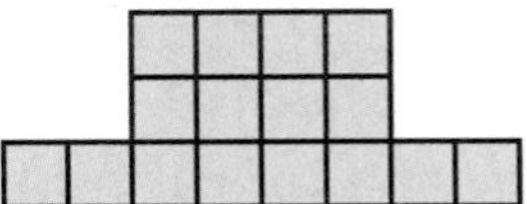

3. 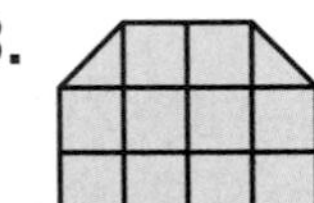

4. A checkerboard has 8 rows and 8 columns of red and black squares. What is the area in square units?

5. Aidan put tiles on his bathroom floor. There are four rows of five tiles and two rows of two tiles. What is the area?

Set C **For each pair, find the perimeter and the area. Tell which figure has the greater area.** (pp. 568–569)

1. A B

2. 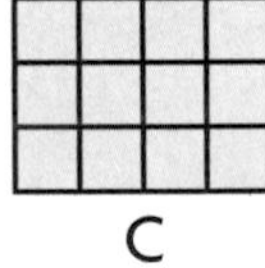 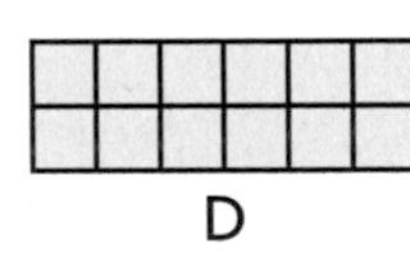

C D

Set D **Use cubes to make each solid. Then write the volume in cubic units.** (pp. 570–571)

1. 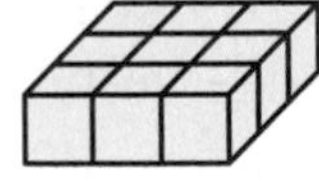

2. 

3. 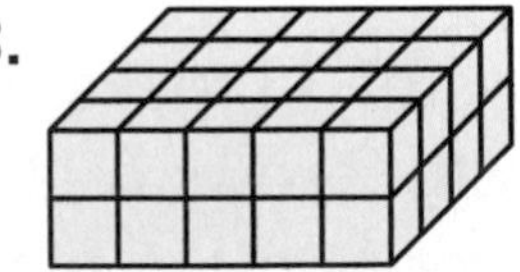

4. Each layer of a prism is 4 cubic units. The volume is 24 cubic units. How many layers are in the prism?

5. The volume of Sam's box is 25 cubic units. There are 5 layers. How many cubes are in each layer?

Technology
Use Harcourt Mega Math, Ice Station Exploration, *Polar Planes*, Levels Q, S.

PRACTICE GAME

Find That Measure

Roll!

3 players

Move!

- Game cards
- 1 number cube
- 3 game pieces

Win!

- Each player places a game piece on either the Perimeter, Area, or Volume space on the gameboard.
- Players take turns tossing a number cube and moving clockwise that number of spaces.
- If a player lands on Perimeter, Area, or Volume, he or she draws a game card and finds the perimeter, area, or volume of the figure on the card.
- The other players check the answer. If it is correct, the player keeps the card and gets another turn.
- If the answer is incorrect, the player returns the card to the bottom of the deck, and play passes to the next player.
- The first player to collect one card each from Perimeter, Area, and Volume wins.

MATH POWER

Perimeter Patterns

Look at the square. Its perimeter is 4 cm. You can use connected squares to form a perimeter pattern.

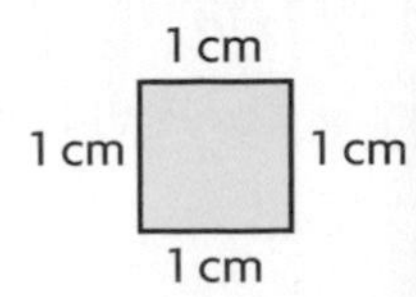

Example

Find the perimeter of 6 connected squares by using a pattern.

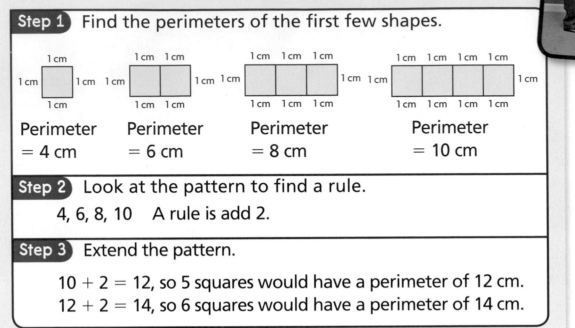

Step 1 Find the perimeters of the first few shapes.

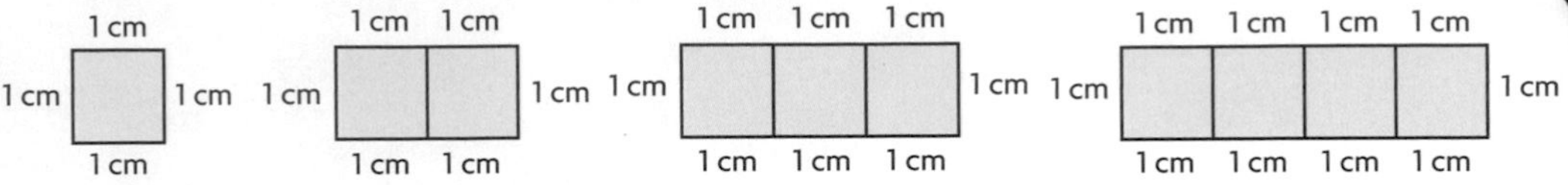

Perimeter = 4 cm | Perimeter = 6 cm | Perimeter = 8 cm | Perimeter = 10 cm

Step 2 Look at the pattern to find a rule.

4, 6, 8, 10 A rule is add 2.

Step 3 Extend the pattern.

$10 + 2 = 12$, so 5 squares would have a perimeter of 12 cm.
$12 + 2 = 14$, so 6 squares would have a perimeter of 14 cm.

So, 6 connected squares have a perimeter of 14 cm.

Try It

Find a pattern. Then use a rule to find the perimeter of 6 connected shapes.

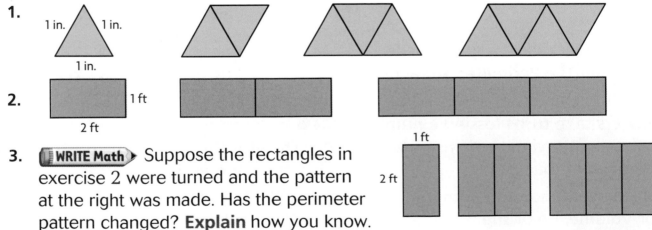

1.

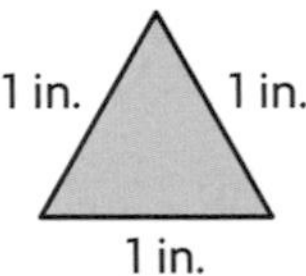

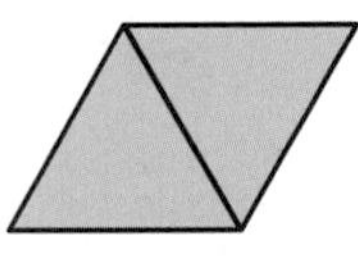

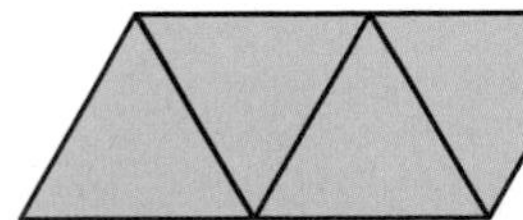

2.

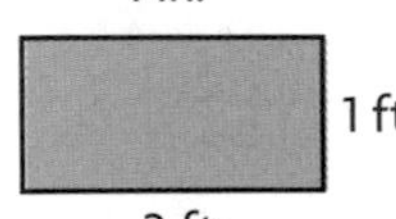

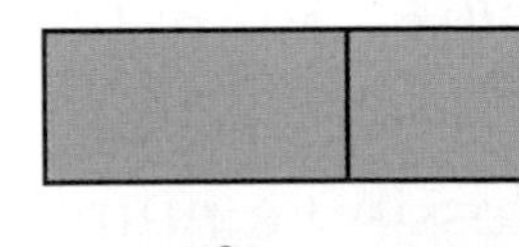

3. WRITE Math Suppose the rectangles in exercise 2 were turned and the pattern at the right was made. Has the perimeter pattern changed? **Explain** how you know.

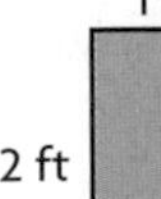

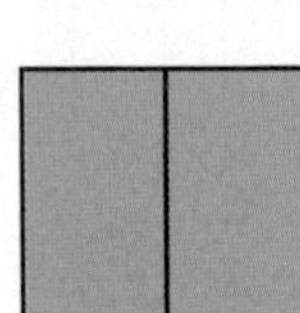

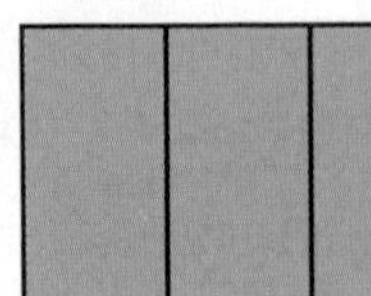

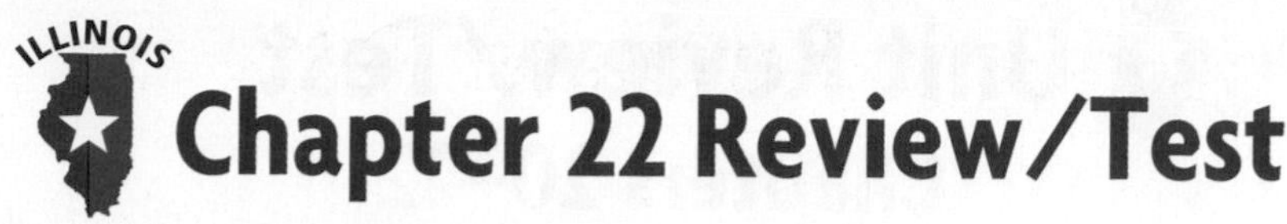

Chapter 22 Review/Test

Check Vocabulary and Concepts

Choose the best term from the box.

VOCABULARY
area
perimeter
volume

1. The __?__ is the amount of space a solid figure takes up. IL 7.3.06 (p. 570)
2. The distance around a figure is the __?__ IL 7.3.03 (p. 560)

Check Skills

Count or multiply to find the area of each figure. Write the answer in square units. IL 7.3.04 (pp. 564–567)

3. 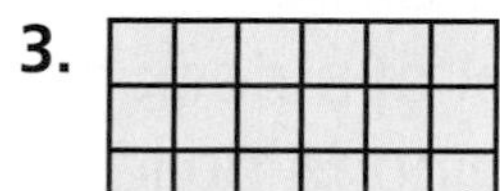

4. 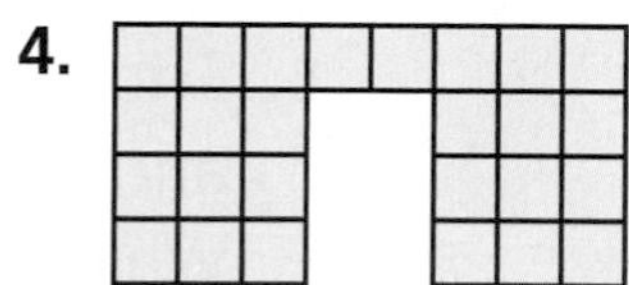

5. 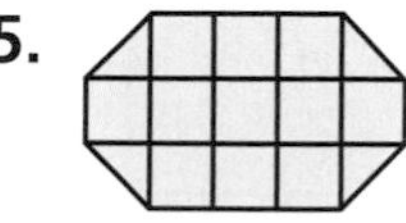

Find the volume of each solid. Write the volume in cubic units. IL 7.3.06 (pp. 570–571)

6. 

7. 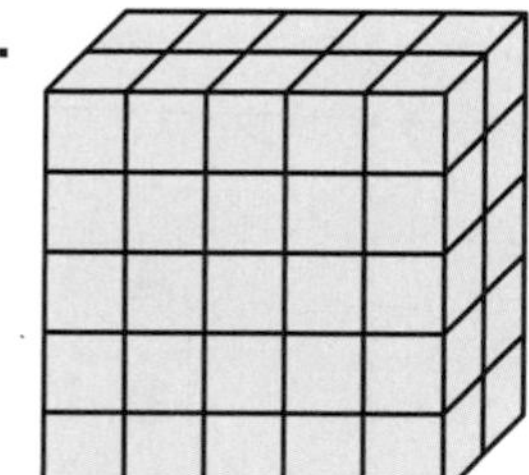

8. 

Check Problem Solving

Solve. IL 7.3.06 (pp. 572–573)

9. Natasha wants to store her souvenir golf balls in a box. The balls are packaged in cube-shaped boxes. Which of the boxes at the right will hold Natasha's 20 golf balls?

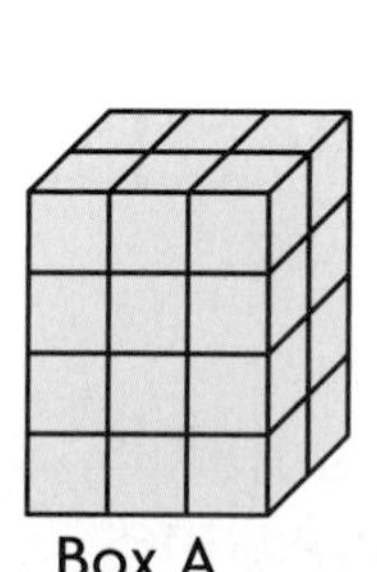

Box A

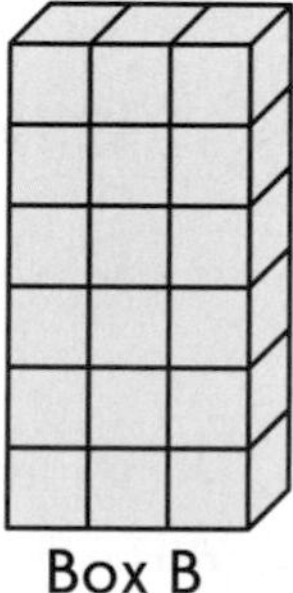

Box B

10. **WRITE Math** **Explain** why a box that has 6 layers of 6 cubes will not hold as much as a box that has 4 layers of 10 cubes.

Technology Use *Online Assessment.*

ILLINOIS

Unit Review/Test
Chapters 20–22

Multiple Choice

1. Angela drew this picture of her vegetable garden. What is the perimeter of her garden? IL 7.3.03 (p. 560)

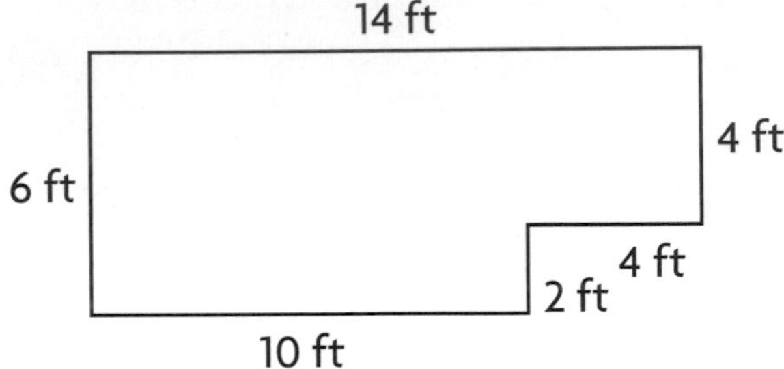

A 24 ft   C 36 ft

B 30 ft   D 40 ft

2. Graham wants to find the mass of a toy car for an experiment. Which is the best estimate of the mass of the toy car? IL 7.3.05 (p. 546)

A 35 g   C 350 g

B 35 kg   D 350 kg

3. Kristin has a roll of string that is 9 yards long. Which shows the length of the roll of string in feet? IL 7.3.07 (p. 540)

A 3 feet

B 18 feet

C 27 feet

D 30 feet

4. Leah's family is driving from Aurora to Chicago. Which unit should they use to measure the distance they will drive? IL 7.3.02 (p. 538)

A centimeters   C meters

B decimeters   D kilometers

5. Eric made this model of a deck he and his father are going to build. Which shows the area of the model? IL 7.3.04 (p. 564)

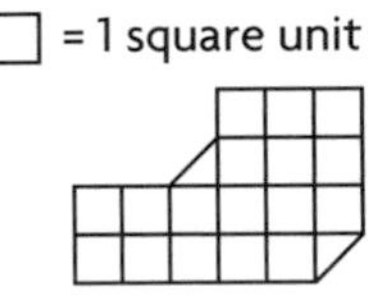

A $17\frac{1}{2}$ square units

B 18 square units

C $20\frac{1}{2}$ square units

D 24 square units

6. Pedro built this figure out of cubes. Which shows the volume of the figure? IL 7.3.06 (p. 570)

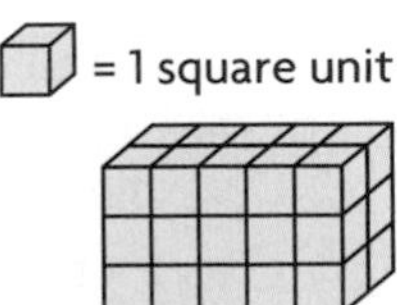

A 10 cubic units

B 15 cubic units

C 22 cubic units

D 30 cubic units

GO ONLINE **Technology** Use *Online Assessment.*

7. Jane is making a design using only figures that are similar to this figure.

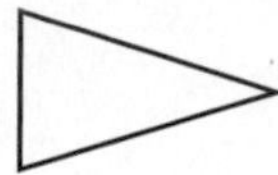

Which of these figures might she use in her design? IL 9.3.10 (p. 388)

A 

C 

B 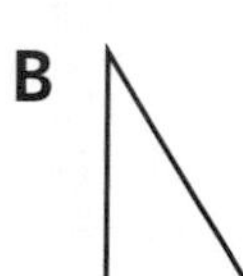

D 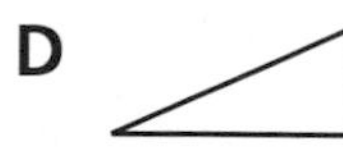

8. Sasha has a box full of apples. There are 8 apples in each layer, and there are 32 apples in the box. Which shows the number of layers of apples in the box? IL 8.3.05 (p. 572)

A 2 layers

B 4 layers

C 8 layers

D 12 layers

9. Simon ate $\frac{4}{10}$ of an orange. Isak ate $\frac{3}{10}$ of the same orange. Which shows the fraction of the orange they ate altogether? IL 6.3.03 (p. 466)

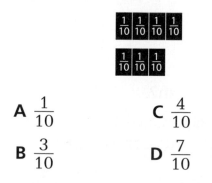

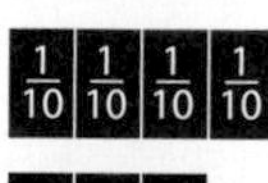

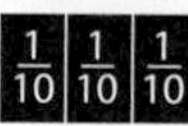

A $\frac{1}{10}$

C $\frac{4}{10}$

B $\frac{3}{10}$

D $\frac{7}{10}$

Short Response

This Venn diagram shows the blocks Peter used to build a castle. IL 10.3.01 (p. 366)

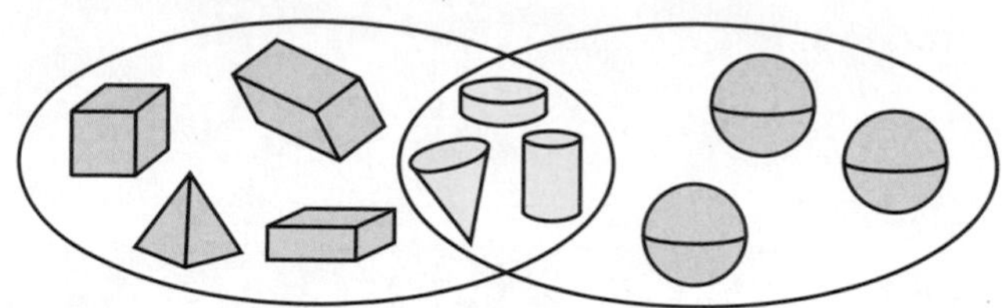

10. How many blocks with curved surfaces did he use? IL 10.3.01 (p. 366)

11. How many blocks with both flat and curved surfaces did he use? IL 10.3.01 (p. 366)

12. How many blocks with only flat surfaces did he use? IL 10.3.01 (p. 366)

Extended Response WRITE Math

13. Alisha has some square tiles with perimeters of 8 cm. She is using her tiles to make this growing pattern:

2 cm

She is using the perimeters of the figures to make a number pattern:

8 cm, 16 cm, 24 cm

Find a rule for each of Alisha's patterns. Then draw the 5th figure in the pattern and find its perimeter. IL 8.3.01 (p. 576)

THE WORLD ALMANAC FOR KIDS

Fish Stories

Great Barrier Reef

The Great Barrier Reef, located off the coast of Australia, is the home of colorful coral and fish. Coral is formed by colonies of tiny sea animals called coral polyps. The Great Barrier Reef has approximately 400 species of coral and 1,500 species of fish.

Some of the fish that live at the Great Barrier Reef are shown on these two pages.

FACT · ACTIVITY

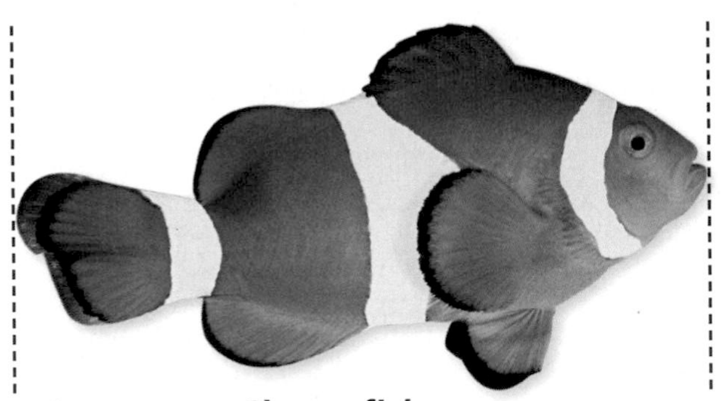

Clown fish

Angelfish

Use a ruler to measure to the nearest centimeter.

1. About how long is the angelfish?
2. About how long is the clown fish?
3. How much shorter is the clown fish than the angelfish?
4. Choose an object that is about the same length as each of these fish. Measure the objects. How do your measurements compare to the lengths of the fish?

ALMANAC **Fact**

The Great Barrier Reef is the world's largest coral reef.

You and the Fish

Has anyone ever told you about "the fish that got away"? When people tell such "fish stories," they sometimes use their hands and arms to show the lengths of fish. It's easier to understand how long something is when you compare it to something familiar, such as the length of your arm span.

FACT • ACTIVITY

For 3–5, use the data on pages 580–581.

1. Copy the chart. Estimate and record each length. Then, with a partner, use a centimeter ruler to measure to the nearest centimeter.

About How Many Centimeters?

Body Unit	Estimate	Actual Measurement
Length of pointer finger		
Length of arm		
Length of foot		

2. How close were your estimates to the actual measurements?
3. Which fish is about as long as your pointer finger?
4. Is the length of your foot greater than or less than the length of the clown fish?
5. Is your height greater than or less than the length of the box jellyfish?
6. WRITE Math Measure the width of your classroom with a meter stick. Then write a number sentence using <, >, or = to compare your measurement with the length of the hammerhead shark.

The hammerhead shark is about 6 meters long.

Including the tentacles, the box jellyfish is 3 meters long!

UNIT

8 Multiply and Divide by 1 Digit

Math on Location

with
Chapter Projects

1

As old computers are taken apart, the number of cases, circuit boards, and keyboards multiply.

2

An equal number of CRT's (cathode ray tubes) are placed on wood pallets for safe handling.

3

Three men can recycle 600 computers a day. That is 75 computers an hour in an 8-hour work day.

VOCABULARY POWER

TALK Math

What math do you see in the **Math on Location** photographs? How is multiplication or division used?

READ Math

REVIEW VOCABULARY You learned the words below when you learned about multiplication and division basic facts. How do these words relate to **Math on Location**?

Commutative Property of Multiplication the property that states that you can multiply two factors in any order and get the same product

quotient the answer in a division problem

dividend the number that is divided in a division problem

WRITE Math

Copy a Venn Diagram like the one below. Use what you know about multiplication and division to add more words.

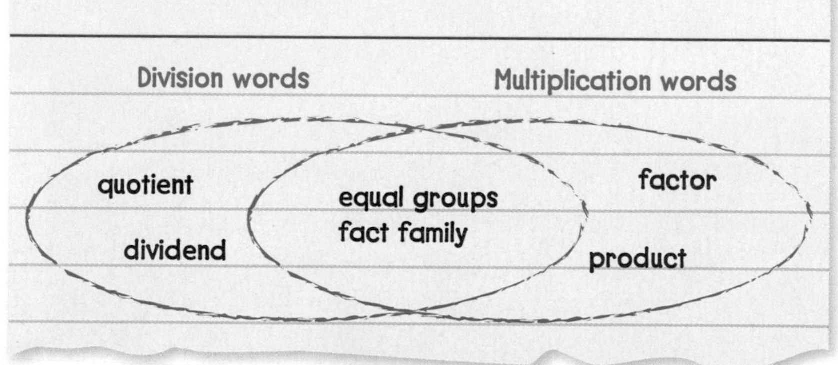

GO ONLINE **Technology**
Multimedia Math Glossary link at
www.harcourtschool.com/hspmath

CHAPTER 23 Multiply by 1 Digit

FAST FACT

A nursery is a place where plants are grown. Some plants have colorful flowers. Scientists group plants by whether or not they have flowers.

Investigate

Some flowers have only 3 petals and some flowers have many petals. Select a flower from the chart. Tell how many petals there would be if you had three of those flowers.

Flowers

Type of Flower	Number of Petals
Sunflower	34
Marigold	12
Daisy	55
Black-eyed Susan	21

Technology
Student pages are available in the Student eBook.

Show What You Know

Check your understanding of important skills needed for success in Chapter 23.

▶ Regroup Ones as Tens

Find the sum.

1. $7 + 9$

2. $15 + 8$

3. $19 + 34$

4. $36 + 27$

5. $23 + 17$

6. $29 + 11$

7. $35 + 37$

8. $32 + 48$

9. $78 + 15 = \blacksquare$

10. $47 + 39 = \blacksquare$

11. $56 + 5 = \blacksquare$

12. $33 + 8 = \blacksquare$

▶ Multiplication Facts Through 10

Find the product.

13. $3 \times 5 = \blacksquare$

14. $7 \times 7 = \blacksquare$

15. $6 \times 4 = \blacksquare$

16. $8 \times 9 = \blacksquare$

17. 6×6

18. 10×8

19. 9×3

20. 5×8

21. 3×2

22. 4×9

23. 8×3

24. 5×4

VOCABULARY POWER

CHAPTER VOCABULARY

array
estimate
factor
multiple
pattern
product

WARM-UP WORDS

estimate A number close to an exact amount

factor A number that is multiplied by another number to find a product

product The answer in a multiplication problem

LESSON 1

ALGEBRA

Multiples of 10 and 100

OBJECTIVE: Use basic facts and patterns to multiply multiples of 10 and 100.

Quick Review

1. 5×3
2. 2×8
3. 7×4
4. 3×6
5. 4×10

Learn

PROBLEM Kyle has 7 yo-yos in his collection. The world record holder for the largest yo-yo collection has about 600 times as many yo-yos as Kyle has. About how many yo-yos does the world record holder have?

You can use basic facts and patterns to multiply multiples of 10 and 100.

Example **Multiply.** 7×600

$7 \times 6 = 42$	← basic fact
$7 \times 60 = 420$	The product has the same
$7 \times 600 = 4{,}200$	number of zeros as the factor.

So, the world record holder has about 4,200 yo-yos.

More Examples

A $5 \times 200 = \blacksquare$

$5 \times 2 = 10$

$5 \times 20 = 100$

$5 \times 200 = 1{,}000$

B $30 \times 3 = \blacksquare$

$3 \times 3 = 9$

$30 \times 3 = 90$

$300 \times 3 = 900$

Math Idea

The product has the same number of zeros as the factor unless the basic fact has a zero in the product.

- Look at Example B. What pattern do you notice with the zeros in the factors and the products? How is Example A different?

Guided Practice

1. What basic fact would you use to find 5×60?

Use a basic fact and patterns to find each product.

2. $3 \times 4 = \blacksquare$
   $3 \times 40 = \blacksquare$
   $3 \times 400 = \blacksquare$

✓3. $8 \times 5 = \blacksquare$
   $80 \times 5 = \blacksquare$
   $800 \times 5 = \blacksquare$

✓4. $6 \times 3 = \blacksquare$
   $6 \times 30 = \blacksquare$
   $6 \times 300 = \blacksquare$

5. **TALK Math** **Explain** how to find the product 9×500.

Independent Practice and Problem Solving

Use a basic fact and patterns to find each product.

6. $7 \times 3 = ■$
$70 \times 3 = ■$
$700 \times 3 = ■$

7. $2 \times 6 = ■$
$2 \times 60 = ■$
$2 \times 600 = ■$

8. $9 \times 9 = ■$
$9 \times 90 = ■$
$9 \times 900 = ■$

Find the product.

9. $60 \times 8 = ■$

10. $5 \times 400 = ■$

11. $■ = 4 \times 200$

12. $30 \times 8 = ■$

13. $■ = 7 \times 80$

14. $6 \times 400 = ■$

15. $■ = 1 \times 70$

16. $■ = 900 \times 3$

17. $300 \times 5 = ■$

USE DATA For 18–19, use the pictograph.

18. The pictograph shows how many yo-yo tricks each student did in 1 minute. How many tricks could Chuck do in 1 hour?
Think: 1 hour = 60 minutes

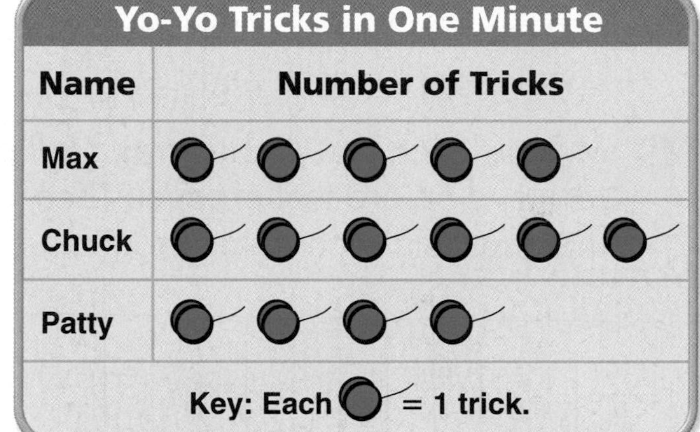

19. Max did yo-yo tricks for 20 minutes. Patty did yo-yo tricks for 30 minutes. Who did more yo-yo tricks? **Explain.**

20. A case contains 3 boxes of yo-yos. Each box holds 100 yo-yos. How many yo-yos are in 6 cases?

21. WRITE Math **What's the Error?** Meg says that $5 \times 800 = 400$. Describe her error. Write the correct answer.

Mixed Review and Test Prep

22. Hugh bought 1.75 pounds of apples, 1.6 pounds of grapes, and 1.58 pounds of peaches. Of which fruit did he buy the greatest amount? (p. 492)

23. How many sides and angles does a hexagon have? (p. 356)

24. **Test Prep** The drama club is selling tickets for the school musical. There are 4 shows. They have 500 tickets for each show. How many tickets are there to sell?

A 200 tickets
B 900 tickets
C 1,000 tickets
D 2,000 tickets

Extra Practice on page 604, Set A

LESSON 2 HANDS ON

Arrays with Tens and Ones

OBJECTIVE: Model multiplication using arrays with base-ten blocks.

Quick Review

1. $5 \times 7 = \blacksquare$
2. $8 \times 3 = \blacksquare$
3. $\blacksquare = 4 \times 4$
4. $10 \times 9 = \blacksquare$
5. $\blacksquare = 2 \times 6$

Molly has a bookcase with 3 shelves. There are 14 books on each shelf. How many books are there in all?

Multiply. 3×14

Investigate

Materials ■ base-ten blocks

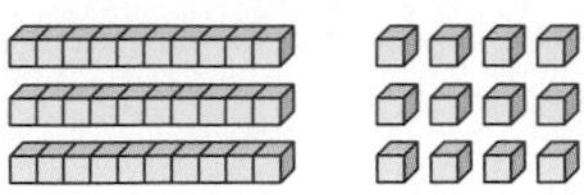

A Use base-ten blocks to model 3×14.

- There are 2 parts to the array. How can you describe each part?

B Multiply each part of the array. Multiply the tens and record that product. Then, multiply the ones and record that product.

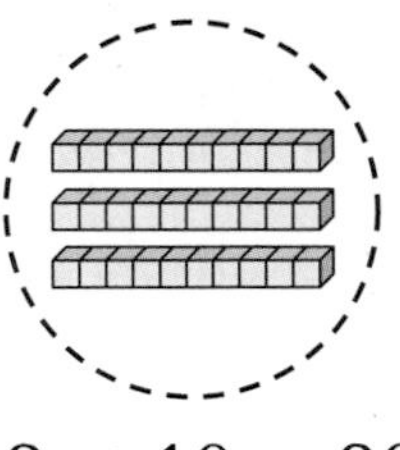

$3 \times 10 = 30$ $3 \times 4 = 12$

C Find the sum of the products. $30 + 12 = 42$

D Now use base-ten blocks to model 2×16. Multiply the tens and ones. Find the product.

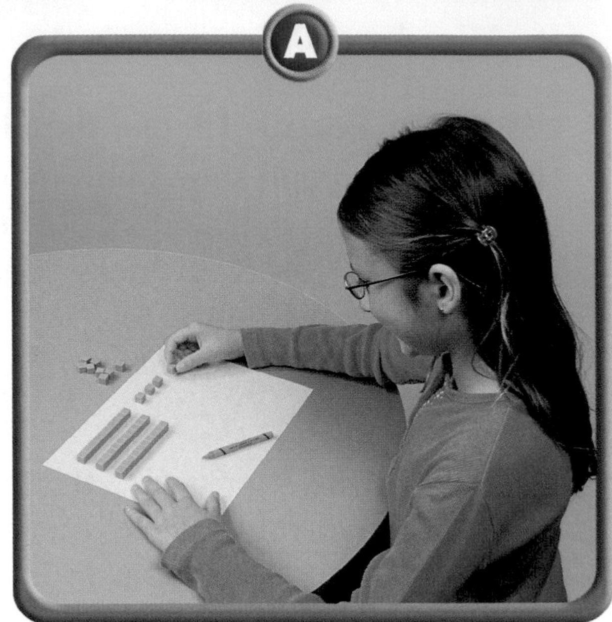

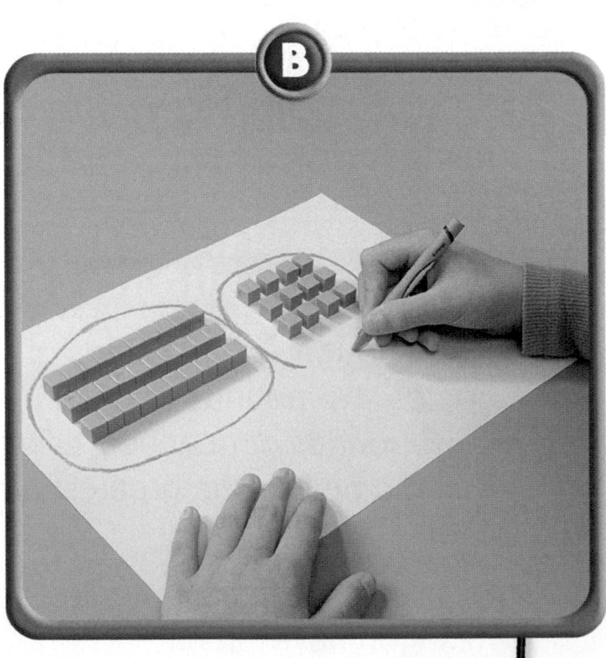

Draw Conclusions

1. Describe the array you made to model 2×16.
2. How would you change the 2×16 array to model 2×26?
3. **Comprehension** One way to model 18 is 1 ten 8 ones. How can knowing this help you find 4×18?

Connect

You can draw arrays on grid paper to model multiplication.

Draw an array to model 3 × 14.

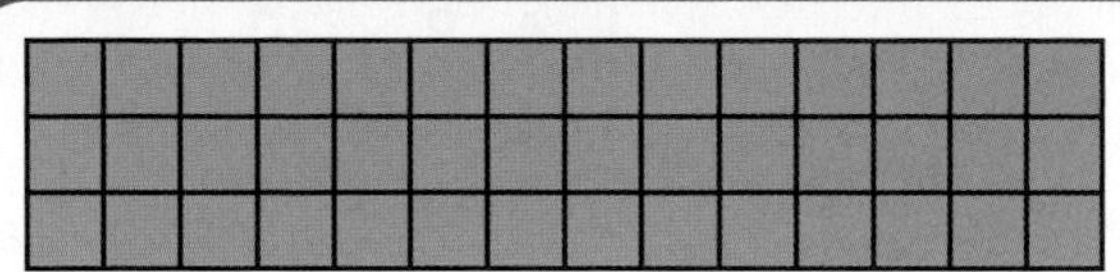

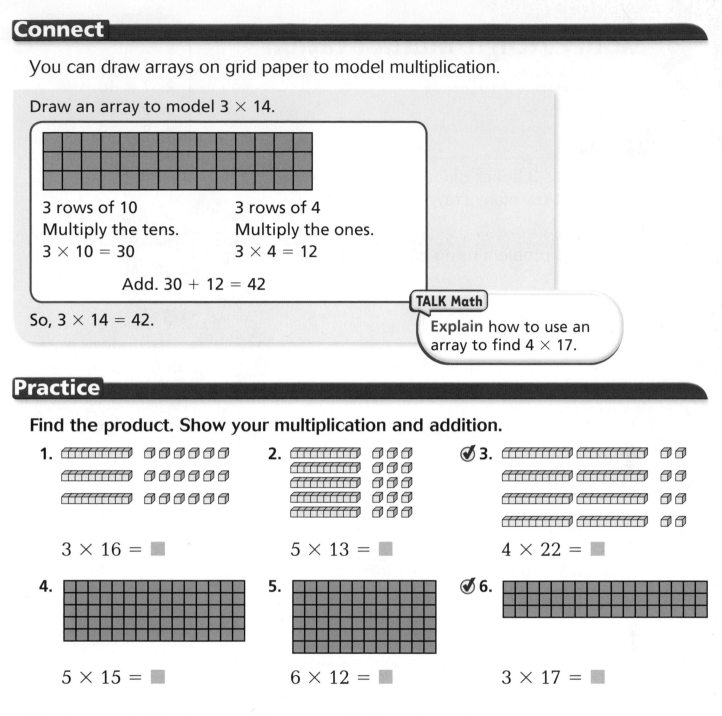

3 rows of 10
Multiply the tens.
3 × 10 = 30

3 rows of 4
Multiply the ones.
3 × 4 = 12

Add. 30 + 12 = 42

So, 3 × 14 = 42.

TALK Math

Explain how to use an array to find 4 × 17.

Practice

Find the product. Show your multiplication and addition.

1. 3 × 16 = ■

2. 5 × 13 = ■

3. 4 × 22 = ■

4. 5 × 15 = ■

5. 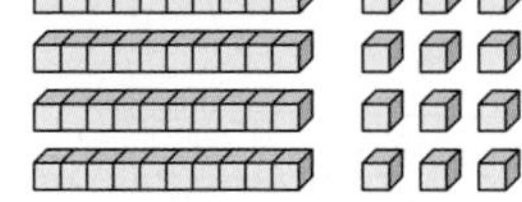

6 × 12 = ■

6. 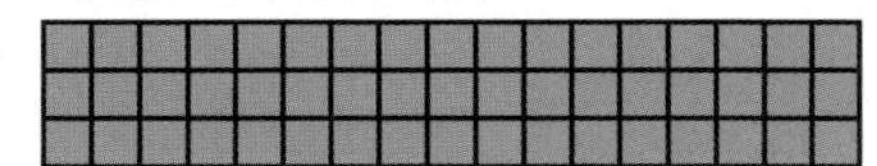

3 × 17 = ■

Use base-ten blocks or grid paper to find each product.

7. 4 × 25 = ■ **8.** 3 × 18 = ■ **9.** 5 × 21 = ■ **10.** 4 × 34 = ■

11. Reasoning The product of two numbers is 48. The sum of the two numbers is 16. What are the two numbers?

12. WRITE Math **Explain** how to use base-ten blocks to find the product 5 × 19.

Model 2-Digit Multiplication

OBJECTIVE: Model 2-digit multiplication with base-ten blocks using place value (partial products) and regrouping.

Quick Review

1. $5 \times 20 = ■$
2. $7 \times 10 = ■$
3. $9 \times 60 = ■$
4. $8 \times 30 = ■$
5. $3 \times 40 = ■$

Learn

PROBLEM Sam has 3 boxes of crayons. Each box holds 24 crayons. How many crayons does Sam have in all?

You can model the problem using base-ten blocks.
Multiply. 3×24

Use place value.

Activity 1

Materials ■ base-ten blocks

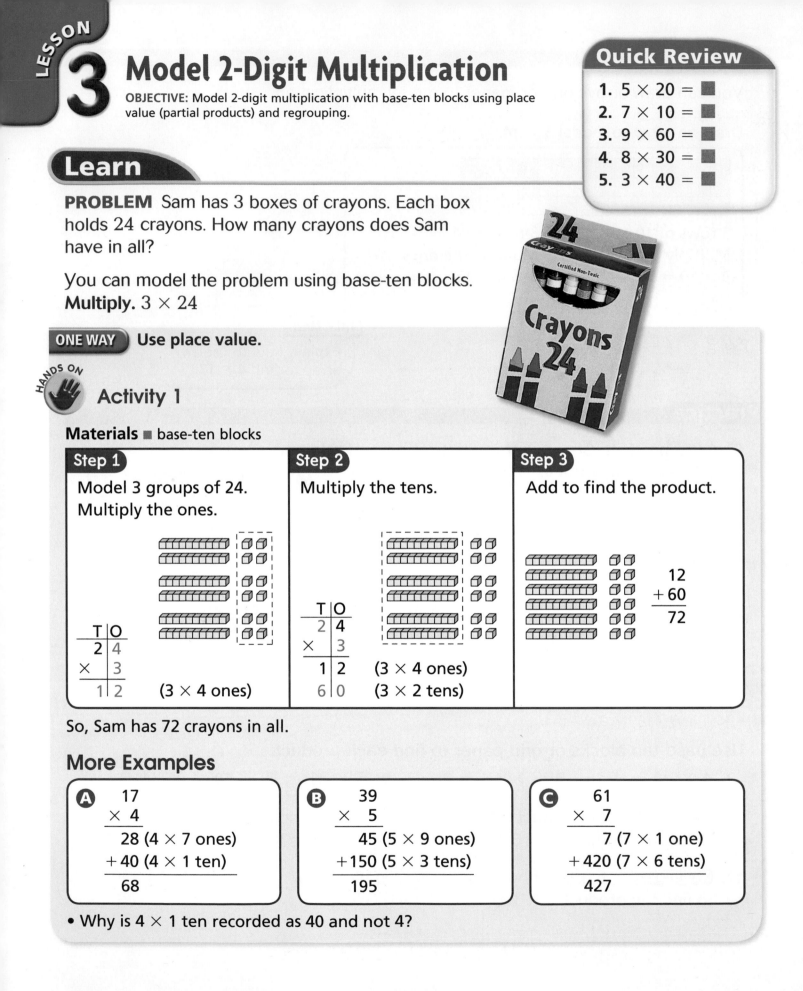

Step 1	Step 2	Step 3
Model 3 groups of 24. Multiply the ones.	Multiply the tens.	Add to find the product.
T O: 2 4 × 3 1 2 (3 × 4 ones)	T O: 2 4 × 3 1 2 (3 × 4 ones) 6 0 (3 × 2 tens)	12 + 60 72

So, Sam has 72 crayons in all.

More Examples

A
$$\begin{array}{r l} 17 & \\ \times\ 4 & \\ \hline 28 & (4 \times 7 \text{ ones}) \\ +40 & (4 \times 1 \text{ ten}) \\ \hline 68 & \end{array}$$

B
$$\begin{array}{r l} 39 & \\ \times\ 5 & \\ \hline 45 & (5 \times 9 \text{ ones}) \\ +150 & (5 \times 3 \text{ tens}) \\ \hline 195 & \end{array}$$

C
$$\begin{array}{r l} 61 & \\ \times\ 7 & \\ \hline 7 & (7 \times 1 \text{ one}) \\ +420 & (7 \times 6 \text{ tens}) \\ \hline 427 & \end{array}$$

- Why is 4×1 ten recorded as 40 and not 4?

ANOTHER WAY Use regrouping.

Activity 2

Materials ■ base-ten blocks

Step 1

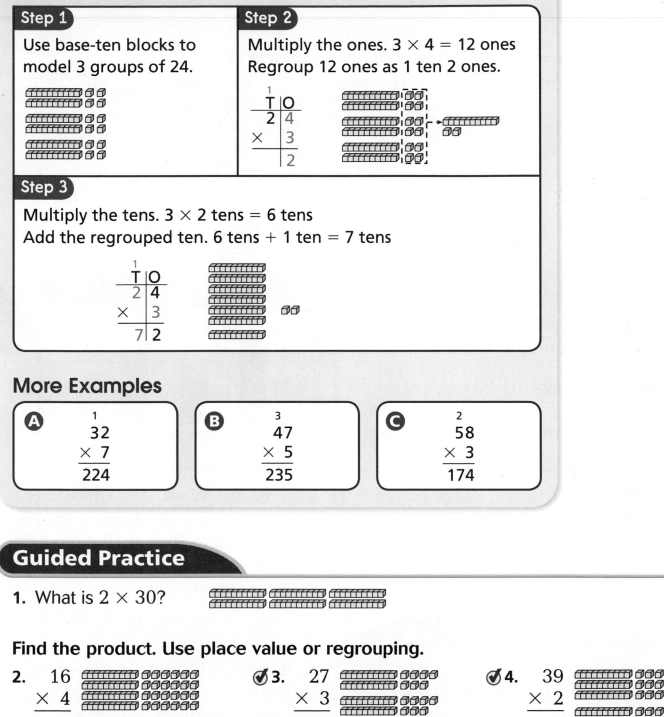

Use base-ten blocks to model 3 groups of 24.

Step 2

Multiply the ones. $3 \times 4 = 12$ ones
Regroup 12 ones as 1 ten 2 ones.

$$\begin{array}{r|l} \multicolumn{1}{r}{^{1}} & \\ T & O \\ 2 & 4 \\ \times & 3 \\ \hline & 2 \end{array}$$

Step 3

Multiply the tens. 3×2 tens $= 6$ tens
Add the regrouped ten. 6 tens + 1 ten = 7 tens

$$\begin{array}{r|l} \multicolumn{1}{r}{^{1}} & \\ T & O \\ 2 & 4 \\ \times & 3 \\ \hline 7 & 2 \end{array}$$

More Examples

A
$$\begin{array}{r} ^{1}\ \ \\ 32 \\ \times\ 7 \\ \hline 224 \end{array}$$

B
$$\begin{array}{r} ^{3}\ \ \\ 47 \\ \times\ 5 \\ \hline 235 \end{array}$$

C
$$\begin{array}{r} ^{2}\ \ \\ 58 \\ \times\ 3 \\ \hline 174 \end{array}$$

Guided Practice

1. What is 2×30?

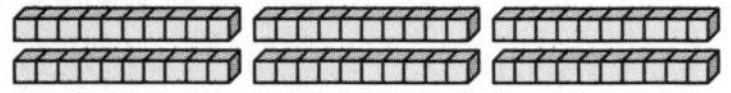

Find the product. Use place value or regrouping.

2. $\begin{array}{r} 16 \\ \times\ 4 \\ \hline \end{array}$

✓3. $\begin{array}{r} 27 \\ \times\ 3 \\ \hline \end{array}$

✓4. $\begin{array}{r} 39 \\ \times\ 2 \\ \hline \end{array}$

5. **TALK Math** Find 3×45 using both place value and regrouping. Tell how the methods are alike and different.

...ependent Practice and Problem Solving

Find the product. Use place value or regrouping.

6. $\begin{array}{r} 25 \\ \times\ 3 \\ \hline \end{array}$

7. $\begin{array}{r} 17 \\ \times\ 4 \\ \hline \end{array}$

8. $\begin{array}{r} 32 \\ \times\ 2 \\ \hline \end{array}$

Multiply. You may wish to use base-ten blocks to help you.

9. $\begin{array}{r} 23 \\ \times\ 6 \\ \hline \end{array}$

10. $\begin{array}{r} 39 \\ \times\ 2 \\ \hline \end{array}$

11. $\begin{array}{r} 45 \\ \times\ 3 \\ \hline \end{array}$

12. $\begin{array}{r} 26 \\ \times\ 4 \\ \hline \end{array}$

13. $\begin{array}{r} 52 \\ \times\ 5 \\ \hline \end{array}$

14. $\begin{array}{r} 31 \\ \times\ 4 \\ \hline \end{array}$

15. $\begin{array}{r} 16 \\ \times\ 5 \\ \hline \end{array}$

16. $\begin{array}{r} 41 \\ \times\ 3 \\ \hline \end{array}$

17. $\begin{array}{r} 18 \\ \times\ 3 \\ \hline \end{array}$

18. $\begin{array}{r} 14 \\ \times\ 8 \\ \hline \end{array}$

Algebra Use base-ten blocks to find the missing factor.

19. $3 \times \blacksquare = 93$
20. $\blacksquare \times 13 = 52$
21. $\blacksquare \times 24 = 72$
22. $5 \times \blacksquare = 80$

USE DATA For 23–24, use the bar graph.

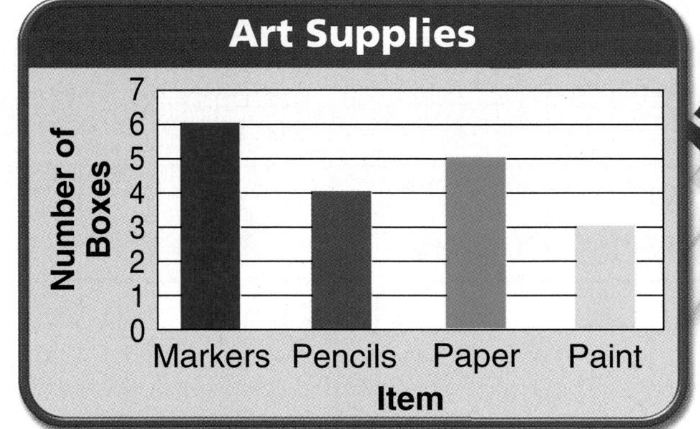

23. There are 16 pencils in each box. How many pencils are in all of the boxes?

24. **Reasoning** There are 20 tubes of paint in each box. If each tube of paint costs \$4, how much did the paint cost altogether?

25. **FAST FACT** The first box of crayons was sold in 1903 and had the same 8 colors that are in an 8-crayon box today. If Holly has 13 of these boxes, how many crayons does she have?

26. **WRITE Math** **What's the Question?** Kate multiplied a 2-digit number by a 1-digit number. She says the product is a four-digit number. Does this make sense? **Explain.**

Mixed Review and Test Prep

27. One pack has 500 sheets of paper. How many sheets are in 4 packs? (p. 586)

28. Chris has a red, a blue, and a green shirt. He has blue and tan pants. How many combinations of 1 shirt and 1 pair of pants are there? (p. 186)

29. **Test Prep** A 3rd grade class went on a field trip. There were 26 students in each of 3 groups. How many students went on the field trip?

A 29 students
B 68 students
C 78 students
D 84 students

 Extra Practice on page 604, Set B

Making Crayons

Identify the Details

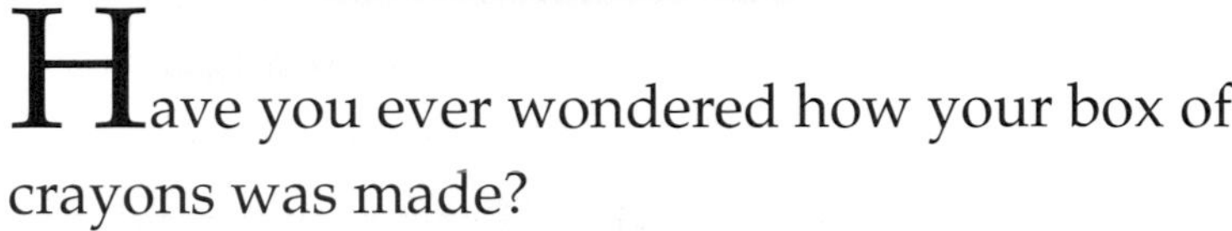

Have you ever wondered how your box of crayons was made?

Two main ingredients are pigment and wax. *Pigment* is another word for *color*. The wax is heated and mixed with pigment and hardening powder. The mixture is poured into a mold.

Cool water is used to cool the mold. After the mold cools, each crayon is wrapped with a paper label. Crayon labels are printed in different languages.

The crayons are separated by color and put into boxes. It can take 3 to 9 minutes to make one crayon.

Identify the details about making crayons:

- 2 main ingredients in crayons
- heated wax is mixed with color
- mixture is poured into mold
- mold is cooled
- crayons are wrapped with paper label
- 3 to 9 minutes to make one crayon

Problem Solving Identify the details to solve the problems.

1. How do crayons get their color?
2. If it takes 7 minutes to make 1 blue crayon, how long would it take to make 25 blue crayons?

4 Estimate Products

OBJECTIVE: Use estimation to find a product.

Quick Review

1. 7×50
2. 4×300
3. 5×800
4. 9×20
5. 6×60

Learn

PROBLEM The Bevilles drove 5 hours from their house to the beach. The family drove at an average speed of 62 miles an hour. About how many miles does the Beville family live from the beach?

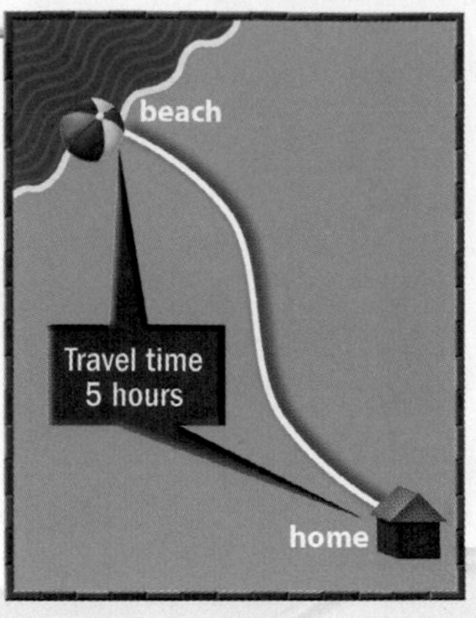

The question asks *about* how many. If you do not need an exact answer, you can find an estimate.
Estimate. 5×62

Example

Step 1

Round 62 to the greatest place value.

5×62
↓
5×60

Step 2

Find the estimated product.

Use a basic fact and pattern of zeros.

$5 \times 6 = 30$
$5 \times 60 = 300$

So, the Beville family lives about 300 miles from the beach.

Remember

To round a number:
- Decide on the place to be rounded.
- Look at the digit to its right.
- If the digit is less than 5, the digit being rounded stays the same.
- If the digit is 5 or more, the digit being rounded is increased by 1.

More Examples

A Round to the nearest ten.

$78 \times 7 \rightarrow 80 \times 7 = 560$

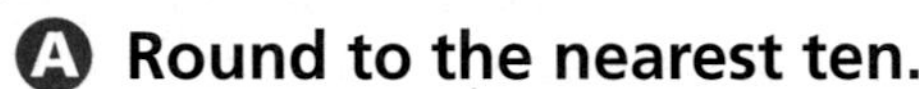

B Round to the nearest hundred.

$284 \times 4 \rightarrow 300 \times 4 = 1{,}200$

Guided Practice

1. Round 718 to the nearest hundred.

Estimate each product. Round to the greatest place value.

2. 3×93
3. 7×826
4. 6×39

5. **TALK Math** **Explain** how to estimate 5×59. Tell whether the exact answer is greater or less than the estimate and why.

Independent Practice and Problem Solving

Estimate each product. Round to the greatest place value.

6. 39×7 **7.** 52×9 **8.** 6×21 **9.** 3×76

10. 641×5 **11.** 8×925 **12.** 4×388 **13.** 872×3

14. $\begin{array}{r} 71 \\ \times\ 4 \\ \hline \end{array}$ **15.** $\begin{array}{r} 48 \\ \times\ 5 \\ \hline \end{array}$ **16.** $\begin{array}{r} 354 \\ \times\ \ \ 8 \\ \hline \end{array}$ **17.** $\begin{array}{r} 216 \\ \times\ \ \ 7 \\ \hline \end{array}$ **18.** $\begin{array}{r} 197 \\ \times\ \ \ 6 \\ \hline \end{array}$

19. $\begin{array}{r} 92 \\ \times\ 8 \\ \hline \end{array}$ **20.** $\begin{array}{r} 461 \\ \times\ \ \ 3 \\ \hline \end{array}$ **21.** $\begin{array}{r} 82 \\ \times\ 4 \\ \hline \end{array}$ **22.** $\begin{array}{r} 167 \\ \times\ \ \ 9 \\ \hline \end{array}$ **23.** $\begin{array}{r} 328 \\ \times\ \ \ 4 \\ \hline \end{array}$

USE DATA For 24–25, use the table.

24. If each room at the Beachfront Suites is filled, and there are 4 people per room, about how many people are staying at the hotel?

25. At the Flamingo, there are about 3 people per room. At the Sand and Surf, there are about 4 people per room. If all the rooms at both hotels are filled, which hotel has more people staying in it? About how many more?

Hotels at the Beach

Name	Number of Rooms
Sand and Surf	52
Flamingo	132
Boardwalk Hotel	87
Beachfront Suites	48

26. Reasoning Marc owns a beach umbrella rental shop. Yesterday, he rented 6 umbrellas. Each umbrella costs \$8 an hour and was rented for 8 hours. About how much did Marc earn yesterday?

27. WRITE Math The Beville family stayed at a hotel that cost \$77 a day. About how much did the hotel cost for 7 days? **Explain.**

Mixed Review and Test Prep

28. Ally brought 4 gallons of juice for the picnic. There are 16 servings in each gallon. How many servings of juice did Ally bring? (p. 590)

29. Oliver has 282 photos in an album and 72 photos that are not in the album. How many photos does Oliver have in all? (p. 58)

30. Test Prep Tom and his friends built 4 birdhouses. They used 177 craft sticks to build each birdhouse. About how many craft sticks did they use in all?

A 300 **C** 600

B 400 **D** 800

Extra Practice on page 604, Set C

Multiply 2-Digit Numbers

OBJECTIVE: Multiply 2-digit numbers using an algorithm.

Quick Review

1. 9×8
2. 3×12
3. 7×5
4. 2×6
5. 4×10

Learn

PROBLEM The cafeteria has 68 tables. Each table has 4 chairs. How many chairs are in the cafeteria?

Multiply. 68×4 **Estimate.** $70 \times 4 = 280$

ONE WAY Use regrouping.

Step 1

Multiply the ones.
4×8 ones $= 32$ ones
Regroup 32 ones as 3 tens 2 ones.

$$\begin{array}{r} {}^{3} \\ 68 \\ \times\ 4 \\ \hline 2 \end{array}$$

Step 2

Multiply the tens.
4×6 tens $= 24$ tens
24 tens + 3 tens = 27 tens
Regroup 27 tens as 2 hundreds 7 tens.

$$\begin{array}{r} {}^{3} \\ 68 \\ \times\ 4 \\ \hline 272 \end{array}$$

ANOTHER WAY Use place value.

Step 1

Multiply the ones. Record.

$$\begin{array}{r} 68 \\ \times\ 4 \\ \hline 32 \end{array} \quad (4 \times 8 = 32)$$

Step 2

Multiply the tens. Record.

$$\begin{array}{r} 68 \\ \times\ 4 \\ \hline 32 \\ 240 \end{array} \quad (4 \times 60 = 240)$$

Step 3

Add the products.

$$\begin{array}{r} 68 \\ \times\ 4 \\ \hline 32 \\ +\,240 \\ \hline 272 \end{array}$$

So, the cafeteria has 272 chairs. Since 272 is close to the estimate, 280, the answer is reasonable.

Guided Practice

1. What is 5×4 tens?

Find each product.

2. $\begin{array}{r} 52 \\ \times\ 6 \\ \hline \end{array}$
3. $\begin{array}{r} 32 \\ \times\ 3 \\ \hline \end{array}$
4. ✓ $\begin{array}{r} 71 \\ \times\ 8 \\ \hline \end{array}$
5. ✓ $\begin{array}{r} 28 \\ \times\ 3 \\ \hline \end{array}$

6. **TALK Math** **Explain** how to find 7×54.

Independent Practice and Problem Solving

Find each product.

7. $\begin{array}{r} 24 \\ \times\ 3 \\ \hline \end{array}$ 8. $\begin{array}{r} 76 \\ \times\ 8 \\ \hline \end{array}$ 9. $\begin{array}{r} 45 \\ \times\ 6 \\ \hline \end{array}$ 10. $\begin{array}{r} 19 \\ \times\ 5 \\ \hline \end{array}$ 11. $\begin{array}{r} 37 \\ \times\ 4 \\ \hline \end{array}$

12. $\begin{array}{r} 37 \\ \times\ 9 \\ \hline \end{array}$ 13. $\begin{array}{r} 93 \\ \times\ 3 \\ \hline \end{array}$ 14. $\begin{array}{r} 31 \\ \times\ 7 \\ \hline \end{array}$ 15. $\begin{array}{r} 82 \\ \times\ 4 \\ \hline \end{array}$ 16. $\begin{array}{r} 63 \\ \times\ 7 \\ \hline \end{array}$

17. 98×5 18. 56×7 19. 9×44 20. 3×76

Algebra Find the missing factor.

21. $12 \times \blacksquare = 36$ 22. $\blacksquare \times 4 = 44$ 23. $16 \times \blacksquare = 64$ 24. $\blacksquare \times 3 = 63$

USE DATA For 25–27, use the bar graph.

25. A box holds 48 cartons of milk. How many cartons of milk does the cafeteria have in all?

26. **Reasoning** If a box holds 32 bottles of juice and 64 bottles of water, does the cafeteria have more bottles of juice or water? **Explain.**

27. The cafeteria sold 58 bottles of lemonade. If one box holds 36 bottles, how many bottles of lemonade are left?

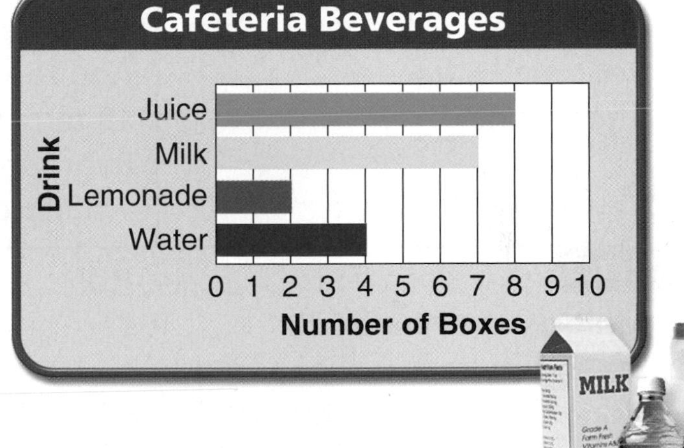

28. **WRITE Math** **What's the Question?** There are 24 bags of pretzels in each box. The answer is 72 bags.

Mixed Review and Test Prep

29. What is the missing addend? (p. 50)

$$12 - \blacksquare = 7$$

30. Nina uses 36 inches of ribbon to make a bow. About how much ribbon will she need to make 8 bows? (p. 594)

31. **Test Prep** Jamie rented three movies. Each movie is 97 minutes long. How long will it take Jamie to watch all three movies?

A 237 minutes **C** 291 minutes
B 271 minutes **D** 480 minutes

Technology CD ROM
Use Harcourt Mega Math, The Number Games, *Up, Up, and Array,* Level J.

Extra Practice on page 604, Set D

Multiply 3-Digit Numbers

OBJECTIVE: Multiply 3-digit numbers using an algorithm.

Quick Review

1. 3×51
2. 6×37
3. 2×72
4. 8×50
5. 7×300

Learn

PROBLEM Mr. Brown walks his dog every day. If he walks 3 miles a day, how many miles will he walk in 1 year? (Hint: 1 year = 365 days)

Multiply. 365×3 **Estimate.** $400 \times 3 = 1{,}200$

ONE WAY Use regrouping.

Step 1

Multiply the ones.
3 × 5 ones = 15 ones
Regroup 15 ones as
1 ten 5 ones.

$$\begin{array}{r} {}^{1} \\ 365 \\ \times \quad 3 \\ \hline 95 \end{array}$$

Step 2

Multiply the tens.
3 × 6 tens = 18 tens
Add the regrouped ten.
18 tens + 1 ten = 19 tens
Regroup 19 tens as
1 hundred 9 tens.

$$\begin{array}{r} {}^{1\,1} \\ 365 \\ \times \quad 3 \\ \hline 95 \end{array}$$

Step 3

Multiply the hundreds.
3 × 3 hundreds = 9 hundreds
Add the regrouped hundred. 9 + 1 = 10
Regroup 10 hundreds as 1 thousand 0 hundreds.

$$\begin{array}{r} {}^{1\,1} \\ 365 \\ \times \quad 3 \\ \hline 1{,}095 \end{array}$$

So, Mr. Brown will walk 1,095 miles in a year. Since 1,095 is close to the estimate, 1,200, the answer is reasonable.

ANOTHER WAY Use place value.

Step 1

Multiply the ones.
Record.

$$\begin{array}{rl} 305 & \\ \times \quad 3 & \\ \hline 15 & (3 \times 5) \end{array}$$

Step 2

Multiply the tens.
Record.

$$\begin{array}{rl} 305 & \\ \times \quad 3 & \\ \hline 15 & (3 \times 5) \\ 0 & (3 \times 0) \end{array}$$

Step 3

Multiply the hundreds.
Record.

$$\begin{array}{rl} 305 & \\ \times \quad 3 & \\ \hline 15 & (3 \times 5) \\ 0 & (3 \times 0) \\ +900 & (3 \times 300) \\ \hline \end{array}$$

Step 4

Add the products.

$$\begin{array}{r} 305 \\ \times \quad 3 \\ \hline 15 \\ 0 \\ +900 \\ \hline 915 \end{array}$$

Guided Practice

1. What is 7×5 hundreds?

Find each product.

2. $\begin{array}{r} 218 \\ \times \quad 4 \\ \hline \end{array}$

3. $\begin{array}{r} 451 \\ \times \quad 6 \\ \hline \end{array}$

4. $\begin{array}{r} 132 \\ \times \quad 3 \\ \hline \end{array}$

5. $\begin{array}{r} 333 \\ \times \quad 4 \\ \hline \end{array}$

6. $\begin{array}{r} 537 \\ \times \quad 5 \\ \hline \end{array}$

7. **TALK Math** **Explain** how to find 4×628.

Independent Practice and Problem Solving

Find each product.

8. $\begin{array}{r} 823 \\ \times \quad 2 \\ \hline \end{array}$

9. $\begin{array}{r} 194 \\ \times \quad 6 \\ \hline \end{array}$

10. $\begin{array}{r} 311 \\ \times \quad 3 \\ \hline \end{array}$

11. $\begin{array}{r} 275 \\ \times \quad 4 \\ \hline \end{array}$

12. $\begin{array}{r} 436 \\ \times \quad 1 \\ \hline \end{array}$

13. $\begin{array}{r} 443 \\ \times \quad 3 \\ \hline \end{array}$

14. $\begin{array}{r} 921 \\ \times \quad 5 \\ \hline \end{array}$

15. $\begin{array}{r} 129 \\ \times \quad 3 \\ \hline \end{array}$

16. $\begin{array}{r} 572 \\ \times \quad 4 \\ \hline \end{array}$

17. $\begin{array}{r} 324 \\ \times \quad 2 \\ \hline \end{array}$

18. 5×204

19. 3×152

20. 6×513

21. 2×789

USE DATA For 22–24, use the chart.

Activity	Calories used per hour*
Playing Piano	76
Swimming	166
Jumping Rope	274

*For 60-pound student

22. A calorie is a unit of energy that food gives you. The chart shows the number of calories used in one hour. Marcus swam for 4 hours. How many calories did he use?

23. **Reasoning** Matt practices the piano 5 times a week for 1 hour each time. How many calories does Matt use in 4 weeks?

24. **WRITE Math** Missy likes to jump rope. How many calories will Missy use by jumping rope for 3 hours? **Explain.**

Mixed Review and Test Prep

25. Monique has 4 quarters, 3 dimes, and 2 nickels. How much money does she have? (p. 110)

26. $8{,}000 - 2{,}768 = \blacksquare$ (p. 88)

27. **Test Prep** Mr. Jackson drives his company truck 417 miles each week. How far does he drive in 6 weeks?

A 2,402 miles
B 2,462 miles
C 2,502 miles
D 2,562 miles

Extra Practice on page 604, Set E

Problem Solving Workshop
Strategy: Solve a Simpler Problem

OBJECTIVE: Solve problems by using the strategy *solve a simpler problem*.

Learn the Strategy

You can use a simpler problem to help you solve more complex problems. You can either break the problem into simpler parts or you can use estimation to help you solve the problem.

Break into Simpler Parts

Kendra uses beads to make necklaces. The beads come in packages of 75. If Kendra buys 6 packages, how many beads will she have?

Break apart 75 into numbers that are easier to multiply.

Rewrite 75 as 70 + 5.

Multiply each addend by 6.

Add the products.

$$\begin{array}{r} 75 \\ \times\ 6 \\ \hline \end{array} = \begin{array}{r} 70 + 5 \\ \times\quad\ 6 \\ \hline 30 \leftarrow 6 \times 5 \\ 420 \leftarrow 6 \times 70 \\ \hline 450 \end{array}$$

So, Kendra will have 450 beads.

Use Estimation

Apples cost $0.99 a pound. Grapes cost $0.89 a pound. Pam bought 4 pounds of apples and 3 pounds of grapes. Did she pay more or less than $5 in all?

$0.99 × 4 → $1 × 4 = $4
$0.89 × 3 → $1 × 3 = $3
$4 + $3 = $7
Pam spent about $7.

So, Pam spent more than $5 in all.

TALK Math

Explain how rounding to the nearest dollar makes the second problem simpler to solve.

Use the Strategy

PROBLEM The students at Lincoln Elementary School are collecting food for the local food pantry. There are 87 third-grade students in the school. Each student brings in 4 cans of food. How many cans do the third-grade students collect altogether?

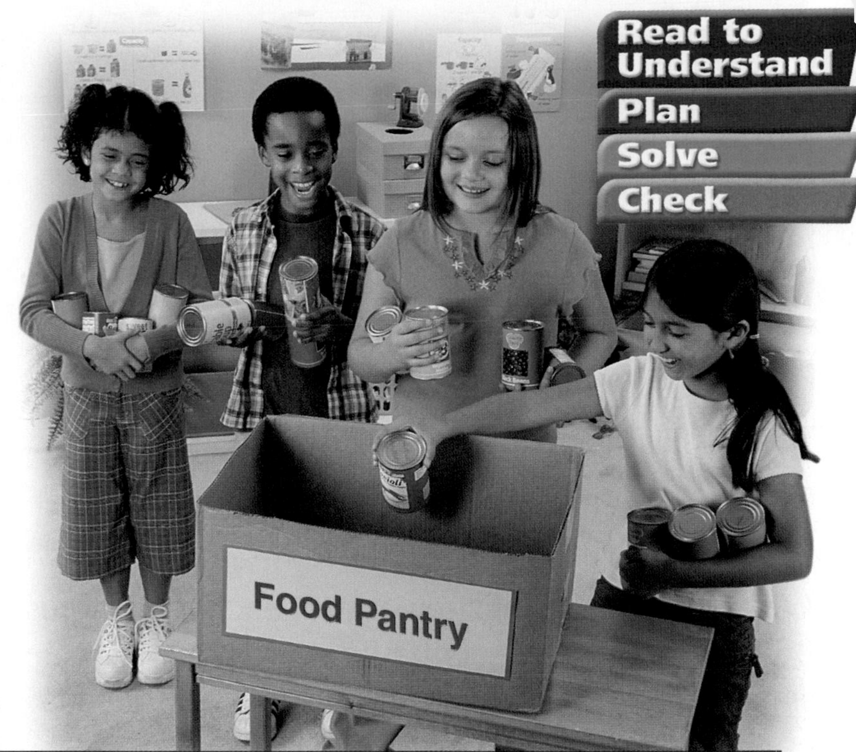

Read to Understand

- **Summarize the problem.**
- **What information is given?**

Plan

- **What strategy can you use to solve the problem?**
  You can solve a simpler problem.

Solve

- **How can you use the strategy to solve the problem?**
  You can find 87×4 by breaking apart 87 into numbers that are easier to multiply.

Rewrite 87 as $80 + 7$.

$$\begin{array}{r} 87 \\ \times\ 4 \\ \hline \end{array} = \begin{array}{r} 80 + 7 \\ \times\quad 4 \\ \hline \end{array}$$

Multiply each addend by 4.

$$\begin{array}{rl} 28 & \leftarrow 4 \times 7 \\ 320 & \leftarrow 4 \times 80 \\ \hline 348 & \end{array}$$

Add the products.

So, the third-grade students collect 348 cans altogether.

Check

- **Look back at the problem. Does the answer make sense for the problem? Explain.**

...ded Problem Solving

Ms. Reynolds volunteers at the food pantry. She organizes the donated food items. She puts the canned food on 5 shelves. Each shelf can hold 58 cans of food. How many cans can fit on the 5 shelves?

First, write a simpler problem.

Then, multiply each addend.

$$\begin{array}{r} 58 \\ \times\ 5 \\ \hline \end{array} = \begin{array}{r} 50 + 8 \\ \times\ \quad 5 \\ \hline \end{array}$$

Finally, add the products to find the total number of cans.

2. **What if** there are 8 shelves and each shelf holds 96 cans of food? Describe how you would use a simpler problem to find the total number of cans on the shelves.

3. The recycling center collected 67 bags of aluminum cans in June and 92 bags of aluminum cans in July. If each bag weighed about 3 pounds, how many pounds of aluminum cans did the center collect in the two months?

Problem Solving Strategy Practice

Use a simpler problem to solve.

4. The science club is collecting glass bottles to raise money for a trip to the planetarium. The students get 5 cents for each bottle they collect. So far the club has collected 96 bottles. How much money, in cents, did the club get for the bottles?

5. **Reasoning** The outdoor club hosted a hike-a-thon. Hikers earned 75 points for every $\frac{1}{2}$ mile they hiked. The course was 3 miles long. If Joe hiked the whole course, how many points did he earn?

6. **WRITE Math** The art club is making a paper chain to decorate the gym for a fund-raiser. Each student makes 8 links for the chain. There are 78 students in the art club. How many links will be on the chain? **Explain** how you found the answer.

Mixed Strategy Practice

USE DATA For 7–9, use the poster.

7. The school band held a car wash to raise money for the local animal shelter. If 36 cars, 8 vans, and 21 trucks came to the car wash, how much money did the band raise?

8. **Pose a Problem** Look back at Problem 7. Write a similar problem by changing the numbers of cars, vans, and trucks.

9. **Open-Ended** In the first two hours of the car wash, the band washed both cars and trucks and raised a total of $48. List a possible combination of cars and trucks that the band washed.

10. A green, a red, a white, and a blue car are in line at the car wash. The red car is not last. The white car is in front of the blue car. The blue car is second. Draw a picture to show the order of the cars.

Choose a STRATEGY

- Solve a Simpler Problem
- Draw a Diagram or Picture
- Make a Model or Act It Out
- Make an Organized List
- Make a Table or Graph
- Predict and Test
- Work Backward
- Find a Pattern
- Write an Equation
- Use Logical Reasoning

Car Wash
SOAP
Friday
2:30 P.M. to 7:00 P.M.
Saturday
9:00 A.M. to 3:00 P.M.
Cars: $3 each
Trucks/Vans: $6 each
All money raised will be donated to the local animal shelter.

CHALLENGE YOURSELF

There are about 5,000 animal shelters nationwide. It costs about $10 a day to care for a cat or dog in a shelter.

11. Vanessa volunteers at her local animal shelter. There are 16 dogs and 24 cats at the shelter. What is the total cost per day to care for the animals?

12. Samuel also volunteers at an animal shelter. At the shelter, there are 12 dogs. Explain how to use a pattern to find the number of dogs nationwide that are in animal shelters if each shelter houses 12 dogs.

Extra Practice

Set A **Use a basic fact and patterns to find each product.** (pp. 586–587)

1. $2 \times 4 = ■$
   $20 \times 4 = ■$
   $200 \times 4 = ■$

2. $6 \times 3 = ■$
   $60 \times 3 = ■$
   $600 \times 3 = ■$

3. $8 \times 5 = ■$
   $8 \times 50 = ■$
   $8 \times 500 = ■$

Find the product.

4. $9 \times 30 = ■$
5. $4 \times 700 = ■$
6. $6 \times 900 = ■$

Set B **Multiply. You may wish to use base-ten blocks to help you.** (pp. 590–593)

1. 43×2
2. 77×5
3. 52×3
4. 80×9
5. 68×8

Set C **Estimate each product. Round to the greatest place value.** (pp. 594–595)

1. 48×6
2. 73×8
3. 62×9
4. 559×4
5. 837×5

6. Some students made 4 paper chains for their classroom. If each chain contained 175 links, about how many links are there in all of the chains?

7. Andy needs to reserve 22 tables for a party. If each table holds 8 people, about how many people will be attending the party?

Set D **Find each product.** (pp. 596–597)

1. 26×4
2. 58×7
3. 94×3
4. 81×6
5. 72×8

6. John's team scored 48 touchdowns in a season. If a touchdown counts as 6 points, how many points in touchdowns did the team score?

7. A jar holds 35 pickles. Dana needs 244 pickles for a school lunch. Are 7 jars enough? Explain.

Set E **Find each product.** (pp. 598–599)

1. 101×4
2. 247×3
3. 658×5
4. 7×431
5. 2×990
6. 3×145
7. 6×203
8. 4×318
9. 5×236

Technology
Use Harcourt Mega Math, The Number Games, *Up, Up, and Array*, Levels I and J.

TECHNOLOGY CONNECTION

Calculator: Multiplication

Use a Calculator for Multiplication

The Drama club sold sandwiches at lunch to raise money for a field trip. There were 6 kinds of sandwiches. They made 45 of each kind. How many sandwiches did they make?

Write a number sentence for the word problem.

$6 \times 45 = \blacksquare$

Use a calculator to solve.

So, the Drama club made 270 sandwiches.

Try It

Use a calculator to multiply. Solve each problem twice to be sure that you have keyed in the correct information.

1. $64 \times 7 = \blacksquare$
2. $32 \times 9 = \blacksquare$
3. $83 \times 4 = \blacksquare$
4. $89 \times 5 = \blacksquare$
5. $55 \times 2 = \blacksquare$
6. $49 \times 3 = \blacksquare$
7. $53 \times 8 = \blacksquare$
8. $77 \times 4 = \blacksquare$
9. $5 \times 42 = \blacksquare$
10. $3 \times 29 = \blacksquare$
11. $7 \times 91 = \blacksquare$
12. $4 \times 52 = \blacksquare$
13. Janet read 9 magazines with 65 pages each during the month of June. How many pages did she read in June?
14. In December, Max read 8 books with 76 pages each. How many pages did he read in December?
15. Angie sold 8 toys for 50¢ each and 6 toys for 75¢ each. How much money, in cents, did she make?
16. **What if** Angie's mother doubled what Angie made? How much money does Angie have now?
17. **Explore More** Heather's piano teacher charges $30 for each half hour of lessons. Heather takes two hour-long lessons each month. How much does she pay each month? If her teacher charged $25 for a half-hour lesson and Heather took four half-hour lessons, would she pay more or less each month? **Explain.**

MATH POWER How Old Are You?

Time Passes

A person's age is usually given in years. Do you know how many days, hours, or minutes old you are? Use a calculator to find out!

Example

Abby was born on February 8, 1998. How old was she on April 3, 2007 in days, hours, and minutes?

Step 1 Multiply Abby's age in years by 365.

$2007 - 1998 = 9$
$9 \times 365 = 3{,}285$

Step 2 Add the number of days from the birthday to the given date.

remaining days in February: 20
days in March: 31
days in April: 3
$20 + 31 + 3 = 54$
$3{,}285 + 54 = 3{,}339$

Step 3 Add one day for each leap year. Leap years are: . . . 1996, 2000, 2004, 2008, . . .

$3{,}339 + 2 = 3{,}341$

So, Abby is 3,341 days old.

Step 4 Multiply Abby's age in days by 24 hours.

$3{,}341 \times 24 = 80{,}184$

So, Abby is 80,184 hours old.

Step 5 Multiply Abby's age in hours by 60 minutes.

$80{,}184 \times 60 = 4{,}811{,}040$

So, Abby was 4,811,040 minutes old.

Try It

Find each age in years, days, hours, and minutes.

1. Jake's birthday is May 25, 1995. Find his age on January 16, 2006.
2. Elsie's birthday is August 3, 2001. Find her age on September 2, 2008.
3. WRITE Math Find your age in days, hours, and minutes. **Explain** how you know.

Chapter 23 Review/Test

Check Concepts

1. Explain how you could use base-ten blocks to help you solve 4×12. IL 6.4.12 (p. 588)
2. What are the steps needed to multiply 23×4? IL 6.4.10 (p. 590)

Check Skills

Find the product. IL 6.3.11 (pp. 586–587)

3. $30 \times 6 = ■$
4. $4 \times 300 = ■$
5. $5 \times 200 = ■$
6. $■ = 7 \times 60$
7. $20 \times 8 = ■$
8. $■ = 3 \times 800$

Find each product. IL 6.4.10 (pp. 596–597, 598–599)

9. 13×3
10. 26×5
11. 49×8
12. 75×9
13. 38×4
14. 51×2
15. 97×6
16. 62×8
17. 43×4
18. 16×7
19. 134×3
20. 309×7
21. 868×6
22. 711×8
23. 299×5

Check Problem Solving

Solve. IL 6.4.10 (pp. 600–603)

24. On a class trip to the zoo, 37 students and 5 teachers each paid $5 admission. How much did they pay in all for admission to the zoo?
25. WRITE Math Lindsay and Jeff live in towns that each have a population of 8 people per square mile. Lindsay's town is 64 square miles. Jeff's town is 120 square miles. How many people in all live in both towns? **Explain.**

GO ONLINE **Technology** Use *Online Assessment.*

Practice for the ISAT
Chapters 1–23

Number and Operations

1. Which statement is true? IL 6.3.05 (p. 28)

   A $78 > 87$

   B $8 < 7$

   C $87 > 78$

   D $807 < 708$

Choose the answer.

See item 2. Multiply to find the answer. If the product does not match one of the answer choices, check your computation.

2. Caroline practices 9 songs on the piano. She spent 9 minutes playing each song. For how many minutes did Caroline practice? IL 6.3.11 (p. 218)

   A 99   C 18

   B 81   D 9

3. **WRITE Math** There are 30 treats in one bag of dog treats. How many treats are in 8 bags? **Explain** your answer. IL 6.3.11 (p. 218)

Algebra

4. Which is the next figure in the pattern? IL 8.3.01 (p. 424)

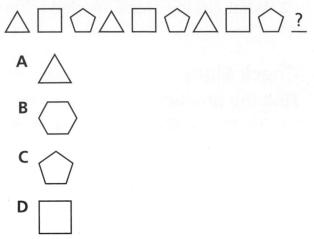

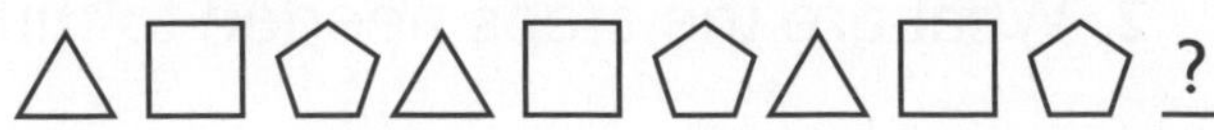

   A (triangle)

   B (hexagon)

   C (pentagon)

   D (square)

5. Which number sentence is in the same fact family as $72 \div 8 = 9$? IL 8.3.03 (p. 286)

   A $8 + 9 = 17$

   B $72 - 8 = 64$

   C $9 \times 8 = 72$

   D $72 \div 12 = 6$

6. **WRITE Math** How many strings are on 6 guitars? **Explain** your answer. IL 8.3.01 (p. 256)

Guitars	1	2	3	4	5	6
Strings	6	12	18	■	■	■

Geometry

7. Jeremy drew a quadrilateral with all sides the same length. Which figure did Jeremy draw? IL 9.3.01 (p. 360)

   A Trapezoid

   B Pentagon

   C Hexagon

   D Square

8. Which figure appears to have only 1 line of symmetry? IL 9.3.04 (p. 386)

   A

   B
   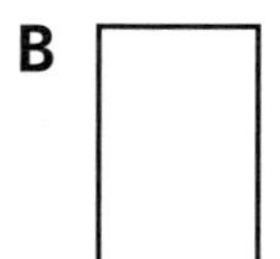

   C

   D
   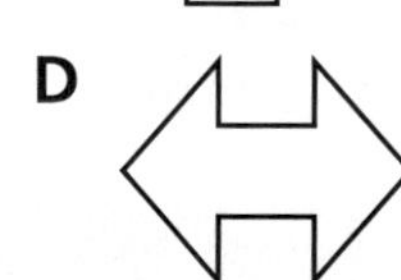

9. **WRITE Math** Which letter shows the location of 33? **Explain** how you know. IL 6.3.07 (p. 6)

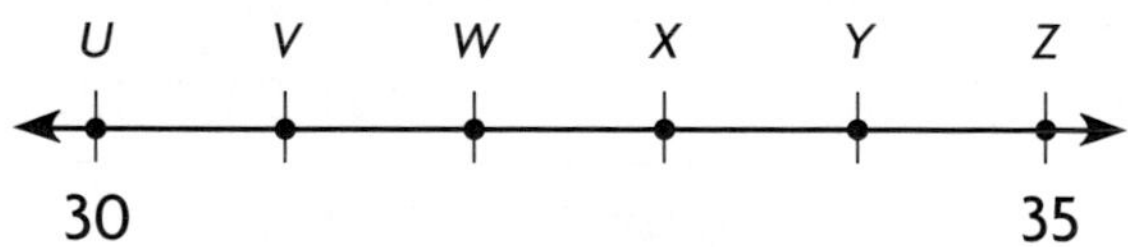

Data Analysis and Probability

10. How many more books did Mark read than Deb? IL 10.3.01 (p. 148)

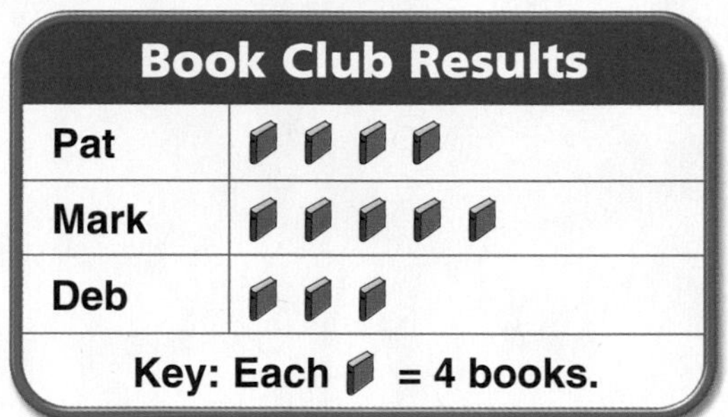

   A 2 **C** 6

   B 4 **D** 8

11. On which day was the greatest number of books sold? IL 10.3.01 (p. 154)

   A Monday **C** Wednesday

   B Tuesday **D** Thursday

12. **WRITE Math** Courtney has 8 blue pencils and 2 red pencils in a drawer. She reaches in the drawer and chooses a pencil without looking. Is she more likely to choose a blue pencil or a red pencil? **Explain.** IL 10.3.04 (p. 178)

24 Divide by 1 Digit

FAST FACT

A pencil can draw a line 35 miles long. If all of the pencils made each year were laid end to end, they would circle the earth about 60 times!

Investigate

Suppose you have $80 to buy art supplies for your school. Use the graph to decide the greatest number and least number of items you could buy. Then choose two items and tell how many of each item you would buy.

Art Supplies

Item	
Box of crayons	1 bill and part of a bill
Box of colored pencils	4 bills
Box of markers	2 bills and part of a bill
Pack of paper	3 bills

Key: Each bill = $2.

Technology
Student pages are available in the Student eBook.

Show What You Know

Check your understanding of important skills needed for success in Chapter 24.

▶ Practice Subtraction Facts

Find the difference.

1. $\begin{array}{r} 8 \\ -2 \\ \hline \end{array}$ **2.** $\begin{array}{r} 36 \\ -\ 9 \\ \hline \end{array}$ **3.** $\begin{array}{r} 42 \\ -\ 5 \\ \hline \end{array}$ **4.** $\begin{array}{r} 61 \\ -\ 7 \\ \hline \end{array}$

▶ Practice Division Facts

Find the quotient.

5. $5\overline{)20}$ **6.** $7\overline{)42}$ **7.** $3\overline{)21}$ **8.** $4\overline{)36}$

▶ Multiplication and Division Facts Through 10

Find the product.

9. $8 \times 2 = ■$ **10.** $9 \times 3 = ■$ **11.** $5 \times 10 = ■$ **12.** $3 \times 8 = ■$

13. $5 \times 7 = ■$ **14.** $6 \times 2 = ■$ **15.** $7 \times 7 = ■$ **16.** $9 \times 4 = ■$

17. $3 \times 9 = ■$ **18.** $5 \times 1 = ■$ **19.** $10 \times 6 = ■$ **20.** $0 \times 9 = ■$

Find the quotient.

21. $6 \div 3 = ■$ **22.** $35 \div 5 = ■$ **23.** $18 \div 2 = ■$ **24.** $54 \div 6 = ■$

25. $4\overline{)36}$ **26.** $7\overline{)70}$ **27.** $5\overline{)25}$ **28.** $8\overline{)72}$

VOCABULARY POWER

CHAPTER VOCABULARY

compatible numbers
dividend
divisor
quotient
remainder

WARM-UP WORDS

dividend The number that is to be divided in a division problem

divisor The number that divides the dividend

remainder The amount left over when a number cannot be divided evenly

Model Division with Remainders

OBJECTIVE: Use counters to model division with remainders.

Quick Review

1. $42 \div 6$
2. $30 \div 5$
3. $81 \div 9$
4. $16 \div 2$
5. $63 \div 7$

Vocabulary

remainder

Learn

PROBLEM Zach has 13 shark teeth. He wants to make 4 necklaces, with the same number of teeth on each necklace. Can Zach divide the 13 teeth equally into 4 groups?

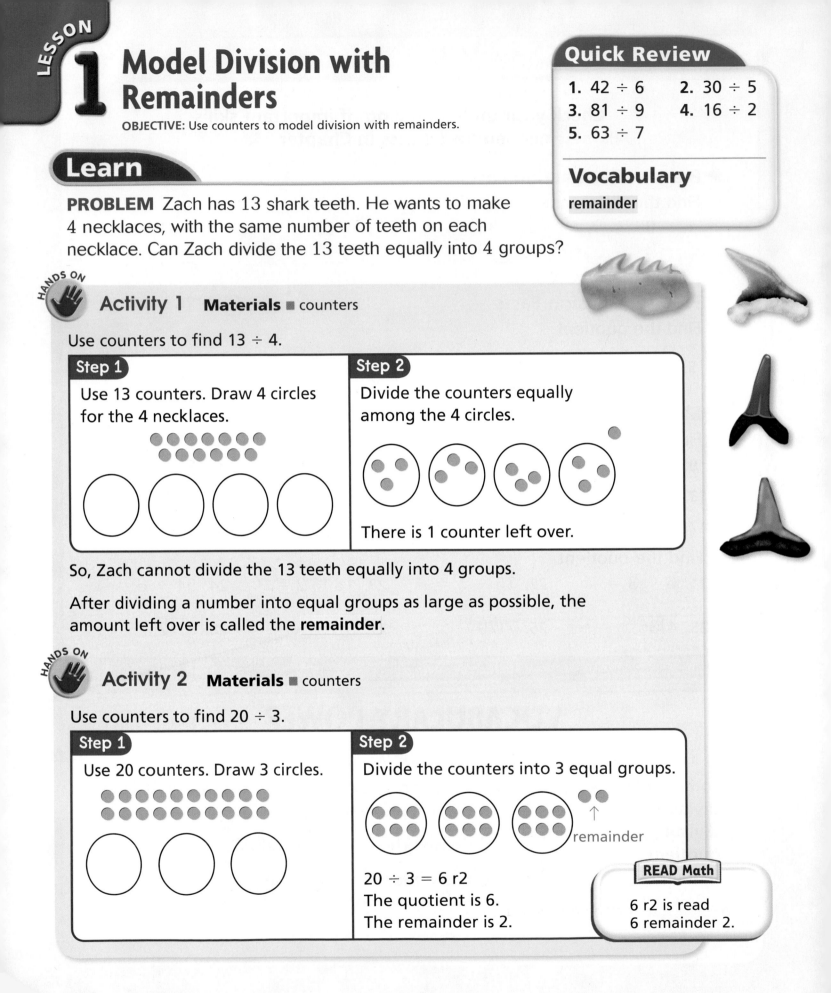

Activity 1 **Materials** ■ counters

Use counters to find $13 \div 4$.

Step 1

Use 13 counters. Draw 4 circles for the 4 necklaces.

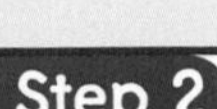

Step 2

Divide the counters equally among the 4 circles.

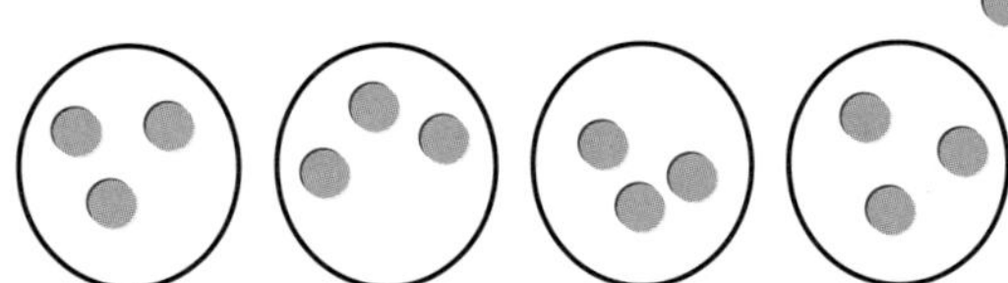

There is 1 counter left over.

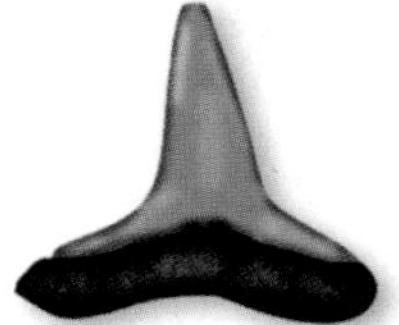

So, Zach cannot divide the 13 teeth equally into 4 groups.

After dividing a number into equal groups as large as possible, the amount left over is called the **remainder**.

Activity 2 **Materials** ■ counters

Use counters to find $20 \div 3$.

Step 1

Use 20 counters. Draw 3 circles.

Step 2

Divide the counters into 3 equal groups.

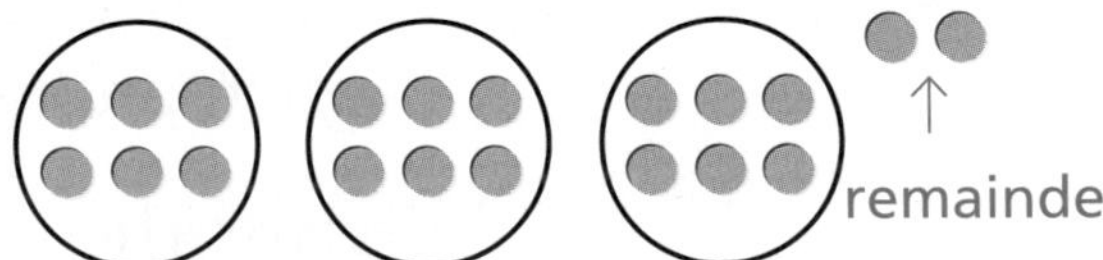

$20 \div 3 = 6$ r2
The quotient is 6.
The remainder is 2.

READ Math

6 r2 is read 6 remainder 2.

Guided Practice

1. Complete the number sentence. $11 \div 2 = \blacksquare$ r $\blacksquare$

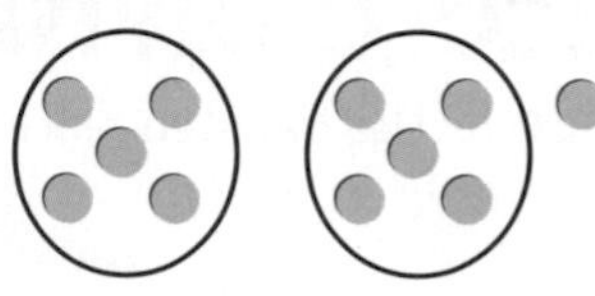

Use counters to find the quotient and remainder.

2. $14 \div 4$
3. $17 \div 2$
4. $13 \div 5$
5. $15 \div 2$
6. $18 \div 5$
7. TALK Math **Explain** why you can't have a remainder of 4 when you divide by 4.

Independent Practice and Problem Solving

Use counters to find the quotient and remainder.

8. $13 \div 2$
9. $22 \div 3$
10. $19 \div 2$
11. $17 \div 7$
12. $23 \div 8$
13. $14 \div 5$
14. $15 \div 2$
15. $16 \div 6$
16. $21 \div 4$
17. $18 \div 4$

Algebra Find the missing number.

18. $19 \div n = 3$ r1
19. $12 \div 5 = n$ r2
20. $11 \div 4 = 2$ rn
21. $n \div 2 = 5$ r1

USE DATA For 22–23, use the graph.

22. **Reasoning** If Zach puts an equal number of tiger shark teeth into 3 boxes, what is the least number of shark teeth he will have left over?
23. WRITE Math If Zach divides the sand shark teeth evenly into 2 boxes, how many will be in each box? How many teeth will be left over? **Explain.**

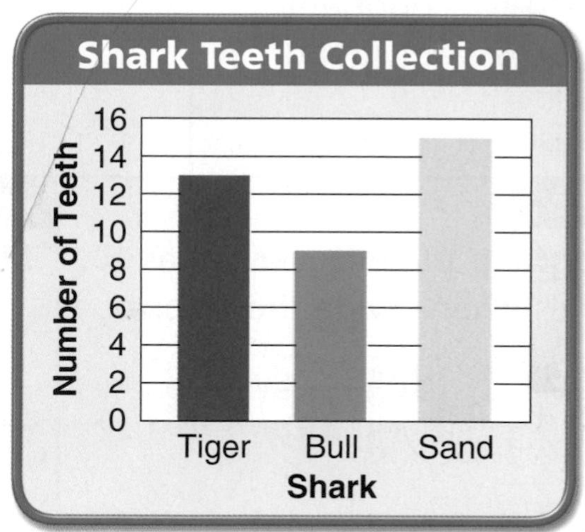

Mixed Review and Test Prep

24. Jake has 17 bull shark teeth and 26 sand shark teeth. How many shark teeth does he have in all? (p. 54)
25. Mary has 9 scarves. Of the scarves, 5 were given to her as presents. What fraction of Mary's scarves were not presents? (p. 450)
26. **Test Prep** Isabel wants to divide 16 lollipops evenly into 3 bags. How many lollipops will be left over?

    A 1   **C** 3

    B 2   **D** 4

Extra Practice on page 624, Set A

LESSON 2

Record Division

OBJECTIVE: Use base-ten blocks to show 2-digit division.

Quick Review

Find the quotient and remainder.

1. 19 ÷ 3 **2.** 14 ÷ 5
3. 18 ÷ 7 **4.** 12 ÷ 5
5. 19 ÷ 4

Learn

PROBLEM Ray is making frozen lemonade popsicles. He has 76 ounces of lemonade. Each popsicle mold holds 6 ounces. How many molds can Ray fill? How many ounces of lemonade will be left over?

Example **Divide.** 76 ÷ 6

Step 1

Use base-ten blocks to model the problem.

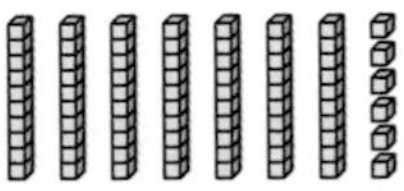

$$\begin{array}{r} \blacksquare \leftarrow \text{quotient} \\ 6\overline{)76} \leftarrow \text{dividend} \end{array}$$

↑ divisor

Step 2

7 > 6, so divide the 7 tens.

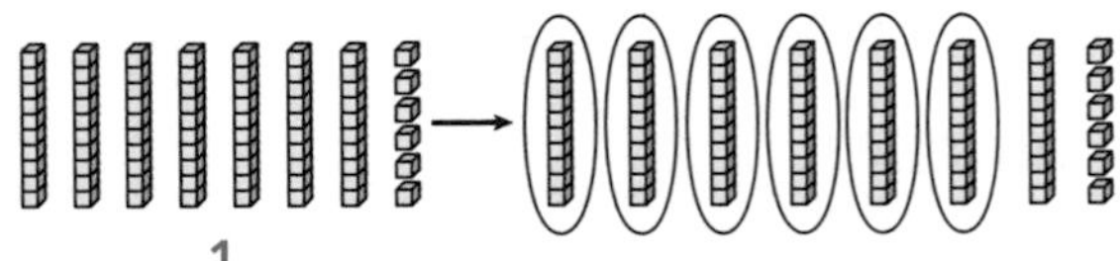

$$\begin{array}{r} 1 \\ 6\overline{)76} \\ -6 \\ \hline 1 \end{array}$$

Divide. 7 ÷ 6
Multiply. 6 × 1
Subtract. 7 − 6
Compare. 1 < 6

Step 3

Regroup the leftover ten as 10 ones. Then divide the 16 ones.

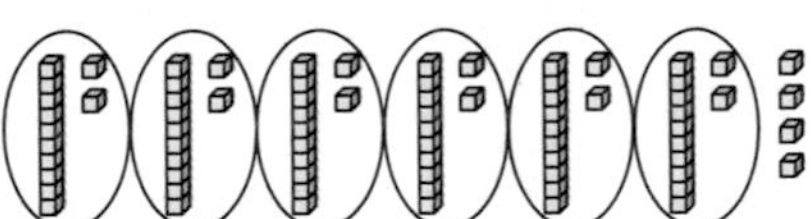

$$\begin{array}{r} 12 \text{ r4} \\ 6\overline{)76} \\ -6\downarrow \\ \hline 16 \\ -12 \\ \hline 4 \end{array} \leftarrow \text{remainder}$$

Divide: 16 ÷ 6
Multiply: 6 × 2
Subtract: 16 − 12
Compare: 4 < 6

Step 4

Multiply to check your answer.

$$\begin{array}{r} 12 \leftarrow \text{quotient} \\ \times\ 6 \leftarrow \text{divisor} \\ \hline 72 \end{array}$$

$$\begin{array}{r} 72 \\ +\ 4 \\ \hline 76 \end{array}$$

+ 4 ← Add the remainder.
76 ← This should equal the dividend.

Math Idea
When checking your answer, use the inverse operation.

So, Ray can fill 12 popsicle molds. He will have 4 ounces of lemonade left over.

- Does a division problem have to have a remainder?

Guided Practice

1. What division problem is modeled here?

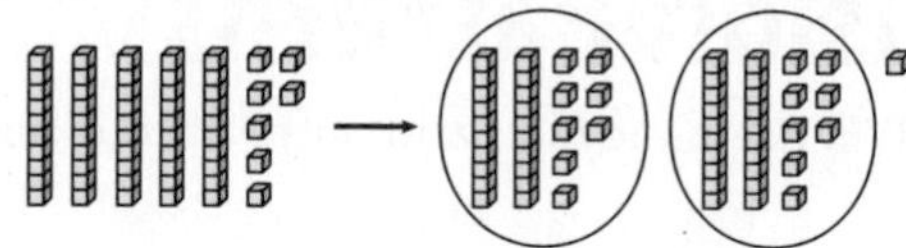

Use base-ten blocks. Write the quotient and remainder.

2. $32 \div 3$ 3. $62 \div 4$ ✓4. $4\overline{)58}$ ✓5. $6\overline{)78}$

6. **TALK Math** **Explain** how to use base-ten blocks to find $85 \div 6$.

Independent Practice and Problem Solving

Use base-ten blocks. Write the quotient and remainder.

7. $48 \div 7$ 8. $82 \div 3$ 9. $2\overline{)46}$ 10. $5\overline{)67}$

11. $6\overline{)85}$ 12. $2\overline{)54}$ 13. $85 \div 3$ 14. $58 \div 4$

Algebra Find the missing digit.

15. $\begin{array}{r} 29 \text{ r}2 \\ 3\overline{)8\blacksquare} \end{array}$ 16. $\begin{array}{r} \blacksquare 5 \text{ r}3 \\ 4\overline{)63} \end{array}$ 17. $\begin{array}{r} 1\blacksquare \text{ r}2 \\ 6\overline{)92} \end{array}$ 18. $\begin{array}{r} 17 \text{ r}\blacksquare \\ 5\overline{)88} \end{array}$

USE DATA For 19-21, use the recipe.

19. Kate poured 1 batch of lemonade equally into 6 tall glasses. How many ounces are in each glass? How many ounces are left over?

20. Erin uses an 8-ounce measuring cup to measure the water. How many times should she fill the cup? How much more water will she need?

21. **Reasoning** Mike made 6 batches of lemonade. He filled 4 pitchers with all of his lemonade. How many ounces of lemon juice are in each pitcher?

22. **WRITE Math** When you subtract in a division problem, why must the difference be less than the divisor? **Explain.**

Mixed Review and Test Prep

23. A bag contains 3 red marbles and 10 blue marbles. One marble is pulled. Name an impossible event. (p. 178)

24. Estimate the product. 4×67 (p. 594)

25. **Test Prep** Paul divided 85 marbles into 4 bags with the same number in each bag. How many marbles were left over?

A 1 **B** 2 **C** 3 **D** 4

Extra Practice on page 624, Set B

LESSON 3

ALGEBRA

Division Patterns

OBJECTIVE: Use basic facts and patterns to divide multiples of 10, 100, and 1,000.

Quick Review

1. 42 ÷ 6
2. 40 ÷ 5
3. 81 ÷ 9
4. 48 ÷ 8
5. 18 ÷ 2

Learn

PROBLEM Rachel took 600 photographs while visiting Chicago. She put the same number of photos in each of 3 albums. How many photos did she put in each one?

Stones from sites in all 50 states and around the world are built into the walls of the Chicago Tribune Building.

You can use basic division facts and patterns to divide multiples of 10, 100, and 1,000.

Example Divide. 600 ÷ 3

dividend ↓	quotient ↓	
6 ÷ 3 = 2		basic fact, no zeros
60 ÷ 3 = 20		1 zero in dividend, 1 zero in quotient
600 ÷ 3 = 200		2 zeros in dividend, 2 zeros in quotient

So, Rachel put 200 photos in each album.

- What do you notice about the number of zeros in the dividend and the number of zeros in the quotient?

More Examples

A Basic fact without a zero

48 ÷ 6 = 8	← basic fact
480 ÷ 6 = 80	← 1 zero
4,800 ÷ 6 = 800	← 2 zeros

B Basic fact with a zero

40 ÷ 8 = 5	← basic fact
400 ÷ 8 = 50	← 1 less zero
4,000 ÷ 8 = 500	← 1 less zero

- **What if** a basic fact already has a zero in the dividend? Explain what happens in the quotient.

Guided Practice

1. What basic fact can you use to help you find 810 ÷ 9?

Use a basic fact and patterns to find each quotient.

2. $32 \div 8 = \blacksquare$; $320 \div 8 = \blacksquare$; $3{,}200 \div 8 = \blacksquare$

3. $56 \div 7 = \blacksquare$; $560 \div 7 = \blacksquare$; $5{,}600 \div 7 = \blacksquare$

✓4. $30 \div 6 = \blacksquare$; $300 \div 6 = \blacksquare$; $3{,}000 \div 6 = \blacksquare$

✓5. $18 \div 9 = \blacksquare$; $180 \div 9 = \blacksquare$; $1{,}800 \div 9 = \blacksquare$

6. TALK Math **Explain** how knowing $42 \div 6 = 7$ can help you find $4{,}200 \div 6$.

Independent Practice and Problem Solving

Use a basic fact and patterns to find each quotient.

7. $16 \div 2 = \blacksquare$; $160 \div 2 = \blacksquare$; $1{,}600 \div 2 = \blacksquare$

8. $72 \div 8 = \blacksquare$; $720 \div 8 = \blacksquare$; $7{,}200 \div 8 = \blacksquare$

9. $18 \div 3 = \blacksquare$; $180 \div 3 = \blacksquare$; $1{,}800 \div 3 = \blacksquare$

10. $50 \div 5 = \blacksquare$; $500 \div 5 = \blacksquare$; $5{,}000 \div 5 = \blacksquare$

Write the basic fact you can use. Then find the quotient.

11. $560 \div 7 = \blacksquare$
12. $\blacksquare = 4{,}500 \div 5$
13. $120 \div 6 = \blacksquare$
14. $\blacksquare = 3{,}600 \div 6$
15. $5{,}000 \div 5 = \blacksquare$
16. $4{,}000 \div 2 = \blacksquare$
17. $\blacksquare = 1{,}800 \div 2$
18. $\blacksquare = 900 \div 3$

Algebra For 19–22, find each value of *n*.

19. $7{,}200 \div 9 = n$
20. $n \div 4 = 70$
21. $2{,}400 \div 8 = n$
22. $1{,}200 \div n = 300$

Solve.

23. **Reasoning** The area of a rectangle is 4,200 square feet. The length is 6 feet. What is the width? What is the perimeter?

24. WRITE Math **What's the Error?** Max says $400 \div 5 = 800$ because 400 has 2 zeros. Describe Max's error.

Mixed Review and Test Prep

25. Mrs. Walters cut a pizza into 8 equal slices. Jan ate 2 slices and Oscar ate 3 slices. What fraction of the pizza is left? (p. 470)

26. Kylie divided 32 cupcakes evenly into 5 boxes. How many cupcakes were left over? (p. 612)

27. **Test Prep** Which basic division fact can be used to find $400 \div 2$?

A $40 \div 5 = 8$
B $40 \div 8 = 5$
C $4 \div 2 = 2$
D $40 \div 10 = 4$

Extra Practice on page 624, Set C

LESSON 4

Estimate Quotients

OBJECTIVE: Use compatible numbers to estimate quotients.

Quick Review

1. 300 ÷ 5
2. 450 ÷ 9
3. 320 ÷ 8
4. 400 ÷ 4
5. 7,200 ÷ 8

Learn

PROBLEM A group of 50 girls have signed up for cheerleading. The girls will be divided into 6 squads. About how many girls will be on each squad?

Compatible numbers are numbers that are easy to compute mentally. When a problem does not need an exact answer, you can estimate by using compatible numbers.

Example 1 Estimate. 50 ÷ 6

Step 1

Think of a number that is close to 50 and easy to divide by 6.

50 ÷ 6
↓
48 ÷ 6

Think: 48 is close to 50.

Step 2

Use the compatible numbers, 48 and 6, to find the estimated quotient.

48 ÷ 6 = 8

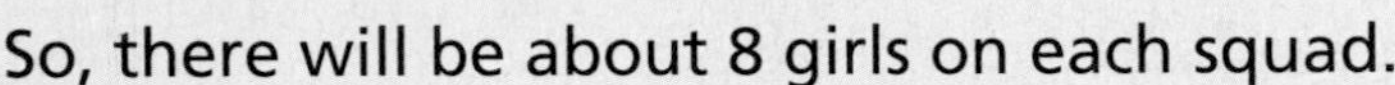

So, there will be about 8 girls on each squad.

- What other compatible numbers could you use to estimate 50 ÷ 6? Explain.

ERROR ALERT

The compatible numbers you choose should divide evenly.

Example 2 Estimate. 418 ÷ 6

Step 1

Look at the first two digits. Think of a number that is close to 41 and easy to divide by 6.

418 ÷ 6
↓
420 ÷ 6

Think: 42 is close to 41. 42 ÷ 6 = 7

Step 2

Estimate using the compatible numbers, 420 and 6.

420 ÷ 6 = 70

So, 418 ÷ 6 is about 70.

Guided Practice

1. What compatible numbers would you use to estimate 29 ÷ 3?

Estimate. Tell the compatible numbers you used for each.

2. $60 \div 9$ **3.** $41 \div 5$ **4.** $293 \div 5$ ✓**5.** $472 \div 7$ ✓**6.** $358 \div 4$

7. TALK Math **Explain** how to estimate $251 \div 3$ using compatible numbers.

Independent Practice and Problem Solving

Estimate. Tell the compatible numbers you used for each.

8. $55 \div 8$ **9.** $37 \div 6$ **10.** $345 \div 7$ **11.** $234 \div 4$ **12.** $119 \div 2$

13. $75 \div 9$ **14.** $32 \div 6$ **15.** $128 \div 3$ **16.** $342 \div 5$ **17.** $226 \div 7$

18. $9\overline{)67}$ **19.** $7\overline{)51}$ **20.** $4\overline{)302}$ **21.** $8\overline{)152}$ **22.** $2\overline{)119}$

USE DATA For 23–26, use the table.

Springfield Recreation League

Sport	Number of Players
Basketball	248
Baseball	216
Soccer	183
Hockey	134
Cheerleading	50

23. The baseball players will be divided into 5 teams. About how many players will be on each team?

24. The soccer players and hockey players are having a combined banquet. Eight players can sit at each table. About how many tables are needed?

25. **Reasoning** The basketball players are divided into 9 teams. The hockey players are divided into 7 teams. Which sport has more players per team? **Explain** how you estimated.

26. WRITE Math Look back at Problem 23. How did you decide which compatible numbers to use? **Explain.**

Mixed Review and Test Prep

27. Morgan has 2 quarters, 6 dimes, 3 nickels and 14 pennies. Caleb has 1 quarter, 9 dimes, 8 nickels and 27 pennies. Who has more money? How much more? (p. 114)

28. If $8 \div 4 = 2$, what is $800 \div 4$? (p. 616)

29. **Test Prep** Sal needs to estimate $57 \div 8$. Which expression shows the best choice of compatible numbers for Sal to use?

A $57 \div 10$
B $60 \div 10$
C $60 \div 8$
D $56 \div 8$

Extra Practice on page 624, Set D

LESSON 5

Divide 2- and 3-Digit Numbers

OBJECTIVE: Divide 2- and 3-digit numbers with and without remainders.

Quick Review

Divide.

1. 15 ÷ 5 **2.** 54 ÷ 9

3. 72 ÷ 8 **4.** 48 ÷ 6

5. 40 ÷ 10

Learn

PROBLEM Miranda's elementary school is visiting the Children's Museum. There are 6 buses for the 288 students going to the museum. How many students will be on each bus?

▲ the Children's Museum in Niantic, Connecticut

Example 1 **Divide.** 288 ÷ 6 or $6\overline{)288}$ **Estimate.** 300 ÷ 6 = 50

Step 1

Decide where to place the first digit.

$$\begin{array}{r} \blacksquare \\ 6\overline{)288} \end{array}$$

2 < 6, so divide the 28 tens.

Step 2

Divide 28 tens by 6.

$$\begin{array}{r} 4 \\ 6\overline{)288} \\ -24 \\ \hline 4 \end{array}$$

Divide. $6\overline{)28}$
Multiply. 6 × 4
Subtract. 28 − 24
Compare. 4 < 6

Step 3

Bring down the 8 ones.
Divide 48 ones by 6.

$$\begin{array}{r} 48 \\ 6\overline{)288} \\ -24\downarrow \\ \hline 48 \\ -48 \\ \hline 0 \end{array}$$

Divide. $6\overline{)48}$
Multiply. 6 × 8
Subtract. 48 − 48
Compare. 0 < 6

So, there will be 48 students on each bus. Since 48 is close to the estimate, 50, the answer is reasonable.

Example 2 **Divide.** 470 ÷ 3 or $3\overline{)470}$

$$\begin{array}{r} 156 \text{ r2} \\ 3\overline{)470}\phantom{\text{ r2}} \\ -3\phantom{\text{ r2}} \\ \hline 17\phantom{\text{ r2}} \\ -15\phantom{\text{ r2}} \\ \hline 20\phantom{\text{ r2}} \\ -18\phantom{\text{ r2}} \\ \hline 2\phantom{\text{ r2}} \end{array}$$

Check your answer by multiplying the quotient by the divisor. Then add the remainder.

$$\begin{array}{r} 156 \\ \times 3 \\ \hline 468 \\ + 2 \\ \hline 470 \end{array}$$

Since the sum, 470, is equal to the dividend, 470, the quotient is correct.

Guided Practice

1. Where should you place the first digit in the quotient for the division problem at the right? **Explain.** $7\overline{)295}$

Divide. Use multiplication to check your answer.

2. $4\overline{)744}$ 3. $5\overline{)423}$ ✓4. $156 \div 6$ ✓5. $679 \div 3$ 6. $278 \div 3$

7. TALK Math **Explain** how you know how many digits are in the quotient $456 \div 2$ without dividing.

Independent Practice and Problem Solving

Divide. Use multiplication to check your answer.

8. $7\overline{)972}$ 9. $3\overline{)269}$ 10. $6\overline{)193}$ 11. $5\overline{)635}$ 12. $2\overline{)415}$

13. $8\overline{)973}$ 14. $2\overline{)374}$ 15. $7\overline{)113}$ 16. $9\overline{)189}$ 17. $6\overline{)286}$

18. $222 \div 6$ 19. $890 \div 7$ 20. $207 \div 5$ 21. $924 \div 9$ 22. $714 \div 8$

23. $261 \div 4$ 24. $632 \div 4$ 25. $644 \div 2$ 26. $742 \div 3$ 27. $398 \div 4$

USE DATA For 28–30, use the graph.

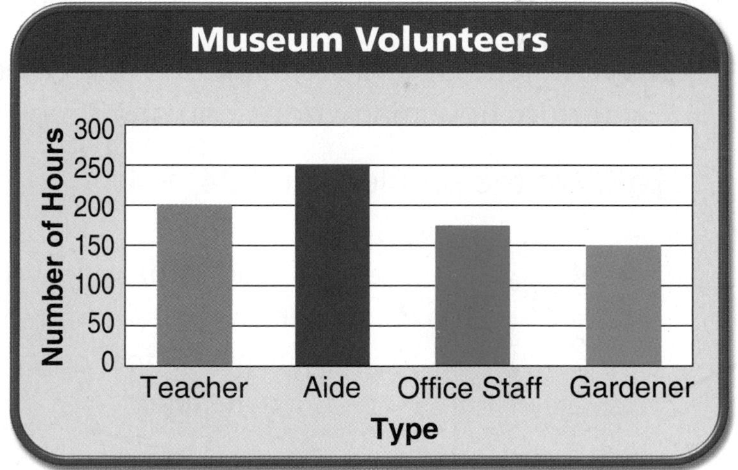

28. At the museum, 5 teachers volunteered the same number of hours. How many hours did each teacher volunteer?

29. Each of the gardening volunteers worked 6 hours. Each of the office staff volunteers worked 7 hours. Were there more gardening volunteers or office staff volunteers? **Explain.**

30. WRITE Math **What's the Question?** Each aide worked 5 hours. The answer is 50.

Mixed Review and Test Prep

31. Gillian's dog weighs 8 pounds. How many ounces does the dog weigh? (pp. 522, 596)

32. Joe buys 4 tickets for $126. About how much does each cost? (p. 618)

33. **Test Prep** What is $431 \div 9$?

A 52 r3 **C** 47 r8

B 48 r1 **D** 31 r7

Extra Practice on page 624, Set E

CD ROM **Technology**
Use Harcourt Mega Math, The Number Games, *Up, Up, and Array,* Levels M, N.

Problem Solving Workshop
Skill: Interpret the Remainder

OBJECTIVE: Solve problems by using the skill *interpret the remainder*.

Read to Understand
Plan
Solve
Check

Read to Understand

PROBLEM Michelle is at a carnival. She needs 49 tickets to go on her favorite rides. The tickets come in packs of 5. How many packs does she need to buy?

When you divide, sometimes you have to decide how to use the remainder to solve the problem.

To solve the problem, find $49 \div 5$.

```
   9 r4
5)49
 -45
   4
```

If Michelle buys 9 packs of tickets, she will only have 45 tickets. The remainder tells her she needs 4 more tickets, so she has to buy 1 more pack of tickets.

So, Michelle needs to buy 10 packs of tickets.

If Michelle has 34 tickets left and she needs 4 tickets for each ride, how many rides can she go on?

To solve the problem, find $34 \div 4$.

```
   8 r2
4)34
 -32
   2
```

If Michelle goes on 8 rides, she will use 32 tickets. The remainder tells her that she will have 2 tickets left. This is not enough for another ride, so drop, or ignore, the remainder.

So, Michelle can go on 8 rides.

TALK Math

Explain how you know when to drop, or ignore, the remainder.

Think and Discuss

Interpret the remainder to solve.

a. Eleven children want to ride a roller coaster at the carnival. Each car holds 3 children. How many cars will the children need?

b. Max uses 6 ounces of caramel to make 1 caramel apple. He has 94 ounces of caramel. How many caramel apples can he make?

Guided Problem Solving

1. Jamie and her family are at the school fair. It takes 5 minutes to make a spin-art picture. How many spin-art pictures can she make in 29 minutes?

   Divide $29 \div 5$.

   What is the quotient? What is the remainder?

   Should you drop the remainder or increase the quotient?

   Solve the problem.

2. **What if** Jamie has 42 minutes to make spin-art pictures? How many pictures could Jamie make?

3. There are 60 children waiting in line at the bumper cars and 9 children can ride at a time. How many times does the ride need to run to give all the children a turn?

Mixed Applications

4. There are 30 picnic tables at the carnival that need to be placed under tents. Only 4 tables will fit under each tent. How many tents are needed?

5. It took Jimmy 35 minutes to get to the fair. Then he rode on 6 rides. Each ride took 8 minutes. How many minutes did Jimmy spend on the rides?

6. Nancy needs 4 tickets to go on the Safari Ride. She needs 3 tickets to go on the Ferris Wheel. Nancy wants to go on each ride 3 times. How many tickets does Nancy need in all?

7. Tommy has $25 to spend on food. He buys a cheese steak for $5.25, a fruit salad for $2.00, and 3 bottles of water for $1.25 each. How much money will Tommy have left?

8. Maggie, Pete, Ryan, and Olivia are waiting in line at the concession stand. Maggie is not last. Pete is behind Olivia. Ryan is first. In what order are the children standing?

9. **Reasoning** Jen rode on 14 rides that each used 5 tickets. Barry rode on 13 rides that each used 6 tickets. Who used more tickets? **Explain.**

10. **WRITE Math** A sheet of 20 tickets costs $23.75. Ned has $50. **Explain** how can he use estimation to decide if he has enough money to buy 2 sheets of tickets.

Extra Practice

Set A **Use counters to find the quotient and remainder.** (pp. 612–613)

1. $18 \div 5$ 2. $15 \div 2$ 3. $34 \div 6$ 4. $22 \div 3$ 5. $27 \div 8$

Set B **Use base-ten blocks. Write the quotient and remainder.** (pp. 614–615)

1. $38 \div 4$ 2. $65 \div 3$ 3. $7\overline{)94}$ 4. $5\overline{)88}$ 5. $6\overline{)95}$

6. $3\overline{)81}$ 7. $4\overline{)97}$ 8. $8\overline{)91}$ 9. $2\overline{)59}$ 10. $6\overline{)77}$

Set C **Use a basic fact and patterns to find each quotient.** (pp. 616–617)

1. $27 \div 3 = \blacksquare$; $270 \div 3 = \blacksquare$; $2{,}700 \div 3 = \blacksquare$
2. $42 \div 6 = \blacksquare$; $420 \div 6 = \blacksquare$; $4{,}200 \div 6 = \blacksquare$
3. $32 \div 4 = \blacksquare$; $320 \div 4 = \blacksquare$; $3{,}200 \div 4 = \blacksquare$
4. $35 \div 7 = \blacksquare$; $350 \div 7 = \blacksquare$; $3{,}500 \div 7 = \blacksquare$

Write the basic fact you can use. Then find the quotient.

5. $140 \div 2 = \blacksquare$ 6. $6{,}400 \div 8 = \blacksquare$ 7. $1{,}800 \div 9 = \blacksquare$ 8. $200 \div 5 = \blacksquare$

Set D **Estimate. Tell the compatible numbers you used for each.** (pp. 618–619)

1. $70 \div 8$ 2. $25 \div 6$ 3. $111 \div 2$ 4. $127 \div 5$ 5. $218 \div 4$

6. $22 \div 3$ 7. $61 \div 7$ 8. $9\overline{)97}$ 9. $6\overline{)176}$ 10. $8\overline{)324}$

11. There are 129 players in a softball league. The league consists of 8 teams. About how many players will be on each team?

12. There are 453 coins in a jar. Gary will divide the coins into 9 equal groups. About how many coins will be in each group?

Set E **Divide. Use multiplication to check your answer.** (pp. 620–621)

1. $4\overline{)128}$ 2. $5\overline{)229}$ 3. $7\overline{)881}$ 4. $365 \div 2$ 5. $547 \div 3$

6. Larissa waters the plants in her garden once every 7 days for 175 days. How many times did Larissa water the plants?

7. Jonathan traveled by train for 3 hours. The train traveled 267 miles. How many miles did the train travel in each hour?

CD ROM **Technology**
Use Harcourt Mega Math, The Number Games, *Up, Up, and Array*, Levels L, M, and N.

PRACTICE GAME

Division Toss

Start

Ready!

2–4 players

Set!

- Two prepared number cubes
- Counter for each player
- Gameboard
- Paper and pencils

Finish

Roll!

- Each player puts a counter on START.
- One player tosses both number cubes.
- The single number showing on one cube is the divisor. The greater number of the same color showing on the other cube is the dividend.
- All players find the quotient.
- The first player to find the quotient calls it out. Other players complete the division and check the first player's quotient. If correct, the player who called it out first moves 1 space.
- The next player tosses the cubes and players try to find the next quotient.
- The first player to reach FINISH wins.

MATH POWER **Divisibility Rules**

Divide and Conquer

A number is divisible by another number if there is no remainder when the numbers are divided. Divisibility rules can be used to find out if one number is divisible by another.

Examples

A A number is divisible by 2 if the ones digit is 0, 2, 4, 6, or 8.

Divisible by 2:	Not divisible by 2:
64 98 412 6,940	65 97 413 6,949

B A number is divisible by 3 if the sum of the digits is divisible by 3.

Divisible by 3:	Not divisible by 3:
$516 \rightarrow 5 + 1 + 6 = 12$	$82 \rightarrow 8 + 2 = 10$
12 is divisible by 3. $12 \div 3 = 4$	10 is not divisible by 3.
So, 516 is divisible by 3.	So, 82 is not divisible by 3.

C A number is divisible by 5 if the ones digit is 0 or 5.

Divisible by 5:	Not divisible by 5:
40 65 230 6,495	41 63 237 6,498

D A number is divisible by 10 if the ones digit is 0.

Divisible by 10:	Not divisible by 10:
20 50 690 8,430	21 53 694 8,437

Try It

List if each number is divisible by 2, 3, 5, or 10.

1. 124 **2.** 875 **3.** 57 **4.** 377

5. 78 **6.** 207 **7.** 444 **8.** 214

9. 3,780 **10.** 6,208 **11.** 163,875 **12.** 119,000

13. WRITE Math Write a 4-digit number. Tell whether your number is divisible by 2, 3, 5, or 10. **Explain** how you know.

Chapter 24 Review/Test

Check Concepts

Explain your answers.

1. What are compatible numbers? IL 6.5.12 (p. 628)
2. How can you use counters or base-ten blocks to find the quotient and remainder of a division problem? IL 6.5.12 (p. 622)
3. What are steps you can use to solve the division problem $144 \div 4$? IL 6.5.12 (p. 630)

Check Skills

Estimate. Tell the compatible numbers you used for each. IL 6.5.12 (pp. 628–629)

4. $50 \div 3$	**5.** $23 \div 5$	**6.** $193 \div 6$	**7.** $276 \div 4$	**8.** $332 \div 8$
9. $2\overline{)79}$	**10.** $7\overline{)385}$	**11.** $9\overline{)101}$	**12.** $5\overline{)243}$	**13.** $6\overline{)455}$

Divide. Use multiplication to check your answer. IL 6.5.12 (pp. 630–631)

14. $4\overline{)96}$	**15.** $7\overline{)266}$	**16.** $2\overline{)731}$	**17.** $8\overline{)304}$	**18.** $9\overline{)482}$
19. $3\overline{)154}$	**20.** $5\overline{)297}$	**21.** $6\overline{)518}$	**22.** $7\overline{)677}$	**23.** $2\overline{)435}$
24. $152 \div 8$	**25.** $203 \div 6$	**27.** $316 \div 2$	**27.** $872 \div 5$	**28.** $399 \div 4$
29. $548 \div 3$	**30.** $260 \div 7$	**31.** $679 \div 9$	**32.** $451 \div 6$	**33.** $735 \div 8$

Check Problem Solving

Solve. IL 6.5.12 (pp. 632–633)

34. A charity offers a movie ticket for 3 cans of food donated to a fundraising event. How many tickets can Desmond receive if he donates 49 cans of food?

35. Kevin bought a case of 580 football cards to distribute to himself and his 7 friends. How many of the 8 boys do not get 73 cards?

36. WRITE Math A concert hall has 355 seats. Are there enough chairs to seat 40 groups of 9 students? If not, how many more seats are needed? **Explain.**

GO ONLINE **Technology** Use *Online Assessment.*

Unit Review/Test
Chapters 23–24

Multiple Choice

1. One ticket to the dinosaur exhibit at the Field Museum costs $28. Which shows about how much 8 tickets will cost? IL 6.3.14 (p. 594)

   A about $300 C about $160
   B about $240 D about $80

2. There are 7 shelves in a bookcase. There are 38 books on each shelf. Which shows how many total books are in the bookcase? IL 8.3.05 (p. 600)

   A 266 C 154
   B 210 D 56

3. One package of white paper has 500 sheets. Which shows the number of sheets in 5 packages? IL 6.3.11 (p. 586)

   A 2,500 C 1,500
   B 2,000 D 1,000

4. There are 236 students going on a field trip. They are taking 6 buses. Which shows about how many students will be on each bus? IL 6.3.14 (p. 618)

   A about 25 C about 35
   B about 30 D about 40

5. There are 417 guests at a school fundraiser. Each table can seat 7 people. Which shows about how many tables are needed for all of the guests? IL 6.3.14 (p. 618)

   A about 60 C about 40
   B about 50 D about 30

6. Katelynn earns $3 every time she waters the garden. This year, she watered the garden 23 times. Which shows how much money Katelynn earned? IL 8.3.05 (p. 600)

   A $19 B $46 C $69 D $75

7. The student theater at Samantha's school has 300 seats. The shows on Thursday, Friday, and Saturday night were all sold out. Which shows how many total tickets were sold for the 3 shows? IL 6.3.11 (p. 586)

   A 9,000 C 90
   B 900 D 9

8. Shawna volunteered for 29 hours last week. For every hour she worked, she planted 9 daffodils. Which shows about how many daffodils Shawna planted last week? IL 6.3.14 (p. 594)

   A about 180 C about 270
   B about 230 D about 320

GO ONLINE **Technology** Use *Online Assessment.*

9. Craig read this thermometer to find the temperature of a glass of water. Which temperature does the thermometer show? IL 7.3.02 (p. 550)

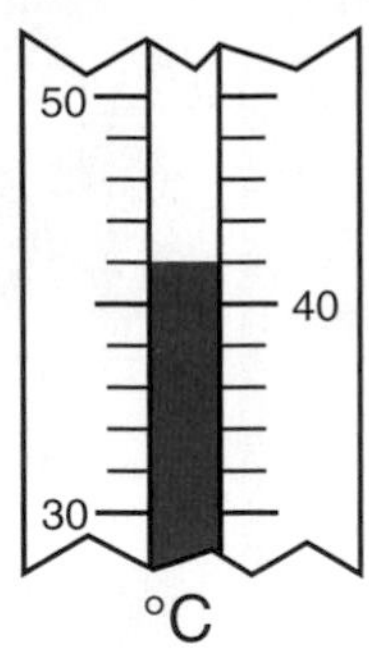

A 33°C
B 40°C
C 42°C
D 45°C

10. The company packs 200 cans of vegetables in one large crate. Last week, the company shipped 8 crates of canned vegetables to a grocery store. Which shows how many total cans of vegetables they shipped to the grocery store last week? IL 6.3.11 (p. 586)

A 1,600
B 1,000
C 800
D 160

11. Jonas painted this repeating pattern on a picture frame. What is the next figure in the pattern? IL 8.3.01 (p. 422)

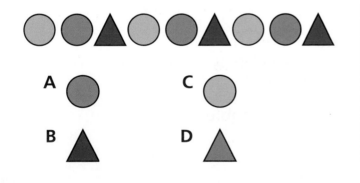

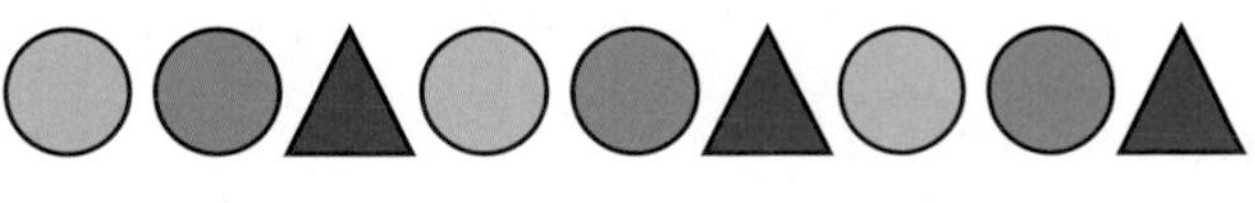

A (circle)
B (triangle)
C (circle)
D (triangle)

Short Response

For 12–14, use the playground grid.

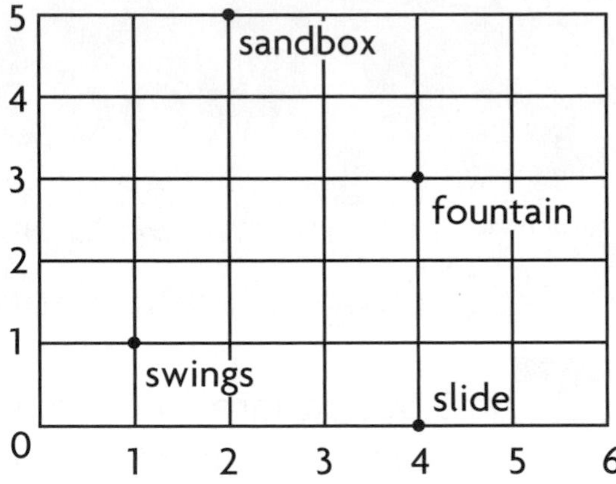

12. What is located at (2, 5)? IL 9.3.03 (p. 166)

13. What is 3 units above the slide? IL 9.3.03 (p. 166)

14. What ordered pair tells the location of the swings? IL 9.3.03 (p. 166)

15. Tristan built a rectangular patio. Its perimeter is 18 meters. Its area is 20 square meters. Draw a picture of the patio and label the sides. IL 7.3.03 (p. 568)

16. Ami wants to measure the distance from his house to the movie theater. What unit, inches or miles, would he use to measure that distance? IL 7.3.02 (p. 538)

THE WORLD ALMANAC FOR KIDS

Model Trains

The Great Train Story

The 3,500 square foot Great Train Story at the Chicago Museum of Science and Industry shows a train's journey across the Western United States from Chicago to Seattle. The exhibit focuses on the materials that a train transports across the country. Some of the materials include fruit, logs, coal, and people.

This exhibit is not just for adults. Children can chop down a tree at the lumberyard, blow up rock to build a tunnel, and load cargo onto the train.

Children can load cargo onto the train.

At the lumberyard, children can cut down a tree.

a real flatcar carrying lumber

FACT·ACTIVITY

Solve.

1. The exhibit designers took an 11-day train trip from Chicago to Seattle to look at the scenery. If it takes the same numbers of day to travel back to Chicago, for how many days were they traveling?
2. The designers tried 25 different layouts for the train exhibit before finding one that worked. If each layout took 1 week, how many days did it take before completing the final layout?
3. There are 192 hand-made buildings in the exhibit. If each team built 6 of them, how many teams would be needed to build all of the buildings?
4. **Pose a Problem** Look at Problem 1. Write a new problem by changing the train trip to last more than 2 weeks.

ALMANAC **Fact**

At the Great Train Story, there are 34 operating trains traveling at one time.

Model Train Layouts

Model train layouts can be built by anyone. Whether young or old, model trains can provide hours of enjoyment. Model train layouts can be as simple as one train with a little scenery, or multiple trains and many different pieces of scenery.

To get started, you need a train, a track, and your imagination.

stone tunnel: 2 per pack, $10

dogs and cats, fire hydrant, trash can: 9 pieces, $12

ready-made trees: 38 per pack, $27

buildings: 3 per pack, $16

FACT • ACTIVITY

Suppose you want to build your own model railroad layout. The pictures show some possible items you can use in addition to the trains and tracks.

- Decide which items and how many packages of each you want in your layout. Find the total number of each item.
- Use the number of packages and the price per package to find the cost of each set of packages you buy. Find your total cost.
- Use grid paper to draw a picture of your model railroad layout.

Student Handbook

ILLINOIS

Review the Illinois Assessment Framework H1

These pages provide review of the Illinois Assessment Framework for your grade. They also help you avoid errors students often make.

Review the Illinois Assessment Framework

Place Value and Numbers to 100,000

6.3.01 Read, write, recognize, and model equivalent representations of whole numbers and their place values up to 100,000.

A number is made up of one or more digits. Each digit has a value. There are different ways to show numbers and the value of each digit.

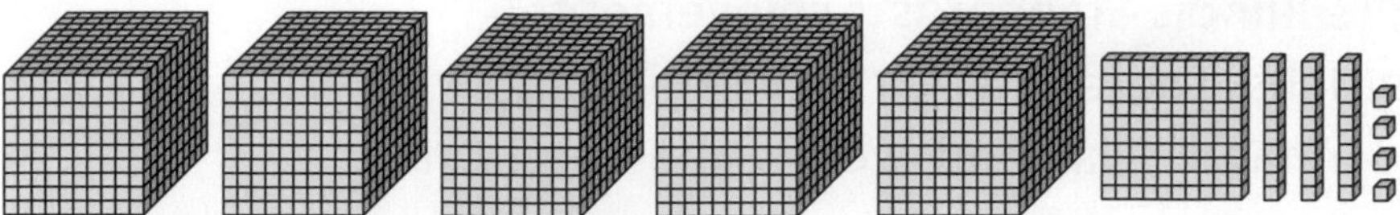

This model shows 5 thousands, 1 hundred, 3 tens, and 4 ones.
This expression shows the the value of each digit: 5,000 + 100 + 30 + 4.
The number is 5,134.

Examples

A What is the value of the digit 4 in 3,428?

THOUSANDS	HUNDREDS	TENS	ONES
3,	4	2	8

Use a place value chart to determine the value of each digit.

The digit 4 has a value of 400.

B Solve.

30,000 + 1,000 + 700 + 5 = ■

The addition sentence shows the value of each digit. Add the values to find the number.

31,705

ERROR ALERT

When you write a number using digits, be sure that each digit has the correct value.

Try It

Write the value of the underlined digit.

1. $3\underline{2},716$ **2.** $2,\underline{8}90$ **3.** $\underline{9}7,218$

4. $8,73\underline{4}$ **5.** $5\underline{1}6$ **6.** $19,\underline{7}01$

Solve.

7. 40,000 + 7,000 + 600 + 10 + 8 = ■

8. 2,000 + 400 + 90 + 3 = ■

9. 60,000 + 100 + 50 + 9 = ■

10. 30,000 + 8,000 + 200 + 90 + 1 = ■

11. Read the problem below. **Explain** why A cannot be the correct answer choice. Then choose the correct answer.

COMMON ERROR

Which number is equal to the expression?

3,000 + 90 + 2

A 3,920
B 3,902
C 3,092
D 392

Review the Illinois Assessment Framework

Read and Write Numbers to 100,000

6.3.02 Identify and write (in words and standard form) whole numbers up to 100,000.

When you write a number number using digits, it is in **standard form**. When you write a number using words, it is in **word form**.

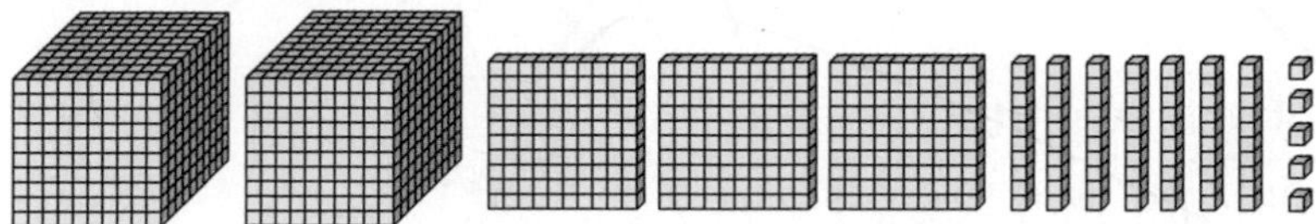

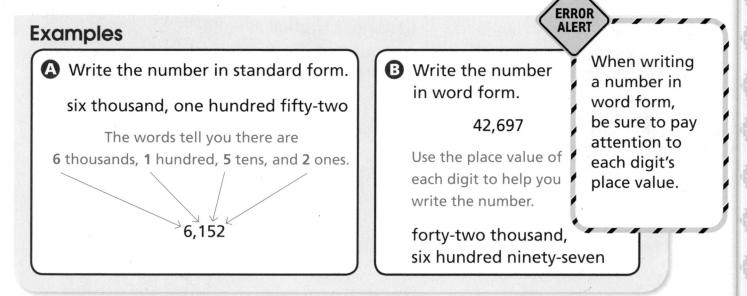

The word form of the number shown by the model is: two thousand, three hundred seventy-five.
The standard form of the number shown by the model is: 2,375.

Examples

A Write the number in standard form.

six thousand, one hundred fifty-two

The words tell you there are **6** thousands, **1** hundred, **5** tens, and **2** ones.

6,152

B Write the number in word form.

42,697

Use the place value of each digit to help you write the number.

forty-two thousand, six hundred ninety-seven

ERROR ALERT When writing a number in word form, be sure to pay attention to each digit's place value.

Try It

Write each number in word form.

1. 25,417
2. 4,032
3. 5,521
4. 49,306

Write each number in standard form.

5. twenty-three thousand, one hundred fifteen
6. eight thousand, five hundred sixty-three
7. ten-thousand, seven hundred forty-eight
8. fifty-five thousand, seventy-four

9. Read the problem below. **Explain** why B cannot be the correct answer choice. Then choose the correct answer. **COMMON ERROR**

   Which shows 8,305 in word form?

   A eight three five

   B eight thousand, three hundred fifty

   C eight thousand, three hundred five

   D eight hundred thirty-five

Review the Illinois Assessment Framework

Recognize Fractions

6.3.03 Recognize a fraction represented with a pictorial model.

A **fraction** is a number that names part of a whole or part of a group.

This figure is divided into 6 equal parts.
Of the 6 equal parts, 5 are yellow.

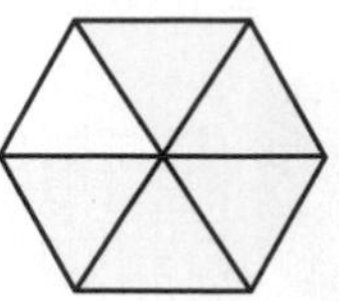

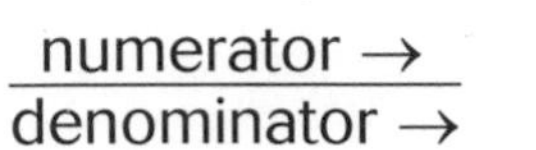

$$\frac{\text{numerator} \rightarrow}{\text{denominator} \rightarrow} \quad \frac{5}{6} \quad \frac{\leftarrow \text{number of yellow parts}}{\leftarrow \text{number of equal parts in the whole}}$$

Write: $\frac{5}{6}$ **Read:** five sixths

ERROR ALERT

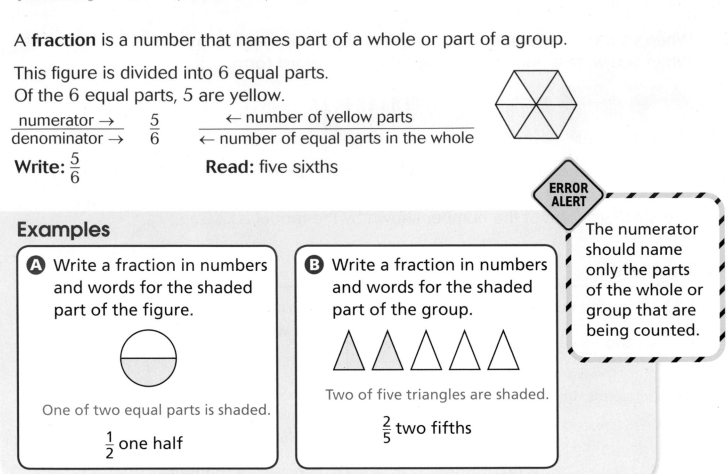

The numerator should name only the parts of the whole or group that are being counted.

Examples

A Write a fraction in numbers and words for the shaded part of the figure.

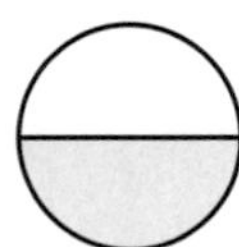

One of two equal parts is shaded.

$\frac{1}{2}$ one half

B Write a fraction in numbers and words for the shaded part of the group.

Two of five triangles are shaded.

$\frac{2}{5}$ two fifths

Try It

Write a fraction in numbers and words to name the shaded part.

1. 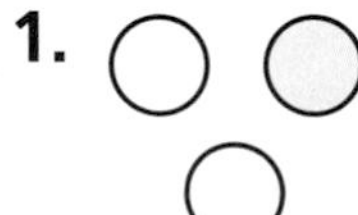

2. 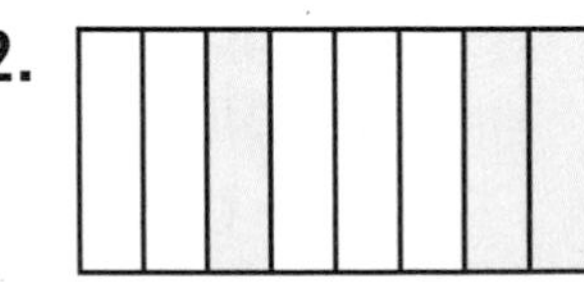

3. 

4. 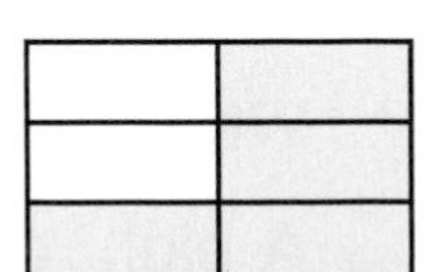

5. 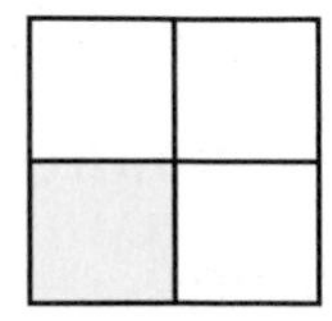

6. 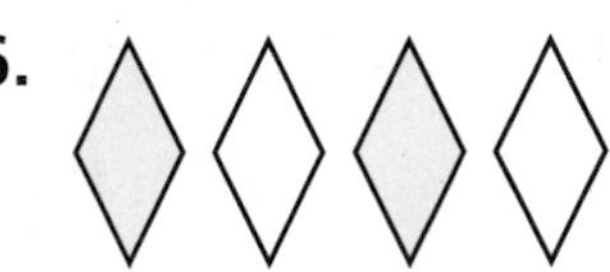

7. Read the problem below. **Explain** why D cannot be the correct answer choice. Then choose the correct answer.

COMMON ERROR

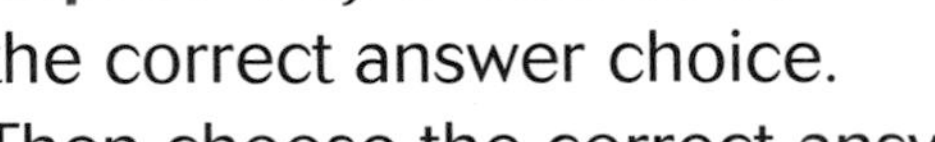

Which fraction names the shaded part?

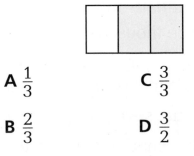

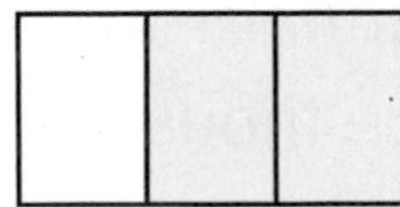

A $\frac{1}{3}$ **C** $\frac{3}{3}$

B $\frac{2}{3}$ **D** $\frac{3}{2}$

Review the Illinois Assessment Framework

Relate Multiplication to Addition

6.3.04 Represent multiplication as repeated addition.

When you have equal groups, you can use addition or multiplication to find out how many you have in all.

Examples

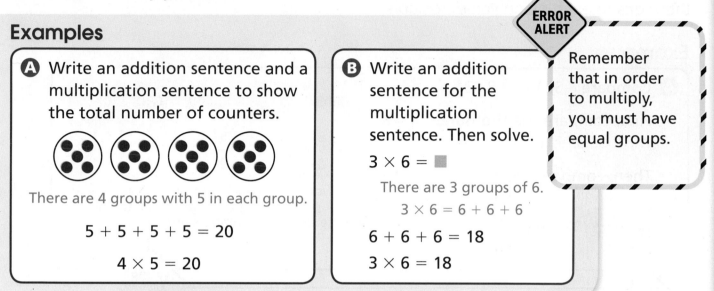

A Write an addition sentence and a multiplication sentence to show the total number of counters.

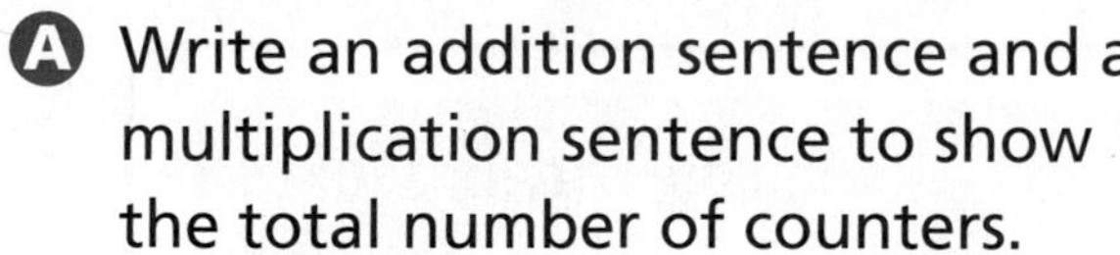

There are 4 groups with 5 in each group.

$5 + 5 + 5 + 5 = 20$

$4 \times 5 = 20$

B Write an addition sentence for the multiplication sentence. Then solve.

$3 \times 6 = ■$

There are 3 groups of 6.

$3 \times 6 = 6 + 6 + 6$

$6 + 6 + 6 = 18$

$3 \times 6 = 18$

ERROR ALERT Remember that in order to multiply, you must have equal groups.

Try It

Write an addition sentence and a multiplication sentence to show the total number of counters.

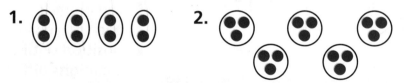

1. 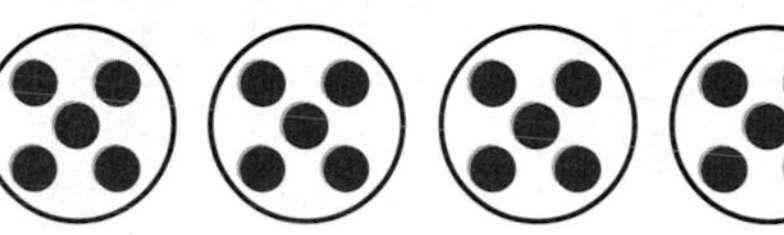

2.   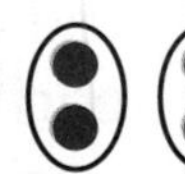 

Write a multiplication sentence for each. Then solve.

3. $7 + 7 + 7 + 7 + 7 + 7 = ■$
4. $10 + 10 = ■$
5. $3 + 3 + 3 + 3 = ■$
6. $9 + 9 + 9 = ■$

Write an addition sentence for each. Then solve.

7. $5 \times 8 = ■$
8. $7 \times 1 = ■$
9. $2 \times 4 = ■$
10. $3 \times 3 = ■$

11. Read the problem below. **Explain** why C cannot be the correct answer choice. Then choose the correct answer. **COMMON ERROR**

Which addition sentence shows the multiplication sentence?

$4 \times 4 = 16$

A $4 + 4 + 3 + 5 = 16$

B $4 + 4 + 4 + 4 = 16$

C $4 + 4 + 2 + 6 = 16$

D $4 + 4 + 8 = 16$

Review the Illinois Assessment Framework

Compare and Order Whole Numbers Up to 10,000

6.3.05 Order and compare whole numbers up to 10,000 using symbols (>, <, or =) and words (e.g., greater (more) than, less than, equal to, between).

A place-value chart can help you compare two numbers by comparing the digits in each place-value position.

Examples

A Compare 8,521 and 8,931.

First, compare the thousands. 8 = 8
The thousands are the same.

Then, compare the hundreds. 5 < 9
5 hundreds are less than 9 hundreds.

So, 8,521 < 8,931.
8,521 is less than 8,931.

THOUSANDS	HUNDREDS	TENS	ONES
8,	5	2	1
8,	9	3	1

Once you know which number is greater, you can stop comparing the digits. If all the digits are the same, the numbers are equal.

B Order 6,320, 6,548, and 6,179 from least to greatest.

First, compare the thousands. 6 = 6 = 6
The thousands are the same.

Then, compare the hundreds. 1 < 3 < 5
1 hundred is less than 3 hundreds, and 3 hundreds are less than 5 hundreds. 3 is between 1 and 5.

6, 3 2 0
6, 5 4 8
6, 1 7 9

So, the numbers from least to greatest are 6,179, 6,320, 6,548.

ERROR ALERT
To compare numbers, start at the left and compare the digits in each place-value position until the digits differ.

Try It

Compare the numbers. Write *is less than, is greater than,* or *is equal to*. Then write <, >, =.

1. 9,186 ● 7,412

2. 5,730 ● 5,673

Write the numbers in order from least to greatest.

3. 7,917; 7,869; 7,123

4. 9,549; 9,262; 9,101

5. Read the problem below. **Explain** why B cannot be the correct answer choice. Then choose the correct answer.

COMMON ERROR

Which number is less than 3,479 but greater than 3,152?

A 3,099 **B** 3,568
C 3,142 **D** 3,285

Review the Illinois Assessment Framework

Compare Money Amounts

6.3.06 Order and compare decimals expressed using monetary units.

You can use place value to compare money amounts.

Line up the decimal points. Then compare the digits in each place value position from left to right.

You can also order money amounts according to place value from least to greatest or from greatest to least.

DOLLARS	.	DIMES	PENNIES
$4	.	8	5
$4	.	8	7

The dollars and dimes are the same. 5 pennies are less than 7 pennies. So, $4.85 < $4.87.

Examples

A Karen bought a crossword puzzle book for $2.99. Wanda bought a crossword puzzle book for $2.75. Who spent the least amount of money?

DOLLARS	.	DIMES	PENNIES
$2	.	9	9
$2	.	7	5

↑ 2 = 2 ↑ 9 > 7

First, compare the dollars. The dollars are the same.

Then, compare the dimes. 7 dimes are less than 9 dimes.

$2.99 > $2.75. Wanda spent the least amount of money.

B Order $7.19, $7.65, and $7.28 from greatest to least.

First, compare the number of dollars. 7 = 7 = 7
The dollars are the same.

Then, compare the number of dimes. 6 > 2 > 1
6 dimes are more than 2 dimes, and 2 dimes are more than 1 dime. 2 is between 6 and 1.

$ 7. 1 9
$ 7. 6 5
$ 7. 2 8

So, the amounts from greatest to least are $7.65, $7.28, and $7.19.

ERROR ALERT

Always work from left to right when comparing and ordering money amounts.

Try It

Use <, >, or = to compare the amounts.

1. $0.39 ● $6.02 **2.** $3.17 ● $3.15

3. $2.92 ● $9.29 **4.** $1.18 ● $1.81

Order the amounts from greatest to least.

5. $3.93, $3.97, $3.77

6. $5.06, $5.80, $5.64

7. Read the problem below. **Explain** why D cannot be the correct answer choice. Then choose the correct answer.

COMMON ERROR

Which amount is greater than $6.39 but less than $6.74?

A $6.58 **C** $6.78

B $6.34 **D** $6.19

Review the Illinois Assessment Framework

Whole Number Addition and Subtraction

6.3.09 Solve problems and number sentences involving addition and subraction with regrouping.

When you add or subtract numbers with more than one digit, begin by adding or subtracting the digits in the ones place. Then move left, adding or subtracting one place value at a time.

Sometimes you need to regroup to solve addition and subtraction problems.

Examples

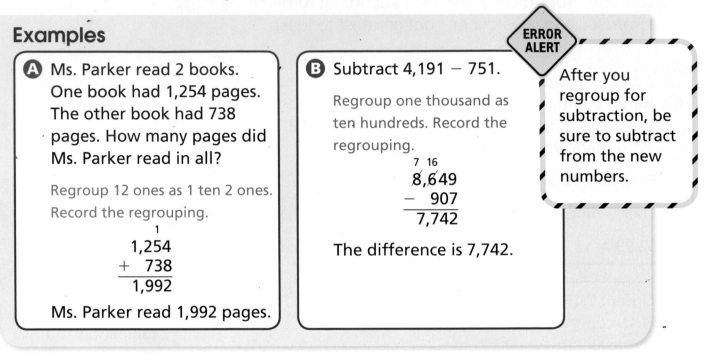

A Ms. Parker read 2 books. One book had 1,254 pages. The other book had 738 pages. How many pages did Ms. Parker read in all?

Regroup 12 ones as 1 ten 2 ones. Record the regrouping.

$$\begin{array}{r} \scriptstyle 1 \\ 1,254 \\ +\ \ 738 \\ \hline 1,992 \end{array}$$

Ms. Parker read 1,992 pages.

B Subtract 4,191 − 751.

Regroup one thousand as ten hundreds. Record the regrouping.

$$\begin{array}{r} \scriptstyle 7\ 16 \\ \not{8},\not{6}49 \\ -\ \ 907 \\ \hline 7,742 \end{array}$$

The difference is 7,742.

ERROR ALERT

After you regroup for subtraction, be sure to subtract from the new numbers.

Try It

Find the sum or difference.

1. 4,619 + 3,811 = ■
2. 8,912 − 4,317 = ■
3. 9,243 + 388 = ■
4. 7,145 + 1,256 = ■
5. 4,987 − 992 = ■
6. 8,329 − 7,492 = ■
7. 8,293 + 1,345 = ■
8. 2,871 − 347 = ■
9. Barbara collected 2,487 bottle caps. Tim collected 1,972 bottle caps. How many more bottle caps did Barbara collect than Tim?
10. Jael has 2,475 round buttons and 4,834 square buttons. How many buttons does Jael have in all?
11. Read the problem below. **Explain** why B cannot be the correct answer choice. Then choose the correct answer. **COMMON ERROR**

    Last week, 3,492 people visited the park and 5,173 people visited the zoo. How many more visitors visited the zoo?

    A 2,781 **C** 1,781

    B 2,681 **D** 1,681

Review the Illinois Assessment Framework

Solve Problems with Bills and Coins

6.3.10 Solve problems involving the value of a collection of bills and coins whose total value is $10.00 or less, and make change.

Change is the money that you get back when you have paid for an item with bills and coins that have a total value greater than the cost of the item.

Norma buys a hat for $2.75. She pays with a $5 bill.
How much change should Norma receive?

Start with the cost of the hat. Count up coins and bills until you reach $5.00.

$$\$2.75 + \$.25 = \$3.00 + \$1.00 = \$4.00 + \$1.00 = \$5.00$$

Then find the total value of the coins and bills you counted up.

$0.25, $1.25, $2.25

Norma should receive $2.25 in change.

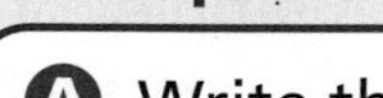

Examples

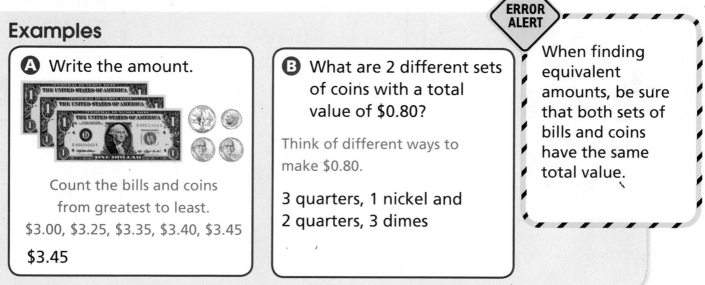

A Write the amount.

Count the bills and coins from greatest to least.

$3.00, $3.25, $3.35, $3.40, $3.45

$3.45

B What are 2 different sets of coins with a total value of $0.80?

Think of different ways to make $0.80.

3 quarters, 1 nickel and
2 quarters, 3 dimes

ERROR ALERT

When finding equivalent amounts, be sure that both sets of bills and coins have the same total value.

Try It

Find two equivalent sets for each. List the bills and coins.

1. $2.25
2. $5.15
3. $0.92

Find the amount of change.

4. Ted buys a book for $3.55. He pays with a $10 bill.
5. Pam buys a juice for $2.60. She pays with a $5 bill.

6. Read the problem below. **Explain** why B cannot be the correct answer choice. Then choose the correct answer.

Which set of coins equal $0.85?

A 1 quarter 3 dimes

B 2 quarters 3 dimes

C 2 quarters 7 nickels

D 7 dimes 1 nickel

Review the Illinois Assessment Framework

Multiplication Facts and Patterns

6.3.11 Model and apply basic multiplication facts (up to 10 × 10), and apply them to related multiples of 10 (e.g., 3 × 4 = 12, 30 × 4 = 120).

When you multiply, you find the total number of items in equal-sized groups. You can model basic multiplication facts in different ways.

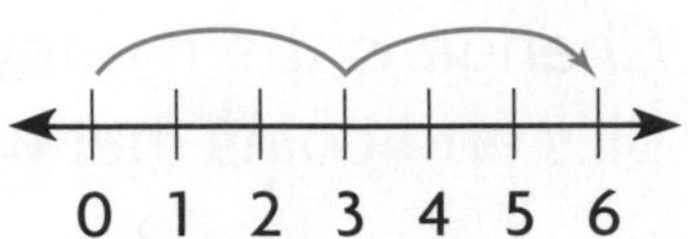

The number line shows 2 × 3 = 6.

You can use basic facts and patterns to find the products of greater factors. When one factor is a multiple of 10, the product will have one zero more than the product in the basic fact.

Examples

A Use models to find 3 × 3.

You can use an array or counters to model the multiplication fact.

Both models show 9 in all.

3 × 3 = 9

B Use a basic fact to find 50 × 4.

First, find the basic fact.
5 × 4 = 20

Then, include the zeros.
50 × 4 = 200

This product has one more zero than the product in the basic fact.

50 × 4 = 200

ERROR ALERT

When using patterns to multiply by multiples of 10, be sure to write the correct number of zeros in the product.

Try It

Find each product.

1. 2 × 9 = ■
2. 6 × 1 = ■
3. 4 × 7 = ■
4. 3 × 5 = ■
5. 8 × 2 = ■
6. 7 × 9 = ■
7. 4 × 10 = ■
8. 5 × 6 = ■

Use a basic fact to find each product.

9. 30 × 2 = ■
10. 4 × 80 = ■
11. 6 × 90 = ■
12. 20 × 7 = ■
13. 50 × 8 = ■
14. 100 × 9 = ■

15. Read the problem below. **Explain** why B cannot be the correct answer choice. Then choose the correct answer. **COMMON ERROR**

What is the product?

50 × 6 = ■

A 25
B 30
C 250
D 300

Review the Illinois Assessment Framework

Elapsed Time

7.3.01 Solve problems involving simple elapsed time in compound units (e.g., hours, minutes, days).

Elapsed time is the amount of time that passes between two events or between the start and end of an event. Count days, hours, and minutes between the start and end of an event.

ERROR ALERT

Make sure to count the hours and minutes separately.

Examples

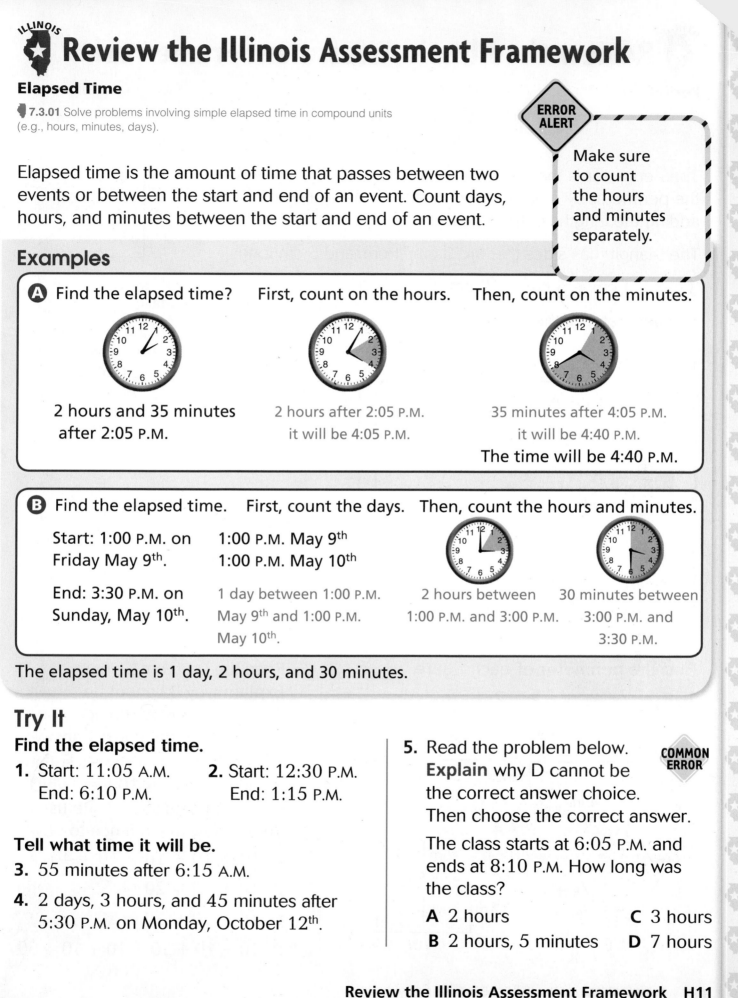

A Find the elapsed time? First, count on the hours. Then, count on the minutes.

2 hours and 35 minutes after 2:05 P.M.

2 hours after 2:05 P.M. it will be 4:05 P.M.

35 minutes after 4:05 P.M. it will be 4:40 P.M.

The time will be 4:40 P.M.

B Find the elapsed time. First, count the days. Then, count the hours and minutes.

Start: 1:00 P.M. on Friday May 9th.

End: 3:30 P.M. on Sunday, May 10th.

1:00 P.M. May 9th
1:00 P.M. May 10th

1 day between 1:00 P.M. May 9th and 1:00 P.M. May 10th.

2 hours between 1:00 P.M. and 3:00 P.M.

30 minutes between 3:00 P.M. and 3:30 P.M.

The elapsed time is 1 day, 2 hours, and 30 minutes.

Try It

Find the elapsed time.

1. Start: 11:05 A.M.
End: 6:10 P.M.

2. Start: 12:30 P.M.
End: 1:15 P.M.

Tell what time it will be.

3. 55 minutes after 6:15 A.M.

4. 2 days, 3 hours, and 45 minutes after 5:30 P.M. on Monday, October 12th.

5. Read the problem below. **Explain** why D cannot be the correct answer choice. Then choose the correct answer.

The class starts at 6:05 P.M. and ends at 8:10 P.M. How long was the class?

A 2 hours
B 2 hours, 5 minutes
C 3 hours
D 7 hours

Review the Illinois Assessment Framework

Perimeter

7.3.03 Solve problems involving the perimeter of a polygon with given side lengths or a given non-standard unit (e.g., paperclip).

The perimeter is the distance around a closed figure. Find the perimeter by measuring each side of the figure and adding the lengths of the sides.

3 cm
5 cm
4 cm

The triangle has sides that are 3 cm, 4 cm, and 5 cm long.

3 cm + 4 cm + 5 cm = 12 cm

The perimeter of the triangle is 12 cm.

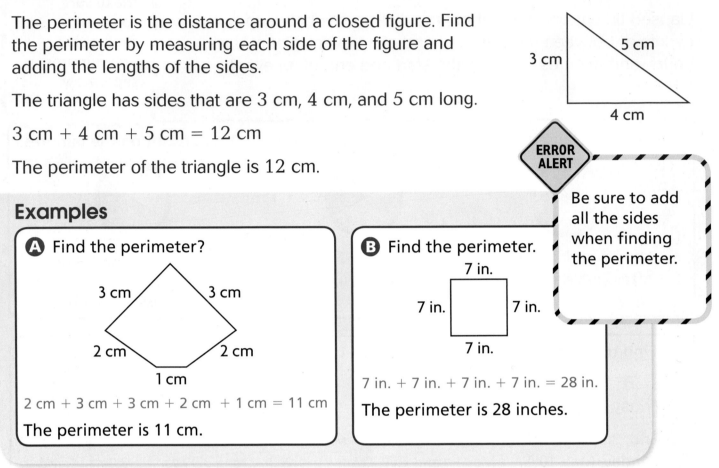

ERROR ALERT

Be sure to add all the sides when finding the perimeter.

Examples

A Find the perimeter?

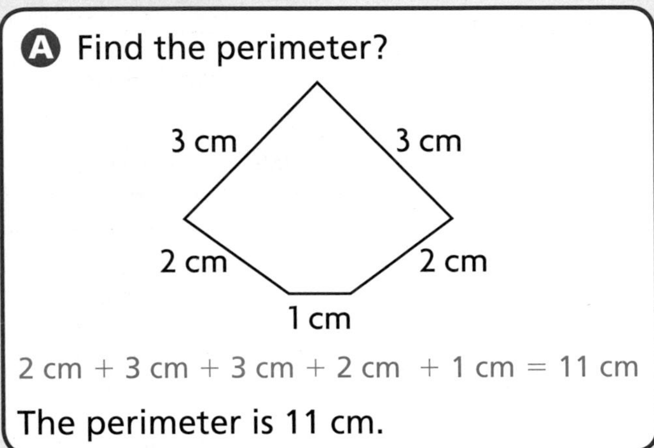

2 cm + 3 cm + 3 cm + 2 cm + 1 cm = 11 cm

The perimeter is 11 cm.

B Find the perimeter.

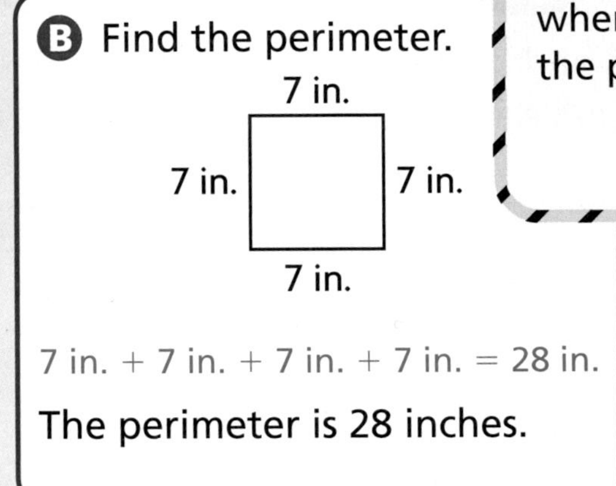

7 in. + 7 in. + 7 in. + 7 in. = 28 in.

The perimeter is 28 inches.

Try It

Find the perimeter of each figure.

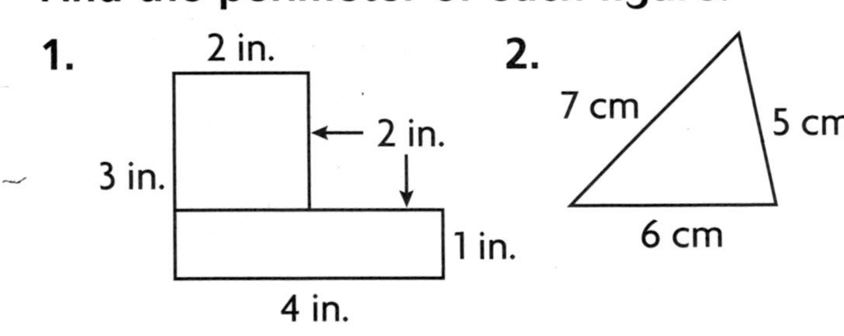

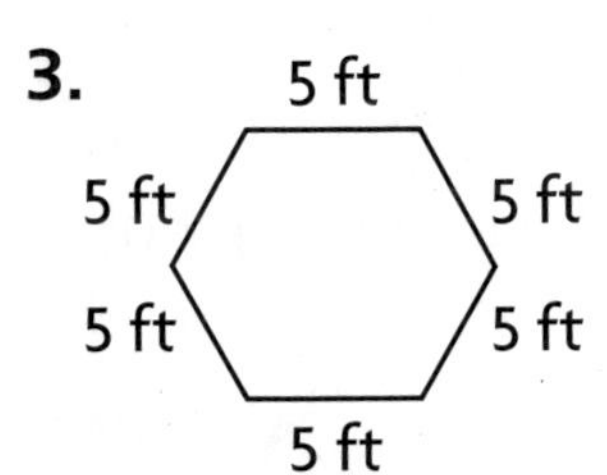

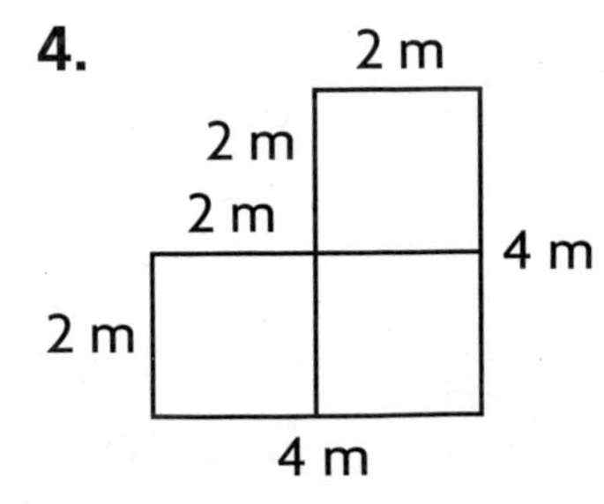

5. Read the problem below. **Explain** why B cannot be the correct answer choice. Then choose the correct answer.

COMMON ERROR

Each side of Mrs. Brown's square garden measures 10 feet. Which measurements should she use to decide how much fence to buy?

A $10 + 10 + 10 + 10 = 40$

B $10 + 10 = 20$

C $10 + 10 + 10 = 30$

D $10 + 10 + 10 + 10 + 10 = 50$

Review the Illinois Assessment Framework

Area

7.3.04 Solve problems involving the area of a figure when whole and half square units are shown within the figure.

The area is the number of square units needed to cover a surface.

The area of the figure is $16\frac{1}{2}$ square units.

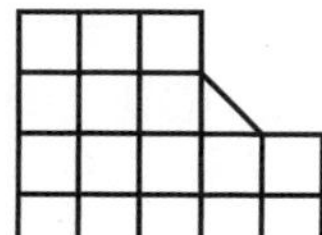

□ = 1 square unit

◺ = $\frac{1}{2}$ square unit

ERROR ALERT

When you multiply to find the area of a rectangle, be sure you are not multiplying the lengths of opposite sides.

Examples

A What is the area of the figure?

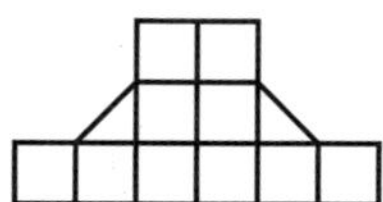

Count the number of square units that cover the figure. Count each half square unit as $\frac{1}{2}$.

The area is 11 square units.

B What is the area of the rectangle?

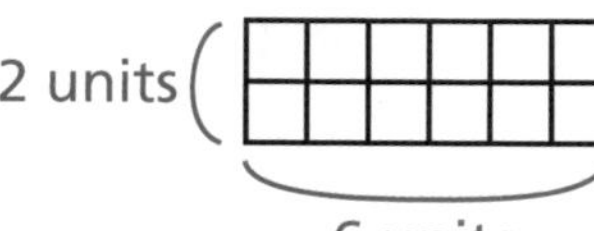

You can multiply to find the area.

2 units × 6 units = 12 square units

The area is 12 square units.

Try It

Find the area of each figure.

□ = 1 square unit

1.  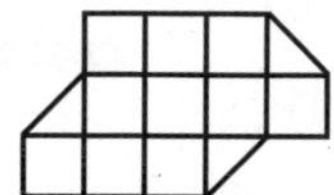

2. 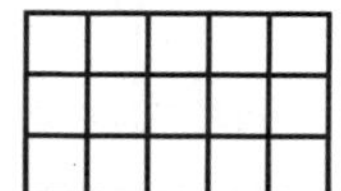

3.  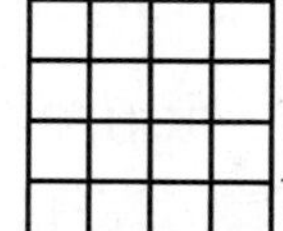

4. 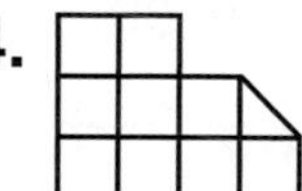

5. 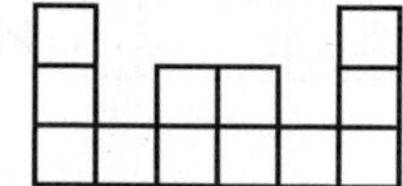

6. 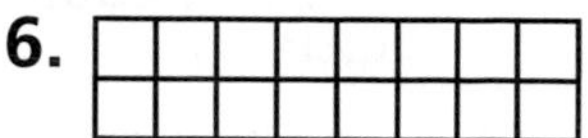

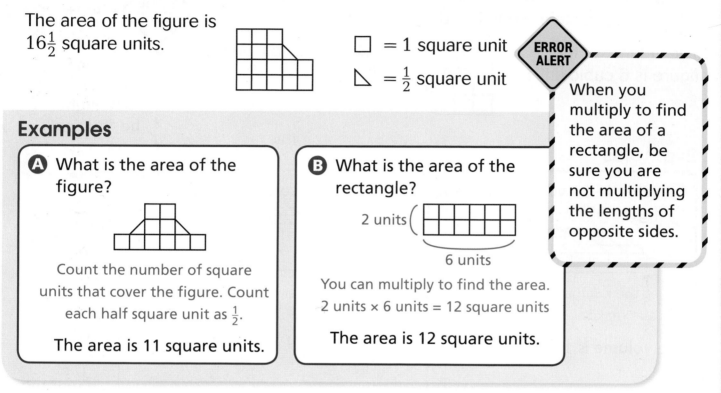

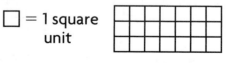

7. Read the problem below. **Explain** why D cannot be the correct answer choice. Then choose the correct answer.

COMMON ERROR

What is the area of the rectangle?

□ = 1 square unit

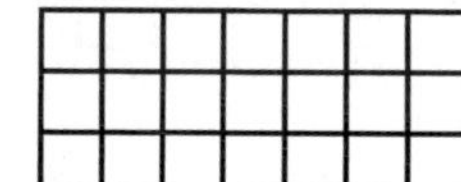

A 9 square units

B 10 square units

C 21 square units

D 49 square units

Review the Illinois Assessment Framework

Volume

7.3.06 Determine the volume of a solid figure that shows cubic units.

Volume is the amount of space a figure occupies and is measured in cubic units. To find the volume, you can count or calculate the number of cubic units.

The volume of the figure is 6 cubic units.

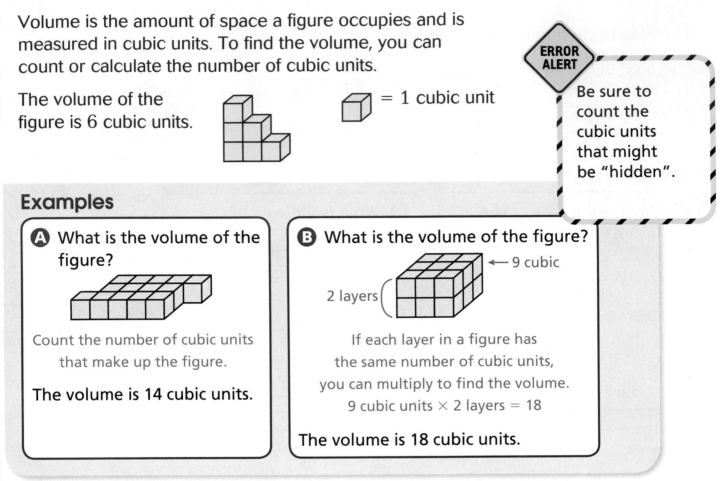

= 1 cubic unit

ERROR ALERT

Be sure to count the cubic units that might be "hidden".

Examples

A What is the volume of the figure?

Count the number of cubic units that make up the figure.

The volume is 14 cubic units.

B What is the volume of the figure?

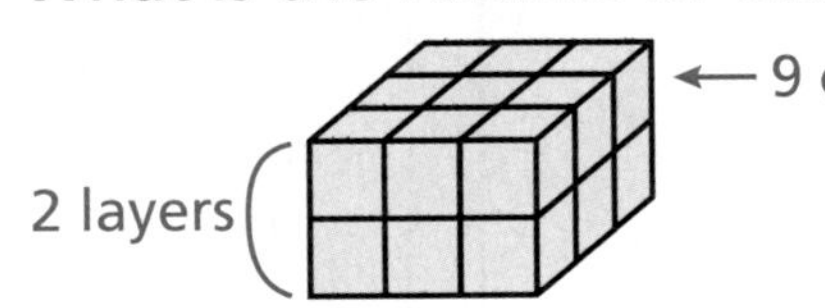

If each layer in a figure has the same number of cubic units, you can multiply to find the volume.

9 cubic units × 2 layers = 18

The volume is 18 cubic units.

Try It

Find the volume of each figure.

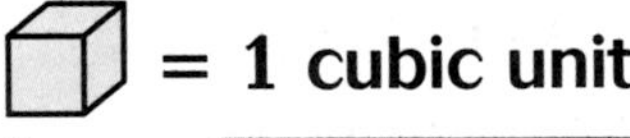

= 1 cubic unit

1. 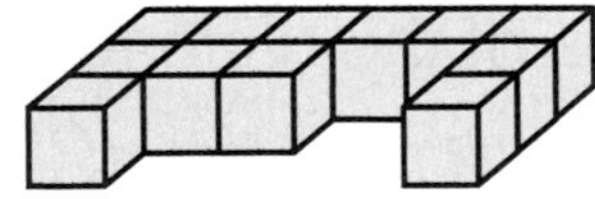

2. 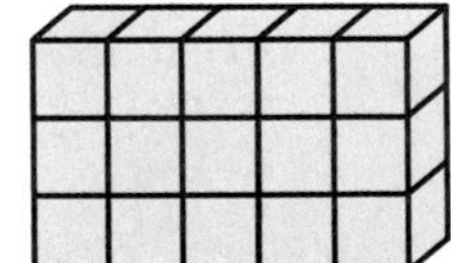

3. 

4. 

5. 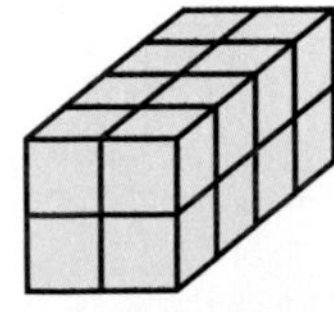

6. 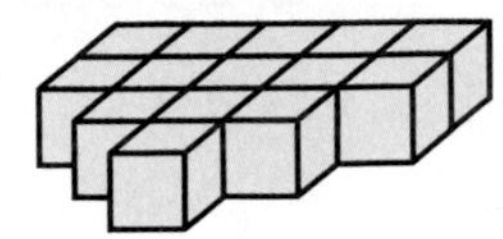

7. Read the problem below. **Explain** why A cannot be the correct answer choice. Then choose the correct answer.

COMMON ERROR

What is the volume of the figure?

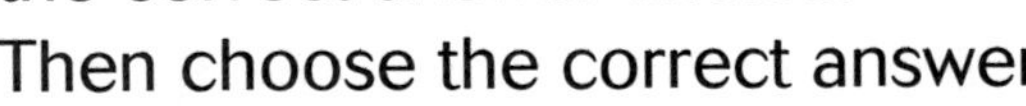

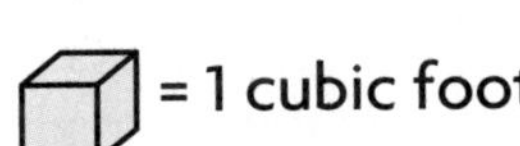

= 1 cubic foot

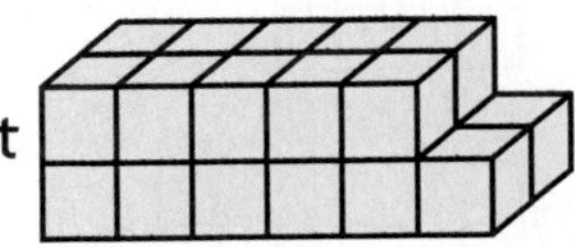

A 12 cubic units

B 22 cubic units

C 24 cubic units

D 28 cubic units

Review the Illinois Assessment Framework

Convert Units of Length and Time

7.3.07 Solve problems involving simple unit conversions within the same measurement system for time and length.

Customary Units of Length
1 ft = 12 in.
1 yd = 3 ft = 36 in.
1 mi = 5,280 ft

Units of Time
60 sec = 1 min
60 min = 1 hr
24 hr = 1 day

Customary and Metric are two different systems of measurement. They use different sets of units to measure length.

You can covert measurements from one unit to another within the same measurement system.

You can also convert units that measure time.

Use multiplication and division to convert units.

Metric Units of Length
1 dm = 10 cm
1 m = 100 cm = 10 dm
1 km = 1,000 m

Examples

A Convert.
5 m = ■ cm
1 m = 100 cm
Multiply the number of meters by 100.
5 × 100 = 500
5 m = 500 cm

B Convert.
48 ft = ■ yd
3 ft = 1 yd
Divide the number of feet by 3.
48 ÷ 3 = 16
48 ft = 16 yd

C Convert.
6 hr = ■ min
1 hour = 60 minutes
Multiply the number of hours by 60.
6 × 60 = 360
6 hr = 360 min

ERROR ALERT
When converting from smaller units into larger units, multiply.

Try It

Convert.

1. 7 m = ■ cm
2. 7 ft = ■ in.
3. 300 cm = ■ m
4. 4 hr = ■ min
5. 20 cm = ■ dm
6. 60 min = ■ hr
7. 2 mi = ■ ft
8. 36 in. = ■ ft
9. 5 yd = ■ ft
10. 48 hr = ■ days
11. 180 sec = ■ min
12. 9 km = ■ m
13. 2 yd = ■ in.
14. 120 min = ■ hr
15. 10 m = ■ cm
16. 3 days = ■ hr

17. Read the problem below. **Explain** why A cannot be the correct answer choice. Then choose the correct answer.

COMMON ERROR

Which length is equal to 50 dm?

A 5 cm
B 50 cm
C 500 cm
D 5,000 cm

Review the Illinois Assessment Framework

Patterns

8.3.01 Determine a missing term in a pattern (sequence), describe a pattern (sequence), and extend a pattern (sequence) when given a description or pattern (sequence).

A pattern is an ordered set of numbers or objects. The picture shows a box with four marbles. If each box has 4 marbles, how many marbles are in 3 boxes? Use a pattern. Count by fours 3 times.

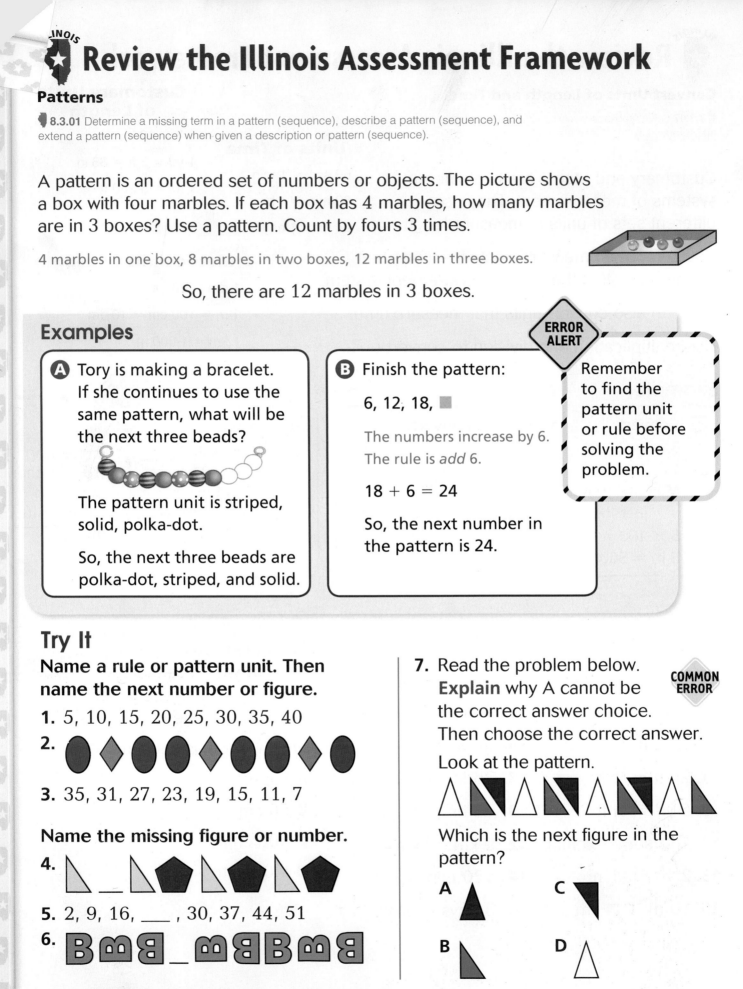

4 marbles in one box, 8 marbles in two boxes, 12 marbles in three boxes.

So, there are 12 marbles in 3 boxes.

Examples

A Tory is making a bracelet. If she continues to use the same pattern, what will be the next three beads?

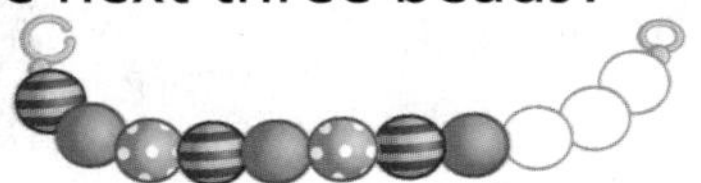

The pattern unit is striped, solid, polka-dot.

So, the next three beads are polka-dot, striped, and solid.

B Finish the pattern:

6, 12, 18, ■

The numbers increase by 6. The rule is *add* 6.

$18 + 6 = 24$

So, the next number in the pattern is 24.

Remember to find the pattern unit or rule before solving the problem.

Try It

Name a rule or pattern unit. Then name the next number or figure.

1. 5, 10, 15, 20, 25, 30, 35, 40
2.
3. 35, 31, 27, 23, 19, 15, 11, 7

Name the missing figure or number.

4. 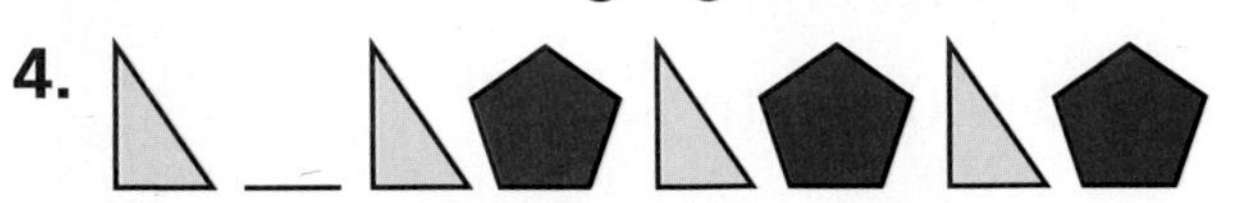
5. 2, 9, 16, ____ , 30, 37, 44, 51
6. B B B _ B B B B B

7. Read the problem below. **Explain** why A cannot be the correct answer choice. Then choose the correct answer.

COMMON ERROR

Look at the pattern.

Which is the next figure in the pattern?

Review the Illinois Assessment Framework

Expressions

8.3.02 Write an expression to represent a given situation.

An expression is made up of numbers, operation signs, and sometimes variables. A variable is a letter or symbol that stands for a number.

$$p + 10$$

If p stands for 5, then the expression is $5 + 10$.

An expression does not have an equal sign.

ERROR ALERT When writing an expression with a variable, be sure to use the correct operation.

Examples

A Luke has 18 apples. He puts an equal number of apples in each of 3 bags. Write an expression representing the number of apples in each bag.

total apples ÷ number of bags

$18 \div 3$

B Replace the x with 118. Then write an equation to solve.

$100 + x$

$100 + 118$

$100 + 188 = 218$

Try It

Write an expression to represent each.

1. a number that is 3 more than r
2. q groups of 5
3. a number that is m less than 10
4. Liz has 12 seashells. She has 8 more seashells than Jenny. Write an expression to represent the number of seashells Jenny has.
5. Ernest has 21 tennis balls. He wants to store them in cans of 3. Write an expression to show the number of cans he will use.
6. There are 6 cartons of eggs in the refrigerator. There are 6 eggs in each carton. Write an expression to show the number of eggs in the refrigerator.
7. Read the problem below. **Explain** why C cannot be the correct answer choice. Then choose the correct answer. **COMMON ERROR**

   Grover bought 8 baseballs for the game. Brent bought 12 baseballs for the game. Which expression shows the number of balls that Grover and Brent bought for the game?

   A $12 + 8$

   B $12 - 8$

   C 12×8

   D $12 \div 8$

Review the Illinois Assessment Framework

Equations and Inequalities

8.3.03 Represent simple mathematical relationships with number sentences (equations and inequalities).

An **equation** always has an equal sign (=) that means the two amounts, or quantities, are equal.

An **inequality** always has a greater-than (>) or less-than (<) sign because one amount is greater or less than another amount.

$4 + 5 = 9$ is an equation.

$4 < 5$ is an inequality.

Examples

A Write the following equation:

Eight plus twelve equals twenty.

Write the addends on one side of the equal sign and the sum on the other side.

$8 + 12 = 20$

B Which of these inequalities is true?

$15 > 9$ or $15 < 9$

$15 > 9$, because 15 is greater than 9.

$15 > 9$ is true.

ERROR ALERT

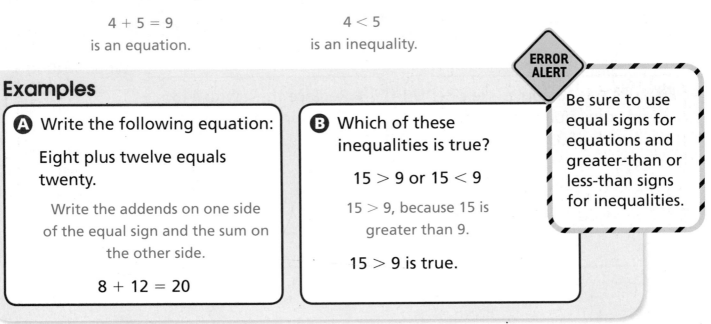

Be sure to use equal signs for equations and greater-than or less-than signs for inequalities.

Try It

Write an equation or inequality to represent each.

1. Seventeen minus three equals fourteen.
2. *p* is less than forty-one.
3. Eight is equal to 72 divided by a number *n*.
4. 9 bags with *c* marbles in each bag.

Compare. Write < or > for each.

5. 900 ● 90
6. 25 ● 40
7. 17 + 8 ● 30 − 6
8. 145 ● 154

9. Read the problem below. **Explain** why C cannot be the correct answer choice. Then choose the correct answer. **COMMON ERROR**

Tim and his family were on vacations for 3 days. Tim wrote 18 postcards. His sister wrote 19 postcards. Which correctly shows the relationship between the number of postcards Tim wrote and the number his sister wrote?

A $18 > 19$ **C** $18 = 19$

B $18 < 19$ **D** $18 > 224$

Review the Illinois Assessment Framework

Missing Numbers and Signs

8.3.04 Solve one-step addition and subtraction equations that have a missing number or missing operation sign (e.g., 3 + □ = 5, 6 □ 1 = 7).

You can use related facts to help you find missing numbers and signs in addition or subtraction equations. Related facts are in the same fact family, and they use the same numbers.

Addition and subtraction are opposite, or inverse operations.

$6 + 9 = 15$, so $15 - 6 = 9$.

Fact families use the same three numbers to make four different equations.

This is the fact family for 2, 5, and 7:

$2 + 5 = 7$ $7 - 2 = 5$
$5 + 2 = 7$ $7 - 5 = 2$

Examples

A Find the missing number.

9 − ■ = 8

8 + 1 = 9, so 9 − 1 = 8

The missing number is 1.

B Find the missing sign.

7 ■ 4 = 11

The fact family for 4, 7, and 11 is:

4 + 7 = 11 11 − 4 = 7
7 + 4 = 11 11 − 7 = 4

The missing sign is +.

ERROR ALERT

Be sure to use the inverse operation to find the missing number in an addition or subtraction fact.

Try It

Find the missing number.

1. ■ + 9 = 13
2. 14 − ■ = 6
3. ■ − 2 = 7
4. ■ + 3 = 4
5. 8 + ■ = 13
6. 11 − ■ = 9

Find the missing sign.

7. 5 ■ 3 = 8
8. 3 ■ 4 = 7
9. 18 ■ 9 = 9
10. 12 ■ 6 = 6
11. 11 ■ 1 = 10
12. 9 ■ 6 = 15

13. Read the problem below. **Explain** why D cannot be the correct answer choice. Then choose the correct answer.

COMMON ERROR

What number completes the sentence?

2 + ■ = 8

A 2
B 4
C 6
D 10

Review the Illinois Assessment Framework

Two-Dimensional Shapes

9.3.01 Identify, describe, and sketch two-dimensional shapes (triangles, squares, rectangles, pentagons, hexagons, and octagons) according to the number of sides, length of sides, and number of vertices.

A polygon is a closed two-dimensional shape with straight sides. It is named by the number of sides and vertices it has. Below are the names and descriptions of some polygons.

Name	Number of Sides	Number of Vertices	Shapes
triangle	3	3	
square	4	4	
rectangle	4	4	
pentagon	5	5	
hexagon	6	6	
octagon	8	8	

Examples

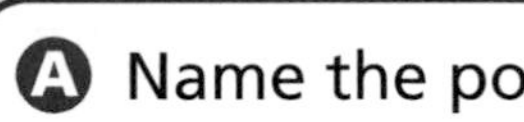

A Name the polygon.

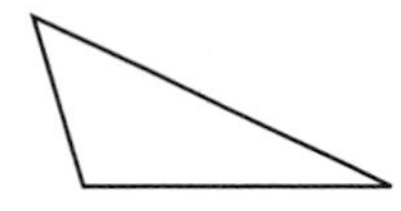

It has 3 sides and 3 vertices.

The polygon is a triangle.

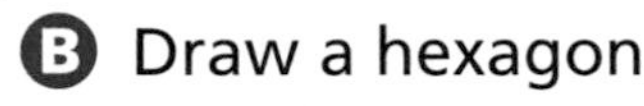

B Draw a hexagon.

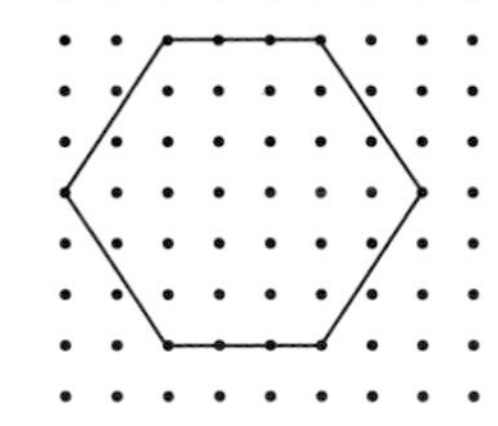

A hexagon is a closed figure with 6 straight sides and 6 vertices.

ERROR ALERT

Count both the sides and vertices when classifying a polygon.

Try It

Name each polygon. Tell how many sides and vertices.

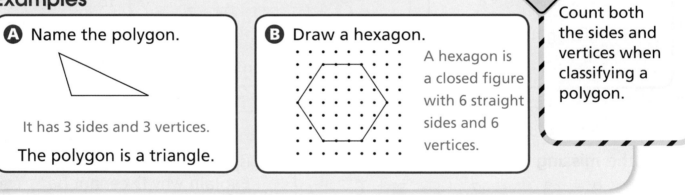

1. 

2. 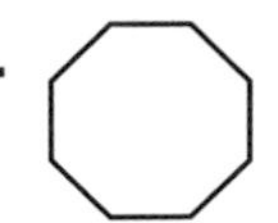

3.

Solve.

4. A ■ has 5 angles.

5. A quadrilateral has ■ sides.

6. Read the problem below. **Explain** why B cannot be the correct answer choice. Then choose the correct answer.

COMMON ERROR

Which figure is a triangle?

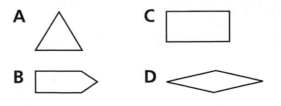

A 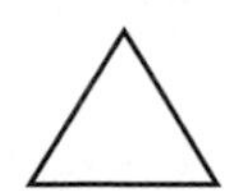

C 

B

D 

Review the Illinois Assessment Framework

Three-Dimensional Shapes

9.3.02 Identify and describe three-dimensional shapes (cubes, spheres, cones, cylinders, prisms, and pyramids) according to their characteristics (faces, edges, vertices).

Three-dimensional figures, or solid figures, have length, width, and height.

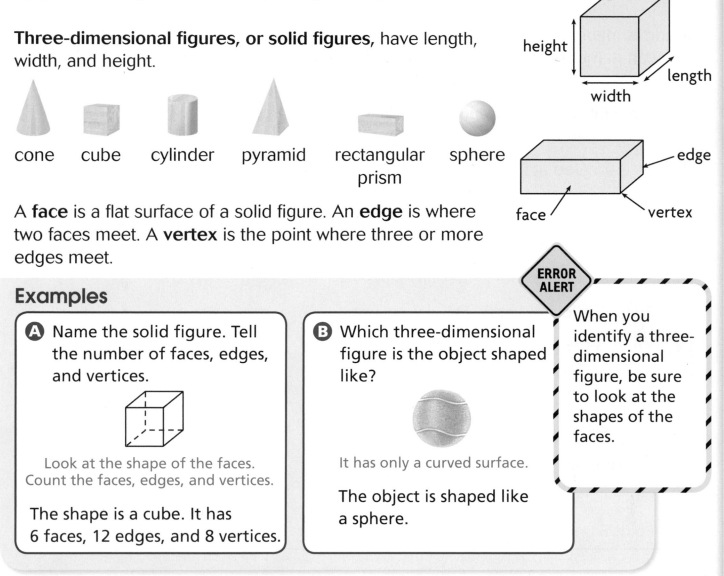

cone

cube

cylinder

pyramid

rectangular prism

sphere

height
length
width

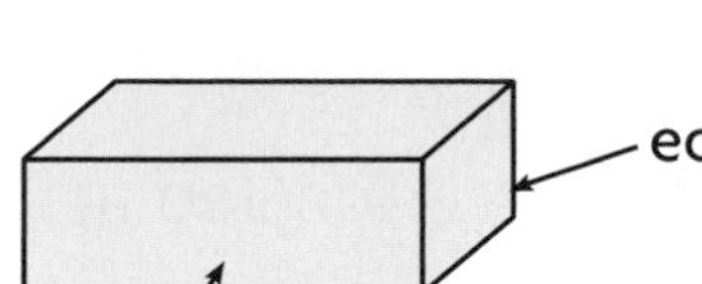

A **face** is a flat surface of a solid figure. An **edge** is where two faces meet. A **vertex** is the point where three or more edges meet.

Examples

A Name the solid figure. Tell the number of faces, edges, and vertices.

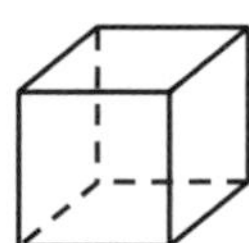

Look at the shape of the faces. Count the faces, edges, and vertices.

The shape is a cube. It has 6 faces, 12 edges, and 8 vertices.

B Which three-dimensional figure is the object shaped like?

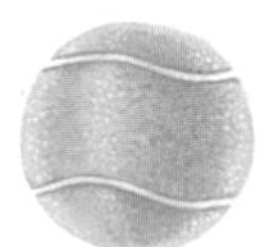

It has only a curved surface.

The object is shaped like a sphere.

ERROR ALERT

When you identify a three-dimensional figure, be sure to look at the shapes of the faces.

Try It

Name the solid figure. Then tell the number of faces, edges, and vertices.

1.  

2. 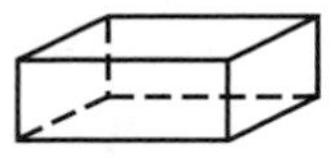

3. 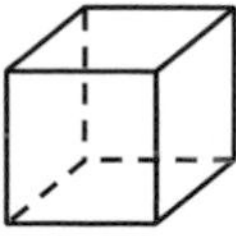

4. 

5. Read the problem below. **Explain** why B cannot be the correct answer choice. Then choose the correct answer.

COMMON ERROR

Which solid figure is the object shaped like?

A cylinder

B cube

C square pyramid

D rectangular prism

ILLINOIS

Review the Illinois Assessment Framework

Locate Points on a Grid

9.3.03 Locate and identify points using numbers and symbols on a grid, and describe how points relate to each other on a grid (e.g., ♥ is 2 units below ✪, point A is 3 units to the right of point B).

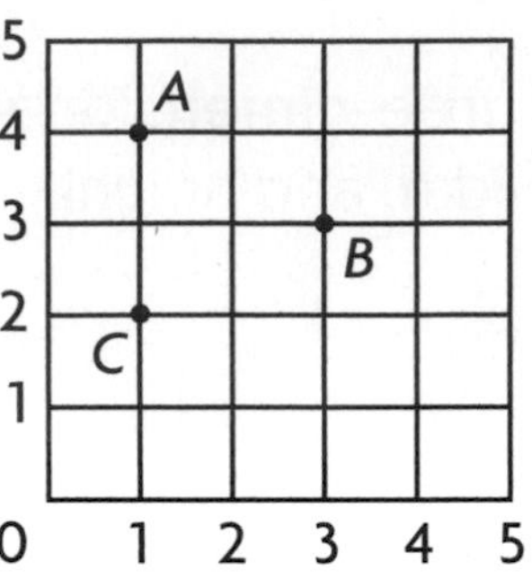

A grid is made up of horizontal and vertical lines. You can name points on a grid using ordered pairs.

The first number tells how many spaces to move from 0 to the right. The second number tells how many spaces to move up.

Point A is located at (1, 4) and is 2 units above point C.

Examples

A Which point on the grid is located at (3, 5)?

Start at 0. Move 3 units to the right. Move 5 units up.

Point D is located at (3, 5).

B What is the location of point F?

Find point F. Look at the number directly below it. Look at the number directly to the left of it.

Point F is located at (3, 3).

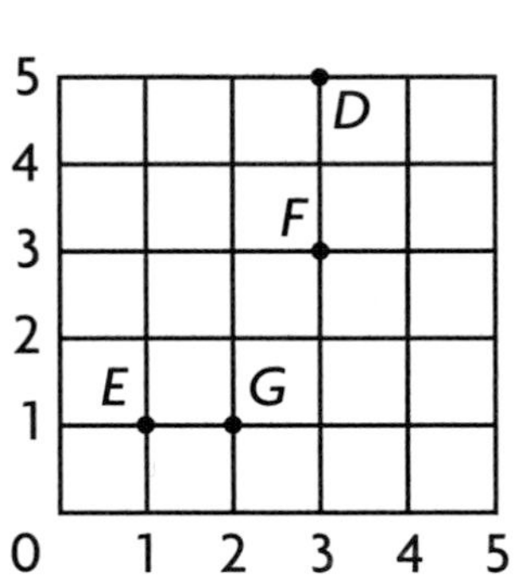

C Which point is 1 unit to the left of point G?

Find point G. Move 1 unit to the left.

Point E is located 1 unit to the left of point G.

ERROR ALERT

When you write ordered pairs, be sure to write the horizontal position before the vertical position.

Try It

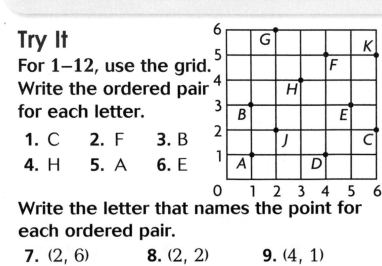

For 1–12, use the grid. Write the ordered pair for each letter.

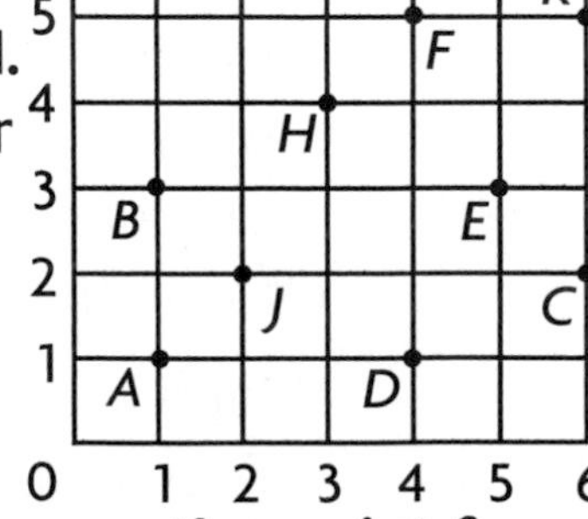

1. C **2.** F **3.** B

4. H **5.** A **6.** E

Write the letter that names the point for each ordered pair.

7. (2, 6) **8.** (2, 2) **9.** (4, 1)

10. Read the problem below. **Explain** why B cannot be the correct answer choice. Then choose the correct answer.

COMMON ERROR

What is the location of point K?

A (5, 5) **C** (6, 5)

B (5, 6) **D** (6, 6)

Review the Illinois Assessment Framework

A Line of Symmetry

9.3.04 Identify whether or not a figure has a line of symmetry, and sketch or identify the line of symmetry.

A figure has **symmetry** if it can be folded along a line so that the two halves are congruent. The line is called the line of symmetry. Some figures have no line of symmetry, and others have one or more lines of symmetry.

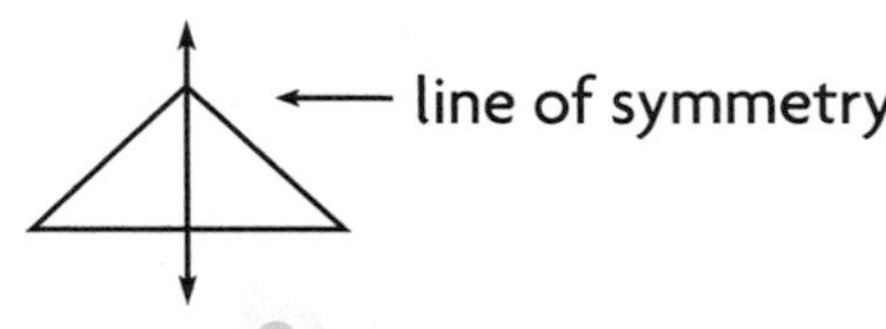

ERROR ALERT

The figures on both sides of the fold must have the exact same size and shape.

Examples

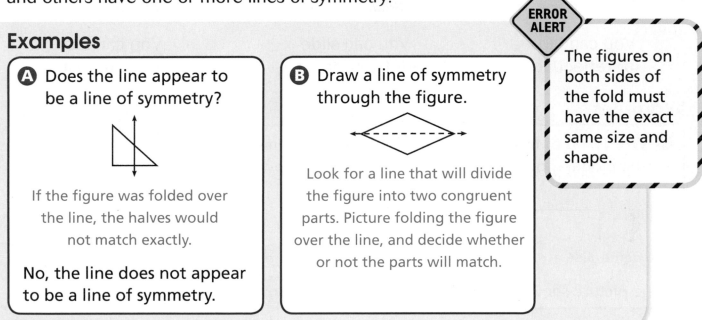

A Does the line appear to be a line of symmetry?

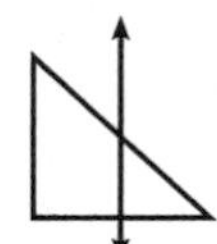

If the figure was folded over the line, the halves would not match exactly.

No, the line does not appear to be a line of symmetry.

B Draw a line of symmetry through the figure.

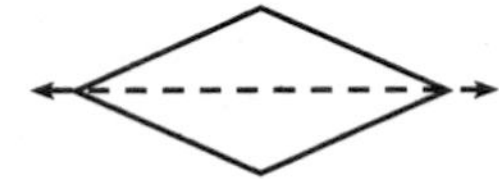

Look for a line that will divide the figure into two congruent parts. Picture folding the figure over the line, and decide whether or not the parts will match.

Try It

Tell if the figures appear to have 0, 1, or more than 1 line of symmetry.

1. 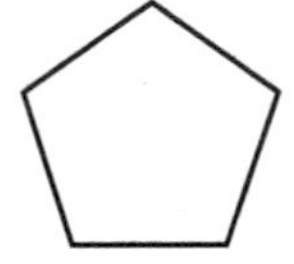

2. 

3. 

4. 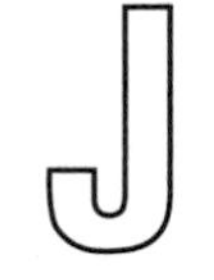

5. 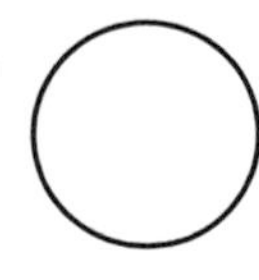

6. 

7. 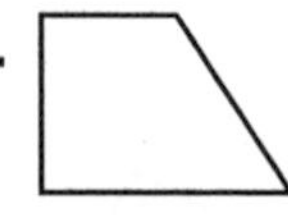

8. 

9. 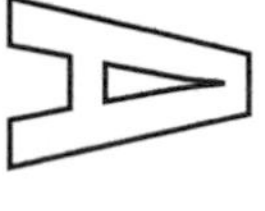

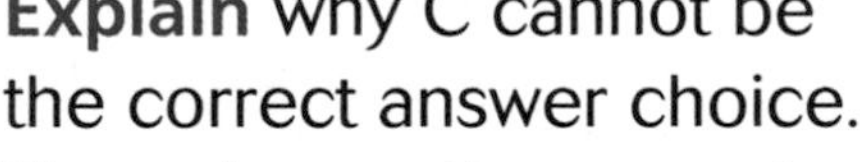

10. Read the problem below. **Explain** why C cannot be the correct answer choice. Then choose the correct answer.

How many lines of symmetry does the figure have?

A 0

B 1

C 2

D 3

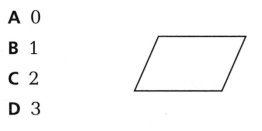

Review the Illinois Assessment Framework

Flips, Slides, and Turns

9.3.05 Identify images resulting from flips (reflections), slides (translations), or turns (rotations).

There are different ways to move a figure without changing its shape or size.

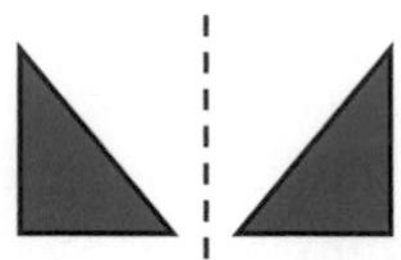

You can **flip** (or **reflect**) it.

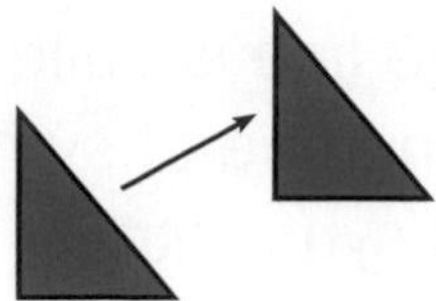

You can **slide** (or **translate**) it.

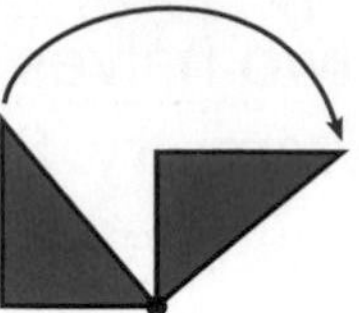

You can **turn** (or **rotate**) it.

Examples

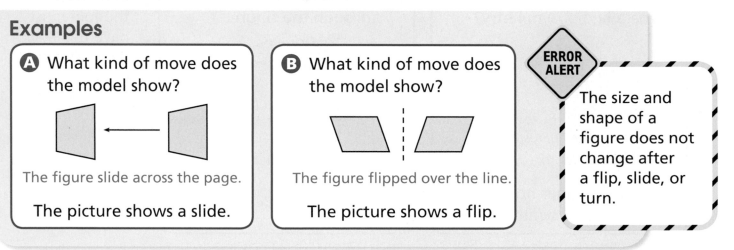

A What kind of move does the model show?

The figure slide across the page.

The picture shows a slide.

B What kind of move does the model show?

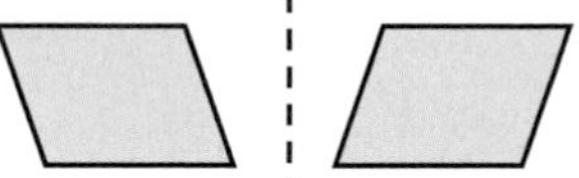

The figure flipped over the line.

The picture shows a flip.

ERROR ALERT

The size and shape of a figure does not change after a flip, slide, or turn.

Try It

Describe how each figure was moved. Write *flip*, *slide*, or *turn*.

1. 

2. 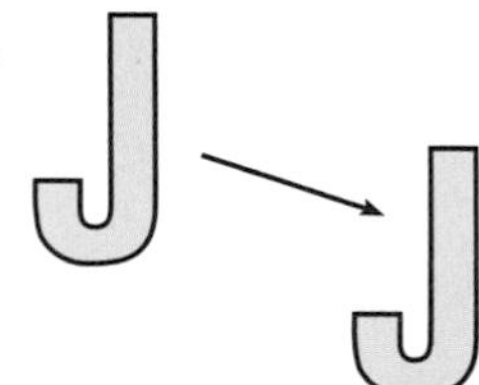

3. 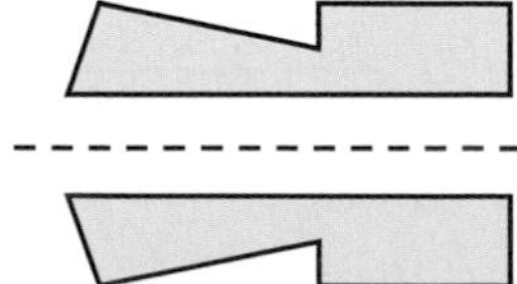

4. 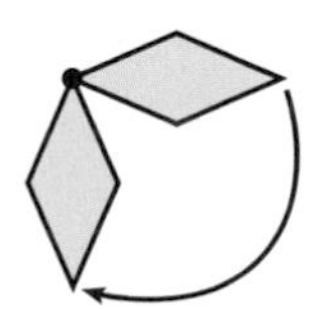

5. 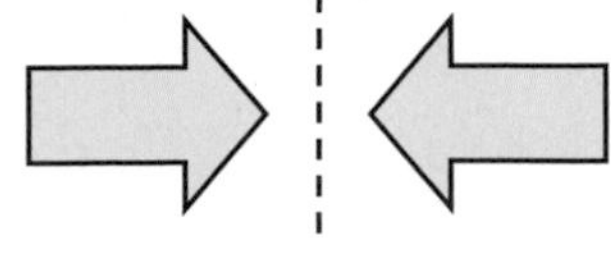

6. 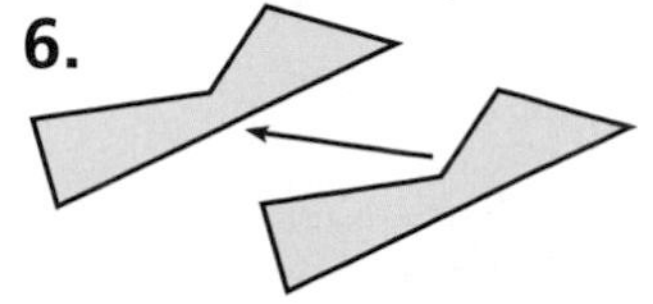

7. Read the problem below. **Explain** why A cannot be the correct answer choice. Then choose the correct answer. **COMMON ERROR**

Which shows the figure after a flip?

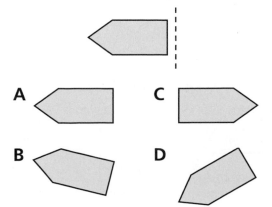

A 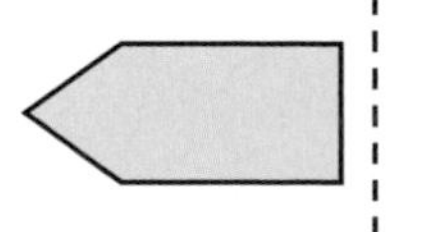

C 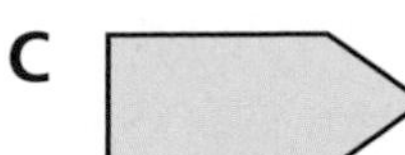

B 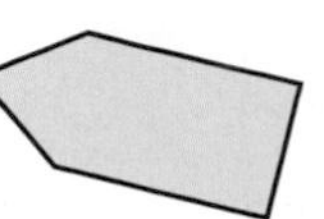

D 

Review the Illinois Assessment Framework

Parallel Lines

9.3.06 Identify parallel lines.

Parallel lines are always the same distance apart, they will never cross and they do not form any angles.

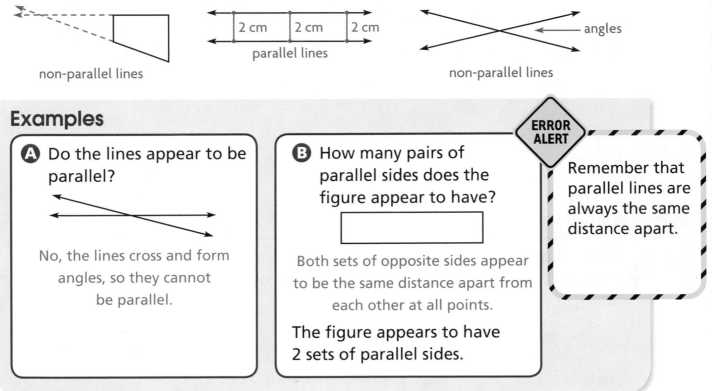

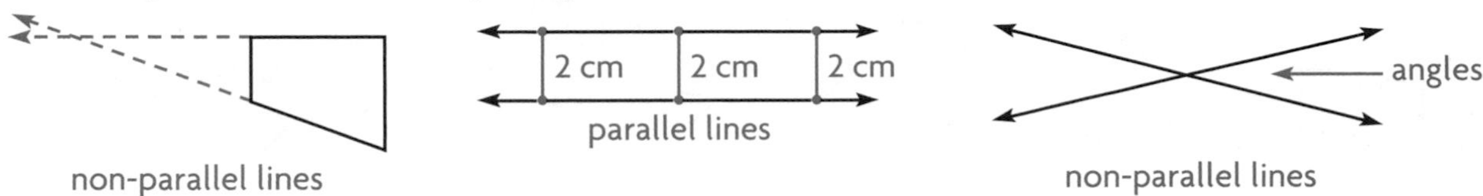

non-parallel lines

non-parallel lines

Examples

A Do the lines appear to be parallel?

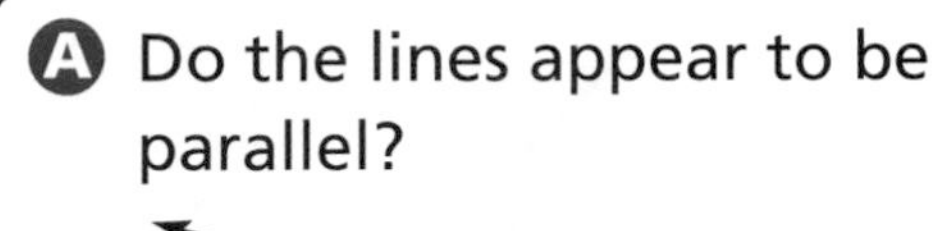

No, the lines cross and form angles, so they cannot be parallel.

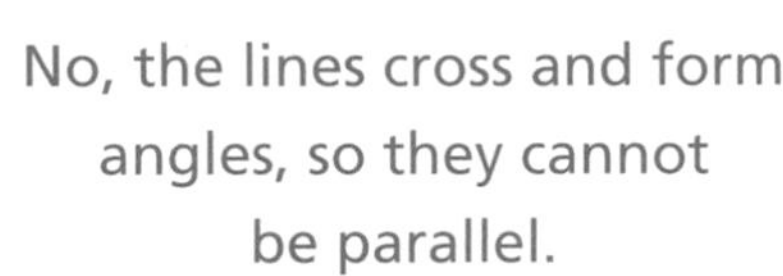

B How many pairs of parallel sides does the figure appear to have?

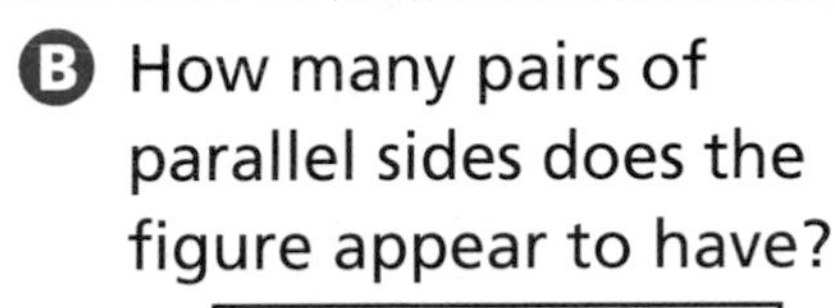

Both sets of opposite sides appear to be the same distance apart from each other at all points.

The figure appears to have 2 sets of parallel sides.

Remember that parallel lines are always the same distance apart.

Try It

Do the lines appear to be parallel? Write *yes* or *no*.

1.

2. **3.**

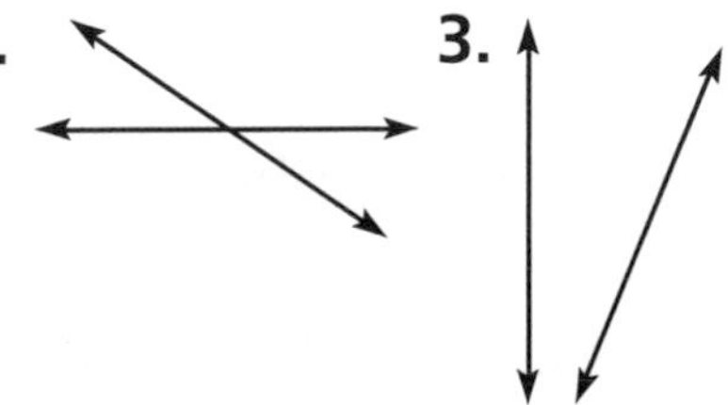

Write 0, 1, or 2 to tell how many pairs of parallel sides each figure appears to have.

4.

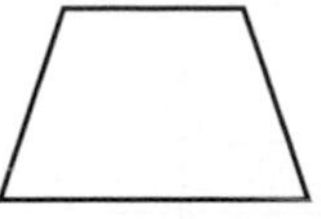

5.

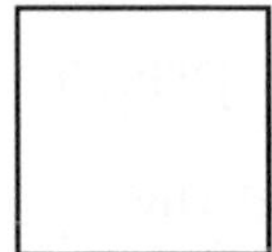

6.

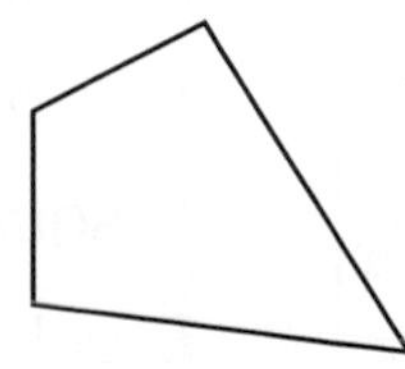

7. Read the problem below. **Explain** why B cannot be the correct answer choice. Then choose the correct answer.

COMMON ERROR

Which set of lines appears to be parallel?

A

C

B

D

Review the Illinois Assessment Framework

Nets

9.3.08 Identify a three-dimensional object from its net.

A net is a two-dimensional pattern of a solid figure. A net is what a solid figure would looks like if you unfolded all the sides and lay them flat.

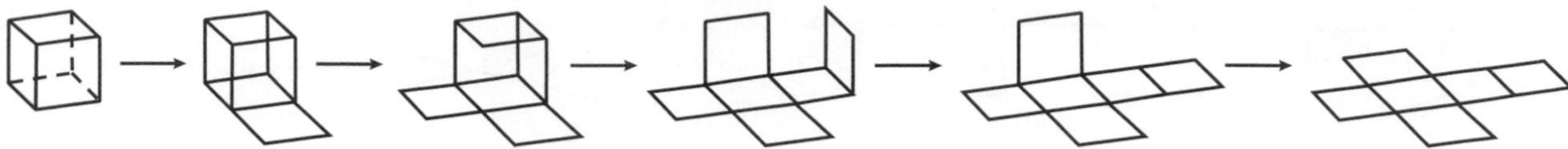

When you unfold a cube, the top view of the net looks like this:

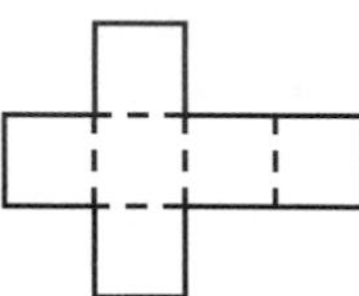

The sides of the cube are all squares, so the net is made up of squares.

ERROR ALERT

Be sure to use the plane shapes of the faces to help you decide what solid can be made from a net.

Examples

A What solid figure can be made from the net?

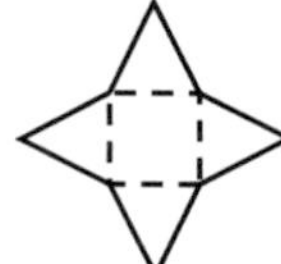

The net is made up of 4 triangles and 1 square

A square pyramid can be made from the net.

B What solid figure can be made from the net?

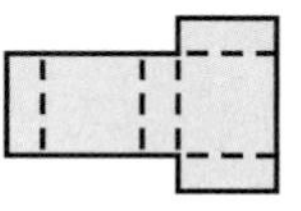

The net is made up of 6 rectangles.

A rectangular prism can be made from the net.

Try It

Identify the solid figure that can be made from each net.

1. 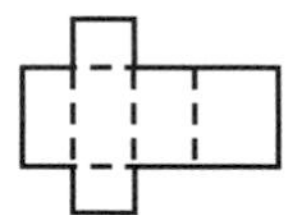

2. 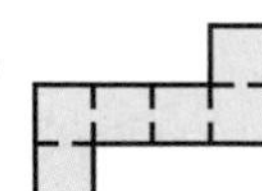

3. 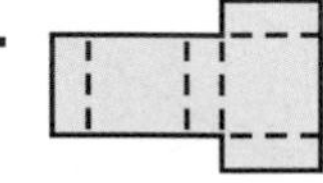

4. 

5. Read the problem below. **Explain** why C cannot be the correct answer choice. Then choose the correct answer.

Which figure can be made from the net?

A cylinder

B rectangular prism

C square pyramid

D cube

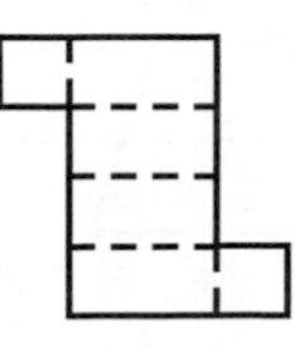

Review the Illinois Assessment Framework

Congruence and Similarity

9.3.10 Identify congruent and similar figures by visual inspection.

Congruent figures have the same shape and size.

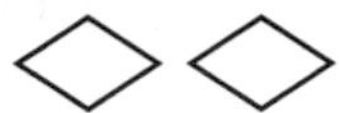

Congruent

The figures have the same shape and the same size.

Not Congruent

The figures have the same shape, but not the same size.

Similar figures have the same shape but may not have the same size.

Similar

The figures have the same shape, but not the same size.

Not Similar

The figures have the same size, but not the same shape.

Examples

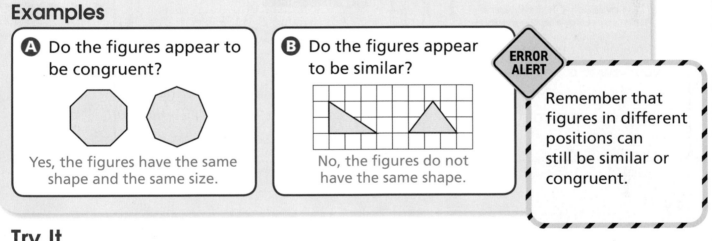

A Do the figures appear to be congruent?

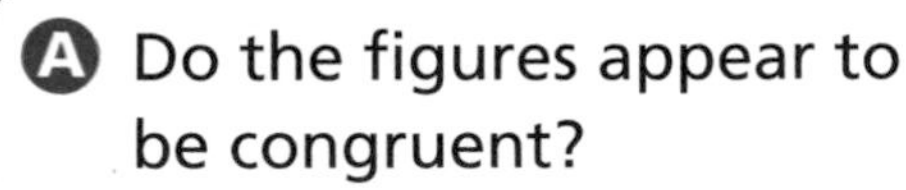

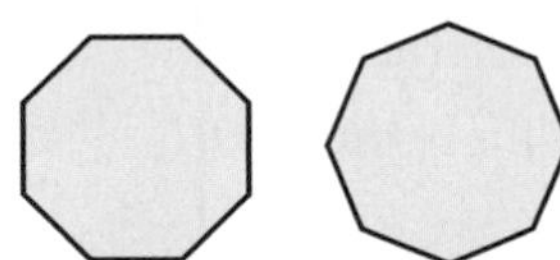

Yes, the figures have the same shape and the same size.

B Do the figures appear to be similar?

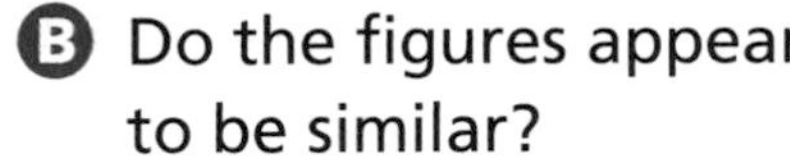

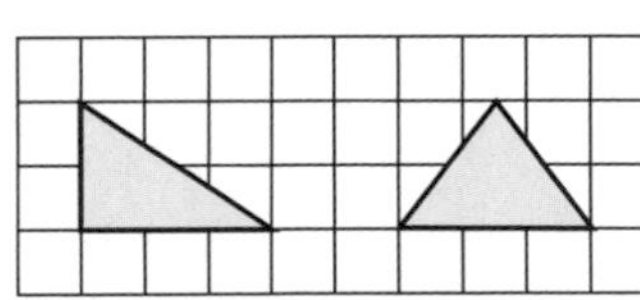

No, the figures do not have the same shape.

ERROR ALERT

Remember that figures in different positions can still be similar or congruent.

Try It

Tell if the figures appear to be congruent. Write *yes* or *no*.

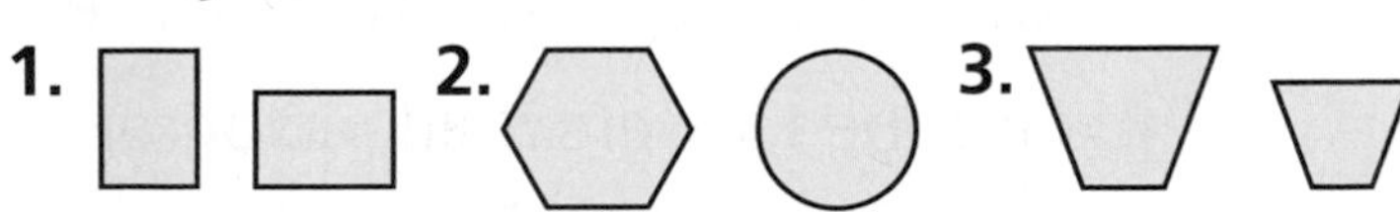

1.

2.

3.

Tell if the figures appear to be similar. Write *yes* or *no*.

4. 

5. 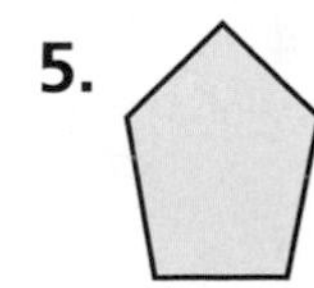 

6. Read the problem below. **Explain** why B cannot be the correct answer choice. Then choose the correct answer.

COMMON ERROR

Which is similar to the figure below?

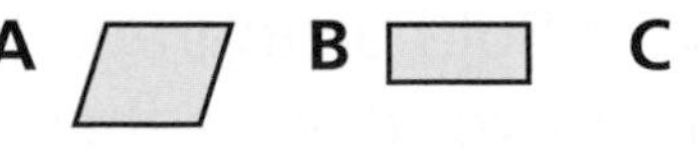

A

B

C 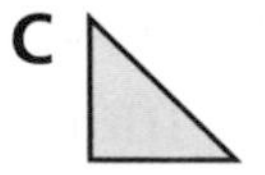

D 

Review the Illinois Assessment Framework

Read and Interpret Data

10.3.01 Read and interpret data represented in a pictograph, bar graph, Venn diagram (with two circles), tally chart, or table.

Flowers Sold	
Flower	**Number**
Rose	20
Tulip	28
Daisy	12

Charts, graphs, tables, and diagrams are all different ways to organize and display data.

This table shows the number of flowers sold at a school flower sale. The graphs on this page show the data from the table in different ways.

Examples

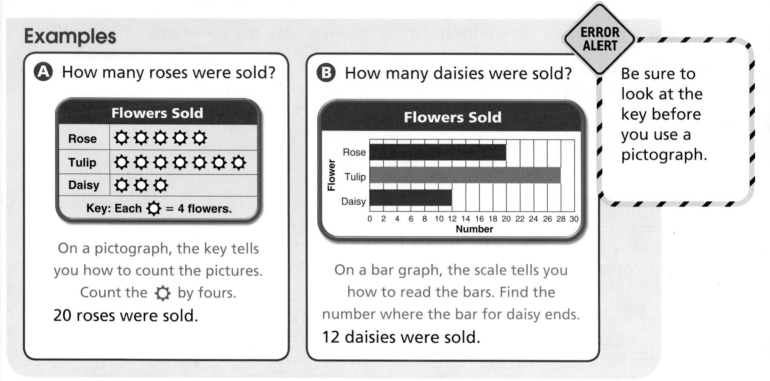

A How many roses were sold?

Flowers Sold	
Rose	
Tulip	
Daisy	
Key: Each = 4 flowers.	

On a pictograph, the key tells you how to count the pictures. Count the by fours.

20 roses were sold.

B How many daisies were sold?

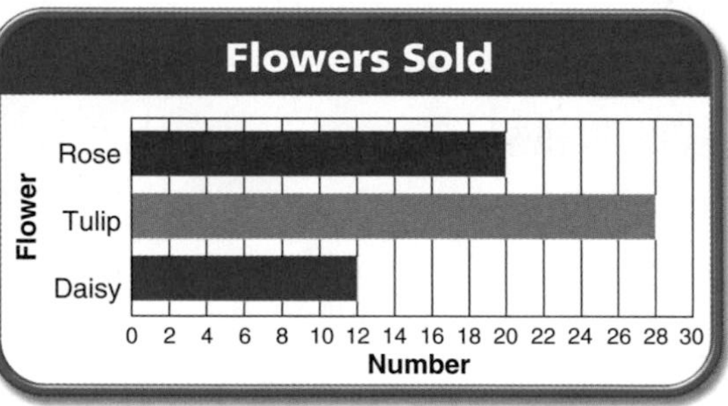

On a bar graph, the scale tells you how to read the bars. Find the number where the bar for daisy ends.

12 daisies were sold.

ERROR ALERT

Be sure to look at the key before you use a pictograph.

Try It

For 1–2, use the Flowers Sold bar graph.

1. Which flower had the lowest sales?
2. Which flower had the highest sales?

For 3–4, use the Flowers Sold table.

3. How many more roses than daisies were sold?
4. How many flowers were sold altogether?
5. Use the Flowers Sold pictograph to find how many fewer daisies than tulips were sold.
6. Read the problem below. **Explain** why A cannot be the correct answer choice. Then choose the correct answer.

COMMON ERROR

Use the Flowers Sold pictograph. How many more tulips than roses were sold?

A 2 **C** 8
B 4 **D** 12

Review the Illinois Assessment Framework

Mode

10.3.03 Determine the mode, given a set of data or a graph.

The **mode** is the number or item found most often in a set of data.

This set of data is shown in a list. It shows a student's test scores.
91, 88, 87, 92, 91, 86, 91, 88, 92

The score 91 appears most often (3), and is the mode.

ERROR ALERT Remember that the mode tells the number or item that appears most often, not the number of times it appears.

Examples

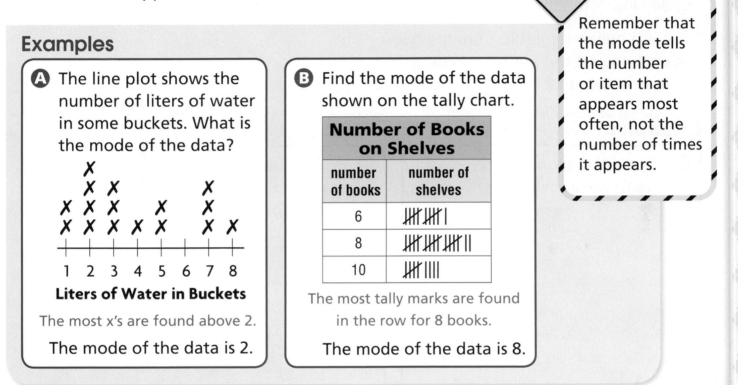

A The line plot shows the number of liters of water in some buckets. What is the mode of the data?

Liters	1	2	3	4	5	6	7	8
X's	XX	XXXX	XXX	X	XX		XXX	X

Liters of Water in Buckets

The most x's are found above 2.

The mode of the data is 2.

B Find the mode of the data shown on the tally chart.

Number of Books on Shelves

number of books	number of shelves
6	卌 卌 |
8	卌 卌 卌 ||
10	卌 ||||

The most tally marks are found in the row for 8 books.

The mode of the data is 8.

Try It

Find the mode of each set of data.

1. 131, 134, 133, 133, 132, 135, 131, 133, 134

2. 2, 4, 6, 7, 4, 7, 7, 8, 4, 2, 6, 4, 7, 2, 6, 6, 4, 8

3. 96, 92, 91, 92, 95, 95, 92, 95, 98, 96, 91, 95

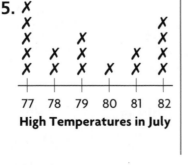

4. **Inches of Snow in Blizzards**

number of inches	number of blizzards
42	卌 卌 ||
43	卌 卌 |||
44	卌 卌 卌 |

5.

Temperature	77	78	79	80	81	82
X's	XXXXX	XX	XXX	X	XX	XXXX

High Temperatures in July

6. Read the problem below. **Explain** why A cannot be the correct answer choice. Then choose the correct answer. **COMMON ERROR**

Which shows the mode of the data?

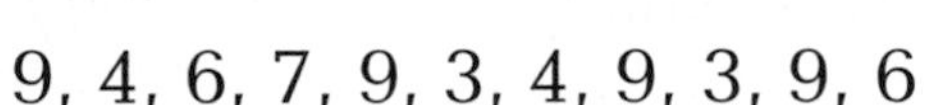
9, 4, 6, 7, 9, 3, 4, 9, 3, 9, 6

A 4

B 6

C 7

D 9

Review the Illinois Assessment Framework

Likelihood

10.3.04 Classify events using words such as certain, most likely, equally likely, least likely, possible, and impossible.

An event is something that happens, like pulling one marble from a bag. **Most likely** means it has a good chance of happening. **Least likely** means it does not have a good chance of happening. **Possible** means it has a chance of happening. **Equally likely** means it has an equal chance of happening.

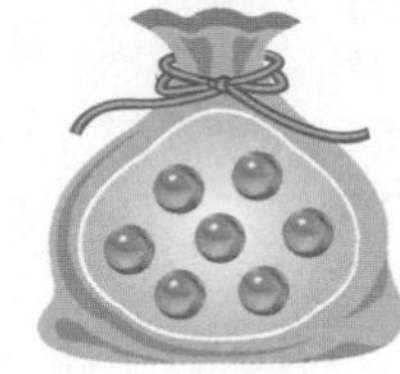

All of the marbles in the bag are green. None of the marbles in the bag are orange.

Greg will pull one marble from the bag.
It is **certain** that the marble will be green.
It is **impossible** that the marble will be orange.

Examples

A Britt will pull one marble. Which events are equally likely?

There are an equal number of red marbles and yellow marbles in the bag. Each has the same chance of being pulled.

Pulling a red marble and pulling a yellow marble are equally likely.

B How would you best describe the likelihood of pulling a red marble?

Most of the marbles in the bag are red. Pulling a red marble is most likely. Pulling a blue marble is least likely.

Pulling a red marble is a likely event.

ERROR ALERT

For an event to be certain, it must be the only possible event.

Try It

For 1–4, use the bag of marbles.

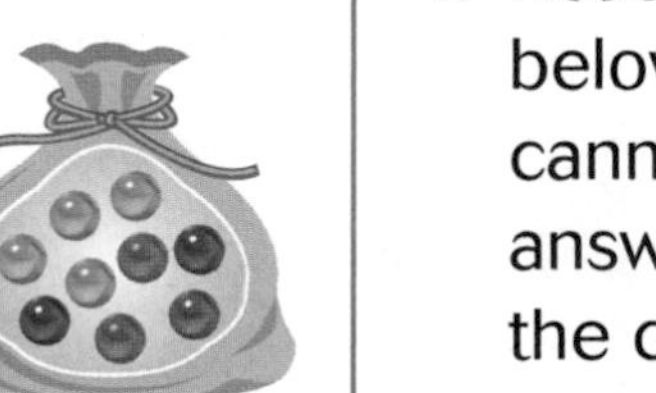

1. Liz will pull one marble. Which two events are equally likely?
2. Theo will pull one marble. What is an impossible event?
3. Sarah will pull one marble. Which marble is most likely to be pulled?
4. Read the problem below. **Explain** why D cannot be the correct answer choice. Then choose the correct answer.

   COMMON ERROR

   Which is the likelihood of pulling a blue marble?

   A impossible **C** most likely
   B least likely **D** certain

Review the Illinois Assessment Framework

Probability and Chance

10.3.05 Describe the chances associated with a context presented visually, including using the response format "3 out of 4."

An **outcome** is the possible result of an event. You can name the chance that a specific outcome will be the result of a single event.

Each section on the spinner is one possible result of one spin. There are 4 equal sized sections. Of those four sections, 2 are circles.

So, the chance of spinning a circle is 2 out of 4.

Examples

A Laurie will spin the spinner. What is the chance that the outcome will be blue?

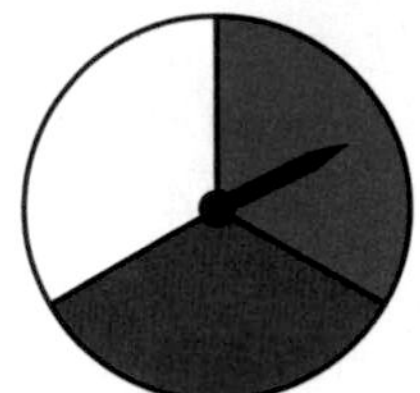

There are 3 equal sized sections.
There is 1 blue section.

The chance of spinning blue is 1 out of 3.

B Jim will pull one marble from the bag. What is the chance that the marble will be yellow?

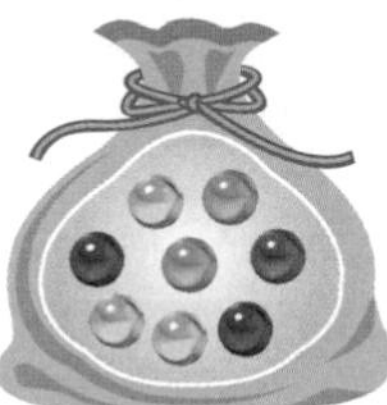

There are 8 marbles in the bag.
There are 3 yellow marbles.

The chance of pulling a yellow marble is 3 out of 8.

ERROR ALERT

When you name the chance of a certain outcome, be sure it is out of the total number of possible outcomes.

Try It

Name the chance of each outcome.
For 1–5, use the spinner.

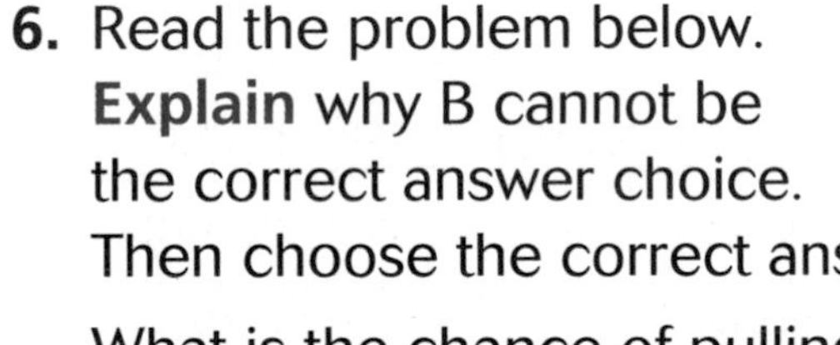

1. spinning yellow
2. spinning white
3. spinning green
4. spinning white or yellow
5. spinning white, yellow, or green

6. Read the problem below. **Explain** why B cannot be the correct answer choice. Then choose the correct answer. **COMMON ERROR**

   What is the chance of pulling a green marble?

   A 1 out of 2
   B 2 out of 6
   C 2 out of 8
   D 6 out of 8

ISAT Test-Taking Strategies

Tips for Taking Math Tests

Being a good test-taker is like being a good problem solver. When you answer test questions, you are solving problems. Remember to UNDERSTAND, PLAN, SOLVE, AND CHECK.

Read to Understand

Read the problem.

- Look for math terms and recall their meanings.
- Reread the problem and think about the question.
- Use the details in the problem and the question.

1

The product of two numbers is 24. One factor is even and one factor is odd. Both factors have one digit. What are the factors?

Ⓐ 1×24 Ⓒ 3×8
Ⓑ 2×12 Ⓓ 4×6

Test Tip **Understand the problem.**

Remember the meanings of *product, factor, even, odd,* and *digit*. Since all choices have a product of 24, look for the choices that have one odd and one even 1-digit number. The answer is **C**.

- Each word is important. Missing a word or reading it incorrectly could cause you to get the wrong answer.
- Pay attention to words that are in **bold** type, all CAPITAL letters, or *italics*.
- Some other words to look for are *round*, *about*, *only*, *best*, or *least to greatest*.

2

Which figure does NOT have $\frac{1}{2}$ shaded?

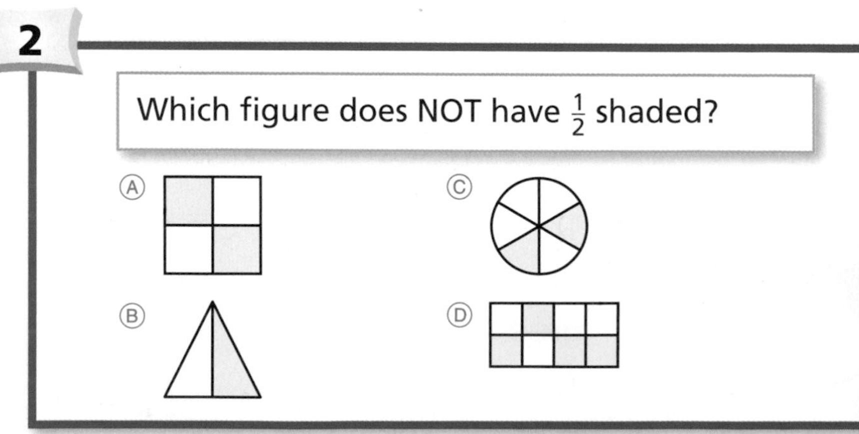

Test Tip **Look for important words.**

The word NOT is important. Without the word NOT, the answers would be A, B, and D. The answer is **C**.

Plan

Think about how you can solve the problem.

- See if you can solve the problem with the information given.
- Pictures, charts, tables, and graphs may have the information you need.
- You may need to think about information you already know.
- The answer choices may have the information you need.

3

How many more girls than boys chose soccer as their favorite sport?

Favorite Sport		
	Boys	**Girls**
Soccer	4	6
Baseball	8	3

Ⓐ 2　　Ⓒ 4

Ⓑ 3　　Ⓓ 5

Test Tip **Get the information you need.**

Use the table to find how many girls and boys chose soccer. Find the difference by subtracting. The answer is **A**.

- You may need to write a number sentence and solve it.
- Some problems have two steps or more.
- In some problems you need to look at relationships instead of computing an answer.
- If the path to the solution isn't clear, choose a problem solving strategy and use it to solve the problem.

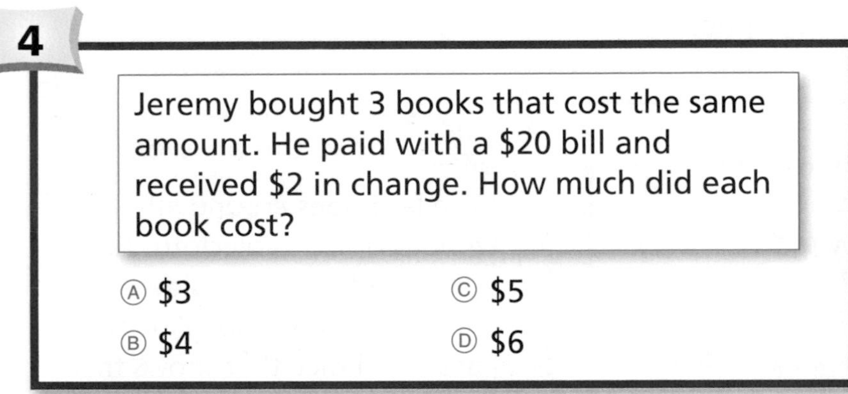

4

Jeremy bought 3 books that cost the same amount. He paid with a $20 bill and received $2 in change. How much did each book cost?

Ⓐ $3　　Ⓒ $5

Ⓑ $4　　Ⓓ $6

Test Tip **Decide on a plan.**

Begin with the amount of change. Subtract the change from $20. Then divide the difference by 3 to find how much each book cost. The answer is **D**.

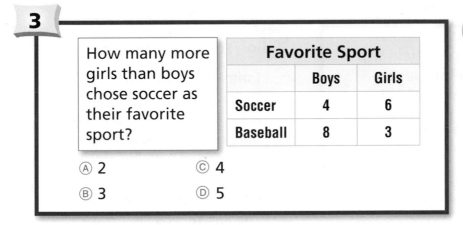

Solve

Follow your plan, working logically and carefully.

- Estimate your answer. Look for unreasonable answer choices.
- Use reasoning to find the most likely choices.
- Solve all steps needed to answer the problem.
- If your answer does not match any answer choice, check your numbers and your computation.

5

Third-grade students went on a field trip on 6 buses. Each bus held 68 students. How many students went on the field trip?

Ⓐ 74 Ⓒ 420

Ⓑ 408 Ⓓ 3,400

Test Tip **Eliminate choices.**

Estimate the product (6×70). The only reasonable answers are B and C. Since 6 times the ones digit 8 is 48, the answer must end in 8. If you are still not certain, multiply and check your answer against B and C. The answer is **B**.

- If your answer still does not match, look for another form of the number, such as a decimal instead of a fraction.
- If answer choices are given as pictures, look at each one by itself while you cover the other three.
- Read answer choices that are statements and relate them to the problem one by one.
- If your strategy isn't working, try a different one.

6

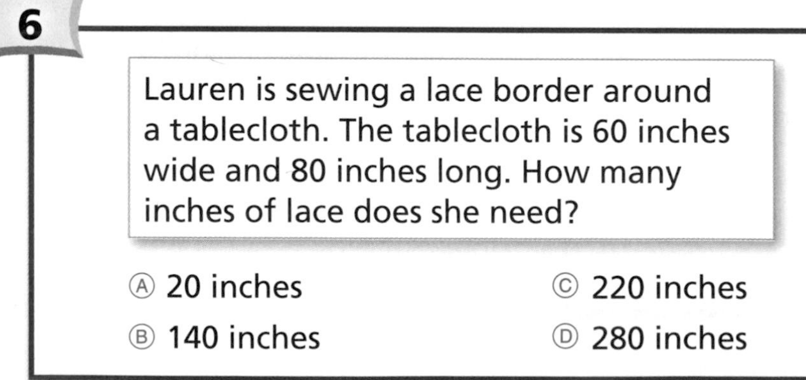

Lauren is sewing a lace border around a tablecloth. The tablecloth is 60 inches wide and 80 inches long. How many inches of lace does she need?

Ⓐ 20 inches Ⓒ 220 inches

Ⓑ 140 inches Ⓓ 280 inches

Test Tip **Choose the answer.**

The lace goes around all 4 sides of the tablecloth. Add the lengths of the 4 sides ($60 + 80 + 60 + 80$). Find the answer choice that shows this sum. The answer is **D**.

Check

Take time to catch your mistakes.

- Be sure you answered the question asked.
- Check for important words you might have missed.
- Did you use all the information you needed?
- Check your computation by using a different method.
- Draw a picture when you are unsure of your answer.

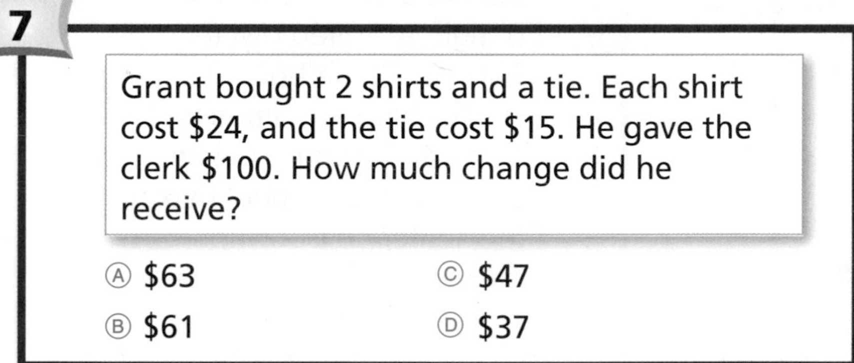

7

Grant bought 2 shirts and a tie. Each shirt cost $24, and the tie cost $15. He gave the clerk $100. How much change did he receive?

Ⓐ $63
Ⓑ $61
Ⓒ $47
Ⓓ $37

Test Tip **Check your work.**

Be sure to find the total cost of both shirts ($2 \times \$24$). Then add the cost of the tie ($\$48 + \$15$) before you subtract. The correct answer is **D**.

Tips for Short-Answer and Extended-Response Items

- Plan to spend from 3 to 5 minutes on each Short-Answer item and from 5 to 15 minutes on each Extended-Response item.
- Read the problem carefully and think about what you are asked to do. Plan how to organize your response.
- Short-Answer items will ask you to find a solution to a problem. Extended-Response items will ask you to use problem solving and reasoning skills to apply something you have learned.
- Think about how you solved the problem. You may be asked to use words, numbers, or pictures to explain how you found your answer.
- Leave time to look back at the problem, check your answer, and correct any mistakes.

Getting Ready for the ISAT

Number Sense

Choose the correct answer.

1

The population of Long Point, IL is 247. What is 247 written in word form?
IL 6.3.02

Ⓐ twenty-four seven
Ⓑ two hundred four seven
Ⓒ two hundred forty-seven
Ⓓ two four-seven

2

The John Hancock Center in Chicago is 1,128 feet tall. The Park Tower is 843 feet tall. Compare the heights of the buildings. What symbol makes the sentence true?
IL 6.3.05

1,128 ● 843

Ⓐ $>$
Ⓑ $<$
Ⓒ $=$
Ⓓ $\div$

3

Erin drove 58 miles from Clinton, IL to Springfield, IL. Erin then drove back to Clinton, IL. How many total miles did Erin drive? IL 6.3.09

Ⓐ 116 miles
Ⓑ 117 miles
Ⓒ 173 miles
Ⓓ 174 miles

4

Alexandra and Portia went to the Field Museum of Natural History. They went to the gift shop and Alexandra bought a stuffed owl for \$40.28. Portia bought a stuffed hippopotamus for \$67.84. Compare the amounts spent. Which symbol makes the sentence true? IL 6.3.06

\$40.28 ● \$67.84

Ⓐ $>$
Ⓑ $<$
Ⓒ $=$
Ⓓ $\div$

5

Michael went on a nature hike and collected 15 leaves. Eight of them were maple leaves and the rest were elm leaves. Which related number sentence can Michael use to solve the problem? IL 6.3.12

$8 + \blacksquare = 15$

Ⓐ $15 + 8 = 23$
Ⓑ $8 - 5 = 3$
Ⓒ $8 + 8 = 16$
Ⓓ $15 - 8 = 7$

6

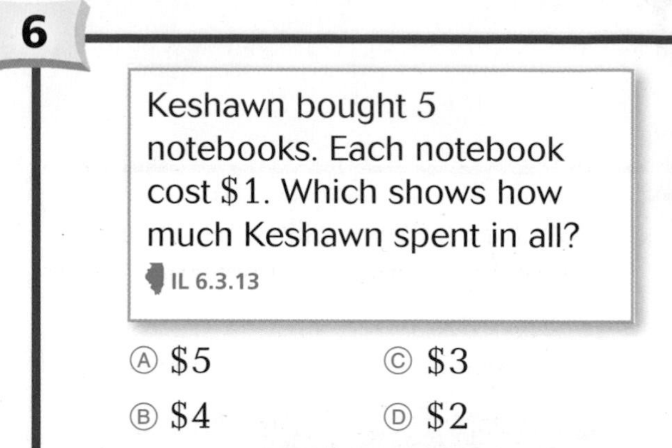

Keshawn bought 5 notebooks. Each notebook cost $1. Which shows how much Keshawn spent in all? IL 6.3.13

Ⓐ $5
Ⓑ $4
Ⓒ $3
Ⓓ $2

7

Tina painted sections of the canvas green. Which names the fraction of the canvas that Tina painted? IL 6.3.03

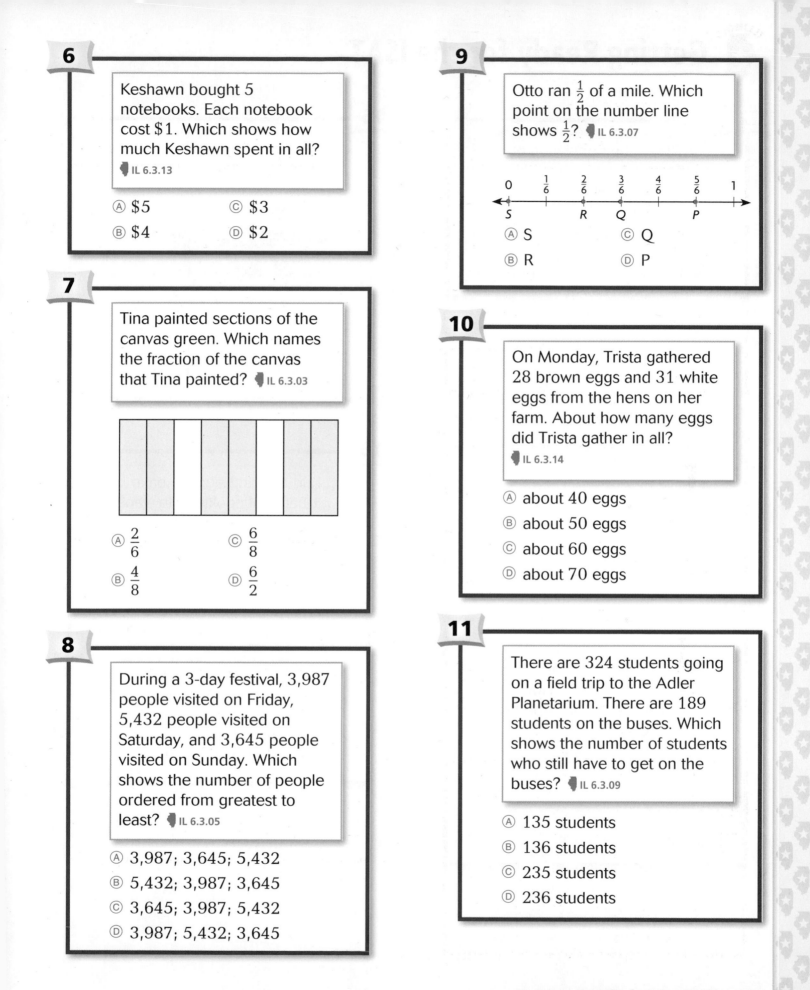

Ⓐ $\frac{2}{6}$
Ⓑ $\frac{4}{8}$
Ⓒ $\frac{6}{8}$
Ⓓ $\frac{6}{2}$

8

During a 3-day festival, 3,987 people visited on Friday, 5,432 people visited on Saturday, and 3,645 people visited on Sunday. Which shows the number of people ordered from greatest to least? IL 6.3.05

Ⓐ 3,987; 3,645; 5,432
Ⓑ 5,432; 3,987; 3,645
Ⓒ 3,645; 3,987; 5,432
Ⓓ 3,987; 5,432; 3,645

9

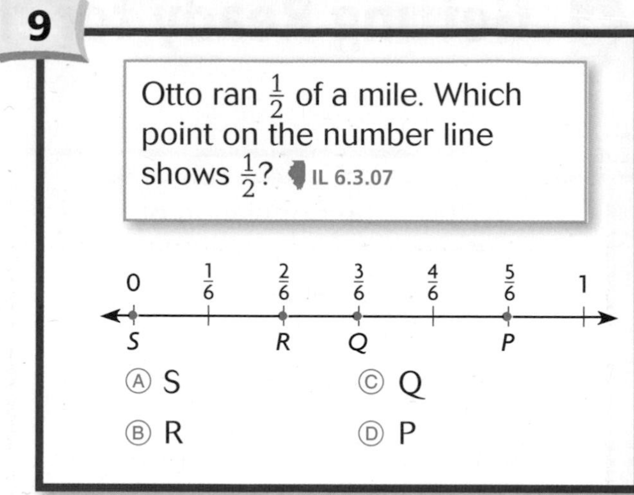

Otto ran $\frac{1}{2}$ of a mile. Which point on the number line shows $\frac{1}{2}$? IL 6.3.07

Ⓐ S
Ⓑ R
Ⓒ Q
Ⓓ P

10

On Monday, Trista gathered 28 brown eggs and 31 white eggs from the hens on her farm. About how many eggs did Trista gather in all? IL 6.3.14

Ⓐ about 40 eggs
Ⓑ about 50 eggs
Ⓒ about 60 eggs
Ⓓ about 70 eggs

11

There are 324 students going on a field trip to the Adler Planetarium. There are 189 students on the buses. Which shows the number of students who still have to get on the buses? IL 6.3.09

Ⓐ 135 students
Ⓑ 136 students
Ⓒ 235 students
Ⓓ 236 students

Getting Ready for the ISAT

12

In 2000, the population of Effingham, IL, was 12,384. What is the value of the digit 1 in 12,384? IL 6.3.01

Ⓐ 100
Ⓑ 1,000
Ⓒ 10,000
Ⓓ 100,000

13

Carla's family made 3 different kinds of tortillas for the fair. They made 200 of each kind. How many tortillas did Carla's family make? IL 6.3.11

Ⓐ 6,000
Ⓑ 600
Ⓒ 500
Ⓓ 60

14

The point on the number line shows how many miles Aris has ridden his bike. How many miles did Aris ride his bike? IL 6.3.07

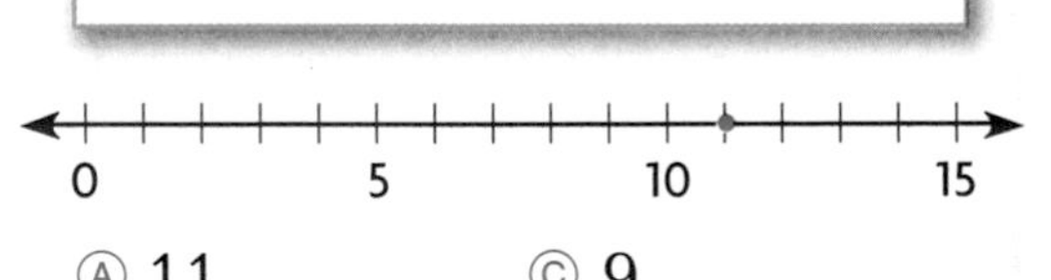

Ⓐ 11
Ⓑ 10
Ⓒ 9
Ⓓ 8

15

Kayla has these bills and coins. How much money does she have? IL 6.3.10

Ⓐ $2.51
Ⓑ $2.76
Ⓒ $2.59
Ⓓ $3.01

16

Kurt needs 2 eggs to bake 1 batch of cookies. He wants to bake 5 batches of cookies. Which addition sentence can Kurt use to solve the multiplication sentence? IL 6.3.04

$2 \times 5 = \blacksquare$

Ⓐ $2 + 5 = 7$
Ⓑ $5 + 5 + 5 + 5 + 5 = 25$
Ⓒ $2 + 2 = 4$
Ⓓ $2 + 2 + 2 + 2 + 2 = 10$

Algebra

Choose the correct answer.

1

A park ranger sold 38 passes to Apple River Canyon State Park in the morning and some more passes in the afternoon. She sold 94 passes in all. Which shows the number of passes the park ranger sold in the afternoon? IL 8.3.05

Ⓐ 18
Ⓑ 56
Ⓒ 76
Ⓓ 130

2

Liza's family drove 360 miles on Monday and 298 miles on Tuesday. Which expression represents the number of miles Liza's family drove? IL 8.3.02

Ⓐ 360×298
Ⓑ $298 - 360$
Ⓒ $360 + 298$
Ⓓ $360 - 298$

3

What is the missing figure in the pattern? IL 8.3.01

?

Ⓐ
Ⓑ
Ⓒ
Ⓓ

4

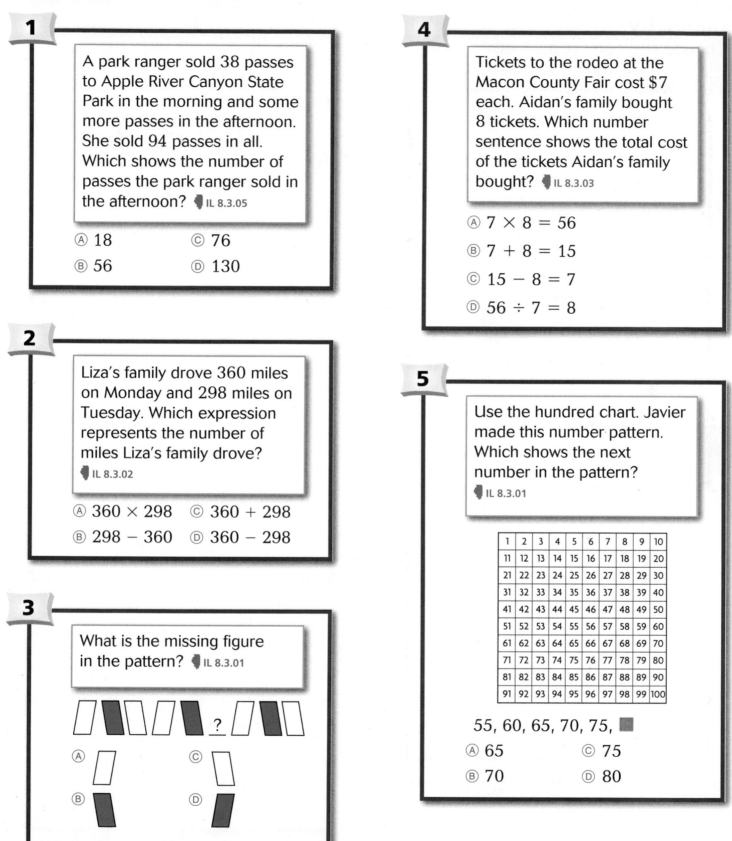

Tickets to the rodeo at the Macon County Fair cost $7 each. Aidan's family bought 8 tickets. Which number sentence shows the total cost of the tickets Aidan's family bought? IL 8.3.03

Ⓐ $7 \times 8 = 56$
Ⓑ $7 + 8 = 15$
Ⓒ $15 - 8 = 7$
Ⓓ $56 \div 7 = 8$

5

Use the hundred chart. Javier made this number pattern. Which shows the next number in the pattern? IL 8.3.01

1	2	3	4	5	6	7	8	9	10
11	12	13	14	15	16	17	18	19	20
21	22	23	24	25	26	27	28	29	30
31	32	33	34	35	36	37	38	39	40
41	42	43	44	45	46	47	48	49	50
51	52	53	54	55	56	57	58	59	60
61	62	63	64	65	66	67	68	69	70
71	72	73	74	75	76	77	78	79	80
81	82	83	84	85	86	87	88	89	90
91	92	93	94	95	96	97	98	99	100

55, 60, 65, 70, 75, ■

Ⓐ 65
Ⓑ 70
Ⓒ 75
Ⓓ 80

Getting Ready for the ISAT

Geometry

Choose the correct answer.

1

Robert drew a figure that has more than 1 line of symmetry. Which figure has more than 1 line of symmetry? IL 9.3.04

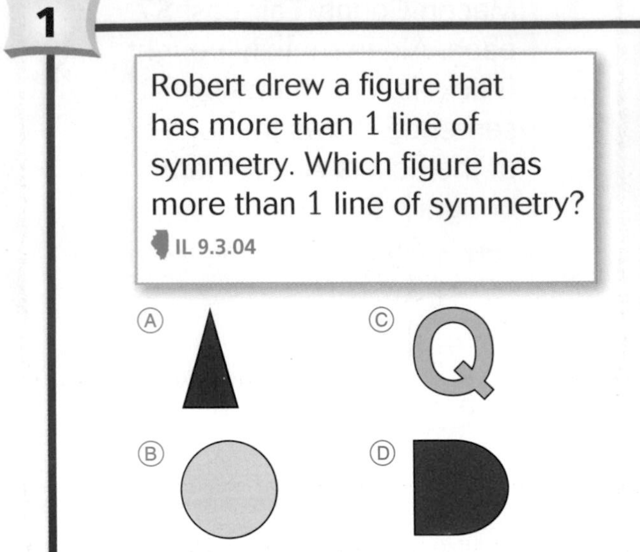

Ⓐ Ⓑ Ⓒ Ⓓ

2

Which figure is similar to the figure below? IL 9.3.10

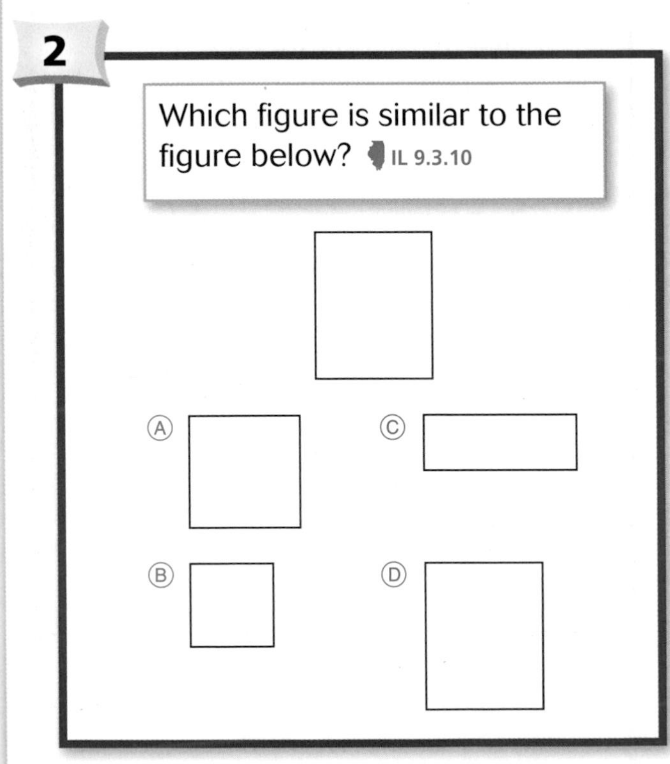

Ⓐ Ⓑ Ⓒ Ⓓ

3

What is the distance between point Q and point X? IL 9.3.11

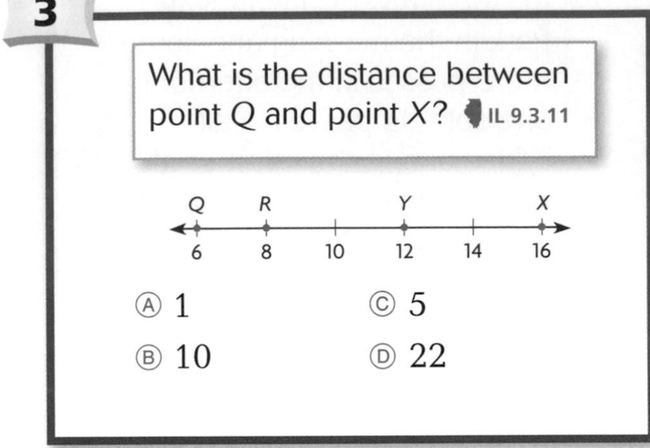

Ⓐ 1 Ⓒ 5

Ⓑ 10 Ⓓ 22

4

Breck placed a cube on a table. Which figure did Breck see when he looked at the side of the cube? IL 9.3.07

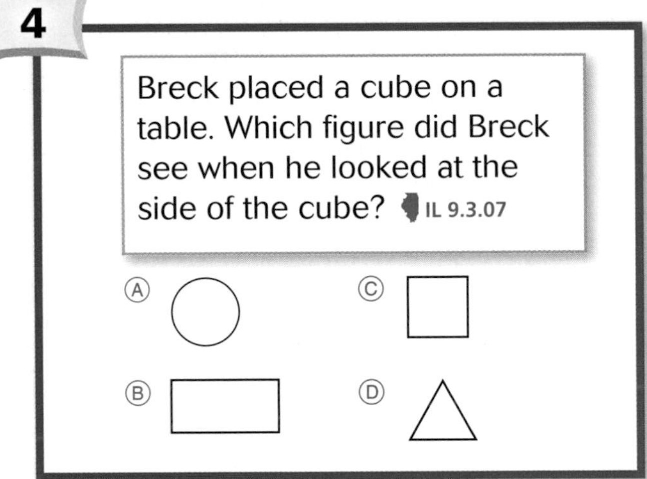

Ⓐ Ⓑ Ⓒ Ⓓ

5

Which term describes the figure? IL 9.3.01

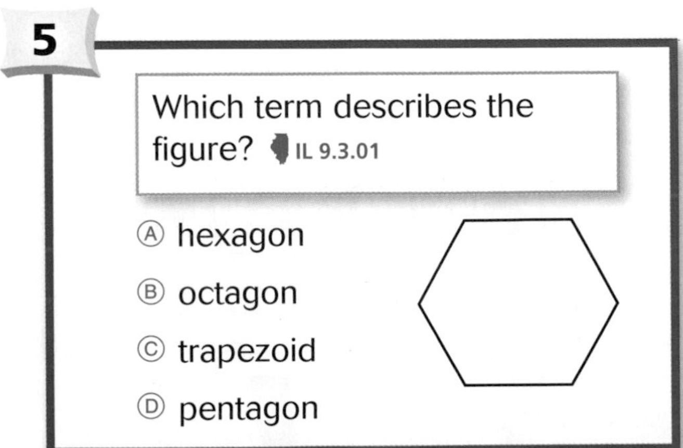

Ⓐ hexagon

Ⓑ octagon

Ⓒ trapezoid

Ⓓ pentagon

6

Connor mapped some of the streets around his house. Which pair of streets appear to be parallel? IL 9.3.06

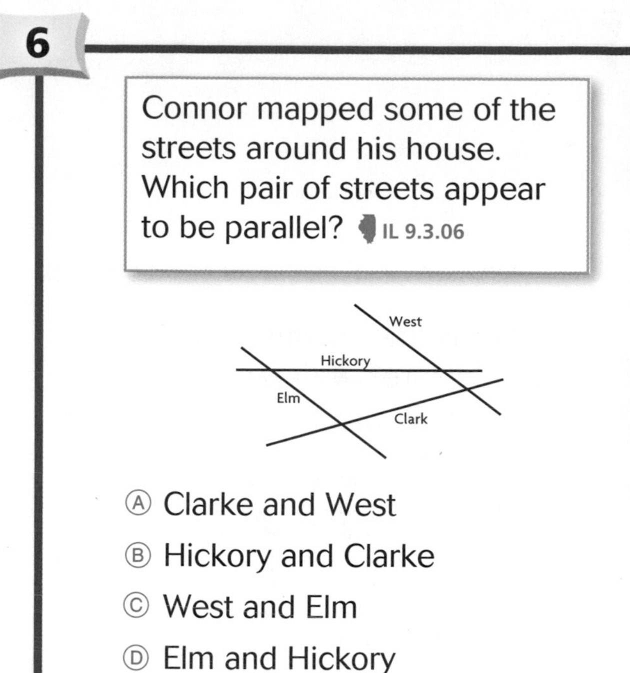

Ⓐ Clarke and West

Ⓑ Hickory and Clarke

Ⓒ West and Elm

Ⓓ Elm and Hickory

7

Tori moved the figure. Which term best describes how Tori moved the figure? IL 9.3.05

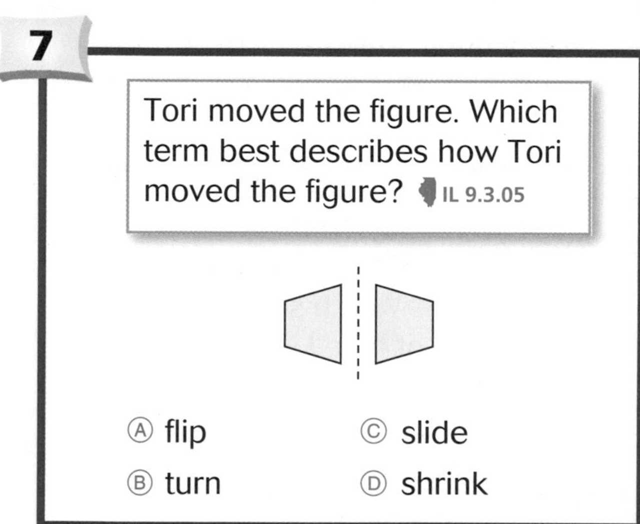

Ⓐ flip

Ⓑ turn

Ⓒ slide

Ⓓ shrink

8

An artist made a net of a solid figure. Which solid figure will the net become when folded? IL 9.3.08

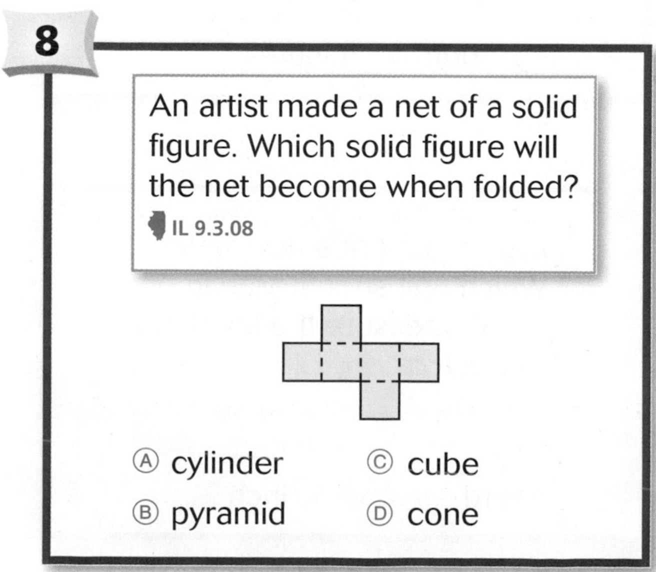

Ⓐ cylinder

Ⓑ pyramid

Ⓒ cube

Ⓓ cone

9

Logan needs shaped like a object should IL 9.3.02

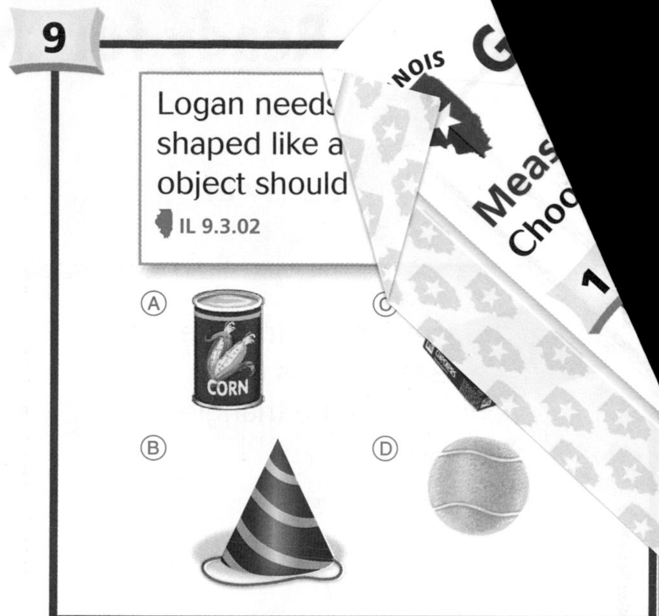

Ⓐ

Ⓑ

Ⓒ

Ⓓ

10

Gracie wants to get a book from the bookshelf. Which ordered pair names the location of the bookshelf? IL 9.3.03

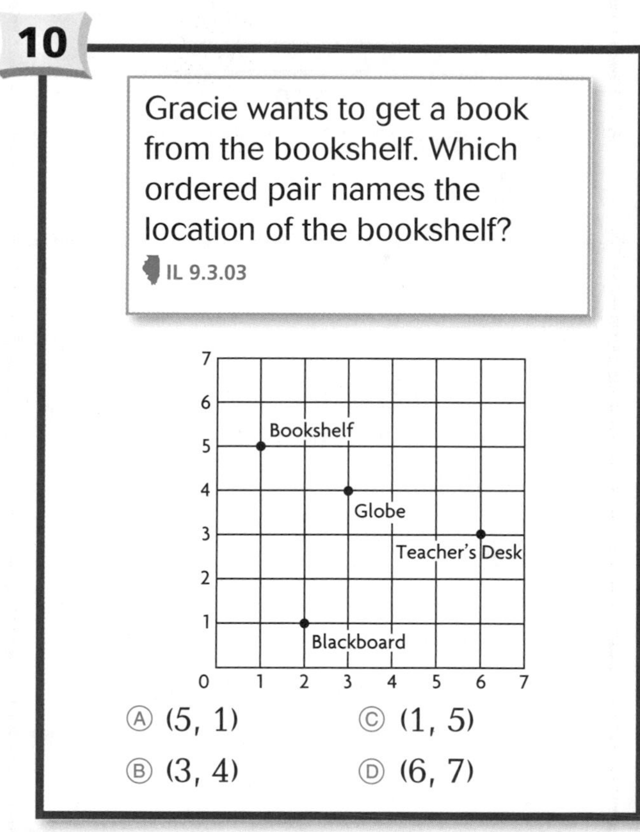

Ⓐ (5, 1)

Ⓑ (3, 4)

Ⓒ (1, 5)

Ⓓ (6, 7)

etting Ready for the ISAT

urement

se the correct answer.

Caroline cut this triangle for a collage. What is the perimeter of the triangle? IL 7.3.03

8 cm
8 cm
5 cm

Ⓐ 15 cm Ⓒ 24 cm
Ⓑ 21 cm Ⓓ 26 cm

2

Bob went to the Illinois State Fair. He was there for 5 hours. Which shows the number of minutes Bob spent at the fair? IL 7.3.07

Ⓐ 30 minutes Ⓒ 300 minutes
Ⓑ 50 minutes Ⓓ 500 minutes

3

Lila has a swimming pool in her backyard. Which is the best estimate for the length of the pool? IL 7.3.05

Ⓐ 5 cm Ⓒ 5 m
Ⓑ 5 dm Ⓓ 5 km

4

What is the volume of the solid figure? IL 7.3.06

= 1 cubic unit

Ⓐ 32 cubic units
Ⓑ 28 cubic units
Ⓒ 14 cubic units
Ⓓ 7 cubic units

5

Liam got to school at 8:45 @.L . He left school at 3:15 O.L . Which shows the amount of time Liam spent at school? IL 7.3.01

Ⓐ 5 hours 30 minutes
Ⓑ 6 hours 30 minutes
Ⓒ 7 hours 15 minutes
Ⓓ 7 hours 45 minutes

6

Marvin bought a new watch. Which unit should Marvin use to measure the length of the watch? IL 7.3.05

Ⓐ mile Ⓒ foot
Ⓑ yard Ⓓ inch

7

Adrian's family drove 9 kilometers from their house to the beach. Which shows the number of meters they drove? IL 7.3.07

Ⓐ 300 meters
Ⓑ 900 meters
Ⓒ 3,000 meters
Ⓓ 9,000 meters

8

Brian left for a track meet at 6:30 A.M. on Saturday. He returned home on Monday at 3:30 P.M. Which shows the amount of time Brian was away from home? IL 7.3.01

Ⓐ 3 days, 9 hours
Ⓑ 3 days, 3 hours
Ⓒ 2 days, 9 hours
Ⓓ 2 days, 3 hours

9

Grady used a thermometer to measure the temperature outside. What temperature is shown on the thermometer?
IL 7.3.02

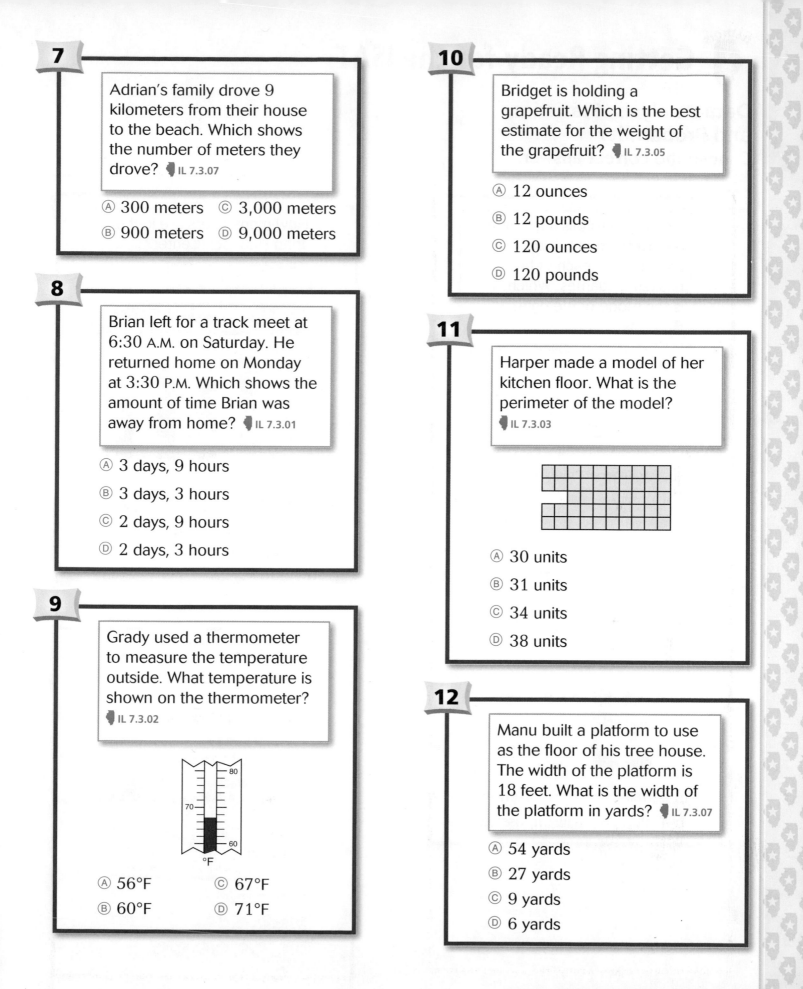

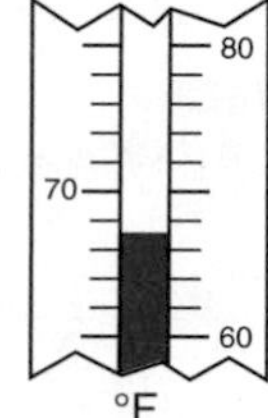

Ⓐ 56°F
Ⓑ 60°F
Ⓒ 67°F
Ⓓ 71°F

10

Bridget is holding a grapefruit. Which is the best estimate for the weight of the grapefruit? IL 7.3.05

Ⓐ 12 ounces
Ⓑ 12 pounds
Ⓒ 120 ounces
Ⓓ 120 pounds

11

Harper made a model of her kitchen floor. What is the perimeter of the model?
IL 7.3.03

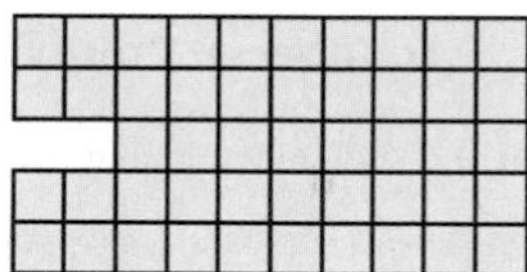

Ⓐ 30 units
Ⓑ 31 units
Ⓒ 34 units
Ⓓ 38 units

12

Manu built a platform to use as the floor of his tree house. The width of the platform is 18 feet. What is the width of the platform in yards? IL 7.3.07

Ⓐ 54 yards
Ⓑ 27 yards
Ⓒ 9 yards
Ⓓ 6 yards

Getting Ready for the ISAT

Data Analysis, Statistics, and Probability

Choose the correct answer.

1

Lindsay used this line plot to record the number of baskets she made in each of her basketball games. Which is the mode of the data?
IL 10.3.03

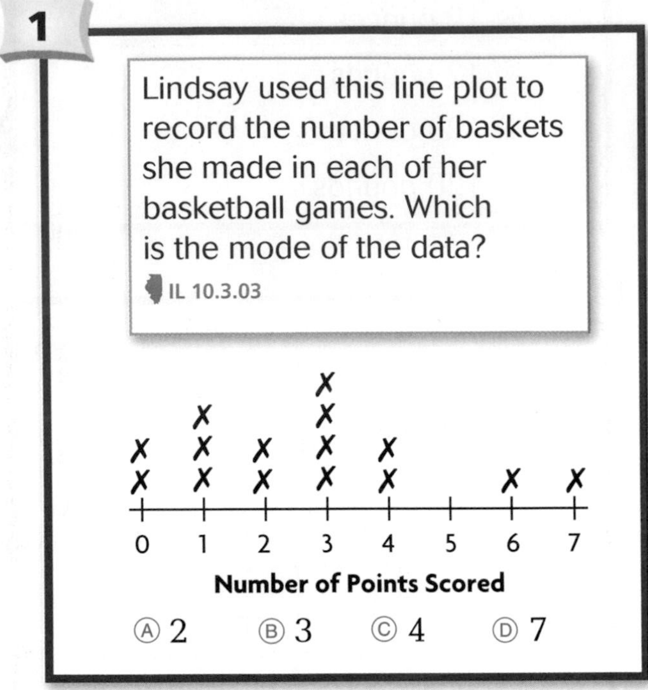

Ⓐ 2 Ⓑ 3 Ⓒ 4 Ⓓ 7

2

Which best describes the probability of pulling a striped sock? IL 10.3.04

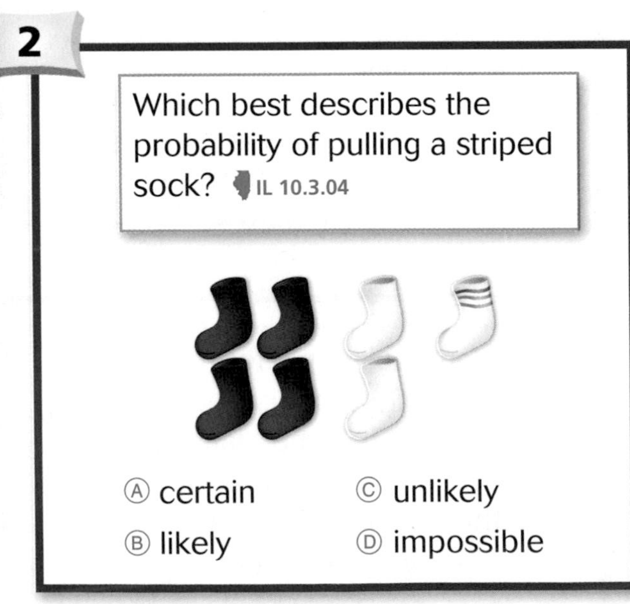

Ⓐ certain
Ⓑ likely
Ⓒ unlikely
Ⓓ impossible

3

How many floors are in the John Hancock Center?
IL 10.3.01

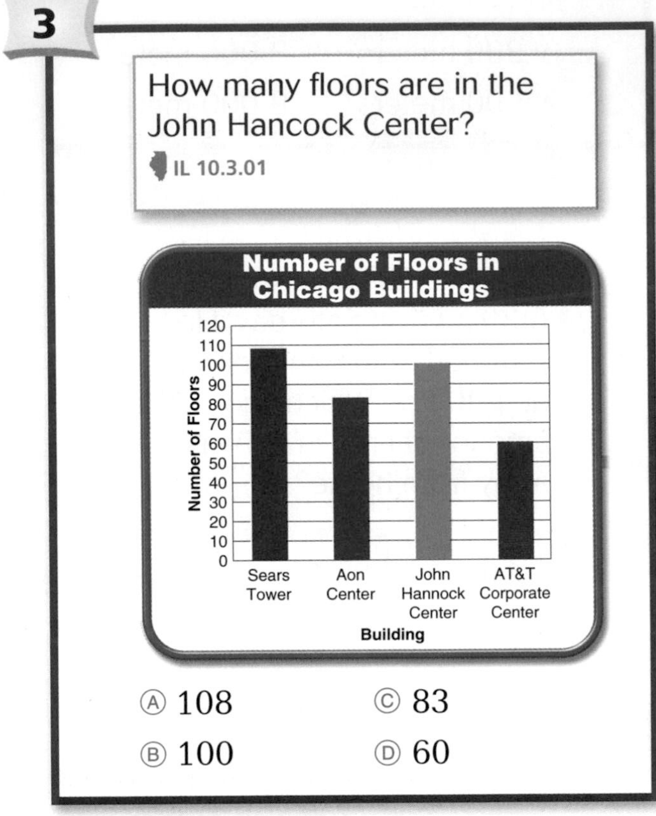

Ⓐ 108
Ⓑ 100
Ⓒ 83
Ⓓ 60

4

Luke wants to add a row to show that Lauren sold 7 bracelets. Which shows what Luke should draw in Lauren's row? IL 10.3.02

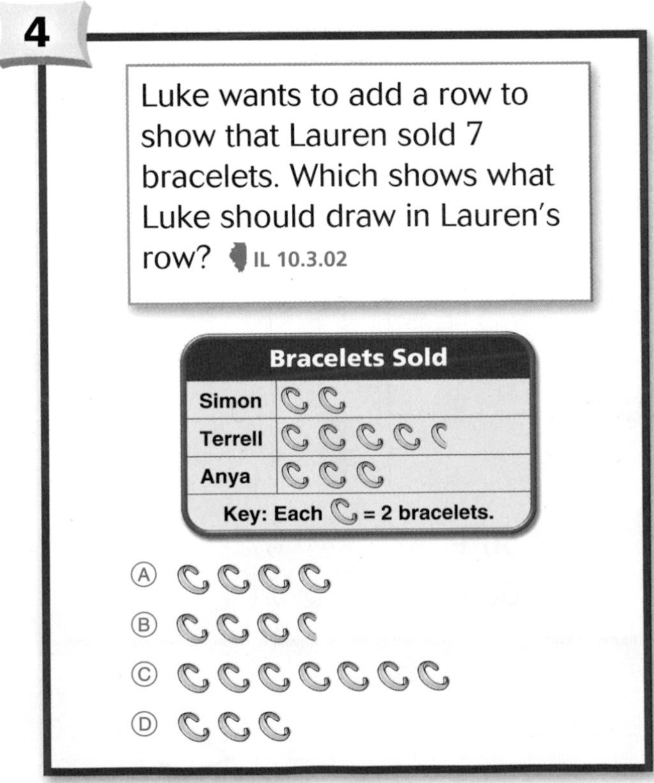

Ⓐ
Ⓑ
Ⓒ
Ⓓ

Extended Response

1

Matt traced each face of a square pyramid on a piece of paper. Draw the plane figures Matt made. Then write the name of each plane figure. IL 9.3.07

2

Last night, Brad finished 29 math problems, Ali finished 32 math problems, and Chen finished 25 math problems. Write an expression to show how many math problems Brad and Chen finished together. Then write an expression to show how many more math problems Ali finished than Chen. IL 8.3.02

3

There are 1,289 girls and 1,248 boys at Vernon High School. There are 1,973 girls and 2,091 boys at Brooktree High School. How many more students go to Brooktree than Vernon High School? IL 6.3.09

4

Helen made this table to record the number of hummingbirds she saw on four different days.

Hummingbirds Seen

Day	Number of Hummingbirds
Monday	3
Tuesday	2
Wednesday	5
Thursday	1

Make a bar graph to show the same data that is shown in Helen's table. IL 10.3.02

5

Maria used square tiles to cover the floor of her bedroom and the floor of the hallway. For the bedroom, she used 8 rows with 6 tiles in each row. For the hallway, she used 11 rows with 4 tiles in each row. Which room has the greater perimeter? Which has the greater area? IL 7.3.05

Addition Facts

	K	L	M	N	O	P	Q	R
A	3 + 2	0 + 6	2 + 4	5 + 9	6 + 1	2 + 5	3 + 10	4 + 4
B	8 + 9	0 + 7	3 + 5	9 + 6	6 + 7	2 + 8	3 + 3	7 + 10
C	4 + 6	9 + 0	7 + 8	4 + 10	3 + 7	7 + 7	4 + 2	7 + 5
D	5 + 7	3 + 9	8 + 1	9 + 5	10 + 5	9 + 8	2 + 6	8 + 7
E	7 + 4	0 + 8	3 + 6	6 + 10	5 + 3	2 + 7	8 + 2	9 + 9
F	2 + 3	1 + 7	6 + 8	5 + 2	7 + 3	4 + 8	10 + 10	6 + 6
G	8 + 3	7 + 2	7 + 0	8 + 5	9 + 1	4 + 7	8 + 4	10 + 8
H	7 + 9	5 + 6	8 + 10	6 + 5	8 + 6	9 + 4	0 + 9	7 + 1
I	4 + 3	5 + 5	6 + 4	10 + 2	7 + 6	8 + 0	6 + 9	9 + 2
J	5 + 8	1 + 9	5 + 4	8 + 8	6 + 2	6 + 3	9 + 7	9 + 10

Subtraction Facts

	K	L	M	N	O	P	Q	R
A	9 − 1	10 − 4	7 − 2	6 − 4	20 − 10	7 − 0	8 − 3	13 − 9
B	9 − 9	13 − 4	7 − 1	11 − 5	9 − 7	6 − 3	15 − 10	6 − 2
C	10 − 2	8 − 8	16 − 8	6 − 5	18 − 10	8 − 7	13 − 3	15 − 6
D	11 − 7	9 − 5	12 − 8	8 − 1	15 − 8	18 − 9	14 − 10	9 − 4
E	9 − 2	7 − 7	10 − 3	8 − 5	16 − 9	11 − 9	14 − 8	12 − 6
F	7 − 3	12 − 10	17 − 9	6 − 0	9 − 6	11 − 8	10 − 9	12 − 2
G	15 − 7	8 − 4	13 − 6	7 − 5	11 − 2	12 − 3	14 − 6	11 − 4
H	7 − 6	13 − 5	12 − 9	10 − 5	13 − 8	11 − 3	16 − 10	14 − 7
I	5 − 0	10 − 8	11 − 6	9 − 3	14 − 5	5 − 4	7 − 7	14 − 9
J	15 − 9	9 − 8	13 − 7	8 − 2	7 − 4	13 − 10	10 − 6	16 − 7

Multiplication Facts

	K	L	M	N	O	P	Q	R
A	2×7	0×6	6×6	9×2	8×3	3×4	2×8	6×1
B	7×7	5×9	2×2	7×5	2×3	10×8	4×10	8×4
C	4×5	5×1	7×0	6×3	3×5	6×8	7×3	9×9
D	0×9	6×4	6×10	1×6	9×8	4×4	3×2	9×3
E	0×7	9×4	1×7	9×7	2×5	7×9	5×6	5×8
F	4×3	6×9	1×9	7×6	7×10	6×0	2×9	10×3
G	5×3	1×5	7×1	3×8	3×6	8×10	3×9	6×7
H	7×4	7×2	3×7	2×4	7×8	4×7	5×10	8×6
I	4×6	5×5	5×7	3×3	9×6	8×0	4×9	8×8
J	8×9	6×2	4×8	9×5	5×4	0×5	10×6	9×10

Division Facts

	K	L	M	N	O	P	Q	R
A	1)1	3)9	2)6	2)4	1)6	3)12	5)15	7)21
B	6)24	8)56	5)40	6)18	6)30	7)42	9)81	5)45
C	5)30	2)16	3)21	7)35	3)15	9)9	8	9)63
D	4)32	9)90	4)8	8)48	9)54	3)18	10)50	6)48
E	7)28	3)0	5)20	4)24	7)14	3)6	5)50	10)60
F	9)18	4)36	5)25	7)63	1)5	8)32	9)45	6)54
G	2)14	8)24	4)4	5)40	3)9	4)12	7)56	8)72
H	5)35	1)4	8)64	5)10	8)40	2)12	6)42	10)70
I	7)49	9)27	10)90	3)27	9)36	4)20	9)72	8)80
J	8)0	4)28	2)10	7)70	1)3	10)80	6)60	10)100

ILLINOIS

Table of Measures

METRIC		CUSTOMARY	
Length			
1 decimeter (dm)	= 10 centimeters (cm)	1 foot (ft)	= 12 inches (in.)
1 meter (m)	= 100 centimeters	1 yard (yd)	= 3 feet, or 36 inches
1 meter (m)	= 10 decimeters	1 mile (mi)	= 1,760 yards, or 5,280 feet
1 kilometer (km)	= 1,000 meters		
Mass/Weight			
1 kilogram (kg)	= 1,000 grams (g)	1 pound (lb)	= 16 ounces (oz)
Capacity			
1 liter (L)	= 1,000 milliliters (mL)	1 pint (pt)	= 2 cups (c)
		1 quart (qt)	= 2 pints
		1 gallon (gal)	= 4 quarts

TIME			
1 minute (min)	= 60 seconds (sec)	1 year (yr)	= 12 months (mo), or about 52 weeks
1 hour (hr)	= 60 minutes	1 year	= 365 days
1 day	= 24 hours	1 leap year	= 366 days
1 week (wk)	= 7 days		

MONEY	
1 penny	= 1 cent (¢)
1 nickel	= 5 cents
1 dime	= 10 cents
1 quarter	= 25 cents
1 half-dollar	= 50 cents
1 dollar ($)	= 100 cents

SYMBOLS
< is less than
> is greater than
= is equal to
°F is degrees Fahrenheit
°C is degrees Celsius

Glossary

Pronunciation Key

a	add, map	f	fit, half	n	nice, tin	p	pit, stop	yōō	fuse, few
ā	ace, rate	g	go, log	ng	ring, song	r	run, poor	v	vain, eve
â(r)	care, air	h	hope, hate	o	odd, hot	s	see, pass	w	win, away
ä	palm, father	i	it, give	ō	open, so	sh	sure, rush	y	yet, yearn
		ī	ice, write	ô	order, jaw	t	talk, sit	z	zest, muse
b	bat, rub	j	joy, ledge	oi	oil, boy	th	thin, both	zh	vision, pleasure
ch	check, catch	k	cool, take	ou	pout, now	t̶h̶	this, bathe		
d	dog, rod	l	look, rule	o͝o	took, full	u	up, done		
e	end, pet	m	move, seem	o͞o	pool, food	û(r)	burn, term		
ē	equal, tree								

ə the schwa, an unstressed vowel representing the sound spelled *a* in above, *e* in sicken, *i* in possible, *o* in melon, *u* in circus

Other symbols:
- • separates words into syllables
- ′ indicates stress on a syllable

acute angle [ə•kyo͞ot′ ang′gəl] **ángulo agudo** An angle that has a measure less than a right angle (p. 350)
Example:

acute triangle [ə•kyo͞ot′ trī′ang•gəl] **triángulo acutángulo** A triangle that has three acute angles (p. 358)

addend [a′dend] **sumando** Any of the numbers that are added (p. 48)
Example: 2 + 3 = 5
↑ ↑
addend addend

addition [ə•di′shən] **suma** The process of finding the total number of items when two or more groups of items are joined; the opposite operation of subtraction (p. 48)

A.M. [ā em] **a.m.** The hours between midnight and noon (p. 128)

analog clock [a′nəl•og kläk] **reloj analógico** A device for measuring time in which hands move around a circle to show hours, minutes, and sometimes seconds (p. 124)
Example:

angle [ang′gəl] **ángulo** A figure formed by two rays that share an endpoint (p. 350)
Example:

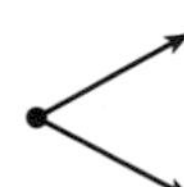

Word History

When the letter *g* is replaced with the letter *k* in the word *angle*, the word becomes *ankle*. Both words come from the same Latin root, *angulus*, which means "a sharp bend."

area [âr′ē•ə] **área** The number of square units needed to cover a flat surface (p. 564)

Example:

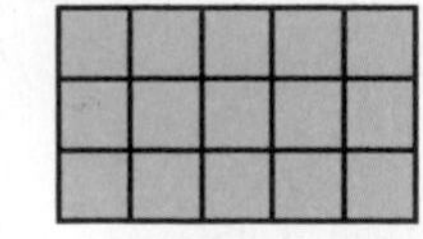

area = 15 square units

arrangement [ə•rānj′•mənt] **ordenación** A choice in which the order of items does matter (p. 194)

array [ə•rā′] **matriz** An arrangement of objects in rows and columns (p. 206)

Example:

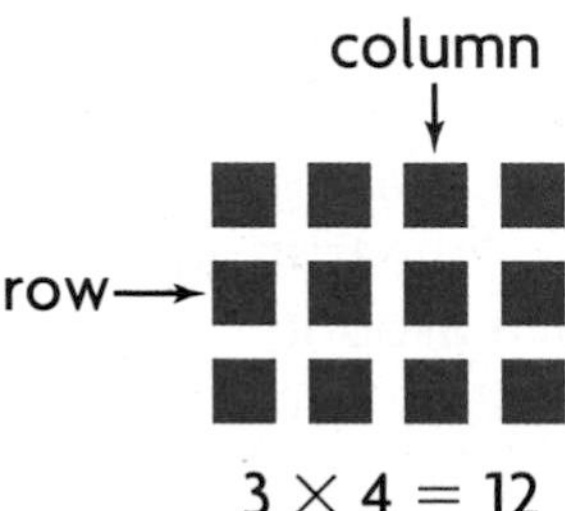

3 × 4 = 12

Associative Property of Addition [ə•sō′shē•ə•tiv prä′pər•tē əv ə•di′shən] **propiedad asociativa de la suma** The property that states that you can group addends in different ways and still get the same sum (p. 48)

Example:

4 + (2 + 5) = 11 and
(4 + 2) + 5 = 11

Associative Property of Multiplication [a•sō′shē•ə•tiv prä′pər•tē əv mul•tə•plə•kā′shən] **propiedad asociativa de la multiplicación** The property that states that when the grouping of factors is changed, the product remains the same (p. 260)

Example:

(3 × 2) × 4 = 24
3 × (2 × 4) = 24

B

bar graph [bär graf] **gráfica de barras** A graph that uses bars to show data (p. 154)

Example:

benchmark numbers [bench′märk num•bərz] **números de referencia** Numbers that help you estimate the number of objects without counting them, such as 25, 50, 100, or 1,000. (p. 42)

C

calendar [ka′lən•dər] **calendario** A chart that shows the days, weeks, and months of a year (p. 132)

capacity [kə•pa′sə•tē] **capacidad** The amount a container can hold (p. 520)

Example:

1 half gallon = 2 quarts

center [sen′tər] **centro** The point in the middle of a circle that is the same distance from anywhere on the circle (p. 364)

Example:

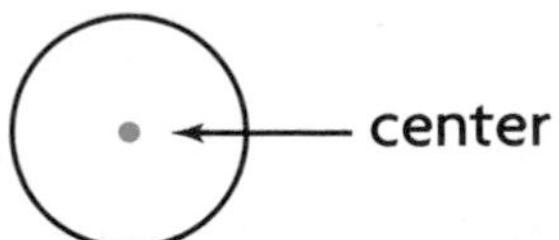

centimeter (cm) [sen′tə•mē•tər] **centímetro** A metric unit that is used to measure length or distance (p. 538)
Example:

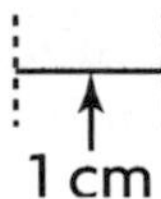

certain [sûr′tən] **seguro** An event is certain if it will always happen. (p. 178)

change [chānj] **cambio** The money you get back if you have paid for an item with coins or bills that have a value greater than the cost of the item (p. 120)

circle [sûr′kəl] **círculo** A closed plane figure made up of points that are the same distance from the center (p. 364)

circle graph [sûr′kəl graf] **gráfica circular** A graph in the shape of a circle that shows data as a whole made up of different parts (p. 172)

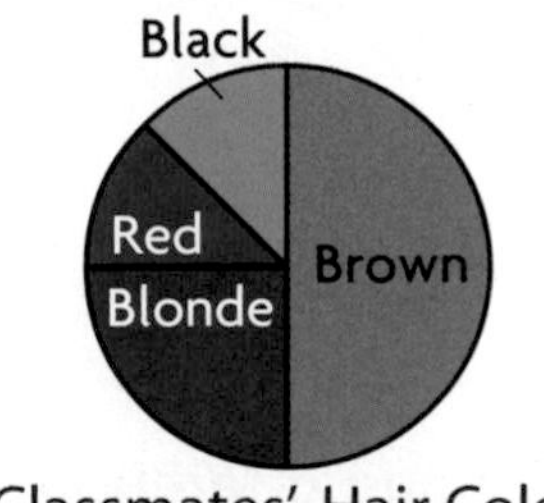

Classmates' Hair Color

circumference [sûr•kum′fər•əns] **circunferencia** The distance around a circle (p. 364)

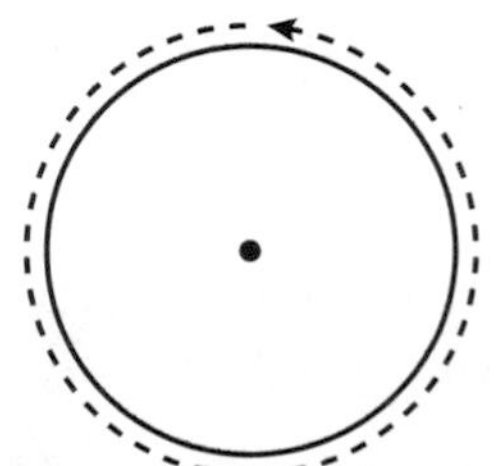

classify [kla′sə•fī] **clasificar** To group pieces of data according to how they are the same; for example, you can classify data by size, color, or shape. (p. 160)

closed figure [klōzd fi′•gyər] **figura cerrada** A shape that begins and ends at the same point (p. 356)
Examples:

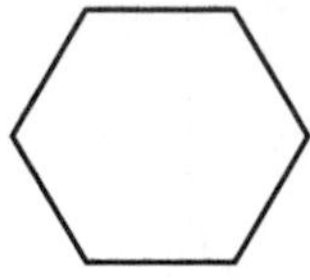

combination [kom•bə•nā′shən] **combinación** A choice in which the order of the items does not matter (p. 186)

Commutative Property of Addition [kə•myo͞o′•tə•tiv prä′pər•tē əv ə•di′shən] **propiedad conmutativa de la suma** The property that states that you can add two or more numbers in any order and get the same sum (p. 48)
Example: $6 + 7 = 13$
$7 + 6 = 13$

Commutative Property of Multiplication [kə•myo͞o•tə•tiv prä′pər•tē əv mul•tə•plə•kā′shən] **propiedad conmutativa de la multiplicación** The property that states that you can multiply two factors in any order and get the same product (p. 206)
Examples: $2 \times 4 = 8$
$4 \times 2 = 8$

compare [kəm•pâr′] **comparar** To describe whether numbers are equal to, less than, or greater than each other (p. 28)

compatible numbers [kəm•pat′ə•bəl num′bərz] **números compatibles** Numbers that are easy to compute mentally (pp. 52, 618)

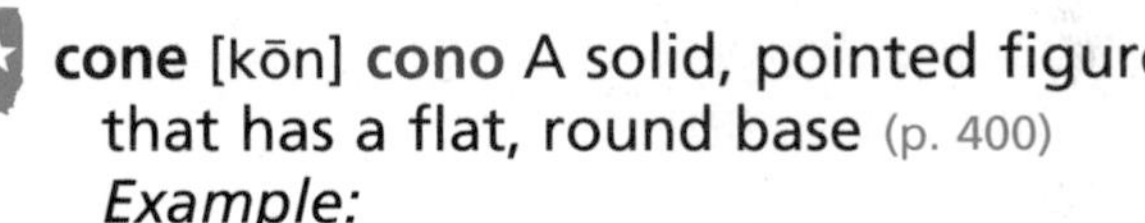

cone [kōn] **cono** A solid, pointed figure that has a flat, round base (p. 400)
Example:

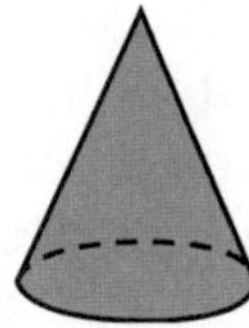

congruent [kən•grōō′ənt] **congruente** Figures that have the same size and shape (p. 378)
Example:

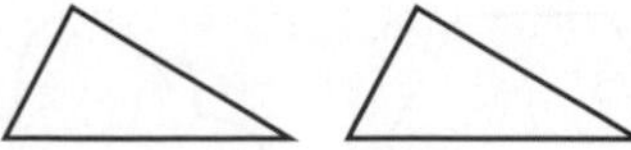

cube [kyōōb] **cubo** A solid figure with six congruent square faces (p. 400)
Example:

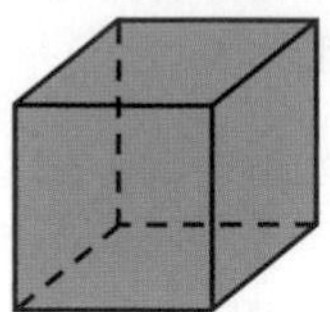

cubic unit [kyōō′bik yōō′nət] **unidad cúbica** A cube with a side length of one unit, used to measure volume (p. 570)

cup (c) [kup] **taza** A customary unit used to measure capacity (p. 520)

cylinder [sil′in•dər] **cilindro** A solid or hollow object that is shaped like a can (p. 400)
Example:

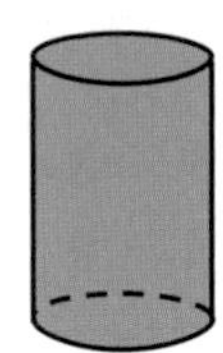

D

data [dā′tə] **datos** Information collected about people or things (p. 146)

decimal [de′sə•məl] **decimal** A number with one or more digits to the right of the decimal point (p. 484)

decimal point [de′sə•məl point] **punto decimal** A symbol used to separate dollars from cents in money and to separate the ones place from the tenths place in decimals (pp. 110, 485)
Examples: \$4.52 0.9
↑ decimal point ↑

decimeter (dm) [de′sə•mē•tər] **decímetro** A metric unit that is used to measure length or distance;
1 decimeter = 10 centimeters (p. 538)

degree Celsius (°C) [di•grē′ sel′sē•əs] **grado Celcius** A metric unit for measuring temperature (p. 550)

degree Fahrenheit (°F) [di•grē′ far′ən•hīt] **grado Fahrenheit** A customary unit for measuring temperature (p. 528)

denominator [di•nä′mə•nā•tər] **denominador** The part of a fraction below the line, which tells how many equal parts there are in the whole or in the group (p. 446)
Example: $\frac{3}{4}$ ← denominator

diameter [dī•am′ə•tər] **diámetro** A line segment that passes through the center of a circle and has its endpoints on the circle (p. 364)
Example:

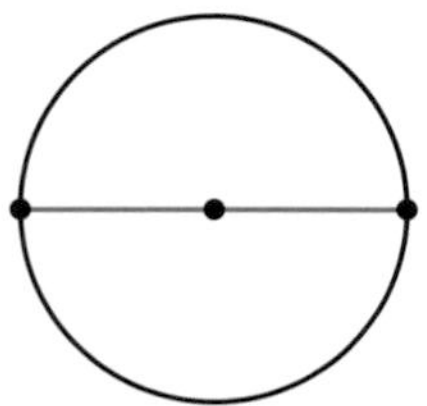

difference [di′frəns] **diferencia** The answer in a subtraction problem (p. 78)
Example: 6 − 4 = 2
↑ difference

digital clock [di′jə•təl kläk] **reloj digital** A clock that shows time to the minute, using digits (p. 124)
Example:

digits [di′jətz] **dígitos** The symbols 0, 1, 2, 3, 4, 5, 6, 7, 8, and 9 (p. 8)

dime [dīm] **moneda de 10¢** A coin worth 10 cents and equal to 10 pennies; 10¢ (p. 110)
Example:

divide [di•vīd′] **dividir** To separate into equal groups; the opposite operation of multiplication (p. 278)

dividend [di′və•dend] **dividendo** The number that is to be divided in a division problem (p. 284)
Example: 35 ÷ 5 = 7
↑ dividend

division [di•vi′zhen] **división** The process of sharing a number of items to find how many groups can be made or how many items will be in a group; the opposite operation of multiplication (p. 278)

divisor [di•vī′zər] **divisor** The number that divides the dividend (p. 284)
Example: 35 ÷ 5 = 7
↑ divisor

dollar [dol′ər] **dólar** Paper money worth 100 cents and equal to 100 pennies; $1.00 (p. 110)
Example:

edge [ej] **arista** A line segment formed where two faces meet (p. 400)
Example:

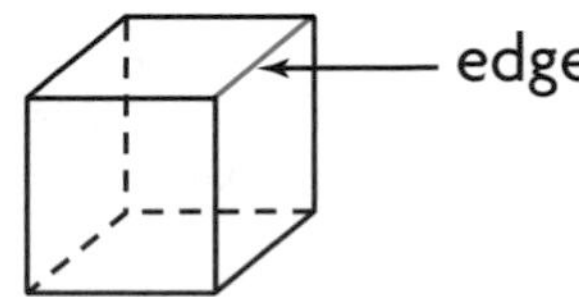

elapsed time [i•lapst′tīm] **tiempo transcurrido** The time that passes from the start of an activity to the end of that activity (p. 130)

equal sign (=) [ē′kwəl sīn] **signo de igualdad** A symbol used to show that two numbers have the same value (p. 28)
Example: 384 = 384

equal to (=) [ē′kwəl to͞o] **igual a** Having the same value (p. 28)
Example: 4 + 4 is equal to 3 + 5

equally likely [ē′kwəl•lē lī′klē] **igualmente probable** Having the same chance of happening (p. 180)

equation [i•kwā′zhən] **ecuación** A number sentence that uses the equal sign to show that two amounts are equal (p. 336)
Examples:
3 + 7 = 10
4 − 1 = 3
6 × 7 = 42

equilateral triangle [ē•kwə•la′tər•əl trī′ang•gəl] **triángulo equilátero** A triangle that has three equal sides and three equal angles (p. 358)
Examples:

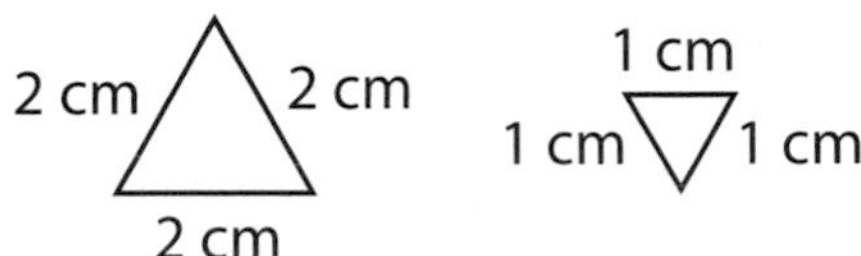

equivalent [ē•kwiv′ə•lənt] **equivalente** Two or more sets that name the same amount (p. 110)

equivalent fractions [ē•kwiv′ə•lənt frak′shənz] **fracciones equivalentes** Two or more fractions that name the same amount (p. 454)
Example:

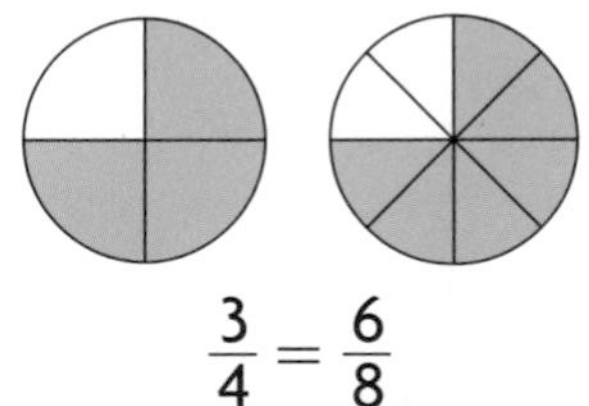

$\frac{3}{4} = \frac{6}{8}$

estimate [es′tə•māt] *verb* **estimar (v)**: To find about how many or how much (p. 52)

estimate [es′tə•mət] *noun* **estimación (s)**: A number close to an exact amount (p. 52)

even [ē′vən] **par** A whole number that has a 0, 2, 4, 6, or 8 in the ones place (p. 4)

event [i•vent′] **suceso** Something that might happen (p. 178)

expanded form [ik•spand′id fôrm] **forma desarrollada** A way to write numbers by showing the value of each digit (p. 8)
Example: 7,201 = 7,000 + 200 + 1

experiment [ik•sper′ə•mənt] **experimento** A test that is done in order to find out something (p. 182)

expression [ik•spre′shən] **expresión** The part of a number sentence that combines numbers and operation signs, but doesn't have an equal sign (p. 336)
Example: 5×6

F

face [fās] **cara** A flat surface of a solid figure (p. 400)
Example:

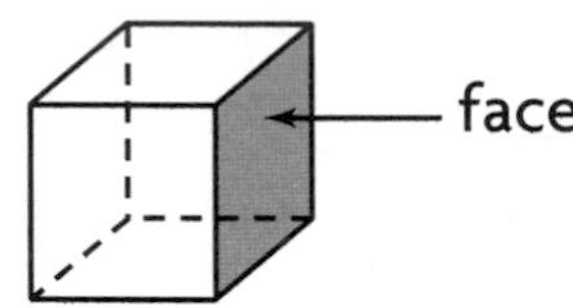

fact family [fakt fam′ə•lē] **familia de operaciones** A set of related addition and subtraction, or multiplication and division, number sentences (pp. 76, 286)
Example:

$4 \times 7 = 28$ $\quad$ $28 \div 7 = 4$
$7 \times 4 = 28$ $\quad$ $28 \div 4 = 7$

factor [fak′tər] **factor** A number that is multiplied by another number to find a product (p. 206)
Example: $3 \times 8 = 24$
↑ factor ↑ factor

flip (reflection) [flip (ri•flek′shən)] **inversión (reflexión)** A movement of a figure to a new position by flipping the figure over a line (p. 390)
Example:

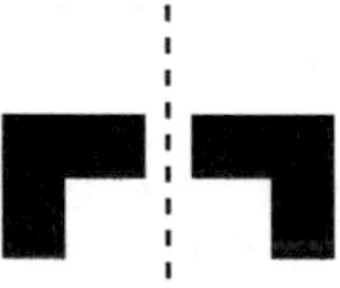

foot (ft) [fo͝ot] **pie** A customary unit used to measure length or distance;
1 foot = 12 inches (p. 512)

fraction [frak′shən] **fracción** A number that names part of a whole or part of a group (p. 446)
Examples:

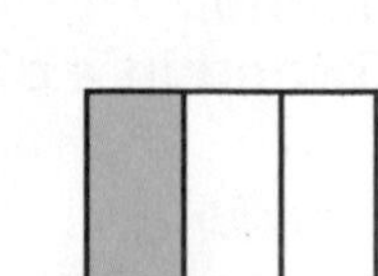

$\frac{1}{3}$

Word History

A *fraction* is part of a whole, or a whole that is broken into pieces. *Fraction* comes from the Latin word *frangere*, which means "to break."

frequency table [frē′kwen•sē tā′bəl] **tabla de frecuencia** A table that uses numbers to record data (p. 146)
Example:

Favorite Color	
Color	**Number**
blue	10
red	7
green	8
yellow	4

G

gallon (gal) [ga′lən] **galón** A customary unit for measuring capacity;
1 gallon = 4 quarts (p. 520)

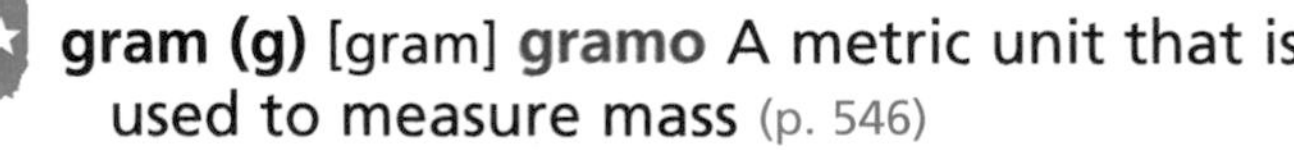

gram (g) [gram] **gramo** A metric unit that is used to measure mass (p. 546)

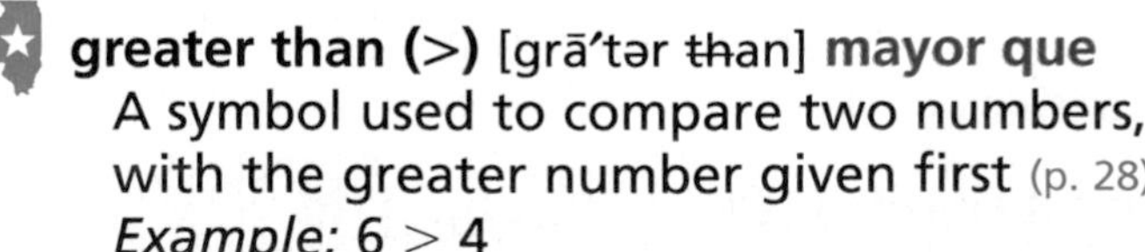

greater than (>) [grā′tər t͟han] **mayor que** A symbol used to compare two numbers, with the greater number given first (p. 28)
Example: $6 > 4$

grid [grid] **cuadrícula** Horizontal and vertical lines on a map (p. 162)

Grouping Property of Addition [grōō′ping prä′pər•tē əv ə•dish′ən] **propiedad de agrupación de la suma** *See* Associative Property of Addition.

Grouping Property of Multiplication [grōō′ping prä′pər•tē əv mul•tə•plə•kā′shən] **propiedad de agrupación de la multiplicación** *See* Associative Property of Multiplication.

growing pattern [grō′ing pa′tern] **patrón acumulativo** A pattern in which the number or number of figures increases by the same amount each time. (p. 424)

half dollar [haf dol′ər] **moneda de 50¢** A coin worth 50 cents and equal to 50 pennies; 50¢ (p. 110)
Example:

half hour [haf our] **media hora** 30 minutes (p. 124)
Example: Between 4:00 and 4:30 is one half hour.

hexagon [hek′sə•gän] **hexágono** A polygon with six sides and six angles (p. 356)
Examples:

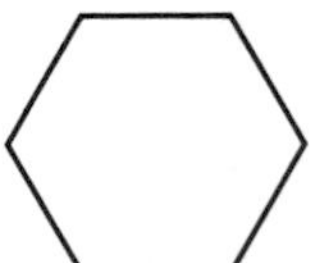

horizontal bar graph [hôr•ə•zän′təl bär graf] **gráfica de barras horizontales** A bar graph in which the bars go from left to right (p. 154)

hour (hr) [our] **hora** A unit used to measure time; in one hour, the hour hand on a clock moves from one number to the next;
1 hour = 60 minutes (p. 124)

hour hand [our hand] **horario** The short hand on an analog clock (p. 124)

hundredth [hun′drədth] **centésimo** One of one hundred equal parts (p. 488)
Example:

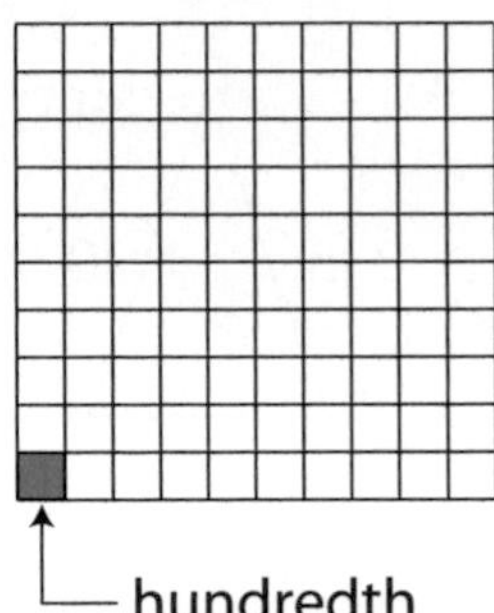

Identity Property of Addition [ī•den′tə•tē prä′pər•tē əv ə•dish′ən] **propiedad de identidad de la suma** The property that states that when you add zero to a number, the result is that number (p. 48)
Example: 24 + 0 = 24

Identity Property of Multiplication [ī•den′tə•tē prä′pər•tē əv mul•tə•plə•kā′shən] **propiedad de identidad de la multiplicación** The property that states that the product of any number and 1 is that number (p. 214)
Examples: $5 \times 1 = 5$
$1 \times 8 = 8$

impossible [im•pä′sə•bəl] **imposible** An event is impossible if it will never happen (p. 178)

inch (in.) [inch] **pulgada** A customary unit used for measuring length or distance (p. 512)
Example:

1 inch

intersecting lines [in•tər•sek′ting līnz] **líneas secantes** Lines that cross (p. 354)
Example:

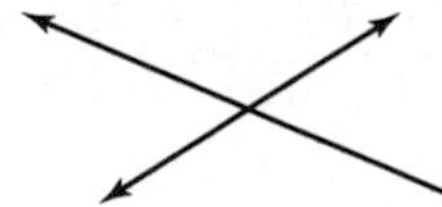

inverse operations [in′vûrs ä•pə•rā′shənz] **operaciones inversas** Opposite operations, or operations that undo each other, such as addition and subtraction or multiplication and division (pp. 76, 284)

isosceles triangle [ī•sä′sə•lēz trī′ang•gəl] **triángulo isósceles** A triangle that has two equal sides (p. 358)
Example:

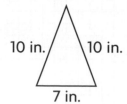

10 in. 10 in. 7 in.

key [kē] **clave** The part of a map or graph that explains the symbols (p. 148)

kilogram (kg) [kil′ə•gram] **kilogramo** A metric unit for measuring mass; 1 kilogram = 1,000 grams (p. 546)

kilometer (km) [kə•lä′mə•tər] **kilómetro** A metric unit for measuring length or distance;
1 kilometer = 1,000 meters (p. 538)

length [leng(k)th] **longitud** The measurement of the distance between two points (p. 512)

less than ($<$) [les *th*an] **menor que** A symbol used to compare two numbers, with the lesser number given first (p. 28)
Example: $3 < 7$

like fractions [līk frak′shənz] **fracciones semejantes** Fractions that have the same denominator (p. 466)
Example: $\frac{3}{8}$ and $\frac{7}{8}$

likely [līk′lē] **probable** An event is likely if it has a good chance of happening. (p. 178)

line [līn] **línea** A straight path extending in both directions with no endpoints (p. 350)
Example:

line graph [līn graf] **gráfica lineal** A graph that uses line segments to show how data change over time (p. 168)

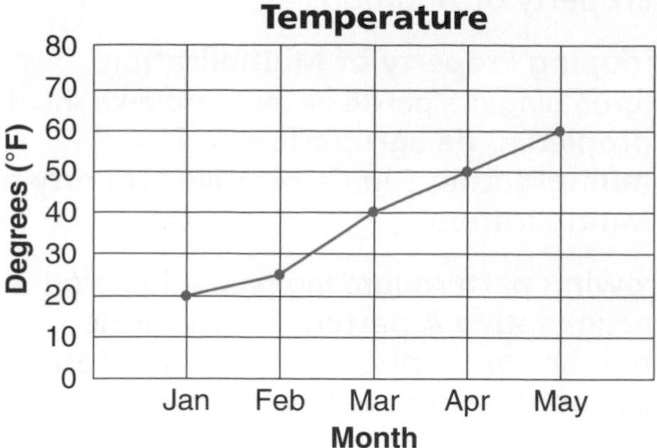

line of symmetry [līn əv si′mə•trē] **eje de simetría** An imaginary line on a figure that when the figure is folded on this line, the two parts match exactly (p. 384)
Example:

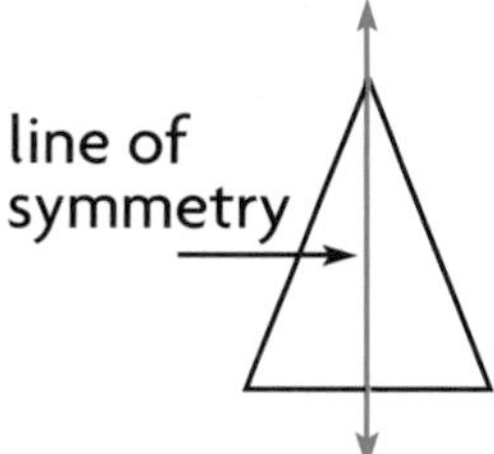

line plot [līn plöt] **diagrama de puntos** A graph that records each piece of data on a number line (p. 162)
Example:

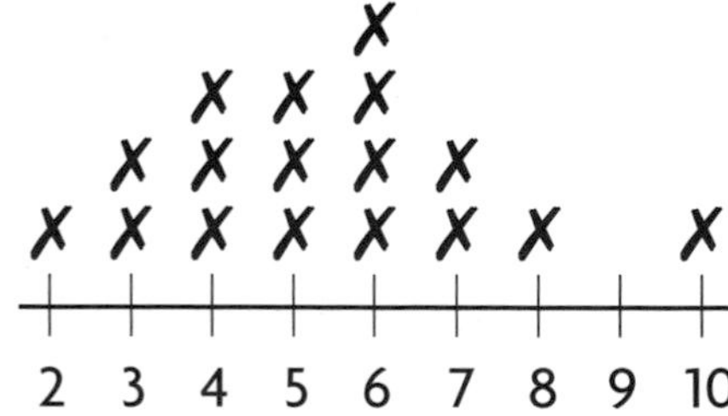

Word History

The word *line* comes from *linen*, a thread spun from the fibers of the flax plant. In early times, thread was held tight to mark a straight line between two points.

line segment [līn seg′mənt] **segmento** A part of a line that includes two points, called endpoints, and all of the points between them (p. 350)
Example:

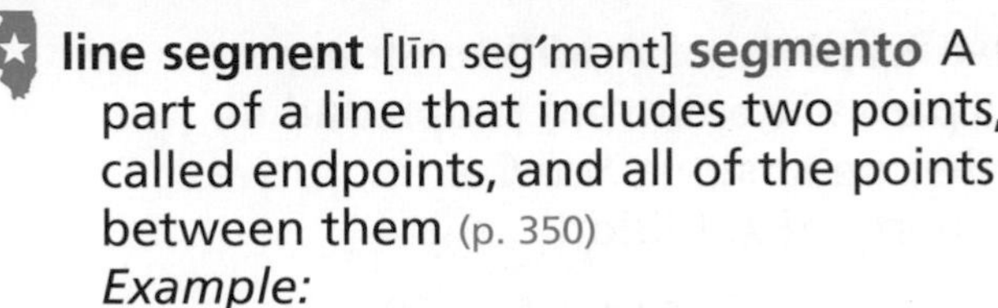

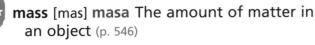

liter (L) [lē′tər] **litro** A metric unit for measuring capacity;
1 liter = 1,000 milliliters (p. 544)

M

mass [mas] **masa** The amount of matter in an object (p. 546)

meter (m) [mē′tər] **metro** A metric unit for measuring length or distance;
1 meter = 100 centimeters (p. 538)

midnight [mid′nīt] **medianoche** 12:00 at night (p. 128)

mile (mi) [mīl] **milla** A customary unit for measuring length or distance;
1 mile = 5,280 feet (p. 512)

milliliter (mL) [mi′lə•lē•tər] **mililitro** A metric unit for measuring capacity (p. 544)

minute (min) [mi′nət] **minuto** A unit used to measure short amounts of time; in one minute, the minute hand moves from one mark to the next (p. 124)

minute hand [mi′nət hand] **minutero** The long hand on an analog clock (p. 124)

mixed number [mikst num′bər] **número mixto** A number represented by a whole number and a fraction (p. 464)
Example: $4\frac{1}{2}$

mode [mōd] **moda** The number or item found most often in a set of data (p. 162)

multiple [mul′tə•pəl] **múltiplo** A number that is the product of a given number and a counting number (p. 234)
Example:

10	10	10	10	counting
× 1	× 2	× 3	× 4	← numbers
10	20	30	40	← multiples of 10

multiplication [mul•tə•plə•kā′shən] **multiplicación** The process of finding the total number of items in two or more equal groups; the opposite operation of division. (p. 204)

multiply [mul′tə•plī] **multiplicar** When you combine equal groups, you can multiply to find how many in all; the opposite operation of division (p. 204)

multistep problem [mul′tē•step prä′bləm] **problema de varios pasos** A problem with more than one step (p. 264)

N

net [net] **plantilla** A two-dimensional pattern of a three-dimensional or solid figure (p. 404)
Example:

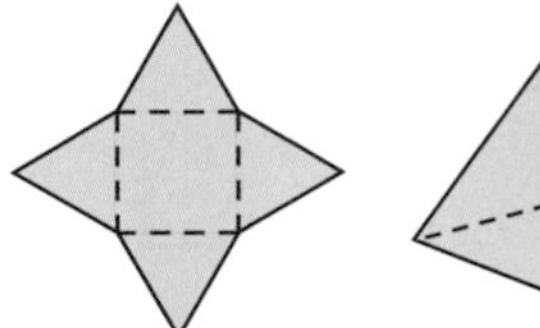

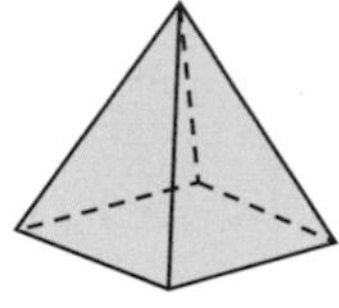

nickel [nik′əl] **moneda de 5¢** A coin worth 5 cents and equal to 5 pennies; 5¢ (p. 110)
Example:

noon [no͞on] **mediodía** 12:00 in the day (p. 128)

number line [num′bər līn] **recta numérica** A line on which numbers can be located (p. 6)
Example:

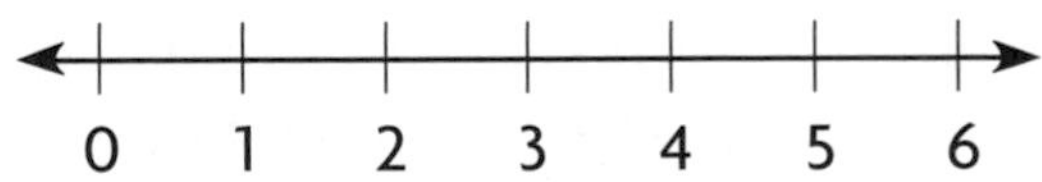

number sentence [num′bər sen′təns] **enunciado numérico** A sentence that includes numbers, operation symbols, and a greater than or less than symbol or an equal sign (p. 290)
Example:
5 + 3 = 8 is a number sentence.

numerator [nōō′mə•rā•tər] **numerador** The part of a fraction above the line, which tells how many parts are being counted (p. 446)
Example: $\frac{3}{4}$ ← numerator

obtuse angle [əb•t(y)ōōs′ ang′gəl] **ángulo obtuso** An angle that has a measure greater than a right angle (p. 350)
Example:

obtuse triangle [əb•t(y)ōōs′ trī′ang•gəl] **triángulo obtusángulo** A triangle that has 1 obtuse angle (p. 358)

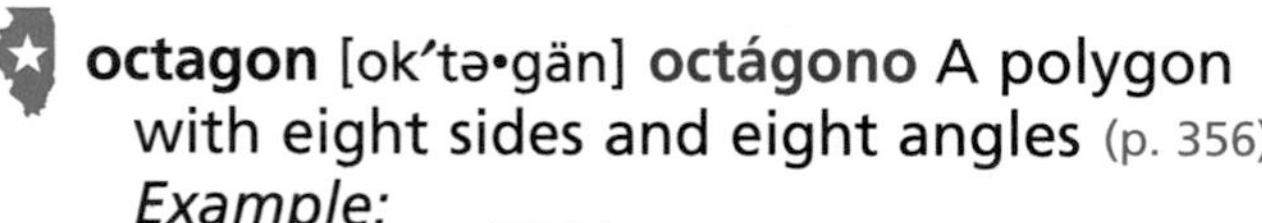

octagon [ok′tə•gän] **octágono** A polygon with eight sides and eight angles (p. 356)
Example:

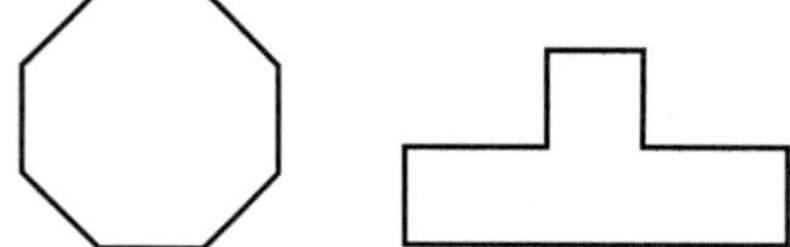

odd [od] **impar** A whole number that has a 1, 3, 5, 7, or 9 in the ones place (p. 4)

open figure [ō′pən fi′gyər] **figura abierta** A figure that does not begin and end at the same point (p. 356)
Examples:

order [ôr′dər] **orden** A particular arrangement or placement of numbers or things, one after another (p. 32)

ordered pair [ôr′dərd pâr] **par ordenado** A pair of numbers that names a point on a grid (p. 166)
Example: (3,4)

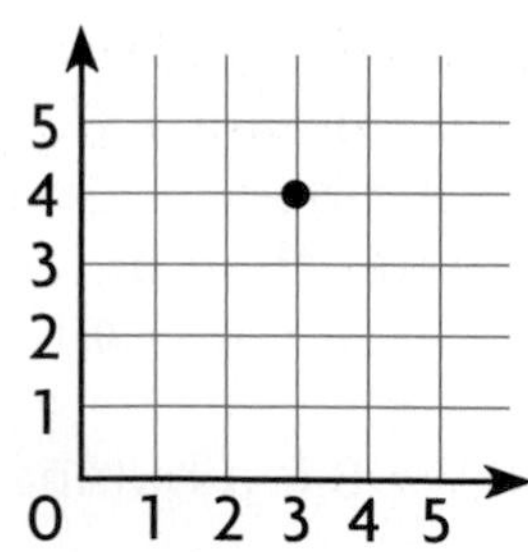

Order Property of Addition [ôr′dər prä′pər•tē əv ə•dish′ən] **propiedad de orden de la suma** *See* Commutative Property of Addition.

Order Property of Multiplication [ôr′dər prä′pər•tē əv mul•tə•plə•kā′shən] **propiedad de orden de la multiplicación** *See* Commutative Property of Multiplication.

ounce (oz) [ouns] **onza** A customary unit for measuring weight (p. 522)

outcome [out′kum] **resultado** A possible result of an experiment (p. 180)

parallel lines [pâr′ə•lel līnz] **líneas paralelas** Lines that never cross; lines that are always the same distance apart (p. 354)
Example:

parallelogram [pâr•ə•le′lə•gram] **paralelogramo** A quadrilateral whose opposite sides are parallel and have the same length (p. 360)
Example:

pattern [pat′ərn] **patrón** An ordered set of numbers or objects; the order helps you predict what will come next. (p. 4)
Examples:
2, 4, 6, 8, 10

pattern unit [pat′ərn yōō′nət] **unidad de patrón** The part of a pattern that repeats (p. 422)
Example:

pentagon [pen′tə•gän] **pentágono** A polygon with five sides and five angles (p. 356)
Example:

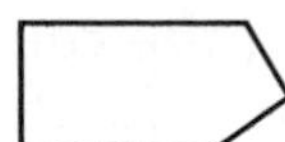

perimeter [pə•ri′mə•tər] **perímetro** The distance around a figure (p. 560)
Example:

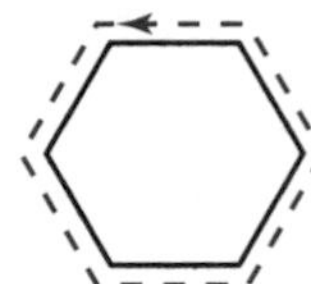

perpendicular [pûr•pən•di′kyə•lər] **perpendicular** A line or plane that makes a right angle with another line or plane (p. 354)

perpendicular lines [pûr•pən•di′kyə•lər līnz] **líneas perpendiculares** Lines that intersect to form right angles (p. 354)
Example:

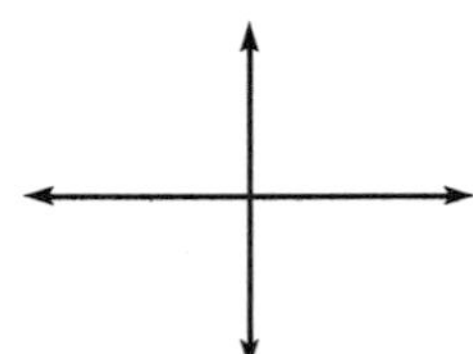

pictograph [pik′tə•graf] **pictografía** A graph that uses pictures to show and compare information (p. 148)
Example:

How We Got To School	
Walk	❀ ❀ ❀
Ride a Bike	❀ ❀ ❀ ❀
Ride a Bus	❀ ❀ ❀ ❀ ❀ ❀
Ride in a Car	❀ ❀
Key: Each ❀ = 10 students.	

pint (pt) [pīnt] **pinta** A customary unit for measuring capacity;
1 pint = 2 cups (p. 520)

place value [plās val′yo͞o] **valor posicional** The value of each digit in a number, based on the location of the digit (p. 8)

plane figure [plān fi′•gyər] **figura plana** A figure in a plane that is formed by lines that are curved, straight, or both (p. 356)
Example:

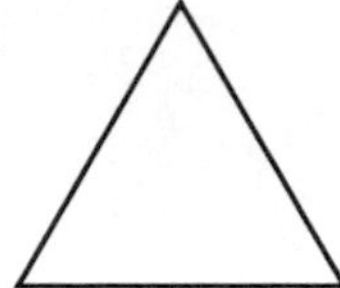

P.M. [pē em] **p.m.** The hours between noon and midnight (p. 128)

point [point] **punto** An exact position or location (p. 350)

polygon [po′lē•gän] **polígono** A closed plane figure with straight sides that are line segments (p. 356)
Examples:

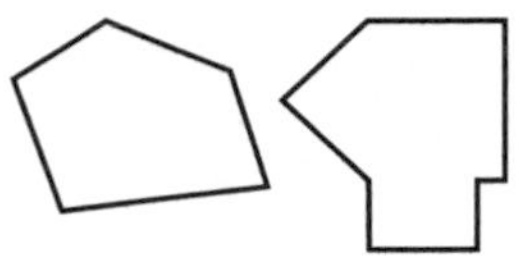

polygons

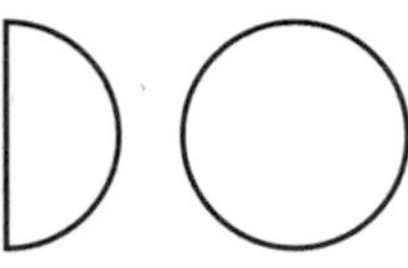

not polygons

Word History

Did you ever notice that a *polygon* looks like a bunch of knees that are bent? This is how the term got its name. *Poly-* is from the Greek root *poli*, which means "many." The ending *-gon* is from the Latin, *gonus*, which means "to bend the knee."

possible [pos′ə•bəl] **posible** Having a chance of happening (p. 180)

possible outcome [pos′ə•bəl out′kəm] **resultado posible** Something that has a chance of happening (p. 180)

pound (lb) [pound] **libra** A customary unit for measuring weight;
1 pound = 16 ounces (p. 522)

predict [pri•dikt′] **predecir** To make a reasonable guess about what will happen (p. 180)

probability [prä•bə•bi′lə•tē] **probabilidad** The chance that a given event will occur (p. 178)
Example:

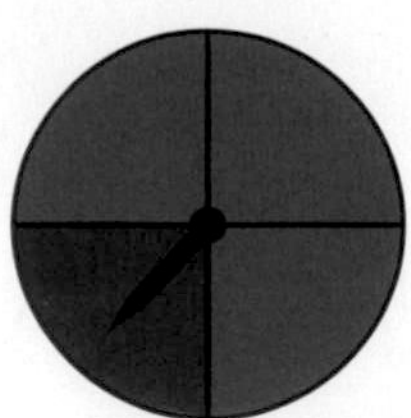

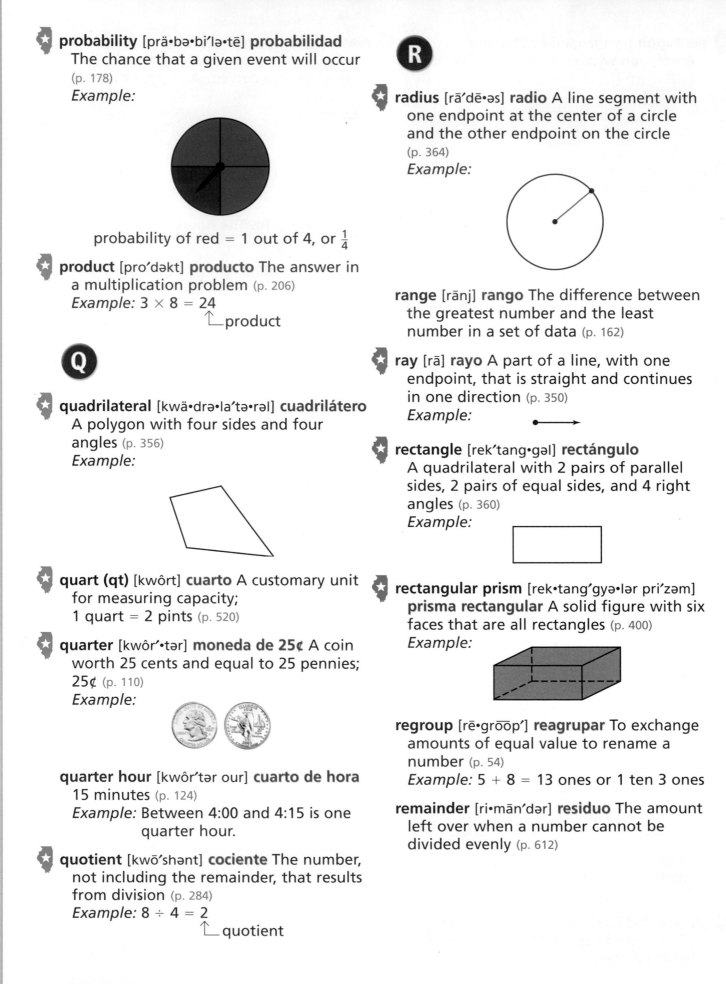

probability of red = 1 out of 4, or $\frac{1}{4}$

product [pro′dəkt] **producto** The answer in a multiplication problem (p. 206)
Example: 3 × 8 = 24
↑product

Q

quadrilateral [kwä•drə•la′tə•rəl] **cuadrilátero** A polygon with four sides and four angles (p. 356)
Example:

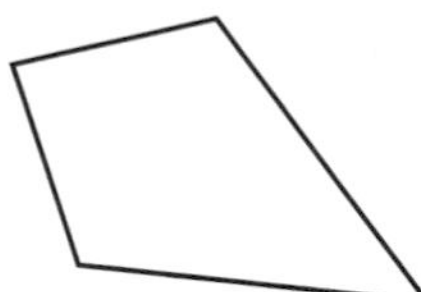

quart (qt) [kwôrt] **cuarto** A customary unit for measuring capacity;
1 quart = 2 pints (p. 520)

quarter [kwôr′•tər] **moneda de 25¢** A coin worth 25 cents and equal to 25 pennies; 25¢ (p. 110)
Example:

quarter hour [kwôr′tər our] **cuarto de hora** 15 minutes (p. 124)
Example: Between 4:00 and 4:15 is one quarter hour.

quotient [kwō′shənt] **cociente** The number, not including the remainder, that results from division (p. 284)
Example: 8 ÷ 4 = 2
↑quotient

R

radius [rā′dē•əs] **radio** A line segment with one endpoint at the center of a circle and the other endpoint on the circle (p. 364)
Example:

range [rānj] **rango** The difference between the greatest number and the least number in a set of data (p. 162)

ray [rā] **rayo** A part of a line, with one endpoint, that is straight and continues in one direction (p. 350)
Example:

rectangle [rek′tang•gəl] **rectángulo** A quadrilateral with 2 pairs of parallel sides, 2 pairs of equal sides, and 4 right angles (p. 360)
Example:

rectangular prism [rek•tang′gyə•lər pri′zəm] **prisma rectangular** A solid figure with six faces that are all rectangles (p. 400)
Example:

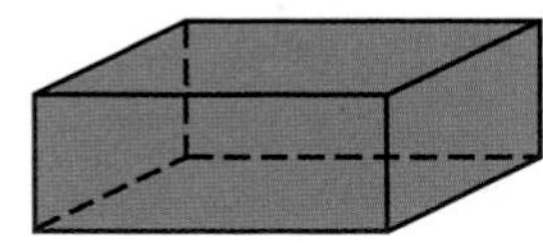

regroup [rē•grōōp′] **reagrupar** To exchange amounts of equal value to rename a number (p. 54)
Example: 5 + 8 = 13 ones or 1 ten 3 ones

remainder [ri•mān′dər] **residuo** The amount left over when a number cannot be divided evenly (p. 612)

repeating pattern [ri•pēt′ing pat′ərn] **patrón que se repite** A pattern which uses the same pattern unit over and over again (p. 424)

results [ri•zults′] **resultados** The answers from a survey (p. 158)

rhombus [räm′bəs] **rombo** A quadrilateral with 2 pairs of parallel sides and 4 equal sides and four angles (p. 360)
Example:

right angle [rīt ang′gəl] **ángulo recto** An angle that forms a square corner (p. 350)
Example:

right triangle [rīt trī′ang•gəl] **triángulo rectángulo** A triangle with one right angle (p. 358)
Example:

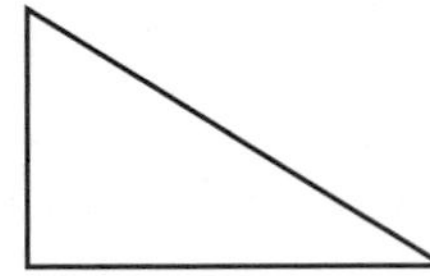

round [round] **redondear** Replace a number with another number that tells about how many or how much (p. 36)

rule [rōōl] **regla** An instruction that tells you the correct way to do something (pp. 256, 424)

S

scale [skāl] **escala** The numbers placed at fixed distances on a graph to help label the graph. (p. 154)

scalene triangle [skā′lēn trī′ang•gəl] **triángulo escaleno** A triangle in which no sides are equal (p. 358)
Example:

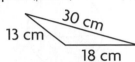

30 cm
13 cm
18 cm

second [se′kənd] **segundo** A small unit of time; (p. 124)
60 seconds = 1 minute

sequence [sē′kwəns] **ordenar** To write events in order (p. 136)

similar [si′mə•lər] **semejante** Having the same shape and the same or different size (p. 388)
Example:

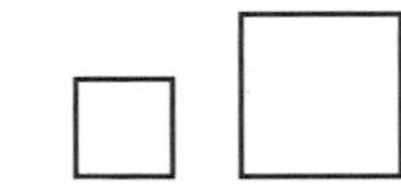

simplest form [sim′pləst fôrm] **mínima expresión** When a fraction is modeled with the largest fraction bar or bars possible (p. 466)

slide (translation) [slīd (trans•lā′shən)] **deslizar (traslación)** A movement of a figure to a new position without turning or flipping it (p. 390)
Example:

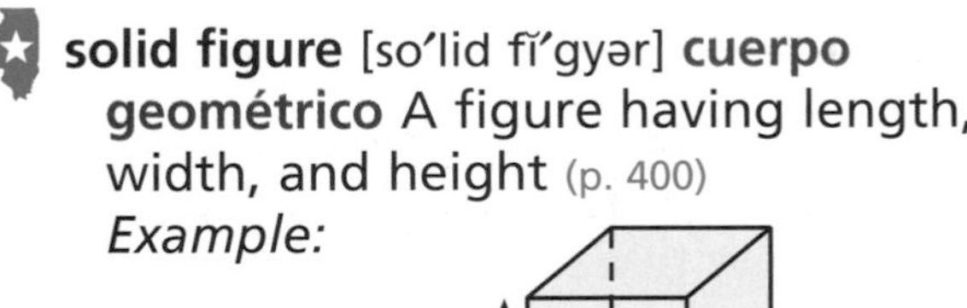

solid figure [so′lid fi′gyər] **cuerpo geométrico** A figure having length, width, and height (p. 400)
Example:

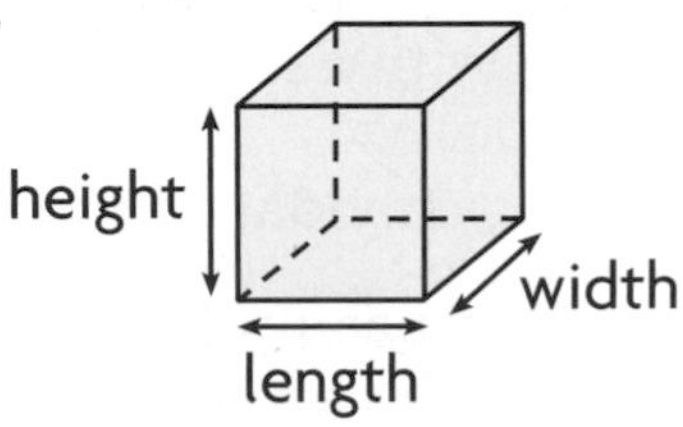

sphere [sfir] **esfera** A solid figure that has the shape of a round ball (p. 400)
Example:

square [skwâr] **cuadrado** A quadrilateral with 2 pairs of parallel sides, 4 equal sides, and 4 right angles (p. 360)
Example:

square number [skwâr num′bər] **número cuadrado** The product of two factors that are the same (p. 206)
Example: $2 \times 2 = 4$, so 4 is a square number

square pyramid [skwâr pir′ə•mid] **pirámide cuadrada** A solid, pointed figure with a flat base that is a square (p. 400)
Example:

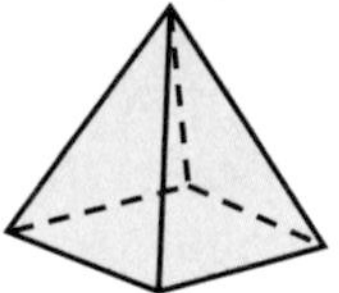

square unit [skwâr yo͞o′nət] **unidad cuadrada** A square with a side length of one unit; used to measure area (p. 564)

standard form [stan′dərd fôrm] **forma normal** A way to write numbers by using the digits 0–9, with each digit having a place value (p. 8)
Example: 345 ← standard form

straight angle [strāt ang′gəl] **ángulo llano** An angle in which two rays point in opposite directions so that they form a line (p. 350)
Example:

subtraction [sub•trak′shən] **resta** The process of finding how many are left when a number of items are taken away from a group of items; the process of finding the difference when two groups are compared; the opposite operation of addition (p. 78)

sum [sum] **suma o total** The answer to an addition problem (p. 48)

survey [sur′vā] **encuesta** A method of gathering information (p. 158)

symmetry [sim′ə•trē] **simetría** A figure has symmetry if it can be folded along a line so that the two parts match exactly; one half of the figure looks like the mirror image of the other half (p. 384)

tally table [ta′lē tā′bəl] **tabla de conteo** A table that uses tally marks to record data (p. 146)
Example:

Favorite Sport	
Sport	Tally
Soccer	𝍸 |||
Baseball	|||
Football	𝍸
Basketball	𝍸 |

tenth [tenth] **décimo** One of ten equal parts (p. 484)
Example:

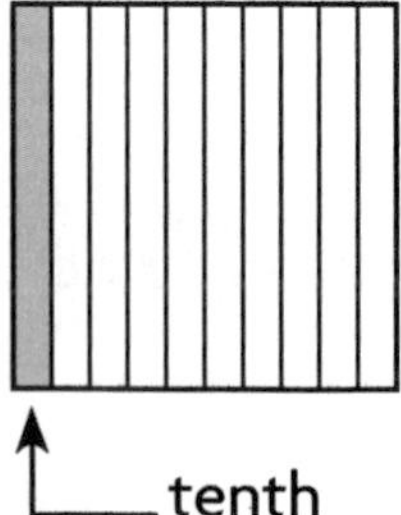

tessellation [te•sə•lā′shən] **teselación** A repeating pattern made of a closed plane figure that covers a surface with no overlapping or empty space (p. 394)
Example:

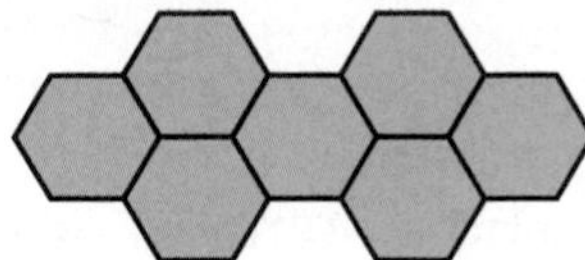

thermometer [thûr•mom′ə•tər] **termómetro** An instrument for measuring temperature (p. 528)

three-dimensional figure [thrē•di•men′shən•əl fig′yər] **figura tridimensional** A figure having length, width, and height (p. 400)
Example:

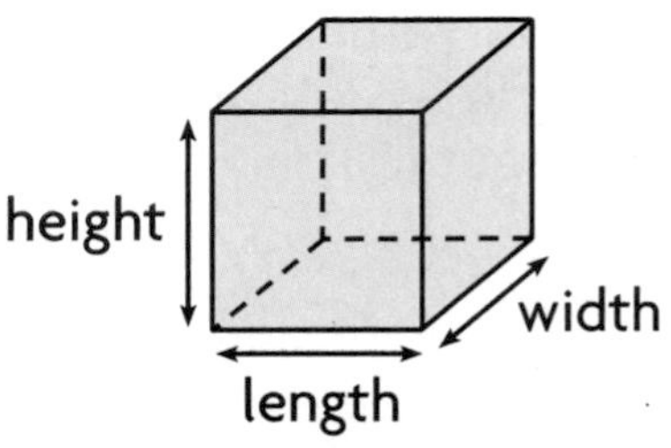

time line [tīm līn] **línea cronológica** A drawing that shows when and in what order events took place (p. 136)

trapezoid [trap′ə•zoid] **trapecio** A quadrilateral with exactly one pair of parallel sides and four angles (p. 360)
Example:

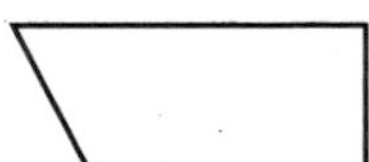

tree diagram [trē dī′ə•gram] **diagrama de árbol** An organized list that shows all possible outcomes of an event (p. 186)
Example:

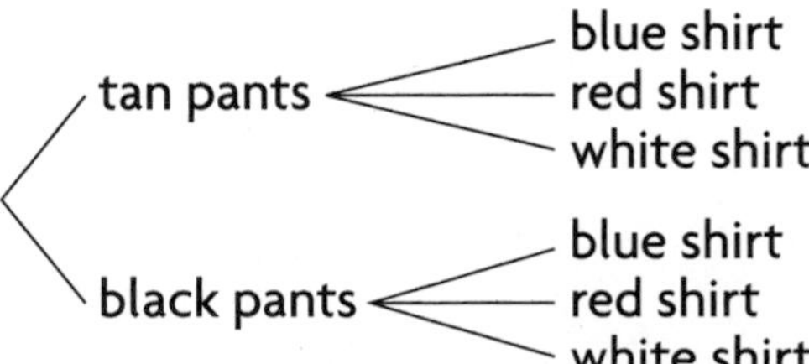

trends [trendz] **tendencias** On a graph, areas where the data increase, decrease, or stay the same over time (p. 168)

triangle [trī′ang′gəl] **triángulo** A polygon with three sides and three angles (p. 356)
Examples:

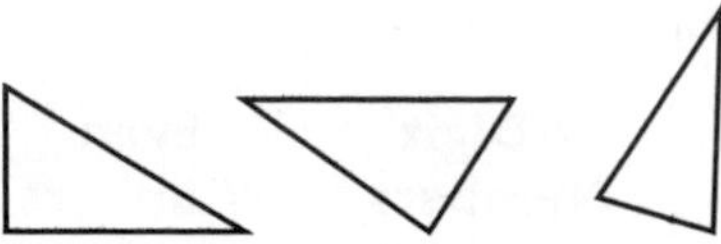

turn (rotation) [tûrn (rō•tā′shən)] **giro (rotación)** A movement of a figure to a new position by rotating the figure around a point (p. 390)
Examples:

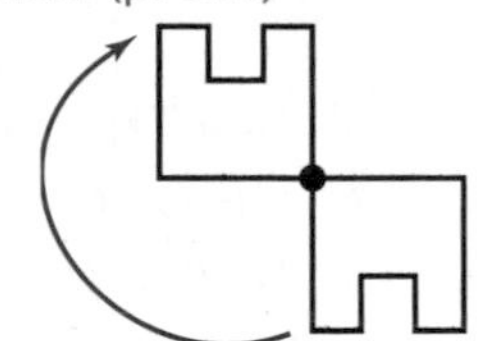

two-dimensional figure [tōō•di•men′shən•əl fig′yer] **figura bidimensional** A figure having length and width (p. 356)
Example:

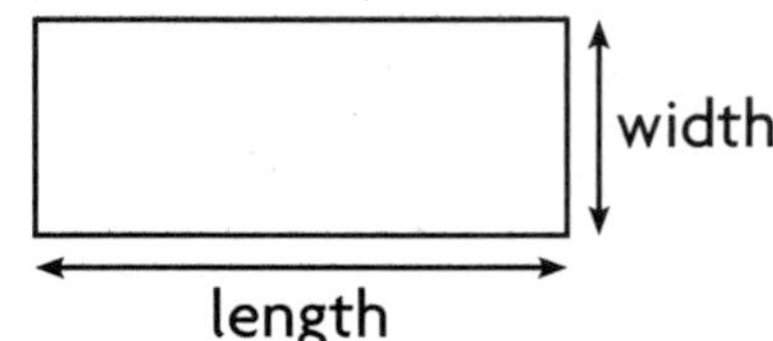

unlikely [un•lī′klē] **poco probable** An event is unlikely if it does not have a good chance of happening. (p. 178)

variable [vâr′ē•ə•bəl] **variable** A symbol or a letter that stands for an unknown number (p. 258)

Word History

Variable The word *vary* comes from the Latin *variabilis*, meaning "changeable." At first, the word applied to changes of color, as in the speckled fur of animals. Eventually, the word was used for things that involve change of any kind.

Venn diagram [ven dī′ə•gram] **diagrama de Venn** A diagram that shows relationships among sets of things (p. 363)
Example:

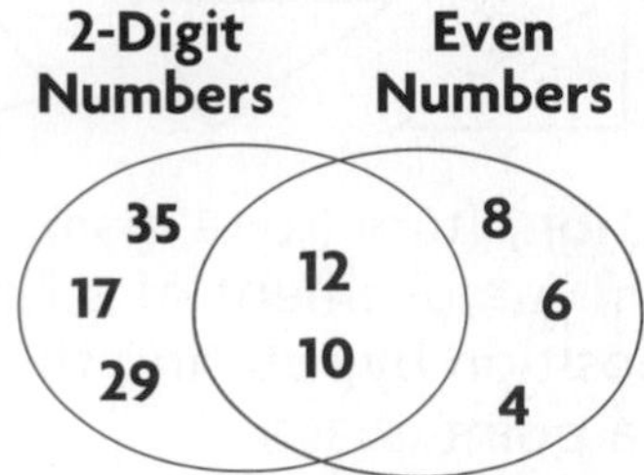

vertex [vûr′teks] **vértice** The point at which two rays of an angle or two (or more) line segments meet in a plane figure or where three or more edges meet in a solid figure (pp. 350, 400)
Examples:

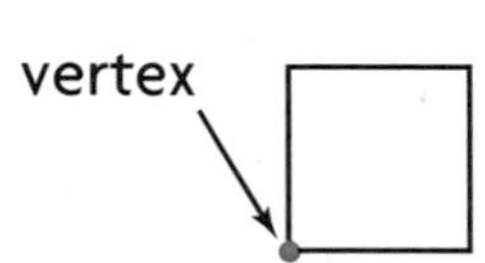

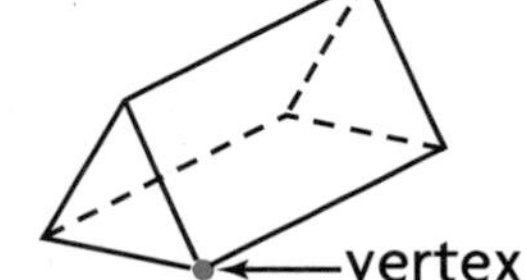

vertical bar graph [vûr′ti•kəl bär graf] **gráfica de barras verticales** A bar graph in which the bars go up from bottom to top (p. 154)

volume [väl′yəm] **volumen** The amount of space a solid figure takes up (p. 570)

weight [wāt] **peso** How heavy an object is (p. 522)

whole number [hōl num′bər] **número entero** One of the numbers 0, 1, 2, 3, 4, ... The set of whole numbers goes on without end.

word form [wûrd fôrm] **en palabras** A way to write numbers by using words (p. 8)
Example: The word form of 212 is two hundred twelve.

yard (yd) [yärd] **yarda** A customary unit for measuring length or distance; 1 yard = 3 feet (p. 512)

Zero Property of Multiplication [zē′rō prä′pər•tē əv mul•tə•plə•kā′shən] **propiedad del cero de la multiplicación** The property that states that the product of zero and any number is zero (p. 214)
Example: $0 \times 6 = 0$

Index

B

C

D

E

F

G

H

I

L

M

N

O

P

Q

R

S

T

U

V

W

Photo Credits

KEY: (t) top, (b) bottom, (l) left, (r) right, (c) center, (bg) background, (fg) foreground

Front Cover: (l) Image100/Alamy; (bg) W. Cody/Corbis ; (r) WoodyStock/Alamy.
Front Endsheets: Digital Vision/Getty Images; Royalty-Free/Corbis.

Back Cover: (l) WoodyStock/Alamy; (r) Ingram Publishing/Alamy.
Back Endsheets: Getty Images; Photodisc Green/Getty Images.

1 (t) The Futures Channel; 1 (c) The Futures Channel; 1 (b) The Futures Channel; 5 (r) John Warden/Getty Images; 8 (cr) Adam Jones Photography; 14 (cr) Gary Crabbe/age footstock; 18 (br) Alamy; 18 (br) Alamy; 26 iStockPhoto; 28 (r) Doris De Witt/Getty Images; 32 (r) Pat Doyle/Corbis; 34 (r) Corbis; 36 (r) Brian Snyder/Reuters Picture Archive; 36 (r) MLB Photos via Getty Images; 36 (r) MLB Photos via Getty Images; 36 (r) Photo File/MLB Photos via Getty Images; 36 (l) Reuters Photo Archive/NewsCom; 43 (bg) Royalty-Free/Corbis; 46 Bob Anderson/Masterfile; 48 (br) Lynn Stone/Index Stock Imagery, Inc.; 49 Alamy; 50 Digital Vision/Getty Images (Royalty-free); 52 ENGER, DON/Animals Animals—Earth Scenes; 53 Getty Images; 54 Hein van den Heuvel/zefa/Corbis; 57 (cr) Frank Siteman/age fotostock; 59 Roy Ooms/Masterfile; 61 (tr) John Giustina/Getty Images; 62 (br) Jeff Greenberg/Age photostock; 63 (r) AP Photo/Don Knight,The Herald Bulletin, Don Knight, File; 64 (br) Chris Cheadle/Getty Images; 66 (br) Alex Maclean/Getty Images; 66 David Zimmerman/Masterfile; 68 (cr) Don Farrall/Getty images; 74 Shah, A&M/Animals Animals-Earth scenes; 80 Royalty-Free/Corbis; 81 Dorling Kindersley; 83 (tr) George Hall/CORBIS; 84 (br) Royalty-Free/Corbis; 87 Mark Erickson/Getty Images; 90 (tr) Royalty-Free/Corbis; 91 (tl) Christopher Groenhout/Getty Images; 91 (inset) Kevin Schafer/CORBIS; 92 (cr) Royalty-Free/Corbis; 92 (cr) Royalty-Free/Corbis; 92 (br) Royalty-Free/Corbis; 93 (tr) ©David Young-Wolff/Photo Edit—All rights reserved.; 93 Royalty-Free/Corbis; 93 (tr) ©David Young-Wolff/Photo Edit—All rights reserved.; 93 Royalty-Free/Corbis; 95 (cr) Jessie Cohen/epa/Corbis; 95 (cr) Jessie Cohen/epa/Corbis; 97 (tr) Michael Newman/Photo Edit; 97 (tr) Michael Newman/Photo Edit; 105 (cr) Richard Cummins/CORBIS; 105 (b) Robert Harding/Getty Images; 107 (t) The Futures Channel; 107 (c) The Futures Channel; 107 (b) The Futures Channel; 108 Pete Saloutos/CORBIS; 113 (r) Matt Baker/iStockPhoto; 113 (tr) Tony Robinson/iStockPhoto; 114 (cr) Creatas/Jupiter Images; 115 (br) iStockPhoto; 115 (br) Stockdisc/Getty Images; 119 (cl) Alaska Stock/PictureQuest; 119 (cl) Americanscapes, Inc./photographersdirect.com; 119 (cl) Lon C. Diehl/Photo Edit; 121 (cr) Spencer Grant/Photo Edit; 122 (tcr) Getty Images; 123 (br) Dorling Kindersley; 123 (br) "Photographer: Tim Ridley Copyright Holder: Dorling Kindersley"; 123 (bc) Tim Swoboda Photography; 124 (cr) Ghislain & Marie David de Lossy/Getty Images; 130 (cr) Wendell Metzen/Index Stock Imagery, Inc.; 136 (cr) Robert J. Bennett/age fotostock; 137 (c) Dorling Kindersley/Getty Images; 144 © Robert Llewellyn/Imagestate; 151 (tr) Masterfile (Royalty Free Div.); 152 (b) Ron Watts/CORBIS; 154 (cr) Joel Rogers; 155 (tr) Joel Rogers; 162 (r) Martin Shields Photography/Photographersdirect.com; 164 (r) Gene Ahrens/SuperStock; 169 (c) Getty Images; 169 (cr) iStockphoto; 176 (bg) Brian Bailey/Getty Images; 190 (br) Tom Bean/Getty Images; 198 (br) Dorling Kindersley/Getty Images; 198 (r) Douglas Plasencia/Courtesy Stack's Rarities; 198 (tr) Douglas Plasencia/Courtesy Stack's Rarities; 198 (cl) Felicia Martinez/PhotoEdit; 198 (c) Felicia Martinez/PhotoEdit; 198 (bl) Getty Images; 198 (bc) Getty Images; 198 (cl) Stockdisc Classic/Alamy; 198 (cr) Stockdisc Classic/Alamy; 198 (r) United States Mint image; 198 (tr) United States Mint image; 199 (b) Sundell Larsen/Getty Images; 201 (t) The Futures Channel; 201 (c) The Futures Channel; 201 (b) The Futures Channel; 202 (t) TIM FITZHARRIS/Minden Pictures; 204 (cr) Alberto Biscaro/Masterfile; 218 (cr) Digital Vision/Getty Images (Royalty-free); 219 (cr) Royalty-Free/Corbis; 221 (tr) Sean Justice/Getty Images; 223 (cr) Getty Images; 230 Chad Ehlers/Index Stock Imagery; 234 (cr) john t. fowler/Alamy; 236 (tc) BERQUIST, PAUL & JOYCE/Animals Animals - Earth Scenes; 237 (br) Larry Fisher/Masterfile; 238 (tr) Purestock/Getty Images (Royalty-free); 239 (cr) USGS/Photo Researchers, Inc.; 240 (cr) Dale C. Spartas/CORBIS; 262 (tr) David Young-Wolff/Photo Edit; 263 (tr) Hemera/age fotostock; 264 (c) Phillip Roberts/Alamy; 265 (cr) 2001 Joel Rogers; 272 (bc) Getty Images; 272 (c) Jupiterimages; 272 (cl) Mark Turner/Jupiterimages; 272 (bl) SuperStock; 275 (t) The Futures Channel; 275 (c) The Futures Channel; 275 (b) The Futures Channel Inc; 276 (t) Stan Liu/Getty Images; 278 (tr) David Toase/Getty Images; 279 (cr) SuperStock, Inc./SuperStock; 284 (cr) Doug Menuez/Getty images (Royalty-free); 302 (cr) Larry Ditto/Bruce Coleman USA; 303 (c) BOB & CLARA CALHOUN/Bruce Coleman USA; 303 (br) Photodisc/Telescope; 312 (tr) Jeff Greenberg/The Image Works; 329 (cr) Stock Connection Distribution/Alamy; 330 (tr) AP Photo/John Bazemore; 331 (cr) Gary Bell/Getty Images; 332 (tr) Altrendo Nature/Getty Images; 334 (br) Bob Bennett/Jupiter Images; 334 (br) John Shaw/NHPA; 334 (cr) Kevin Schafer/CORBIS; 334 (br) Rosemary Calvert/Jupiter Images; 344 (t) Inga Spence/Index Stock Imagery; 345 (cl) age fotostock; 345 (bl) Alamy; 345 (tl) Corbis; 345 (cl) Dinodia Images/Alamy; 345 (tl) Index Stock Imagery; 345 (b) Joanna B Pinneo/Getty Images; 345 (bl) NASA/SCIENCE PHOTO LIBRARY; 347 (t) The Futures Channel; 347 (c) The Futures Channel; 347 (b) The Futures Channel; 348 (bg) Alan Schein/zefa/Corbis; 350 (bc) Jeremy Edwards/iStockPhoto; 350 (bl) Nicole Waring/Shutterstock; 350 (bl) Riccardo Bissacco/iStockPhoto; 352 (c) John C. Panella Jr./Shutterstock; 357 (c) Harris Shiffman/iStockPhoto; 357 (cl) photolibrary.com pty. ltd./Index Stock Imagery, Inc.; 357 (cr) photolibrary.com pty. ltd./Index Stock Imagery, Inc.; 358 (cr) n/a; 360 (cr) Andrew McKim/Masterfile; 376 (bg) Jim Brandenburg/Minden Pictures; 38 Chris Wood-Tank; 401 (b) Brand X Pictures/Alamy; 401 (b) Comstock Images/Alamy; 401 (bl) Image Source/Alamy; 402 (tl) konrad lew/Istock Photo; 407 (cl) Terry Wilson/iStockphoto; 411 iStockphoto; 413 (br) iStockphoto; 413 (cr) LaHeather Massengale/iStockphoto; 420 Julie Gang; 440 (tr) Bill Boch/Jupiterimages; 440 (br) Brian Hagiwara/JupiterImages; 440 (tr) Courtesy of Yuri Raskin; 440 (bc) Solzberg Studios/StockFood; 441 (br) Brian Hagiwara/JupiterImages; 441 (cl) Courtesy of Pictures of Record; 441 (bl) Courtesy of Pictures of Record; 441 (b) Courtesy of Texas Archaeological Research Laboratory, The University of Texas at Austin, cat.# 16SA48-C101; 441 (tr) Marilyn Angel Wynn/Nativestock; 441 (br) Photo by D. E. Hurlbert; 441 (tr) University of Virginia Museum; 482 AP Photo/Enid News & Eagle, Kyle Nosal; 482 Steve Bloom/Getty Images; 487 (b) iStockphoto; 487 (b) Raymond Kasprzak/Shutterstock; 487 (b) S.T. Yiap/Alamy; 487 (t) WireImageStock/Masterfile; 495 (tr) PNC/Getty Images; 506 (c) Anna Peisl/zefa/Corbis; 506 (cr) Corbis; 506 (b) Getty Images; 506 (c) Getty Images; 506 (l) Getty Images; 506 (cl) Michael Prince/Corbis; 506 (r) Rob Howard/CORBIS; 509 (b) Rare Coin Wholesalers/The Futures Channel; 509 (b) Rare Coin Wholesalers/The Futures Channel; 509 (t) The Futures Channel; 509 (c) The Futures Channel; 509 (b) The Futures Channel; 509 (t) The Futures Channel; 509 (c) The Futures Channel; 512 (bl) George Doyle & Ciaran Griffin/Getty Images; 512 (bc) Siede Preis/Getty Images; 512 (bc) Siede Preis/Getty Images; 512 (br) Asger Carlsen/Getty Images; 513 (tr) Alamy; 520 (tcl) David Young-Wolff/Photoedit; 520 (tcr) iStockphoto; 520 (tr) Tetra Images/Alamy; 526 (br) Brian Bevan/ardea London; 527 (cl) iStockphoto; 527 (cr) iStockphoto; 527 (br) Jan Tyler/RM; 527 (bl) Perfect Picture Parts/Alamy; 530 (br) David Young-Wolff/Getty Images; 535 (bc) iStockphoto; 541 (tl) MARY GODLESKI/Associated Press; 548 (br) Duncan Usher/Alamy; 558 Joseph Sohm; ChromoSohm Inc./CORBIS; 565 (b) Corbis; 580 (cl) Corbis; 580 (tr) Douglas David Seifert/Ardea; 580 (cr) Randy Faris/CORBIS; 581 (cr) Amos Nachoum/CORBIS; 581 (br) David Fleetham/Visuals Unlimited; 581 (b) Gary Bell/Getty Images; 583 (t) The futures Channel; 583 (c) The Futures Channel; 583 (b) The Futures Channel; 584 Justin Kase/Alamy; 593 (tl) AP Photo/Rick Smith; 593 (tc) AP Photo/Steve Rasmussen; 593 (cr) Michael Newman/Photo Edit; 593 (tr) William Thomas Cain/Getty Images; 597 (r) Andy Crawford/Getty Images; 597 (c) Felicia Martinez/Photo Edit; 598 (r) Corbis; 603 Michael Newman/Photo Edit; 616 Andrew Leyerle/Getty Images; 618 Tim Pannell/Masterfile; 620 (tr) Photo Courtesy of The Children's Museum of Southeastern, CT; 622 Digital Vision/Getty Images; 630 (tr) Alaska Stock Inc.; 630 (br) Reino Hanninen/Alamy; 630 (tr) The Great Train Story, Museum of Science and Industry, Chicago; 630 (cr) The Great Train Story, Museum of Science and Industry, Chicago; 630 (bg) vario images GmbH & Co.KG/Alamy; 631 (tl) Jeff Kieffer Photography/photographersdirect; 631 (tc) John Rattle/photographersdirect; 631 (bc) NiKreationS/Alamy; 631 (bl) Rodney Todt Photography/PhotographersDirect; 631 (tc) Thomas Stevenson Grant/photographersdirect; (tr) © Bettmann/CORBIS; (bg) © Brand X/SuperStock; (t) Don Farrall/Getty images; (br) Dorling Kindersley/Getty Images; (br) Getty Images; (tr) GK Hart/Vikki Hart/Getty Images (Royalty-free); (l) Image100/Alamy; (r) Ingram Publishing/Alamy; (tc) Martin Harvey/CORBIS; (br) RubberBall Productions/Jupiter Images; (tr) RubberBall Productions/Jupiter Images (l) W. Cody/Corbis; (r) WoodyStock/Alamy;

All other photos © Harcourt School Publishers. Harcourt Photos provided by the Harcourt Index, Harcourt IPR, and Harcourt photographers; Weronica Ankarorn, Eric Camden, Don, Couch, Doug Dukane, Ken Kinzie, April Riehm, and Steve Williams.